STEPS IN THE ACCOUNTING CYCLE

Source Documents

2 → GENERAL JOURNAL

3 → GENERAL LEDGER

8, 9 →

4

10

1

8

9

Adjusting

Name of Company
Work Sheet
For Period Ended

5 **6** →

Name of Company
Trial Balance
For Period Ended

Closing

7

Name of Company
Income Statement
For Period Ended

7

Name of Company
Statement of Owner's Equity
For Period Ended

7

Name of Company
Balance Sheet
Date

Steps in the Accounting Cycle

During Accounting Period:
1. Analyze source documents.
2. Journalize the transactions.
3. Post to the ledger accounts.

End of Accounting Period:
4. Prepare a trial balance.
5. Determine and prepare the needed adjustments on the work sheet.
6. Complete an end-of-period work sheet.
7. Prepare an income statement, statement of owner's equity, and balance sheet.
8. Journalize and post the adjusting entries.
9. Journalize and post the closing entries.
10. Prepare a post-closing trial balance.

16TH EDITION

COLLEGE

ACCOUNTING

CHAPTERS 1–28

James A. Heintz, DBA, CPA
Professor of Accounting
University of Kansas
Lawrence, Kansas

Robert W. Parry, Jr., PhD
Professor of Accounting
Indiana University
Bloomington, Indiana

SOUTH-WESTERN College Publishing

An International Thomson Publishing Company

Publishing Team Director:	Richard Lindgren, CPA
Acquisitions Editor:	Alex Von Rosenberg
Developmental Editors:	Sara Wilson, CPA, Katherine Meisenheimer
Production Editor:	Marcella Dechter
Production House:	Navta Associates, Inc.
Cover Design and Store Photography:	Matulionis Photography and Design
Additional Cover Photography:	at 1998, The Stock Market
Internal Design:	Barbara Libby
Manufacturing Coordinator:	Gordon Woodside
Marketing Manager:	Matthew Filimonov

Copyright © 1999
by South-Western College Publishing
Cincinnati, Ohio

Library of Congress Cataloging-in-Publication Data:
Heintz, James A.
     College accounting.   Chapters 1-28 / James A. Heintz,
Robert W. Parry, Jr. -- 16th ed.
          p.   cm.
     Includes index.
     ISBN 0-538-87668-9 (alk. paper)
     1. Accounting.   I. Parry, Robert W., 1950-   . II. Title.
     HF5635.H444 1998
657'.044—dc21   98-14633
                                                        CIP

Student Edition, Chapters 1–28	ISBN: 0-538-87668-9
Student Edition, Chapters 1–15	ISBN: 0-538-88599-8
Student Edition, Chapters 1–10	ISBN: 0-538-88600-5

4 5 6 7 8 9 TRP 5 4 3 2 1 0 9
Printed in Canada

I(T)P®
International Thomson Publishing
South-Western College Publishing is an ITP Company.
The ITP trademark is used under license.

Dedication

We are grateful to our wives

Celia Heintz and Jane Parry

and our children

Andrea Heintz, John Heintz, Jessica Jane Parry, and Mitch Parry

for their love, support, and assistance during the creation
of this sixteenth edition. We especially appreciate
Jessie Parry's willingness to let us use her name
throughout the first six chapters.

PREFACE

SIMPLY THE BEST

What qualifies a College Accounting text as simply the best?

For some, it's a thorough, readable style that helps students get good jobs by building practical accounting skills. For others, it's a solid approach supported by a learning package that makes the most of class preparation.

We think it's both of these qualities... and more.

We think it's the total educational environment of *College Accounting, 16e*. This text presents concepts **simply** and ensures **the best**, most accurate coverage. The step-by-step, straightforward approach has made accounting accessible to millions of students, from accounting and business majors to students in business administration, office technology, computer science, paralegal programs, and other disciplines.

As we updated this text, we were guided by a commitment to creating a text that is unsurpassed. The new 16th edition delivers on its promises with...

▶ **Simply the best approach.**   Heintz/Parry helps your students by not rushing into financial statements or overloading them with theory. The concise, richly illustrated text helps students master one topic before moving to the next.

▶ **Simply the best improvements.**   We responded to instructors' feedback to ensure that this text meets changing classroom needs. New Internet assignments, for example, show how this technology can be used as an accounting resource.

▶ **Simply the best pedagogy.**   Solid, proven educational techniques are used to enhance student understanding.

▶ **Simply the best package.**   The extensive supplement package includes an enhanced instructor's resource manual, transparencies, PowerPoint® slides, and much more.

▶ **Simply the best service.**   South-Western has a professional team—from your ITP sales representative, to the Academic Resource Center staff, to the authors—that is committed to helping you.

Take a closer look at *College Accounting, 16e,* and see for yourself why it's simply the best.

What makes our approach simply the best?

College Accounting, 16e, doesn't rush students into financial statements or overwhelm them with theory. The text presents simple concepts first, and builds to the more advanced. And in each chapter students focus on only one major topic or procedure, ensuring that they master each new concept before moving on.

▶ *Real-world skills* are developed to help students get jobs after graduation.

▶ *Careful development of topics* prevents "information overload."

▶ *Repetition of key topics* throughout helps students master important concepts and procedures.

▶ *Narrative approach* covers the simpler example of a service business first before moving on to a merchandising business.

▶ *Demonstration problems* can be used as study aids or in-class examples.

▶ *Comprehensive problems* provide important opportunities to review skills.

▶ *Three versions* of the text (10, 15, or 28 chapters) create a custom fit for *your* course.

What makes our improved presentation simply the best?

We've incorporated many user requests and suggestions into this edition, making a great text even better. Skill development and mastery are encouraged and assisted by a number of features.

New! **Chapter Openers** present the topic in context. For Chapters 1–7, the continuing scenario deals with a sole-proprietor service business; for Chapters 8–19, a sole-proprietor retail business; for Chapter 20, a partnership; and for Chapters 21–28, a small retail corporation that includes manufacturing. Each scenario presents a realistic company and ties its development to the main concepts of each chapter.

John Zenith recently opened a sports equipment and clothing shop named Be A Sport in West Springfield, MA. To protect and properly manage cash, John uses a checking account. All cash and checks received from customers are deposited promptly. All bills are paid by check. In this way, John can use the deposit slips and monthly bank statement to verify his records of cash received. Similarly, cancelled checks and the monthly bank statement can be used to verify John's records of cash payments. Complete and accurate records of cash receipts and cash payments help John control this important asset and plan for future cash needs.

At the end of the month, the balance in the cash account in John's books differs from the cash balance shown on the bank statement. In trying to reconcile the two amounts, how should John treat the checks he wrote during the month that have not yet been presented to the bank for payment?

> Note what happens if the accounts payable ledger is posted daily and the general ledger is posted at the end of the month. The accounts payable ledger total will equal the general ledger Accounts Payable total only at the end of the month.

New!   **Margin Notes**, used widely throughout the text, enrich students' understanding of concepts and terms beyond what is contained in the text narrative.

New!   **A Broader View**, found in each chapter, provides students with interesting examples of actual events or situations that tie to accounting.

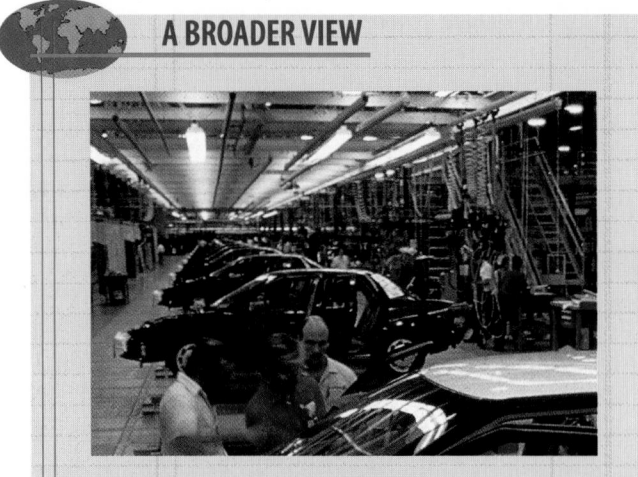

A BROADER VIEW

ASSETS AND THE COST OF PRODUCTS WE BUY

Next time you buy something, think of all the assets that a company needs to produce that product. If the product comes from a "capital-intensive" industry, one that requires heavy investments in assets, the company must price the product high enough to cover the cost of using the assets and replacing them when they wear out. For example, General Motors recently reported that the cost of property, plant, and equipment used for operating purposes came to over $100 billion.

New!   **Computers and Accounting Modules,** written by James A. Hall of Lehigh University, expand the coverage of computers, reflecting their increasing importance in businesses. There are two modules:

- ▶ **Module 1,** following Chapter 6, describes how the computer is used in bookkeeping.

- ▶ **Module 2,** after Chapter 10, explains the computer's use in payroll accounting.

- ▶ **Module 3,** after Chapter 28, explores the computer's company-wide influence in corporate and manufacturing environments.

COMPUTERS AND ACCOUNTING

Principles of Computer-Based Accounting Systems

Modern organizations use computer technology to perform many of their routine accounting tasks. While the accounting principles discussed in this text still apply, computer-based accounting systems also make use of unique transaction processing techniques that accountants should understand at a conceptual level. Our discussion will focus on three computerized accounting approaches: batch processing, real-time processing, and systems that combine both batch and real-time features. Before we enter into this material, however, the relationship between traditional accounting records and their computerized counterparts needs to be addressed.

Computerized Accounting Records

File Structures. Financial information in a computerized accounting system is represented by a three-level format or structure: data, records, and files. We will use accounts receivable to illustrate this structure, which is shown in Figure 1. *Data* are individual facts that help describe a financial entity. For instance, the customer's

Expanded! **Color coding** enhances understanding by highlighting accounts in a consistent color scheme. Assets are shown in blue, liabilities in yellow, owner- ship equity in purple, revenues in green, expenses in light red, and drawing accounts in mauve. All journals are on blue rulings to differentiate those chronological records from ledgers and other processing documents, which are shown in yellow. Financial statements are white. Source documents vary in color, in the same manner as real-life documents.

New end-of-chapter coverage broadens the learning experience:

New! **Reflection: Answering the Opening Question** provides the answer to the question posed in the opening scenario.

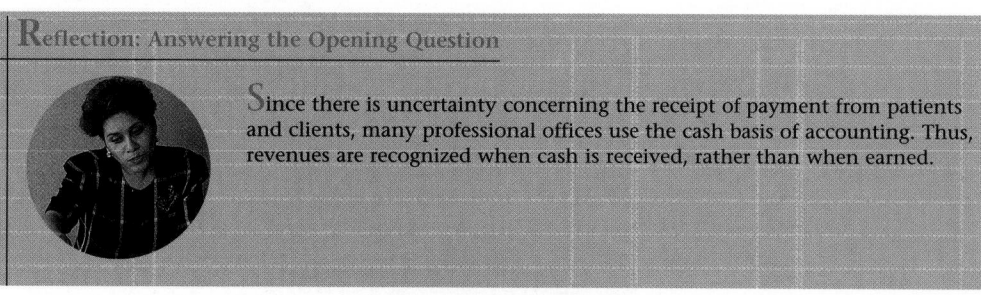

Reflection: Answering the Opening Question

Since there is uncertainty concerning the receipt of payment from patients and clients, many professional offices use the cash basis of accounting. Thus, revenues are recognized when cash is received, rather than when earned.

New! **Ethics Cases,** written by Kim Belden of Daytona Beach Community College, help students think through what they would do in various situa- tions. Case problems for individual and group use allow students to weigh the merits of various ethical considerations related to accounting.

ETHICS CASE

Ethics

Jason Tierro, an inventory clerk at Lexmar Company, is responsible for taking a physical count of the goods on hand at the end of the year. He has been performing this duty for several years. This year Jason was very busy due to a shortage of personnel at the company, so he decided to just estimate the amount of ending inventory instead of doing an accurate count. He reasoned that he could come very close to the true amount because of his past experience working with inventory. Besides, he was sure that the sophisticated computer program that Lexmar had just invested in kept an accurate record of inventory on hand.

1. What is your opinion of Jason's reasoning?

2. If Jason underestimates the dollar amount of ending inventory, what effect will it have on net income for the current accounting period?

3. Write a short paragraph explaining why a physical inventory should be taken at least once a year.

New! **Web Work** assignments expose students to the business applications of the Internet by directing them to Internet sites, where they obtain information to complete an assignment. The Heintz/Parry Web site (http://heintz.swcollege.com) provides easy access to assignment resources. This central site will be updated should any of the original addresses listed in the text become unavailable.

WEB WORK

As mentioned in the Chapter 11 question, many retailers are going on-line. More banks are on-line too. Many paychecks are direct deposited and people are seeing less and less physical currency. What happens to cash accounting when there is no more cash? If this sounds farfetched, look at the following site.

PNC Bank is only one of many banks that offers on-line banking:

http://www.pncbank.com

(http://heintz.swcollege.com)

New! **Inc. Online** in Chapters 21–28 (corporate accounting), direct students to an Internet site where they can read related articles from Inc. magazine. These articles provide a current, real-world perspective on a variety of business and accounting topics.

Inc.
ONLINE

"The Cash-Flow Quagmire"
(http://heintz.swcollege.com)
Why is a thriving company failing?

New! **Self-Study Test Questions**, found at the end of each chapter, allow students to assess their understanding of chapter material to determine if further study is required before proceeding to the next chapter. Answers to the questions are provided at the end of the text.

Self-Study Test Questions

True/False

1. To debit an account is to enter an amount on the left side of the account.
2. Liability accounts normally have debit balances.

Multiple Choice

1. A common example of an asset is

   (a) Professional Fees.
   (b) Rent Expense.
   (c) Accounts Receivable.
   (d) Accounts Payable.

Why is our pedagogy simply the best?

This text facilitates student learning by employing a classroom-proven pedagogy.

Learning Objectives, located at the beginning of each chapter, preview the skills that will be learned and mastered in that chapter.

"There is plenty for students to do. I always assign the review questions for writing practice. The exercises and problems are representative of real life. The mastery problems, appendices, and comprehensive problems are all good."

Virginia Choate
American Commercial
College, Abilene, TX

LEARNING OBJECTIVES:
Careful study of this chapter should enable you to:

LO 1 **Prepare end-of-period adjustments.**

LO 2 **Prepare a work sheet.**

LO 3 **Describe methods for finding errors on the work sheet.**

LO 4 **Journalize adjusting entries.**

Learning Keys emphasize important new points and are an excellent way to prepare for tests.

> **LEARNING KEY:** The voucher system contains elements of internal control such as segregation of duties, authorization to order the goods and prepare the voucher, and accounting procedures that require prenumbering and accounting for the supporting documents.

Profiles in Accounting feature real people who have used *College Accounting* and are now successfully working and using their skills.

PROFILES in ACCOUNTING

Jeanette Anderson, Factory Accounting Clerk

Jeanette Anderson earned a 4.0 GPA and membership in Phi Theta Kappa while completing her Associate Degree in Business at Eastern Wyoming College. While on campus, she held a work-study job as an Instructor Assistant. In this position Jeanette demonstrated a sound work ethic, an ability to get along well with others, and competence.

After graduation, she went to work for Imperial/Holly Sugar Corp. in Torrington, WY. Her duties include working with automated accounts payable, accounts receivable, and inventory control. During the annual harvest campaign, she supervises data entry clerks.

Jeanette believes the key to her success has been her understanding of double-entry accounting combined with her computer skills. Possessing problem-solving skills and being flexible are also important.

Source: Jack Kappeler, Eastern Wyoming College

Key Steps, incorporated frequently throughout the text, demonstrate steps to accomplish specific objectives—such as how to prepare a bank reconciliation or work sheet, how to post subsidiary and general ledger accounts, and how to find the cause of errors in a bank reconciliation or trial balance.

STEP 2   **Enter the debit.** Cash is entered on the first line at the extreme left of the Description column. The amount of the debit, $2,000, is entered on the same line in the Debit column. Since this is not a formal financial statement, dollar signs are not used.

	DATE		DESCRIPTION	POST REF.	DEBIT	CREDIT	
1	20-- June	1	Cash		2 0 0 0 00		1
2							2

GENERAL JOURNAL   PAGE 1

Illustrations are used often, especially when any new accounting principle or procedure is introduced. A wealth of accounting documents and records, diagrams, and flow charts help students visualize important concepts. Some examples include:

▶ Transactions reflected in the accounting equation (Page 18)
▶ The interaction of the key financial statements (Page 29)
▶ Owner's equity umbrella (Page 50)
▶ Source documents (Page 90)

▶ General Journal and General Ledger relationship (Page 99)

▶ Work sheet development (Page 142G)

▶ Linkages between the work sheet and the financial statements (Pages 177 and 179)

▶ Tax forms (Pages 300–302 and 337–342)

Accounting forms are presented on rulings to emphasize structure and help students quickly learn how to prepare these documents.

Multi-layer presentation **work sheet acetates** (Chapter 5) show step-by-step progress.

The **statement of cash flows** coverage reflects its importance today. Students learn the basics about this financial statement in an appendix to Chapter 6.

The most current **payroll** information is presented in two chapters (Chapters 9 and 10) to take advantage of the natural break between employee and employer taxes and related issues.

The topics of **sales and cash receipts** and **purchases and cash payments** are presented consecutively in Chapters 11 and 12. This organization promotes a clear understanding of how these important concepts tie together.

Voucher system coverage (Chapter 13) immediately follows purchases and cash payments (Chapter 12) so that students can see the voucher system as a natural expansion of accounting for purchases.

Accounts receivable and **notes receivable** are presented in this order to enhance student comprehension. The simpler subject of accounts receivable is covered first (Chapter 16) so that students can better understand notes receivable (Chapter 17).

Depreciation methods are introduced in Chapter 5 with some detailing in that chapter's appendix. A more in-depth study occurs in Chapter 19, when long-term assets are covered.

Arrow pointers and text pointers emphasize the sources and calculations of numbers.

Chapter-ending activities reinforce learning.

Key Points provide an effective review of important information covered in each chapter.

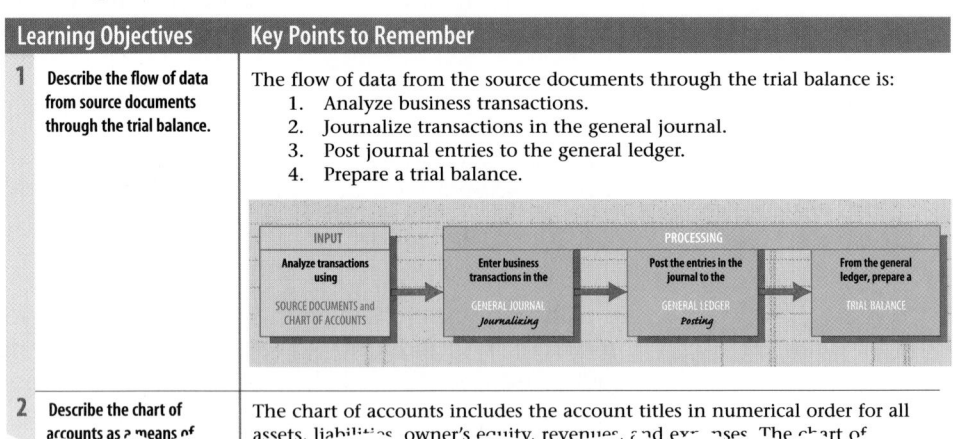

Learning Objectives	Key Points to Remember
1 Describe the flow of data from source documents through the trial balance.	The flow of data from the source documents through the trial balance is: 1. Analyze business transactions. 2. Journalize transactions in the general journal. 3. Post journal entries to the general ledger. 4. Prepare a trial balance.
2 Describe the chart of accounts as a means of	The chart of accounts includes the account titles in numerical order for all assets, liabilities, owner's equity, revenues, and expenses. The chart of

Key Terms are defined at the end of each chapter, and the page of their first appearance is listed.

The **Demonstration Problem** brings together key concepts and principles. Students can work through the problems and solutions independently to gain confidence before working the homework assignments. The problems are also effective for in-class examples. Selected problems may be solved using the General Ledger Software: these are designated by an icon.

Review Questions for each chapter help students understand and assimilate the important points covered and determine where additional review is required.

Managing Your Writing, introduced in a Chapter 1 module, guides students through an easy-to-follow, 12-step process for honing writing skills. An assignment at the end of each chapter allows students to apply critical thinking and writing skills to issues raised by material in that chapter.

W & D

A & B Exercises and Problems, keyed to chapter learning objectives, provide a range of instructional choices. One set can be used in class and the other for assignments. Alternatively, both sets can be used for practice for students needing extra assistance. Selected problems may be solved using the General Ledger Software. These are designated by an icon that is labeled with a "W" if solvable using the Windows®-based version and "W" and "D" if solvable using either the Windows®-based or the DOS-based software.

Mastery Problems challenge students to apply the essential elements introduced in the chapter. Selected problems may be solved using the General Ledger Software: these are designated by an icon.

What makes our package simply the best?

With this edition, you have access to an unsurpassed, total teaching and learning package. All materials have been verified multiple times to guarantee an accurate, error-free text and package. The wide array of materials makes it easy to tailor this text to your class.

> "I have used your text and supporting materials for many years and continue to find it to be superior to anything on the market that crosses my desk."
> Greg Marcarelli
> The Westchester Business Institute,
> Pearl River, NY

FOR THE INSTRUCTOR

The expanded **Instructor's Resource Guide**, written by Mary Elizabeth Ray of Indiana Business College, contains a wealth of resources to help instructors augment the classroom experience, including enhanced chapter outlines, references to exhibits, suggested enrichments and activities, pretests, transparency masters of the PowerPoint® Presentation slides, and check figures. The check figures are also available separately in packages of 25.

The **Solutions Manual** provides complete, carefully verified solutions for Review Questions, Managing Your Writing Activities, Ethics Cases, Series A & B Exercises and Problems, Mastery Problems, and Comprehensive Problems. Solutions are shown on accounting rulings where appropriate. These are also the solutions to the working papers.

Solutions Transparencies are available for Series A & B Exercises and Problems, Mastery Problems, and Comprehensive Problems. Where appropriate, solutions appear on accounting rulings.

Study Guide Solutions are available for the instructor. They may be packaged with the study guide at the instructor's discretion. The solutions to all study guide review questions, exercises, and problems are included. The end-of-chapter/working paper solutions are not included.

A printed **Test Bank and two electronic versions** simplify test preparation. The Test Bank resource has been doubled, offering instructors twice as many options with a selection of multiple choice, true-false, matching, fill-in-the-blank, and short problems. Windows® and DOS versions of the computerized test banks are also available.

Achievement Tests and Keys, written by Tabitha Hosty of Bradford School, are available. These contain A and B tests for each chapter.

Teaching Transparencies provide many of the text illustrations for use in classroom presentations.

New!   **PowerPoint® Presentations,** created by John Woeste of Miami-Jacobs College, provide a continuing story that illustrates the concepts being presented in Chapters 2–10. For maximum student interest, this ongoing accounting study is based on the development of a rock band which starts out as a service business. A PowerPoint® viewer is included with the software. The transparency masters for these slides are included in the Instructor's Resource Guide.

Videos are available for Chapters 1–15 of the text. The videos highlight key points of each chapter and present a problem and solution that correlates with the topics addressed in the chapter.

COMPREHENSIVE STUDENT PACKAGE

Study Guide and Working Papers are combined into one convenient resource with this edition. Students have a variety of aids at their fingertips, including chapter outlines tied to the learning objectives, review questions, exercises, problems, and accounting rulings and forms tailored to the text's end-of-chapter assignments. Separate books are available for Chapters 1–10, Chapters 1–15, and Chapters 1–28.

General Ledger Software, developed by Klooster, Allen, and Allen, is available for use with selected problems. As students use the opening balances, chart of accounts, and set-up functions to complete problems, they gain valuable, hands-on experience with full-functioning general ledger software. (An Inspector Disk is available for instructors.)

Peachtree 5.0 for College Accounting, developed by Warren Allen, is available for use with selected problems. This product allows students to learn how to use real-world accounting software while working through assignments. A student instruction book accompanies the software.

Tutorial Software reinforces concepts, allowing students to review text material for studying and preparing for tests.

Practice Sets contain realistic source documents to help simulate simple accounting cycles for service and retail business in a sole proprietorship environment. Both practice sets can be solved either manually or with the Practice Set General Ledger Software, packaged free with each copy of the practice sets. The GL software contains both DOS and Windows® versions and a Key is available with an Inspector Disk.

Star Express Cleaning Service, by Janet Caruso of Briarcliffe College, is a sole-proprietorship service business simulation for use after Chapter 8. It reviews the accounting cycle, the combination journal, and accounting for cash.

Best Bargain TV & Appliances, by Toni R. Hartley, Laurel Business Institute, is a sole-proprietorship merchandising business. This set, for use after Chapter 15, emphasizes payroll and the use of special journals and subsidiary ledgers.

Sun Coast Surf Products, Inc., by Kim Belden of Daytona Beach Community College, gives students hands-on experience with a departmentalized wholesaler operating as a corporation. The set, for use after Chapter 26, requires preparation of financial statements and ratio analysis.

Check Figures for Series A & B Exercises and Problems and Mastery Problems are also available on separate printed sheets, packaged in sets of 25 copies.

OTHER CLASSROOM AIDS

As the world leader in accounting publishing, South-Western College Publishing offers a variety of resources designed to enhance the *College Accounting* course.

▶ **Accounting for a Legal Office** and **Accounting for a Medical Office** provide additional coverage of specialized accounting procedures for students preparing for a career in the legal or medical fields.

▶ **Integrated Accounting**, available for Windows® or DOS, provides accounting applications for proprietorships, partnerships, and corporations; service and merchandising businesses; departmentalized and nondepartmentalized businesses; and voucher systems.

▶ **Using QuickBooks** is the first text of its kind to provide a self-paced environment where students use a commercially-available software product to analyze, interpret, and investigate accounting information to make business decisions.

▶ **BusinessLink Videos**, one for financial accounting and one for managerial accounting, present segments on the following topics: financial—internal controls, inventory, long-term assets, accounting information systems, financing through debt and equity, and financial statement analysis; managerial—activity-based costing, just-in-time principles, incremental analysis, performance evaluation, and quality control. Real companies are featured. A student workbook and a related instructor's manual are available for each of the videos.

WHAT MAKES OUR SERVICE SIMPLY THE BEST?

"I have taught for 22 years and have used your textbook for at least 15 of these years. The support your company gives is wonderful."

Thomas E. Lynch
Hocking College,
The Plains, OH

The entire Heintz/Parry team is ready to help **instructors**.

▶ **Your South-Western Representative** is always available to provide individualized assistance.

▶ The **Heintz/Parry Web site** at http://heintz.swcollege.com gives you access to supplement downloads, a help line, teaching ideas, hot links, and more.

▶ Call the **Academic Resource Center** for desk copies and product information:
   Career College Customers: 800-477-3692
   Community College or University Customers: 800-423-0563

▶ Call the **Preferred Accounting Customer Hotline** for special requests:
   800-342-8798

▶ **E-mail the authors** through the hot link at http://heintz.swcollege.com

ACKNOWLEDGMENTS

We thank the following individuals for their helpful contributions in assisting us in the revision of *College Accounting*.

Rosemarie D. Afflick
College of the Desert
Joanne K. Anderson
Mount Marty College and Lake Area Technical Institute
Linda Bath
Hinds Community College
Janet L. Batman
Indian Hills Community College
Paul E. Bayes
East Tennessee State University
Kim Belden
Daytona Beach Community College
Susan Bowers
South Hills Business School
Suzanne Bradford
Angelina College
Terry M. Brown
Cincinnati College of Mortuary Science
Madelyn Bruning
Pueblo Community College
Anita Carbone
Ohlone College
Janet Caruso
Briarcliffe College
Virginia Choate
American Commercial College
Stan Chow
Mission College
Diana V. Cole
University of New Mexico
Joyce M. Collins
Holmes Community College——Grenada
Karley R. Cooper
Louisiana Technical College
Marcus E. Crawford
Hillsborough Community College
Richard Crutcher
Kilgore College
Jean Danner
Orangeburg-Calhoun Technical College
Richard Dugger
Kilgore College
Diane Emery-Jackson
Camelot Career College
Bill Faulk
Northwestern Michigan College
Valerie Fisher
Southern Illinois University
Rebecca M. Floor
Greenville Technical College

Harry Gray
Ivy Tech State College
James A. Guyos
St. Clair County Community College
James A. Hall
Lehigh University
James Halstead
Clatsop Community College
Douglas S. Hamilton
Berkeley College
Judith Hansen
Waukesha County Technical College
Juanita Hanson
North Iowa Area Community College
Toni R. Hartley
Laurel Business Institute
Sueann Hely
Paducah Community College
Sandra Herkowitz
Mildred Elley Business School
Nancy Hicks
Tallahassee Community College
Tabitha L. Hosty
Bradford School
Dawn A. Humburg
Iowa Central Community College
Gerald F. Jedlicka
Trinity Valley Community College
Charlie L. Jones
National Business College
Jack Kappeler
Eastern Wyoming College
Lolita Keck
Globe College of Business
Linda G. Kennedy
College of the Sequoias
Judy Kidder
Mohave Community College
S. B. Klopp
Palm Beach Community College
Sam Lanzafame
Bryant & Stratton
Keith R. Leeseberg
Manatee Community College
Judy Lingo
Lane Community College
Thomas E. Lynch
Hocking College
Fred McCracken
Indiana Business College
Linda F. McIlwain
Louisiana Technical College

Marvin F. Mai
Empire College

Greg Marcarelli
The Westchester Business Institute

Ruth Marin
National Business College

Jerry May
Northwest Arkansas Community College

Alan W. Middleton
Commonwealth College

Lorraine W. Minton
Caldwell Community College and Technical Institute

Paul Muller
Western Nevada Community College

Al Nelson
Nicolet Area Technical College

Patricia Olson
Moraine Park Technical College

Frank A. Paliotta
Berkeley College

Dana Pepper
Western Dakota Technical Institute

Erick G. Pifer
Lake Michigan College

Pat Prugh
East Central College

Tianay Rabb
Cisco Junior College

Mary Elizabeth Ray
Indiana Business College

James R. Reap
Indian River Community College

Mary Beth Robbins
Herzing College

Eugene G. Saatmann
Eastern Arizona College

Roman S. Salazar
Modesto Junior College

John H. Scott
National Business College

J. Curt Sharp
Lakeshore Technical College

Alice Sineath
Forsyth Technical College

Paul Siragusa
Delgado College

Jeannine M. Sparks
Eldorado College

Thomas F. Stander
Southern Ohio College

Michelle Stobnicke
Santa Fe Community College

Mary Ann Swindelhurst
Carroll Community College

Ivan D. Terrill
Gateway Technical College

Edwin J. Thieman
Kilgore College

Jim D. Thomas
Cosumnes River College

Mary Jane Thomson
Alpena Community College

Thomas H. Tolan
Plaza Business Institute

Richard Tuttrup
Fresno City College

Sheila Viel
University of Wisconsin-Milwaukee

Al Walczak
Linn-Benton Community College

Cynthia Weiske
Duluth Business University

Nancy T. Weller
Grand Rapids Community College

Mary Ann Whitehurst
Griffin Technical Institute

John Woeste
Miami-Jacobs College

Douglas R. Yost
Crown College

Special thanks to Carmen Leichty, David Daniels, Jane Parry, and Andrea Heintz for assistance in the development of this text.

Through 15 editions, *College Accounting* has helped millions of students understand and employ basic accounting skills. But we know we can't rest on past success. The business world continues to change. And so do we. To prepare today's generation for a lifetime of accounting skills, the solution is simple. Depend on the text that's **simply the best.**

College Accounting, 16e. From the leader in college accounting, you wouldn't expect anything less.

—*Jim Heintz*
—*Rob Parry*

CONTENTS
IN BRIEF

CONTENTS

PART 2   SPECIALIZED ACCOUNTING PROCEDURES FOR SERVICE BUSINESSES AND PROPRIETORSHIPS

PART 4 SPECIALIZED ACCOUNTING PROCEDURES FOR MERCHANDISING BUSINESSES AND PARTNERSHIPS

PART 1

Accounting for a Service Business

1

Introduction to Accounting

LEARNING OBJECTIVES:
Careful study of this chapter should enable you to:

LO 1 Describe the purpose of accounting.

LO 2 Describe the accounting process.

LO 3 Define three types of business ownership structures.

LO 4 Classify different types of businesses by activities.

LO 5 Identify career opportunities in accounting.

So, you have decided to study accounting. Good decision. A solid foundation in accounting concepts and techniques will be helpful. This is true whether you take a professional position in accounting or business, or simply want to better understand your personal finances and dealings with businesses.

Throughout Chapters 2 through 6, we will introduce Jessie Jane's Campus Delivery service. By studying Jessie's business transactions and accounting techniques, you will learn about business and accounting. This is a major advantage of studying accounting. While studying accounting, you also learn a lot about business.

Knowledge of how accounting works will help you evaluate the financial health of businesses and other organizations. It will also give you a solid approach to dealing with financial and business transactions in your personal life. How do you plan to use the accounting skills developed in this class?

Accounting is the language of business. You must learn this language to understand the impact of economic events on a specific company. Common, everyday terms have very precise meanings when used in accounting. For example, you have probably heard terms like asset, liability, revenue, expense, and net income. Take a moment to jot down how you would define each of these terms. After reading and studying Chapter 2, compare your definitions with those developed in this text. This comparison will show whether you can trust your current understanding of accounting terms. Whether you intend to pursue a career in accounting or simply wish to understand the impact of business transactions, you need a clear understanding of this language.

THE PURPOSE OF ACCOUNTING

LO 1   Describe the purpose of accounting.

The purpose of accounting is to provide financial information about the current operations and financial condition of a business to individuals, agencies, and organizations. As shown in Figure 1-1, owners, managers, creditors, and government agencies all need accounting information. Other users of accounting information include customers, clients, labor unions, stock exchanges, and financial analysts.

FIGURE 1-1 Users of Accounting Information

USER	INFORMATION NEEDED	DECISIONS MADE BY USERS
Owners— Present and future	Company's profitability and current financial condition.	If business is good, owners may consider making additional investments for growth. If business is poor, they may want to talk to management to find out why and may consider closing the business.
Managers— May or may not own business	Detailed measures of business performance.	Managers need to make operating decisions. How much and what kinds of inventory should be carried? Is business strong enough to support higher wages for employees?
Creditors— Present and future	Company's profitability, debt outstanding, and assets that could be used to secure debt.	Should a loan be granted to this business? If so, what amount of debt can the business support and what interest rate should be charged?
Government Agencies— National, state, and local	Company's profitability, cash flows, and overall financial condition.	The IRS will decide how much income tax the business must pay. Local governments may be willing to adjust property taxes paid by the business to encourage it to stay in town.

THE ACCOUNTING PROCESS

LO 2   Describe the accounting process.

Accounting is a system of gathering financial information about a business and reporting this information to users. The six major steps of the accounting process are analyzing, recording, classifying, summarizing, reporting, and interpreting (Figure 1-2). Computers are often used in the recording, classifying, summarizing, and reporting steps. Whether or not computers are used, the accounting concepts and techniques are the same. Information entered into the computer system must reflect a proper application of these concepts. Otherwise, the output will be meaningless.

FIGURE 1-2 The Accounting Process

▶ **Analyzing** is looking at events that have taken place and thinking about how they affect the business.

▶ **Recording** is entering financial information about events into the accounting system. Although this can be done with paper and pencil, most businesses use computers to perform routine record-keeping operations.

▶ **Classifying** is sorting and grouping similar items together rather than merely keeping a simple, diary-like record of numerous events.

▶ **Summarizing** is bringing the various items of information together to determine a result.

▶ **Reporting** is telling the results. In accounting, it is common to use tables of numbers to report results.

▶ **Interpreting** is deciding the meaning and importance of the information in various reports. This may include percentage analyses and the use of ratios to help explain how pieces of information relate to one another.

Generally accepted accounting principles (GAAP) are followed during the accounting process. The Financial Accounting Standards Board develops these accounting rules, called GAAP, to provide procedures and guidelines to be followed in the accounting and reporting process. These rules provide some assurance that companies are reporting business activities in a similar manner. This allows users of financial statements to evaluate a company's financial performance and make comparisons with other companies.

THREE TYPES OF OWNERSHIP STRUCTURES

LO 3   Define three types of business ownership structures.

One or more persons may own a business. Businesses are classified according to who owns them and the specific way they are organized. Three types of ownership structures are (1) sole proprietorship, (2) partnership, and (3) corporation (Figure 1-3). Accountants provide information to owners of all three types of ownership structures.

Sole Proprietorship

A **sole proprietorship** is owned by one person. The owner is often called a proprietor. The proprietor often manages the business. The owner assumes all risks for the business, and personal assets can be taken to pay creditors. The advantage of a sole proprietorship is that the owner can make all decisions.

FIGURE 1-3 Types of Ownership Structures—Advantages and Disadvantages

Partnership

A **partnership** is owned by more than one person. One or more partners may manage the business. Like proprietors, partners assume the risks for the business, and their assets may be taken to pay creditors. An advantage of a partnership is that owners share risks and decision making. A disadvantage is that partners may disagree about the best way to run the business.

Corporation

A **corporation** is owned by stockholders (or shareholders). Corporations may have many owners, and they usually employ professional managers. The owners' risk is usually limited to their initial investment, and they often have very little influence on the business decisions.

> Most businesses in the United States operate as sole proprietorships or partnerships. However, corporations earn the highest amount of revenue. The largest corporations in the United States are known as the "Fortune 500."

TYPES OF BUSINESSES

LO 4 Classify different types of businesses by activities.

Businesses are classified according to the type of service or product provided. Some businesses provide a service. Others sell a product. A business that provides a service is called a **service business**. A business that buys a product from another business to sell to customers is called a **merchandising business**. A business that makes a product to sell is called a **manufacturing business**. You will learn about all three types of businesses in this book. Figure 1-4 lists examples of types of businesses organized by activity.

FIGURE 1-4 Types and Examples of Businesses Organized by Activities

SERVICES	MERCHANDISING	MANUFACTURING
Travel Agency	Department Store	Automobile Manufacturer
Computer Consultant	Pharmacy	Furniture Maker
Physician	Jewelry Store	Toy Factory

A BROADER VIEW

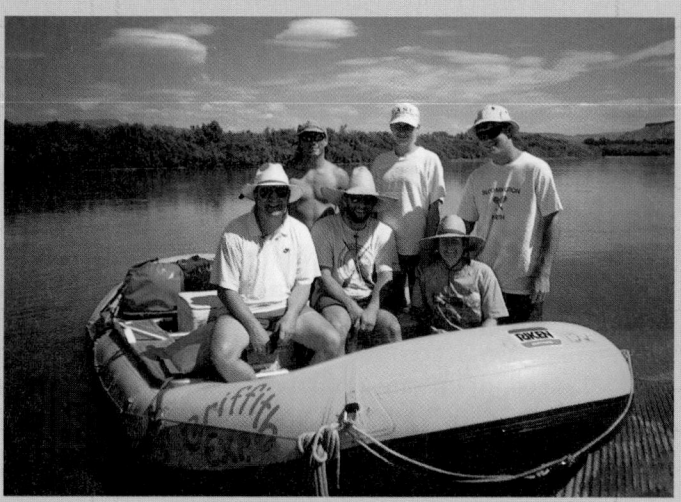

ALL KINDS OF BUSINESSES NEED ACCOUNTING SYSTEMS

Even small businesses like the one that took the Parry family on a two-day, white-water rafting trip down the Colorado River need good accounting systems. Proper records must be maintained for the cost of the rafts, food served, tour guides' salaries (second and third from left), and office expenses. Without this information, the company would not know how much to charge and whether a profit is made on these trips.

CAREER OPPORTUNITIES IN ACCOUNTING

LO 5 Identify career opportunities in accounting.

ACCOUNTING CLERK
Travel agency is looking for an accounting clerk to handle bookkeeping tasks. 1–3 years experience with an automated accounting system required.

Accounting offers many career opportunities. The positions described below require varying amounts of education, experience, and technological skill.

Accounting Clerks

Businesses with large quantities of accounting tasks to perform daily often employ **accounting clerks** to record, sort, and file accounting information. Often accounting clerks will specialize in cash, payroll, accounts receivable, accounts payable, inventory, or purchases. As a result, they are involved with only a small portion of the total accounting responsibilities for the firm. Accounting clerks usually have at least one year of accounting education.

Bookkeepers and Para-Accountants

BOOKKEEPING/ACCOUNTING
Service company has an opening for a full charge bookkeeper/accountant. Previous accounting experience with an associate degree preferred. Salary commensurate with experience. Excellent knowledge of LOTUS 1-2-3® or Excel® required.

Bookkeepers generally supervise the work of accounting clerks, help with daily accounting work, and summarize accounting information. In small-to-medium-sized businesses, the bookkeeper may also help managers and owners interpret the accounting information. Bookkeepers usually have one to two years of accounting education and experience as an accounting clerk.

Para-accountants provide many accounting, auditing, or tax services under the direct supervision of an accountant. A typical para-accountant has a two-year degree or significant accounting and bookkeeping experience.

Accountants

ACCOUNTANT
Responsibilities include accounts receivable, accounts payable, and general ledger. Familiarity with computerized systems a must. Supervisory experience a plus.

The difference between accountants and bookkeepers is not always clear, particularly in smaller companies where bookkeepers also help interpret the accounting information. In large companies, the distinction is clearer. Bookkeepers focus on the processing of accounting data. **Accountants** design the accounting information system and focus on analyzing and interpreting information. They also look for important trends in the data and study the impact of alternative decisions.

Most accountants enter the field with a college degree in accounting. Accountants are employed in public accounting, private (managerial) accounting, and in governmental and not-for-profit accounting (Figure 1-5).

FIGURE 1-5 Accounting Careers

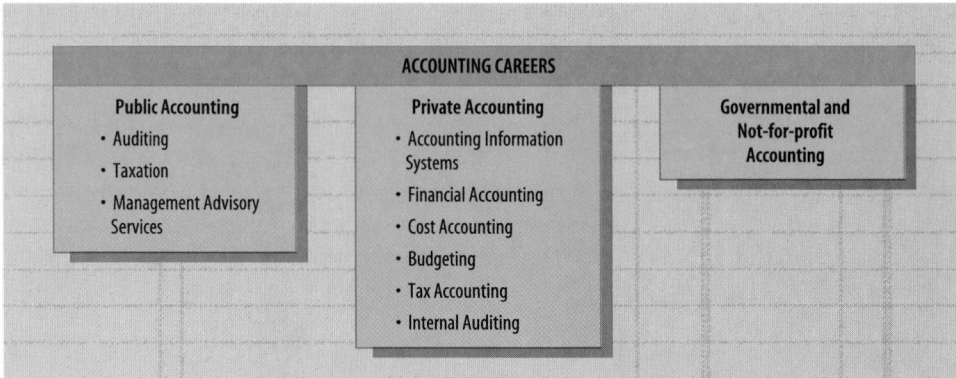

ACCOUNTING CAREERS		
Public Accounting	**Private Accounting**	**Governmental and Not-for-profit Accounting**
• Auditing	• Accounting Information Systems	
• Taxation	• Financial Accounting	
• Management Advisory Services	• Cost Accounting	
	• Budgeting	
	• Tax Accounting	
	• Internal Auditing	

Public Accounting. Public accountants offer services in much the same way as doctors and lawyers. The public accountant can achieve professional recognition as a **Certified Public Accountant** (CPA). This is done by meeting certain educational and experience requirements as determined by each state, and passing a uniform examination prepared by the American Institute of Certified Public Accountants.

Many CPAs work alone, while others work for local, regional, or national accounting firms that vary in scope and size. The largest public accounting firms in the United States are known as the "Big Six." They are Arthur Andersen & Co., Coopers and Lybrand, Deloitte and Touche, Ernst & Young, KPMG Peat Marwick, and Price Waterhouse & Co.

Services offered by public accountants are listed below.

▶ **Auditing.** Auditing involves the application of standard review and testing procedures to be certain that proper accounting policies and practices have been followed. The purpose of the audit is to provide an independent opinion that the financial information about a business is fairly presented in a manner consistent with generally accepted accounting principles.

▶ **Taxation.** Tax specialists advise on tax planning, prepare tax returns, and represent clients before governmental agencies such as the Internal Revenue Service.

▶ **Management Advisory Services.** Given the financial training and business experience of public accountants, many businesses seek their advice on a wide variety of managerial issues. Often, accounting firms are involved in designing computerized accounting systems.

Private (Managerial) Accounting. Many accountants are employees of private business firms. The **controller** oversees the entire accounting process and is the principal accounting officer of the company. Private or managerial accountants perform a wide variety of services for the business. These services are listed below.

▶ **Accounting Information Systems.** Accountants in this area design and implement manual and computerized accounting systems.

▶ **Financial Accounting.** Based on the accounting data prepared by the bookkeepers and accounting clerks, accountants prepare various reports and financial statements and help in analyzing operating, investing, and financing decisions.

▶ **Cost Accounting.** The cost of producing specific products or providing services must be measured. Further analysis is also done to determine whether the products and services are produced in the most cost-effective manner.

▶ **Budgeting.** In the budgeting process, accountants help managers develop a financial plan.

▶ **Tax Accounting.** Instead of hiring a public accountant, a company may have its own accountants. They focus on tax planning, preparation of tax returns, and dealing with the Internal Revenue Service and other governmental agencies.

▶ **Internal Auditing.** Internal auditors review the operating and accounting control procedures adopted by management to make sure the controls are adequate and are being followed. They also monitor the accuracy and timeliness of the reports provided to management and to external parties.

A managerial accountant can achieve professional status as a **Certified Management Accountant** (CMA). This is done by passing a uniform examination offered by the Institute of Management Accountants. An internal auditor can achieve professional recognition as a **Certified Internal Auditor** (CIA) by passing the uniform examination offered by the Institute of Internal Auditors.

Governmental and Not-for-Profit Accounting. Thousands of governmental and not-for-profit organizations (states, cities, schools, churches, and hospitals) gather and report financial information. These organizations employ a large number of accountants. Since these entities are not profit-oriented, the rules are somewhat different for governmental and not-for-profit organizations. However, many accounting procedures are similar to those found in profit-seeking enterprises.

CONTROLLER
$45,000–$50,000
Service company seeks financial manager to oversee all general accounting and financial reporting. PC skills important. 4+ years in corporate or public accounting will qualify.

ACCOUNTANT
Assist fiscal officer in not-for-profit accounting. Experience in payroll, payroll taxes, and LOTUS 1-2-3 or Excel helpful. Qualifications: accounting degree or equivalent. $25–$28K.

Job Opportunities

Job growth in some areas will be much greater than in others. Newspaper advertisements often indicate that accountants and accounting clerks are expected to have computer skills. Computer skills definitely increase the opportunities available to you in your career. Almost every business needs accountants, accounting clerks, and bookkeepers. Figure 1-6 shows the expected growth for different types of businesses. Notice that growth will be greatest in the service businesses. Chapters 2 through 10 introduce accounting skills that you will need to work in a service business. Chapter 11 begins the discussion of merchandising businesses. Accounting for manufacturing businesses is addressed in the last chapters of the book.

Figure 1-7 shows the expected demand for accounting skills. Although a small drop in demand is expected for bookkeeping, accounting, and auditing clerks, these types of positions will offer the highest number of job opportunities over the next several years. The next highest demand is for accountants and auditors and this demand is expected to increase over the next several years.

FIGURE 1-6 Expected Growth   **FIGURE 1-7** Expected Demand

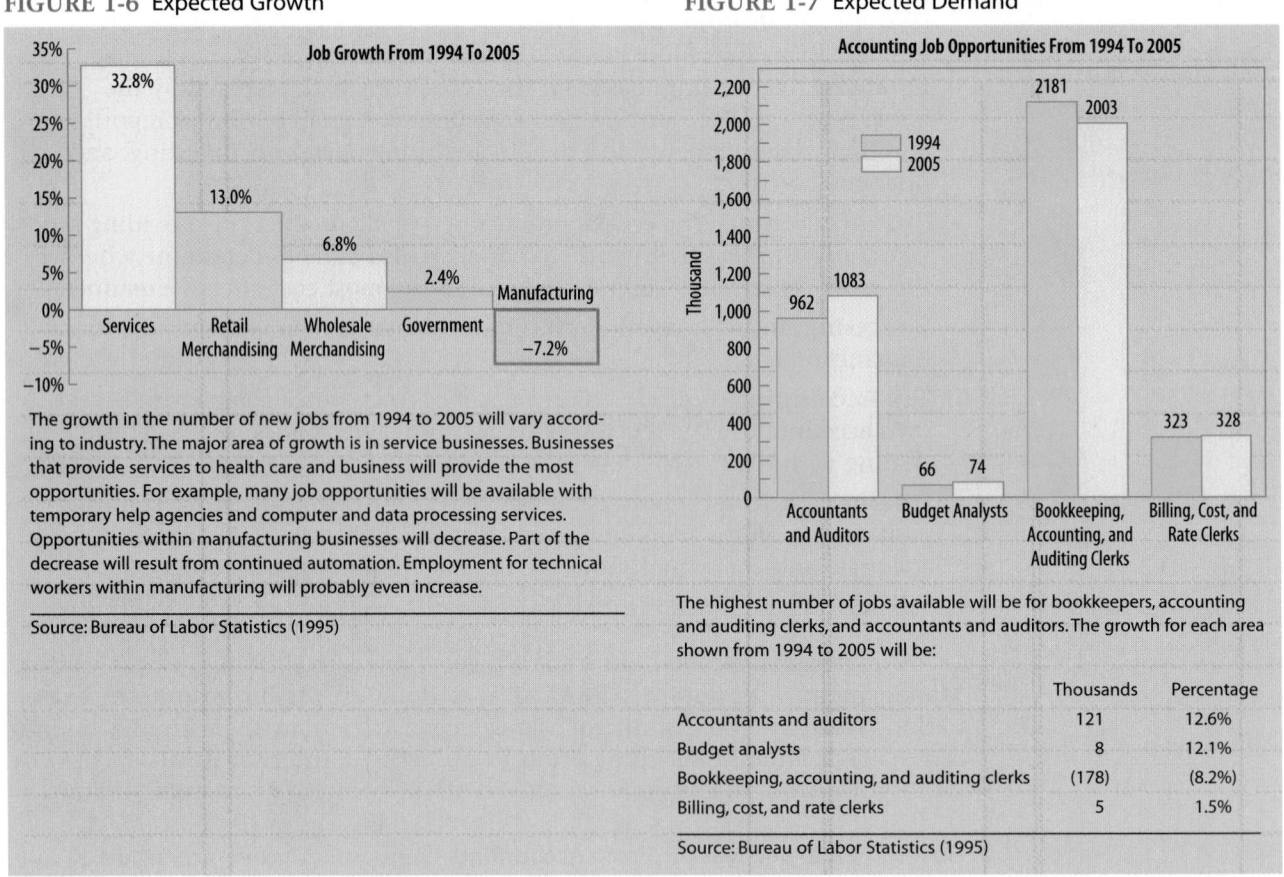

The growth in the number of new jobs from 1994 to 2005 will vary according to industry. The major area of growth is in service businesses. Businesses that provide services to health care and business will provide the most opportunities. For example, many job opportunities will be available with temporary help agencies and computer and data processing services. Opportunities within manufacturing businesses will decrease. Part of the decrease will result from continued automation. Employment for technical workers within manufacturing will probably even increase.

Source: Bureau of Labor Statistics (1995)

The highest number of jobs available will be for bookkeepers, accounting and auditing clerks, and accountants and auditors. The growth for each area shown from 1994 to 2005 will be:

	Thousands	Percentage
Accountants and auditors	121	12.6%
Budget analysts	8	12.1%
Bookkeeping, accounting, and auditing clerks	(178)	(8.2%)
Billing, cost, and rate clerks	5	1.5%

Source: Bureau of Labor Statistics (1995)

Regardless of the type of career you desire, writing skills are important in business and your personal life. Becoming a good writer requires practice and a strategy for the process used to prepare memos, letters, and other documents. On pages 9 and 10, Ken Davis offers an excellent approach to managing your writing. Take a moment to read Ken's tips. Then, practice his approach by completing the writing assignments as you finish each chapter.

MANAGING YOUR WRITING

Ken Davis

*H*ere's a secret: the business writing that you and I do—the writing that gets the world's work done—requires no special gift. It can be *managed*, like any other business process.

Managing writing is largely a matter of managing time. Writing is a process, and like any process it can be done efficiently or inefficiently. Unfortunately, most of us are pretty inefficient writers. That's because we try to get each word, each sentence, right the first time. Given a letter to write, we begin with the first sentence. We think about that sentence, write it, revise it, even check its spelling, before going on to the second sentence. In an hour of writing, we might spend 45 or 50 minutes doing this kind of detailed drafting. We spend only a few minutes on overall planning at the beginning and only a few minutes on overall revising at the end.

That approach to writing is like building a house by starting with the front door: planning, building, finishing—even washing the windows—before doing anything with the rest of the house. No wonder most of us have so much trouble writing.

Efficient, effective writers take better charge of their writing time. They *manage* their writing. Like building contractors, they spend time planning before they start construction. Once construction has started, they don't try to do all of the finishing touches as they go.

As the illustration below shows, many good writers break their writing process into three main stages: planning, drafting, and revising. They spend more time at the first and third stages than at the second. They also build in some "management" time at the beginning and the end, and some break time in the middle. To manage *your* writing time, try the following steps.

At the MANAGING stage (perhaps two or three minutes for a one-hour writing job), remind yourself that writing *can* be managed and that it's largely a matter of managing time. Plan your next hour.

At the PLANNING stage (perhaps 20 minutes out of the hour):

1. **Find the "we."** Define the community to which you and your reader belong. Then ask, "How are my reader and I alike and different?"—in knowledge, attitudes, and circumstances.

2. **Define your purpose.** Remember the advice a consultant once gave Stanley Tool executives: "You're not in the business of making drills; you're in the business of making holes." Too many of us lose sight of the difference between making drills and making holes when we write letters and memos. We focus on the piece of writing—the tool itself—not its purpose. The result: our writing often misses the chance to be as effective as it could be. When you're still at the planning stage, focus on the outcome you want, not on the means you will use to achieve it.

3. **Get your stuff together.** Learn from those times when you've turned a one-hour home-improvement project into a three- or four-hour job by having to make repeated trips to the hardware store for tools or parts. Before you start the drafting stage of writing, collect the information you need.

4. **Get your ducks in a row.** Decide on the main points you want to make. Then, make a list or rough outline placing your points in the most logical order.

At the DRAFTING stage (perhaps 5 minutes out of the hour):

5. **Do it wrong the first time.** Do a "quick and dirty" draft, without editing. Think of your draft as a "prototype," written not for the end user but for your own testing and improvement. Stopping to edit while you draft breaks your train of thought and keeps you from being a good writer. (Hint: if you are writing at a computer, try turning off the monitor during the drafting stage.)

At the BREAK stage (perhaps 5 minutes):

6. **Take a break and change hats.** Get away from your draft, even if for only a few minutes. Come back with a fresh perspective—the reader's perspective.

At the REVISING stage (perhaps 25 minutes):

7. **Signal your turns.** Just as if you were driving a car, you're leading your reader through new territory. Use "turn signals"—*and, in addition, but, however, or, therefore, because, for example*—to guide your reader from sentence to sentence.

8. **Say what you mean.** Put the point of your sentences in the subjects and verbs. For example, revise "There are drawbacks to using this accounting method" to "This accounting method has some drawbacks." You'll be saying what you mean, and you'll be a more effective communicator.

9. **Pay by the word.** Reading your memo requires work. If your sentences are wordy and you are slow to get to the point, the reader may decide that it is not worth the effort. Pretend you are paying the reader by the word to read your memo. Then, revise your memo to make it as short and to the point as possible.

10. **Translate into English.** Keep your words simple. (Lee Iacocca put both these tips in one "commandment of good management": "Say it in English and keep it short.") Remember that you write to express, not impress.

11. **Finish the job.** Check your spelling, punctuation, and mechanics.

Finally, at the MANAGING stage again (2 to 3 minutes):

12. **Evaluate your writing process.** Figure out how to improve it next time.

By following these 12 steps, you can take charge of your writing time. Begin today to *manage your writing.* As a United Technologies Corporation advertisement in *The Wall Street Journal* admonished, "If you want to manage somebody, manage yourself. Do that well and you'll be ready to stop managing and start leading."

Dr. Ken Davis is Professor of English and coordinator of the Applied Writing Group at Indiana University-Purdue University at Indianapolis. He is president of Komei, Inc., a global communication consulting company.

Learning Objectives	Key Points to Remember
1 Describe the purpose of accounting.	The purpose of accounting is to provide financial information about a business to individuals and organizations.
2 Describe the accounting process.	The six major steps of the accounting process are analyzing, recording, classifying, summarizing, reporting, and interpreting.
3 Define three types of business ownership structures.	Three types of business ownership structures are sole proprietorship, partnership, and corporation.
4 Classify different types of businesses by activities.	Different types of businesses classified by activities are a service business, a merchandising business, and a manufacturing business.
5 Identify career opportunities in accounting.	Career opportunities in accounting include work in public accounting, private accounting, and governmental and not-for-profit accounting.

Reflection: Answering the Opening Question

Of course, your answer to the opening question depends on your specific plans. In general, though, accounting skills are helpful in all kinds of business, nonprofit, and personal activities. As discussed in the chapter, accounting knowledge is important when working in all types of businesses: service, merchandising, and manufacturing. It is also helpful regardless of the ownership structure: sole proprietorship, partnership, or corporation.

KEY TERMS

accountant, (6)   Designs the accounting information system and focuses on analyzing and interpreting information.

accounting, (3)   A system of gathering financial information about a business and reporting this information to users.

accounting clerk, (5)   Records, sorts, and files accounting information.

accounting information systems, (7)   Accountants in this area design and implement manual and computerized accounting systems.

analyzing, (3)   Looking at events that have taken place and thinking about how they affect the business.

auditing, (7)   Reviewing and testing to be certain that proper accounting policies and practices have been followed.

bookkeeper, (6)   Generally supervises the work of accounting clerks, helps with daily accounting work, and summarizes accounting information.

budgeting, (7)   The process in which accountants help managers develop a financial plan.

Certified Internal Auditor, (7)   An internal auditor who has achieved professional recognition by passing the uniform examination offered by the Institute of Internal Auditors.

Certified Management Accountant, (7)   An accountant who has passed an examination offered by the Institute of Management Accountants.

Certified Public Accountant, (6)   A public accountant who has met certain educational and experience requirements and has passed an examination prepared by the American Institute of Certified Public Accountants.

classifying, (3)   Sorting and grouping similar items together rather than merely keeping a simple, diary-like record of numerous events.

controller, (7)   The accountant who oversees the entire accounting process and is the principal accounting officer of a company.

corporation, (4)   A type of ownership structure in which stockholders own the business. The owners' risk is usually limited to their initial investment, and they usually have very little influence on the business decisions.

cost accounting, (7)   Determining the cost of producing specific products or providing services and analyzing for cost effectiveness.

financial accounting, (7)   Includes preparing various reports and financial statements and analyzing operating, investing, and financing decisions.

generally accepted accounting principles (GAAP), (3)   Procedures and guidelines developed by the Financial Accounting Standards Board to be followed in the accounting and reporting process.

internal auditing, (7)   Reviewing the operating and accounting control procedures adopted by management to make sure the controls are adequate and being followed; assuring that accurate and timely information is provided.

interpreting, (3)   Deciding the meaning and importance of the information in various reports.

management advisory services, (7)   Providing advice to businesses on a wide variety of managerial issues.

manufacturing business, (4)   A business that makes a product to sell.

merchandising business, (4)   A business that buys products to sell.

para-accountant, (6)   A paraprofessional who provides many accounting, auditing, or tax services under the direct supervision of an accountant.

partnership, (4)   A type of ownership structure in which more than one person owns the business.

recording, (3)   Entering financial information about events affecting the company into the accounting system.

reporting, (3)   Telling the results of the financial information.

service business, (4)   A business that provides a service.

sole proprietorship, (4)   A type of ownership structure in which one person owns the business.

summarizing, (3)   Bringing the various items of information together to determine a result.

tax accounting, (7)   Focusing on tax planning, preparing tax returns, and dealing with the Internal Revenue Service and other governmental agencies.

taxation, (7)   See tax accounting.

REVIEW QUESTIONS

1. What is the purpose of accounting?

2. Identify four user groups normally interested in financial information about a business.

3. Identify the six major steps of the accounting process and explain each step.

4. Identify the three types of ownership structures and discuss the advantages and disadvantages of each.

5. Identify three types of businesses according to activities.

6. What are the main functions of an accounting clerk?

7. Name and describe three areas of specialization for a public accountant.

8. Name and describe six areas of specialization for a managerial accountant.

MANAGING YOUR WRITING

1. Prepare a one-page memo to your instructor that explains what you hope to learn in this course and how this knowledge will be useful to you.

2. If you started a business, what would it be? Prepare a one-page memo that describes the type of business you would enjoy the most. Would it be a service, merchandising, or manufacturing business? Explain what form of ownership you would prefer and why.

SERIES A EXERCISES

EXERCISE 1A-1 (LO 1) PURPOSE OF ACCOUNTING Match the following users with the information needed.

1. Owners

2. Managers

3. Creditors

4. Government agencies

a. Whether the firm can pay its bills on time

b. Detailed, up-to-date information to measure business performance (and plan for future operations)

c. To determine taxes to be paid and whether other regulations are met

d. The firm's current financial condition

EXERCISE 1A-2 (LO 2) ACCOUNTING PROCESS List the six major steps of the accounting process in order (1–6) and define each.

2	Recording
4	Summarizing
5	Reporting
1	Analyzing
6	Interpreting
3	Classifying

SERIES B EXERCISES

EXERCISE 1B-1 (LO 1) PURPOSE OF ACCOUNTING Describe the kind of information needed by the users listed.

Owners (present and future)

Managers

Creditors (present and future)

Government agencies

EXERCISE 1B-2 (LO 2) ACCOUNTING PROCESS Match the following steps of the accounting process with their definitions.

Analyzing	a.	Telling the results
Recording	b.	Looking at events that have taken place and thinking about how they affect the business
Classifying		
Summarizing	c.	Deciding the importance of the various reports
Reporting	d.	Bringing together information to explain a result
Interpreting	e.	Sorting and grouping like items together
	f.	Entering financial information into the accounting system

2

Analyzing Transactions: The Accounting Equation

LEARNING OBJECTIVES:
Careful study of this chapter should enable you to:

LO 1 Define the accounting elements.

LO 2 Construct the accounting equation.

LO 3 Analyze business transactions.

LO 4 Show the effects of business transactions on the accounting equation.

LO 5 Prepare and describe the purposes of a simple income statement, statement of owner's equity, and balance sheet.

LO 6 Define the three basic phases of the accounting process.

Have you ever heard the expression "garbage in, garbage out"? Computer users commonly use it to mean that if input to the computer system is not correctly entered, the output from the system will be worthless. The same expression applies in accounting. In this chapter Jessica Jane enters into many transactions while running her delivery business. For example, she purchases a motor scooter to make deliveries. To understand the impact of this event, Jessie needs to know how to properly measure the cost of the asset, estimate its useful life, and keep records of whether she paid cash or promised to make payments in the future. If Jessie does not understand the economic events affecting her delivery business and their impact on the accounting equation, the events will not be correctly entered into the accounting system. This will make the outputs from the system (the financial statements) worthless. What kinds of questions do you think Jessie should ask herself to improve her understanding of an event and its impact on the business?

The entire accounting process is based on one simple equation, called the accounting equation. In this chapter, you will learn how to use this equation to analyze business transactions. You also will learn how to prepare financial statements that report the effect of these transactions on the financial condition of a business.

THE ACCOUNTING ELEMENTS

LO 1 Define the accounting elements.

Before the accounting process can begin, the entity to be accounted for must be defined. A **business entity** is an individual, association, or organization that engages in economic activities and controls specific economic resources. This definition allows the personal and business finances of an owner to be accounted for separately.

Three basic accounting elements exist for every business entity: assets, liabilities, and owner's equity. These elements are defined below.

LEARNING KEY: Pay close attention to the definitions for the basic accounting elements. A clear understanding of these definitions will help you analyze even the most complex business transactions.

Assets

Assets are items that are owned by a business and will provide future benefits. Examples of assets include cash, merchandise, furniture, fixtures, machinery, buildings, and land. Businesses may also have an asset called **accounts receivable**. This asset represents the amount of money owed to the business by its customers as a result of making sales "on account," or "on credit." Making sales on account simply means that the customers have promised to pay sometime in the future.

Liabilities

Liabilities represent something owed to another business entity. The amount owed represents a probable future outflow of assets as a result of a past event or transaction. Liabilities are debts or obligations of the business that can be paid with cash, goods, or services.

The most common liabilities are accounts payable and notes payable. An **account payable** is an unwritten promise to pay a supplier for assets purchased or services received. Acquiring assets or services by promising to make payments in the future is referred to as making a purchase "on account," or "on credit." Formal written promises to pay suppliers or lenders specified sums of money at definite future times are known as **notes payable**.

A BROADER VIEW

ASSETS AND THE COST OF PRODUCTS WE BUY

Next time you buy something, think of all the assets that a company needs to produce that product. If the product comes from a "capital-intensive" industry, one that requires heavy investments in assets, the company must price the product high enough to cover the cost of using the assets and replacing them when they wear out. For example, General Motors recently reported that the cost of property, plant, and equipment used for operating purposes came to over $100 billion.

Owner's Equity

Owner's equity is the amount by which the business assets exceed the business liabilities. Other terms used for owner's equity include **net worth** and **capital**. If there are no business liabilities, the owner's equity is equal to the total assets.

The owner of a business may have business assets and liabilities as well as nonbusiness assets and liabilities. For example, the business owner probably owns a home, clothing, and a car, and perhaps owes the dentist for dental service. These are personal, nonbusiness assets and liabilities. According to the **business entity concept**, nonbusiness assets and liabilities are not included in the business entity's accounting records.

LEARNING KEY: The business entity's assets and liabilities are separate from the owner's nonbusiness assets and liabilities.

If the owner invests money or other assets in the business, the item invested is reclassified from a nonbusiness asset to a business asset. If the owner withdraws money or other assets from the business for personal use, the item withdrawn is reclassified from a business asset to a nonbusiness asset. These distinctions are important and allow the owner to make decisions based on the financial condition and results of the business apart from nonbusiness activities.

THE ACCOUNTING EQUATION

LO 2   Construct the accounting equation.

> The accounting equation is a very important tool to help in understanding and analyzing transactions.

The relationship between the three basic accounting elements—assets, liabilities, and owner's equity—can be expressed in the form of a simple equation known as the **accounting equation**.

Assets	=	Liabilities	+	Owner's Equity

This equation reflects the fact that both outsiders and insiders have an interest in all of the assets of a business. *Liabilities represent the outside interests of creditors. Owner's equity represents the inside interests of owners. When two elements are known, the third can always be calculated.* For example, assume that assets on December 31 total $60,400. On that same day, the business liabilities consist of $5,400 owed for equipment. Owner's equity is calculated by subtracting total liabilities from total assets, $60,400 – $5,400 = $55,000.

> The left side of the equation represents the assets. The right side of the equation shows where the money came from to buy the assets.

Assets	=	Liabilities	+	Owner's Equity
$60,400	=	$5,400	+	$55,000
$60,400	=	$60,400		

LEARNING KEY: If you know two accounting elements, you can calculate the third element.

Total assets	$60,400
Total liabilities	–5,400
Owner's equity	$55,000

ANALYZING BUSINESS TRANSACTIONS

LO 3   Analyze business transactions.

A **business transaction** is an economic event that has a direct impact on the business. A business transaction almost always requires an exchange between the business and another outside entity. We must be able to measure this exchange in dollars. Examples of business transactions include buying goods and services, selling goods and services, buying and selling assets, making loans, and borrowing money.

All business transactions affect the accounting equation through specific accounts. An **account** is a separate record used to summarize changes in each asset, liability, and owner's equity of a business. **Account titles** provide a description of the particular type of asset, liability, or owner's equity affected by a transaction.

Three basic questions must be answered when analyzing the effects of a business transaction on the accounting equation.

1. **What happened?**

   ▶ Make certain you understand the event that has taken place.

2. **Which accounts are affected?**

   ▶ Identify the accounts that are affected.

   ▶ Classify these accounts as assets, liabilities, or owner's equity.

3. **How is the accounting equation affected?**

   ▶ Determine which accounts have increased or decreased.

   ▶ Make certain that the accounting equation remains in balance after the transaction has been entered.

EFFECT OF TRANSACTIONS ON THE ACCOUNTING EQUATION

LO 4   Show the effects of business transactions on the accounting equation.

Each transaction affects one or more of the three basic accounting elements. A transaction increases or decreases specific asset, liability, or owner's equity accounts. Assume that the following transactions occurred during June 20--, the first month of operations for Jessie Jane's Campus Delivery.

Transaction (a): Investment by owner

> Remember, capital does not mean cash. The cash is shown in the cash account.

An Increase in an Asset Offset by an Increase in Owner's Equity. Jessica Jane opened a bank account with a deposit of $2,000 for her business. The new business now has $2,000 of the asset Cash. Since Jessie contributed the asset, the owner's equity element, Jessica Jane, Capital, increases by the same amount.

Assets (Items Owned)	=	Liabilities (Amounts Owed)	+	Owner's Equity (Owner's Investment)
Cash	=			Jessica Jane, Capital
(a) $2,000	=			$2,000

Transaction (b): Purchase of an asset for cash

An Increase in an Asset Offset by a Decrease in Another Asset. Jessie decided that the fastest and easiest way to get around campus and find parking is on a motor scooter. Thus, she bought a motor scooter (delivery equipment) for $1,200 cash. Jessie exchanged one asset, cash, for another, delivery equipment. This transaction reduces Cash and creates a new asset, Delivery Equipment.

Assets (Items Owned)			=	Liabilities (Amounts Owed)	+	Owner's Equity (Owner's Investment)
Cash	+	Delivery Equipment	=			Jessica Jane, Capital
(b) $2,000 −1,200		+1,200				$2,000
$800	+	$1,200				$2,000
$2,000			=			$2,000

LEARNING KEY: If transactions are entered correctly, the accounting equation always remains in balance.

Transaction (c): Purchase of an asset on account

An Increase in an Asset Offset by an Increase in a Liability. Jessie hired a friend to work for her, which meant that a second scooter would be needed. Given Jessie's limited cash, she bought the dealer's demonstration model for $900. The seller agreed to allow Jessie to spread the payments over the next three months. This transaction increased an asset, Delivery Equipment, by $900 and increased the liability, Accounts Payable, by an equal amount.

	Assets (Items Owned)			=	Liabilities (Amounts Owed)	+	Owner's Equity (Owner's Investment)
	Cash	+	Delivery Equipment	=	Accounts Payable	+	Jessica Jane, Capital
(c)	$ 800		$1,200 + 900		+ $900		$2,000
	$ 800	+	$2,100	=	$900	+	$2,000
	$2,900			=		**$2,900**	

Transaction (d): Payment on a loan

A Decrease in an Asset Offset by a Decrease in a Liability. Jessie paid the first installment on the scooter of $300 (see transaction (c)). This payment decreased the asset, Cash, and the liability, Accounts Payable, by $300.

	Assets (Items Owned)			=	Liabilities (Amounts Owed)	+	Owner's Equity (Owner's Investment)
	Cash	+	Delivery Equipment	=	Accounts Payable	+	Jessica Jane, Capital
(d)	$ 800 −300		$2,100		$900 −300		$2,000
	$ 500	+	$2,100	=	$600	+	$2,000
	$2,600			=		**$2,600**	

Expanding the Accounting Equation: Revenues, Expenses, and Withdrawals

In the preceding sections, three key accounting elements of every business entity were defined and explained: assets, liabilities, and owner's equity. To complete the explanation of the accounting process, three additional elements must be added to the discussion: revenues, expenses, and withdrawals.

Revenues. Revenues represent the amount a business charges customers for products sold or services performed. Customers generally pay with cash or a credit card, or they promise to pay at a later date. Most businesses recognize revenues when earned, even if cash has not yet been received. Separate accounts are used to recognize different types of revenue. Examples include Delivery Fees;

Consulting Fees; Rent Revenue, if the business rents space to others; Interest Revenue, for interest earned on bank deposits; and Sales, for sales of merchandise. *Revenues increase both assets and owner's equity.*

Expenses. **Expenses** represent the decrease in assets (or increase in liabilities) as a result of efforts made to produce revenues. Common examples of expenses are rent, salaries, supplies consumed, and taxes. As with revenues, separate accounts are used to maintain records for each different type of expense. Expenses are "incurred" as assets are consumed (such as supplies), cash is paid for services performed for the business, or a promise is made to pay cash at a future date for services performed for the business (such as wages). The promise to pay in the future represents a liability. *Expenses either decrease assets or increase liabilities. Expenses always reduce owner's equity.*

 LEARNING KEY: It is important to remember that expenses do not always reduce cash and revenues do not always increase cash right away.

The main purposes of recognizing an expense are to keep track of the amount and types of expenses incurred and to show the reduction in owner's equity. Note that an expense can cause a reduction in assets or an increase in liabilities. Wages earned by employees is a good example. If paid, the expense reduces an asset, Cash. If not paid, it increases a liability, Wages Payable. Either way, owner's equity is reduced.

If total revenues exceed total expenses of the period, the excess is the **net income** or net profit for the period.

Revenues Greater than Expenses = Net Income

On the other hand, if expenses exceed revenues of the period, the excess is a **net loss** for the period.

Expenses Greater than Revenues = Net Loss

The owner can determine the time period used in the measurement of net income or net loss. It may be a month, a quarter (three months), a year, or some other time period. The concept that income determination can be made on a periodic basis is known as the **accounting period concept**. Any accounting period of twelve months is called a **fiscal year**. The fiscal year frequently coincides with the calendar year.

Withdrawals. **Withdrawals**, or **drawing**, reduce owner's equity as a result of the owner taking cash or other assets out of the business for personal use. Since earnings are expected to offset withdrawals, this reduction is viewed as temporary.

The accounting equation is expanded to include revenues, expenses, and withdrawals. Note that revenues increase owner's equity, while expenses and drawing reduce owner's equity.

 LEARNING KEY:

Owner's Equity	
Decrease	Increase
Expenses	Revenues
Drawing	Investments

Assets (Items Owned)			=	Liabilities (Amounts Owed)	+	Owner's Equity (Owner's Investment + Earnings)				
	Cash	+ Delivery Equipment	=	Accounts Payable	+ Jessica Jane, Capital	− Jessica Jane, Drawing	+ Revenues	− Expenses		
Balance	$ 500 +	$2,100	=	$600	+ $2,000					
	$2,600		=				**$2,600**			

Effect of Revenue, Expense, and Withdrawal Transactions on the Accounting Equation

To show the effects of revenue, expense, and withdrawal transactions, the example of Jessie Jane's Campus Delivery will be continued. Assume that the following transactions took place in Jessie's business during June 20--.

Transaction (e): Delivery revenues earned in cash

An Increase in an Asset Offset by an Increase in Owner's Equity Resulting from Revenue. Jessie received $500 cash from clients for delivery services. This transaction increased the asset, Cash, and increased owner's equity by $500. The increase in owner's equity is shown by increasing the revenue account, Delivery Fees, by $500.

Assets (Items Owned)			=	Liabilities (Amounts Owed)	+	Owner's Equity (Owner's Investment + Earnings)				
	Cash	+ Delivery Equipment	=	Accounts Payable	+ Jessica Jane, Capital	− Jessica Jane, Drawing	+ Revenues	− Expenses	Description
	$ 500	$2,100		$600	$2,000				
(e)	+500						+$500		Deliv. Fees
	$1,000 +	$2,100	=	$600	+ $2,000		+ $500		
	$3,100		=				**$3,100**		

Transaction (f): Paid rent for month

A Decrease in an Asset Offset by a Decrease in Owner's Equity Resulting from an Expense. Jessie rents a small office on campus. She paid $200 for office rent for June. This transaction decreased both Cash and owner's equity by $200. The decrease in owner's equity is shown by increasing an expense called Rent Expense by $200. An increase in an expense decreases owner's equity.

Assets (Items Owned)			=	Liabilities (Amounts Owed)	+	Owner's Equity (Owner's Investment + Earnings)				
	Cash	+ Delivery Equipment	=	Accounts Payable	+ Jessica Jane, Capital	− Jessica Jane, Drawing	+ Revenues	− Expenses	Description
	$1,000	$2,100		$600	$2,000		$500		
(f)	−200							+200	Rent Exp.
	$ 800 +	$2,100	=	$600	+ $2,000		+ $500 −	$200	
	$2,900		=				**$2,900**		

Transaction (g): Paid telephone bill

A Decrease in an Asset Offset by a Decrease in Owner's Equity Resulting from an Expense. Jessie paid $50 in cash for telephone service. This transaction, like the previous one, decreased both Cash and owner's equity. This decrease in owner's equity is shown by increasing an expense called Telephone Expense by $50.

Assets (Items Owned)		=	Liabilities (Amounts Owed)	+	Owner's Equity (Owner's Investment + Earnings)				
Cash	+	Delivery Equipment	=	Accounts Payable	+	Jessica Jane, Capital	−	Jessica Jane, Drawing	+	Revenues	−	Expenses	Description

Cash	+	Delivery Equipment	=	Accounts Payable	+	Jessica Jane, Capital	− Jessica Jane, Drawing	+ Revenues	− Expenses	Description
$ 800		$2,100		$600		$2,000		$500	$200	
(g) −50									+50	Tel. Expense
$ 750 +		$2,100	=	$600	+	$2,000	+	$500 −	$250	
		$2,850	=				$2,850			

Transaction (h): Delivery revenues earned on account

An Increase in an Asset Offset by an Increase in Owner's Equity Resulting from Revenue. Jessie extends credit to regular customers. Often delivery services are performed for which payment will be received later. Since revenues are recognized when earned, an increase in owner's equity must be reported by increasing the revenue account. Since no cash is received at this time, Cash cannot be increased. Instead, an increase is reported for another asset, Accounts Receivable. *The total of Accounts Receivable at any point in time reflects the amount owed to Jessie by her customers.* Deliveries made on account amounted to $600. Accounts Receivable and Delivery Fees are increased.

Assets (Items Owned)					=	Liabilities (Amounts Owed)	+	Owner's Equity (Owner's Investment + Earnings)					
Cash	+	Accounts Receivable	+	Delivery Equipment	=	Accounts Payable	+	Jessica Jane, Capital	− Jessica Jane, Drawing	+ Revenues	− Expenses	Description
$ 750				$2,100		$600		$2,000		$ 500	$250	
(h)		+600								+600		Deliv. Fees
$ 750 +		$ 600 +		$2,100	=	$600	+	$2,000	+	$1,100 −	$250	
		$3,450			=				$3,450			

 LEARNING KEY: Revenue is recognized even though cash is not received.

Transaction (i): Purchase of supplies

An Increase in an Asset Offset by a Decrease in an Asset. Jessie bought pens, paper, delivery envelopes, and other supplies for $80 cash. These supplies should last for several months. Since they will generate future benefits, the supplies should be recorded as an asset. The accounting equation will show an increase in an asset, Supplies, and a decrease in Cash.

Assets (Items Owned)					=	Liabilities (Amounts Owed)		+	Owner's Equity (Owner's Investment + Earnings)				
Cash +	Accounts Receivable +	Supplies +		Delivery Equipment =		Accounts Payable	+	Jessica Jane, Capital	– Jessica Jane, Drawing	+ Revenues	– Expenses	Description	
$ 750 (i) – 80	$ 600	+$80		$2,100		$600		$2,000		$1,100	$250		
$ 670 +	$ 600 +	$80 +		$2,100 =		$600	+	$2,000		+ $1,100	– $250		
$3,450					=	**$3,450**							

Transaction (j): Payment of insurance premium

An Increase in an Asset Offset by a Decrease in an Asset. Since Jessie plans to graduate and sell the business next January, she paid $200 for an eight-month liability insurance policy. Insurance is paid in advance and will provide future benefits. Thus, it is treated as an asset. We must expand the equation to include another asset, Prepaid Insurance, and show that Cash has been reduced.

Assets (Items Owned)						=	Liabilities (Amounts Owed)		+	Owner's Equity (Owner's Investment + Earnings)				
Cash +	Accounts Receivable +	Supplies +	Prepaid Insurance +	Delivery Equipment =			Accounts Payable	+	Jessica Jane, Capital	– Jessica Jane, Drawing	+ Revenues	– Expenses	Description	
$ 670 (j) – 200	$ 600	$80	+$200	$2,100			$600		$2,000		$1,100	$250		
$ 470 +	$ 600 +	$80 +	$200 +	$2,100 =			$600	+	$2,000		+ $1,100	– $250		
$3,450						=	**$3,450**							

 LEARNING KEY: Both supplies and insurance are recorded as assets because they will last for several months.

> *As shown in transactions i, j, and k, transactions do not always affect both sides of the accounting equation.*

Transaction (k): Cash receipts from prior sales on account

An Increase in an Asset Offset by a Decrease in an Asset. Jessie received $570 in cash for delivery services performed for customers earlier in the month (see transaction (h)). Receipt of this cash increases the cash account and reduces the amount due from customers reported in the accounts receivable account. *Notice that owner's equity is not affected in this transaction. Owner's equity increased in transaction (h) when revenue was recognized as it was earned, rather than now when cash is received.*

Assets (Items Owned)						=	Liabilities (Amounts Owed)		+	Owner's Equity (Owner's Investment + Earnings)				
Cash +	Accounts Receivable +	Supplies +	Prepaid Insurance +	Delivery Equipment =			Accounts Payable	+	Jessica Jane, Capital	– Jessica Jane, Drawing	+ Revenues	– Expenses	Description	
$ 470 (k) +570	$ 600 – 570	$80	$200	$2,100			$600		$2,000		$1,100	$250		
$1,040 +	$ 30 +	$80 +	$200 +	$2,100 =			$600	+	$2,000		+ $1,100	– $250		
$3,450						=	**$3,450**							

Transaction (l): Purchase of an asset on account making a partial payment

An Increase in an Asset Offset by a Decrease in an Asset and an Increase in a Liability. With business increasing, Jessie hired a second employee and bought a third motor scooter. The scooter cost $1,500. Jessie paid $300 in cash and will spread the remaining payments over the next four months. The asset Delivery Equipment increases by $1,500, Cash decreases by $300, and the liability Accounts Payable increases by $1,200. *Note that this transaction changes three accounts. Even so, the accounting equation remains in balance.*

	Assets (Items Owned)					=	Liabilities (Amounts Owed)	+	Owner's Equity (Owner's Investment + Earnings)					
Cash	+ Accounts Receivable	+ Supplies	+ Prepaid Insurance	+ Delivery Equipment	=		Accounts Payable	+ Jessica Jane, Capital	− Jessica Jane, Drawing	+ Revenues	− Expenses	Description		
$1,040	$30	$80	$200	$2,100			$ 600	$2,000		$1,100	$250			
(l) −300				+1,500			+1,200							
$ 740 +	$30 +	$80 +	$200 +	$3,600	=		$1,800	+ $2,000		+ $1,100 −	$250			
	$4,650					=			**$4,650**					

Transaction (m): Payment of wages

A Decrease in an Asset Offset by a Decrease in Owner's Equity Resulting from an Expense. Jessie paid her part-time employees $650 in wages. This represents an additional business expense. As with other expenses, Cash is reduced and owner's equity is reduced by increasing an expense.

	Assets (Items Owned)					=	Liabilities (Amounts Owed)	+	Owner's Equity (Owner's Investment + Earnings)				
Cash	+ Accounts Receivable	+ Supplies	+ Prepaid Insurance	+ Delivery Equipment	=		Accounts Payable	+ Jessica Jane, Capital	− Jessica Jane, Drawing	+ Revenues	− Expenses	Description
$740	$30	$80	$200	$3,600			$1,800	$2,000		$1,100	$250	
(m) − 650											+650	Wages Exp.
$ 90 +	$30 +	$80 +	$200 +	$3,600	=		$1,800	+ $2,000		+ $1,100 −	$900	
	$4,000					=			**$4,000**			

Transaction (n): Deliveries made for cash and on account

An Increase in Two Assets Offset by an Increase in Owner's Equity. Total delivery fees for the remainder of the month amounted to $1,050: $430 in cash and $620 on account. Since all of these delivery fees have been earned, the revenue account increases by $1,050. Also, Cash increases by $430 and Accounts Receivable increases by $620. Thus, revenues increase assets and owner's equity. Note, once again, that one event impacts three accounts while the equation remains in balance.

	Assets (Items Owned)					=	Liabilities (Amounts Owed)	+	Owner's Equity (Owner's Investment + Earnings)					
	Cash +	Accounts Receivable +	Supplies +	Prepaid Insurance +	Delivery Equipment =		Accounts Payable	+	Jessica Jane, Capital	– Jessica Jane, Drawing	+ Revenues	– Expenses	Description
(n)	$ 90 +430	$ 30 +620	$80	$200	$3,600		$1,800		$2,000		$1,100 +1,050	$900	Deliv. Fees
	$520 +	$650 +	$80 +	$200 +	$3,600 =		$1,800	+	$2,000	+	$2,150	– $900	
			$5,050			=				$5,050			

Transaction (o): Withdrawal of cash from business

A Decrease in an Asset Offset by a Decrease in Owner's Equity Resulting from a Withdrawal by the Owner. At the end of the month, Jessie took $150 in cash from the business to purchase books for her classes. Since the books are not business related, this is a withdrawal. Withdrawals can be viewed as the opposite of investments by the owner. Both owner's equity and Cash decrease.

	Assets (Items Owned)					=	Liabilities (Amounts Owed)	+	Owner's Equity (Owner's Investment + Earnings)					
	Cash +	Accounts Receivable +	Supplies +	Prepaid Insurance +	Delivery Equipment =		Accounts Payable	+	Jessica Jane, Capital	– Jessica Jane, Drawing	+ Revenues	– Expenses	Description
(o)	$ 520 –150	$650	$80	$200	$3,600		$1,800		$2,000	+$150	$2,150	$900	
	$370 +	$650 +	$80 +	$200 +	$3,600 =		$1,800	+	$2,000 –	$150	+ $2,150	– $900	
			$4,900			=				$4,900			

LEARNING KEY: Withdrawals by the owner are reported in the drawing account. Withdrawals are the opposite of investments by the owner. Recall the business entity concept. The owner of the business and the business are separate economic entities. Thus, personal transactions must not be included with those of the business. If this is allowed, it will be very difficult to evaluate the performance of the business.

Figure 2-1 shows a summary of the transactions. Use this summary to test your understanding of transaction analysis by describing the economic event represented by each transaction. At the bottom of Figure 2-1, the asset accounts and their totals are compared with the liability and owner's equity accounts and their totals.

FIGURE 2-1   Summary of Transactions Illustrated

Trans-action	Cash	+ Accounts Receivable	+ Supplies	+ Prepaid Insurance	+ Delivery Equipment	= Accounts Payable	+ Jessica Jane, Capital	− Jessica Jane, Drawing	+ Revenues	− Expenses	Description
Balance											
(a)	2,000						2,000				
Balance	2,000						2,000				
(b)	(1,200)				1,200						
Balance	800				1,200		2,000				
(c)					900	900					
Balance	800				2,100	900	2,000				
(d)	(300)					(300)					
Balance	500				2,100	600	2,000				
(e)	500								500		Deliv. Fees
Balance	1,000				2,100	600	2,000		500		
(f)	(200)									200	Rent Exp.
Balance	800				2,100	600	2,000		500	200	
(g)	(50)									50	Tele. Exp.
Balance	750				2,100	600	2,000		500	250	
(h)		600							600		Deliv. Fees
Balance	750	600			2,100	600	2,000		1,100	250	
(i)	(80)		80								
Balance	670	600	80		2,100	600	2,000		1,100	250	
(j)	(200)			200							
Balance	470	600	80	200	2,100	600	2,000		1,100	250	
(k)	570	(570)									
Balance	1,040	30	80	200	2,100	600	2,000		1,100	250	
(l)	(300)				1,500	1,200					
Balance	740	30	80	200	3,600	1,800	2,000		1,100	250	
(m)	(650)									650	Wages Exp.
Balance	90	30	80	200	3,600	1,800	2,000		1,100	900	
(n)	430	620							1,050		Deliv. Fees
Balance	520	650	80	200	3,600	1,800	2,000		2,150	900	
(o)	(150)							150			
Balance	370 +	650 +	80 +	200 +	3,600 =	1,800 +	2,000 −	150 +	2,150 −	900	

Cash	$ 370	Accounts Payable	$ 1,800
Accounts Receivable	650	Jessica Jane, Capital	2,000
Supplies	80	Jessica Jane, Drawing	(150)
Prepaid Insurance	200	Delivery Fees	2,150
Delivery Equipment	3,600	Rent Expense	(200)
Total assets	$ 4,900	Telephone Expense	(50)
		Wages Expense	(650)
		Total liabilities and owner's equity	$ 4,900

Amounts in ( ) are subtracted

LEARNING KEY: As with the running totals in the table, the listing immediately below the table provides proof that the accounting equation is in balance.

FINANCIAL STATEMENTS

LO 5 Prepare a simple income statement, statement of owner's equity, and balance sheet.

Three financial statements commonly prepared by a business entity are the income statement, statement of owner's equity, and balance sheet. The transaction information gathered and summarized in the accounting equation may be used to prepare these financial statements. Figure 2-2 shows the following:

1. A summary of the specific revenue and expense transactions and the ending totals for the asset, liability, capital, and drawing accounts from the accounting equation.

2. The financial statements and their linkages with the accounting equation and each other.

Note that each of the financial statements in Figure 2-2 has a heading consisting of:

HEADING FOR FINANCIAL STATEMENTS	
1. The name of the company	Jessie Jane's Campus Delivery
2. The title of the statement	Income Statement, Statement of Owner's Equity, or Balance Sheet
3. The time period covered or the date of the statement	For Month Ended June 30, 20--, or June 30, 20--

The income statement and statement of owner's equity provide information concerning events covering a period of time, in this case, *the month ended* June 30, 20--. The balance sheet, on the other hand, offers a picture of the business *on a specific date*, June 30, 20--.

The Income Statement

> The income statement reports the following:
> Revenues   xxx
> Expenses   (xx)
> Net income   xx

The **income statement**, sometimes called the **profit and loss statement** or **operating statement**, reports the profitability of business operations for a specific period of time. Jessie's income statement shows the revenues earned for the month of June. Next, the expenses incurred as a result of the efforts made to earn these revenues are deducted. If the revenues are greater than the expenses, net income is reported. If the expenses are greater than the revenue, a net loss is reported.

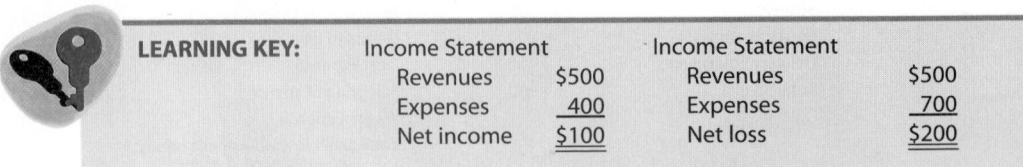

LEARNING KEY:	Income Statement		Income Statement	
	Revenues	$500	Revenues	$500
	Expenses	400	Expenses	700
	Net income	$100	Net loss	$200

By carefully studying the income statement, it is clear that Jessie earns revenues in only one way: by making deliveries. If other types of services were offered, these revenues would also be identified on the statement. Further, the reader can see the kinds of expenses that were incurred. The reader can make a

FIGURE 2-2 Summary and Financial Statements

Assets (Items Owned)					=	Liabilities (Amounts Owed)	+	Owner's Equity (Owner's Investment + Earnings)				
Trans-action	Cash	+ Accounts Receivable	+ Supplies	+ Prepaid Insurance	+ Delivery Equipment =	Accounts Payable	+ Jessica Jane, Capital	− Jessica Jane, Drawing	+ Revenues	− Expenses	Description
(e)									500		Deliv. Fees
(f)										200	Rent Exp.
(g)										50	Tele. Exp.
(h)									600		Deliv. Fees
(m)										650	Wages Exp.
(n)									1,050		Deliv. Fees
Balance	370 +	650 +	80 +	200 +	3,600 =	1,800 +	2,000 −	150 +	2,150 −	900	

Jessie Jane's Campus Delivery
Income Statement
For Month Ended June 30, 20 --

Revenues		
Delivery fees		$2 1 5 0 00
Expenses		
Wages expense	$ 6 5 0 00	
Rent expense	2 0 0 00	
Telephone expense	5 0 00	
Total expenses		9 0 0 00
Net income		$1 2 5 0 00

$ at top of columns

Subtotal underline

Jessie Jane's Campus Delivery
Statement of Owner's Equity
For Month Ended June 30, 20 - -

Jessica Jane, capital, June 1, 20 - -		$2 0 0 0 00
Net income for June	$1 2 5 0 00	
Less withdrawals for June	1 5 0 00	
Increase in capital		1 1 0 0 00
Jessica Jane, capital, June 30, 20 - -		$3 1 0 0 00

$ on total

Jessie Jane's Campus Delivery
Balance Sheet
June 30, 20 - -

Assets		Liabilities	
Cash	$ 3 7 0 00	Accounts payable	$1 8 0 0 00
Accounts receivable	6 5 0 00		
Supplies	8 0 00	Owner's Equity	
Prepaid insurance	2 0 0 00	Jessica Jane, capital	3 1 0 0 00
Delivery equipment	3 6 0 0 00		
		Total liabilities and	
Total assets	$4 9 0 0 00	owner's equity	$4 9 0 0 00

Double underline totals

judgment as to whether these seem reasonable given the amount of revenue earned. Finally, the most important number on the statement is the net income. This is known as the "bottom line."

The Statement of Owner's Equity

The **statement of owner's equity** illustrated in Figure 2-2 reports on these activities for the month of June. Jessie started her business with an investment of $2,000. During the month of June she earned $1,250 in net income and withdrew $150 for personal expenses. This resulted in a net increase in Jessie's capital of $1,100. Jessie's $2,000 original investment, plus the net increase of $1,100, results in her ending capital of $3,100.

Note that Jessie's original investment and later withdrawal are taken from the accounting equation. *The net income figure could have been computed from information in the accounting equation. However, it is easier to simply transfer net income as reported on the income statement to the statement of owner's equity.* This is an important linkage between the income statement and statement of owner's equity.

If Jessie had a net loss of $500 for the month, the statement of owner's equity would be prepared as shown in Figure 2-3.

FIGURE 2-3 Statement of Owner's Equity with Net Loss

> *Owner's equity is affected by two basic types of activities:*
> *1. Investments and withdrawals by the owner, and*
> *2. Profits and losses generated through operations.*
> *This information is reported on the statement of owner's equity.*

Jessie Jane's Campus Delivery Statement of Owner's Equity For Month Ended June 30, 20 - -												
Jessica Jane, capital, June 1, 20 - -									$2	0	0	0	00
Less: Net loss for June	$	5	0	0	00								
Withdrawals for June		1	5	0	00								
Decrease in capital							6	5	0	00			
Jessica Jane, capital, June 30, 20 - -							$1	3	5	0	00		

The Balance Sheet

> **Balance Sheet**
>
> | Assets | Liabilities + Owner's Equity |
> |---|---|
> | xxx | xxx |

The **balance sheet** reports a firm's assets, liabilities, and owner's equity on a specific date. It is called a balance sheet because it confirms that the accounting equation has remained in balance. It is also referred to as a **statement of financial position** or **statement of financial condition**.

As illustrated in Figure 2-2, the asset and liability accounts are taken from the accounting equation and reported on the balance sheet. *The total of Jessie's capital account on June 30 could have been computed from the owner's equity accounts in the accounting equation ($2,000 − $150 + $2,150 − $900). However, it is simpler to take the June 30, 20--, capital as computed on the statement of owner's equity and transfer it to the balance sheet.* This is an important linkage between these two statements.

Most firms also prepare a statement of cash flows. Given the complexity of this statement, we will postpone its discussion until later in this text.

GUIDELINES FOR PREPARING FINANCIAL STATEMENTS

1. Financial statements are prepared primarily for users not associated with the company. To make a good impression and enhance understanding, financial statements must follow a standard form with careful attention to placement, spacing, and indentations.
2. All statements have a heading with the name of the company, name of the statement, and accounting period or date.
3. Single rules (lines) indicate that the numbers above the line have been added or subtracted. Double rules (double underlines) indicate a total.
4. Dollar signs are used at the top of columns and for the first amount entered in a column beneath a ruling.
5. On the income statement, a common practice is to list expenses from highest to lowest dollar amount, with miscellaneous expense listed last.
6. On the balance sheet, assets are listed from most liquid to least liquid. **Liquidity** measures the ease with which the asset will be converted to cash. Liabilities are listed from most current to least current.

OVERVIEW OF THE ACCOUNTING PROCESS

LO 6   Define the three basic phases of the accounting process.

Figure 2-4 shows the three basic phases of the accounting process in terms of input, processing, and output.

▶ **Input.** Business transactions provide the necessary **input**.

▶ **Processing.** Recognizing the effect of these transactions on the assets, liabilities, owner's equity, revenues, and expenses of a business is the **processing** function.

▶ **Output.** The financial statements are the **output**.

FIGURE 2-4   Input, Processing, and Output

Learning Objectives	Key Points to Remember
1 **Define the accounting elements.**	The three key accounting elements are assets, liabilities, and owner's equity. Owner's equity is expanded to include revenues, expenses, and drawing.
2 **Construct the accounting equation.**	The accounting equation is: Assets = Liabilities + Owner's Equity
3 **Analyze business transactions.**	Three questions must be answered in analyzing business transactions: 1. What happened? 2. Which accounts are affected? 3. How is the accounting equation affected?
4 **Show the effects of business transactions on the accounting equation.**	Each transaction affects one or more of the three basic accounting elements. The transactions described in this chapter can be classified into five groups: 1. Increase in an asset offset by an increase in owner's equity. 2. Increase in an asset offset by a decrease in another asset. 3. Increase in an asset offset by an increase in a liability. 4. Decrease in an asset offset by a decrease in a liability. 5. Decrease in an asset offset by a decrease in owner's equity.
5 **Prepare and describe the purposes of a simple income statement, statement of owner's equity, and balance sheet.**	The purposes of the income statement, statement of owner's equity, and balance sheet can be summarized as follows:

STATEMENT	PURPOSE
Income statement	Reports net income or loss Revenues – Expenses = Net Income or Loss
Statement of owner's equity	Shows changes in the owner's capital account Beginning Capital + Investments + Net Income – Withdrawals = Ending Capital
Balance sheet	Verifies balance of accounting equation Assets = Liabilities + Owner's Equity

6 **Define the three basic phases of the accounting process.**	The three basic phases of the accounting process are shown below. ▶ **Input.** Business transactions provide the necessary input. ▶ **Processing.** Recognizing the effect of these transactions on the assets, liabilities, owner's equity, revenues, and expenses of a business is the processing function. ▶ **Output.** The financial statements are the output.

Reflection: Answering the Opening Question

1. What happened?

2. Which accounts are affected?

3. How is the accounting equation affected?

KEY TERMS

account, (18)   A separate record used to summarize changes in each asset, liability, and owner's equity of a business.

account payable, (16)   An unwritten promise to pay a supplier for assets purchased or services rendered.

account receivable, (16)   An amount owed to a business by its customers as a result of the sale of goods or services.

account title, (18)   Provides a description of the particular type of asset, liability, owner's equity, revenue, or expense.

accounting equation, (18)   The accounting equation consists of the three basic accounting elements: assets = liabilities + owner's equity.

accounting period concept, (21)   The concept that income determination can be made on a periodic basis.

asset, (16)   An item that is owned by a business and will provide future benefits.

balance sheet, (30)   Reports assets, liabilities, and owner's equity on a specific date. It is called a balance sheet because it confirms that the accounting equation is in balance.

business entity, (16)   An individual, association, or organization that engages in economic activities and controls specific economic resources.

business entity concept, (17)   The concept that nonbusiness assets and liabilities are not included in the business entity's accounting records.

business transaction, (18)   An economic event that has a direct impact on the business.

capital, (17)   Another term for owner's equity, the amount by which the business assets exceed the business liabilities.

drawing, (21)   Withdrawals that reduce owner's equity as a result of the owner taking cash or other assets out of the business for personal use.

expenses, (21)   The decrease in assets (or increase in liabilities) as a result of efforts to produce revenues.

fiscal year, (21)   Any accounting period of twelve months' duration.

income statement, (28)   Reports the profitability of business operations for a specific period of time. (Also called the profit and loss statement or operating statement.)

input, (31)   Business transactions provide the necessary input for the accounting information system.

liability, (16)   Something owed to another business entity.

net income, (21)   The excess of total revenues over total expenses for the period.

net loss, (21)   The excess of total expenses over total revenues for the period.

net worth, (17)   Another term for owner's equity, the amount by which the business assets exceed the business liabilities.

note payable, (16)   A formal written promise to pay a supplier or lender a specified sum of money at a definite future time.

operating statement, (28)   Another name for the income statement, which reports the profitability of business operations for a specific period of time.

output, (31)   The financial statements are the output of the accounting information system.

owner's equity, (17)   The amount by which the business assets exceed the business liabilities.

processing, (31)   Recognizing the effect of transactions on the assets, liabilities, owner's equity, revenues, and expenses of a business.

profit and loss statement, (28)   Another name for the income statement, which reports the profitability of business operations for a specific period of time.

revenues, (20)   The amount a business charges customers for products sold or services performed.

statement of financial condition, (30)   Another name for the balance sheet, which reports assets, liabilities, and owner's equity on a specific date.

statement of financial position, (30)   Another name for the balance sheet, which reports assets, liabilities, and owner's equity on a specific date.

statement of owner's equity, (30)   Reports beginning capital plus net income less withdrawals to compute ending capital.

withdrawals, (21)   Reduce owner's equity as a result of the owner taking cash or other assets out of the business for personal use.

DEMONSTRATION PROBLEM

Damon Young has started his own business, Home and Away Inspections. He inspects property for buyers and sellers of real estate. Young rents office space and has a part-time assistant to answer the phone and help with inspections. The transactions for the month of September are as follows:

(a) On the first day of the month, Young invested cash by making a deposit in a bank account for the business, $15,000.

(b) Paid rent for September, $300.

(c) Bought a used truck for cash, $8,000.

(d) Purchased tools on account from Crafty Tools, $3,000.

(e) Paid electricity bill, $50.

(f) Paid two-year premium for liability insurance on truck, $600.

(g) Received cash from clients for service performed, $2,000.

(h) Paid part-time assistant (wages) for first half of month, $200.

(i) Performed inspection services for clients on account, $1,000.

(j) Paid telephone bill, $35.

(k) Bought office supplies costing $300. Paid $100 cash and will pay the balance next month, $200.

(l) Received cash from clients for inspections performed on account in (i), $300.

(m) Paid part-time assistant (wages) for last half of month, $250.

(n) Made partial payment on tools bought in (d), $1,000.

(o) Earned additional revenues amounting to $2,000: $1,400 in cash and $600 on account.

(p) Young withdrew cash at the end of the month for personal expenses, $500.

REQUIRED   1. Enter the transactions in an accounting equation similar to the one illustrated below. After each transaction, show the new amount for each account.

Assets (Items Owned)						=	Liabilities (Amounts Owed)	+	Owner's Equity (Owner's Investment + Earnings)				
Cash +	Accounts Receivable +	Supplies +	Prepaid Insurance +	Tools +	Van =		Accounts Payable	+	Lisa Vozniak, Capital	– Lisa Vozniak, Drawing	+ Revenues	– Expenses	Description

2. Compute the ending balances for all accounts.

3. Prepare an income statement for Home and Away Inspections for the month of September 20--.

4. Prepare a statement of owner's equity for Home and Away Inspections for the month of September 20--.

5. Prepare a balance sheet for Home and Away Inspections as of September 30, 20--.

(continued)

Solution

1, 2.

	Cash	+ Accounts Receivable	+ Supplies	+ Prepaid Insurance	+ Tools	+ Truck	= Accounts Payable	+ Damon Young, Capital	− Damon Young, Drawing	+ Revenues	− Expenses	Description
Bal.												
(a)	15,000							15,000				
Bal.	15,000							15,000				
(b)	(300)										300	Rent Exp.
Bal.	14,700							15,000			300	
(c)	(8,000)					8,000						
Bal.	6,700					8,000		15,000			300	
(d)					3,000		3,000					
Bal.	6,700				3,000	8,000	3,000	15,000			300	
(e)	(50)										50	Utilities Exp.
Bal.	6,650				3,000	8,000	3,000	15,000			350	
(f)	(600)			600								
Bal.	6,050			600	3,000	8,000	3,000	15,000			350	
(g)	2,000									2,000		Inspect. Fees
Bal.	8,050			600	3,000	8,000	3,000	15,000		2,000	350	
(h)	(200)										200	Wages Exp.
Bal.	7,850			600	3,000	8,000	3,000	15,000		2,000	550	
(i)		1,000								1,000		Inspect. Fees
Bal.	7,850	1,000		600	3,000	8,000	3,000	15,000		3,000	550	
(j)	(35)										35	Tele. Exp.
Bal.	7,815	1,000		600	3,000	8,000	3,000	15,000		3,000	585	
(k)	(100)		300				200					
Bal.	7,715	1,000	300	600	3,000	8,000	3,200	15,000		3,000	585	
(l)	300	(300)										
Bal.	8,015	700	300	600	3,000	8,000	3,200	15,000		3,000	585	
(m)	(250)										250	Wages Exp.
Bal.	7,765	700	300	600	3,000	8,000	3,200	15,000		3,000	835	
(n)	(1,000)						(1,000)					
Bal.	6,765	700	300	600	3,000	8,000	2,200	15,000		3,000	835	
(o)	1,400	600								2,000		Inspect. Fees
Bal.	8,165	1,300	300	600	3,000	8,000	2,200	15,000		5,000	835	
(p)	(500)								500			
Bal.	7,665 +	1,300 +	300 +	600 +	3,000 +	8,000 =	2,200 +	15,000 −	500 +	5,000 −	835	

3.

Home and Away Inspections Income Statement For Month Ended September 30, 20 --										
Revenues										
Inspection fees							$5	0	0	0	00
Expenses										
Wages expense	$	4	5	0	00					
Rent expense		3	0	0	00					
Utilities expense			5	0	00					
Telephone expense			3	5	00					
Total expenses								8	3	5	00
Net income							$4	1	6	5	00

4.

Home and Away Inspections Statement of Owner's Equity For Month Ended September 30, 20 - -										
Damon Young, capital, September 1, 20 - -							$15	0	0	0	00
Net income for September	$4	1	6	5	00					
Less withdrawals for September		5	0	0	00					
Increase in capital								3	6	6	5	00
Damon Young, capital, September 30, 20 - -							$18	6	6	5	00

5.

Home and Away Inspections Balance Sheet September 30, 20 - -										
Assets						**Liabilities**				
Cash	$ 7	6	6	5	00	Accounts payable	$ 2	2	0	0	00
Accounts receivable	1	3	0	0	00					
Supplies		3	0	0	00	**Owner's Equity**				
Prepaid insurance		6	0	0	00	Damon Young, capital	18	6	6	5	00
Tools	3	0	0	0	00					
Truck	8	0	0	0	00	Total liabilities and				
Total assets	$20	8	6	5	00	owner's equity	$20	8	6	5	00

REVIEW QUESTIONS

1. Why is it necessary to distinguish between business assets and liabilities and nonbusiness assets and liabilities of a single proprietor?

2. List the three basic questions that must be answered when analyzing the effects of a business transaction on the accounting equation.

3. Name and define the six major elements of the accounting equation.

4. What is the function of an income statement?

5. What is the function of a statement of owner's equity?

6. What is the function of a balance sheet?

7. What are the three basic phases of the accounting process?

MANAGING YOUR WRITING

Write a brief memo that explains the differences and similarities between expenses and withdrawals.

SERIES A EXERCISES

EXERCISE 2A-1 (LO 1) ACCOUNTING ELEMENTS Label each of the following accounts as an asset (A), a liability (L), or owner's equity (OE), using the following format.

Item	Account	Classification
Money in bank	Cash	
Office supplies	Supplies	
Money owed	Accounts Payable	
Office chairs	Office Furniture	
Net worth of owner	John Smith, Capital	
Money withdrawn by owner	John Smith, Drawing	
Money owed by customers	Accounts Receivable	

EXERCISE 2A-2 (LO 2) THE ACCOUNTING EQUATION Using the accounting equation, compute the missing elements.

Assets	=	Liabilities	+	Owner's Equity
_____	=	$24,000	+	$10,000
$25,000	=	$18,000	+	_____
$40,000	=	_____	+	$15,000

EXERCISE 2A-3 (LO 3/4) EFFECTS OF TRANSACTIONS (BALANCE SHEET ACCOUNTS) Alice Stern started a business. During the first month (February 20--), the following transactions occurred. Show the effect of each transaction on the accounting equation: *Assets = Liabilities + Owner's Equity.* After each transaction, show the new account totals.

(a) Invested cash in the business, $20,000.

(b) Bought office equipment on account, $3,500.

(c) Bought office equipment for cash, $1,200.

(d) Paid cash on account to supplier in (b), $1,500.

EXERCISE 2A-4 (LO 3/4) EFFECTS OF TRANSACTIONS (REVENUE, EXPENSE, WITHDRAWALS Assume Alice Stern completed the following additional transactions during February. Show the effect of each transaction on the basic elements of the expanded accounting equation: *Assets = Liabilities + Owner's Equity [Capital – Drawing + Revenues – Expenses].* After each transaction show the new account totals.

(e) Received cash from a client for professional services, $2,500.

(f) Paid office rent for February, $900.

(g) Paid February telephone bill, $73.

(h) Withdrew cash for personal use, $500.

(i) Performed services for clients on account, $1,000.

(j) Paid wages to part-time employee, $600.

(k) Received cash for services performed on account in (i), $600.

EXERCISE 2A-5 (LO 1/5) FINANCIAL STATEMENT ACCOUNTS Label each of the following accounts as an asset (A), liability (L), owner's equity (OE), revenue (R), or expense (E). Indicate the financial statement on which the account belongs — income statement (IS), statement of owner's equity (SOE), or balance sheet (B) — in a format similar to the following.

Account	Classification	Financial Statement
Cash		
Rent Expense		
Accounts Payable		
Service Fees		
Supplies		
Wages Expense		
Ramon Martinez, Drawing		
Ramon Martinez, Capital		
Prepaid Insurance		
Accounts Receivable		

EXERCISE 2A-6 (LO 5) STATEMENT OF OWNER'S EQUITY REPORTING NET INCOME Betsy Ray started an accounting service on June 1, 20--, by investing $20,000. Her net income for the month was $10,000 and she withdrew $8,000. Prepare a statement of owner's equity for the month of June.

EXERCISE 2A-7 (LO 5) STATEMENT OF OWNER'S EQUITY REPORTING NET LOSS Based on the information provided in Exercise 2A-6, prepare a statement of owner's equity assuming Ray had a net loss of $3,000.

SERIES A PROBLEMS

PROBLEM 2A-1 (LO 1/2) THE ACCOUNTING EQUATION Dr. John Schleper is a chiropractor. As of December 31, he owned the following property that related to his professional practice:

Cash	$ 4,750
Office Equipment	$ 6,200
X-ray Equipment	$11,680
Laboratory Equipment	$ 7,920

He also owes the following business suppliers:

Chateau Gas Company	$2,420
Aloe Medical Supply Company	$3,740

REQUIRED

1. From the preceding information, compute the accounting elements and enter them in the accounting equation shown as follows.

Assets	=	Liabilities	+	Owner's Equity
	=	_____	+	

2. During January, the assets increase by $7,290, and the liabilities increase by $4,210. Compute the resulting accounting equation.

3. During February, the assets decrease by $2,920, and the liabilities increase by $2,200. Compute the resulting accounting equation.

PROBLEM 2A-2 (LO 3/4) EFFECT OF TRANSACTIONS ON ACCOUNTING EQUATION Jay Pembroke started a business. During the first month (April 20--), the following transactions occurred:

(a) Invested cash in business, $18,000.

(b) Bought office supplies for $4,600: $2,000 in cash and $2,600 on account.

(c) Paid one-year insurance premium, $1,200.

(d) Earned revenues totaling $3,300: $1,300 in cash and $2,000 on account.

(e) Paid cash on account to the company that supplied the office supplies in (b), $2,300.

(f) Paid office rent for the month, $750.

(g) Withdrew cash for personal use, $100.

REQUIRED   Show the effect of each transaction on the basic elements of the accounting equation: *Assets = Liabilities + Owner's Equity [Capital – Drawing + Revenues – Expenses]*. After each transaction, show the new account totals.

PROBLEM 2A-3 (LO 5) INCOME STATEMENT Based on Problem 2A-2, prepare an income statement for Jay Pembroke for the month of April 20--.

PROBLEM 2A-4 (LO 5) STATEMENT OF OWNER'S EQUITY Based on Problem 2A-2, prepare a statement of owner's equity for Jay Pembroke for the month of April 20--.

PROBLEM 2A-5 (LO 5) BALANCE SHEET Based on Problem 2A-2, prepare a balance sheet for Jay Pembroke as of April 30, 20--.

SERIES B EXERCISES

EXERCISE 2B-1 (LO 1) ACCOUNTING ELEMENTS Label each of the following accounts as an asset (A), liability (L), or owner's equity (OE) using the following format.

Account	Classification
Cash	
Accounts Payable	
Supplies	
Bill Jones, Drawing	
Prepaid Insurance	
Accounts Receivable	
Bill Jones, Capital	

EXERCISE 2B-2 (LO 2) THE ACCOUNTING EQUATION Using the accounting equation, compute the missing elements.

Assets	=	Liabilities	+	Owner's Equity
_____	=	$20,000	+	$5,000
$30,000	=	$15,000	+	_____
$20,000	=	_____	+	$10,000

EXERCISE 2B-3 (LO 3/4) EFFECTS OF TRANSACTIONS (BALANCE SHEET ACCOUNTS) Jon Wallace started a business. During the first month (March 20--), the following transactions occurred. Show the effect of each transaction on the accounting equation: *Assets = Liabilities + Owner's Equity*. After each transaction, show the new account totals.

(a) Invested cash in the business, $30,000.

(b) Bought office equipment on account, $4,500.

(c) Bought office equipment for cash, $1,600.

(d) Paid cash on account to supplier in (b), $2,000.

EXERCISE 2B-4 (LO 3/4) EFFECTS OF TRANSACTIONS (REVENUE, EXPENSE, WITHDRAWALS) Assume Jon Wallace completed the following additional transactions during March. Show the effect of each transaction on the basic elements of the expanded accounting equation: *Assets = Liabilities + Owner's Equity [Capital – Drawing + Revenues – Expenses]*. After each transaction show the new account totals.

(e) Performed services and received cash, $3,000.

(f) Paid rent for March, $1,000.

(g) Paid March telephone bill, $68.

(h) Jon Wallace withdrew cash for personal use, $800.

(i) Performed services for clients on account, $900.

(j) Paid wages to part-time employee, $500.

(k) Received cash for services performed on account in (i), $500.

EXERCISE 2B-5 (LO 1/5) FINANCIAL STATEMENT ACCOUNTS Label each of the following accounts as an asset (A), liability (L), owner's equity (OE), revenue (R), or expense (E). Indicate the financial statement on which the account belongs—income statement (IS), statement of owner's equity (SOE), or balance sheet (B)—in a format similar to the following.

Account	Classification	Financial Statement
Cash		
Rent Expense		
Accounts Payable		
Service Fees		
Supplies		
Wages Expense		
Amanda Wong, Drawing		
Amanda Wong, Capital		
Prepaid Insurance		
Accounts Receivable		

EXERCISE 2B-6 (LO 5) STATEMENT OF OWNER'S EQUITY REPORTING NET INCOME Efran Lopez started a financial consulting service on June 1, 20--, by investing $15,000. His net income for the month was $6,000 and he withdrew $7,000 for personal use. Prepare a statement of owner's equity for the month of June.

EXERCISE 2B-7 (LO 5) STATEMENT OF OWNER'S EQUITY REPORTING NET LOSS Based on the information provided in Exercise 2B-6, prepare a statement of owner's equity assuming Lopez had a net loss of $2,000.

SERIES B PROBLEMS

PROBLEM 2B-1 (LO 1/2) THE ACCOUNTING EQUATION Dr. Patricia Parsons is a dentist. As of January 31, Parsons owned the following property that related to her professional practice:

Cash	$3,560
Office Equipment	$4,600
X-ray Equipment	$8,760
Laboratory Equipment	$5,940

She also owes the following business suppliers:

Cupples Gas Company	$1,815
Swan Dental Lab	$2,790

REQUIRED

1. From the preceding information, compute the accounting elements and enter them in the accounting equation as shown below.

Assets	=	Liabilities	+	Owner's Equity
_____	=	_____	+	_____

2. During February, the assets increase by $4,565, and the liabilities increase by $3,910. Compute the resulting accounting equation.

3. During March, the assets decrease by $2,190, and the liabilities increase by $1,650. Compute the resulting accounting equation.

PROBLEM 2B-2 (LO 3/4) EFFECT OF TRANSACTIONS ON ACCOUNTING EQUATION David Segal started a business. During the first month (October 20--), the following transactions occurred.

(a) Invested cash in the business, $15,000.

(b) Bought office supplies for $3,800: $1,800 in cash and $2,000 on account.

(c) Paid one-year insurance premium, $1,000.

(d) Earned revenues amounting to $2,700: $1,700 in cash and $1,000 on account.

(e) Paid cash on account to the company that supplied the office supplies in (b), $1,800.

(f) Paid office rent for the month, $650.

(g) Withdrew cash for personal use, $150.

REQUIRED Show the effect of each transaction on the basic elements of the accounting equation: *Assets = Liabilities + Owner's Equity [Capital – Drawing + Revenues – Expenses]*. After each transaction, show the new account totals.

PROBLEM 2B-3 (LO 5) INCOME STATEMENT Based on Problem 2B-2, prepare an income statement for David Segal for the month of October 20--.

PROBLEM 2B-4 (LO 5) STATEMENT OF OWNER'S EQUITY Based on Problem 2B-2, prepare a statement of owner's equity for David Segal for the month of October 20--.

PROBLEM 2B-5 (LO 5) BALANCE SHEET Based on Problem 2B-2, prepare a balance sheet for David Segal as of October 31, 20--.

MASTERY PROBLEM

Lisa Vozniak started her own business, We Do Windows. She offers interior and exterior window cleaning for local area residents. Lisa rents a garage to store her tools and cleaning supplies and has a part-time assistant to answer the phone and handle third-story work. (Lisa is afraid of heights.) The transactions for the month of July are as follows:

(a) On the first day of the month, Vozniak invested cash by making a deposit in a bank account for the business, $8,000.

(b) Paid rent for July, $150.

(c) Purchased a used van for cash, $5,000.

(d) Purchased tools on account from Clean Tools, $600.

(e) Purchased cleaning supplies that cost $300. Paid $200 cash and will pay the balance next month, $100.

(f) Paid part-time assistant (wages) for first half of month, $100.

(g) Paid for advertising, $75.

(h) Paid two-year premium for liability insurance on van, $480.

(i) Received cash from clients for services performed, $800.

(j) Performed cleaning services for clients on account, $500.

(k) Paid telephone bill, $40.

(l) Received cash from clients for window cleaning performed on account in (j), $200.

(m) Paid part-time assistant (wages) for last half of month, $150.

(n) Made partial payment on tools purchased in (d), $200.

(o) Earned additional revenues amounting to $800: $600 in cash and $200 on account.

(p) Vozniak withdrew cash at the end of the month for personal expenses, $100.

REQUIRED

1. Enter the above transactions in an accounting equation similar to the one illustrated below. After each transaction, show the new amount for each account.

Assets (Items Owned)						=	Liabilities (Amounts Owed)	+	Owner's Equity (Owner's Investment + Earnings)				
Cash	+ Accounts Receivable	+ Supplies	+ Prepaid Insurance	+ Tools	+ Truck =		Accounts Payable	+	Damon Young, Capital	– Damon Young, Drawing	+ Revenues	– Expenses	Description

2. Compute the ending balances for all accounts.

3. Prepare an income statement for We Do Windows for the month of July 20--.

4. Prepare a statement of owner's equity for We Do Windows for the month of July 20--.

5. Prepare a balance sheet for We Do Windows as of July 31, 20--.

Self-Study Test Questions

True/False

1. Assets are items that are owned by the business and are expected to provide future benefits. _____

2. Accounts Payable is an example of an asset account. _____

3. According to the business entity concept, nonbusiness assets and liabilities are not included in the business's accounting records. _____

4. The accounting equation (assets = liabilities + owner's equity) must always be in balance. _____

5. When an asset increases, a liability must also increase. _____

6. When total revenues exceed total expenses, the difference is called net loss. _____

7. Expenses represent outflows of assets or increases in liabilities as a result of efforts to produce revenues. _____

Multiple Choice

1. An increase to which of these accounts will increase owner's equity? _____

   (a) Accounts Payable   (c) Client Fees
   (b) Drawing   (d) Rent Expense

2. When delivery revenue is earned in cash, which accounts increase and decrease? _____

   (a) Cash increases; Revenue increases.
   (b) Cash decreases; Revenue increases.
   (c) Cash decreases; Revenue decreases.
   (d) Cash does not change; owner's equity increases.

3. When delivery revenue is earned on account, which accounts increase and decrease? _____

   (a) Cash increases; Revenue increases.
   (b) Accounts Receivable increases; Revenue increases.
   (c) Accounts Receivable increases; Revenue decreases.
   (d) Accounts Receivable decreases; Revenue decreases.

4. When payment is made on an existing debt, which accounts increase and decrease? _____

   (a) Cash increases; Accounts Receivable increases.
   (b) Cash decreases; Accounts Payable increases.
   (c) Cash increases; Accounts Payable increases.
   (d) Cash decreases; Accounts Payable decreases.

5. The process of entering information into the accounting system is called _____

   (a) analyzing.   (c) classifying.
   (b) recording.   (d) summarizing.

The answers to the Self-Study Test Questions are at the end of the text.

3

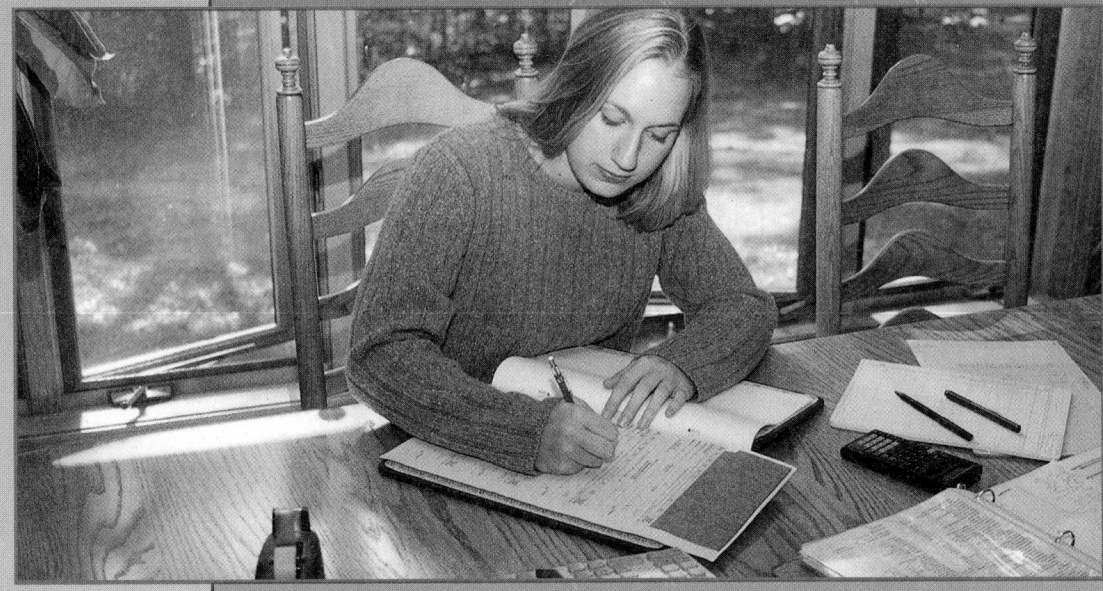

The Double-Entry Framework

LEARNING OBJECTIVES:
Careful study of this chapter should enable you to:

LO 1 Define the parts of a T account.

LO 2 Foot and balance a T account.

LO 3 Describe the effects of debits and credits on specific types of accounts.

LO 4 Use T accounts to analyze transactions.

LO 5 Prepare a trial balance and explain its purposes and linkages with the financial statements.

How do you keep track of your personal finances? Perhaps you make a list of your earnings and other cash inflows. Then you prepare a list of how the money was spent. Jessie needs to do this, too. However, since businesses earn and spend money in many different ways, and enter thousands of transactions, a systematic approach must be followed. This is called the double-entry framework. Could you use this double-entry system for your personal finances, or for a small business that you might start?

The terms asset, liability, owner's equity, revenue, and expense were explained in Chapter 2. Examples showed how individual business transactions change one or more of these basic accounting elements. Each transaction had a dual effect. An increase or decrease in any asset, liability, owner's equity, revenue, or expense was *always* accompanied by an offsetting change within the basic accounting elements. The fact that each transaction has a dual effect upon the accounting elements provides the basis for what is called **double-entry accounting.** To understand double-entry accounting, it is important to learn how T accounts work and the role of debits and credits in accounting.

THE T ACCOUNT

LO 1   Define the parts of a T account.

The assets of a business may consist of a number of items, such as cash, accounts receivable, equipment, buildings, and land. The liabilities may consist of one or more items, such as accounts payable and notes payable. Similarly, owner's equity may consist of the owner's investments and various revenue and expense items. A separate account is used to record the increases and decreases in each type of asset, liability, owner's equity, revenue, and expense.

The T account gets its name from the fact that it resembles the letter T. As shown below, there are three major parts of an account:

1.   the title,

2.   the debit, or left side, and

3.   the credit, or right side.

Title	
Debit = Left	Credit = Right

The debit side is always on the left and the credit side is always on the right. This is true for all types of asset, liability, owner's equity, revenue, and expense accounts.

LEARNING KEY: Debit means left and credit means right.

BALANCING A T ACCOUNT

LO 2   Foot and balance a T account.

To determine the balance of a T account at any time, simply total the dollar amounts on the debit and credit sides. These totals are known as **footings.** The difference between the footings is called the **balance** of the account. This amount is then written on the side with the larger footing.

In Chapter 2, the accounting equation was used to analyze business transactions. This required columns in which to record the increases and decreases in various accounts. Let's compare this approach with the use of a T account for the transactions affecting cash. When a T account is used, increases in cash are recorded on the debit side and decreases are recorded on the credit side. Transactions for Jessie Jane's Campus Delivery are shown in Figure 3-1.

FIGURE 3-1 Cash T account

COLUMNAR SUMMARY (From Chapter 2, page 27)		T ACCOUNT FORM				

COLUMNAR SUMMARY
(From Chapter 2, page 27)

Transaction	Cash
(a)	2,000
(b)	(1,200)
(d)	(300)
(e)	500
(f)	(200)
(g)	(50)
(i)	(80)
(j)	(200)
(k)	570
(l)	(300)
(m)	(650)
(n)	430
(o)	(150)
Balance	370

T ACCOUNT FORM

Cash

(a)	2,000	(b)	1,200
(e)	500	(d)	300
(k)	570	(f)	200
(n)	430	(g)	50
footing → 3,500		(i)	80
		(j)	200
		(l)	300
		(m)	650
		(o)	150
Balance → 370		3,130 ← footing

DEBITS AND CREDITS

LO 3 Describe the effects of debits and credits on specific types of accounts.

Abbreviations: Often debit and credit are abbreviated as:

Dr. = Debit
Cr. = Credit

(based on the Latin terms "debere" and "credere")

To **debit** an account means to enter an amount on the left or debit side of the account. To **credit** an account means to enter an amount on the right or credit side of the account. *Debits may increase **or** decrease the balances of specific accounts. This is also true for credits. To learn how to use debits and credits, it is best to reflect on the accounting equation.*

Assets		=	Liabilities		+	Owner's Equity	
Debit	Credit		Debit	Credit		Debit	Credit
+	–		–	+		–	+

Assets

Assets are on the left side of the accounting equation. Therefore, increases are entered on the left (debit) side of an asset account and decreases are entered on the right (credit) side.

Liabilities and Owner's Equity

Liabilities and owner's equity are on the right side of the equation. Therefore, increases are entered on the right (credit) side and decreases are entered on the left (debit) side.

LEARNING KEY: Debits increase assets and decrease liabilities and owner's equity. Credits decrease assets and increase liabilities and owner's equity.

Normal Balances

A **normal balance** is the side of an account that is increased. Since assets are debited for increases, these accounts normally have **debit balances**. Since liability and owner's equity accounts are credited for increases, these accounts normally have **credit balances**. Figure 3-2 shows the relationship between normal balances and debits and credits.

FIGURE 3-2 Normal Balances

ACCOUNT	SIDE OF ACCOUNTING EQUATION	INCREASE	DECREASE	NORMAL BALANCE
Assets	Left	Debit	Credit	Debit
Liabilities	Right	Credit	Debit	Credit
Owner's Equity	Right	Credit	Debit	Credit

Expanding the accounting equation helps illustrate the use of debits and credits for revenue, expense, and drawing accounts. Since these accounts affect owner's equity, they are shown under the "umbrella" of owner's equity in the accounting equation in Figure 3-3.

FIGURE 3-3 The Accounting Equation and the Owner's Equity Umbrella

Revenues

Revenues increase owner's equity. Revenues could be recorded directly on the credit side of the owner's capital account. However, readers of financial statements are interested in the specific types of revenues earned. Therefore, specific revenue accounts, like Delivery Fees, Sales, and Service Fees, are used. These specific accounts are credited when revenue is earned.

Expenses

Expenses decrease owner's equity. Expenses could be recorded on the debit side of the owner's capital account. However, readers of financial statements want to see the types of expenses incurred during the accounting period. Thus, specific expense accounts are maintained for items like rent, wages, advertising, and utilities. These specific accounts are debited as expenses are incurred.

LEARNING KEY: You could credit the owner's capital account for revenues and debit the capital account for expenses and withdrawals. However, this is not a good idea. Using specific accounts provides additional information. Remember: an increase in an expense decreases owner's equity.

Drawing

Withdrawals of cash and other assets by the owner for personal reasons decrease owner's equity. Withdrawals could be debited directly to the owner's capital account. However, readers of financial statements want to know the amount of withdrawals for the accounting period. Thus, this information is kept in a separate account.

Normal Balances for the Owner's Equity Umbrella

Since expense and drawing accounts are debited for increases, these accounts normally have debit balances. Since revenue accounts are credited for increases, these accounts normally have credit balances. Figure 3-4 shows the normal balances for the owner's equity accounts.

FIGURE 3-4 Normal Balances for the Owner's Equity Umbrella

ACCOUNT	SIDE OF OWNER'S EQUITY UMBRELLA	INCREASE	DECREASE	NORMAL
Revenues	Right	Credit	Debit	Credit
Expenses	Left	Debit	Credit	Debit
Drawing	Left	Debit	Credit	Debit

TRANSACTION ANALYSIS

LO 4 Use T accounts to analyze transactions.

In Chapter 2, you learned how to analyze transactions by using the accounting equation. Here, we continue to use the accounting equation, but add debits and credits by using T accounts. As shown in Figure 3-5, the three basic questions that must be answered when analyzing a transaction are essentially the same, but are expanded slightly to address the use of the owner's equity umbrella and T accounts. You must determine the location of the account within the accounting equation and/or the owner's equity umbrella. You must also determine whether the accounts should be debited or credited.

FIGURE 3-5 Steps in Transaction Analysis

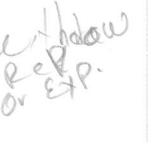

1. **What happened?**
   Make certain you understand the event that has taken place.

2. **Which accounts are affected?**
   Once you have determined what happened, you must:
   ▶ Identify the accounts that are affected.
   ▶ Classify these accounts as assets, liabilities, owner's equity, revenues, or expenses.
   ▶ Identify the location of the accounts in the accounting equation and/or the owner's equity umbrella—left or right.

3. **How is the accounting equation affected?**
   ▶ Determine whether the accounts have increased or decreased.
   ▶ Determine whether the accounts should be debited or credited.
   ▶ Make certain that the accounting equation remains in balance after the transaction has been entered.
   (1) Assets = Liabilities + Owner's Equity.
   (2) Debits = Credits for every transaction.

LEARNING KEY: If you have a debit, you must always have at least one credit. If you have a credit, you must always have at least one debit.

Debits and Credits: Asset, Liability, and Owner's Equity Accounts

Transactions (a) through (d) from Jessie Jane's Campus Delivery (Chapter 2) demonstrate the double-entry process for transactions affecting asset, liability, and owner's equity accounts.

As you study each transaction, answer the three questions: (1) What happened? (2) Which accounts are affected? and (3) How is the accounting equation affected? The transaction statement tells you what happened. The analysis following the illustration of each transaction tells which accounts are affected. The illustration shows you how the accounting equation is affected.

Transaction (a): Investment by owner

Jessica Jane opened a bank account with a deposit of $2,000 for her business (Figure 3-6).

Analysis: As a result of this transaction, the business acquired an asset, Cash. In exchange for the asset, the business gave Jessica Jane owner's equity. The owner's equity account is called Jessica Jane, Capital. The transaction is entered as an increase in an asset and an increase in owner's equity. Debit Cash and credit Jessica Jane, Capital for $2,000.

FIGURE 3-6 Transaction (a): Investment by Owner

Assets		=	Liabilities		+	Owner's Equity	
Debit	**Credit**		**Debit**	**Credit**		**Debit**	**Credit**
+	–		–	+		–	+
Cash						Jessica Jane, Capital	
(a) 2,000							(a) 2,000
$2,000		=				**$2,000**	

ACCOUNT AFFECTED	CLASSIFICATION	LOCATION IN EQUATION	INCREASE OR DECREASE	DEBIT OR CREDIT
Cash	Asset	Left	Increase	Debit
Capital	Owner's Equity	Right	Increase	Credit

Transaction (b): Purchase of an asset for cash

Jessie bought a motor scooter (delivery equipment) for $1,200 cash (Figure 3-7).

Analysis: Jessie exchanged one asset, Cash, for another, Delivery Equipment. Debit Delivery Equipment and credit Cash for $1,200. Notice that the total assets are still $2,000 as they were following transaction (a). Transaction (b) shifted assets from cash to delivery equipment, but total assets remained the same.

FIGURE 3-7 Transaction (b): Purchase of an Asset for Cash

Assets		=	Liabilities		+	Owner's Equity	
Debit	**Credit**		**Debit**	**Credit**		**Debit**	**Credit**
+	–		–	+		–	+
Cash						Jessica Jane, Capital	
Bal. 2,000							Bal. 2,000
	(b) 1,200						
Bal. 800							
Delivery Equipment							
(b) 1,200							
$2,000		=				**$2,000**	

ACCOUNT AFFECTED	CLASSIFICATION	LOCATION IN EQUATION	INCREASE OR DECREASE	DEBIT OR CREDIT
Delivery Equipment	Asset	Left	Increase	Debit
Cash	Asset	Left	Decrease	Credit

Transaction (c): Purchase of an asset on account
Jessie bought a second motor scooter on account for $900 (Figure 3-8).

Analysis: The asset, Delivery Equipment, increases by $900 and the liability, Accounts Payable, increases by the same amount. Thus, debit Delivery Equipment and credit Accounts Payable for $900.

FIGURE 3-8 Transaction (c): Purchase of an Asset on Account

Assets		=	Liabilities		+	Owner's Equity	
Debit +	Credit −		Debit −	Credit +		Debit −	Credit +
Cash			Accounts Payable			Jessica Jane, Capital	
Bal. 800				(c) 900			Bal. 2,000
Delivery Equipment							
Bal. 1,200							
(c) 900							
Bal. 2,100							
$2,900		=				$2,900	

ACCOUNT AFFECTED	CLASSIFICATION	LOCATION IN EQUATION	INCREASE OR DECREASE	DEBIT OR CREDIT
Delivery Equipment	Asset	Left	Increase	Debit
Accounts Payable	Liability	Right	Increase	Credit

Transaction (d): Payment on a loan
Jessie made the first $300 payment on the scooter purchased in transaction (c) (Figure 3-9).

Analysis: This payment decreases the asset, Cash, and decreases the liability, Accounts Payable. Debit Accounts Payable and credit Cash for $300.

FIGURE 3-9 Transaction (d): Payment on a Loan

Assets		=	Liabilities		+	Owner's Equity	
Debit	**Credit**		**Debit**	**Credit**		**Debit**	**Credit**
+	−		−	+		−	+
Cash			Accounts Payable			Jessica Jane, Capital	
Bal. 800				Bal. 900			Bal. 2,000
	(d) 300		(d) 300				
Bal. 500				Bal. 600			
Delivery Equipment							
Bal. 2,100							
$2,600		=				**$2,600**	

ACCOUNT AFFECTED	CLASSIFICATION	LOCATION IN EQUATION	INCREASE OR DECREASE	DEBIT OR CREDIT
Accounts Payable	Liability	Right	Decrease	Debit
Cash	Asset	Left	Decrease	Credit

Notice that for transactions (a) through (d), the debits equal credits and the accounting equation is in balance. Review transactions (a) through (d). Again, identify the accounts that were affected and how they were classified (assets, liabilities, or owner's equity). Finally, note each account's location within the accounting equation.

Debits and Credits: Including Revenues, Expenses, and Drawing

Transactions (a) through (d) involved only assets, liabilities, and the owner's capital account. To complete the illustration of Jessie Jane's Campus Delivery, the equation is expanded to include revenues, expenses, and drawing. Remember, revenues increase owner's equity and are shown under the credit side of the capital account. Expenses and drawing decrease owner's equity and are shown under the debit side of the capital account. The expanded equation is shown in Figure 3-10.

LEARNING KEY: Credits increase the capital account. Revenues increase capital. Thus, revenues are shown under the credit side of the capital account. Debits decrease the capital account. Expenses and drawing reduce owner's equity. Thus, they are shown under the debit side of the capital account.

FIGURE 3-10 The Expanded Accounting Equation

Assets		=	Liabilities		+	Owner's Equity (Jessica Jane, Capital)		
Debit	Credit		Debit	Credit		Debit		Credit
+	–		–	+		–		+

			Drawing		Expenses		Revenues	
			Debit	Credit	Debit	Credit	Debit	Credit
			+	–	+	–	–	+

Transaction (e): Delivery revenues earned in cash

Jessie made deliveries and received $500 cash from clients (Figure 3-11).

Analysis: The asset, Cash, and the revenue, Delivery Fees, increase. Debit Cash and credit Delivery Fees for $500.

FIGURE 3-11 Transaction (e): Delivery Revenues Earned in Cash

Assets		=	Liabilities		+	Owner's Equity	
Debit	Credit		Debit	Credit		Debit	Credit
+	–		–	+		–	+

Cash: Bal. 500; (e) 500; Bal. 1,000
Delivery Equipment: Bal. 2,100
Accounts Payable: Bal. 600
Jessica Jane, Capital: Bal. 2,000

Drawing		Expenses		Revenues	
Debit	Credit	Debit	Credit	Debit	Credit
+	–	+	–	–	+

Delivery Fees: (e) 500

$3,100 = $3,100

ACCOUNT AFFECTED	CLASSIFICATION	LOCATION IN EQUATION	INCREASE OR DECREASE	DEBIT OR CREDIT
Cash	Asset	Left	Increase	Debit
Delivery Fees	Revenue	Right O.E.—Right Side	Increase	Credit

Transaction (f): Paid rent for month
Jessie paid $200 for office rent for June (Figure 3-12).

Analysis: Rent Expense increases and Cash decreases. Debit Rent Expense and credit Cash for $200.

A debit to an expense account increases that expense and decreases owner's equity. Notice that the placement of the plus and minus signs for expenses are opposite the placement of the signs for owner's equity. Note also that expenses are located on the left (debit) side of the owner's equity umbrella.

FIGURE 3-12 Transaction (f): Paid Rent for Month

Assets		=	Liabilities		+	Owner's Equity			
Debit	Credit		Debit	Credit		Debit		Credit	
+	−		−	+		−		+	

Cash
Bal. 1,000	
	(f) 200
Bal. 800	

Accounts Payable
| | Bal.   600 |

Jessica Jane, Capital
| | Bal. 2,000 |

Delivery Equipment
| Bal. 2,100 | |

Drawing		Expenses		Revenues	
Debit	Credit	Debit	Credit	Debit	Credit
+	−	+	−	−	+

Rent Expense
| (f)   200 | |

Delivery Fees
| | Bal.   500 |

$2,900   = $2,900

ACCOUNT AFFECTED	CLASSIFICATION	LOCATION IN EQUATION	INCREASE OR DECREASE	DEBIT OR CREDIT
Rent Expense	Expense	Right O.E.—Left Side	Exp.— Increases; O.E.— Decreases	Debit
Cash	Asset	Left	Decrease	Credit

Transaction (g): Paid telephone bill
Jessie paid for telephone service, $50 (Figure 3-13).

Analysis: This transaction, like the previous one, increases an expense and decreases an asset. Debit Telephone Expense and credit Cash for $50.

FIGURE 3-13 Transaction (g): Paid Telephone Bill

Assets		=	Liabilities		+	Owner's Equity		
Debit	Credit		Debit	Credit		Debit		Credit
+	–		–	+		–		+

Cash			Accounts Payable			Jessica Jane, Capital		
Bal. 800				Bal. 600				Bal. 2,000
	(g) 50							
Bal. 750								

Delivery Equipment	
Bal. 2,100	

Drawing		Expenses		Revenues	
Debit	Credit	Debit	Credit	Debit	Credit
+	–	+	–	–	+

		Rent Expense		Delivery Fees	
		Bal. 200			Bal. 500
		Telephone Expense			
		(g) 50			

$2,850	=	**$2,850**

ACCOUNT AFFECTED	CLASSIFICATION	LOCATION IN EQUATION	INCREASE OR DECREASE	DEBIT OR CREDIT
Tele. Expense	Expense	Right O.E.—Left Side	Exp.— Increases; O.E.— Decreases	Debit
Cash	Asset	Left	Decrease	Credit

Transaction (h): Delivery revenues earned on account
Jessie made deliveries on account for $600 (Figure 3-14).

Analysis: As discussed in Chapter 2, delivery services are performed for which payment will be received later. This is called offering services "on account" or "on credit." Instead of receiving cash, Jessie receives a promise that her customers will pay cash in the future. Therefore, the asset, Accounts Receivable, increases. Since revenues are recognized when earned, the revenue account, Delivery Fees, also increases. Debit Accounts Receivable and credit Delivery Fees for $600.

FIGURE 3-14 Transaction (h): Delivery Revenues Earned on Account

Assets		=	Liabilities		+	Owner's Equity	
Debit	Credit		Debit	Credit		Debit	Credit
+	–		–	+		–	+

Cash
Bal. 750

Accounts Receivable
(h) 600

Delivery Equipment
Bal. 2,100

$3,450

=

Accounts Payable
Bal. 600

Jessica Jane, Capital
Bal. 2,000

Drawing		Expenses		Revenues	
Debit	Credit	Debit	Credit	Debit	Credit
+	–	+	–	–	+

Rent Expense
Bal. 200

Delivery Fees
Bal. 500
(h) 600
Bal. 1,100

Telephone Expense
Bal. 50

$3,450

ACCOUNT AFFECTED	CLASSIFICATION	LOCATION IN EQUATION	INCREASE OR DECREASE	DEBIT OR CREDIT
Accounts Rec.	Asset	Left	Increase	Debit
Delivery Fees	Revenue	Right O.E.—Right Side	Increase	Credit

Review transactions (e) through (h). Two of these transactions are expenses and two are revenue transactions. Each of these transactions affected the owner's equity umbrella. Three transactions affected Cash and one transaction affected Accounts Receivable. Keep in mind that expense and revenue transactions do not always affect cash.

Notice that the debits equal credits and the accounting equation is in balance after each transaction. As you review transactions (e) through (h), identify the accounts that were affected and classify each account (assets, liabilities, owner's equity, revenue, or expense). Notice each account's location within the accounting equation and the owner's equity umbrella.

Upcoming transactions (i) and (j) both involve an exchange of cash for another asset. As you analyze these two transactions and answer the three questions about these transactions, you may wonder why prepaid insurance and supplies are assets while the rent and telephone bill in transactions (f) and (g) are expenses. Prepaid insurance and supplies are assets because they will last for more than one month. Jessie pays her rent and her telephone bill each month so they are classified as expenses. If Jessie paid her rent only once every three months, she would need to set up an asset account called Prepaid Rent. She would debit this account when she paid the rent.

Transaction (i): Purchase of supplies

Jessie bought pens, paper, delivery envelopes, and other supplies for $80 cash (Figure 3-15).

Analysis: These supplies will last for several months. Since they will generate future benefits, the supplies should be recorded as an asset. An asset, Supplies, increases, and an asset, Cash, decreases. Debit Supplies and credit Cash for $80.

FIGURE 3-15 Transaction (i): Purchase of Supplies

Assets		=	Liabilities		+	Owner's Equity	
Debit	**Credit**		**Debit**	**Credit**		**Debit**	**Credit**
+	–		–	+		–	+

Cash
Bal. 750	
	(i) 80
Bal. 670	

Accounts Receivable
| Bal. 600 | |

Supplies
| (i)   80 | |

Delivery Equipment
| Bal. 2,100 | |

Accounts Payable
| | Bal.   600 |

Jessica Jane, Capital
| | Bal. 2,000 |

Drawing		Expenses		Revenues	
Debit	**Credit**	**Debit**	**Credit**	**Debit**	**Credit**
+	–	+	–	–	+

Rent Expense
| Bal.   200 | |

Telephone Expense
| Bal.   50 | |

Delivery Fees
| | Bal. 1,100 |

$3,450 = $3,450

ACCOUNT AFFECTED	CLASSIFICATION	LOCATION IN EQUATION	INCREASE OR DECREASE	DEBIT OR CREDIT
Supplies	Asset	Left	Increase	Debit
Cash	Asset	Left	Decrease	Credit

A BROADER VIEW

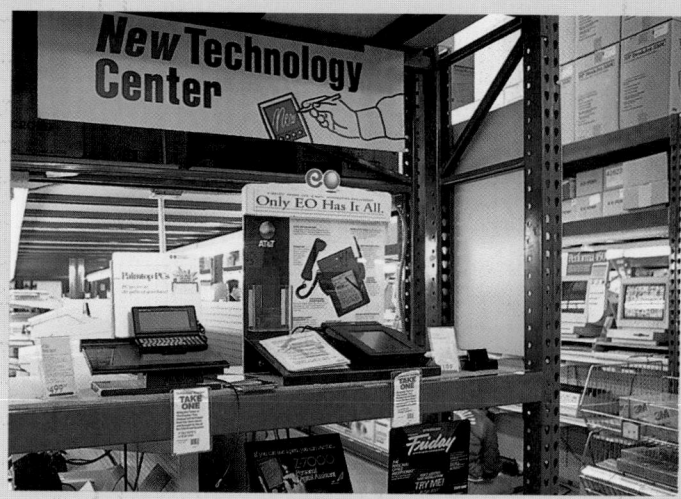

SUPPLIES—ASSET OR EXPENSE?

When businesses buy office supplies from Staples or other suppliers, the supplies are initially recorded as assets. This is done because the supplies will provide future benefits. Those still remaining at the end of the accounting period are reported on the balance sheet as assets. Supplies actually used during the period are recognized as an expense on the income statement. We will discuss how to account for the expense in Chapter 5.

Transaction (j): Payment of insurance premium

Jessie paid $200 for an eight-month liability insurance policy (Figure 3-16).

Analysis: Since insurance is paid in advance and will provide future benefits, it is treated as an asset. Therefore, one asset, Prepaid Insurance, increases and another, Cash, decreases. Debit Prepaid Insurance and credit Cash for $200.

PROFILES in ACCOUNTING

Jeanette Anderson, Factory Accounting Clerk

Jeanette Anderson earned a 4.0 GPA and membership in Phi Theta Kappa while completing her Associate Degree in Business at Eastern Wyoming College. While on campus, she held a work-study job as an Instructor Assistant. In this position Jeanette demonstrated a sound work ethic, an ability to get along well with others, and competence.

After graduation, she went to work for Imperial/Holly Sugar Corp. in Torrington, WY. Her duties include working with automated accounts payable, accounts receivable, and inventory control. During the annual harvest campaign, she supervises data entry clerks.

Jeanette believes the key to her success has been her understanding of double-entry accounting combined with her computer skills. Possessing problem-solving skills and being flexible are also important.

Source: Jack Kappeler, Eastern Wyoming College

FIGURE 3-16 Transaction (j): Payment of Insurance Premium

Assets		=	Liabilities		+	Owner's Equity	
Debit	**Credit**		**Debit**	**Credit**		**Debit**	**Credit**
+	**–**		**–**	**+**		**–**	**+**

Cash		Accounts Payable		Jessica Jane, Capital	
Bal. 670			Bal. 600		Bal. 2,000
	(j) 200				
Bal. 470					

Accounts Receivable	
Bal. 600	

	Drawing		Expenses		Revenues	
	Debit	**Credit**	**Debit**	**Credit**	**Debit**	**Credit**
	+	**–**	**+**	**–**	**–**	**+**

Supplies	
Bal. 80	

Rent Expense		Delivery Fees	
Bal. 200			Bal. 1,100

Prepaid Insurance	
(j) 200	

Telephone Expense	
Bal. 50	

Delivery Equipment	
Bal. 2,100	

$3,450 = $3,450

ACCOUNT AFFECTED	CLASSIFICATION	LOCATION IN EQUATION	INCREASE OR DECREASE	DEBIT OR CREDIT
Prepaid Insurance	Asset	Left	Increase	Debit
Cash	Asset	Left	Decrease	Credit

Transaction (k): Cash receipts from prior sales on account

Jessie received $570 in cash for delivery services performed for customers earlier in the month (see transaction (h)) (Figure 3-17).

Analysis: This transaction increases Cash and reduces the amount due from customers reported in Accounts Receivable. Debit Cash and credit Accounts Receivable $570.

As you analyze transaction (k), notice which accounts are affected and the location of these accounts in the accounting equation. Jessie received cash, but this transaction did not affect revenue. The revenue was recorded in transaction (h). Transaction (k) is an exchange of one asset (Accounts Receivable) for another asset (Cash).

FIGURE 3-17 Transaction (k): Cash Receipts from Prior Sales on Account

Assets		=	Liabilities		+	Owner's Equity	
Debit	**Credit**		**Debit**	**Credit**		**Debit**	**Credit**
+	–		–	+		–	+

Cash		Accounts Payable		Jessica Jane, Capital	
Bal. 470			Bal. 600		Bal. 2,000
(k) 570					
Bal. 1,040					

Accounts Receivable	
Bal. 600	
	(k) 570
Bal. 30	

	Drawing		Expenses		Revenues	
	Debit	**Credit**	**Debit**	**Credit**	**Debit**	**Credit**
	+	–	+	–	–	+

Supplies	
Bal. 80	

Rent Expense		Delivery Fees	
Bal. 200			Bal. 1,100

Prepaid Insurance	
Bal. 200	

Telephone Expense	
Bal. 50	

Delivery Equipment	
Bal. 2,100	

$3,450	=	$3,450

ACCOUNT AFFECTED	CLASSIFICATION	LOCATION IN EQUATION	INCREASE OR DECREASE	DEBIT OR CREDIT
Cash	Asset	Left	Increase	Debit
Accounts Rec.	Asset	Left	Decrease	Credit

As you analyze transactions (l) through (o), make certain that you understand what has happened in each transaction. Identify the accounts that are affected and the locations of these accounts within the accounting equation. Notice that the accounting equation remains in balance after every transaction and debits equal credits for each transaction.

Transaction (l): Purchase of an asset on credit making a partial payment

Jessie bought a third motor scooter for $1,500. Jessie made a down payment of $300 and spread the remaining payments over the next four months (Figure 3-18).

Analysis: The asset, Delivery Equipment, increases by $1,500, Cash decreases by $300, and the liability, Accounts Payable, increases by $1,200. Thus, debit Delivery Equipment for $1,500, credit Cash for $300, and credit Accounts Payable for $1,200. This transaction requires one debit and two credits. Even so, total debits ($1,500) equal the total credits ($1,200 + $300) and the accounting equation remains in balance.

FIGURE 3-18 Transaction (l): Purchase of an Asset on Credit Making a Partial Payment

Assets		=	Liabilities		+	Owner's Equity	
Debit	**Credit**		**Debit**	**Credit**		**Debit**	**Credit**
+	−		−	+		−	+

Cash			Accounts Payable	
Bal. 1,040				Bal. 600
	(l) 300			(l) 1,200
Bal. 740				Bal. 1,800

Accounts Receivable	
Bal. 30	

Supplies	
Bal. 80	

Prepaid Insurance	
Bal. 200	

Delivery Equipment	
Bal. 2,100	
(l) 1,500	
Bal. 3,600	

Jessica Jane, Capital — Bal. 2,000

	Drawing		Expenses		Revenues	
	Debit	**Credit**	**Debit**	**Credit**	**Debit**	**Credit**
	+	−	+	−	−	+

Rent Expense		Delivery Fees	
Bal. 200			Bal. 1,100

Telephone Expense	
Bal. 50	

$4,650   = $4,650

ACCOUNT AFFECTED	CLASSIFICATION	LOCATION IN EQUATION	INCREASE OR DECREASE	DEBIT OR CREDIT
Delivery Equip.	Asset	Left	Increase	Debit
Cash	Asset	Left	Decrease	Credit
Accounts Payable	Liability	Right	Increase	Credit

Transaction (m): Payment of wages

Jessie paid her part-time employees $650 in wages (Figure 3-19).

Analysis: This is an additional business expense. Expenses increase and Cash decreases. Debit Wages Expense and credit Cash for $650.

FIGURE 3-19 Transaction (m): Payment of Wages

ACCOUNT AFFECTED	CLASSIFICATION	LOCATION IN EQUATION	INCREASE OR DECREASE	DEBIT OR CREDIT
Wages Expense	Expense	Right O.E.— Left Side	Exp.— Increases; O.E.— Decreases	Debit
Cash	Asset	Left	Decrease	Credit

Transaction (n): Deliveries made for cash and credit

Total delivery fees for the remainder of the month amounted to $1,050: $430 in cash and $620 on account (Figure 3-20).

Analysis: Since the delivery fees have been earned, the revenue account increases by $1,050. Also, Cash increases by $430 and Accounts Receivable increases by $620. Note once again that one event impacts three accounts. This time we have debits of $430 to Cash and $620 to Accounts Receivable, and a credit of $1,050 to Delivery Fees. As before, the total debits ($430 + $620) equal the total credits ($1,050) and the accounting equation remains in balance.

FIGURE 3-20 Transaction (n): Deliveries Made for Cash and Credit

Assets		=	Liabilities		+	Owner's Equity	
Debit	**Credit**		**Debit**	**Credit**		**Debit**	**Credit**
+	–		–	+		–	+

Cash			Accounts Payable			Jessica Jane, Capital	
Bal. 90				Bal. 1,800			Bal. 2,000
(n) 430							
Bal. 520							

Accounts Receivable

| Bal. 30 |
| (n) 620 |
| Bal. 650 |

Supplies

| Bal. 80 |

Prepaid Insurance

| Bal. 200 |

Delivery Equipment

| Bal. 3,600 |

Drawing		Expenses		Revenues	
Debit	**Credit**	**Debit**	**Credit**	**Debit**	**Credit**
+	–	+	–	–	+

		Rent Expense		Delivery Fees	
		Bal. 200			Bal. 1,100
					(n) 1,050
					Bal. 2,150

Telephone Expense

| Bal. 50 |

Wages Expense

| Bal. 650 |

$5,050 = $5,050

ACCOUNT AFFECTED	CLASSIFICATION	LOCATION IN EQUATION	INCREASE OR DECREASE	DEBIT OR CREDIT
Cash	Asset	Left	Increase	Debit
Accounts Rec.	Asset	Left	Increase	Debit
Delivery Fees	Revenue	Right O.E.—Right Side	Increase	Credit

Transaction (o): Withdrawal of cash from business

At the end of the month, Jessie withdrew $150 in cash from the business to purchase books for her classes (Figure 3-21).

Analysis: Cash withdrawals decrease owner's equity and decrease cash. Debit Jessica Jane, Drawing and credit Cash for $150.

FIGURE 3-21 Transaction (o): Withdrawal of Cash from Business

Assets		=	Liabilities		+	Owner's Equity		
Debit	**Credit**		**Debit**	**Credit**		**Debit**		**Credit**
+	–		–	+		–		+

Cash			Accounts Payable	
Bal. 520				Bal. 1,800
	(o) 150			
Bal. 370				

Jessica Jane, Capital
Bal. 2,000

Accounts Receivable	
Bal. 650	

	Drawing		Expenses		Revenues	
	Debit	**Credit**	**Debit**	**Credit**	**Debit**	**Credit**
	+	–	+	–	–	+

Supplies	
Bal. 80	

Jessica Jane, Drawing		Rent Expense		Delivery Fees	
(o) 150		Bal. 200			Bal. 2,150

Prepaid Insurance	
Bal. 200	

Telephone Expense
Bal. 50

Delivery Equipment	
Bal. 3,600	

Wages Expense
Bal. 650

$4,900 = $4,900

ACCOUNT AFFECTED	CLASSIFICATION	LOCATION IN EQUATION	INCREASE OR DECREASE	DEBIT OR CREDIT
Drawing	Drawing	Right O.E.— Left Side	Drawing— Increases; O.E.— Decreases	Debit
Cash	Asset	Left	Decrease	Credit

Withdrawals are reported in the drawing account. Withdrawals by an owner are the opposite of an investment. You could debit the owner's capital account for withdrawals. However, using a specific account tells the user of the accounting information how much was withdrawn for the period.

Summary of Transactions

In illustrating transactions (a) through (o), each T account for Jessie Jane's Campus Delivery shows a balance before and after each transaction. To focus your attention on the transaction being explained, only a single entry was shown. In practice, this is not done. Instead, each account gathers all transactions for a period. Jessie's accounts, with all transactions listed, are shown in Figure 3-22. Note the following:

1. The footings are directly under the debit (left) and credit (right) sides of the T account for those accounts with more than one debit or credit.

2. The balance is shown on the side with the larger footing.

3. The footing serves as the balance for accounts with entries on only one side of the account.

4. If an account has only a single entry, it is not necessary to enter a footing or balance.

FIGURE 3-22 Summary of Transactions (a) Through (o)

Assets		=	Liabilities		+	Owner's Equity	
Debit +	**Credit** –		**Debit** –	**Credit** +		**Debit** –	**Credit** +

Cash

(a)	2,000	(b)	1,200
(e)	500	(d)	300
(k)	570	(f)	200
(n)	430	(g)	50
	3,500	(i)	80
		(j)	200
		(l)	300
		(m)	650
		(o)	150
			3,130
Bal.	370		

Accounts Receivable

(h)	600	(k)	570
(n)	620		
	1,220		
Bal.	650		

Supplies

(i)	80	

Prepaid Insurance

(j)	200	

Delivery Equipment

(b)	1,200	
(c)	900	
(l)	1,500	
Bal.	3,600	

Accounts Payable

(d)	300	(c)	900
		(l)	1,200
			2,100
		Bal.	1,800

Jessica Jane, Capital

	(a)	2,000

Drawing		Expenses		Revenues	
Debit +	**Credit** –	**Debit** +	**Credit** –	**Debit** –	**Credit** +

Jessica Jane, Drawing

(o)	150	

Rent Expense

(f)	200	

Delivery Fees

	(e)	500
	(h)	600
	(n)	1,050
	Bal.	2,150

Telephone Expense

(g)	50	

Wages Expense

(m)	650	

$4,900 = $4,900

THE TRIAL BALANCE

LO 5   Prepare a trial balance and explain its purposes and linkages with the financial statements.

Recall the two very important rules in double-entry accounting:

1. The sum of the debits must equal the sum of the credits. This means that at least two accounts are affected by each transaction. This rule is so important that many computer accounting programs will not permit a transaction to be entered into the accounting system unless the debits equal the credits.

2. The accounting equation must remain in balance.

In illustrating the transactions for Jessie Jane's Campus Delivery, the equality of the accounting equation was verified after each transaction. Because of the large number of transactions entered each day, this is not done in practice. Instead, a trial balance is prepared periodically to determine the equality of the debits and credits. A **trial balance** is a list of all accounts showing the title and balance of each account. By totaling the debits and credits, their equality can be tested.

A trial balance of Jessie's accounts, taken on June 30, 20--, is shown in Figure 3-23. This date is shown on the third line of the heading. The trial balance shows that the debit and credit totals are equal in amount. This is proof that (1) in entering transactions (a) through (o), the total of the debits was equal to the total of the credits, and (2) the accounting equation has remained in balance.

 LEARNING KEY: A trial balance provides proof that total debits equal total credits and shows that the accounting equation is in balance.

A trial balance is not a formal statement or report. Normally, only the accountant sees it. As shown in Figure 3-24, a trial balance can be used as an aid in preparing the financial statements.

FIGURE 3-23 Trial Balance

Since a trial balance is not a formal statement, dollar signs are not used.

ACCOUNT TITLE	DEBIT BALANCE	CREDIT BALANCE
Cash	3 7 0 00	
Accounts Receivable	6 5 0 00	
Supplies	8 0 00	
Prepaid Insurance	2 0 0 00	
Delivery Equipment	3 6 0 0 00	
Accounts Payable		1 8 0 0 00
Jessica Jane, Capital		2 0 0 0 00
Jessica Jane, Drawing	1 5 0 00	
Delivery Fees		2 1 5 0 00
Rent Expense	2 0 0 00	
Telephone Expense	5 0 00	
Wages Expense	6 5 0 00	
	5 9 5 0 00	5 9 5 0 00

Jessie Jane's Campus Delivery
Trial Balance
June 30, 20--

FIGURE 3-24 Linkages Between the Trial Balance and Financial Statements

Jessie Jane's Campus Delivery
Trial Balance
June 30, 20 - -

ACCOUNT TITLE	DEBIT BALANCE	CREDIT BALANCE
Cash	3 7 0 00	
Accounts Receivable	6 5 0 00	
Supplies	8 0 00	
Prepaid Insurance	2 0 0 00	
Delivery Equipment	3 6 0 0 00	
Accounts Payable		1 8 0 0 00
Jessica Jane, Capital		2 0 0 0 00
Jessica Jane, Drawing	1 5 0 00	
Delivery Fees		2 1 5 0 00
Rent Expense	2 0 0 00	
Telephone Expense	5 0 00	
Wages Expense	6 5 0 00	
	5 9 5 0 00	5 9 5 0 00

Jessie Jane's Campus Delivery
Income Statement
For Month Ended June 30, 20 --

Revenue:		
Delivery fees		$2 1 5 0 00
Expenses:		
Wages expense	$ 6 5 0 00	
Rent expense	2 0 0 00	
Telephone expense	5 0 00	
Total expenses		9 0 0 00
Net income		$1 2 5 0 00

Jessie Jane's Campus Delivery
Statement of Owner's Equity
For Month Ended June 30, 20 - -

Jessica Jane, capital, June 1, 20 - -		$2 0 0 0 00
Net income for June	$1 2 5 0 00	
Less withdrawals for June	1 5 0 00	
Increase in capital		1 1 0 0 00
Jessica Jane, capital, June 30, 20 - -		$3 1 0 0 00

Jessie Jane's Campus Delivery
Balance Sheet
June 30, 20 - -

Assets		Liabilities	
Cash	$ 3 7 0 00	Accounts payable	$1 8 0 0 00
Accounts receivable	6 5 0 00		
Supplies	8 0 00	Owner's Equity	
Prepaid insurance	2 0 0 00	Jessica Jane, capital	3 1 0 0 00
Delivery equipment	3 6 0 0 00		
		Total liabilities and	
Total assets	$4 9 0 0 00	owner's equity	$4 9 0 0 00

Learning Objectives	Key Points to Remember
1 **Define the parts of a T account.**	The parts of a T account are: 1. the title, 2. the debit or left side, and 3. the credit or right side.

Title

Debit = Left	Credit = Right

2 **Foot and balance a T account.**	Rules for footing and balancing T accounts are: 1. The footings are directly under the debit (left) and credit (right) sides of the T account for those accounts with more than one debit or credit. 2. The balance is shown on the side with the larger footing. 3. The footing serves as the balance for accounts with entries on only one side of the account. 4. If an account has only a single entry, it is not necessary to enter a footing or balance.
3 **Describe the effects of debits and credits on specific types of accounts.**	Rules for debits and credits. (See illustration below.) 1. Assets are on the left side of the accounting equation. Therefore, increases are entered on the left (debit) side of an asset account and decreases are entered on the right (credit) side. 2. Liabilities and owner's equity are on the right side of the accounting equation. Therefore, increases are entered on the right (credit) side and decreases are entered on the left (debit) side. 3. Revenues are on the right side of the owner's equity umbrella. Therefore, increases are entered on the right (credit) side and decreases are entered on the left (debit) side. 4. Expenses and drawing are on the left side of the owner's equity umbrella. Therefore, increases are entered on the left (debit) side and decreases are entered on the right (credit) side.

Accounting Equation with Owner's Equity Umbrella

Assets		=	Liabilities		+	Owner's Equity Jessica Jane, Capital	
Debit	**Credit**		**Debit**	**Credit**		**Debit**	**Credit**
+	–		–	+		–	+

Drawing		Revenues	
Debit	**Credit**	**Debit**	**Credit**
+	–	–	+

Expenses	
Debit	**Credit**
+	–

Learning Objectives	Key Points to Remember
4 **Use T accounts to analyze transactions.**	Picture the accounting equation in your mind as you analyze transactions. When entering transactions in T accounts: 1. The sum of the debits must equal the sum of the credits. 2. At least two accounts are affected by each transaction. 3. When finished, the accounting equation must remain in balance.
5 **Prepare a trial balance and explain its purposes and linkages with the financial statements.**	A trial balance shows that the debit and credit totals are equal. A trial balance also can be used in preparing the financial statements.

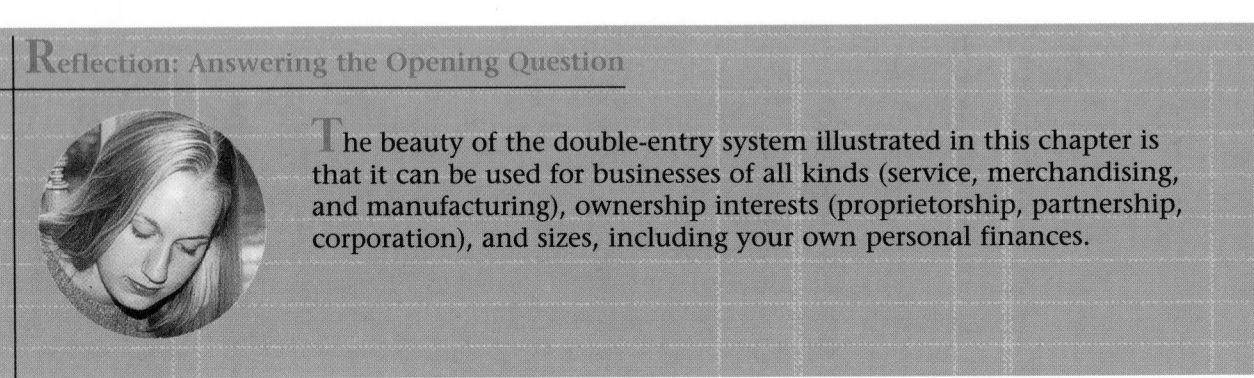

Reflection: Answering the Opening Question

The beauty of the double-entry system illustrated in this chapter is that it can be used for businesses of all kinds (service, merchandising, and manufacturing), ownership interests (proprietorship, partnership, corporation), and sizes, including your own personal finances.

KEY TERMS

balance, (48)   The difference between the footings of an account.

credit, (49)   To enter an amount on the right side of an account.

credit balance, (50)   The normal balance of liability, owner's equity, and revenue accounts.

debit, (49)   To enter an amount on the left side of an account.

debit balance, (50)   The normal balance of asset, expense, and drawing accounts.

double-entry accounting, (48)   A system in which each transaction has a dual effect on the accounting elements.

footings, (48)   The total dollar amounts on the debit and credit sides of an account.

normal balance, (50)   The side of an account that is increased.

trial balance, (69)   A list of accounts, showing the title and balance of each account, used to prove that the debits equal the credits in the general ledger.

DEMONSTRATION PROBLEM

Celia Pints opened We-Buy, You-Pay Shopping Services. For a fee that is based on the amount of research and shopping time required, Pints and her associates will shop for almost anything from groceries to home furnishings. Business is particularly heavy around Christmas and in early summer. The business operates from a rented store front. The associates receive a commission based on the revenues they produce and a mileage reimbursement for the use of their personal automobiles for shopping trips. Pints decided to use the following accounts to record transactions:

Assets	Owner's Equity
Cash	Celia Pints, Capital
Accounts Receivable	Celia Pints, Drawing
Office Equipment	Revenue
Computer Equipment	Shopping Fees
Liabilities	Expenses
Accounts Payable	Rent Expense
Notes Payable	Telephone Expense
	Commissions Expense
	Utilities Expense
	Travel Expense

The following transactions are for the month of December 20--.

(a) Pints invested cash in the business, $30,000.

(b) Bought office equipment for $10,000. Paid $2,000 in cash and promised to pay the balance over the next four months.

(c) Paid rent for December, $500.

(d) Provided shopping services for customers on account, $5,200.

(e) Paid telephone bill, $90.

(f) Borrowed cash from the bank by signing a note payable, $5,000.

(g) Bought a computer and printer, $4,800.

(h) Collected cash from customers for services performed on account, $4,000.

(i) Paid commissions to associates for revenues generated during the first half of the month, $3,500.

(j) Paid utility bill, $600.

(k) Paid cash on account for the office equipment purchased in transaction (b), $2,000.

(l) Earned shopping fees of $13,200: $6,000 in cash and $7,200 on account.

(m) Paid commissions to associates for last half of month, $7,000.

(n) Paid mileage reimbursements for the month, $1,500.

(o) Paid cash on note payable to bank, $1,000.

(p) Pints withdrew cash for personal use, $2,000.

(continued)

1. Enter the transactions for December in T accounts. Use the accounting equation as a guide for setting up the T accounts.

2. Foot the T accounts and determine their balances as necessary.

3. Prepare a trial balance of the accounts as of December 31 of the current year.

4. Prepare an income statement for the month ended December 31 of the current year.

5. Prepare a statement of owner's equity for the month ended December 31 of the current year.

6. Prepare a balance sheet as of December 31 of the current year.

Solution

1, 2.

Assets		=	Liabilities		+	Owner's Equity	
Debit	**Credit**		**Debit**	**Credit**		**Debit**	**Credit**
+	–		–	+		–	+

Cash

(a) 30,000	(b) 2,000
(f) 5,000	(c) 500
(h) 4,000	(e) 90
(l) 6,000	(g) 4,800
45,000	(i) 3,500
	(j) 600
	(k) 2,000
	(m) 7,000
	(n) 1,500
	(o) 1,000
	(p) 2,000
	24,990
Bal. 20,010	

Accounts Receivable

(d) 5,200	(h) 4,000
(l) 7,200	
12,400	
Bal. 8,400	

Office Equipment

(b) 10,000	

Computer Equipment

(g) 4,800	

Accounts Payable

(k) 2,000	(b) 8,000
	Bal. 6,000

Notes Payable

(o) 1,000	(f) 5,000
	Bal. 4,000

Celia Pints, Capital

	(a) 30,000

Drawing		Expenses		Revenues	
Debit	**Credit**	**Debit**	**Credit**	**Debit**	**Credit**
+	–	+	–	–	+

Celia Pints, Drawing

(p) 2,000	

Rent Expense

(c) 500	

Telephone Expense

(e) 90	

Commissions Expense

(i) 3,500	
(m) 7,000	
Bal. 10,500	

Utilities Expense

(j) 600	

Travel Expense

(n) 1,500	

Shopping Fees

	(d) 5,200
	(l) 13,200
	Bal. 18,400

$43,210	=	**$43,210**

3.

We-Buy, You-Pay Shopping Services **Trial Balance** **December 31, 20 - -**										
ACCOUNT TITLE	DEBIT BALANCE					CREDIT BALANCE				
Cash	20	0	1	0	00					
Accounts Receivable	8	4	0	0	00					
Office Equipment	10	0	0	0	00					
Computer Equipment	4	8	0	0	00					
Accounts Payable						6	0	0	0	00
Notes Payable						4	0	0	0	00
Celia Pints, Capital						30	0	0	0	00
Celia Pints, Drawing	2	0	0	0	00					
Shopping Fees						18	4	0	0	00
Rent Expense		5	0	0	00					
Telephone Expense			9	0	00					
Commissions Expense	10	5	0	0	00					
Utilities Expense		6	0	0	00					
Travel Expense	1	5	0	0	00					
	58	4	0	0	00	58	4	0	0	00

4.

We-Buy, You-Pay Shopping Services **Income Statement** **For Month Ended December 31, 20 - -**										
Revenue:										
Shopping fees						$18	4	0	0	00
Expenses:										
Commissions expense	$10	5	0	0	00					
Travel expense	1	5	0	0	00					
Utilities expense		6	0	0	00					
Rent expense		5	0	0	00					
Telephone expense			9	0	00					
Total expenses						13	1	9	0	00
Net income						$ 5	2	1	0	00

5.

We-Buy, You-Pay Shopping Services **Statement of Owner's Equity** **For Month Ended December 31, 20 - -**										
Celia Pints, capital, December 1, 20 - -						$30	0	0	0	00
Net income for December	$5	2	1	0	00					
Less withdrawals for December	2	0	0	0	00					
Increase in capital						3	2	1	0	00
Celia Pints, capital, December 31, 20 - -						$33	2	1	0	00

(continued)

6.

We-Buy, You-Pay Shopping Services Balance Sheet December 31, 20 - -												
Assets						**Liabilities**						
Cash	$ 20	0	1	0	00	Accounts payable	$ 6	0	0	0	00
Accounts receivable	8	4	0	0	00	Notes payable	4	0	0	0	00
Office equipment	10	0	0	0	00	Total liabilities	$10	0	0	0	00
Computer equipment	4	8	0	0	00						
						Owner's Equity					
						Celia Pints, capital	33	2	1	0	00
						Total liabilities and					
Total assets	$43	2	1	0	00	owner's equity	$43	2	1	0	00

REVIEW QUESTIONS

1. What are the three major parts of a T account?

2. What is the left side of the T account called? the right side?

3. What is a footing?

4. What is the relationship between the revenue and expense accounts and the owner's equity account?

5. What is the function of the trial balance?

MANAGING YOUR WRITING

Write a one-page memo to your instructor explaining how you could use the double-entry system to maintain records of your personal finances. What types of accounts would you use for the accounting elements?

SERIES A EXERCISES

EXERCISE 3A-1 (LO 2) FOOT AND BALANCE A T ACCOUNT Foot and balance the cash T account shown.

Cash

500	100
400	200
600	

2000   *300*

1,700.00

EXERCISE 3A-2 (LO 3) DEBIT AND CREDIT ANALYSIS Complete the following questions using either "debit" or "credit."

(a) The cash account is increased with a _____.

(b) The owner's capital account is increased with a _____.

(c) The delivery equipment account is increased with a _____.

(d) The cash account is decreased with a _____.

(e) The liability account Accounts Payable is increased with a _____.

(f) The revenue account Delivery Fees is increased with a _____.

(g) The asset account Accounts Receivable is increased with a _____.

(h) The rent expense account is increased with a _____.

(i) The owner's drawing account is increased with a _____.

EXERCISE 3A-3 (LO 2/3/4) ANALYSIS OF T ACCOUNTS Jim Arnold began a business called Arnold's Shoe Repair.

1. Create T accounts for Cash; Supplies; Jim Arnold, Capital; and Utilities Expense. Identify the following transactions by letter and place them on the proper side of the T accounts.

(a) Arnold invested cash in the business, $5,000.

(b) Purchased supplies for cash, $800.

(c) Paid utility bill, $1,500.

2. Foot the T account for cash and enter the ending balance.

EXERCISE 3A-4 (LO 3) NORMAL BALANCE OF ACCOUNT Indicate the normal balance (debit or credit) for each of the following accounts.

1. Cash   *debit*

2. Wages Expense   *debit*

3. Accounts Payable *credit*

4. Owner's Drawing *Debit*

5. Supplies   *Debit*

6. Owner's Capital *Credit*

7. Equipment   *Debit*

EXERCISE 3A-5 (LO 4) TRANSACTION ANALYSIS Sheryl Hansen started a business on May 1, 20--. Analyze the following transactions for the first month of business using T accounts. Label each T account with the title of the account affected and then place the transaction letter and the dollar amount on the debit or credit side.

(a) Hansen invested cash in the business, $4,000.

(b) Bought equipment for cash, $500.

(c) Bought equipment on account, $800.

(continued)

(d) Paid cash on account for equipment purchased in transaction (c), $300.

(e) Hansen withdrew cash for personal use, $700.

EXERCISE 3A-6 (LO 2) FOOT AND BALANCE A T ACCOUNT Foot and balance the cash T account prepared in Exercise 3A-5.

EXERCISE 3A-7 (LO 2/4) ANALYSIS OF TRANSACTIONS Charles Chadwick opened a business called Charlie's Detective Service in January 20--. Set up T accounts for the following accounts: Cash; Accounts Receivable; Office Supplies; Computer Equipment; Office Furniture; Accounts Payable; Charles Chadwick, Capital; Charles Chadwick, Drawing; Professional Fees; Rent Expense; and Utilities Expense.

The following transactions occurred during the first month of business. Record these transactions in T accounts. After all transactions are recorded, foot and balance the accounts if necessary.

(a) Chadwick invested cash in the business, $30,000.

(b) Bought office supplies for cash, $300.

(c) Bought office furniture for cash, $5,000.

(d) Purchased computer and printer on account, $8,000.

(e) Received cash from clients for services, $3,000.

(f) Paid cash on account for computer and printer purchased in transaction (d), $4,000.

(g) Earned professional fees on account during the month, $9,000.

(h) Paid cash for office rent for January, $1,500.

(i) Paid utility bills for the month, $800.

(j) Received cash from clients billed in transaction (g), $6,000.

(k) Chadwick withdrew cash for personal use, $3,000.

EXERCISE 3A-8 (LO 5) TRIAL BALANCE Based on the transactions recorded in Exercise 3A-7, prepare a trial balance for Charlie's Detective Service as of January 31, 20--.

EXERCISE 3A-9 (LO 5) TRIAL BALANCE The following accounts have normal balances. Prepare a trial balance for Juanita's Delivery Service as of September 30, 20--.

Cash	$ 5,000
Accounts Receivable	3,000
Supplies	800
Prepaid Insurance	600
Delivery Equipment	8,000
Accounts Payable	2,000
Juanita Raye, Capital	10,000
Juanita Raye, Drawing	1,000
Delivery Fees	9,400
Wages Expense	2,100
Rent Expense	900

EXERCISE 3A-10 (LO 5) INCOME STATEMENT From the information in Exercise 3A-9, prepare an income statement for Juanita's Delivery Service for the month ended September 30, 20--.

EXERCISE 3A-11 (LO 5) STATEMENT OF OWNER'S EQUITY From the information in Exercise 3A-9, prepare a statement of owner's equity for Juanita's Delivery Service for the month ended September 30, 20--.

EXERCISE 3A-12 (LO 5) BALANCE SHEET From the information in Exercise 3A-9, prepare a balance sheet for Juanita's Delivery Service as of September 30, 20--.

SERIES A PROBLEMS

PROBLEM 3A-1 (LO 2/4/5) T ACCOUNTS AND TRIAL BALANCE Harold Long started a business in May 20-- called Harold's Home Repair. Long hired a part-time college student as an assistant. Long has decided to use the following accounts for recording transactions:

Assets	Owner's Equity
Cash	Harold Long, Capital
Accounts Receivable	Harold Long, Drawing
Office Supplies	Revenue
Prepaid Insurance	Service Fees
Equipment	Expenses
Van	Rent Expense
Liabilities	Wages Expense
Accounts Payable	Telephone Expense
	Gas and Oil Expense

The following transactions occurred during May:

(a) Long invested cash in the business, $20,000.

(b) Purchased a used van for cash, $7,000.

(c) Purchased equipment on account, $5,000.

(d) Received cash for services rendered, $6,000.

(e) Paid cash on account owed from transaction (c), $2,000.

(f) Paid rent for the month, $900.

(g) Paid telephone bill, $200.

(h) Earned revenue on account, $4,000.

(i) Purchased office supplies for cash, $120.

(j) Paid wages to student, $600.

(k) Purchased insurance, $1,200.

(l) Received cash from services performed in transaction (h), $3,000.

(m) Paid cash for gas and oil expense on the van, $160.

(continued)

(n) Purchased additional equipment for $3,000, paying $1,000 cash and spreading the remaining payments over the next 10 months.

(o) Service fees earned for the remainder of the month amounted to $3,200: $1,800 in cash and $1,400 on account.

(p) Long withdrew cash at the end of the month, $2,800.

REQUIRED
1. Enter the transactions in T accounts, identifying each transaction with its corresponding letter.

2. Foot and balance the accounts where necessary.

3. Prepare a trial balance as of May 31, 20--.

PROBLEM 3A-2 (LO 5) NET INCOME AND CHANGE IN OWNER'S EQUITY Refer to the trial balance of Harold's Home Repair in Problem 3A-1 to determine the following information. Use the format provided below.

1. a. Total revenue for the month _____

   b. Total expenses for the month _____

   c. Net income for the month _____

2. a. Harold Long's original investment in the business _____

      + the net income for the month _____

      – owner's drawing _____

      Increase (decrease) in capital _____

      = ending owner's equity _____

   b. End of month accounting equation:

Assets	=	Liabilities	+	Owner's Equity
_____	=	_____	+	_____

PROBLEM 3A-3 (LO 5) FINANCIAL STATEMENTS Refer to the trial balance in Problem 3A-1 and to the analysis of the change in owner's equity in Problem 3A-2.

REQUIRED
1. Prepare an income statement for Harold's Home Repair for the month ended May 31, 20--.

2. Prepare a statement of owner's equity for Harold's Home Repair for the month ended May 31, 20--.

3. Prepare a balance sheet for Harold's Home Repair as of May 31, 20--.

SERIES B EXERCISES

EXERCISE 3B-1 (LO 2) FOOT AND BALANCE A T ACCOUNT Foot and balance the accounts payable T account shown.

Accounts Payable	
300	450
250	350
	150

EXERCISE 3B-2 (LO 3) DEBIT AND CREDIT ANALYSIS Complete the following questions using either "debit" or "credit."

(a) The asset account Prepaid Insurance is increased with a _Debit_.

(b) The owner's drawing account is increased with a _Debit_.

(c) The asset account Accounts Receivable is decreased with a _Credit_.

(d) The liability account Accounts Payable is decreased with a _Debit_.

(e) The owner's capital account is increased with a _Credit_.

(f) The revenue account Professional Fees is increased with a _Credit_

(g) The expense account Repair Expense is increased with a _Debit_.

(h) The asset account Cash is decreased with a _Credit_.

(i) The asset account Delivery Equipment is decreased with a _Credit_.

EXERCISE 3B-3 (LO 2/3/4) ANALYSIS OF T ACCOUNTS Roberto Alvarez began a business called Roberto's Fix-It Shop.

1. Create T accounts for Cash; Supplies; Roberto Alvarez, Capital; and Utilities Expense. Identify the following transactions by letter and place them on the proper side of the T accounts.

    (a) Alvarez invested cash in the business, $6,000.

    (b) Purchased supplies for cash, $1,200.

    (c) Paid utility bill, $900.

2. Foot the T account for cash and enter the ending balance.

EXERCISE 3B-4 (LO 3) NORMAL BALANCE OF ACCOUNT Indicate the normal balance (debit or credit) for each of the following accounts.

1. Cash   _Debit_

2. Rent Expense   _Debit_

3. Notes Payable   _Credit_

4. Owner's Drawing   _Debit_

5. Accounts Receivable   _Debit_

6. Owner's Capital   _Credit_

7. Tools   _Debit_

EXERCISE 3B-5 (LO 4) TRANSACTION ANALYSIS George Atlas started a business on June 1, 20--. Analyze the following transactions for the first month of business using T accounts. Label each T account with the title of the account affected and then place the transaction letter and the dollar amount on the debit or credit side.

(a) Atlas invested cash in the business, $7,000.

(b) Purchased equipment for cash, $900.

(c) Purchased equipment on account, $1,500.

(d) Paid cash on account for equipment purchased in transaction (c), $800.

(e) Atlas withdrew cash for personal use, $1,100.

EXERCISE 3B-6 (LO 2) FOOT AND BALANCE A T ACCOUNT Foot and balance the cash T account prepared in Exercise 3B-5.

EXERCISE 3B-7 (LO 2/4) ANALYSIS OF TRANSACTIONS Nicole Lawrence opened a business called Nickie's Neat Ideas in January 20--. Set up T accounts for the following accounts: Cash; Accounts Receivable; Office Supplies; Computer Equipment; Office Furniture; Accounts Payable; Nicole Lawrence, Capital; Nicole Lawrence, Drawing; Professional Fees; Rent Expense; and Utilities Expense.

The following transactions occurred during the first month of business. Record these transactions in T accounts. After all transactions have been recorded, foot and balance the accounts if necessary.

(a) Lawrence invested cash in the business, $18,000.

(b) Purchased office supplies for cash, $500.

(c) Purchased office furniture for cash, $8,000.

(d) Purchased computer and printer on account, $5,000.

(e) Received cash from clients for services, $4,000.

(f) Paid cash on account for computer and printer purchased in transaction (d), $2,000.

(g) Earned professional fees on account during the month, $7,000.

(h) Paid office rent for January, $900.

(i) Paid utility bills for the month, $600.

(j) Received cash from clients that were billed previously in transaction (g), $3,000.

(k) Lawrence withdrew cash for personal use, $4,000.

EXERCISE 3B-8 (LO 5) TRIAL BALANCE Based on the transactions recorded in Exercise 3B-7, prepare a trial balance for Nickie's Neat Ideas as of January 31, 20--.

EXERCISE 3B-9 (LO 5) TRIAL BALANCE The following accounts have normal balances. Prepare a trial balance for Bill's Delivery Service as of September 30, 20--.

Cash	$ 7,000
Accounts Receivable	4,000
Supplies	600
Prepaid Insurance	900

Delivery Equipment	9,000
Accounts Payable	3,000
Bill Swift, Capital	12,000
Bill Swift, Drawing	2,000
Delivery Fees	12,500
Wages Expense	3,000
Rent Expense	1,000

EXERCISE 3B-10 (LO 5) INCOME STATEMENT From the information in Exercise 3B-9, prepare an income statement for Bill's Delivery Service for the month ended September 30, 20--.

EXERCISE 3B-11 (LO 5) STATEMENT OF OWNER'S EQUITY From the information in Exercise 3B-9, prepare a statement of owner's equity for Bill's Delivery Service for the month ended September 30, 20--.

EXERCISE 3B-12 (LO 5) BALANCE SHEET From the information in Exercise 3B-9, prepare a balance sheet for Bill's Delivery Service as of September 30, 20--.

SERIES B PROBLEMS

PROBLEM 3B-1 (LO 2/4/5) T ACCOUNTS AND TRIAL BALANCE Sue Jantz started a business in August 20-- called Jantz Plumbing Service. Jantz hired a part-time college student as an administrative assistant. Jantz has decided to use the following accounts:

Assets	Owner's Equity
Cash	Sue Jantz, Capital
Accounts Receivable	Sue Jantz, Drawing
Office Supplies	Revenue
Prepaid Insurance	Service Fees
Plumbing Equipment	Expenses
Van	Rent Expense
Liabilities	Wages Expense
Accounts Payable	Telephone Expense
	Advertising Expense

The following transactions occurred during August:

(a) Jantz invested cash in the business, $30,000.

(b) Purchased a used van for cash, $8,000.

(c) Purchased plumbing equipment on account, $4,000.

(d) Received cash for services rendered, $3,000.

(e) Paid cash on account owed from transaction (c), $1,000.

(f) Paid rent for the month, $700.

(g) Paid telephone bill, $100.

(h) Earned revenue on account, $4,000.

(i) Purchased office supplies for cash, $300.

(continued)

(j) Paid wages to student, $500.

(k) Purchased insurance, $800.

(l) Received cash from services performed in transaction (h), $3,000.

(m) Paid cash for advertising expense, $2,000.

(n) Purchased additional plumbing equipment for $2,000, paying $500 cash and spreading the remaining payments over the next six months.

(o) Revenue earned from services for the remainder of the month amounted to $2,800: $1,100 in cash and $1,700 on account.

(p) Jantz withdrew cash at the end of the month, $3,000.

REQUIRED   1. Enter the transactions in T accounts, identifying each transaction with its corresponding letter.

2. Foot and balance the accounts where necessary.

3. Prepare a trial balance as of August 31, 20--.

PROBLEM 3B-2 (LO 5) NET INCOME AND CHANGE IN OWNER'S EQUITY Refer to the trial balance of Jantz Plumbing Service in Problem 3B-1 to determine the following information. Use the format provided below.

1. a. Total revenue for the month   _____

    b. Total expenses for the month   _____

    c. Net income for the month   _____

2. a. Sue Jantz's original investment   _____
        in the business

            + the net income for the month   _____

            – owner's drawing   _____

            Increase (decrease) in capital   _____

            = ending owner's equity   _____

    b. End of month accounting equation:

Assets	=	Liabilities	+	Owner's Equity
_____	=	_____	+	_____

PROBLEM 3B-3 (LO 5) FINANCIAL STATEMENTS Refer to the trial balance in Problem 3B-1 and to the analysis of the change in owner's equity in Problem 3B-2.

REQUIRED   1. Prepare an income statement for Jantz Plumbing Service for the month ended August 31, 20--.

2. Prepare a statement of owner's equity for Jantz Plumbing Service for the month ended August 31, 20--.

3. Prepare a balance sheet for Jantz Plumbing Service as of August 31, 20--.

MASTERY PROBLEM

Craig Fisher started a lawn service called Craig's Quick Cut to earn money over the summer months. Fisher has decided to use the following accounts for recording transactions:

Assets
    Cash
    Accounts Receivable
    Mowing Equipment
    Lawn Tools
Liabilities
    Accounts Payable
    Notes Payable
Owner's Equity
    Craig Fisher, Capital
    Craig Fisher, Drawing

Revenue
    Lawn Fees
Expenses
    Rent Expense
    Wages Expense
    Telephone Expense
    Gas and Oil Expense
    Transportation Expense

Transactions for the month of June are listed below.

(a) Fisher invested cash in the business, $3,000.

(b) Bought mowing equipment for $1,000: paid $200 in cash and promised to pay the balance over the next four months.

(c) Paid garage rent for June, $50.

(d) Provided lawn services for customers on account, $520.

(e) Paid telephone bill, $30.

(f) Borrowed cash from the bank by signing a note payable, $500.

(g) Bought lawn tools, $480.

(h) Collected cash from customers for services performed on account in transaction (d), $400.

(i) Paid associates for lawn work done during the first half of the month, $350.

(j) Paid for gas and oil for the equipment, $60.

(k) Paid cash on account for the mowing equipment purchased in transaction (b), $200.

(l) Earned lawn fees of $1,320: $600 in cash and $720 on account.

(m) Paid associates for last half of month, $700.

(n) Reimbursed associates for expenses associated with using their own vehicles for transportation, $150.

(o) Paid on note payable to bank, $100.

(p) Fisher withdrew cash for personal use, $200.

REQUIRED
1. Enter the transactions for June in T accounts. Use the accounting equation as a guide for setting up the T accounts.

2. Foot and balance the T accounts where necessary.

3. Prepare a trial balance of the accounts as of June 30, 20--.

4. Prepare an income statement for the month ended June 30, 20--.

5. Prepare a statement of owner's equity for the month ended June 30, 20--.

6. Prepare a balance sheet as of June 30, 20--.

Self-Study Test Questions

True/False

1. To debit an account is to enter an amount on the left side of the account. _____

2. Liability accounts normally have debit balances. _____

3. Increases in owner's equity are entered as credits. _____

4. Revenue accounts normally have debit balances. _____

5. To credit an account is to enter an amount on the right side of the account. _____

6. A debit to an asset account will decrease it. _____

Multiple Choice

1. A common example of an asset is _____

   (a) Professional Fees.
   (b) Rent Expense.
   (c) Accounts Receivable.
   (d) Accounts Payable.

2. To record the payment of rent expense, an accountant would _____

   (a) debit Cash; credit Rent Expense.
   (b) debit Rent Expense; debit Cash.
   (c) debit Rent Expense; credit Cash.
   (d) credit Rent Expense; credit Cash.

3. The accounting equation may be expressed as _____

   (a) Assets = Liabilities – Owner's Equity.
   (b) Assets = Liabilities + Owner's Equity.
   (c) Liabilities = Owner's Equity – Assets.
   (d) all of the above.

4. Liability, owner's equity, and revenue accounts normally have _____

   (a) debit balances.
   (b) large balances.
   (c) negative balances.
   (d) credit balances.

5. An investment of cash by the owner will _____

   (a) increase assets and owner's equity.
   (b) increase assets and liabilities.
   (c) increase liabilities and owner's equity.
   (d) increase owner's equity; decrease liabilities.

The answers to the Self-Study Test Questions are at the end of the text.

4

Journalizing and Posting Transactions

Since Jessie has not studied accounting, she has hired an accounting student, Mitch, to help her "keep the books." One day Jessie was catching up with some work at the office when she decided to take a look at the entries that Mitch had made earlier in the day. "Kelly, come here," called Jessie. "Look at the way Mitch entered this transaction. What was he thinking? Why does he make these entries in ink? Do you have an ink eraser?" Should Jessie try to correct Mitch's error by erasing his work and reentering the transaction?

The double-entry framework of accounting was explained and illustrated in Chapter 3. To demonstrate the use of debits and credits, business transactions were entered directly into T accounts. Now we will take a more detailed look at the procedures used to account for business transactions.

FLOW OF DATA

LO 1   Describe the flow of data from source documents through the trial balance.

This chapter traces the flow of financial data from the source documents through the accounting information system. This process includes the following steps:

1. Analyze what happened by using information from source documents and the firm's chart of accounts.

2. Enter business transactions in the general journal in the form of journal entries.

3. Post these journal entries to the accounts in the general ledger.

4. Prepare a trial balance.

The flow of data from the source documents through the preparation of a trial balance is shown in Figure 4-1.

FIGURE 4-1 Flow of Data from Source Documents through Trial Balance

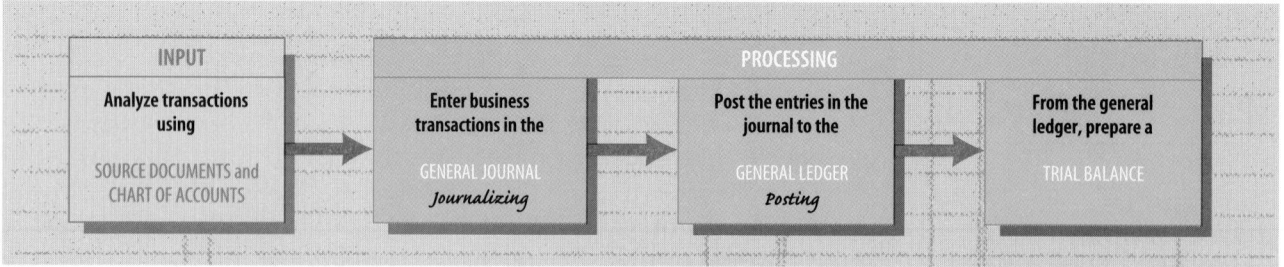

THE CHART OF ACCOUNTS

LO 2   Describe the chart of accounts as a means of classifying financial information.

You learned in Chapters 2 and 3 that there are three basic questions that must be answered when analyzing transactions:

1. What happened?

2. Which accounts are affected?

3. How is the accounting equation affected?

To determine which accounts are affected (step 2), the accountant must know the accounts being used by the business. A list of all accounts used by a business is called a **chart of accounts.**

The chart of accounts includes the account titles in numeric order for all assets, liabilities, owner's equity, revenues, and expenses. The numbering should follow a consistent pattern. In Jessie Jane's Campus Delivery, asset accounts begin with "1," liability accounts begin with "2," owner's equity accounts begin with "3," revenue accounts begin with "4," and expense accounts begin with "5." Jessie uses three-digit numbers for all accounts.

A chart of accounts for Jessie Jane's Campus Delivery is shown in Figure 4-2. Jessie would not need many accounts initially because the business is new. Additional accounts can easily be added as needed. Note that the accounts are arranged according to the accounting equation.

FIGURE 4-2 Chart of Accounts

JESSIE JANE'S CAMPUS DELIVERY CHART OF ACCOUNTS			
Assets	**(100–199)**	**Revenues**	**(400–499)**
101	Cash	401	Delivery Fees
122	Accounts Receivable		
141	Supplies	**Expenses**	**(500–599)**
145	Prepaid Insurance	511	Wages Expense
185	Delivery Equipment	521	Rent Expense
		525	Telephone Expense
Liabilities	**(200–299)**		
202	Accounts Payable		
Owner's Equity	**(300–399)**		
311	Jessica Jane, Capital		
312	Jessica Jane, Drawing		

Assets begin with 1
Liabilities begin with 2
Owner's Equity begin with 3
Revenues begin with 4
Expenses begin with 5

SOURCE DOCUMENTS

LO 3 Describe and explain the purpose of source documents.

Almost any document that provides information about a business transaction can be called a **source document**. A source document triggers the analysis of what happened. It begins the process of entering transactions in the accounting system. Examples of source documents are shown in Figure 4-3. These source documents provide information that is useful in determining the effect of business transactions on specific accounts.

In addition to serving as input for transaction analysis, source documents serve as objective evidence of business transactions. If anyone questions the accounting records, these documents may be used as objective, verifiable evidence of the accuracy of the accounting records. For this reason, source documents are filed for possible future reference. *Having objective, verifiable evidence that a transaction occurred is an important accounting concept.*

FIGURE 4-3 Source Documents

SOURCE DOCUMENTS	
Example	**Provides Information About**
1. Check stubs or copies of checks	Cash payments
2. Receipt stubs, copies of receipts, cash register tapes, or memos of cash register totals	Cash receipts
3. Copies of sales tickets or sales invoices issued to customers or clients	Sales of goods or services
4. Purchase invoices received from suppliers	Purchases of goods or services

THE GENERAL JOURNAL

LO 4 Journalize transactions.

A day-by-day listing of the transactions of a business is called a **journal**. The purpose of a journal is to provide a record of all transactions completed by the business. The journal shows the date of each transaction, titles of the accounts to be debited and credited, and the amounts of the debits and credits.

> **LEARNING KEY:** A journal provides a day-by-day listing of all transactions completed by the business.

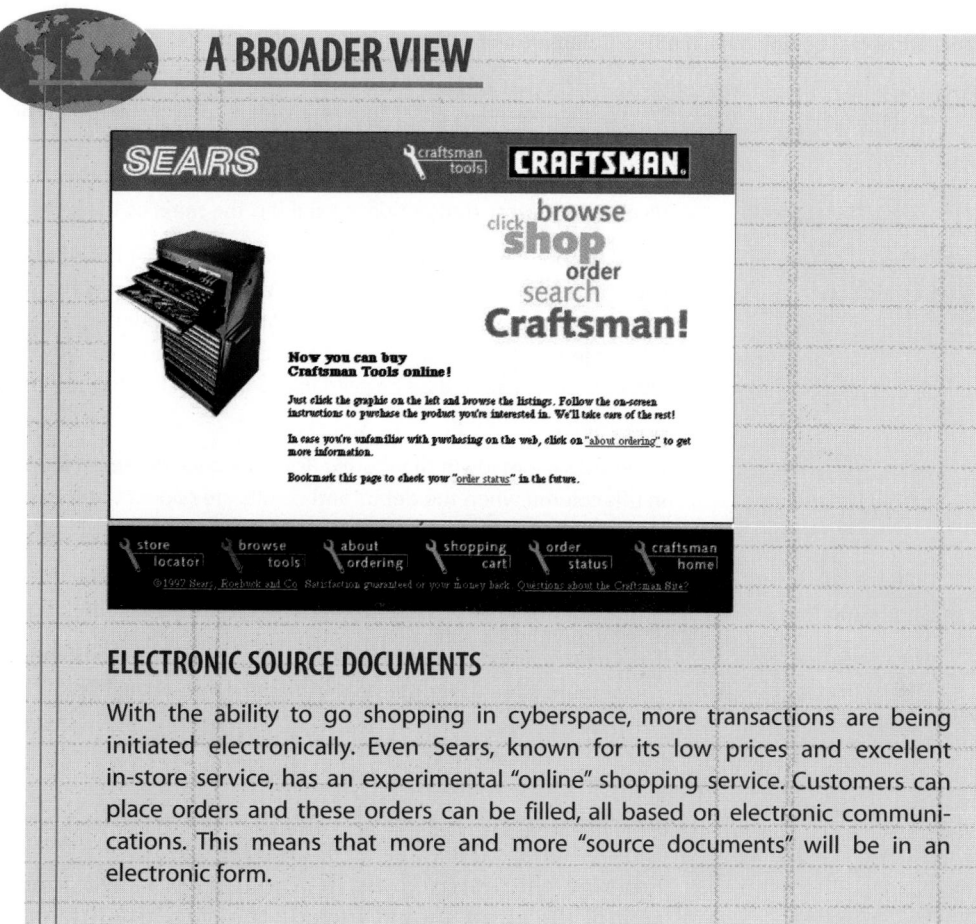

ELECTRONIC SOURCE DOCUMENTS

With the ability to go shopping in cyberspace, more transactions are being initiated electronically. Even Sears, known for its low prices and excellent in-store service, has an experimental "online" shopping service. Customers can place orders and these orders can be filled, all based on electronic communications. This means that more and more "source documents" will be in an electronic form.

A journal is commonly referred to as a **book of original entry** because it is here that the first formal accounting record of a transaction is made. Although many types of journals are used in business, the simplest journal form is a two-column general journal (Figure 4-4). Any kind of business transaction may be entered into a general journal.

FIGURE 4-4   Two-Column General Journal

	DATE	DESCRIPTION	POST REF.	DEBIT	CREDIT	
	20—					
1	1	2	3	4	5	1
2						2
3						3

GENERAL JOURNAL   PAGE 1

A **two-column general journal** is so-named because it has only two amount columns, one for debit amounts and one for credit amounts. Journal pages are numbered in the upper right-hand corner. The five column numbers in Figure 4-4 are explained in Figure 4-5.

FIGURE 4-5 The Columns in a Two-Column General Journal

Column 1 Date	The year is entered in small figures at the top of the column immediately below the column heading. The year is repeated only at the top of each new page. The month is entered for the first entry on the page and for the first transaction of the month. The day of the month is recorded for every transaction, even if it is the same as the prior entry.
Column 2 Description	The *Description* or *Explanation* column is used to enter the titles of the accounts affected by each transaction, and to provide a very brief description of the transaction. Each transaction affects two or more accounts. The account(s) to be debited are entered first at the extreme left of the column. The account(s) to be credited are listed after the debits and indented. The description should be entered immediately following the last credit entry with an additional indentation.
Column 3 Posting Reference	No entries are made in the *Posting Reference column* during journalizing. Entries are made in this column when the debits and credits are copied to the proper accounts in the ledger. This process will be explained in detail later in this chapter.
Column 4 Debit Amount	The *Debit amount column* is used to enter the amount to be debited to an account. The amount should be entered on the same line as the title of that account.
Column 5 Credit Amount	The *Credit amount column* is used to enter the amount to be credited to an account. The amount should be entered on the same line as the title of that account.

Journalizing

Entering the transactions in a journal is called **journalizing.** For every transaction, the entry should include the date, the title of each account affected, the amounts, and a brief description.

To illustrate the journalizing process, transactions for the first month of operations of Jessie Jane's Campus Delivery will be journalized. The transactions are listed in Figure 4-6. Since you analyzed these transactions in Chapters 2 and 3, the journalizing process should be easier to understand. Let's start with a close look at the steps followed when journalizing the first transaction, Jessie's initial investment of $2,000.

LEARNING KEY: When journalizing, the exact account titles shown in the chart of accounts must be used. Refer to the chart of accounts in Figure 4-2 as you review the entries for Jessie Jane's Campus Delivery.

FIGURE 4-6   Summary of Transactions

		Summary of Transactions Jessie Jane's Campus Delivery
Transaction		
(a)	June 1	Jessica Jane invested cash in her business, $2,000.
(b)	3	Bought delivery equipment for cash, $1,200.
(c)	5	Bought delivery equipment on account from Big Red Scooters, $900.
(d)	6	Paid first installment from transaction (c) to Big Red Scooters, $300.
(e)	6	Received cash for delivery services rendered, $500.
(f)	7	Paid cash for June office rent, $200.
(g)	15	Paid telephone bill, $50.
(h)	15	Made deliveries on account for a total of $600: Accounting Department ($400) and the School of Music ($200).
(i)	16	Bought supplies for cash, $80.
(j)	18	Paid cash for an eight-month liability insurance policy, $200. Coverage began on June 1.
(k)	20	Received $570 in cash for services performed in transaction (h): $400 from the Accounting Department and $170 from the School of Music.
(l)	25	Bought a third scooter from Big Red Scooters, $1,500. Paid $300 cash, with the remaining payments expected over the next four months.
(m)	27	Paid wages of part-time employees, $650.
(n)	30	Earned delivery fees for the remainder of the month amounting to $1,050: $430 in cash and $620 on account. Deliveries on account: Accounting Department ($250) and Athletic Ticket Office ($370).
(o)	30	Jessie withdrew cash for personal use, $150.

Transaction (a)

June 1   Jessica Jane opened a bank account with a deposit of $2,000 for her business.

STEP 1   **Enter the date.** Since this is the first entry on the journal page, the year is entered on the first line of the Date column (in small print at the top of the line). The month and day are entered on the same line, below the year, in the Date column.

	DATE		DESCRIPTION	POST REF.	DEBIT	CREDIT	
	20--						
1	June	1					1
2							2

GENERAL JOURNAL   PAGE 1

STEP 2   **Enter the debit.** Cash is entered on the first line at the extreme left of the Description column. The amount of the debit, $2,000, is entered on the same line in the Debit column. Since this is not a formal financial statement, dollar signs are not used.

	DATE		DESCRIPTION	POST REF.	DEBIT	CREDIT	
			GENERAL JOURNAL			PAGE 1	
1	20-- June	1	Cash		2 0 0 0 00		1
2							2

STEP 3   **Enter the credit.** The title of the account to be credited, Jessica Jane, Capital, is entered on the second line, indented one-half inch from the left side of the Description column. The amount of the credit, $2,000, is entered on the same line in the Credit column.

	DATE		DESCRIPTION	POST REF.	DEBIT	CREDIT	
			GENERAL JOURNAL			PAGE 1	
1	20-- June	1	Cash		2 0 0 0 00		1
2			Jessica Jane, Capital			2 0 0 0 00	2

STEP 4   **Enter the explanation.** The explanation of the entry is entered on the next line, indented an additional one-half inch. The second line of the explanation, if needed, is also indented the same distance as the first.

	DATE		DESCRIPTION	POST REF.	DEBIT	CREDIT	
			GENERAL JOURNAL			PAGE 1	
1	20-- June	1	Cash		2 0 0 0 00		1
2			Jessica Jane, Capital			2 0 0 0 00	2
3			Owner's original investment in				3
4			delivery business				4

To enter transaction (b), the purchase of a motor scooter for $1,200 cash, we skip a line and follow the same four steps. *To help prevent inappropriate changes to entries, you probably would not skip a line in practice.* Note that the month and year do not need to be repeated. The day of the month must, however, be entered.

GENERAL JOURNAL — PAGE 1

	DATE		DESCRIPTION	POST REF.	DEBIT					CREDIT					
	20--														
1	June	1	Cash		2	0	0	0	00						1
2			Jessica Jane, Capital							2	0	0	0	00	2
3			Owner's original investment in												3
4			delivery business												4
5															5
6		3	Delivery Equipment		1	2	0	0	00						6
7			Cash							1	2	0	0	00	7
8			Purchased delivery equipment for cash												8

Skip a line → (points to line 5)

The journal entries for the month of June are shown in Figure 4-7. Note that the entries on June 25 and June 30 affect more than two accounts. Entries requiring more than one debit and/or one credit are called **compound entries**. The entry on June 25 has two credits. The credits are listed after the debit, indented and listed one under the other. The entry on June 30 has two debits. They are aligned with the left margin of the Description column and listed one under the other. In both cases, the debits equal the credits.

FIGURE 4-7 General Journal Entries

GENERAL JOURNAL — PAGE 1

	DATE		DESCRIPTION	POST REF.	DEBIT					CREDIT					
	20--														
1	June	1	Cash		2	0	0	0	00						1
2			Jessica Jane, Capital							2	0	0	0	00	2
3			Owner's original investment in												3
4			delivery business												4
5															5
6			Delivery Equipment		1	2	0	0	00						6
7			Cash							1	2	0	0	00	7
8			Purchased delivery equipment for cash												8
9															9
10		5	Delivery Equipment			9	0	0	00						10
11			Accounts Payable								9	0	0	00	11
12			Purchased delivery equipment on account												12
13			from Big Red Scooters												13
14															14
15		6	Accounts Payable			3	0	0	00						15
16			Cash								3	0	0	00	16
17			Made partial payment to Big Red Scooters												17
18															18
19		6	Cash			5	0	0	00						19
20			Delivery Fees								5	0	0	00	20
21			Received cash for delivery services												21

(Annotation callouts:)
- List debits first
- List credits second and indented.
- Explanation is third and indented.
- Space to make entries easier to read. To prevent improper changes to entries, the extra spacing might not be used in practice.

FIGURE 4-7 General Journal Entries *(continued)*

		GENERAL JOURNAL				PAGE 1	
	DATE	DESCRIPTION	POST REF.	DEBIT	CREDIT		
23	7	Rent Expense		2 0 0 00			23
24		Cash			2 0 0 00		24
25		Paid office rent for June					25
26							26
27	15	Telephone Expense		5 0 00			27
28		Cash			5 0 00		28
29		Paid telephone bill for June					29
30							30
31	15	Accounts Receivable		6 0 0 00			31
32		Delivery Fees			6 0 0 00		32
33		Deliveries made on account for Accounting					33
34		Department ($400) and School of Music ($200)					34
35							35

			GENERAL JOURNAL				PAGE 2	
	DATE		DESCRIPTION	POST REF.	DEBIT	CREDIT		
	20--							
1	June	16	Supplies		8 0 00			1
2			Cash			8 0 00		2
3			Purchased supplies for cash					3
4								4
5		18	Prepaid Insurance		2 0 0 00			5
6			Cash			2 0 0 00		6
7			Paid premium for eight-month					7
8			insurance policy					8
9								9
10		20	Cash		5 7 0 00			10
11			Accounts Receivable			5 7 0 00		11
12			Received cash on account from Accounting					12
13			Department ($400) and School of Music ($170)					13
14								14
15		25	Delivery Equipment		1 5 0 0 00			15
16			Accounts Payable			1 2 0 0 00		16
17			Cash			3 0 0 00		17
18			Purchased scooter with down payment;					18
19			balance on account with Big Red Scooters					19
20								20
21		27	Wages Expense		6 5 0 00			21
22			Cash			6 5 0 00		22
23			Paid employees					23
24								24

Compound entry

Line up credits

Debits = Credits

FIGURE 4-7 General Journal Entries *(continued)*

	DATE	DESCRIPTION	POST REF.	DEBIT	CREDIT	
25	30	Cash		4 3 0 00		25
26		Accounts Receivable		6 2 0 00		26
27		Delivery Fees			1 0 5 0 00	27
28		Deliveries made for cash and on account to				28
29		Accounting Department ($250) and				29
30		Athletic Ticket Office ($370)				30
31						31
32	30	Jessica Jane, Drawing		1 5 0 00		32
33		Cash			1 5 0 00	33
34		Owner's withdrawal				34

GENERAL JOURNAL — PAGE 2

Line up debits · *Compound entry* · *Debits = Credits*

THE GENERAL LEDGER

LO 5 Post to the general ledger.

The journal provides a day-by-day record of business transactions. To determine the current balance of specific accounts, however, the information in the journal must be transferred to accounts similar to the T accounts illustrated in Chapter 3. This process is called **posting.**

A complete set of all the accounts used by a business is known as the **general ledger.** The general ledger accumulates a complete record of the debits and credits made to each account as a result of entries made in the journal. The accounts are numbered and arranged in the same order as the chart of accounts. That is, accounts are numbered and grouped by classification: assets, liabilities, owner's equity, revenues, and expenses.

LEARNING KEY: While the journal provides a day-by-day record of business transactions, the ledger provides a record of the transactions entered in each account.

Four-Column Account

For purposes of illustration, the T account was introduced in Chapter 3. In practice, businesses are more likely to use a version of the account called the **four-column account.** Figure 4-8 compares the cash T account from Chapter 3 for Jessie Jane's Campus Delivery and a four-column cash account summarizing the same cash transactions. A four-column account contains columns for the debit or credit transaction and columns for the debit or credit running balance. In addition, there are columns for the date, description of the item, and posting reference. The Item column is used to provide descriptions of special entries. For example, "Balance" is written in this column when the balance of an account is transferred to a new page. The Posting Reference column is used to indicate the journal page from which an entry was posted, or a check mark (✔) is inserted to indicate that no posting was required.

As shown in Figure 4-8, the primary advantage of the T account is that the debit and credit sides of the account are easier to identify. Thus, for demonstration purposes and analyzing what happened, T accounts are very helpful. However, computing the balance of a T account is cumbersome. The primary advantage of the four-column account is that it maintains a running balance.

Note that the heading for the four-column account has the account title and an account number. The account number is taken from the chart of accounts and is used in the posting process.

FIGURE 4-8 Comparison of T Account and Four-Column Account

Cash			
(a)	2,000	(b)	1,200
(e)	500	(d)	300
(k)	570	(f)	200
(n)	430	(g)	50
	3,500	(i)	80
		(j)	200
		(l)	300
		(m)	650
		(o)	150
Bal.	370		3,130

GENERAL LEDGER

ACCOUNT: Cash　　　　ACCOUNT NO. 101

DATE	ITEM	POST REF.	DEBIT	CREDIT	BALANCE DEBIT	BALANCE CREDIT
20-- June 1			2 0 0 0 00		2 0 0 0 00	
3				1 2 0 0 00	8 0 0 00	
6				3 0 0 00	5 0 0 00	
6			5 0 0 00		1 0 0 0 00	
7				2 0 0 00	8 0 0 00	
15				5 0 00	7 5 0 00	
16				8 0 00	6 7 0 00	
18				2 0 0 00	4 7 0 00	
20			5 7 0 00		1 0 4 0 00	
25				3 0 0 00	7 4 0 00	
27				6 5 0 00	9 0 00	
30			4 3 0 00		5 2 0 00	
30				1 5 0 00	3 7 0 00	

└── **Transaction Amount** ──┘ └── **Running Balances** ──┘

LEARNING KEY: The four-column account is similar to the T account, but makes it easier to maintain a running balance.

Posting to the General Ledger

The process of copying the debits and credits from the journal to the ledger accounts is known as **posting.** All amounts entered in the journal must be posted to the general ledger accounts.

LEARNING KEY: Posting is simply the copying of the exact dates and dollar amounts from the journal to the ledger.

Posting from the journal to the ledger is done daily or at frequent intervals. There are five steps.

Steps in the Posting Process

In the ledger account:

STEP 1   Enter the date of the transaction in the Date column. There is no need to repeat the month and year, but the day must be entered even if it is the same date as in the previous transaction.

STEP 2   Enter the amount of the debit or credit in the Debit or Credit column.

STEP 3   Enter the new balance in the Balance columns under Debit or Credit. If the balance of the account is zero, draw a line through the debit and credit columns.

STEP 4   Enter the journal page number from which each transaction is posted in the Posting Reference column.

In the journal:

STEP 5   Enter the ledger account number in the Posting Reference column of the journal for each transaction that is posted.

Step 5 is the last step in the posting process. After this step is completed, the posting references will indicate which journal entries have been posted to the ledger accounts. This is very helpful, particularly if you are interrupted during the posting process. The information in the Posting Reference columns of the journal and ledger provides a link between the journal and ledger known as a **cross-reference.**

 LEARNING KEY: Posting references indicate that a journal entry has been posted to the general ledger.

To illustrate the posting process, the first journal entry for Jessie Jane's Campus Delivery will be posted step-by-step. First, let's post the debit to Cash (Figure 4-9).

FIGURE 4-9   Posting a Debit

In the ledger account:

STEP 1   Enter the year, "20--," the month, "June," and the day, "1," in the Date column of the cash account.

STEP 2   Enter the amount, "$2,000," in the Debit column. Again, since this is not a formal financial statement, dollar signs are not used.

STEP 3   Enter the $2,000 balance in the Balance columns under Debit.

STEP 4   Enter "J1" in the Posting Reference column since the posting came from page 1 of the *Journal*.

   The Item column is left blank, except for special reasons such as indicating the beginning balance.

In the journal:

STEP 5   Enter the account number for cash, 101 (see chart of accounts in Figure 4-2 on page 89), in the Posting Reference column of the journal on the same line as the debit to Cash for $2,000.

   Now let's post the credit portion of the first entry (Figure 4-10).

FIGURE 4-10   Posting a Credit

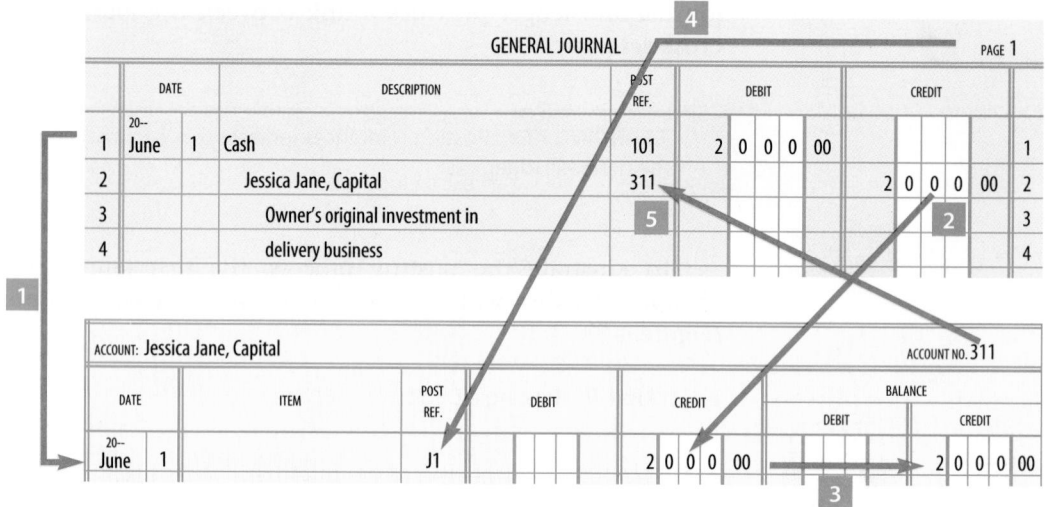

In the ledger account:

STEP 1   Enter the year, "20--," the month, "June," and the day, "1," in the Date column of the Jessica Jane, Capital account.

STEP 2   Enter the amount, "$2,000," in the Credit column.

STEP 3   Enter the $2,000 balance in the Balance columns under Credit.

STEP 4   Enter "J1" in the Posting Reference column since the posting came from Page 1 of the *Journal*.

In the journal:

STEP 5   Enter the account number for Jessica Jane, Capital, 311, in the Posting Reference column.

After posting the journal entries for Jessie Jane's Campus Delivery for the month of June, the general journal and general ledger should appear as illustrated in Figures 4-11 and 4-12 on pages 101–104. *Note that the Posting Reference column of the journal has been filled in because the entries have been posted.*

FIGURE 4-11   General Journal After Posting

	DATE		DESCRIPTION	POST REF.	DEBIT	CREDIT	
	20--						
1	June	1	Cash	101	2 0 0 0 00		1
2			Jessica Jane, Capital	311		2 0 0 0 00	2
3			Owner's original investment in				3
4			delivery business				4
5							5
6		3	Delivery Equipment	185	1 2 0 0 00		6
7			Cash	101		1 2 0 0 00	7
8			Purchased delivery equipment for cash				8
9							9
10		5	Delivery Equipment	185	9 0 0 00		10
11			Accounts Payable	202		9 0 0 00	11
12			Purchased delivery equipment on account				12
13			from Big Red Scooters				13
14							14
15		6	Accounts Payable	202	3 0 0 00		15
16			Cash	101		3 0 0 00	16
17			Made partial payment to Big Red Scooters				17
18							18
19		6	Cash	101	5 0 0 00		19
20			Delivery Fees	401		5 0 0 00	20
21			Received cash for delivery services				21
22							22
23		7	Rent Expense	521	2 0 0 00		23
24			Cash	101		2 0 0 00	24
25			Paid office rent for June				25
26							26
27		15	Telephone Expense	525	5 0 00		27
28			Cash	101		5 0 00	28
29			Paid telephone bill for June				29
30							30
31		15	Accounts Receivable	122	6 0 0 00		31
32			Delivery Fees	401		6 0 0 00	32
33			Deliveries made on account for Accounting				33
34			Department ($400) and School of Music ($200)				34
35							35

GENERAL JOURNAL   PAGE 1

FIGURE 4-11 General Journal After Posting *(continued)*

	DATE		DESCRIPTION	POST REF.	DEBIT					CREDIT					
1	20-- June	16	Supplies	141			8	0	00						1
2			Cash	101								8	0	00	2
3			Purchased supplies for cash												3
4															4
5		18	Prepaid Insurance	145		2	0	0	00						5
6			Cash	101							2	0	0	00	6
7			Paid premium for eight-month												7
8			insurance policy												8
9															9
10		20	Cash	101		5	7	0	00						10
11			Accounts Receivable	122							5	7	0	00	11
12			Received cash on account from Accounting												12
13			Department ($400) and School of Music ($170)												13
14															14
15		25	Delivery Equipment	185	1	5	0	0	00						15
16			Accounts Payable	202						1	2	0	0	00	16
17			Cash	101							3	0	0	00	17
18			Purchased scooter with down payment;												18
19			balance on account with Big Red Scooters												19
20															20
21		27	Wages Expense	511		6	5	0	00						21
22			Cash	101							6	5	0	00	22
23			Paid employees												23
24															24
25		30	Cash	101		4	3	0	00						25
26			Accounts Receivable	122		6	2	0	00						26
27			Delivery Fees	401						1	0	5	0	00	27
28			Deliveries made for cash and on account to												28
29			Accounting Department ($250) and												29
30			Athletic Ticket Office ($370)												30
31															31
32		30	Jessica Jane, Drawing	312		1	5	0	00						32
33			Cash	101							1	5	0	00	33
34			Owner's withdrawal												34

FIGURE 4-12   General Ledger After Posting

GENERAL LEDGER

ACCOUNT: Cash   **ACCOUNT NO. 101**

DATE		ITEM	POST REF.	DEBIT	CREDIT	BALANCE DEBIT	BALANCE CREDIT
20-- June	1		J 1	2 0 0 0 00		2 0 0 0 00	
	3		J 1		1 2 0 0 00	8 0 0 00	
	6		J 1		3 0 0 00	5 0 0 00	
	6		J 1	5 0 0 00		1 0 0 0 00	
	7		J 1		2 0 0 00	8 0 0 00	
	15		J 1		5 0 00	7 5 0 00	
	16		J 2		8 0 00	6 7 0 00	
	18		J 2		2 0 0 00	4 7 0 00	
	20		J 2	5 7 0 00		1 0 4 0 00	
	25		J 2		3 0 0 00	7 4 0 00	
	27		J 2		6 5 0 00	9 0 00	
	30		J 2	4 3 0 00		5 2 0 00	
	30		J 2		1 5 0 00	3 7 0 00	

ACCOUNT: Accounts Receivable   **ACCOUNT NO. 122**

DATE		ITEM	POST REF.	DEBIT	CREDIT	BALANCE DEBIT	BALANCE CREDIT
20-- June	15		J 1	6 0 0 00		6 0 0 00	
	20		J 2		5 7 0 00	3 0 00	
	30		J 2	6 2 0 00		6 5 0 00	

ACCOUNT: Supplies   **ACCOUNT NO. 141**

DATE		ITEM	POST REF.	DEBIT	CREDIT	BALANCE DEBIT	BALANCE CREDIT
20-- June	16		J 2	8 0 00		8 0 00	

ACCOUNT: Prepaid Insurance   **ACCOUNT NO. 145**

DATE		ITEM	POST REF.	DEBIT	CREDIT	BALANCE DEBIT	BALANCE CREDIT
20-- June	18		J 2	2 0 0 00		2 0 0 00	

ACCOUNT: Delivery Equipment   **ACCOUNT NO. 185**

DATE		ITEM	POST REF.	DEBIT	CREDIT	BALANCE DEBIT	BALANCE CREDIT
20-- June	3		J 1	1 2 0 0 00		1 2 0 0 00	
	5		J 1	9 0 0 00		2 1 0 0 00	
	25		J 2	1 5 0 0 00		3 6 0 0 00	

FIGURE 4-12 General Ledger After Posting *(continued)*

ACCOUNT: Accounts Payable   ACCOUNT NO. 202

DATE	ITEM	POST REF.	DEBIT	CREDIT	BALANCE DEBIT	BALANCE CREDIT
20-- June 5		J1		9 0 0 00		9 0 0 00
6		J1	3 0 0 00			6 0 0 00
25		J2		1 2 0 0 00		1 8 0 0 00

ACCOUNT: Jessica Jane, Capital   ACCOUNT NO. 311

DATE	ITEM	POST REF.	DEBIT	CREDIT	BALANCE DEBIT	BALANCE CREDIT
20-- June 1		J1		2 0 0 0 00		2 0 0 0 00

ACCOUNT: Jessica Jane, Drawing   ACCOUNT NO. 312

DATE	ITEM	POST REF.	DEBIT	CREDIT	BALANCE DEBIT	BALANCE CREDIT
20-- June 30		J2	1 5 0 00		1 5 0 00	

ACCOUNT: Delivery Fees   ACCOUNT NO. 401

DATE	ITEM	POST REF.	DEBIT	CREDIT	BALANCE DEBIT	BALANCE CREDIT
20-- June 6		J1		5 0 0 00		5 0 0 00
15		J1		6 0 0 00		1 1 0 0 00
30		J2		1 0 5 0 00		2 1 5 0 00

ACCOUNT: Wages Expense   ACCOUNT NO. 511

DATE	ITEM	POST REF.	DEBIT	CREDIT	BALANCE DEBIT	BALANCE CREDIT
20-- June 27		J2	6 5 0 00		6 5 0 00	

ACCOUNT: Rent Expense   ACCOUNT NO. 521

DATE	ITEM	POST REF.	DEBIT	CREDIT	BALANCE DEBIT	BALANCE CREDIT
20-- June 7		J1	2 0 0 00		2 0 0 00	

ACCOUNT: Telephone Expense   ACCOUNT NO. 525

DATE	ITEM	POST REF.	DEBIT	CREDIT	BALANCE DEBIT	BALANCE CREDIT
20-- June 15		J1	5 0 00		5 0 00	

The Trial Balance

In Chapter 3, a **trial balance** was used to prove that the totals of the debit and credit balances in the T accounts were equal. In this chapter, a trial balance is used to prove the equality of the debits and credits in the ledger accounts. A trial balance can be prepared daily, weekly, monthly, or whenever desired. Before preparing a trial balance, all transactions should be journalized and posted so that the effect of all transactions will be reflected in the ledger accounts.

The trial balance for Jessie Jane's Campus Delivery shown in Figure 4-13 was prepared from the balances in the general ledger in Figure 4-12. The accounts are listed in the order used in the chart of accounts. This order is also often used when preparing financial statements. In Chapter 2, we pointed out that many firms list expenses from highest to lowest amounts. Some firms list expenses according to the chart of accounts, which is the method we will follow.

 LEARNING KEY: The chart of accounts determines the order for listing accounts in the general ledger and trial balance. This order may also be used when preparing financial statements.

FIGURE 4-13   Trial Balance

ACCOUNT TITLE	ACCOUNT NO.	DEBIT BALANCE	CREDIT BALANCE
Jessie Jane's Campus Delivery **Trial Balance** **June 30, 20 - -**			
Cash	101	3 7 0 00	
Accounts Receivable	122	6 5 0 00	
Supplies	141	8 0 00	
Prepaid Insurance	145	2 0 0 00	
Delivery Equipment	185	3 6 0 0 00	
Accounts Payable	202		1 8 0 0 00
Jessica Jane, Capital	311		2 0 0 0 00
Jessica Jane, Drawing	312	1 5 0 00	
Delivery Fees	401		2 1 5 0 00
Wages Expense	511	6 5 0 00	
Rent Expense	521	2 0 0 00	
Telephone Expense	525	5 0 00	
		5 9 5 0 00	5 9 5 0 00

Even though the trial balance indicates that the ledger is in balance, the ledger can still contain errors. For example, if a journal entry was made debiting or crediting the wrong accounts, or if an item was posted to the wrong account, the ledger will still be in balance. It is important, therefore, to be very careful in preparing the journal entries and in posting them to the ledger accounts.

FINDING AND CORRECTING ERRORS IN THE TRIAL BALANCE

LO 6 Explain how to find and correct errors.

Tips are available to help if your trial balance has an error. Figure 4-14 offers hints for finding the error when your trial balance does not balance.

FIGURE 4-14 Tips for Finding Errors in the Trial Balance

1. Double check your addition.

2. Find the difference between the debits and the credits.

   a. If the difference is equal to the amount of a specific transaction, perhaps you forgot to post the debit or credit portion of this transaction.

   b. Divide the difference by *2*. If the difference is evenly divisible by 2, you may have posted two debits or two credits for a transaction. If a debit were posted as a credit, it would mean that one transaction had two credits and no debits. The difference between the total debits and credits would be twice the amount of the debit that was posted as a credit.

   c. Divide the difference by *9*. If the difference is evenly divisible by 9, you may have committed a **slide error** or a **transposition error**. A slide occurs when debit or credit amounts "slide" a digit or two to the left or right when entered. For example, if *$250* was entered as *$25*:

$250	–	25	=	$225
$225	÷	9	=	$25

   The difference is evenly divisible by 9.

   A transposition occurs when two digits are reversed. For example, if *$250* was entered as *$520*:

$520	–	250	=	$270
$270	÷	9	=	$30

   Again, the difference is evenly divisible by 9.

If the tips in Figure 4-14 don't work, you must retrace your steps through the accounting process. Double check your addition for the ledger accounts. Also trace all postings. Be patient as you search for your error. Use this process as an opportunity to reinforce your understanding of the flow of information through the accounting system. Much can be learned while looking for an error.

Once you have found an error, there are two methods of making the correction. Although you may want to erase when correcting your homework, this is not acceptable in practice. An erasure may suggest that you are trying to hide something. Instead you should use the ruling method or make a correcting entry.

Ruling Method

The **ruling method** should be used to correct two types of errors:

1. When an incorrect journal entry has been made, but not yet posted.

2. When a proper entry has been made but posted to the wrong account or for the wrong amount.

When using the ruling method, draw a single line through the incorrect account title or amount and write the correct information directly above the line. Corrections should be initialed by someone authorized to make such changes. This is done so the source and reason for the correction can be traced. This type of correction may be made in the journal or ledger accounts, as shown in Figure 4-15.

FIGURE 4-15   Ruling Method of Making a Correction

	DATE		DESCRIPTION	POST REF.	DEBIT	CREDIT	
1	20-- Sept.	17	~~Wages Expense MP~~ ~~Entertainment Expense~~		6 5 0 00		1
2			Cash			6 5 0 00	2
3			Paid employees				3
4							4
5		18	Prepaid Insurance		MP 2 0 0 00 ~~2 0 00~~		5
6			Cash			MP 2 0 0 00 ~~2 0 00~~	6
7			Paid premium for eight-month				7
8			insurance policy				8
9							9

GENERAL JOURNAL · PAGE 2

Slide

GENERAL LEDGER

ACCOUNT: Accounts Payable · ACCOUNT NO. 202

DATE		ITEM	POST REF.	DEBIT	CREDIT	BALANCE DEBIT	BALANCE CREDIT
20-- Sept.	8		J1		7 0 0 00		7 0 0 00
	15		J1	2 0 0 00			5 0 0 00
	25		J2		~~1 2 0 0 00~~ MP ~~2 1 0 0 00~~		MP 1 7 0 0 00 ~~2 6 0 0 00~~

Transposition

Correcting Entry Method

If an incorrect entry has been journalized and posted to the wrong account, a **correcting entry** should be made. For example, assume that a $400 payment for Rent Expense was incorrectly debited to Repair Expense and correctly credited to Cash. This requires a correcting entry and explanation as shown in Figure 4-16. Figure 4-17 shows the effects of the correcting entry on the ledger accounts. Generally, "Correcting" is written in the Item column of the general ledger account.

FIGURE 4-16 Correcting Entry Method

	DATE		DESCRIPTION	POST REF.	DEBIT	CREDIT	
			GENERAL JOURNAL			PAGE 6	
1	20-- Sept.	25	Rent Expense	521	4 0 0 00		1
2			Repair Expense	537		4 0 0 00	2
3			To correct error in which payment for rent				3
4			was debited to Repair Expense				4
5							5

FIGURE 4-17 Effects of Correcting Entry on Ledger Accounts

GENERAL LEDGER

ACCOUNT: Rent Expense — ACCOUNT NO. 521

DATE		ITEM	POST REF.	DEBIT	CREDIT	BALANCE	
						DEBIT	CREDIT
20-- Sept.	25	Correcting	J 6	4 0 0 00		4 0 0 00	

ACCOUNT: Repair Expense — ACCOUNT NO. 537

DATE		ITEM	POST REF.	DEBIT	CREDIT	BALANCE	
						DEBIT	CREDIT
20-- Sept.	10		J 5	5 0 00		5 0 00	
	15		J 5	4 0 0 00		4 5 0 00	
	25	Correcting	J 6		4 0 0 00	5 0 00	

Learning Objectives	Key Points to Remember
1 **Describe the flow of data from source documents through the trial balance.**	The flow of data from the source documents through the trial balance is: 1. Analyze business transactions. 2. Journalize transactions in the general journal. 3. Post journal entries to the general ledger. 4. Prepare a trial balance.

INPUT		PROCESSING	
Analyze transactions using SOURCE DOCUMENTS and CHART OF ACCOUNTS	**Enter business transactions in the** GENERAL JOURNAL *Journalizing*	**Post the entries in the journal to the** GENERAL LEDGER *Posting*	**From the general ledger, prepare a** TRIAL BALANCE

Learning Objectives	Key Points to Remember
2 **Describe the chart of accounts as a means of classifying financial information.**	The chart of accounts includes the account titles in numerical order for all assets, liabilities, owner's equity, revenues, and expenses. The chart of accounts is used in classifying information about transactions.
3 **Describe and explain the purpose of source documents.**	Source documents trigger the analysis of business transactions and the entries into the accounting system.
4 **Journalize transactions.**	A journal provides a day-by-day listing of transactions. The journal shows the date, titles of the accounts to be debited or credited, and the amounts of the debits and credits. The steps in the journalizing process are: 1. Enter the date. 2. Enter the debit. Accounts to be debited are entered first. 3. Enter the credit. Accounts to be credited are entered after the debits and are indented one-half inch. 4. Enter the explanation. A brief explanation of the transaction should be entered in the description column on the line following the last credit. The explanation should be indented an additional one-half inch.
5 **Post to the general ledger.**	The general ledger is a complete set of all accounts used by the business. The steps in posting from the general journal to the general ledger are: In the general ledger: 1. Enter the date of each transaction. 2. Enter the amount of each debit or credit in the Debit or Credit column. 3. Enter the new balance. 4. Enter the journal page number from which each transaction is posted in the Posting Reference column. In the journal: 5. Enter the account number to which each transaction is posted in the Posting Reference column.
6 **Explain how to find and correct errors.**	Errors may be found by verifying your addition, by dividing the difference between the debits and credits by 2 or 9, and by retracing your steps through the accounting process. Use the ruling method or the correcting entry method to correct the error.

Reflection: Answering the Opening Question

Corrections should not be made by erasing the original entry. Erasing could create suspicion over what was changed and the reasons for the change. Instead, use the ruling method or make a correcting entry as discussed in the chapter.

KEY TERMS

book of original entry, (91)   The journal or the first formal accounting record of a transaction.

chart of accounts, (88)   A list of all accounts used by a business.

compound entry, (95)   A general journal entry that affects more than two accounts.

correcting entry, (107)   An entry to correct an incorrect entry that has been journalized and posted to the wrong account.

cross-reference, (99)   The information in the Posting Reference columns of the journal and ledger that provides a link between the journal and ledger.

four-column account, (97)   An account with columns for the debit or credit transaction and columns for the debit or credit running balance.

general ledger, (97)   A complete set of all the accounts used by a business. The general ledger accumulates a complete record of the debits and credits made to each account as a result of entries made in the journal.

journal, (90)   A day-by-day listing of the transactions of a business.

journalizing, (92)   Entering the transactions in a journal.

posting, (97)   Copying the debits and credits from the journal to the ledger accounts.

ruling method, (106)   A method of correcting an entry in which a line is drawn through the error and the correct information is placed above it.

slide error, (106)   An error that occurs when debit or credit amounts "slide" a digit or two to the left or right.

source document, (89)   Any document that provides information about a business transaction.

transposition error, (106)   An error that occurs when two digits are reversed.

trial balance, (105)   A list used to prove that the totals of the debit and credit balances in the ledger accounts are equal.

two-column general journal, (91)   A journal with only two amount columns, one for debit amounts and one for credit amounts.

DEMONSTRATION PROBLEM

George Fielding is a financial planning consultant. He provides budgeting, estate planning, tax planning, and investing advice for professional golfers. He developed the following chart of accounts for his business.

Assets	Revenues
101 Cash	401 Professional Fees
142 Office Supplies	

Liabilities	Expenses
202 Accounts Payable	511 Wages Expense
	521 Rent Expense
Owner's Equity	525 Telephone Expense
311 George Fielding, Capital	533 Utilities Expense
312 George Fielding, Drawing	534 Charitable Contributions Expense
	538 Automobile Expense

The following transactions took place during the month of December of the current year.

Dec. 1   Fielding invested cash to start the business, $20,000.

   3   Paid Bollhorst Real Estate for December office rent, $1,000.

   4   Received cash from Aaron Patton, a client, for services, $2,500.

   6   Paid T. Z. Anderson Electric for December heating and light, $75.

   7   Received cash from Andrew Conder, a client, for services, $2,000.

   12   Paid Fichter's Super Service for gasoline and oil purchases for the company car, $60.

   14   Paid Hillenburg Staffing for temporary secretarial services during the past two weeks, $600.

   17   Bought office supplies from Bowers Office Supply on account, $280.

   20   Paid Mitchell Telephone Co. for business calls during the past month, $100.

   21   Fielding withdrew cash for personal use, $1,100.

   24   Made donation to the National Multiple Sclerosis Society, $100.

   27   Received cash from Billy Walters, a client, for services, $2,000.

   28   Paid Hillenburg Staffing for temporary secretarial services during the past two weeks, $600.

   29   Made payment on account to Bowers Office Supply, $100.

REQUIRED   1.   Record the preceding transactions in a general journal.

   2.   Post the entries to the general ledger.

   3.   Prepare a trial balance.

(continued)

Solution

1.

	DATE		DESCRIPTION	POST REF.	DEBIT					CREDIT					
	20--														
1	Dec.	1	Cash	101	20	0	0	0	00						1
2			George Fielding, Capital	311						20	0	0	0	00	2
3			Owner's original investment in												3
4			consulting business												4
5															5
6		3	Rent Expense	521	1	0	0	0	00						6
7			Cash	101						1	0	0	0	00	7
8			Paid rent for December												8
9															9
10		4	Cash	101	2	5	0	0	00						10
11			Professional Fees	401						2	5	0	0	00	11
12			Received cash for services rendered												12
13															13
14		6	Utilities Expense	533			7	5	00						14
15			Cash	101								7	5	00	15
16			Paid utilities												16
17															17
18		7	Cash	101	2	0	0	0	00						18
19			Professional Fees	401						2	0	0	0	00	19
20			Received cash for services rendered												20
21															21
22		12	Automobile Expense	538			6	0	00						22
23			Cash	101								6	0	00	23
24			Paid for gas and oil												24
25															25
26		14	Wages Expense	511		6	0	0	00						26
27			Cash	101							6	0	0	00	27
28			Paid temporary secretaries												28
29															29
30		17	Office Supplies	142		2	8	0	00						30
31			Accounts Payable	202							2	8	0	00	31
32			Purchased office supplies on account from												32
33			Bowers Office Supply												33
34															34
35															35

GENERAL JOURNAL PAGE 1

GENERAL JOURNAL   PAGE 2

	DATE		DESCRIPTION	POST REF.	DEBIT	CREDIT	
1	20-- Dec.	20	Telephone Expense	525	1 0 0 00		1
2			Cash	101		1 0 0 00	2
3			Paid telephone bill				3
4							4
5		21	George Fielding, Drawing	312	1 1 0 0 00		5
6			Cash	101		1 1 0 0 00	6
7			Owner's withdrawal				7
8							8
9		24	Charitable Contributions Expense	534	1 0 0 00		9
10			Cash	101		1 0 0 00	10
11			Contribution to National Multiple				11
12			Sclerosis Society				12
13							13
14		27	Cash	101	2 0 0 0 00		14
15			Professional Fees	401		2 0 0 0 00	15
16			Received cash for services rendered				16
17							17
18		28	Wages Expense	511	6 0 0 00		18
19			Cash	101		6 0 0 00	19
20			Paid temporary secretaries				20
21							21
22		29	Accounts Payable	202	1 0 0 00		22
23			Cash	101		1 0 0 00	23
24			Payment on account to Bowers Office Supply				24

2.

GENERAL LEDGER

ACCOUNT: Cash   ACCOUNT NO. 101

DATE		ITEM	POST REF.	DEBIT	CREDIT	BALANCE DEBIT	BALANCE CREDIT
20-- Dec.	1		J 1	20 0 0 0 00		20 0 0 0 00	
	3		J 1		1 0 0 0 00	19 0 0 0 00	
	4		J 1	2 5 0 0 00		21 5 0 0 00	
	6		J 1		7 5 00	21 4 2 5 00	
	7		J 1	2 0 0 0 00		23 4 2 5 00	
	12		J 1		6 0 00	23 3 6 5 00	
	14		J 1		6 0 0 00	22 7 6 5 00	
	20		J 2		1 0 0 00	22 6 6 5 00	
	21		J 2		1 1 0 0 00	21 5 6 5 00	
	24		J 2		1 0 0 00	21 4 6 5 00	
	27		J 2	2 0 0 0 00		23 4 6 5 00	
	28		J 2		6 0 0 00	22 8 6 5 00	
	29		J 2		1 0 0 00	22 7 6 5 00	

(continued)

ACCOUNT: Office Supplies   ACCOUNT NO. 142

DATE	ITEM	POST REF.	DEBIT	CREDIT	BALANCE DEBIT	BALANCE CREDIT
20-- Dec. 17		J1	2 8 0 00		2 8 0 00	

ACCOUNT: Accounts Payable   ACCOUNT NO. 202

DATE	ITEM	POST REF.	DEBIT	CREDIT	BALANCE DEBIT	BALANCE CREDIT
20-- Dec. 17		J1		2 8 0 00		2 8 0 00
29		J2	1 0 0 00			1 8 0 00

ACCOUNT: George Fielding, Capital   ACCOUNT NO. 311

DATE	ITEM	POST REF.	DEBIT	CREDIT	BALANCE DEBIT	BALANCE CREDIT
20-- Dec. 1		J1		20 0 0 0 00		20 0 0 0 00

ACCOUNT: George Fielding, Drawing   ACCOUNT NO. 312

DATE	ITEM	POST REF.	DEBIT	CREDIT	BALANCE DEBIT	BALANCE CREDIT
20-- Dec. 21		J2	1 1 0 0 00		1 1 0 0 00	

ACCOUNT: Professional Fees   ACCOUNT NO. 401

DATE	ITEM	POST REF.	DEBIT	CREDIT	BALANCE DEBIT	BALANCE CREDIT
20-- Dec. 4		J1		2 5 0 0 00		2 5 0 0 00
7		J1		2 0 0 0 00		4 5 0 0 00
27		J2		2 0 0 0 00		6 5 0 0 00

ACCOUNT: Wages Expense   ACCOUNT NO. 511

DATE	ITEM	POST REF.	DEBIT	CREDIT	BALANCE DEBIT	BALANCE CREDIT
20-- Dec. 14		J1	6 0 0 00		6 0 0 00	
28		J2	6 0 0 00		1 2 0 0 00	

ACCOUNT: Rent Expense   ACCOUNT NO. 521

DATE	ITEM	POST REF.	DEBIT	CREDIT	BALANCE DEBIT	BALANCE CREDIT
20-- Dec. 3		J1	1 0 0 0 00		1 0 0 0 00	

ACCOUNT: Telephone Expense   ACCOUNT NO. 525

DATE	ITEM	POST REF.	DEBIT	CREDIT	BALANCE DEBIT	BALANCE CREDIT
20-- Dec. 20		J 2	1 0 0 00		1 0 0 00	

ACCOUNT: Utilities Expense   ACCOUNT NO. 533

DATE	ITEM	POST REF.	DEBIT	CREDIT	BALANCE DEBIT	BALANCE CREDIT
20-- Dec. 6		J 1	7 5 00		7 5 00	

ACCOUNT: Charitable Contributions Expense   ACCOUNT NO. 534

DATE	ITEM	POST REF.	DEBIT	CREDIT	BALANCE DEBIT	BALANCE CREDIT
20-- Dec. 24		J 2	1 0 0 00		1 0 0 00	

ACCOUNT: Automobile Expense   ACCOUNT NO. 538

DATE	ITEM	POST REF.	DEBIT	CREDIT	BALANCE DEBIT	BALANCE CREDIT
20-- Dec. 12		J 1	6 0 00		6 0 00	

3.

George Fielding, Financial Planning Consultant
Trial Balance
December 31, 20 - -

ACCOUNT TITLE	ACCOUNT NO.	DEBIT BALANCE	CREDIT BALANCE
Cash	101	22 7 6 5 00	
Office Supplies	142	2 8 0 00	
Accounts Payable	202		1 8 0 00
George Fielding, Capital	311		20 0 0 0 00
George Fielding, Drawing	312	1 1 0 0 00	
Professional Fees	401		6 5 0 0 00
Wages Expense	511	1 2 0 0 00	
Rent Expense	521	1 0 0 0 00	
Telephone Expense	525	1 0 0 00	
Utilities Expense	533	7 5 00	
Charitable Contributions Expense	534	1 0 0 00	
Automobile Expense	538	6 0 00	
		26 6 8 0 00	26 6 8 0 00

REVIEW QUESTIONS

1. Trace the flow of accounting information through the accounting system.

2. Explain the purpose of a chart of accounts.

3. Name the five types of financial statement classifications for which it is ordinarily desirable to keep separate accounts.

4. Name a source document that provides information about each of the following types of business transactions:
   a. Cash payment
   b. Cash receipt
   c. Sale of goods or services
   d. Purchase of goods or services

5. Where is the first formal accounting record of a business transaction usually made?

6. Describe the four steps required to journalize a business transaction in a general journal.

7. In what order are the accounts customarily placed in the ledger?

8. Explain the primary advantage of a four-column ledger account.

9. Explain the five steps required when posting the journal to the ledger.

10. What information is entered in the Posting Reference column of the journal as an amount is posted to the proper account in the ledger?

11. Explain why the ledger can still contain errors even though the trial balance is in balance. Give examples of two such types of errors.

12. What is a slide error?

13. What is a transposition error?

14. What is the ruling method of correcting an error?

15. What is the correcting entry method?

MANAGING YOUR WRITING

You are a public accountant with many small business clients. During a recent visit to a client's business, the bookkeeper approached you with a problem. The columns of the trial balance were not equal. You helped the bookkeeper find and correct the error, but believe you should go one step further. Write a memo to all of your clients that explains the purpose of the double-entry framework, the importance of maintaining the equality of the accounting equation, the errors that might cause an inequality, and suggestions for finding the errors.

SERIES A EXERCISES

EXERCISE 4A-1 (LO 3) SOURCE DOCUMENTS Source documents trigger the analysis of events requiring an accounting entry. Match the following source documents with the type of information they provide.

1. Check stubs or check register

2. Purchase invoice from suppliers (vendors)

3. Sales tickets or invoices to customers

4. Receipts or cash register tapes

a. A good or service has been sold.

b. Cash has been received by the business.

c. Cash has been paid by the business.

d. Goods or services have been purchased by the business.

EXERCISE 4A-2 (LO 4) GENERAL JOURNAL ENTRIES For each of the following transactions, list the account to be debited and the account to be credited in the general journal.

1. Invested cash in the business, $5,000.

2. Paid office rent, $500.

3. Purchased office supplies on account, $300.

4. Received cash for services rendered (fees), $400.

5. Paid cash on account, $50.

6. Rendered services on account, $300.

7. Received cash for an amount owed by a customer, $100.

EXERCISE 4A-3 (LO 5) GENERAL LEDGER ACCOUNTS Set up T accounts for each of the general ledger accounts needed for Exercise 4A-2 and post debits and credits to the accounts. Foot the accounts and enter the balances. Prove that total debits equal total credits.

EXERCISE 4A-4 (LO 4) GENERAL JOURNAL ENTRIES Jean Jones has opened Jones Consulting. Journalize the following transactions that occurred during January of the current year. Use the following journal pages: January 1–10, page 1 and January 11–29, page 2. Use the chart of accounts provided below.

Chart of Accounts

Assets	Revenues
101 Cash	401 Consulting Fees
142 Office Supplies	
181 Office Equipment	Expenses
	511 Wages Expense
Liabilities	521 Rent Expense
202 Accounts Payable	525 Telephone Expense
	533 Utilities Expense
Owner's Equity	549 Miscellaneous Expense
311 Jean Jones, Capital	
312 Jean Jones, Drawing	

(continued)

Jan. 1 Jones invested cash in the business, $10,000.

2 Paid office rent, $500.

3 Purchased office equipment on account, $1,500.

5 Received cash for services rendered, $750.

8 Paid telephone bill, $65.

10 Paid for a magazine subscription (miscellaneous expense), $15.

11 Purchased office supplies on account, $300.

15 Made a payment on account (see Jan. 3 transaction), $150.

18 Paid part-time employee, $500.

21 Received cash for services rendered, $350.

25 Paid utilities bill, $85.

27 Jones withdrew cash for personal use, $100.

29 Paid part-time employee, $500.

EXERCISE 4A-5 (LO 5) GENERAL LEDGER ACCOUNTS; TRIAL BALANCE Set up four-column general ledger accounts using the chart of accounts provided in Exercise 4A-4. Post the transactions from Exercise 4A-4 to the general ledger accounts and prepare a trial balance.

EXERCISE 4A-6 FINANCIAL STATEMENTS From the information in Exercises 4A-4 and 4A-5, prepare an income statement, a statement of owner's equity, and a balance sheet.

EXERCISE 4A-7 FINANCIAL STATEMENTS From the following trial balance taken after one month of operation, prepare an income statement, a statement of owner's equity, and a balance sheet. Assume that TJ Ulza made no additional investments in the business during the month.

TJ's Paint Service
Trial Balance
July 31, 20 - -

ACCOUNT TITLE	ACCOUNT NO.	DEBIT BALANCE	CREDIT BALANCE
Cash	101	4 3 0 0 00	
Accounts Receivable	122	1 1 0 0 00	
Supplies	141	8 0 0 00	
Paint Equipment	183	9 0 0 00	
Accounts Payable	202		2 1 5 0 00
TJ Ulza, Capital	311		3 2 0 5 00
TJ Ulza, Drawing	312	5 0 0 00	
Painting Fees	401		3 6 0 0 00
Wages Expense	511	9 0 0 00	
Rent Expense	521	2 5 0 00	
Telephone Expense	525	5 0 00	
Transportation Expense	526	6 0 00	
Utilities Expense	533	7 0 00	
Miscellaneous Expense	549	2 5 00	
		8 9 5 5 00	8 9 5 5 00

EXERCISE 4A-8 (LO 6) FINDING AND CORRECTING ERRORS Joe Adams bought $500 worth of office supplies on account. The following entry was recorded on May 17. Find the error(s) and correct it (them) using the ruling method.

14											14
15	20– May	17	Office Equipment		4 0 0 00				15
16			Cash				4 0 0 00		16
17			Purchased copy paper						17

On May 25, after the transactions had been posted, Adams discovered that the following entry contains an error. The cash received represents a collection on account, rather than new service fees. Correct the error in the general journal using the correcting entry method.

22								22
23	20– May	23	Cash	101	1 0 0 0 00			23
24			Service Fees	401		1 0 0 0 00		24
25			Received cash for services previously earned					25

SERIES A PROBLEMS

PROBLEM 4A-1 (LO 4/5) JOURNALIZING AND POSTING TRANSACTIONS Jim Andrews opened a delivery business in March. He rented a small office and has a part-time assistant. His trial balance shows accounts for the first three months of business.

	Jim's Quick Delivery Trial Balance May 31, 20 - -			
ACCOUNT TITLE	ACCOUNT NO.	DEBIT BALANCE	CREDIT BALANCE
Cash	101	3 8 2 6 00	
Accounts Receivable	122	1 2 1 2 00	
Office Supplies	142	6 4 8 00	
Office Equipment	181	2 1 0 0 00	
Delivery Truck	185	8 0 0 0 00	
Accounts Payable	202		6 0 0 0 00
Jim Andrews, Capital	311		4 4 7 8 00
Jim Andrews, Drawing	312	1 8 0 0 00	
Delivery Fees	401		9 8 8 0 00
Wages Expense	511	1 2 0 0 00	
Advertising Expense	512	9 0 00	
Rent Expense	521	9 0 0 00	
Telephone Expense	525	1 2 6 00	
Electricity Expense	533	9 8 00	
Charitable Contributions Expense	534	6 0 00	
Gas and Oil Expense	538	1 8 6 00	
Miscellaneous Expense	549	1 1 2 00	
		20 3 5 8 00	20 3 5 8 00

(continued)

Andrews' transactions for the month of June are as follows:

June 1 Paid rent, $300.

2 Performed delivery services for $300: $100 in cash and $200 on account.

4 Paid for newspaper advertising, $15.

6 Purchased office supplies on account, $180.

7 Received cash for delivery services rendered, $260.

9 Paid cash on account (truck payment), $200.

10 Purchased a copier (office equipment) for $700: paid $100 in cash and put $600 on account.

11 Made a contribution to the Red Cross (charitable contributions), $20.

12 Received cash for delivery services rendered, $380.

13 Received cash on account for services previously rendered, $100.

15 Paid a part-time worker, $200.

16 Paid electric bill, $36.

18 Paid telephone bill, $46.

19 Received cash on account for services previously rendered, $100.

20 Andrews withdrew cash for personal use, $200.

21 Paid for gas and oil, $32.

22 Made payment on account (for office supplies), $40.

24 Received cash for services rendered, $340.

26 Paid for a magazine subscription (miscellaneous expense), $15.

27 Received cash for services rendered, $180.

27 Received cash on account for services previously rendered, $100.

29 Paid for gasoline, $24.

30 Paid a part-time worker, $200.

REQUIRED 1. Set up four-column general ledger accounts by entering the balances as of June 1.

2. Journalize the transactions for June in a two-column general journal. Use the following journal pages: June 1–10, page 7; June 11–20, page 8; June 21–30, page 9.

3. Post the entries from the general journal.

4. Prepare a trial balance.

W & D

PROBLEM 4A-2 (LO 4/5) JOURNALIZING AND POSTING TRANSACTIONS
Annette Creighton opened Creighton Consulting. She rented a small office and paid a part-time worker to answer the telephone and make deliveries. Her chart of accounts is as follows:

Chart of Accounts

Assets	Revenues
101 Cash	401 Consulting Fees
142 Office Supplies	
181 Office Equipment	Expenses
	511 Wages Expense
Liabilities	512 Advertising Expense
202 Accounts Payable	521 Rent Expense
	525 Telephone Expense
Owner's Equity	526 Transportation Expense
311 Annette Creighton, Capital	533 Utilities Expense
312 Annette Creighton, Drawing	549 Miscellaneous Expense

Creighton's transactions for the first month of business are as follows:

Jan. 1   Creighton invested cash in the business, $10,000.

1   Paid rent, $500.

2   Purchased office supplies on account, $300.

4   Purchased office equipment on account, $1,500.

6   Received cash for services rendered, $580.

7   Paid telephone bill, $42.

8   Paid utilities bill, $38.

10   Received cash for services rendered, $360.

12   Made payment on account, $50.

13   Paid for car rental while visiting an out-of-town client (transportation expense), $150.

15   Paid part-time worker, $360.

17   Received cash for services rendered, $420.

18   Creighton withdrew cash for personal use, $100.

20   Paid for a newspaper ad, $26.

22   Reimbursed part-time employee for cab fare incurred delivering materials to clients (transportation expense), $35.

24   Paid for books on consulting practices (miscellaneous expense), $28.

25   Received cash for services rendered, $320.

27   Made payment on account for office equipment purchased, $150.

29   Paid part-time worker, $360.

30   Received cash for services rendered, $180.

(continued)

REQUIRED

1. Set up four-column general ledger accounts from the chart of accounts.

2. Journalize the transactions for January in a two-column general journal. Use the following journal page numbers: January 1–10, page 1; January 12–24, page 2; January 25–30, page 3.

3. Post the transactions from the general journal.

4. Prepare a trial balance.

5. Prepare an income statement and a statement of owner's equity for the month of January, and a balance sheet as of January 31, 20--.

PROBLEM 4A-3 (LO 6) CORRECTING ERRORS Assuming that all entries have been posted, prepare correcting entries for each of the following errors:

1. The following entry was made to record the purchase of $500 in supplies on account:

Supplies	142	500
Cash	101	500

2. The following entry was made to record the payment of $300 in wages:

Rent Expense	521	300
Cash	101	300

3. The following entry was made to record a $200 payment to a supplier on account:

Supplies	142	100
Cash	101	100

SERIES B EXERCISES

EXERCISE 4B-1 (LO 3) SOURCE DOCUMENTS What type of information is found on each of the following source documents?

1. Cash register tape

2. Sales ticket (issued to customer)

3. Purchase invoice (received from supplier or vendor)

4. Check stub

EXERCISE 4B-2 (LO 4) GENERAL JOURNAL ENTRIES For each of the following transactions, list the account to be debited and the account to be credited in the general journal.

1. Invested cash in the business, $1,000.

2. Performed services on account, $200.

3. Purchased office equipment on account, $500.

4. Received cash on account for services previously rendered, $200.

5. Made a payment on account, $100.

EXERCISE 4B-3 (LO 5) GENERAL LEDGER ACCOUNTS Set up T accounts for each of the general ledger accounts needed for Exercise 4B-2 and post debits and credits to the accounts. Foot the accounts and enter the balances. Prove that total debits equal total credits.

EXERCISE 4B-4 (LO 4) GENERAL JOURNAL ENTRIES Sengel Moon opened The Bike Doctor. Journalize the following transactions that occurred during the month of October of the current year. Use the following journal pages: October 1–12, page 1 and October 14–29, page 2. Use the chart of accounts provided below.

Chart of Accounts

Assets	Revenues
101 Cash	401 Repair Fees
141 Bicycle Parts	
142 Office Supplies	Expenses
	511 Wages Expense
Liabilities	521 Rent Expense
202 Accounts Payable	525 Telephone Expense
	533 Utilities Expense
Owner's Equity	549 Miscellaneous Expense
311 Sengel Moon, Capital	
312 Sengel Moon, Drawing	

Oct. 1 Moon invested cash in the business, $15,000.

2 Paid shop rental for the month, $300.

3 Purchased bicycle parts on account, $2,000.

5 Purchased office supplies on account, $250.

8 Paid telephone bill, $38.

9 Received cash for services, $140.

11 Paid a sports magazine subscription (miscellaneous expense), $15.

12 Made payment on account (see Oct. 3 transaction), $100.

14 Paid part-time employee, $300.

15 Received cash for services, $350.

16 Paid utilities bill, $48.

19 Received cash for services, $250.

23 Moon withdrew cash for personal use, $50.

25 Made payment on account (see Oct. 5 transaction), $50.

29 Paid part-time employee, $300.

EXERCISE 4B-5 (LO 5) GENERAL LEDGER ACCOUNTS; TRIAL BALANCE Set up four-column general ledger accounts using the chart of accounts provided in Exercise 4B-4. Post the transactions from Exercise 4B-4 to the general ledger accounts and prepare a trial balance.

EXERCISE 4B-6 FINANCIAL STATEMENTS From the information in Exercises 4B-4 and 4B-5, prepare an income statement, a statement of owner's equity, and a balance sheet.

EXERCISE 4B-7 FINANCIAL STATEMENTS From the following trial balance taken after one month of operation, prepare an income statement, a statement of owner's equity, and a balance sheet. Assume that no additional investments were made during the month.

AT's Speaker's Bureau Trial Balance March 31, 20 - -											
ACCOUNT TITLE	ACCOUNT NO.	DEBIT BALANCE					CREDIT BALANCE				
Cash	101	6	6	0	0	00					
Accounts Receivable	122	2	8	0	0	00					
Office Supplies	142	1	0	0	0	00					
Office Equipment	181	1	5	0	0	00					
Accounts Payable	202						3	0	0	0	00
AT Speaker, Capital	311						6	0	9	8	00
AT Speaker, Drawing	312		8	0	0	00					
Speaking Fees	401						4	8	0	0	00
Wages Expense	511		4	0	0	00					
Rent Expense	521		2	0	0	00					
Telephone Expense	525			3	5	00					
Travel Expense	526		4	5	0	00					
Utilities Expense	533			8	8	00					
Miscellaneous Expense	549			2	5	00					
		13	8	9	8	00	13	8	9	8	00

EXERCISE 4B-8 (LO 6) FINDING AND CORRECTING ERRORS Mary Smith purchased $350 worth of office equipment on account. The following entry was recorded on April 6. Find the error(s) and correct it (them) using the ruling method.

7												7
8	20-- Apr.	6	Office Supplies			5	3	0	00				8
9			Cash							5	3	0	00	9
10			Purchased office equipment										10

On April 25, after the transactions had been posted, Smith discovered the following entry contains an error. When her customer received services, Cash was debited, but no cash was received. Correct the error in the journal using the correcting entry method.

27												27
28	20-- Apr.	21	Cash	101		3	0	0	00				28
29			Service Fees	401						3	0	0	00	29
30			Revenue earned from services										30
31			previously rendered										31

SERIES B PROBLEMS

PROBLEM 4B-1 (LO 4/5) JOURNALIZING AND POSTING TRANSACTIONS Ann Tailor owns a suit tailoring shop. She opened business in September. She rented a small work space and has an assistant to receive job orders and process claim tickets. Her trial balance shows her account balances for the first two months of business.

Tailor Tailoring Trial Balance October 31, 20 - -			
ACCOUNT TITLE	ACCOUNT NO.	DEBIT BALANCE	CREDIT BALANCE
Cash	101	6 2 1 1 00	
Accounts Receivable	122	4 8 4 00	
Tailoring Supplies	141	1 0 0 0 00	
Tailoring Equipment	183	3 8 0 0 00	
Accounts Payable	202		4 1 2 5 00
Ann Tailor, Capital	311		6 1 3 0 00
Ann Tailor, Drawing	312	8 0 0 00	
Tailoring Fees	401		3 6 0 0 00
Wages Expense	511	8 0 0 00	
Advertising Expense	512	3 4 00	
Rent Expense	521	6 0 0 00	
Telephone Expense	525	6 0 00	
Electricity Expense	533	4 4 00	
Miscellaneous Expense	549	2 2 00	
		13 8 5 5 00	13 8 5 5 00

Tailor's transactions for November are as follows:

Nov. 1 Paid rent, $300.

2 Purchased tailoring supplies on account, $150.

3 Purchased a new button hole machine on account, $300.

5 Earned first week's revenue, $400: $100 in cash and $300 on account.

8 Paid for newspaper advertising, $13.

9 Paid telephone bill, $28.

10 Paid electric bill, $21.

11 Received cash on account from customers, $200.

12 Earned second week's revenue, $450: $200 in cash and $250 on account.

15 Paid assistant, $400.

16 Made payment on account, $100.

17 Paid for magazine subscription (miscellaneous expense), $12.

19 Earned third week's revenue, $450: $300 in cash, $150 on account.

23 Received cash on account from customers, $300.

24 Paid for newspaper advertising, $13.

(continued)

26 Paid for postage (miscellaneous expense), $12.

27 Earned fourth week's revenue, $600: $200 in cash and $400 on account.

30 Received cash on account from customers, $400.

REQUIRED
1. Set up four-column general ledger accounts by entering the balances as of November 1, 20--.

2. Journalize the transactions for November in a two-column general journal. Use the following journal page numbers: November 1–11, page 7; November 12–24, page 8; November 26–30, page 9.

3. Post the entries from the general journal.

4. Prepare a trial balance.

PROBLEM 4B-2 (LO 4/5) JOURNALIZING AND POSTING TRANSACTIONS Benito Mendez opened Mendez Appraisals. He rented office space and has a part-time secretary to answer the telephone and make appraisal appointments. His chart of accounts is as follows:

Chart of Accounts

Assets	Revenues
101 Cash	401 Appraisal Fees
122 Accounts Receivable	
142 Office Supplies	Expenses
181 Office Equipment	511 Wages Expense
	512 Advertising Expense
Liabilities	521 Rent Expense
202 Accounts Payable	525 Telephone Expense
	526 Transportation Expense
Owner's Equity	533 Electricity Expense
311 Benito Mendez, Capital	549 Miscellaneous Expense
312 Benito Mendez, Drawing	

Mendez's transactions for the first month of business are as follows:

May 1 Mendez invested cash in the business, $5,000.

2 Paid rent, $500.

3 Purchased office supplies, $100.

4 Purchased office equipment on account, $2,000.

5 Received cash for services rendered, $280.

8 Paid telephone bill, $38.

9 Paid electric bill, $42.

10 Received cash for services rendered, $310.

13 Paid part-time employee, $500.

14 Paid car rental for out-of-town trip, $200.

15 Paid for newspaper ad, $30.

18 Received cash for services rendered, $620.

19   Paid mileage reimbursement for part-time employee's use of personal car for business deliveries (transportation expense), $22.

21   Mendez withdrew cash for personal use, $50.

23   Made payment on account for office equipment purchased earlier, $200.

24   Earned appraisal fee, which will be paid in a week, $500.

26   Paid for newspaper ad, $30.

27   Paid for local softball team sponsorship (miscellaneous expense), $15.

28   Paid part-time employee, $500.

29   Received cash on account, $250.

30   Received cash for services rendered, $280.

31   Paid cab fare (transportation expense), $13.

REQUIRED   1.   Set up four-column general ledger accounts from the chart of accounts.

2.   Journalize the transactions for May in a two-column general journal. Use the following journal page numbers: May 1–10, page 1; May 13–24, page 2; May 26–31, page 3.

3.   Post the transactions from the general journal.

4.   Prepare a trial balance.

5.   Prepare an income statement and a statement of owner's equity for the month of May, and a balance sheet as of May 31, 20--.

PROBLEM 4B-3 (LO 6) CORRECTING ERRORS Assuming that all entries have been posted, prepare correcting entries for each of the following errors:

1.   The following entry was made to record the purchase of $400 in equipment on account:

| Supplies | 142 | 400 | |
| Cash | 101 | | 400 |

2.   The following entry was made to record the payment of $200 for advertising:

| Repair Expense | 537 | 200 | |
| Cash | 101 | | 200 |

3.   The following entry was made to record a $600 payment to a supplier on account:

| Prepaid Insurance | 145 | 400 | |
| Cash | 101 | | 400 |

MASTERY PROBLEM

Barry Bird opened the Barry Bird Basketball Camp for children ages 10 through 18. Campers typically register for one week in June or July, arriving on Sunday and returning home the following Saturday. College players serve as cabin counselors and assist the local college and high school coaches who run the practice sessions. The registration fee includes a room, meals at a nearby restaurant, and basketball instruction. In the off-season, the facilities are used for weekend retreats and coaching clinics. Bird developed the following chart of accounts for his service business.

Chart of Accounts

Assets	Revenues
101 Cash	401 Registration Fees
142 Office Supplies	
183 Athletic Equipment	Expenses
184 Basketball Facilities	511 Wages Expense
	512 Advertising Expense
Liabilities	524 Food Expense
202 Accounts Payable	525 Telephone Expense
	533 Utilities Expense
Owner's Equity	536 Postage Expense
311 Barry Bird, Capital	
312 Barry Bird, Drawing	

The following transactions took place during the month of June.

June 1   Bird invested cash in the business, $10,000.

1   Purchased basketballs and other athletic equipment, $3,000.

2   Paid Hite Advertising for fliers that had been mailed to prospective campers, $5,000.

2   Collected registration fees, $15,000.

2   Rogers Construction completed work on a new basketball court that cost $12,000. Arrangements were made to pay the bill in July.

5   Purchased office supplies on account from Gordon Office Supplies, $300.

6   Received bill from Magic's Restaurant for meals served to campers on account, $5,800.

7   Collected registration fees, $16,200.

10   Paid wages to camp counselors, $500.

14   Collected registration fees, $13,500.

14   Received bill from Magic's Restaurant for meals served to campers on account, $6,200.

17   Paid wages to camp counselors, $500.

18   Paid postage, $85.

21   Collected registration fees, $15,200.

22   Received bill from Magic's Restaurant for meals served to campers on account, $6,500.

24   Paid wages to camp counselors, $500.

28   Collected registration fees, $14,000.

30   Received bill from Magic's Restaurant for meals served to campers on account, $7,200.

30   Paid wages to camp counselors, $500.

30   Paid Magic's Restaurant on account, $25,700.

30   Paid utility bill, $500.

30   Paid telephone bill, $120.

30   Bird withdrew cash for personal use, $2,000.

REQUIRED   1.   Enter the above transactions in a general journal. Use the following journal pages: June 1–6, page 1; June 7–22, page 2; June 24–30, page 3.

2.   Post the entries to the general ledger.

3.   Prepare a trial balance.

Self-Study Test Questions

True/False

1. Source documents serve as historical evidence of business transactions. _____

2. No entries are made in the Posting Reference column at the time of journalizing. _____

3. When entering the credit item in a general journal, it should be listed after all debits and indented. _____

4. The chart of accounts lists capital accounts first, followed by liabilities, assets, expenses, and revenue. _____

5. When an incorrect entry has been journalized and posted to the wrong account, a correcting entry should be made. _____

Multiple Choice

1. The process of copying debits and credits from the journal to the ledger is called _____

   (a) journalizing.   (c) cross-referencing.
   (b) posting.   (d) sliding.

2. To purchase an asset such as office equipment on account, you would credit which account? _____

   (a) Cash   (c) Accounts Payable
   (b) Accounts Receivable   (d) Capital

3. When fees are earned but will be paid later, which account is debited? _____

   (a) Cash   (c) Accounts Payable
   (b) Accounts Receivable   (d) Capital

4. When the correct numbers are used but are in the wrong order, the error is called a _____

   (a) transposition.   (c) ruling.
   (b) slide.   (d) correcting entry.

5. A revenue account will begin with the number _____ in the chart of accounts. _____

   (a) 1   (c) 3
   (b) 2   (d) 4

The answers to the Self-Study Test Questions are at the end of the text.

5

Adjusting Entries and the Work Sheet

LEARNING OBJECTIVES:
Careful study of this chapter should enable you to:

LO 1 Prepare end-of-period adjustments.

LO 2 Prepare a work sheet.

LO 3 Describe methods for finding errors on the work sheet.

LO 4 Journalize adjusting entries.

LO 5 Post adjusting entries to the general ledger.

At the end of the first month of operations, Jessie and Mitch were looking over the trial balance. "These accounts don't look right," said Jessie. "Don't worry, I just need to make a few adjustments before we prepare the financial statements," replied Mitch. Does it seem appropriate to make adjustments prior to issuing financial statements?

Up to this point, you have learned how to journalize business transactions, post to the ledger, and prepare a trial balance. Now it is time to learn how to make end-of-period adjustments to the accounts listed in the trial balance. This chapter explains the need for adjustments and illustrates how they are made using a work sheet.

END-OF-PERIOD ADJUSTMENTS

LO 1   Prepare end-of-period adjustments.

> *Transactions are entered as they occur throughout the year. Adjustments are made to reflect changes in account balances that are not the direct result of an exchange with an outside party. Adjustments are made at the end of the accounting period.*

Throughout the accounting period, business transactions are entered in the accounting system. These transactions are based on exchanges between the business and other companies and individuals. During the accounting period, other changes occur that affect the business's financial condition. For example, equipment is wearing out, prepaid insurance and supplies are being used up, and employees are earning wages that have not yet been paid. Since these events have not been entered into the accounting system, they must be entered as adjustments prior to the preparation of financial statements.

The **matching principle** in accounting requires the matching of revenues earned during an accounting period with the expenses incurred to produce the revenues. This approach offers the best measure of net income. The income statement reports earnings for a specific period of time and the balance sheet reports the assets, liabilities, and owner's equity on a specific date. Thus, to follow the matching principle, the accounts must be brought up to date before financial statements are prepared. This requires adjusting some of the accounts listed in the trial balance. Figure 5-1 lists reasons to adjust the trial balance.

 LEARNING KEY: Matching revenues earned with expenses incurred as a result of efforts to produce those revenues offers the best measure of net income.

FIGURE 5-1 Reasons to Adjust the Trial Balance

1. To report all revenues earned during the accounting period.
2. To report all expenses incurred to produce the revenues earned in this accounting period.
3. To accurately report the assets on the balance sheet date. Some assets may have been used up during the accounting period.
4. To accurately report the liabilities on the balance sheet date. Expenses may have been incurred but not yet paid.

Generally, adjustments are made and financial statements prepared at the end of a twelve-month period called a **fiscal year.** This period does not need to be the same as a calendar year. In fact, many businesses schedule their fiscal year end for a time when business is slow. In this chapter we continue the illustration of Jessie Jane's Campus Delivery and will prepare adjustments at the end of the first month of operations. We will focus on the following accounts: Supplies, Prepaid Insurance, Delivery Equipment, and Wages Expense.

ADJUSTING ENTRIES

Are adjusting entries important? The Walt Disney Company and Mattel, Inc. probably think so. The Walt Disney Company granted Mattel, Inc. the right to make and sell toys based on Disney characters. In return, Mattel agreed to make payments to Disney as the toys were sold. One of the issues in a court case was whether Mattel should have made an adjusting entry when it fell behind on these payments. The entry would have been:

Royalty Expense on Disney Characters	17,000,000	
Accounts Payable (Disney)		17,000,000

This adjusting entry would have reduced Mattel's fourth quarter earnings for that year by more than 15%. Following an investigation by the Securities and Exchange Commission, Mattel eventually agreed to make an adjustment to later financial statements.

Supplies

During June, Jessie purchased supplies consisting of paper, pens, and delivery envelopes for $80. *Since these supplies were expected to provide future benefits, Supplies, an asset, was debited at the time of the purchase.* No other entries were made to the supplies account during June. As reported on the trial balance in Figure 5-2, the $80 balance remains in the supplies account at the end of the month.

FIGURE 5-2 Trial Balance

ACCOUNT TITLE	ACCOUNT NO.	DEBIT BALANCE					CREDIT BALANCE				
Cash	101		3	7	0	00					
Accounts Receivable	122		6	5	0	00					
Supplies	141			8	0	00					
Prepaid Insurance	145		2	0	0	00					
Delivery Equipment	185	3	6	0	0	00					
Accounts Payable	202						1	8	0	0	00
Jessica Jane, Capital	311						2	0	0	0	00
Jessica Jane, Drawing	312		1	5	0	00					
Delivery Fees	401						2	1	5	0	00
Wages Expense	511		6	5	0	00					
Rent Expense	521		2	0	0	00					
Telephone Expense	525			5	0	00					
		5	9	5	0	00	5	9	5	0	00

Jessie Jane's Campus Delivery
Trial Balance
June 30, 20 - -

As supplies are used, an expense is incurred. However, it is not practical to make a journal entry to recognize this expense and the reduction in the supplies account every time someone uses an envelope. It is more efficient to wait until the end of the accounting period to make one adjusting entry to reflect the expense incurred for the use of supplies for the entire month.

LEARNING KEY: Since it is not practical to make a journal entry for supplies expense each time supplies are used, one adjusting entry is made at the end of the accounting period.

At the end of the month, an inventory, or physical count, of the remaining supplies is taken. The inventory shows that supplies costing $20 were still unused at the end of June. Since Jessie bought supplies costing $80, and only $20 worth remain, supplies costing $60 must have been used ($80 – $20 = $60). Thus, supplies expense for the month is $60. (Trial balance is abbreviated as TB in Figure 5-3 and other T account illustrations.)

Since $60 worth of supplies have been used, Supplies Expense is debited and Supplies (asset) is credited for $60 (Figure 5-3). Thus, as shown in Figure 5-4, supplies with a cost of $20 will be reported as an asset on the balance sheet and a supplies expense of $60 will be reported on the income statement. The adjusting entry affected an income statement account (Supplies Expense) and a balance sheet account (Supplies).

FIGURE 5-3 Adjustment for Supplies

Assets		=	Liabilities		+	Owner's Equity							
Debit	Credit		Debit	Credit		Debit					Credit		
+	–		–	+		–					+		
							Drawing		Expenses		Revenues		
							Debit	Credit	Debit	Credit	Debit	Credit	
							+	–	+	–	–	+	

Supplies				Supplies Expense	
TB 80				Adj. 60	
	Adj. 60				
Bal. 20					

FIGURE 5-4 Effect of Adjusting Entry for Supplies on Financial Statements

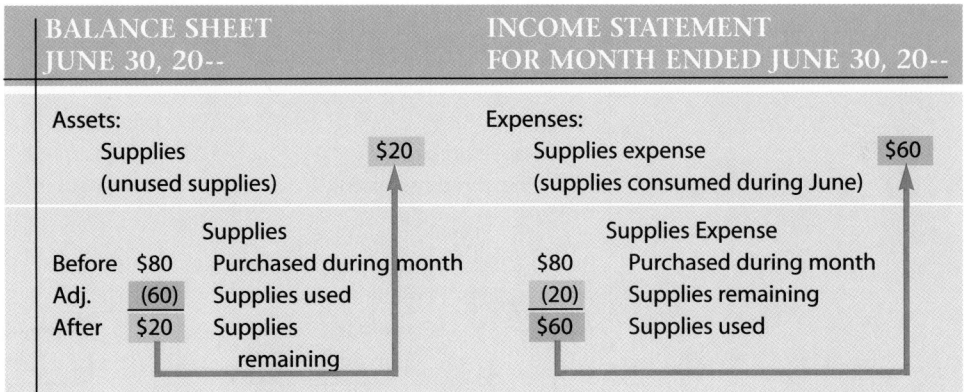

LEARNING KEY: By making an adjusting entry that debits Supplies Expense and credits Supplies, you are taking the amount of supplies used out of Supplies and putting it in Supplies Expense.

Prepaid Insurance

On June 18, Jessie paid $200 for an eight-month liability insurance policy with coverage beginning on June 1. *Prepaid Insurance, an asset, was debited because the insurance policy is expected to provide future benefits.* The $200 balance is reported on the trial balance. As the insurance policy expires with the passage of time, the asset should be reduced and an expense recognized.

Since the $200 premium covers eight months, the cost of the expired coverage for June is $25 ($200 ÷ 8 months). As shown in Figure 5-5, the adjusting entry is to debit Insurance Expense for $25 and credit Prepaid Insurance for $25. Figure 5-6 shows that the unexpired portion of the insurance premium will be reported on the balance sheet as Prepaid Insurance of $175. The expired portion will be reported on the income statement as Insurance Expense of $25.

LEARNING KEY: The $200 premium covers eight months. The cost for June is $25 ($200 ÷ 8 months).

FIGURE 5-5 Adjustment for Expired Insurance

FIGURE 5-6 Effect of Adjusting Entry for Prepaid Insurance on Financial Statements

Wages Expense

Jessie paid her part-time employees $650 on June 27. Since then, they have earned an additional $50, but have not yet been paid. The additional wages expense must be recognized.

Since the employees have not been paid, Wages Payable, a liability, should be established. Thus, Wages Expense is debited and Wages Payable is credited for $50 in Figure 5-7. Note in Figure 5-8 that Wages Expense of $700 is reported on the income statement and Wages Payable of $50 is reported on the balance sheet.

PROFILES in ACCOUNTING

Jeff Clifton, Account Supervisor

Jeff Clifton maintained a 4.0 GPA with nearly perfect attendance while earning an Associate Degree in Accounting Automation. He performed an externship with Brooke County Taxing Authority and then began working as an accounts receivable clerk with the DeBartolo Properties Management, Inc., in Youngstown, OH.

He was promoted and is now an account supervisor. His duties include managing accounts receivable for 20 development properties across the United States, supervising five employees, and interviewing prospective employees.

According to Jeff, being self-motivated is the main key to success. You need to work hard and success will come. Accounting interested Jeff because he enjoys working with numbers and considers himself to be very analytical.

FIGURE 5-7 Adjustment for Unpaid Wages

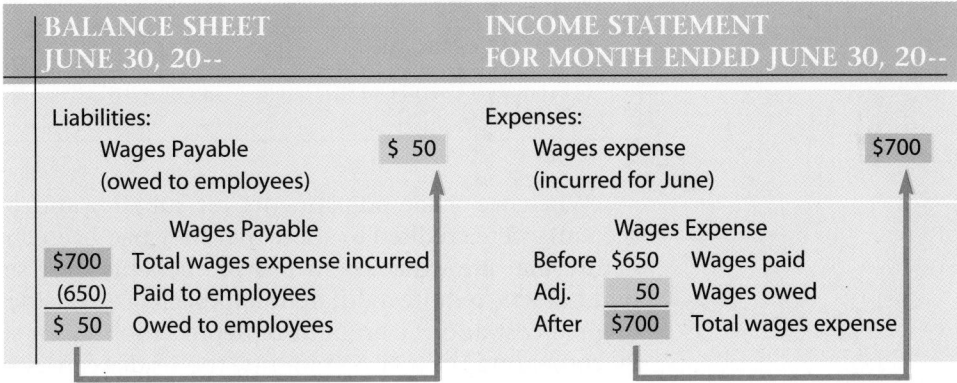

Assets		=	Liabilities		+	Owner's Equity		
Debit	Credit		Debit	Credit		Debit		Credit
+	−		−	+		−		+

	Drawing		Expenses		Revenues	
	Debit	Credit	Debit	Credit	Debit	Credit
	+	−	+	−	−	+

Wages Payable		Wages Expense	
	Adj. 50	TB 650	
		Adj. 50	
		Bal. 700	

FIGURE 5-8 Effect of Adjusting Entry for Wages on Financial Statements

BALANCE SHEET
JUNE 30, 20--

INCOME STATEMENT
FOR MONTH ENDED JUNE 30, 20--

Liabilities:		Expenses:	
Wages Payable	$ 50	Wages expense	$700
(owed to employees)		(incurred for June)	

Wages Payable			Wages Expense		
$700	Total wages expense incurred		Before	$650	Wages paid
(650)	Paid to employees		Adj.	50	Wages owed
$ 50	Owed to employees		After	$700	Total wages expense

Depreciation Expense

During the month of June, Jessie purchased three motor scooters. Since the scooters will provide future benefits, they were recorded as assets in the delivery equipment account. Under the **historical cost principle**, assets are recorded at their actual cost, in this case $3,600. This cost remains on the books as long as the business owns the asset. No adjustments are made for changes in the market value of the asset. It does not matter whether the firm got a "good buy" or paid "too much" when the asset was purchased.

LEARNING KEY: The historical cost principle is an important accounting concept. Assets are recorded at their actual cost. This historical cost is not adjusted for changes in market values.

The period of time that an asset is expected to help produce revenues is called its **useful life**. The asset's useful life expires as a result of wear and tear or because it no longer satisfies the needs of the business. For example, as Jessie adds miles to her scooters, they will become less reliable and will eventually fail to run. As this happens, depreciation expense should be recognized and the value of the asset should be reduced. **Depreciation** is a method of *matching* an asset's original

> *Depreciation expense is based on estimates of useful lives and salvage values.*

cost against the revenues produced over its useful life. There are many depreciation methods. In our example, we will use the **straight-line method**.

Let's assume that Jessie's motor scooters have estimated useful lives of three years and will have no salvage value at the end of that time period. **Salvage value** (also called scrap value, or residual value) is the expected **market value** or selling price of the asset at the end of its useful life. The **depreciable cost** of these scooters is the original cost, less salvage value, or $3,600. It is this amount that is subject to depreciation. Let's also assume that a full month's depreciation is recognized in the month in which an asset is purchased.

The depreciable cost is spread over 36 months (3 years × 12 months). Thus, the straight-line depreciation expense for the month of June is $100 ($3,600 ÷ 36 months).

Straight-Line Depreciation				
Original Cost	−	Salvage Value	=	Depreciable Cost
$\dfrac{\text{Depreciable Cost}}{\text{Estimated Useful Life}}$	=	$\dfrac{\$3,600}{36 \text{ months}}$	=	$100 per month

When we made adjustments for supplies and prepaid insurance, the asset accounts were credited to show that they had been consumed. Assets of a durable nature that are expected to provide benefits over several years or more, called **plant assets**, require a different approach. The business maintains a record of the original cost and the amount of depreciation taken since the asset was acquired. By comparing these two amounts, the reader can estimate the relative age of the assets. Thus, instead of crediting Delivery Equipment for the amount of depreciation, a contra-asset account, Accumulated Depreciation—Delivery Equipment, is credited. "Contra" means opposite or against. Thus, a **contra-asset** has a credit balance (the opposite of an asset) and is deducted from the related asset account on the balance sheet.

LEARNING KEY: Depreciable assets provide benefits over more than one year. Therefore, the historical cost of the asset remains in the asset account. To show that it has been depreciated, a *contra-asset* account is used.

As shown in Figure 5-9, the appropriate adjusting entry consists of a debit to Depreciation Expense—Delivery Equipment and a credit to Accumulated Depreciation—Delivery Equipment. Note the position of the accumulated depreciation account in the accounting equation. It is shown in the asset section, directly beneath Delivery Equipment. Contra-asset accounts should always be shown along with the related asset account. Therefore, Delivery Equipment and Accumulated Depreciation—Delivery Equipment are shown together.

FIGURE 5-9 Adjustment for Depreciation of Delivery Equipment

Assets		=	Liabilities		+	Owner's Equity					
Debit	**Credit**		**Debit**	**Credit**		**Debit**				**Credit**	
+	–		–	+		–				+	
Delivery Equipment						**Drawing**		**Expenses**		**Revenues**	
						Debit	**Credit**	**Debit**	**Credit**	**Debit**	**Credit**
TB 3,600						+	–	+	–	–	+
Accumulated Depreciation–Delivery Equipment								Depreciation Expense– Delivery Equipment			
	Adj. 100							Adj. 100			

The same concept is used on the balance sheet. Note in Figure 5-10 that Accumulated Depreciation is reported immediately beneath Delivery Equipment as a deduction. The difference between these accounts is known as the **book value**, or **undepreciated cost**, of the delivery equipment. Book value simply means the value carried on the books or in the accounting records. It does *not* represent the market value, or selling price, of the asset.

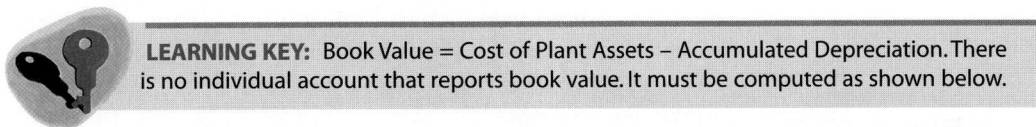

LEARNING KEY: Book Value = Cost of Plant Assets – Accumulated Depreciation. There is no individual account that reports book value. It must be computed as shown below.

FIGURE 5-10 Effect of Adjusting Entry for Depreciation on Financial Statements for June

BALANCE SHEET JUNE 30, 20--			INCOME STATEMENT FOR MONTH ENDED JUNE 30, 20--	
Assets:			Expenses:	
Delivery equipment	$3,600		Depreciation expense	$100
Less: Accumulated			(Expired cost for June)	
depreciation	100	$3,500		
		(Book value)		

If no delivery equipment is bought or sold during the next month, the same adjusting entry would be made at the end of July. If an income statement for the month of July and a balance sheet as of July 31 were prepared, the amounts shown in Figure 5-11 would be reported for the delivery equipment.

FIGURE 5-11 Effect of Adjusting Entry for Depreciation on Financial Statements for July

BALANCE SHEET JULY 31, 20--		INCOME STATEMENT FOR MONTH ENDED JULY 31, 20--	
Assets:		Expenses:	
Delivery equipment	$3,600	Depreciation expense	$100
Less: Accumulated		(Expired cost for July)	
depreciation	200 $3,400		
	(Book value)		

The cost ($3,600) remains unchanged, but the accumulated depreciation has increased to $200. This represents *the depreciation that has accumulated* since the delivery equipment was purchased ($100 in June and $100 in July). The depreciation expense for July is $100, the same as reported for June. Depreciation expense is reported for a specific time period. It does not accumulate across reporting periods.

Expanded Chart of Accounts

Several new accounts were needed to make the adjusting entries. New accounts are easily added to the chart of accounts, as shown in Figure 5-12. Note the close relationship between assets and contra-assets in the numbering of the accounts. Contra-accounts carry the same number as the related asset account with a ".1" suffix. For example, Delivery Equipment is account number 185 and the contra-asset account, Accumulated Depreciation—Delivery Equipment, is account number 185.1.

FIGURE 5-12 Expanded Chart of Accounts

JESSIE JANE'S CAMPUS DELIVERY CHART OF ACCOUNTS			
Assets		**Revenue**	
101	Cash	401	Delivery Fees
122	Accounts Receivable		
141	Supplies	**Expenses**	
145	Prepaid Insurance	511	Wages Expense
185	Delivery Equipment	521	Rent Expense
185.1	Accumulated Depr.—	523	Supplies Expense
	Delivery Equipment	525	Telephone Expense
		535	Insurance Expense
Liabilities		541	Depr. Expense—
202	Accounts Payable		Delivery Equipment
219	Wages Payable		
Owner's Equity			
311	Jessica Jane, Capital		
312	Jessica Jane, Drawing		

THE WORK SHEET

LO 2   Prepare a work sheet.

A **work sheet** pulls together all of the information needed to enter adjusting entries and prepare the financial statements. Work sheets are not financial statements and are not a formal part of the accounting system. Ordinarily, only the accountant uses a work sheet. For this reason, a work sheet is usually prepared in pencil or as a spreadsheet on a computer.

The Ten-Column Work Sheet

Although a work sheet can take several forms, a common format has a column for account titles and ten amount columns grouped into five pairs. The work sheet format and the five steps in preparing the work sheet are illustrated in Figure 5-13. As with financial statements, the work sheet has a heading consisting of the name of the company, name of the working paper, and the date of the accounting period just ended. The five major column headings for the work sheet are Trial Balance, Adjustments, Adjusted Trial Balance, Income Statement, and Balance Sheet.

Preparing the Work Sheet

Let's apply the five steps required for the preparation of a work sheet to Jessie Jane's Campus Delivery.

STEP 1   **Prepare the Trial Balance.** As shown in Figure 5-14, the first pair of amount columns is for the trial balance. The trial balance assures the equality of the debits and credits before the adjustment process begins. The columns should be double ruled to show that they are equal.

> You are already familiar with a trial balance. Here we are simply copying a trial balance to a different form, called a work sheet.

Note that all accounts listed in the expanded chart of accounts are included in the Trial Balance columns of the work sheet. This is done even though some accounts have zero balances. The accounts with zero balances could be added to the bottom of the list as they are needed for adjusting entries. However, it is easier to include them now, especially if preparing the work sheet on an electronic spreadsheet. Listing the accounts within their proper classifications (assets, liabilities, etc.) also makes it easier to extend the amounts to the proper columns.

STEP 2   **Prepare the Adjustments.** As shown in Figure 5-15, the second pair of amount columns is used to prepare the adjusting entries. Enter the adjustments directly in these columns. When an account is debited or credited, the amount is entered on the same line as the name of the account and in the appropriate Adjustments Debit or Credit column. A small letter in parentheses identifies each adjusting entry made on the work sheet.

> **LEARNING KEY:** For adjustments (a), (b), and (d), we are simply recognizing that assets have been used. When this happens, the asset must be decreased and an expense recognized. Note that the reported amount for delivery equipment is reduced by crediting a contra-asset.

ADJUSTMENT (a):
Supplies costing $60 were used during June.

	Debit	Credit
Supplies Expense	60	
Supplies		60

ADJUSTMENT (b):
One month's insurance premium has expired.

	Debit	Credit
Insurance Expense	25	
Prepaid Insurance		25

ADJUSTMENT (c):
Employees earned $50 that has not yet been paid.

	Debit	Credit
Wages Expense	50	
Wages Payable		50

 LEARNING KEY: Adjustment (c) recognizes an economic event that has not required an actual transaction yet. Employees earned wages, but have not been paid. The adjustment recognizes an expense and a liability.

ADJUSTMENT (d):
Depreciation on the motor scooters is recognized.

	Debit	Credit
Depreciation Expense—Delivery Equipment	100	
Accumulated Depreciation—Delivery Equipment		100

When all adjustments have been entered on the work sheet, each column should be totaled to assure that the debits equal the credits for all entries. After balancing the columns, they should be double ruled.

STEP 3   **Prepare the Adjusted Trial Balance.** As shown in Figure 5-16, the third pair of amount columns on the work sheet are the **Adjusted Trial Balance Columns**. When an account balance is not affected by entries in the Adjustments columns, the amount in the Trial Balance columns is extended directly to the Adjusted Trial Balance columns. *When affected by an entry in the Adjustments columns, the balance to be entered in the Adjusted Trial Balance columns increases or decreases by the amount of the adjusting entry.*

For example, in Jessica Jane's business, Supplies is listed in the Trial Balance Debit column as $80. Since the entry of $60 is in the Adjustments Credit column, the amount extended to the Adjusted Trial Balance Debit column is $20 ($80 – $60).

Wages Expense is listed in the Trial Balance Debit column as $650. Since $50 is in the Adjustments Debit column, the amount extended to the Adjusted Trial Balance Debit column is $700 ($650 + $50).

After all extensions have been made, the Adjusted Trial Balance columns are totaled to prove the equality of the debits and the credits. Once balanced, the columns are double ruled.

FIGURE 5-13 Steps in Preparing the Work Sheet

Name of Company
Work Sheet
For Month Ended June 30, 20 - -

ACCOUNT TITLE	TRIAL BALANCE		ADJUSTMENTS		ADJUSTED TRIAL BALANCE		INCOME STATEMENT		BALANCE SHEET	
	DEBIT	CREDIT	DEBIT	CREDIT	DEBIT	CREDIT	DEBIT	CREDIT	DEBIT	CREDIT

Insert ledger account titles

STEP 1 — Prepare the trial balance
STEP 2 — Prepare the adjustments
STEP 3 — Prepare the adjusted trial balance
STEP 4 — Extend adjusted account balances

Trial Balance: Assets (Debit), Liabilities (Credit), Drawing (Debit), Capital (Credit), Expenses (Debit), Revenues (Credit)

Adjusted Trial Balance: Assets (Debit), Liabilities (Credit), Drawing (Debit), Capital (Credit), Expenses (Debit), Revenues (Credit)

Income Statement: Expenses (Debit), Revenues (Credit)

Balance Sheet: Assets (Debit), Liabilities (Credit), Drawing (Debit), Capital (Credit)

STEP 5 — Complete the work sheet
1. Sum columns
2. Compute net income (loss)

Income Statement: Net Income (Debit), Net Loss (Credit)
Balance Sheet: Net Loss (Debit), Net Income (Credit)

FIGURE 5-14 Step 1—Prepare the Trial Balance

Jessica Jane's Campus Delivery
Work Sheet
For Month Ended June 30, 20 - -

	ACCOUNT TITLE	TRIAL BALANCE DEBIT	TRIAL BALANCE CREDIT	ADJUSTMENTS DEBIT	ADJUSTMENTS CREDIT	ADJUSTED TRIAL BALANCE DEBIT	ADJUSTED TRIAL BALANCE CREDIT	INCOME STATEMENT DEBIT	INCOME STATEMENT CREDIT	BALANCE SHEET DEBIT	BALANCE SHEET CREDIT	
1	Cash	3 7 0 00										1
2	Accounts Receivable	6 5 0 00										2
3	Supplies	8 0 00										3
4	Prepaid Insurance	2 0 0 00										4
5	Delivery Equipment	3 6 0 0 00										5
6	Accum. Depr.—Delivery Equipment											6
7	Accounts Payable		1 8 0 0 00									7
8	Wages Payable											8
9	Jessica Jane, Capital		2 0 0 0 00									9
10	Jessica Jane, Drawing	1 5 0 00										10
11	Delivery Fees		2 1 5 0 00									11
12	Wages Expense	6 5 0 00										12
13	Rent Expense	2 0 0 00										13
14	Supplies Expense											14
15	Telephone Expense	5 0 00										15
16	Insurance Expense											16
17	Depr. Expense—Delivery Equipment											17
18		5 9 5 0 00	5 9 5 0 00									18
19												19
20												20
21												21
22												22
23												23
24												24
25												25
26												26
27												27
28												28
29												29
30												30

STEP 1

Preparing the Work Sheet

STEP 1 **Prepare the Trial Balance.**

▲ Write the heading, account titles, and the debit and credit amounts from the general ledger.

▲ Place a single rule across the Trial Balance columns and total the debit and credit amounts.

▲ Place a double rule under the columns to show that they are equal.

STEP 2 **Prepare the Adjustments.**

▲ Record the adjustments.

Hint: Make certain that each adjustment is on the same line as the account name and in the appropriate column.

Hint: Identify each adjusting entry by a letter in parentheses.

▲ Rule the Adjusted Trial Balance columns.

▲ Total the debit and credit columns and double rule the columns to show equality.

STEP 3 **Prepare the Adjusted Trial Balance.**

▲ Extend those debits and credits that are not adjusted directly to the appropriate Adjusted Trial Balance column.

▲ Enter the adjusted balances in the appropriate Adjusted Trial Balance column.

Hint: If an account has a debit and a credit, subtract the adjustment. If an account has two debits or two credits, add the adjustment.

▲ Single rule the Adjusted Trial Balance columns. Total and double rule the debit and credit columns.

STEP 4 **Extend Adjusted Balances to the Income Statement and Balance Sheet Columns.**

▲ Extend all revenue accounts to the Income Statement Credit column.

▲ Extend all expense accounts to the Income Statement Debit column.

▲ Extend the asset and drawing accounts to the Balance Sheet Debit column.

▲ Extend the liability and owner's capital accounts to the Balance Sheet Credit column.

STEP 5 **Complete the Work Sheet.**

▲ Rule and total the Income Statement and Income Statement Debit and Credit columns. Calculate the difference between the Balance Sheet Debit and Credit columns.

▲ Calculate the difference between the Balance Sheet Debit and Credit columns.

Hint: If the Income Statement credits exceed debits, net income has occurred; otherwise a net loss has occurred. If the Balance Sheet debits exceed the credits, the difference is net income; otherwise a net loss has occurred.

Hint: The difference between the Balance Sheet columns and the difference between the Income Statement columns should be the same.

▲ Add the net income to the Income Statement Debit column or add the net loss to the Income Statement Credit column. Add the net income to the Balance Sheet Credit column or the net loss to the Balance Sheet Debit column.

▲ Total and double rule the columns.

STEP 4   **Extend Adjusted Balances to the Income Statement and Balance Sheet Columns.** As shown in Figure 5-17, each account listed in the Adjusted Trial Balance must be extended to either the Income Statement or Balance Sheet columns. The **Income Statement columns** show the amounts that will be reported in the income statement. All revenue accounts are extended to the Income Statement Credit column and expense accounts are extended to the Income Statement Debit column.

The asset, liability, drawing, and capital accounts are extended to the **Balance Sheet columns.** Although called the Balance Sheet columns, these columns of the work sheet show the amounts that will be reported in the balance sheet and the statement of owner's equity. The asset and drawing accounts are extended to the Balance Sheet Debit column. The liability and owner's capital accounts are extended to the Balance Sheet Credit column.

LEARNING KEY: The Balance Sheet columns show the amounts for both the balance sheet and the statement of owner's equity.

STEP 5   **Complete the Work Sheet.** To complete the work sheet, first total the Income Statement columns. If the total of the credits (revenues) exceeds the total of the debits (expenses), the difference represents net income. If the total of the debits exceeds the total of the credits, the difference represents a net loss.

The Income Statement columns of Jessie's work sheet in Figure 5-18 show total credits of $2,150 and total debits of $1,135. The difference, $1,015, is the net income for the month of June. This amount should be added to the debit column to balance the Income Statement columns. "Net Income" should be written on the same line in the Account Title column. If the business had a net loss, the amount of the loss would be added to the Income Statement Credit column and the words "Net Loss" would be written in the Account Title column. Once balanced, the columns should be double ruled.

Finally, the Balance Sheet columns are totaled. The difference between the totals of these columns also is the amount of net income or net loss for the accounting period. If the total debits exceed the total credits, the difference is net income. If the total credits exceed the total debits, the difference is a net loss. This difference should be the same as the difference we found for the Income Statement columns.

LEARNING KEY: In the Balance Sheet columns of the work sheet, total debits minus total credits equals net _income_ if greater than zero and equals net _loss_ if less than zero.

The Balance Sheet columns of Jessie's work sheet show total debits of $4,965 and total credits of $3,950. The difference of $1,015 represents the amount of net income for the month. This amount is added to the credit column to balance the Balance Sheet columns. If the business had a net loss, this amount would be added to the Balance Sheet Debit column. Once balanced, the columns should be double ruled.

A trick for remembering the appropriate placement of the net income and net loss is the following: Net Income *apart*; Net Loss *together*. Figure 5-19 illustrates this learning aid.

FIGURE 5-19   Net Income Apart, Net Loss Together

	INCOME STATEMENT		BALANCE SHEET				INCOME STATEMENT		BALANCE SHEET	
	DEBIT	CREDIT	DEBIT	CREDIT			DEBIT	CREDIT	DEBIT	CREDIT
Net Income	1 1 3 5 00	2 0 0 0 00	4 8 1 5 00	3 9 5 0 00		**Net Loss**	2 5 0 0 00	2 0 0 0 00	5 0 1 5 00	5 5 1 5 00
	8 6 5 00			8 6 5 00				5 0 0 00	5 0 0 00	
	2 0 0 0 00	2 0 0 0 00	4 8 1 5 00	4 8 1 5 00			2 5 0 0 00	2 5 0 0 00	5 5 1 5 00	5 5 1 5 00

— Apart —   — Together —

FINDING ERRORS ON THE WORK SHEET

LO 3   Describe methods for finding errors on the work sheet.

If any of the columns on the work sheet do not balance, you must find the error before you continue. Once you are confident that the work sheet is accurate, you are ready to journalize the adjusting entries and prepare financial statements. Figure 5-20 offers tips for finding errors on the work sheet.

FIGURE 5-20   Finding Errors on the Work Sheet

TIPS FOR FINDING ERRORS ON THE WORK SHEET

1. Check the addition of all columns.

2. Check the addition and subtraction required when extending to the Adjusted Trial Balance columns.

3. Make sure the adjusted account balances have been extended to the appropriate columns.

4. Make sure that the net income or net loss has been added to the appropriate columns.

JOURNALIZING ADJUSTING ENTRIES

LO 4   Journalize adjusting entries.

Keep in mind that the work sheet simply helps the accountant organize the end-of-period work. *Writing the adjustments on the work sheet has no effect on the ledger accounts in the accounting system. The only way to change the balance of a ledger account is to make a journal entry.* Once the adjustments have been entered on the work sheet, simply copy the adjustments from the work sheet to the journal.

Jessie's adjusting entries are illustrated in Figure 5-21 as they would appear in a general journal. Note that the last day of the accounting period, June 30, has been entered in the date column and *"Adjusting Entries"* is written in the Description column prior to the first adjusting entry. No explanation is required in the Description column for individual adjusting entries. We simply label them as adjusting entries.

POSTING ADJUSTING ENTRIES

LO 5 Post adjusting entries to the general ledger.

Adjusting entries are posted to the general ledger in the same manner as all other entries, except that *"Adjusting"* is written in the Item column of the general ledger. Figure 5-22 shows the posting of the adjusting entry for supplies. The posting reference numbers are inserted as each entry is posted.

FIGURE 5-21 Adjusting Entries

	DATE		DESCRIPTION	POST REF.	DEBIT	CREDIT	
1			**Adjusting Entries**				1
2	20-- June	30	Supplies Expense	523	6 0 00		2
3			Supplies	141		6 0 00	3
4							4
5		30	Insurance Expense	535	2 5 00		5
6			Prepaid Insurance	145		2 5 00	6
7							7
8		30	Wages Expense	511	5 0 00		8
9			Wages Payable	219		5 0 00	9
10							10
11		30	Depr. Expense — Delivery Equipment	541	1 0 0 00		11
12			Accum. Depr. — Delivery Equipment	185.1		1 0 0 00	12

GENERAL JOURNAL — PAGE 3

FIGURE 5-22 Posting the Adjusting Entry for Supplies

GENERAL LEDGER

ACCOUNT: Supplies — ACCOUNT NO. 141

DATE		ITEM	POST REF.	DEBIT	CREDIT	BALANCE DEBIT	BALANCE CREDIT
20-- June	16		J1	8 0 00		8 0 00	
	30	Adjusting	J3		6 0 00	2 0 00	

ACCOUNT: Supplies Expense — ACCOUNT NO. 523

DATE		ITEM	POST REF.	DEBIT	CREDIT	BALANCE DEBIT	BALANCE CREDIT
20-- June	30	Adjusting	J3	6 0 00		6 0 00	

Learning Objectives	Key Points to Remember
1 Prepare end-of-period adjustments.	End-of-period adjustments are necessary to bring the general ledger accounts up to date prior to preparing financial statements. Reasons to adjust the trial balance are: 1. To report all revenues earned during the accounting period. 2. To report all expenses incurred to produce the revenues during the accounting period. 3. To accurately report the assets on the balance sheet date. Some may have been used during the accounting period. 4. To accurately report the liabilities on the balance sheet date. Expenses may have been incurred, but not yet paid.
2 Prepare a work sheet.	Steps in preparing the work sheet are: 1. Prepare the trial balance. 2. Prepare the adjustments. 3. Prepare the adjusted trial balance. 4. Extend the adjusted account balances to the Income Statement and Balance Sheet columns. 5. Total the Income Statement and Balance Sheet columns to compute the net income or net loss.
3 Describe methods for finding errors on the work sheet.	Tips for finding errors on the work sheet include: 1. Check the addition of all columns. 2. Check the addition and subtraction required when extending to the Adjusted Trial Balance columns. 3. Make sure the adjusted account balances have been extended to the appropriate columns. 4. Make sure that the net income or net loss has been added to the appropriate columns.
4 Journalize adjusting entries.	The adjustments are copied from the work sheet to the journal. The last day of the accounting period is entered in the Date column and "Adjusting Entries" is written in the Description column.
5 Post adjusting entries to the general ledger.	Adjusting entries are posted to the general ledger in the same manner as all other entries, except that "Adjusting" is written in the Item column of the general ledger.

Reflection: Answering the Opening Question

As discussed in the chapter, it is essential to make appropriate adjustments prior to the preparation of financial statements.

KEY TERMS

Adjusted Trial Balance columns, (142)   The third pair of amount columns on the work sheet. They are used to prove the equality of the debits and credits in the general ledger accounts after making all end-of-period adjustments.

Balance Sheet columns, (142H)   The work sheet columns that show the amounts that will be reported in the balance sheet and the statement of owner's equity.

book value, (139)   The difference between the asset account and its related accumulated depreciation account. The value reflected by the accounting records.

contra-asset, (138)   An account with a credit balance that is deducted from the related asset account on the balance sheet.

depreciable cost, (138)   The cost of an asset that is subject to depreciation.

depreciation, (137)   A method of matching an asset's original cost against the revenues produced over its useful life.

fiscal year, (132)   A twelve-month period for which financial reports are prepared.

historical cost principle, (137)   A principle that requires assets to be recorded at their actual cost.

Income Statement columns, (142H)   The work sheet columns that show the amounts that will be reported in the income statement.

market value, (138)   The amount an item can be sold for under normal economic conditions.

matching principle, (132)   A principle that requires the matching of revenues earned during an accounting period with the expenses incurred to produce the revenues.

plant assets, (138)   Assets of a durable nature that will be used for operations over several years. Examples include buildings and equipment.

salvage value, (138)   The expected market value of an asset at the end of its useful life.

straight-line method, (138)   A depreciation method in which the depreciable cost is divided by the estimated useful life.

undepreciated cost, (139)   The difference between the asset account and its related accumulated depreciation account. Also known as book value.

useful life, (137)   The period of time that an asset is expected to help produce revenues.

work sheet, (141)   A form used to pull together all of the information needed to enter adjusting entries and prepare the financial statements.

DEMONSTRATION PROBLEM

W & D

Justin Park is a lawyer specializing in corporate tax law. He began his practice on January 1. A chart of accounts and trial balance taken on December 31, 20-- are provided below.

Information for year-end adjustments:

(a) Office supplies on hand at year end amounted to $300.

(b) On January 1, 20--, Park purchased office equipment costing $15,000 with an expected life of five years and no salvage value.

(c) Computer equipment costing $6,000 with an expected life of three years and no salvage value was purchased on July 1, 20--. Assume that Park computes depreciation to the nearest full month.

(d) A premium of $1,200 for a one-year insurance policy was paid on December 1, 20--.

(e) Wages earned by Park's part-time secretary, which have not yet been paid, amount to $300.

REQUIRED
1. Prepare the work sheet for the year ended December 31, 20--.

2. Prepare adjusting entries in a general journal.

JUSTIN PARK LEGAL SERVICES
CHART OF ACCOUNTS

Assets			Revenue	
101	Cash		401	Client Fees
142	Office Supplies			
145	Prepaid Insurance		**Expenses**	
181	Office Equipment		511	Wages Expense
181.1	Accumulated Depr.—		521	Rent Expense
	Office Equipment		523	Office Supplies Expense
187	Computer Equipment		525	Telephone Expense
187.1	Accumulated Depr.—		533	Utilities Expense
	Computer Equipment		535	Insurance Expense
Liabilities			541	Depr. Expense—
201	Notes Payable			Office Equipment
202	Accounts Payable		542	Depr. Expense—
219	Wages Payable			Computer Equipment
Owner's Equity				
311	Justin Park, Capital			
312	Justin Park, Drawing			

(continued)

		Justin Park Legal Services Trial Balance December 31, 20 - -										
ACCOUNT TITLE	ACCOUNT NO.	DEBIT BALANCE					CREDIT BALANCE				
Cash	101	7	0	0	0	00					
Office Supplies	142		8	0	0	00					
Prepaid Insurance	145	1	2	0	0	00					
Office Equipment	181	15	0	0	0	00					
Computer Equipment	187	6	0	0	0	00					
Notes Payable	201						5	0	0	0	00
Accounts Payable	202							5	0	0	00
Justin Park, Capital	311						11	4	0	0	00
Justin Park, Drawing	312	5	0	0	0	00					
Client Fees	401						40	0	0	0	00
Wages Expense	511	12	0	0	0	00					
Rent Expense	521	5	0	0	0	00					
Telephone Expense	525	1	0	0	0	00					
Utilities Expense	533	3	9	0	0	00					
		56	9	0	0	00	56	9	0	0	00

Solution

1.

Justin Park Legal Services
Work Sheet
For Month Ended December 31, 20--

#	ACCOUNT TITLE	TRIAL BALANCE DEBIT	TRIAL BALANCE CREDIT	ADJUSTMENTS DEBIT	ADJUSTMENTS CREDIT	ADJUSTED TRIAL BALANCE DEBIT	ADJUSTED TRIAL BALANCE CREDIT	INCOME STATEMENT DEBIT	INCOME STATEMENT CREDIT	BALANCE SHEET DEBIT	BALANCE SHEET CREDIT
1	Cash	7 0 0 0 00				7 0 0 0 00				7 0 0 0 00	
2	Office Supplies	8 0 0 00			(a) 5 0 0 00	3 0 0 00				3 0 0 00	
3	Prepaid Insurance	1 2 0 0 00			(d) 1 0 0 00	1 1 0 0 00				1 1 0 0 00	
4	Office Equipment	15 0 0 0 00				15 0 0 0 00				15 0 0 0 00	
5	Accum. Depr.—Office Equip.				(b) 3 0 0 00		3 0 0 00				3 0 0 00
6	Computer Equipment	6 0 0 0 00				6 0 0 0 00				6 0 0 0 00	
7	Accum. Depr.—Computer Equip.				(c) 1 0 0 00		1 0 0 00				1 0 0 00
8	Notes Payable		5 0 0 0 00				5 0 0 0 00				5 0 0 0 00
9	Accounts Payable		5 0 0 00				5 0 0 00				5 0 0 00
10	Wages Payable				(e) 3 0 0 00		3 0 0 00				3 0 0 00
11	Justin Park, Capital		11 4 0 0 00				11 4 0 0 00				11 4 0 0 00
12	Justin Park, Drawing	5 0 0 0 00				5 0 0 0 00				5 0 0 0 00	
13	Client Fees		40 0 0 0 00				40 0 0 0 00		40 0 0 0 00		
14	Wages Expense	12 0 0 0 00		(e) 3 0 0 00		12 3 0 0 00		12 3 0 0 00			
15	Rent Expense	5 0 0 0 00				5 0 0 0 00		5 0 0 0 00			
16	Office Supplies Expense			(a) 5 0 0 00		5 0 0 00		5 0 0 00			
17	Telephone Expense	1 0 0 0 00				1 0 0 0 00		1 0 0 0 00			
18	Utilities Expense	3 9 0 0 00				3 9 0 0 00		3 9 0 0 00			
19	Insurance Expense			(d) 1 0 0 00		1 0 0 00		1 0 0 00			
20	Depr. Expense—Office Equip.			(b) 3 0 0 00		3 0 0 00		3 0 0 00			
21	Depr. Expense—Computer Equip.			(c) 1 0 0 00		1 0 0 00		1 0 0 00			
22		56 9 0 0 00	56 9 0 0 00	4 9 0 0 00	4 9 0 0 00	61 2 0 0 00	61 2 0 0 00	26 8 0 0 00	40 0 0 0 00	34 4 0 0 00	21 2 0 0 00
23	Net Income							13 2 0 0 00			13 2 0 0 00
24								40 0 0 0 00	40 0 0 0 00	34 4 0 0 00	34 4 0 0 00

(continued)

2.

				GENERAL JOURNAL												PAGE 11	
	DATE			DESCRIPTION	POST REF.		DEBIT					CREDIT						
1				Adjusting Entries														1
2	20--Dec.	31		Office Supplies Expense				5	0	0	00							2
3				Office Supplies										5	0	0	00	3
4																		4
5		31		Depr. Expense—Office Equipment			3	0	0	0	00							5
6				Accum. Depr.—Office Equipment									3	0	0	0	00	6
7																		7
8		31		Depr. Expense—Computer Equipment			1	0	0	0	00							8
9				Accum. Depr—Computer Equipment									1	0	0	0	00	9
10																		10
11		31		Insurance Expense				1	0	0	00							11
12				Prepaid Insurance										1	0	0	00	12
13																		13
14		31		Wages Expense				3	0	0	00							14
15				Wages Payable										3	0	0	00	15

REVIEW QUESTIONS

1. Explain the matching principle.

2. Explain the historical cost principle.

3. Describe a plant asset.

4. What is a contra-asset?

5. What is the useful life of an asset?

6. What is the purpose of depreciation?

7. What is an asset's depreciable cost?

8. What is the book value of an asset?

9. Explain the purpose of the work sheet.

10. Identify the five major column headings on a work sheet.

11. List the five steps taken in preparing a work sheet.

12. Describe four tips for finding errors on the work sheet.

MANAGING YOUR WRITING

Delia Alvarez, owner of Delia's Lawn Service, wants to borrow money to buy new lawn equipment. A local bank has asked for financial statements. Alvarez has asked you to prepare financial statements for the year ended December 31, 20--. You have been given the unadjusted trial balance shown below and suspect that Alvarez expects you to base your statements on this information. You are concerned, however, that some of the account balances may need to be adjusted. Write a memo to Alvarez explaining what additional information you need before you can prepare the financial statements. Alvarez is not familiar with accounting issues. Therefore, explain in your memo why you need this information, the potential impact of this information on the financial statements, and the importance of making these adjustments before approaching the bank for a loan.

Delia's Lawn Service
Trial Balance
December 31, 20 - -

ACCOUNT TITLE	ACCOUNT NO.	DEBIT BALANCE	CREDIT BALANCE
Cash	101	7 7 0 00	
Accounts Receivable	122	1 7 0 0 00	
Supplies	142	2 8 0 00	
Prepaid Insurance	145	4 0 0 00	
Lawn Equipment	183	13 8 0 0 00	
Accounts Payable	202		2 2 0 0 00
Delia Alvarez, Capital	311		3 0 0 0 00
Delia Alvarez, Drawing	312	3 5 0 00	
Lawn Cutting Fees	401		52 4 0 0 00
Wages Expense	511	35 8 5 0 00	
Rent Expense	521	1 2 0 0 00	
Gas and Oil Expense	538	3 2 5 0 00	
		57 6 0 0 00	57 6 0 0 00

SERIES A EXERCISES

EXERCISE 5A-1 (LO 1) ADJUSTMENT FOR SUPPLIES On December 31, the trial balance indicates that the supplies account has a balance, prior to the adjusting entry, of $320. A physical count of the supplies inventory shows that $90 of supplies remain. Analyze this adjustment for supplies using T accounts, and then formally enter this adjustment in the general journal.

EXERCISE 5A-2 (LO 1) ADJUSTMENT FOR INSURANCE On December 1, a six-month liability insurance policy was purchased for $900. Analyze the required adjustment as of December 31 using T accounts, and then formally enter this adjustment in the general journal.

EXERCISE 5A-3 (LO 1) ADJUSTMENT FOR WAGES On December 31, the trial balance shows wages expense of $600. An additional $200 of wages was earned by the employees, but has not yet been paid. Analyze this adjustment for wages, and then formally enter this adjustment in the general journal.

EXERCISE 5A-4 (LO 1) ADJUSTMENT FOR DEPRECIATION OF ASSET On December 1, delivery equipment was purchased for $7,200. The delivery equipment has an estimated useful life of 4 years (48 months) and no salvage value. Using the straight-line depreciation method, prepare the necessary adjusting entry as of December 31 (one month), and then formally enter this adjustment in the general journal.

EXERCISE 5A-5 (LO 1) CALCULATION OF BOOK VALUE On June 1, 20--, a depreciable asset was acquired for $5,400. The asset has an estimated useful life of 5 years (60 months) and no salvage value. Using the straight-line depreciation method, calculate the book value as of December 31, 20--.

EXERCISE 5A-6 (LO 1) ANALYSIS OF ADJUSTING ENTRY FOR SUPPLIES Analyze each situation and indicate the correct dollar amount for the adjusting entry. (Trial balance is abbreviated as TB.)

1. Ending inventory of supplies is $130.

(Balance Sheet) Supplies		(Income Statement) Supplies Expense	
TB	460		
	Adj. _____	Adj. _____	
Bal. _____			

2. Amount of supplies used is $320.

(Balance Sheet) Supplies		(Income Statement) Supplies Expense	
TB	545		
	Adj. _____	Adj. _____	
Bal. _____			

EXERCISE 5A-7 (LO 1) ANALYSIS OF ADJUSTING ENTRY FOR INSURANCE Analyze each situation and indicate the correct dollar amount for the adjusting entry.

1. Amount of insurance expired is $900.

(Balance Sheet) Prepaid Insurance		(Income Statement) Insurance Expense	
TB	1,300		
	Adj. _____	Adj. _____	
Bal. _____			

2. Amount of unexpired insurance is $185.

(Balance Sheet) Prepaid Insurance		(Income Statement) Insurance Expense	
TB	860		
	Adj. _____	Adj. _____	
Bal. _____			

EXERCISE 5A-8 (LO 2) WORK SHEET AND ADJUSTING ENTRIES A partial work sheet for Jim Jacob's furniture repair is shown as follows. Indicate by letters (a) through (d) the four adjustments in the Adjustments columns of the work sheet, properly matching each debit and credit. Complete the Adjustments columns.

Jim Jacob's Furniture Repair
Work Sheet (Partial)
For Month Ended December 31, 20 - -

	ACCOUNT TITLE	TRIAL BALANCE DEBIT	TRIAL BALANCE CREDIT	ADJUSTMENTS DEBIT	ADJUSTMENTS CREDIT	ADJUSTED TRIAL BALANCE DEBIT	ADJUSTED TRIAL BALANCE CREDIT	
1	Cash	1 0 0 00				1 0 0 00		1
2	Supplies	8 5 0 00				2 0 0 00		2
3	Prepaid Insurance	9 0 0 00				3 0 0 00		3
4	Delivery Equipment	3 6 0 0 00				3 6 0 0 00		4
5	Accum. Depr.— Delivery Equipment		6 0 0 00				8 0 0 00	5
6	Wages Payable						1 0 0 00	6
7	Jim Jacob, Capital		4 0 0 0 00				4 0 0 0 00	7
8	Repair Fees		1 6 5 0 00				1 6 5 0 00	8
9	Wages Expense	6 0 0 00				7 0 0 00		9
10	Advertising Expense	2 0 0 00				2 0 0 00		10
11	Supplies Expense					6 5 0 00		11
12	Insurance Expense					6 0 0 00		12
13	Depr. Expense—Delivery Equipment					2 0 0 00		13
14		6 2 5 0 00	6 2 5 0 00			6 5 5 0 00	6 5 5 0 00	14

EXERCISE 5A-9 (LO 4) JOURNALIZING ADJUSTING ENTRIES From the adjustments columns in Exercise 5A-8, journalize the four adjusting entries, as of December 31, in proper general journal format.

EXERCISE 5A-10 (LO 2) EXTENDING ADJUSTED BALANCES TO THE INCOME STATEMENT AND BALANCE SHEET COLUMNS Indicate with an "x" whether each account total should be extended to the Income Statement Debit or Credit or to the Balance Sheet Debit or Credit columns on the work sheet.

	Income Statement Debit	Income Statement Credit	Balance Sheet Debit	Balance Sheet Credit
Cash				
Accounts Receivable				
Supplies				
Prepaid Insurance				
Delivery Equipment				
Accum. Depr.—Delivery Equipment				
Accounts Payable				
Wages Payable				
Owner, Capital				
Owner, Drawing				
Delivery Fees				
Wages Expense				
Rent Expense				
Supplies Expense				
Insurance Expense				
Depr. Exp.—Delivery Equipment				

EXERCISE 5A-11 (LO 2) ANALYSIS OF NET INCOME OR NET LOSS ON THE WORK SHEET Indicate with an "x" in which columns, Income Statement Debit or Credit or Balance Sheet Debit or Credit, a net income or a net loss would appear on a work sheet.

	Income Statement		Balance Sheet	
	Debit	Credit	Debit	Credit
Net Income	_____	_____	_____	_____
Net Loss	_____	_____	_____	_____

EXERCISE 5A-12 (LO 5) POSTING ADJUSTING ENTRIES Two adjusting entries are in the following general journal. Post these adjusting entries to the four general ledger accounts. The following account numbers were taken from the chart of accounts: 141, Supplies; 219, Wages Payable; 511, Wages Expense; and 523, Supplies Expense. If you are not using the working papers that accompany this text, enter the following balances before posting the entries: Supplies, $200 Dr.; Wages Expense, $1,200 Dr.

		GENERAL JOURNAL				PAGE 9
	DATE	DESCRIPTION	POST REF.	DEBIT	CREDIT	
1		Adjusting Entries				1
2	20-- Dec.	31 Supplies Expense		8 5 00		2
3		Supplies			8 5 00	3
4						4
5	Dec.	31 Wages Expense		2 2 0 00		5
6		Wages Payable			2 2 0 00	6

SERIES A PROBLEMS

PROBLEM 5A-1 (LO 1/2) ADJUSTMENTS AND WORK SHEET SHOWING NET INCOME The trial balance after one month of operation for Mason's Delivery Service as of September 30, 20--, is shown below. Data to complete the adjustments are as follows:

(a) Supplies inventory as of September 30, $165.
(b) Insurance expired (used), $800.
(c) Depreciation on delivery equipment, $400.
(d) Wages earned by employees, but not paid as of September 30, $225.

REQUIRED 1. Enter the adjustments in the Adjustments columns of the work sheet.

2. Complete the work sheet.

Mason's Delivery Service
Work Sheet
For Month Ended September 30, 20 - -

	ACCOUNT TITLE	TRIAL BALANCE		ADJUSTMENTS		
		DEBIT	CREDIT	DEBIT	CREDIT	
1	Cash	1 6 0 0 00				1
2	Accounts Receivable	9 4 0 00				2
3	Supplies	6 3 5 00				3
4	Prepaid Insurance	1 2 0 0 00				4
5	Delivery Equipment	6 4 0 0 00				5
6	Accum. Depr.—Delivery Equipment					6
7	Accounts Payable		1 2 2 0 00			7
8	Wages Payable					8
9	Jill Mason, Capital		8 0 0 0 00			9
10	Jill Mason, Drawing	1 4 0 0 00				10
11	Delivery Fees		6 2 0 0 00			11
12	Wages Expense	1 5 0 0 00				12
13	Advertising Expense	4 6 0 00				13
14	Rent Expense	8 0 0 00				14
15	Supplies Expense					15
16	Telephone Expense	1 6 5 00				16
17	Insurance Expense					17
18	Repair Expense	2 3 0 00				18
19	Oil and Gas Expense	9 0 00				19
20	Depr. Expense—Delivery Equipment					20
21		15 4 2 0 00	15 4 2 0 00			21

PROBLEM 5A-2 (LO 1/2) ADJUSTMENTS AND WORK SHEET SHOWING A NET LOSS Jason Armstrong started a business called Campus Escort Service. After the first month of operations, the trial balance as of November 30, 20--, is as shown on the next page.

REQUIRED 1. Analyze the following adjustments and enter them on the work sheet.

(a) Ending inventory of supplies on November 30, $185.

(b) Unexpired (remaining) insurance as of November 30, $800.

(c) Depreciation expense on van, $300.

(d) Wages earned, but not paid as of November 30, $190.

2. Complete the work sheet.

(continued)

Campus Escort Service
Work Sheet
For Month Ended November 30, 20 - -

	ACCOUNT TITLE	TRIAL BALANCE		ADJUSTMENTS		
		DEBIT	CREDIT	DEBIT	CREDIT	
1	Cash	9 8 0 00				1
2	Accounts Receivable	5 9 0 00				2
3	Supplies	5 7 5 00				3
4	Prepaid Insurance	1 3 0 0 00				4
5	Van	5 8 0 0 00				5
6	Accum. Depr.—Van					6
7	Accounts Payable		9 6 0 00			7
8	Wages Payable					8
9	Jason Armstrong, Capital		10 0 0 0 00			9
10	Jason Armstrong, Drawing	6 0 0 00				10
11	Escort Fees		2 6 0 0 00			11
12	Wages Expense	1 8 0 0 00				12
13	Advertising Expense	3 8 0 00				13
14	Rent Expense	9 0 0 00				14
15	Supplies Expense					15
16	Telephone Expense	2 2 0 00				16
17	Insurance Expense					17
18	Repair Expense	3 1 5 00				18
19	Oil and Gas Expense	1 0 0 00				19
20	Depr. Expense—Van					20
21		13 5 6 0 00	13 5 6 0 00			21

PROBLEM 5A-3 (LO 4/5) JOURNALIZE AND POST ADJUSTING ENTRIES FROM THE WORK SHEET Refer to Problem 5A-2 and the following additional information.

Account Name	Account Number	Balance in Account Before Adjusting Entry
Supplies	141	$ 575
Prepaid Insurance	145	1,300
Accum. Depr.—Van	185.1	0
Wages Payable	219	0
Wages Expense	511	1,800
Supplies Expense	523	0
Insurance Expense	535	0
Depr. Expense—Van	541	0

REQUIRED

1. Journalize the adjusting entries on page 5 of the general journal.

2. Post the adjusting entries to the general ledger. (If you are not using the working papers that accompany this text, enter the balances provided in this problem before posting the adjusting entries.)

PROBLEM 5A-4 (LO 3) CORRECTING WORK SHEET WITH ERRORS A beginning accounting student tried to complete a work sheet for Joyce Lee's Tax Service. The following adjusting entries were to have been analyzed and entered onto the work sheet. The worksheet is shown on page 158.

(a) Ending inventory of supplies as of March 31, $160.

(b) Unexpired insurance as of March 31, $520.

(c) Depreciation of office equipment, $275.

(d) Wages earned, but not paid as of March 31, $110.

REQUIRED   The accounting student made a number of errors. Review the work sheet for addition mistakes, transpositions, and other errors and make all necessary corrections.

SERIES B EXERCISES

EXERCISE 5B-1 (LO 1) ADJUSTMENT FOR SUPPLIES On July 31, the trial balance indicates that the supplies account has a balance, prior to the adjusting entry, of $430. A physical count of the supplies inventory shows that $120 of supplies remain. Analyze the adjustment for supplies using T accounts, and then formally enter this adjustment in the general journal.

EXERCISE 5B-2 (LO 1) ADJUSTMENT FOR INSURANCE On July 1, a six-month liability insurance policy was purchased for $750. Analyze the required adjustment as of July 31 using T accounts, and then formally enter this adjustment in the general journal.

EXERCISE 5B-3 (LO 1) ADJUSTMENT FOR WAGES On July 31, the trial balance shows wages expense of $800. An additional $150 of wages was earned by the employees but has not yet been paid. Analyze the required adjustment using T accounts, and then formally enter this adjustment in the general journal.

EXERCISE 5B-4 (LO 1) ADJUSTMENT FOR DEPRECIATION OF ASSET On July 1, delivery equipment was purchased for $4,320. The delivery equipment has an estimated useful life of 3 years (36 months) and no salvage value. Using the straight-line depreciation method, prepare the necessary adjusting entry as of July 31 (one month), and then formally enter this adjustment in the general journal.

EXERCISE 5B-5 (LO 1) CALCULATION OF BOOK VALUE On January 1, 20--, a depreciable asset was acquired for $5,760. The asset has an estimated useful life of 4 years (48 months) and no salvage value. Use the straight-line depreciation method to calculate the book value as of July 1, 20--.

PROBLEM 5A-4

Joyce Lee's Tax Service
Work Sheet
For Month Ended March 31, 20 - -

	Trial Balance		Adjustments		Adjusted Trial Balance		Income Statement		Balance Sheet	
Account Title	Debit	Credit	Debit	Credit	Debit	Credit	Debit	Credit	Debit	Credit
1 Cash	1 725 00				1 725 00				1 752 00	
2 Accounts Receivable	960 00				960 00				960 00	
3 Supplies	525 00			(a) 160 00	365 00				365 00	
4 Prepaid Insurance	930 00			(b) 410 00	540 00				540 00	
5 Office Equipment	5 450 00			(c) 275 00	5 175 00				5 175 00	
6 Accum. Depr.—Office Equipment										
7 Accounts Payable		480 00				480 00				480 00
8 Wages Payable				(d) 110 00		110 00		110 00		
9 Joyce Lee, Capital		7 500 00				7 500 00				7 500 00
10 Joyce Lee, Drawing	1 125 00				1 125 00				1 125 00	
11 Professional Fees		5 700 00				5 700 00		5 700 00		
12 Wages Expense	1 420 00		(d) 110 00		1 420 00		1 420 00			
13 Advertising Expense	350 00				350 00		350 00			
14 Rent Expense	700 00				700 00		700 00			
15 Supplies Expense			(a) 160 00		160 00		160 00			
16 Telephone Expense	130 00				130 00		130 00			
17 Utilities Expense	190 00				190 00		190 00			
18 Insurance Expense			(b) 410 00		410 00		410 00			
19 Depr. Expense—Office Equipment			(c) 275 00		275 00		275 00			
20 Miscellaneous Expense	175 00				175 00		175 00			
21										
22	13 680 00	13 680 00	955 00	955 00	13 160 00	13 790 00	4 560 00	5 810 00	9 508 00	7 980 00
23							1 250 00			1 528 00
24							5 810 00	5 810 00	9 508 00	9 508 00

This work sheet contains errors.

EXERCISE 5B-6 (LO 1) ANALYSIS OF ADJUSTING ENTRY FOR SUPPLIES Analyze each situation and indicate the correct dollar amount for the adjusting entry.

1. Ending inventory of supplies is $95.

2. Amount of supplies used is $280.

(Balance Sheet) Supplies		(Income Statement) Supplies Expense	
TB 540	Adj. _____	Adj. _____	
Bal. _____			

(Balance Sheet) Supplies		(Income Statement) Supplies Expense	
TB 330	Adj. _____	Adj. _____	
Bal. _____			

EXERCISE 5B-7 (LO 1) ANALYSIS OF ADJUSTING ENTRY FOR INSURANCE Analyze each situation and indicate the correct dollar amount for the adjusting entry.

1. Amount of insurance expired (used) is $830.

2.

(Balance Sheet) Prepaid Insurance		(Income Statement) Insurance Expense	
TB 960	Adj. _____	Adj. _____	
Bal. _____			

Amount of unexpired (remaining) insurance is $340.

(Balance Sheet) Prepaid Insurance		(Income Statement) Insurance Expense	
TB 1,135	Adj. _____	Adj. _____	
Bal. _____			

EXERCISE 5B-8 (LO 2) WORK SHEET AND ADJUSTING ENTRIES Page 160 shows a partial work sheet for Jasmine Kah's Auto Detailing. Indicate by letters (a) through (d) the four adjustments in the Adjustments columns of the work sheet, properly matching each debit and credit. Complete the Adjustments columns.

(continued)

Jasmine Kah's Auto Detailing
Work Sheet (Partial)
For Month Ended June 30, 20 - -

	ACCOUNT TITLE	TRIAL BALANCE		ADJUSTMENTS		ADJUSTED TRIAL BALANCE		
		DEBIT	CREDIT	DEBIT	CREDIT	DEBIT	CREDIT	
1	Cash	1 5 0 00				1 5 0 00		1
2	Supplies	5 2 0 00				9 0 00		2
3	Prepaid Insurance	7 5 0 00				2 0 0 00		3
4	Cleaning Equipment	5 4 0 0 00				5 4 0 0 00		4
5	Accum. Depr.— Cleaning Equipment		8 5 0 00				1 1 5 0 00	5
6	Wages Payable						2 5 0 00	6
7	Jasmine Kah, Capital		4 6 0 0 00				4 6 0 0 00	7
8	Detailing Fees		2 2 2 0 00				2 2 2 0 00	8
9	Wages Expense	7 0 0 00				9 5 0 00		9
10	Advertising Expense	1 5 0 00				1 5 0 00		10
11	Supplies Expense					4 3 0 00		11
12	Insurance Expense					5 5 0 00		12
13	Depr. Expense—Cleaning Equipment					3 0 0 00		13
14		7 6 7 0 00	7 6 7 0 00			8 2 2 0 00	8 2 2 0 00	14

EXERCISE 5B-9 (LO 4) JOURNALIZING ADJUSTING ENTRIES From the Adjustments columns in Exercise 5B-8, journalize the four adjusting entries as of June 30, in proper general journal format.

EXERCISE 5B-10 (LO 2) EXTENDING ADJUSTED BALANCES TO THE INCOME STATEMENT AND BALANCE SHEET COLUMNS Indicate with an "x" whether each account total should be extended to the Income Statement Debit or Credit or to the Balance Sheet Debit or Credit columns on the work sheet.

	Income Statement Debit	Income Statement Credit	Balance Sheet Debit	Balance Sheet Credit
Cash	___	___	___	___
Accounts Receivable	___	___	___	___
Supplies	___	___	___	___
Prepaid Insurance	___	___	___	___
Automobile	___	___	___	___
Accum. Depr.—Automobile	___	___	___	___
Accounts Payable	___	___	___	___
Wages Payable	___	___	___	___
Owner, Capital	___	___	___	___
Owner, Drawing	___	___	___	___
Service Fees	___	___	___	___
Wages Expense	___	___	___	___
Supplies Expense	___	___	___	___
Utilities Expense	___	___	___	___
Insurance Expense	___	___	___	___
Depr. Exp.—Automobile	___	___	___	___

EXERCISE 5B-11 (LO 2) ANALYSIS OF NET INCOME OR NET LOSS ON THE WORK SHEET Insert the dollar amounts where the net income or net loss would appear on the work sheet.

	Income Statement		Balance Sheet	
	Debit	Credit	Debit	Credit
Net Income: $2,500	_____	_____	_____	_____
Net Loss: $1,900	_____	_____	_____	_____

EXERCISE 5B-12 (LO 5) POSTING ADJUSTING ENTRIES Two adjusting entries are shown in the following general journal. Post these adjusting entries to the four general ledger accounts. The following account numbers were taken from the chart of accounts: 145, Prepaid Insurance; 183.1, Accumulated Depreciation—Cleaning Equipment; 541, Depreciation Expense—Cleaning Equipment; and 535, Insurance Expense. If you are not using the working papers that accompany this text, enter the following balances before posting the entries: Prepaid Insurance, $960 Dr.; Accumulated Depr.—Cleaning Equip., $870 Cr.

	DATE		DESCRIPTION	POST REF.	DEBIT	CREDIT	
1			Adjusting Entries				1
2	20-- July	31	Insurance Expense		3 2 0 00		2
3			Prepaid Insurance			3 2 0 00	3
4							4
5		31	Depr. Expense—Cleaning Equipment		1 4 5 00		5
6			Accum. Depr.—Cleaning Equipment			1 4 5 00	6

GENERAL JOURNAL   PAGE 7

SERIES B PROBLEMS

PROBLEM 5B-1 (LO 1/2) ADJUSTMENTS AND WORK SHEET SHOWING NET INCOME Louie Long started a business called Louie's Lawn Service. The trial balance as of March 31, after the first month of operation, is shown below.

Louie's Lawn Service
Work Sheet
For Month Ended March 31, 20 - -

	ACCOUNT TITLE	TRIAL BALANCE		ADJUSTMENTS		
		DEBIT	CREDIT	DEBIT	CREDIT	
1	Cash	1 3 7 5 00				1
2	Accounts Receivable	8 8 0 00				2
3	Supplies	4 9 0 00				3
4	Prepaid Insurance	8 0 0 00				4
5	Lawn Equipment	5 7 0 0 00				5
6	Accum. Depr.—Lawn Equipment					6
7	Accounts Payable		7 8 0 00			7
8	Wages Payable					8
9	Louie Long, Capital		6 5 0 0 00			9
10	Louie Long, Drawing	1 2 5 0 00				10
11	Lawn Service Fees		6 1 0 0 00			11
12	Wages Expense	1 1 4 5 00				12
13	Advertising Expense	5 4 0 00				13
14	Rent Expense	7 2 5 00				14
15	Supplies Expense					15
16	Telephone Expense	1 6 0 00				16
17	Insurance Expense					17
18	Repair Expense	2 5 0 00				18
19	Depr. Expense—Lawn Equipment					19
20	Miscellaneous Expense	6 5 00				20
21		13 3 8 0 00	13 3 8 0 00			21

REQUIRED
1. Analyze the following adjustments and enter them on a work sheet.

   (a) Ending supplies inventory as of March 31, $165.

   (b) Insurance expired (used), $100.

   (c) Depreciation of lawn equipment, $200.

   (d) Wages earned, but not paid as of March 31, $180.

2. Complete the work sheet.

PROBLEM 5B-2 (LO 1/2) ADJUSTMENTS AND WORK SHEET SHOWING A NET LOSS Val Nolan started a business called Nolan's Home Appraisals. The trial balance as of October 31, after the first month of operations, is shown below.

Nolan's Home Appraisals
Work Sheet
For Month Ended October 31, 20 - -

	ACCOUNT TITLE	TRIAL BALANCE DEBIT	TRIAL BALANCE CREDIT	ADJUSTMENTS DEBIT	ADJUSTMENTS CREDIT	
1	Cash	8 3 0 00				1
2	Accounts Receivable	7 6 0 00				2
3	Supplies	6 2 5 00				3
4	Prepaid Insurance	9 5 0 00				4
5	Automobile	6 5 0 0 00				5
6	Accum. Depr.—Automobile					6
7	Accounts Payable		1 5 0 0 00			7
8	Wages Payable					8
9	Val Nolan, Capital		9 9 0 0 00			9
10	Val Nolan, Drawing	1 1 0 0 00				10
11	Appraisal Fees		3 0 0 0 00			11
12	Wages Expense	1 5 6 0 00				12
13	Advertising Expense	4 2 0 00				13
14	Rent Expense	1 0 5 0 00				14
15	Supplies Expense					15
16	Telephone Expense	2 5 5 00				16
17	Insurance Expense					17
18	Repair Expense	2 7 0 00				18
19	Oil and Gas Expense	8 0 00				19
20	Depr. Expense—Automobile					20
21		14 4 0 0 00	14 4 0 0 00			21

REQUIRED
1. Analyze the following adjustments and enter them on the work sheet.

   (a) Supplies inventory as of October 31, $210.

   (b) Unexpired (remaining) insurance as of October 31, $800.

   (c) Depreciation of automobile, $250.

   (d) Wages earned, but not paid as of October 31, $175.

2. Complete the work sheet.

W & D

PROBLEM 5B-3 (LO 4/5) JOURNALIZE AND POST ADJUSTING ENTRIES FROM THE WORK SHEET Refer to Problem 5B-2 and the following additional information.

Account Name	Account Number	Balance in Account Before Adjusting Entry
Supplies	141	$ 625
Prepaid Insurance	145	950
Accum. Depr.—Automobile	185.1	0
Wages Payable	219	0
Wages Expense	511	1,560
Supplies Expense	523	0
Insurance Expense	535	0
Depr. Expense—Automobile	541	0

REQUIRED

1. Journalize the adjusting entries on page 3 of the general journal.

2. Post the adjusting entries to the general ledger. (If you are not using the working papers that accompany this text, enter the balances provided in this problem before posting the adjusting entries.)

PROBLEM 5B-4 (LO 3) CORRECTING WORK SHEET WITH ERRORS A beginning accounting student tried to complete a work sheet for Dick Ady's Bookkeeping Service. The following adjusting entries were to have been analyzed and entered in the work sheet.

(a) Ending inventory of supplies on July 31, $130.

(b) Unexpired insurance on July 31, $420.

(c) Depreciation of office equipment, $325.

(d) Wages earned, but not paid as of July 31, $95.

REQUIRED

Review the work sheet shown on page 165 for addition mistakes, transpositions, and other errors and make all necessary corrections.

PROBLEM 5B-4

Dick Ady's Bookkeeping Service
Work Sheet
For Month Ended July 31, 20--

	ACCOUNT TITLE	TRIAL BALANCE DEBIT	TRIAL BALANCE CREDIT	ADJUSTMENTS DEBIT	ADJUSTMENTS CREDIT	ADJUSTED TRIAL BALANCE DEBIT	ADJUSTED TRIAL BALANCE CREDIT	INCOME STATEMENT DEBIT	INCOME STATEMENT CREDIT	BALANCE SHEET DEBIT	BALANCE SHEET CREDIT	
1	Cash	1 3 6 5 00				1 3 6 5 00				1 3 5 6 00		1
2	Accounts Receivable	8 4 5 00				8 4 5 00			8 4 5 00			2
3	Supplies	6 2 0 00			(a) 4 9 0 00	1 3 0 00				1 3 0 00		3
4	Prepaid Insurance	1 1 5 00			(b) 4 2 0 00	7 3 0 00				7 3 0 00		4
5	Office Equipment	6 4 0 0 00			(c) 3 2 5 00	6 7 2 5 00				6 7 2 5 00		5
6	Accum. Depr.—Office Equipment											6
7	Accounts Payable		7 3 5 00				7 3 5 00				7 3 5 00	7
8	Wages Payable				(d) 9 5 00		9 5 00				5 9 00	8
9	Dick Ady, Capital		7 8 0 0 00				7 8 0 0 00				7 8 0 0 00	9
10	Dick Ady, Drawing	1 2 0 0 00				1 2 0 0 00				1 2 0 0 00		10
11	Professional Fees		6 3 5 0 00				6 3 5 0 00		6 3 5 0 00			11
12	Wages Expense	1 4 9 5 00		(d) 9 5 00		1 5 9 0 00		1 5 9 0 00				12
13	Advertising Expense	3 8 0 00				3 8 0 00		3 8 0 00				13
14	Rent Expense	8 5 0 00				8 5 0 00		8 5 0 00				14
15	Supplies Expense			(a) 4 9 0 00		4 9 0 00		4 9 0 00				15
16	Telephone Expense	2 0 5 00				2 0 5 00		2 5 0 00				16
17	Utilities Expense	2 8 5 00				2 8 5 00		2 8 5 00				17
18	Insurance Expense			(b) 4 2 0 00		4 2 0 00		4 2 0 00				18
19	Depr. Expense—Office Equipment			(c) 3 2 5 00		3 2 5 00		3 2 5 00				19
20	Miscellaneous Expense	9 0 00				9 0 00		9 0 00				20
21		14 8 8 5 00	14 8 8 5 00	1 3 3 0 00	1 3 3 0 00	15 6 3 0 00	14 9 8 0 00	4 8 8 0 00	7 1 9 5 00	10 1 4 1 00	8 5 9 4 00	21
22	Net Income							2 3 1 5 00			1 5 4 7 00	22
23								7 1 9 5 00	7 1 9 5 00	10 1 4 1 00	10 1 4 1 00	23

This work sheet contains errors.

MASTERY PROBLEM

W & D

Kristi Williams offers family counseling services specializing in financial and marital problems. A chart of accounts and a trial balance taken on December 31, 20-1, are provided below.

KRISTI WILLIAMS FAMILY COUNSELING SERVICES
CHART OF ACCOUNTS

Assets		Revenue	
101	Cash	401	Client Fees
142	Office Supplies		
145	Prepaid Insurance	**Expenses**	
181	Office Equipment	511	Wages Expense
181.1	Accumulated Depr.—	521	Rent Expense
	Office Equipment	523	Office Supplies Expense
187	Computer Equipment	533	Utilities Expense
187.1	Accumulated Depr.—	535	Insurance Expense
	Computer Equipment	541	Depr. Expense—
			Office Equipment
Liabilities		542	Depr. Expense—
201	Notes Payable		Computer Equipment
202	Accounts Payable	549	Miscellaneous Expense
Owner's Equity			
311	Kristi Williams, Capital		
312	Kristi Williams, Drawing		

Kristi Williams Family Counseling Services
Trial Balance
December 31, 20 - 1

ACCOUNT TITLE	ACCOUNT NO.	DEBIT BALANCE	CREDIT BALANCE
Cash	101	8 7 3 0 00	
Office Supplies	142	7 0 0 00	
Prepaid Insurance	145	6 0 0 00	
Office Equipment	181	18 0 0 0 00	
Computer Equipment	187	6 0 0 0 00	
Notes Payable	201		8 0 0 0 00
Accounts Payable	202		5 0 0 00
Kristi Williams, Capital	311		11 4 0 0 00
Kristi Williams, Drawing	312	3 0 0 0 00	
Client Fees	401		35 8 0 0 00
Wages Expense	511	9 5 0 0 00	
Rent Expense	521	6 0 0 0 00	
Utilities Expense	533	2 1 7 0 00	
Miscellaneous Expense	549	1 0 0 0 00	
		55 7 0 0 00	55 7 0 0 00

Information for year-end adjustments:

(a) Office supplies on hand at year end amounted to $100.

(b) On January 1, 20-1, Williams purchased office equipment that cost $18,000. It has an expected useful life of ten years and no salvage value.

(c) On July 1, 20-1, Williams purchased computer equipment costing $6,000. It has an expected useful life of four years and no salvage value. Assume that Williams computes depreciation to the nearest full month.

(d) On December 1, 20-1, Williams paid a premium of $600 for a six-month insurance policy.

REQUIRED 1. Prepare the work sheet for the year ended December 31, 20-1.

2. Prepare adjusting entries in a general journal.

Self-Study Test Questions

True/False

1. The matching principle in accounting requires the matching of debits and credits. _____

2. Adjusting entries are required at the end of the accounting period because of mistakes in the journal and ledger. _____

3. As part of the adjustment of supplies, an expense account is debited and Supplies is credited for the amount of supplies used during the accounting period. _____

4. Depreciable cost is the difference between the original cost of the asset and its accumulated depreciation. _____

5. The purpose of depreciation is to record the asset's market value in the accounting records. _____

Multiple Choice

1. The purpose of depreciation is to _____

   (a) spread the cost of an asset over its useful life.
   (b) show the current market value of an asset.
   (c) set up a reserve fund to purchase a new asset.
   (d) expense the asset in the year it was purchased.

2. Depreciable cost is the _____

   (a) difference between original cost and accumulated depreciation.
   (b) difference in actual cost and true market value.
   (c) difference between original cost and estimated salvage value.
   (d) difference between estimated salvage value and the actual salvage value.

3. Book value is the _____

   (a) difference between market value and estimated value.
   (b) difference between market value and historical cost.
   (c) difference between original cost and salvage value.
   (d) difference between original cost and accumulated depreciation.

4. The adjustment for wages earned but not yet paid is _____

   (a) debit Wages Payable and credit Wages Expense.
   (b) debit Wages Expense and credit Cash.
   (c) debit Wages Expense and credit Wages Payable.
   (d) debit Wages Expense and credit Accounts Receivable.

5. The first step in preparing a work sheet is to _____
   (a) prepare the trial balance.
   (b) prepare the adjustments.
   (c) prepare the adjusted trial balance.
   (d) extend the amounts from the Adjusted Trial Balance to the Income Statement and Balance Sheet columns.

The answers to the Self-Study Test Questions are at the end of the text.

CHAPTER 5 APPENDIX

Depreciation Methods

LEARNING OBJECTIVES:
Careful study of this appendix should enable you to:

LO 1 Prepare a depreciation schedule using the straight-line method.

LO 2 Prepare a depreciation schedule using the sum-of-the-years'-digits method.

LO 3 Prepare a depreciation schedule using the double-declining-balance method.

LO 4 Prepare a depreciation schedule for tax purposes using the Modified Accelerated Cost Recovery System.

In Chapter 5, we introduced the straight-line method of depreciation. Here, we will review this method and illustrate three others: sum-of-the-years'-digits; double-declining-balance; and, for tax purposes, the Modified Accelerated Cost Recovery System. For all illustrations, we will assume that a delivery van was purchased for $40,000. It has a five-year useful life and salvage value of $4,000.

STRAIGHT-LINE METHOD

LO1 Prepare a depreciation schedule using the straight-line method.

Under the straight-line method, an equal amount of depreciation will be taken each period. First, compute the depreciable cost by subtracting the salvage value from the cost of the asset. This is done because we expect to sell the asset for $4,000 at the end of its useful life. Thus, the total cost to be recognized as an expense over the five years is $36,000, not $40,000.

Cost	–	Salvage Value	=	Depreciable Cost
$40,000	–	$4,000	=	$36,000

Next, we divide the depreciable cost by the expected life of the asset, 5 years.

Depreciation Expense per Year	=	$\dfrac{\text{Depreciable Cost}}{\text{Years of Life}}$
$7,200 per year	=	$\dfrac{\$36,000}{5 \text{ years}}$

When preparing a depreciation schedule, it is often convenient to use a depreciation rate per year. In this case it would be 20% (100% ÷ 5 years of life). Figure 5A-1 shows the depreciation expense, accumulated depreciation, and book value for each of the five years.

FIGURE 5A-1 Depreciation Schedule Using Straight-Line Method

| | **STRAIGHT-LINE DEPRECIATION** | | | | | |
| | Depreciable | | | Depreciation | Accumulated Depreciation | Book Value[c] |
Year	Cost[a]	×	Rate[b]	= Expense	(End of Year)	(End of Year)
1	$36,000		20%	$7,200	$ 7,200	$32,800
2	36,000		20%	7,200	14,400	25,600
3	36,000		20%	7,200	21,600	18,400
4	36,000		20%	7,200	28,800	11,200
5	36,000		20%	7,200	36,000	4,000

[a] Depreciable Cost = Cost – Salvage Value ($40,000 – $4,000 = $36,000)
[b] Rate = 1 year ÷ 5 years of life × 100 = 20%
[c] Book Value = Cost ($40,000) – Accumulated Depreciation

SUM-OF-THE-YEARS'-DIGITS

LO2 Prepare a depreciation schedule using the sum-of-the-years'-digits method.

Under the sum-of-the-years'-digits method, depreciation is determined by multiplying the depreciable cost by a schedule of fractions. The numerator of the fraction for a specific year is the number of years of remaining useful life for the asset, measured from the beginning of the year. The denominator for all fractions is determined by adding the digits that represent the years of the estimated life of the asset. The calculation for our delivery van with a five-year useful life is shown below.

Sum-of-the-Years'-Digits = 5 + 4 + 3 + 2 + 1 = 15

A depreciation schedule using these fractions is shown in Figure 5A-2.

FIGURE 5A-2 Depreciation Schedule Using Sum-of-the-Years'-Digits Method

| | **SUM-OF-THE-YEARS'-DIGITS** | | | | | |
| | Depreciable | | | Depreciation | Accumulated Depreciation | Book Value[c] |
Year	Cost[a]	×	Rate[b]	= Expense	(End of Year)	(End of Year)
1	$36,000		5/15	$12,000	$12,000	$28,000
2	36,000		4/15	9,600	21,600	18,400
3	36,000		3/15	7,200	28,800	11,200
4	36,000		2/15	4,800	33,600	6,400
5	36,000		1/15	2,400	36,000	4,000

[a] Depreciable Cost = Cost – Salvage Value ($40,000 – $4,000 = $36,000)
[b] Rate = Number of Years of Remaining Useful Life ÷ Sum-of-the-Years'-Digits
[c] Book Value = Cost ($40,000) – Accumulated Depreciation

DOUBLE-DECLINING-BALANCE METHOD

LO3   Prepare a depreciation schedule using the double-declining-balance method.

Under this method, the book value is multiplied by a fixed rate, often double the straight-line rate. The van has a five-year life, so the straight-line rate is 1 ÷ 5, or 20%. Double the straight-line rate is 2 × 20%, or 40%. The double-declining-balance depreciation schedule is shown in Figure 5A-3. Note that the rate is applied to the book value of the asset. Once the book value is reduced to the expected salvage value, $4,000, no more depreciation may be recognized.

FIGURE 5A-3 Depreciation Schedule Using Double-Declining-Balance Method

	DOUBLE-DECLINING-BALANCE METHOD					
Year	**Book Value[a] (Beginning of Year)**	**×**	**Rate[b]**	**Depreciation = Expense**	**Accumulated Depreciation (End of Year)**	**Book Value[a] (End of Year)**
1	$40,000		40%	$16,000	$16,000	$24,000
2	24,000		40%	9,600	25,600	14,400
3	14,400		40%	5,760	31,360	8,640
4	8,640		40%	3,456	34,816	5,184
5	5,184			1,184	36,000	4,000

[a] Book Value = Cost ($40,000) – Accumulated Depreciation
[b] Rate = Double the straight-line rate (1/5 × 2 = 2/5 or 40%)

LEARNING KEY: Double means double the straight-line rate. Declining-balance means that the rate is multiplied by the *book value* (not depreciable cost) at the beginning of each year. This amount is *declining* each year.

MODIFIED ACCELERATED COST RECOVERY SYSTEM

LO4   Prepare a depreciation schedule for tax purposes using the Modified Accelerated Cost Recovery System.

For assets purchased since 1986, many firms use the Modified Accelerated Cost Recovery System (MACRS) for tax purposes. Under this method, the Internal Revenue Service (IRS) classifies various assets according to useful life and sets depreciation rates for each year of the asset's life. These rates are then multiplied by the cost of the asset. Even though the van is expected to have a useful life of five years, and a salvage value of $4,000, the IRS schedule, shown in Figure 5A-4, spreads the depreciation over a six-year period and assumes no salvage value.

FIGURE 5A-4 Depreciation Schedule Using Modified Accelerated Cost Recovery System

MODIFIED ACCELERATED COST RECOVERY SYSTEM

Year	Cost	×	Rate[a]	=	Depreciation Expense	Accumulated Depreciation (End of Year)	Book Value[b] (End of Year)
1	$40,000		20.00%		$ 8,000	$ 8,000	$32,000
2	40,000		32.00%		12,800	20,800	19,200
3	40,000		19.20%		7,680	28,480	11,520
4	40,000		11.52%		4,608	33,088	6,912
5	40,000		11.52%		4,608	37,696	2,304
6	40,000		5.76%		2,304	40,000	0

[a] Rates set by IRS
[b] Book Value = Cost ($40,000) − Accumulated Depreciation

SERIES A EXERCISES

EXERCISE 5ApxA-1 (LO 1) STRAIGHT-LINE DEPRECIATION A small delivery truck was purchased on January 1 at a cost of $25,000. It has an estimated useful life of 4 years and an estimated salvage value of $5,000. Prepare a depreciation schedule showing the depreciation expense, accumulated depreciation, and book value for each year under the straight-line method.

EXERCISE 5ApxA-2 (LO 2) SUM-OF-THE-YEARS'-DIGITS DEPRECIATION Using the information given in Exercise 5ApxA-1, prepare a depreciation schedule showing the depreciation expense, accumulated depreciation, and book value for each year under the sum-of-the-years'-digits method.

EXERCISE 5ApxA-3 (LO 3) DOUBLE-DECLINING-BALANCE DEPRECIATION Using the information given in Exercise 5ApxA-1, prepare a depreciation schedule showing the depreciation expense, accumulated depreciation, and book value for each year under the double-declining-balance method.

EXERCISE 5ApxA-4 (LO 4) MODIFIED ACCELERATED COST RECOVERY SYSTEM Using the information given in Exercise 5ApxA-1 and the rates shown in Figure 5A-4, prepare a depreciation schedule showing the depreciation expense, accumulated depreciation, and book value for each year under the Modified Accelerated Cost Recovery System. For tax purposes, assume that the truck has a useful life of 5 years. (The IRS schedule will spread depreciation over 6 years.)

SERIES B EXERCISES

EXERCISE 5ApxB-1 (LO 1) STRAIGHT-LINE DEPRECIATION A computer was purchased on January 1 at a cost of $5,000. It has an estimated useful life of 5 years and an estimated salvage value of $500. Prepare a depreciation schedule showing the depreciation expense, accumulated depreciation, and book value for each year under the straight-line method.

EXERCISE 5ApxB-2 (LO 2) SUM-OF-THE-YEARS'-DIGITS DEPRECIATION Using the information given in Exercise 5ApxB-1, prepare a depreciation schedule showing the depreciation expense, accumulated depreciation, and book value for each year under the sum-of-the-years'-digits method.

EXERCISE 5ApxB-3 (LO 3) DOUBLE-DECLINING-BALANCE DEPRECIATION Using the information given in Exercise 5ApxB-1, prepare a depreciation schedule showing the depreciation expense, accumulated depreciation, and book value for each year under the double-declining-balance method.

EXERCISE 5ApxB-4 (LO 4) MODIFIED ACCELERATED COST RECOVERY SYSTEM Using the information given in Exercise 5ApxB-1 and the rates shown in Figure 5A-4, prepare a depreciation schedule showing the depreciation expense, accumulated depreciation, and book value for each year under the Modified Accelerated Cost Recovery System. For tax purposes, assume that the truck has a useful life of 5 years. (The IRS schedule will spread depreciation over 6 years.)

6

Financial Statements and the Closing Process

LEARNING OBJECTIVES:
Careful study of this chapter should enable you to:

LO1 Prepare financial statements with the aid of a work sheet.

LO2 Journalize and post closing entries.

LO3 Prepare a post-closing trial balance.

LO4 List and describe the steps in the accounting cycle.

"Come on Jessie, let's get busy. We have to close the books before we go to the New Year's Eve party," said Mitch. But after seeing the disappointed look on Jessie's face, Mitch changed his mind. "What the heck. Let's do it on the 2nd, while we recover from watching all of those bowl games." "Great," said Jessie, "let's get out of here." Will Mitch and Jessie be in trouble for not closing the books before the end of the year?

The work sheet, introduced in Chapter 5, is used for three major end-of-period activities:

1. journalizing adjusting entries,
2. preparing financial statements, and
3. journalizing closing entries.

This chapter illustrates the use of the work sheet for preparing financial statements and closing entries. In addition, the post-closing trial balance is explained and illustrated. All of these activities take place at the end of the firm's fiscal year. However, to continue our illustration of Jessie Jane's Campus Delivery, we demonstrate these activities at the end of the first month of operations.

THE FINANCIAL STATEMENTS

LO 1 Prepare financial statements with the aid of a work sheet.

Since Jessie made no additional investments during the month, the work sheet prepared in Chapter 5 supplies all of the information needed to prepare an income statement, a statement of owner's equity, and a balance sheet. The statements and work sheet columns from which they are derived for Jessie Jane's Campus Delivery are shown in Figures 6-1 and 6-2.

As you refer to the financial statements in Figures 6-1 and 6-2, notice the placement of dollar signs, single rulings, and double rulings. Dollar signs are placed at the top of each column and beneath rulings. Single rulings indicate addition or subtraction, and double rulings are placed under totals. Notice that each statement heading contains three lines: (1) company name, (2) statement title, and (3) period ended or date.

The Income Statement

> Multiple columns are used on the financial statements to make them easier to read. There are no debit or credit columns on the financial statements.

Figure 6-1 shows how the Income Statement columns of the work sheet provide the information needed to prepare an income statement. Revenue is shown first, followed by an itemized and totaled list of expenses. Then, net income is calculated to double check the accuracy of the work sheet. It is presented with a double ruling as the last item in the statement.

The expenses could be listed in the same order that they appear in the chart of accounts or in descending order by dollar amount. The second approach helps the reader identify the most important expenses.

FIGURE 6-1 Linkages Between the Work Sheet and Income Statement

Jessie Jane's Campus Delivery
Work Sheet (Partial)
For Month Ended June 30, 20--

ACCOUNT TITLE	INCOME STATEMENT	
	DEBIT	CREDIT
1 Cash		
2 Accounts Receivable		
3 Supplies		
4 Prepaid Insurance		
5 Delivery Equipment		
6 Accum. Depr.—Delivery Equipment		
7 Accounts Payable		
8 Wages Payable		
9 Jessica Jane, Capital		
10 Jessica Jane, Drawing		
11 Delivery Fees		2 1 5 0 00
12 Wages Expense	7 0 0 00	
13 Rent Expense	2 0 0 00	
14 Supplies Expense	6 0 0 00	
15 Telephone Expense	5 0 00	
16 Insurance Expense	2 5 00	
17 Depr. Expense—Delivery Equipment	1 0 0 00	
18	1 1 3 5 00	2 1 5 0 00
19 Net Income	1 0 1 5 00	2 1 5 0 00
20		
21		
22		
23		
24		
25		
26		
27		
28		
29		

Prepare the Income Statement first.

Jessie Jane's Campus Delivery
Income Statement
For Month Ended June 30, 20--

Revenue:			
Delivery Fees			$ 2 1 5 0 00
Expenses:			
Wages Expense	$ 7 0 0 00		
Rent Expense	2 0 0 00		
Supplies Expense	6 0 0 00		
Telephone Expense	5 0 00		
Insurance Expense	2 5 00		
Depr. Expense—Delivery Equip.	1 0 0 00		
Total Expenses			1 1 3 5 00
Net Income			$ 1 0 1 5 00

Name of company
Title of statement
Accounting period ended

Revenues listed first

Expenses listed second by amount (largest to smallest), or in chart of accounts order. Amounts are itemized in left column, subtotaled in right column.

Dollar signs used at top of columns and under rulings.

Single rulings indicate addition or subtraction.

Double rulings indicate totals.

The Statement of Owner's Equity

Figure 6-2 shows that the Balance Sheet columns of the work sheet provide the information needed to prepare a statement of owner's equity. Jessie's capital account balance and the drawing account balance are in the Balance Sheet columns of the work sheet. The net income for the year can be found either on the work sheet at the bottom of the Income Statement (see Figure 6-1) and Balance Sheet columns or on the income statement. With these three items of information, the statement of owner's equity can be prepared.

Be careful when using the capital account balance reported in the balance sheet columns of the work sheet. This account balance is the beginning balance *plus any additional investments made during the period.* Since Jessie made no additional investments during June, the $2,000 balance may be used as the beginning balance on the statement of owner's equity.

LEARNING KEY: The owner's capital account in the general ledger must be reviewed to determine if additional investments were made during the accounting period.

The Balance Sheet

As shown in Figure 6-2, the work sheet and the statement of owner's equity are used to prepare Jessie's balance sheet. The asset and liability amounts can be found in the Balance Sheet columns of the work sheet. The ending balance in Jessica Jane, Capital has been computed on the statement of owner's equity. This amount should be copied from the statement of owner's equity to the balance sheet.

Two important features of the balance sheet in Figure 6-2 should be noted. First, it is a **report form of balance sheet**, which means that the liabilities and owner's equity sections are shown below the assets section. It differs from an **account form of balance sheet** in which the assets are on the left and the liabilities and owner's equity sections are on the right. (See Jessie's balance sheet illustrated in Figure 2-2 on page 29 in Chapter 2.)

Second, it is a **classified balance sheet**, which means that similar items are grouped together on the balance sheet. Assets are classified as current assets and property, plant, and equipment. Similarly, liabilities are broken down into current and long-term sections. The following major balance sheet classifications are generally used.

Current Assets. Current assets include cash and assets that will be converted into cash or consumed within either one year or the normal operating cycle of the business, whichever is longer. Examples include cash, accounts receivable, supplies, and prepaid insurance. An **operating cycle** is the period of time required to purchase supplies and services and convert them back into cash.

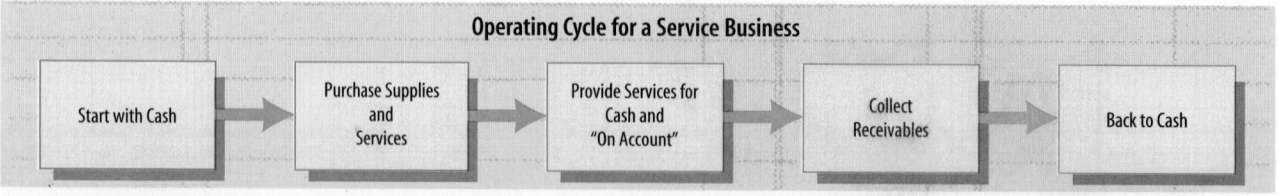

FIGURE 6-2 Linkages Between the Work Sheet, Statement of Owner's Equity and Balance Sheet

Note: The Statement of Owner's Equity is prepared before the Balance Sheet. The S.O.E. is shown below the B.S. to enhance the illustration of the linkages between the work sheet and financial statements.

Jessie Jane's Campus Delivery
Work Sheet (Partial)
For Month Ended June 30, 20--

	ACCOUNT TITLE	BALANCE SHEET	
		DEBIT	CREDIT
1	Cash	3 7 0 00	
2	Accounts Receivable	6 5 0 00	
3	Supplies	2 0 00	
4	Prepaid Insurance	1 7 5 00	
5	Delivery Equipment	3 6 0 0 00	
6	Accum. Depr.—Delivery Equip.		1 0 0 00
7	Accounts Payable		1 8 0 0 00
8	Wages Payable		5 0 00
9	Jessica Jane, Capital		2 0 0 0 00
10	Jessica Jane, Drawing	1 5 0 00	
11	Delivery Fees		
12	Wages Expense		
13	Rent Expense		
14	Supplies Expense		
15	Telephone Expense		
16	Insurance Expense		
17	Depr. Expense—Delivery Equip.		
18		4 9 6 5 00	3 9 5 0 00
19	Net Income		1 0 1 5 00
20		4 9 6 5 00	4 9 6 5 00
21			

Prepare the Balance Sheet third.

Jessie Jane's Campus Delivery
Balance Sheet
June 30, 20--

Assets			
Current Assets			
Cash	$	3 7 0 00	
Accounts Receivable		6 5 0 00	
Supplies		2 0 00	
Prepaid Insurance		1 7 5 00	
Total current assets			$ 1 2 1 5 00
Property, Plant and Equipment			
Delivery Equipment	$3	6 0 0 00	
Accum. Depr. —Delivery Equipment		1 0 0 00	3 5 0 0 00
Total assets			$ 4 7 1 5 00
Liabilities			
Current Liabilities			
Accounts Payable	$1	8 0 0 00	
Wages Payable		5 0 00	
Total current liabilities			$ 1 8 5 0 00
Owner's Equity			
Jessica Jane, capital			2 8 6 5 00
Total liabilities and owner's equity			$ 4 7 1 5 00

Prepare the Statement of Owner's Equity second.

Jessie Jane's Campus Delivery
Statement of Owner's Equity
For Month Ended June 30, 20--

Jessica Jane, capital, June 1, 20--			$ 2 0 0 0 00
Net income for June	$ 1 0 1 5 00		
Less withdrawals for June	1 5 0 00		
Increase in capital			8 6 5 00
Jessica Jane, capital, June 30, 20--			$ 2 8 6 5 00

Name of company
Title of statement
Accounting period ended

Current assets: cash and items that will be converted to cash or consumed within a year.

Property, plant and equipment: durable assets that will help produce revenues for several years.

Current liabilities: amounts owed that will be paid within a year (will require the use of current assets).

Ending capital is not taken from work sheet. It is computed on the statement of owner's equity.

Dollar signs used at top of columns and beneath rulings.

Single rulings indicate addition or subtraction.

Double rulings indicate totals.

Property, Plant, and Equipment. Property, plant, and equipment, also called **plant assets** or **long-term assets**, represent assets that are expected to serve the business for many years. Examples include land, buildings, and equipment.

Current Liabilities. Current liabilities are due within either one year or the normal operating cycle of the business, whichever is longer. They will be paid out of current assets. Accounts payable and wages payable are classified as current liabilities.

Long-Term Liabilities. Long-term liabilities, or **long-term debt**, are obligations that are not expected to be paid within a year and do not require the use of current assets. A mortgage on an office building is an example of a long-term liability. Jessie has no long-term debts. If she did, they would be listed on the balance sheet in the long-term liabilities section immediately following the current liabilities.

A BROADER VIEW

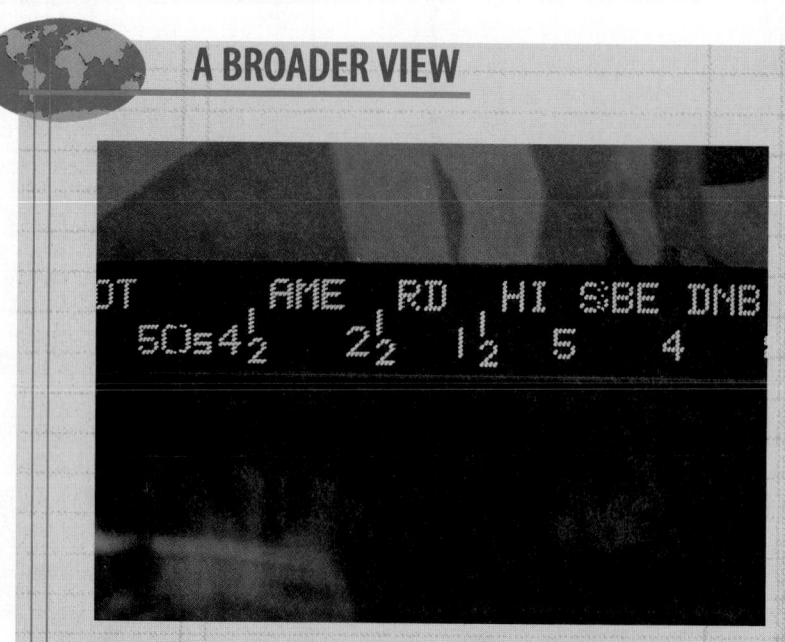

IMPORTANCE OF EARNINGS TO THE STOCK MARKET

Investors in the stock market pay close attention to earnings reported on the income statement. This information is so important that corporate officials often announce expected earnings before the financial statements are actually distributed to the public. If the announcement is different from what investors are expecting, the price of the stock may go up or down. For example, when Aetna, a leader in the managed health care industry, warned that earnings would be about 27% lower than expected by stock analysts, its stock price fell more than 10%.

Additional Investments by the Owner

If the owner of a business made additional investments during the accounting period, the owner's capital reported in the Balance Sheet columns of the work sheet would represent the beginning balance plus any additional investments made during the accounting period. If this amount were used as the beginning balance on the statement of owner's equity, it would not equal the ending balance from last period and would create confusion for those comparing the two statements. In addition, the statement would not reflect all of the activities affecting the owner's capital account during the period.

Thus, we must also review the owner's capital account in the general ledger to get the information needed to prepare the statement of owner's equity. Figure 6-3 illustrates this situation for another business, Ramon's Shopping Service. The $5,000 balance of July 1, 20--, in Ramon Balboa's general ledger capital account is used as the beginning balance on the statement of owner's equity. Note that this is also the ending balance on June 30, 20--. The additional investment of $3,000 made on July 5 and posted to Balboa's general ledger capital account is reported by writing "add additional investments" on the line immediately after the beginning balance. The beginning balance plus the additional investment equals the total investment by the owner in the business and is the amount reported in the Balance Sheet columns of the work sheet. From this point, the preparation of the statement is the same as for businesses without additional investments.

FIGURE 6-3 Statement of Owner's Equity with Additional Investment

THE CLOSING PROCESS

LO 2   Journalize and post closing entries.

Assets, liabilities, and the owner's capital account accumulate information across accounting periods. Their balances are brought forward for each new period. For example, the amount of cash at the end of one accounting period must be the same as the amount of cash at the beginning of the next period. Thus, the balance reported for Cash is a result of all cash transactions since the business first opened. This is true for all accounts reported on the balance sheet. For this reason, they are called **permanent accounts**.

 LEARNING KEY: Permanent accounts contain the results of all transactions since the business started. Their balances are carried forward to each new accounting period.

Revenue, expense, and drawing accounts accumulate information *for a specific accounting period*. At the end of the fiscal year, these accounts must be *closed*. The **closing process** gives these accounts zero balances so they are prepared to accumulate new information for the next accounting period. Since these accounts do not accumulate information across accounting periods, they are called **temporary accounts**. The drawing account and all accounts reported in the income statement are temporary accounts and must be closed at the end of each accounting period.

 LEARNING KEY: Temporary accounts contain information for one accounting period. These accounts are closed at the end of each accounting period.

The income summary account is not really needed for the closing process. Some businesses simply close the revenue and expense accounts directly to the owner's capital account. One benefit of using the income summary account is that its balance before closing to the capital account equals the net income or net loss for the period. Thus, it can serve as a check of the accuracy of the closing entries for revenues and expenses. Of course, computer programs post the closing entries to the owner's capital account automatically.

The closing process is most clearly demonstrated by returning to the accounting equation and T accounts. As shown in Figure 6-4, revenue, expense, and drawing accounts impact owner's equity and should be considered "under the umbrella" of the capital account. The effect of these accounts on owner's equity is formalized at the end of the accounting period when the balances of the temporary accounts are transferred to the owner's capital account (a permanent account) during the closing process.

The four basic steps in the closing process are illustrated in Figure 6-4. As you can see, a new account, **Income Summary**, is used in the closing process. This account may also be called *Expense and Revenue Summary*. This temporary account is used to close the revenue and expense accounts. After closing the revenues and expenses to Income Summary, the balance of this account is equal to the net income. This is why it is called Income Summary. Income Summary is opened during the closing process. Then it is closed to the owner's capital account. It does not appear on any financial statement. The four steps in the closing process are explained starting on the next page.

FIGURE 6-4 The Closing Process

STEPS IN THE CLOSING PROCESS

STEP 1   **Close Revenue Accounts to Income Summary.** Revenues have credit balances and increase owner's equity. Therefore, the revenue account is debited to create a zero balance. Income Summary is credited for the same amount.

STEP 2   **Close Expense Accounts to Income Summary.** Expenses have debit balances and reduce owner's equity. Therefore, the expense accounts are credited to create a zero balance. Income Summary must be debited for the total of the expenses.

STEP 3   **Close Income Summary to Capital.** The balance in Income Summary represents the net income (credit balance) or net loss (debit balance) for the period. This balance is transferred to the owner's capital account. If net income has been earned, Income Summary is debited to create a zero balance, and the owner's capital account is credited. If a net loss has been incurred, the owner's capital account is debited and Income Summary is credited to create a zero balance. Figure 6-5 shows examples for closing net income and net loss.

FIGURE 6-5 Step 3: Closing Net Income and Closing Net Loss

NET INCOME				NET LOSS			
Capital				**Capital**			
		1,000	(Net Income) STEP 3	STEP 3	(Net Loss)	2,000	
Income Summary				**Income Summary**			
(Expenses)	4,000	5,000	(Revenues)	(Expenses)	6,000	4,000	(Revenues)
STEP 3	1,000					2,000	STEP 3

STEP 4   **Close Drawing to Capital.** Drawing has a debit balance and reduces owner's equity. Therefore, it is credited to create a zero balance. The owner's capital account is debited.

> **LEARNING KEY:** The owner can make withdrawals from the business for any amount and at any time, as long as the assets are available. These withdrawals are for personal reasons and have nothing to do with measuring the profitability of the firm. Thus, they are closed directly to the owner's capital account.

Upon completion of these four steps, all temporary accounts have zero balances. The earnings and withdrawals for the period have been transferred to the owner's capital account.

Journalize Closing Entries

Of course, to actually change the ledger accounts, the closing entries must be journalized and posted to the general ledger. As shown in Figure 6-6, the balances of the accounts to be closed are readily available from the Income Statement and Balance Sheet columns of the work sheet. These balances are used to illustrate the closing entries for Jessie Jane's Campus Delivery, in T account and general journal form, in Figures 6-7 and 6-8, respectively. Remember: Closing entries are made at

FIGURE 6-6 Role of the Work Sheet in the Closing Process

Rulings are entered on the debit and credit sides of the T accounts to indicate a zero balance.

the end of the *fiscal year*. Closing entries made at the end of June are illustrated here so you can see the completion of the accounting cycle for Jessie Jane's Campus Delivery.

Like adjusting entries, the closing entries are made on the last day of the accounting period. "Closing Entries" is written in the Description column before the first entry and no explanations are required. Note that it is best to make one compound entry to close the expense accounts.

FIGURE 6-7 Closing Entries in T Account Form

Assets		=	Liabilities		+	Owner's Equity	
Debit	**Credit**		**Debit**	**Credit**		**Debit**	**Credit**
+	–		–	+		–	+

Jessica Jane, Capital

(4)	150	2000	
		1015	(3)

Income Summary

(2)	1135	2150	(1)
(3)	1015	1015	Bal.

Drawing		Expenses		Revenues	
Debit	**Credit**	**Debit**	**Credit**	**Debit**	**Credit**
+	–	+	–	–	+

Jessica Jane, Drawing		Wages Expense		Delivery Fees	
Bal. 150	150 (4)	Bal. 700	700 (2)	(1) 2150	Bal. 2150

Rent Expense

Bal.	200	200	(2)

Supplies Expense

Bal.	60	60	(2)

Telephone Expense

Bal.	50	50	(2)

Insurance Expense

Bal.	25	25	(2)

Depreciation Exp.—
Delivery Equipment

Bal.	100	100	(2)

LEARNING KEY: Each individual revenue, expense, and drawing account must be closed.

FIGURE 6-8 Closing Entries in General Journal

	DATE		DESCRIPTION	POST REF.	DEBIT	CREDIT	
			GENERAL JOURNAL			PAGE 4	
1			Closing Entries				1
2	20-- June	30	Delivery Fees	401	2 1 5 0 00		2
3			Income Summary	313		2 1 5 0 00	3
4							4
5		30	Income Summary	313	1 1 3 5 00		5
6			Wages Expense	511		7 0 0 00	6
7			Rent Expense	521		2 0 0 00	7
8			Supplies Expense	523		6 0 00	8
9			Telephone Expense	525		5 0 00	9
10			Insurance Expense	535		2 5 00	10
11			Depr. Expense—Delivery Equipment	541		1 0 0 00	11
12							12
13		30	Income Summary	313	1 0 1 5 00		13
14			Jessica Jane, Capital	311		1 0 1 5 00	14
15							15
16		30	Jessica Jane, Capital	311	1 5 0 00		16
17			Jessica Jane, Drawing	312		1 5 0 00	17
18							18
19							19

STEP 1 — row 2

STEP 2 — row 5

Compund Entry — (points to rows 6–11)

STEP 3 — row 13

STEP 4 — row 16

No explanations are necessary — (points to row 17)

Post the Closing Entries

The account numbers have been entered in the Posting Reference column of the journal to show that the entries have been posted to the ledger accounts illustrated in Figure 6-9. Note that "Closing" has been written in the Item column of each account to identify the closing entries. Zero account balances are recorded by drawing a line in both the debit and credit Balance columns.

LEARNING KEY: Once the closing entries are posted, the general ledger account balances will agree with the amounts reported on the balance sheet.

FIGURE 6-9 Closing Entries Posted to the General Ledger

GENERAL LEDGER

ACCOUNT: Jessica Jane, Capital   ACCOUNT NO. 311

DATE		ITEM	POST REF.	DEBIT	CREDIT	BALANCE DEBIT	BALANCE CREDIT
20-- June	1		J1		2 0 0 0 00		2 0 0 0 00
	30	Closing	J4		1 0 1 5 00		3 0 1 5 00
	30	Closing	J4	1 5 0 00			2 8 6 5 00

ACCOUNT: Jessica Jane, Drawing   ACCOUNT NO. 312

DATE		ITEM	POST REF.	DEBIT	CREDIT	BALANCE DEBIT	BALANCE CREDIT
20-- June	30		J2	1 5 0 00		1 5 0 00	
	30	Closing	J4		1 5 0 00		

ACCOUNT: Income Summary   ACCOUNT NO. 313

DATE		ITEM	POST REF.	DEBIT	CREDIT	BALANCE DEBIT	BALANCE CREDIT
20-- June	30	Closing	J4		2 1 5 0 00		2 1 5 0 00
	30	Closing	J4	1 1 3 5 00			1 0 1 5 00
	30	Closing	J4	1 0 1 5 00			

ACCOUNT: Delivery Fees   ACCOUNT NO. 401

DATE		ITEM	POST REF.	DEBIT	CREDIT	BALANCE DEBIT	BALANCE CREDIT
20-- June	6		J1		5 0 0 00		5 0 0 00
	15		J1		6 0 0 00		1 1 0 0 00
	30		J2		1 0 5 0 00		2 1 5 0 00
	30	Closing	J4	2 1 5 0 00			

ACCOUNT: Wages Expense   ACCOUNT NO. 511

DATE		ITEM	POST REF.	DEBIT	CREDIT	BALANCE DEBIT	BALANCE CREDIT
20-- June	27		J2	6 5 0 00		6 5 0 00	
	30	Adjusting	J3	5 0 00		7 0 0 00	
	30	Closing	J4		7 0 0 00		

ACCOUNT: Rent Expense   ACCOUNT NO. 521

DATE		ITEM	POST REF.	DEBIT	CREDIT	BALANCE DEBIT	BALANCE CREDIT
20-- June	7		J1	2 0 0 00		2 0 0 00	
	30	Closing	J4		2 0 0 00		

ACCOUNT: Supplies Expense   ACCOUNT NO. 523

DATE		ITEM	POST REF.	DEBIT	CREDIT	BALANCE DEBIT	BALANCE CREDIT
20-- June	30	Adjusting	J3	6 0 00		6 0 00	
	30	Closing	J4		6 0 00		

FIGURE 6-9 Closing Entries Posted to the General Ledger *(continued)*

ACCOUNT: Telephone Expense   ACCOUNT NO. 525

DATE		ITEM	POST REF.	DEBIT	CREDIT	BALANCE DEBIT	BALANCE CREDIT
20-- June	15		J 1	5 0 00		5 0 00	
	30	Closing	J 4		5 0 00		

ACCOUNT: Insurance Expense   ACCOUNT NO. 535

DATE		ITEM	POST REF.	DEBIT	CREDIT	BALANCE DEBIT	BALANCE CREDIT
20-- June	30	Adjusting	J 3	2 5 00		2 5 00	
	30	Closing	J 4		2 5 00		

ACCOUNT: Depreciation Expense—Delivery Equipment   ACCOUNT NO. 541

DATE		ITEM	POST REF.	DEBIT	CREDIT	BALANCE DEBIT	BALANCE CREDIT
20-- June	30	Adjusting	J 3	1 0 0 00		1 0 0 00	
	30	Closing	J 4		1 0 0 00		

POST-CLOSING TRIAL BALANCE

LO 3 Prepare a post-closing trial balance.

After posting the closing entries, a **post-closing trial balance** should be prepared to prove the equality of the debit and credit balances in the general ledger accounts. The ending balance of each general ledger account that remains open at the end of the year is listed. Remember: Only the permanent accounts remain open after the closing process is completed. Figure 6-10 shows the post-closing trial balance for Jessie's ledger.

FIGURE 6-10 Post-Closing Trial Balance

Jessie Jane's Campus Delivery
Post-Closing Trial Balance
June 30, 20 - -

ACCOUNT TITLE	ACCOUNT NO.	DEBIT BALANCE	CREDIT BALANCE
Cash	101	3 7 0 00	
Accounts Receivable	122	6 5 0 00	
Supplies	141	2 0 00	
Prepaid Insurance	145	1 7 5 00	
Delivery Equipment	185	3 6 0 0 00	
Accumulated Depreciation—Delivery Equipment	185.1		1 0 0 00
Accounts Payable	202		1 8 0 0 00
Wages Payable	219		5 0 00
Jessica Jane, Capital	311		2 8 6 5 00
		4 8 1 5 00	4 8 1 5 00

Note that all amounts reflected on the post-closing trial balance are the same as reported in the Balance Sheet columns of the work sheet except Drawing and Owner's Capital. Drawing was closed. Owner's Capital was updated to reflect revenues, expenses, and drawing for the accounting period.

THE ACCOUNTING CYCLE

LO 4   List and describe the steps in the accounting cycle.

The steps involved in accounting for all of the business activities during an accounting period are called the **accounting cycle**. The cycle begins with the analysis of source documents and ends with a post-closing trial balance. A brief summary of the steps in the cycle follows.

STEPS IN THE ACCOUNTING CYCLE

During Accounting Period

STEP 1   Analyze source documents.

STEP 2   Journalize the transactions.

STEP 3   Post to the ledger accounts.

End of Accounting Period

STEP 4   Prepare a trial balance.

STEP 5   Determine and prepare the needed adjustments on the work sheet.

STEP 6   Complete an end-of-period work sheet.

STEP 7   Prepare an income statement, statement of owner's equity, and balance sheet.

STEP 8   Journalize and post the adjusting entries.

STEP 9   Journalize and post the closing entries.

STEP 10   Prepare a post-closing trial balance.

 LEARNING KEY: Properly analyzing and journalizing transactions is very important. A mistake made in step 1 is carried through the entire accounting cycle.

Steps 4 through 10 in the preceding list are performed *as of* the last day of the accounting period. This does not mean that they are actually done on the last day. The accountant may not be able to do any of these things until the first few days (sometimes weeks) of the next period. Nevertheless, the work sheet, statements, and entries are prepared as of the closing date.

COMPUTERS AND ACCOUNTING

Principles of Computer-Based Accounting Systems—James Hall

Modern organizations use computer technology to perform many of their routine accounting tasks. While the accounting principles discussed in this text still apply, computer-based accounting systems also make use of unique transaction processing techniques that accountants should understand at a conceptual level. Our discussion will focus on three computerized accounting approaches: batch processing, real-time processing, and systems that combine both batch and real-time features. Before we enter into this material, however, the relationship between traditional accounting records and their computerized counterparts needs to be addressed.

Computerized Accounting Records

File Structures. Financial information in a computerized accounting system is represented by a three-level format or structure: data, records, and files. We will use accounts receivable to illustrate this structure, which is shown in Figure 1. *Data* are individual facts that help describe a financial entity. For instance, the customer's name, address, amount owed, and line-of-credit are some of the data that describe an account receivable. The entire set of data needed to describe a single customer's account is an account receivable *record*. All the customer records taken together form the accounts receivable *file*. Every record in the accounts receivable file contains the same types of data, but each record is unique because the data values for individual customers are different. Examples of other accounting files structured in this way include accounts payable, inventory, cash receipts, and payroll.

Types of Computer Files. Two different types of files are mainly used in transaction processing systems: transaction files and master files. *Transaction files* are like groups of source documents. Cash receipts, sales invoices, and purchase orders for the day are examples of transaction files. Each transaction is captured as a unique record in the appropriate transaction file. To illustrate, Figure 2 shows the file structure of a sales invoice transaction file. The file contains a record for the credit

Figure 1

Data, Records, and Files

Accounts Receivable Data
Customer Account Number (Key)
Customer Name
Customer Address
Current Balance of Account
Customer Credit Limit

= Accounts Receivable Record

All Accounts Receivable Records

Accounts Receivable Record 1 2 3 n

= Accounts Receivable File

Figure 2   **Relationship Between Transactions and Master Files**

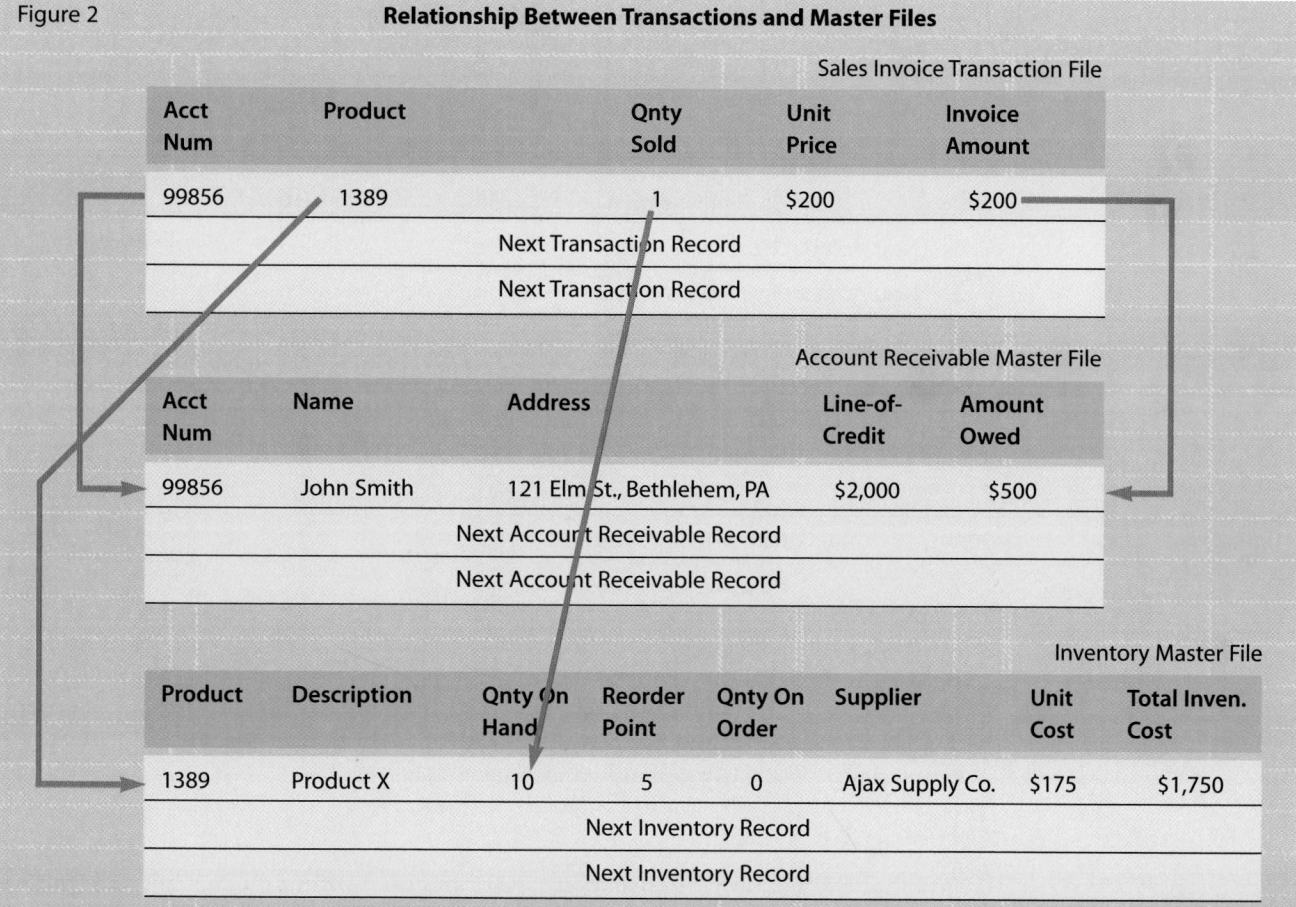

Sales Invoice Transaction File

Acct Num	Product	Qnty Sold	Unit Price	Invoice Amount
99856	1389	1	$200	$200
Next Transaction Record				
Next Transaction Record				

Account Receivable Master File

Acct Num	Name	Address	Line-of-Credit	Amount Owed
99856	John Smith	121 Elm St., Bethlehem, PA	$2,000	$500
Next Account Receivable Record				
Next Account Receivable Record				

Inventory Master File

Product	Description	Qnty On Hand	Reorder Point	Qnty On Order	Supplier	Unit Cost	Total Inven. Cost
1389	Product X	10	5	0	Ajax Supply Co.	$175	$1,750
Next Inventory Record							
Next Inventory Record							

sale of one unit of product "1389" for $200 to John Smith, whose account number is 99856. For simplicity, the illustration shows a file containing only one record. In fact, depending on the size of the company, a transaction file may contain dozens, hundreds, or even thousands of records called a *batch*. A batch represents the transactions for a period of time. For example, an entire day's sales orders may be assembled into a batch and entered into a transaction file. The task of creating a transaction file from a batch of source documents is called *data entry*. We will examine data entry in more detail later.

Master files are made up of the subsidiary ledger and general ledger records of the organization. Figure 2 shows two master files: Accounts Receivable and Inventory. Master files records contain data values that are changed by transaction records during data processing. Each transaction record will change data values contained in two or more master file records. In our example, the invoice amount data in the sales invoice transaction record will increase the amount owed in John Smith's accounts receivable record from its current balance of $500 to the new balance of $700. Similarly, the quantity sold data in the sales invoice transaction will reduce, by one unit, the quantity-on-hand data for product "1389" in the inventory subsidiary master file. (See Figure 3.) Later we see how this task is accomplished.

Where is the Journal? Since subsidiary ledger and general ledger accounts are updated directly from source documents, journals do not play the same role in computerized systems that they do in manual systems. In fact, journals do not exist in some computer-based accounting systems. However, many organizations prefer a computerized accounting system that is like the traditional environment.

Figure 3   **Master Files After Being Updated by the Transaction**

Account Receivable Master File

Acct Num	Name	Address	Line-of-Credit	Amount Owed
99856	John Smith	121 Elm St., Bethlehem, PA	$2,000	$700
		Next Account Receivable Record		
		Next Account Receivable Record		

Beginning balances have been changed by the transaction

Inventory Master File

Product	Description	Qnty On Hand	Reorder Point	Qnty On Order	Supplier	Unit Cost	Total Inven. Cost
1389	Product X	9	5	0	Ajax Supply Co.	$175	$1,575
			Next Inventory Record				
			Next Inventory Record				

In such a case, a special master file (sometimes called an archive file) will be created to store traditional journal entries. Under this approach, the period's transaction records are summarized and added as a separate record to the file. Records in the journal master file can thus be used for auditing purposes and for routine reconciliation with the general ledger master file.

Computer-Based Accounting Systems

Now that the relationship between traditional accounting records and computer files has been explained, we are in position to examine transaction processing techniques. The following discussion reviews key features of three approaches.

Batch Systems

Batch processing involves assembling transactions into groups (batches) for processing. A typical batch system will have the following features:

▶ *File maintenance* involves adding (or deleting) records to the master file. For example, when a new customer is approved for a department store credit card, the customer's record must be added to the accounts receivable master file before any transactions can be processed. Most computerized accounting systems allow this to be done quite easily. For instance, from a computer terminal connected to the accounting system, the accounting clerk selects the "File Maintenance" option from the menu. A data input screen appears allowing the clerk to enter the necessary data about the customer, which is taken from the approved credit application. Since a master file should contain only active accounts, a menu option will also exist for deleting the records of customers who have canceled their credit cards. File maintenance is performed on all types of master files. Inventory, accounts payable, and payroll files regularly have records added to and deleted from them to keep the files current.

▶ *Data entry* is the task of converting a batch of source documents into a transaction file. Typical source documents include the day's sales invoices, employee time cards, or cash receipts from customers. From the computer terminal, the clerk selects the appropriate data entry task (e.g., "Enter Sales Invoices") from the screen menu. In well-designed systems, the data input screen that appears will resemble very closely the physical source documents being entered by the clerk. As the cursor on the data input screen moves from field to field, the clerk's eyes track the corresponding data in the physical source document. This makes data entry much easier and less prone to error.

In a manual system, a single transaction must be recorded several times. It is captured on the source document, entered into the journal, posted to two or more subsidiary ledgers, and then summarized and entered into the general ledger. Each recording task takes effort and is an opportunity for error. A key feature of computerized accounting systems is that they use the "single entry" approach. The clerk enters each transaction only once into the transaction file, and the necessary processing is performed automatically by the computer. In some systems, the processing task is initiated by the data entry clerk who selects the "Run" option from the screen menu after the data entry step is completed. In other systems, the processing is scheduled by the computer to run automatically the same time each day.

The processing phase of a batch system is a series of computer programs called *runs*. The following describes a typical sequence of batch runs.

▶ First, a program called an *edit run* reads the transaction file and checks it for clerical errors. Any records with detected errors are rejected and placed in a separate error file to be corrected and resubmitted later by the clerk. After editing, the valid records remain in the transaction file and are passed to the next program.

▶ A *file update run* posts the transaction data to the appropriate subsidiary ledger master files.

▶ A *balancing run* summarizes the transactions, reconciles debits and credits, creates a journal entry, and posts to the general ledger accounts.

▶ Finally, a *report run* produces various reports, such as lists of transactions and account status reports.

Time Lag. The task of gathering transactions into batches creates a time lag between the point at which the transaction occurs and when it is posted to the accounts. The amount of lag depends on the frequency of batch processing, which can range from several minutes to weeks. For some applications in some companies, time lags pose a serious problem. In other situations, lags pose no problem at all. Payroll processing is a typical example of a batch system. Work occurs continuously throughout the pay period, but the employee paychecks are prepared and the accounts are updated only at the end of the pay period.

Real-Time Systems

Real-time systems process and post transactions to all accounts as the events occur. There is no gathering of transactions to produce a transaction file. In a sense, these systems process a batch of one. An example of real-time processing is an airline reservation system, which processes requests for services from each traveler while he or she waits. Real-time systems permit the data entry clerk to edit the transaction as it is being entered into the system thus eliminating the need to correct and resubmit erroneous transactions. The real-time environment provides managers and other users with immediate access to current financial information and transaction status, thus streamlining the organization's business processes.

Systems with Batch and Real-Time Features

Many accounting systems have both batch and real-time features. For example, consider an order entry system for a catalogue sales company in which customers place telephone orders with many different sales clerks. At any point in time, each clerk needs to know what inventory is in stock and the exact quantities on hand. When inventory is sold by one clerk, this information must be available to the others. In this setting, inventory records need to be updated in real time as orders are taken. Other records, such as accounts receivable and general ledger accounts, however, need not be updated in real time. In fact, to do so may tie up the system and slow customer service. Some accounting can, therefore, be performed in batch mode at the end of the day.

In Summary

Transaction files are equivalent to batches of source documents in a manual system, and master files constitute the subsidiary ledger and general ledger accounts. Computer-based systems may not use traditional journals. Transaction processing involves updating master file records from data contained in transaction records. The update process can be either batch, real-time, or a combination of both.

Dr. James Hall is an Associate Professor of Accounting at Lehigh University in Bethlehem, PA and the author of Accounting Information Systems, 2nd edition.

Learning Objectives	Key Points to Remember
1 **Prepare financial statements with the aid of a work sheet.**	The work sheet is used as an aid in preparing: 1. adjusting entries, 2. financial statements, and 3. closing entries The following classifications are used for accounts reported on the balance sheet. ▶ *Current assets* include cash and assets that will be converted into cash or consumed within either one year or the normal operating cycle of the business, whichever is longer. An *operating cycle* is the time required to purchase supplies and services and convert them back into cash. ▶ *Property, plant, and equipment*, also called *plant assets* or *long-term assets*, represent assets that are expected to serve the business for many years. ▶ *Current liabilities* are liabilities that are due within either one year or the normal operating cycle of the business, whichever is longer, and that are to be paid out of current assets. ▶ *Long-term liabilities*, or *long-term debt*, are obligations that are not expected to be paid within a year and do not require the use of current assets.
2 **Journalize and post closing entries.**	Steps in the closing process are: 1. Close revenue accounts to Income Summary. 2. Close expense accounts to Income Summary. 3. Close Income Summary to Capital. 4. Close Drawing to Capital.

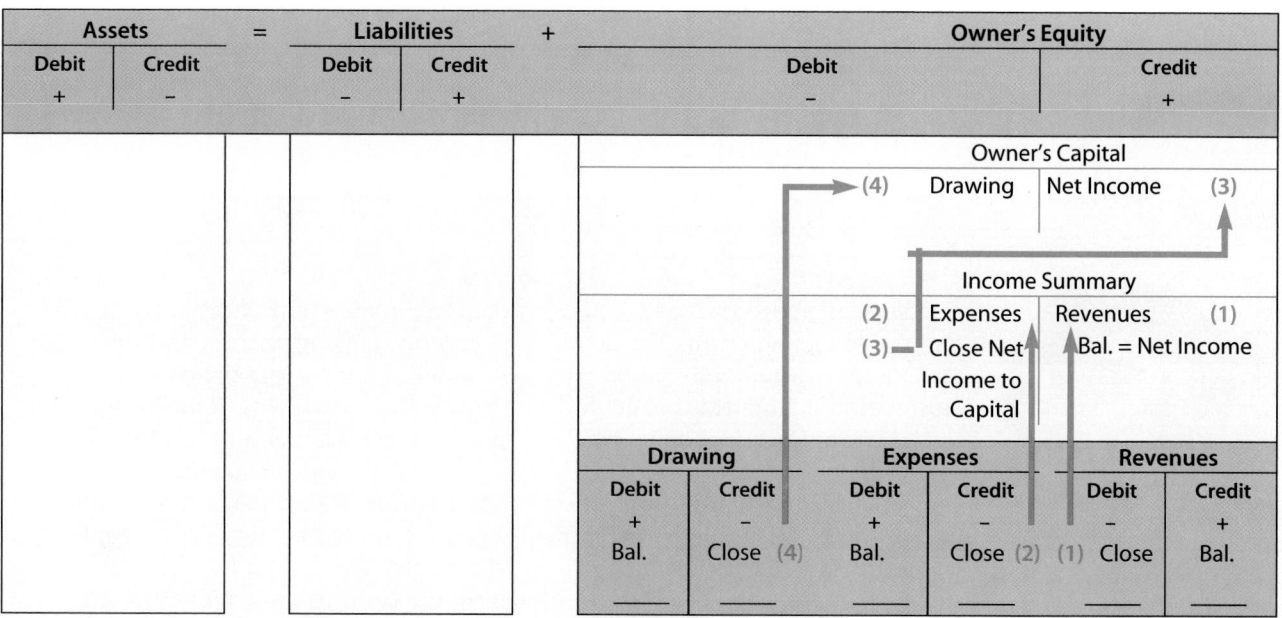

Learning Objectives	Key Points to Remember
3 **Prepare a post-closing trial balance.**	After posting the closing entries, a post-closing trial balance should be prepared to prove the equality of the debit and credit balances in the general ledger accounts. The accounts shown in the post-closing trial balance are the permanent accounts.
4 **List and describe the steps in the accounting cycle.**	Steps in the accounting cycle are: *During Accounting Period* 1. Analyze source documents. 2. Journalize the transactions. 3. Post to the ledger accounts. *End of Accounting Period* 4. Prepare a trial balance. 5. Determine and prepare the needed adjustments on the work sheet. 6. Complete an end-of-period work sheet. 7. Prepare an income statement, statement of owner's equity, and balance sheet. 8. Journalize and post the adjusting entries. 9. Journalize and post the closing entries. 10. Prepare a post-closing trial balance.

Reflection: Answering the Opening Question

The accounting records are closed "as of" December 31, or another fiscal year end chosen by the firm. The actual adjustments, closing entries, and financial statements are generally prepared several weeks after the official closing date. However, it is important to include all transactions occurring prior to year end in the current year's financial statements. Similarly, transactions taking place after year end must be included in the next year's financial statements. Improper timing of the recognition of transactions taking place around the end of the year can have major effects on the reported profits. For example, some firms have been found to "leave the books open" for a few days to include a major sale, or other profitable transactions, that actually took place after the end of the year. If undetected, the good news could be reported on the current year's statements, rather than in the following year. Similarly, a firm could be tempted to "close early" to avoid recognizing unprofitable events occurring during the last few days of the year. Thus, proper treatment of transactions taking place around the end of the year is carefully monitored by auditors.

KEY TERMS

account form of balance sheet, (178)   A balance sheet in which the assets are on the left and the liabilities and the owner's equity sections are on the right.

accounting cycle, (189)   The steps involved in accounting for all of the business activities during an accounting period.

classified balance sheet, (178)   A balance sheet with separate categories for current assets; property, plant, and equipment; current liabilities; and long-term liabilities.

closing process, (182)   The process of giving zero balances to the temporary accounts so that they can accumulate information for the next accounting period.

current assets, (178)   Cash and assets that will be converted into cash or consumed within either one year or the normal operating cycle of the business, whichever is longer.

current liabilities, (180)   Liabilities that are due within either one year or the normal operating cycle of the business, whichever is longer, and that are to be paid out of current assets.

Income Summary, (182)   A temporary account used in the closing process to summarize the effects of all revenue and expense accounts.

long-term assets, (180)   See property, plant, and equipment.

long-term debt, (180)   See long-term liabilities.

long-term liabilities, (180)   Obligations that are not expected to be paid within a year and do not require the use of current assets. Also called long-term debt.

operating cycle, (178)   The period of time required to purchase supplies and services and convert them back into cash.

permanent accounts, (182)   Accounts that accumulate information across accounting periods; all accounts reported on the balance sheet.

plant assets, (180)   See property, plant, and equipment.

post-closing trial balance, (188)   Prepared after posting the closing entries to prove the equality of the debit and credit balances in the general ledger accounts.

property, plant, and equipment, (180)   Assets that are expected to serve the business for many years. Also called plant assets or long-term assets.

report form of balance sheet, (178)   A balance sheet in which the liabilities and the owner's equity sections are shown below the assets section.

temporary accounts, (182)   Accounts that do not accumulate information across accounting periods but are closed, such as the drawing account and all income statement accounts.

DEMONSTRATION PROBLEM

Timothy Chang owns and operates Hard Copy Printers. A work sheet for the year ended December 31, 20--, is provided on the next page. Chang made no additional investments during the year.

REQUIRED   1.   Prepare financial statements.

2.   Prepare closing entries.

Hard Copy Printers
Work Sheet
For Year Ended December 31, 20--

	Trial Balance Debit	Trial Balance Credit	Adjustments Debit	Adjustments Credit	Adjusted Trial Balance Debit	Adjusted Trial Balance Credit	Income Statement Debit	Income Statement Credit	Balance Sheet Debit	Balance Sheet Credit
1 Cash	1 180 00				1 180 00				1 180 00	
2 Paper Supplies	3 600 00			(a) 3 550 00	50 00				50 00	
3 Prepaid Insurance	1 000 00			(b) 505 00	495 00				495 00	
4 Printing Equipment	5 800 00				5 800 00				5 800 00	
5 Accum. Depr.—Printing Equipment		500 00		(d) 1 200 00		1 700 00				1 700 00
6 Accounts Payable		1 000 00				1 000 00				1 000 00
7 Wages Payable				(c) 30 00		30 00				30 00
8 Timothy Chang, Capital		9 000 00				9 000 00				9 000 00
9 Timothy Chang, Drawing	13 000 00				13 000 00				13 000 00	
10 Printing Fees		35 100 00				35 100 00		35 100 00		
11 Wages Expense	11 970 00		(c) 30 00		12 000 00		12 000 00			
12 Rent Expense	7 500 00				7 500 00		7 500 00			
13 Paper Supplies Expense			(a) 3 550 00		3 550 00		3 550 00			
14 Telephone Expense	550 00				550 00		550 00			
15 Utilities Expense	1 000 00				1 000 00		1 000 00			
16 Insurance Expense			(b) 505 00		505 00		505 00			
17 Depr. Expense—Printing Equipment			(d) 1 200 00		1 200 00		1 200 00			
18	45 600 00	45 600 00	5 285 00	5 285 00	46 830 00	46 830 00	26 305 00	35 100 00	20 525 00	11 730 00
19 Net Income							8 795 00			8 795 00
20							35 100 00	35 100 00	20 525 00	20 525 00

Solution

1.

Hard Copy Printers
Income Statement
For Year Ended December 31, 20 - -

Revenue:										
Printing fees						$ 35	1	0	0	00
Expenses:										
Wages expense	$ 12	0	0	0	00					
Rent expense	7	5	0	0	00					
Paper supplies expense	3	5	5	0	00					
Telephone expense		5	5	0	00					
Utilities expense	1	0	0	0	00					
Insurance expense		5	0	5	00					
Depreciation expense—printing equipment	1	2	0	0	00					
Total expenses						26	3	0	5	00
Net income						$ 8	7	9	5	00

Hard Copy Printers
Statement of Owner's Equity
For Year Ended December 31, 20 - -

Timothy Chang, capital, Jan. 1, 20 - -						$ 10	0	0	0	00
Net income for 20 - -	$ 8	7	9	5	00					
Less withdrawals for 20 - -	13	0	0	0	00					
Decrease in capital						(4	2	0	5	00)
Timothy Chang, capital, Dec. 31, 20 - -						$ 5	7	9	5	00

Hard Copy Printers
Balance Sheet
December 31, 20 - -

Assets										
Current Assets:										
Cash	$ 1	1	8	0	00					
Paper supplies			5	0	00					
Prepaid insurance		4	9	5	00					
Total current assets						$ 1	7	2	5	00
Property, plant and equipment:										
Printing equipment	$ 5	8	0	0	00					
Less accumulated depreciation	1	2	0	0	00	4	6	0	0	00
Total assets						$ 6	3	2	5	00
Liabilities										
Current liabilities:										
Accounts payable	$	5	0	0	00					
Wages payable			3	0	00					
Total current liabilities						$	5	3	0	00
Owner's Equity										
Timothy Chang, capital							5	7	9	5	00
Total liabilities and owner's equity						$ 6	3	2	5	00

2.

	DATE		DESCRIPTION	POST. REF.	DEBIT						CREDIT						
1			Closing Entries														1
2	20-- Dec.	31	Printing Fees		35	1	0	0	00								2
3			Income Summary								35	1	0	0	00		3
4		.															4
5		31	Income Summary		26	3	0	5	00								5
6			Wages Expense								12	0	0	0	00		6
7			Rent Expense								7	5	0	0	00		7
8			Paper Supplies Expense								3	5	5	0	00		8
9			Telephone Expense									5	5	0	00		9
10			Utilities Expense								1	0	0	0	00		10
11			Insurance Expense									5	0	5	00		11
12			Depr. Expense—Printing Equipment								1	2	0	0	00		12
13																	13
14		31	Income Summary		8	7	9	5	00								14
15			Timothy Chang, Capital								8	7	9	5	00		15
16																	16
17		30	Timothy Chang, Capital		13	0	0	0	00								17
18			Timothy Chang, Drawing								13	0	0	0	00		18
19																	19

GENERAL JOURNAL — PAGE 4

REVIEW QUESTIONS

1. Identify the source of the information needed to prepare the income statement.

2. Describe two approaches to listing the expenses in the income statement.

3. Identify the sources of the information needed to prepare the statement of owner's equity.

4. If additional investments were made during the year, what information in addition to the work sheet would be needed to prepare the statement of owner's equity?

5. Identify the sources of the information needed to prepare the balance sheet.

6. What is a permanent account? On which financial statement are permanent accounts reported?

7. Name three types of temporary accounts.

8. List the four steps for closing the temporary accounts.

9. Describe the net effect of the four closing entries on the balance of the owner's capital account. Where else is this same amount calculated?

10. What is the purpose of the post-closing trial balance?

11. List the ten steps in the accounting cycle.

MANAGING YOUR WRITING

At lunch, two bookkeepers got into a heated discussion about whether closing entries should be made before or after preparing the financial statements. They have come to you to resolve this issue and have agreed to accept your position. Write a memo explaining the purpose of closing entries and whether they should be made before or after preparing the financial statements.

SERIES A EXERCISES

EXERCISE 6A-1 (LO 1) INCOME STATEMENT From the partial work sheet for Case Advising, prepare an income statement.

Case Advising
Work Sheet (Partial)
For Month Ended January 31, 20- -

	ACCOUNT TITLE	INCOME STATEMENT DEBIT	INCOME STATEMENT CREDIT	BALANCE SHEET DEBIT	BALANCE SHEET CREDIT	
1	Cash			1 2 1 2 00		1
2	Accounts Receivable			8 9 6 00		2
3	Supplies			4 8 2 00		3
4	Prepaid Insurance			9 0 0 00		4
5	Office Equipment			3 0 0 0 00		5
6	Accum. Depr.—Office Equipment				1 0 0 00	6
7	Accounts Payable				1 0 0 0 00	7
8	Wages Payable				2 0 0 00	8
9	Bill Case, Capital				4 0 0 0 00	9
10	Bill Case, Drawing			8 0 0 00		10
11	Advising Fees		3 7 9 3 00			11
12	Wages Expense	8 0 0 00				12
13	Advertising Expense	8 0 00				13
14	Rent Expense	5 0 0 00				14
15	Supplies Expense	1 2 0 00				15
16	Telephone Expense	5 8 00				16
17	Electricity Expense	4 4 00				17
18	Insurance Expense	3 0 00				18
19	Gas and Oil Expense	3 8 00				19
20	Depr. Expense—Office Equipment	1 0 0 00				20
21	Miscellaneous Expense	3 3 00				21
22		1 8 0 3 00	3 7 9 3 00	7 2 9 0 00	5 3 0 0 00	22
23	Net Income	1 9 9 0 00			1 9 9 0 00	23
24		3 7 9 3 00	3 7 9 3 00		7 2 9 0 00	24

EXERCISE 6A-2 (LO 1) STATEMENT OF OWNER'S EQUITY From the partial work sheet in Exercise 6A-1, prepare a statement of owner's equity, assuming no additional investment was made by the owner.

EXERCISE 6A-3 (LO 1) BALANCE SHEET From the partial work sheet in Exercise 6A-1, prepare a balance sheet.

EXERCISE 6A-4 (LO 2) CLOSING ENTRIES (NET INCOME) Set up T accounts for Case Advising based on the work sheet in Exercise 6A-1 and the chart of accounts provided below. Enter the existing balance for each account. Prepare closing entries in general journal form. Then post the closing entries to the T accounts.

Chart of Accounts

Assets		Revenues	
101	Cash	401	Advising Fees
122	Accounts Receivable		
141	Supplies	**Expenses**	
145	Prepaid Insurance	511	Wages Expense
181	Office Equipment	512	Advertising Expense
181.1	Accum. Depr.—Office Equip.	521	Rent Expense
		524	Supplies Expense
Liabilities		525	Telephone Expense
202	Accounts Payable	533	Electricity Expense
219	Wages Payable	535	Insurance Expense
		538	Gas and Oil Expense
Owner's Equity		541	Depr. Exp.—Office Equip.
311	Bill Case, Capital	549	Miscellaneous Expense
312	Bill Case, Drawing		
313	Income Summary		

EXERCISE 6A-5 (LO 2) CLOSING ENTRIES (NET LOSS) Using the following T accounts, prepare closing entries in general journal form dated January 31, 20--. Then post the closing entries to the T accounts.

Accum. Depr.—Del. Equip. 185.1		Wages Expense 511		Electricity Expense 533	
	Bal. 100	Bal. 1,800		Bal. 44	

Wages Payable 219		Advertising Expense 512		Insurance Expense 535	
	Bal. 200	Bal. 80		Bal. 30	

Saburo Goto, Capital 311		Rent Expense 521		Gas and Oil Expense 538	
	Bal. 4,000	Bal. 500		Bal. 38	

Saburo Goto, Drawing 312		Supplies Expense 523		Depr. Exp.—Del. Equip. 541	
Bal. 800		Bal. 120		Bal. 100	

Income Summary 313		Telephone Expense 525		Miscellaneous Expense 549	
		Bal. 58		Bal. 33	

Delivery Fees 401	
	Bal. 2,200

SERIES A PROBLEMS

PROBLEM 6A-1 (LO 1) FINANCIAL STATEMENTS The following page shows a work sheet for Monte's Repairs. No additional investments were made by the owner during the month.

REQUIRED
1. Prepare an income statement.

2. Prepare a statement of owner's equity.

3. Prepare a balance sheet.

PROBLEM 6A-2 (LO 1) STATEMENT OF OWNER'S EQUITY The capital account for Autumn Chou, including an additional investment, and a partial work sheet are shown below.

REQUIRED
Prepare a statement of owner's equity.

GENERAL LEDGER

ACCOUNT: Autumn Chou, Capital   ACCOUNT NO. 311

DATE		ITEM	POST REF.	DEBIT	CREDIT	BALANCE DEBIT	BALANCE CREDIT
20-- Jan.	1	Balance	✔				4 8 0 0 00
	18		J1		1 2 0 0 00		6 0 0 0 00

Autumn's Home Designs
Work Sheet (Partial)
For Month Ended January 31, 20 - -

	ACCOUNT TITLE	INCOME STATEMENT DEBIT	INCOME STATEMENT CREDIT	BALANCE SHEET DEBIT	BALANCE SHEET CREDIT	
1	Cash			3 2 0 0 00		1
2	Accounts Receivable			1 6 0 0 00		2
3	Supplies			8 0 0 00		3
4	Prepaid Insurance			9 0 0 00		4
5	Office Equipment			2 5 0 0 00		5
6	Accum. Depr.—Office Equipment				5 0 00	6
7	Accounts Payable				1 9 5 0 00	7
8	Wages Payable				1 8 0 00	8
9	Autumn Chou, Capital				6 0 0 0 00	9
10	Autumn Chou, Drawing			1 0 0 0 00		10
11	Design Fees		4 8 6 6 00			11
12	Wages Expense	1 9 0 0 00				12
13	Advertising Expense	2 1 00				13
14	Rent Expense	6 0 0 00				14
15	Supplies Expense	2 0 0 00				15
16	Telephone Expense	8 5 00				16
17	Electricity Expense	4 8 00				17
18	Insurance Expense	6 0 00				18
19	Gas and Oil Expense	3 2 00				19
20	Depr. Expense—Office Equipment	5 0 00				20
21	Miscellaneous Expense	5 0 00				21
22		3 0 4 6 00	4 8 6 6 00	10 0 0 0 00	8 1 8 0 00	22
23	Net Income	1 8 2 0 00			1 8 2 0 00	23
24		4 8 6 6 00	4 8 6 6 00	10 0 0 0 00	10 0 0 0 00	24

(PROBLEM 6A-1)

Monte's Repairs
Work Sheet
For Month Ended January 31, 20 - -

	ACCOUNT TITLE	TRIAL BALANCE DEBIT	TRIAL BALANCE CREDIT	ADJUSTMENTS DEBIT	ADJUSTMENTS CREDIT	ADJUSTED TRIAL BALANCE DEBIT	ADJUSTED TRIAL BALANCE CREDIT	INCOME STATEMENT DEBIT	INCOME STATEMENT CREDIT	BALANCE SHEET DEBIT	BALANCE SHEET CREDIT	
1	Cash	3 0 8 0 00				3 0 8 0 00				3 0 8 0 00		1
2	Accounts Receivable	1 2 0 0 00				1 2 0 0 00				1 2 0 0 00		2
3	Supplies	8 0 0 00			(a) 2 0 0 00	6 0 0 00				6 0 0 00		3
4	Prepaid Insurance	9 0 0 00			(b) 1 0 0 00	8 0 0 00				8 0 0 00		4
5	Delivery Equipment	3 0 0 0 00				3 0 0 0 00				3 0 0 0 00		5
6	Accum. Depr.—Delivery Equipment				(d) 3 0 00		3 0 00				3 0 00	6
7	Accounts Payable		1 1 0 0 00				1 1 0 0 00				1 1 0 0 00	7
8	Wages Payable				(c) 1 5 0 00		1 5 0 00				1 5 0 00	8
9	Monte Eli, Capital		7 0 0 0 00				7 0 0 0 00				7 0 0 0 00	9
10	Monte Eli, Drawing	1 0 0 0 00				1 0 0 0 00				1 0 0 0 00		10
11	Repair Fees		4 2 3 0 00				4 2 3 0 00		4 2 3 0 00			11
12	Wages Expense	1 6 5 0 00		(c) 1 5 0 00		1 8 0 0 00		1 8 0 0 00				12
13	Advertising Expense	1 7 0 00				1 7 0 00		1 7 0 00				13
14	Rent Expense	4 2 0 00				4 2 0 00		4 2 0 00				14
15	Supplies Expense			(a) 2 0 0 00		2 0 0 00		2 0 0 00				15
16	Telephone Expense	4 9 00				4 9 00		4 9 00				16
17	Insurance Expense			(b) 1 0 0 00		1 0 0 00		1 0 0 00				17
18	Gas and Oil Expense	3 3 00				3 3 00		3 3 00				18
19	Depr. Expense—Delivery Equipment			(d) 3 0 00		3 0 00		3 0 00				19
20	Miscellaneous Expense	2 8 00				2 8 00		2 8 00				20
21		12 3 3 0 00	12 3 3 0 00	4 8 0 00	4 8 0 00	12 5 1 0 00	12 5 1 0 00	2 8 3 0 00	4 2 3 0 00	9 6 8 0 00	8 2 8 0 00	21
22	Net Income							1 4 0 0 00			1 4 0 0 00	22
23								4 2 3 0 00	4 2 3 0 00	9 6 8 0 00	9 6 8 0 00	23
24												24
25												25
26												26
27												27
28												28
29												29
30												30

PROBLEM 6A-3 (LO 2/3) CLOSING ENTRIES AND POST-CLOSING TRIAL BALANCE Refer to the work sheet in Problem 6A-1 for Monte's Repairs. The trial balance amounts (before adjustments) have been entered in the ledger accounts provided in the working papers. If you are not using the working papers that accompany this book, set up ledger accounts and enter these balances as of January 31, 20--. A chart of accounts is provided below.

Monte's Repairs
Chart of Accounts

Assets		Revenues	
101	Cash	401	Repair Fees
122	Accounts Receivable		
141	Supplies	Expenses	
145	Prepaid Insurance	511	Wages Expense
185	Delivery Equipment	512	Advertising Expense
185.1	Accum. Depr.—Delivery Equip.	521	Rent Expense
		523	Supplies Expense
Liabilities		525	Telephone Expense
202	Accounts Payable	535	Insurance Expense
219	Wages Payable	538	Gas and Oil Expense
		541	Depr. Exp.—Delivery Equip.
Owner's Equity		549	Miscellaneous Expense
311	Monte Eli, Capital		
312	Monte Eli, Drawing		
313	Income Summary		

REQUIRED

1. Journalize (page 10) and post the adjusting entries

2. Journalize (page 11) and post the closing entries.

3. Prepare a post-closing trial balance.

SERIES B EXERCISES

EXERCISE 6B-1 (LO 1) INCOME STATEMENT From the partial work sheet for Adams' Shoe Shine on the next page, prepare an income statement.

EXERCISE 6B-2 (LO 1) STATEMENT OF OWNER'S EQUITY From the partial work sheet in Exercise 6B-1, prepare a statement of owner's equity, assuming no additional investment was made by the owner.

EXERCISE 6B-3 (LO 1) BALANCE SHEET From the partial work sheet in Exercise 6B-1, prepare a balance sheet for Adams' Shoe Shine.

(EXERCISE 6B-1)

Adams' Shoe Shine
Work Sheet (Partial)
For Month Ended June 30, 20 - -

	ACCOUNT TITLE	INCOME STATEMENT		BALANCE SHEET		
		DEBIT	CREDIT	DEBIT	CREDIT	
1	Cash			3 2 6 2 00		1
2	Accounts Receivable			1 2 4 4 00		2
3	Supplies			8 0 0 00		3
4	Prepaid Insurance			6 4 0 00		4
5	Office Equipment			2 1 0 0 00		5
6	Accum. Depr.—Office Equipment				1 1 0 00	6
7	Accounts Payable				1 8 5 0 00	7
8	Wages Payable				2 6 0 00	8
9	Mary Adams, Capital				6 0 0 0 00	9
10	Mary Adams, Drawing			2 0 0 0 00		10
11	Service Fees		4 8 1 3 00			11
12	Wages Expense	1 0 8 0 00				12
13	Advertising Expense	3 4 00				13
14	Rent Expense	9 0 0 00				14
15	Supplies Expense	3 2 2 00				15
16	Telephone Expense	1 3 3 00				16
17	Utilities Expense	1 0 2 00				17
18	Insurance Expense	1 2 0 00				18
19	Gas and Oil Expense	8 8 00				19
20	Depr. Expense—Office Equipment	1 1 0 00				20
21	Miscellaneous Expense	9 8 00				21
22		2 9 8 7 00	4 8 1 3 00	10 0 4 6 00	8 2 2 0 00	22
23	Net Income	1 8 2 6 00			1 8 2 6 00	23
24		4 8 1 3 00	4 8 1 3 00	10 0 4 6 00	10 0 4 6 00	24

EXERCISE 6B-4 (LO 2) CLOSING ENTRIES (NET INCOME) Set up T accounts for Adams' Shoe Shine based on the work sheet in Exercise 6B-1 and the chart of accounts provided below. Enter the existing balance for each account. Prepare closing entries in general journal form. Then, post the closing entries to the T accounts.

Chart of Accounts

Assets
101 Cash
122 Accounts Receivable
141 Supplies
145 Prepaid Insurance
181 Office Equipment
181.1 Accum. Depr.—Office Equip.

Liabilities
202 Accounts Payable
219 Wages Payable

Owner's Equity
311 Mary Adams, Capital
312 Mary Adams, Drawing
313 Income Summary

Revenues
401 Service Fees

Expenses
511 Wages Expense
512 Advertising Expense
521 Rent Expense
523 Supplies Expense
525 Telephone Expense
533 Utilities Expense
535 Insurance Expense
538 Gas and Oil Expense
542 Depr. Exp.—Office Equip.
549 Miscellaneous Expense

EXERCISE 6B-5 (LO 2) CLOSING ENTRIES (NET LOSS) Using the following T accounts, prepare closing entries in general journal form dated June 30, 20--. Then post the closing entries to the T accounts.

Accum. Depr.— Office Equip. 181.1		Wages Expense 511		Utilities Expense 533	
	Bal. 110	Bal. 1,080		Bal. 102	

Wages Payable 219		Advertising Expense 512		Insurance Expense 535	
	Bal. 260	Bal. 34		Bal. 120	

Raquel Zapata, Capital 311		Rent Expense 521		Gas and Oil Expense 538	
	Bal. 6,000	Bal. 900		Bal. 88	

Raquel Zapata, Drawing 312		Supplies Expense 523		Depr. Exp.— Office Equip. 541	
Bal. 2,000		Bal. 322		Bal. 110	

Income Summary 313		Telephone Expense 525		Miscellaneous Expense 549	
		Bal. 133		Bal. 98	

Referral Fees 401	
	Bal. 2,813

SERIES B PROBLEMS

PROBLEM 6B-1 (LO 1) FINANCIAL STATEMENTS A work sheet for Juanita's Consulting is shown on the following page. There were no additional investments made by the owner during the month.

REQUIRED   1.   Prepare an income statement.

2.   Prepare a statement of owner's equity.

3.   Prepare a balance sheet.

(PROBLEM 6B-1)

Juanita's Consulting
Work Sheet
For Month Ended June 30, 20--

	Account Title	Trial Balance Debit	Trial Balance Credit	Adjustments Debit	Adjustments Credit	Adjusted Trial Balance Debit	Adjusted Trial Balance Credit	Income Statement Debit	Income Statement Credit	Balance Sheet Debit	Balance Sheet Credit	
1	Cash	5 2 8 5 00				5 2 8 5 00				5 2 8 5 00		1
2	Accounts Receivable	1 0 7 5 00				1 0 7 5 00				1 0 7 5 00		2
3	Supplies	7 5 0 00			(a) 2 5 0 00	5 0 0 00				5 0 0 00		3
4	Prepaid Insurance	5 0 0 00			(b) 1 0 0 00	4 0 0 00				4 0 0 00		4
5	Office Equipment	2 2 0 0 00				2 2 0 0 00				2 2 0 0 00		5
6	Accum. Depr.—Office Equipment				(d) 1 1 0 00		1 1 0 00				1 1 0 00	6
7	Accounts Payable		1 5 0 0 00				1 5 0 0 00				1 5 0 0 00	7
8	Wages Payable				(c) 2 0 0 00		2 0 0 00				2 0 0 00	8
9	Juanita Alvarez, Capital		7 0 0 0 00				7 0 0 0 00				7 0 0 0 00	9
10	Juanita Alvarez, Drawing	8 0 0 00				8 0 0 00				8 0 0 00		10
11	Consulting Fees		4 2 0 4 00				4 2 0 4 00		4 2 0 4 00			11
12	Wages Expense	1 4 0 0 00		(c) 2 0 0 00		1 6 0 0 00		1 6 0 0 00				12
13	Advertising Expense	6 0 00				6 0 00		6 0 00				13
14	Rent Expense	5 0 0 00				5 0 0 00		5 0 0 00				14
15	Supplies Expense			(a) 2 5 0 00		2 5 0 00		2 5 0 00				15
16	Telephone Expense	4 6 00				4 6 00		4 6 00				16
17	Electricity Expense	3 9 00				3 9 00		3 9 00				17
18	Insurance Expense			(b) 1 0 0 00		1 0 0 00		1 0 0 00				18
19	Gas and Oil Expense	2 8 00				2 8 00		2 8 00				19
20	Depr. Expense—Office Equipment			(d) 1 1 0 00		1 1 0 00		1 1 0 00				20
21	Miscellaneous Expense	2 1 00				2 1 00		2 1 00				21
22		12 7 0 4 00	12 7 0 4 00	6 6 0 00	6 6 0 00	13 0 1 4 00	13 0 1 4 00	2 7 5 4 00	4 2 0 4 00	10 2 6 0 00	8 8 1 0 00	22
23	Net Income							1 4 5 0 00			1 4 5 0 00	23
24								4 2 0 4 00	4 2 0 4 00	10 2 6 0 00	10 2 6 0 00	24
25												25
26												26
27												27
28												28
29												29
30												30

PROBLEM 6B-2 (LO 1) STATEMENT OF OWNER'S EQUITY The capital account for Minta's Editorial Services, including an additional investment, and a partial work sheet are shown below.

GENERAL LEDGER

ACCOUNT: Minta Berry, Capital   ACCOUNT NO. 311

DATE		ITEM	POST REF.	DEBIT	CREDIT	BALANCE DEBIT	BALANCE CREDIT
20-- Jan.	1	Balance	✔				3 6 0 0 00
	22		J1		2 9 0 0 00		6 5 0 0 00

Minta's Editorial Services
Work Sheet (Partial)
For Month Ended January 31, 20 - -

	ACCOUNT TITLE	INCOME STATEMENT DEBIT	INCOME STATEMENT CREDIT	BALANCE SHEET DEBIT	BALANCE SHEET CREDIT	
1	Cash			3 8 0 0 00		1
2	Accounts Receivable			2 2 0 0 00		2
3	Supplies			1 0 0 0 00		3
4	Prepaid Insurance			9 5 0 00		4
5	Computer Equipment			4 5 0 0 00		5
6	Accum. Depr.—Computer Equipment				2 2 5 00	6
7	Accounts Payable				2 1 0 0 00	7
8	Wages Payable				1 5 0 00	8
9	Minta Berry, Capital				6 5 0 0 00	9
10	Minta Berry, Drawing			1 7 0 0 00		10
11	Editing Fees		7 0 1 2 00			11
12	Wages Expense	6 0 0 00				12
13	Advertising Expense	4 9 00				13
14	Rent Expense	4 5 0 00				14
15	Supplies Expense	2 8 8 00				15
16	Telephone Expense	4 4 00				16
17	Utilities Expense	3 8 00				17
18	Insurance Expense	1 2 5 00				18
19	Depr. Expense—Computer Equipment	2 2 5 00				19
20	Miscellaneous Expense	1 8 00				20
21		1 8 3 7 00	7 0 1 2 00	14 1 5 0 00	8 9 7 5 00	21
22	Net Income	5 1 7 5 00			5 1 7 5 00	22
23		7 0 1 2 00	7 0 1 2 00	14 1 5 0 00	14 1 5 0 00	23

REQUIRED   Prepare a statement of owner's equity.

PROBLEM 6B-3 (LO 2/3) CLOSING ENTRIES AND POST-CLOSING TRIAL BALANCE Refer to the work sheet for Juanita's Consulting in Problem 6B-1. The trial balance amounts (before adjustments) have been entered in the ledger accounts provided in the working papers. If you are not using the working papers that accompany this book, set up ledger accounts and enter these balances as of June 30, 20--. A chart of accounts is provided below.

Juanita's Consulting
Chart of Accounts

Assets		Revenues	
101	Cash	401	Consulting Fees
122	Accounts Receivable		
141	Supplies		Expenses
145	Prepaid Insurance	511	Wages Expense
181	Office Equipment	512	Advertising Expense
181.1	Accum. Depr.—Office Equip.	521	Rent Expense
		523	Supplies Expense
Liabilities		525	Telephone Expense
202	Accounts Payable	533	Electricity Expense
219	Wages Payable	535	Insurance Expense
		538	Gas and Oil Expense
Owner's Equity		541	Depr. Exp.—Office Equip.
311	Juanita Alvarez, Capital	549	Miscellaneous Expense
312	Juanita Alvarez, Drawing		
313	Income Summary		

REQUIRED

1. Journalize (page 10) and post the adjusting entries.

2. Journalize (page 11) and post the closing entries.

3. Prepare a post-closing trial balance.

MASTERY PROBLEM

Elizabeth Soltis owns and operates Aunt Ibby's Styling Salon. A year-end work sheet is provided on the next page. Using this information, prepare financial statements and closing entries. Soltis made no additional investments during the year.

Aunt Ibby's Styling Salon
Work Sheet
For Year Ended December 31, 20- -

	ACCOUNT TITLE	TRIAL BALANCE DEBIT	TRIAL BALANCE CREDIT	ADJUSTMENTS DEBIT	ADJUSTMENTS CREDIT	ADJUSTED TRIAL BALANCE DEBIT	ADJUSTED TRIAL BALANCE CREDIT	INCOME STATEMENT DEBIT	INCOME STATEMENT CREDIT	BALANCE SHEET DEBIT	BALANCE SHEET CREDIT	
1	Cash	9 4 0 0 00				9 4 0 0 00				9 4 0 0 00		1
2	Styling Supplies	1 5 0 0 00			(a) 1 4 5 0 00	5 0 00				5 0 00		2
3	Prepaid Insurance	8 0 0 00			(b) 6 5 0 00	1 5 0 00				1 5 0 00		3
4	Salon Equipment	4 5 0 0 00				4 5 0 0 00				4 5 0 0 00		4
5	Accum. Depr.—Salon Equipment				(d) 9 0 0 00		9 0 0 00				9 0 0 00	5
6	Accounts Payable		2 2 5 00				2 2 5 00				2 2 5 00	6
7	Wages Payable				(c) 4 0 00		4 0 00				4 0 00	7
8	Elizabeth Soltis, Capital		2 7 6 5 00				2 7 6 5 00				2 7 6 5 00	8
9	Elizabeth Soltis, Drawing	12 0 0 0 00				12 0 0 0 00				12 0 0 0 00		9
10	Styling Fees		32 0 0 0 00				32 0 0 0 00		32 0 0 0 00			10
11	Wages Expense	8 0 0 0 00		(c) 4 0 00		8 0 4 0 00		8 0 4 0 00				11
12	Rent Expense	6 0 0 0 00				6 0 0 0 00		6 0 0 0 00				12
13	Styling Supplies Expense			(a) 1 4 5 0 00		1 4 5 0 00		1 4 5 0 00				13
14	Telephone Expense	4 5 0 00				4 5 0 00		4 5 0 00				14
15	Utilities Expense	8 0 0 00				8 0 0 00		8 0 0 00				15
16	Insurance Expense			(b) 6 5 0 00		6 5 0 00		6 5 0 00				16
17	Depr. Expense—Salon Equipment			(d) 9 0 0 00		9 0 0 00		9 0 0 00				17
18		34 9 9 0 00	34 9 9 0 00	3 0 4 0 00	3 0 4 0 00	35 9 3 0 00	35 9 3 0 00	18 2 9 0 00	32 0 0 0 00	17 6 4 0 00	3 9 3 0 00	18
19	Net Income							13 7 1 0 00			13 7 1 0 00	19
20								32 0 0 0 00	32 0 0 0 00	17 6 4 0 00	17 6 4 0 00	20
21												21
22												22
23												23
24												24
25												25
26												26
27												27
28												28
29												29
30												30

Self-Study Test Questions

True/False

1. Expenses are listed on the income statement as they appear in the chart of accounts or in descending order (by dollar amount). _____

2. Additional investments of capital during the month are not reported on the statement of owner's equity. _____

3. The income statement cannot be prepared using the work sheet alone. _____

4. A classified balance sheet groups similar items together such as current assets. _____

5. Temporary accounts are closed at the end of each accounting period. _____

Multiple Choice

1. Which of these types of accounts is considered a "permanent" account? _____

   (a) Revenue   (c) Drawing
   (b) Asset   (d) Expense

2. Which of these accounts is considered a "temporary" account? _____

   (a) Cash   (c) J. Jones, Capital
   (b) Accounts Payable   (d) J. Jones, Drawing

3. Which of these is the first step in the closing process? _____

   (a) Close revenue account(s).
   (b) Close expense accounts.
   (c) Close the income summary account.
   (d) Close the drawing account.

4. The _____ is prepared after closing entries are posted to prove the equality of debit and credit balances. _____

   (a) balance sheet   (c) post-closing trial balance
   (b) income statement   (d) statement of owner's equity

5. Steps that begin with analyzing source documents and conclude with the post-closing trial balance are called the _____ . _____

   (a) closing process   (c) adjusting entries
   (b) accounting cycle   (d) journalizing transactions

The answers to the Self-Study Test Questions are at the end of the text.

CHAPTER **6** APPENDIX

Statement of Cash Flows

LEARNING OBJECTIVES:
Careful study of this appendix should enable you to:

LO 1 Classify business transactions as operating, investing, or financing.

LO 2 Prepare a statement of cash flows by analyzing and categorizing a series of business transactions.

Thus far, we have discussed three financial statements: the income statement, the statement of owner's equity, and the balance sheet. A fourth statement, the statement of cash flows, is also very important. It explains what the business did to generate cash and how the cash was used. This is done by categorizing all cash transactions into three types of activities: operating, investing, and financing.

TYPES OF BUSINESS ACTIVITIES

LO1 Classify business transactions as operating, investing, or financing.

Cash flows from **operating activities** are related to the revenues and expenses reported on the income statement. Examples include cash received for services performed and the payment of cash for expenses.

 LEARNING KEY: There are three types of business activities: operating, investing, and financing.

Investing activities are those transactions involving the purchase and sale of long-term assets, lending money, and collecting the principal on the related loans.

Financing activities are those transactions dealing with the exchange of cash between the business and its owners and creditors. Examples include cash received from the owner to finance the operations and cash paid to the owner as withdrawals. Financing activities also include borrowing cash and repaying the loan principal.

LEARNING KEY: Lending money to another entity is an outflow of cash from investing activities. The collection of the principal when the loan is due is an inflow of cash from investing activities. Borrowing cash is an inflow from financing activities. Repayment of the loan principal is an outflow from financing activities.

Figure 6A-1 provides a review of the transactions for Jessie Jane's Campus Delivery for the month of June. The transactions are classified as operating, investing, or financing, and an explanation for the classification is provided.

213

FIGURE 6A-1 Summary of Transactions for Jessie Jane's Campus Delivery

SUMMARY OF TRANSACTIONS FOR JESSIE JANE'S CAMPUS DELIVERY	TYPE OF TRANSACTION	EXPLANATION
(a) Jessica Jane invested cash in her business, $2,000.	Financing	Cash received from the owner is an inflow from financing activities. Don't be fooled by the word "invested." From the company's point of view, this is a way to *finance* the business.
(b) Purchased delivery equipment for cash, $1,200.	Investing	Purchases of long-term assets are investments.
(c) Purchased delivery equipment on account from Big Red Scooters, $900. (Note: Big Red has loaned Jane $900.)	No cash involved	This transaction will not affect the main sections of the statement of cash flows. (This is a noncash investing and financing activity.)
(d) Paid first installment to Big Red Scooters, $300. (See transaction (c).)	Financing	Repayments of loans are financing activities.
(e) Received cash for delivery services rendered, $500.	Operating	Cash received as a result of providing services is classified as an operating activity.
(f) Paid cash for June office rent, $200.	Operating	Cash payments for expenses are classified as operating activities.
(g) Paid telephone bill, $50.	Operating	Cash payments for expenses are classified as operating activities.
(h) Made deliveries on account for a total of $600: $400 for the Accounting Department and $200 for the School of Music.	No cash involved	This transaction will not affect the statement of cash flows.
(i) Purchased supplies for cash, $80.	Operating	Cash payments for expenses are classified as operating activities. Most of these supplies were used up. Those that remain will be used in the near future. These are not long-term assets and, thus, do not qualify as investments.
(j) Paid cash for an eight-month liability insurance policy, $200. Coverage began on June 1.	Operating	Cash payments for expenses are classified as operating activities. Prepaid Insurance is not considered a long-term asset and, thus, does not qualify as an investment.
(k) Received $570 in cash for services performed in transaction (h): $400 from the Accounting Department and $170 from the School of Music.	Operating	Cash received as a result of providing services is classified as an operating activity.
(l) Purchased a third scooter from Big Red Scooters, $1,500. A down payment of $300 was made with the remaining payments expected over the next four months.	Investing	Purchases of long-term assets are investments. Only the $300 cash paid will be reported on the statement of cash flows.
(m) Paid wages of part-time employees, $650.	Operating	Cash payments for expenses are classified as operating activities.
(n) Earned delivery fees for the remainder of the month amounting to $1,050: $430 in cash and $620 on account. Deliveries on account: $250 for the Accounting Department and $370 for the Athletic Ticket Office.	Operating	Cash received ($430) as a result of providing services is classified as an operating activity.
(o) Jane withdrew cash for personal use, $150.	Financing	Cash payments to owners are classified as a financing activity.

PREPARING THE STATEMENT OF CASH FLOWS

LO2   Prepare a statement of cash flows by analyzing and categorizing a series of business transactions.

The classifications of the cash transactions for Jessie Jane's Campus Delivery are summarized in the expanded cash T account shown in Figure 6A-2. Using this information, we can prepare a statement of cash flows. As shown in Figure 6A-3 on page 214, the heading is similar to that used for the income statement. Since the statement of cash flows reports on the flow of cash for a period of time, the statement is dated for the month ended June 30, 20--.

FIGURE 6A-2 Cash T Account for Jessie Jane's Campus Delivery with Classifications of Cash Transactions

CASH

Event	Classification	Amount	Amount	Classification	Event
(a) Investment by Jessie.	Financing	2,000	1,200	Investing	Purchased delivery equipment. (b)
(e) Cash received for services.	Operating	500	300	Financing	Made payment on loan. (d)
(k) Cash received for services.	Operating	570	200	Operating	Paid office rent. (f)
(n) Cash received for services.	Operating	430	50	Operating	Paid telephone bill. (g)
		3,500	80	Operating	Purchased supplies. (i)
			200	Operating	Paid for insurance. (j)
			300	Investing	Purchased delivery equipment. (l)
			650	Operating	Paid wages. (m)
			150	Financing	Withdrawal by owner. (o)
			3,130		
	Bal.	370			

FIGURE 6A-3 Statement of Cash Flows for Jessie Jane's Campus Delivery

Jessie Jane's Campus Delivery Statement of Cash Flows For Month Ended June 30, 20 - -										
Cash flows from operating activities:										
Cash received from customers for delivery services							$1	5	0	0	00
Cash paid for wages	$	(6	5	0	00)					
Cash paid for rent		(2	0	0	00)					
Cash paid for supplies			(8	0	00)					
Cash paid for telephone			(5	0	00)					
Cash paid for insurance		(2	0	0	00)					
Total cash paid for operations						(1	1	8	0	00)
Net cash provided by operating activities						$	3	2	0	00
Cash flows from investing activities:										
Cash paid for delivery equipment	$(1	5	0	0	00)					
Net cash used for investing activities						(1	5	0	0	00)
Cash flows from financing activities:										
Cash investment by owner	$2	0	0	0	00					
Cash withdrawal by owner		(1	5	0	00)					
Payment made on loan		(3	0	0	00)					
Net cash provided by financing activities						1	5	5	0	00
Net increase in cash						$	3	7	0	00

The main body of the statement is arranged in three sections: operating, investing, and financing activities. First, cash received from customers is listed under operating activities. Then, cash payments for operating activities are listed and totaled. The net amount is reported as net cash provided by operating activities. Since this is the main purpose of the business, it is important to be able to generate positive cash flows from operating activities.

The next two sections list the inflows and outflows from investing and financing activities. Debits to the cash account are inflows and credits are outflows. Note that there was an outflow, or net use of cash, from investing activities resulting from the purchase of the motor scooters. In addition, cash was provided from financing activities because Jessie's initial investment more than covered her withdrawal and the payment on the loan. These investing and financing activities are typical for a new business.

The sum of the inflows and outflows from operating, investing, and financing activities equals the net increase (or decrease) in the cash account during the period. Since this is a new business, the cash account had a beginning balance of zero. The ending balance is $370. This agrees with the net increase in cash of $370 reported on the statement of cash flows.

 LEARNING KEY: To prove the accuracy of the statement of cash flows, compare the net increase or decrease reported on the statement with the change in the balance of the cash account.

This appendix introduces you to the purpose and format of the statement of cash flows. Here, we classified entries made to the cash account as operating, investing, or financing. These classifications were then used to prepare the statement. Businesses have thousands of entries to the cash account. Thus, this approach to preparing the statement is not really practical. Other approaches to preparing the statement will be discussed in Chapter 24. However, the purpose and format of the statements are the same.

Learning Objectives	Key Points to Remember
1 **Classify business transactions as operating, investing, or financing.**	The purpose of the statement of cash flows is to report what the firm did to generate cash and how the cash was used. Business transactions are classified as operating, investing, and financing activities. *Operating activities* are those transactions related to the revenues and expenses reported on the income statement. *Investing activities* are those transactions involving the purchase and sale of long-term assets, lending money, and collecting the principal on the related loans. *Financing activities* are those transactions dealing with the exchange of cash between the business and its owners and creditors.
2 **Prepare a statement of cash flows by analyzing and categorizing a series of business transactions.**	The main body of the statement of cash flows consists of three sections: operating, investing, and financing activities.

Name of Business Statement of Cash Flows For Period Ended Date											
Cash flows from operating activities:											
Cash received from customers							$x	x	x	x	xx
List cash paid for various expenses	$	(x	x	x	xx)							
Total cash paid for operations							(x	x	x	x	xx)
Net cash provided by (used for) operating activities							$	x	x	x	xx
Cash flows from investing activities:											
List cash received from the sale of long-term assets and other investing activities	$x	x	x	x	xx							
List cash paid for the purchase of long-term assets and other investing activities	(x	x	x	x	xx)							
Net cash provided by (used for) investing activities							x	x	x	x	xx
Cash flows from financing activities:											
List cash received from owners and creditors	$x	x	x	x	xx							
List cash paid to owners and creditors		(x	x	x	xx)							
Net cash provided by (used for) financing activities							x	x	x	x	xx
Net increase (decrease) in cash							$	x	x	x	xx

KEY TERMS

financing activities, (211)   Those transactions dealing with the exchange of cash between the business and its owners and creditors.

investing activities, (211)   Those transactions involving the purchase and sale of long-term assets, lending money, and collecting the principal on the related loans.

operating activities, (211)   Those transactions related to the revenues and expenses reported on the income statement.

REVIEW QUESTIONS

1. Explain the purpose of the statement of cash flows.

2. Define and provide examples of the three types of business activities.

SERIES A EXERCISE

EXERCISE 6ApxA-1 (LO 1) CLASSIFYING BUSINESS TRANSACTIONS Dolores Lopez opened a new consulting business. The following transactions occurred during January of the current year. Classify each transaction as an operating, investing, or financing activity.

(a) Invested cash in the business, $10,000.

(b) Paid office rent, $500.

(c) Purchased office equipment. Paid $1,500 cash and agreed to pay the balance of $2,000 in four monthly installments.

(d) Received cash for services rendered, $900.

(e) Paid telephone bill, $65.

(f) Made payment on loan in transaction (c), $500.

(g) Paid wages to part-time employee, $500.

(h) Received cash for services rendered, $800.

(i) Paid electricity bill, $85

(j) Withdrew cash for personal use, $100.

(k) Paid wages to part-time employee, $500.

SERIES A PROBLEM

PROBLEM 6ApxA-1 (LO 2) PREPARING A STATEMENT OF CASH FLOWS Prepare a statement of cash flows based on the transactions reported in Exercise 6ApxA-1.

SERIES B EXERCISE

EXERCISE 6ApxB-1 (LO 1) CLASSIFYING BUSINESS TRANSACTIONS Bob Jacobs opened an advertising agency. The following transactions occurred during January of the current year. Classify each transaction as an operating, investing, or financing activity.

(a) Invested cash in the business, $5,000.

(b) Purchased office equipment. Paid $2,500 cash and agreed to pay the balance of $2,000 in four monthly installments.

(c) Paid office rent, $400.

(d) Received cash for services rendered, $700.

(e) Paid telephone bill, $95.

(f) Received cash for services rendered, $600.

(g) Made payment on loan in transaction (b), $500.

(h) Paid wages to part-time employee, $800.

(i) Paid electricity bill, $100.

(j) Withdrew cash for personal use, $500.

(k) Paid wages to part-time employee, $600.

SERIES B PROBLEM

PROBLEM 6ApxB-1 (LO 2) PREPARING A STATEMENT OF CASH FLOWS Prepare a statement of cash flows based on the transactions reported in Exercise 6ApxB-1.

COMPREHENSIVE PROBLEM 1: THE ACCOUNTING CYCLE

Bob Night opened "The General's Favorite Fishing Hole." The fishing camp is open from April through September and attracts many famous college basketball coaches during the off-season. Guests typically register for one week, arriving on Sunday afternoon and returning home the following Saturday afternoon. The registration fee includes room and board, the use of fishing boats, and professional instruction in fishing techniques. The chart of accounts for the camping operations is provided below.

The General's Favorite Fishing Hole
Chart of Accounts

Assets		Revenues	
101	Cash	401	Registration Fees
142	Office Supplies		
144	Food Supplies	Expenses	
145	Prepaid Insurance	511	Wages Expense
181	Fishing Boats	521	Rent Expense
181.1	Accum. Depr.—Fishing Boats	523	Office Supplies Expense
		524	Food Supplies Expense
Liabilities		525	Telephone Expense
202	Accounts Payable	533	Utilities Expense
219	Wages Payable	535	Insurance Expense
		536	Postage Expense
		542	Depr. Exp.—Fishing Boats
Owner's Equity			
311	Bob Night, Capital		
312	Bob Night, Drawing		
313	Income Summary		

The following transactions took place during April 20--.

Apr. 1 Night invested cash in business, $90,000.

1 Paid insurance premium for camping season, $9,000.

2 Paid rent for lodge and campgrounds for the month of April, $40,000.

2 Deposited registration fees, $35,000.

2 Purchased ten fishing boats on account for $60,000. The boats have estimated useful lives of five years, at which time they will be donated to a local day camp. Arrangements were made to pay for the boats in July.

3 Purchased food supplies from Acme Super Market on account, $7,000.

5 Purchased office supplies from Gordon Office Supplies on account, $500.

7 Deposited registration fees, $38,600.

10 Purchased food supplies from Acme Super Market on account, $8,200.

10 Paid wages to fishing guides, $10,000.

14 Deposited registration fees, $30,500.

16 Purchased food supplies from Acme Super Market on account, $9,000.

17 Paid wages to fishing guides, $10,000.

18	Paid postage, $150.
21	Deposited registration fees, $35,600.
24	Purchased food supplies from Acme Super Market on account, $8,500.
24	Paid wages to fishing guides, $10,000.
28	Deposited registration fees, $32,000.
29	Paid wages to fishing guides, $10,000.
30	Purchased food supplies from Acme Super Market on account, $6,000.
30	Paid Acme Super Market on account, $32,700.
30	Paid utilities bill, $2,000.
30	Paid telephone bill, $1,200.
30	Bob Night withdrew cash for personal use, $6,000.

Adjustment information for the end of April is provided below.

(a) Office supplies remaining on hand, $100.

(b) Food supplies remaining on hand, $8,000.

(c) Insurance expired during the month of April, $1,500.

(d) Depreciation on the fishing boats for the month of April, $1,000.

(e) Wages earned, but not yet paid, at the end of April, $500.

REQUIRED

1. Enter the above transactions in a general journal. Enter transactions from April 1–5 on page 1, April 7–18 on page 2, April 21–29 and the first two entries for April 30 on page 3, and the remaining entries for April 30 on page 4.

2. Post the entries to the general ledger. (If you are not using the working papers that accompany this text, you will need to enter the account titles and account numbers in the general ledger accounts.)

3. Prepare a trial balance on a work sheet.

4. Complete the work sheet.

5. Prepare the income statement.

6. Prepare the statement of owner's equity.

7. Prepare the balance sheet.

8. Journalize the adjusting entries (page 5).

9. Post the adjusting entries to the general ledger.

10. Journalize the closing entries (pages 5 and 6).

11. Post the closing entries to the general ledger.

12. Prepare a post-closing trial balance.

P A R T 2

Specialized Accounting Procedures for Service Businesses and <u>Proprietorships</u>

7

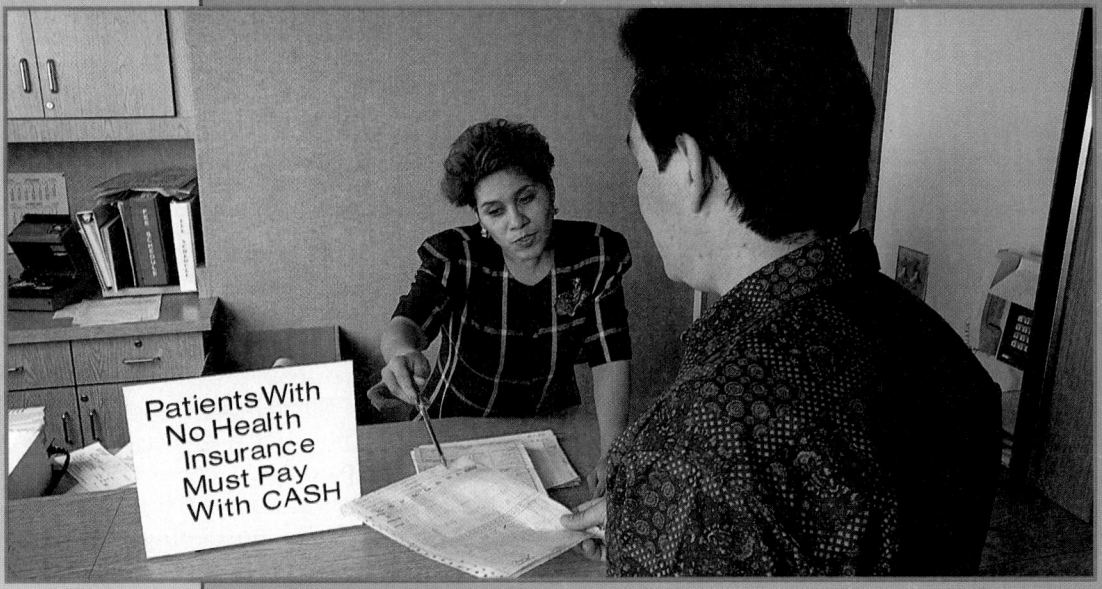

Accounting for a Professional Service Business: The Combination Journal

LEARNING OBJECTIVES:
Careful study of this chapter should enable you to:

LO 1 Explain the cash, modified cash, and accrual bases of accounting.

LO 2 Describe special records for a professional service business using the modified cash basis.

LO 3 Describe and use a combination journal to record transactions of a professional service business.

LO 4 Post from the combination journal to the general ledger.

LO 5 Prepare a work sheet, financial statements, and adjusting and closing entries for a professional service business.

Jessie's friend has just been hired to work in a doctor's office as a bookkeeper. She has been observing general office procedures and is a bit confused about when to record revenues. Some patients pay cash as they leave the office. Others submit forms that are filed with insurance companies. Sometimes the insurance companies pay the entire amount. Other times, only a portion of the bill is paid, with the balance being billed to the patient. Generally, the patients pay the balance, but occasionally they don't. Finally, there are some patients who never seem to pay. This all seems very confusing. When should she recognize revenues?

The accrual basis of accounting offers the best matching of revenues and expenses. Throughout the first six chapters, the accrual basis was demonstrated for a service business. For simplicity, we used a general journal as the book of original entry. However, not all businesses use the accrual basis of accounting and many use manual or computerized specialized journals. In this chapter we explain the cash basis and modified cash basis of accounting. In addition, we demonstrate the advantages of using a combination journal as the book of original entry.

ACCRUAL BASIS VERSUS CASH BASIS

LO 1 Explain the cash, modified cash, and accrual bases of accounting.

Under the **accrual basis of accounting**, revenues are recorded when earned. Revenues are considered earned when a service is provided or a product sold, regardless of whether cash is received. If cash is not received, a receivable is set up. The accrual basis also assumes that expenses are recorded when incurred. Expenses are incurred when a service is received or an asset consumed, regardless of when cash is paid. If cash is not paid when a service is received, a payable is set up. When assets are consumed, prepaid assets are decreased or long-term assets are depreciated. Since the accrual basis accounts for long-term assets, prepaid assets, receivables, and payables, it is the most comprehensive system and best method of measuring income for the vast majority of businesses.

LEARNING KEY:

Accrual Basis

Accounting for:		
Revenues and Expenses	**Assets and Liabilities**	
Record revenue when earned.	Accounts receivable:	Yes
Record expenses when incurred.	Accounts payable:	Yes
	Prepaid assets:	Yes
	Long-term assets:	Yes

Under the **cash basis of accounting**, revenues are recorded when cash is received and expenses are recorded when cash is paid. This is appropriate when there are few receivables or payables or when the collection of the receivables is uncertain. As shown in Figure 7-1, the cash and accrual bases can result in very different measures of net income if a business has significant amounts of receivables, payables, and assets.

LEARNING KEY:

Cash Basis

Accounting for:		
Revenues and Expenses	**Assets and Liabilities**	
Record revenue when cash is received.	Accounts receivable:	No
Record expenses when cash is paid.	Accounts payable:	No
	Prepaid assets:	No
	Long-term assets:	No

FIGURE 7-1 Cash Versus Accrual Accounting

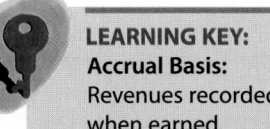

ENTRIES MADE FOR EXPENSES AND REVENUES

| | | Method of Accounting | | | |
| | | Accrual Basis | | Cash Basis | |
Transaction		Expense	Revenue	Expense	Revenue
(a)	Provided services on account, $600.		$600		
(b)	Paid wages, $300.	$300		$300	
(c)	Received cash for services performed on account last month, $200.				$200
(d)	Received cleaning bill for month, $250.	250			
(e)	Paid on account for last month's advertising, $100.			100	
(f)	Purchase of supplies, $50.			50	
(g)	Supplies used during month, $40.	40			
		$590	$600	$450	$200
Revenue			$600		$200
Expense			590		450
Net Income (Loss)			$ 10		($250)
Revenues are recognized when:			earned		cash is received
Expenses are recognized when:			incurred		cash is paid

A third method of accounting combines aspects of the cash and accrual methods. With the **modified cash basis**, a business uses the cash basis for recording revenues and most expenses. Exceptions are made when cash is paid for assets with useful lives greater than one accounting period. For example, under a strict cash basis, if cash is paid for equipment, buildings, supplies, or insurance, the amount is immediately recorded as an expense. This approach would cause major distortions when measuring net income. Under the modified cash basis, cash payments like these are recorded as assets, and adjustments are made each period as under the accrual basis. Liabilities associated with the acquisition of these assets are also recognized.

Although similar to the accrual basis, the modified cash basis does not account for receivables or for payables for services received. Thus, the modified cash basis is a combination of the cash and accrual methods of accounting. The differences and similarities among the cash, modified cash, and accrual methods of accounting are demonstrated in Figure 7-2.

FIGURE 7-2 Comparison of Cash, Modified Cash, and Accrual Methods

ENTRIES MADE UNDER EACH ACCOUNTING METHOD

Event	Cash	Modified Cash	Accrual
Revenues: Perform services for cash	Cash Professional Fees	Cash Professional Fees	Cash Professional Fees
Perform services on account	No entry	No entry	Accounts Receivable Professional Fees
Expenses: Pay cash for operating expenses: wages, advertising, rent, telephone, etc.	Expense Cash	Expense Cash	Expense Cash
Pay cash for prepaid items: insurance, supplies, etc.	Expense Cash	Prepaid Asset Cash	Prepaid Asset Cash
Pay cash for property, plant, and equipment (PP&E)	Expense Cash	PP&E Asset Cash	PP&E Asset Cash
Receive bill for services received	No entry	No entry	Expense Accounts Payable
End-of-period adjustments: Wages earned by employees but not paid	No entry	No entry	Wages Expense Wages Payable
Prepaid items used	No entry	Expense Prepaid Asset	Expense Prepaid Asset
Depreciation on property, plant, and equipment	No entry	Depreciation Expense Accumulated Depreciation	Depreciation Expense Accumulated Depreciation
Other: Purchase of assets on account	No entry	Asset Accounts Payable	Asset Accounts Payable
Payments for assets purchased on account	Expense Cash	Accounts Payable Cash	Accounts Payable Cash

LEARNING KEY: Shaded area shows that sometimes the modified cash basis is the same as the cash basis and sometimes it is the same as the accrual basis. For some transactions, all methods are the same.

If all businesses were the same, only one method of accounting would be needed. However, businesses vary in their need for major assets like buildings and equipment, the amount of customer receivables, and payables to suppliers. For example, if a business were rather small with no major assets, receivables, or payables, it would be simpler to use the cash basis of accounting. In addition, under these circumstances, the difference in net income under the accrual and cash bases of accounting would be small. Most individuals fit this description and use the cash basis on their tax returns.

Businesses with buildings and equipment, but few receivables and payables, might use the modified cash basis. Again, the accounting would be a little simpler and differences between net income computed under the modified cash and accrual bases would be small.

A BROADER VIEW

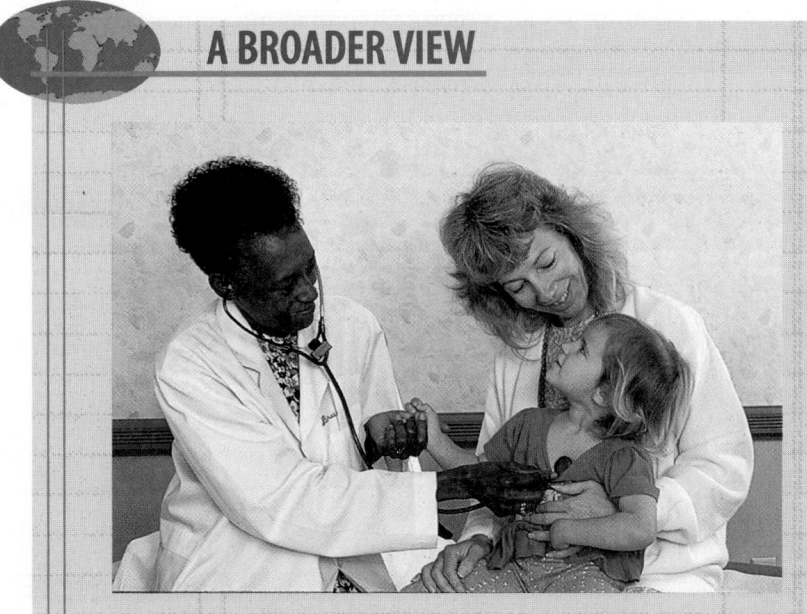

THE MODIFIED CASH BASIS

Many professional and small service businesses use the modified cash basis of accounting. Under this method, revenues are recognized when cash is received. Accounts receivable are not entered into the accounting system. Doctors do this because they are somewhat uncertain about the actual amount of revenue earned at the time they have completed a visit with a patient. Insurance companies pay different amounts for various procedures. Sometimes this is the same as the amount charged by the doctor, but not always. Some doctors simply accept what the insurance company pays. Others bill the patient for the difference. And, of course, not all patients pay their bills. Thus, it is better to wait until the cash is received to recognize revenue.

Finally, businesses with buildings and equipment, and receivables and payables, should use the accrual basis of accounting to achieve the best matching of revenues and expenses. The following sections will focus primarily on the modified cash basis of accounting.

ACCOUNTING FOR A PROFESSIONAL SERVICE BUSINESS

LO 2 Describe special records for a professional service business using the modified cash basis.

Many small professional service businesses use the modified cash basis of accounting. Professional service businesses include law, dentistry, medicine, optometry, architecture, engineering, and accounting.

FIGURE 7-3 Appointment Record

Date: 6/4/--

Time	Patient	Medical Service	Fees	Payments
8:00	Dennis Rogan	OV	40.00	40.00
15				
30	Rick Cosier	OV;EKG	120.00	
45				
9:00	George Hettenhouse	OV;MISC	50.00	
15				
30	Sam Frumer	OV;LAB	75.00	75.00
45				
10:00	Dan Dalton	OV	40.00	
15				
30	Louis Biagioni	OV;X	65.00	
45				
11:00	Mike Groomer	X	40.00	40.00
15				
30				
45				
12:00				
15				
30				
45				
1:00	Mike Tiller	OV;LAB	80.00	
15				
30	Peggy Hite	OV;PHYS	190.00	
45				
2:00				
15				
30				
45				
3:00	Vivian Winston	OV;MISC	40.00	
15				
30				
45				
4:00	Hank Davis	OV	40.00	40.00
15				
30				
45				
	Bill Sharp			150.00
	Phil Jones			80.00
	Diane Gallagher			200.00
			780.00	625.00

Look again at Figure 7-2. There are two primary differences between the accrual basis and the modified cash basis. First, under the modified cash basis, no adjusting entries are made for accrued wages expense. Second, under the modified cash basis, revenues from services performed on account are not recorded until cash is received. Thus, no accounts receivable are entered in the accounting system. This means that other records must be maintained to keep track of amounts owed by clients and patients. These records generally include an appointment record and a client or patient ledger record. These records are illustrated in Figures 7-3 and 7-4.

The appointment record is used to schedule appointments and to maintain a record of the services rendered, fees charged, and payments received. It also serves as a source document for the patient ledger records, which show the amount owed by each client or patient for services performed. A copy of this record may also be used for billing purposes.

FIGURE 7-4 Client or Patient Ledger Account

Patient Name	Dennis Rogan				
Address	1542 Hamilton Avenue Cincinnati OH 45240-5524				
Phone Number	555-1683				

Date	Service Rendered	Time	Debit	Credit	Balance
20-- June 4	Office Visit	8:00	40.00		40.00
4				40.00	—

THE COMBINATION JOURNAL

LO 3   Describe and use a combination journal to record transactions of a professional service business.

The two-column general journal illustrated in Chapter 4 can be used to enter every transaction of a business. However, in most businesses, there are many similar transactions that involve the same account or accounts. Cash receipts and payments are good examples. Suppose that in a typical month there are 30 transactions that result in an increase in cash and 40 transactions that cause a decrease in cash. In a two-column general journal, this would require entering the account Cash 70 times, using a journal line each time.

A considerable amount of time and space is saved if a journal contains **special columns** for cash debits and cash credits. At the end of the month, the special columns for cash debits and credits are totaled. The total of the Cash Debit column is posted as one amount to the debit side of the cash account and the total of the Cash Credit column is posted as one amount to the credit side of the cash account. Thus, instead of receiving 70 postings, Cash receives only two: one debit and one credit. This method requires much less time and reduces the risk of making posting errors.

LEARNING KEY: The totals of special journal columns are posted as one amount to the account. This saves time and reduces the possibility of posting errors.

If other accounts are used frequently, special columns can be added for these accounts. **General Debit** and **General Credit columns** are used for accounts not affected by many transactions. A journal with such special and general columns is called a **combination journal**.

Many small professional enterprises use a combination journal to record business transactions. To demonstrate the use of a combination journal, let's consider the medical practice of Dr. Ray Bonita. Bonita uses the modified cash basis of accounting. The chart of accounts for his medical practice is shown in Figure 7-5. The transactions for the month of June, his first month in practice, are provided in Figure 7-6.

A combination journal for Bonita's medical practice is illustrated in Figure 7-7 on page 232. Note that special columns were set up for Cash (Debit and Credit), Medical Fees (Credit), Wages Expense (Debit), Laboratory Expense (Debit), Medical Supplies (Debit), and Office Supplies (Debit). Special columns were set up for these accounts because they will be used frequently in this business. Other businesses might set up special columns for different accounts depending on the frequency of their use. Of course, General Debit and Credit columns for transactions affecting other accounts are also needed.

LEARNING KEY: Set up special columns for the most frequently used accounts.

FIGURE 7-5 Chart of Accounts

RAY BONITA, M.D. CHART OF ACCOUNTS				
Assets			**Revenue**	
101	Cash		401	Medical Fees
141	Medical Supplies			
142	Office Supplies		**Expenses**	
145	Prepaid Insurance		511	Wages Expense
182	Office Furniture		521	Rent Expense
182.1	Accum. Depr. —Office Furn.		523	Office Supplies Expense
185	Medical Equipment		524	Medical Supplies Expense
185.1	Accum. Depr.—Med. Equip.		525	Telephone Expense
			526	Laboratory Expense
Liabilities			535	Insurance Expense
202	Accounts Payable		541	Depr. Exp.—Office Furn.
			542	Depr. Exp.—Med. Equip.
Owner's Equity				
311	Ray Bonita, Capital			
312	Ray Bonita, Drawing			
313	Income Summary			

FIGURE 7-6 Summary of Transactions for Ray Bonita's Medical Practice

June 1	Ray Bonita invested cash to start a medical practice, $50,000.
2	Paid for a one-year liability insurance policy, $6,000. Coverage began on June 1.
3	Purchased medical equipment for cash, $22,000.
4	Paid bill for laboratory work, $300.
5	Purchased office furniture on credit from Bittle's Furniture, $9,000.
6	Received cash from patients and insurance companies for medical services rendered, $5,000.
7	Paid June office rent, $2,000.
8	Paid part-time wages, $3,000.
9	Purchased medical supplies for cash, $250.
15	Paid telephone bill, $150.
15	Received cash from patients and insurance companies for medical services rendered, $10,000.
16	Paid bill for laboratory work, $280.
17	Paid part-time wages, $3,000.
19	Purchased office supplies for cash, $150.
20	Received cash from patients and insurance companies for medical services rendered, $3,200.
22	Paid the first installment to Bittle's Furniture, $3,300.
23	Purchased medical supplies for cash, $200.
24	Paid bill for laboratory work, $400.
25	Purchased additional furniture from Bittle's Furniture, $4,000. A down payment of $500 was made, with the remaining payments expected over the next four months.
27	Paid part-time wages, $2,500.
30	Received cash from patients and insurance companies for medical services rendered, $7,000.
30	Bonita withdrew cash for personal use, $10,000.

Journalizing in a Combination Journal

The following procedures were used to enter the transactions for Bonita for June.

General Columns. Enter transactions in the *general columns* in a manner similar to that used for the *general journal*. Look at the entry for June 5 in Figure 7-7.

a.   Enter the name of the debited account (Office Furniture) first at the extreme left of the Description column.

b.   Enter the amount in the General Debit column.

c.   Enter the name of the account credited (Accounts Payable—Bittle's Furniture) on the next line, indented.

d.   Enter the amount in the General Credit column.

FIGURE 7-7   Combination Journal: Modified Cash Basis

COMBINATION JOURNAL   PAGE 1

#	DATE	CASH Debit	CASH Credit	DESCRIPTION	POST REF.	GENERAL Debit	GENERAL Credit	MEDICAL FEES Credit	WAGES EXPENSE Debit	LABORATORY EXPENSE Debit	MEDICAL SUPPLIES Debit	OFFICE SUPPLIES Debit
1	20— June 1	50 0 0 0 00		Ray Bonita, Capital	311		50 0 0 0 00					
2	2		6 0 0 00	Prepaid Insurance	145	6 0 0 00						
3	3		22 0 0 00	Medical Equipment	185	22 0 0 00						
4	4			Office Furniture	182	9 0 0 00				3 0 0 00		
5	5		3 0 0 00									
6	6	5 0 0 00		Accounts Payable—Bittle's Furn.	202		9 0 0 00	5 0 0 0 00				
7	7		2 0 0 00	Rent Expense	521	2 0 0 0 00						
8	8		3 0 0 00		—							
9	9		2 5 0 00		—							
10	10		1 5 0 00	Telephone Expense	525	1 5 0 00					2 5 0 00	
11	11				—							
12	12	10 0 0 00			—			10 0 0 0 00				
13	13		2 8 0 00		—				3 0 0 0 00			
14	14		3 0 0 00		—					2 8 0 00		
15	15		1 5 0 00		—							1 5 0 00
16	16			Accounts Payable—Bittle's Furniture	202	3 3 0 00		3 2 0 0 00				
17	17		3 0 0 00		—				3 0 0 0 00			
18	18				—							
19	19		1 5 0 00	Office Furniture	182	4 0 0 00				4 0 0 00		2 0 0 00
20	20	3 2 0 00		Accounts Payable—Bittle's Furn.	202		3 5 0 0 00					
21	21		5 0 0 00		—	4 0 0 00						
22	22		3 3 0 00		—				2 5 0 0 00			
23	23		2 0 0 00		—			7 0 0 0 00				
24	24		4 0 0 00	Ray Bonita, Drawing	312	10 0 0 00						
25	25	7 0 0 00	10 0 0 00						8 5 0 0 00	9 8 0 00	4 5 0 00	1 5 0 00
26		75 2 0 0 00	54 0 3 0 00			56 4 5 0 00	62 5 0 0 00	25 2 0 0 00	8 5 0 0 00	9 8 0 00	4 5 0 00	1 5 0 00

Totals: (1 0 1) (1 0 1) | (✓) (✓) | (4 0 1) | (5 1 1) | (5 2 6) | (1 4 1) | (1 4 2)

Proving the Combination Journal

Debit Columns		Credit Columns	
Cash	75,200	Cash	54,030
General	56,450	General	62,500
Wages Expense	8,500	Medical Fees	25,200
Laboratory Expense	980		141,730
Medical Supplies	450		
Office Supplies	150		
	141,730		

Note: The account numbers in the Posting Reference Column and at the bottom of the Special Columns are inserted as posting is completed. The same is true for the (✓) at the bottom of the General Debit and Credit Columns.

General and Special Accounts. Some transactions affect both a *general account and a special account.* Look at the entry for June 1 in Figure 7-7.

a. Enter the name of the general account in the Description column.

b. Enter the amount in the General Debit or Credit column.

c. Enter the amount of the debit or credit for the special account in the appropriate special column.

Enter all of this information on the same line.

Special Accounts. Many transactions affect only *special accounts*. Look at the entry for June 6 in Figure 7-7.

a. Enter the amounts in the appropriate special debit and credit columns.

b. Do not enter anything in the Description column.

c. Place a dash in the Posting Reference column to indicate that this amount is not posted individually. It will be posted as part of the total of the special column at the end of the month. (The posting process is described later in this chapter.)

Description Column. In general, the **Description column** is used for the following:

a. To enter the account titles for the General Debit and General Credit columns.

b. To identify specific creditors when assets are purchased on account (see entry for June 5).

   NOTE: For firms using the accrual basis of accounting, this column also would be used to identify specific customers receiving services on account (accounts receivable) and specific businesses that provided services on account (accounts payable).

c. To identify amounts forwarded. When more than one page is required during an accounting period, amounts from the previous page are brought forward. In this situation, "Amounts Forwarded" is entered in the Description column on the first line.

Proving the Combination Journal

At the end of the accounting period, all columns of the combination journal should be totaled and ruled. The sum of the debit columns should be compared with the sum of the credit columns to verify that they are equal. The proving of Bonita's combination journal for the month of June is shown at the bottom of Figure 7-7 on page 232.

POSTING FROM THE COMBINATION JOURNAL

LO 4   Post from the combination journal to the general ledger.

The procedures for posting a special column are different from the procedures used when posting a general column. Accounts debited or credited in the general columns are posted individually in the same manner as that followed for the general journal. A different procedure is used for special columns. Figure 7-8 describes the procedures to follow in posting from the combination journal.

FIGURE 7-8   Posting from a Combination Journal

GENERAL COLUMNS	Since a combination journal is being used, enter "CJ" and the page number in each general ledger account's **Posting Reference column**. Once the amount has been posted to the general ledger account, the account number is entered in the Posting Reference column of the combination journal. Accounts in the general column should be posted daily. The check marks at the bottom of the General Debit and Credit columns indicate that these totals should not be posted.
SPECIAL COLUMNS	1. Post the totals of the special columns to the appropriate general ledger accounts. 2. Once posted, enter the account number (in parentheses) beneath the column.

LEARNING KEY: Amounts in the General column are posted individually. Only the totals of the special columns are posted.

The general ledger accounts for Cash, Accounts Payable, and Medical Fees are shown in Figure 7-9 to illustrate the effects of this posting process.

FIGURE 7-9   The General Ledger After Posting

GENERAL LEDGER

ACCOUNT: **Cash**   ACCOUNT NO. 101

DATE	ITEM	POST REF.	DEBIT	CREDIT	BALANCE DEBIT	BALANCE CREDIT
20-- June 30		CJ1	75 2 0 0 00		75 2 0 0 00	
30		CJ1		54 0 3 0 00	21 1 7 0 00	

ACCOUNT: **Accounts Payable**   ACCOUNT NO. 202

DATE	ITEM	POST REF.	DEBIT	CREDIT	BALANCE DEBIT	BALANCE CREDIT
20-- June 5		CJ1		9 0 0 0 00		9 0 0 0 00
22		CJ1	3 3 0 0 00			5 7 0 0 00
25		CJ1		3 5 0 0 00		9 2 0 0 00

FIGURE 7-9 The General Ledger After Posting *(continued)*

ACCOUNT: Medical Fees												ACCOUNT NO. 401		
											BALANCE			
DATE		ITEM	POST REF.	DEBIT		CREDIT			DEBIT			CREDIT		
20-- June	30		C J 1			25	2 0 0	00				25	2 0 0	00

To see the advantages of posting a combination journal compared with the general journal, simply compare the accounts in Figure 7-9 with the same accounts in Chapter 4, Figure 4-12. Note the number of postings required for the general journal and combination journal.

	Number of Postings		
	General Journal	Combination Journal	
Cash	13	2	(Special columns for cash)
Accounts Payable	3	3	(No special column)
Delivery/Medical Fees	3	1	(Special column for Medical Fees)

Clearly, using the combination journal can be quite efficient.

Determining the Cash Balance

The debits and credits to Cash are not posted until the end of the accounting period. Therefore, the cash balance must be computed when this information is needed. The cash balance may be computed at any time during the month by taking the beginning balance, adding total cash debits and subtracting total cash credits to date. Figure 7-10 shows the calculation of Bonita's cash balance on June 15.

LEARNING KEY:

Beginning cash balance
+ Cash debits to date
− Cash credits to date
Current cash balance

FIGURE 7-10 Determining the Cash Balance

COMBINATION JOURNAL
PAGE 1

DATE		DESCRIPTION	POST REF.	CASH DEBIT	CASH CREDIT	GENERAL DEBIT	GENERAL CREDIT	MEDICAL FEES CREDIT	WAGES EXPENSE DEBIT	LABORATORY EXPENSE DEBIT	MEDICAL SUPPLIES DEBIT	OFFICE SUPPLIES DEBIT	
20— June	1	Ray Bonita, Capital	311	50 0 0 0 00			50 0 0 0 00						1
	2	Prepaid Insurance	145		6 0 0 0 00	6 0 0 0 00							2
	3	Medical Equipment	185		22 0 0 0 00	22 0 0 0 00							3
	4		—		3 0 0 00					3 0 0 00			4
	5	Office Furniture	182			9 0 0 0 00							5
	6	Accounts Payable—Bittles's Furn.	202				9 0 0 0 00						6
	7	Rent Expense	521		2 0 0 0 00	2 0 0 0 00							7
	8		—		3 0 0 0 00				3 0 0 0 00				8
	9		—	5 0 0 0 00				5 0 0 0 00					9
	10		—		2 5 0 00						2 5 0 00		10
	11	Telephone Expense	525		1 5 0 00	1 5 0 00							11
	12		—	10 0 0 0 00				10 0 0 0 00					12
	13			65 0 0 0 00	33 7 0 0 00								13

Beginning balance	$ 0
Add cash debits	65,000
Total	$65,000
Less cash credits	33,700
Cash balance, June 15	$31,300

PERFORMING END-OF-PERIOD WORK FOR A PROFESSIONAL SERVICE BUSINESS

LO 5   Prepare a work sheet, financial statements, and adjusting and closing entries for a professional service business.

Once the combination journal has been posted to the general ledger, the end-of-period work sheet is prepared in the same way as described in Chapter 5. Recall that financial statements are prepared and end-of-period work is normally performed at the end of the fiscal year. For illustration purposes, we will perform these activities at the end of Bonita's first month of operations.

Preparing the Work Sheet

Bonita's work sheet is illustrated in Figure 7-11 on page 238. Adjustments were made for the following items:

(a) Medical supplies remaining on June 30, $350.

(b) Office supplies remaining on June 30, $100.

(c) Prepaid insurance expired during June, $500.

(d) Depreciation on office furniture for June, $200.

(e) Depreciation on medical equipment for June, $300.

Preparing Financial Statements

Dr. Bonita made no additional investment during June. Thus, as we saw in Chapter 6, the financial statements can be prepared directly from the work sheet. Recall that if Bonita had made an additional investment, this amount would be identified by reviewing Bonita's capital account and would need to be reported in the statement of owner's equity. Bonita's financial statements are illustrated in Figure 7-12 on page 239.

PROFILES in ACCOUNTING

Amy Butler, Office Manager

Amy Butler earned an Associate Degree in Travel/Hospitality Management. After completing her externship with the Clubhouse Inn, Amy worked for Design Coatings as a receptionist. After eight months, she accepted an office manager's position with EMI, a database consulting firm.

Amy's duties include accounts payable and receivable, payroll, word processing, filing, and supervising and training eight employees.

She considers being professional at all times the key to success.

FIGURE 7-11 Work Sheet for Ray Bonita, M.D.

Ray Bonita, M.D.
Worksheet
For Month Ended June 30, 20 --

#	Account Title	Trial Balance Debit	Trial Balance Credit	Adjustments Debit	Adjustments Credit	Adjusted Trial Balance Debit	Adjusted Trial Balance Credit	Income Statement Debit	Income Statement Credit	Balance Sheet Debit	Balance Sheet Credit
1	Cash	21 1 7 0 00				21 1 7 0 00				21 1 7 0 00	
2	Medical Supplies	4 5 0 00			(a) 1 0 0 00	3 5 0 00				3 5 0 00	
3	Office Supplies	1 5 0 00			(b) 5 0 00	1 0 0 00				1 0 0 00	
4	Prepaid Insurance	6 0 0 0 00			(c) 5 0 0 00	5 5 0 0 00				5 5 0 0 00	
5	Office Furniture	13 0 0 0 00				13 0 0 0 00				13 0 0 0 00	
6	Accum. Depr.—Office Furniture				(d) 2 0 0 00		2 0 0 00				2 0 0 00
7	Medical Equipment	22 0 0 0 00				22 0 0 0 00				22 0 0 0 00	
8	Accum. Depr.—Medical Equipment				(e) 3 0 0 00		3 0 0 00				3 0 0 00
9	Accounts Payable		9 2 0 0 00				9 2 0 0 00				9 2 0 0 00
10	Ray Bonita, Capital		50 0 0 0 00				50 0 0 0 00				50 0 0 0 00
11	Ray Bonita, Drawing	10 0 0 0 00				10 0 0 0 00				10 0 0 0 00	
12	Medical Fees		25 2 0 0 00				25 2 0 0 00		25 2 0 0 00		
13	Wages Expense	8 5 0 0 00				8 5 0 0 00		8 5 0 0 00			
14	Rent Expense	2 0 0 0 00				2 0 0 0 00		2 0 0 0 00			
15	Office Supplies Expense			(b) 5 0 00		5 0 00		5 0 00			
16	Medical Supplies Expense			(a) 1 0 0 00		1 0 0 00		1 0 0 00			
17	Telephone Expense	1 5 0 00				1 5 0 00		1 5 0 00			
18	Laboratory Expense	9 8 0 00				9 8 0 00		9 8 0 00			
19	Insurance Expense			(c) 5 0 0 00		5 0 0 00		5 0 0 00			
20	Depr. Expense—Office Furniture			(d) 2 0 0 00		2 0 0 00		2 0 0 00			
21	Depr. Expense—Medical Equipment			(e) 3 0 0 00		3 0 0 00		3 0 0 00			
22		84 4 0 0 00	84 4 0 0 00	1 1 5 0 00	1 1 5 0 00	84 9 0 0 00	84 9 0 0 00	12 7 8 0 00	25 2 0 0 00	72 1 2 0 00	59 7 0 0 00
23	Net Income							12 4 2 0 00			12 4 2 0 00
24								25 2 0 0 00	25 2 0 0 00	72 1 2 0 00	72 1 2 0 00
25											
26											
27											
28											
29											
30											

FIGURE 7-12 Financial Statements for Ray Bonita, M.D.

Ray Bonita, M.D. Income Statement For Month Ended June 30, 20 - -										
Revenue:										
Medical fees						$ 25	2	0	0	00
Expenses:										
Wages expense	$ 8	5	0	0	00					
Rent expense	2	0	0	0	00					
Office supplies expense			5	0	00					
Medical supplies expense		1	0	0	00					
Telephone expense		1	5	0	00					
Laboratory expense		9	8	0	00					
Insurance expense		5	0	0	00					
Depreciation expense—office furniture		2	0	0	00					
Depreciation expense—medical equipment		3	0	0	00					
Total expenses						12	7	8	0	00
Net income						$12	4	2	0	00

Ray Bonita, M.D. Statement of Owner's Equity For Month Ended June 30, 20 - -										
Ray Bonita, capital, June 1, 20 - -						$50	0	0	0	00
Net income for June	$12	4	2	0	00					
Less withdrawals for June	10	0	0	0	00					
Increase in capital						2	4	2	0	00
Ray Bonita, capital, June 30, 20 - -						$52	4	2	0	00

Ray Bonita, M.D. Balance Sheet June 30, 20 - -										
Assets										
Current assets:										
Cash	$21	1	7	0	00					
Medical supplies		3	5	0	00					
Office supplies		1	0	0	00					
Prepaid insurance	5	5	0	0	00					
Total current assets						$27	1	2	0	00
Property, plant, and equipment:										
Office furniture	$13	0	0	0	00					
Less accumulated depreciation		2	0	0	00	12	8	0	0	00
Medical equipment	$22	0	0	0	00					
Less accumulated depreciation		3	0	0	00	21	7	0	0	00
Total assets						$61	6	2	0	00
Liabilities										
Current liabilities:										
Accounts payable						$ 9	2	0	0	00
Owner's Equity										
Ray Bonita, capital						52	4	2	0	00
Total liabilities and owner's equity						$61	6	2	0	00

Preparing Adjusting and Closing Entries

Adjusting and closing entries are made in the combination journal in the same manner demonstrated for the general journal in Chapter 6. We simply use the Description and General Debit and Credit columns. These posted entries are illustrated in Figures 7-13 and 7-14.

FIGURE 7-13 Adjusting Entries

COMBINATION JOURNAL

	DATE		CASH DEBIT	CASH CREDIT	DESCRIPTION	POST REF.	GENERAL DEBIT	GENERAL CREDIT	
1					Adjusting Entries				1
2	20-- June	30			Medical Supplies Expense	524	1 0 0 00		2
3					Medical Supplies	141		1 0 0 00	3
4		30			Office Supplies Expense	523	5 0 00		4
5					Office Supplies	142		5 0 00	5
6		30			Insurance Expense	535	5 0 0 00		6
7					Prepaid Insurance	145		5 0 0 00	7
8		30			Depr. Expense—Office Furniture	541	2 0 0 00		8
9					Accum. Depr.—Office Furn.	182.1		2 0 0 00	9
10		30			Depr. Expense—Medical Equip.	542	3 0 0 00		10
11					Accum. Depr.—Medical Equip.	185.1		3 0 0 00	11

FIGURE 7-14 Closing Entries

COMBINATION JOURNAL

	DATE		CASH DEBIT	CASH CREDIT	DESCRIPTION	POST REF.	GENERAL DEBIT	GENERAL CREDIT	
12									12
13					Closing Entries				13
14	20-- June	30			Medical Fees	401	25 2 0 0 00		14
15					Income Summary	313		25 2 0 0 00	15
16		30			Income Summary	313	12 7 8 0 00		16
17					Wages Expense	511		8 5 0 0 00	17
18					Rent Expense	521		2 0 0 0 00	18
19					Office Supplies Expense	523		5 0 00	19
20					Medical Supplies Expense	524		1 0 0 00	20
21					Telephone Expense	525		1 5 0 00	21
22					Laboratory Expense	526		9 8 0 00	22
23					Insurance Expense	535		5 0 0 00	23
24					Depr. Expense—Office Furn.	541		2 0 0 00	24
25					Depr. Expense—Med. Equip.	542		3 0 0 00	25
26		30			Income Summary	313	12 4 2 0 00		26
27					Ray Bonita, Capital	311		12 4 2 0 00	27
28		30			Ray Bonita, Capital	311	10 0 0 0 00		28
29					Ray Bonita, Drawing	312		10 0 0 0 00	29

Learning Objectives	Key Points to Remember
1 Explain the cash, modified cash, and accrual bases of accounting.	There are three bases of accounting: cash, modified cash, and accrual. Differences in the recording of revenues, expenses, assets, and liabilities are listed below. **Recording revenues** Cash: when cash is received Modified cash: when cash is received Accrual: when earned **Recording expenses** Cash: when cash is paid Modified cash: when cash is paid, except for property, plant, and equipment and prepaid items Accrual: when incurred **Recording assets and liabilities**

Recording assets and liabilities:

	Cash Basis	Modified Cash Basis	Accrual Basis
Accounts receivable	No	No	Yes
Payables			
for purchase of assets	No	Yes	Yes
for services received (wages payable)	No	No	Yes
Prepaid assets	No	Yes	Yes
Long-term assets	No	Yes	Yes

Learning Objectives	Key Points to Remember
2 Describe special records for a professional service business using the modified cash basis.	Special records are required for a professional service business using the modified cash basis. Since accounts receivable are not entered in the accounting system, other records must be maintained to keep track of amounts owed by clients and patients. These records generally include an appointment record and a client or patient ledger record.
3 Describe and use a combination journal to record transactions of a professional service business.	A combination journal is used by some businesses to improve the efficiency of recording and posting transactions. It includes general and special columns. The headings for a typical combination journal for a doctor's office are shown below.

COMBINATION JOURNAL   PAGE 1

DATE	CASH DEBIT	CASH CREDIT	DESCRIPTION	POST REF.	GENERAL DEBIT	GENERAL CREDIT	MEDICAL FEES CREDIT	WAGES EXPENSE DEBIT	LABORATORY EXPENSE DEBIT	MEDICAL SUPPLIES DEBIT	OFFICE SUPPLIES DEBIT

Learning Objectives	Key Points to Remember
4 Post from the combination journal to the general ledger.	Rules for posting a combination journal: 1. Amounts entered in the general columns are posted individually to the general ledger on a daily basis. 2. The totals of the special columns are posted to the general ledger at the end of the month.
5 Prepare a work sheet, financial statements, and adjusting and closing entries for a professional service business.	The work sheet, financial statements, adjusting entries, and closing entries are prepared in the same manner as discussed in Chapters 5 and 6. Remember, however, that under the modified cash basis, adjustments are made only for prepaid items and depreciation of plant and equipment.

Reflection: Answering the Opening Question

Since there is uncertainty concerning the receipt of payment from patients and clients, many professional offices use the cash basis of accounting. Thus, revenues are recognized when cash is received, rather than when earned.

KEY TERMS

accrual basis of accounting, (224)   A method of accounting under which revenues are recorded when earned and expenses are recorded when incurred.

cash basis of accounting, (224)   A method of accounting under which revenues are recorded when cash is received and expenses are recorded when cash is paid.

combination journal, (230)   A journal with special and general columns.

Description column, (233)   The column in the combination journal used to enter the account titles for the General Debit and General Credit columns, to identify specific creditors when assets are purchased on account, and to identify amounts forwarded.

General Credit column, (230)   The column in the combination journal used to credit accounts that are used infrequently.

General Debit column, (230)   The column in the combination journal used to debit accounts that are used infrequently.

modified cash basis, (225)   A method of accounting that combines aspects of the cash and accrual methods. It uses the cash basis for recording revenues and most expenses. Exceptions are made when cash is paid for assets with useful lives greater than one accounting period.

Posting Reference column, (234)   The column in the combination journal where the account number is entered after posting.

special columns, (229)   Columns in journals for frequently used accounts.

DEMONSTRATION PROBLEM

Maria Vietor is a financial planning consultant. She developed the following chart of accounts for her business.

Vietor Financial Planning
Chart of Accounts

Assets	Revenues
101 Cash	401 Professional Fees
142 Office Supplies	
	Expenses
Liabilities	511 Wages Expense
202 Accounts Payable	521 Rent Expense
	523 Office Supplies Expense
Owner's Equity	525 Telephone Expense
311 Maria Vietor, Capital	526 Automobile Expense
312 Maria Vietor, Drawing	533 Utilities Expense
313 Income Summary	534 Charitable Contributions Expense

Vietor completed the following transactions during the month of December of the current year:

Dec. 1   Vietor invested cash to start a consulting business, $20,000.

3   Paid December office rent, $1,000.

4   Received a check from Aaron Bisno, a client, for services, $2,500.

6   Paid Union Electric for December heating and light, $75.

7   Received a check from Will Carter, a client, for services, $2,000.

12   Paid Smith's Super Service for gasoline and oil purchases, $60.

14   Paid Comphelp for temporary secretarial services obtained through them during the past two weeks, $600.

17   Purchased office supplies on account from Cleat Office Supply, $280.

20   Paid Cress Telephone Co. for local and long-distance business calls during the past month, $100.

21   Vietor withdrew cash for personal use, $1,100.

24   Made donation to the National Multiple Sclerosis Society, $100.

27   Received a check from Ellen Thaler, a client, for services, $2,000.

28   Paid Comphelp for temporary secretarial services obtained through them during the past two weeks, $600.

29   Made payment on account to Cleat Office Supply, $100.

REQUIRED   1. Enter the transactions in a combination journal. Establish special columns for Professional Fees, Wages Expense, and Automobile Expense. Vietor uses the modified cash basis of accounting. (Refer to the Chapter 4 Demonstration Problem to see how similar transactions were recorded in a general journal. Notice that the combination journal is much more efficient.)

2. Prove the combination journal.

3. Post these transactions to a general ledger.

4. Prepare a trial balance.

(continued)

Solution

1, 2.

COMBINATION JOURNAL — PAGE 1

DATE	CASH DEBIT	CASH CREDIT	DESCRIPTION	POST REF	GENERAL DEBIT	GENERAL CREDIT	PROFESSIONAL FEES CREDIT	WAGES EXPENSE DEBIT	AUTOMOBILE EXPENSE DEBIT
20-- Dec. 1	20 0 0 0 00		Maria Vietor, Capital	311		20 0 0 0 00			
3		1 0 0 0 00	Rent Expense	521	1 0 0 0 00				
4	2 5 0 0 00			—			2 5 0 0 00		
6		7 5 00	Utilities Expense	533	7 5 00				
7	2 0 0 0 00			—			2 0 0 0 00		
12		6 0 0 00		—				6 0 0 00	
14		6 0 0 00		—				6 0 0 00	
17			Office Supplies	142	2 8 0 00				
17			Accounts Payable—Cleat Office Supply	202		2 8 0 00			
20		1 0 0 00	Telephone Expense	525	1 0 0 00				
21		1 0 0 0 00	Maria Vietor, Drawing	312	1 0 0 0 00				
24		1 0 0 00	Charitable Contributions Expense	534	1 0 0 00				
27	2 0 0 0 00			—			2 0 0 0 00		
28		6 0 00		—					6 0 00
29		2 0 0 00	Accounts Payable—Cleat Office Supply	202	2 0 0 00				
	26 5 0 0 00	3 7 3 5 00			2 7 5 5 00	20 2 8 0 00	6 5 0 0 00	1 2 0 0 00	6 0 00
	(1 0 1)	(1 0 1)			(✓)	(✓)	(4 0 1)	(5 1 1)	(5 2 6)

Proving the Combination Journal

Debit Columns		Credit Columns	
Cash	26,500	Cash	3,735
General	2,755	General	20,280
Wages Expense	1,200	Professional Fees	6,500
Auto. Expense	60		
	30,515		30,515

3.

GENERAL LEDGER

ACCOUNT: Cash   ACCOUNT NO. 101

DATE		ITEM	POST REF.	DEBIT	CREDIT	BALANCE	
						DEBIT	CREDIT
20-- Dec.	31		CJ1	26 5 0 0 00		26 5 0 0 00	
	31		CJ1		3 7 3 5 00	22 7 6 5 00	

ACCOUNT: Office Supplies   ACCOUNT NO. 142

DATE		ITEM	POST REF.	DEBIT	CREDIT	BALANCE	
						DEBIT	CREDIT
20-- Dec.	17		CJ1	2 8 0 00		2 8 0 00	

ACCOUNT: Accounts Payable   ACCOUNT NO. 202

DATE		ITEM	POST REF.	DEBIT	CREDIT	BALANCE	
						DEBIT	CREDIT
20-- Dec.	17		CJ1		2 8 0 00		2 8 0 00
	29		CJ1	1 0 0 00			1 8 0 00

ACCOUNT: Maria Vietor, Capital   ACCOUNT NO. 311

DATE		ITEM	POST REF.	DEBIT	CREDIT	BALANCE	
						DEBIT	CREDIT
20-- Dec.	1		CJ1		20 0 0 0 00		20 0 0 0 00

ACCOUNT: Maria Vietor, Drawing   ACCOUNT NO. 312

DATE		ITEM	POST REF.	DEBIT	CREDIT	BALANCE	
						DEBIT	CREDIT
20-- Dec.	21		CJ1	1 1 0 0 00		1 1 0 0 00	

ACCOUNT: Income Summary   ACCOUNT NO. 313

DATE		ITEM	POST REF.	DEBIT	CREDIT	BALANCE	
						DEBIT	CREDIT
20--							

ACCOUNT: Professional Fees   ACCOUNT NO. 401

DATE		ITEM	POST REF.	DEBIT	CREDIT	BALANCE	
						DEBIT	CREDIT
20-- Dec.	31		CJ1		6 5 0 0 00		6 5 0 0 00

ACCOUNT: Wages Expense   ACCOUNT NO. 511

DATE		ITEM	POST REF.	DEBIT	CREDIT	BALANCE	
						DEBIT	CREDIT
20-- Dec.	31		CJ1	1 2 0 0 00		1 2 0 0 00	

(continued)

3.

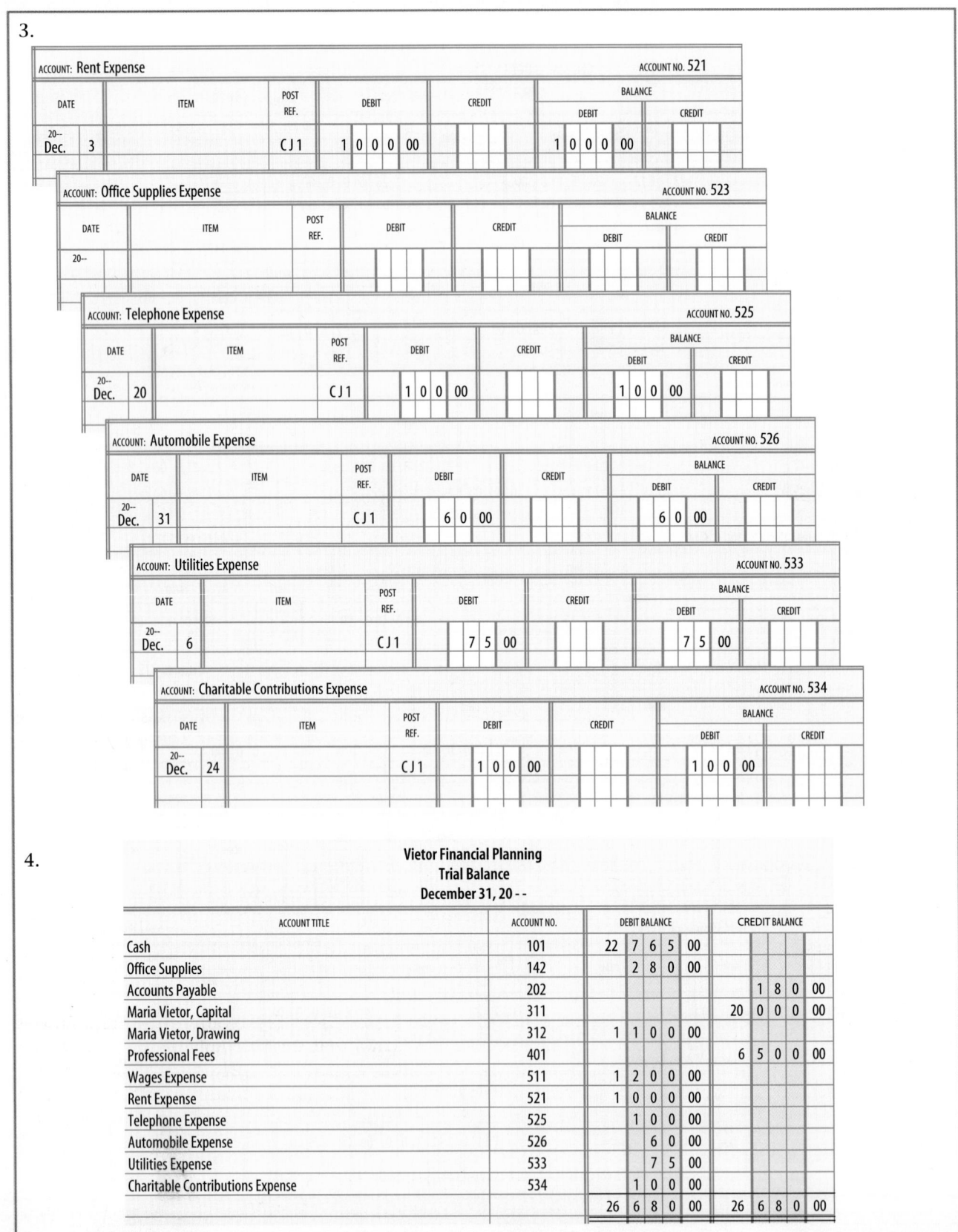

ACCOUNT: Rent Expense — **ACCOUNT NO.** 521

DATE	ITEM	POST REF.	DEBIT	CREDIT	BALANCE DEBIT	BALANCE CREDIT
20-- Dec. 3		CJ1	1 0 0 0 00		1 0 0 0 00	

ACCOUNT: Office Supplies Expense — **ACCOUNT NO.** 523

DATE	ITEM	POST REF.	DEBIT	CREDIT	BALANCE DEBIT	BALANCE CREDIT
20--						

ACCOUNT: Telephone Expense — **ACCOUNT NO.** 525

DATE	ITEM	POST REF.	DEBIT	CREDIT	BALANCE DEBIT	BALANCE CREDIT
20-- Dec. 20		CJ1	1 0 0 00		1 0 0 00	

ACCOUNT: Automobile Expense — **ACCOUNT NO.** 526

DATE	ITEM	POST REF.	DEBIT	CREDIT	BALANCE DEBIT	BALANCE CREDIT
20-- Dec. 31		CJ1	6 0 00		6 0 00	

ACCOUNT: Utilities Expense — **ACCOUNT NO.** 533

DATE	ITEM	POST REF.	DEBIT	CREDIT	BALANCE DEBIT	BALANCE CREDIT
20-- Dec. 6		CJ1	7 5 00		7 5 00	

ACCOUNT: Charitable Contributions Expense — **ACCOUNT NO.** 534

DATE	ITEM	POST REF.	DEBIT	CREDIT	BALANCE DEBIT	BALANCE CREDIT
20-- Dec. 24		CJ1	1 0 0 00		1 0 0 00	

4.

Vietor Financial Planning
Trial Balance
December 31, 20 - -

ACCOUNT TITLE	ACCOUNT NO.	DEBIT BALANCE	CREDIT BALANCE
Cash	101	22 7 6 5 00	
Office Supplies	142	2 8 0 00	
Accounts Payable	202		1 8 0 00
Maria Vietor, Capital	311		20 0 0 0 00
Maria Vietor, Drawing	312	1 1 0 0 00	
Professional Fees	401		6 5 0 0 00
Wages Expense	511	1 2 0 0 00	
Rent Expense	521	1 0 0 0 00	
Telephone Expense	525	1 0 0 00	
Automobile Expense	526	6 0 00	
Utilities Expense	533	7 5 00	
Charitable Contributions Expense	534	1 0 0 00	
		26 6 8 0 00	26 6 8 0 00

REVIEW QUESTIONS

1. Explain when revenues are recorded under the cash basis, modified cash basis, and accrual basis of accounting.

2. Explain when expenses are recorded under the cash basis, modified cash basis, and accrual basis of accounting.

3. Explain the purpose of an appointment record.

4. Explain the purpose of a patient ledger account.

5. Explain the purpose of a special column in the combination journal.

6. Explain the purpose of the General columns in the combination journal.

7. How does the use of the combination journal save time and space in entering cash transactions?

8. Explain the purpose of the Description column in the combination journal.

9. What is the purpose of proving the totals in the combination journal?

10. When an entry is posted from the combination journal to a ledger account, what information is entered in the Posting Reference column of the combination journal? in the Posting Reference column of the ledger account?

MANAGING YOUR WRITING

Your friend is planning to start her own business and has asked you for advice. In particular, she is concerned about which method of accounting she should use. She has heard about the cash, modified cash, and accrual methods of accounting. However, she does not really understand the differences. Write a memo that explains each method and the type of business for which each method is most appropriate.

ETHICS CASE

Nancy Bowles, the owner of Bowles Services, a sole proprietorship, rushed into the office late Monday morning carrying a deposit receipt from the bank. Upon handing the receipt to Sarah, the accountant, she instructed her to debit cash and credit professional fees for the full $10,000. When Sarah examined the source document she saw that the cash had come from the account of Richard Bowles, Nancy's father. Nancy explained to Sarah that she was applying for a bank loan and needed to "show that her company earned more year-to-date income than it actually had." Nancy used the rationale that the company would earn at least $10,000 in revenue during the next few months but the financial statements the bank required were as of the end of this month.

1. Does Nancy's explanation make sense? Is it ethical?

2. How should this transaction be entered in Bowles Services' books? Does it matter whether the cash basis or accrual basis of accounting is used?

(continued)

3. Make a written list of all the consequences Nancy might face as a result of recording this transaction as a debit to cash and a credit to professional fees.

4. Break up into groups of two and role play Nancy and Sarah's points of view in this situation.

WEB WORK

For some other views on accrual and cash accounting, check out these web pages. What are some differences between cash and accrual accounting? Can businesses use one method for internal record keeping and another method for tax reporting?

American Express offers a small business services page at

http://www.americanexpress.com/smallbusiness.

Choose Business Planning and Resources, and then Managing Your Business. Small Office/Home Office has information at

http://www.toolkit.cch.com/text/P06_1340.htm.

Note: All Web sites referred to in the Web Work assignments in this text can be accessed through the Heintz/Parry Web site at

http://heintz.swcollege.com.

Also, if a Web Work address becomes unavailable, the corrected link will be posted on our site.

SERIES A EXERCISES

EXERCISE 7A-1 (LO 1) CASH, MODIFIED CASH, AND ACCRUAL BASES OF ACCOUNTING Prepare the entry for each of the following transactions, using the (a) cash basis, (b) modified cash basis, and (c) accrual basis of accounting.

1. Purchase supplies on account.

2. Make payment on asset previously purchased.

3. Purchase supplies for cash.

4. Purchase insurance for cash.

5. Pay cash for wages.

6. Pay cash for telephone expense.

7. Pay cash for new equipment.

End-of-Period Adjusting Entries:

8. Wages earned but not paid.

9. Prepaid item purchased, partly used.

10. Depreciation on long-term assets.

EXERCISE 7A-2 (LO 1/3) JOURNAL ENTRIES Jean Akins opened a consulting business. Journalize the following transactions that occurred during the month of January of the current year using the modified cash basis and a combination journal. Set up special columns for Consulting Fees (credit) and Wages Expense (debit).

Jan. 1   Invested cash in the business, $10,000.

  2   Paid office rent, $500.

  3   Purchased office equipment on account from Business Machines, Inc., $1,500.

  5   Received cash for services rendered, $750.

  8   Paid telephone bill, $65.

  10   Paid for a magazine subscription (miscellaneous expense), $15.

  11   Purchased office supplies on account from Leo's Office Supplies, $300.

  15   Paid for one-year liability insurance policy, $150.

  18   Paid part-time help, $500.

  21   Received cash for services rendered, $350.

  25   Paid electricity bill, $85.

  27   Withdrew cash for personal use, $100.

  29   Paid part-time help, $500.

EXERCISE 7A-3 (LO 1/3) JOURNAL ENTRIES Bill Rackes opened a bicycle repair shop. Journalize the following transactions that occurred during the month of October of the current year. Use the modified cash basis and a combination journal with special columns for Repair Fees (credit) and Wages Expense (debit). Prove the combination journal.

Oct. 1   Invested cash in the business, $15,000.

  2   Paid shop rental for the month, $300.

  3   Purchased bicycle parts on account from Tracker's Bicycle Parts, $2,000.

  5   Purchased office supplies on account from Downtown Office Supplies, $250.

  8   Paid telephone bill, $38.

  9   Received cash for services, $140.

  11   Paid for a sports magazine subscription (miscellaneous expense), $15.

  12   Made payment on account for parts previously purchased, $100.

  14   Paid part-time help, $300.

  15   Received cash for services, $350.

  16   Paid electricity bill, $48.

  19   Received cash for services, $250.

  23   Withdrew cash for personal use, $50.

  25   Made payment on account for office supplies previously purchased, $50.

  29   Paid part-time help, $300.

SERIES A PROBLEMS

PROBLEM 7A-1 (LO 3/4/5) JOURNALIZING AND POSTING TRANSACTIONS AND PREPARING A TRIAL BALANCE Angela McWharton opened an on-call nursing services business. She rented a small office space and pays a part-time worker to answer the telephone. Her chart of accounts is shown below.

Angela McWharton Nursing Services
Chart of Accounts

Assets	Revenues
101 Cash	401 Nursing Care Fees
142 Office Supplies	
181 Office Equipment	Expenses
	511 Wages Expense
Liabilities	512 Advertising Expense
202 Accounts Payable	521 Rent Expense
	525 Telephone Expense
Owner's Equity	526 Transportation Expense
311 Angela McWharton, Capital	533 Electricity Expense
312 Angela McWharton, Drawing	549 Miscellaneous Expense
313 Income Summary	

McWharton's transactions for the first month of business are as follows:

Jan. 1 Invested cash in the business, $10,000.

1 Paid January rent, $500.

2 Purchased office supplies on account from Crestline Office Supplies, $300.

4 Purchased office equipment on account from Office Technology, Inc., $1,500.

6 Received cash for nursing services rendered, $580.

7 Paid telephone bill, $42.

8 Paid electricity bill, $38.

10 Received cash for nursing services rendered, $360.

12 Made payment on account for office supplies previously purchased, $50.

13 Reimbursed part-time worker for use of personal automobile (transportation expense), $150.

15 Paid part-time worker, $360.

17 Received cash for nursing services rendered, $420.

18 Withdrew cash for personal use, $100.

20 Paid for newspaper advertising, $26.

22 Paid for gas and oil, $35.

24 Paid subscription for journal on nursing care practices (miscellaneous expense), $28.

25 Received cash for nursing services rendered, $320.

27 Made payment on account for office equipment previously purchased, $150.

29 Paid part-time worker, $360.

30 Received cash for nursing services rendered, $180.

REQUIRED   1. Journalize the transactions for January using the modified cash basis and page 1 of a combination journal. Set up special columns for Nursing Care Fees (credit), Wages Expense (debit), and Transportation Expense (debit).

2. Determine the cash balance as of January 12 (using the combination journal).

3. Prove the combination journal.

4. Set up four-column general ledger accounts from the chart of accounts and post the transactions from the combination journal.

5. Prepare a trial balance.

PROBLEM 7A-2 (LO 3/4/5) JOURNALIZING AND POSTING TRANSACTIONS AND PREPARING FINANCIAL STATEMENTS Sue Reyton owns a suit tailoring shop. She opened her business in September. She rents a small work space and has an assistant to receive job orders and process claim tickets. Her trial balance shows her account balances for the first two months of business (September and October). No adjustments were made in September or October.

Sue Reyton Tailors Trial Balance October 31, 20 - -											
ACCOUNT TITLE	ACCOUNT NO.	DEBIT BALANCE					CREDIT BALANCE				
Cash	101	5	7	1	1	00					
Tailoring Supplies	141	1	0	0	0	00					
Office Supplies	142		4	8	5	00					
Prepaid Insurance	145		1	0	0	00					
Tailoring Equipment	188	3	8	0	0	00					
Accumulated Depreciation—Tailoring Equipment	188.1										
Accounts Payable	202							4	1	2	5	00
Sue Reyton, Capital	311							5	4	3	0	00
Sue Reyton, Drawing	312		5	0	0	00					
Tailoring Fees	401							3	6	0	0	00
Wages Expense	511		8	0	0	00					
Advertising Expense	512			3	3	00					
Rent Expense	521		6	0	0	00					
Telephone Expense	525			6	0	00					
Utilities Expense	533			4	4	00					
Miscellaneous Expense	549			2	2	00					
		13	1	5	5	00	13	1	5	5	00

Reyton's transactions for November are as follows:

Nov. 1 Paid November rent, $300.

2 Purchased tailoring supplies on account from Sew Easy Supplies, $150.

3 Purchased a new button hole machine on account from Seam's Sewing Machines, $3,000.

5 Earned first week's revenue: $400 in cash.

8 Paid for newspaper advertising, $13.

9 Paid telephone bill, $28.

(continued)

10 Paid electricity bill, $21.

12 Earned second week's revenue: $200 in cash, $300 on account.

15 Paid part-time worker, $400.

16 Made payment on account for tailoring supplies, $100.

17 Paid for magazine subscription (miscellaneous expense), $12.

19 Earned third week's revenue: $450 in cash.

21 Paid for prepaid insurance for the year, $500.

23 Received cash from customers (previously owed), $300.

24 Paid for newspaper advertising, $13.

26 Paid for special delivery fee (miscellaneous expense), $12.

29 Earned fourth week's revenue: $600 in cash.

Additional accounts needed are as follows:

313 Income Summary
523 Office Supplies Expense
524 Tailoring Supplies Expense
535 Insurance Expense
542 Depreciation Expense—Tailoring Equipment

Nov. 30 Adjustments:

(a) Tailoring supplies on hand, $450.

(b) Office supplies on hand, $285.

(c) Prepaid insurance expired over past three months, $150.

(d) Depreciation on tailoring equipment for the last three months, $300.

REQUIRED

1. Journalize the transactions for November using the modified cash basis and page 5 of a combination journal. Set up special columns for Tailoring Fees (credit), Wages Expense (debit), and Advertising Expense (debit).

2. Determine the cash balance as of November 12.

3. Prove the combination journal.

4. Set up four-column general ledger accounts, including the additional accounts listed above, entering the balances as of November 1, 20--. Post the entries from the combination journal.

5. Prepare a work sheet for the three months ended November 30, 20--.

6. Prepare an income statement and statement of owner's equity for the three months ended November 30, and a balance sheet as of November 30, 20--. (Assume that Reyton made an investment of $5,430 on September 1, 20--.)

7. Record the adjusting and closing entries on page 6 of the combination journal and post to the general ledger accounts.

SERIES B EXERCISES

EXERCISE 7B-1 (LO 1) CASH, MODIFIED CASH, AND ACCRUAL BASES OF ACCOUNTING For each journal entry shown below, indicate the accounting method(s) for which the entry would be appropriate. If the journal entry is not appropriate for a particular accounting method, explain the proper accounting treatment for that method.

1. Office Equipment
      Cash
         Purchased equipment for cash

2. Office Equipment
      Accounts Payable
         Purchased equipment on account

3. Cash
      Revenue
         Cash receipts for week

4. Accounts Receivable
      Revenue
         Services performed on account

5. Prepaid Insurance
      Cash
         Purchased prepaid asset

6. Supplies
      Accounts Payable
         Purchased prepaid asset

7. Telephone Expense
      Cash
         Paid telephone bill

8. Wages Expense
      Cash
         Paid wages for month

9. Accounts Payable
      Cash
         Payment on account

   Adjusting Entries:

10. Supplies Expense
       Supplies

11. Wages Expense
       Wages Payable

12. Depreciation Expense—Office Equipment
       Accumulated Depreciation—Office Equipment

EXERCISE 7B-2 (LO 1/3) JOURNAL ENTRIES Bill Miller opened a bookkeeping service business. Journalize the following transactions that occurred during the month of March of the current year. Use the modified cash basis and a combination journal with special columns for Bookkeeping Fees (credit) and Wages Expense (debit).

Mar. 1   Invested cash in the business, $7,500.

3   Paid March office rent, $500.

5   Purchased office equipment on account from Desk Top Office Equipment, $800.

6   Received cash for services rendered, $400.

8   Paid telephone bill, $48.

10   Paid for a magazine subscription (miscellaneous expense), $25.

11   Purchased office supplies, $200.

14   Received cash for services rendered, $520.

16   Paid for a one-year insurance policy, $200.

18   Paid part-time worker, $400.

21   Received cash for services rendered, $380.

22   Made payment on account for office equipment previously purchased, $100.

24   Paid electricity bill, $56.

27   Withdrew cash for personal use, $200.

29   Paid part-time worker, $400.

30   Received cash for services rendered, $600.

EXERCISE 7B-3 (LO 1/3) JOURNAL ENTRIES Amy Anjelo opened a delivery service. Journalize the following transactions that occurred in January of the current year. Use the modified cash basis and a combination journal with special columns for Delivery Fees (credit) and Wages Expense (debit). Prove the combination journal.

Jan. 1   Invested cash in the business, $10,000.

2   Paid shop rental for the month, $400.

3   Purchased a delivery cart on account from Walt's Wheels, $1,000.

5   Purchased office supplies, $250.

6   Paid telephone bill, $51.

8   Received cash for delivery services, $428.

11   Paid electricity bill, $37.

12   Paid part-time employee, $480.

13   Paid for postage stamps (miscellaneous expense), $29.

15   Received cash for delivery services, $382.

18   Made payment on account for delivery cart previously purchased, $90.

21   Withdrew cash for personal use, $250.

24   Paid for a one-year liability insurance policy, $180.

26   Received cash for delivery services, $292.

29   Paid part-time employee, $480.

SERIES B PROBLEMS

PROBLEM 7B-1 (LO 3/4/5) JOURNALIZING AND POSTING TRANSACTIONS AND PREPARING A TRIAL BALANCE J. B. Hoyt opened a training center at the marina where he provides private water-skiing lessons. He rented a small building at the marina and has a part-time worker to assist him. His chart of accounts is shown below.

Water Walking by Hoyt
Chart of Accounts

Assets	Revenues
101 Cash	401 Training Fees
142 Office Supplies	
183 Skiing Equipment	Expenses
	511 Wages Expense
Liabilities	521 Rent Expense
202 Accounts Payable	525 Telephone Expense
	526 Transportation Expense
Owner's Equity	533 Electricity Expense
311 J. B. Hoyt, Capital	537 Repair Expense
312 J. B. Hoyt, Drawing	549 Miscellaneous Expense
313 Income Summary	

Transactions for the first month of business are as follows:

July 1   Invested cash in the business, $5,000.

2   Paid rent for the month, $250.

3   Purchased office supplies, $150.

4   Purchased skiing equipment on account from Water Fun, Inc., $2,000.

6   Paid telephone bill, $36.

7   Received cash for skiing lessons, $200.

10   Paid electricity bill, $28.

12   Paid part-time worker, $250.

14   Received cash for skiing lessons, $300.

16   Paid for gas and oil (transportation expense), $60.

17   Received cash for skiing lessons, $250.

20   Paid for repair to ski rope, $20.

21   Made payment on account for skiing equipment previously purchased, $100.

24   Received cash for skiing lessons, $310.

(continued)

26   Paid for award certificates (miscellaneous expense), $18.

28   Paid part-time worker, $250.

30   Received cash for skiing lessons, $230.

31   Paid for repair to life jacket, $20.

REQUIRED
1. Journalize the transactions for July using the modified cash basis and page 1 of a combination journal. Set up special columns for Training Fees (credit), Wages Expense (debit), and Repair Expense (debit).

2. Determine the cash balance as of July 14, 20--.

3. Prove the combination journal.

4. Set up four-column general ledger accounts from the chart of accounts and post the transactions from the combination journal.

5. Prepare a trial balance.

PROBLEM 7B-2 (LO 3/4/5) JOURNALIZING AND POSTING TRANSACTIONS AND PREPARING FINANCIAL STATEMENTS Molly Claussen owns a lawn care business. She opened her business in April. She rents a small shop area where she stores her equipment and has an assistant to receive orders and process accounts. Her trial balance shows her account balances for the first two months of business (April and May). No adjustments were made at the end of April or May.

Molly Claussen's Green Thumb Trial Balance May 31, 20 - -												
ACCOUNT TITLE	ACCOUNT NO.	DEBIT BALANCE					CREDIT BALANCE					
Cash	101	4	6	0	4	00						
Lawn Care Supplies	141		5	8	8	00						
Office Supplies	142		2	4	3	00						
Prepaid Insurance	145		1	5	0	00						
Lawn Care Equipment	189	2	4	0	8	00						
Accumulated Depreciation—Lawn Care Equipment	189.1											
Accounts Payable	202							1	0	8	0	00
Molly Claussen, Capital	311							5	0	0	0	00
Molly Claussen, Drawing	312		8	0	0	00						
Lawn Care Fees	401							4	0	3	3	00
Wages Expense	511		6	0	0	00						
Rent Expense	521		4	0	0	00						
Telephone Expense	525			8	8	00						
Electricity Expense	533			6	2	00						
Repair Expense	537			5	0	00						
Gas and Oil Expense	538		1	2	0	00						
		10	1	1	3	00	10	1	1	3	00	

Transactions for June are as follows:

June 1   Paid shop rent, $200.

2   Purchased office supplies, $230.

3   Purchased new landscaping equipment on account from Earth Care, Inc., $1,000.

5   Paid telephone bill, $31.

6   Received cash for lawn care fees, $640.

8   Paid electricity bill, $31.

10   Paid part-time worker, $300.

11   Received cash for lawn care fees, $580.

12   Paid for a one-year insurance policy, $200.

14   Made payment on account for landscaping equipment previously purchased, $100.

15   Paid for gas and oil, $40.

19   Paid for mower repairs, $25.

21   Received $310 cash for lawn care fees and earned $480 on account.

24   Withdrew cash for personal use, $100.

26   Paid for edging equipment repairs, $20.

28   Received cash from customers (previously owed), $480.

29   Paid part-time worker, $300.

Additional accounts needed are as follows:

313   Income Summary
523   Office Supplies Expense
524   Lawn Care Supplies Expense
535   Insurance Expense
542   Depreciation Expense—Lawn Care Equipment

June 30 Adjustments:

(a) Office supplies on hand, $273.

(b) Lawn care supplies on hand, $300.

(c) Prepaid insurance expired over past three months, $100.

(d) Depreciation on lawn care equipment for past three months, $260.

REQUIRED   1.   Journalize the transactions for June using the modified cash basis and page 5 of a combination journal. Set up special columns for Lawn Care Fees (credit), Repair Expense (debit), and Wages Expense (debit).

2.   Determine the cash balance as of June 12.

3.   Prove the combination journal.

(continued)

4. Set up four-column general ledger accounts including the additional accounts listed above, entering balances as of June 1, 20--. Post the entries from the combination journal.

5. Prepare a work sheet for the three months ended June 30, 20--.

6. Prepare an income statement and statement of owner's equity for the three months ended June 30, and a balance sheet as of June 30, 20--. Assume that Claussen invested $5,000 on April 1, 20--.

7. Record the adjusting and closing entries on page 6 of the combination journal and post to the general ledger accounts.

MASTERY PROBLEM

John McRoe opened a tennis resort in June 20--. Most guests register for one week, arriving on Sunday afternoon and returning home the following Saturday afternoon. Guests stay at an adjacent hotel. The tennis resort provides lunch and dinner. Dining and exercise facilities are provided in a building rented by McRoe. A dietitian, masseuse, physical therapist, and athletic trainers are on call to assure the proper combination of diet and exercise. The chart of accounts and transactions for the month of June are provided below. McRoe uses the modified cash basis of accounting.

McRoe Tennis Resort
Chart of Accounts

Assets		Revenue	
101	Cash	401	Registration Fees
142	Office Supplies		
144	Food Supplies		**Expenses**
184	Tennis Facilities	511	Wages Expense
184.1	Accum. Depr.—Tennis Facilities	521	Rent Expense
186	Exercise Equipment	523	Office Supplies Expense
186.1	Accum. Depr.—Exercise Equip.	524	Food Supplies Expense
		525	Telephone Expense
Liabilities		533	Utilities Expense
202	Accounts Payable	535	Insurance Expense
		536	Postage Expense
Owner's Equity		541	Depr. Exp.—Tennis Facilities
311	John McRoe, Capital	542	Depr. Exp.—Exercise Equip.
312	John McRoe, Drawing		
313	Income Summary		

June 1   McRoe invested cash in the business, $90,000.

     1   Paid for new exercise equipment, $9,000.

     2   Deposited registration fees in the bank, $15,000.

     2   Paid rent for month of June on building and land, $2,500.

     2   Rogers Construction completed work on new tennis courts that cost $70,000. The estimated useful life of the facility is five years, at which time the courts will have to be resurfaced. Arrangements were made to pay the bill in July.

3   Purchased food supplies on account from Au Naturel Foods, $5,000.

5   Purchased office supplies on account from Gordon Office Supplies, $300.

7   Deposited registration fees in the bank, $16,200.

10   Purchased food supplies on account from Au Naturel Foods, $6,200.

10   Paid wages to staff, $500.

14   Deposited registration fees in the bank, $13,500.

16   Purchased food supplies on account from Au Naturel Foods, $4,000.

17   Paid wages to staff, $500.

18   Paid postage, $85.

21   Deposited registration fees in the bank, $15,200.

24   Purchased food supplies on account from Au Naturel Foods, $5,500.

24   Paid wages to staff, $500.

28   Deposited registration fees in the bank, $14,000.

30   Purchased food supplies on account from Au Naturel Foods, $6,000.

30   Paid wages to staff, $500.

30   Paid Au Naturel Foods on account, $28,700.

30   Paid utility bill, $500.

30   Paid telephone bill, $120.

30   McRoe withdrew cash for personal use, $1,500.

REQUIRED   1.   Enter the transactions in a combination journal (page 1). Establish special columns for Registration Fees (credit), Wages Expense (debit), and Food Supplies (debit).

2.   Prove the combination journal.

3.   Post these transactions to a general ledger.

4.   Prepare a trial balance as of June 30.

Self-Study Test Questions

True/False

1. Under the accrual basis of accounting, revenues are recorded when earned. _____

2. The cash basis of accounting is used by most large businesses. _____

3. The modified cash basis uses the accrual basis when recording revenues and expenses. _____

4. The modified cash basis is a combination of the cash and accrual methods of accounting. _____

5. Many small professional service businesses use the modified cash basis. _____

Multiple Choice

1. Which of these would make the best "special column" in a combination journal? _____

   (a) Office Equipment   (c) Revenue
   (b) Prepaid Insurance   (d) Telephone Expense

2. Verifying that debit column totals equal credit column totals is the process of _____

   (a) debiting.   (c) closing.
   (b) proving.   (d) adjusting.

3. Posting from the combination journal is accomplished by placing a " _____ " and _____
   page number in the Posting Reference column of the general ledger account.

   (a) G   (c) J
   (b) DJ   (d) CJ

4. Using the modified cash basis, when a business provides services on account, _____
   _____ is debited.

   (a) No entry   (c) Cash
   (b) Accounts Receivable (d) Owner's Equity

5. Using the modified cash basis, when wages are earned but not paid, _____ is debited. _____

   (a) Wages Expense   (c) Wages Payable
   (b) No entry   (d) Accrued Wages

The answers to the Self-Study Test Questions are at the end of the text.

8

Accounting for Cash

LEARNING OBJECTIVES:
Careful study of this chapter should enable you to:

LO 1 Describe how to open and use a checking account.

LO 2 Prepare a bank reconciliation and related journal entries.

LO 3 Establish and use a petty cash fund.

LO 4 Use the cash short and over account.

John Zenith recently opened a sports equipment and clothing shop named Be A Sport in West Springfield, MA. To protect and properly manage cash, John uses a checking account. All cash and checks received from customers are deposited promptly. All bills are paid by check. In this way, John can use the deposit slips and monthly bank statement to verify his records of cash received. Similarly, cancelled checks and the monthly bank statement can be used to verify John's records of cash payments. Complete and accurate records of cash receipts and cash payments help John control this important asset and plan for future cash needs.

At the end of the month, the balance in the cash account in John's books differs from the cash balance shown on the bank statement. In trying to reconcile the two amounts, how should John treat the checks he wrote during the month that have not yet been presented to the bank for payment?

Cash is an asset that is quite familiar and important to all of us. We generally think of **cash** as the currency and coins in our pockets and the money we have in our checking accounts. To a business, cash also includes checks received from customers, money orders, and bank cashier's checks.

Because it plays such a central role in operating a business, cash must be carefully managed and controlled. A business should have a system of **internal control**—a set of procedures designed to ensure proper accounting for transactions. For good internal control of cash transactions, all cash received should be deposited daily in a bank. All disbursements, except for payments from petty cash, should be made by check.

CHECKING ACCOUNT

LO 1   Describe how to open and use a checking account.

The key documents and forms required in opening and using a checking account are the signature card, deposit tickets, checks, and bank statements.

Opening a Checking Account

To open a checking account, each person authorized to sign checks must complete and sign a **signature card** (Figure 8-1). The bank uses this card to verify the depositor's signature on any banking transactions. The depositor's social security number or employer identification number (EIN) is shown on the card to identify the depositor. An EIN can be obtained from the Internal Revenue Service.

FIGURE 8-1 Signature Card

LAST NAME, FIRST NAME, MIDDLE INITIAL	ACCT #	
	TYPE	
	DATE	INIT.
STREET ADDRESS TOWN	STATE	ZIP
I CERTIFY THAT THE NUMBER SHOWN ON THIS FORM IS MY CORRECT TAXPAYER IDENTIFICATION NUMBER AND THAT I AM NOT SUBJECT TO BACKUP WITHHOLDING.		
SIGNATURE 1	DATE OF BIRTH / /	SOCIAL SECURITY NO.
SIGNATURE 2		
SIGNATURE 3		

Making Deposits

A **deposit ticket** (Figure 8-2) is a detailed listing of items being deposited. Currency, coins, and checks are listed separately. Each check should be identified by its **ABA (American Bankers Association) Number**. This number is the small fraction printed in the upper right-hand corner of each check. The number is used to sort and route checks throughout the U.S. banking system. Normally, only the numerator of the fraction is used in identifying checks on the deposit ticket.

FIGURE 8-2 Deposit Ticket

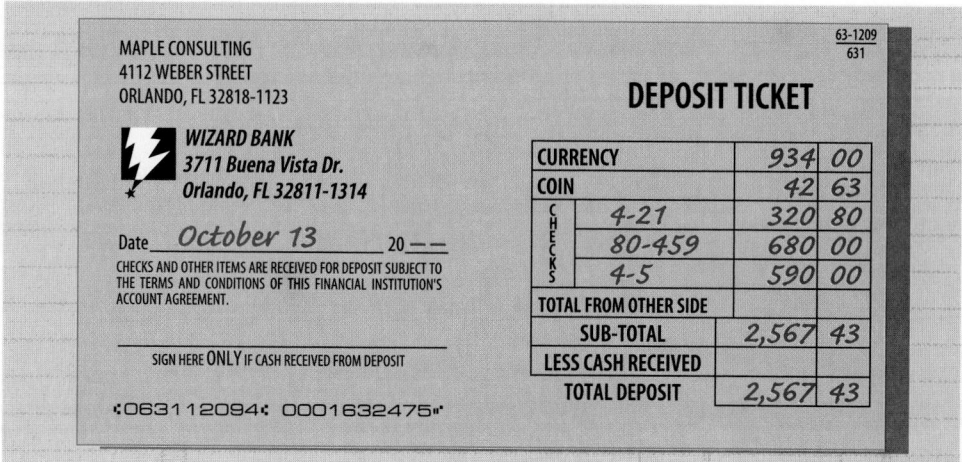

The depositor delivers or mails the deposit ticket and all items being deposited to the bank. The bank then gives or mails a receipt to the depositor.

Endorsements. Each check being deposited must be endorsed by the depositor. The **endorsement** consists of stamping or writing the depositor's name and sometimes other information on the back of the check, near the left end. There are two basic types of endorsements:

1. **Blank endorsement**—the depositor simply signs the back of the check. This makes the check payable to any bearer.

2. **Restrictive endorsement**—the depositor adds words such as "For deposit," "Pay to any bank," or "Pay to Daryl Beck only" to restrict the payment of the check.

Businesses commonly use a rubber stamp to endorse checks for deposit. The check shown in Figure 8-3 has been stamped with a restrictive endorsement.

FIGURE 8-3 Restrictive Endorsement

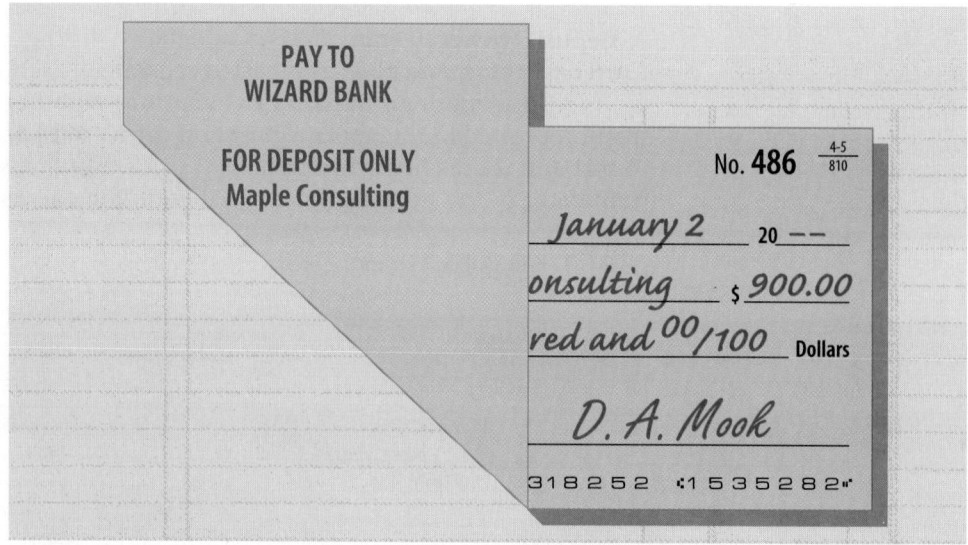

Automated Teller Machines. Many banks now make **automated teller machines (ATMs)** available at all times to depositors for making deposits or withdrawals. Each depositor has a plastic card (Figure 8-4) and a personal identification number (PIN). The depositor inserts the card, keys in the PIN, indicates whether the transaction is a withdrawal or a deposit, and enters the amount. The machine has a drawer or door for the withdrawal or deposit.

It is important for the depositor to keep an accounting record of ATM withdrawals and deposits. This is done on the check stub or register described in the following section, and with an appropriate journal entry.

FIGURE 8-4 Automated Teller Machine Card

Writing Checks

A **check** is a document ordering a bank to pay cash from a depositor's account. There are three parties to every check:

1. **Drawer**—the depositor who orders the bank to pay the cash.

2. **Drawee**—the bank on which the check is drawn.

3. **Payee**—the person being paid the cash.

Checks used by businesses are usually bound in the form of a book. In some checkbooks, each check is attached to a **check stub** (Figure 8-5) that contains space to record all relevant information about the check. Other checkbooks are accompanied by a small register book in which the relevant information is noted. If a financial computer software package is used, both the check and the register can be prepared electronically.

Use the following three steps in preparing a check.

STEP 1   Complete the check stub or register.

STEP 2   Enter the date, payee name, and amount on the check.

STEP 3   Sign the check.

The check stub is completed first so that the drawer retains a record of each check issued. This information is needed to determine the proper journal entry for the transaction.

The payee name is entered on the first long line on the check, followed by the amount in figures. The amount in words is then entered on the second long line. If the amount in figures does not agree with the amount in words, the bank usually contacts the drawer for the correct amount or returns the check unpaid.

The most critical point in preparing a check is signing it, and this should be done last. The signature authorizes the bank to pay cash from the drawer's account. The check signer should make sure that all other aspects of the check are correct before signing it.

Note that the check stubs in Figure 8-5 contain space to record amounts deposited. It generally is a good idea also to indicate the date of the deposit, as shown on check stub No. 108.

The payee and amount written in words should be followed by something, such as a line, to make it difficult to alter the payee or the amount.

It is sometimes necessary to void a check. Proper procedures for doing so are to tear off or deface the signature box and to file the voided check numerically with the cancelled checks.

PROFILES in ACCOUNTING

Lisa Davis, Legal Coordinator

Lisa Davis began working as a part-time legal secretary with Zegarelli Associates. Lisa continued her career with this company after earning an Associate Degree in Legal Office Management.

After graduation, Lisa was hired as a legal assistant and later promoted to legal coordinator. Her duties include budgeting, accounts receivable, supervising two employees, coordinating schedules, researching, and dealing with clients on a daily basis.

According to Lisa, dependability, initiative, and loyalty lead to success. Lisa chose the legal filed because she always had an interest in law and wanted to work in a fast-paced environment.

FIGURE 8-5 Checks and Check Stubs

Bank Statement

A statement of account issued by a bank to each depositor once a month is called a **bank statement**. Figure 8-6 is a bank statement for a checking account. The statement shows:

1. The balance at the beginning of the period.

2. Deposits and other amounts added during the period.

3. Checks and other amounts subtracted during the period.

4. The balance at the end of the period.

With the bank statement, the bank normally sends to the depositor:

1. **Cancelled checks**—the depositor's checks paid by the bank during the period. (Some banks send cancelled checks only upon request of the depositor.)

2. Any other forms representing items added to or subtracted from the account.

FIGURE 8-6 Bank Statement

RECONCILING THE BANK STATEMENT

LO 2 Prepare a bank reconciliation and related journal entries.

On any given day, the balance in the cash account on the depositor's books (the book balance) is unlikely to be the same as that on the bank's books (the bank balance). This difference can be due to errors, but it usually is caused by timing. Transactions generally are recorded by the business at a time that is different from when the bank records them.

Deposits

Suppose there are cash receipts of $600.00 on April 30. These cash receipts would be recorded on the depositor's books on April 30 and a deposit of $600.00 would be sent to the bank. The deposit would not reach the bank, however, until at least the following day, May 1. This timing difference in recording the $600.00 of cash receipts is illustrated in Figure 8-7. Notice that on April 30, the balances in the depositor's books and in the bank's books would be different.

FIGURE 8-7 Depositor and Bank Records—Deposits

Cash Payments

Similar timing differences occur with cash payments. Suppose a check for $350.00 is written on April 30. This cash payment would be recorded on the depositor's books on April 30 and the check mailed to the payee. The check probably would not be received by the payee until May 3. If the payee deposited the check promptly, it still would not clear the bank until May 4. This timing difference in recording the $350.00 cash payment is illustrated in Figure 8-8. Notice once again that on April 30, the balances in the depositor's books and in the bank's books would be different.

FIGURE 8-8 Depositor and Bank Records—Cash Payments

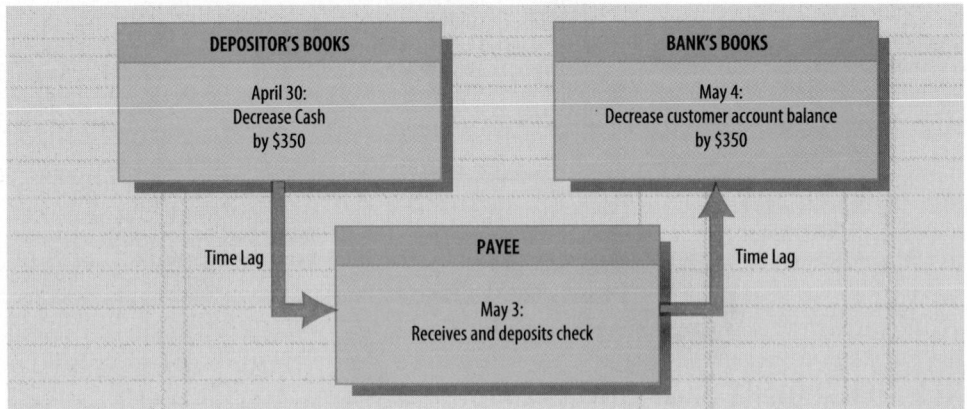

Reasons for Differences Between Bank and Book Balances

When the bank statement is received, the depositor examines the records to identify the items that explain the difference between the book and bank balances. This process of bringing the book and bank balances into agreement is called preparing a **bank reconciliation**.

The most common reasons for differences between the book and bank balances are the following:

1. **Outstanding checks.** Checks issued during the period that have not been presented to the bank for payment before the statement is prepared.

2. **Deposits in transit.** Deposits that have not reached or been recorded by the bank before the statement is prepared.

3. **Service charges.** Bank charges for services such as check printing and processing.

4. **Collections.** Collections of promissory notes or charge accounts made by the bank on behalf of the depositor.

5. **Not sufficient funds (NSF) checks.** Checks deposited by the depositor that are not paid because the drawer did not have sufficient funds.

6. **Errors.** Errors made by the bank or the depositor in recording cash transactions.

Steps in Preparing the Bank Reconciliation

Use the following three steps in preparing the bank reconciliation:

STEP 1　Identify deposits in transit and any related errors.

STEP 2　Identify outstanding checks and any related errors.

STEP 3　Identify additional reconciling items.

Deposits in Transit and Related Errors. Follow these steps:

STEP 1　Compare deposits listed on the bank statement with deposits in transit on last month's bank reconciliation. All of last month's deposits in transit should appear on the current month's bank statement.

STEP 2　Compare the remaining deposits on the bank statement with deposits listed in the accounting records. Any deposits listed in the accounting records but not on the bank statement are deposits in transit on the current bank reconciliation.

STEP 3　Compare the individual deposit amounts on the bank statement and in the accounting records. If they differ, the error needs to be corrected.

Outstanding Checks and Related Errors. Follow these steps:

STEP 1　Compare cancelled checks with the bank statement and the accounting records. If the amounts differ, the error needs to be corrected.

STEP 2　As each cancelled check is compared with the accounting records, place a check mark on the check stub or other accounting record to indicate that the check has cleared.

STEP 3　Any checks written that have not been checked off represent outstanding checks on the bank reconciliation.

Additional Reconciling Items. Compare any additions and deductions on the bank statement that are not deposits or checks with the accounting records. Items that the bank adds to the account are called **credit memos**. Items that the bank deducts from the account are called **debit memos**. Remember that a depositor's account is a liability to the bank. Thus, a credit memo increases this liability; a debit memo reduces the liability. Any of these items not appearing in the accounting records represent additional items on the bank reconciliation.

Illustration of a Bank Reconciliation

A general format for the bank reconciliation is shown in Figure 8-9. Not every item shown in this illustration would be in every bank reconciliation, but this format is helpful in determining where to put items. A bank reconciliation form also can be found on the back of most bank statements.

FIGURE 8-9 Bank Reconciliation Format

BANK RECONCILIATION		
Bank statement balance		$xxxx
Add: Deposits in transit	$xxxx	
Bank errors	xxxx	xxxx
		$xxxx
Deduct: Outstanding checks	$xxxx	
Bank errors	xxxx	xxxx
Adjusted bank balance		$xxxx
Book balance		$xxxx
Add: Bank credit memos	$xxxx	
Book errors	xxxx	xxxx
		$xxxx
Deduct: Bank debit memos	$xxxx	
Book errors	xxxx	xxxx
Adjusted book balance		$xxxx

To illustrate the preparation of a bank reconciliation, we will use the Maple Consulting bank statement shown in Figure 8-6. That statement shows a balance of $1,748.09 as of November 21. The balance in Maple's check stubs and general ledger cash account is $2,393.23. The three steps described on page 269 were used to identify the following items, and the reconciliation in Figure 8-10 was prepared.

1. A deposit of $637.02 recorded on November 21 had not been received by the bank. Maple has received the funds but the amount has not yet been counted by the bank. This deposit in transit is added to the bank statement balance.

2. Check numbers 219, 224, and 227 are outstanding. The funds have been disbursed by Maple but have not yet been paid out by the bank. The amount of these outstanding checks is subtracted from the bank statement balance.

3. Check number 214 was written for $18.98, but was entered on the check stub and on the books as $19.88. This $.90 error is added to the book balance because $.90 too much had been deducted from the book balance.

4. Maple made an ATM withdrawal of $100.00 on November 13 for personal use but did not record the withdrawal on the books. The bank has reduced Maple's balance by this amount. Thus, this amount is deducted from the book balance.

5. The bank returned an NSF check of $200.00. This was a check received by Maple from a customer. The bank has reduced Maple's balance by $200.00 but Maple has not yet recorded it. This amount is deducted from the book balance.

6. The bank service charge was $1.80. The bank has reduced Maple's balance by this amount but Maple has not yet recorded it. This amount is deducted from the book balance.

FIGURE 8-10 Bank Reconciliation

Maple Consulting											
Bank Reconciliation											
November 21, 20 - -											
Bank statement balance, November 21							$1	7	4	8	09
Add deposit in transit								6	3	7	02
							$2	3	8	5	11
Deduct outstanding checks:											
No. 219	$	2	0	0	00						
No. 224			2	5	00						
No. 227			6	7	78			2	9	2	78
Adjusted bank balance							$2	0	9	2	33
Book balance, November 21							$2	3	9	3	23
Add error on check no. 214											90
							$2	3	9	4	13
Deduct:											
Unrecorded ATM withdrawal	$	1	0	0	00						
NSF check		2	0	0	00						
Bank service charge				1	80			3	0	1	80
Adjusted book balance							$2	0	9	2	33

Requires journal entry ▷

Require journal entries ▷

Reconciled balances ◁

A BROADER VIEW

FRAUD—A REAL THREAT TO SMALL BUSINESS

The bookkeeper for Kramer Iron, Inc., in Hamden, CT, embezzled $213,539 from the company over a four-year period. She used two schemes. One was to alter the number of the dollar amount printed on checks payable to her. The other technique involved putting her own name on the "pay to" line on checks intended for other parties.

This fraud shows the importance of two procedures described in this chapter: (1) Make sure that all aspects of a check are correct before signing it. (2) In preparing the bank reconciliation, compare cancelled checks with the accounting records.

Journal Entries

Only two kinds of items appearing on a bank reconciliation require journal entries:

1. Errors in the books.

2. Bank additions and deductions that do not already appear in the accounting records.

LEARNING KEY: Journal entries are needed to correct errors in the books and to record bank additions and deductions that are not in the accounting records.

Figure 8-11 contains a detailed list of items that require journal entries.

FIGURE 8-11 Bank Reconciliation Items that Require Journal Entries

ADDITIONS TO CASH BALANCE	DEDUCTIONS FROM CASH BALANCE

* Unrecorded deposits (including ATM)
 * Note collected by bank
 * Interest earned
 * Errors:
   1. Added too little as a deposit
   2. Deducted too much as a check
	* Unrecorded ATM withdrawals
	 * NSF checks
	 * Bank service charges
	 * Deposits recorded twice
	 * Unrecorded checks
	 * Loan payments
	 * Interest payments
	 * Errors:
	   1. Added too much as a deposit
	   2. Deducted too little as a check

Note the four items in the lower portion of the bank reconciliation in Figure 8-10. A journal entry always is required for each item in this portion of the bank reconciliation.

The $.90 item is an error in the accounting records that occurred when the check amount was incorrectly entered. Assume the $18.98 was in payment of an account payable which had been incorrectly debited for $19.88. The entry to correct this error is:

4			Cash						90						4
5			Accounts Payable											90	5
6			Error in recording check												6

The $100.00 ATM withdrawal has been deducted from Maple's account by the bank. Maple has not yet recorded the withdrawal. Maple withdrew the funds for personal use, so the following journal entry is required:

8			James Maple, Drawing			1	0	0	00						8
9			Cash								1	0	0	00	9
10			Unrecorded ATM withdrawal												10

The $200.00 NSF check is a deduction by the bank for a check deposited by Maple that proved to be worthless. This amount must be deducted from the book balance. Assuming the $200.00 was received from a customer on account, the following journal entry is required:

12		Accounts Receivable					2	0	0	00							12
13		Cash										2	0	0	00		13
14		Unrecorded NSF check															14

The $1.80 bank service charge is a fee for bank services received by Maple. The bank has deducted this amount from Maple's account. Bank service charges are usually small and are charged to Miscellaneous Expense.

16		Miscellaneous Expense							1	80							16
17		Cash												1	80		17
18		Bank service charge															18

Electronic Funds Transfer

Electronic funds transfer (EFT) uses a computer rather than paper checks to complete transactions with the bank. This technique is being used increasingly today. Applications of EFT include payrolls, social security payments, retail purchases, mortgage payments, and the ATM transactions described earlier in the chapter.

Heavy use of EFT can present a challenge in preparing bank reconciliations. Many of the documents handled in a purely manual environment disappear when EFT is used. Bank accounts are just one of many areas where computers require accountants to think in new ways. Regardless of what system is used, the key point to remember is that the accounting records must be correctly updated.

THE PETTY CASH FUND

LO 3   Establish and use a petty cash fund.

For good control over cash, payments generally should be made by check. Unfortunately, payments of very small amounts by check can be both inconvenient and inefficient. For example, the time and cost required to write a check for $.70 to mail a letter might be greater than the cost of the postage. Therefore, businesses customarily establish a **petty cash fund** to pay for small items with cash. "Petty" means small, and both the amount of the fund and the maximum amount of any bill that can be paid from the fund are small.

Establishing a Petty Cash Fund

To establish a petty cash fund, a check is written to the petty cash custodian for the amount to be set aside in the fund. The amount may be $50.00, $100.00, $200.00, or any amount considered necessary. The journal entry to establish a petty cash fund of $100.00 would be as follows:

4		Petty Cash					1	0	0	00							4
5		Cash										1	0	0	00		5
6		Establish petty cash fund															6

Petty cash is an asset that is listed immediately below Cash on the balance sheet.

The custodian cashes the check and places the money in a petty cash box. For good control, the custodian should be the only person authorized to make payments from the fund. The custodian should be able to account for the full amount of the fund at any time.

Making Payments from a Petty Cash Fund

A receipt called a **petty cash voucher** (Figure 8-12) should be prepared for every payment from the fund. The voucher shows the name of the payee, the purpose of the payment, and the account to be charged for the payment. Each voucher should be signed by the custodian and by the person receiving the cash. The vouchers should be numbered consecutively so that all vouchers can be accounted for.

FIGURE 8-12 Petty Cash Voucher

Petty Cash Payments Record

When a petty cash fund is maintained, a formal record is often kept of all payments from the fund. The **petty cash payments record** (Figure 8-13) is a special multi-column record that supplements the regular accounting records. It is not a journal. The headings of the Distribution of Payments columns may vary, depending upon the types of expenditures.

The petty cash payments record of Maple Consulting is shown in Figure 8-13 on page 276. A narrative of the petty cash transactions shown in Figure 8-13 is as follows:

Dec. 1   Maple issued a check for $200.00 payable to Tina Blank, Petty Cash Custodian. Blank cashed the check and placed the money in a secure cash box.

A notation of the amount received is made in the Description column of the petty cash payments record. In addition, this transaction is entered in the journal as follows:

8	Dec. 1	Petty Cash			2	0	0	00						8
9		Cash								2	0	0	00	9
10		Establish petty cash fund												10

During the month of December, the following payments were made from the petty cash fund:

Dec. 5   Paid $32.80 to Jerry's Auto for servicing the company automobile. Voucher No. 1.

8   Reimbursed Maple $15.75 for the amount spent for lunch with a client. Voucher No. 2.

9   Gave Maple $30.00 for personal use. Voucher No. 3.

There is no special Distribution column for entering amounts withdrawn by the owner for personal use. Therefore this payment is entered by writing the account name in the Account column and $30.00 in the Amount column at the extreme right of the petty cash payments record.

15   Paid $28.25 for typewriter repairs. Voucher No. 4.

17   Reimbursed Maple $14.50 for travel expenses. Voucher No. 5.

19   Paid $8.00 to Big Red Car Care for washing the company automobile. Voucher No. 6.

22   Paid $9.50 for mailing a package. Voucher No. 7.

29   Paid $30.00 for postage stamps. Voucher No. 8.

Replenishing the Petty Cash Fund

The petty cash fund should be replenished whenever the fund runs low and at the end of each accounting period, so that the accounts are brought up to date. The amount columns of the petty cash payments record are totaled to verify that the total of the Total Amount column equals the total of the Distribution columns. The amount columns are then ruled as shown in Figure 8-13.

The information in the petty cash payments record is then used to replenish the petty cash fund. On December 31, a check for $168.80 is issued to the petty cash custodian. The journal entry to record the replenishment of the fund is as follows:

18	Dec.	31	Automobile Expense					4	0	80								18
19			Postage Expense					3	9	50								19
20			Travel and Entertainment Expense					3	0	25								20
21			Miscellaneous Expense					2	8	25								21
22			James Maple, Drawing					3	0	00								22
23			Cash										1	6	8	80		23
24			Replenishment of petty cash fund															24

Note two important aspects of the functioning of a petty cash fund:

1.   Once the fund is established by debiting Petty Cash and crediting Cash, no further entries are made to Petty Cash. Notice in the journal entry to replenish the fund that the debits are to appropriate expense accounts and the credit is to Cash. Only if the amount of the fund itself is being changed would there be a debit or credit to Petty Cash.

2.   The petty cash payments record is strictly a supplement to the regular accounting records. Because it is not a journal, no posting is done from this record. A separate entry must by made in the journal to replenish the fund and update the expense accounts.

FIGURE 8-13 Maple Consulting's Petty Cash Payments Record

PETTY CASH PAYMENTS FOR THE MONTH OF December 20— PAGE 1

DAY		DESCRIPTION		VOU. NO.	TOTAL AMOUNT	AUTO EXP.	POST. EXP.	TRAVEL/ ENTERT. EXP.	MISC. EXP.	ACCOUNT	AMOUNT	
						DISTRIBUTION OF PAYMENTS						
1	1	Received in fund	200.00									1
2	5	Automobile repairs		1	3 2 80	3 2 80						2
3	8	Client luncheon		2	1 5 75			1 5 75				3
4	9	James Maple, personal use		3	3 0 00					James Maple, Drawing	3 0 00	4
5	15	Typewriter repairs		4	2 8 25				2 8 25			5
6	17	Traveling expenses		5	1 4 50			1 4 50				6
7	19	Washing automobile		6	8 00	8 00						7
8	22	Postage expense		7	9 50		9 50					8
9	29	Postage stamps		8	3 0 00		3 0 00					9
10					1 6 8 80	4 0 80	3 9 50	3 0 25	2 8 25		3 0 00	10
11	31	Balance	31.20									11
12	31	Replenished fund	168.80									12
13		Total	200.00									13
14												14
15												15
16												16
17												17
18												18
19												19
20												20
21												21
22												22
23												23
24												24
25												25
26												26
27												27
28												28

Credit to replenish petty cash fund

Debits to replenish petty cash fund

LEARNING KEY: Once the petty cash fund is established, an entry is made to Petty Cash only if the amount of the fund is being changed.

CASH SHORT AND OVER

LO 4   Use the cash short and over account.

Businesses generally must be able to make change when customers pay for goods or services received. An unavoidable part of this change-making process is that errors can occur. It is important to know whether such errors have occurred and how to account for them.

Businesses commonly use cash registers with tapes that accumulate a record of the day's receipts. The amount of cash according to the tapes can be compared with the amount of cash in the register to determine any error. For example, assume a cash shortage is identified for June 19.

Receipts per register tapes	$963.00
Cash count	961.00
Cash shortage	$ 2.00

Similarly, assume a cash overage is identified for June 20.

Receipts per register tapes	$814.00
Cash count	815.00
Cash overage	$ 1.00

We account for such errors by using an account called Cash Short and Over. In T account form, Cash Short and Over appears as follows:

Cash Short and Over	
Shortage (Expense)	Overage (Revenue)

The register tapes on June 19 showed receipts of $963.00, but only $961.00 in cash was counted. The journal entry on June 19 to record the revenues and cash shortage would be:

18	June	19	Cash		9 6 1 00				18
19			Cash Short and Over		2 00				19
20			Service Fees				9 6 3 00		20
21			Record cash shortage						21

The entry on June 20 to record the revenues and cash overage would be:

23	June	20	Cash		8 1 5 00				23
24			Service Fees				8 1 4 00		24
25			Cash Short and Over				1 00		25
26			Record cash overage						26

The cash short and over account is used to accumulate cash shortages and overages throughout the accounting period. At the end of the period, a debit balance in the account (a net shortage) is treated as an expense. A credit balance in the account (a net overage) is treated as revenue.

Learning Objectives	Key Points to Remember
1 Describe how to open and use a checking account.	Three steps to follow in preparing a check are: 1. Complete the check stub or register. 2. Enter the date, payee name, and amount on the check. 3. Sign the check.
2 Prepare a bank reconciliation and related journal entries.	The most common reasons for differences between the book and bank cash balances are: 1. Outstanding checks 2. Deposits in transit 3. Bank service charges 4. Bank collections for the depositor 5. NSF checks 6. Errors by the bank or the depositor Three steps to follow in preparing a bank reconciliation are: 1. Identify deposits in transit and any related errors. 2. Identify outstanding checks and any related errors. 3. Identify additional reconciling items. Only two kinds of items on a bank reconciliation require journal entries: 1. Errors on the depositor's books. 2. Bank additions and deductions that do not already appear in the accounting records.
3 Establish and use a petty cash fund.	Two important aspects of the functioning of a petty cash fund are: 1. Once the fund is established, subsequent entries do not affect the petty cash account balance, unless the size of the fund itself is being changed. 2. The petty cash payments record is supplemental to the regular accounting records. No posting is done from this record.
4 Use the cash short and over account.	Cash shortages and overages are accounted for using the cash short and over account. A debit balance in this account represents expense; a credit balance represents revenue.

Reflection: Answering the Opening Question

Checks John wrote that have not been presented to the bank for payment are considered outstanding checks. In reconciling the book and bank balances, outstanding checks are subtracted from the bank statement balance to determine the adjusted bank balance. If the outstanding checks are not subtracted correctly on the bank reconciliation, John could overstate his cash balance and risk writing a check for funds he does not have in the bank. This would harm John's credibility with both the bank and his creditors.

KEY TERMS

ABA (American Bankers Association) Number, (263)   The small fraction printed in the upper right-hand corner of each check.

automated teller machines (ATMs), (264)   Machines used by depositors to make withdrawals or deposits at any time.

bank reconciliation, (268)   Bringing the book and bank balances into agreement.

bank statement, (265)   A statement of account issued by a bank to each depositor once a month.

blank endorsement, (263)   The depositor signs the back of the check, making the check payable to any bearer.

cancelled checks, (265)   The depositor's checks paid by the bank during the bank statement period.

cash, (262)   To a business, cash includes currency, coins, checks received from customers, money orders, and bank cashier's checks.

check, (264)   A document ordering a bank to pay cash from a depositor's account.

check stub, (264)   In some checkbooks, each check is attached to a stub that contains space for relevant information.

credit memos, (269)   Items that the bank adds to the account.

debit memos, (269)   Items that the bank deducts from the account.

deposit ticket, (263)   A detailed listing of items being deposited.

deposits in transit, (268)   Deposits that have not reached or been recorded by the bank before the bank statement is prepared.

drawee, (264)   The bank on which the check is drawn.

drawer, (264)   The depositor who orders the bank to pay the cash.

electronic funds transfer (EFT), (273)   Using a computer rather than paper checks to complete transactions with the bank.

endorsement, (263)   Stamping or writing the depositor's name and sometimes other information on the back of the check.

internal control, (262)   A set of procedures designed to ensure proper accounting for transactions.

not sufficient funds (NSF) checks, (269)   Checks deposited by the depositor that are not paid because the drawer did not have sufficient funds.

outstanding checks, (268)   Checks issued during the bank statement period that have not been presented to the bank for payment before the statement is prepared.

payee, (264)   The person being paid the cash.

petty cash fund, (273) A fund established to pay for small items with cash.

petty cash payments record, (274) A special multi-column record that supplements the regular accounting records.

petty cash voucher, (274) A receipt that is prepared for every payment from the petty cash fund.

restrictive endorsement, (263) The depositor adds words such as "For deposit" to restrict the payment of the check.

service charges, (268) Bank charges for services such as check printing and processing.

signature card, (262) A card that is completed and signed by each person authorized to sign checks.

DEMONSTRATION PROBLEM

Jason Kuhn's check stubs indicated a balance of $4,673.12 on March 31. This included a record of a deposit of $926.10 mailed to the bank on March 30, but not credited to Kuhn's account until April 1. In addition, the following checks were outstanding on March 31:

No. 462,	$524.26
No. 465,	$213.41
No. 473,	$543.58
No. 476,	$351.38
No. 477,	$197.45

The bank statement showed a balance of $5,419.00 as of March 31. The bank statement included a service charge of $4.10 with the date of March 29. In matching the cancelled checks and record of deposits with the stubs, it was discovered that check no. 456, to Office Suppliers, Inc., for $93.00 was erroneously recorded on the stub for $39.00. This caused the bank balance on that stub and those following to be $54.00 too large. It was also discovered that an ATM withdrawal of $100.00 for personal use was not recorded on the books.

Kuhn maintains a $200.00 petty cash fund. His petty cash payments record showed the following totals at the end of March of the current year.

Automobile expense	$ 32.40
Postage expense	27.50
Charitable contributions expense	35.00
Telephone expense	6.20
Travel and entertainment expense	38.60
Miscellaneous expense	17.75
Jason Kuhn, Drawing	40.00
Total	$197.45

This left a balance of $2.55 in the petty cash fund.

REQUIRED

1. Prepare a bank reconciliation for Jason Kuhn as of March 31, 20--.

2. Journalize the entries that should be made by Kuhn on his books as of March 31, 20--: (a) as a result of the bank reconciliation and (b) to replenish the petty cash fund.

3. Show proof that, after these entries, the total of the cash and petty cash account balances equals $4,715.02.

Solution

1.

Kuhn's Wilderness Outfitters
Bank Reconciliation
March 31, 20 - -

Bank statement balance, March 31						$5 4 1 9	00
Add deposit in transit						9 2 6	10
						$6 3 4 5	10
Deduct outstanding checks:							
No. 462	$ 5 2 4	26					
No. 465	2 1 3	41					
No. 473	5 4 3	58					
No. 476	3 5 1	38					
No. 477	1 9 7	45			1 8 3 0	08	
Adjusted bank balance						$4 5 1 5	02
Book balance, March 31						$4 6 7 3	12
Deduct: Bank service charge	$ 4	10					
Error on check no. 456	5 4	00					
Unrecorded ATM withdrawal	1 0 0	00			1 5 8	10	
Adjusted book balance						$4 5 1 5	02

2a.

3						3
4	20-- Mar.	31	Miscellaneous Expense	4 10		4
5			Accounts Payable—Office Supp., Inc	5 4 00		5
6			Jason Kuhn, Drawing	1 0 0 00		6
7			Cash		1 5 8 10	7
8			Bank transactions for March			8
9						9

b.

10		31	Automobile Expense	3 2 40		10
11			Postage Expense	2 7 50		11
12			Charitable Contributions Expense	3 5 00		12
13			Telephone Expense	6 20		13
14			Travel and Entertainment Expense	3 8 60		14
15			Miscellaneous Expense	1 7 75		15
16			Jason Kuhn, Drawing	4 0 00		16
17			Cash		1 9 7 45	17
18			Replenishment of petty cash			18
19			fund			19
20						20
21						21

3. Cash in bank:

Check stub balance, March 31	$4,673.12
Less bank charges	158.10
Adjusted cash in bank	$4,515.02

Cash on hand:

Petty cash fund	$ 2.55
Add replenishment	197.45
Adjusted cash on hand	$ 200.00
Total cash in bank and petty cash on hand	$4,715.02

REVIEW QUESTIONS

1. Why must a signature card be filled out and signed to open a checking account?

2. Explain the difference between a blank endorsement and a restrictive endorsement.

3. Who are the three parties to every check?

4. What are the three steps to follow in preparing a check?

5. What are the most common reasons for differences between the book and bank cash balances?

6. What are the three steps to follow in preparing a bank reconciliation?

7. What two kinds of items on a bank reconciliation require journal entries?

8. Name four applications of electronic funds transfer in current use.

9. What is the purpose of a petty cash fund?

10. What should be prepared every time a petty cash payment is made?

11. At what two times should the petty cash fund be replenished?

12. From what source is the information obtained for issuing a check to replenish the petty cash fund?

13. What does a debit balance in the cash short and over account represent? What does a credit balance in this account represent?

MANAGING YOUR WRITING

The current month's bank statement for your account arrives in the mail. In reviewing the statement, you notice a deposit listed for $400.00 that you did not make. It has been credited in error to your account.

Discuss whether you have an ethical or legal obligation to inform the bank of the error. What action should you take?

ETHICS CASE

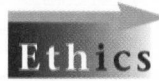

Ben Thomas works as a teller for First National Bank. When he arrived at work on Friday, the branch manager, Frank Mills, asked him to get his cash drawer out early because the head teller, Naomi Ray, was conducting a surprise cash count for all the tellers. Surprise cash counts are usually done four or five times a year by the branch manager or the head teller and once or twice a year by internal auditors. Ben's drawer was $100.00 short and his reconciliation tape showed that he was in balance on Thursday night. Naomi asked Ben for an explanation, and Ben immediately took $100.00 out of his pocket and handed it to her. He went on to explain he needed the cash to buy prescriptions for his son and pay for groceries and intended to put the $100.00 back in his cash drawer on Monday, which was pay day. He also told Naomi that this was the first time he had ever "borrowed" money from his cash drawer and that he would never do it again.

1. What are the ethical considerations in this case from both Ben's and Naomi's perspectives?

2. What options does Naomi have to address this problem?

3. Assume Naomi chooses to inform the branch manager. Write a short incident report describing the findings.

4. In small groups come up with as many ideas as possible on how to safeguard cash on hand in a bank (petty cash, teller drawer cash, and vault cash) from employee theft and mismanagement.

WEB WORK

Your business will, at some point in time, need to write a check to pay a vendor or an employee, or to cover an unforeseen expense. What do you need to do to open an account? What are some of the costs and restrictions a business owner needs to be aware of? Check out these sites for information on checking accounts:

http://www.bofa.com/b-banking/bb_checkov.html
http://www.edc-sea.org/textonly/seafirst/bizbank.html
(http://heintz.swcollege.com)

SERIES A EXERCISES

EXERCISE 8A-1 (LO 1) CHECKING ACCOUNT TERMS Match the following words with their definitions.

1. An endorsement where the depositor simply signs on the back of the check

2. An endorsement that contains words like "For Deposit Only" together with the signature

3. A card filled out and signed by each person authorized to sign checks on an account

4. The depositor who orders the bank to pay cash from the depositor's account

5. The bank on which the check is drawn

6. The person being paid the cash

7. A check that has been paid by the bank and is being returned to the depositor

a. signature card

b. cancelled check

c. blank endorsement

d. drawer

e. restrictive endorsement

f. drawee

g. payee

EXERCISE 8A-2 (LO 1) PREPARE DEPOSIT TICKET Based on the following information, prepare a deposit ticket.

Date:		January 15, 20--
Currency:		$334.00
Coin:		26.00
Checks:	No. 4-11	311.00
	No. 80-322	108.00
	No. 3-9	38.00

EXERCISE 8A-3 (LO 1) PREPARE CHECK AND STUB Based on the following information, prepare a check and stub.

Date:	January 15, 20--
Balance brought forward:	$2.841.50
Deposit:	(from Exercise 8A-2)
Check to:	J.M. Suppliers
Amount:	$150.00
For:	Office Supplies
Signature:	Sign your name

EXERCISE 8A-4 (LO 2) BANK RECONCILIATION TERMINOLOGY In a format similar to the following, indicate whether the action at the left will result in an addition to (+) or subtraction from (–) the ending bank balance or the ending checkbook balance.

	Ending Bank Balance	Ending Checkbook Balance
1. Deposits in transit to the bank		
2. Error in checkbook: check recorded as $32.00 but was actually for $23.00		
3. Service fee charged by bank		
4. Outstanding checks		
5. NSF check deposited earlier		
6. Error in checkbook: check recorded as $22.00 but was actually for $220.00		
7. Bank credit memo advising they collected a note for us		

EXERCISE 8A-5 (LO 2) PREPARE JOURNAL ENTRIES FOR BANK RECONCILIATION Based on bank reconciliation information shown on the next page, prepare the journal entries.

EXERCISE 8A-6 (LO 3) PETTY CASH JOURNAL ENTRIES Based on the following petty cash information, prepare (a) the journal entry to establish a petty cash fund, and (b) the journal entry to replenish the petty cash fund.

On January 1, 20--, a check was written in the amount of $200.00 to establish a petty cash fund. During January, the following vouchers were written for cash removed from the petty cash drawer:

Voucher No.	Account Debited	Amount
1	Telephone Expense	$17.50
2	Automobile Expense	33.00
3	Joseph Levine, Drawing	70.00
4	Postage Expense	12.50
5	Charitable Contributions Expense	15.00
6	Miscellaneous Expense	49.00

(FOR EXERCISE 8A-5)

Lisa Choy Associates Bank Reconciliation July 31, 20 - -								
Bank statement balance, July 31						$2 7 6 4 40
Add deposits in transit	$ 2 5 0 00					
		9 8 00		3 4 8 00	
				$3 1 1 2 40	
Deduct outstanding checks:					
No. 387	$ 3 5 3 50				
No. 393	1 7 80				
No. 398	3 3 20		4 0 4 50	
Adjusted bank balance				$2 7 0 7 90	
Book balance, July 31				$3 1 3 0 90	
Deduct: Error on check no. 394*	$ 2 3 00				
NSF check	3 9 0 00				
Bank service charge	1 0 00		4 2 3 00	
Adjusted book balance				$2 7 0 7 90	
*Accounts Payable was debited in original entry.					

EXERCISE 8A-7 (LO 4) CASH SHORT AND OVER ENTRIES Based on the following information, prepare the weekly entries for cash receipts from service fees and cash short and over.

Date	Cash Register Receipt Amount	Actual Cash Counted
April 2	$268.50	$266.50
9	237.75	233.50
16	309.25	311.00
23	226.50	224.00
30	318.00	322.00

SERIES A PROBLEMS

PROBLEM 8A-1 (LO 2) BANK RECONCILIATION AND RELATED JOURNAL ENTRIES The balance in the checking account of Violette Enterprises as of October 31 is $4,765.00. The bank statement shows an ending balance of $4,235.00. The following information is discovered by (1) tracing last month's deposits in transit to this month's bank statement, (2) comparing checks deposited and written per books and per bank in the current month, and (3) noting service charges and other debit and credit memos shown on the bank statement.

Deposits in transit:	10/26	$175.00
	10/28	334.00
Outstanding checks:	No. 1764	$47.00
	No. 1767	146.00
	No. 1781	369.00

(continued)

Unrecorded ATM withdrawal*:	180.00
Bank service charge:	43.00
NFS check:	370.00
Error on check no. 1754	Checkbook shows it was for $72.00, but was actually written for $62.00. Accounts Payable was debited.

*Funds were withdrawn by Guy Violette for personal use.

REQUIRED
1. Prepare a bank reconciliation as of October 31, 20--.
2. Prepare the required journal entries.

PROBLEM 8A-2 (LO 2) BANK RECONCILIATION AND RELATED JOURNAL ENTRIES The balance in the checking account of Lyle's Salon as of November 30 is $3,282.95. The bank statement shows an ending balance of $2,127.00. By examining last month's bank reconciliation, comparing the checks deposited and written per books and per bank in November, and noting the service charges and other debit and credit memos shown on the bank statement, the following were found:

a. An ATM withdrawal of $150.00 on November 18 by Lyle for personal use was not recorded on the books.

b. A bank debit memo issued for an NSF check from a customer of $19.50.

c. A bank credit memo issued for interest of $19.00 earned during the month.

d. On November 30, a deposit of $1,177.00 was made, which is not shown on the bank statement.

e. A bank debit memo issued for $17.50 for bank service charges.

f. Checks for the amounts of $185.00, $21.00, and $9.40 were written during November but have not yet been received by the bank.

g. The reconciliation from the previous month showed outstanding checks of $271.95. One of those checks for $18.65 has not yet been received by the bank.

h. Check No. 523 written to a creditor in the amount of $372.90 was recorded in the books as $327.90.

REQUIRED
1. Prepare a bank reconciliation as of November 30.
2. Prepare the required journal entries.

PROBLEM 8A-3 (LO 3) PETTY CASH RECORD AND JOURNAL ENTRIES On May 1, a petty cash fund was established for $150.00. The following vouchers were issued during May:

Date	Voucher No.	Purpose	Amount
May 1	1	postage due	$3.50
3	2	office supplies	11.00
5	3	auto repair (miscellaneous)	22.00
7	4	drawing (Joy Adams)	25.00
11	5	donation (Red Cross)	10.00

15	6	travel expenses	28.00
22	7	postage stamps	3.50
26	8	telephone call	5.00
30	9	donation (Boy Scouts)	30.00

REQUIRED

1. Prepare the journal entry to establish the petty cash fund.

2. Record the vouchers in the petty cash record. Total and rule the petty cash record.

3. Prepare the journal entry to replenish the petty cash fund. Make the appropriate entry in the petty cash record.

PROBLEM 8A-4 (LO 4) CASH SHORT AND OVER ENTRIES Listed below are the weekly cash register tape amounts for service fees and the related cash counts during the month of July.

Date	Cash Register Receipt Amount	Actual Cash Counted
July 2	$289.50	$287.00
9	311.50	311.50
16	306.00	308.50
23	317.50	315.00
30	296.00	299.50

REQUIRED

1. Prepare the journal entries to record the cash service fees and cash short and over for each of the five weeks.

2. Post to the cash short and over account (use account no. 573).

3. Determine the ending balance of the cash short and over account. Does it represent an expense or revenue?

SERIES B EXERCISES

EXERCISE 8B-1 (LO 1) CHECKING ACCOUNT TERMS Match the following words with their definitions.

1. Banking number used to identify checks for deposit tickets

2. A card filled out to open a checking account

3. A machine from which withdrawals can be taken or deposits made to accounts

4. A place where relevant information is recorded about a check

5. A set of procedures designed to ensure proper accounting for transactions

6. A statement of account issued to each depositor once a month

7. A detailed listing of items being deposited to an account

a. bank statement

b. deposit ticket

c. signature card

d. internal control

e. check stub

f. ATM

g. ABA number

EXERCISE 8B-2 (LO 1) PREPARE DEPOSIT TICKET Based on the following information, prepare a deposit ticket.

Date:		November 15, 20--
Currency:		$283.00
Coin:		19.00
Checks:	No. 3-22	201.00
	No. 19-366	114.00
	No. 3-2	28.00

EXERCISE 8B-3 (LO 1) PREPARE CHECK AND STUB Based on the following information, prepare a check and stub.

Date:	November 15, 20--
Balance brought forward:	$3,181.00
Deposit:	(from Exercise 8B-2)
Check to:	R.J. Smith Co.
Amount:	$120.00
For:	Payment on account
Signature:	Sign your name

EXERCISE 8B-4 (LO 2) BANK RECONCILIATION TERMINOLOGY In a format similar to the following, indicate whether the action at the left will result in an addition to (+) or subtraction from (–) the ending bank balance or the ending checkbook balance.

	Ending Bank Balance	Ending Checkbook Balance
1. Service fee of $12 charged by bank	_____	_____
2. Outstanding checks	_____	_____
3. Error in checkbook: check recorded as $36.00 was actually for $28.00	_____	_____
4. NSF check deposited earlier	_____	_____
5. Bank credit memo advising they collected a note for us	_____	_____
6. Deposits in transit to the bank	_____	_____
7. Error in checkbook: check recorded as $182.00 was actually for $218.00	_____	_____

EXERCISE 8B-5 (LO 2) PREPARE JOURNAL ENTRIES FOR BANK RECONCILIATION Based on the bank reconciliation information that appears on the next page, prepare the journal entries.

EXERCISE 8B-6 (LO 3) PETTY CASH JOURNAL ENTRIES Based on the following petty cash information, prepare (a) the journal entry to establish a petty cash fund, and (b) the journal entry to replenish the petty cash fund.

(FOR EXERCISE 8B-5)

Regina D'Alfonso Associates
Bank Reconciliation
July 31, 20 - -

Bank statement balance, July 31				$1 7 8 4 00	
Add deposits in transit	$ 4 1 8 50				
	1 0 0 50		5 1 9 00		
			$2 3 0 3 00		
Deduct outstanding checks:					
No. 185	$ 2 0 6 50				
No. 203	3 1 7 40				
No. 210	5 6 10	5 8 0 00			
Adjusted bank balance			$1 7 2 3 00		
Book balance, July 31			$1 7 9 4 00		
Add error on check no. 191*			1 0 00		
			$1 8 0 4 00		
Deduct: NSF check	$ 6 6 00				
Bank service charge	1 5 00	8 1 00			
Adjusted book balance			$1 7 2 3 00		
*Accounts Payable was debited in original entry.					

On October 1, 20--, a check was written in the amount of $200.00 to establish a petty cash fund. During October, the following vouchers were written for cash taken from the petty cash drawer:

Voucher No.	Account Debited	Amount
1	Postage Expense	$13.00
2	Miscellaneous Expense	17.00
3	John Flanagan, Drawing	45.00
4	Telephone Expense	36.00
5	Charitable Contributions Expense	50.00
6	Automobile Expense	29.00

EXERCISE 8B-7 (LO 4) CASH SHORT AND OVER ENTRIES Based on the following information, prepare the weekly entries for cash receipts from service fees and cash short and over.

Date	Cash Register Receipt Amount	Actual Cash Counted
June 1	$330.00	$333.00
8	297.00	300.00
15	233.00	231.00
22	302.00	296.50
29	316.00	312.00

SERIES B PROBLEMS

PROBLEM 8B-1 (LO 2) BANK RECONCILIATION AND RELATED JOURNAL ENTRIES The balance in the checking account of Kyros Enterprises as of November 30 is $3,004.00. The bank statement shows an ending balance of $2,525.00. The following information is discovered by (1) tracing last month's deposits in transit to this month's bank statement, (2) comparing checks deposited and written per books and per bank in the current month, and (3) noting service charges and other debit and credit memos shown on the bank statement.

Deposits in transit:	11/21	$125.00
	11/26	200.00
Outstanding checks:	No. 322	17.00
	No. 324	105.00
	No. 327	54.00
Unrecorded ATM withdrawal*:		100.00
Bank service charge:		25.00
NSF check:		185.00
Error on check no. 321	Checkbook shows it was for $44.00, but was actually written for $64.00. Accounts Payable was debited.	

*Funds were withdrawn by Steve Kyros for personal use.

REQUIRED
1. Prepare a bank reconciliation as of November 30, 20--.

2. Prepare the required journal entries.

PROBLEM 8B-2 (LO 2) BANK RECONCILIATION AND RELATED JOURNAL ENTRIES The balance in the checking account of Tori's Health Center as of April 30 is $4,690.30. The bank statement shows an ending balance of $3,275.60. By examining last month's bank reconciliation, comparing the checks deposited and written per books and per bank in April, and noting the service charges and other debit and credit memos shown on the bank statement, the following were found:

a. An ATM withdrawal of $200.00 on April 20 by Tori for personal use was not recorded on the books.

b. A bank debit memo issued for an NSF check from a customer of $29.10.

c. A bank credit memo issued for interest of $28.00 earned during the month.

d. On April 30, a deposit of $1,592.00 was made, which is not shown on the bank statement.

e. A bank debit memo issued for $24.50 for bank service charges.

f. Checks for the amounts of $215.00, $71.00, and $24.30 were written during April but have not yet been received by the bank.

g. The reconciliation from the previous month showed outstanding checks of $418.25. One of these checks for $38.60 has not yet been received by the bank.

h. Check No. 422 written to a creditor in the amount of $217.90 was recorded in the books as $271.90.

REQUIRED   1.   Prepare a bank reconciliation as of April 30.

2.   Prepare the required journal entries.

PROBLEM 8B-3 (LO 3) PETTY CASH RECORD AND JOURNAL ENTRIES On July 1, a petty cash fund was established for $100.00. The following vouchers were issued during July:

Date	Voucher No.	Purpose	Amount
July 1	1	office supplies	$ 3.00
3	2	donation (Goodwill)	15.00
5	3	travel expenses	5.00
7	4	postage due	2.00
8	5	office supplies	4.00
11	6	postage due	3.50
15	7	telephone call	5.00
21	8	travel expenses	11.00
25	9	withdrawal by owner (L. Ortiz)	20.00
26	10	copier repair (miscellaneous)	18.50

REQUIRED   1.   Prepare the journal entry to establish the petty cash fund.

2.   Record the vouchers in the petty cash record. Total and rule the petty cash record.

3.   Prepare the journal entry to replenish the petty cash fund. Make the appropriate entry in the petty cash record.

PROBLEM 8B-4 (LO 4) CASH SHORT AND OVER ENTRIES Listed below are the weekly cash register tape amounts for service fees and the related cash counts during the month of July.

Date	Cash Register Receipt Amount	Actual Cash Counted
Aug. 1	$292.50	$295.00
8	305.00	301.50
15	286.00	286.00
22	330.25	332.75
29	298.50	295.00

REQUIRED   1.   Prepare the journal entries to record the cash service fees and cash short and over for each of the five weeks.

2.   Post to the cash short and over account. (Use account no. 573.)

3.   Determine the ending balance of the cash short and over account. Does it represent an expense or revenue?

MASTERY PROBLEM

Turner Excavation maintains a checking account and has decided to open a petty cash fund. The following petty cash fund transactions occurred during July.

July 2   Established a petty cash fund by issuing check no. 301 for $100.00.

5   Paid $25.00 from the petty cash fund for postage. Voucher no. 1.

7   Paid $30.00 from the petty cash fund for delivery of flowers for the secretaries (Miscellaneous Expense). Voucher no. 2.

8   Paid $20.00 from the petty cash fund to repair a tire on the company truck. Voucher no. 3.

12   Paid $22.00 from the petty cash fund for a newspaper advertisement. Voucher no. 4.

13   Issued check no. 303 to replenish the petty cash fund. (Total and rule the petty cash payments record. Record the balance and the amount needed to replenish the fund in the Description column of the petty cash payments record.)

20   Paid $26.00 from the petty cash fund to reimburse an employee for expenses incurred to repair the company truck. Voucher no. 5.

24   Paid $12.50 from the petty cash fund for telephone calls made from a phone booth. Voucher no. 6.

28   Paid $25.00 from the petty cash fund as a contribution to the YMCA. Voucher no. 7.

31   Issued check no. 308 to replenish the petty cash fund. (Total and rule the petty cash payments record. Record the balance and the amount needed to replenish the fund in the Description column of the petty cash payments record.)

The following additional transactions occurred during July.

July 5   Issued check no. 302 to pay office rent, $650.00.

15   Issued check no. 304 for office equipment, $525.00.

17   Issued check no. 305 for the purchase of supplies, $133.00.

18   Issued check no. 306 to pay attorney fees, $1,000.00.

30   Issued check no. 307 to pay newspaper for an advertisement, $200.20.

REQUIRED   1. Record the petty cash transactions in a petty cash payments record.

2. Make all required general journal entries for the cash transactions. (Note: The petty cash fund was established and replenished twice during July.)

3. The following bank statement (Figure 8-14) was received in the mail. Deposits were made on July 6 for $3,500.00 and on July 29 for $2,350.00. The checkbook balance on July 31 is $4,331.55. Notice the discrepancy in check no. 302 that cleared the bank for $655.00. This check was written on July 5 for rent expense, but was incorrectly entered on the check stub and in the journal as $650.00. Prepare a bank reconciliation and make any necessary journal entries as of July 31.

FIGURE 8-14 Bank Statement

STATEMENT						**M** erchant's **N** ational Bank

| TURNER EXCAVATION
220 MAIN STREET
OAKHURST, NJ 07755-1461 | | **TE** | | Reference Number 16 3247 5
Statement Date July 21, 20--
Statement Instructions | | Page Number |

Beginning Balance	No. of Deposits and Credits	We have added these deposits and credits totaling	No. of withdrawals and charges	We have subtracted these withdrawals and charges totaling	Resulting in a statement balance of
$1,250.25	1	$3,500.00	6	$1,512.50	$3,237.75

Document Count	Average Daily Balance this Statement Period	Minimum Balance this Statement Period	Date	Amount

If Your Account does not Balance, Please See Reverse Side and Report any Discrepancies to our Customer Service Department.

7/1	Beginning Balance		1,250.25
7/5	Check No. 301	−100.00	1,150.25
7/8	Check No. 302	−655.00	495.25
7/9	Deposit	3,500.00	3,995.25
7/15	Check No. 303	−97.00	3,898.25
7/20	Check No. 304	−525.00	3,373.25
7/28	Check No. 305	−133.00	3,240.25
7/31	Service Charge	−2.50	3,237.75

EC – Error Correction	OD – Overdrawn	RC – Return Check Charge
ATM – Automated Teller Machine	TR – Wire Transfer	D/N – Day/Night

Depositor Agrees and Bank Accepts Business Upon the Terms and Conditions of Bank's Rules and Regulations Now in Effect or as May be Hereafter Adopted.

Self-Study Test Questions

True/False

1. The primary purpose of a bank reconciliation is to detect and correct errors made by the bank in its records. _____

2. NSF checks are subtracted from the bank's ending balance on the bank reconciliation. _____

3. The bank service charge requires a journal entry to record its effects on the cash account. _____

4. Unrecorded ATM withdrawals are added to the checkbook balance on the bank reconciliation. _____

5. The petty cash record is a journal of original entry (entries are posted from it to the general ledger accounts). _____

Multiple Choice

1. To establish a petty cash fund, which account is debited? _____

   (a) Cash   (c) Miscellaneous Expense
   (b) Petty Cash   (d) Revenue

2. When the cash short and over account has a debit balance at the end of the month, it is considered _____

   (a) an expense.   (c) revenue.
   (b) an asset.   (d) a liability.

3. Which of these could be *added* to the ending checkbook balance? _____

   (a) service charges   (c) checkbook errors
   (b) NSF check   (d) outstanding checks

4. Which of these is *subtracted* from the ending checkbook balance? _____

   (a) deposits in transit   (c) note collection
   (b) service charges   (d) bank errors

5. Which of these is *added* to the ending bank statement balance? _____

   (a) outstanding checks   (c) checkbook errors
   (b) service charges   (d) deposits in transit

The answers to the Self-Study Test Questions are at the end of the text.

9

Payroll Accounting: Employee Earnings and Deductions

LEARNING OBJECTIVES:
Careful study of this chapter should enable you to:

LO 1 Distinguish between employees and independent contractors.

LO 2 Calculate employee earnings and deductions.

LO 3 Describe and prepare payroll records.

LO 4 Account for employee earnings and deductions.

LO 5 Describe various payroll record-keeping methods.

Six months after opening the Be A Sport shop described at the beginning of Chapter 8, John Zenith is pleased to find that the business is doing very well. John has hired a student who is studying accounting at the local college as a part-time bookkeeper. He also has added an employee to help in the shop during peak periods and to keep the inventory organized. He knows he needs to keep a record of the hours worked so that he can compute the employees' earnings. His new bookkeeper says he also needs to withhold certain taxes from the employees' wages. What taxes must John withhold from his employees' wages? How does he determine the correct amounts to withhold?

The only contact most of us have with payroll is receiving a paycheck. Few of us have seen the large amount of record keeping needed to produce that paycheck.

Employers maintain complete payroll accounting records for two reasons. First, payroll costs are major expenditures for most companies. Payroll accounting records provide data useful in analyzing and controlling these expenditures. Second, federal, state, and local laws require employers to keep payroll records. Companies must accumulate payroll data both for the business as a whole and for each employee.

There are two major types of payroll taxes: those paid by the employee and those paid by the employer. In this chapter we discuss employee taxes. In Chapter 10 we address payroll taxes paid by the employer.

EMPLOYEES AND INDEPENDENT CONTRACTORS

LO 1 Distinguish between employees and independent contractors.

Not every person who performs services for a business is considered an employee. An **employee** works under the control and direction of an employer. Examples include secretaries, maintenance workers, salesclerks, and plant supervisors. In contrast, an **independent contractor** performs a service for a fee and does not work under the control and direction of the company paying for the service. Examples of independent contractors include public accountants, real estate agents, and lawyers.

The distinction between an employee and an independent contractor is very important for payroll purposes. Government laws and regulations regarding payroll are much more complex for employees than for independent contractors. Employers must deduct certain taxes, maintain payroll records, and file numerous reports for all employees. Only one form (Form 1099) must be filed for independent contractors. The payroll accounting procedures described in this chapter apply only to employer/employee relationships.

EMPLOYEE EARNINGS AND DEDUCTIONS

LO 2 Calculate employee earnings and deductions.

Three steps are required to determine how much to pay an employee for a pay period:

1. Calculate total earnings.

2. Determine the amounts of deductions.

3. Subtract deductions from total earnings to compute net pay.

Salaries and Wages

Compensation for managerial or administrative services usually is called **salary**. A salary normally is expressed in biweekly (every two weeks), monthly, or annual terms. Compensation for skilled or unskilled labor usually is referred to as **wages**. Wages ordinarily are expressed in terms of hours, weeks, or units produced. The terms "salaries" and "wages" often are used interchangeably in practice.

The **Fair Labor Standards Act (FLSA)** requires employers to pay overtime at 1½ times the regular rate to any hourly employee who works over 40 hours in a week. Some companies pay a higher rate for hours worked on Saturday or Sunday, but this is not required by the FLSA. Some salaried employees are exempt from the FLSA rules and are not paid overtime.

Computing Total Earnings

Compensation usually is based on the time worked during the payroll period. Sometimes earnings are based on sales or units of output during the period. When compensation is based on time, a record must be kept of the time worked by each employee. Time cards (Figure 9-1) are helpful for this purpose. In large businesses with computer-based timekeeping systems, plastic cards or badges with special barcodes (Figure 9-2) can be used.

FIGURE 9-1 Time Card

FIGURE 9-2 Barcode Time Card

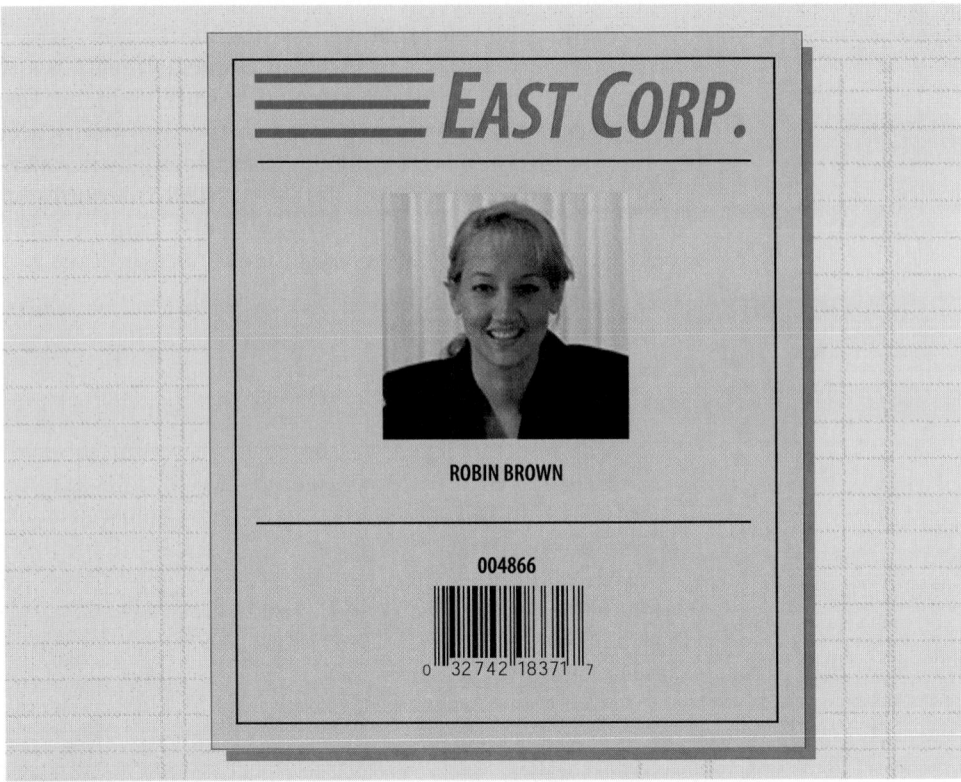

To illustrate the computation of total earnings, look at the time card of Helen Kuzmik in Figure 9-1. The card shows that Kuzmik worked 55 hours for the week:

Regular hours	40 hours
Overtime	11
Double time	4
Total hours worked	55 hours

Kuzmik's regular rate of pay is $12 per hour. She is paid 1½ times the regular rate for hours in excess of 40 per week, and twice the regular rate for hours on Sunday. Kuzmik's total earnings for the week ended December 19 are computed as follows:

40 hours × $12	$480
11 hours × $18 (1½ × $12 = $18)	198
4 hours (on Sunday) × $24 (2 × $12 = $24)	96
Total earnings for the week	$774

An employee who is paid a salary may also be entitled to premium pay for overtime. If this is the case, it is necessary to compute the regular hourly rate of pay before computing the overtime rate. To illustrate, assume that Linda Swaney has a salary of $2,288 a month plus 1½ times the regular hourly rate for hours in excess of 40 per week. Swaney's overtime rate of pay is computed as follows:

> There are 52 weeks in each year but not 4 weeks in each month. That is why monthly salaries must be annualized in order to determine the hourly rate.

$2,288 × 12 months	$27,456 annual pay
$27,456 ÷ 52 weeks	$528.00 pay per week
$528.00 ÷ 40 hours	$13.20 pay per regular hour
$13.20 × 1½	$19.80 overtime pay per hour

If Swaney worked 50 hours during the week ended December 19, her total earnings for the week would be computed as follows:

40 hours × $13.20	$528.00
10 hours × $19.80	198.00
Total earnings for the week	$726.00

Deductions from Total Earnings

An employee's total earnings are called **gross pay**. Various deductions are made from gross pay to yield take-home or **net pay**. Deductions from gross pay fall into three major categories:

1. Federal (and possibly state and city) income tax withholding

2. Employee FICA tax withholding

3. Voluntary deductions

Income Tax Withholding. Federal law requires employers to withhold certain amounts from the total earnings of each employee. These withholdings are applied toward the payment of the employee's federal income tax. Four factors determine the amount to be withheld from an employee's gross pay each pay period:

1. Total earnings

2. Marital status

3. Number of withholding allowances claimed

4. Length of the pay period

Withholding Allowances. Each employee is required to furnish the employer an Employee's Withholding Allowance Certificate, Form W-4 (Figure 9-3). The marital status of the employee and the number of allowances claimed on Form W-4 determine the dollar amount of earnings subject to withholding. A **withholding allowance** exempts a specific dollar amount of an employee's gross pay from federal income tax withholding. In general, each employee is permitted one personal withholding allowance, one for a spouse who does not also claim an allowance, and one for each dependent.

A withholding certificate completed by Ken Istone is shown in Figure 9-3. Istone is married, has a spouse who does not claim an allowance, and has four dependent children. On line 5 of the W-4 form, Istone claims 6 allowances, calculated as follows:

Personal allowance	1
Spouse allowance	1
Allowances for dependents	4
Total withholding allowances	6

FIGURE 9-3 Employee's Withholding Allowance Certificate (Form W-4)

Form **W-4** Department of the Treasury Internal Revenue Service	**Employee's Withholding Allowance Certificate** ▶ For Privacy Act and Paperwork Reduction Act Notice, see page 2.	OMB No. 1545-0010 **1998**

1 Type or print your first name and middle initial	Last name	2 Your social security number
Ken M.	*Istone*	*393 : 58 : 8194*

Home address (number and street or rural route)
1546 Swallow Drive

3 ☐ Single ☒ Married ☐ Married, but withhold at higher Single rate.
Note: *If married, but legally separated, or spouse is a nonresident alien, check the Single box.*

City or town, state, and Zip code
St. Louis, MO 63144-4752

4 If your last name differs from that on your social security card, check here and call 1-800-772-1213 for a new card . . . . . ▶ ☐

5 Total number of allowances you are claiming (from line H above or from the worksheets on page 2 if they apply) . . | 5 | *6*

6 Additional amount, if any, you want withheld from each paycheck . . . . | 6 | $

7 I claim exemption from withholding for 1998, and I certify that I meet **BOTH** of the following conditions for exemption:
• Last year I had a right to a refund of **ALL** Federal income tax withheld because I had **NO** tax liability **AND**
• This year I expect a refund of **ALL** Federal income tax withheld because I expect to have **NO** tax liability.
If you meet both conditions, enter "EXEMPT" here . . . . ▶ | 7 |

Under penalties of perjury, I certify that I am entitled to the number of withholding allowances claimed on this certificate or entitled to claim exempt status.

Employee's signature ▶ *Ken M. Istone*   Date ▶ *January 3* , 19--

8 Employer's name and address (Employer: Complete 8 and 10 only if sending to IRS) | 9 Office code (optional) | 10 Employer identification number

Cat. No. 10220Q

Wage-Bracket Method. Employers generally use the **wage-bracket method** to determine the amount of tax to be withheld from an employee's pay. The employee's gross pay for a specific time period is traced into the appropriate wage-bracket table provided by the Internal Revenue Service (IRS). These tables cover various time periods, and there are separate tables for single and married taxpayers. Copies are provided in *Circular E—Employer's Tax Guide*, which may be obtained from any local IRS office.

Portions of weekly income tax wage-bracket withholding tables for single and married persons are illustrated in Figure 9-4. Assume that Ken Istone (who claims 6 allowances) had gross earnings of $545 for the week ending December 19, 19--. The table for married persons is used as follows:

1. Find the row for wages of "at least $540, but less than $550."

2. Find the column headed "6 withholding allowances."

3. Where the row and column cross, $16.00 is given as the amount to be withheld.

LEARNING KEY: 1. Find the row for wages.
2. Find the column for withholding allowances.
3. Find the amount where they cross.

For state or city income taxes, withholding generally is handled in one of two ways: (1) forms and tables similar to those provided by the IRS are used or (2) an amount equal to a percentage of the federal withholding amount is withheld.

FIGURE 9-4 Federal Withholding Tax Table: Single Persons

SINGLE Persons—WEEKLY Payroll Period
(For Wages Paid in 1998)

At least	But less than	0	1	2	3	4	5	6	7	8	9	10
$300	$310	38	30	23	15	7	0	0	0	0	0	0
310	320	40	32	24	16	8	1	0	0	0	0	0
320	330	41	33	26	18	10	2	0	0	0	0	0
330	340	43	35	27	19	11	4	0	0	0	0	0
340	350	44	36	29	21	13	5	0	0	0	0	0
350	360	46	38	30	22	14	7	0	0	0	0	0
360	370	47	39	32	24	16	8	0	0	0	0	0
370	380	49	41	33	25	17	10	2	0	0	0	0
380	390	50	42	35	27	19	11	3	0	0	0	0
390	400	52	44	36	28	20	13	5	0	0	0	0
400	410	53	45	38	30	22	14	6	0	0	0	0
410	420	55	47	39	31	23	16	8	0	0	0	0
420	430	56	48	41	33	25	17	9	2	0	0	0
430	440	58	50	42	34	26	19	11	3	0	0	0
440	450	59	51	44	36	28	20	12	5	0	0	0
450	460	61	53	45	37	29	22	14	6	0	0	0
460	470	62	54	47	39	31	23	15	8	0	0	0
470	480	64	56	48	40	32	25	17	9	1	0	0
480	490	65	57	50	42	34	26	18	11	3	0	0
490	500	67	59	51	43	35	28	20	12	4	0	0
500	510	68	60	53	45	37	29	21	14	6	0	0
510	520	70	62	54	46	38	31	23	15	7	0	0
520	530	72	63	56	48	40	32	24	17	9	1	0
530	540	75	65	57	49	41	34	26	18	10	3	0
540	550	78	66	59	51	43	35	27	20	12	4	0
550	560	81	68	60	52	44	37	29	21	13	6	0
560	570	83	69	62	54	46	38	30	23	15	7	0
570	580	86	72	63	55	47	40	32	24	16	9	1
580	590	89	74	65	57	49	41	33	26	18	10	2
590	600	92	77	66	58	50	43	35	27	19	12	4
600	610	95	80	68	60	52	44	36	29	21	13	5
610	620	97	83	69	61	53	46	38	30	22	15	7
620	630	100	86	71	63	55	47	39	32	24	16	8
630	640	103	88	74	64	56	49	41	33	25	18	10
640	650	106	91	77	66	58	50	42	35	27	19	11
650	660	109	94	79	67	59	52	44	36	28	21	13
660	670	111	97	82	69	61	53	45	38	30	22	14
670	680	114	100	85	70	62	55	47	39	31	24	16
680	690	117	102	88	73	64	56	48	41	33	25	17
690	700	120	105	91	76	65	58	50	42	34	27	19
700	710	123	108	93	79	67	59	51	44	36	28	20
710	720	125	111	96	82	68	61	53	45	37	30	22
720	730	128	114	99	84	70	62	54	47	39	31	23
730	740	131	116	102	87	73	64	56	48	40	33	25
740	750	134	119	105	90	76	65	57	50	42	34	26
750	760	137	122	107	93	78	67	59	51	43	36	28
760	770	139	125	110	96	81	68	60	53	45	37	29
770	780	142	128	113	98	84	70	62	54	46	39	31
780	790	145	130	116	101	87	72	63	56	48	40	32
790	800	148	133	119	104	90	75	65	57	49	42	34
800	810	151	136	121	107	92	78	66	59	51	43	35
810	820	153	139	124	110	95	81	68	60	52	45	37
820	830	156	142	127	112	98	83	69	62	54	46	38
830	840	159	144	130	115	101	86	72	63	55	48	40
840	850	162	147	133	118	104	89	74	65	57	49	41
850	860	165	150	135	121	106	92	77	66	58	51	43
860	870	167	153	138	124	109	95	80	68	60	52	44
870	880	170	156	141	126	112	97	83	69	61	54	46
880	890	173	158	144	129	115	100	86	71	63	55	47
890	900	176	161	147	132	118	103	88	74	64	57	49
900	910	179	164	149	135	120	106	91	77	66	58	50
910	920	181	167	152	138	123	109	94	80	67	60	52
920	930	184	170	155	140	126	111	97	82	69	61	53
930	940	187	172	158	143	129	114	100	85	71	63	55
940	950	190	175	161	146	132	117	102	88	73	64	56
950	960	193	178	163	149	134	120	105	91	76	66	58
960	970	195	181	166	152	137	123	108	94	79	67	59
970	980	198	184	169	154	140	125	111	96	82	69	61
980	990	201	186	172	157	143	128	114	99	85	70	62
990	1,000	204	189	175	160	146	131	116	102	87	73	64
1,000	1,010	207	192	177	163	148	134	119	105	90	76	65
1,010	1,020	209	195	180	166	151	137	122	108	93	78	67
1,020	1,030	212	198	183	168	154	139	125	110	96	81	68
1,030	1,040	215	200	186	171	157	142	128	113	99	84	70
1,040	1,050	218	203	189	174	160	145	130	116	101	87	72
1,050	1,060	221	206	191	177	162	148	133	119	104	90	75
1,060	1,070	223	209	194	180	165	151	136	122	107	92	78
1,070	1,080	226	212	197	182	168	153	139	124	110	95	81
1,080	1,090	229	214	200	185	171	156	142	127	113	98	84
1,090	1,100	232	217	203	188	174	159	144	130	115	101	86
1,100	1,110	235	220	205	191	176	162	147	133	118	104	89
1,110	1,120	238	223	208	194	179	165	150	136	121	106	92
1,120	1,130	241	226	211	196	182	167	153	138	124	109	95
1,130	1,140	244	228	214	199	185	170	156	141	127	112	98
1,140	1,150	247	231	217	202	188	173	158	144	129	115	100
1,150	1,160	250	234	219	205	190	176	161	147	132	118	103
1,160	1,170	253	237	222	208	193	179	164	150	135	120	106
1,170	1,180	256	240	225	210	196	181	167	152	138	123	109
1,180	1,190	259	243	228	213	199	184	170	155	141	126	112
1,190	1,200	262	246	231	216	202	187	172	158	143	129	114
1,200	1,210	266	249	233	219	204	190	175	161	146	132	117
1,210	1,220	269	253	236	222	207	193	178	164	149	134	120
1,220	1,230	272	256	240	224	210	195	181	166	152	137	123
1,230	1,240	275	259	243	227	213	198	184	169	155	140	126
1,240	1,250	278	262	246	230	216	201	186	172	157	143	128

FIGURE 9-4 Federal Withholding Tax Table: *(continued)* Married Persons

MARRIED Persons—WEEKLY Payroll Period
(For Wages Paid in 1998)

If the wages are—		And the number of withholding allowances claimed is—										
At least	But less than	0	1	2	3	4	5	6	7	8	9	10
		The amount of income tax to be withheld is—										
$290	$300	26	18	10	2	0	0	0	0	0	0	0
300	310	27	19	12	4	0	0	0	0	0	0	0
310	320	29	21	13	5	0	0	0	0	0	0	0
320	330	30	22	15	7	0	0	0	0	0	0	0
330	340	32	24	16	8	0	0	0	0	0	0	0
340	350	33	25	18	10	2	0	0	0	0	0	0
350	360	35	27	19	11	3	0	0	0	0	0	0
360	370	36	28	21	13	5	0	0	0	0	0	0
370	380	38	30	22	14	6	0	0	0	0	0	0
380	390	39	31	24	16	8	0	0	0	0	0	0
390	400	41	33	25	17	9	2	0	0	0	0	0
400	410	42	34	27	19	11	3	0	0	0	0	0
410	420	44	36	28	20	12	5	0	0	0	0	0
420	430	45	37	30	22	14	6	0	0	0	0	0
430	440	47	39	31	23	15	8	0	0	0	0	0
440	450	48	40	33	25	17	9	1	0	0	0	0
450	460	50	42	34	26	18	11	3	0	0	0	0
460	470	51	43	36	28	20	12	4	0	0	0	0
470	480	53	45	37	29	21	14	6	0	0	0	0
480	490	54	46	39	31	23	15	7	0	0	0	0
490	500	56	48	40	32	24	17	9	1	0	0	0
500	510	57	49	42	34	26	18	10	3	0	0	0
510	520	59	51	43	35	27	20	12	4	0	0	0
520	530	60	52	45	37	29	21	13	6	0	0	0
530	540	62	54	46	38	30	23	15	7	0	0	0
540	550	63	55	48	40	32	24	16	9	1	0	0
550	560	65	57	49	41	33	26	18	10	2	0	0
560	570	66	58	51	43	35	27	19	12	4	0	0
570	580	68	60	52	44	36	29	21	13	5	0	0
580	590	69	61	54	46	38	30	22	15	7	0	0
590	600	71	63	55	47	39	32	24	16	8	1	0
600	610	72	64	57	49	41	33	25	18	10	2	0
610	620	74	66	58	50	42	35	27	19	11	4	0
620	630	75	67	60	52	44	36	28	21	13	5	0
630	640	77	69	61	53	45	38	30	22	14	7	0
640	650	78	70	63	55	47	39	31	24	16	8	0
650	660	80	72	64	56	48	41	33	25	17	10	2
660	670	81	73	66	58	50	42	34	27	19	11	3
670	680	83	75	67	59	51	44	36	28	20	13	5
680	690	84	76	69	61	53	45	37	30	22	14	6
690	700	86	78	70	62	54	47	39	31	23	16	8
700	710	87	79	72	64	56	48	40	33	25	17	9
710	720	89	81	73	65	57	50	42	34	26	19	11
720	730	90	82	75	67	59	51	43	36	28	20	12
730	740	92	84	76	68	60	53	45	37	29	22	14
740	750	93	85	78	70	62	54	46	39	31	23	15
750	760	95	87	79	71	63	56	48	40	32	25	17
760	770	96	88	81	73	65	57	49	42	34	26	18
770	780	98	90	82	74	66	59	51	43	35	28	20
780	790	99	91	84	76	68	60	52	45	37	29	21
790	800	101	93	85	77	69	62	54	46	38	31	23
800	810	102	94	87	79	71	63	55	48	40	32	24
810	820	104	96	88	80	72	65	57	49	41	34	26
820	830	105	97	90	82	74	66	58	51	43	35	27
830	840	107	99	91	83	75	68	60	52	44	37	29
840	850	108	100	93	85	77	69	61	54	46	38	30
850	860	110	102	94	86	78	71	63	55	47	40	32
860	870	111	103	96	88	80	72	64	57	49	41	33
870	880	113	105	97	89	81	74	66	58	50	43	35
880	890	114	106	99	91	83	75	67	60	52	44	36
890	900	116	108	100	92	84	77	69	61	53	46	38
900	910	118	109	102	94	86	78	70	63	55	47	39
910	920	121	111	103	95	87	80	72	64	56	49	41
920	930	124	112	105	97	89	81	73	66	58	50	42
930	940	126	114	106	98	90	83	75	67	59	52	44
940	950	129	115	108	100	92	84	76	69	61	53	45
950	960	132	117	109	101	93	86	78	70	62	55	47
960	970	135	120	111	103	95	87	79	72	64	56	48
970	980	138	123	112	104	96	89	81	73	65	58	50
980	990	140	126	114	106	98	90	82	75	67	59	51
990	1,000	143	129	115	107	99	92	84	76	68	61	53
1,000	1,010	146	131	117	109	101	93	85	78	70	62	54
1,010	1,020	149	134	120	110	102	95	87	79	71	64	56
1,020	1,030	152	137	122	112	104	96	88	81	73	65	57
1,030	1,040	154	140	125	113	105	98	90	82	74	67	59
1,040	1,050	157	143	128	115	107	99	91	84	76	68	60
1,050	1,060	160	145	131	116	108	101	93	85	77	70	62
1,060	1,070	163	148	134	119	110	102	94	87	79	71	63
1,070	1,080	166	151	136	122	111	104	96	88	80	73	65
1,080	1,090	168	154	139	125	113	105	97	90	82	74	66
1,090	1,100	171	157	142	128	114	107	99	91	83	76	68
1,100	1,110	174	159	145	130	116	108	100	93	85	77	69
1,110	1,120	177	162	148	133	119	110	102	94	86	79	71
1,120	1,130	180	165	150	136	121	111	103	96	88	80	72
1,130	1,140	182	168	153	139	124	113	105	97	89	82	74
1,140	1,150	185	171	156	142	127	114	106	99	91	83	75
1,150	1,160	188	173	159	144	130	116	108	100	92	85	77
1,160	1,170	191	176	162	147	133	118	109	102	94	86	78
1,170	1,180	194	179	164	150	135	121	111	103	95	88	80
1,180	1,190	196	182	167	153	138	124	112	105	97	89	81
1,190	1,200	199	185	170	156	141	126	114	106	98	91	83
1,200	1,210	202	187	173	158	144	129	115	108	100	92	84
1,210	1,220	205	190	176	161	147	132	117	109	101	94	86
1,220	1,230	208	193	178	164	149	135	120	111	103	95	87
1,230	1,240	210	196	181	167	152	138	123	112	104	97	89
1,240	1,250	213	199	184	170	155	140	126	114	106	98	90
1,250	1,260	216	201	187	172	158	143	129	115	107	100	92
1,260	1,270	219	204	190	175	161	146	131	117	109	101	93
1,270	1,280	222	207	192	178	163	149	134	120	110	103	95
1,280	1,290	224	210	195	181	166	152	137	123	112	104	96

When the Social Security program was established in 1937, the tax was 1% on earnings up to $3,000 per year!

Employee FICA Tax Withholding. The Federal Insurance Contributions Act requires employers to withhold **FICA taxes** from employees' earnings. FICA taxes include amounts for both Social Security and Medicare programs. Social Security provides pensions and disability benefits. Medicare provides health insurance.

Congress has frequently changed the tax rates and the maximum amounts of earnings subject to FICA taxes. For 1998, the Social Security rate is 6.2% on maximum earnings of $68,400. The Medicare rate is 1.45% on all earnings; there is no maximum.

To illustrate the calculation of FICA taxes, assume the following earnings for Sarah Cadrain:

	Earnings	
Pay Period	Week	Year-to-Date
Dec. 6–12	$1,200	$67,740
Dec. 13–19	$1,260	$69,000

For the week of December 6–12, FICA taxes on Cadrain's earnings would be:

Gross Pay	×	Tax Rate		=	Tax
$1,200		Social Security	6.2%		$74.40
		Medicare	1.45%		17.40
					$91.80

During the week of December 13–19, Cadrain's earnings for the calendar year went over the $68,400 Social Security maximum by $600 ($69,000 − $68,400). Therefore, $600 of her $1,260 earnings for the week would not be subject to the Social Security tax.

Year-to-date earnings	$69,000
Social Security maximum	68,400
Amount not subject to Social Security tax	$ 600

The Social Security tax on Cadrain's December 13–19 earnings would be:

Gross pay	$1,260.00
Amount not subject to Social Security tax	600.00
Amount subject to Social Security tax	660.00
Tax rate	6.2%
Social Security tax	$ 40.92

Since there is no Medicare maximum, all of Cadrain's December 13–19 earnings would be subject to the Medicare tax.

Gross pay	$1,260.00
Tax rate	1.45%
Medicare tax	$ 18.27

The total FICA tax would be:

Social Security tax	$40.92
Medicare tax	18.27
Total FICA tax	$59.19

For the rest of the calendar year through December 31, Cadrain's earnings would be subject only to Medicare taxes.

Voluntary Deductions. In addition to the mandatory deductions from employee earnings for income and FICA taxes, many other deductions are possible. These deductions are usually voluntary and depend on specific agreements between the employee and employer. Examples of voluntary deductions are:

1. United States savings bond purchases

2. Health insurance premiums

3. Credit union deposits

4. Pension plan payments

5. Charitable contributions

Computing Net Pay

To compute an employee's net pay for the period, subtract all tax withholdings and voluntary deductions from the gross pay. Ken Istone's net pay for the week ended December 19 would be calculated as follows:

Gross pay		$545.00
Deductions:		
Federal income tax withholding	$16.00	
Social Security tax withholding	33.79	
Medicare tax withholding	7.90	
Health insurance premiums	10.00	
Total deductions		67.69
Net pay		$477.31

FIGURE 9-5 Payroll Register (left side)

PAYROLL

	NAME	ALLOWANCES	MARITAL STATUS	EARNINGS REGULAR	EARNINGS OVERTIME	EARNINGS TOTAL	CUMULATIVE TOTAL	TAXABLE EARNINGS UNEMPLOYMENT COMPENSATION	TAXABLE EARNINGS SOCIAL SECURITY	
1	Cadrain, Sarah	4	M	1 1 0 0 00	1 6 0 00	1 2 6 0 00	69 0 0 0 00		6 6 0 00	1
2	Guder, James	1	S	8 6 0 00	4 0 00	9 0 0 00	43 4 0 0 00		9 0 0 00	2
3	Istone, Ken	6	M	5 4 5 00		5 4 5 00	27 0 2 5 00		5 4 5 00	3
4	Kuzmik, Helen	2	M	4 8 0 00	2 9 4 00	7 7 4 00	31 0 0 0 00		7 7 4 00	4
5	Lee, Hoseoup	3	M	4 4 0 00		4 4 0 00	22 3 4 0 00		4 4 0 00	5
6	Swaney, Linda	2	S	5 2 8 00	1 9 8 00	7 2 6 00	27 5 0 0 00		7 2 6 00	6
7	Tucci, Paul	5	M	4 9 0 00		4 9 0 00	25 0 5 0 00		4 9 0 00	7
8	Wiles, Harry	1	S	3 0 0 00		3 0 0 00	6 3 0 0 00	3 0 0 00	3 0 0 00	8
9				4 7 4 3 00	6 9 2 00	5 4 3 5 00	251 6 1 5 00	3 0 0 00	4 8 3 5 00	9

Time cards, pay rates

Prior period total + current period earnings

Current below $7,000 cumul. total

Current below $68,400 cumul. total

PAYROLL RECORDS

LO 3   Describe and prepare payroll records.

Payroll records should provide the following information for each employee:

1. Name, address, occupation, social security number, marital status, and number of withholding allowances

2. Gross amount of earnings, date of payment, and period covered by each payroll

3. Gross amount of earnings accumulated for the year

4. Amounts of taxes and other items withheld

Three types of payroll records are used to accumulate this information:

1. The payroll register

2. The payroll check with earnings statement attached

3. The employee earnings record

These records can be prepared by either manual or automated methods. The illustrations in this chapter are based on a manual system. The forms and procedures illustrated are equally applicable to both manual and automated systems.

Payroll Register

A **payroll register** is a form used to assemble the data required at the end of each payroll period. Figure 9-5 illustrates Westly, Inc.'s payroll register for the payroll period ended December 19, 19--. Detailed information on earnings, taxable earnings, deductions, and net pay is provided for each employee. Column headings for deductions may vary, depending on which deductions are commonly used by a particular business. The sources of key information in the register are indicated in Figure 9-5 below.

FIGURE 9-5 Payroll Register (right side)

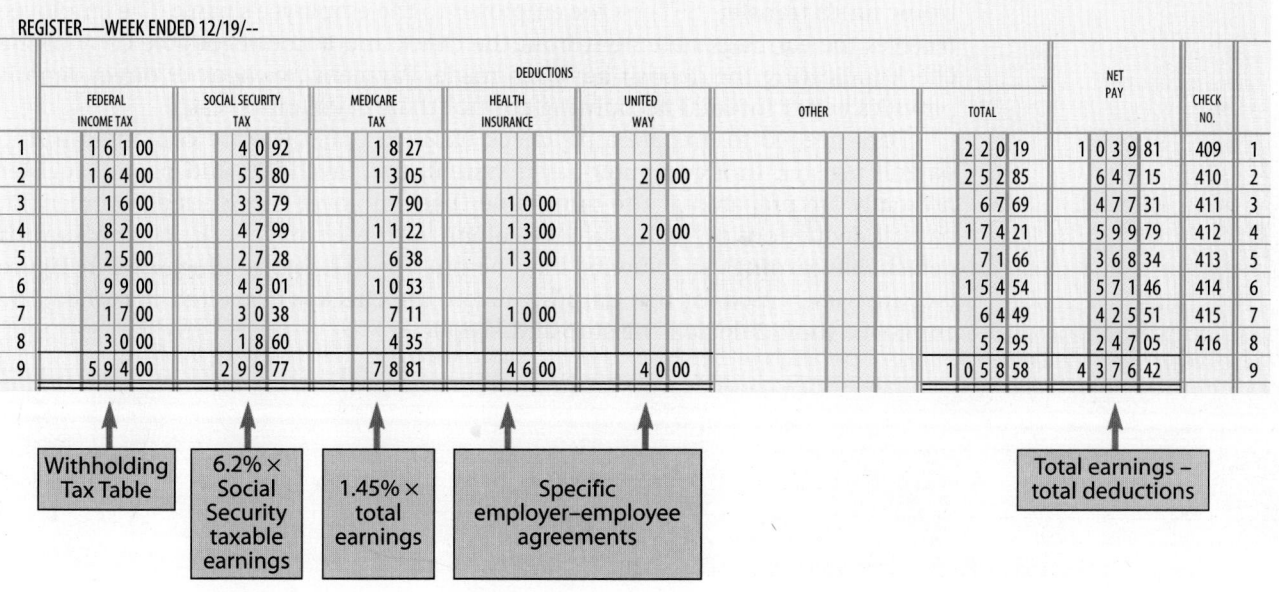

Westly, Inc., has eight employees. The first $68,400 of earnings of each employee is subject to Social Security tax. The Cumulative Total column, under the Earnings category, shows that Sarah Cadrain has exceeded this limit during the period. Thus only $660 of her earnings for this pay period is subject to Social Security tax, as shown in the Taxable Earnings columns. The Taxable Earnings columns are needed for determining the Social Security tax and the employer's payroll taxes. Employers must pay unemployment tax on the first $7,000 of employee earnings and Social Security tax on the first $68,400. Employer payroll taxes are discussed in Chapter 10.

Regular deductions are made from employee earnings for federal income tax and Social Security and Medicare taxes. In addition, voluntary deductions are made for health insurance and United Way contributions, based on agreements with individual employees.

After the data for each employee have been entered, the amount columns in the payroll register should be totaled and the totals verified as follows:

Regular earnings		$4,743.00
Overtime earnings		692.00
Gross earnings		$5,435.00
Deductions:		
Federal income tax	$594.00	
Social Security tax	299.77	
Medicare tax	78.81	
Health insurance premiums	46.00	
United Way	40.00	1,058.58
Net amount of payroll		$4,376.42

In a computerized accounting system, the payroll software performs this proof. An error in the payroll register could cause the payment of an incorrect amount to an employee. It also could result in sending an incorrect amount to the government or other agencies for whom funds are withheld.

Payroll Check

Employees may be paid in cash or by check. In some cases, the employee does not even handle the paycheck. Rather, payment is made by **direct deposit** or electronic funds transfer (EFT) by the employer to the employee's bank. The employee receives the earnings statement from the check and a nonnegotiable copy of the check indicating the deposit has been made. Payment by check or direct deposit provides better internal accounting control than payment by cash.

Data needed to prepare a paycheck for each employee are contained in the payroll register. In a computer-based system, the paychecks and payroll register normally are prepared at the same time. The employer furnishes a statement of payroll deductions to each employee along with each paycheck. Paychecks with detachable earnings statements, like the one for Ken Istone illustrated in Figure 9-6, are widely used for this purpose. Before the check is deposited or cashed, the employee should detach the stub and keep it.

FIGURE 9-6 Paycheck and Earnings Statement

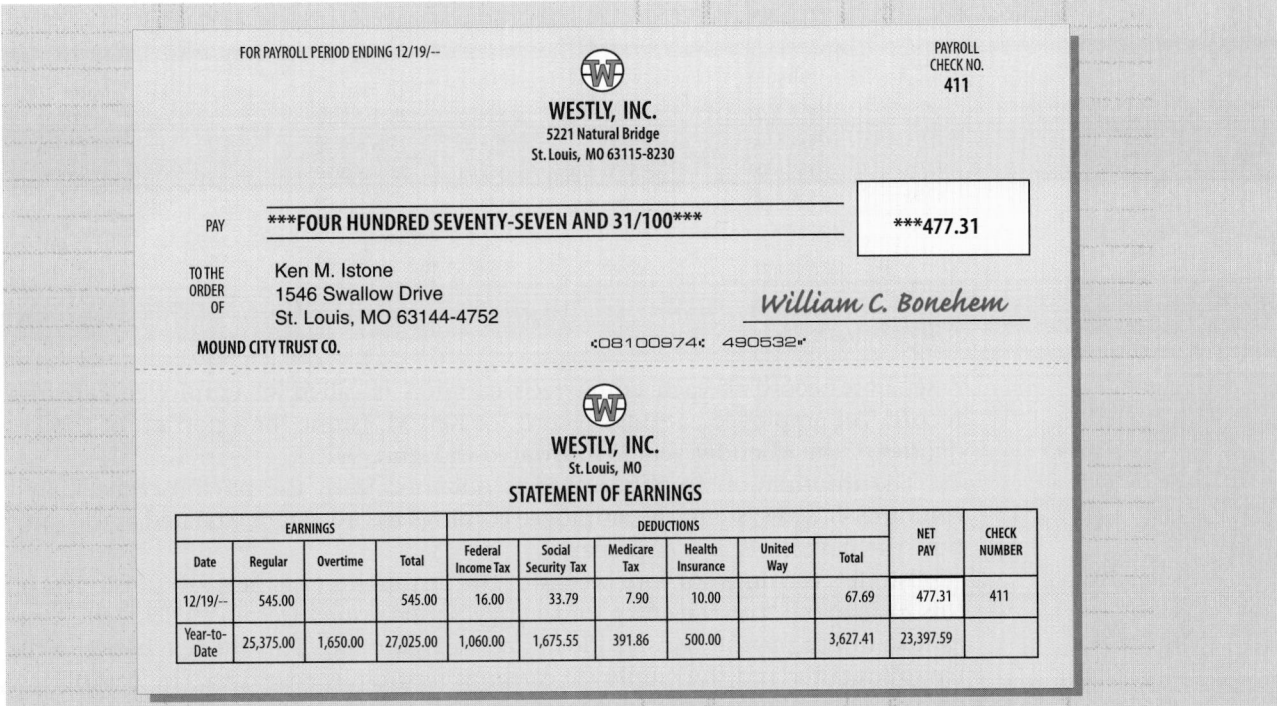

FOR PAYROLL PERIOD ENDING 12/19/--

PAYROLL CHECK NO. **411**

WESTLY, INC.
5221 Natural Bridge
St. Louis, MO 63115-8230

PAY ***FOUR HUNDRED SEVENTY-SEVEN AND 31/100***   ***477.31

TO THE ORDER OF Ken M. Istone
1546 Swallow Drive
St. Louis, MO 63144-4752

William C. Bonehem

MOUND CITY TRUST CO.   ⑆08100974⑆ 490532⑈

WESTLY, INC.
St. Louis, MO
STATEMENT OF EARNINGS

	EARNINGS			DEDUCTIONS						NET PAY	CHECK NUMBER
Date	Regular	Overtime	Total	Federal Income Tax	Social Security Tax	Medicare Tax	Health Insurance	United Way	Total		
12/19/--	545.00		545.00	16.00	33.79	7.90	10.00		67.69	477.31	411
Year-to-Date	25,375.00	1,650.00	27,025.00	1,060.00	1,675.55	391.86	500.00		3,627.41	23,397.59	

A BROADER VIEW

PAYROLL FRAUD—PAYING FOR GHOSTS

A supervisor at Haas Transfer Warehouse embezzled $12,000 from the company by collecting paychecks for former employees. When an employee left the company, the supervisor continued to submit a department time report for the employee. This caused a paycheck to be generated for the "ghost" employee. The supervisor then simply kept this paycheck when others were distributed to actual employees.

This fraud shows the importance of two procedures that appear in this chapter: (1) a time card, plastic card, or badge should be used for each employee to keep an accurate record of time worked and (2) payment by direct deposit or electronic funds transfer to the employee's bank is a good internal control.

FIGURE 9-7 Employee Earnings Record (left side)

		EARNINGS								TAXABLE EARNINGS			
PERIOD ENDED		REGULAR		OVERTIME		TOTAL		CUMULATIVE TOTAL		UNEMPLOYMENT COMPENSATION		SOCIAL SECURITY	
11/28		5 4 5	00	7 5	00	6 2 0	00	25 2 4 0	00			6 2 0	00
12/5		5 4 5	00	7 5	00	6 2 0	00	25 8 6 0	00			6 2 0	00
12/12		5 4 5	00	7 5	00	6 2 0	00	26 4 8 0	00			6 2 0	00
12/19		5 4 5	00			5 4 5	00	27 0 2 5	00			5 4 5	00

GENDER		DEPARTMENT	OCCUPATION	SOCIAL SECURITY NUMBER	MARITAL STATUS	ALLOWANCES
M ✓	F	Maintenance	Service	393-58-8194	M	6

EMPLOYEE EARNINGS RECORD

Employee Earnings Record

A separate record of each employee's earnings is called an **employee earnings record**. An employee earnings record for Ken M. Istone for a portion of the last quarter of the calendar year is illustrated in Figure 9-7.

The information in this record is obtained from the payroll register. In a computer-based system, the employee earnings record can be updated at the same time the payroll register is prepared.

Istone's earnings for four weeks of the last quarter of the year are shown on this form. Note that the entry for the pay period ended December 19 is the same as that in the payroll register illustrated in Figure 9-5. This linkage between the payroll register and the employee earnings record always exists. The payroll register provides a summary of the earnings of all employees for each pay period. The earnings record provides a summary of the annual earnings of an individual employee.

The earnings record illustrated in Figure 9-7 is designed to accumulate both quarterly and annual totals. The employer needs this information to prepare several reports. These reports will be discussed in Chapter 10.

ACCOUNTING FOR EMPLOYEE EARNINGS AND DEDUCTIONS

LO 4   Account for employee earnings and deductions.

The payroll register described in the previous section provides complete payroll data for each pay period. But the payroll register is not a journal. We still need to make a journal entry for payroll.

Journalizing Payroll Transactions

The totals at the bottom of the columns of the payroll register in Figure 9-5 show the following information.

Regular earnings		$4,743.00
Overtime earnings		692.00
Gross earnings		$5,435.00
Deductions:		
Federal income tax	$594.00	
Social Security tax	299.77	
Medicare tax	78.81	
Health insurance premiums	46.00	
United Way contributions	40.00	1,058.58
Net amount of payroll		$4,376.42

FIGURE 9-7 Employee Earnings Record (right side)

FOR PERIOD ENDED					19--			

FEDERAL INCOME TAX	SOCIAL SECURITY TAX	MEDICARE TAX	HEALTH INSURANCE	UNITED WAY	OTHER	TOTAL	CHECK NO.	AMOUNT
2 8 00	3 8 44	8 99	1 0 00			8 5 43	387	5 3 4 57
2 8 00	3 8 44	8 99	1 0 00			8 5 43	395	5 3 4 57
2 8 00	3 8 44	8 99	1 0 00			8 5 43	403	5 3 4 57
1 6 00	3 3 79	7 90	1 0 00			6 7 69	411	4 7 7 31

PAY RATE	DATE OF BIRTH	DATE HIRED	NAME/ADDRESS	EMPLOYEE NUMBER
$545/wk	8/17/64	1/3/87	Ken M. Istone 1546 Swallow Drive St. Louis, MO 63144-4752	3

The payroll register column totals thus provide the basis for recording the payroll. If the employee paychecks are written from the regular bank account, the following journal entry is made:

5	Dec.	19	Wages and Salaries Expense	5 4 3 5 00		5
6			Employee Income Tax Payable		5 9 4 00	6
7			Social Security Tax Payable		2 9 9 77	7
8			Medicare Tax Payable		7 8 81	8
9			Health Insurance Premiums Payable		4 6 00	9
10			United Way Contributions Payable		4 0 00	10
11			Cash		4 3 7 6 42	11
12			Payroll for week ended Dec. 19			12

Employee paychecks also can be written from a special payroll bank account. Large businesses with many employees commonly use a payroll bank account. If Westly used a payroll bank account, it first would have made the following entry on December 19 to transfer funds from the regular bank account to the payroll bank account:

5	19-- Dec.	19	Payroll Cash	4 3 7 6 42		5
6			Cash		4 3 7 6 42	6
7			Cash for Dec. 19 payroll			7

Then, the payroll entry shown above would be made, except that the credit of $4,376.42 would be to Payroll Cash rather than Cash.

If a payroll bank account is used, individual checks totaling $4,376.42 are written to the employees from that account. Otherwise, individual checks totaling that amount are written to the employees from the regular bank account.

Notice two important facts about the payroll entry. First, Wages and Salaries Expense is debited for the gross pay of the employees. The expense to the employer is the gross pay, not the employees' net pay after deductions. Second, a separate account is kept for each deduction.

LEARNING KEY: Wages and Salaries Expense is debited for the gross pay. A separate account is kept for each earnings deduction. Cash is credited for the net pay.

The accounts needed in entering deductions depend upon the deductions involved. To understand the accounting for these deductions, consider what the employer is doing. By deducting amounts from employees' earnings, the employer is simply serving as an agent for the government and other groups. Amounts that are deducted from an employee's gross earnings must be paid by the employer to these groups. Therefore, a separate account should be kept for the liability for each type of deduction.

To help us understand the journal entry for payroll, let's examine the accounts involved. The seven accounts affected by the payroll entry shown on page 15 are as follows:

ACCOUNT	CLASSIFICATION
Wages and Salaries Expense	Expense
Employee Income Tax Payable	Liability
Social Security Tax Payable	Liability
Medicare Tax Payable	Liability
Health Insurance Premiums Payable	Liability
United Way Contributions Payable	Liability
Cash (or Payroll Cash)	Asset

Wages and Salaries Expense

This account is debited for the gross pay of all employees for each pay period. Sometimes separate expense accounts are kept for the employees of different departments. Thus separate accounts may be kept for Office Salaries Expense, Sales Salaries Expense, and Factory Wages Expense.

Wages and Salaries Expense

Debit	Credit
gross pay of employees for each pay period	

Employee Income Tax Payable

This account is credited for the total federal income tax withheld from employees' earnings. The account is debited for amounts paid to the IRS. When all of the income taxes withheld have been paid, the account will have a zero balance. A state or city income tax payable account is used in a similar manner.

Employee Income Tax Payable

Debit	Credit
payment of income tax previously withheld	federal income tax withheld from employees' earnings

Social Security and Medicare Taxes Payable

These accounts are credited for (1) the Social Security and Medicare tax withheld from employees' earnings and (2) the Social Security and Medicare taxes imposed on the employer. Social Security and Medicare taxes imposed on the employer are discussed in Chapter 10. The accounts are debited for amounts paid to the IRS. When all of the Social Security and Medicare taxes have been paid, the accounts will have zero balances.

Social Security Tax Payable

Debit	Credit
payment of Social Security tax previously withheld or imposed	Social Security taxes (1) withheld from employees' earnings and (2) imposed on the employer

Medicare Tax Payable

Debit	Credit
payment of Medicare tax previously withheld or imposed	Medicare taxes (1) withheld from employees' earnings and (2) imposed on the employer

Other Deductions

Health Insurance Premiums Payable is credited for health insurance contributions deducted from an employee's pay. The account is debited for the subsequent payment of these amounts to the health insurer. United Way Contributions Payable is handled in a similar manner.

PAYROLL RECORD-KEEPING METHODS

LO 5   Describe various payroll record-keeping methods.

You probably noticed that the same information appears in several places in the payroll records—in the payroll register, paycheck and stub, and employee earnings records. If all records are prepared by hand (a **manual system**), the same information would be recorded several times. Unless an employer has only a few employees, this can be very inefficient. Various approaches are available to make payroll accounting more efficient and accurate.

> *Payroll typically is one of the first functions to be computerized by businesses.*

Both medium- and large-size businesses commonly use two approaches for payroll record keeping: payroll processing centers and electronic systems. A **payroll processing center** is a business that sells payroll record-keeping services. The employer provides the center with all basic employee data and each period's report of hours worked. The processing center maintains all payroll records and prepares each period's payroll checks. Payroll processing center fees tend to be much less than the cost to an employer of handling payroll internally.

An **electronic system** is a computer system based on a software package that performs all payroll record keeping and prepares payroll checks. In this system, only the employee number and hours worked need to be entered into a computer each pay period, as shown in Figure 9-8. All other payroll data needed to prepare the payroll records can be stored in the computer. The computer uses the employee number and hours worked to determine the gross pay, deductions, and net pay. The payroll register, checks, and employee earnings records are provided as outputs.

FIGURE 9-8 Electronic Payroll System

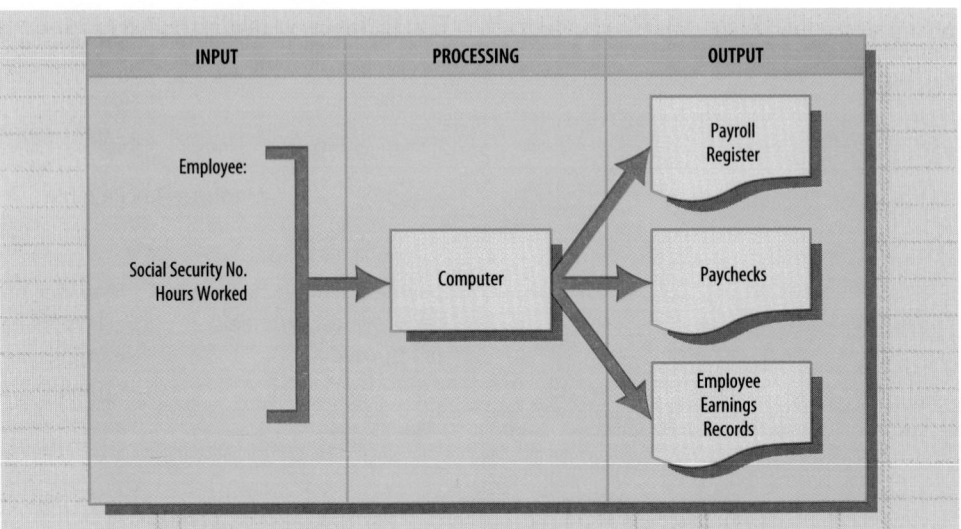

The same inputs and outputs are required in all payroll systems. Even with a computer, the data required for payroll processing have to be entered into the system at some point. The outputs—the payroll register, paychecks, and employee earnings records—are basically the same under each system.

Learning Objectives	Key Points to Remember
1 Distinguish between employees and independent contractors.	Employees work under the control and direction of an employer. Independent contractors perform a service for a fee and do not work under the control and direction of the company paying for the service. Payroll accounting procedures apply only to employees, not to independent contractors.
2 Calculate employee earnings and deductions.	Three steps are required to determine how much to pay an employee for a pay period: 1. Calculate total earnings. 2. Determine the amounts of deductions. 3. Subtract deductions from total earnings to compute net pay. Deductions from gross pay fall into three categories: 1. Income tax withholding. 2. Employee Social Security and Medicare taxes withholding. 3. Voluntary deductions. Four factors determine the amount to be withheld from an employee's gross pay each pay period: 1. Total earnings 2. Marital status 3. Number of withholding allowances claimed 4. Length of the pay period
3 Describe and prepare payroll records.	The payroll register and the employee earnings record are linked. The payroll register provides a summary of earnings of all employees for each pay period. The earnings record provides a summary of the annual earnings of an individual employee.
4 Account for employee earnings and deductions.	The totals at the bottom of the columns of the payroll register provide the basis for the journal entry for payroll. Amounts withheld or deducted by the employer from employee earnings are credited to liability accounts. The employer must pay these amounts to the proper government groups and other appropriate groups.
5 Describe various payroll record-keeping methods.	In a manual payroll system, the same information may need to be recorded several times. An electronic payroll system is much more efficient.

Reflection: Answering the Opening Questions

John must withhold amounts for federal (and possibly city and state) income taxes and for FICA taxes (Social Security and Medicare). To determine the correct amount of income tax withholding, the employee must complete Form W-4. Based on the number of withholding allowances claimed, John can use the withholding tables to determine the amount to withhold. These tables are provided in *Circular E—Employer's Tax Guide*. FICA tax should be withheld at a rate of 6.2% for Social Security and 1.45% for Medicare. *Circular E* also provides guidance regarding FICA taxes. John's bookkeeper should be able to handle all of these payroll matters.

KEY TERMS

direct deposit, (306)   The employee does not handle the paycheck; payment is made by the employer directly to the employee's bank.

electronic system, (312)   A computer system based on a software package that performs all payroll record keeping and prepares payroll checks.

employee, (296)   Works under the control and direction of an employer.

employee earnings record, (308)   A separate record of each employee's earnings.

Fair Labor Standards Act (FLSA), (297)   Requires employers to pay overtime at 1½ times the regular rate to any hourly employee who works over 40 hours in a week.

FICA taxes, (303)   Payroll taxes withheld to provide Social Security and Medicare benefits.

gross pay, (299)   An employee's total earnings.

independent contractor, (296)   Performs a service for a fee and does not work under the control and direction of the company paying for the service.

manual system, (311)   Payroll system in which all records are prepared by hand.

net pay, (299)   Gross pay less mandatory and voluntary deductions.

payroll processing center, (311)   A business that sells payroll record-keeping services.

payroll register, (305)   A form used to assemble the data required at the end of each payroll period.

salary, (297)   Compensation for managerial or administrative services.

wage-bracket method, (300)   Employers determine the amount to withhold from an employee's gross pay for a specific time period from the appropriate wage-bracket table provided by the Internal Revenue Service.

wages, (297)   Compensation for skilled or unskilled labor.

withholding allowance, (299)   Exempts a specific dollar amount of an employee's gross pay from federal income tax withholding.

DEMONSTRATION PROBLEM

Carole Vohsen operates a pet grooming salon called Canine Coiffures. She has five employees, all of whom are paid on a weekly basis. Canine Coiffures uses a payroll register, individual employee earnings records, a journal, and a general ledger.

The payroll data for each employee for the week ended January 21, 19--, are given below. Employees are paid 1½ times the regular rate for work over 40 hours a week and double time for work on Sunday.

Name	Employee No.	No. of Allowances	Marital Status	Total Hours Worked Jan. 15–21	Rate	Total Earnings Jan. 1–14
DeNourie, Katie	1	2	S	44	$11.50	$1,058.00
Garriott, Pete	2	1	M	40	12.00	1,032.00
Martinez, Sheila	3	3	M	39	12.50	987.50
Parker, Nancy	4	4	M	42	11.00	957.00
Shapiro, John	5	2	S	40	11.50	931.50

Sheila Martinez is the manager of the Shampooing Department. Her Social Security number is 500-88-4189, and she was born April 12, 1969. She lives at 46 Darling Crossing; Norwich, CT 06360. Martinez was hired September 1 of last year.

Canine Coiffures uses a federal income tax withholding table. A portion of this weekly table is provided in Figure 9-4 on pages 301 and 302. Social Security tax is withheld at the rate of 6.2% of the first $68,400 earned. Medicare tax is withheld at the rate of 1.45%, and city earnings tax at the rate of 1%, both applied to gross pay. Garriott and Parker each have $14.00 and Denourie and Martinez each have $4.00 withheld for health insurance. DeNourie, Martinez, and Shapiro each have $15.00 withheld to be invested in the groomers' credit union. Garriott and Shapiro each have $18.75 withheld under a savings bond purchase plan.

Canine Coiffures' payroll is met by drawing checks on its regular bank account. This week, the checks were issued in sequence, beginning with no. 811.

REQUIRED
1. Prepare a payroll register for Canine Coiffures for the week ended January 21, 19--. (In the Taxable Earnings/Unemployment Compensation column, enter the same amounts as in the Social Security column.) Total the amount columns, verify the totals, and rule with single and double lines.

2. Prepare an employee earnings record for Sheila Martinez for the week ended January 21, 19--.

3. Assuming that the wages for the week ended January 21 were paid on January 23, prepare the journal entry for the payment of this payroll.

4. Post the entry in requirement 3 to the affected accounts in the ledger of Canine Coiffures. Do not enter any amounts in the Balance columns. Use account numbers as follows: Cash–101; Employee Income Tax Payable—211; Social Security Tax Payable—212; Medicare Tax Payable—213; City Earnings Tax Payable—215; Health Insurance Premiums Payable—216; Credit Union Payable—217; Savings Bond Deductions Payable—218; Wages and Salaries Expense—511.

(continued)

Solution

1.

PAYROLL

	NAME	EMPLOYEE NO.	ALLOWANCES	MARITAL STATUS	EARNINGS REGULAR	EARNINGS OVERTIME	EARNINGS TOTAL	CUMULATIVE TOTAL	TAXABLE EARNINGS UNEMPLOYMENT COMPENSATION	TAXABLE EARNINGS SOCIAL SECURITY	
1	DeNourie, Katie	1	2	S	460 00	69 00	529 00	1587 00	529 00	529 00	1
2	Garriott, Pete	2	1	M	480 00		480 00	1512 00	480 00	480 00	2
3	Martinez, Sheila	3	3	M	487 50		487 50	1475 00	487 50	487 50	3
4	Parker, Nancy	4	4	M	440 00	33 00	473 00	1430 00	473 00	473 00	4
5	Shapiro, John	5	2	S	460 00		460 00	1391 50	460 00	460 00	5
6					2327 50	102 00	2429 50	7395 50	2429 50	2429 50	6
7											7

REGISTER—WEEK ENDED January 21, 19--

	FEDERAL INCOME TAX	SOCIAL SECURITY TAX	MEDICARE TAX	CITY TAX	HEALTH INSURANCE	CREDIT UNION	OTHER		TOTAL	NET PAY	CHECK NO.	
1	56 00	32 80	7 67	5 29	4 00	15 00			120 76	408 24	811	1
2	46 00	29 76	6 96	4 80	14 00		U.S. Savings Bond	18 75	120 27	359 73	812	2
3	31 00	30 23	7 07	4 88	4 00	15 00			92 18	395 32	813	3
4	21 00	29 33	6 86	4 73	14 00				75 92	397 08	814	4
5	47 00	28 52	6 67	4 60		15 00	U.S. Savings Bond	18 75	120 54	339 46	815	5
6	201 00	150 64	35 23	24 30	36 00	45 00		37 50	529 67	1899 83		6
7												7

2.

EMPLOYEE EARNINGS RECORD

19-- PERIOD ENDED	EARNINGS REGULAR	EARNINGS OVERTIME	EARNINGS TOTAL	CUMULATIVE TOTAL	TAXABLE EARNINGS UNEMPLOYMENT COMPENSATION	TAXABLE EARNINGS SOCIAL SECURITY
1/7						
1/14						
1/21	487 50		487 50	1475 00	487 50	487 50
1/28						

GENDER	DEPARTMENT	OCCUPATION	SOCIAL SECURITY NUMBER	MARITAL STATUS	ALLOWANCES
M F ✔	Shampooing	Manager	500-88-4189	M	3

FOR PERIOD ENDED   19--

FEDERAL INCOME TAX	SOCIAL SECURITY TAX	MEDICARE TAX	CITY TAX	HEALTH INSURANCE	CREDIT UNION	OTHER	TOTAL	CHECK NO.	AMOUNT
31 00	30 23	7 07	4 88	4 00	15 00		92 18	813	395 32

PAY RATE	DATE OF BIRTH	DATE HIRED	NAME/ADDRESS	EMPLOYEE NUMBER
$12.50	4/12/69	9/1/--	Sheila Martinez 46 Darling Crossing Norwich, CT 06360	3

3.

GENERAL JOURNAL   PAGE 1

	DATE		DESCRIPTION	POST REF.	DEBIT	CREDIT	
1	19-- Jan.	23	Wages and Salaries Expense	511	2 4 2 9 50		1
2			Employee Income Tax Payable	211		2 0 1 00	2
3			Social Security Tax Payable	212		1 5 0 64	3
4			Medicare Tax Payable	213		3 5 23	4
5			City Earnings Tax Payable	215		2 4 30	5
6			Health Insurance Premiums Payable	216		3 6 00	6
7			Credit Union Payable	217		4 5 00	7
8			Savings Bond Deductions Payable	218		3 7 50	8
9			Cash	101		1 8 9 9 83	9
10			Payroll for week ended Jan. 21				10

GENERAL LEDGER

ACCOUNT: Cash   **ACCOUNT NO. 101**

DATE	ITEM	POST REF.	DEBIT	CREDIT	BALANCE DEBIT	BALANCE CREDIT
19-- Jan. 23		J 1		1 8 9 9 83		

ACCOUNT: Employee Income Tax Payable   **ACCOUNT NO. 211**

DATE	ITEM	POST REF.	DEBIT	CREDIT	BALANCE DEBIT	BALANCE CREDIT
19-- Jan. 23		J 1		2 0 1 00		

ACCOUNT: Social Security Tax Payable   **ACCOUNT NO. 212**

DATE	ITEM	POST REF.	DEBIT	CREDIT	BALANCE DEBIT	BALANCE CREDIT
19-- Jan. 23		J 1		1 5 0 64		

ACCOUNT: Medicare Tax Payable   **ACCOUNT NO. 213**

DATE	ITEM	POST REF.	DEBIT	CREDIT	BALANCE DEBIT	BALANCE CREDIT
19-- Jan. 23		J 1		3 5 23		

ACCOUNT: City Earnings Tax Payable   **ACCOUNT NO. 215**

DATE	ITEM	POST REF.	DEBIT	CREDIT	BALANCE DEBIT	BALANCE CREDIT
19-- Jan. 23		J 1		2 4 30		

ACCOUNT: Health Insurance Premiums Payable   **ACCOUNT NO. 216**

DATE	ITEM	POST REF.	DEBIT	CREDIT	BALANCE DEBIT	BALANCE CREDIT
19-- Jan. 23		J 1		3 6 00		

(continued)

ACCOUNT: Credit Union Payable							ACCOUNT NO. 217	
DATE	ITEM	POST REF.	DEBIT	CREDIT	BALANCE			
					DEBIT		CREDIT	
19-- Jan. 23		J1		4 5 00				

ACCOUNT: Savings Bond Deductions Payable							ACCOUNT NO. 218	
DATE	ITEM	POST REF.	DEBIT	CREDIT	BALANCE			
					DEBIT		CREDIT	
19-- Jan. 23		J1		3 7 50				

ACCOUNT: Wages and Salaries Expense							ACCOUNT NO. 511	
DATE	ITEM	POST REF.	DEBIT	CREDIT	BALANCE			
					DEBIT		CREDIT	
19-- Jan. 23		J1	2 4 2 9 50					

REVIEW QUESTIONS

1. Why is it important for payroll accounting purposes to distinguish between an employee and an independent contractor?

2. Name three major categories of deductions from an employee's gross pay.

3. Identify the four factors that determine the amount of federal income tax that is withheld from an employee's pay each pay period.

4. In general, an employee is entitled to withholding allowances for what purposes?

5. Identify the three payroll records usually needed by an employer.

6. Describe the information contained in the payroll register.

7. Why is it important to total and verify the totals of the payroll register after the data for each employee have been entered?

8. Distinguish between the payroll register and the employee earnings record.

9. Explain what an employer does with the amounts withheld from an employee's pay.

10. Explain why payroll processing centers and electronic systems are commonly used in payroll accounting.

MANAGING YOUR WRITING

The minimum wage originally was only 25 cents an hour. Today it is $5.15 an hour. Assume that Congress is considering raising the minimum wage again and your United States representative is asking for public opinion on this issue. Write a letter to your representative with arguments for and against a higher minimum wage.

ETHICS CASE

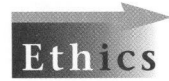

Maura Lowe is a payroll accountant for N & L Company. She prepares and processes the company's payroll on a weekly basis and has been at N & L for only three months. All employees are paid on Friday. On Wednesday afternoon, Simon Lentz, one of the company's top sales associates, asks Maura to not take out any payroll deductions from his pay this week. He explains that he is short of cash and needs the full amount of his gross salary just to put food on the table and make his past-due car payment. He promises Maura that she can catch up on the deductions over the next month. The deductions include employee income tax, Social Security tax, Medicare tax, and health insurance premiums.

1. Is Simon's request of Maura ethical? Why or why not?

2. If this were the first pay period of the year and Maura agreed not to take out deductions from Simon's pay, what effect would this have on the liabilities section of the balance sheet?

3. Write a short paragraph from Maura to Simon explaining how omitting deductions from a pay period will cause errors in the company's financial statements.

4. In small groups, discuss what action Maura should take regarding Simon's request.

WEB WORK

Most people receive paychecks; they don't issue them. The bottom line and the benefits are noted and grumbled about, but what really goes into a person's paycheck? What are various benefits and compensation strategies?
For general compensation reviews across the nation, look here:

http://jobsmart.org/tools/salary/surv-gen.htm

For an explanation of some benefits, check out

http://www.bestjobsusa.com/erframe.htm
(http://heintz/swcollege.com)

SERIES A EXERCISES

EXERCISE 9A-1 (LO 2) COMPUTING NET PAY Mary Sue Guild works for a company that pays its employees 1½ times the regular rate for all hours worked in excess of 40 per week. Guild's pay rate is $10.00 per hour. Her wages are subject to deductions for federal income tax, Social Security tax, and Medicare tax. She is married and claims 4 withholding allowances. Guild has a ½-hour lunch break during an 8½-hour day. Her time card is shown on the next page.

Name	Mary Sue Guild						
Week Ending		March 30, 19--					
Day	In	Out	In	Out	Hours Worked		
					Regular	Overtime	
M	7:57	12:05	12:35	4:33	8		
T	7:52	12:09	12:39	5:05	8	½	
W	7:59	12:15	12:45	5:30	8	1	
T	8:00	12:01	12:30	6:31	8	2	
F	7:56	12:05	12:34	4:30	8		
S	8:00	10:31				2½	

Complete the following:

a) _____ regular hours × $10.00 per hour $_____

b _____ overtime hours × $15.00 per hour $_____

c) Total gross wages $_____

d) Federal income tax withholding (from tax tables in Figure 9-4, pages 301 and 302) $_____

e) Social Security withholding at 6.2% $_____

f) Medicare withholding at 1.45% $_____

g) Total withholding $_____

h) Net pay $_____

EXERCISE 9A-2 (LO 2) COMPUTING WEEKLY GROSS PAY Ryan Lawrence's regular hourly rate is $15.00. He receives 1½ times the regular rate for any hours worked over 40 a week and double the rate for work on Sunday. During the past week, Lawrence worked 8 hours each day Monday through Thursday, 10 hours on Friday, and 5 hours on Sunday. Compute Lawrence's gross pay for the past week.

EXERCISE 9A-3 (LO 2) COMPUTING OVERTIME RATE OF PAY AND GROSS WEEKLY PAY Rebecca Huang receives a regular salary of $2,600 a month and is paid 1½ times the regular hourly rate for hours worked in excess of 40 per week.

a) Calculate Huang's overtime rate of pay.

b) Calculate Huang's total gross weekly pay if she works 45 hours during the week.

EXERCISE 9A-4 (LO 2) COMPUTING FEDERAL INCOME TAX Using the table in Figure 9-4 on pages 301 and 302, determine the amount of federal income tax an employer should withhold weekly for employees with the following marital status, earnings, and withholding allowances.

	Marital Status	Total Weekly Earnings	Number of Allowances	Amount of Withholding
a)	S	$327.90	2	_____
b)	S	$410.00	1	_____
c)	M	$438.16	5	_____
d)	S	$518.25	0	_____
e)	M	$603.98	6	_____

EXERCISE 9A-5 (LO 2) CALCULATING SOCIAL SECURITY AND MEDICARE TAXES
Assume a Social Security tax rate of 6.2% is applied to maximum earnings of
$68,400 and a Medicare tax rate of 1.45% is applied to all earnings. Calculate the
Social Security and Medicare tax for the following situations.

Cumul. Pay Before Current Weekly Payroll	Current Gross Pay	Year-to-Date Earnings	Soc. Sec. Maximum	Amount Over Max. Soc. Sec.	Amount Subject to Soc. Sec.	Soc. Sec. Tax Withheld	Medicare Tax Withheld
$22,000	$1,200	_____	$68,400	_____	_____	_____	_____
$54,000	$4,200	_____	$68,400	_____	_____	_____	_____
$65,800	$3,925	_____	$68,400	_____	_____	_____	_____
$67,800	$4,600	_____	$68,400	_____	_____	_____	_____

EXERCISE 9A-6 (LO 4) JOURNALIZING PAYROLL TRANSACTIONS On December
31, the payroll register of Hamstreet Associates indicated the following information:

Wages and Salaries Expense	$8,700.00
Employee Income Tax Payable	920.00
United Way Contributions Payable	200.00
Earnings subject to Social Security tax	8,000.00

Determine the amount of Social Security and Medicare taxes to be withheld and
record the journal entry for the payroll, crediting Cash for the net pay.

EXERCISE 9A-7 (LO 4) PAYROLL JOURNAL ENTRY Journalize the following data
taken from the payroll register of University Printing as of April 15, 19--.

Regular earnings	$5,418.00
Overtime earnings	824.00
Deductions:	
Federal income tax	593.00
Social Security tax	387.00
Medicare tax	90.51
Pension plan	90.00
Health insurance premiums	225.00
United Way contributions	100.00

SERIES A PROBLEMS

PROBLEM 9A-1 (LO 2/4) GROSS PAY, DEDUCTIONS, AND NET PAY Donald Chin works for Northwest Supplies. His rate of pay is $8.50 per hour, and he is paid 1½ times the regular rate for all hours worked in excess of 40 per week. During the last week of January of the current year he worked 48 hours. Chin is married and claims 4 withholding allowances on his W-4 form. His weekly wages are subject to the following deductions:

a) Employee income tax (use Figure 9-4 on pages 301 and 302)

b) Social Security tax at 6.2%

c) Medicare tax at 1.45%

d) Health insurance premium, $85.00

e) Credit union, $125.00

f) United Way contribution, $10.00

REQUIRED

1. Compute Chin's regular pay, overtime pay, gross pay, and net pay.

2. Journalize the payment of his wages for the week ended January 31, crediting Cash for the net amount.

PROBLEM 9A-2 (LO 2/3/4) PAYROLL REGISTER AND PAYROLL JOURNAL ENTRY Don McCullum operates a travel agency called Don's Luxury Travel. He has five employees, all of whom are paid on a weekly basis. The travel agency uses a payroll register, individual employee earnings records, and a general journal.

Don's Luxury Travel uses a weekly federal income tax withholding table. The payroll data for each employee for the week ended March 22, 19--, are given below. Employees are paid 1½ times the regular rate for working over 40 hours a week.

Name	No. of Allowances	Marital Status	Total Hours Worked Mar. 16–22	Rate	Total Earnings Jan. 1–Mar. 15
Ali, Loren	4	M	45	$11.00	$5,280.00
Carson, Judy	1	S	40	12.00	5,760.00
Hernandez, Maria	3	M	43	9.50	4,560.00
Knox, Wayne	1	S	39	11.00	5,125.50
Paglione, Jim	2	M	40	10.50	4,720.50

Social Security tax is withheld from the first $68,400 of earnings at the rate of 6.2%. Medicare tax is withheld at the rate of 1.45%, and city earnings tax at the rate of 1%, both applied to gross pay. Ali and Knox have $15.00 withheld and Carson and Hernandez have $5.00 withheld for health insurance. Ali and Knox have $20.00 withheld to be invested in the travel agencies' credit union. Carson has $38.75 withheld and Hernandez $18.75 withheld under a savings bond purchase plan.

Don's Luxury Travel's payroll is met by drawing checks on its regular bank account. The checks were issued in sequence, beginning with check no. 423.

REQUIRED

1. Prepare a payroll register for Don's Luxury Travel for the week ended March 22, 19--. (In the Taxable Earnings/Unemployment Compensation column, enter the same amounts as in the Social Security column.) Total the amount columns, verify the totals, and rule with single and double lines.

2. Assuming that the wages for the week ended March 22 were paid on March 24, prepare the journal entry for the payment of the payroll.

PROBLEM 9A-3 (LO 3) EMPLOYEE EARNINGS RECORD Don's Luxury Travel in Problem 9A-2 keeps employee earnings records. Judy Carson, employee number 62, is employed as a manager in the ticket sales department. She was born on May 8, 1959, and was hired on June 1 of last year. Her Social Security number is 544-67-1283. She lives at 28 Quarry Drive, Vernon, CT 06066.

REQUIRED   For the week ended March 22, complete an employee earnings record for Judy Carson. (Insert earnings data only for the week of March 22.)

SERIES B EXERCISES

EXERCISE 9B-1 (LO 2) COMPUTING NET PAY Tom Hallinan works for a company that pays its employees 1½ times the regular rate for all hours worked in excess of 40 per week. Hallinan's pay rate is $12.00 per hour. His wages are subject to deductions for federal income tax, Social Security tax, and Medicare tax. He is married and claims 5 withholding allowances. Hallinan has a ½-hour lunch break during an 8½-hour day. His time card is shown below.

Name	Tom Hallinan						
Week Ending	March 30, 19--						
Day	In	Out	In	Out	Hours Worked		
					Regular	Overtime	
M	7:55	12:02	12:32	5:33	8	1	
T	7:59	12:04	12:34	6:05	8	1½	
W	7:59	12:05	12:35	4:30	8		
T	8:00	12:01	12:30	5:01	8	½	
F	7:58	12:02	12:31	5:33	8	1	
S	7:59	9:33				1½	

4

Complete the following:

a) ____40____ regular hours × $12.00 per hour $ __480__   5.5418

b) ____6.5____ overtime hours × $18.00 per hour $ __98__   0

c) Total gross wages $ __579__

d) Federal income tax withholding (from tax tables in Figure 9-4, pages 301 and 302) $ __29__

e) Social Security withholding at 6.2% $ __35.90__

f) Medicare withholding at 1.45% $ __8.40__

(continued)

g) Total withholding $ _73 30_

h) Net pay $ _505.70_

EXERCISE 9B-2 (LO 2) COMPUTING WEEKLY GROSS PAY Manuel Soto's regular hourly rate is $12.00. He receives 1½ times the regular rate for hours worked in excess of 40 a week and double the rate for work on Sunday. During the past week, Soto worked 8 hours each day Monday through Thursday, 11 hours on Friday, and 6 hours on Sunday. Compute Soto's gross pay for the past week.

EXERCISE 9B-3 (LO 2) COMPUTING OVERTIME RATE OF PAY AND GROSS WEEKLY PAY Mike Fritz receives a regular salary of $3,250 a month and is paid 1½ times the regular hourly rate for hours worked in excess of 40 per week.

a) Calculate Fritz's overtime rate of pay. (Compute to the nearest half cent.)

b) Calculate Fritz's total gross weekly pay if he works 46 hours during the week.

EXERCISE 9B-4 (LO 2) COMPUTING FEDERAL INCOME TAX Using the table in Figure 9-4 on pages 301 and 302, determine the amount of federal income tax an employer should withhold weekly for employees with the following marital status, earnings, and withholding allowances.

	Marital Status	Total Weekly Earnings	Number of Allowances	Amount of Withholding
a)	M	$346.32	4	_____
b)	M	$390.00	3	_____
c)	S	$461.39	2	_____
d)	M	$522.88	6	_____
e)	S	$612.00	0	_____

EXERCISE 9B-5 (LO 2) CALCULATING SOCIAL SECURITY AND MEDICARE TAXES Assume a Social Security tax rate of 6.2% is applied to maximum earnings of $68,400 and a Medicare tax rate of 1.45% is applied to all earnings. Calculate the Social Security and Medicare tax for the following situations.

Cumul. Pay Before Current Weekly Payroll	Current Gross Pay	Year-to-Date Earnings	Soc. Sec. Maximum	Amount Over Max. Soc. Sec.	Amount Subject to Soc. Sec.	Soc. Sec. Tax Withheld	Medicare Tax Withheld
$31,000	$1,500	_____	$68,400	_____	_____	_____	_____
$53,000	$2,860	_____	$68,400	_____	_____	_____	_____
$65,500	$3,140	_____	$68,400	_____	_____	_____	_____
$67,800	$2,920	_____	$68,400	_____	_____	_____	_____

EXERCISE 9B-6 (LO 4) JOURNALIZING PAYROLL TRANSACTIONS On November 30, the payroll register of Webster & Smith indicated the following information:

Wages and Salaries Expense	$9,400.00
Employee Income Tax Payable	985.00
United Way Contributions Payable	200.00
Earnings subject to Social Security tax	9,400.00

Determine the amount of Social Security and Medicare taxes to be withheld and record the journal entry for the payroll, crediting Cash for the net pay.

EXERCISE 9B-7 (LO 4) PAYROLL JOURNAL ENTRY Journalize the following data taken from the payroll register of Himes Bakery as of June 12, 19--.

Regular earnings	$6,520.00
Overtime earnings	950.00
Deductions:	
Federal income tax	782.00
Social Security tax	463.14
Medicare tax	108.32
Pension plan	80.00
Health insurance premiums	190.00
United Way contributions	150.00

SERIES B PROBLEMS

PROBLEM 9B-1 (LO 2/4) GROSS PAY, DEDUCTIONS, AND NET PAY Elyse Lin works for Columbia Industries. Her rate of pay is $9.00 per hour, and she is paid 1½ times the regular rate for all hours worked in excess of 40 per week. During the last week of January of the current year she worked 46 hours. Lin is married and claims 5 withholding allowances on her W-4 form. Her weekly wages are subject to the following deductions:

a) Employee income tax (use Figure 9-4 on pages 301 and 302)

b) Social Security tax at 6.2%

c) Medicare tax at 1.45%

d) Health insurance premium, $92.00

e) Credit union, $110.00

f) United Way contribution, $5.00

REQUIRED
1. Compute Lin's regular pay, overtime pay, gross pay, and net pay.

2. Journalize the payment of her wages for the week ended January 31, crediting Cash for the net amount.

PROBLEM 9B-2 (LO 2/3/4) PAYROLL REGISTER AND PAYROLL JOURNAL ENTRY Karen Jolly operates a bakery called Karen's Cupcakes. She has five employees, all of whom are paid on a weekly basis. Karen's Cupcakes uses a payroll register, individual employee earnings records, and a general journal.

(continued)

Karen's Cupcakes uses a weekly federal income tax withholding table. The payroll data for each employee for the week ended February 15, 19--, are given below. Employees are paid 1½ times the regular rate for working over 40 hours a week.

Name	No. of Allowances	Marital Status	Total Hours Worked Feb. 9–15	Rate	Total Earnings Jan. 1–Feb. 15
Barone, William	1	S	40	$10.00	$2,400.00
Hastings, Gene	4	M	45	12.00	3,360.00
Nitobe, Isako	3	M	46	8.75	2,935.00
Smith, Judy	4	M	42	11.00	2,745.00
Tarshis, Dolores	1	S	39	10.50	2,650.75

Social Security tax is withheld from the first $68,400 of earnings at the rate of 6.2%. Medicare tax is withheld at the rate of 1.45%, and city earnings tax at the rate of 1%, both applied to gross pay. Hastings and Smith have $35.00 withheld and Nitobe and Tarshis have $15.00 withheld for health insurance. Nitobe and Tarshis have $25.00 withheld to be invested in the bakers' credit union. Hastings has $18.75 withheld and Smith $43.75 withheld under a savings bond purchase plan.

Karen's Cupcakes payroll is met by drawing checks on its regular bank account. The checks were issued in sequence, beginning with no. 365.

REQUIRED

1. Prepare a payroll register for Karen's Cupcakes for the week ended February 15, 19--. (In the Taxable Earnings/Unemployment Compensation column, enter the same amounts as in the Social Security column.) Total the amount columns, verify the totals, and rule with single and double lines.

2. Assuming that the wages for the week ended February 15 were paid on February 17, prepare the journal entry for the payment of this payroll.

PROBLEM 9B-3 (LO 3) EMPLOYEE EARNINGS RECORD Karen's Cupcakes in Problem 9B-2 keeps employee earnings records. William Barone, employee number 19, is employed as a baker in the desserts department. He was born on August 26, 1959, and was hired on October 1 of last year. His Social Security number is 342-73-4681. He lives at 30 Timber Lane, Willington, CT 06279.

REQUIRED   For the week ended February 15, complete an employee earnings record for William Barone. (Insert earnings data only for the week of February 15.)

MASTERY PROBLEM

Abigail Trenkamp owns and operates the Trenkamp Collection Agency. Listed below are the name, number of allowances claimed, marital status, information from time cards on hours worked each day, and the hourly rate of each employee. All hours worked in excess of 40 hours for Monday through Friday are paid at 1½ times the regular rate. All weekend hours are paid at double the regular rate.

Trenkamp uses a weekly federal income tax withholding table (see Figure 9-4 on pages 301 and 302). Social Security tax is withheld at the rate of 6.2% for the first $68,400 earned. Medicare tax is withheld at 1.45% and state income tax at 3.5%. Each employee has $5.00 withheld for health insurance. All employees use payroll deduction to the credit union for varying amounts as listed on the next page.

Trenkamp Collection Agency
Payroll Information for the Week Ended November 18, 19--

Name	Employee No.	No. of Allow.	Marital Status	Regular Hours Worked							Hourly Rate	Credit Union Deposit	Total Earnings 1/1–11/11
				S	S	M	T	W	T	F			
Berling, James	1	3	M	2	2	9	8	8	9	10	$12.00	$149.60	$24,525.00
Merz, Linda	2	4	M	4	3	8	8	8	8	11	10.00	117.00	20,480.00
Goetz, Ken	3	5	M	0	0	6	7	8	9	10	11.00	91.30	21,500.00
Menick, Judd	4	2	M	8	8	0	0	8	8	9	11.00	126.50	22,625.00
Morales, Eva	5	3	M	0	0	8	8	8	6	8	13.00	117.05	24,730.00
Heimbrock, Jacob	6	2	S	0	0	8	8	8	8	8	30.00	154.25	67,600.00
Townsley, Sarah	7	2	M	4	0	6	6	6	6	4	9.00	83.05	21,425.00
Salzman, Ben	8	4	M	6	2	8	8	6	6	6	11.00	130.00	6,635.00
Layton, Esther	9	4	M	0	0	8	8	8	8	8	11.00	88.00	5,635.00
Thompson, David	10	5	M	0	2	10	9	7	7	10	11.00	128.90	21,635.00
Vadillo, Carmen	11	2	S	8	0	4	8	8	8	9	13.00	139.11	24,115.00

The Trenkamp Collection Agency follows the practice of drawing a single check for the net amount of the payroll and depositing the check in a special payroll account at the bank. Individual checks issued were numbered consecutively, beginning with no. 331.

REQUIRED

1. Prepare a payroll register for Trenkamp Collection Agency for the week ended November 18, 19--. (In the Taxable Earnings/Unemployment Compensation column, enter $365 for Salzman and $440 for Layton. Leave this column blank for all other employees.) Total the amount columns, verify the totals, and rule with single and double lines.

2. Assuming that the wages for the week ended November 18 were paid on November 21, prepare the journal entry for the payment of this payroll.

3. The current employee earnings record for Ben Salzman is provided in the working papers. Update Salzman's earnings record to reflect the November 18 payroll. Although this information should have been entered earlier, complete the required information on the earnings record. The necessary information is provided below.

Name	Ben F. Salzman
Address	12 Windmill Lane
	Trumbull, CT 06611
Employee No.	8
Gender	Male
Department	Administration
Occupation	Office Manager
Social Security No.	446-46-6321
Marital Status	Married
Allowances	4
Pay Rate	$11.00 per hour
Date of Birth	4/5/64
Date Hired	7/22/--

Self-Study Test Questions

True/False

1. An independent contractor is one who works under the control and direction of an employer. _____

2. Government laws and regulations regarding payroll are more complex for employees than for independent contractors. _____

3. Compensation for skilled or unskilled labor expressed in terms of hours, weeks, or units is called salary. _____

4. An employee's total earnings is called gross pay. _____

5. A payroll register is a multi-column form used to assemble the data required at the end of each payroll period. _____

Multiple Choice

1. Jack Smith is married, has a spouse who is not employed, has five dependent children, and does not anticipate large itemized deductions. How many withholding allowances is Smith entitled to? _____

    (a) 5   (c) 7
    (b) 6   (d) 8

2. A separate record of each employee's earnings is called a(n) _____

    (a) payroll register.   (c) W-4.
    (b) employee earnings record.   (d) earnings statement.

3. Nancy Summers worked 44 hours during the past week. She is entitled to 1½ times her regular pay for all hours worked in excess of 40 during the week. Her regular rate of pay is $12.00. Social Security tax is withheld at the rate of 6.2% and Medicare tax is withheld at the rate of 1.45%; federal income tax withheld is $68; and $5 of union dues are withheld. Her net pay for the week is _____

    (a) $440.89.   (c) $552.00.
    (b) $472.00.   (d) $436.78.

4. Social Security Tax Payable and Medicare Tax Payable are classified as _____

    (a) liabilities.   (c) owner's equity.
    (b) assets.   (d) expenses.

5. Which of the following is *not* a factor that determines the amount of federal income tax to be withheld from an employee's gross pay? _____

    (a) marital status   (c) total earnings
    (b) number of withholding allowances claimed (d) age of employee

The answers to the Self-Study Test Questions are at the end of the text.

10

Payroll Accounting: Employer Taxes and Reports

John Zenith's new shop assistant has worked out extremely well. Be A Sport is better organized and customers receive more direct attention. Having worked in a similar store in Connecticut, the new hire also was able to help John obtain accounts with two new vendors. The only negative feature of having the new employee has been the cost. Based on 25 hours per week at $8 an hour, John had budgeted a cost of $200 per week for the help. In fact, as John's bookkeeper had warned him, the cost is substantially higher. In simple terms, John has discovered that he must pay numerous payroll taxes, in addition to the basic wages of the employee. What payroll taxes must John pay as an employer? Assuming the employee works a full year and is paid $10,400 (52 weeks × $200), what is the total payroll cost to John of having this employee?

The taxes we discussed in Chapter 9 had one thing in common—they all were levied on the employee. The employer withheld them from employees' earnings and paid them to the government. They did not add anything to the employer's payroll expenses.

In this chapter, we will examine several taxes that are imposed directly on the employer. All of these taxes represent additional payroll expenses.

EMPLOYER PAYROLL TAXES

LO 1 Describe and calculate employer payroll taxes.

Most employers must pay FICA taxes, FUTA (Federal Unemployment Tax Act) taxes, and SUTA (State Unemployment Tax) taxes.

Employer's FICA Taxes

> Both the employer and employee must pay Social Security and Medicare taxes. The employer FICA tax equals the employee FICA tax and the employer Medicare tax equals the employee Medicare tax.

Employer FICA taxes are levied on employers at the same rates and on the same earnings bases as the employee FICA taxes. As explained in Chapter 9, for 1998 the Social Security component is 6.2% on maximum earnings of $68,400 for each employee. Since there is no maximum on the Medicare component, this tax is 1.45% on all earnings.

The payroll register we saw in Chapter 9 is a key source of information for computing employer payroll taxes. That payroll register is reproduced in Figure 10-1. The Taxable Earnings Social Security column shows that $4,835 of employee earnings were subject to Social Security tax for the pay period. The employer's Social Security tax on these earnings is computed as follows:

Social Security Taxable Earnings	×	Tax Rate	=	Tax
$4,835		.062		$299.77

FIGURE 10-1 Payroll Register (left side)

LEARNING KEY: Use the information in the payroll register to compute employer payroll taxes.

The Medicare tax applies to the total earnings of $5,435. The employer's Medicare tax on these earnings is computed as follows:

Total Earnings	×	Tax Rate	=	Tax
$5,435		.0145		$78.81

These amounts plus the employees' Social Security and Medicare taxes withheld must be paid by the employer to the Internal Revenue Service (IRS).

Self-Employment Tax

> The self-employment tax rate is about double the employee and employer Social Security and Medicare rates because the self-employed person is considered both the employer and employee.

Individuals who own and run their own business are considered self-employed. These individuals can be viewed as both employer and employee. They do not receive salary or wages from the business, but they do have earnings in the form of the business net income. **Self-employment income** is the net income of a trade or business run by an individual. Currently, persons earning self-employment income of $400 or more must pay a **self-employment tax**. Self-employment tax is a contribution to the FICA program. The tax rates are about double the Social Security and Medicare rates. They are applied to the same income bases as those used for the Social Security and Medicare taxes.

One half of the self-employment tax is a personal expense of the owner of the business. The other half is similar to the employer Social Security and Medicare taxes paid for each employee. This portion of the tax is considered a business expense and is debited to Self-Employment Tax.

FIGURE 10-1 Payroll Register (right side)

REGISTER—WEEK ENDED 12/19/--

	FEDERAL INCOME TAX	SOCIAL SECURITY TAX	MEDICARE TAX	HEALTH INSURANCE	UNITED WAY	OTHER	TOTAL	NET PAY	CHECK NO.	
1	1 6 1 00	4 0 92	1 8 27				2 2 0 19	1 0 3 9 81	409	1
2	1 6 4 00	5 5 80	1 3 05		2 0 00		2 5 2 85	6 4 7 15	410	2
3	1 6 00	3 3 79	7 90	1 0 00			6 7 69	4 7 7 31	411	3
4	8 2 00	4 7 99	1 1 22	1 3 00	2 0 00		1 7 4 21	5 9 9 79	412	4
5	2 5 00	2 7 28	6 38	1 3 00			7 1 66	3 6 8 34	413	5
6	9 9 00	4 5 01	1 0 53				1 5 4 54	5 7 1 46	414	6
7	1 7 00	3 0 38	7 11	1 0 00			6 4 49	4 2 5 51	415	7
8	3 0 00	1 8 60	4 35				5 2 95	2 4 7 05	416	8
9	5 9 4 00	2 9 9 77	7 8 81	4 6 00	4 0 00		1 0 5 8 58	4 3 7 6 42		9

Withholding Tax Table

6.2% × Social Security taxable earnings

1.45% × total earnings

Specific employer–employee agreements

Total earnings – total deductions

Employer's FUTA Tax

The **FUTA (Federal Unemployment Tax Act) tax** is levied only on employers. It is not deducted from employees' earnings. The purpose of this tax is to raise funds to administer the combined federal/state unemployment compensation program. The maximum amount of earnings subject to the FUTA tax and the tax rate can be changed by Congress. The current rate is 6.2% applied to maximum earnings of $7,000 for each employee. But employers are allowed a credit of up to 5.4% for participation in state unemployment programs. Thus, the effective federal rate is commonly 0.8%.

Gross FUTA rate	6.2%
Credit for state	
unemployment taxes	5.4%
Net FUTA rate	0.8%

To illustrate the computation of the FUTA tax, refer to Figure 10-1. The Taxable Earnings Unemployment Compensation column shows that only $300 of employee earnings were subject to the FUTA tax. This amount is so low because the payroll period is late in the calendar year (December 19, 19—). It is common for most employees to exceed the $7,000 earnings limit by this time. The FUTA tax is computed as shown in Figure 10-2.

FIGURE 10-2 Computation of FUTA Tax

Employer's SUTA Tax

The **SUTA (State Unemployment Tax) tax** is also levied only on employers in most states. The purpose of this tax is to raise funds to pay unemployment benefits. Tax rates and unemployment benefits vary among the states. The most common rate is 5.4% applied to maximum earnings of $7,000 for each employee. Most states have a **merit-rating system** to encourage employers to provide regular employment to workers. If an employer has very few former employees receiving unemployment compensation, the employer qualifies for a lower state unemployment tax rate. If an employer qualifies for a lower state rate, the full credit of 5.4% would still be allowed in computing the federal unemployment tax due.

Refer to the payroll register in Figure 10-1. As we saw with the FUTA tax, only $300 of employee earnings for this pay period are subject to the state unemployment tax. The tax is computed as shown in Figure 10-3.

FIGURE 10-3 Computation of SUTA Tax

	UNEMPLOYMENT COMPENSATION		State Unemployment Taxable Earnings × Tax Rate = Tax
5			
6			
7			$300 5.4% $16.20
8	3 0 0 00		
9	3 0 0 00		
10			

ACCOUNTING FOR EMPLOYER PAYROLL TAXES

LO 2 Account for employer payroll taxes expense.

Now that we have computed the employer payroll taxes, we need to journalize them. It is common to debit all employer payroll taxes to a single account—Payroll Taxes Expense. However, we usually credit separate liability accounts for Social Security, Medicare, FUTA, and SUTA taxes payable.

Journalizing Employer Payroll Taxes

The employer payroll taxes computed in the previous section can be summarized as follows:

Employer's Social Security tax	$299.77
Employer's Medicare tax	78.81
FUTA tax	2.40
SUTA tax	16.20
Total employer payroll taxes	$397.18

These amounts provide the basis for the following journal entry:

5	Dec.	19	Payroll Taxes Expense		3 9 7 18			5
6			Social Security Tax Payable			2 9 9 77		6
7			Medicare Tax Payable			7 8 81		7
8			FUTA Tax Payable			2 40		8
9			SUTA Tax Payable			1 6 20		9
10			Employer payroll taxes for week ended Dec. 19					10

The steps needed to prepare this journal entry for employer payroll taxes are:

STEP 1 Obtain the taxable earnings amounts from the Taxable Earnings columns of the payroll register. In this case, Social Security taxable earnings were $4,835; Unemployment Compensation taxable earnings were $300.

STEP 2 Compute the amount of employer Social Security tax by multiplying the Social Security taxable earnings by 6.2%.

STEP 3 Compute the amount of Medicare tax by multiplying total earnings by 1.45%.

STEP 4 Compute the amount of FUTA tax by multiplying the Unemployment Taxable earnings by 0.8%.

STEP 5 Compute the amount of SUTA tax by multiplying the Unemployment Taxable earnings by 5.4%.

STEP 6 Prepare the appropriate journal entry using the amounts computed in steps 2–5.

To understand the journal entry for employer payroll taxes, let's examine the accounts involved.

Payroll Taxes Expense

The Social Security, Medicare, FUTA, and SUTA taxes imposed on the employer are expenses of doing business. Each of the employer taxes is debited to Payroll Taxes Expense.

Payroll Taxes Expense

Debit	Credit
Social Security, Medicare, FUTA, and SUTA taxes imposed on the employer	

Social Security and Medicare Taxes Payable

These are the same liability accounts used in Chapter 9 to record the Social Security and Medicare taxes withheld from employees' earnings. The accounts are credited to enter the Social Security and Medicare taxes imposed on the employer. They are debited when the taxes are paid to the IRS. When all of the Social Security and Medicare taxes have been paid, the accounts will have zero balances.

Social Security Tax Payable

Debit	Credit
payment of Social Security tax	Social Security taxes (1) with-held from employees' earnings and (2) imposed on the employer

Medicare Tax Payable

Debit	Credit
payment of Medicare tax	Medicare taxes (1) with-held from employees' earnings and (2) imposed on the employer

 LEARNING KEY: Employer and employee Social Security and Medicare taxes are credited to the same liability accounts because both of these taxes are due and will be paid to the IRS.

FUTA Tax Payable

A separate liability account entitled FUTA Tax Payable is kept for the employer's FUTA tax. This account is credited for the tax imposed on employers under the Federal Unemployment Tax Act. The account is debited when this tax is paid. When all of the FUTA taxes have been paid, the account will have a zero balance.

FUTA Tax Payable

Debit	Credit
payment of FUTA tax	FUTA tax imposed on the employer

SUTA Tax Payable

A separate liability account entitled SUTA Tax Payable is kept for the state unemployment tax. This account is credited for the tax imposed on employers under the state unemployment compensation laws. The account is debited when this tax is paid. When all of the state unemployment taxes have been paid, the account will have a zero balance.

SUTA Tax Payable

Debit	Credit
payment of SUTA tax	SUTA tax imposed on the employer

Total Payroll Cost of an Employee

It is interesting to note what it really costs to employ a person. The employer must, of course, pay the gross wages of an employee. In addition, the employer must pay payroll taxes on employee earnings up to certain dollar limits.

To illustrate, assume that an employee earns $26,000 a year. The total cost of this employee to the employer is calculated as follows:

Gross wages	$26,000
Employer Social Security tax, 6.2% of $26,000	1,612
Employer Medicare tax, 1.45% of $26,000	377
State unemployment tax, 5.4% of $7,000	378
FUTA tax, 0.8% of $7,000	56
	$28,423

Thus, the total payroll cost of employing a person whose stated compensation is $26,000 is $28,423. Employer payroll taxes clearly are a significant cost of doing business. Employer-paid medical insurance and pension plans can further increase total payroll costs.

REPORTING AND PAYMENT RESPONSIBILITIES

LO 3   Describe employer reporting and payment responsibilities.

Employer payroll reporting and payment responsibilities fall into five areas:

1. Federal income tax withholding and Social Security and Medicare taxes

2. FUTA taxes

3. SUTA taxes

4. Employee Wage and Tax Statement (Form W-2)

5. Summary of employee wages and taxes

Federal Income Tax Withholding and Social Security and Medicare Taxes

Three important aspects of employer reporting and payment responsibilities for federal income tax withholding and Social Security and Medicare taxes are:

1. Determining when payments are due

2. Use of Form 8109, Federal Tax Deposit Coupon

3. Use of Form 941, Employer's Quarterly Federal Tax Return

When Payments are Due. The date by which federal income tax withholding and Social Security and Medicare taxes must be paid depends on the amount of these taxes. Figure 10-4 summarizes the deposit rules stated in *Circular E—Employer's Tax Guide*. In general, the larger the amount that needs to be deposited, the more frequently payments must be made. For simplicity, we will assume that deposits must be made 15 days after the end of each month.

FIGURE 10-4 Summary of Deposit Rules

Deposit Amount	Deposit Due
1. Less than $500 at the end of the current quarter	1. Pay with Form 941 at end of the month following end of the quarter
2. $500 or more at the end of the current quarter and $50,000 or less in total during the lookback period*	2. Deposit 15 days after end of the month
3. $500 or more at the end of the current quarter and more than $50,000 in total during the lookback period*	3. Deposit every other Wednesday or Friday, depending on day of the week payroll payments are made
4. $100,000 or more on any day during the current quarter	4. Deposit by the end of the next banking day

*Lookback period is the four quarters beginning July 1, two years ago, and ending June 30, one year ago.

Form 8109. Deposits are made at a Federal Reserve Bank or other authorized commercial bank using Form 8109, Federal Tax Deposit Coupon (Figure 10-5). The **Employer Identification Number (EIN)** shown on this form is obtained by the employer from the IRS. This number identifies the employer and must be shown on all payroll forms and reports filed with the IRS.

FIGURE 10-5 Federal Tax Deposit Coupon (Form 8109)

The $5,850.88 deposit shown in Figure 10-5 for Westly, Inc. was for the following taxes:

Employees' income tax withheld from wages		$2,526.80
Social Security tax:		
Withheld from employees' wages	$1,346.24	
Imposed on employer	1,346.24	2,692.48
Medicare tax:		
Withheld from employees' wages	$ 315.80	
Imposed on employer	315.80	631.60
Amount of check		$5,850.88

The journal entry for this deposit would be:

5	Dec.	19	Employee Income Tax Payable	2 5 2 6 80			5
6			Social Security Tax Payable	2 6 9 2 48			6
7			Medicare Tax Payable	6 3 1 60			7
8			Cash		5 8 5 0 88		8
9			Deposit of employee federal income tax and				9
10			Social Security and Medicare taxes				10

Form 941. Form 941, Employer's Quarterly Federal Tax Return, must be filed with the IRS at the end of the month following each calendar quarter. This form reports the following taxes for the quarter:

1. Employee federal income tax withheld

2. Employee Social Security and Medicare taxes withheld

3. Employer Social Security and Medicare taxes

A completed form for Westly, Inc. for the first quarter of the calendar year is shown in Figure 10-6. Instructions for completing the form are provided with the form and in *Circular E*.

FIGURE 10-6 Employer's Quarterly Federal Tax Return (Form 941)

Form **941** (Rev. January 1997) Department of the Treasury Internal Revenue Service

4141

Employer's Quarterly Federal Tax Return
▶ See separate instructions for information on completing this return.
Please type or print.

Enter state code for state in which deposits made . ▶ M:O (see page 3 of instructions).

Name (as distinguished from trade name)

Trade name, if any
Westly, Inc

Address (number and street)
5221 Natural Bridge

Date quarter ended
March 30, 19--

Employer identification number
43-0211630

City, state, and ZIP code
St. Louis, Mo 63115-8230

OMB No. 1545-0029

T	
FF	
FD	
FP	
I	
T	

If address is different from prior return, check here ▶

IRS Use

1 1 1 1 1 1 1 1 1 1   2   3 3 3 3 3   4 4 4

5 5 5   6   7   8 8 8 8 8   9 9   10 10 10 10 10 10 10 10 10 10

If you do not have to file returns in the future, check here ▶ ☐ and enter date final wages paid ▶
If you are a seasonal employer, see **Seasonal employers** on page 1 of the instructions and check here ▶ ☐

1	Number of employees (except household) employed in the pay period that includes March 12th ▶	1	8	
2	Total wages and tips, plus other compensation	2	65,160	00
3	Total income tax withheld from wages, tips, and sick pay	3	7,595	80
4	Adjustment of withheld income tax for preceding quarters of calendar year	4	0	
5	Adjusted total of income tax withheld (line 3 as adjusted by line 4—see instructions)	5	7,595	80

6	Taxable social security wages	6a $ 65,160 00 × 12.4% (.124) =	6b	8,079	84
	Taxable social security tips	6c $ 0 × 12.4% (.124) =	6d	0	
7	Taxable Medicare wages and tips . . .	7a $ 65,160 00 × 2.9% (.029) =	7b	1,889	64
8	Total social security and Medicare taxes (add lines 6b, 6d, and 7b). Check here if wages are not subject to social security and/or Medicare tax . . . . ▶ ☐		8	9,969	48
9	Adjustment of social security and Medicare taxes (see instructions for required explanation) Sick Pay $ _____ ± Fractions of Cents $ _____ ± Other $ _____ =		9	0	
10	Adjusted total of social security and Medicare taxes (line 8 as adjusted by line 9—see instructions)		10	9,969	48
11	**Total taxes** (add lines 5 and 10)		11	17,565	28
12	Advance earned income credit (EIC) payments made to employees		12		
13	Net taxes (subtract line 12 from line 11). **This should equal line 17, column (d) below** (or line D of Schedule B (Form 941))		13	17,565	28
14	Total deposits for quarter, including overpayment applied from a prior quarter		14	'17,565	28
15	**Balance due** (subtract line 14 from line 13). See instructions		15		

16 **Overpayment,** if line 14 is more than line 13, enter excess here ▶ $ _____
and check if to be: ☐ Applied to next return **OR** ☐ Refunded.

● **All filers:** If line 13 is less than $500, you need not complete line 17 or Schedule B.
● **Semiweekly schedule depositors:** Complete Schedule B and check here . . . . ▶ ☐
● **Monthly schedule depositors:** Complete line 17, columns (a) through (d), and check here . . . . ▶ ☒

17	Monthly Summary of Federal Tax Liability			
(a) First month liability	(b) Second month liability	(c) Third month liability	(d) Total liability for quarter
5,850.88	5,690.77	6,023.63	17,565.28

Sign Here

Under penalties of perjury, I declare that I have examined this return, including accompanying schedules and statements, and to the best of my knowledge and belief, it is true, correct, and complete.

Signature ▶ *William P. Jones* Print Your Name and Title ▶ *Treasurer* Date ▶ 4/30/--

For Paperwork Reduction Act Notice, see page 1 of separate instructions. Cat. No. 17001Z Form **941** (Rev. 1-97)

FUTA Taxes

Federal unemployment taxes must be calculated on a quarterly basis. If the accumulated liability exceeds $100, the total must be paid to a Federal Reserve Bank or other authorized commercial bank. The total is due by the end of the month following the close of the quarter. If the liability is $100 or less, no deposit is necessary. The amount is simply added to the amount to be deposited for the next quarter. FUTA taxes are deposited using Form 8109 (Figure 10-5).

Assume that Westly, Inc.'s accumulated FUTA tax liability for the first quarter of the calendar year is $408. Westly would use Form 8109 to deposit this amount on April 30. The journal entry for this transaction would be as follows:

15	Apr.	30	FUTA Tax Payable		4 0 8 00			15
16			Cash			4 0 8 00		16
17			Paid federal unemployment tax					17

Form 940. In addition to making quarterly deposits, employers are required to file an annual report of federal unemployment tax using Form 940. This form must be filed with the IRS by January 31 following the end of the calendar year. Figure 10-7 shows a completed Form 940 for Westly, Inc. Instructions for completing the form are provided with the form and in *Circular E.*

FIGURE 10-7 Employer's Annual Federal Unemployment (FUTA) Tax Return (Form 940)

FIGURE 10-7　Employer's Annual Federal Unemployment (FUTA) Tax Return (Form 940) *(continued)*

Form 940 (1997)　　　Page **2**

Part II　**Tax Due or Refund**

1	Gross FUTA tax. Multiply the wages in Part I, line 5, by .062	**1**		3,453 40
2	Maximum credit. Multiply the wages in Part I, line 5, by .054 . . .	**2**	3,007 80	

3　**Computation of tentative credit** (Note: *All taxpayers must complete the applicable columns.*)

(a) Name of state	(b) State reporting number(s) as shown on employer's state contribution returns	(c) Taxable payroll (as defined in state act)	(d) State experience rate period		(e) State experience rate	(f) Contributions if rate had been 5.4% (col. (c) x .054)	(g) Contributions payable at experience rate (col. (c) x col. (e))	(h) Additional credit (col. (f) minus col.(g)). If 0 or less, enter -0-.	(i) Contributions actually paid – to state
			From	To					
MO	36112	55,700.00	1/1/--	12/31/--	.054	3,007.80	3,007.80	-0-	3,007.80

3a	Totals . . . ▶	55,700.00			
3b	**Total tentative credit** (add line 3a, columns (h) and (i) only—see instructions for limitations on late payments) ▶				3,007 80
4					
5					
6	**Credit:** Enter the smaller of the amount in Part II, line 2 or line 3b	**6**		3,007 80
7	**Total FUTA tax** (subtract line 6 from line 1)	**7**		445 60
8	Total FUTA tax deposited for the year, including any overpayment applied from a prior year . .	**8**		427 60
9	**Balance due** (subtract line 8 from line 7). This should be $100 or less. Pay to the Internal Revenue Service. See page 4 of the **Instructions for Form 940** for details . . . . ▶	**9**		18 00
10	**Overpayment** (subtract line 7 from line 8). Check if it is to be: ☐ **Applied to next return** or ☐ **Refunded** . . . . ▶	**10**		

Part III　**Record of Quarterly Federal Unemployment Tax Liability** *(Do not include state liability.)* Complete only if line 7 is over $100.

Quarter	First (Jan. 1–Mar. 31)	Second (Apr. 1–June 30)	Third (July 1–Sept. 30)	Fourth (Oct. 1–Dec. 31)	Total for year
Liability for quarter	408.00	26.00	5.60	6.00	445.60

Under penalties of perjury, I declare that I have examined this return, including accompanying schedules and statements, and to the best of my knowledge and belief, it is true, correct, and complete, and that no part of any payment made to a state unemployment fund claimed as a credit was, or is to be, deducted from the payments to employees.

Signature ▶ *William P. Jones*　Title (Owner, etc.) ▶ *Treasurer*　　　Date ▶ *1/31/--*

SUTA Taxes

Deposit rules and forms for state unemployment taxes vary among the states. Deposits usually are required on a quarterly basis. Assume that Westly's accumulated state unemployment liability for the first quarter of the calendar year is $2,754. The journal entry for the deposit of this amount with the state on April 30 would be:

19	Apr.	30	SUTA Tax Payable		2 7 5 4 00			19
20			Cash			2 7 5 4 00		20
21			Paid state unemployment tax					21

Employee Wage and Tax Statement

By January 31 of each year, employers must furnish each employee with a Wage and Tax Statement, Form W-2 (Figure 10-8). This form shows the total amount of wages paid to the employee and the amounts of taxes withheld during the preceding taxable year. The employee earnings record contains the information needed to complete this form.

FIGURE 10-8 Wage and Tax Statement (Form W-2)

a Control number		OMB No. 1545-0008		
b Employer's identification number 43-0211630		**1** Wages, tips, other compensation 27,645.00	**2** Federal income tax withheld 1,088.00	
c Employer's name, address, and ZIP code Westly, Inc. 5221 Natural Bridge St. Louis, MO 63115-8230		**3** Social security wages 27,645.00	**4** Social security tax withheld 1,713.99	
		5 Medicare wages and tips 27,645.00	**6** Medicare tax withheld 400.85	
		7 Social security tips	**8** Allocated tips	
d Employee's social security number 393-58-8194		**9** Advance EIC payment	**10** Dependent care benefits	
e Employee's name, address, and ZIP code Ken M. Istone 1546 Swallow Dr. St. Louis, MO 63144-4752		**11** Nonqualified plans	**12** Benefits included in box 1	
		13 See Instrs. for Form W-2	**14** Other	
		15 Statutory employee ☐ Deceased ☐ Pension plan ☐ Legal rep. ☐ Hshld. emp. ☐ Subtotal ☐ Deferred compensation ☐		
16 State Employer's state I.D. No.	**17** State wages, tips, etc.	**18** State income tax	**19** Locality name **20** Local wages, tips, etc.	**21** Local income tax

Department of the Treasury—Internal Revenue Service

For Paperwork Reduction Act Notice, see separate instructions.

Form **W-2** Wage and Tax Statement **1997**

Copy D For Employer

Multiple copies of Form W-2 are needed for the following purposes:

▶ Copy A—Employer sends to Social Security Administration

▶ Copy B—Employee attaches to federal income tax return

▶ Copy C—Employee retains for his or her own records

▶ Copy D—Employer retains for business records

▶ Copy 1—Employer sends to state or local tax department

▶ Copy 2—Employee attaches to state or local income tax return

Summary of Employee Wages and Taxes

Employers send Form W-3, Transmittal of Wage and Tax Statements (Figure 10-9), with Copy A of Forms W-2 to the Social Security Administration. Form W-3 must be filed by the last day of February following the end of each taxable year. This form summarizes the employee earnings and tax information presented on Forms W-2 for the year. Information needed to complete Form W-3 is contained in the employee earnings records.

FIGURE 10-9 Transmittal of Wage and Tax Statements (Form W-3)

a Control number		OMB No. 1545-0008		
b **Kind of Payer** ▶ 941 ☒ Military ☐ 943 ☐ CT-1 ☐ Hshld. ☐ Medicare govt. emp. ☐		1 Wages, tips, other compensation 249,815.00	2 Federal income tax withheld 29,100.00	
		3 Social security wages 247,955.00	4 Social security tax withheld 15,373.21	
c Total number of statements 8	d Establishment number	5 Medicare wages and tips 249,815.00	6 Medicare tax withheld 3,622.32	
e Employer's identification number 43-0211630		7 Social security tips	8 Allocated tips	
f Employer's name Westly, Inc.		9 Advance EIC payments	10 Dependent care benefits	
5221 Natural Bridge St. Louis, MO 63115-8230 YOUR COPY KEEP FOR YOUR RECORDS		11 Nonqualified plans 247,955.00	12 Deferred compensation	
		13		
		14		
g Employer's address and ZIP code				
h Other EIN used this year		15 Income tax withheld by third-party payer		
i Employer's state I.D. No. 21686001				

Form **W-3 Transmittal of Wage and Tax Statements 1997**   Department of the Treasury Internal Revenue Service

Summary of Reports and Payments

The complexity of payroll reports, deposit rules, and due dates is a major reason that small businesses often hire an accountant or an outside company to handle payroll.

Keeping track of the many payroll reports, deposits, and due dates can be a challenge for an employer. Figure 10-10 shows a calendar that highlights the due dates for the various reports and deposits. The calendar assumes the following for an employer:

1. Undeposited FIT (federal income tax) and Social Security and Medicare taxes of $500 at the end of each quarter and less than $50,000 during the look-back period.

2. Undeposited FUTA taxes of more than $100 at the end of each quarter.

3. SUTA taxes deposited quarterly.

FIGURE 10-10 Payroll Calendar

Color Key

File Forms 940, 941, state unemployment tax report, and send W-2 to employees.	File Form 941 and state unemployment tax report.
File form W-3 with Copy A of W-2s.	Deposit FIT and Social Security and Medicare taxes from previous month.

A BROADER VIEW

DEALING WITH PAYROLL COMPLEXITY—LET SOMEONE ELSE DO IT

A common way for both small and large businesses to deal with the complexity of payroll reports, deposit rules, and due dates is to hire an outside company to handle the payroll. Payroll processing companies have combined payroll expertise with the power of computers to create a major business enterprise based on the efficient and effective provision of payroll services.

To give you some idea of the extent to which businesses have turned to outside companies to handle payroll, consider Automatic Data Processing, Inc. (ADP), the world's largest provider of payroll services. ADP currently processes payrolls for more than 350,000 employers, with over 20 million employees in North America plus several million in Europe. ADP prepares employee paychecks, journals, and summary reports; collects and remits funds for federal, state, and local payroll taxes; and files all required forms with government taxing authorities.

FIGURE 10-10 Payroll Calendar *(continued)*

January

S	M	T	W	T	F	S
			1	2	3	4
5	6	7	8	9	10	11
12	13	14	15	16	17	18
19	20	21	22	23	24	25
26	27	28	29	30	31	

February

S	M	T	W	T	F	S
						1
2	3	4	5	6	7	8
9	10	11	12	13	14	15
16	17	18	19	20	21	22
23	24	25	26	27	28	29

March

S	M	T	W	T	F	S
1	2	3	4	5	6	7
8	9	10	11	12	13	14
15	16	17	18	19	20	21
22	23	24	25	26	27	28
29	30	31				

April

S	M	T	W	T	F	S
			1	2	3	4
5	6	7	8	9	10	11
12	13	14	15	16	17	18
19	20	21	22	23	24	25
26	27	28	29	30		

May

S	M	T	W	T	F	S
					1	2
3	4	5	6	7	8	9
10	11	12	13	14	15	16
17	18	19	20	21	22	23
24	25	26	27	28	29	30
31						

June

S	M	T	W	T	F	S
	1	2	3	4	5	6
7	8	9	10	11	12	13
14	15	16	17	18	19	20
21	22	23	24	25	26	27
28	29	30				

July

S	M	T	W	T	F	S
			1	2	3	4
5	6	7	8	9	10	11
12	13	14	15	16	17	18
19	20	21	22	23	24	25
26	27	28	29	30	31	

August

S	M	T	W	T	F	S
						1
2	3	4	5	6	7	8
9	10	11	12	13	14	15
16	17	18	19	20	21	22
23	24	25	26	27	28	29
30	31					

September

S	M	T	W	T	F	S
		1	2	3	4	5
6	7	8	9	10	11	12
13	14	15	16	17	18	19
20	21	22	23	24	25	26
27	28	29	30			

October

S	M	T	W	T	F	S
				1	2	3
4	5	6	7	8	9	10
11	12	13	14	15	16	17
18	19	20	21	22	23	24
25	26	27	28	29	30	31

November

S	M	T	W	T	F	S
1	2	3	4	5	6	7
8	9	10	11	12	13	14
15	16	17	18	19	20	21
22	23	24	25	26	27	28
29	30					

December

S	M	T	W	T	F	S
		1	2	3	4	5
6	7	8	9	10	11	12
13	14	15	16	17	18	19
20	21	22	23	24	25	26
27	28	29	30	31		

WORKERS' COMPENSATION INSURANCE

LO 4 Describe and account for workers' compensation insurance.

Most states require employers to carry workers' compensation insurance. **Workers' compensation insurance** provides insurance for employees who suffer a job-related illness or injury.

The employer usually pays the entire cost of workers' compensation insurance. The cost of the insurance depends on the number of employees, riskiness of the job, and the company's accident history. For example, the insurance premium for workers in a chemical plant could be higher than for office workers. Employers generally obtain the insurance either from the state in which they operate or from a private insurance company.

The employer usually pays the premium at the beginning of the year, based on the estimated payroll for the year. At the end of the year, after the actual amount of payroll is known, an adjustment is made. If the employer has overpaid, a credit is received from the state or insurance company. If the employer has underpaid, an additional premium is paid.

To illustrate the accounting for workers' compensation insurance, assume that Lockwood Co. expects its payroll for the year to be $210,000. If Lockwood's insurance premium rate is 0.2%, its payment for workers' compensation insurance at the beginning of the year would be $420:

Estimated Payroll	×	Rate	=	Estimated Insurance Premium
$210,000		.002		$420.00

The journal entry for the payment of this $420 premium would be:

7		Workers' Compensation Insurance Expense		4 2 0 00			7
8		Cash			4 2 0 00		8
9		Paid insurance premium					9

If Lockwood's actual payroll for the year is $220,000, Lockwood would owe an additional premium of $20 at year end:

Actual Payroll	×	Rate	=	Insurance Premium
$220,000		.002		$440.00
Less premium paid				420.00
Additional premium due				$ 20.00

The adjusting entry at year end for this additional expense would be:

11	Dec.	31	Workers' Compensation Insur. Exp.		2 0 00			11
12			Workers' Compensation Insur. Pay.			2 0 00		12
13			Adjustment for insurance premium					13

In T account form, the total Workers' Compensation Insurance Expense of $440.00 would look like this:

Workers' Compensation Insurance Expense

Debit	Credit
420.00	
20.00	
440.00	

If Lockwood's actual payroll for the year is only $205,000, Lockwood would be due a refund of $10:

Payroll	×	Rate	=	Insurance Premium
$205,000		.002		$410.00
Less premium paid				420.00
Refund due				$(10.00)

The adjusting entry at year end for this refund due would be:

16	Dec.	31	Insurance Refund Receivable			1	0	00					16
17			Workers' Compensation Insur. Exp.						1	0	00		17
18			Adjustment for insurance premium										18

In T account form, the total Workers' Compensation Insurance Expense of $410 would look like this:

Workers' Compensation Insurance Expense

Debit	Credit
420.00	10.00
410.00	

COMPUTERS AND ACCOUNTING

Computer-Based Payroll Systems—James Hall

Basic payroll systems consist of two primary functions: the *employee master file maintenance* system and the *payroll processing* system. Key features of each of these are discussed below. Also, two alternative approaches to payroll processing are reviewed.

Master File Maintenance System

Employee master records contain personal data such as hourly pay rate, earnings to date, marital status, number of dependents, and other W-4 details needed for payroll processing. The master file maintenance system allows the payroll clerk to revise employee records when changes in status occur. This system is also used to add new employees to the master file and to remove terminated employees from the file. For internal control purposes, the maintenance task is often performed as a scheduled batch job. Once each pay period, prior to the payroll processing run, changes in status and additions and deletions to the master file are formally

COMPUTERS AND ACCOUNTING (continued)

approved by the appropriate manager and processed. This maintenance activity ensures that the information used for preparing payroll checks is accurate and complete.

Payroll Processing System

The complex task of preparing the payroll is made easy by computerization. At the end of the pay period, the payroll clerk simply enters each employee's time card information through the computer terminal to produce a transaction file. From this file and personal data contained in the employee master file, the system calculates gross pay, net pay, taxes, and withholdings for each employee. The employee records, taxes payable, expense accounts, and general ledger accounts are updated automatically and the paychecks are written by the computer. For internal control purposes, paychecks should be deposited into the employees' bank accounts or distributed directly to the employees by an authorized manager. This ensures that each employee receives his or her paycheck and that no unauthorized checks were printed and unaccounted for.

Outside Service Bureau

The technical complexities of payroll processing make it a prime candidate for computerization in all but the smallest organizations. Processing payroll manually is labor intensive and invites errors. Some firms discover that delegating their payroll responsibility to an outside service bureau is an economically better option than investing in the computer technology and the staff needed to perform the task in-house. The service bureau collects employee time cards from their client, maintains all the accounting records, prepares the paychecks, and provides the client with detailed reports, transaction information, and account balances.

Human Resource Management System

Moderate-sized and large organizations often integrate payroll processing within the *human resource management (HRM)* system. The HRM system captures and processes a wide range of personnel-related data, including employee benefits, labor resource planning, employee relations, employee education and job skills, personnel actions (promotion and disciplinary action), as well as payroll information. HRM systems provide real-time access to personnel files for purposes of direct inquiries and recording changes in employee status. In addition to payroll preparation, this broader perspective of the human resource allows management to more effectively manage labor costs, allocate the work force, plan employee training, coordinate employee vacation and plant maintenance, and plan employee recruiting to accommodate future labor needs.

Learning Objectives	Key Points to Remember
1 **Describe and calculate employer payroll taxes.** **2** **Account for employer payroll taxes expense.**	Employer payroll taxes include FICA, FUTA, and SUTA taxes. These taxes represent additional payroll expenses of the employer. The journal entry for payroll taxes is

8		Payroll Taxes Expense	x x x xx				8
9		Social Security Tax Payable		x x x xx			9
10		Medicare Tax Payable		x x x xx			10
11		FUTA Tax Payable		x x x xx			11
12		SUTA Tax Payable		x x x xx			12

The steps to be followed in preparing this journal entry are:

1. Obtain the taxable earnings amounts from the Taxable Earnings columns of the payroll register.

2. Compute the amount of employer Social Security tax by multiplying the Social Security taxable earnings by 6.2%.

3. Compute the amount of Medicare tax by multiplying total earnings by 1.45%.

4. Compute the amount of FUTA tax by multiplying the Unemployment Taxable earnings by 0.8%.

5. Compute the amount of SUTA tax by multiplying the Unemployment Taxable earnings by 5.4%.

6. Prepare the appropriate journal entry using the amounts computed in steps 2–5.

Learning Objectives	Key Points to Remember
3 **Describe employer reporting and payment responsibilities.**	Employer payroll reporting and payment responsibilities fall into five areas:

1. Federal income tax withholding and Social Security and Medicare taxes

2. FUTA taxes

3. SUTA taxes

4. Employee Wage and Tax Statement (Form W-2)

5. Summary of employee wages and taxes

Key forms needed in reporting and paying employer payroll taxes are:

1. Form 8109, Federal Tax Deposit Coupon

2. Form 941, Employer's Quarterly Federal Tax Return

3. Form 940, Employer's Annual Federal Unemployment Tax Return

By January 31 of each year, employers must provide each employee with a Wage and Tax Statement, Form W-2.

By February 28 of each year, employers must file Form W-3 and Copy A of Forms W-2 with the Social Security Administration.

Learning Objectives	Key Points to Remember
4 **Describe and account for workers' compensation insurance.**	Workers' compensation insurance provides insurance for employees who suffer a job-related illness or injury. Employers generally are required to carry and pay the entire cost of this insurance.

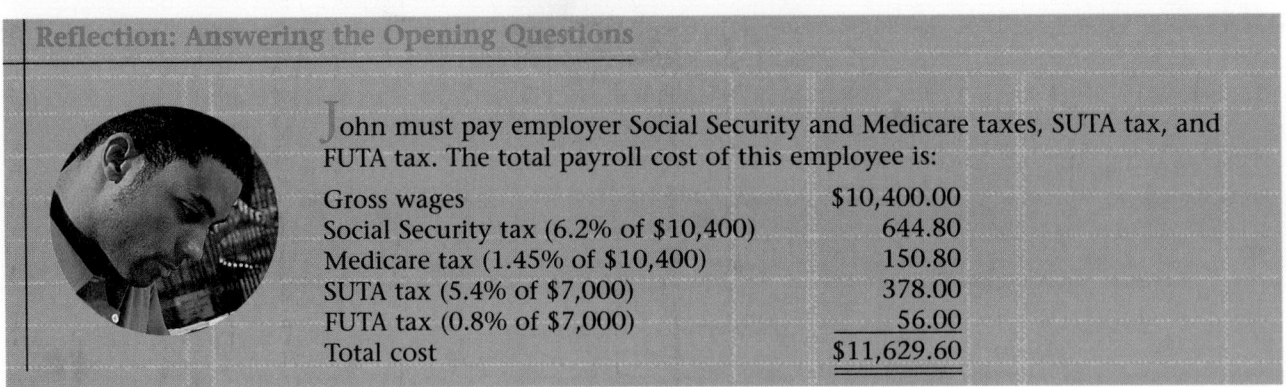

Reflection: Answering the Opening Questions

John must pay employer Social Security and Medicare taxes, SUTA tax, and FUTA tax. The total payroll cost of this employee is:

Gross wages	$10,400.00
Social Security tax (6.2% of $10,400)	644.80
Medicare tax (1.45% of $10,400)	150.80
SUTA tax (5.4% of $7,000)	378.00
FUTA tax (0.8% of $7,000)	56.00
Total cost	$11,629.60

KEY TERMS

employer FICA taxes, (330)   Taxes levied on employers at the same rates and on the same earnings bases as the employee FICA taxes.

Employer Identification Number (EIN), (336)   A number that identifies the employer on all payroll forms and reports filed with the IRS.

FUTA (Federal Unemployment Tax Act) tax, (332)   A tax levied on employers to raise funds to administer the federal/state unemployment compensation program.

merit-rating system, (332)   A system to encourage employers to provide regular employment to workers.

self-employment income, (331)   The net income of a trade or business run by an individual.

self-employment tax, (331)   A contribution to the FICA program.

SUTA (state unemployment tax) tax, (332)   A tax levied on employers to raise funds to pay unemployment benefits.

workers' compensation insurance, (344)   Provides insurance for employees who suffer a job-related illness or injury.

DEMONSTRATION PROBLEM

The totals line from Hart Company's payroll register for the week ended December 31, 19--, is as follows:

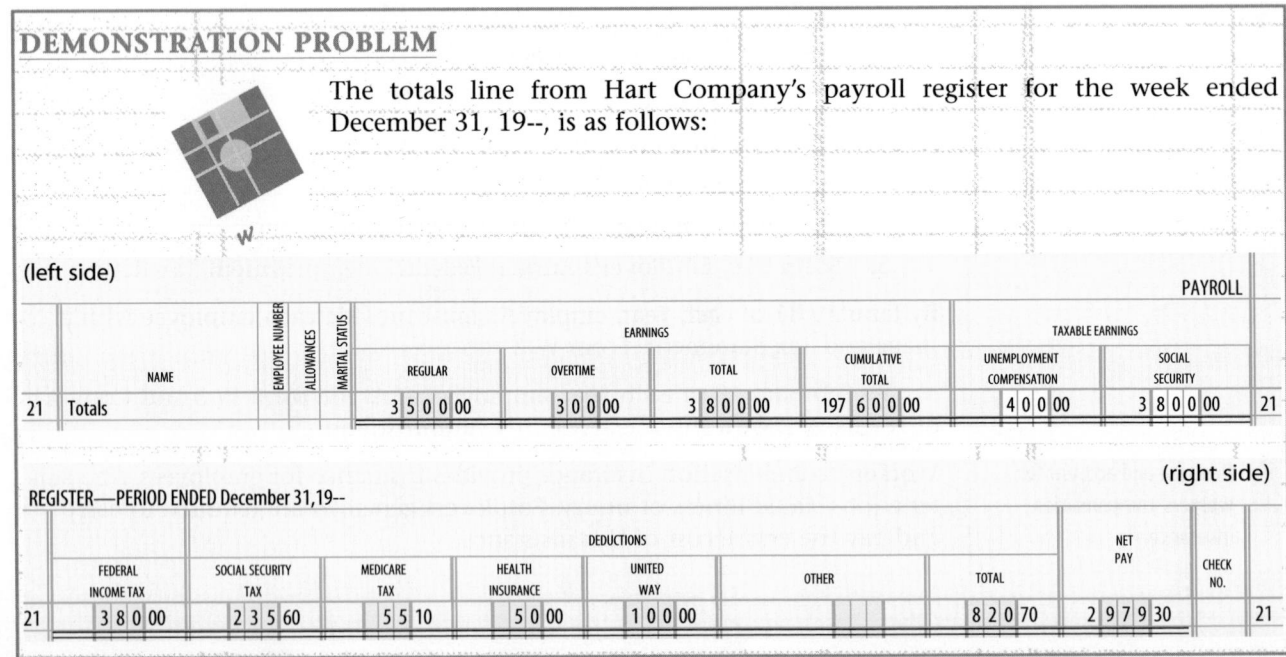

(left side)

PAYROLL

	NAME	EMPLOYEE NUMBER	ALLOWANCES	MARITAL STATUS	EARNINGS REGULAR	EARNINGS OVERTIME	EARNINGS TOTAL	CUMULATIVE TOTAL	TAXABLE EARNINGS UNEMPLOYMENT COMPENSATION	TAXABLE EARNINGS SOCIAL SECURITY	
21	Totals				3 5 0 0 00	3 0 0 00	3 8 0 0 00	197 6 0 0 00	4 0 0 00	3 8 0 0 00	21

(right side)

REGISTER—PERIOD ENDED December 31,19--

	FEDERAL INCOME TAX	SOCIAL SECURITY TAX	MEDICARE TAX	HEALTH INSURANCE	UNITED WAY	OTHER	TOTAL	NET PAY	CHECK NO.	
21	3 8 0 00	2 3 5 60	5 5 10	5 0 00	1 0 0 00		8 2 0 70	2 9 7 9 30		21

Payroll taxes are imposed as follows: Social Security, 6.2%; Medicare, 1.45%; FUTA, 0.8%; and SUTA, 5.4%.

REQUIRED
1. a. Prepare the journal entry for payment of this payroll on December 31, 19--.

   b. Prepare the journal entry for the employer's payroll taxes for the period ended December 31, 19--.

2. Hart Company had the following balances in its general ledger *after* the entries for requirement (1) were made:

Employee Income Tax Payable	$1,520.00
Social Security Tax Payable	1,847.00
Medicare Tax Payable	433.00
FUTA Tax Payable	27.20
SUTA Tax Payable	183.60

   a. Prepare the journal entry for payment of the liabilities for employee federal income taxes and Social Security and Medicare taxes on January 15, 19--.

   b. Prepare the journal entry for payment of the liability for FUTA tax on January 31, 19--.

   c. Prepare the journal entry for payment of the liability for SUTA tax on January 31, 19--.

3. Hart Company paid a premium of $280 for workers' compensation insurance based on estimated payroll as of the beginning of the year. Based on actual payroll as of the end of the year, the premium is $298. Prepare the adjusting entry to reflect the underpayment of the insurance premium.

Solution

1.

GENERAL JOURNAL   PAGE 1

	DATE		DESCRIPTION	POST REF.	DEBIT	CREDIT	
1	19-- Dec.	31	Wages and Salaries Expense		3 8 0 0 00		1
2			Employee Income Tax Payable			3 8 0 00	2
3			Social Security Tax Payable			2 3 5 60	3
4			Medicare Tax Payable			5 5 10	4
5			Health Insurance Premiums Payable			5 0 00	5
6			United Way Contributions Payable			1 0 0 00	6
7			Cash			2 9 7 9 30	7
8			To record Dec. 31 payroll				8
9							9
10	Dec.	31	Payroll Taxes Expense		3 1 5 50		10
11			Social Security Tax Payable			2 3 5 60	11
12			Medicare Tax Payable			5 5 10	12
13			FUTA Tax Payable			3 20	13
14			SUTA Tax Payable			2 1 60	14
15			Employer payroll taxes for week ended Dec. 31				15

(continued)

2, 3.

18	Jan.	15	Employee Income Tax Payable		1	5	2	0	00								18
19			Social Security Tax Payable		1	8	4	7	00								19
20			Medicare Tax Payable			4	3	3	00								20
21			Cash								3	8	0	0	00		21
22			Deposit of employee federal income tax and														22
23			Social Security and Medicare taxes														23
24																	24
25	Jan.	31	FUTA Tax Payable			2	7	20									25
26			Cash									2	7	20			26
27			Paid FUTA tax														27
28																	28
29	Jan.	31	SUTA Tax Payable		1	8	3	60									29
30			Cash								1	8	3	60			30
31			Paid SUTA tax														31
32																	32
33	Dec.	31	Workers' Compensation Insurance Expense			1	8	00									33
34			Workers' Compensation Insurance Payment									1	8	00			34
35			Adjustment for insurance premium														35

REVIEW QUESTIONS

1. Why do employer payroll taxes represent an additional expense to the employer, whereas the various employee payroll taxes do not?

2. At what rate and on what earnings base is the employer's Social Security tax levied?

3. What is the purpose of the FUTA tax and who must pay it?

4. What is the purpose of the state unemployment tax and who must pay it?

5. What accounts are affected when employer payroll tax expenses are properly recorded?

6. Identify all items that are debited or credited to Social Security Tax Payable and to Medicare Tax Payable.

7. Explain why an employee whose gross salary is $20,000 costs an employer more than $20,000 to employ.

8. What is the purpose of Form 8109, Federal Tax Deposit Coupon?

9. What is the purpose of Form 941, Employer's Quarterly Federal Tax Return?

10. What is the purpose of Form 940, Employer's Annual Federal Unemployment Tax Return?

11. What information appears on Form W-2, the employee's Wage and Tax Statement?

12. What is the purpose of workers' compensation insurance and who must pay for it?

MANAGING YOUR WRITING

The Director of the Art Department, Wilson Watson, wants to hire new office staff. His boss tells him that to do so he must find in his budget not only the base salary for this position but an additional 30% for "fringe benefits." Wilson explodes: "How in the world can there be 30% in fringe benefits?" Write a memo to Wilson Watson explaining the costs that probably make up these fringe benefits.

ETHICS CASE

Bob Estes works at Cliffrock Company in the central receiving department. He unpacks incoming shipments and verifies quantities of goods received. Over the weekend, Bob pulled a muscle in his back while playing basketball. When he came to work on Monday and started unpacking shipments, his back started to hurt again. Bob called the Human Resources Department and told them he hurt his back lifting a package at work. He was told to fill out an accident report and sent to an orthopedic clinic with a workers' compensation form. The doctor at the clinic told Bob not to lift anything heavy for two weeks and to stay home from work for at least one week.

1. Is Bob entitled to workers' compensation? Why or why not?

2. What effect will Bob's claim have on Cliffrock Company's workers' compensation insurance premium?

3. Write a short memo from the Human Resources Department to Cliffrock Company's employees explaining the purpose of worker's compensation.

4. In small groups discuss the job-related illness or injury risks of a computer input operator and measures an employer might take to minimize these risks.

WEB WORK

How long are employers required to keep employment tax records? For this and other tax advice, go to the IRS business resource page at

http://www.irs.ustreas.gov/prod/bus_info/index.html.
(http://heintz.swcollege.com)

Choose Tax Topics for Business, then Recordkeeping.

SERIES A EXERCISES

EXERCISE 10A-1 (LO 1/2) JOURNAL ENTRY FOR EMPLOYER PAYROLL TAXES
Portions of the payroll register for Barney's Bagels for the week ended July 15 are shown below. The SUTA tax rate is 5.4% and the FUTA tax rate is 0.8%, both of which are levied on the first $7,000 of earnings. The Social Security tax rate is 6.2% on the first $68,400 of earnings. The Medicare rate is 1.45% on gross earnings.

(continued)

Barney's Bagels
Payroll Register
Total Taxable Earnings of All Employees

Total Earnings	Unemployment Compensation	Social Security
$12,200	$10,500	$12,200

Calculate the employer's payroll taxes expense and prepare the journal entry to record the employer's payroll taxes expense for the week ended July 15 of the current year.

EXERCISE 10A-2 (LO 1/2) EMPLOYER PAYROLL TAXES Earnings for several employees for the week ended March 12, 19--, are as follows:

		Taxable Earnings	
Employee Name	Total Earnings	Unemployment Compensation	Social Security
Aus, Glenn E.	$ 700	$200	$ 700
Diaz, Charles K.	350	350	350
Knapp, Carol S.	1,200	—	1,200
Mueller, Deborah F.	830	125	830
Yeager, Jackie R.	920	35	920

Calculate the employer's payroll taxes expense and prepare the journal entry as of March 12, 19--, assuming that FUTA tax is 0.8%, SUTA tax is 5.4%, Social Security tax is 6.2%, and Medicare tax is 1.45%.

EXERCISE 10A-3 (LO 1/2) TAXABLE EARNINGS AND EMPLOYER'S PAYROLL TAXES JOURNAL ENTRY Selected information from the payroll register of Raynette's Boutique for the week ended September 14, 19--, is as follows. Social Security tax is 6.2% on the first $68,400 of earnings for each employee. Medicare tax is 1.45% of gross earnings. FUTA tax is 0.8% and SUTA tax is 5.4% on the first $7,000 of earnings.

			Taxable Earnings	
Employee Name	Cumulative Pay Before Current Earnings	Current Gross Pay	Unemployment Compensation	Social Security
Burgos, Juan	$ 6,800	$1,250		
Ellis, Judy A.	6,300	1,100		
Lewis, Arlene S.	54,200	2,320		
Mason, Jason W.	53,900	2,270		
Yates, Ruby L.	27,650	1,900		
Zielke, Ronald M.	66,530	2,680		

Calculate the amount of taxable earnings for unemployment, Social Security, and Medicare taxes, and prepare the journal entry to record the employer's payroll taxes as of September 14, 19--.

EXERCISE 10A-4 (LO 1/2) TOTAL COST OF EMPLOYEE J. B. Kenton employs Sharla Knox at a salary of $32,000 a year. Kenton is subject to employer Social Security taxes at a rate of 6.2% and Medicare taxes at a rate of 1.45% on Knox's salary. In addition, Kenton must pay SUTA tax at a rate of 5.4% and FUTA tax at a rate of 0.8% on the first $7,000 of Knox's salary.

Compute the total cost to Kenton of employing Knox for the year.

EXERCISE 10A-5 (LO 3) JOURNAL ENTRY FOR PAYMENT OF EMPLOYER'S PAY-ROLL TAXES Angel Ruiz owns a business called Ruiz Construction Co. He does his banking at Citizens National Bank in Portland, Oregon. The amounts in his general ledger for payroll taxes and the employees' withholding of Social Security, Medicare, and federal income tax payable as of April 15 of the current year are as follows:

Social Security tax payable (includes both employer and employee)	$3,750
Medicare tax payable (includes both employer and employee)	875
FUTA tax payable	200
SUTA tax payable	1,350
Employee income tax payable	2,275

Journalize the payment of the Form 941 deposit (i.e., Social Security, Medicare, and federal income tax) to Citizens National Bank and the payment of the SUTA tax to the state of Oregon as of April 15, 19--.

EXERCISE 10A-6 (LO 4) WORKERS' COMPENSATION INSURANCE AND ADJUST-MENT General Manufacturing estimated that its total payroll for the coming year would be $425,000. The workers' compensation insurance premium rate is 0.2%.

REQUIRED
1. Calculate the estimated workers' compensation insurance premium and prepare the journal entry for the payment as of January 2, 19--.

2. Assume that General Manufacturing's actual payroll for the year is $432,000. Calculate the total insurance premium owed and prepare a journal entry as of December 31, 19--, to record the adjustment for the underpayment. The actual payment of the additional premium will take place in January of the next year.

SERIES A PROBLEMS

PROBLEM 10A-1 (LO 1/2) CALCULATING PAYROLL TAXES EXPENSE AND PREPARING JOURNAL ENTRY Selected information from the payroll register of Anderson's Dairy for the week ended May 7, 19--, is shown below. SUTA tax is withheld at the rate of 5.4% and the FUTA tax at the rate of 0.8%, both on the first $7,000 of earnings. Social Security tax on the employer is 6.2% on the first $68,400 of earnings and Medicare tax is 1.45% on gross earnings.

			Taxable Earnings	
Employee Name	Cumulative Pay Before Current Earnings	Current Weekly Earnings	Unemployment Compensation	Social Security
Barnum, Alex	$ 6,750	$ 820		
Duel, Richard	6,340	725		
Hunt, J. B.	23,460	1,235		
Larson, Susan	6,950	910		
Mercado, Denise	67,050	2,520		
Swan, Judy	15,470	1,125		
Yates, Keith	28,675	1,300		

REQUIRED
1. Calculate the total employer payroll taxes for these employees.

2. Prepare the journal entry to record the employer payroll taxes as of May 7, 19--.

w

PROBLEM 10A-2 (LO 2) JOURNALIZING AND POSTING PAYROLL ENTRIES The Cascade Company has four employees. All are paid on a monthly basis. The fiscal year of the business is July 1 to June 30. Payroll taxes are imposed as follows:

1. Social Security tax of 6.2% withheld from employees' wages on the first $68,400 of earnings and Medicare tax withheld at 1.45% of gross earnings.

2. Social Security tax of 6.2% imposed on the employer on the first $68,400 of earnings and Medicare tax of 1.45% on gross earnings.

3. SUTA tax of 5.4% imposed on the employer on the first $7,000 of earnings.

4. FUTA tax of 0.8% imposed on the employer on the first $7,000 of earnings.

The accounts kept by Cascade include the following:

Account Number	Title	Balance on July 1
101	Cash	$50,200
211	Employee Income Tax Payable	1,015
212	Social Security Tax Payable	1,458
213	Medicare Tax Payable	342
218	Savings Bond Deductions Payable	350
221	FUTA Tax Payable	164
222	SUTA Tax Payable	810
511	Wages and Salaries Expense	0
530	Payroll Taxes Expense	0

The following transactions relating to payrolls and payroll taxes occurred during July and August.

July 15 Paid $2,815 covering the following June taxes:

Social Security tax	$ 1,458
Medicare tax	342
Employee income tax withheld	1,015
Total	$ 2,815

31 July payroll:

Total wages and salaries expense		$12,000
Less amounts withheld:		
Social Security tax	$ 744	
Medicare tax	174	
Employee income tax	1,020	
Savings bond deductions	350	2,288
Net amount paid		$ 9,712

31 Purchased savings bonds for employees, $700

31 Data for completing employer's payroll taxes expense for July:

Social Security taxable wages	$12,000
Unemployment taxable wages	3,000

Aug. 15 Paid $2,856 covering the following July taxes:

Social Security tax	$ 1,488
Medicare tax	348
Employee income tax withheld	1,020
Total	$ 2,856

15 Paid SUTA tax for the quarter, $972

15 Paid FUTA tax, $188

REQUIRED   1. Journalize the preceding transactions using a general journal.

2. Open T accounts for the payroll expenses and liabilities. Enter the beginning balances and post the transactions recorded in the journal.

PROBLEM 10A-3 (LO 4) WORKERS' COMPENSATION INSURANCE AND ADJUSTMENT Willamette Manufacturing estimated that its total payroll for the coming year would be $650,000. The workers' compensation insurance premium rate is 0.3%.

REQUIRED   1. Calculate the estimated workers' compensation insurance premium and prepare the journal entry for the payment as of January 2, 19--.

2. Assume that Willamette Manufacturing's actual payroll for the year was $672,000. Calculate the total insurance premium owed and prepare a journal entry as of December 31, 19--, to record the adjustment for the underpayment. The actual payment of the additional premium will take place in January of the next year.

3. Assume instead that Willamette Manufacturing's actual payroll for the year was $634,000. Prepare a journal entry as of December 31, 19--, for the total amount that should be refunded. The refund will not be received until the next year.

SERIES B EXERCISES

EXERCISE 10B-1 (LO 1/2) JOURNAL ENTRY FOR EMPLOYER PAYROLL TAXES Portions of the payroll register for Kathy's Cupcakes for the week ended June 21 are shown below. The SUTA tax rate is 5.4% and the FUTA tax rate is 0.8%, both on the first $7,000 of earnings. The Social Security tax rate is 6.2% on the first $68,400 of earnings. The Medicare rate is 1.45% on gross earnings.

72,600

Kathy's Cupcakes
Payroll Register
Total Taxable Earnings of All Employees

Total Earnings	Unemployment Compensation	Social Security
$15,680	$12,310	$15,680

Calculate the employer's payroll taxes expense and prepare the journal entry to record the employer's payroll taxes expense for the week ended June 21 of the current year.

EXERCISE 10B-2 (LO 1/2) EMPLOYER PAYROLL TAXES Earnings for several employees for the week ended April 7, 19--, are as follows:

		Taxable Earnings	
Employee Name	Total Earnings	Unemployment Compensation	Social Security
Boyd, Glenda L.	$ 850	$300	$ 850
Evans, Sheryl N.	970	225	970
Fox, Howard J.	830	830	830
Jacobs, Phyllis J.	1,825	—	1,825
Roh, William R.	990	25	990

Calculate the employer's payroll taxes expense and prepare the journal entry as of April 7, 19--, assuming that FUTA tax is 0.8%, SUTA tax is 5.4%, Social Security tax is 6.2%, and Medicare tax is 1.45%.

EXERCISE 10B-3 (LO 1/2) TAXABLE EARNINGS AND EMPLOYER'S PAYROLL TAXES JOURNAL ENTRY Selected information from the payroll register of Howard's Cutlery for the week ended October 7, 19--, is presented below. Social Security tax is 6.2% on the first $68,400 of earnings for each employee. Medicare tax is 1.45% on gross earnings. FUTA tax is 0.8% and SUTA tax is 5.4% on the first $7,000 of earnings.

			Taxable Earnings	
Employee Name	Cumulative Pay Before Current Earnings	Current Gross Pay	Unemployment Compensation	Social Security
Carlson, David J.	$ 6,635	$ 950		
Delgado, Luisa	6,150	1,215		
Lewis, Arlene S.	54,375	2,415		
Nixon, Robert R.	53,870	1,750		
Shippe, Lance W.	24,830	1,450		
Watts, Brandon Q.	67,000	2,120		

Calculate the amount of taxable earnings for unemployment, Social Security, and Medicare taxes, and prepare the journal entry to record the employer's payroll taxes as of October 7, 19--.

EXERCISE 10B-4 (LO 1/2) TOTAL COST OF EMPLOYEE B.F Goodson employs Eduardo Gonzales at a salary of $46,000 a year. Goodson is subject to employer Social Security taxes at a rate of 6.2% and Medicare taxes at a rate of 1.45% on Gonzales' salary. In addition, Goodson must pay SUTA tax at a rate of 5.4% and FUTA tax at a rate of 0.8% on the first $7,000 of Gonzales' salary.

Compute the total cost to Goodson of employing Gonzales for the year.

EXERCISE 10B-5 (LO 3) JOURNAL ENTRY FOR PAYMENT OF EMPLOYER'S PAYROLL TAXES Francis Baker owns a business called Baker Construction Co. She does her banking at the American National Bank in Seattle, Washington. The amounts in her general ledger for payroll taxes and employees' withholding of Social Security, Medicare, and federal income tax payable as of July 15 of the current year are as follows:

Social Security tax payable (includes both employer and employee)	$6,375
Medicare tax payable (includes both employer and employee)	1,500
FUTA tax payable	336
SUTA tax payable	2,268
Employee federal income tax payable	4,830

Journalize the payment of the Form 941 deposit (i.e., Social Security, Medicare, and federal income tax) to the American National Bank and the payment of the state unemployment tax to the state of Washington as of July 15, 19--.

EXERCISE 10B-6 (LO 4) WORKERS' COMPENSATION INSURANCE AND ADJUSTMENT Columbia Industries estimated that its total payroll for the coming year would be $385,000. The workers' compensation insurance premium rate is 0.2%.

REQUIRED

1. Calculate the estimated workers' compensation insurance premium and prepare the journal entry for the payment as of January 2, 19--.

2. Assume that Columbia Industries' actual payroll for the year is $396,000. Calculate the total insurance premium owed and prepare a journal entry as of December 31, 19--, to record the adjustment for the underpayment. The actual payment of the additional premium will take place in January of the next year.

SERIES B PROBLEMS

PROBLEM 10B-1 (LO 1/2) CALCULATING PAYROLL TAXES EXPENSE AND PREPARING JOURNAL ENTRY Selected information from the payroll register of Wray's Drug Store for the week ended July 7, 19--, is shown below. SUTA tax is withheld at the rate of 5.4% and FUTA tax at the rate of 0.8%, both on the first $7,000 of earnings. Social Security tax on the employer is 6.2% on the first $68,400 of earnings and Medicare tax is 1.45% on gross earnings.

| | Cumulative Pay Before Current Earnings | Current Weekly Earnings | Taxable Earnings | |
| | | | Unemployment Compensation | Social Security |
Employee Name				
Ackers, Alice	$ 6,460	$ 645		
Conley, Dorothy	27,560	1,025		
Davis, James	6,850	565		
Lawrence, Kevin	52,850	2,875		
Rawlings, Judy	16,350	985		
Tanaka, Sumio	22,320	835		
Vadillo, Raynette	66,560	2,540		

REQUIRED

1. Calculate the total employer payroll taxes for these employees.

2. Prepare the journal entry to record the employer payroll taxes as of July 7, 19--.

PROBLEM 10B-2 (LO 2) JOURNALIZING AND POSTING PAYROLL ENTRIES The Oxford Company has five employees. All are paid on a monthly basis. The fiscal year of the business is June 1 to May 31. Payroll taxes are imposed as follows:

1. Social Security tax of 6.2% to be withheld from employees' wages on the first $68,400 of earnings and Medicare tax of 1.45% on gross earnings.

2. Social Security tax of 6.2% imposed on the employer on the first $68,400 of earnings and Medicare tax of 1.45% on gross earnings.

3. SUTA tax of 5.4% imposed on the employer on the first $7,000 of earnings.

4. FUTA tax of 0.8% imposed on the employer on the first $7,000 of earnings.

The accounts kept by the Oxford Company include the following:

Account Number	Title	Balance on June 1
101	Cash	$48,650
211	Employee Income Tax Payable	1,345
212	Social Security Tax Payable	1,823
213	Medicare Tax Payable	427
218	Savings Bond Deductions Payable	525
221	FUTA Tax Payable	360
222	SUTA Tax Payable	920
511	Wages and Salaries Expense	0
530	Payroll Taxes Expense	0

The following transactions relating to payrolls and payroll taxes occurred during June and July.

(continued)

June 15   Paid $3,595.00 covering the following May taxes:

Social Security tax	$ 1,823.00
Medicare tax	427.00
Employee income tax withheld	1,345.00
Total	$ 3,595.00

30   June payroll:

Total wages and salaries expense		$14,700.00
Less amounts withheld:		
Social Security tax	$ 911.40	
Medicare tax	213.15	
Employee income tax	1,280.00	
Savings bond deductions	525.00	2,929.55
Net amount paid		$11,770.45

30   Purchased savings bonds for employees, $1,050.00

30   Data for completing employer's payroll taxes expense for June:

Social Security taxable wages	$14,700.00
Unemployment taxable wages	4,500.00

July 15   Paid $3,529.10 covering the following June taxes:

Social Security tax	$ 1,822.80
Medicare tax	426.30
Employee income tax withheld	1,280.00
Total	$ 3,529.10

15   Paid SUTA tax for the quarter, $1,163.00

15   Paid FUTA tax, $396.00

REQUIRED   1. Journalize the preceding transactions using a general journal.

2. Open T accounts for the payroll expenses and liabilities. Enter the beginning balances and post the transactions recorded in the journal.

PROBLEM 10B-3 (LO 4) WORKERS' COMPENSATION INSURANCE AND ADJUSTMENT Multnomah Manufacturing estimated that its total payroll for the coming year would be $540,000. The workers' compensation insurance premium rate is 0.2%.

REQUIRED   1. Calculate the estimated workers' compensation insurance premium and prepare the journal entry for the payment as of January 2, 19--.

2. Assume that Multnomah Manufacturing's actual payroll for the year was $562,000. Calculate the total insurance premium owed and prepare a journal entry as of December 31, 19--, to record the adjustment for the underpayment. The actual payment of the additional premium will take place in January of the next year.

3. Assume instead that Multnomah Manufacturing's actual payroll for the year was $532,000. Prepare a journal entry as of December 31, 19--, for the total amount that should be refunded. The refund will not be received until the next year.

MASTERY PROBLEM

W

The totals line from Nix Company's payroll register for the week ended March 31, 19--, is as follows:

(left side)

PAYROLL

	NAME	EMPLOYEE NUMBER	ALLOWANCES	MARITAL STATUS	EARNINGS			CUMULATIVE TOTAL	TAXABLE EARNINGS		
					REGULAR	OVERTIME	TOTAL		UNEMPLOYMENT COMPENSATION	SOCIAL SECURITY	
21	Totals				5 4 0 0 00	1 0 0 00	5 5 0 0 00	71 5 0 0 00	5 0 0 0 00	5 5 0 0 00	21

(right side)

REGISTER—PERIOD ENDED December 31,19--

	DEDUCTIONS								NET PAY	CHECK NO.	
	FEDERAL INCOME TAX	SOCIAL SECURITY TAX	MEDICARE TAX	HEALTH INSURANCE	LIFE INSURANCE	OTHER		TOTAL			
21	5 0 0 00	3 4 1 00	7 9 75	1 6 5 00	2 0 0 00			1 2 8 5 75	4 2 1 4 25		21

Payroll taxes are imposed as follows: Social Security tax, 6.2%; Medicare tax, 1.45%; FUTA tax 0.8%, and SUTA tax, 5.4%.

REQUIRED

1. a. Prepare the journal entry for payment of this payroll on March 31, 19--.

   b. Prepare the journal entry for the employer's payroll taxes for the period ended March 31, 19--.

2. Nix Company had the following balances in its general ledger before the entries for requirement (1) were made:

Employee income tax payable	$2,500
Social Security tax payable	2,008
Medicare tax payable	470
FUTA tax payable	520
SUTA tax payable	3,510

   a. Prepare the journal entry for payment of the liabilities for federal income taxes and Social Security and Medicare taxes on April 15, 19--.

   b. Prepare the journal entry for payment of the liability for FUTA tax on April 30, 19--.

   c. Prepare the journal entry for payment of the liability for SUTA tax on April 30, 19--.

3. Nix Company paid a premium of $420 for workers' compensation insurance based on the estimated payroll as of the beginning of the year. Based on actual payroll as of the end of the year, the premium is only $400. Prepare the adjusting entry to reflect the overpayment of the insurance premium at the end of the year (December 31, 19--).

Self-Study Test Questions

True/False

1. Employer payroll taxes are deducted from the employee's pay. _____

2. The payroll register is a key source of information for computing employer payroll taxes. _____

3. Self-employment income is the net income of a trade or business owned and run by an individual. _____

4. The FUTA tax is levied only on the employees. _____

5. The W-4, which shows total annual earnings and deductions for federal and state income taxes, must be completed by the employer and given to the employee by January 31. _____

Multiple Choice

1. The general ledger accounts commonly used to record the employer's Social Security, Medicare, FUTA, and SUTA taxes are classified as _____

   (a) assets.
   (b) liabilities.
   (c) expenses.
   (d) owner's equity.

2. Joyce Lee earns $30,000 a year. Her employer pays a matching Social Security tax of 6.2% on the first $68,400 in earnings, a Medicare tax of 1.45% on gross earnings, and a FUTA tax of 0.8% and a SUTA tax of 5.4%, both on the first $7,000 in earnings. What is the total cost of Joyce Lee to her employer? _____

   (a) $32,250
   (b) $30,000
   (c) $30,434
   (d) $32,729

3. The Form 941 tax deposit includes which of the following types of taxes withheld from the employee and paid by the employer? _____

   (a) Federal income tax and FUTA tax
   (b) Federal income tax and Social Security and Medicare taxes
   (c) Social Security and Medicare taxes and SUTA tax
   (d) FUTA tax and SUTA tax

4. Workers' compensation provides insurance for employees who _____

   (a) are unemployed due to a layoff.
   (b) are unemployed due to a plant closing.
   (c) are underemployed and need additional compensation.
   (d) suffer a job-related illness or injury.

5. The journal entry at the end of the year that recognizes an additional premium owed under workers' compensation insurance will include a _____

   (a) debit to Workers' Compensation Insurance Expense.
   (b) debit to Cash.
   (c) debit to Workers' Compensation Insurance Payable.
   (d) credit to Workers' Compensation Insurance Expense.

The answers to the Self-Study Test Questions are at the end of the text.

P A R T 3

Accounting for a Merchandising Business

11

Accounting for Sales and Cash Receipts

When John Zenith opened Be A Sport, he accepted only cash and personal checks from customers. Soon he had several customers asking to make large purchases of merchandise on account. John refused because he thought his business was too small to carry such receivables and he was unsure about the credit risk of some customers. John had a similar attitude toward bank credit cards, such as MasterCard and Visa. A friend with a store near Hartford, Connecticut encouraged him to reconsider. He said bank credit card sales are "just like cash" and can provide a major boost in sales. How are bank credit card sales "just like cash"? How should John's bookkeeper account for such sales?

Over the last ten chapters, we have learned how to account for a service business. We are now ready to consider accounting for a different kind of business—merchandising. A **merchandising business** purchases merchandise such as clothing, furniture, or computers, and sells that merchandise to customers. For example, John Zenith buys shirts from vendors and manufacturers and sells them to his customers at Be A Sport.

This chapter examines how to account for the sale of merchandise using the accrual basis of accounting. We will learn how to use four new accounts, two special journals, and a subsidiary ledger.

MERCHANDISE SALES TRANSACTIONS

LO 1 Describe merchandise sales transactions.

A **sale** is a transfer of merchandise from one business or individual to another in exchange for cash or a promise to pay cash. Sales procedures and documents vary greatly, depending on the nature and size of the business.

Retailer

Retail businesses generally sell to customers who enter the store, select the merchandise they want, and bring it to a salesclerk. The salesclerk enters the sale in some type of electronic cash register that generates a receipt for the customer. A copy of the receipt is retained in the register. Most registers can print a summary of the day's sales activity, like the one in Figure 11-1. This summary can be used to journalize sales in the accounting records.

FIGURE 11-1 Cash Register Tape Summary

```
              (1)
CASH SALES        327.79  *
              (3)
MCARD/VISA        550.62  *
              (6)
LAYAWAY            79.50  *
TOTAL CASH        957.91  *
              (2)
CHARGE SALES      543.84  *
              (5)
APPROVAL          126.58  *
TOTAL CHARGE      670.42  *

TOTAL SALES     1,628.33 G*
SALES TAX          81.42  *
                   81.42  *

REC'D ON ACCT.    324.51  *
                  324.51  *

PAID OUT           76.51  *
                   76.51  *

NO SALE             0.00  *
                    0.00  *

 *     SUB-TOTAL
G*     GRAND TOTAL
```

An additional document often created as evidence of a sale in a retail business is a **sales ticket** (Figure 11-2). One copy of the sales ticket is given to the customer and the other copy is sent to accounting.

FIGURE 11-2 Sales Ticket

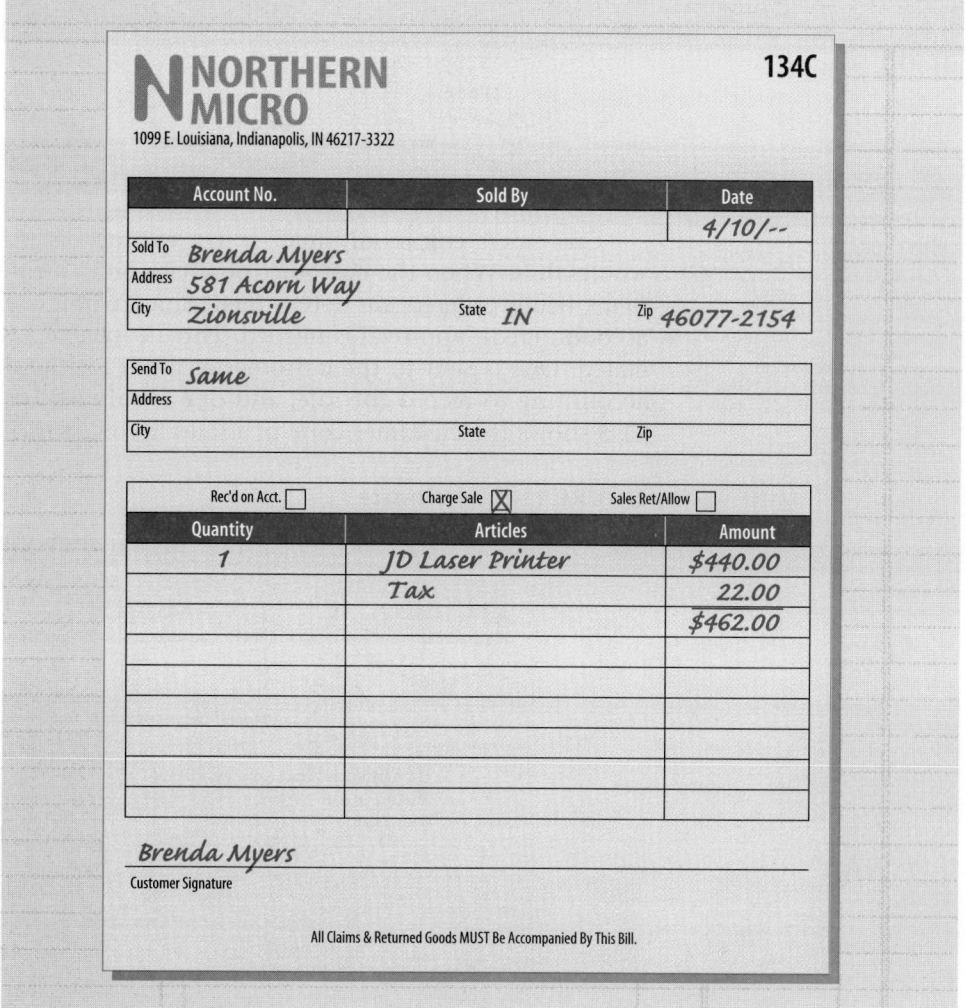

Wholesaler

Figure 11-3 shows how the wholesaler plays a different role than the retailer in the marketing chain. Retailers usually sell to final consumers, whereas wholesalers tend to sell to retailers. This causes the wholesale sales transaction process to differ, as shown in Figure 11-4.

FIGURE 11-3 Marketing Chain

FIGURE 11-4 Wholesale Sales Transaction Process

Customers commonly mail or fax written orders to buy merchandise from wholesalers. When the customer purchase order arrives, the customer name and items being ordered are determined. Since wholesalers typically make sales on account, credit approval is needed. Three copies of a **sales invoice** are then generated. One is sent to the customer as a bill for the merchandise, one is sent to accounting to record the sale, and one is shipped with the merchandise. Figure 11-5 shows the customer copy of a sales invoice for Aladdin Electric Supply.

FIGURE 11-5 Sales Invoice

	Sales Invoice		No. 513

Aladdin Electric Supply
204 Main St., Hartford, CT 06103

CUSTOMER: Crafters Builders
P.O. Box 502
Storrs, CT 06268

DATE: May 5, 20--

TERMS: 2/10, n/30

QUANTITY	DESCRIPTION	UNIT PRICE	AMOUNT
6	#DC-26-AB Fixtures	$25	$150.00
5	#HPS-50-P Fixtures	$50	250.00
TOTAL			$400.00

Credit Memorandum

Both retailers and wholesalers sometimes have customers return goods or seek price reductions for damaged goods. Merchandise returned by a customer for a refund is called a **sales return**. Price reductions granted by the seller because of defects or other problems with the merchandise are called **sales allowances**. When credit is given for merchandise returned or for an allowance, a **credit memo** is issued for the amount involved. This document is called a credit memo because the customer's account receivable is *credited* to reduce the amount the customer owes. One copy of the credit memo is given to the customer and one copy is sent to accounting. Figure 11-6 shows a credit memo issued by Northern Micro for merchandise returned by a customer.

FIGURE 11-6 Credit Memo

MERCHANDISE SALES ACCOUNTS

LO 2   Describe and use merchandise sales accounts.

To account for merchandise sales transactions, we will use four new accounts:

1. Sales
2. Sales Tax Payable
3. Sales Returns and Allowances
4. Sales Discounts

Sales Account

The sales account is a revenue account used to record sales of merchandise. The account is credited for the selling price of merchandise sold during the period.

Sales

Debit	Credit
	to enter the selling price of merchandise sold

If a $100 sale is made for cash, the following entry is made:

5		Cash		1 0 0 00			5
6		Sales			1 0 0 00		6
7		Made cash sale					7

If the same sale is made on account, the entry is:

5		Accounts Receivable/Customer		1 0 0 00			5
6		Sales			1 0 0 00		6
7		Made credit sale					7

Accounts Receivable is followed by a slash and the name of the specific customer who now owes money on account.

Sales Tax Payable Account

When sales tax is imposed on merchandise sold, a separate account for Sales Tax Payable is kept. This is a liability account that is credited for the taxes imposed on sales. The account is debited for sales taxes paid to the proper taxing authority or for sales taxes on merchandise returned by customers. A credit balance in the account indicates the amount owed to the taxing authority for taxes collected.

Sales Tax Payable

Debit	Credit
to enter payment of tax to taxing authority or adjustment of tax on merchandise returned by customers	to enter tax imposed on sales

If a cash sale for $100 plus 5% sales tax (5% × $100 = $5) occurs, the following entry is made:

10		Cash		1 0 5 00			10
11		Sales			1 0 0 00		11
12		Sales Tax Payable			5 00		12
13		Made cash sale					13

If the same sale is made on account, the entry is:

10		Accounts Receivable/Customer			1	0	5	00					10
11		Sales							1	0	0	00	11
12		Sales Tax Payable									5	00	12
13		Made credit sale											13

The debit to Accounts Receivable indicates that the amount owed by customers to the business has increased. Since the buyer has accepted the merchandise and promised to pay for it, revenue is recognized by crediting Sales. Sales Tax Payable is credited because the amount of sales tax owed to the taxing authority has increased.

Sales Returns and Allowances Account

Sales Returns and Allowances is a contra-revenue account to which sales returns and sales allowances are debited. As shown in Figure 11-7, this account is reported as a deduction from Sales on the income statement. Returns and allowances are debited to a separate account rather than directly to Sales so that the business can more readily keep track of this activity.

Sales Returns and Allowances

Debit	Credit
to enter returns and allowances	

Look at the credit memo in Figure 11-6 on page 367. The entry for the return of these printer ribbons by Susan Chang would be:

19		Sales Returns and Allowances			4	0	00						19
20		Sales Tax Payable				2	00						20
21		Accounts Receivable/Susan Chang								4	2	00	21
22		Issued credit memo for returned merchandise											22

Note carefully the parts of this entry. Sales Returns and Allowances is debited for the amount of the sale, *excluding* the sales tax. Sales Tax Payable is debited separately for the sales tax on the original sale amount. Accounts Receivable is credited for the total amount originally billed to Chang.

LEARNING KEY: To record returns and allowances, debit Sales Returns and Allowances for the amount of the sale excluding the sales tax.

FIGURE 11-7 Sales Returns and Allowances on the Income Statement

Sales	$38,500.00
Less sales returns and allowances	200.00
Net sales	$38,300.00

Sales Discounts Account

Some businesses offer **cash discounts** to encourage prompt payment by customers who buy merchandise on account. Some possible credit terms are shown in Figure 11-8.

FIGURE 11-8 Credit Terms

TERMS	MEANING
2/10, n/30*	2% discount off sales price if paid within 10 days
	Total amount due within 30 days
1/10, n/30	Same as 2/10, n/30, except 1% discount instead of 2%
2/eom, n/60	2% discount if paid before end of month
	Total amount due within 60 days
3/10 eom, n/60	3% discount if paid within 10 days after end of month
	Total amount due within 60 days

* See Figure 11-5. A discount of $8 (2% × $400) is allowed if this invoice is paid by May 15 (invoice date of May 5 + 10 days).

To the seller, cash discounts are considered **sales discounts**. Sales Discounts is a contra-revenue account to which cash discounts allowed are debited. Like Sales Returns and Allowances, this account is reported as a deduction from Sales on the income statement, as shown in Figure 11-9.

Sales Discounts

Debit	Credit
to enter cash discounts	

If merchandise is sold for $100 with credit terms of 2/10, n/30, and cash is received within the discount period, the following entries are made.

At time of sale:

26		Accounts Receivable/Customer		1 0 0 00			26
27		Sales			1 0 0 00		27
28		Made sale on account					28

At time of collection:

30		Cash		9 8 00			30
31		Sales Discounts		2 00			31
32		Accounts Receivable/Customer			1 0 0 00		32
33		Received cash on account					33

> If any merchandise has been returned, the sales discount is calculated on the sale amount after deducting the amount of the return. If there is a sales tax, the discount is calculated on the sale amount excluding the sales tax.

FIGURE 11-9 Sales Discounts on the Income Statement

Sales		$38,500.00
Less: Sales returns and allowances	$200.00	
Sales discounts	140.00	340.00
Net sales		$38,160.00

JOURNALIZING AND POSTING SALES TRANSACTIONS

LO 3   Describe and use the sales journal and accounts receivable ledger.

To illustrate the journalizing and posting of sales transactions, we use Northern Micro, a retail computer business. Assume that the following sales transactions occurred during April, 20--.

April 4   Made sale no. 133C on account to Enrico Lorenzo, $1,520 plus $76 sales tax.

10   Made sale no. 134C on account to Brenda Myers, $440 plus $22 sales tax.

18   Made sale no. 105D on account to Edith Walton, $980 plus $49 sales tax.

21   Made sale no. 202B on account to Susan Chang, $620 plus $31 sales tax.

24   Made sale no. 162A on account to Heidi Schwitzer, $1,600 plus $80 sales tax.

These transactions could be entered in a general journal as shown in Figure 11-10.

FIGURE 11-10 Sales Entered in General Journal

4	Apr.	4	Accounts Receivable/E. Lorenzo		1	5	9	6	00						4
5			Sales								1	5	2	0	00	5
6			Sales Tax Payable										7	6	00	6
7			Sale No. 133C													7
8																8
9		10	Accounts Receivable/B. Meyers			4	6	2	00							9
10			Sales									4	4	0	00	10
11			Sales Tax Payable										2	2	00	11
12			Sale No. 134C													12
13																13
14		18	Accounts Receivable/E. Walton		1	0	2	9	00						14
15			Sales									9	8	0	00	15
16			Sales Tax Payable										4	9	00	16
17			Sale No. 105D													17
18																18
19		21	Accounts Receivable/S. Chang			6	5	1	00							19
20			Sales									6	2	0	00	20
21			Sales Tax Payable										3	1	00	21
22			Sale No. 202B													22
23																23
24		24	Accounts Receivable/H. Schwitzer		1	6	8	0	00						24
25			Sales									1	6	0	0	00	25
26			Sales Tax Payable										8	0	00	26
27			Sale No. 162A													27

Notice that each of these five entries involved the same three accounts. The same account titles were recorded five times. Similarly, to post these entries to the general ledger, five separate postings would be made to each of the three accounts, a total of fifteen postings.

This repetition is inefficient. Fortunately, there is a much more efficient way to record sales on account. This is done by using a **special journal** designed for recording only certain kinds of transactions.

Sales Journal

A **sales journal** is a special journal used to record only sales on account. By using a sales journal, we streamline the journalizing and posting of sales on account.

 LEARNING KEY: Use a sales journal only for recording sales on account.

To illustrate, reconsider the five sales made on account by Northern Micro. They are entered in the sales journal in Figure 11-11. The sales journal provides separate columns for Accounts Receivable Debit, Sales Credit, and Sales Tax Payable Credit, the three accounts used repeatedly in the general journal in Figure 11-10. A sale is recorded in the sales journal by entering the following information:

1. Date

2. Sale number

3. Customer

4. Dollar amounts

There is no need to enter any general ledger account titles.

FIGURE 11-11 Northern Micro Sales Journal

	DATE		SALE NO.	TO WHOM SOLD	POST REF.	ACCOUNTS RECEIVABLE DEBIT	SALES CREDIT	SALES TAX PAYABLE CREDIT	
	20—								
1	Apr.	4	133C	Enrico Lorenzo		1 5 9 6 00	1 5 2 0 00	7 6 00	1
2		10	134C	Brenda Myers		4 6 2 00	4 4 0 00	2 2 00	2
3		18	105D	Edith Walton		1 0 2 9 00	9 8 0 00	4 9 00	3
4		21	202B	Susan Chang		6 5 1 00	6 2 0 00	3 1 00	4
5		24	162A	Heidi Schwitzer		1 6 8 0 00	1 6 0 0 00	8 0 00	5

The sales journal in Figure 11-11 is designed for a company, like Northern Micro, that charges sales tax. For a wholesaler or any other company that does not charge sales tax, a sales journal like that in Figure 11-12 would be sufficient. In this case, there is only a single amount column headed Accounts Receivable Debit/Sales Credit. With no sales tax, the Accounts Receivable Debit and Sales Credit amounts are identical for each sale. Thus only a single column is needed.

FIGURE 11-12 Sales Journal Without Sales Tax

	DATE		SALE NO.	TO WHOM SOLD	POST REF.	ACCOUNTS RECEIVABLE DEBIT/ SALES CREDIT	

Posting from the Sales Journal

The illustrations of posting sales here and of posting cash receipts later in the chapter are for a manual accounting system. With a computerized system, the journal, general ledger, and any subsidiary ledger can be updated simultaneously when a transaction is entered.

Posting from the sales journal also is very efficient. Each general ledger account used in the sales journal requires only one posting each period. Figure 11-13 illustrates the general ledger posting process for Northern Micro's sales journal for the month of April.

The following steps are used to post from the sales journal to the general ledger at the end of each month, as indicated in Figure 11-13.

STEP 1   Total the amount columns, verify that the total of the debit column equals the total of the credit columns, and rule the columns.

STEP 2   Post the column totals to the general ledger accounts indicated in the column headings.

STEP 3   Insert the date in the Date column and the initial "S" and the sales journal page number in the Posting Reference column of each ledger account.

STEP 4   Insert the general ledger account numbers immediately below the column totals.

FIGURE 11-13 Posting the Sales Journal to the General Ledger

The accounts receivable ledger also can be posted from the source document used to make the sales journal entry. For example, sales ticket #134C (see Figure 11-2) could be used to post that sale to Brenda Myers' account in the accounts receivable ledger. In this case, 134C would be inserted in the Posting Reference column of her account.

The sales and accounts receivable accounts in the general ledger are now up to date. But at this point Northern Micro has no complete record of the account receivable from *individual customers*. To run the business properly, Northern Micro needs this information.

A common approach to keeping a record of each customer's account receivable is to use a subsidiary **accounts receivable ledger**. This is a separate ledger containing an individual account receivable for each customer. If there are many customer accounts, it is good practice to assign each customer an account number. The subsidiary ledger accounts are kept in either alphabetical or numerical order, depending on whether customer accounts are identified by number. A summary accounts receivable account called a **controlling account** is still maintained in the general ledger. The accounts receivable ledger is "subsidiary" to this account.

Figure 11-14 illustrates the use of the accounts receivable ledger. The accounts receivable ledger is posted *daily* so that current information is available for each customer at all times. The following steps are used to post from the sales journal to the accounts receivable ledger, as shown in Figure 11-14.

STEP 1   Post the individual sale amount to the customer's account on the date the sale occurs.

STEP 2   Insert the date in the Date column and the initial "S" and the sales journal page number in the Posting Reference column of each customer account.

STEP 3   Insert a check mark (✔) in the Posting Reference column of the sales journal to indicate that the amount has been posted.

Note the relationship between the sales journal, accounts receivable ledger, and general ledger. All individual entries in the sales journal are posted to the accounts receivable ledger. The totals of all entries in the sales journal are posted to the general ledger accounts. After the posting of the accounts receivable ledger and the general ledger is completed, the total of the accounts receivable ledger balances should equal the Accounts Receivable balance in the general ledger. Remember, the accounts receivable ledger is simply a detailed listing of the same information that is summarized in Accounts Receivable in the general ledger.

LEARNING KEY: The total of the accounts receivable ledger balances must equal the Accounts Receivable balance in the general ledger.

FIGURE 11-14 Posting the Sales Journal to the Accounts Receivable Ledger

SALES JOURNAL — Page 6

Date	Sale No.	To Whom Sold	Post Ref.	Accounts Receivable Debit	Sales Credit	Sales Tax Payable Credit
20--						
Apr. 4	133C	Enrico Lorenzo	✔	1,596.00	1,520.00	76.00
10	134C	Brenda Myers	✔	462.00	440.00	22.00
18	105D	Edith Walton	✔	1,029.00	980.00	49.00
21	202B	Susan Chang	✔	651.00	620.00	31.00
24	162A	Heidi Schwitzer	✔	1,680.00	1,600.00	80.00
			3	5,418.00	5,160.00	258.00
				(122)	(401)	(231)

ACCOUNTS RECEIVABLE LEDGER

NAME Helen Avery
ADDRESS 1739 Woodsage Trace, Indianapolis, IN 46237-1199

Date	Item	Post Ref.	Debit	Credit	Balance
20--					
Apr. 1	Bal.	✔			2,302.00

NAME Susan Chang
ADDRESS 337 Elm Street, Noblesville, IN 46060-3377

Date	Item	Post Ref.	Debit	Credit	Balance
20--					
Apr. 21		S6	651.00		651.00

NAME Enrico Lorenzo
ADDRESS 5240 Tousley Court, Indianapolis, IN 46224-5678

Date	Item	Post Ref.	Debit	Credit	Balance
20--					
Apr. 4		S6	1,596.00		1,596.00

NAME Brenda Myers
ADDRESS 581 Acorn Way, Zionsville, IN 46077-2154

Date	Item	Post Ref.	Debit	Credit	Balance
20--					
Apr. 10		S6	462.00		462.00

NAME Heidi Schwitzer
ADDRESS 5858 Wildflower Cir., Bloomington, IN 47401-6209

Date	Item	Post Ref.	Debit	Credit	Balance
20--					
Apr. 1	Bal.	✔			1,883.00
24		S6	1,680.00		3,563.00

NAME Ken Ulmet
ADDRESS 5260 Eagle Creek, Indianapolis, IN 46254-8275

Date	Item	Post Ref.	Debit	Credit	Balance
20--					
Apr. 1	Bal.	✔			3,315.00

NAME Edith Walton
ADDRESS 1113 Stones Crossing, Zionsville, IN 46077-6601

Date	Item	Post Ref.	Debit	Credit	Balance
20--					
Apr. 18		S6	1,029.00		1,029.00

NAME Vivian Winston
ADDRESS 124 Main St., Zionsville, IN 46077-1358

Date	Item	Post Ref.	Debit	Credit	Balance
20--					
Apr. 1	Bal.	✔			4,500.00

GENERAL LEDGER (Partial)

ACCOUNT Accounts Receivable   **ACCOUNT NO.** 122

Date	Item	Post Ref.	Debit	Credit	Balance Debit	Balance Credit
20--						
Apr. 1	Bal.	✔			12,000.00	
30		S6	5,418.00		17,418.00	

ACCOUNT Sales Tax Payable   **ACCOUNT NO.** 231

Date	Item	Post Ref.	Debit	Credit	Balance Debit	Balance Credit
20--						
Apr. 30		S6		258.00		258.00

ACCOUNT Sales   **ACCOUNT NO.** 401

Date	Item	Post Ref.	Debit	Credit	Balance Debit	Balance Credit
20--						
Apr. 1	Bal.	✔				27,000.00
30		S6		5,160.00		32,160.00

Sales Returns and Allowances

If a customer returns merchandise or is given an allowance for damaged merchandise, a general journal entry is required. Remember, the sales journal can be used only to enter sales on account. On May 5, Susan Chang returned two printer ribbons costing $40 plus $2 sales tax (Figure 11-6, page 367). Figure 11-15 shows the general journal entry, general ledger posting, and accounts receivable ledger posting for this transaction.

FIGURE 11-15 Accounting for Sales Returns and Allowances

LEARNING KEY: Enter sales returns and allowances in the general journal.

The general journal entry is made in the usual manner. The postings are made daily using the following steps:

STEP 1   Post the Sales Returns and Allowances and Sales Tax Payable debits to the general ledger accounts. Insert the date in the Date column and the general journal posting reference (J4) in the Posting Reference column of each ledger account.

STEP 2   Insert the general ledger account numbers in the Posting Reference column of the general journal.

Posting the Accounts Receivable credit requires special attention, as follows:

STEP 3   Post the Accounts Receivable credit to the general ledger account. Insert the date in the Date column and the general journal posting reference (J4) in the Posting Reference column.

STEP 4   Post the same amount to the customer account in the accounts receivable subsidiary ledger. Insert the same date in the Date column and posting reference (J4) in the Posting Reference column.

STEP 5   To indicate that the general ledger has been posted, insert the account number (122) and a slash (/) in the Posting Reference column of the general journal.

STEP 6   To indicate that the customer account has been posted, insert a check mark (✔) following the slash in the Posting Reference column of the general journal.

JOURNALIZING AND POSTING CASH RECEIPTS

LO 4   Describe and use the cash receipts journal and accounts receivable ledger.

Like sales transactions, cash receipt transactions occur frequently in most businesses. Sales on account lead to cash receipts, which could be entered in the general journal. For example, assume that Northern Micro receives cash from Enrico Lorenzo for sale no. 133C on April 14. The transaction could be recorded in the general journal as follows:

25	Apr.	14	Cash		1 5 9 6 00		25
26			Accounts Receivable/E. Lorenzo			1 5 9 6 00	26
27			Received cash on account				27

Most businesses also regularly make cash sales. A general journal can be used to record cash sales. The following entry shows cash sales of $500 recorded in the general journal on May 5.

3	May	5	Cash		5 0 0 00		3
4			Sales			5 0 0 00	4
5			Made cash sales				5

In addition, an increasing amount of sales today are made using bank credit cards. Bank credit card sales are similar to cash sales because the cash is available to the business as soon as an electronic deposit is made at the end of the day. The credit card company makes the electronic deposit to the merchandiser's bank account for the gross amount of credit card sales less a processing fee. The fee is based on the gross amount of the sale, including the sales tax. Thus, on a sale of $100 plus sales tax of $5, the credit card fee at 4% would be $4.20 (4% × $105). The following entry shows this credit card sale recorded on May 6.

8	May	6	Cash			1	0	0	80						8
9			Bank Credit Card Expense				4	20							9
10			Sales								1	0	0	00	10
11			Sales Tax Payable									5	00		11
12			Made credit card sale												12

Note two important features of the three journal entries illustrated above:

1. Each involves a debit to Cash.

2. Each occurs frequently in a business.

If the general journal were used to record all such transactions, the journalizing and posting process would be repetitive and inefficient.

The previous section of this chapter showed how sales on account could be journalized and posted more efficiently by using a sales journal. Using a special journal to record cash receipts transactions also increases efficiency.

Cash Receipts Journal

A **cash receipts journal** is a special journal used to record only cash receipts transactions. To illustrate its use, we continue with the transactions of Northern Micro. Northern Micro's cash receipts journal for the month of April is shown in Figure 11-16, with the following transactions.

Apr. 14 Received cash on account from Enrico Lorenzo for sale no. 133C, $1,596.

20 Received cash on account from Brenda Myers for sale no. 134C, $462.

28 Received cash on account from Edith Walton for sale no. 105D, $1,029.

30 Cash sales for the month are $3,600 plus tax of $180.

30 Bank credit card sales for the month are $2,500 plus tax of $125. Bank credit card expenses on these sales are $100.

FIGURE 11-16 Northern Micro Cash Receipts Journal (left side)

	DATE		ACCOUNT CREDITED	POST REF.	GENERAL CREDIT					
1	20-- Apr.	14	Enrico Lorenzo							1
2		20	Brenda Myers							2
3		28	Edith Walton							3
4		30								4
5		30								5
6		30	Rent Revenue			6	0	0	00	6
7		30	Notes Payable		3	0	0	0	00	7
8										8

30   Received cash for rent revenue, $600.

30   Borrowed cash from the bank by signing a note, $3,000.

 LEARNING KEY: Use a cash receipts journal to streamline journalizing and posting of cash receipts.

Northern Micro's cash receipts journal provides separate columns for Accounts Receivable Credit, Sales Credit, Sales Tax Payable Credit, Bank Credit Card Expense Debit, and Cash Debit. These are the accounts most frequently affected by Northern Micro's cash receipts transactions. In addition, a General Credit column is provided for credits to any other accounts affected by cash receipts transactions.

A cash receipt is recorded in the cash receipts journal by entering the following information:

1.   Date

2.   Account credited (if applicable)

3.   Dollar amounts

The Account Credited column is used for two purposes:

1.   To identify the customer name for any collection on account. This column is used whenever the Accounts Receivable Credit column is used.

2.   To enter the appropriate account name whenever the General Credit column is used.

The Account Credited column is left blank whenever the entry is for cash sales or bank credit card sales.

The cash receipts journal in Figure 11-16 is designed for a company like Northern Micro, which charges sales tax, makes bank credit card sales, and offers no cash discounts. For a wholesaler who does not charge sales tax, makes no bank credit card sales, and offers cash discounts, a cash receipts journal like the one in Figure 11-17 would be used. Recall that a special journal should be designed with column headings for frequently used accounts. Thus, the cash receipts journal in

FIGURE 11-16 Northern Micro Cash Receipts Journal (right side)

PAGE 7

	ACCOUNTS RECEIVABLE CREDIT	SALES CREDIT	SALES TAX PAYABLE CREDIT	BANK CREDIT CARD EXPENSE DEBIT	CASH DEBIT	
1	1 5 9 6 00				1 5 9 6 00	1
2	4 6 2 00				4 6 2 00	2
3	1 0 2 9 00				1 0 2 9 00	3
4		3 6 0 0 00	1 8 0 00		3 7 8 0 00	4
5		2 5 0 0 00	1 2 5 00	1 0 0 00	2 5 2 5 00	5
6					6 0 0 00	6
7					3 0 0 0 00	7
8						8

Figure 11-17 has no Sales Tax Payable Credit or Bank Credit Card Expense Debit column. Instead, a Sales Discounts Debit column is provided. In this way, the common cash receipts transactions of the wholesaler can be easily and efficiently recorded.

FIGURE 11-17 Cash Receipts Journal Without Sales Tax

	DATE	ACCOUNT CREDITED	POST REF.	GENERAL CREDIT	ACCOUNTS RECEIVABLE CREDIT	SALES CREDIT	SALES DISCOUNTS DEBIT	CASH DEBIT	
		SALES JOURNAL						PAGE 1	
1									1

A BROADER VIEW

IS THIS SALE FOR REAL?

U.S. businesses lose billions of dollars annually because of credit card fraud and bad checks. To reduce credit card fraud, cashiers should do two things: (1) Watch the customer sign the credit card slip and match it to the signature on the card. (2) Obtain an approval code on all credit card transactions. To reduce bad check losses, cashiers should accept only a driver's license as identification. They should compare the picture with the customer, watch the check being signed, and match the check signature with that on the driver's license.

Posting from the Cash Receipts Journal

Figure 11-18 illustrates the general ledger posting process for Northern Micro's cash receipts journal.
    On a daily basis:

STEP 1   Post each amount in the General Credit column to the appropriate general ledger account.

STEP 2   Insert the date in the Date column and the initials "CR" and the cash receipts journal page number in the Posting Reference column of each ledger account.

STEP 3   Insert the general ledger account numbers in the Posting Reference column of the cash receipts journal.

FIGURE 11-18 Posting the Cash Receipts Journal to the General Ledger

CASH RECEIPTS JOURNAL Page 7

Date	Account Credited	Post Ref.	General Credit	Accounts Receivable Credit	Sales Credit	Sales Tax Payable Credit	Bank Credit Card Expense Debit	Cash Debit
20--								
Apr. 14	Enrico Lorenzo	8		1,596.00				1,596.00
20	Brenda Myers			462.00				462.00
28	Edith Walton			1,029.00				1,029.00
30		✔			3,600.00	180.00		3,780.00
30		✔			2,500.00	125.00	100.00	2,525.00
30	Rent Revenue	412	600.00					600.00
30	Notes Payable	201	3,000.00					3,000.00
		3	3,600.00	3,087.00	6,100.00	305.00	100.00	12,992.00
		8	(✔)	(122)	(401)	(231)	(513)	(101)

4

7

GENERAL LEDGER (Partial)

ACCOUNT Cash ACCOUNT NO. 101

Date	Item	Post Ref.	Debit	Credit	Balance Debit	Balance Credit
20--						
Apr. 1	Bal.	✔			20,000.00	
30		CR7	12,992.00		32,992.00	

6

ACCOUNT Accounts Receivable ACCOUNT NO. 122

Date	Item	Post Ref.	Debit	Credit	Balance Debit	Balance Credit
20--						
Apr. 1	Bal.	✔			12,000.00	
30		S6	5,418.00		17,418.00	
30		CR7		3,087.00	14,331.00	

1   6   5

ACCOUNT Notes Payable ACCOUNT NO. 201

Date	Item	Post Ref.	Debit	Credit	Balance Debit	Balance Credit
20--						
Apr. 1	Bal.	✔				6,000.00
30		CR7		3,000.00		9,000.00

2

ACCOUNT Sales Tax Payable ACCOUNT NO. 231

Date	Item	Post Ref.	Debit	Credit	Balance Debit	Balance Credit
20--						
Apr. 30		S6		258.00		258.00
30		CR7		305.00		563.00

6

ACCOUNT Sales ACCOUNT NO. 401

Date	Item	Post Ref.	Debit	Credit	Balance Debit	Balance Credit
20--						
Apr. 1	Bal.	✔				27,000.00
30		S6		5,160.00		32,160.00
30		CR7		6,100.00		38,260.00

6

ACCOUNT Rent Revenue ACCOUNT NO. 412

Date	Item	Post Ref.	Debit	Credit	Balance Debit	Balance Credit
20--						
Apr. 1	Bal.	✔				1,800.00
30		CR7		600.00		2,400.00

2

ACCOUNT Bank Credit Card Expense ACCOUNT NO. 513

Date	Item	Post Ref.	Debit	Credit	Balance Debit	Balance Credit
20--						
Apr. 1	Bal.	✔			430.00	
30		CR7	100.00		530.00	

6

4 Debit total: $ 100
            12,992
           $13,092

Credit total: $ 3,600
              3,087
              6,100
                305
            $13,092

At the end of each month:

STEP 4   Total the amount columns, verify that the total of the debit columns equals the total of the credit columns, and rule the columns.

STEP 5   Post each column total except the General Credit column to the general ledger account indicated in the column headings.

STEP 6   Insert the date in the Date column and the initials "CR" and the cash receipts journal page number in the Posting Reference column of each ledger account.

STEP 7   Insert the general ledger account numbers immediately below each column total except the General Credit column.

STEP 8   Insert a check mark (✔) in the Posting Reference column of the cash receipts journal for the cash sales and bank credit card sales and immediately below the General Credit column.

The general ledger accounts affected by the cash receipts transactions are now up to date. Postings to the accounts receivable ledger also must be made. These postings are made daily. Figure 11-19 illustrates the posting procedures, as follows:

STEP 1   Post the individual cash receipt to the customer's account on the date the receipt occurs.

STEP 2   Insert the date in the Date column and the initials "CR" and the cash receipts journal page number in the Posting Reference column of each customer account.

STEP 3   Insert a check mark (✔) in the Posting Reference column of the cash receipts journal to indicate that the amount has been posted.

SCHEDULE OF ACCOUNTS RECEIVABLE

LO 5   Prepare a schedule of accounts receivable.

All postings to the general ledger and accounts receivable ledger are now complete. At this point, the Accounts Receivable balance in the general ledger should equal the sum of the customer balances in the accounts receivable ledger.

To verify that the sum of the accounts receivable ledger balances equals the Accounts Receivable balance, a **schedule of accounts receivable** is prepared. This is an alphabetical or numerical listing of customer accounts and balances, usually prepared at the end of the month. The schedule of accounts receivable for Northern Micro as of April 30 is illustrated in Figure 11-20.

FIGURE 11-20   Schedule of Accounts Receivable

Northern Micro Schedule of Accounts Receivable April 30, 20--						
Helen Avery	$ 2	3	0	2	00
Susan Chang		6	5	1	00
Heidi Schwitzer	3	5	6	3	00
Ken Ulmet	3	3	1	5	00
Vivian Winston	4	5	0	0	00
Total	$14	3	3	1	00

FIGURE 11-19 Posting the Cash Receipts Journal to the Accounts Receivable Ledger

CASH RECEIPTS JOURNAL Page 7

Date	Account Credited	Post Ref.	General Credit	Accounts Receivable Credit	Sales Credit	Sales Tax Payable Credit	Bank Credit Card Expense Debit	Cash Debit
20-- Apr. 14	Enrico Lorenzo	✔		1,596.00				1,596.00
20	Brenda Myers	✔		462.00				462.00
28	Edith Walton	✔		1,029.00				1,029.00
30		✔			3,600.00	180.00		3,780.00
30		✔			2,500.00	125.00	100.00	2,525.00
30	Rent Revenue	412	600.00					600.00
30	Notes Payable	201	3,000.00					3,000.00
			3,600.00	3,087.00	6,100.00	305.00	100.00	12,992.00
			(✔)	(122)	(401)	(231)	(513)	(101)

3

1

2

ACCOUNTS RECEIVABLE LEDGER

NAME Helen Avery
ADDRESS 1739 Woodsage Trace, Indianapolis, IN 46237-1199

Date	Item	Post Ref.	Debit	Credit	Balance
20-- Apr. 1	Bal.	✔			2,302.00

NAME Susan Chang
ADDRESS 337 Elm Street, Noblesville, IN 46060-3377

Date	Item	Post Ref.	Debit	Credit	Balance
20-- Apr. 21		S6	651.00		651.00

NAME Enrico Lorenzo
ADDRESS 5240 Tousley Court, Indianapolis, IN 46224-5678

Date	Item	Post Ref.	Debit	Credit	Balance
20-- Apr. 4		S6	1,596.00		1,596.00
14		CR7		1,596.00	—

NAME Brenda Myers
ADDRESS 581 Acorn Way, Zionsville, IN 46077-2154

Date	Item	Post Ref.	Debit	Credit	Balance
20-- Apr. 10		S6	462.00		462.00
20		CR7		462.00	—

NAME Heidi Schwitzer
ADDRESS 5858 Wildflower Cir., Bloomington, IN 47401-6209

Date	Item	Post Ref.	Debit	Credit	Balance
20-- Apr. 1	Bal.	✔			1,883.00
24		S6	1,680.00		3,563.00

NAME Ken Ulmet
ADDRESS 5260 Eagle Creek, Indianapolis, IN 46254-8275

Date	Item	Post Ref.	Debit	Credit	Balance
20-- Apr. 1	Bal.	✔			3,315.00

NAME Edith Walton
ADDRESS 1113 Stones Crossing, Zionsville, IN 46077-6601

Date	Item	Post Ref.	Debit	Credit	Balance
20-- Apr. 18		S6	1,029.00		1,029.00
28		CR7		1,029.00	—

NAME Vivian Winston
ADDRESS 124 Main St., Zionsville, IN 46077-1358

Date	Item	Post Ref.	Debit	Credit	Balance
20-- Apr. 1	Bal.	✔			4,500.00

GENERAL LEDGER (Partial)

ACCOUNT Cash **ACCOUNT NO.** 101

Date	Item	Post Ref.	Debit	Credit	Balance Debit	Balance Credit
20-- Apr. 1	Bal.	✔			20,000.00	
30		CR7	12,992.00		32,992.00	

ACCOUNT Accounts Receivable **ACCOUNT NO.** 122

Date	Item	Post Ref.	Debit	Credit	Balance Debit	Balance Credit
20-- Apr. 1	Bal.	✔			12,000.00	
30		S6	5,418.00		17,418.00	
30		CR7		3,087.00	14,331.00	

ACCOUNT Notes Payable **ACCOUNT NO.** 201

Date	Item	Post Ref.	Debit	Credit	Balance Debit	Balance Credit
20-- Apr. 1	Bal.	✔				6,000.00
30		CR7		3,000.00		9,000.00

ACCOUNT Sales Tax Payable **ACCOUNT NO.** 231

Date	Item	Post Ref.	Debit	Credit	Balance Debit	Balance Credit
20-- Apr. 30		S6		258.00		258.00
30		CR7		305.00		563.00

ACCOUNT Sales **ACCOUNT NO.** 401

Date	Item	Post Ref.	Debit	Credit	Balance Debit	Balance Credit
20-- Apr. 1	Bal.	✔				27,000.00
30		S6		5,160.00		32,160.00
30		CR7		6,100.00		38,260.00

ACCOUNT Rent Revenue **ACCOUNT NO.** 412

Date	Item	Post Ref.	Debit	Credit	Balance Debit	Balance Credit
20-- Apr. 1	Bal.	✔				1,800.00
30		CR7		600.00		2,400.00

ACCOUNT Bank Credit Card Expense **ACCOUNT NO.** 513

Date	Item	Post Ref.	Debit	Credit	Balance Debit	Balance Credit
20-- Apr. 1	Bal.	✔			430.00	
30		CR7	100.00		530.00	

This schedule is prepared from the list of customer accounts in the accounts receivable ledger. The total calculated in the schedule is compared with the balance in Accounts Receivable in the general ledger. Note that the $14,331 total listed in the schedule equals the Accounts Receivable balance shown in Figure 11-19. If the schedule total and the Accounts Receivable balance do not agree, the error must be located and corrected. To find the error, use the following procedures.

STEP 1   Verify the total of the schedule.

STEP 2   Verify the postings to the accounts receivable ledger.

STEP 3   Verify the totals in the sales and cash receipts journals.

STEP 4   Verify the postings to Accounts Receivable in the general ledger.

Learning Objectives	Key Points to Remember
1 Describe merchandise sales transactions.	A merchandising business buys and sells merchandise. Retailers generally make sales in the store. Important accounting documents are cash register tapes and sales tickets. Wholesalers generally ship merchandise to retailers. A key accounting document is the sales invoice. When customers return merchandise or obtain price adjustments, a credit memo is issued.
2 Describe and use merchandise sales accounts.	Four accounts are used in accounting for merchandise sales transactions: 1. Sales 2. Sales Tax Payable 3. Sales Returns and Allowances 4. Sales Discounts
3 Describe and use the sales journal and accounts receivable ledger.	A sales journal is a special journal for recording sales on account. A sale is recorded by entering the following: 1. Date 2. Sale number 3. Customer 4. Dollar amounts To post from the sales journal to the general ledger: 1. Total, verify the equality of, and rule the amount columns. 2. Post column totals to the general ledger accounts. 3. Insert the date and posting reference in the ledger accounts. 4. Insert the account numbers below the column totals in the sales journal. An accounts receivable ledger is a separate ledger containing an individual account receivable for each customer. To post from the sales journal to the accounts receivable ledger: 1. Post individual sale amounts to customer accounts. 2. Insert the date and posting reference in the customer accounts.

Learning Objectives	Key Points to Remember
	3. Insert a check mark (✔) in the Posting Reference column of the sales journal. Sales returns and allowances are recorded in the general journal.
4 **Describe and use the cash receipts journal and accounts receivable ledger.**	A cash receipts journal is a special journal for recording cash receipts. A cash receipt is recorded by entering the following: 1. Date 2. Account credited (if applicable) 3. Dollar amounts To post from the cash receipts journal to the general ledger: On a daily basis: 1. Post General Credit column amounts to the general ledger. 2. Insert the date and posting reference in the accounts. 3. Insert the account numbers in the Posting Reference column of the cash receipts journal. At the end of each month: 4. Total, verify the equality of, and rule the amount columns. 5. Post specific account column totals to the general ledger. 6. Insert the date and posting reference in the accounts. 7. Insert the account numbers below the specific account column totals. 8. Insert a check mark (✔) in the Posting Reference column for the cash sales and bank credit card sales and below the General Credit column. To post from the cash receipts journal to the accounts receivable ledger: 1. Post individual cash receipts to customer accounts. 2. Insert the date and posting reference in the customer accounts. 3. Insert a check mark (✔) in the Posting Reference column of the cash receipts journal.
5 **Prepare a schedule of accounts receivable.**	The schedule of accounts receivable is used to verify that the sum of the accounts receivable ledger balances equals the Accounts Receivable balance.

Reflection: Answering the Opening Question

Bank credit card sales are similar to cash sales because the cash is available to the business as soon as an electronic deposit is made to the merchandiser's bank account by the credit card company at the end of the day. The cash available is the gross amount of the sale less a processing fee. The bookkeeper should account for such sales by crediting Sales for the gross amount of the sale, debiting Bank Credit Card Expense for the bank fee, and debiting Cash for the net proceeds.

KEY TERMS

accounts receivable ledger, (374)   A separate ledger containing an individual account receivable for each customer, kept in either alphabetical or numerical order.

cash discounts, (370)   Discounts to encourage prompt payment by customers who buy merchandise on account.

cash receipts journal, (378)   A special journal used to record only cash receipts transactions.

controlling account, (374)   A summary account maintained in the general ledger with a subsidiary ledger (for example, the accounts receivable ledger).

credit memo, (366)   A document issued when credit is given for merchandise returned or for an allowance.

merchandising business, (364)   Purchases merchandise such as clothing, furniture, or computers, and sells that merchandise to its customers.

sale, (364)   A transfer of merchandise from one business or individual to another in exchange for cash or a promise to pay cash.

sales allowances, (366)   Reductions in the price of merchandise granted by the seller because of defects or other problems with the merchandise.

sales discounts, (370)   To the seller, cash discounts are considered sales discounts.

sales invoice, (366)   A document that is generated to bill the customer who made the purchase.

sales journal, (372)   A special journal used to record only sales on account.

sales return, (366)   Merchandise returned by a customer for a refund.

sales ticket, (365)   A document created as evidence of a sale in a retail business.

schedule of accounts receivable, (382)   An alphabetical or numerical listing of customer accounts and balances, usually prepared at the end of the month.

special journal, (372)   A journal designed for recording only certain kinds of transactions.

DEMONSTRATION PROBLEM

Karen Hunt operates Hunt's Audio-Video Store. The books include a sales journal, a cash receipts journal, and a general journal. The following transactions related to sales on account and cash receipts occurred during April 20--.

April 3   Sold merchandise on account to Susan Haberman, $159.50 plus tax of $11.17. Sale no. 41.

4   Sold merchandise on account to Goro Kimura, $299.95 plus tax of $21.00. Sale no. 42.

6   Received payment from Tera Scherrer on account, $69.50.

7   Issued a credit memo to Kenneth Watt for merchandise returned that had been sold on account, $42.75 including tax of $2.80.

10   Received payment from Kellie Cokley on account, $99.95.

11   Sold merchandise on account to Victor Cardona, $499.95 plus tax of $35.00. Sale no. 43.

14   Received payment from Kenneth Watt in full settlement of account, $157.00.

17   Sold merchandise on account to Susan Haberman, $379.95 plus tax of $26.60. Sale no. 44.

19   Sold merchandise on account to Tera Scherrer, $59.95 plus tax of $4.20. Sale no. 45.

21   Issued a credit memo to Goro Kimura for merchandise returned that had been sold on account, $53.45 including tax of $3.50.

24   Received payment from Victor Cardona on account, $299.95.

25   Sold merchandise on account to Kellie Cokley, $179.50 plus tax of $12.57. Sale no. 46.

26   Received payment from Susan Haberman on account, $250.65.

28   Sold merchandise on account to Kenneth Watt, $49.95 plus tax of $3.50. Sale no. 47.

30   Bank credit card sales for the month, $1,220.00 plus tax of $85.40. Bank credit card expense on these sales, $65.27.

30   Cash sales for the month, $2,000.00 plus tax of $140.00.

Hunt had the following general ledger account balances as of April 1:

Account Title	Account No.	General Ledger Balance on April 1
Cash	101	$5,000.00
Accounts Receivable	122	1,208.63
Sales Tax Payable	231	72.52
Sales	401	8,421.49
Sales Returns and Allowances	401.1	168.43
Bank Credit Card Expense	513	215.00

Hunt also had the following accounts receivable ledger account balances as of April 1:

Customer	Accounts Receivable Balance
Victor Cardona 6300 Washington Blvd. St. Louis, MO 63130-9523	$299.95
Kellie Cokley 4220 Kingsbury Blvd. St. Louis, MO 63130-1645	$99.95
Susan Haberman 9421 Garden Ct. Kirkwood, MO 63122-1878	$79.98
Goro Kimura 6612 Arundel Pl. Clayton, MO 63150-9266	$379.50
Tera Scherrer 315 W. Linden St. Webster Groves, MO 63119-9881	$149.50
Kenneth Watt 11742 Fawnridge Dr. St. Louis, MO 63131-1726	$199.75

(continued)

REQUIRED

1. Open four-column general ledger accounts and three-column accounts receivable ledger accounts for Hunt's Audio-Video Store as of April 1, 20--. Enter the April 1 balance in each of the accounts.

2. Enter each transaction either in a three-column sales journal (page 5), a six-column cash receipts journal (page 8), or a general journal (page 7).

3. Post directly from each of the three journals to the proper customers' accounts in the accounts receivable ledger. Each subsidiary ledger account should show the initials "S," "CR," or "J," followed by the appropriate journal page number as a posting reference for each transaction.

4. Enter the totals and rule the sales journal and the cash receipts journal. Complete the summary posting of the cash receipts and sales journals and the individual posting of the general journal to the proper general ledger accounts. Each general ledger account should show the initials "S," "CR," or "J," followed by the appropriate journal page number as a posting reference for each transaction.

5. Prove the balance of the summary accounts receivable account by preparing a schedule of accounts receivable as of April 30, based on the accounts receivable ledger.

Solution

1, 3, 4.

ACCOUNTS RECEIVABLE LEDGER

NAME: Victor Cardona

DATE		ITEM	POST REF.	DEBIT	CREDIT	BALANCE
20-- Apr.	1	Bal.	✔			2 9 9 95
	11		S5	5 3 4 95		8 3 4 90
	24		CR8		2 9 9 95	5 3 4 95

NAME: Kellie Cokley

DATE		ITEM	POST REF.	DEBIT	CREDIT	BALANCE
20-- Apr.	1	Bal.	✔			9 9 95
	10		CR8		9 9 95	--
	25		S5	1 9 2 07		1 9 2 07

NAME: Susan Haberman

DATE		ITEM	POST REF.	DEBIT	CREDIT	BALANCE
20-- Apr.	1	Bal.	✔			7 9 98
	3		S5	1 7 0 67		2 5 0 65
	17		S5	4 0 6 55		6 5 7 20
	26		CR8		2 5 0 65	4 0 6 55

NAME: Goro Kimura

DATE		ITEM	POST REF.	DEBIT	CREDIT	BALANCE
20— Apr.	1	Bal.	✔			3 7 9 50
	4		S5	3 2 0 95		7 0 0 45
	21		J7		5 3 45	6 4 7 00

NAME: Tera Scherrer

DATE		ITEM	POST REF.	DEBIT	CREDIT	BALANCE
20— Apr.	1	Bal.	✔			1 4 9 50
	6		CR8		6 9 50	8 0 00
	19		S5	6 4 15		1 4 4 15

NAME: Kenneth Watt

DATE		ITEM	POST REF.	DEBIT	CREDIT	BALANCE
20— Apr.	1	Bal.	✔			1 9 9 75
	7		J7		4 2 75	1 5 7 00
	14		CR8		1 5 7 00	--
	28		S5	5 3 45		5 3 45

GENERAL LEDGER

ACCOUNT: Cash   ACCOUNT NO. 101

DATE		ITEM	POST REF.	DEBIT	CREDIT	BALANCE DEBIT	BALANCE CREDIT
20— Apr.	1	Bal.	✔			5 0 0 0 00	
	30		CR8	4 2 5 7 18		9 2 5 7 18	

ACCOUNT: Accounts Receivable   ACCOUNT NO. 122

DATE		ITEM	POST REF.	DEBIT	CREDIT	BALANCE DEBIT	BALANCE CREDIT
20— Apr.	1	Bal.	✔			1 2 0 8 63	
	7		J7		4 2 75	1 1 6 5 88	
	21		J7		5 3 45	1 1 1 2 43	
	30		S5	1 7 4 2 79		2 8 5 5 22	
	30		CR8		8 7 7 05	1 9 7 8 17	

(continued)

1, 3, 4.

ACCOUNT: Sales Tax Payable — ACCOUNT NO. 231

DATE		ITEM	POST REF.	DEBIT	CREDIT	BALANCE DEBIT	BALANCE CREDIT
20-- Apr.	1	Bal.	✔				7 2 52
	7		J7	2 80			6 9 72
	21		J7	3 50			6 6 22
	30		S5		1 1 4 04		1 8 0 26
	30		CR8		2 2 5 40		4 0 5 66

ACCOUNT: Sales — ACCOUNT NO. 401

DATE		ITEM	POST REF.	DEBIT	CREDIT	BALANCE DEBIT	BALANCE CREDIT
20-- Apr.	1	Bal.	✔				8 4 2 1 49
	30		S5		1 6 2 8 75		10 0 5 0 24
	30		CR8		3 2 2 0 00		13 2 7 0 24

ACCOUNT: Sales Returns and Allowances — ACCOUNT NO. 401.1

DATE		ITEM	POST REF.	DEBIT	CREDIT	BALANCE DEBIT	BALANCE CREDIT
20-- Apr.	1	Bal.	✔			1 6 8 43	
	7		J7	3 9 95		2 0 8 38	
	21		J7	4 9 95		2 5 8 33	

ACCOUNT: Bank Credit Card Expense — ACCOUNT NO.. 513

DATE		ITEM	POST REF.	DEBIT	CREDIT	BALANCE DEBIT	BALANCE CREDIT
20-- Apr.	1	Bal.	✔			2 1 5 00	
	30		CR8	6 5 27		2 8 0 27	

2.

GENERAL JOURNAL — PAGE 7

	DATE		DESCRIPTION	POST REF.	DEBIT	CREDIT	
1	20-- Apr.	7	Sales Returns and Allowances	401.1	3 9 95		1
2			Sales Tax Payable	231	2 80		2
3			Accounts Receivable/K. Watt	122		4 2 75	3
4							4
5		21	Sales Returns and Allowances	401.1	4 9 95		5
6			Sales Tax Payable	231	3 50		6
7			Accounts Receivable/G. Kimura	122		5 3 45	7

2, 3, 4.

				CASH RECEIPTS JOURNAL																PAGE 8	
	DATE	ACCOUNT CREDITED	POST REF.	GENERAL CREDIT				ACCOUNTS RECEIVABLE CREDIT			SALES CREDIT			SALES TAX PAYABLE CREDIT			BANK CREDIT CARD EXPENSE DEBIT			CASH DEBIT		
1	20-- Apr 6	Tera Scherrer	✔			1	1		6 9 50											6 9 50	1
2	10	Kellie Cokley	✔			2	2		9 9 95											9 9 95	2
3	14	Kenneth Watt	✔			3	3	1 5 7 00											1 5 7 00		3
4	24	Victor Cardona	✔			4	4	2 9 9 95											2 9 9 95		4
5	26	Susan Haberman	✔			5	5	2 5 0 65											2 5 0 65		5
6	30		✔			6	6			1 2 2 0 00			8 5 40		6 5 27	1 2 4 0 13			6
7	30		✔			7	7			2 0 0 0 00			1 4 0 00				2 1 4 0 00		7
8						8	8	8 7 7 05		3 2 2 0 00			2 2 5 40		6 5 27	4 2 5 7 18			8
9						9	9	(1 22)		(4 01)			(2 31)		(5 13)		(1 01)			9
10						10	10													10

2, 3, 4.

					SALES JOURNAL						PAGE 5	
	DATE	SALE NO.	TO WHOM SOLD	POST REF.	ACCOUNTS RECEIVABLE DEBIT		SALES CREDIT		SALES TAX PAYABLE CREDIT			
1	20-- Apr. 3	41	Susan Haberman	✔	1 7 0 67	1 5 9 50		1 1 17			1
2	4	42	Goro Kimura	✔	3 2 0 95	2 9 9 95		2 1 00			2
3	11	43	Victor Cardona	✔	5 3 4 95	4 9 9 95		3 5 00			3
4	17	44	Susan Haberman	✔	4 0 6 55	3 7 9 95		2 6 60			4
5	19	45	Tera Scherrer	✔	6 4 15	5 9 95		4 20			5
6	25	46	Kellie Cokley	✔	1 9 2 07	1 7 9 50		1 2 57			6
7	28	47	Kenneth Watt	✔	5 3 45	4 9 95		3 50			7
8					1 7 4 2 79	1 6 2 8 75		1 1 4 04			8
9					(1 22)	(4 01)		(2 31)			9

5.

Hunt's Audio-Video Store
Schedule of Accounts Receivable
April 30, 20--

Victor Cardona		5	3	4	95
Kellie Cokley		1	9	2	07
Susan Haberman		4	0	6	55
Goro Kimura		6	4	7	00
Tera Scherrer		1	4	4	15
Kenneth Watt			5	3	45
Total	1	9	7	8	17

REVIEW QUESTIONS

1. Identify the sales documents commonly used in retail and wholesale businesses.

2. What is the purpose of a credit memo?

3. Describe how each of the following accounts is used: (1) Sales, (2) Sales Tax Payable, (3) Sales Returns and Allowances, and (4) Sales Discounts.

4. List four items of information about each sale entered in the sales journal.

5. What steps are followed in posting from the sales journal to the general ledger?

6. What steps are followed in posting from the sales journal to the accounts receivable ledger?

7. How is the posting of Sales Returns and Allowances from the general journal to the general ledger and accounts receivable ledger different from the normal posting process?

8. List three items of information about each cash receipt entered in the cash receipts journal.

9. What steps are followed in posting from the cash receipts journal to the general ledger?

10. What steps are followed in posting from the cash receipts journal to the accounts receivable ledger?

11. If the total of the schedule of accounts receivable does not agree with the Accounts Receivable balance, what procedures should be used to search for the error?

MANAGING YOUR WRITING

You and your spouse have separate charge accounts at a local department store. When you tried to use your card last week, you were told that you were over your credit limit. This puzzled you because you had paid the entire account balance several weeks ago. When the monthly statements arrived yesterday, the error was clear. The store had credited your payment to your spouse's account.

Your account was treated as over the limit, and the store charged you interest on the unpaid balance. You suspect that part of the problem is that you and your spouse use the same last name (Morales) and have similar first names (Carmen and Carmelo).

Write a letter to the store requesting correction of your accounts and suggesting a way to identify your accounts so that this error does not happen again.

ETHICS CASE

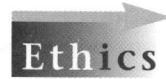

Wholesale Health Supply sells a variety of medical equipment and supplies to retailers. When a new retailer is approved for credit, one of the criteria is that the retailer must have been in business for at least six months. Good Earth Foods placed a large order with Wholesale Health Supply and requested credit terms. Wholesale Health Supply faxed a credit request form to Good Earth Foods and the buyer at Good Earth Foods faxed the completed form back to Wholesale Health Supply. Robin Sylvester, the Sales Manager at Wholesale Health Supply, saw the credit application and noticed Good Earth Foods had only been in business for two months. Thinking she might lose the order if Good Earth Foods wasn't extended credit, Robin authorized the shipment. She figured by the time the credit department rejected the application, Good Earth Foods would have received the order and the Vice President would override the rejection to keep a new customer. Robin was sure that everything would turn out alright.

1. Do you think Robin's decision to ship the order was unethical? Why or why not?

2. What would you have done if you were in Robin's position?

3. Write a memo from the Credit Department Manager to Robin Sylvester explaining the reasoning behind requiring a new credit customer to be in business for at least six months.

4. In small groups discuss ways to prevent a situation like this from happening.

WEB WORK

1. Not only is mail-order big business, but Internet retailing is expanding at a tremendous rate. Companies like Sears (**http://www.sears.com**), J. C. Penney (**http://www.jcpenney.com**) and L.L. Bean (**http://www.llbean.com**) are on the Net, as are millions of other retailers. How would their sales journals differ, if at all, for Internet sales versus mail order? What new challenges or problems might Internet sales present for record keeping? (**http://heintz.swcollege.com**)

2. E-business is not just for major players.

   http://www.accountantsledger.com/ebusiness/u125eb.htm

   (**http://heintz.swcollege.com**)

SERIES A EXERCISES

EXERCISE 11A-1 (LO1) SALES DOCUMENTS For each document or procedure listed below, indicate whether it would be used for a retail business or a wholesale business, as described in the chapter.

1. sales ticket	4. cash register tape summary
2. sales invoice	5. credit memo
3. credit approval	6. customer purchase order

EXERCISE 11A-2 (LO2) SALES TRANSACTIONS AND ACCOUNTS Using T accounts for Cash, Accounts Receivable, Sales Tax Payable, Sales, Sales Returns and Allowances, and Sales Discounts, enter the following sales transactions. Use a new set of accounts for each part, 1–5.

1. No sales tax.

    (a) Merchandise is sold for $300 cash.

    (b) Merchandise is sold on account for $285.

    (c) Payment is received for merchandise sold on account.

2. 5% sales tax.

    (a) Merchandise is sold for $300 cash plus sales tax.

    (b) Merchandise is sold on account for $285 plus sales tax.

    (c) Payment is received for merchandise sold on account.

3. Cash and credit sales, with returned merchandise.

    (a) Merchandise is sold for $325 cash.

    (b) $25 of merchandise sold for $325 is returned for refund.

    (c) Merchandise is sold on account for $350.

    (d) $35 of merchandise sold for $350 is returned for a credit.

    (e) Payment is received for balance owed on merchandise sold on account.

4. 5% sales tax, with returned merchandise.

    (a) Merchandise is sold on account for $400 plus sales tax.

    (b) Merchandise totaling $40 is returned for a credit.

    (c) Balance on account is paid in cash.

    (d) Merchandise is sold for $280 cash plus sales tax.

    (e) $20 of merchandise sold for $280 cash is returned for a refund.

5. Sales on account, with 2/10, n/30 cash discount terms.

    (a) Merchandise is sold on account for $350.

    (b) The balance is paid within the discount period.

EXERCISE 11A-3 (LO2) COMPUTING NET SALES Based on the following information, compute net sales.

Gross sales	$3,580
Sales returns and allowances	428
Sales discounts	73

EXERCISE 11A-4 (LO 3) JOURNALIZING SALES TRANSACTIONS Enter the following transactions (a) in a general journal and (b) in a sales journal. Use a 6% sales tax rate.

May 1 Sold merchandise on account to J. Adams, $2,000 plus sales tax. Sale no 488.

   4 Sold merchandise on account to B. Clark, $1,800 plus sales tax. Sale no. 489.

   8 Sold merchandise on account to A. Duck, $1,500 plus sales tax. Sale no. 490.

   11 Sold merchandise on account to E. Hill, $1,950 plus sales tax. Sale no. 491.

EXERCISE 11A-5 (LO 3) JOURNALIZING SALES RETURNS AND ALLOWANCES Enter the following transactions in a general journal and post them to the appropriate general ledger and accounts receivable ledger accounts. Use account numbers as shown in the chapter. Beginning balance in Accounts Receivable is $4,200. Beginning balances in customer accounts are: Abramowitz, $850; Perez, $1,018; and Gruder, $428.

June 1 John B. Abramowitz returned merchandise previously purchased on account (sale no. 329), $73.

   6 Marie L. Perez returned merchandise previously purchased on account (sale no. 321), $44.

   8 L. B. Gruder returned merchandise previously purchased on account (sale no. 299), $24.

EXERCISE 11A-6 (LO 4) JOURNALIZING CASH RECEIPTS Enter the following transactions (a) in a general journal and (b) in a cash receipts journal.

July 6 James Adler made payment on account, $643.

   10 Cash sales for the week, $2,320

   14 Betty Havel made payment on account, $430.

   15 J. L. Borg made payment on account, $117.

   17 Cash sales for the week, $2,237.

EXERCISE 11A-7 (LO 5) SCHEDULE OF ACCOUNTS RECEIVABLE From the accounts receivable ledger shown, prepare a schedule of accounts receivable for Pheng Co. as of August 31, 20--.

ACCOUNTS RECEIVABLE LEDGER																			
NAME	**B & G Distributors**																		
ADDRESS	2628 Burlington Avenue, Chicago, IL 60604-1329																		
DATE		ITEM	POST REF.	DEBIT					CREDIT					BALANCE					
20-- Aug.	3		S1	1	3	8	0	00						1	3	8	0	00		
	8		J1							1	4	0	00	1	2	4	0	00		

(continued)

NAME	M. Chang								
ADDRESS	1422 SW Pacific, Chicago, IL 60603-8596								
DATE		ITEM	POST REF.	DEBIT		CREDIT		BALANCE	
20-- Aug.	5		S1	2 1 3 6 00				2 1 3 6 00	
	11		CR1			2 1 3 6 00			

NAME	B. J. Hinschliff & Co.								
ADDRESS	133 College Blvd., Des Plaines, IL 60611-4431								
DATE		ITEM	POST REF.	DEBIT		CREDIT		BALANCE	
20-- Aug.	15		S1	1 1 0 6 00				1 1 0 6 00	
	21		S1	3 8 4 00				1 4 9 0 00	

NAME	Sally M. Pitts								
ADDRESS	213 East 29th Place, Chicago, IL 60601-6287								
DATE		ITEM	POST REF.	DEBIT		CREDIT		BALANCE	
20-- Aug.	21		S1	8 3 8 00				8 3 8 00	

NAME	Trendsetter, Inc.								
ADDRESS	29 Industrial Way, Chicago, IL 60600-5918								
DATE		ITEM	POST REF.	DEBIT		CREDIT		BALANCE	
20-- Aug.	28		S1	1 0 1 8 00				1 0 1 8 00	

SERIES A PROBLEMS

PROBLEM 11A-1 (LO 3) SALES JOURNAL J. K. Bijan owns a retail business and made the following sales during the month of August 20--. There is a 6% sales tax on all sales.

Aug. 1 Sale no. 213 to Jung Manufacturing Co., $1,200 plus sales tax.

3 Sale no. 214 to Hassad Co., $3,600 plus sales tax.

7 Sale no. 215 to Helsinki, Inc., $1,400 plus sales tax. (Open a new account for this customer. Address is 125 Fishers Dr., Noblesville, IN 47870-8867.)

11 Sale no. 216 to Ardis Myler, $1,280 plus sales tax.

18 Sale no. 217 to Hassad Co., $4,330 plus sales tax.

22 Sale no. 218 to Jung Manufacturing Co., $2,000 plus sales tax.

30 Sale no. 219 to Ardis Myler, $1,610 plus sales tax.

REQUIRED
1. Record the transactions in the sales journal. Total and verify the column totals and rule the columns.

2. Post from the sales journal to the general ledger accounts and to the accounts receivable ledger accounts. Use account numbers as shown in the chapter.

PROBLEM 11A-2 (LO 4) CASH RECEIPTS JOURNAL Zebra Imaginarium, a retail business, had the following cash receipts during December 20--. The sales tax is 6%.

Dec. 1 Received payment on account from Michael Anderson, $1,360.

2 Received payment on account from Ansel Manufacturing, $382.

7 Cash sales for the week, $3,160 plus tax. Bank credit card sales for the week, $1,000 plus tax. Bank credit card fee is 3%.

8 Received payment on account from J. Gorbea, $880.

11 Michael Anderson returned merchandise for a credit, $60 plus tax.

14 Cash sales for the week, $2,800 plus tax. Bank credit card sales for the week, $800 plus tax. Bank credit card fee is 3%.

20 Received payment on account from Tom Wilson, $1,110.

21 Ansel Manufacturing returned merchandise for a credit, $22 plus tax.

21 Cash sales for the week, $3,200 plus tax.

24 Received payment on account from Rachel Carson, $2,000.

Beginning general ledger account balances were:

Cash	$9,862
Accounts Receivable	$9,352

Beginning customer account balances were:

M. Anderson	$2,480
Ansel Manufacturing	982
J. Gorbea	880
R. Carson	3,200
T. Wilson	1,810

REQUIRED

1. Record the transactions in the cash receipts journal. Total and verify column totals and rule the columns. Use the general journal to record sales returns and allowances.

2. Post the journals to the general ledger and to the accounts receivable ledger accounts. Use account numbers as shown in the chapter.

W & D

PROBLEM 11A-3 (LO 3/4) SALES JOURNAL, CASH RECEIPTS JOURNAL, AND GENERAL JOURNAL Owens Distributors is a retail business. The following sales, returns, and cash receipts occurred during March 20--. There is an 8% sales tax. Beginning general ledger account balances were: Cash, $9,741.00; and Accounts Receivable, $1,058.25. Beginning customer account balances were: Thompson Group, $1,058.25.

March 1 Sale no. 33C to Able & Co., $1,800 plus sales tax.

3 Sale no. 33D to R. J. Kalas, Inc., $2,240 plus sales tax.

5 Able & Co. returned merchandise from sale no. 33C for a credit (credit memo no. 66), $30 plus sales tax.

7 Cash sales for the week, $3,160 plus sales tax.

10 Received payment from Able & Co. for sale no. 33C less credit memo no. 66.

(continued)

11   Sale no. 33E to Blevins Bakery, $1,210 plus sales tax.

13   Received payment from R. J. Kalas for sale no. 33D.

14   Cash sales for the week, $4,200 plus sales tax.

16   Blevins Bakery returned merchandise from sale no. 33E for a credit (credit memo no. 67), $44 plus sales tax.

18   Sale no. 33F to R. J. Kalas, Inc., $2,620 plus sales tax.

20   Received payment from Blevins Bakery for sale no. 33E less credit memo no. 67.

21   Cash sales for the week, $2,400 plus sales tax.

25   Sale no. 33G to Blevins Bakery, $1,915 plus sales tax.

27   Sale no. 33H to Thompson Group, $2,016 plus sales tax.

28   Cash sales for the week, $3,500 plus sales tax.

REQUIRED   1.   Record the transactions in the sales journal, the cash receipts journal, and the general journal. Total, verify, and rule the columns where appropriate at the end of the month.

2.   Post from the journals to the general ledger and accounts receivable ledger accounts. Use account numbers as shown in the chapter.

PROBLEM 11A-4 (LO 5) SCHEDULE OF ACCOUNTS RECEIVABLE Based on the information provided in Problem 11A-3, prepare a schedule of accounts receivable for Owens Distributors as of March 31, 20--. Verify that the accounts receivable account balance in the general ledger agrees with the schedule of accounts receivable total.

SERIES B EXERCISES

EXERCISE 11B-1 (LO 1) SALES DOCUMENTS Indicate whether each of the following documents or procedures is for a retail business or for a wholesale business, as described in the chapter.

1.   A cash register receipt is given to the customer.

2.   Credit approval is required since sales are almost always "on account."

3.   Three copies of the sales invoice are prepared: one for shipping, one for the customer (as a bill), and one for accounting.

4.   A sales ticket is given to a customer and another copy is sent to accounting.

5.   The sales process begins with a customer purchase order.

6.   The sales invoice itemizes what is sold, its cost, and the total amount owed.

EXERCISE 11B-2 (LO 2) SALES TRANSACTIONS AND ACCOUNTS Using T accounts for Cash, Accounts Receivable, Sales Tax Payable, Sales, Sales Returns and Allowances, and Sales Discounts, enter the following sales transactions. Use a new set of accounts for each part, 1–5.

1.   No sales tax.

    (a) Merchandise is sold for $250 cash.

    (b) Merchandise is sold on account for $225.

    (c) Payment is received for merchandise sold on account.

2. 6% sales tax.

    (a) Merchandise is sold for $250 cash plus sales tax.

    (b) Merchandise is sold on account for $225 plus sales tax.

    (c) Payment is received for merchandise sold on account.

3. Cash and credit sales, with returned merchandise.

    (a) Merchandise is sold for $481 cash.

    (b) $18 of merchandise sold for $481 is returned for a refund.

    (c) Merchandise is sold on account for $388.

    (d) $24 of merchandise sold for $388 is returned for a credit.

    (e) Payment is received for balance owed on merchandise sold on account.

4. 6% sales tax, with returned merchandise.

    (a) Merchandise is sold on account for $480 plus sales tax.

    (b) Merchandise totaling $30 is returned.

    (c) The balance on the account is paid in cash.

    (d) Merchandise is sold for $300 cash plus sales tax.

    (e) $30 of merchandise sold for $300 cash is returned for a refund.

5. Sales on account, with 2/10, n/30 cash discount terms.

    (a) Merchandise is sold on account for $280.

    (b) The balance is paid within the discount period.

EXERCISE 11B-3 (LO 2) COMPUTING NET SALES Based on the following information, compute net sales.

Gross sales	$2,880
Sales returns and allowances	322
Sales discounts	56

EXERCISE 11B-4 (LO 3) JOURNALIZING SALES TRANSACTIONS Enter the following transactions (a) in a general journal and (b) in a sales journal. Use a 5% sales tax rate.

Sept. 1 Sold merchandise on account to K. Smith, $1,800 plus sales tax. Sale no. 228.

    3 Sold merchandise on account to J. Arnes, $3,100 plus sales tax. Sale no. 229.

    5 Sold merchandise on account to M. Denison, $2,800 plus sales tax. Sale no. 230.

    7 Sold merchandise on account to B. Marshall, $1,900 plus sales tax. Sale no. 231

EXERCISE 11B-5 (LO 3) JOURNALIZING SALES RETURNS AND ALLOWANCES Enter the following transactions in a general journal and post them to the appropriate general ledger and accounts receivable ledger accounts. Use account numbers as shown in the chapter. Beginning balance in Accounts Receivable is $3,900. Beginning balances in customer accounts are: Phillips, $1,018; Adams, $850; and Green, $428.

(continued)

June 1 Marie L. Phillips returned merchandise previously purchased on account (sale no. 33), $43.

11 John B. Adams returned merchandise previously purchased on account (sale no. 34), $59.

15 L. B. Greene returned merchandise previously purchased on account (sale no. 35), $21.

EXERCISE 11B-6 (LO 4) JOURNALIZING CASH RECEIPTS Enter the following transactions (a) in the general journal and (b) in a cash receipts journal.

Nov. 1 Jean Haghighat made payment on account, $750.

12 Marc Antonoff made payment on account, $464.

15 Cash sales, $3,763.

18 Will Mossein made payment on account, $241.

25 Cash sales, $2,648.

EXERCISE 11B-7 (LO 5) SCHEDULE OF ACCOUNTS RECEIVABLE From the accounts receivable ledger shown, prepare a schedule of accounts receivable for Gelph Co. as of November 30, 20--.

ACCOUNTS RECEIVABLE LEDGER

NAME James L. Adams Co.

ADDRESS 24481 McAdams Road, Dallas, TX 77001-3465

DATE		ITEM	POST REF.	DEBIT	CREDIT	BALANCE
20-- Nov.	1		S11	3 1 8 0 00		3 1 8 0 00
	5		J8		1 8 0 00	3 0 0 0 00
	7		S11	2 0 0 00		3 2 0 0 00

NAME Trish Berens

ADDRESS 34 West 55th Avenue, Fort Worth, TX 76310-8182

DATE		ITEM	POST REF.	DEBIT	CREDIT	BALANCE
20-- Nov.	3		S11	1 3 6 0 00		1 3 6 0 00

NAME M and T Jenkins, Inc.

ADDRESS 100 NW Richfield, Austin, TX 78481-3791

DATE		ITEM	POST REF.	DEBIT	CREDIT	BALANCE
20-- Nov.	5		S11	2 6 2 8 00		2 6 2 8 00
	12		CR11		2 6 2 8 00	--

NAME R & J Travis

ADDRESS 288 Beacon Street, Dallas, TX 79301-6642

DATE		ITEM	POST REF.	DEBIT	CREDIT	BALANCE
20-- Nov.	22		S11	1 8 4 2 00		1 8 4 2 00

SERIES B PROBLEMS

PROBLEM 11B-1 (LO 3) SALES JOURNAL T. M. Maxwell owns a retail business and made the following sales during the month of July 20--. There is a 5% sales tax on all sales.

July 1   Sale no. 101 to Saga, Inc., $1,200 plus sales tax.

8   Sale no. 102 to Vinnie Ward, $2,100 plus sales tax.

15   Sale no. 103 to Dvorak Manufacturing, $4,300 plus sales tax.

21   Sale no. 104 to Vinnie Ward, $1,800 plus sales tax.

24   Sale no. 105 to Zapata Co., $1,600 plus sales tax. (Open a new account for this customer. Address is 789 N. Stafford Dr., Bloomington, IN 47401-6201.)

29   Sale no. 106 to Saga, Inc., $1,450 plus sales tax.

REQUIRED

1. Record the transactions in the sales journal. Total and verify the column totals and rule the columns.

2. Post the sales journal to the general ledger accounts and to the accounts receivable ledger accounts. Use account numbers as shown in the chapter.

PROBLEM 11B-2 (LO 4) CASH RECEIPTS JOURNAL Color Florists, a retail business, had the following cash receipts during January 20--. The sales tax is 5%.

Jan. 1   Received payment on account from Ray Boyd, $880.

3   Received payment on account from Clint Hassell, $271.

5   Cash sales for the week, $2,800 plus tax. Bank credit card sales for the week, $1,200 plus tax. Bank credit card fee is 3%.

8   Received payment on account from Jan Sowada, $912.

11   Ray Boyd returned merchandise for a credit, $40 plus tax.

12   Cash sales for the week, $3,100 plus tax. Bank credit card sales for the week, $1,900 plus tax. Bank credit card fee is 3%.

15   Received payment on account from Robert Zehnle, $1,100.

18   Robert Zehnle returned merchandise for a credit, $31 plus tax.

19   Cash sales for the week, $2,230 plus tax.

25   Received payment on account from Dazai Manufacturing, $318.

Beginning general ledger account balances were:

| Cash | $2,890.75 |
| Accounts Receivable | 6,300.00 |

Beginning customer account balances were:

R. Boyd	$1,400
Dazai Manufacturing	318
C. Hassell	815
J. Sowada	1,481
R. Zehnle	2,286

(continued)

REQUIRED
1. Record the transactions in the cash receipts journal. Total and verify the column totals and rule the columns. Use the general journal to record sales returns and allowances.

2. Post the journals to the general ledger and to the accounts receivable ledger accounts. Use account numbers as shown in the chapter.

PROBLEM 11B-3 (LO 3/4) SALES JOURNAL, CASH RECEIPTS JOURNAL, GENERAL JOURNAL Paul Jackson owns a retail business. The following sales, returns, and cash receipts are for April 20--. There is a 7% sales tax.

April 1 Sale no. 111 to O. L. Meyers, $2,100 plus sales tax.

3 Sale no. 112 to Andrew Plaa, $1,000 plus sales tax.

6 O. L. Meyers returned merchandise from sale no. 111 for a credit (credit memo no. 42), $50 plus sales tax.

7 Cash sales for the week, $3,240 plus sales tax.

9 Received payment from O. L. Meyers for sale no. 111 less credit memo no. 42.

12 Sale no. 113 to Melissa Richfield, $980 plus sales tax.

14 Cash sales for the week, $2,180 plus sales tax.

17 Melissa Richfield returned merchandise from sale no. 113 for a credit (credit memo no. 43), $40 plus sales tax.

19 Sale no. 114 to Kelsay Munkres, $1,020 plus sales tax.

21 Cash sales for the week, $2,600 plus sales tax.

24 Sale no. 115 to O. L. Meyers, $920 plus sales tax.

27 Sale no. 116 to Andrew Plaa, $1,320 plus sales tax.

28 Cash sales for the week, $2,800 plus sales tax.

Beginning general ledger account balances were:

Cash	$2,864.54
Accounts Receivable	2,726.25

Beginning customer account balances were:

O. L. Meyers	$2,186.00
K. Munkres	482.00
M. Richfield	58.25

REQUIRED
1. Record the transactions in the sales journal, the cash receipts journal, and the general journal. Total, verify, and rule the columns where appropriate at the end of the month.

2. Post from the journals to the general ledger and accounts receivable ledger accounts. Use account numbers as shown in the chapter.

PROBLEM 11B-4 (LO 5) SCHEDULE OF ACCOUNTS RECEIVABLE Based on the information provided in Problem 11B-3, prepare a schedule of accounts receivable for Paul Jackson as of April 30, 20--. Verify that the accounts receivable account balance in the general ledger agrees with the schedule of accounts receivable total.

MASTERY PROBLEM

W & D

Geoff and Sandy Harland own and operate Wayward Kennel and Pet Supply. Their motto is, "If your pet is not becoming to you, he should be coming to us." The Harlands maintain a sales tax payable account throughout the month to account for the 6% sales tax. They use a sales journal, a cash receipts journal, and a general journal. The following sales and cash collections took place during the month of September.

Sept. 2   Sold a fish aquarium on account to Ken Shank, $125.00 plus tax of $7.50, terms n/30. Sale no. 101.

3   Sold dog food on account to Nancy Truelove, $68.25 plus tax of $4.10, terms n/30. Sale no. 102.

5   Sold a bird cage on account to Jean Warkentin, $43.95 plus tax of $2.64, terms n/30. Sale no. 103.

8   Cash sales for the week, $2,332.45 plus tax of $139.95.

10   Received cash for boarding and grooming services, $625.00 plus tax of $37.50.

11   Jean Warkentin stopped by the store to point out a minor defect in the bird cage purchased in sale no. 103. The Harlands offered a sales allowance of $10.00 plus tax on the price of the cage which satisfied Warkentin.

12   Sold a cockatoo on account to Tully Shaw, $1,200.00 plus tax of $72.00, terms n/30. Sale no. 104.

14   Received cash on account from Rosa Alanso, $256.00

15   Rosa Alanso returned merchandise, $93.28 including tax of $5.28.

15   Cash sales for the week, $2,656.85 plus tax of $159.41.

16   Received cash on account from Nancy Truelove, $58.25.

18   Received cash for boarding and grooming services, $535.00 plus tax of $32.10.

19   Received cash on account from Ed Cochran, $63.25.

20   Sold pet supplies on account to Susan Hays, $83.33 plus tax of $5.00, terms n/30. Sale no. 105.

21   Sold three Labrador Retriever puppies to All American Day Camp, $375.00 plus tax of $22.50, terms n/30. Sale no. 106.

22   Cash sales for the week, $3,122.45 plus tax of $187.35.

23   Received cash for boarding and grooming services, $515.00 plus tax of $30.90.

25   Received cash on account from Ken Shank, $132.50.

26   Received cash on account from Nancy Truelove, $72.35.

27   Received cash on account from Joe Gloy, $273.25.

28   Borrowed cash to purchase a pet limousine, $11,000.00.

29   Cash sales for the week, $2,835.45 plus tax of $170.13.

30   Received cash for boarding and grooming services, $488.00 plus tax of $29.28.

(continued)

Wayward had the following general ledger account balances as of September 1:

Account Title	Account No.	General Ledger Balance on Sept. 1
Cash	101	$23,500.25
Accounts Receivable	122	850.75
Notes Payable	201	2,500.00
Sales Tax Payable	231	909.90
Sales	401	13,050.48
Sales Returns and Allowances	401.1	86.00
Boarding and Grooming Revenue	402	2,115.00

Wayward also had the following accounts receivable ledger balances as of September 1:

Customer	Accounts Receivable Balance
Rosa Alanso 2541 East 2nd Street Bloomington, IN 47401-5356	$456.00
Ed Cochran 2669 Windcrest Drive Bloomington, IN 47401-5446	$63.25
Joe Gloy 1458 Parnell Avenue Muncie, IN 47304-2682	$273.25
Nancy Truelove 2300 E. National Road Cumberland, IN 46229-4824	$58.25

New customers opening accounts during September were:

All American Day Camp
3025 Old Mill Run
Bloomington, IN 47408-1080

Tully Shaw
3315 Longview Avenue
Bloomington, IN 47401-7223

Susan Hays
1424 Jackson Creek Road
Nashville, IN 47448-2245

Jean Warkentin
1813 Deep Well Court
Bloomington, IN 47401-5124

Ken Shank
6422 E. Bender Road
Bloomington, IN 47401-7756

REQUIRED

1. Enter the transactions for the month of September in the proper journals.

2. Enter the totals and rule the journals where appropriate.

3. Post the entries to the general and subsidiary ledgers. Open new accounts for any customers who did not have a balance as of September 1.

4. Prepare a schedule of accounts receivable.

5. Compute the net sales for the month of September.

Self-Study Test Questions

True/False

1. All sales, for cash or on credit, are recorded in the sales journal. _____

2. Reductions in the price of merchandise granted by the seller because of defects or other problems with the merchandise are called sales allowances. _____

3. Sales Tax Payable is a liability account that is credited for the amount of tax imposed on sales. _____

4. Sales Returns and Allowances is debited for the amount of the sale, including the sales tax on that amount. _____

5. Cash discounts are offered to encourage prompt payment by customers who buy on account. _____

Multiple Choice

1. A credit sale of $250 plus a 6 percent sales tax would require a debit to Accounts Receivable of _____

    (a) $15.
    (b) $280.
    (c) $30.
    (d) $265.

2. When $25 of merchandise is returned for a credit on account, what is the amount of the credit to Accounts Receivable, assuming a 6 percent sales tax rate? _____

    (a) $1.50
    (b) $25.00
    (c) $26.50
    (d) $31.00

3. When $300, plus sales tax of 6 percent, is received for an amount previously owed, Cash is debited for what amount? _____

    (a) $18
    (b) $318
    (c) $300
    (d) $282

4. When credit sales are $325 plus sales tax of 5 percent, and there is a bank credit card fee of 3 percent, what is the debit to Bank Credit Card Expense? _____

    (a) $16.25
    (b) $10.24
    (c) $341.25
    (d) $331.01

5. In the cash receipts journal, each amount in the General Credit column is posted _____

    (a) daily.
    (b) weekly.
    (c) end of month.
    (d) not posted.

The answers to the Self-Study Test Questions are at the end of the text.

12

Accounting for Purchases and Cash Payments

LEARNING OBJECTIVES:
Careful study of this chapter should enable you to:

LO 1 Define merchandise purchases transactions.

LO 2 Describe and use merchandise purchases accounts.

LO 3 Describe and use the purchases journal and accounts payable ledger.

LO 4 Describe and use the cash payments journal and accounts payable ledger.

LO 5 Prepare a schedule of accounts payable.

In the early months of operating Be A Sport, John Zenith paid for his purchases by issuing a check to the vendors who delivered the items to his store. His store was new, so manufacturers and vendors would not sell to him on account. Accounting for such purchases was simple. As the business succeeded, John was able to buy on account and have merchandise shipped to him. He had to pay the freight charges on such shipments. He also found that he was eligible for various discounts on his purchases and could return items for credit on his account. Accounting for purchases has become much more complicated. How should John's bookkeeper account for items like freight charges, discounts, and credits for purchases that he returns to the manufacturer or vendor?

Chapter 11 demonstrated how to account for sales in a merchandising business. This chapter continues the study of the merchandising business by examining how to account for merchandise purchases. We will learn how to use four new accounts, two more special journals, and another subsidiary ledger.

MERCHANDISE PURCHASES TRANSACTIONS

LO 1   Define merchandise purchases transactions.

In everyday language, purchases can refer to almost anything we have bought. For a merchandising business, however, **purchases** refers to merchandise acquired for resale. These are the goods a business buys for the sole purpose of selling them to its customers.

Purchasing procedures and documents vary, depending on the nature and size of a business. For example, in a small business, the owner or an employee might do the buying on a part-time basis. In a large business, there might be a separate purchasing department with a full-time manager and staff. In addition, the procedures and documents used can be affected by whether purchases are made on account or for cash.

The flowchart in Figure 12-1 shows some of the major documents used in the purchasing process of a merchandising business. In discussing the purchasing process, we will assume that the business makes purchases on account and has a purchasing department.

FIGURE 12-1 Purchasing Process Documents

Purchase Requisition

A **purchase requisition** is a form used to request the purchase of merchandise or other property. Any authorized person or department can prepare this form and submit it to the purchasing department. Figure 12-2 shows a purchase requisition used by Northern Micro. One copy of this form is sent to the purchasing department, one to the accounting department, and one is kept by the department that prepared the requisition.

FIGURE 12-2 Purchase Requisition

Purchase Order

The purchasing department reviews and approves the purchase requisition and prepares a purchase order. A **purchase order** is a written order to buy goods from a specific vendor (supplier). Figure 12-3 shows a purchase order prepared by Northern Micro based on the purchase requisition in Figure 12-2. One copy of the purchase order is sent to the vendor to order the goods, one to the accounting department, and one copy is kept in the purchasing department. Other copies may be sent to the department that prepared the purchase requisition, and to the receiving area.

FIGURE 12-3 Purchase Order

Receiving Report and Purchase Invoice

When the merchandise is received, a **receiving report** indicating what has been received is prepared. The receiving report can be a separate form, or one can be created from the vendor's purchase invoice. Figure 12-4 shows a vendor invoice on which a rubber stamp has been used to imprint a type of receiving report. The receiving clerk has indicated on the form the date and condition of the goods received.

FIGURE 12-4 Purchase Invoice

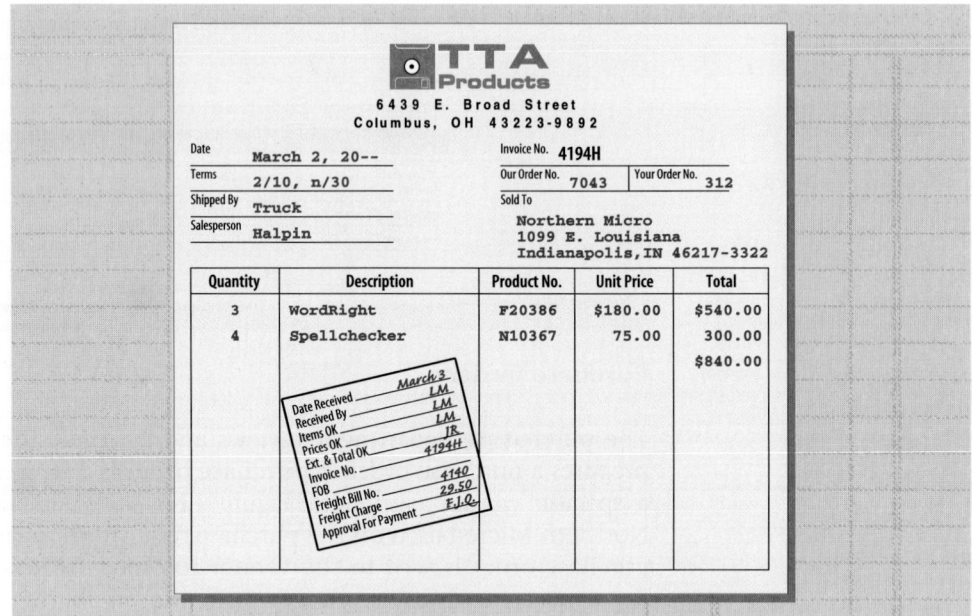

An **invoice** is a document prepared by the seller as a bill for the merchandise shipped. To the seller, this is a sales invoice, as explained in Chapter 11. To the buyer, this is a **purchase invoice**. Figure 12-4 shows an invoice sent by TTA Products to Northern Micro for the goods ordered with the purchase order in Figure 12-3.

The accounting department compares the purchase invoice with the purchase requisition, purchase order, and receiving report. If the invoice is for the goods ordered and the correct price, the invoice is paid by the due date.

This is an example of good internal control. The procedure helps ensure that the business pays only for goods it ordered and received, and at the correct price.

Cash and Trade Discounts

Notice that the invoice in Figure 12-4 shows terms of 2/10, n/30. These are the same credit terms discussed in Chapter 11. A discount is available if the bill is paid within the discount period. The only difference is that we are now looking from the buyer's point of view rather than the seller's. We will see how to account for these discounts later in the chapter.

Another type of discount, called a **trade discount**, is often offered by manufacturers and wholesalers. This discount is a reduction from the list or catalog price offered to different classes of customers. By simply adjusting the trade discount percentages, companies can avoid the cost of reprinting catalogs every time there is a change in prices. Trade discounts are usually shown as a deduction from the total amount of the invoice. For example, the invoice in Figure 12-5 includes a trade discount of 10%. The amount to be entered in the accounting records for this invoice is $756, the net amount after deducting the trade discount of $84. Trade discounts represent a reduction in the price of the merchandise and should not be entered in the accounts of either the seller or the buyer.

FIGURE 12-5 Purchase Invoice with Trade Discount

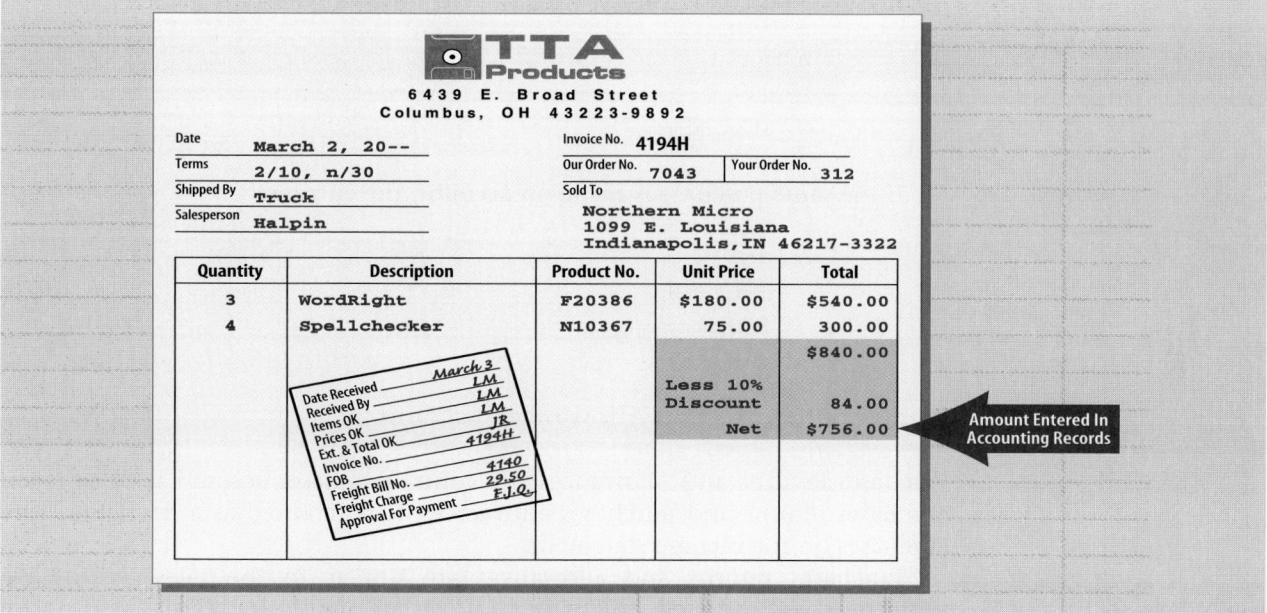

We need to be careful in computing the cash discount when an invoice has both cash and trade discounts. The cash discount applies to the *net amount* after deducting the trade discount. For example, the cash discount and amount to be paid on the invoice in Figure 12-5 would be calculated as follows:

Gross amount	$840.00
Less 10% trade discount	84.00
Net amount	$756.00
Less 2% cash discount	15.12
Amount to be paid	$740.88

MERCHANDISE PURCHASES ACCOUNTS

LO 2   Describe and use merchandise purchases accounts.

To account for merchandise purchases transactions, we will use four new accounts:

1. Purchases

2. Purchases Returns and Allowances

3. Purchases Discounts

4. Freight-In

Purchases Account

The purchases account is used to record the cost of merchandise purchased.

Purchases

Debit	Credit
to enter the cost of merchandise purchased	

If a $100 purchase is made for cash, the following entry is made:

5		Purchases	1 0 0 00		5
6		Cash		1 0 0 00	6
7		Made cash purchase			7

If the same purchase is made on account, the entry is:

5		Purchases	1 0 0 00		5
6		Accounts Payable		1 0 0 00	6
7		Made purchase on account			7

Purchases Returns and Allowances Account

Purchases Returns and Allowances is a contra-purchases account used to record purchases returns and purchases allowances. It is reported as a deduction from Purchases on the income statement.

Purchases returns and allowances are similar to the sales returns and allowances we discussed in Chapter 11. We are simply looking at returns and allowances from the buyer's point of view. If merchandise is returned to a supplier, or the supplier grants a price reduction because of defects or other problems with merchandise purchased, Purchases Returns and Allowances is credited.

Purchases Returns and Allowances

Debit	Credit
	to enter returns and allowances

If merchandise that was purchased on account for $200 is defective and is returned to the supplier, the following entry is made:

9		Accounts Payable	2 0 0 00		9
10		Purchases Returns and Allowances		2 0 0 00	10
11		Returned merchandise			11

If the same merchandise is retained but the supplier grants a price reduction of $45 because of the defects, the entry is:

9		Accounts Payable	4 5 00		9
10		Purchases Returns and Allowances		4 5 00	10
11		Allowance for defective merchandise			11

Purchases Discounts Account

Purchases Discounts is a contra-purchases account used to record cash discounts allowed on purchases. Like Purchases Returns and Allowances, it is reported as a deduction from Purchases on the income statement.

Purchases Discounts

Debit	Credit
	for cash discounts taken

If merchandise is purchased for $100 on account, with credit terms of 2/10, n/30, the following entry is made:

14	Purchases		1 0 0 00		14
15	Accounts Payable			1 0 0 00	15
16	Made purchase on account				16

If payment for the merchandise is subsequently made within the discount period, the entry is:

18	Accounts Payable		1 0 0 00		18
19	Cash			9 8 00	19
20	Purchases Discounts			2 00	20
21	Made payment on account				21

Note the parts of this entry. Accounts Payable is debited for $100, the full amount of the invoice, because the entire debt has been satisfied. Cash is credited for only $98 because that is all that was required to pay the debt. The difference of $2 ($100 – $98) is credited to Purchases Discounts, which represents a reduction in the purchase price of the merchandise. That is why Purchases Discounts is deducted from Purchases on the income statement.

> This approach to accounting for purchases discounts is known as the "gross-price method." The "net-price method" is described in the Appendix.

Freight-In Account

Freight-In is an adjunct-purchases account used to record transportation charges on merchandise purchases. It is added to Purchases on the income statement.

Freight-In

Debit	Credit
for transportation charges on merchandise purchases	

Transportation charges are expressed in FOB (free on board) terms that indicate who is responsible for paying the freight costs. **FOB shipping point** means that transportation charges are paid by the buyer. **FOB destination** means that transportation charges are paid by the seller.

When the terms are FOB shipping point, either the freight charges will be listed separately on the purchase invoice or a separate freight bill will be sent.

Assume Northern Micro receives an invoice for $400 plus freight charges of $38. The entry for this purchase is:

25	Purchases		4	0	0	00						25
26	Freight-In			3	8	00						26
27	Accounts Payable							4	3	8	00	27
28	Made purchase on account											28

Assume instead that Northern Micro receives an invoice for $400 for the same merchandise, shipped FOB shipping point. Northern Micro then receives a separate bill from the transportation company for $38. These two transactions are entered as follows:

30	Purchases		4	0	0	00						30
31	Accounts Payable							4	0	0	00	31
32	Made purchase on account											32
33												33
34	Freight-In			3	8	00						34
35	Accounts Payable								3	8	00	35
36	Freight charges on merchandise purchase											36

When the terms are FOB destination, generally no freight charges appear on the purchase invoice. The buyer simply records the purchase at the amount of the invoice. The freight-in account is not used in recording this purchase.

Computation of Gross Profit

> Goods available for sale include beginning inventory plus the cost of all goods purchased during the year.

An important step in determining net income for a merchandising business is the calculation of its gross profit. **Gross profit** (also called **gross margin**) is the difference between net sales and cost of goods sold. **Cost of goods sold** (also called **cost of merchandise sold**) is the difference between the goods available for sale and the ending inventory. It indicates the cost of the goods sold during the period. Gross profit provides very important information. It tells management the amount of sales dollars available to cover expenses, after covering the cost of the goods sold.

LEARNING KEY: Net sales − cost of goods sold = gross profit.

To compute gross profit, we use two of the four new accounts described in Chapter 11, the four new accounts described above, and the merchandise inventory balances. Assume that Northern Micro has the following sales, purchases, and merchandise inventory balances for the year ended December 31, 20--.

From Chapter 11		
	Sales	$200,500
	Sales returns and allowances	1,200

From Chapter 12		
	Purchases	105,000
	Purchases returns and allowances	800
	Purchases discounts	1,000
	Freight-In	300
	Merchandise inventory, January 1, 20--	26,000
	Merchandise inventory, December 31, 20--	18,000

Figure 12-6 uses these balances to compute net sales, net purchases, cost of goods sold, and gross profit. The following four steps in computing gross profit are labeled in the figure.

STEP 1   Compute net sales.

(Sales – sales returns and allowances)

STEP 2   Compute goods available for sale.

(Beginning inventory + cost of goods purchased)

STEP 3   Compute cost of goods sold.

(Goods available for sale – ending inventory)

STEP 4   Compute gross profit.

(Net sales – cost of goods sold)

FIGURE 12-6 Computation of Gross Profit

Sales					$200 5 0 0 00		
Less sales returns and allowances					1 2 0 0 00		
Step 1 ▷ **Net sales**						$199 3 0 0 00	
Cost of goods sold:							
Merchandise inventory, Jan. 1					$ 26 0 0 0 00		
Purchases			$105 0 0 0 00				
Less: Purchases returns and allowances	$ 8 0 0 00						
Purchases discounts	1 0 0 0 00		1 8 0 0 00				
Net purchases			$103 2 0 0 00				
Add freight-in			3 0 0 00				
Cost of goods purchased					103 5 0 0 00		
Step 2 ▷ **Goods available for sale**					$129 5 0 0 00		
Less merchandise inventory, Dec. 31					18 0 0 0 00		
Step 3 ▷ **Cost of goods sold**						111 5 0 0 00	
Step 4 ▷ **Gross profit**						$ 87 8 0 0 00	

A BROADER VIEW

CASH MANAGEMENT—THOSE DISCOUNTS MATTER

If a business makes a $2,000 purchase on account, with terms of 2/10, n/30, the available discount is only $40 ($2,000 × .02). On the surface, this seems unimportant, like "small change." But take a closer look. If the business does not pay $1,960 ($2,000 − $40) within 10 days, it must pay $2,000 within 30 days. This means that the business would pay $40 for the use of $1,960 for 20 more days. If we assume a 360-day year, the approximate annual interest rate for using the $1,960 for 20 days is 36%.

The innocent looking 2% cash discount represents a very high rate of interest. If a business regularly misses cash discount opportunities, the annual dollar cost can be substantial. For sound cash management, take advantage of discounts.

> In Chapter 17 we discuss how to compute interest. There you will learn to compute the exact interest rate.

JOURNALIZING AND POSTING PURCHASES TRANSACTIONS

LO 3   Describe and use the purchases journal and accounts payable ledger.

To illustrate the journalizing and posting of purchases transactions, we will continue with the transactions of Northern Micro. Assume the following purchases on account occurred during the month of April.

April 4   Purchased merchandise from Compucraft, Inc., $3,300. Invoice no. 631, dated April 2, terms, n/30.

8   Purchased merchandise from Datasoft, $2,500. Invoice no. 927D, dated April 6, terms, n/30.

11   Purchased merchandise from EZX Corp., $8,700. Invoice no. 804, dated April 9, terms, 1/15, n/30.

17   Purchased merchandise from Printpro Corp., $800.
Invoice no. 611, dated April 16, terms, n/30.

23   Purchased merchandise from Televax, Inc., $5,300.
Invoice no. 1465, dated April 22, terms, 1/10, n/30.

These transactions could be entered in a general journal as shown in Figure 12-7.

FIGURE 12-7 Purchases Entered in General Journal

	DATE		DESCRIPTION	POST REF.	DEBIT	CREDIT	
1	20-- Apr.	4	Purchases		3 3 0 0 00		1
2			Accounts Payable/Compucraft			3 3 0 0 00	2
3			Invoice no. 631				3
4							4
5		8	Purchases		2 5 0 0 00		5
6			Accounts Payable/Datasoft			2 5 0 0 00	6
7			Invoice no. 927D				7
8							8
9		11	Purchases		8 7 0 0 00		9
10			Accounts Payable/EZX			8 7 0 0 00	10
11			Invoice no. 804				11
12							12
13		17	Purchases		8 0 0 00		13
14			Accounts Payable/Printpro			8 0 0 00	14
15			Invoice no. 611				15
16							16
17		23	Purchases		5 3 0 0 00		17
18			Accounts Payable/Televax			5 3 0 0 00	18
19			Invoice no. 1465				19

GENERAL JOURNAL   PAGE 1

The same problem occurs with this approach to recording purchases that occurred in Chapter 11 with sales transactions. The same account titles had to be recorded five times to make these five entries. Similarly, to post these entries to the general ledger, five separate postings would have to be made to each of the two accounts, a total of ten postings.

Fortunately, there is a more efficient way to record purchases on account. A purchases journal is used.

Purchases Journal

A **purchases journal** is a special journal used to record only purchases of merchandise on account. By using a purchases journal, both journalizing and posting of purchases on account is much more efficient.

To illustrate, reconsider the five purchases on account of Northern Micro. They are entered in the purchases journal in Figure 12-8. Northern Micro's pur-

LEARNING KEY: Use a purchases journal only for recording purchases of merchandise on account.

chases journal has a single column for Purchases Debit/Accounts Payable Credit, the two accounts used repeatedly in the general journal in Figure 12-7. A purchase is recorded in the purchases journal by entering the following information:

1. Date

2. Invoice number

3. Supplier (from whom purchased)

4. Dollar amount

There is no need to enter any general ledger account titles, since they appear in the column heading.

FIGURE 12-8 Northern Micro Purchases Journal

							PURCHASES JOURNAL				PAGE 8	
	DATE		INVOICE NO.	FROM WHOM PURCHASED				POST REF.		PURCHASES DEBIT/ACCOUNTS PAYABLE CREDIT			
1	20-- Apr.	4	631	Compucraft, Inc.						3 3 0 0	00		1
2		8	927D	Datasoft						2 5 0 0	00		2
3		11	804	EZX Corp.						8 7 0 0	00		3
4		17	611	Printpro Corp.						8 0 0	00		4
5		23	1465	Televax, Inc.						5 3 0 0	00		5
6										20 6 0 0	00		6

The purchases journal in Figure 12-8 is designed for a company like Northern Micro, whose suppliers generally pay freight charges. For a company that frequently pays freight charges as part of the purchase price of merchandise, a purchases journal like the one in Figure 12-9 would be used. In this case, there are three columns: (1) Purchases Debit, (2) Freight-In Debit, and (3) Accounts Payable Credit. Each special journal should be designed for the particular needs of the company using it.

FIGURE 12-9 Purchases Journal with Freight-In Column

							PURCHASES JOURNAL						
	DATE		INVOICE NO.	FROM WHOM PURCHASED			POST REF.		PURCHASES DEBIT		FREIGHT-IN DEBIT		ACCOUNTS PAYABLE CREDIT

Posting the Purchases Journal

Each general ledger account used in the purchases journal requires only one posting each period. Figure 12-10 illustrates the general ledger posting process for Northern Micro's purchases journal for the month of April.

FIGURE 12-10 Posting the Purchases Journal to the General Ledger

PURCHASES JOURNAL   Page 8

Date	Invoice No.	From Whom Purchased	Post Ref.	Purchases Debit/ Accounts Payable Credit
20--				
Apr. 4	631	Compucraft, Inc.		3,300.00
8	927D	Datasoft		2,500.00
11	804	EZX Corp.		8,700.00
17	611	Printpro Corp.		800.00
23	1465	Televax, Inc.		5,300.00
				20,600.00 **1**
				(501) (202) **3** **1**

GENERAL LEDGER (Partial)

ACCOUNT   Accounts Payable   ACCOUNT NO. 202

	Date	Item	Post Ref.	Debit	Credit	Balance Debit	Balance Credit
	20--						
	Apr. 1	Bal.	✔				4,800.00
2	30		P8		20,600.00		25,400.00

ACCOUNT   Purchases   ACCOUNT NO. 501

	Date	Item	Post Ref.	Debit	Credit	Balance Debit	Balance Credit
	20--						
	Apr. 1	Bal.	✔			17,400.00	
2	30		P8	20,600.00		38,000.00	

The following three steps are used to post from the purchases journal to the general ledger at the end of each month, as indicated in Figure 12-10.

STEP 1   Total and rule the amount column and post the total to the Purchases and Accounts Payable accounts in the general ledger.

STEP 2   Insert the date in the Date column and the initial "P" and the purchases journal page number in the Posting Reference column of each ledger account.

STEP 3   Insert the Purchases and Accounts Payable account numbers in parentheses immediately below the column total in the purchases journal.

The Purchases and Accounts Payable resulting from merchandise purchases on account are now up to date in the general ledger. A record can be kept of the amount owed to each supplier by using a subsidiary **accounts payable ledger.** This is a separate ledger containing an individual account payable for each supplier. If there are many supplier accounts, it is a good practice to assign each supplier an account number. The subsidiary ledger accounts are kept in either alphabetical or numerical order, depending on whether the supplier accounts are identified by number. A summary accounts payable account called a controlling account is maintained in the general ledger. The accounts payable ledger is "subsidiary" to this account.

Figure 12-11 illustrates the use of the accounts payable ledger. The following three steps are used to post from the purchases journal to the accounts payable ledger, as shown in Figure 12-11.

STEP 1   Post the individual purchase amount to the supplier's account on the date the purchase occurs.

FIGURE 12-11 Posting the Purchases Journal to the Accounts Payable Ledger

STEP 2   Insert the date in the Date column and the initial "P" and the purchases journal page number in the Posting Reference column of each supplier account.

STEP 3   Insert a check mark (✔) in the Posting Reference column of the purchases journal to indicate that the amount has been posted.

Note what happens if the accounts payable ledger is posted daily and the general ledger is posted at the end of the month. The accounts payable ledger total will equal the general ledger Accounts Payable total only at the end of the month.

After the posting of the accounts payable ledger and general ledger is completed, the total of the accounts payable ledger balances should equal the Accounts Payable balance in the general ledger.

Purchases Returns and Allowances

If a buyer returns merchandise or is given an allowance for damaged merchandise, a general journal entry is required. Remember, the purchases journal can only be used to enter purchases on account. Assume that on May 4, Northern Micro returns $200 of merchandise to Televax, Inc. These goods were part of the purchase made on April 23. Figure 12-12 shows the general journal entry, general ledger posting, and accounts payable ledger posting for this transaction.

LEARNING KEY: Enter purchases returns and allowances in the general journal.

FIGURE 12-12 Accounting for Purchases Returns and Allowances

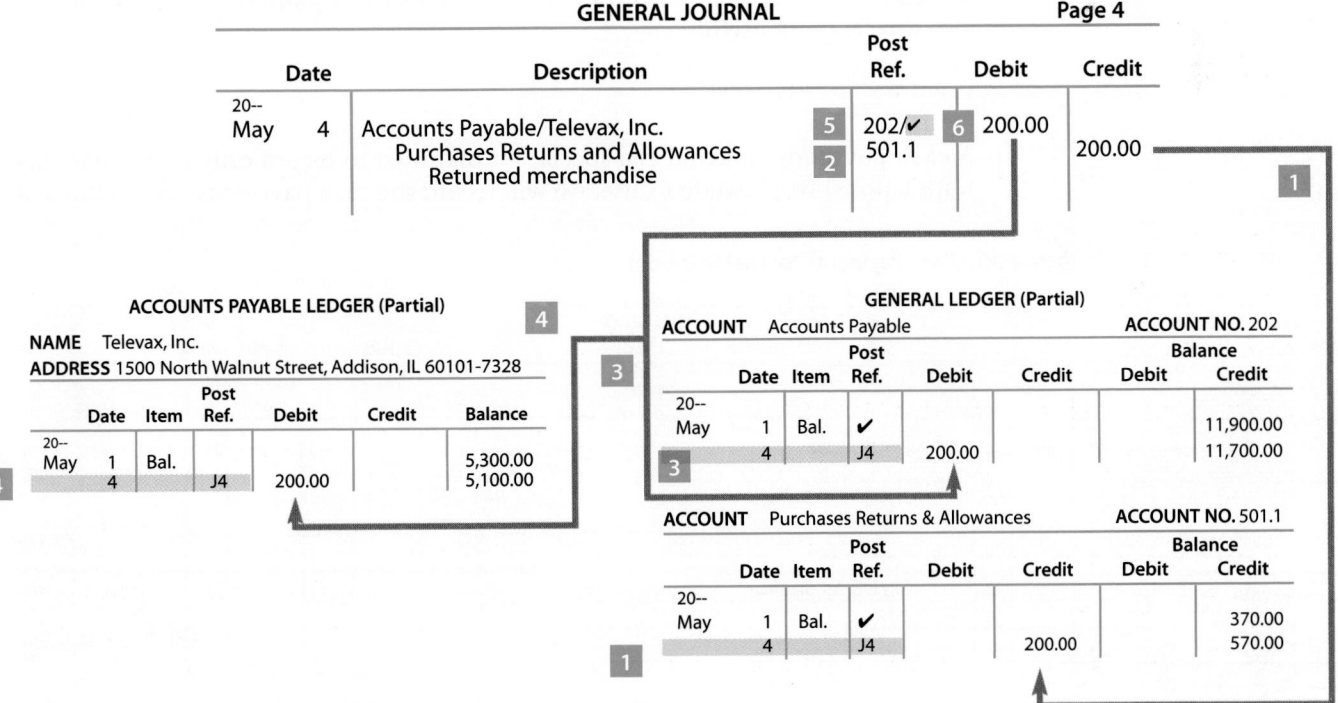

The general journal entry is made in the usual manner. The postings are made daily, using the following six steps:

STEP 1 Post the Purchases Returns and Allowances credit to the general ledger account. Insert the date in the Date column and the general journal reference (J4) in the Posting Reference column.

STEP 2 Insert the general ledger account number in the Posting Reference column of the general journal.

The Accounts Payable debit requires special attention, as follows:

STEP 3 Post the Accounts Payable debit to the general ledger account and insert the date in the Date column and the general journal posting reference (J4) in the Posting Reference column.

STEP 4 Post the same amount to the supplier account in the accounts payable ledger and insert the same date in the Date column and posting reference (J4) in the Posting Reference column.

STEP 5 To indicate that the general ledger has been posted, insert the account number (202) and a slash (/) in the Posting Reference column of the general journal.

STEP 6 To indicate that the supplier account has been posted, insert a check mark (✔) following the slash in the Posting Reference column of the general journal.

JOURNALIZING AND POSTING CASH PAYMENTS

LO 4 Describe and use the cash payments journal and accounts payable ledger.

Chapter 11 demonstrated how a cash receipts journal can be used to efficiently record cash receipts transactions. Cash payments transactions generally occur just as frequently as cash receipts transactions, so a special journal for cash payments also can be quite useful.

Cash Payments Journal

A **cash payments journal** is a special journal used to record only cash payments transactions. To illustrate its use, we will record the cash payments transactions of

FIGURE 12-13 Northern Micro Cash Payments Journal (left side)

	DATE		CK. NO.	ACCOUNT DEBITED	POST REF.	GENERAL DEBIT					
1	Apr.	2	307	Rent Expense		2	4	0	0	00	1
2		4	308								2
3		10	309	B. B. Small							3
4		14	310	Notes Payable		2	0	0	0	00	4
5		22	311	Gary L. Fishel, Drawing		1	6	0	0	00	5
6		24	312	EZX Corp.							6
7						6	0	0	0	00	7

LEARNING KEY: Use a cash payments journal to streamline journalizing and posting of cash payments.

Northern Micro. Northern Micro's cash payments journal for the month of April is shown in Figure 12-13. Five types of cash payments transactions are shown:

1. Payment of an expense (April 2)

2. Cash purchase (April 4)

3. Payment of an account payable (April 10 and 24)

4. Payment of a note payable (April 14)

5. Withdrawal by the owner (April 22)

Northern Micro's cash payments journal provides separate columns for Accounts Payable Debit, Purchases Debit, Purchases Discounts Credit, and Cash Credit. These are the accounts most frequently affected by Northern Micro's cash payments transactions. In addition, a General Debit column is provided for debits to any other accounts affected by cash payments transactions. For good internal control over cash payments, all payments (except out of petty cash) should be made by check. Therefore, the cash payments journal also includes a Check No. column.

A cash payment is recorded in the cash payments journal by entering the following information:

1. Date

2. Check number

3. Account debited (if applicable)

4. Dollar amounts

The Account Debited column is used for two purposes:

1. To identify the supplier name for any payment on account. This column is used whenever the Accounts Payable Debit column is used.

2. To enter the appropriate account name whenever the General Debit column is used.

Note that the column is left blank if the entry is for cash purchases.

FIGURE 12-13 Northern Micro Cash Payments Journal (right side)

	ACCOUNTS PAYABLE DEBIT	PURCHASES DEBIT	PURCHASES DISCOUNTS CREDIT	CASH CREDIT	
1				2 4 0 0 00	1
2		1 4 0 0 00		1 4 0 0 00	2
3	4 8 0 0 00			4 8 0 0 00	3
4				2 0 0 0 00	4
5				1 6 0 0 00	5
6	8 7 0 0 00		8 7 00	8 6 1 3 00	6
7	13 5 0 0 00	1 4 0 0 00	8 7 00	20 8 1 3 00	7

Posting the Cash Payments Journal

Figure 12-14 illustrates the general ledger posting process for Northern Micro's cash payments journal.

On a daily basis:

STEP 1   Post each amount in the General Debit column to the appropriate general ledger account.

STEP 2   Insert the date in the Date column and the initials "CP" and the cash payments journal page number in the Posting Reference column of each ledger account.

STEP 3   Insert the general ledger account numbers in the Posting Reference column of the cash payments journal.

At the end of each month:

STEP 4   Total the amount columns, verify that the total of the debit columns equals the total of the credit columns, and rule the columns.

STEP 5   Post each column total except the General Debit column to the general ledger account indicated in the column headings.

STEP 6   Insert the date in the Date column and the initials "CP" and the cash payments journal page number in the Posting Reference column of each ledger account.

STEP 7   Insert the general ledger account numbers below each column total except the General Debit column.

STEP 8   Insert a check mark (✔) in the Posting Reference column for the cash purchases and below the General Debit column.

Postings from the cash payments journal to the accounts payable ledger also must be made. These postings are made daily. Posting procedures are as follows, as shown in Figure 12-15 on page 426.

STEP 1   Post the individual cash payment to the supplier's account on the date the payment occurs.

STEP 2   Insert the date in the Date column and the initials "CP" and the cash payments journal page number in the Posting Reference column of each supplier account.

STEP 3   Insert a check mark (✔) in the Posting Reference column of the cash payments journal to indicate that the amount has been posted.

FIGURE 12-14 Posting the Cash Payments Journal to the General Ledger

CASH PAYMENTS JOURNAL   Page 12

Date	Check No.	Account Debited	Post Ref.	General Debit	Accounts Payable Credit	Purchases Debit	Purchases Discounts Credit	Cash Credit
20--								
Apr. 2	307	Rent Expense	521	2,400.00				2,400.00
4	308		✔			1,400.00		1,400.00
10	309	B. B. Small			4,800.00			4,800.00
14	310	Notes Payable	201	2,000.00				2,000.00
22	311	Gary L. Fishel, Drawing	312	1,600.00				1,600.00
24	312	EZX Corp.			8,700.00		87.00	8,613.00
				6,000.00	13,500.00	1,400.00	87.00	20,813.00
				(✔)	(202)	(501)	(501.2)	(101)

4 Debit total: $ 6,000
13,500
1,400
$20,900

Credit total: $ 87
20,813
$20,900

GENERAL LEDGER (Partial)

ACCOUNT   Cash   ACCOUNT NO. 101

Date	Item	Post Ref.	Debit	Credit	Balance Debit	Balance Credit
20--						
Apr. 1	Bal.	✔			20,000.00	
30		CR7	12,992.00		32,992.00	
30		CP12		20,813.00	12,179.00	

ACCOUNT   Notes Payable   ACCOUNT NO. 201

Date	Item	Post Ref.	Debit	Credit	Balance Debit	Balance Credit
20--						
Apr. 1	Bal.	✔				6,000.00
14		CP12	2,000.00			4,000.00

ACCOUNT   Accounts Payable   ACCOUNT NO. 202

Date	Item	Post Ref.	Debit	Credit	Balance Debit	Balance Credit
20--						
Apr. 1	Bal.	✔				4,800.00
30		P8		20,600.00		25,400.00
30		CP12	13,500.00			11,900.00

ACCOUNT   Gary L. Fishel, Drawing   ACCOUNT NO. 312

Date	Item	Post Ref.	Debit	Credit	Balance Debit	Balance Credit
20--						
Apr. 1	Bal.	✔			4,500.00	
22		CP12	1,600.00		6,100.00	

ACCOUNT   Purchases   ACCOUNT NO. 501

Date	Item	Post Ref.	Debit	Credit	Balance Debit	Balance Credit
20--						
Apr. 1	Bal.	✔			17,400.00	
30		P8	20,600.00		38,000.00	
30		CP12	1,400.00		39,400.00	

ACCOUNT   Purchases Discounts   ACCOUNT NO. 501.2

Date	Item	Post Ref.	Debit	Credit	Balance Debit	Balance Credit
20--						
Apr. 1	Bal.	✔				330.00
30		CP12		87.00		417.00

ACCOUNT   Rent Expense   ACCOUNT NO. 521

Date	Item	Post Ref.	Debit	Credit	Balance Debit	Balance Credit
20--						
Apr. 1	Bal.	✔			6,600.00	
2		CP12	2,400.00		9,000.00	

FIGURE 12-15 Posting the Cash Payments Journal to the Accounts Payable Ledger

CASH PAYMENTS JOURNAL   Page 12

Date	Check No.	Account Debited	Post Ref.	General Debit	Accounts Payable Credit	Purchases Debit	Purchases Discounts Credit	Cash Credit
20--								
Apr. 2	307	Rent Expense	521	2,400.00				2,400.00
4	308		✔			1,400.00		1,400.00
10	309	B. B. Small	✔		4,800.00			4,800.00
14	310	Notes Payable	201	2,000.00				2,000.00
22	311	Gary L. Fishel, Drawing	312	1,600.00				1,600.00
24	312	EZX Corp.	✔		8,700.00		87.00	8,613.00
				6,000.00	13,500.00	1,400.00	87.00	20,813.00
				(✔)	(202)	(501)	(501.2)	(101)

1

ACCOUNTS PAYABLE LEDGER (Partial)

NAME B. B. Small
ADDRESS 2323 High Street, Gurnee, IL 60031-5524

Date	Item	Post Ref.	Debit	Credit	Balance
20--					
Apr. 1	Bal.	✔			4,800.00
2 10		CP12	4,800.00		—

NAME Compucraft, Inc.
ADDRESS 2100 West Main Street, Muncie, IN 47304-8139

Date	Item	Post Ref.	Debit	Credit	Balance
20--					
Apr. 4		P8		3,300.00	3,300.00

NAME Datasoft
ADDRESS 210 Kirkwood, Bloomington, IN 47408-4346

Date	Item	Post Ref.	Debit	Credit	Balance
20--					
Apr. 8		P8		2,500	2,500.00

NAME EZX Corp.
ADDRESS 2928 Rhodes Ave., Chicago, IL 60658-5036

Date	Item	Post Ref.	Debit	Credit	Balance
20--					
Apr. 11		P8		8,700.00	8,700.00
2 24		CP12	8,700.00		—

NAME Printpro Corp.
ADDRESS 1200 Chambers Pike, Lincolnwood, IL 60648-2417

Date	Item	Post Ref.	Debit	Credit	Balance
20--					
Apr. 17		P8		800.00	800.00

NAME Televax, Inc.
ADDRESS 1500 North Walnut Street, Addison, IL 60101-7328

Date	Item	Post Ref.	Debit	Credit	Balance
20--					
Apr. 23		P8		5,300.00	5,300.00

GENERAL LEDGER (Partial)

ACCOUNT Cash   **ACCOUNT NO.** 101

Date	Item	Post Ref.	Debit	Credit	Balance Debit	Balance Credit
20--						
Apr. 1	Bal.	✔			20,000.00	
30		CR7	12,992.00		32,992.00	
30		CP12		20,813.00	12,179.00	

ACCOUNT Notes Payable   **ACCOUNT NO.** 201

Date	Item	Post Ref.	Debit	Credit	Balance Debit	Balance Credit
20--						
Apr. 1	Bal.	✔				6,000.00
14		CP12	2,000.00			4,000.00

ACCOUNT Accounts Payable   **ACCOUNT NO.** 202

Date	Item	Post Ref.	Debit	Credit	Balance Debit	Balance Credit
20--						
Apr. 1	Bal.	✔				4,800.00
30		P8		20,600.00		25,400.00
30		CP12	13,500.00			11,900.00

ACCOUNT Gary L. Fishel, Drawing   **ACCOUNT NO.** 312

Date	Item	Post Ref.	Debit	Credit	Balance Debit	Balance Credit
20--						
Apr. 1	Bal.	✔			4,500.00	
22		CP12	1,600.00		6,100.00	

ACCOUNT Purchases   **ACCOUNT NO.** 501

Date	Item	Post Ref.	Debit	Credit	Balance Debit	Balance Credit
20--						
Apr. 1	Bal.	✔			17,400.00	
30		P8	20,600.00		38,000.00	
30		CP12	1,400.00		39,400.00	

ACCOUNT Purchases Discounts   **ACCOUNT NO.** 501.2

Date	Item	Post Ref.	Debit	Credit	Balance Debit	Balance Credit
20--						
Apr. 1	Bal.	✔				330.00
30		CP12		87.00		417.00

ACCOUNT Rent Expense   **ACCOUNT NO.** 521

Date	Item	Post Ref.	Debit	Credit	Balance Debit	Balance Credit
20--						
Apr. 1	Bal.	✔			6,600.00	
2		CP12	2,400.00		9,000.00	

SCHEDULE OF ACCOUNTS PAYABLE

LO 5   Prepare a schedule of accounts payable.

All postings to the general ledger and accounts payable ledger are now complete. At this point, the Accounts Payable balance in the general ledger should equal the sum of the supplier balances in the accounts payable ledger.

To verify that the sum of the accounts payable ledger balances equals the Accounts Payable balance, a **schedule of accounts payable** is prepared. This is an alphabetical or numerical listing of supplier accounts and balances, usually prepared at the end of the month. Note that suppliers whose account balance is zero are not included. Figure 12-16 shows the schedule of accounts payable for Northern Micro as of April 30.

FIGURE 12-16   Schedule of Accounts Payable

Northern Micro Schedule of Accounts Payable April 30, 20--					
Compucraft, Inc.	$ 3	3	0	0	00
Datasoft	2	5	0	0	00
Printpro Corp.		8	0	0	00
Televax, Inc.	5	3	0	0	00
	$11	9	0	0	00

This schedule is prepared from the list of supplier accounts in the accounts payable ledger. The total calculated in the schedule is compared with the balance in Accounts Payable in the general ledger. Note that the $11,900 total listed in the schedule equals the Accounts Payable balance shown in Figure 12-15. If the schedule total and the Accounts Payable balance do not agree, the error must be located and corrected. To find the error, use the following procedures:

STEP 1   Verify the total of the schedule.

STEP 2   Verify the postings to the accounts payable ledger.

STEP 3   Verify the totals in the purchases and cash payments journals.

STEP 4   Verify the postings to Accounts Payable in the general ledger.

PROFILES in ACCOUNTING

Christy Rankin, Accounts Payable Representative

Christy Rankin credits good training and a willingness to continue to learn for her success as an accounts payable representative for a home builder. After 18 months at Davis Homes LLC, Christy finds her job challenging and rewarding. She uses what she learned in her college accounting classes, including computer accounting, every day at work.

This is Christy's first job since graduating with an Associate Degree in Business Management. She firmly believes her degree, along with the skills she learned in college, has helped her earn a better salary and will continue to pay off in the future.

Christy believes her college education provided her with a foundation and she feels that she is building her skills each day. Asked if she had any advice for today's students, Christy said "stick with it."

Learning Objectives	Key Points to Remember
1 Define merchandise purchases transactions.	For a merchandising business, purchases refers to merchandise acquired for resale. Major documents used in the purchasing process are the purchase requisition, purchase order, receiving report, and purchase invoice.
2 Describe and use merchandise purchases accounts.	Four accounts are used in accounting for merchandise purchases transactions: 1. Purchases 2. Purchases Returns and Allowances 3. Purchases Discounts 4. Freight-In
3 Describe and use the purchases journal and accounts payable ledger.	A purchases journal is a special journal for recording purchases on account. A purchase is recorded by entering the following: 1. Date 2. Invoice number 3. Supplier 4. Dollar amount To post from the purchases journal to the general ledger: 1. Total and rule the amount column and post the total to Purchases and Accounts Payable in the general ledger. 2. Insert the date and posting reference in the ledger accounts. 3. Insert the Purchases and Accounts Payable account numbers below the column total in the purchases journal. An accounts payable ledger is a separate ledger containing an individual account payable for each supplier. To post from the purchases journal to the accounts payable ledger: 1. Post individual purchase amounts to supplier accounts. 2. Insert the date and posting reference in the supplier accounts. 3. Insert a check mark (✔) in the Posting Reference column of the purchases journal. Purchases returns and allowances are recorded in the general journal.
4 Describe and use the cash payments journal and accounts payable ledger.	A cash payments journal is a special journal for recording cash payments. A cash payment is recorded by entering the following: 1. Date 2. Check number 3. Account debited (if applicable) 4. Dollar amounts To post from the cash payments journal to the general ledger:

Learning Objectives	Key Points to Remember
	On a daily basis:
	1. Post General Debit column amounts to the general ledger.
	2. Insert the date and posting reference in the accounts.
	3. Insert the account numbers in the Posting Reference column of the cash payments journal.
	At the end of each month:
	4. Foot, verify the equality of, and rule the amount columns.
	5. Post account column totals to the appropriate general ledger accounts.
	6. Insert the date and posting reference in the accounts.
	7. Insert the account numbers below the specific account column totals.
	8. Insert a check mark (✔) in the Posting Reference column for the cash purchases and below the General Debit column.
	To post from the cash payments journal to the accounts payable ledger:
	1. Post individual cash payments to supplier accounts.
	2. Insert the date and posting reference in the supplier accounts.
	3. Insert a check mark (✔) in the Posting Reference column of the cash payments journal.
5 Prepare a schedule of accounts payable.	The schedule of accounts payable is used to verify that the sum of the accounts payable ledger balances equals the Accounts Payable balance.

Reflection: Answering the Opening Question

Freight charges should be debited to Freight-In and added to the cost of the purchases. Trade discounts should not be entered in the accounts. Purchases should be debited for the net amount paid for the items after deducting trade discounts. Cash discounts should be credited to Purchases Discounts and deducted from the cost of the purchases. The amount of returned purchases should be credited to Purchases Returns and Allowances and deducted from the cost of the purchases.

KEY TERMS

accounts payable ledger, (419)   A separate ledger containing an individual account payable for each supplier.

cash payments journal, (422)   A special journal used to record only cash payments transactions.

cost of goods sold, (414)   The difference between the goods available for sale and the ending inventory.

cost of merchandise sold, (414) See cost of goods sold.

FOB destination, (413) Transportation charges are paid by the seller.

FOB shipping point, (413) Transportation charges are paid by the buyer.

gross margin, (414) See gross profit.

gross profit, (414) The difference between net sales and cost of goods sold.

invoice, (410) A document prepared by the seller as a bill for the merchandise shipped. To the seller, this is a sales invoice. To the buyer, this is a purchase invoice.

purchase invoice, (410) A document prepared by the seller as a bill for the merchandise shipped. To the buyer, this is a purchase invoice.

purchase order, (409) A written order to buy goods from a specific vendor (supplier).

purchase requisition, (408) A form used to request the purchase of merchandise or other property.

purchases, (408) Merchandise acquired for resale to customers.

purchases journal, (417) A special journal used to record only purchases of merchandise on account.

receiving report, (410) A report indicating what has been received.

schedule of accounts payable, (427) An alphabetical or numerical listing of supplier accounts and balances, usually prepared at the end of the month.

trade discount, (410) A reduction from the list or catalog price offered to different classes of customers.

DEMONSTRATION PROBLEM

Jodi Rutman operates a retail pharmacy called Rutman Pharmacy. The books of original entry include a purchases journal in which purchases of merchandise on account are entered, a cash payments journal in which all cash payments (except petty cash) are entered, and a general journal in which entries such as purchases returns and allowances are made. A subsidiary ledger is used for accounts payable. The following are the transactions related to purchases and cash payments for the month of June 20--.

June 1 Purchased merchandise from Sullivan Co. on account, $234.20. Invoice no. 71 dated June 1, terms 2/10, n/30.

2 Issued check no. 536 for payment of June rent (Rent Expense), $1,000.00.

5 Purchased merchandise from Amfac Drug Supply on account, $562.40. Invoice no. 196 dated June 2, terms 1/15, n/30.

7 Purchased merchandise from University Drug Co. on account, $367.35. Invoice no. 914A dated June 5, terms 3/10 eom, n/30.

9 Issued check no. 537 to Sullivan Co. in payment of invoice no. 71 less 2% discount.

12 Received a credit memo from Amfac Drug Supply for merchandise returned that was purchased on June 5, $46.20.

14 Purchased merchandise from Mutual Drug Co. on account, $479.40. Invoice no. 745 dated June 14, terms 2/10, n/30.

15   Received a credit memo from University Drug Co. for merchandise returned that was purchased on June 7, $53.70.

16   Issued check no. 538 to Amfac Drug Supply in payment of invoice no. 196 less the credit memo of June 12 and less 1% discount.

23   Issued check no. 539 to Mutual Drug Co. in payment of invoice no. 745 less 2% discount.

27   Purchased merchandise from Flites Pharmaceuticals on account, $638.47. Invoice no. 675 dated June 27, terms 2/10 eom, n/30.

29   Issued check no. 540 to Dolgin Candy Co. for a cash purchase of merchandise, $270.20.

30   Issued check no. 541 to Vashon Medical Supply in payment of invoice no. 416, $1,217.69. No discount allowed.

REQUIRED   1.   Enter the transactions in a purchases journal, a five-column cash payments journal, and a general journal. Total and rule the purchases and cash payments journals. Prove the cash payments journal.

2.   Post from the journals to the general ledger accounts and the accounts payable ledger. Then, update the account balances.

3.   Prepare a schedule of accounts payable from the accounts payable ledger in the problem. Verify that the total of accounts payable in the schedule equals the June 30 balance of Accounts Payable in the general ledger.

Solution

1,2.

Proof of Cash Payments Journal:

Debit total:		Credit total:	
	$1,000.00		$ 19.43
	2,447.49		3,698.26
	270.20		$3,717.69
	$3,717.69		

(continued)

Cash Payments Journal (left side)

	DATE		CK. NO.	ACCOUNT DEBITED	POST REF.	GENERAL DEBIT		
						CASH PAYMENTS JOURNAL		
1	20-- June	2	536	Rent Expense	521	1 0 0 0 00	1
2		9	537	Sullivan Co.	✔		2
3		16	538	Amfac Drug Supply	✔		3
4		23	539	Mutual Drug Co.	✔		4
5		29	540		✔		5
6		30	541	Vashon Medical Supply	✔		6
7						1 0 0 0 00	7
8						(✔)	8

Cash Payments Journal (right side)

PAGE 4

	ACCOUNTS PAYABLE DEBIT				PURCHASES DEBIT				PURCHASES DISCOUNTS CREDIT			CASH CREDIT				
1												1	0	0	0	00	1
2	2	3	4	20						4	68	2	2	9	52	2
3	5	1	6	20						5	16	5	1	1	04	3
4	4	7	9	40						9	59	4	6	9	81	4
5					2	7	0	20				2	7	0	20	5
6	1	2	1	7 69								1	2	1	7 69	6
7	2	4	4	7 49	2	7	0	20	1	9	43	3	6	9	8 26	7
8	(202)				(501)				(501.2)			(101)				8

	DATE		INVOICE NO.	FROM WHOM PURCHASED	POST REF.	PURCHASES DEBIT/ACCOUNTS PAYABLE CREDIT		
				PURCHASES JOURNAL		PAGE 2		
1	20-- June	1	71	Sullivan Co.	✔	2 3 4 20	1
2		5	196	Amfac Drug Supply	✔	5 6 2 40	2
3		7	914A	University Drug Co.	✔	3 6 7 35	3
4		14	745	Mutual Drug Co.	✔	4 7 9 40	4
5		27	675	Flites Pharmaceuticals	✔	6 3 8 47	5
6						2 2 8 1 82	6
7						(501) (202)	7

	DATE		DESCRIPTION	POST REF.	DEBIT		CREDIT		
			GENERAL JOURNAL				PAGE 4		
1	20-- June	12	Accts. Payable/Amfac Drug Supply	202/✔	4 6 20			1
2			Purchases Returns and Allow.	501.1			4 6 20	2
3			Returned merchandise					3
4								4
5		15	Accts. Payable/University Drug Co.	202/✔	5 3 70			5
6			Purchases Returns and Allow.	501.1			5 3 70	6
7			Returned merchandise					7

2.

GENERAL LEDGER

ACCOUNT: Cash   ACCOUNT NO. 101

DATE		ITEM	POST REF.	DEBIT	CREDIT	BALANCE DEBIT	BALANCE CREDIT
20-- June	1	Balance	✔			9 1 8 0 00	
	30		CP4		3 6 9 8 26	5 4 8 1 74	

ACCOUNT: Accounts Payable   ACCOUNT NO. 202

DATE		ITEM	POST REF.	DEBIT	CREDIT	BALANCE DEBIT	BALANCE CREDIT
20-- June	1	Balance	✔				1 2 1 7 69
	12		J4	4 6 20			1 1 7 1 49
	15		J4	5 3 70			1 1 1 7 79
	30		P2		2 2 8 1 82		3 3 9 9 61
	30		CP4	2 4 4 7 49			9 5 2 12

ACCOUNT: Purchases   ACCOUNT NO. 501

DATE		ITEM	POST REF.	DEBIT	CREDIT	BALANCE DEBIT	BALANCE CREDIT
20-- June	1	Bal.	✔			13 8 2 6 25	
	30		P2	2 2 8 1 82		16 1 0 8 07	
	30		CP4	2 7 0 20		16 3 7 8 27	

ACCOUNT: Purchases Returns and Allowances   ACCOUNT NO. 501.1

DATE		ITEM	POST REF.	DEBIT	CREDIT	BALANCE DEBIT	BALANCE CREDIT
20-- June	1	Balance	✔				3 1 2 63
	12		J4		4 6 20		3 5 8 83
	15		J4		5 3 70		4 1 2 53

ACCOUNT: Purchases Discounts   ACCOUNT NO. 501.2

DATE		ITEM	POST REF.	DEBIT	CREDIT	BALANCE DEBIT	BALANCE CREDIT
20-- June	1	Balance	✔				2 1 1 45
	30		CP4		1 9 43		2 3 0 88

ACCOUNT: Rent Expense   ACCOUNT NO. 521

DATE		ITEM	POST REF.	DEBIT	CREDIT	BALANCE DEBIT	BALANCE CREDIT
20-- June	1	Balance	✔			5 0 0 0 00	
	2		CP4	1 0 0 0 00		6 0 0 0 00	

ACCOUNTS PAYABLE LEDGER

NAME: Amfac Drug Supply

DATE		ITEM	POST REF.	DEBIT	CREDIT	BALANCE
20-- June	5		P2		5 6 2 40	5 6 2 40
	12		J4	4 6 20		5 1 6 20
	16		CP4	5 1 6 20		--

(continued)

NAME: Flites Pharmaceuticals

DATE		ITEM	POST REF.	DEBIT	CREDIT	BALANCE
20-- June	27		P2		6 3 8 47	6 3 8 47

NAME: Mutual Drug Co.

DATE		ITEM	POST REF.	DEBIT	CREDIT	BALANCE
20-- June	14		P2		4 7 9 40	4 7 9 40
	23		CP4	4 7 9 40		--

NAME: Sullivan Co.

DATE		ITEM	POST REF.	DEBIT	CREDIT	BALANCE
20-- June	1		P2		2 3 4 20	2 3 4 20
	9		CP4	2 3 4 20		--

NAME: University Drug Co.

DATE		ITEM	POST REF.	DEBIT	CREDIT	BALANCE
20-- June	7		P2		3 6 7 35	3 6 7 35
	15		J4	5 3 70		3 1 3 65

NAME: Vashon Medical Supply

DATE		ITEM	POST REF.	DEBIT	CREDIT	BALANCE
20-- June	1	Balance	✔			1 2 1 7 69
	30		CP4	1 2 1 7 69		--

3.

Rutman Pharmacy
Schedule of Accounts Payable
June 30, 20--

Flites Pharmaceuticals	$	6	3	8	47
University Drug Co.		3	1	3	65
	$	9	5	2	12
Proof					
Balance of Accounts Payable, June 30	$	9	5	2	12

REVIEW QUESTIONS

1. Identify the major documents commonly used in the purchasing process.

2. Distinguish between a cash discount and a trade discount.

3. Describe how each of the following accounts is used: (1) Purchases, (2) Purchases Returns and Allowances, (3) Purchases Discounts, and (4) Freight-In.

4. How are cost of goods sold and gross profit computed?

5. List four items of information about each purchase entered in the purchases journal.

6. What steps are followed in posting from the purchases journal to the general ledger?

7. What steps are followed in posting from the purchases journal to the accounts payable ledger?

8. What steps are used to post Purchases Returns and Allowances from the general journal to the general ledger and accounts payable ledger?

9. List four items of information about each cash payment entered in the cash payments journal.

10. What steps are followed in posting from the cash payments journal to the general ledger?

11. What steps are followed in posting from the cash payments journal to the accounts payable ledger?

12. If the total of the schedule of accounts payable does not agree with the Accounts Payable balance, what procedures should be used to search for the error?

MANAGING YOUR WRITING

You have a part-time job as a bookkeeper at a local office supply store. The accounting records consist of a general journal and general ledger. The manager is concerned about efficiency and feels that too much time is spent recording transactions. In addition, there sometimes is difficulty determining the amount owed to specific suppliers. The manager knows you are an accounting student and asks for your suggestions to improve the accounting function.

Write a memo to the manager describing how to increase efficiency and accuracy by using different accounting records.

ETHICS CASE

Bob's Discount Auto Parts receives a cash discount of 2 percent from Auto Warehouse if they pay an invoice within 10 days. Bob, the owner, consistently sends payments 15 to 20 days after receiving the invoice and still deducts the amount of the discount. Last week Bob received a call from Auto Warehouse reminding him that in order to get the discount, an invoice must be paid within 10 days. When Bob received the next invoice, he dated the check exactly 10 days from the date of the invoice but didn't mail the check for another week. The Receivables Manager from Auto Warehouse called Bob and again reminded him that the check should be mailed by the 10th day in order to receive the 2 percent discount. When Bob received the next invoice he mailed it on time but postdated the check for the following week.

1. Are Bob's attempts to extend the discount period unethical?

2. What alternatives can Auto Warehouse take to prevent Bob's Discount Auto Parts from stretching the discount period?

3. Write a short note from Auto Warehouse to Bob's Discount Auto Parts explaining cash discounts and credit terms.

4. In small groups make a list of the advantages and disadvantages of offering cash discounts.

WEB WORK

As mentioned in the Chapter 11 question, many retailers are going on-line. More banks are on-line too. Many paychecks are direct deposited and people are seeing less and less physical currency. What happens to cash accounting when there is no more cash? If this sounds farfetched, look at the following site.

PNC Bank is only one of many banks that offers on-line banking:

http://www.pncbank.com
(http://heintz.swcollege.com)

SERIES A EXERCISES

EXERCISE 12A-1 (LO 1) PURCHASING DOCUMENTS AND FLOWCHART LABELING A partially completed flowchart showing some of the major documents commonly used in the purchasing function of a merchandise business is presented below. Identify documents 1, 3, and 4.

EXERCISE 12A-2 (LO 1) TRADE DISCOUNT AND CASH DISCOUNTS Merchandise was purchased on account from Jacob's Distributors on May 17. The purchase price was $2,000, subject to a 10% trade discount and credit terms of 2/10, n/30.

1. Calculate the net amount to record the invoice, subject to the 10% trade discount.

2. Calculate the amount to be paid on this invoice within the discount period.

3. Journalize the purchase of the merchandise on May 17 in a general journal. Journalize the payment on May 27 (within the discount period).

EXERCISE 12A-3 (LO 2) PURCHASE TRANSACTIONS AND T ACCOUNTS Using T accounts for Cash, Accounts Payable, Purchases, Purchases Returns and Allowances, Purchases Discounts, and Freight-In, enter the following purchase transactions. Identify each transaction with its corresponding letter. Use a new set of T accounts for each set of transactions, 1–4.

1. Purchase of merchandise with cash.

   (a) Merchandise is purchased for cash, $1,500.

   (b) Merchandise listed at $3,500, subject to a trade discount of 15%, is purchased for cash.

2. Purchase of merchandise on account with credit terms.

   (a) Merchandise is purchased on account, credit terms 2/10, n/30, $2,000.

   (b) Merchandise is purchased on account, credit terms 3/10, n/30, $1,200.

   (c) Payment is made on invoice (a) within the discount period.

   (d) Payment is made on invoice (b) too late to receive the cash discount.

3. Purchase of merchandise on account with return of merchandise.

   (a) Merchandise is purchased on account, credit terms 2/10, n/30, $4,000.

   (b) Merchandise is returned for credit before payment is made, $500.

   (c) Payment is made within the discount period.

4. Purchase of merchandise with freight-in.

   (a) Merchandise is purchased on account, $2,500 plus freight charges of $100. Terms of the sale were FOB shipping point.

   (b) Payment is made for the cost of merchandise and the freight charge.

EXERCISE 12A-4 (LO 2) GROSS PROFIT The following data were taken from the accounts of Delhi Hardware, a small retail business. Determine the gross profit.

Sales	$113,000
Sales returns and allowances	800
Merchandise inventory, January 1	34,000
Purchases during the period	76,000
Purchases returns and allowances during the period	4,000
Purchases discounts taken during the period	3,000
Freight-in on merchandise purchased during the period	1,500
Merchandise inventory, December 31	30,000

EXERCISE 12A-5 (LO 3) JOURNALIZING TRANSACTIONS IN PURCHASES JOURNAL AND GENERAL JOURNAL

1. Journalize the following transactions in a general journal.

May 3   Purchased merchandise from Cintron, $6,500. Invoice no. 321, dated May 1, terms n/30.

9   Purchased merchandise from Mitsui, $2,300. Invoice no. 614, dated May 8, terms 2/10, n/30.

18   Purchased merchandise from Aloha Distributors, $4,200. Invoice no. 180, dated May 15, terms 1/15, n/30.

23   Purchased merchandise from Soto, $6,300. Invoice no. 913, dated May 22, terms 1/10, n/30.

2. Journalize the transactions in a purchases journal like the one below.

		PURCHASES JOURNAL		PAGE 5
DATE	INVOICE NO.	FROM WHOM PURCHASED	POST REF.	PURCHASES DEBIT/ACCOUNTS PAYABLE CREDIT

EXERCISE 12A-6 (LO 3) JOURNALIZE PURCHASES RETURNS AND ALLOWANCES AND POST TO GENERAL LEDGER AND ACCOUNTS PAYABLE LEDGER Using page 3 of a general journal and the following general ledger and accounts payable ledger accounts, journalize and post the following transactions.

July 7   Merchandise returned to Starcraft Industries, $700.

15   Merchandise returned to XYZ, Inc., $450.

27   Merchandise returned to Datamagic, $900.

General Ledger

Account No.	Account	Balance July 1, 20--
202	Accounts Payable	$10,650
501.1	Purchases Returns and Allowances	

Accounts Payable Ledger

Name	Balance, July 1, 20--
Datamagic	$2,600
Starcraft Industries	4,300
XYZ, Inc.	3,750

EXERCISE 12A-7 (LO 4) CASH PAYMENTS JOURNAL Landmark Industries uses a cash payments journal. Prepare a cash payments journal using the same format and account titles as illustrated in the chapter. Record the following payments for merchandise purchased.

Sept. 5   Issued check no. 318 to Clinton Corp. for merchandise purchased August 28, $6,000, terms 2/10, n/30. Payment is made within the discount period.

12   Issued check no. 319 to Mitchell Company for merchandise purchased September 2, $7,500, terms 1/10, n/30. Received a credit memo from Mitchell Company for merchandise returned, $500. Payment is made within the discount period after deduction for the return dated September 8.

19   Issued check no. 320 to Expert Systems for merchandise purchased August 19, $4,100, terms n/30.

27   Issued check no. 321 to Graphic Data for merchandise purchased September 17, $9,000, terms 2/10, n/30. Payment is made within the discount period.

EXERCISE 12A-8 (LO 5) PREPARATION OF SCHEDULE OF ACCOUNTS PAYABLE Ryan's Express, a retail business, had the following beginning balances and purchases and payments activity in its accounts payable ledger during October. Prepare a schedule of accounts payable for Ryan's Express as of October 31, 20--.

Accounts Payable Ledger

Name	Balance Oct. 1, 20--	Purchases	Payments
Columbia Products	$4,350	$3,060	$2,060
Favorite Fashions	4,910	1,970	2,600
Rustic Legends	5,130	2,625	3,015

SERIES A PROBLEMS

PROBLEM 12A-1 (LO 3) PURCHASES JOURNAL J. B. Speck, owner of Speck's Galleria, made the following purchases of merchandise on account during the month of September.

Sept. 3   Purchase invoice no. 415, $2,650, from Smith Distributors.

8   Purchase invoice no. 132, $3,830, from Michaels Wholesaler.

11   Purchase invoice no. 614, $3,140, from J. B. Sanders & Co.

18   Purchase invoice no. 329, $2,250, from Bateman & Jones, Inc.

23   Purchase invoice no. 167, $4,160, from Smith Distributors.

27   Purchase invoice no. 744, $1,980, from Anderson Company.

30   Purchase invoice no. 652, $2,780, from Michaels Wholesaler.

REQUIRED

1. Record the transactions in the purchases journal. Total and rule the journal.

2. Post from the purchases journal to the general ledger accounts and to the accounts payable ledger accounts. Use account numbers as shown in the chapter.

PROBLEM 12A-2 (LO 3) PURCHASES JOURNAL, GENERAL LEDGER, AND ACCOUNTS PAYABLE LEDGER The purchases journal of Kevin's Kettle, a small retail business, is as follows:

	PURCHASES JOURNAL					PAGE 1	
	DATE	INVOICE NO.	FROM WHOM PURCHASED	POST REF.	PURCHASES DEBIT/ACCOUNTS PAYABLE CREDIT		
1	20-- Jan. 2	101	Ruiz Imports		3 0 0 0 00		1
2	3	621	Helmut's Hair Supply		2 4 8 0 00		2
3	7	195	Viola's Boutique		4 3 6 0 00		3
4	12	267	Royal Flush		1 9 5 0 00		4
5	18	903	Maria's Melodies		4 7 0 0 00		5
6	25	680	Helmut's Hair Supply		1 7 6 0 00		6
7					18 2 5 0 00		7

REQUIRED

1. Post the total of the purchases journal to the appropriate general ledger accounts. Use account numbers as shown in the chapter.

2. Post the individual purchase amounts to the accounts payable ledger.

PROBLEM 12A-3 (LO 4) CASH PAYMENTS JOURNAL, ACCOUNTS PAYABLE LEDGER, AND GENERAL LEDGER Sam Santiago operates a retail variety store. The books include a cash payments journal and an accounts payable ledger. All cash payments (except petty cash) are entered in the cash payments journal.

Selected account balances on May 1 are as follows:

(continued)

General Ledger

Cash	$40,000
Accounts Payable	20,000

Accounts Payable Ledger

Fantastic Toys	$5,200
Goya Outlet	3,800
Mueller's Distributors	3,600
Van Kooning	7,400

The following are the transactions related to cash payments for the month of May:

May 1   Issued check no. 426 in payment of May rent (Rent Expense), $2,400.

3   Issued check no. 427 to Mueller's Distributors in payment of merchandise purchased on account, $3,600 less a 3% discount. Check was written for $3,492.

7   Issued check no. 428 to Van Kooning in partial payment of merchandise purchased on account, $5,500. A cash discount was not allowed.

12   Issued check no. 429 to Fantastic Toys for merchandise purchased on account, $5,200, less a 1% discount. Check was written for $5,148.

15   Issued check no. 430 to City Power and Light (Utilities Expense), $1,720.

18   Issued check no. 431 to A-1 Warehouse for a cash purchase of merchandise, $4,800.

26   Issued check no. 432 to Goya Outlet for merchandise purchased on account, $3,800, less a 2% discount. Check was written for $3,724.

30   Issued check no. 433 to Mercury Transit Company for freight charges on merchandise purchased (Freight-In), $1,200.

31   Issued check no. 434 to Town Merchants for a cash purchase of merchandise, $3,000.

REQUIRED   1.   Enter the transactions in a cash payments journal. Total, rule, and prove the cash payments journal.

2.   Post from the cash payments journal to the general ledger and the accounts payable ledger. Use general ledger account numbers as shown in the chapter.

PROBLEM 12A-4 (LO 3/4) PURCHASES JOURNAL, CASH PAYMENTS JOURNAL, GENERAL JOURNAL, GENERAL LEDGER, AND ACCOUNTS PAYABLE LEDGER
Freddy Flint owns a small retail business called Flint's Fantasy. The cash account has a balance of $20,000 on July 1. The following transactions occurred during July.

July 1   Issued check no. 414 in payment of July rent, $1,500.

1   Purchased merchandise on account from Tang's Toys, invoice no. 311, $2,700, terms 2/10, n/30.

3   Purchased merchandise on account from Sillas & Company, invoice no. 812, $3,100, terms 1/10, n/30.

5   Returned merchandise purchased from Tang's Toys, receiving a credit memo on the amount owed, $500.

8   Purchased merchandise on account from Daisy's Dolls, invoice no. 139, $1,900, terms 2/10, n/30.

11   Issued check no. 415 to Tang's Toys for merchandise purchased on account, less return of July 5 and less 2% discount.

13   Issued a check no. 416 to Sillas & Company for merchandise purchased on account, less 1% discount.

15   Returned merchandise purchased from Daisy's Dolls, receiving a credit memo on the amount owed, $400.

18   Issued check no. 417 to Daisy's Dolls for merchandise purchased on account, less return of July 15 and less 2% discount.

25   Purchased merchandise on account from Allied Business, invoice no. 489, $2,450, terms n/30.

26   Purchased merchandise on account from Tang's Toys, invoice no. 375, $1,980, terms 2/10, n/30.

29   Purchased merchandise on account from Sillas & Company, invoice no. 883, $3,460, terms 1/10, n/30.

31   Freddy Flint withdrew cash for personal use, $2,000. Issued check no. 418.

31   Issued check no. 419 to Glisan Distributors for a cash purchase of merchandise, $975.

REQUIRED   1.   Enter the transactions in a purchases journal, a cash payments journal, and a general journal. Total and rule the purchases and cash payments journals. Prove the cash payments journal.

2.   Post from the journals to the general ledger and accounts payable ledger accounts. Use general ledger account numbers as shown in the chapter.

PROBLEM 12A-5 (LO 5) SCHEDULE OF ACCOUNTS PAYABLE Based on the information provided in Problem 12A-4, prepare a schedule of accounts payable for Flint's Fantasy as of July 31, 20--. Verify that the accounts payable account balance in the general ledger agrees with the schedule of accounts payable total.

SERIES B EXERCISES

EXERCISE 12B-1 (LO 1) PURCHASING DOCUMENTS AND FLOWCHART LABELING A flowchart showing some of the major documents commonly used in the purchasing function of a merchandise business is presented below. Briefly describe each document.

EXERCISE 12B-2 (LO 1) TRADE DISCOUNT AND CASH DISCOUNTS Merchandise was purchased on account from Grant's Distributors on June 12. The purchase price was $5,000, subject to a 10% trade discount and credit terms of 3/10, n/30.

1. Calculate the net amount to record the invoice, subject to the 10% trade discount.

2. Calculate the amount to be paid on this invoice within the discount period.

3. Journalize the purchase of the merchandise on June 12 and the payment on June 22 (within the discount period) in a general journal.

EXERCISE 12B-3 (LO 2) PURCHASE TRANSACTIONS AND T ACCOUNTS Using T accounts for Cash, Accounts Payable, Purchases, Purchases Returns and Allowances, Purchases Discounts, and Freight-In, enter the following purchase transactions. Identify each transaction with its corresponding letter. Use a new set of T accounts for each set of transactions, 1–4.

1. Purchase of merchandise with cash.

    (a) Merchandise is purchased for cash, $2,300.

    (b) Merchandise listed at $4,000, subject to a trade discount of 10%, is purchased for cash.

2. Purchase of merchandise on account with credit terms.

    (a) Merchandise is purchased on account, credit terms 2/10, n/30, $4,000.

    (b) Merchandise is purchased on account, credit terms 3/10, n/30, $2,800.

    (c) Payment is made on invoice (a) within the discount period.

    (d) Payment is made on invoice (b) too late to receive the cash discount.

3. Purchase of merchandise on account with return of merchandise.

    (a) Merchandise is purchased on account, credit terms 2/10, n/30, $5,600.

    (b) Merchandise is returned for credit before payment is made, $600.

    (c) Payment is made within the discount period.

4. Purchase of merchandise with freight-in.

    (a) Merchandise is purchased on account, $3,800 plus freight charges of $200. Terms of the sale were FOB shipping point.

    (b) Payment is made for the cost of merchandise and the freight charge.

EXERCISE 12B-4 (LO 2) GROSS PROFIT The following data were taken from the accounts of Burnside Bedknobs, a retail business. Determine the gross profit.

Sales	$116,500
Sales returns and allowances	1,100
Merchandise inventory, January 1	30,000
Purchases during the period	100,000
Purchases returns and allowances during the period	2,000
Purchases discounts taken during the period	2,800
Freight-in on merchandise purchased during the period	1,500
Merchandise inventory, December 31	50,000

EXERCISE 12B-5 (LO 3) JOURNALIZING TRANSACTIONS IN PURCHASES JOURNAL AND GENERAL JOURNAL

1. Journalize the following transactions in a general journal.

Jan. 3   Purchased merchandise from Feng, $6,000. Invoice no. 416, dated January 1, terms 2/10, n/30.

12   Purchased merchandise from Miranda, $9,000. Invoice no. 624, dated January 10, terms n/30.

19   Purchased merchandise from J. B. Barba, $6,400. Invoice no. 190, dated January 18, terms 1/10, n/30.

26   Purchased merchandise from Ramirez, $3,700. Invoice no. 923, dated January 25, terms 1/15, n/30.

2. Journalize the transactions in a purchases journal like the one below.

		PURCHASES JOURNAL		PAGE 5
DATE	INVOICE NO.	FROM WHOM PURCHASED	POST REF.	PURCHASES DEBIT/ACCOUNTS PAYABLE CREDIT

EXERCISE 12B-6 (LO 3) JOURNALIZE PURCHASES RETURNS AND ALLOWANCES AND POST TO GENERAL LEDGER AND ACCOUNTS PAYABLE LEDGER Using page 3 of a general journal and the following general ledger accounts and accounts payable ledger accounts, journalize and post the following transactions.

Mar. 5   Merchandise returned to Tower Industries, $500.

11   Merchandise returned to A & D Arms, $625.

23   Merchandise returned to Mighty Mansion, $275.

General Ledger

Account No.	Account	Balance Mar. 1, 20--
202	Accounts Payable	$8,350
501.1	Purchases Returns and Allowances	

Accounts Payable Ledger

Name	Balance, Mar. 1, 20--
A & D Arms	$2,300
Mighty Mansion	1,450
Tower Industries	4,600

EXERCISE 12B-7 (LO 4) ENTRIES IN A CASH PAYMENTS JOURNAL Sandcastles Northwest uses a cash payments journal. Prepare a cash payments journal using the same format and account titles as illustrated in the chapter. Record the following payments for merchandise purchased.

April 5   Issued check no. 429 to Standard Industries for merchandise purchased April 3, $8,000, terms 2/10, n/30. Payment is made within the discount period.

19   Issued check no. 430 to Finest Company for merchandise purchased April 10, $5,300, terms 1/10, n/30. Received a credit memo from Finest Company for merchandise returned, $300. Payment is made within the discount period after deduction for the return dated April 12.

(continued)

21 Issued check no. 431 to Funny Follies for merchandise purchased March 21, $3,250, terms n/30.

29 Issued check no. 432 to Classic Data for merchandise purchased April 20, $7,000, terms 2/10, n/30. Payment is made within the discount period.

EXERCISE 12B-8 (LO 5) PREPARATION OF SCHEDULE OF ACCOUNTS PAYABLE Crystal's Candles, a retail business, had the following balances and purchases and payments activity in its accounts payable ledger during November. Prepare a schedule of accounts payable for Crystal's Candles as of November 30, 20--.

Accounts Payable Ledger

Name	Balance Nov. 1, 20--	Purchases	Payments
Carl's Candle Wax	$4,135	$ 955	$1,610
Handy Supplies	3,490	1,320	1,850
Wishy Wicks	3,300	1,905	1,080

SERIES B PROBLEMS

PROBLEM 12B-1 (LO 3) PURCHASES JOURNAL Ann Benton, owner of Benton's Galleria, made the following purchases of merchandise on account during the month of October.

Oct. 2 Purchase invoice no. 321, $1,950, from Boggs Distributors.

7 Purchase invoice no. 152, $2,915, from Wolfs Wholesaler.

10 Purchase invoice no. 634, $3,565, from Komuro & Co.

16 Purchase invoice no. 349, $2,845, from Fritz & McCord, Inc.

24 Purchase invoice no. 187, $3,370, from Boggs Distributors.

26 Purchase invoice no. 764, $2,240, from Sanderson Company.

31 Purchase invoice no. 672, $1,630, from Wolfs Wholesaler.

REQUIRED
1. Record the transactions in the purchases journal. Total and rule the journal.

2. Post from the purchases journal to the general ledger accounts and to the accounts payable ledger accounts. Use account numbers as shown in the chapter.

PROBLEM 12B-2 (LO 3) PURCHASES JOURNAL, GENERAL LEDGER, AND ACCOUNTS PAYABLE LEDGER The purchases journal of Ryan's Rats Nest, a small retail business, is as follows:

				PURCHASES JOURNAL				PAGE 1			
	DATE	INVOICE NO.		FROM WHOM PURCHASED	POST REF.	PURCHASES DEBIT/ACCOUNTS PAYABLE CREDIT					
1	20-- Jan. 3	121		Sandra's Sweets		4	4	9	0	00	1
2	5	641		Amelia & Vincente		5	9	2	0	00	2
3	9	215		Nobuko's Nature Store		2	6	8	0	00	3
4	15	227		Smith and Johnson Company		6	5	6	0	00	4
5	21	933		Hidemi Inc.		1	3	0	0	00	5
6	30	650		Amelia & Vincente		1	8	9	0	00	6
7						22	8	4	0	00	7

REQUIRED
1. Post the total of the purchases journal to the appropriate general ledger accounts. Use account numbers as shown in the chapter.

2. Post the individual purchase amounts to the accounts payable ledger.

PROBLEM 12B-3 (LO 4) CASH PAYMENTS JOURNAL, ACCOUNTS PAYABLE LEDGER, AND GENERAL LEDGER Kay Zembrowski operates a retail variety store. The books include a cash payments journal and an accounts payable ledger. All cash payments (except petty cash) are entered in the cash payments journal. Selected account balances on May 1 are as follows:

General Ledger

Cash	$40,000
Accounts Payable	20,000

Accounts Payable Ledger

Cortez Distributors	$4,200
Indra & Velga	6,800
Toy Corner	4,600
Troutman Outlet	4,400

The following are the transactions related to cash payments for the month of May.

May 1   Issued check no. 326 in payment of May rent (Rent Expense), $2,600.

4   Issued check no. 327 to Cortez Distributors in payment of merchandise purchased on account, $4,200 less a 3% discount. Check was written for $4,074.

7   Issued check no. 328 to Indra & Velga in partial payment of merchandise purchased on account, $6,200. A cash discount was not allowed.

11   Issued check no. 329 to Toy Corner for merchandise purchased on account, $4,600 less a 1% discount. Check was written for $4,554.

15   Issued check no. 330 to County Power and Light (Utilities Expense), $1,500.

19   Issued check no. 331 to Builders Warehouse for a cash purchase of merchandise, $3,500.

25   Issued check no. 332 to Troutman Outlet for merchandise purchased on account, $4,400 less a 2% discount. Check was written for $4,312.

30   Issued check no. 333 to Rapid Transit Company for freight charges on merchandise purchased (Freight-In), $800.

31   Issued check no. 334 to City Merchants for a cash purchase of merchandise, $2,350.

REQUIRED
1. Enter the transactions in a cash payments journal. Total, rule, and prove the cash payments journal.

2. Post from the cash payments journal to the general ledger and the accounts payable ledger.

PROBLEM 12B-4 (LO 3/4) PURCHASES JOURNAL, CASH PAYMENTS JOURNAL, GENERAL JOURNAL, GENERAL LEDGER, AND ACCOUNTS PAYABLE LEDGER Debbie Mueller owns a small retail business called Debbie's Doll House. The cash account has a balance of $20,000 on July 1. The following transactions occurred during July.

(continued)

July 1   Issued check no. 314 for July rent, $1,400.

      1   Purchased merchandise on account from Topper's Toys, invoice no. 211, $2,500, terms 2/10, n/30.

      3   Purchased merchandise on account from Jones & Company, invoice no. 812, $2,800, terms 1/10, n/30

      5   Returned merchandise purchased from Topper's Toys receiving a credit memo on the amount owed, $400.

      8   Purchased merchandise on account from Downtown Merchants, invoice no. 159, $1,600, terms 2/10, n/30.

     11   Issued check no. 315 to Topper's Toys for merchandise purchased on account, less return of July 5 and less 2% discount.

     13   Issued check no. 316 to Jones & Company for merchandise purchased on account, less 1% discount.

     15   Returned merchandise purchased from Downtown Merchants receiving a credit memo on the amount owed, $600.

     18   Issued check no. 317 to Downtown Merchants for merchandise purchased on account, less return of July 15 and less 2% discount.

     25   Purchased merchandise on account from Columbia Products, invoice no. 468, $3,200, terms n/30.

     26   Purchased merchandise on account from Topper's Toys, invoice no. 395, $1,430, terms 2/10, n/30.

     29   Purchased merchandise on account from Jones & Company, invoice no. 853, $2,970 terms 1/10, n/30.

     31   Mueller withdrew cash for personal use, $2,500. Issued check no. 318.

     31   Issued check no. 319 to Burnside Warehouse for a cash purchase of merchandise, $1,050.

REQUIRED   1. Enter the transactions in a purchases journal, a cash payments journal, and a general journal. Total and rule the purchases and cash payments journals. Prove the cash payments journal.

           2. Post from the journals to the general ledger and accounts payable ledger accounts. Use general ledger account numbers as shown in the chapter.

PROBLEM 12B-5 (LO 5) SCHEDULE OF ACCOUNTS PAYABLE Based on the information provided in Problem 12B-4, prepare a schedule of accounts payable for Debbie's Doll House as of July 31, 20--. Verify that the accounts payable account balance in the general ledger agrees with the schedule of accounts payable total.

MASTERY PROBLEM

Michelle French owns and operates Books and More, a retail book store. Selected account balances on June 1 are as follows:

General Ledger

Cash	$32,200.00
Accounts Payable	2,000.00
Michelle French, Drawing	18,000.00
Purchases	67,021.66
Purchases Returns and Allowances	2,315.23
Purchases Discounts	905.00
Freight-In	522.60

Rent Expense	3,125.00
Utilities Expense	1,522.87

Accounts Payable Ledger

North-Eastern Publishing Co.	$2,000.00

The following purchases and cash payment transactions took place during the month of June:

June 1   Purchased books on account from Irving Publishing Company, $2,100. Invoice no. 101, terms 2/10, n/30, FOB destination.

2   Issued check no. 300 to North-Eastern Publishing Company for goods purchased on May 23, terms 2/10, n/30, $1,960 (the $2,000 invoice amount less the 2% discount).

3   Purchased books on account from Broadway Publishing, Inc., $2,880. Invoice no. 711, subject to 20% trade discount, and invoice terms of 3/10, n/30, FOB shipping point.

3   Issued check no. 301 to Mayday Shipping for delivery from Broadway Publishing Company, $250.

4   Issued check no. 302 for June rent, $625.

8   Purchased books on account from North-Eastern Publishing Company, $5,825. Invoice no. 268, terms 2/eom, n/60, FOB destination.

10   Received a credit memo from Irving Publishing Company, $550. Books had been returned because the covers were on upside down.

13   Issued check no. 304 to Broadway Publishing, Inc., for the purchase made on June 3. (Check no. 303 was voided because an error was made in preparing it.)

28   Made the following purchases:

Invoice No.	Company	Amount	Terms
579	Broadway Publishing, Inc.	$2,350	2/10, n/30 FOB destination
406	North-Eastern Publishing Co.	4,200	2/eom, n/60 FOB destination
964	Riley Publishing Co.	3,450	3/10, n/30 FOB destination

30   Issued check no. 305 to Taylor County Utility Co., for June utilities, $325.

30   French withdrew cash for personal use, $4,500. Issued check no. 306.

30   Issued check no. 307 to Irving Publishing Company for purchase made on June 1 less returns made on June 10.

30   Issued check no. 308 to North-Eastern Publishing Company for purchase made on June 8.

30   Issued check no. 309 for books purchased at an auction, $1,328.

REQUIRED   1.   Enter the above transactions in the appropriate journals.

2.   Total and rule the purchases journal and cash payments journal. Prove the cash payments journal.

3.   Post from the journals to the general ledger accounts and the accounts payable ledger.

4.   Prepare a schedule of accounts payable.

5.   If merchandise inventory was $35,523 on January 1 and $42,100 as of June 30, prepare the cost of goods sold section of the income statement for the six months ended June 30, 20--.

Self-Study Test Questions

True/False

1. In the purchasing process, the purchase invoice is the first document prepared. _____

2. A sales invoice prepared by the seller is called a purchase invoice by the buyer. _____

3. A trade discount is a reduction from the list or catalog price offered to different classes of customers. _____

4. Purchases Returns and Allowances is debited when merchandise is returned for credit. _____

5. FOB shipping point means that transportation charges are paid by the seller. _____

Multiple Choice

1. In the cash payments journal, each amount in the General Debit column is _____

   (a) posted daily.
   (b) posted weekly.
   (c) posted at the end of month.
   (d) not posted.

2. The journal that should be used to record the return of merchandise for credit is the _____

   (a) purchases journal.
   (b) cash payments journal.
   (c) general journal.
   (d) accounts payable ledger.

3. The difference between net sales and cost of goods sold is called _____

   (a) gross profit.
   (b) net purchases.
   (c) goods available for sale.
   (d) the bottom line.

4. The difference between merchandise available for sale and the end-of-period merchandise inventory is called _____

   (a) gross profit.
   (b) net purchases.
   (c) net sales.
   (d) cost of goods sold.

5. A purchase invoice for $1,200 with credit terms 2/10, n/30, and a return of $300 received by the seller prior to payment, is paid within the discount period. A check should be sent for _____

   (a) $1,200.
   (b) $882.
   (c) $900.
   (d) $810.

The answers to the Self-Study Test Questions are at the end of the text.

CHAPTER 12 APPENDIX

The Net-Price Method of Recording Purchases

LEARNING OBJECTIVES:
Careful study of this appendix should enable you to:

LO 1 Describe the net-price method of recording purchases.

LO 2 Record purchases and cash payments using the net-price method.

NET-PRICE METHOD

LO 1 Describe the net-price method of recording purchases.

In this chapter, purchases were recorded using the **gross-price method**. Under this method, purchases are recorded at the gross amount, regardless of available cash discounts. An alternative approach to accounting for purchases is the **net-price method**. Under this method, purchases are recorded at the net amount, assuming that all available cash discounts will be taken.

RECORDING WITH THE NET-PRICE METHOD

LO 2 Record purchases and cash payments using the net-price method.

To compare the two methods, reconsider the purchase for $100 on account, with credit terms of 2/10, n/30, on page 413. At the time of the purchase, the following entries are made under the two methods:

Gross-Price		Net-Price		
Purchases	100.00	Purchases	98.00*	
Accounts Payable		100.00	Accounts Payable		98.00

*$100 – $2 (2% cash discount)

If the payment for the merchandise is made within the discount period, the entries are:

Gross-Price			Net-Price		
Accounts Payable	100.00		Accounts Payable	98.00	
Cash		98.00	Cash		98.00
Purchases Discounts		2.00			

If payment for the merchandise is not made until after the discount period, the entries are:

Gross-Price			Net-Price		
Accounts Payable	100.00		Accounts Payable	98.00	
Cash		100.00	Purchases Discounts Lost	2.00	
			Cash		100.00

Note that under the net-price method a new account, Purchases Discounts Lost, is used. Purchases Discounts Lost is a temporary owners' equity account used to record cash discounts lost on purchases.

Purchases Discounts Lost

Debit	Credit
for discounts lost because of late payment of invoices	

Purchases Discounts Lost represents a finance charge for postponing the payment for merchandise. If the balance in this account is large relative to the amount of gross purchases, management should review its cash payment procedures. Purchases Discounts Lost is reported as an expense on the income statement.

Learning Objectives	Key Points to Remember
1 Describe the net-price method of recording purchases.	Under the net-price method, purchases are recorded at the net amount, assuming all available cash discounts will be taken.
2 Record purchases and cash payments using the net-price method.	Assume a purchase is made for $100 on account, with credit terms of 2/10, n/30. Under the net-price method, the entry at the time of purchase is:

Purchases   98.00
    Accounts Payable   98.00

If payment is made within the discount period, the entry is:

Accounts Payable   98.00
    Cash   98.00

If payment is not made until after the discount period, the entry is:

Accounts Payable   98.00
Purchases Discounts Lost   2.00
    Cash   100.00

KEY TERMS

gross-price method, (449)   Under this method, purchases are recorded at the gross amount.

net-price method, (449)   Under this method, purchases are recorded at the net amount, assuming all available cash discounts are taken.

SERIES A EXERCISE

EXERCISE 12ApxA-1 (LO 2) PURCHASES TRANSACTIONS—GROSS PRICE AND NET-PRICE METHODS Romero's Heating and Cooling had the following transactions during April:

April 2   Purchased merchandise on account from Alanon Valve for $1,000, terms 2/10, n/30.

5   Purchased merchandise on account from Leon's Garage for $1,400, terms 1/10, n/30.

11   Paid the amount due to Alanon Valve for the purchase on April 2.

25   Paid the amount due to Leon's Garage for the purchase on April 5.

1.   Prepare general journal entries for these transactions using the gross-price method.

2.   Prepare general journal entries for these transactions using the net-price method.

SERIES B EXERCISE

EXERCISE 12ApxB-1 (LO 2) PURCHASES TRANSACTIONS—GROSS-PRICE AND NET-PRICE METHODS Gloria's Repair Shop had the following transactions during May:

May 2 Purchased merchandise on account from Delgado's Supply for $900, terms 2/10, n/30.

6 Purchased merchandise on account from Goro's Auto Care for $1,200, terms 1/10, n/30.

11 Paid the amount due to Delgado's Supply for the purchase on May 2.

27 Paid the amount due to Goro's Auto Care for the purchase on May 6.

1. Prepare general journal entries for these transactions using the gross-price method.

2. Prepare general journal entries for these transactions using the net-price method.

13

The Voucher System

By the end of the first year of operations of Be a Sport, John Zenith finds that revenues and expenses have become much larger than in the early months. John feels comfortable with control over revenues. He has developed a good feel for what sales should be on a weekly and even a daily basis in most cases. All cash is deposited daily in the bank and he regularly monitors his inventory.

For expenditures, John personally signs all checks after reviewing any bills or other supporting paper work. He is unaware of any errors having occurred. Still, John wonders whether he has adequate control over his expenditures. His bookkeeper says that she learned in one of her recent courses that a voucher system is a good way to control expenditures. John is interested in such a system. What is a voucher system? Would a voucher system be a good idea for John's business?

Chapter 12 demonstrated how merchandise purchased on account can be efficiently recorded in a purchases journal. In this chapter, we will learn to use a special journal for recording all purchases of assets and services of any kind. Chapter 12 also demonstrated how cash payments can be efficiently recorded in a cash payments journal. In this chapter, we will learn to use another type of journal for recording cash payments.

The two new journals introduced in this chapter provide more than an efficient way to record transactions. These journals are an important part of what is called a voucher system.

INTERNAL CONTROL OF EXPENDITURES

LO 1 Describe how a voucher system is used to control expenditures.

Internal controls are important in every business, regardless of its size. The main effect of size on internal controls is that in larger businesses, the internal controls need to be more formal and tend to be more costly.

To be successful, management must have adequate control of the operations of the business. When we think of controlling business operations, most of us tend to emphasize ways to control revenues. For example, when a sale occurs, we want to be sure the sales clerk puts the cash in the register. In fact, it is just as important to control the expenditure process.

Management needs to see that expenditures are made only for goods and services needed by the business and at a fair price. In a small business, management does so by direct involvement with the expenditure process. But as a business grows larger, management cannot continue such direct involvement. Instead, in medium- and large-size businesses, management controls expenditures by using an appropriate internal control system.

Elements of Internal Control

Internal controls are the set of procedures used to ensure that there is proper accounting for all activities of the business. A full discussion of internal controls is a subject for an advanced text. Our attention will be limited to three elements of internal control that are particularly important for expenditures:

1. Segregation of duties

2. Authorization procedures and related responsibilities

3. Adequate documents and records

   Segregation of duties means that:

1. Different employees should be responsible for different parts of a transaction; and

2. Employees who account for transactions should not also have custody of the assets.

   For example, one employee should be responsible for ordering goods and a different employee should be responsible for issuing the check to pay for them. Similarly, one employee should be responsible for recording the purchase of goods and a different employee should be responsible for receiving and placing the goods in inventory. This segregation of duties provides a built-in check by one employee on another. One employee cannot obtain goods for personal use without being caught by another employee.

Authorization procedures and related responsibilities means that every business activity should be properly authorized. In addition, it should be possible to identify who is responsible for every activity that has occurred. For example, to acquire new equipment, a signed document should authorize the purchase. After the purchase is made, this signed document shows who is responsible for the action.

Adequate documents and records means that accounting documents and records should be used so that all business transactions are recorded. For example, every purchase that occurs should be supported by a document. These documents should be prenumbered, used in sequence, and subsequently accounted for. In this way, the business can be sure that it has made a record of each transaction.

Voucher System

A formal voucher system is most appropriate for medium- and large-size businesses. The volume of transactions in a business must be sufficient to warrant the cost of such a system.

The three elements of internal control described above can be combined to control expenditures by using a voucher system. A **voucher system** is a control technique that requires that every acquisition and subsequent payment be supported by an approved voucher. A **voucher** is a document that shows that an acquisition is proper and that payment is authorized.

Figure 13-1 is a simplified illustration of how the purchasing portion of a voucher system operates. The purchase requisition, purchase order, receiving report, and purchase invoice were explained and illustrated in Chapter 12. Recall that an authorized person or department prepares a purchase requisition to indicate the need for goods. The purchasing department reviews and approves the purchase requisition and prepares a purchase order to send to the supplier. When the goods are received, a receiving report is prepared. A copy of each of these documents is sent to the vouchers payable section in the accounting department.

FIGURE 13-1 Voucher System—Purchasing Process

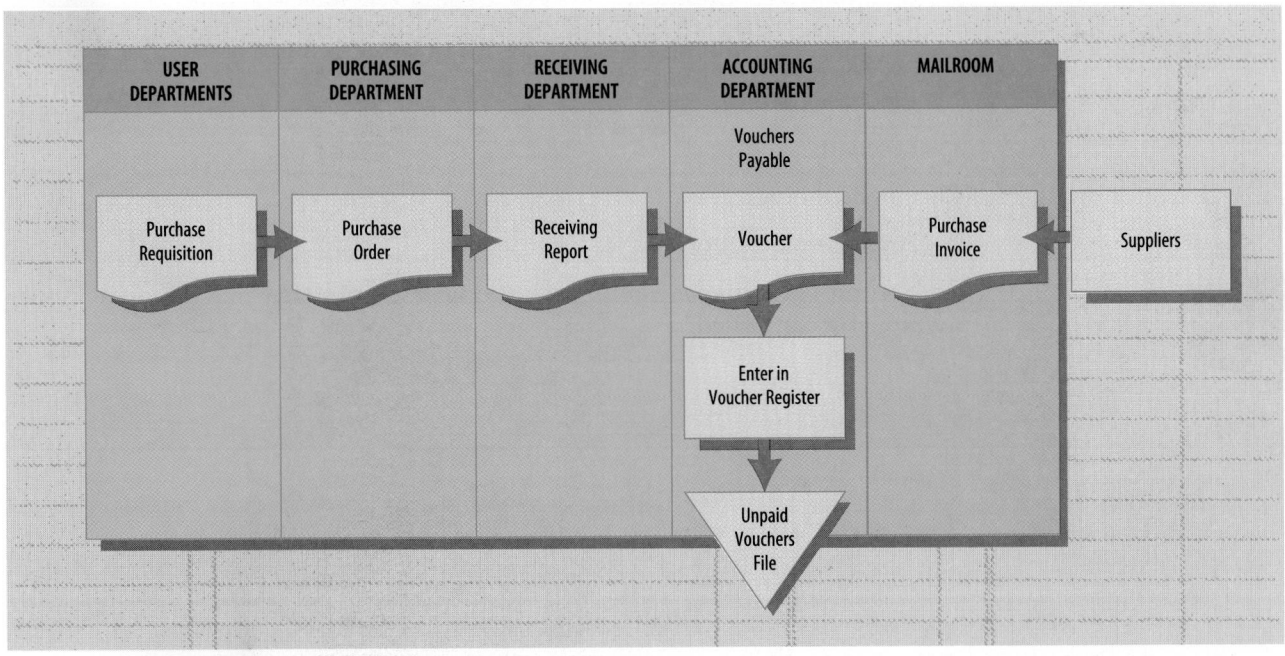

When the purchase invoice arrives, it is compared with the purchase requisition, purchase order, and receiving report. If the purchase invoice is

▶ for the goods ordered (purchase requisition and purchase order),

▶ at the correct price (purchase order),

▶ and for the correct quantity (receiving report),

then a voucher (see Figure 13-3, page 458) is prepared. This is the first key control provided by the voucher system. If any aspect of the purchase is improper, it will be caught when the voucher is prepared.

After the voucher is prepared and approved, it is entered in a special journal called a voucher register. It then is filed by due date.

The completed voucher provides the basis for paying the supplier's invoice on the due date. This is the second key control provided by the voucher system. *No payment may be made without an approved voucher.* The payment process will be discussed later in this chapter.

LEARNING KEY: The voucher system contains elements of internal control such as segregation of duties, authorization to order the goods and prepare the voucher, and accounting procedures that require prenumbering and accounting for the supporting documents.

Notice how the three elements of internal control can be seen in this system. (1) *Duties are segregated* because different employees order, receive, and record the purchases. (2) *Authorization* is required to order the goods and to prepare the voucher. (3) The *documents and records* include purchase requisitions, purchase orders, receiving reports, and vouchers that are prenumbered and accounted for. This means that every recorded purchase is supported by the following five documents:

1. Voucher

2. Purchase invoice

3. Receiving report

4. Purchase order

5. Purchase requisition

This provides management with strong assurance that purchasing activities are properly controlled.

PREPARING A VOUCHER

LO 2   Prepare a voucher.

To illustrate the preparation of a voucher and how a voucher system works, we extend the Northern Micro transactions from Chapter 12. In this chapter, we assume that Northern Micro uses a voucher system, and several transactions are added.

When a purchase invoice (Figure 13-2) is received from a supplier, the following procedures are performed in the voucher section:

STEP 1   Compare the invoice with the purchase requisition, purchase order, and receiving report to determine that:

    a.   the quantity was requisitioned (purchase requisition), ordered (purchase order), and received (receiving report)

    b.   the price and credit terms are proper (purchase order)

STEP 2   Judge whether the purchase is appropriate for the business.

STEP 3   Verify all computations on the invoice (quantity × price, and any discounts).

Note how the voucher section thus provides a final, independent check on the entire purchasing process. If any aspect is improper, it can be caught before payment is made.

FIGURE 13-2   Purchase Invoice

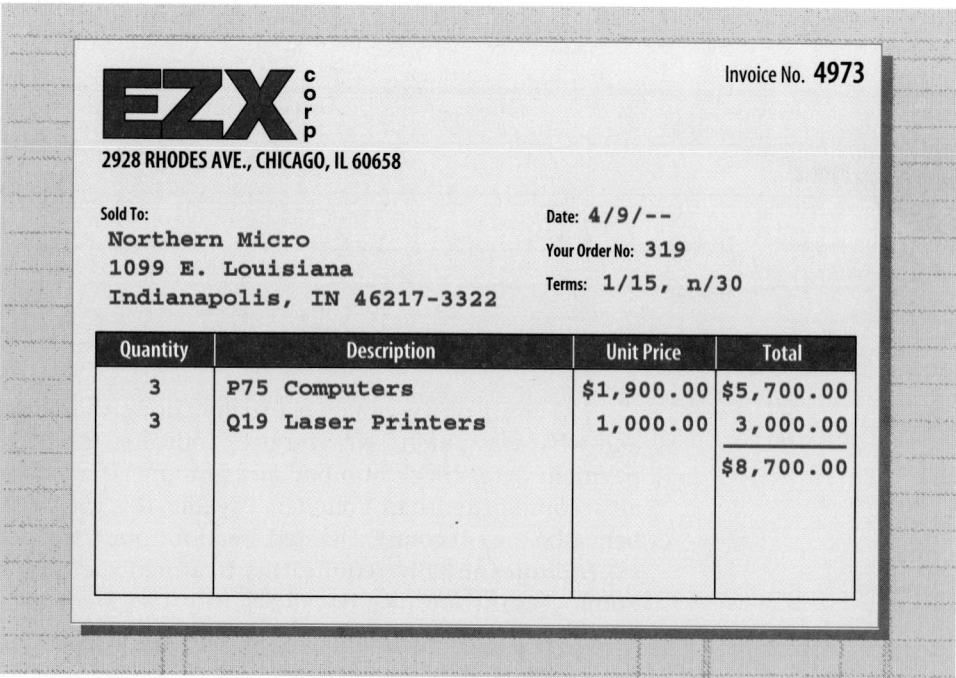

After performing these procedures, the voucher is prepared. Many acceptable formats for vouchers can be used. Figure 13-3 illustrates a commonly used form. This voucher was prepared based on the purchase invoice in Figure 13-2.

FIGURE 13-3 Voucher

NORTHERN MICRO
1099 E. Louisiana, Indianapolis, IN 46217-3322

Date 4/11/--   Terms: 1/15, n/30   Due: 4/24/--
To: EZX Corp.
     2928 Rhodes Ave.
     Chicago, IL 60658

Voucher No. **111**

Invoice Date	Invoice No.	Description	Amount
4/9/--	4973	P75 Computers-3	$5,700.00
		Q19 Laser Printers-3	3,000.00
			$8,700.00

Authorization ___J. Jensen___ (Supervisor)   Prepared By ___B. Zimmer___ (Clerk)

Front

Voucher No. **111**

Account Debited	Account No.	Amount	Summary	
Purchases	501	$8,700.00	Invoice	$8,700.00
			Discount	87.00
			Net	$8,613.00

Payment   Date 4/24/--   Check No. 437   Amount $8,613.00

Approved   Distribution ___J. G.___   Payment _____

Back

The front of the voucher usually shows the voucher number, date, supplier, and what was purchased. The back indicates the accounts to be debited and the payment date, check number, and amount. If an expenditure requires a credit to an account other than Vouchers Payable, this can be shown as a separate notation beneath the Account Debited section on the back of the voucher. Payroll expenditures usually require this treatment because of the related liabilities for Employees Income Tax, Social Security Tax, Medicare Tax, etc.

The prenumbered voucher in Figure 13-3 was prepared using the following steps:

STEP 1   On the front of the voucher, insert

a.   voucher date

b.   invoice terms

c.   due date

d.   supplier name and address

e.   invoice date

f.   description of items purchased

g.   invoice amount

STEP 2   On the back, insert the accounts and amounts to be debited.

After these steps are completed, the voucher clerk (B. Zimmer) signs the voucher and has it approved by the voucher section supervisor (J. Jensen). On the back of the voucher, the "Distribution" (the accounts to which the expenditure is charged) is approved by the accounting supervisor (J. G.). The "Payment" approval is not completed until the voucher is paid on the due date. The $87 purchases discount will be recorded when the voucher is paid.

VOUCHER REGISTER

LO 3   Describe and use a voucher register.

After the voucher is completed and approved, it is entered in a voucher register. A **voucher register** is a special journal used to record purchases of all types of assets and services. You can think of a voucher register as an expanded purchases journal like the one we saw in Chapter 12. In fact, if a voucher register is used, it replaces the purchases journal.

LEARNING KEY: Use the voucher register to record all types of purchases.

Figure 13-4 illustrates Northern Micro's voucher register. It has four debit columns—Purchases, Supplies, Wages Expense, and General Debit—and a credit column for Vouchers Payable. The General Debit column is used for transactions affecting account titles other than those with special column headings. To allow for credits to accounts other than Vouchers Payable, the General Debit column can be expanded to include General Debit and Credit columns. The additional accounts and amounts would be listed in these columns of the voucher register. The voucher register also has a Payment column that is used when the voucher is paid. As with any special journal, the exact number and types of debit and credit columns used depends on the nature of the business.

The transaction on 4/15/-- for payroll actually would require a debit to Payroll and credits to Vouchers Payable, Employee Income Tax Payable, Social Security Tax Payable, and Medicare Tax Payable. To simplify the illustrations in this chapter, all payroll transactions are shown as a debit to Wages Expense and credit to Vouchers Payable for a single amount.

FIGURE 13-4 Voucher Register (left side)

	DATE	VOUCHER NO.	ISSUED TO	PURCHASES DEBIT					
1	4/2/--	106	Triumph Leasing						1
2	4/4/--	107	Sam's Cyberware	1	4	0	0	00	2
3	4/4/--	108	Compucraft, Inc.	3	3	0	0	00	3
4	4/8/--	109	Datasoft	2	5	0	0	00	4
5	4/9/--	110	Bemon Office Supply						5
6	4/11/--	111	EZX Corp.	8	7	0	0	00	6
7	4/15/--	112	Payroll						7
15				23	5	6	0	00	15

A voucher is recorded in the voucher register by entering the following information:

1. Date

2. Voucher number

3. Person or business to whom the voucher is issued

4. Dollar amounts of debits and credits

The entry for Voucher No. 111 (Figure 13-3) was made on April 11.

Filing Unpaid Vouchers

After the voucher is entered in the voucher register, the voucher and supporting documents (purchase requisition, purchase order, receiving report, and purchase invoice) are stapled together. This "voucher packet" is then filed in an **unpaid vouchers file**, normally by due date. Alternatively, vouchers can be filed by supplier name. Filing by due date is preferred because this helps management plan for cash needs. It also helps ensure that vouchers are paid on the due date and cash discounts are taken.

The unpaid vouchers file functions as an accounts payable ledger. However, payables are grouped by due date rather than by supplier.

LEARNING KEY: When a voucher system is used, the unpaid vouchers file can serve as an accounts payable ledger.

Posting from the Voucher Register

Both individual and summary postings are required from the voucher register to the general ledger. Figure 13-5 illustrates the posting process for Northern Micro's voucher register for April, as follows:

FIGURE 13-4 Voucher Register (right side)

	SUPPLIES DEBIT			WAGES EXPENSE DEBIT			GENERAL DEBIT				VOUCHERS PAYABLE CREDIT		PAYMENT		
							ACCOUNT	POST. REF.	AMOUNT				DATE	CHECK NO.	
1							Rent Exp.		2 4 0 0	00	2 4 0 0	00	4/2/- -	421	1
2											1 4 0 0	00	4/4/- -	423	2
3											3 3 0 0	00			3
4											2 5 0 0	00			4
5	1 6 0	00									1 6 0	00	4/25/- -	438	5
6											8 7 0 0	00	4/24/- -	437	6
7				8 3 0	00						8 3 0	00	4/15/- -	430	7
15	2 8 0	00	1 7 0 0	00					5 9 0 0	00	31 4 4 0	00			15

PAGE 4

On a daily basis:

STEP 1   Post each amount from the General Debit column to the appropriate general ledger account. (Note that only the first half of the month is shown in Figure 13-5. The rest of the month would be posted in a similar manner.)

STEP 2   Insert the date in the Date column and the initials "VR" and the voucher register page number in the Posting Reference column of each general ledger account.

STEP 3   Insert the general ledger account numbers in the Posting Reference column of the General Debit column of the voucher register.

At the end of each month:

STEP 4   Total the amount columns, verify that the total of the debit columns equals the total of the credit column, and rule the columns.

STEP 5   Post each column total except the General Debit column to the general ledger account indicated in the column headings.

STEP 6   Insert the date in the Date column and the initials "VR" and the voucher register page number in the Posting Reference column of each ledger account.

STEP 7   Insert the general ledger account numbers immediately below each column total except the General Debit column.

STEP 8   Insert a check mark (✓) immediately below the General Debit column total.

Note that the payables account in Figure 13-5 may be called either Vouchers Payable or Accounts Payable. Even with a voucher system, many businesses still use the Accounts Payable title. On the balance sheet, the Accounts Payable title is almost always used.

No posting to an accounts payable ledger is necessary for Northern Micro. They use the unpaid vouchers file as their accounts payable ledger. The unpaid vouchers file was updated when the vouchers were filed after being entered in the voucher register.

FIGURE 13-5 Posting Voucher Register to General Ledger

						General Debit			Vouchers	Payment	
Date	Voucher No.	Issued To	Purchases Debit	Supplies Debit	Wages Expense Debit	Account	Post Ref.	Amount	Payable Credit	Date	Check No.
4/2/--	106	Triumph Leasing				Rent Exp.	521	2,400.00	2,400.00	4/2/--	421
4/4/--	107	Sam's Cyberware	1,400.00						1,400.00	4/4/--	423
4/4/--	108	Compucraft, Inc.	3,300.00						3,300.00		
4/8/--	109	Datasoft	2,500.00						2,500.00		
4/9/--	110	Bemon Office Supply		160.00					160.00	4/25/--	438
4/11/--	111	EZX Corp.	8,700.00						8,700.00	4/24/--	437
4/15/--	112	Payroll			830.00				830.00	4/15/--	430
TOTALS			23,560.00	280.00	1,700.00				5,900.00	31,440.00	
			(501)	(141)	(511)				(✓)	(202)	

VOUCHER REGISTER PAGE 4

Debit total: $23,560
280
1,700
5,900
$31,440

Credit total: $31,440

ACCOUNT Supplies   **ACCOUNT NO.** 141

Date	Item	Post Ref.	Debit	Credit	Balance Debit	Balance Credit
20-- Apr. 1	Bal.	✓			210.00	
30		VR4	280.00		490.00	

ACCOUNT Vouchers Payable   **ACCOUNT NO.** 202

Date	Item	Post Ref.	Debit	Credit	Balance Debit	Balance Credit
20-- Apr. 1	Bal.	✓				4,800.00
30		VR4		31,440.00		36,240.00

ACCOUNT Purchases   **ACCOUNT NO.** 501

Date	Item	Post Ref.	Debit	Credit	Balance Debit	Balance Credit
20-- Apr. 1	Bal.	✓			17,400.00	
30		VR4	23,560.00		40,960.00	

ACCOUNT Wages Expense   **ACCOUNT NO.** 511

Date	Item	Post Ref.	Debit	Credit	Balance Debit	Balance Credit
20-- Apr. 1	Bal.	✓			5,900.00	
30		VR4	1,700.00		7,600.00	

ACCOUNT Rent Expense   **ACCOUNT NO.** 521

Date	Item	Post Ref.	Debit	Credit	Balance Debit	Balance Credit
20-- Apr. 1	Bal.	✓			6,600.00	
2		VR4	2,400.00		9,000.00	

THE PAYMENT PROCESS USING A VOUCHER SYSTEM

LO 4   Describe the payment process using a voucher system.

Figure 13-6 illustrates the payment process when a voucher system is used. On the due date, the voucher is pulled from the unpaid vouchers file. The voucher is given to the person responsible for preparing and signing checks (for Northern Micro, the cashier). The cashier reviews each voucher and supporting documents to see that the expenditure is proper. The cashier then prepares and signs the check and sends it to the supplier. It is important for internal control that no check be prepared without a supporting voucher and that the check be mailed as soon as it is signed.

FIGURE 13-6 Voucher System—Payment Process

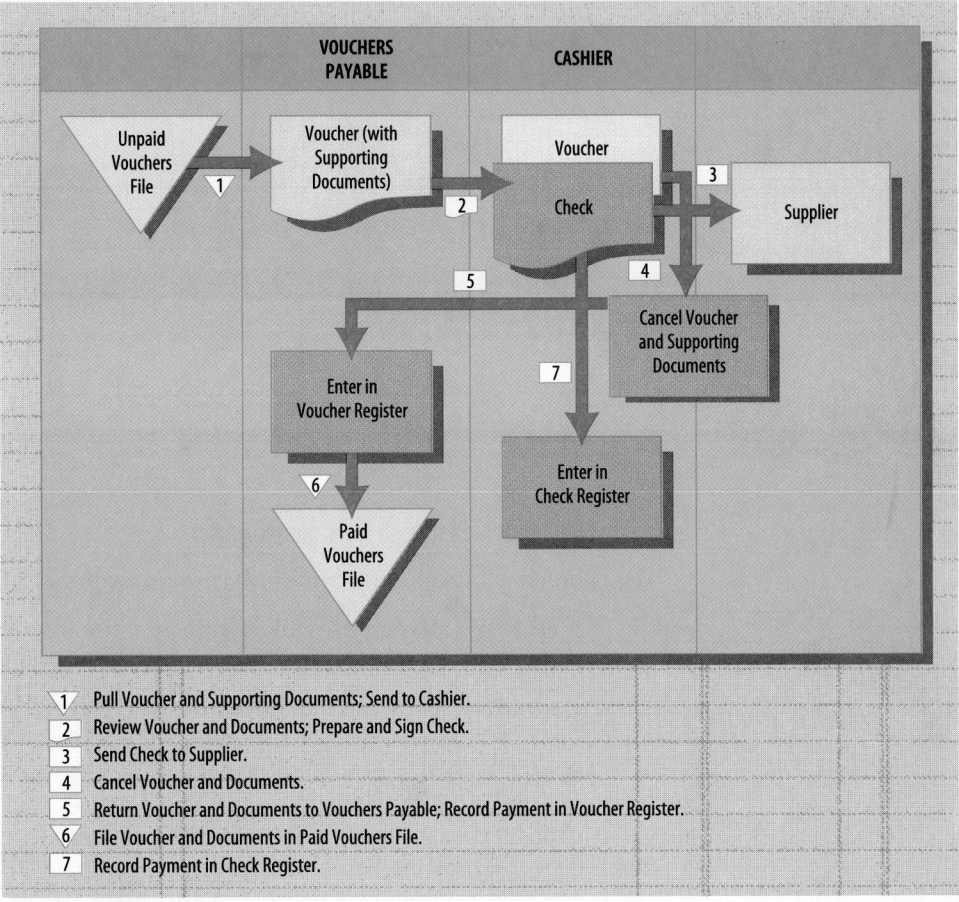

1	Pull Voucher and Supporting Documents; Send to Cashier.
2	Review Voucher and Documents; Prepare and Sign Check.
3	Send Check to Supplier.
4	Cancel Voucher and Documents.
5	Return Voucher and Documents to Vouchers Payable; Record Payment in Voucher Register.
6	File Voucher and Documents in Paid Vouchers File.
7	Record Payment in Check Register.

Ordinary checks may be used to make payments, but under the voucher system, voucher checks often are used. A **voucher check** is a check with space for entering data about the voucher being paid. Figure 13-7 shows Northern Micro's voucher check to pay Voucher No. 111 (Figure 13-3).

FIGURE 13-7 Voucher Check

The voucher check has two parts:

1. The check itself, which is similar to an ordinary check, and

2. An attached statement, which indicates the invoice being paid and any deductions.

In addition, the voucher check stub identifies the voucher number being paid.

After the voucher has been paid, the cashier completes the "Payment" approval on the back of the voucher. The voucher and supporting documents are then cancelled to indicate payment. The cancelling can be done with a rubber stamp, by perforating, or by simply writing "paid" on all relevant documents. This prevents a voucher from being processed again to create a duplicate payment. The cancelled voucher and supporting documents are then returned to the vouchers payable section. The cancelled voucher is used to record the payment of the voucher in the voucher register. The voucher and supporting documents are then filed either numerically or by supplier in a **paid vouchers file**. In either case, the numerical sequence should be accounted for to identify possible missing or duplicate vouchers.

A BROADER VIEW

FRAUD CAN MEAN EXPENSIVE SUPPLIES

A computer systems worker at Mobil Chemical Co. in Stratford, Connecticut, stole $522,000 by paying for purchases of supplies that did not exist. First, the worker established a false company. At Mobil, he prepared purchase orders to purchase supplies from this company. He then prepared receiving reports for supplies that were never delivered. When he sent bills from the company to Mobil, they were paid based on the bogus receiving reports and purchase orders. Checks issued to pay for the supplies were sent to a post office box where the worker collected them.

This fraud shows the importance of segregation of duties and use of a voucher system as described in this chapter. This worker was able to control too many parts of this purchase transaction. In addition, payment was made without an approved voucher with all supporting documents.

CHECK REGISTER

LO 5   Describe and use a check register.

A copy of the check is used to enter the payment in a check register. A **check register** is a special journal used to record all checks written in a voucher system. Figure 13-8 illustrates Northern Micro's check register.

A check register is similar to the cash payments journal we saw in Chapter 12 (Figure 12-13). A key difference is that the check register has only three amount columns—Vouchers Payable Debit, Purchases Discounts Credit, and Cash Credit. Recall that in a voucher system, every purchase of assets or services must be supported by a voucher. This means that every purchase has been recorded in a voucher register before any payment can be made. Thus, the debit in the check register is to Vouchers Payable, and the credits are to Purchases Discounts and Cash. When a business uses the voucher system and a voucher register, the check register replaces the cash payments journal.

FIGURE 13-8 Check Register

	DATE	CHECK NO.	PAYEE	VOUCHERS PAYABLE DR. NO.	AMOUNT	PURCHASES DISCOUNTS CREDIT	CASH CREDIT	
								PAGE 4
1	4/1/- -	420	Payroll	105	8 7 0 00		8 7 0 00	1
2	4/2/- -	421	Triumph Leasing	106	2 4 0 0 00		2 4 0 0 00	2
19	4/24/- -	437	EZX Corp.	111	8 7 0 0 00	8 7 00	8 6 1 3 00	19
20	4/25/- -	438	Bemon Office Supply	110	1 6 0 00		1 6 0 00	20
21	4/29/- -	443	TTA Products	115	1 5 0 0 00		1 5 0 0 00	21
22	TOTALS				24 3 4 0 00	1 7 9 00	24 1 6 1 00	22

LEARNING KEY: There are only three amount columns in the check register: Vouchers Payable Debit, Purchases Discounts Credit, and Cash Credit.

A check is recorded in the check register by entering the following information:

1. Date
2. Check number
3. Payee
4. Voucher number
5. Dollar amounts

The entry on April 24 is for the voucher check in Figure 13-7.

The check entering process also affects the voucher register. As shown in the diagram in Figure 13-6, the canceled voucher is used to enter the payment of the vouchers in the voucher register. A portion of the voucher register in Figure 13-4 is reproduced in Figure 13-9, with the Payment column filled in for voucher no. 111. Both the date of payment and the check number are inserted to indicate that the voucher has been paid.

FIGURE 13-9 Partial Voucher Register (left side)

	DATE	VOUCHER NO.	ISSUED TO	PURCHASES DEBIT	
					VOUCHER REGISTER
6	4/11/- -	111	EZX Corp.	8 7 0 0 00	6
7					7
8					8

Posting from the Check Register

Only monthly summary postings are required from the check register to the general ledger. Figure 13-10 illustrates the posting process for Northern Micro's check register at the end of April, as follows:

STEP 1   Total the amount columns, verify that the total of the debit column equals the total of the credit columns, and rule the columns.

STEP 2   Post each column total to the general ledger account indicated in the column headings.

STEP 3   Insert the date in the Date column and the initials "CK" and the check register page number in the Posting Reference column of each ledger account.

STEP 4   Insert the general ledger account numbers immediately below each column total.

Schedule of Vouchers Payable

It was explained earlier that most businesses that use a voucher system do not keep an accounts payable ledger. It is still desirable, however, to verify each month that the sum of the individual amounts owed to creditors equals the Vouchers Payable balance. For this purpose, a schedule of vouchers payable (Figure 13-11) is prepared. Note that the $11,900 total listed in the schedule equals the vouchers payable balance shown in Figure 13-10.

This schedule is prepared from either the voucher register or the unpaid vouchers file. Every blank in the Payment column of the voucher register represents an unpaid voucher to include in the schedule. Similarly, each voucher in the unpaid vouchers file should be included in the schedule.

If the schedule total and the Vouchers Payable balance do not agree, the error must be located and corrected. To find the error, use the following procedures:

STEP 1   Verify the total of the schedule.

STEP 2   Review the voucher register or the unpaid vouchers file to be sure no vouchers were missed or counted twice.

STEP 3   Verify the totals in the voucher register and check register.

STEP 4   Verify the postings to Vouchers Payable in the general ledger.

FIGURE 13-9 Partial Voucher Register (right side)

FIGURE 13-10 Posting Check Register to General Ledger

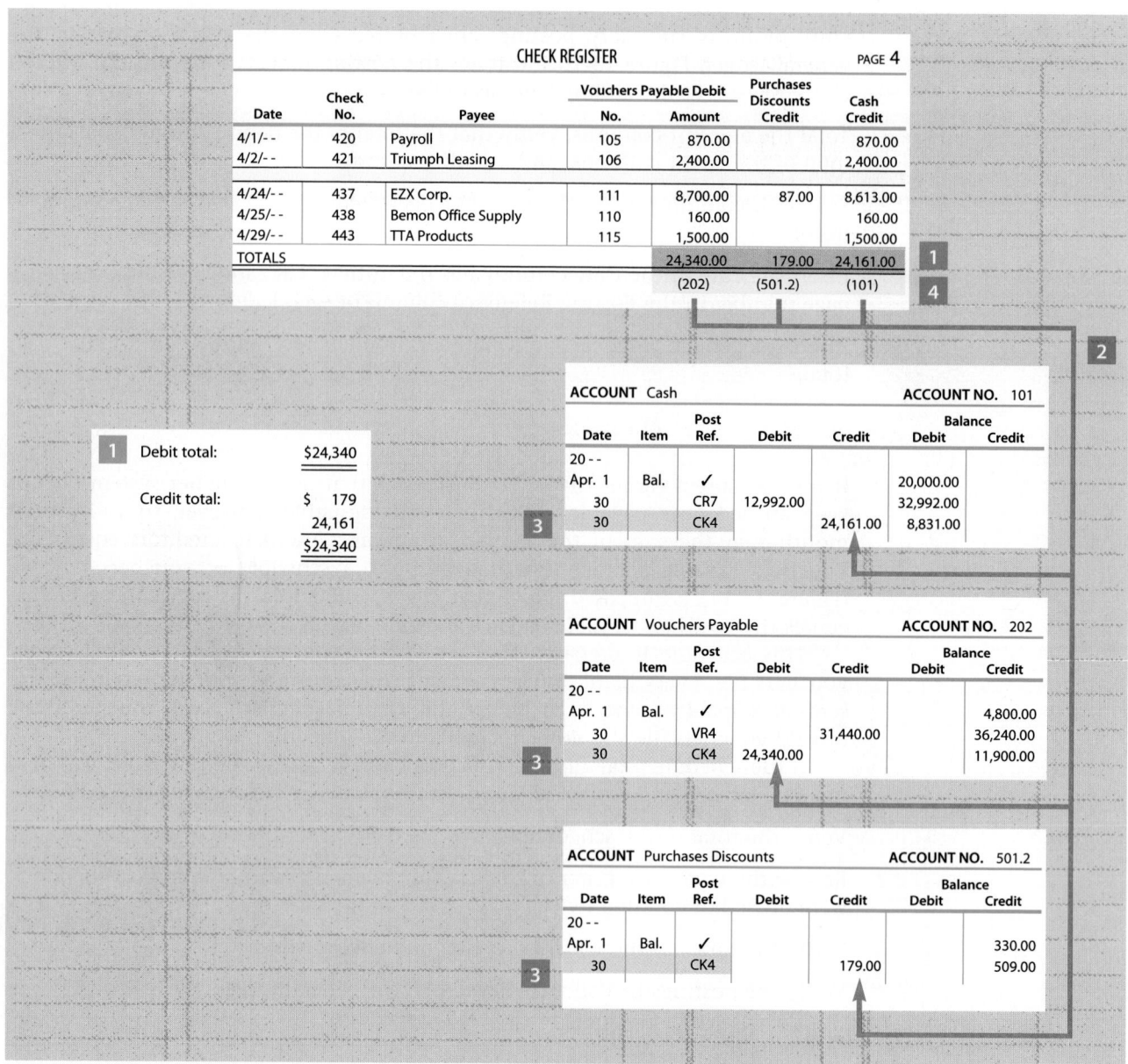

FIGURE 13-11 Schedule of Vouchers Payable

Northern Micro Schedule of Vouchers Payable April 30, 20 - -					
Compucraft, Inc.	$ 3	3	0	0	00
Datasoft	2	5	0	0	00
Printpro		8	0	0	00
Televax	5	3	0	0	00
	$11	9	0	0	00

Accounting for Returns, Allowances, and Partial Payments

For a voucher system to provide good control of expenditures, vouchers must be carefully handled and recorded. This includes both the initial creation and recording of the voucher as well as its subsequent payment. Because the voucher is such an important control device, special procedures are needed when the amount of the voucher needs to be changed.

Purchases Returns and Allowances. If a complete return is made of merchandise costing $670 and a credit memo is received from the supplier, the following procedures are performed:

1. Note the return on the voucher, attach the credit memo, and place the voucher in the paid vouchers file.

2. Note the return in the Payment column of the voucher register by inserting the date of the return and an R (for "Return") in the Check No. column.

	DATE	VOUCHER NO.	ISSUED TO	PURCHASES DEBIT	VOUCHERS PAYABLE CREDIT	PAYMENT DATE	CHECK NO.	
1	5/6/--	121	Compumax	6 7 0 00	6 7 0 00	5/9/--	R	1

3. Make a general journal entry to record the return.

5		Vouchers Payable/Compumax	6 7 0 00		5
6		Purchases Returns and Allowances		6 7 0 00	6
7		Returned merchandise			7

If a partial return is made of $250 of merchandise costing $670 and a credit memo is received, the following procedures are performed:

1. Note the return on the voucher, attach the credit memo, and return the voucher to the unpaid vouchers file.

2. Note the return in the voucher register in the Payment column, as follows:

	DATE	VOUCHER NO.	ISSUED TO	PURCHASES DEBIT	VOUCHERS PAYABLE CREDIT	PAYMENT DATE	CHECK NO.	
1	5/6/--	121	Compumax	6 7 0 00	6 7 0 00	5/9/--	R/250	1

Notice that both the return and the dollar amount are indicated. This distinguishes the partial return from a complete return.

3. Make a general journal entry to record the return.

8		Vouchers Payable/Compumax	2 5 0 00		8
9		Purchases Returns and Allowances		2 5 0 00	9
10		Returned merchandise			10

4. When the voucher is paid for the original amount less the return, note the payment in the Payment column of the voucher register, as follows:

	DATE	VOUCHER NO.	ISSUED TO	PURCHASES DEBIT		VOUCHERS PAYABLE CREDIT	PAYMENT DATE	CHECK NO.	
1	5/6/--	121	Compumax	6 7 0 00		6 7 0 00	5/9/-- 5/21/--	R/250 451	1

Partial Payments. If partial payments (installments) are planned at the time a purchase is made, a separate voucher is prepared for each payment. Each voucher and payment is then recorded in the voucher register and check register in the normal manner.

If a partial payment is made after a voucher is created and entered, the original voucher is cancelled and new vouchers are created. Assume that merchandise is purchased for $600. Subsequently, a partial payment of only $200 is made. The following procedures are used to account for these events:

1. Make a general journal entry to cancel the original voucher.

12			Vouchers Payable/PC -Time			6 0 0 00				12
13			Purchases				6 0 0 00			13
14			Cancelled voucher							14

2. Make a notation in the Payment column of the voucher register.

	DATE	VOUCHER NO.	ISSUED TO	PURCHASES DEBIT		VOUCHERS PAYABLE CREDIT	PAYMENT DATE	CHECK NO.	
1	5/3/--	118	PC - Time	6 0 0 00		6 0 0 00	5/7/--	V122/ 123	1

3. Prepare two new vouchers for $200 and $400 and enter them in the voucher register. Note the payment of the $200 voucher in the Payment column.

	DATE	VOUCHER NO.	ISSUED TO	PURCHASES DEBIT		VOUCHERS PAYABLE CREDIT	PAYMENT DATE	CHECK NO.	
1	5/7/--	122	PC - Time	2 0 0 00		2 0 0 00	5/7/--	447	1
2	5/7/--	123	PC - Time	4 0 0 00		4 0 0 00			2

Learning Objectives	Key Points to Remember
1 Describe how a voucher system is used to control expenditures.	The three elements of internal control that are combined to control expenditures in a voucher system are: 1. Segregation of duties 2. Authorization procedures and related responsibilities 3. Adequate documents and records
2 Prepare a voucher.	In a voucher system, every acquisition and subsequent payment must be supported by a voucher. When a purchase invoice arrives, the voucher section verifies the quantity, price, and computations on the invoice. In addition, the appropriateness of the purchase is evaluated before preparing the voucher.

3 Describe and use a voucher register.	A voucher is recorded in a voucher register by entering the following information:
	1. Date
	2. Voucher number
	3. Person or business to whom the voucher is issued
	4. Dollar amounts of debits and credits
	     After entry in the voucher register, vouchers are filed in an unpaid vouchers file, normally by due date.
	     The voucher register is posted to the general ledger as follows:
	On a daily basis:
	1. Post General Debit amounts to the general ledger.
	2. Insert the date and posting reference in the accounts.
	3. Insert the account numbers in the posting reference column of the voucher register.
	At the end of each month:
	4. Total, verify the equality of, and rule the amount columns.
	5. Post specific account column totals to the general ledger accounts.
	6. Insert the date and posting reference in the accounts.
	7. Insert the account numbers below the specific account column totals in the voucher register.
	8. Insert a check mark below the General Debit column.

4 Describe the payment process using a voucher system.	On the due date, the voucher and supporting documents are reviewed by the check signer, who prepares and signs the check and sends it to the supplier. After a voucher is paid, the voucher and supporting documents are cancelled to prevent processing them again to create a duplicate payment.

5 Describe and use a check register.	A check is recorded in the check register by entering the following information:
	1. Date
	2. Check number
	3. Payee
	4. Voucher number
	5. Dollar amounts
	The check register is posted to the general ledger as follows:
	1. Total, verify the equality of, and rule the amount columns.
	2. Post column totals to the general ledger accounts.
	3. Insert the date and posting reference in the accounts.
	4. Insert the account numbers below the column totals in the check register.
	     To verify that the sum of the individual amounts owed to creditors equals the Vouchers Payable balance, a schedule of unpaid vouchers is prepared.
	     Special procedures are required when purchases returns and allowances or partial payments occur in a voucher system.

Reflection: Answering the Opening Questions

A voucher system is a control technique requiring every acquisition and subsequent payment to be supported by an approved document called a voucher. A voucher system is most appropriate for medium- and large-size businesses. The volume of transactions in John's business probably is not sufficient to warrant the cost of a voucher system.

KEY TERMS

check register, (465)   A special journal used to record all checks written in a voucher system.

internal controls, (454)   The set of procedures used to ensure that there is proper accounting for all activities of the business.

paid vouchers file, (464)   Contains vouchers paid and cancelled and filed either numerically or by supplier.

unpaid vouchers file, (460)   Vouchers and supporting documents stapled together and filed either by due date (preferred) or by supplier until paid.

voucher, (455)   A document which shows that an acquisition is proper and that payment is authorized.

voucher check, (463)   A check with space for entering data about the voucher being paid.

voucher register, (459)   A special journal used to record purchases of all types of assets and services.

voucher system, (455)   A control technique which requires that every acquisition and subsequent payment be supported by an approved voucher.

DEMONSTRATION PROBLEM

Harpo, Inc., is a retail novelty store. The following transactions relate to operations for the month of March.

March 2   Issued voucher no. 313 to Tremont Rental for March rent, $500.

2   Issued check no. 450 to Tremont Rental, $500. Voucher no. 313.

3   Purchased merchandise from Gail's Gags, $550, terms 2/15, n/60. Voucher no. 314.

4   Purchased merchandise from Silly Sam's, $200, terms 2/10, n/60. Voucher no. 315.

10   Issued check no. 451 to Jerry's Jokes, $500 less $10 discount. Voucher no. 310.

12   Received a credit memo from Silly Sam's for returned merchandise that was purchased on March 4, $100.

14   Issued check no. 452 to Resource Supplies, $250. Voucher no. 311.

16   Purchased merchandise from Giggles, $700, terms 2/10, n/30. Voucher no. 316.

18   Issued check no. 453 to Gail's Gags for purchase made on March 3 less 2% discount. Voucher no. 314.

19   Issued check no. 454 to Donnelley's, $750. Voucher no. 312.

21   Purchased merchandise from Creations, $870, terms 3/15, n/50. Voucher no. 317.

25   Purchased supplies from Hal's Supply, $120, terms 3/10, n/30. Voucher no. 318.

31   Issued check no. 455 to Silly Sam's for purchase made on March 4 less returns made on March 12. Voucher no. 315.

31   Issued voucher no. 319 to Payroll in payment of March wages, $1,250.

31   Issued check no. 456 to Payroll, $1,250. Voucher no. 319.

REQUIRED   Selected general ledger accounts and their opening balances as well as a portion of the voucher register for February are shown below.

1.   Enter the transactions in the voucher register, check register, and general journal. Total, rule, and prove the voucher register and check register.

2.   Post the transactions to the general ledger accounts.

3.   Prepare a schedule of vouchers payable and compare the March 31 balance to the balance of Vouchers Payable in the general ledger.

GENERAL LEDGER

ACCOUNT: **Cash**   ACCOUNT NO. **101**

DATE	ITEM	POST REF.	DEBIT	CREDIT	BALANCE DEBIT	BALANCE CREDIT
20-- Mar. 1	Balance	✓			6 0 0 0 00	

ACCOUNT: **Supplies**   ACCOUNT NO. **141**

DATE	ITEM	POST REF.	DEBIT	CREDIT	BALANCE DEBIT	BALANCE CREDIT
20-- Mar. 1	Balance	✓			4 0 0 00	

ACCOUNT: **Vouchers Payable**   ACCOUNT NO. **202**

DATE	ITEM	POST REF.	DEBIT	CREDIT	BALANCE DEBIT	BALANCE CREDIT
20-- Mar. 1	Balance	✓				1 5 0 0 00

(continued)

ACCOUNT: Purchases   ACCOUNT NO. 501

DATE	ITEM	POST REF.	DEBIT	CREDIT	BALANCE DEBIT	BALANCE CREDIT
20-- Mar. 1	Balance	✓			4 2 5 0 00	

ACCOUNT: Purchases Returns and Allowances   ACCOUNT NO. 501.1

DATE	ITEM	POST REF.	DEBIT	CREDIT	BALANCE DEBIT	BALANCE CREDIT
20-- Mar. 1	Balance	✓				1 0 0 00

ACCOUNT: Purchases Discounts   ACCOUNT NO. 501.2

DATE	ITEM	POST REF.	DEBIT	CREDIT	BALANCE DEBIT	BALANCE CREDIT
20-- Mar. 1	Balance	✓				5 0 00

VOUCHER REGISTER

	DATE	VOUCHER NO.	ISSUED TO	PURCHASES DEBIT	
1	2/24/--	310	Jerry's Jokes	5 0 0 00	1
2	2/26/--	311	Resource Supplies		2
3	2/26/--	312	Donnelly's	7 5 0 00	3
4					4
5					5

Solution

1.

VOUCHER REGISTER

	DATE	VOUCHER NO.	ISSUED TO	PURCHASES DEBIT	
1	2/24/--	310	Jerry's Jokes	5 0 0 00	1
2	2/26/--	311	Resource Supplies		2
3	2/26/--	312	Donnelly's	7 5 0 00	3
4					4
5					5

ACCOUNT: Wages Expense							ACCOUNT NO. 511	
DATE	ITEM	POST REF.	DEBIT	CREDIT	BALANCE			
					DEBIT		CREDIT	
20-- Mar. 1	Balance	✓			2 5 0 0 00			

ACCOUNT: Rent Expense							ACCOUNT NO. 521	
DATE	ITEM	POST REF.	DEBIT	CREDIT	BALANCE			
					DEBIT		CREDIT	
20-- Mar. 1	Balance	✓			1 0 0 0 00			

PAGE 6

	SUPPLIES DEBIT	WAGES EXPENSE DEBIT	GENERAL DEBIT			VOUCHERS PAYABLE CREDIT	PAYMENT		
			ACCOUNT	POST. REF.	AMOUNT		DATE	CHECK NO.	
1						5 0 0 00			1
2	2 5 0 00					2 5 0 00			2
3						7 5 0 00			3
4									4
5									5

PAGE 6

	SUPPLIES DEBIT	WAGES EXPENSE DEBIT	GENERAL DEBIT			VOUCHERS PAYABLE CREDIT	PAYMENT		
			ACCOUNT	POST. REF.	AMOUNT		DATE	CHECK NO.	
1						5 0 0 00	3/10/--	451	1
2	2 5 0 00					2 5 0 00	3/14/--	452	2
3						7 5 0 00	3/19/--	454	3
4									4
5									5

(continued)

1.

VOUCHER REGISTER

	DATE	VOUCHER NO.	ISSUED TO	PURCHASES DEBIT	
1	3/2/--	313	Tremont Rental		1
2	3/3/--	314	Gail's Gags	5 5 0 00	2
3	3/4/--	315	Silly Sam's	2 0 0 00	3
4	3/16/--	316	Giggles	7 0 0 00	4
5	3/21/--	317	Creations	8 7 0 00	5
6	3/25/--	318	Hal's Supply		6
7	3/31/--	319	Payroll		7
8				2 3 2 0 00	8
9				(501)	9
10					10

CHECK REGISTER   PAGE 6

	DATE	CHECK NO.	PAYEE	VOUCHERS PAYABLE DR. NO.	VOUCHERS PAYABLE DR. AMOUNT	PURCHASES DISCOUNTS CREDIT	CASH CREDIT	
1	3/2/--	450	Tremont Rental	313	5 0 0 00		5 0 0 00	1
2	3/10/--	451	Jerry's Jokes	310	5 0 0 00	1 0 00	4 9 0 00	2
3	3/14/--	452	Resource Supplies	311	2 5 0 00		2 5 0 00	3
4	3/18/--	453	Gail's Gags	314	5 5 0 00	1 1 00	5 3 9 00	4
5	3/19/--	454	Donnelly's	312	7 5 0 00		7 5 0 00	5
6	3/31/--	455	Silly Sam's	315	1 0 0 00		1 0 0 00	6
7	3/31/--	456	Payroll	319	1 2 5 0 00		1 2 5 0 00	7
8					3 9 0 0 00	2 1 00	3 8 7 9 00	8
9					(202)	(501.2)	(101)	9

GENERAL JOURNAL   PAGE 3

	DATE	DESCRIPTION	POST REF.	DEBIT	CREDIT	
1	20-- Mar. 12	Vouchers Payable/Silly Sam's	202	1 0 0 00		1
2		Purchases Returns & Allowances	501.1		1 0 0 00	2
3		Received credit memo from Silly Sam's				3
4						4
5						5
6						6
7						7
8						8
9						9
10						10

PAGE 7

	SUPPLIES DEBIT			WAGES EXPENSE DEBIT			GENERAL DEBIT					VOUCHERS PAYABLE CREDIT			PAYMENT			
							ACCOUNT	POST. REF.		AMOUNT					DATE	CHECK NO.	
1							Rent Exp.	521	5 0 0	00		5 0 0	00	3/2/- -	450	1
2												5 5 0	00	3/18/- -	453	2
3												2 0 0	00	3/12/- - 3/31/- -	R/100 455	3
4												7 0 0	00			4
5												8 7 0	00			5
6	1 2 0	00										1 2 0	00			6
7			1 2 5 0	00								1 2 5 0	00	3/31/- -	456	7
8	1 2 0	00	1 2 5 0	00				5 0 0	00		4 1 9 0	00			8
9	(141)		(511)					(✓)			(202)				9
10																10

2.

GENERAL LEDGER

ACCOUNT: **Cash**　　　　ACCOUNT NO. 101

DATE		ITEM	POST REF.	DEBIT	CREDIT	BALANCE	
						DEBIT	CREDIT
20-- Mar.	1	Balance	✓			6 0 0 0 00	
	31		CK6		3 8 7 9 00	2 1 2 1 00	

ACCOUNT: **Supplies**　　　　ACCOUNT NO. 141

DATE		ITEM	POST REF.	DEBIT	CREDIT	BALANCE	
						DEBIT	CREDIT
20-- Mar.	1	Balance	✓			4 0 0 00	
	31		VR7	1 2 0 00		5 2 0 00	

ACCOUNT: **Vouchers Payable**　　　　ACCOUNT NO. 202

DATE		ITEM	POST REF.	DEBIT	CREDIT	BALANCE	
						DEBIT	CREDIT
20-- Mar.	1	Balance	✓				1 5 0 0 00
	12		J3	1 0 0 00			1 4 0 0 00
	31		VR7		4 1 9 0 00		5 5 9 0 00
	31		CK6	3 9 0 0 00			1 6 9 0 00

ACCOUNT: **Purchases**　　　　ACCOUNT NO. 501

DATE		ITEM	POST REF.	DEBIT	CREDIT	BALANCE	
						DEBIT	CREDIT
20-- Mar.	1	Balance	✓			4 2 5 0 00	
	31		VR7	2 3 2 0 00		6 5 7 0 00	

(continued)

2.

ACCOUNT: Purchases Returns and Allowances   ACCOUNT NO. 501.1

DATE		ITEM	POST REF.	DEBIT	CREDIT	BALANCE DEBIT	BALANCE CREDIT
20-- Mar.	1	Balance	✓				1 0 0 00
	12		J3		1 0 0 00		2 0 0 00

ACCOUNT: Purchases Discounts   ACCOUNT NO. 501.2

DATE		ITEM	POST REF.	DEBIT	CREDIT	BALANCE DEBIT	BALANCE CREDIT
20-- Mar.	1	Balance	✓				5 0 00
	31		CK6		2 1 00		7 1 00

ACCOUNT: Wages Expense   ACCOUNT NO. 511

DATE		ITEM	POST REF.	DEBIT	CREDIT	BALANCE DEBIT	BALANCE CREDIT
20-- Mar.	1	Balance	✓			2 5 0 0 00	
	31		VR7	1 2 5 0 00		3 7 5 0 00	

ACCOUNT: Rent Expense   ACCOUNT NO. 521

DATE		ITEM	POST REF.	DEBIT	CREDIT	BALANCE DEBIT	BALANCE CREDIT
20-- Mar.	1	Balance	✓			1 0 0 0 00	
	2		VR7	5 0 0 00		1 5 0 0 00	

3.

Harpo, Inc.
Schedule of Vouchers Payable
March 31, 20 - -

Giggles	$	7	0	0	00
Creations		8	7	0	00
Hal's Supply		1	2	0	00
	$1	6	9	0	00

REVIEW QUESTIONS

1. What three elements of internal control are particularly important for controlling expenditures?

2. What two key controls over expenditures are provided by the voucher system?

3. When a purchase invoice is received from a supplier, what procedures are performed by the voucher section?

4. List four items of information about each voucher entered in the voucher register.

5. Why is it desirable to file unpaid vouchers by due date?

6. What steps are followed in posting from the voucher register to the general ledger?

7. After a voucher is paid, what should be done with the voucher and supporting documents? Why?

8. List five items of information about each check entered in the check register.

9. What steps are followed in posting from the check register to the general ledger?

10. If the total of the schedule of vouchers payable does not equal the Vouchers Payable balance, what procedures should be used to search for the error?

11. If a partial return of merchandise is made, what procedures are used in a voucher system?

12. If a partial payment is made after a voucher has been created and entered for the full amount of a purchase, what procedures are used in a voucher system?

MANAGING YOUR WRITING

The major fund raiser for a local youth center traditionally has been a variety show put on by the members of the center. Tickets for the show are sold primarily by the members. The tickets are available in boxes at the center, and members simply take them as needed. Money is then turned in for whatever tickets are sold. The new manager of the center is concerned about whether all of the money from ticket sales is being turned in and is seeking your advice. Write a memo to the manager explaining how to control the tickets and money to ensure that both are being accounted for.

ETHICS CASE

Earl Farr, Mandy Wells, and Ron Good are clerks in a busy doctor's office. One of Earl's responsibilities is to reconcile the bank statement. (He isn't involved in authorizing payments, writing checks, or making deposits.) Ron is the accounts receivable clerk. He posts all payments and makes bank deposits. Occasionally, when he gets busy, Earl asks Ron to perform the monthly bank reconciliation. After it is reconciled, Earl initials it as though he had done it. Mandy, who is in charge of accounts payable, has been observing Earl and Ron and is considering saying something to their supervisor, the office manager. Mandy is sure the office manager is unaware of what is going on.

1. Is what Earl and Ron are doing unethical? Would your answer be different if Ron were stealing money?

2. If Mandy chooses not to say anything to the office manager, is she being unethical?

3. Write a short memo from the office manager to Earl, Mandy, and Ron explaining the importance of the segregation of duties.

4. In pairs, play the roles of Mandy and the office manager, assuming Mandy decides to tell the office manager about the situation.

WEB WORK

Vouchers are part of a system of checks and balances that reduce loss to employee theft and embezzling.

Where can loss occur, and what are possible preventative techniques? Check out the following Web pages for some answers:

http://www.oregonmbi.com/controls.htm
http://www.commercepark.com/AAAA/bulletin/2_28_97/intro.html
(http://heintz.swcollege.com)

SERIES A EXERCISES

EXERCISE 13A-1 (LO 1) PURCHASING PROCESS USING A VOUCHER SYSTEM In the flowchart below, identify the documents and records that illustrate the voucher process.

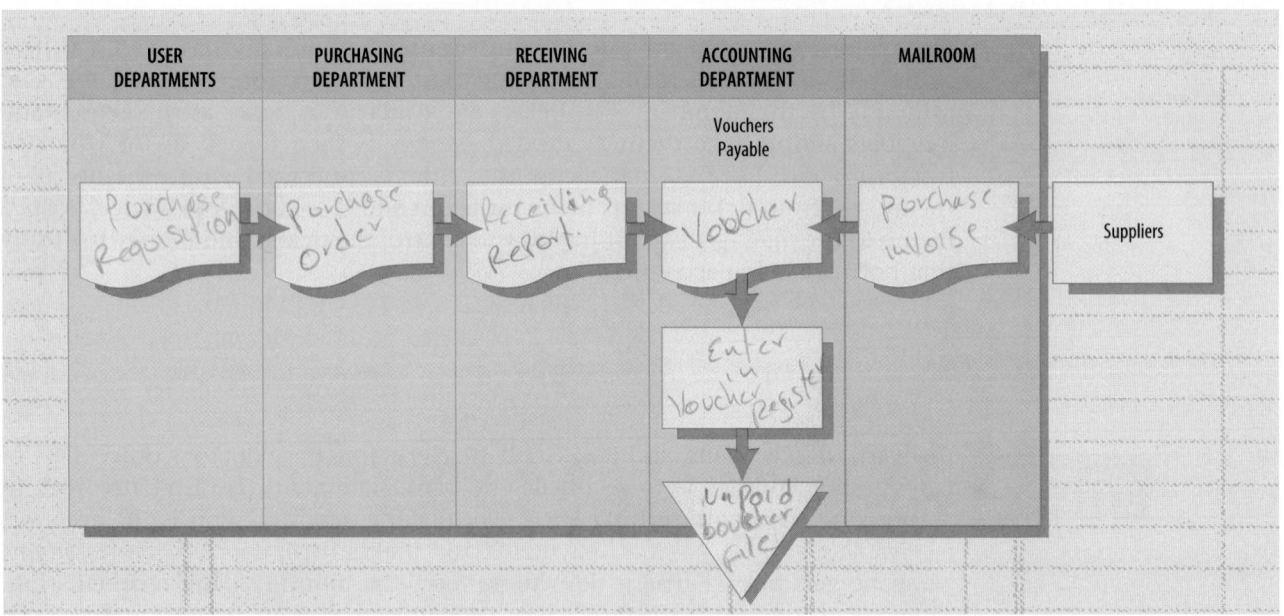

EXERCISE 13A-2 (LO 2) PREPARING A VOUCHER Prepare voucher no. 164 on May 8, similar to the one shown in Figure 13-3 in the chapter, from the purchase invoice shown on page 481.

The supplier, Sportime Corp., sent 12 Prince Spectrum rackets with a unit price of $130 and 2 DuraLink nets with a unit price of $110. Assume that the cash discount will be taken. Indicate that the voucher was prepared by you and authorized by J. Jenkins and that distribution was approved by B. Zimmer.

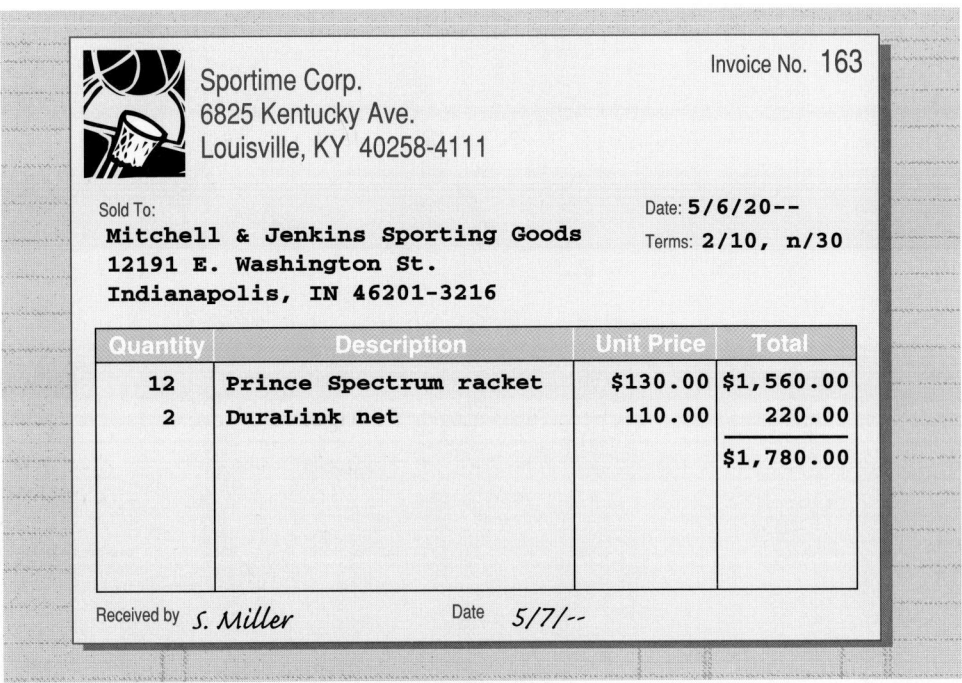

Sportime Corp.
6825 Kentucky Ave.
Louisville, KY 40258-4111

Invoice No. 163

Sold To:
Mitchell & Jenkins Sporting Goods
12191 E. Washington St.
Indianapolis, IN 46201-3216

Date: **5/6/20--**
Terms: **2/10, n/30**

Quantity	Description	Unit Price	Total
12	Prince Spectrum racket	$130.00	$1,560.00
2	DuraLink net	110.00	220.00
			$1,780.00

Received by *S. Miller*   Date *5/7/--*

EXERCISE 13A-3 (LO 3) VOUCHER REGISTER Enter the following vouchers and payments into a voucher register.

Date	Voucher No.	Issued To	Amount	Purpose
6/1	331	Middleton Assoc.	$1,200	June rent
6/5	332	Guzman Distributors	960	Merchandise on account
6/9	333	MicroLabs, Inc.	1,400	Merchandise on account
6/11	334	Miller Office Supply	244	Prepaid office supplies
6/13	335	Bradham Products	1,604	Merchandise on account
6/15	336	Payroll	6,000	Bimonthly paychecks
6/21	337	Guzman Distributors	1,700	Merchandise on account

The following vouchers were paid:

Date Paid	Voucher No.	Check No.
6/10	331	498
6/14	332	499
6/15	336	500
6/18	333	501
6/20	335	502
6/30	337	503

EXERCISE 13A-4 (LO 4) PAYMENT PROCESS USING A VOUCHER SYSTEM In the following flowchart, identify the documents and records that illustrate the payment process using a voucher system.

(continued)

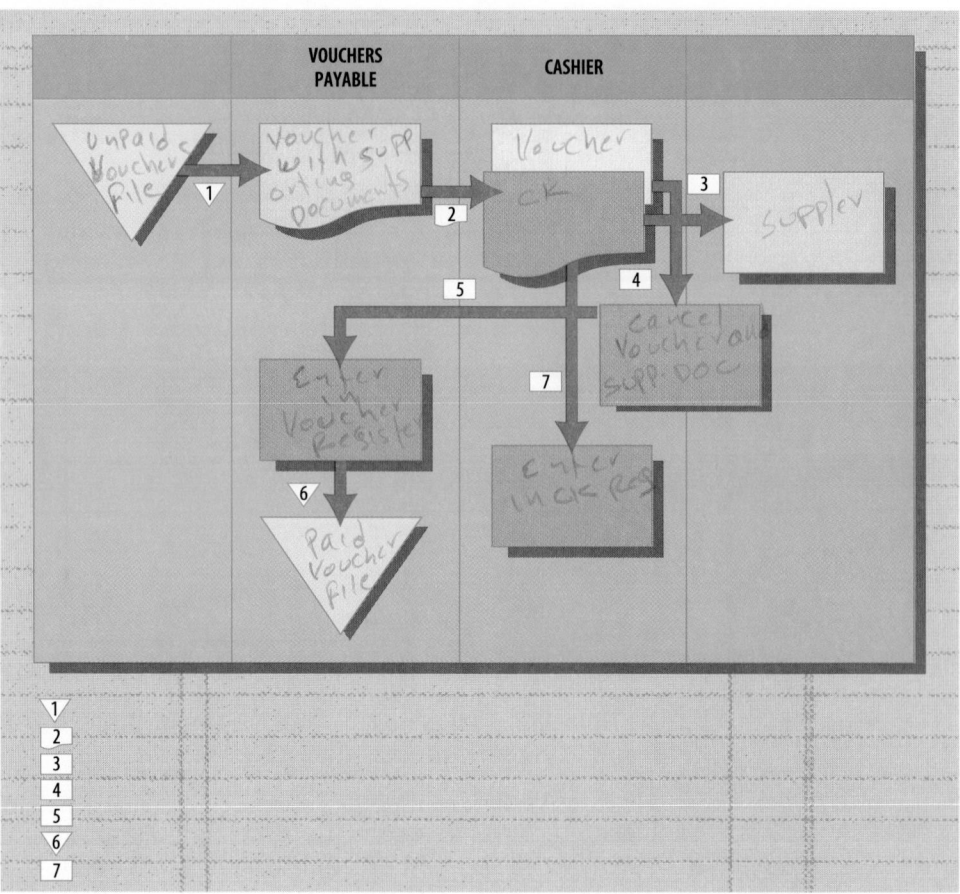

EXERCISE 13A-5 (LO 5) CHECK REGISTER The following information, taken from the voucher register, is evidenced by unpaid vouchers. Enter the appropriate information into a check register. The discount amounts shown should be deducted from the voucher amounts. Total and rule the register.

Date	Voucher No.	Pay To	Amount	Check No.	Purpose	Discount Amount
8/5	111	Armos Bros.	$1,600	406	Merchandise on account	$16.00
8/7	108	H & L Realty	1,000	407	August rent	
8/11	113	Excel Products	760	408	Merchandise on account	15.20
8/13	109	Bell & Mason	1,280	409	Merchandise on account	25.60
8/15	115	Payroll	4,000	410	Bimonthly paychecks	
8/19	117	C. P. Delgado	1,776	411	Merchandise on account	35.52
8/25	119	Office Pro, Inc.	500	412	Office supplies	
8/31	120	Payroll	4,000	413	Bimonthly paychecks	

EXERCISE 13A-6 (LO 5) SCHEDULE OF VOUCHERS PAYABLE Prepare a schedule of vouchers payable for Randalls Appliances, based on information found in the following register.

Voucher Register—left side

	DATE	VOUCHER NO.	ISSUED TO	PURCHASES DEBIT	
1	1/1/--	101	Alomar, Inc.	6 0 0 00	1
2	1/3/--	102	Bremer Office Supplies		2
3	1/6/--	103	Kettles and Kabrus	2 8 0 00	3
4	1/7/--	104	Moore & Johnson		4
5	1/11/--	105	Kitchen Kaboodle	3 0 0 00	5
6	1/13/--	106	Alomar, Inc.	3 7 5 00	6
7	1/16/--	107	Payroll		7
8	1/21/--	108	Rich & Associates	4 0 0 00	8
9	1/29/--	109	Darin Elwood Co.	2 1 9 00	9
10				2 1 7 4 00	10

Voucher Register—right side

PAGE 1

	SUPPLIES DEBIT	WAGES EXPENSE DEBIT	ACCOUNT	POST. REF.	GENERAL DEBIT AMOUNT	VOUCHERS PAYABLE CREDIT	PAYMENT DATE	CHECK NO.	
1						6 0 0 00	1/11/--	2	1
2	1 1 8 00					1 1 8 00			2
3						2 8 0 00	1/24/--	4	3
4			Rent Exp.		5 0 0 00	5 0 0 00	1/7/--	1	4
5						3 0 0 00			5
6						3 7 5 00			6
7		1 0 0 0 00				1 0 0 0 00	1/16/--	3	7
8						4 0 0 00			8
9						2 1 9 00			9
10	1 1 8 00	1 0 0 0 00			5 0 0 00	3 7 9 2 00			10

EXERCISE 13A-7 (LO 5) RETURN OF MERCHANDISE AND PARTIAL PAYMENTS
Enter the following merchandise returns and partial payments in a general journal and in a voucher register like the one on the next page, as appropriate.

Sept. 10   Merchandise purchased from XYZ Co. for $800, voucher no. 203, is returned. A credit memo is received, attached to the voucher, and the voucher is placed in the paid vouchers file.

20   A partial return of merchandise purchased from Trizon Suppliers is made for $200, voucher no. 206. A credit memo is received, attached to the voucher, and the voucher is returned to the unpaid vouchers file.

24   A partial payment for merchandise purchased from F. B. Jones Co. is made for $300 on voucher no. 208, which was for $600. Plan to pay the remaining $300 in two weeks (new vouchers are issued). Check no. 682.

(continued)

28 A partial return of merchandise purchased from Arbiters, Inc. is made for $80, voucher no. 204. A credit memo is received, attached to the voucher, and the voucher is returned to the unpaid vouchers file.

Voucher Register—left side

	DATE	VOUCHER NO.	ISSUED TO	PURCHASES DEBIT	
1	9/6/- -	202	Briggs Store	6 0 0 00	1
2	9/8/- -	203	XYZ Co.	8 0 0 00	2
3	9/10/- -	204	Arbiters, Inc.	7 0 0 00	3
4	9/11/- -	205	Paper Traders		4
5	9/15/- -	206	Trizon Suppliers	3 5 0 00	5
6	9/16/- -	207	Payroll		6
7	9/18/- -	208	F. B. Jones Co.	6 0 0 00	7
8					8

VOUCHER REGISTER

Voucher Register—right side

PAGE 1

	SUPPLIES DEBIT	WAGES EXPENSE DEBIT	GENERAL DEBIT			VOUCHERS PAYABLE CREDIT	PAYMENT		
			ACCOUNT	POST. REF.	AMOUNT		DATE	CHECK NO.	
1						6 0 0 00	9/8/- -	681	1
2						8 0 0 00			2
3						7 0 0 00			3
4	1 8 6 00					1 8 6 00			4
5						3 5 0 00			5
6		1 2 0 0 00				1 2 0 0 00			6
7						6 0 0 00			7
8									8

SERIES A PROBLEMS

PROBLEM 13A-1 (LO 3) VOUCHER REGISTER AND POSTING TO GENERAL LEDGER Escribano Electronics had the following transactions for the month of July 20--:

Date	Voucher No.	Issued To	Amount	Purpose	Date Paid	Check No.
7/1	206	Parkhouse, Inc.	$ 600	July rent	7/1	318
7/3	207	G. B. Fiorucci	1,700	Merchandise	7/18	320
7/5	208	Richardson's	240	Office supplies		
7/9	209	Soto Supply	1,800	Merchandise	7/19	321
7/15	210	Payroll	2,000	Paychecks	7/15	319
7/21	211	Pressman's	1,160	Merchandise		
7/28	212	T. R. Canady Co.	1,240	Merchandise		
7/30	213	Excelsior Ltd.	656	Merchandise		
7/31	214	Payroll	2,000	Paychecks	7/31	322

REQUIRED
1. Enter the transactions for July 20-- on page 7 of the voucher register. Total, rule, and prove the register.

2. Post the voucher register to the general ledger. Use account numbers as shown in the chapter.

3. Prepare a schedule of vouchers payable.

PROBLEM 13A-2 (LO 5) CHECK REGISTER AND POSTING TO GENERAL LEDGER
The following transactions occurred during August 20--. A voucher register is used. Assume terms of 2/10, n/30 for purchases on account and assume that all discounts are taken. General ledger account balances on August 1 were: Cash, $9,862; and Vouchers Payable, $8,482.

Date	Check No.	Pay To	Voucher No.	Amount	Purpose
8/3	111	M. Pearson	108	$ 800	August rent
8/5	112	K. B. Adams Co.	109	550	Merchandise on account
8/8	113	Quality Paper	111	300	Office supplies
8/11	114	Paulson Group	113	600	Merchandise on account
8/15	115	Payroll	115	2,000	Bimonthly payroll
8/17	116	Peerson, Inc.	116	720	Merchandise on account
8/22	117	K. B. Adams Co.	118	380	Merchandise on account
8/25	118	Wilson's	121	440	Merchandise on account
8/31	119	Payroll	123	2,000	Bimonthly payroll

REQUIRED
1. Enter the transactions for August 20-- in the check register (page 8). Total, rule, and prove the register.

2. Post the check register totals to the general ledger. Use account numbers as shown in the chapter.

PROBLEM 13A-3 (LO 3/5) VOUCHER REGISTER, CHECK REGISTER, POSTING, AND SCHEDULE OF VOUCHERS PAYABLE Betty Classic owns the Classic Candle Shop. The following transactions occurred during April 20--. The Classic Candle Shop uses a voucher register, a check register, and a general ledger. Unpaid vouchers are filed and listed at the end of the month. General ledger account balances on April 1 were: Cash, $5,189; and Supplies, $408.

Date	Voucher No.	Issued To	Amount	Purpose	Terms
4/1	1101	Landmark Realty	$ 500	April rent	
4/3	1102	Wax House	280	Merchandise	2/10, n/30
4/5	1103	Designs West	490	Merchandise	2/10, n/30
4/9	1104	Crane Stationers	180	Office supplies	
4/11	1105	Magic Solutions	600	Merchandise	2/10, n/30
4/15	1106	Payroll	1,500	Bimonthly payroll	
4/23	1107	Wax House	510	Merchandise	1/10, n/30
4/25	1108	Baskets & More	440	Merchandise	2/10, n/30
4/28	1109	Magic Solutions	450	Merchandise	2/10, n/30
4/30	1110	Payroll	1,500	Bimonthly payroll	

(continued)

Checks issued:

Date	Check No.	Payee	Voucher No.	Amount
4/1	928	Landmark Realty	1101	$ 500
4/9	929	Crane Stationers	1104	180
4/11	930	Wax House	1102	280
4/15	931	Payroll	1106	1,500
4/19	932	Designs West	1103	490
4/30	933	Payroll	1110	1,500

REQUIRED
1. Enter the transactions for April in the voucher register. Total, rule, and prove the register. Update the Payment column when vouchers are paid.

2. Enter the transactions for April in the check register. Be sure to take discounts where appropriate. Total, rule, and prove the register.

3. Post the voucher register and the check register to the general ledger. Use account numbers as shown in the chapter.

4. Prepare a schedule of vouchers payable.

PROBLEM 13A-4 (LO 3/5) VOUCHER REGISTER, CHECK REGISTER, AND GENERAL JOURNAL (RETURNS AND PARTIAL PAYMENTS) Richard Harris owns Harris's Appliance Store. The following transactions occurred during May 20--. Harris's Appliance Store uses a voucher register, a check register, and a general journal.

May 1   Issued voucher no. 208 to McPherson's Co. for May rent, $800.

1   Issued check no. 411 to McPherson's Co., $800. Voucher no. 208.

3   Purchased merchandise from Welding Supply Co., $280, terms 2/10, n/30. Voucher no. 209.

5   Received a credit memo from Welding Supply Co. for returned merchandise that was purchased on May 3, $40.

7   Purchased supplies from Quality Office Supply, $118. Voucher no. 210.

7   Issued check no. 412 to Quality Office Supply, $118. Voucher no. 210.

10   Purchased merchandise from Piper's Inc., $440, terms 2/10, n/30. Voucher no. 211.

10   Received a credit memo from Piper's Inc., for returned merchandise that was purchased on May 10, $440.

11   Issued check no. 413 to Welding Supply Co. for purchase made on May 3, less return made on May 5 less 2% discount. Voucher no. 209.

12   Purchased merchandise from Moreno's Wholesale, $620, terms 2/10, n/30. Voucher no. 212.

15   Issued voucher no. 213 to Payroll in payment of bimonthly wages, $1,000.

15   Issued check no. 414 to Payroll, $1,000. Voucher no. 213.

19   Purchased merchandise from Welding Supply Co., $860, terms 2/10, n/30. Voucher no. 214.

21   Issued check no. 415 to Welding Supply Co., in partial payment of goods purchased on May 19, $430 less 2% discount. Voucher no. 214. Issued new vouchers no. 215 and 216.

22   Purchased supplies from Quality Office Supply, $210. Voucher no. 217.

23   Issued check no. 416 to Moreno's Wholesale, $620. Voucher no. 212.

25   Purchased merchandise from Regional Distributors, $460, terms 1/10, n/30. Voucher no. 218.

28   Purchased merchandise from Pringle's & Co., $600, terms 2/10, n/30. Voucher no. 219.

31   Issued voucher no. 220 to Payroll in payment of bimonthly wages, $1,000.

31   Issued check no. 417 to Payroll, $1,000. Voucher no. 220.

REQUIRED   Enter the transactions in a voucher register (page 5), check register (page 5), or general journal (page 5), as appropriate. Total, rule, and prove the voucher register and check register.

SERIES B EXERCISES

EXERCISE 13B-1 (LO 1) PURCHASING PROCESS USING A VOUCHER SYSTEM In the following flowchart, identify the departments and other sources of the documents and records that illustrate the voucher process.

EXERCISE 13B-2 (LO 2) PREPARING A VOUCHER Prepare voucher no. 193 on May 18, similar to the one shown in Figure 13-3 in the chapter, from the purchase invoice shown below.

The supplier, Sportime Corp., sent 33 cases of Sport tennis balls at $30 a case and 14 Wilke racket covers at $25 each. Assume that the cash discount will be taken. Indicate that the voucher was prepared by you and authorized by J. Jenkins and that distribution was approved by B. Zimmer.

EXERCISE 13B-3 (LO 3) VOUCHER REGISTER Enter the following vouchers and payments into a voucher register.

Date	Voucher No.	Issued To	Amount	Purpose
7/1	431	Katz Management	$ 200	July rent
7/5	432	Garcia Distributors	340	Merchandise on account
7/9	433	Mirror Labs, Inc.	150	Merchandise on account
7/11	434	Owens Office Supply	55	Prepaid office supplies
7/13	435	Richards Products	176	Merchandise on account
7/15	436	Payroll	1,250	Bimonthly paychecks
7/21	437	Garcia Distributors	175	Merchandise on account

The following vouchers were paid:

Date Paid	Voucher No.	Check No.
7/10	431	598
7/14	432	599
7/15	436	600
7/18	433	601
7/20	435	602

EXERCISE 13B-4 (LO 4) PAYMENT PROCESS USING A VOUCHER SYSTEM The following flowchart illustrates the payment process using a voucher system. Briefly describe each document and file.

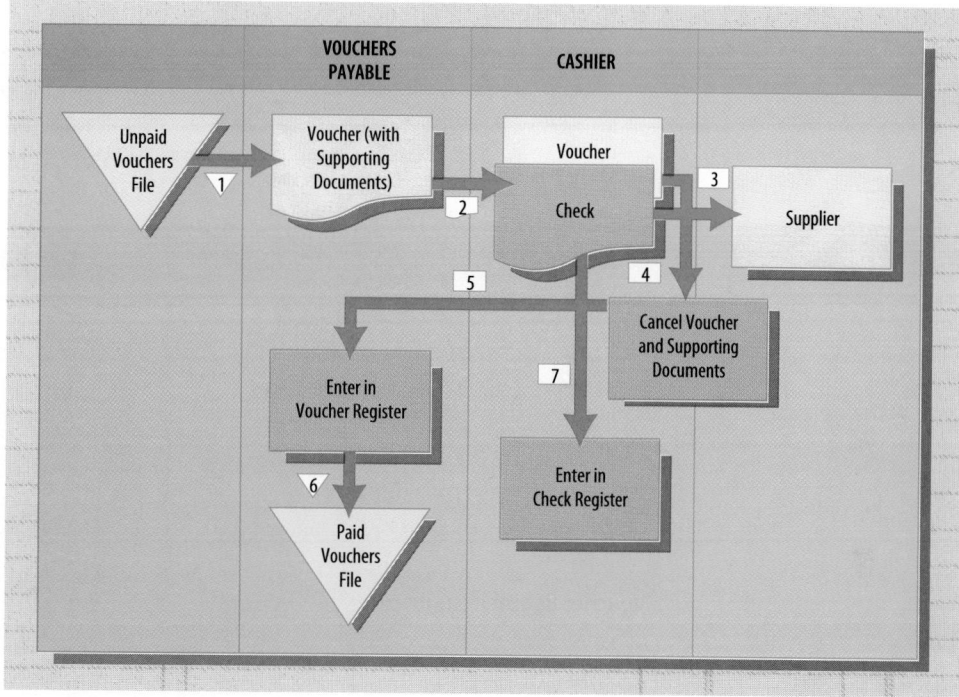

EXERCISE 13B-5 (LO 5) CHECK REGISTER The following information, taken from the voucher register, is evidenced by unpaid vouchers. Enter the appropriate information into a check register. The discount amounts shown should be deducted from the voucher amounts. Total and rule the register.

Date	Voucher No.	Pay To	Amount	Check No.	Purpose	Discount Amount
9/5	1111	Mendel Bros.	$ 300	2814	Merchandise on account	$3.00
9/7	1108	B & J Realty	200	2815	September rent	
9/11	1113	Trycl Products	140	2816	Merchandise on account	$2.80
9/13	1114	Myro & Smith	270	2817	Merchandise on account	$5.40
9/15	1109	Payroll	1,100	2818	Bimonthly paychecks	
9/19	1117	T. M. Kingley	244	2819	Merchandise on account	$2.44
9/25	1123	Bly Stationers	75	2820	Office supplies	
9/30	1120	Payroll	1,100	2821	Bimonthly paychecks	

EXERCISE 13B-6 (LO 5) SCHEDULE OF VOUCHERS PAYABLE Prepare a schedule of vouchers payable for M. B. Jacobs, based on information found in the following voucher register.

Voucher Register—left side

	DATE	VOUCHER NO.	ISSUED TO	PURCHASES DEBIT	
1	3/1/--	306	Richland Associates		1
2	3/4/--	307	Carlson & Daughter	8 0 0 00	2
3	3/6/--	308	Wu Office Supplies		3
4	3/9/--	309	Black & Brewer	6 0 0 00	4
5	3/12/--	310	Kreklow Company	3 8 0 00	5
6	3/16/--	311	Payroll		6
7	3/21/--	312	Anderson Enterprises	2 6 0 00	7
8	3/24/--	313	Carlson & Daughter	4 1 0 00	8
9	3/28/--	314	Wu Office Supplies		9
10	3/31/--	315	Payroll		10
11				2 4 5 0 00	11

Voucher Register—right side

PAGE 3

	SUPPLIES DEBIT	WAGES EXPENSE DEBIT	GENERAL DEBIT			VOUCHERS PAYABLE CREDIT	PAYMENT		
			ACCOUNT	POST. REF.	AMOUNT		DATE	CHECK NO.	
1			Rent Exp.		3 0 0 00	3 0 0 00	3/2/--	806	1
2						8 0 0 00	3/11/--	808	2
3	1 8 0 00					1 8 0 00	3/8/--	807	3
4						6 0 0 00			4
5						3 8 0 00	3/18/--	810	5
6		1 0 0 0 00				1 0 0 0 00	3/16/--	809	6
7						2 6 0 00			7
8						4 1 0 00			8
9	9 8 00					9 8 00			9
10		1 0 0 0 00				1 0 0 0 00	3/31/--	811	10
11	2 7 8 00	2 0 0 0 00			3 0 0 00	5 0 2 8 00			11

EXERCISE 13B-7 (LO 5) RETURN OF MERCHANDISE AND PARTIAL PAYMENTS Enter the following merchandise returns and partial payments in a general journal and in a voucher register like the one on the next page, as appropriate.

Sept. 15 Merchandise purchased from Arbiters, Inc. for $700, voucher no. 204, is returned. A credit memo is received, attached to the voucher, and the voucher is placed in the paid vouchers file.

20 A partial return of merchandise purchased from XYZ Co. is made for $300, voucher no. 203. A credit memo is received, attached to the voucher, and the voucher is returned to the unpaid vouchers file.

25   A partial payment for merchandise purchased from Trizon Suppliers is made for $150 on voucher no. 206, which was for $350. Plan to pay the remaining $200 in two weeks (new vouchers are issued). Check no. 682.

30   A partial return of merchandise purchased from F. B. Jones Co. is made for $20, voucher no. 208. A credit memo is received, attached to the voucher, and the voucher is returned to the unpaid vouchers file.

Voucher Register—left side

VOUCHER REGISTER

	DATE	VOUCHER NO.	ISSUED TO	PURCHASES DEBIT	
1	9/6/--	202	Briggs Store	6 0 0 00	1
2	9/8/--	203	XYZ Co.	8 0 0 00	2
3	9/10/--	204	Arbiters, Inc.	7 0 0 00	3
4	9/11/--	205	Paper Traders		4
5	9/15/--	206	Trizon Suppliers	3 5 0 00	5
6	9/16/--	207	Payroll		6
7	9/18/--	208	F. B. Jones Co.	6 0 0 00	7
8					8

Voucher Register—right side

PAGE 1

	SUPPLIES DEBIT	WAGES EXPENSE DEBIT	ACCOUNT	POST. REF.	AMOUNT	VOUCHERS PAYABLE CREDIT	DATE	CHECK NO.	
1						6 0 0 00	9/8/--	681	1
2						8 0 0 00			2
3						7 0 0 00			3
4	1 8 6 00					1 8 6 00			4
5						3 5 0 00			5
6		1 2 0 0 00				1 2 0 0 00			6
7						6 0 0 00			7
8									8

SERIES B PROBLEMS

PROBLEM 13B-1 (LO 3) VOUCHER REGISTER AND POSTING TO GENERAL LEDGER Stodolski Sounds had the following transactions for the month of July 20--:

Date	Voucher No.	Issued To	Amount	Purpose	Date Paid	Check No.
7/1	771	Milltown Realty	$1,000	July rent	7/1	330
7/4	772	Khalaf Electronics	1,700	Merchandise	7/11	332
7/7	773	Phak's	640	Office supplies	7/8	331
7/11	774	Breck Sound Supply	760	Merchandise	7/21	334
7/15	775	Payroll	3,000	Bimonthly paychecks	7/15	333
7/21	776	Clear Tone Disks	1,360	Merchandise		
7/28	777	Khalaf Electronics	820	Merchandise		
7/29	778	Phak's	456	Office supplies		
7/31	779	Payroll	3,000	Bimonthly paychecks	7/31	335

REQUIRED

1. Enter the transactions for July 20-- in the voucher register (page 7). Total, rule, and prove the voucher register.

2. Post the voucher register to the general ledger. Use account numbers as shown in the chapter.

3. Prepare a schedule of vouchers payable.

PROBLEM 13B-2 (LO 5) CHECK REGISTER AND POSTING TO GENERAL LEDGER The following transactions were for the month of August 20--. A voucher register is used. Assume terms of 2/10, n/30 for purchases on account, and assume that all discounts are taken. General ledger account balances on August 1 were: Cash, $9,862; and Vouchers Payable, $8,482.

Date	Check No.	Pay To	Voucher No.	Amount	Purpose
8/2	211	Realty Co.	108	$600	August rent
8/5	212	Tri-Cities Co.	111	238	Merchandise on account
8/8	213	Miller's	112	412	Merchandise on account
8/10	214	A & E Office Co.	115	108	Office supplies
8/15	215	Payroll	114	900	Bimonthly payroll
8/18	216	Blythe Mill	118	620	Merchandise on account
8/22	217	Tri-Cities Co.	119	512	Merchandise on account
8/27	218	Miller's	122	816	Merchandise on account
8/31	219	Payroll	123	900	Bimonthly payroll

REQUIRED

1. Enter the transactions for August 20-- in the check register (page 8). Total, rule, and prove the register.

2. Post the check register totals to the general ledger. Use account numbers as shown in the chapter.

W & D

PROBLEM 13B-3 (LO 3/5) VOUCHER REGISTER, CHECK REGISTER, POSTING, AND SCHEDULE OF VOUCHERS PAYABLE Jane Hledik is owner of Hledik Lawn Supply. The following transactions occurred during April 20--. Hledik Lawn Supply uses a voucher register, a check register, and a general ledger. Unpaid vouchers are filed and listed at the end of the month. General ledger account balances on April 1 were: Cash, $5,189; and Supplies, $408.

Vouchers issued:

Date	Voucher No.	Issued To	Amount	Purpose	Terms
4/2	662	Brenner's	$600	April rent	
4/4	663	Lawn Care Wholesale	300	Merchandise	2/10, n/30
4/7	664	Southern Supply	128	Office supplies	
4/10	665	Clay's Chemicals	420	Merchandise	1/20, n/30
4/13	666	Mendel & Son	530	Merchandise	2/10, n/30
4/15	667	Payroll	950	Bimonthly payroll	
4/19	668	Lawn Care Wholesale	570	Merchandise	1/10, n/30
4/27	669	Southern Supply	99	Office supplies	
4/29	670	Lakeside Fertilizer	280	Merchandise	2/10, n/30
4/30	671	Payroll	950	Bimonthly payroll	

Checks issued:

Date	Check No.	Payee	Voucher No.	Amount
4/2	748	Brenner's	662	$600
4/7	749	Southern Supply	664	128
4/11	750	Lawn Care Wholesale	663	300
4/15	751	Payroll	667	950
4/20	752	Mendel & Son	666	530
4/30	753	Payroll	671	950

REQUIRED

1. Enter the transactions for April in the voucher register. Total, rule, and prove the register. Update the Payment column when vouchers are paid.

2. Enter the transactions for April in the check register. Be sure to take discounts where appropriate. Total, rule, and prove the register.

3. Post the voucher register and the check register to the general ledger. Use account numbers as shown in the chapter.

4. Prepare a schedule of vouchers payable.

PROBLEM 13B-4 (LO 3/5) VOUCHER REGISTER, CHECK REGISTER, AND GENERAL JOURNAL (RETURNS AND PARTIAL PAYMENTS) Michael Blake owns Blake's Appliance Store. The following transactions occurred during May 20--. Blake's Appliance Store uses a voucher register, a check register, and a general journal.

May 1   Issued voucher no. 308 to Johnson & Smith for May rent, $500.

1   Issued check no. 411 to Johnson & Smith in payment of May rent, $500. Voucher no. 308.

3   Purchased merchandise from Wilson Supply Co., $380, terms 2/10, n/30. Voucher no. 309.

5   Received a credit memo from Wilson Supply Co. for returned merchandise that was purchased May 3, $50.

(continued)

7   Purchased supplies from B & J Office Supply, $138. Voucher no. 310.

7   Issued check no. 412 to B & J Office Supply, $138. Voucher no. 310.

10   Purchased merchandise from P. T. Benkley Co., $540, terms 2/10, n/30. Voucher no. 311.

11   Received a credit memo from P. T. Benkley Co. for returned merchandise that was purchased May 10, $540.

11   Issued check no. 413 to Wilson Supply Co. for purchase made on May 3 less returns made on May 5 less 2% discount. Voucher no. 309.

12   Purchased merchandise from Wesley's Wholesale, $720, terms 2/10, n/30. Voucher no. 312.

15   Issued voucher no. 313 to Payroll in payment of bimonthly wages, $1,000.

15   Issued check no. 414 to Payroll, $1,000. Voucher no. 313.

19   Purchased merchandise from Wilson Supply Co., $660, terms 2/10, n/30. Voucher no. 314.

21   Issued check no. 415 to Wilson Supply Co. in partial payment for goods purchased on May 19, $330 less 2% discount. Voucher no. 314. Issued new vouchers no. 315 and 316.

22   Purchased supplies from B & J Office Supply, $120. Voucher no. 317.

23   Issued check no. 416 to Wesley's Wholesale, $720. Voucher no. 312.

25   Purchased merchandise from Eastern Distributors, $360, terms 1/10, n/30. Voucher no. 318.

28   Purchased merchandise from Torres & Co., $400, terms 2/10, n/30. Voucher no. 319.

31   Issued voucher no. 320 to Payroll in payment of bimonthly wages, $1,000.

31   Issued check no. 417 to Payroll, $1,000. Voucher no. 320.

REQUIRED   Enter the transactions in a voucher register (page 5), check register (page 5), or general journal (page 5), as appropriate. Total, rule, and prove the voucher register and check register.

MASTERY PROBLEM

Sunshine Flower Shop began operations in the month of July. The following transactions occurred during the first month of the business.

July 1   Purchased merchandise from Thorny Wholesale, $600. Voucher no. 1.

2   Issued check no. 1 to Strongs Rental for July rent, $1,000. Voucher no. 2

3   Purchased merchandise from Flowerbed, Inc., $470, terms 2/15, n/60, FOB shipping point. Voucher no. 3.

7   Issued check no. 2 to Thorny Wholesale in partial payment for goods purchased on July 1, $300. Voucher no. 1. Issued new vouchers no. 4 and 5.

9   Issued check no. 3 to Charlie's Trucking for shipping charges, $20. Voucher no. 6.

15   Issued check no. 4 to Payroll for wages, $600. Voucher no. 7.

16   Purchased merchandise from Petals Co., $377, terms 2/15, n/30. Voucher no. 8.

17   Purchased merchandise from Weeds Plus, $436, terms 3/15, n/60. Voucher no. 9.

18   Issued check no. 5 to Flowerbed, Inc., for goods purchased on July 3 less discount. Voucher no. 3.

23   Purchased supplies from Staples Supply, $150. Voucher no. 10

25   Received a credit memo from Weeds Plus for returned merchandise that was purchased on July 17, $80.

31   Issued check no. 6 to Petals Co. for goods purchased on July 16 less discount. Voucher no. 8.

31   Issued check no. 7 to Payroll for wages, $600. Voucher no. 11.

REQUIRED   The general ledger accounts are listed below. The $6,000 with which the Flower Shop began business is entered in the cash account. Only this account has a beginning balance.

Cash	101
Supplies	141
Vouchers Payable	202
Purchases	501
Purchases Returns and Allowances	501.1
Purchases Discounts	501.2
Freight-In	502
Wages Expense	511
Rent Expense	521

1.   Enter all transactions in the voucher register, check register, and general journal. Total, rule, and prove the voucher register and check register.

2.   Post the transactions to the general ledger.

3.   Prepare a schedule of vouchers payable and compare the July 31 total to the balance of Vouchers Payable in the general ledger.

Self-Study Test Questions

True/False

1. The voucher system is a control technique that requires every acquisition and subsequent payment to be supported by an approved voucher.

2. A voucher is prepared after the check is issued for payment of an invoice.

3. Segregation of duties, authorization procedures, and adequate documents and records are examples of internal controls.

4. The total of the schedule of vouchers payable should be the same as the total of the vouchers with a blank in the Payment column of the voucher register.

5. A voucher register is used together with a cash payments journal and a purchases journal.

Multiple Choice

1. The check register takes the place of the

   (a) voucher register.   (c) purchases journal.
   (b) cash payments journal.   (d) sales journal.

2. The unpaid vouchers file often replaces the

   (a) voucher register.
   (b) purchases journal.
   (c) cash payments journal.
   (d) accounts payable ledger.

3. In the check register, _____ is always debited.

   (a) Vouchers Payable   (c) Purchases
   (b) Accounts Payable   (d) Cash

4. When merchandise is returned and a credit memo is received and attached to the unpaid voucher, _____ is credited.

   (a) Vouchers Payable
   (b) Accounts Payable
   (c) Purchases Returns and Allowances
   (d) Purchases Discounts

5. When a partial payment is made for merchandise, the original voucher is cancelled, and _____ is credited.

   (a) Cash   (c) Accounts Payable
   (b) Purchases   (d) Vouchers Payable

The answers to the Self-Study Test Questions are at the end of the text.

14

Adjustments and the Work Sheet for a Merchandising Business

Often we are expected to pay in advance for goods and services. This is true for season tickets for sporting events, magazine subscriptions, or tickets for popular operas or rock concerts. In return, we expect to receive the goods or services. Often, John Zenith receives cash deposits on large orders. How should these cash receipts be treated by his business?

LEARNING OBJECTIVES:
Careful study of this chapter should enable you to:

LO 1   Prepare an adjustment for merchandise inventory.

LO 2   Prepare an adjustment for unearned revenue.

LO 3   Prepare a work sheet for a merchandising business.

LO 4   Journalize adjusting entries for a merchandising business.

In Chapters 11 through 13, we learned how to account for the day-to-day transactions of a merchandising business. In this chapter, we focus on end-of-period adjustments and the preparation of the work sheet. Finally, in Chapter 15, we will complete the accounting cycle by preparing financial statements and closing entries.

A work sheet for a merchandising business is similar to the work sheet prepared for a service business (Chapter 5). It is used to prepare adjustments for supplies, prepaid insurance, wages earned but not paid, depreciation, and other necessary year-end adjustments. A merchandising business must also make an adjustment to properly report the amount of merchandise inventory held at the end of the accounting period. While revisiting the work sheet, we will also introduce a new adjustment for unearned revenue.

ADJUSTMENT FOR MERCHANDISE INVENTORY

LO 1   Prepare an adjustment for merchandise inventory.

Figure 14-1 provides a review of the entries made when a business buys and sells merchandise. Note that the merchandise inventory account is not debited or credited during the year.

FIGURE 14-1   Review of Entries for Purchase and Sale of Merchandise

TRANSACTION	ENTRY		
Purchase of merchandise	Purchases	xxx	
	Accounts Payable or Cash		xxx
Sale of merchandise	Accounts Receivable or Cash	xxx	
	Sales		xxx

Since sales and purchases have taken place during the year, the beginning balance of the merchandise inventory account no longer provides an accurate picture of the inventory held at the end of the year. Thus, an adjustment must be made to remove the beginning inventory and enter the ending inventory in the merchandise inventory account. The quantity of inventory on hand at the end of the accounting period is determined by taking a physical count of the goods on hand. This process is referred to as a **physical inventory**. The cost of these goods is determined by reviewing the accounting records. Of course, this year's ending inventory becomes next year's beginning inventory.

To illustrate the adjustment for merchandise inventory, let's assume that Ponder's Bike Parts had a beginning merchandise inventory of $25,000. During the year, the entries shown in Figure 14-1 were made as merchandise was purchased and sold. At the end of the accounting period, a physical inventory of the merchandise determined that merchandise costing $30,000 was still on hand. This indicates that the cost of the merchandise purchased exceeded cost of goods sold by $5,000.

LEARNING KEY: To adjust the merchandise inventory account, take out the old and bring in the new.

As shown in Figure 14-2, the inventory adjustment is made in two steps:

STEP 1 In adjustment (a), the beginning inventory ($25,000) is removed by crediting Merchandise Inventory. Income Summary is debited because this amount is used in the calculation of cost of goods sold. "Cost of goods sold" is an expense on the income statement.

STEP 2 In adjustment (b), the ending inventory ($30,000) is entered by debiting Merchandise Inventory. Income Summary is credited because this amount also is used in the calculation of cost of goods sold. After making the second adjustment, the balance of $30,000 in Merchandise Inventory reflects the inventory on hand at the end of the accounting period.

 LEARNING KEY: Income Summary is used to adjust Merchandise Inventory. It is also used when closing the temporary owner's equity accounts.

FIGURE 14-2 Two-Step Adjustment for Merchandise Inventory

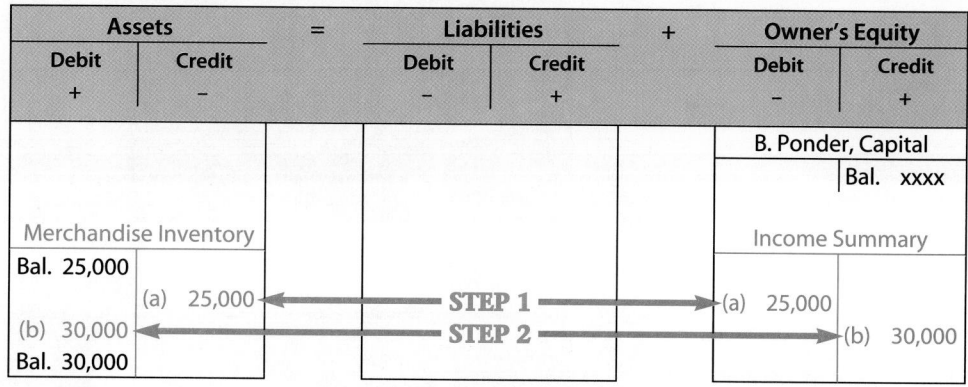

The two-step adjustment process is a bit unusual. Perhaps the best way to explain the reason for this approach is by illustrating how these adjustments are made on the work sheet and how the work sheet information is used to prepare the income statement. Figure 14-3 illustrates a partial work sheet for Ponder's Bike Parts and the cost of goods sold section of the income statement.

The inventory adjustments are made following the two-step process described above.

Step 1	Income Summary	25,000	
	Merchandise Inventory		25,000
Step 2	Merchandise Inventory	30,000	
	Income Summary		30,000

Both the debit of $25,000 and the credit of $30,000 made to the income summary account are extended to the Adjusted Trial Balance and Income Statement columns. *This is the only time that the individual figures, rather than the net amount, are extended on the work sheet.* It is done in this case because the individual amounts are needed for the calculation of cost of goods sold on the income statement. As shown in Figure 14-3, all of the information needed for the preparation of the income statement is in the Income Statement columns of the work sheet. This is the result of using the two-step adjustment process for inventory and extending both the debit and credit made to Income Summary.

> **LEARNING KEY:** Both the debit and credit amounts on the income summary line are extended. This is because both amounts are needed to prepare the income statement. The amount in the debit column is the beginning inventory. The amount in the credit column is the ending inventory.

A BROADER VIEW

THE IMPORTANCE OF INVENTORY

Note the important role of the ending inventory in the calculation of cost of goods sold in Figure 14-3. If the ending inventory is overstated for any reason, net income will also be overstated. Given this important relationship, auditors observe and verify the accuracy of the physical inventory. However, unethical managers, desperate to improve profits, have on occasion found ways to mislead auditors.

In one case, managers overstated inventory counts for items that the auditors had not physically verified. In another case, auditors found a barrel whose contents had been valued by management at thousands of dollars. It actually contained floor sweepings. Finally, there was a case where management called the auditor, the day after the inventory audit, to report that additional inventory had arrived and should be included in the inventory count. The auditor never verified that the inventory was real. It turned out to be a scam that helped the company double its reported profits for the year. These unfortunate events highlight the reason auditors must exercise great care when conducting an inventory audit.

FIGURE 14-3 Calculation of Cost of Goods Sold Using Information in the Income Statement Columns of the Work Sheet

Ponder's Bike Parts
Work Sheet
For Year Ended December 31, 20 - -

ACCOUNT TITLE	TRIAL BALANCE DEBIT	TRIAL BALANCE CREDIT	ADJUSTMENTS DEBIT	ADJUSTMENTS CREDIT	ADJUSTED TRIAL BALANCE DEBIT	ADJUSTED TRIAL BALANCE CREDIT	INCOME STATEMENT DEBIT	INCOME STATEMENT CREDIT	BALANCE SHEET DEBIT	BALANCE SHEET CREDIT	
											1
											2
											3
											4
Merchandise Inventory	25 0 0 0 00		(b) 30 0 0 0 00	(a) 25 0 0 0 00	30 0 0 0 00			Ending Inventory 30 0 0 0 00	30 0 0 0 00		5
Income Summary			(a) 25 0 0 0 00	(b) 30 0 0 0 00		30 0 0 0 00	Beginning Inventory 25 0 0 0 00	30 0 0 0 00			6
Purchases	80 0 0 0 00				80 0 0 0 00		Purchases 80 0 0 0 00				7
Purchases Returns and Allowances		1 0 0 0 00				1 0 0 0 00		1 0 0 0 00	Purchases Returns & Allow.		8
Purchases Discounts		5 0 0 00				5 0 0 00		5 0 0 00	Purchases Discounts		9
Freight-In	7 0 0 00				7 0 0 00		Freight-In 7 0 0 00				10
											11
											12
											13
											14

Cost of goods sold:
Merchandise inventory, January 1			$ 25 0 0 0 00	
Purchases		$ 80 0 0 0 00		
Less: Purchases returns and allowances	$ 1 0 0 0 00			
Purchases discounts	5 0 0 00	1 5 0 0 00		
Net purchases		$ 78 5 0 0 00		
Add freight-in		7 0 0 00		
Cost of goods purchased			79 2 0 0 00	
Goods available for sale			$104 2 0 0 00	
Less merchandise inventory, December 31			30 0 0 0 00	
Cost of goods sold				$ 74 2 0 0 00

ADJUSTMENT FOR UNEARNED REVENUE

LO 2 Prepare an adjustment for unearned revenue.

Some businesses require payment before delivering a product or performing a service. Examples include insurance companies, magazine publishers, apartment complexes, college food services, and professional sports and theater companies that sell season tickets. The cash received in advance is called **unearned revenue**. Since the cash has been received in advance, the company owes the customers the product or service, or must refund their money. Thus, unearned revenue is reported as a *liability* on the balance sheet.

LEARNING KEY: Remember, under the accrual basis of accounting, revenue is recorded when *earned* regardless of when cash is received.

To illustrate, let's assume that the Brown County Playhouse sells season tickets for five plays produced throughout the year. Tickets sell for $10 for each play ($50 for a season ticket) and a maximum of 1,000 seats can be sold for each play. For simplicity, let's assume that all shows sell out during the first week that season tickets are available for sale. As shown below and in Figure 14-4, the sale of the tickets would be recorded as follows:

8	(1) Cash	50 0 0 0 00			8
9	Unearned Ticket Revenue		50 0 0 0 00		9
10	Season ticket sales				10
11	($10 × 1,000 seats × 5 shows)				11

To prepare financial statements following production of the third show, an adjusting entry is needed to recognize that $30,000 ($10 × 1,000 seats × 3 shows) in ticket revenue has been earned. To do this, the following adjusting entry is made:

13	Adjusting Entries				13
14	(Adj) Unearned Ticket Revenue	30 0 0 0 00			14
15	Ticket Revenue		30 0 0 0 00		15

The remaining balance of $20,000 in Unearned Ticket Revenue is reported as a current liability on the balance sheet.

FIGURE 14-4 Entries for Unearned Revenue

Assets		=	Liabilities		+	Owner's Equity	
Debit	**Credit**		**Debit**	**Credit**		**Debit**	**Credit**
+	−		−	+		−	+

Expanded Chart of Accounts

Let's take a look at where the new accounts for a merchandising business fit into a chart of accounts. Recall that the chart of accounts follows the form of the accounting equation (Assets = Liabilities + Owner's Equity + Revenues − Expenses). A chart of accounts for Northern Micro is provided in Figure 14-5. Note the classification of the new accounts introduced in Chapters 11 and 12 for a merchandising firm.

Merchandise Inventory is listed as a current asset. Since Northern Micro sells subscriptions to a computer magazine that it produces, Unearned Subscriptions Revenue is listed as a current liability, and Subscriptions Revenue is listed as a revenue. Sales Returns and Allowances and Sales Discounts are **contra-revenue accounts**. Recall, however, that Northern Micro does not offer sales discounts.

Purchases, Purchases Returns and Allowances, Purchases Discounts, and Freight-In are used to compute cost of goods sold. Thus, they are listed under this heading. Purchases Returns and Allowances and Purchases Discounts are often called **contra-cost accounts** or contra-purchases accounts.

Interest Expense is classified as "Other Expense" instead of being listed under Operating Expenses. This is because it represents the expense of obtaining money to do business, rather than an expense directly associated with operating the business.

FIGURE 14-5 Chart of Accounts for Northern Micro

NORTHERN MICRO
CHART OF ACCOUNTS

Assets			Revenue		
Current Assets			401	Sales	
101	Cash		401.1	Sales Returns and	
122	Accounts Receivable			Allowances	
131	Merchandise Inventory		**Other Revenue**		
141	Supplies		411	Interest Revenue	
145	Prepaid Insurance		412	Rent Revenue	
			413	Subscriptions Revenue	
Property, Plant, and Equipment			**Expenses**		
161	Land		**Cost of Goods Sold**		
171	Building		501	Purchases	
171.1	Accumulated Depreciation—		501.1	Purchases Returns and	
	Building			Allowances	
181	Store Equipment		501.2	Purchases Discounts	
181.1	Accumulated Depreciation—		502	Freight-In	
	Store Equipment		**Operating Expenses**		
Liabilities			511	Wages Expense	
Current Liabilities			512	Advertising Expense	
201	Notes Payable		513	Bank Credit Card	
202	Accounts Payable			Expense	
219	Wages Payable		521	Rent Expense	
231	Sales Tax Payable		523	Supplies Expense	
241	Unearned Subscriptions		525	Telephone Expense	
	Revenue		533	Utilities Expense	
Long-Term Liabilities			535	Insurance Expense	
251	Mortgage Payable		540	Depreciation Expense—	
				Building	
Owner's Equity			541	Depreciation Expense—	
311	Gary L. Fishel, Capital			Store Equipment	
312	Gary L. Fishel, Drawing		549	Miscellaneous Expense	
			Other Expenses		
313	Income Summary		551	Interest Expense	

PREPARING A WORK SHEET FOR A MERCHANDISING BUSINESS

LO 3   Prepare a work sheet for a merchandising business.

The work sheet for a merchandising business is similar to the one shown in Chapter 5 for a service business. Recall the five steps taken to prepare a work sheet:

STEP 1   Prepare the trial balance.

STEP 2   Prepare the adjustments.

STEP 3   Prepare the adjusted trial balance.

STEP 4   Extend the adjusted trial balance to the Income Statement and Balance Sheet columns.

STEP 5   Complete the work sheet by totaling the Income Statement and Balance Sheet columns to compute the net income or net loss.

The work sheet format and the five steps taken when preparing the work sheet are illustrated in Figure 14-6. Note that the new accounts introduced for a merchandising firm and the unearned revenue account are highlighted so that you can see their proper placement and extensions. (The abbreviation BI stands for beginning inventory; EI stands for ending inventory.) Pay particular attention to the extension of Income Summary. Both the debit and credit amounts for this account must be extended.

Adjustments for Northern Micro

Before preparing a work sheet for Northern Micro, let's review the preparation of adjustments in T account form. Figure 14-7 provides year-end adjustment information for Northern Micro. Figure 14-8 shows adjusting entries based on this information. The unadjusted balances for these accounts were taken from Northern Micro's trial balance.

Preparing a Work Sheet for Northern Micro

Let's prepare a work sheet for Northern Micro following the five steps illustrated in Figure 14-6.

STEP 1   In Figure 14-9, the Trial Balance columns are completed by copying the balances of all accounts from the general ledger (not shown).

STEP 2   In Figure 14-10, the adjustments are entered. These entries are exactly the same as those made in T account form in Figure 14-8.

STEP 3   In Figure 14-11, extensions are made to the Adjusted Trial Balance columns. Note that both the debit and credit amounts for Income Summary are extended.

STEP 4   In Figure 14-12, the Adjusted Trial Balance amounts are extended to the Income Statement and Balance Sheet columns.

STEP 5   In Figure 14-12, the work sheet is completed by totaling the Income Statement and Balance Sheet columns. The difference between the debits and credits for each pair of columns represents the net income or net loss.

FIGURE 14-6 Overview of Work Sheet for a Merchandising Business

Name of Company
Work Sheet
For Month Ended June 30, 20 - -

Row	ACCOUNT TITLE	TRIAL BALANCE DEBIT	TRIAL BALANCE CREDIT	ADJUSTMENTS DEBIT	ADJUSTMENTS CREDIT	ADJUSTED TRIAL BALANCE DEBIT	ADJUSTED TRIAL BALANCE CREDIT	INCOME STATEMENT DEBIT	INCOME STATEMENT CREDIT	BALANCE SHEET DEBIT	BALANCE SHEET CREDIT
		Step 1: Prepare a Trial Balance		Step 2: Prepare the Adjustments		Step 3: Prepare the Adjusted Trial Balance			Step 4: Extend Adjusted Account Balances		
1	- - - - - - -										
2	- - - - - - -										
3	(Insert Ledger Account Titles)	Assets				Assets				Assets	
4											
5		Mdse. Inv. (BI)		EI	BI	Mdse. Inv. (EI)				Mdse. Inv. (EI)	
6			Liabilities				Liabilities				Liabilities
7			Unearned				Unearned				Unearned
8			Revenues				Revenues				Revenues
9											
10			Capital				Capital				Capital
11		Drawing				Drawing				Drawing	
12											
13	Income Summary			BI	EI	BI	EI	BI	EI		
14	- - - - - - -										
15			Revenues				Revenues		Revenues		
16			Sales				Sales		Sales		
17		Sales R&A				Sales R&A		Sales R&A			
18		Sales Discounts				Sales Discounts		Sales Discounts			
19											
20		Expenses				Expenses		Expenses			
21		Purchases				Purchases		Purchases			
22			Purch. R&A				Purch. R&A		Purch. R&A		
23			Purch. Discounts				Purch. Discounts		Purch. Discounts		
24		Freight-In				Freight-In		Freight-In			
25											
26								Step 5: Complete the work sheet			
27								1) Sum columns			
28								2) Compute net income (loss)			
29											
30								Net	Net	Net	Net
31								Income	Loss	Loss	Income
32											

B I = Beginning Inventory
E I = Ending Inventory

FIGURE 14-7 Year-End Adjustment Data for Northern Micro

YEAR-END ADJUSTMENT DATA FOR NORTHERN MICRO

(a, b)	A physical count showed that merchandise inventory costing $18,000 is on hand as of December 31.
(c)	Supplies remaining at the end of the year, $400.
(d)	Unexpired insurance on December 31, $600.
(e)	Depreciation expense on the building for the year, $4,000.
(f)	Depreciation expense on the store equipment for the year, $3,000.
(g)	Wages earned but not paid as of December 31, $450.
(h)	Northern Micro publishes a computer magazine. Subscribers pay in advance. Unearned subscriptions revenue as of December 31, $2,000.

FIGURE 14-8 Adjusting Entries for Northern Micro

FIGURE 14-9 Step 1: Completion of the Trial Balance Columns

Northern Micro
Work Sheet
For Month Ended December 31, 20--

#	ACCOUNT TITLE	TRIAL BALANCE DEBIT	TRIAL BALANCE CREDIT
1	Cash	20 0 0 0 00	
2	Accounts Receivable	15 0 0 0 00	
3	Merchandise Inventory	26 0 0 0 00	
4	Supplies	1 8 0 0 00	
5	Prepaid Insurance	2 4 0 0 00	
6	Land	10 0 0 0 00	
7	Building	90 0 0 0 00	
8	Accum. Depr.—Building		16 0 0 0 00
9	Store Equipment	50 0 0 0 00	
10	Accum. Depr.—Store Equipment		15 0 0 0 00
11	Notes Payable		5 0 0 0 00
12	Accounts Payable		10 0 0 0 00
13	Wages Payable		
14	Sales Tax Payable		1 5 0 0 00
15	Unearned Subscriptions Revenue		12 0 0 0 00
16	Mortgage Payable		30 0 0 0 00
17	Gary L. Fishel, Capital		114 4 0 0 00
18	Gary L. Fishel, Drawing	20 0 0 0 00	
19	Income Summary		
20	Sales		214 0 0 0 00
21	Sales Returns and Allowances	1 2 0 0 00	
22	Interest Revenue		9 0 0 00
23	Rent Revenue		8 0 0 00
24	Subscriptions Revenue		
25	Purchases	105 0 0 0 00	
26	Purchases Returns and Allowances		8 0 0 00
27	Purchases Discounts		1 0 0 00
28	Freight-In	3 0 0 00	
29	Wages Expense	42 0 0 0 00	
30	Advertising Expense	2 5 0 0 00	
31	Bank Credit Card Expense	1 5 0 0 00	
32	Rent Expense	20 0 0 0 00	
33	Supplies Expense		
34	Telephone Expense	3 5 0 0 00	
35	Utilities Expense	12 0 0 0 00	
36	Insurance Expense		
37	Depr. Expense—Building		
38	Depr. Expense—Store Equipment		
39	Miscellaneous Expense	2 2 5 0 00	
40	Interest Expense	3 1 5 0 00	
41		428 6 0 0 00	428 6 0 0 00
42			

Column headings (unfilled): ADJUSTMENTS (Debit, Credit); ADJUSTED TRIAL BALANCE (Debit, Credit); INCOME STATEMENT (Debit, Credit); BALANCE SHEET (Debit, Credit).

STEP 1

FIGURE 14-10 Step 2: Preparation of the Adjustments

Northern Micro
Work Sheet
For Month Ended December 31, 20- -

#	Account Title	Trial Balance Debit	Trial Balance Credit	Adjustments Debit	Adjustments Credit	Adjusted Trial Balance Debit	Adjusted Trial Balance Credit	Income Statement Debit	Income Statement Credit	Balance Sheet Debit	Balance Sheet Credit
1	Cash	20 0 0 0 00									
2	Accounts Receivable	15 0 0 0 00									
3	Merchandise Inventory	26 0 0 0 00		(b) 18 0 0 0 00	(a) 26 0 0 0 00						
4	Supplies	1 8 0 0 00			(c) 1 4 0 0 00						
5	Prepaid Insurance	2 4 0 0 00			(d) 1 8 0 0 00						
6	Land	10 0 0 0 00									
7	Building	90 0 0 0 00									
8	Accum. Depr.—Building		16 0 0 0 00		(e) 4 0 0 0 00						
9	Store Equipment	50 0 0 0 00									
10	Accum. Depr.—Store Equipment		15 0 0 0 00		(f) 3 0 0 0 00						
11	Notes Payable		5 0 0 0 00								
12	Accounts Payable		10 0 0 0 00								
13	Wages Payable				(g) 4 5 0 0 00						
14	Sales Tax Payable		1 5 0 0 00								
15	Unearned Subscriptions Revenue		12 0 0 0 00	(h) 10 0 0 0 00							
16	Mortgage Payable		30 0 0 0 00								
17	Gary L. Fishel, Capital		114 4 0 0 00								
18	Gary L. Fishel, Drawing	20 0 0 0 00									
19	Income Summary			(a) 26 0 0 0 00	(b) 18 0 0 0 00						
20	Sales		214 0 0 0 00								
21	Sales Returns and Allowances	1 2 0 0 00									
22	Interest Revenue		9 0 0 00								
23	Rent Revenue		8 0 0 00								
24	Subscriptions Revenue				(h) 10 0 0 0 00						
25	Purchases	105 0 0 0 00									
26	Purchases Returns and Allowances		8 0 0 0 00								
27	Purchases Discounts		1 0 0 0 00								
28	Freight-In	3 0 0 0 00									
29	Wages Expense	42 0 0 0 00		(g) 4 5 0 0 00							
30	Advertising Expense	2 5 0 0 00									
31	Bank Credit Card Expense	1 5 0 0 00									
32	Rent Expense	20 0 0 0 00									
33	Supplies Expense	3 5 0 0 00		(c) 1 4 0 0 00							
34	Telephone Expense										
35	Utilities Expense	12 0 0 0 00									
36	Insurance Expense			(d) 1 8 0 0 00							
37	Depr. Expense—Building			(e) 4 0 0 0 00							
38	Depr. Expense—Store Equipment			(f) 3 0 0 0 00							
39	Miscellaneous Expense	2 2 5 0 0 00									
40	Interest Expense	3 1 5 0 0 00									
41		428 6 0 0 0 00	428 6 0 0 0 00	64 6 5 0 00	64 6 5 0 00						
42											

STEP 1   STEP 2

FIGURE 14-11 Step 3: Extensions to the Adjusted Trial Balance Columns

Northern Micro
Work Sheet
For Month Ended December 31, 20--

FIGURE 14-12 Step 4: Extensions to the Income Statement and Balance Sheet Columns   Step 5: Completing the Work Sheet and Computing Net Income

Northern Micro
Work Sheet
For Year Ended December 31, 20- -

#	ACCOUNT TITLE	TRIAL BALANCE DEBIT	TRIAL BALANCE CREDIT	ADJUSTMENTS DEBIT	ADJUSTMENTS CREDIT	ADJUSTED TRIAL BALANCE DEBIT	ADJUSTED TRIAL BALANCE CREDIT	INCOME STATEMENT DEBIT	INCOME STATEMENT CREDIT	BALANCE SHEET DEBIT	BALANCE SHEET CREDIT
1	Cash	20 0 0 0 00				20 0 0 0 00				20 0 0 0 00	
2	Accounts Receivable	15 0 0 0 00				15 0 0 0 00				15 0 0 0 00	
3	Merchandise Inventory	26 0 0 0 00		(b) 18 0 0 0 00	(a) 26 0 0 0 00	18 0 0 0 00				18 0 0 0 00	
4	Supplies	1 8 0 0 00			(c) 1 4 0 0 00	4 0 0 00				4 0 0 00	
5	Prepaid Insurance	2 4 0 0 00			(d) 1 8 0 0 00	6 0 0 00				6 0 0 00	
6	Land	10 0 0 0 00				10 0 0 0 00				10 0 0 0 00	
7	Building	90 0 0 0 00				90 0 0 0 00				90 0 0 0 00	
8	Accum. Depr.—Building		16 0 0 0 00		(e) 4 0 0 0 00		20 0 0 0 00				20 0 0 0 00
9	Store Equipment	50 0 0 0 00				50 0 0 0 00				50 0 0 0 00	
10	Accum. Depr.—Store Equipment		15 0 0 0 00		(f) 3 0 0 0 00		18 0 0 0 00				18 0 0 0 00
11	Notes Payable		5 0 0 0 00				5 0 0 0 00				5 0 0 0 00
12	Accounts Payable		10 0 0 0 00				10 0 0 0 00				10 0 0 0 00
13	Wages Payable				(g) 4 5 0 00		4 5 0 00				4 5 0 00
14	Sales Tax Payable		1 5 0 0 00				1 5 0 0 00				1 5 0 0 00
15	Unearned Subscriptions Revenue		12 0 0 0 00	(h) 10 0 0 0 00			2 0 0 0 00				2 0 0 0 00
16	Mortgage Payable		30 0 0 0 00				30 0 0 0 00				30 0 0 0 00
17	Gary L. Fishel, Capital		114 4 0 0 00				114 4 0 0 00				114 4 0 0 00
18	Gary L. Fishel, Drawing	20 0 0 0 00				20 0 0 0 00				20 0 0 0 00	
19	Income Summary			(a) 26 0 0 0 00	(b) 18 0 0 0 00	26 0 0 0 00	18 0 0 0 00	26 0 0 0 00	18 0 0 0 00		
20	Sales		214 0 0 0 00				214 0 0 0 00		214 0 0 0 00		
21	Sales Returns and Allowances	1 2 0 0 00				1 2 0 0 00		1 2 0 0 00			
22	Interest Revenue		9 0 0 00				9 0 0 00		9 0 0 00		
23	Rent Revenue		8 0 0 0 00				8 0 0 0 00		8 0 0 0 00		
24	Subscriptions Revenue				(h) 10 0 0 0 00		10 0 0 0 00		10 0 0 0 00		
25	Purchases	105 0 0 0 00				105 0 0 0 00		105 0 0 0 00			
26	Purchases Returns and Allowances		8 0 0 0 00				8 0 0 0 00		8 0 0 0 00		
27	Purchases Discounts		1 0 0 0 00				1 0 0 0 00		1 0 0 0 00		
28	Freight-In	3 0 0 0 00				3 0 0 0 00		3 0 0 0 00			
29	Wages Expense	42 0 0 0 00		(g) 4 5 0 00		42 4 5 0 00		42 4 5 0 00			
30	Advertising Expense	2 5 0 0 00				2 5 0 0 00		2 5 0 0 00			
31	Bank Credit Card Expense	1 5 0 0 00				1 5 0 0 00		1 5 0 0 00			
32	Rent Expense	20 0 0 0 00				20 0 0 0 00		20 0 0 0 00			
33	Supplies Expense			(c) 1 4 0 0 00		1 4 0 0 00		1 4 0 0 00			
34	Telephone Expense	3 5 0 0 00				3 5 0 0 00		3 5 0 0 00			
35	Utilities Expense	12 0 0 0 00				12 0 0 0 00		12 0 0 0 00			
36	Insurance Expense			(d) 1 8 0 0 00		1 8 0 0 00		1 8 0 0 00			
37	Depr. Expense—Building			(e) 4 0 0 0 00		4 0 0 0 00		4 0 0 0 00			
38	Depr. Expense—Store Equipment			(f) 3 0 0 0 00		3 0 0 0 00		3 0 0 0 00			
39	Miscellaneous Expense	2 2 5 0 00				2 2 5 0 00		2 2 5 0 00			
40	Interest Expense	3 1 5 0 00				3 1 5 0 00		3 1 5 0 00			
41		428 6 0 0 00	428 6 0 0 00	64 6 5 0 00	64 6 5 0 00	454 0 5 0 00	454 0 5 0 00	230 0 5 0 00	252 7 0 0 00	224 0 0 0 00	201 3 5 0 00
42	Net Income							22 6 5 0 00			22 6 5 0 00
43								252 7 0 0 00	252 7 0 0 00	224 0 0 0 00	224 0 0 0 00

STEP 1   STEP 2   STEP 3   STEPS 4 AND 5

ADJUSTING ENTRIES

LO 4   Journalize adjusting entries for a merchandising business.

Recall that making the adjustments on the work sheet has no effect on the actual accounts in the general ledger. Journal entries must be made to enter the adjustments into the accounting system. Figure 14-13 shows the adjusting entries for Northern Micro.

 LEARNING KEY: Recall that the work sheet is just a planning tool. The adjusting entries must be entered in the general journal.

FIGURE 14-13 Adjusting Entries for Northern Micro

GENERAL JOURNAL   PAGE 3

	DATE		DESCRIPTION	POST REF.	DEBIT	CREDIT	
1			Adjusting Entries				1
2	20-- Dec.	31	Income Summary		26 0 0 0 00		2
3			Merchandise Inventory			26 0 0 0 00	3
4							4
5		31	Merchandise Inventory		18 0 0 0 00		5
6			Income Summary			18 0 0 0 00	6
7							7
8		31	Supplies Expense		1 4 0 0 00		8
9			Supplies			1 4 0 0 00	9
10							10
11		31	Insurance Expense		1 8 0 0 00		11
12			Prepaid Insurance			1 8 0 0 00	12
13							13
14		31	Depr. Expense—Building		4 0 0 0 00		14
15			Accumulated Depr.—Building			4 0 0 0 00	15
16							16
17		31	Depr. Expense—Store Equipment		3 0 0 0 00		17
18			Accumulated Depr.—Store Equipment			3 0 0 0 00	18
19							19
20		31	Wages Expense		4 5 0 00		20
21			Wages Payable			4 5 0 00	21
22							22
23		31	Unearned Subscriptions Revenue		10 0 0 0 00		23
24			Subscriptions Revenue			10 0 0 0 00	24
25							25

Learning Objectives	Key Points to Remember
1 **Prepare an adjustment for merchandise inventory.**	Extra care is required for the end-of-period adjustment for merchandise inventory and the related extensions on the work sheet. The two-step adjustment process in T account form and the work sheet treatment for Northern Micro are reviewed in Figures 14-14 and 14-15 below and on page 514.

FIGURE 14-14 Two-Step Adjustment for Merchandise Inventory in T Account Form

Assets		=	Liabilities		+	Owner's Equity	
Debit	**Credit**		**Debit**	**Credit**		**Debit**	**Credit**
+	−		−	+		−	+

						Gary L. Fishel, Capital	
							Bal. xxx
Merchandise Inventory						Income Summary	
Bal. 26,000							
	Adj. 26,000			◀—— STEP 1 ——▶		Adj. 26,000	
Adj. 18,000 ◀				——— STEP 2 ———▶			Adj. 18,000

Learning Objectives	Key Points to Remember
2 **Prepare an adjustment for unearned revenue.**	Some firms receive cash before providing a service or selling a product. This cash is considered a liability, unearned revenue, until earned. The adjusting entry to recognize that unearned revenue has become earned is:

    Unearned Revenue   xxx
        Revenue   xxx |
| **3** **Prepare a work sheet for a merchandising business.** | Steps to follow when preparing a work sheet:
   1. Prepare the trial balance.
   2. Prepare the adjustments.
   3. Prepare the adjusted trial balance.
   4. Extend the adjusted trial balance amounts to the Income Statement and Balance Sheet columns.
   5. Total the Income Statement and Balance Sheet columns to compute the net income or net loss. |
| **4** **Journalize adjusting entries for a merchandising business.** | The work sheet is a useful tool when preparing end-of-period adjustments and financial statements. Remember: The work sheet is NOT a formal part of the accounting system. Adjustments made on the work sheet must be entered in a journal and posted to the ledger. |

KEY TERMS

contra-cost accounts, (503)   Accounts that are deducted from the Purchases account when computing cost of goods sold—Purchases Returns and Allowances and Purchases Discounts.

contra-revenue accounts, (503)   Accounts that are deducted from Sales on the income statement—Sales Returns and Allowances and Sales Discounts.

physical inventory, (498)   A physical count of the goods on hand.

unearned revenue, (502)   Cash received in advance of delivering a product or performing a service.

FIGURE 14-15 Work Sheet Adjustment and Extension for Merchandise Inventory and Calculation of Cost of Goods Sold Using Information in the Income Statement Columns of the Work Sheet

Northern Micro
Work Sheet
For Year Ended December 31, 20- -

DEMONSTRATION PROBLEM

W & D

Aaron Patton owns and operates Patton's Bait Shop and Boat Rental. A year-end trial balance is shown on the next page.

Year-end adjustment data for Patton's Bait Shop and Boat Rental is as follows:

(a, b) A physical count shows that merchandise inventory costing $15,000 is on hand as of December 31, 20--.

(c)   Supplies remaining at the end of the year, $200.

(d)   Unexpired insurance on December 31, $300.

(e)   Depreciation expense on the building for 20--, $2,000.

(f)   Depreciation expense on the store equipment for 20--, $1,500.

(g)   Wages earned but not paid as of December 31, $225.

(h)   Unearned boat rental revenue as of December 31, $1,000.

REQUIRED   1. Prepare a year-end work sheet.

2. Journalize the adjusting entries.

Patton's Bait Shop and Boat Rental
Trial Balance
December 31, 20 - -

ACCOUNT TITLE	DEBIT BALANCE					CREDIT BALANCE				
Cash	10	0	0	0	00					
Accounts Receivable	7	5	0	0	00					
Merchandise Inventory	19	0	0	0	00					
Supplies		9	0	0	00					
Prepaid Insurance	1	2	0	0	00					
Land	5	0	0	0	00					
Building	45	0	0	0	00					
Accumulated Depreciation—Building						8	0	0	0	00
Store Equipment	25	0	0	0	00					
Accumulated Depreciation—Store Equipment						7	5	0	0	00
Notes Payable						2	5	0	0	00
Accounts Payable						5	0	0	0	00
Wages Payable										
Unearned Boat Rental Revenue						11	0	0	0	00
Aaron Patton, Capital						77	9	0	0	00
Aaron Patton, Drawing	10	0	0	0	00					
Income Summary										
Sales						100	2	5	0	00
Sales Returns and Allowances		6	0	0	00					
Boat Rental Revenue										
Purchases	52	5	0	0	00					
Purchases Returns and Allowances							4	0	0	00
Purchases Discounts							5	0	0	00
Freight-In		1	5	0	00					
Wages Expense	21	0	0	0	00					
Advertising Expense	3	7	5	0	00					
Supplies Expense										
Telephone Expense	1	7	5	0	00					
Utilities Expense	6	0	0	0	00					
Insurance Expense										
Depreciation Expense—Building										
Depreciation Expense—Store Equipment										
Miscellaneous Expense	3	6	2	5	00					
Interest Expense			7	5	00					
	213	0	5	0	00	213	0	5	0	00

Solution

1.

Patton's Bait Shop and Boat Rental
Work Sheet
For Year Ended December 31, 20--

#	ACCOUNT TITLE	Trial Balance Debit	Trial Balance Credit	Adjustments Debit	Adjustments Credit	Adjusted Trial Balance Debit	Adjusted Trial Balance Credit	Income Statement Debit	Income Statement Credit	Balance Sheet Debit	Balance Sheet Credit
1	Cash	10 0 0 0 00				10 0 0 0 00				10 0 0 0 00	
2	Accounts Receivable	7 5 0 0 00				7 5 0 0 00				7 5 0 0 00	
3	Merchandise Inventory	19 0 0 0 00		(b) 15 0 0 0 00	(a) 19 0 0 0 00	15 0 0 0 00				15 0 0 0 00	
4	Supplies	9 0 0 0 00			(c) 7 0 0 0 00	2 0 0 0 00				2 0 0 0 00	
5	Prepaid Insurance	12 0 0 0 00			(d) 9 0 0 0 00	3 0 0 0 00				3 0 0 0 00	
6	Land	5 0 0 0 00				5 0 0 0 00				5 0 0 0 00	
7	Building	45 0 0 0 00				45 0 0 0 00				45 0 0 0 00	
8	Accum. Depr.—Building		8 0 0 0 00		(e) 2 0 0 0 00		10 0 0 0 00				10 0 0 0 00
9	Store Equipment	25 0 0 0 00				25 0 0 0 00				25 0 0 0 00	
10	Accum. Depr.—Store Equipment		7 5 0 0 00		(f) 1 5 0 0 00		9 0 0 0 00				9 0 0 0 00
11	Notes Payable		2 5 0 0 00				2 5 0 0 00				2 5 0 0 00
12	Accounts Payable		5 0 0 0 00				5 0 0 0 00				5 0 0 0 00
13	Wages Payable				(g) 2 2 5 00		2 2 5 00				2 2 5 00
14	Unearned Boat Rental Revenue		11 0 0 0 00	(h) 10 0 0 0 00			1 0 0 0 00				1 0 0 0 00
15	Aaron Patton, Capital		77 9 0 0 00				77 9 0 0 00				77 9 0 0 00
16	Aaron Patton, Drawing	10 0 0 0 00				10 0 0 0 00				10 0 0 0 00	
17	Income Summary			(a) 19 0 0 0 00	(b) 15 0 0 0 00	19 0 0 0 00	15 0 0 0 00	19 0 0 0 00	15 0 0 0 00		
18	Sales		100 2 5 0 00				100 2 5 0 00		100 2 5 0 00		
19	Sales Returns and Allowances	6 0 0 0 00				6 0 0 0 00		6 0 0 0 00			
20	Boat Rental Revenue				(h) 10 0 0 0 00		10 0 0 0 00		10 0 0 0 00		
21	Purchases	52 5 0 0 00				52 5 0 0 00		52 5 0 0 00			
22	Purchases Returns and Allowances		4 0 0 0 00				4 0 0 0 00		4 0 0 0 00		
23	Purchases Discounts		5 0 0 00				5 0 0 00		5 0 0 00		
24	Freight-In	1 5 0 0 00				1 5 0 0 00		1 5 0 0 00			
25	Wages Expense	21 0 0 0 00		(g) 2 2 5 00		21 2 2 5 00		21 2 2 5 00			
26	Advertising Expense	3 7 5 0 00				3 7 5 0 00		3 7 5 0 00			
27	Supplies Expense			(c) 7 0 0 0 00		7 0 0 0 00		7 0 0 0 00			
28	Telephone Expense	1 7 5 0 00				1 7 5 0 00		1 7 5 0 00			
29	Utilities Expense	6 0 0 0 00				6 0 0 0 00		6 0 0 0 00			
30	Insurance Expense			(d) 9 0 0 0 00		9 0 0 0 00		9 0 0 0 00			
31	Depr. Expense—Building			(e) 2 0 0 0 00		2 0 0 0 00		2 0 0 0 00			
32	Depr. Expense—Store Equipment			(f) 1 5 0 0 00		1 5 0 0 00		1 5 0 0 00			
33	Miscellaneous Expense	3 6 2 5 00				3 6 2 5 00		3 6 2 5 00			
34	Interest Expense	7 5 0 00				7 5 0 00		7 5 0 00			
35		213 0 5 0 00	213 0 5 0 00	49 3 2 5 00	49 3 2 5 00	231 7 7 5 00	231 7 7 5 00	113 7 7 5 00	126 1 5 0 00	118 0 0 0 00	105 6 2 5 00
36	Net Income							12 3 7 5 00			12 3 7 5 00
37								126 1 5 0 00	126 1 5 0 00	118 0 0 0 00	118 0 0 0 00

(continued)

2.

			GENERAL JOURNAL					PAGE 3	
	DATE		DESCRIPTION	POST REF.	DEBIT		CREDIT		
1			**Adjusting Entries**						1
2	20-- Dec.	31	Income Summary		19 0 0 0 00				2
3			Merchandise Inventory				19 0 0 0 00		3
4									4
5		31	Merchandise Inventory		15 0 0 0 00				5
6			Income Summary				15 0 0 0 00		6
7									7
8		31	Supplies Expense		7 0 0 00				8
9			Supplies				7 0 0 00		9
10									10
11		31	Insurance Expense		9 0 0 00				11
12			Prepaid Insurance				9 0 0 00		12
13									13
14		31	Depr. Expense—Building		2 0 0 0 00				14
15			Accumulated Depr.—Building				2 0 0 0 00		15
16									16
17		31	Depr. Expense—Store Equipment		1 5 0 0 00				17
18			Accumulated Depr.—Store Equipment				1 5 0 0 00		18
19									19
20		31	Wages Expense		2 2 5 00				20
21			Wages Payable				2 2 5 00		21
22									22
23		31	Unearned Boat Rental Revenue		10 0 0 0 00				23
24			Boat Rental Revenue				10 0 0 0 00		24
25									25

REVIEW QUESTIONS

1. What work sheet amounts are used to compute cost of goods sold?

2. Why are both the debit and credit amounts in the Adjustments columns on the Income Summary line of the work sheet extended to the Adjusted Trial Balance columns?

3. What is an unearned revenue?

4. Give three examples of unearned revenues.

5. List the five steps taken to prepare a work sheet.

6. What does the difference between the totals of the Income Statement columns represent? What does the difference between the Balance Sheet column totals represent?

MANAGING YOUR WRITING

A friend of yours recently opened Abracadabra, a sportswear shop specializing in monogrammed athletic gear. Most merchandise is special ordered for customers. However, a small inventory is on hand. Your friend does not understand why a physical inventory is necessary before preparing the financial statements. She knows how much she paid for all merchandise purchased. Why not simply use this amount for cost of goods sold? After all, it has been paid for. Write a brief memo explaining the purpose of the physical inventory and why she should not use the cost of purchases as cost of goods sold.

ETHICS CASE

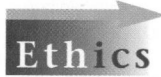

Jason Tierro, an inventory clerk at Lexmar Company, is responsible for taking a physical count of the goods on hand at the end of the year. He has been performing this duty for several years. This year Jason was very busy due to a shortage of personnel at the company, so he decided to just estimate the amount of ending inventory instead of doing an accurate count. He reasoned that he could come very close to the true amount because of his past experience working with inventory. Besides, he was sure that the sophisticated computer program that Lexmar had just invested in kept an accurate record of inventory on hand.

1. What is your opinion of Jason's reasoning?

2. If Jason underestimates the dollar amount of ending inventory, what effect will it have on net income for the current accounting period?

3. Write a short paragraph explaining why a physical inventory should be taken at least once a year.

4. In groups of three or four make a list of possible reasons that the actual ending inventory might not agree with the ending inventory according to a computer system.

WEB WORK

Visit Sears' homepage for a look at their annual report. Notice that their inventory fluctuated over the last five years. What reasons could there be for the larger increases and decreases?

http://www.sears.com/company/annrep/indexa.htm
(http://heintz.swcollege.com)

SERIES A EXERCISES

EXERCISE 14A-1 (LO 1) ADJUSTMENT FOR MERCHANDISING INVENTORY USING T ACCOUNTS Sam Baker owns a business called Sam's Sporting Goods. His beginning inventory as of January 1, 20--, was $47,000 and his ending inventory as of December 31, 20--, was $53,000. Set up T accounts for Merchandise Inventory and Income Summary and perform the year-end adjustment for Merchandise Inventory.

EXERCISE 14A-2 (LO 1) CALCULATION OF COST OF GOODS SOLD Prepare the cost of goods sold section for Adams Gift Shop. The following amounts are known:

Beginning merchandise inventory	$26,000
Ending merchandise inventory	23,000
Purchases	71,000
Purchases returns and allowances	3,500
Purchases discounts	5,500
Freight-in	200

EXERCISE 14A-3 (LO 2) ADJUSTMENT FOR UNEARNED REVENUES USING T ACCOUNTS Set up T accounts for Cash, Unearned Ticket Revenue, and Ticket Revenue. Post the following two transactions to the appropriate accounts, indicating each transaction by letter.

(a) Sold 1,500 season tickets at $30 each, receiving cash of $45,000.

(b) An end-of-period adjustment is needed to recognize that $35,000 in ticket revenue has been earned.

EXERCISE 14A-4 (LO 3) WORK SHEET EXTENSIONS FOR MERCHANDISE INVENTORY ADJUSTMENTS The following partial work sheet is taken from Kevin's Gift Shop for the year ended December 31, 20--. The ending merchandise inventory is $50,000.

1. Complete the Adjustments columns for the merchandise inventory.

2. Extend the merchandise inventory to the Adjusted Trial Balance, Income Statement, and Balance Sheet columns.

3. Extend the remaining accounts to the Adjusted Trial Balance and Income Statement columns.

4. Prepare a cost of goods sold section from the partial work sheet.

Kevin's Gift Shop
Work Sheet (Partial)
For Year Ended December 31, 20 - -

	ACCOUNT TITLE	TRIAL BALANCE		ADJUSTMENTS		
		DEBIT	CREDIT	DEBIT	CREDIT	
1	Merchandise Inventory	40 0 0 0 00				1
12	Income Summary					12
13	Purchases	90 0 0 0 00				13
14	Purchases Returns and Allowances		2 0 0 0 00			14
15	Purchases Discounts		3 0 0 0 00			15
16	Freight-In	5 0 0 00				16
17						17
18						18

EXERCISE 14A-5 (LO 3) DETERMINING THE BEGINNING AND ENDING INVENTORY FROM A PARTIAL WORK SHEET From the following partial work sheet, indicate the dollar amount of beginning and ending merchandise inventory.

	ACCOUNT TITLE	ADJUSTMENTS DEBIT	ADJUSTMENTS CREDIT	ADJUSTED TRIAL BALANCE DEBIT	ADJUSTED TRIAL BALANCE CREDIT	INCOME STATEMENT DEBIT	INCOME STATEMENT CREDIT	BALANCE SHEET DEBIT	BALANCE SHEET CREDIT	
1	Merchandise Inventory	(b) 60 0 0 0 00	(a) 55 0 0 0 00	60 0 0 0 00				60 0 0 0 00		1
2	Income Summary	(a) 55 0 0 0 00	(b) 60 0 0 0 00	55 0 0 0 00	60 0 0 0 00	55 0 0 0 00	60 0 0 0 00			2

EXERCISE 14A-6 (LO 4) JOURNALIZE ADJUSTING ENTRIES FOR A MERCHAN-DISING BUSINESS The following partial work sheet is taken from the books of Kelly's Kittens, a local pet kennel, for the year ended December 31, 20--. Journalize the adjustments in a general journal.

Kelly's Kittens
Work Sheet (Partial)
For Year Ended December 31, 20 - -

	ACCOUNT TITLE	TRIAL BALANCE DEBIT	TRIAL BALANCE CREDIT	ADJUSTMENTS DEBIT	ADJUSTMENTS CREDIT	
1	Merchandise Inventory	45 0 0 0 00		(b) 50 0 0 0 00	(a) 45 0 0 0 00	1
2	Supplies	10 0 0 0 00			(d) 7 0 0 0 00	2
3	Building	60 0 0 0 00				3
4	Accum. Depr.—Building		15 0 0 0 00		(e) 5 0 0 0 00	4
5	Wages Payable				(f) 1 2 0 0 00	5
6	Unearned Grooming Revenue		3 0 0 0 00	(c) 2 0 0 0 00		6
7	Income Summary			(a) 45 0 0 0 00	(b) 50 0 0 0 00	7
8	Grooming Revenue		20 0 0 0 00		(c) 2 0 0 0 00	8
9	Wages Expense	37 0 0 0 00		(f) 1 2 0 0 00		9
10	Supplies Expense			(d) 7 0 0 0 00		10
11	Depr. Expense—Building			(e) 5 0 0 0 00		11
12				110 2 0 0 00	110 2 0 0 00	12
13						13

SERIES A PROBLEMS

W & D

PROBLEM 14A-1 (LO 1/2/3/4) COMPLETION OF A WORK SHEET SHOWING A NET INCOME The trial balance for the Seaside Kite Shop, a business owned by Joyce Kennington, is shown on page 522. Year-end adjustment information is as follows:

(a, b) Merchandise inventory costing $30,000 is on hand as of December 31, 20--.

(c)   Supplies remaining at the end of the year, $2,700.

(d)   Unexpired insurance on December 31, $2,900.

(e)   Depreciation expense on the building for 20--, $5,000.

(f)   Depreciation expense on the store equipment for 20--, $3,200.

(g)   Unearned rent revenue as of December 31, $2,200.

(h)   Wages earned but not paid as of December 31, $900.

(continued)

REQUIRED

1. Complete the Adjustments columns, identifying each adjustment with its corresponding letter.

2. Complete the work sheet.

3. Enter the adjustments in a general journal.

Seaside Kite Shop
Trial Balance
December 31, 20 - -

ACCOUNT TITLE	DEBIT BALANCE					CREDIT BALANCE				
Cash	20	0	0	0	00					
Accounts Receivable	14	0	0	0	00					
Merchandise Inventory	25	0	0	0	00					
Supplies	8	0	0	0	00					
Prepaid Insurance	5	4	0	0	00					
Land	30	0	0	0	00					
Building	50	0	0	0	00					
Accumulated Depreciation—Building						20	0	0	0	00
Store Equipment	35	0	0	0	00					
Accumulated Depreciation—Store Equipment						14	0	0	0	00
Accounts Payable						9	6	0	0	00
Wages Payable										
Sales Tax Payable						5	9	0	0	00
Unearned Rent Revenue						8	9	0	0	00
Mortgage Payable						45	0	0	0	00
Joyce Kennington, Capital						65	4	1	0	00
Joyce Kennington, Drawing	26	0	0	0	00					
Income Summary										
Sales						118	0	0	0	00
Sales Returns and Allowances	1	7	0	0	00					
Rent Revenue										
Purchases	27	0	0	0	00					
Purchases Returns and Allowances						1	4	0	0	00
Purchases Discounts						1	8	0	0	00
Freight-In	2	1	0	0	00					
Wages Expense	32	0	0	0	00					
Advertising Expense	3	6	0	0	00					
Supplies Expense										
Telephone Expense	1	3	5	0	00					
Utilities Expense	8	0	0	0	00					
Insurance Expense										
Depreciation Expense —Building										
Depreciation Expense —Store Equipment										
Miscellaneous Expense		8	6	0	00					
	290	0	1	0	00	290	0	1	0	00

W & D

PROBLEM 14A-2 (LO 1/2/3/4) COMPLETION OF A WORK SHEET SHOWING A NET LOSS The trial balance for Cascade Bicycle Shop, a business owned by David Lamond, is shown below. Year-end adjustment information is provided below.

(a, b)   Merchandise inventory costing $22,000 is on hand as of December 31, 20--.

(c)   Supplies remaining at the end of the year, $2,400.

(d)   Unexpired insurance on December 31, $1,750.

(e)   Depreciation expense on the building for 20--, $4,000.

(f)   Depreciation expense on the store equipment for 20--, $3,600.

(g)   Unearned storage revenue as of December 31, $1,950.

(h)   Wages earned but not paid as of December 31, $750.

Cascade Bicycle Shop
Trial Balance
December 31, 20 - -

ACCOUNT TITLE	DEBIT BALANCE	CREDIT BALANCE
Cash	23 0 0 0 00	
Accounts Receivable	15 0 0 0 00	
Merchandise Inventory	31 0 0 0 00	
Supplies	7 2 0 0 00	
Prepaid Insurance	4 6 0 0 00	
Land	28 0 0 0 00	
Building	53 0 0 0 00	
Accumulated Depreciation—Building		17 0 0 0 00
Store Equipment	27 0 0 0 00	
Accumulated Depreciation—Store Equipment		9 0 0 0 00
Accounts Payable		3 8 0 0 00
Wages Payable		
Sales Tax Payable		3 0 5 0 00
Unearned Storage Revenue		5 6 0 0 00
Mortgage Payable		42 0 0 0 00
David Lamond, Capital		165 7 6 0 00
David Lamond, Drawing	33 0 0 0 00	
Income Summary		
Sales		51 0 0 0 00
Sales Returns and Allowances	2 4 0 0 00	
Storage Revenue		
Purchases	21 0 0 0 00	
Purchases Returns and Allowances		1 3 0 0 00
Purchases Discounts		1 9 0 0 00
Freight-in	1 8 0 0 00	
Wages Expense	35 0 0 0 00	
Advertising Expense	5 7 0 0 00	
Supplies Expense		
Telephone Expense	2 2 0 0 00	
Utilities Expense	9 6 0 0 00	
Insurance Expense		
Depreciation Expense —Building		
Depreciation Expense —Store Equipment		
Miscellaneous Expense	9 1 0 00	
	300 4 1 0 00	300 4 1 0 00

(continued)

REQUIRED
1. Complete the Adjustments columns, identifying each adjustment with its corresponding letter.

2. Complete the work sheet.

3. Enter the adjustments in the general journal.

PROBLEM 14A-3 (LO 1/2/4) WORKING BACKWARD FROM ADJUSTED TRIAL BALANCE TO DETERMINE ADJUSTING ENTRIES The partial work sheet shown on page 525 is taken from the books of Stark Street Computers, a business owned by Logan Cowart, for the year ended December 31, 20--.

REQUIRED
1. Determine the adjusting entries by analyzing the difference between the adjusted trial balance and the trial balance.

2. Journalize the adjusting entries in a general journal.

PROBLEM 14A-4 (LO 1/2/3/4) WORKING BACKWARD FROM THE INCOME STATEMENT AND BALANCE SHEET COLUMNS OF THE WORK SHEET TO DETERMINE ADJUSTED TRIAL BALANCE AND ADJUSTING ENTRIES The partially completed work sheet from the books of Lewis Music Store, a business owned by Hugo Lewis, for the year ended December 31, 20--, is shown on page 526.

REQUIRED
1. Analyze the work sheet and determine the adjusted trial balance and the adjusting entries by working backward from the Income Statement and Balance Sheet columns.

2. Journalize the adjusting entries in a general journal.

3. Prepare the cost of goods sold section of the income statement for Lewis Music Store.

SERIES B EXERCISES

EXERCISE 14B-1 (LO 1) ADJUSTMENT FOR MERCHANDISE INVENTORY USING T ACCOUNTS Sandra Owens owns a business called Sandra's Sporting Goods. Her beginning inventory as of January 1, 20--, was $33,000 and her ending inventory as of December 31, 20--, was $36,000. Set up T accounts for Merchandise Inventory and Income Summary and perform the year-end adjustment for Merchandise Inventory.

EXERCISE 14B-2 (LO 1) CALCULATION OF COST OF GOODS SOLD Prepare the cost of goods sold section for Havens Gift Shop. The following amounts are known:

Beginning merchandise inventory	$29,000
Ending merchandise inventory	27,000
Purchases	62,000
Purchases returns and allowances	2,800
Purchases discounts	3,400
Freight-in	300

Stark Street Computers
Work Sheet (Partial)
For Year Ended December 31, 20 - -

	ACCOUNT TITLE	TRIAL BALANCE DEBIT	TRIAL BALANCE CREDIT	ADJUSTMENTS DEBIT	ADJUSTMENTS CREDIT	ADJUSTED TRIAL BALANCE DEBIT	ADJUSTED TRIAL BALANCE CREDIT	
1	Cash	18 000 00				18 000 00		1
2	Accounts Receivable	11 000 00				11 000 00		2
3	Merchandise Inventory	25 000 00				35 000 00		3
4	Supplies	8 000 00				2 820 00		4
5	Prepaid Insurance	5 400 00				1 225 00		5
6	Land	27 000 00				27 000 00		6
7	Building	48 000 00				48 000 00		7
8	Accum. Depr.—Building		20 000 00				27 000 00	8
9	Store Equipment	33 000 00				33 000 00		9
10	Accum. Depr.—Store Equipment		8 700 00				12 800 00	10
11	Accounts Payable		6 400 00				6 400 00	11
12	Wages Payable						1 300 00	12
13	Sales Tax Payable		5 700 00				5 700 00	13
14	Unearned Repair Revenue		8 200 00				1 800 00	14
15	Mortgage Payable		44 000 00				44 000 00	15
16	Logan Cowart, Capital		80 025 00				80 025 00	16
17	Logan Cowart, Drawing	35 000 00				35 000 00		17
18	Income Summary					25 000 00	35 000 00	18
19	Sales		122 000 00				122 000 00	19
20	Sales Returns and Allowances	2 250 00				2 250 00		20
21	Repair Revenue						6 400 00	21
22	Purchases	29 750 00				29 750 00		22
23	Purchases Returns and Allowances		1 850 00				1 850 00	23
24	Purchases Discounts		1 425 00				1 425 00	24
25	Freight-In	3 200 00				3 200 00		25
26	Wages Expense	37 000 00				38 300 00		26
27	Advertising Expense	4 125 00				4 125 00		27
28	Supplies Expense					5 180 00		28
29	Telephone Expense	1 650 00				1 650 00		29
30	Utilities Expense	9 150 00				9 150 00		30
31	Insurance Expense					4 175 00		31
32	Depr. Expense—Building					7 000 00		32
33	Depr. Expense—Store Equipment					4 100 00		33
34	Miscellaneous Expense	775 00				775 00		34
35		298 300 00	298 300 00			345 700 00	345 700 00	35

EXERCISE 14B-3 (LO 2) ADJUSTMENT FOR UNEARNED REVENUES USING T ACCOUNTS Set up T accounts for Cash, Unearned Ticket Revenue, and Ticket Revenue. Post the following two transactions to the appropriate accounts, indicating each transaction by letter.

(a) Sold 1,200 season tickets at $20 each, receiving cash of $24,000.

(b) An end-of-period adjustment is needed to recognize that $19,000 in ticket revenue has been earned.

PROBLEM 14A-4

Lewis Music Store
Work Sheet
For Year Ended December 31, 20 - -

#	ACCOUNT TITLE	TRIAL BALANCE DEBIT	TRIAL BALANCE CREDIT	ADJUSTMENTS DEBIT	ADJUSTMENTS CREDIT	ADJUSTED TRIAL BALANCE DEBIT	ADJUSTED TRIAL BALANCE CREDIT	INCOME STATEMENT DEBIT	INCOME STATEMENT CREDIT	BALANCE SHEET DEBIT	BALANCE SHEET CREDIT
1	Cash	27 0 0 0 00								27 0 0 0 00	
2	Accounts Receivable	13 3 0 0 00								13 3 0 0 00	
3	Merchandise Inventory	34 0 0 0 00								38 0 0 0 00	
4	Supplies	5 3 0 0 00								1 5 0 0 00	
5	Prepaid Insurance	6 1 0 0 00								1 7 8 5 00	
6	Land	31 0 0 0 00								31 0 0 0 00	
7	Building	52 0 0 0 00								52 0 0 0 00	
8	Accum. Depr.—Building		17 0 0 0 00								21 1 4 5 00
9	Store Equipment	39 0 0 0 00								39 0 0 0 00	
10	Accum. Depr.—Store Equipment		11 9 0 0 00								14 8 7 5 00
11	Accounts Payable		6 2 5 0 00								6 2 5 0 00
12	Wages Payable										8 7 5 00
13	Sales Tax Payable		6 2 0 0 00								6 2 0 0 00
14	Unearned Rent Revenue		7 4 0 0 00								3 1 7 5 00
15	Mortgage Payable		46 0 0 0 00								46 0 0 0 00
16	Hugo Lewis, Capital		111 6 2 0 00								111 6 2 0 00
17	Hugo Lewis, Drawing	37 0 0 0 00								37 0 0 0 00	
18	Income Summary							34 0 0 0 00	38 0 0 0 00		
19	Sales		136 0 0 0 00						136 0 0 0 00		
20	Sales Returns and Allowances	3 5 0 0 00						3 5 0 0 00			
21	Rent Revenue								4 2 2 5 00		
22	Purchases	39 0 0 0 00						39 0 0 0 00			
23	Purchases Returns and Allowances		2 5 3 0 00						2 5 3 0 00		
24	Purchases Discounts		1 9 7 5 00						1 9 7 5 00		
25	Freight-In	2 6 5 0 00						2 6 5 0 00			
26	Wages Expense	42 0 0 0 00						42 8 7 5 00			
27	Advertising Expense	4 1 7 5 00						4 1 7 5 00			
28	Supplies Expense							3 8 0 0 00			
29	Telephone Expense	1 9 8 0 00						1 9 8 0 00			
30	Utilities Expense	7 9 4 5 00						7 9 4 5 00			
31	Insurance Expense							4 3 1 5 00			
32	Depr. Expense—Building							4 1 4 5 00			
33	Depr. Expense—Store Equipment							2 9 7 5 00			
34	Miscellaneous Expense	9 2 5 00						9 2 5 00			
35		346 8 7 5 00	346 8 7 5 00					152 2 8 5 00	182 7 3 0 00	240 5 8 5 00	210 1 4 0 00
36	Net Income							30 4 4 5 00			30 4 4 5 00
37								182 7 3 0 00	182 7 3 0 00	240 5 8 5 00	240 5 8 5 00

EXERCISE 14B-4 (LO 3) WORK SHEET EXTENSIONS FOR MERCHANDISE INVENTORY ADJUSTMENTS The following partial work sheet is taken from Nicole's Gift Shop for the year ended December 31, 20--. The ending merchandise inventory is $37,000.

1. Complete the Adjustments columns for the merchandise inventory.

2. Extend the merchandise inventory to the Adjusted Trial Balance, Income Statement, and Balance Sheet columns.

3. Extend the remaining accounts to the Adjusted Trial Balance and Income Statement columns.

4. Prepare a cost of goods sold section from the partial work sheet.

Nicole's Gift Shop
Work Sheet (Partial)
For Year Ended December 31, 20 - -

	ACCOUNT TITLE	TRIAL BALANCE DEBIT	TRIAL BALANCE CREDIT	ADJUSTMENTS DEBIT	ADJUSTMENTS CREDIT	
1	Merchandise Inventory	30 0 0 0 00				1
12	Income Summary					12
13	Purchases	85 0 0 0 00				13
14	Purchases Returns and Allowances		2 2 0 0 00			14
15	Purchases Discounts		2 5 0 0 00			15
16	Freight-In	1 0 0 0 00				16
17						17
18						18

EXERCISE 14B-5 (LO 3) DETERMINING THE BEGINNING AND ENDING INVENTORY FROM A PARTIAL WORK SHEET From the following partial work sheet, indicate the dollar amount of beginning and ending merchandise inventory.

	ACCOUNT TITLE	ADJUSTMENTS DEBIT	ADJUSTMENTS CREDIT	ADJUSTED TRIAL BALANCE DEBIT	ADJUSTED TRIAL BALANCE CREDIT	INCOME STATEMENT DEBIT	INCOME STATEMENT CREDIT	BALANCE SHEET DEBIT	BALANCE SHEET CREDIT	
1	Merchandise Inventory	(b) 45 0 0 0 00	(a) 49 0 0 0 00	45 0 0 0 00				45 0 0 0 00		1
2	Income Summary	(a) 49 0 0 0 00	(b) 45 0 0 0 00	49 0 0 0 00	45 0 0 0 00	49 0 0 0 00	45 0 0 0 00			2

EXERCISE 14B-6 (LO 4) JOURNALIZE ADJUSTING ENTRIES FOR A MERCHAN-DISING BUSINESS The following partial work sheet is taken from the books of Carmen's Collies, a local pet kennel, for the year ended December 31, 20--. Journalize the adjustments in a general journal.

Carmen's Collies
Work Sheet (Partial)
For Year Ended December 31, 20 - -

	ACCOUNT TITLE	TRIAL BALANCE DEBIT	TRIAL BALANCE CREDIT	ADJUSTMENTS DEBIT	ADJUSTMENTS CREDIT	
1	Merchandise Inventory	35 0 0 0 00		(b) 30 0 0 0 00	(a) 35 0 0 0 00	1
2	Supplies	4 5 0 0 00			(d) 3 1 0 0 00	2
3	Building	50 0 0 0 00				3
4	Accum. Depr.—Building		23 0 0 0 00		(e) 6 0 0 0 00	4
5	Wages Payable				(f) 1 3 0 0 00	5
6	Unearned Grooming Revenue		7 0 0 0 00	(c) 5 5 0 0 00		6
7	Income Summary			(a) 35 0 0 0 00	(b) 30 0 0 0 00	7
8	Grooming Revenue		24 0 0 0 00		(c) 5 5 0 0 00	8
9	Wages Expense	41 0 0 0 00		(f) 1 3 0 0 00		9
10	Supplies Expense			(d) 3 1 0 0 00		10
11	Depr. Expense—Building			(e) 6 0 0 0 00		11
12				80 9 0 0 00	80 9 0 0 00	12
13						13

SERIES B PROBLEMS

PROBLEM 14B-1 (LO 1/2/3/4) COMPLETION OF A WORK SHEET SHOWING A NET INCOME A trial balance for the Basket Corner, a business owned by Linda Palermo, is shown on page 529. Year-end adjustment information is provided below.

(a, b) Merchandise inventory costing $24,000 is on hand as of December 31, 20--.

(c) Supplies remaining at the end of the year, $2,100.

(d) Unexpired insurance on December 31, $2,600.

(e) Depreciation expense on the building for 20--, $5,300.

(f) Depreciation expense on the store equipment for 20--, $3,800.

(g) Unearned decorating revenue as of December 31, $1,650.

(h) Wages earned but not paid as of December 31, $750.

REQUIRED
1. Complete the Adjustments columns, identifying each adjustment with its corresponding letter.

2. Complete the work sheet.

3. Enter the adjustments in a general journal.

Basket Corner
Trial Balance
December 31, 20 - -

ACCOUNT TITLE	DEBIT BALANCE					CREDIT BALANCE				
Cash	25	0	0	0	00					
Accounts Receivable	8	1	0	0	00					
Merchandise Inventory	32	0	0	0	00					
Supplies	7	1	0	0	00					
Prepaid Insurance	3	6	0	0	00					
Land	40	0	0	0	00					
Building	45	0	0	0	00					
Accumulated Depreciation—Building						16	0	0	0	00
Store Equipment	27	0	0	0	00					
Accumulated Depreciation—Store Equipment						5	5	0	0	00
Accounts Payable						3	6	0	0	00
Wages Payable										
Sales Tax Payable						6	2	0	0	00
Unearned Decorating Revenue						6	3	0	0	00
Mortgage Payable						36	0	0	0	00
Linda Palermo, Capital						112	0	5	0	00
Linda Palermo, Drawing	31	0	0	0	00					
Income Summary										
Sales						125	0	0	0	00
Sales Returns and Allowances	2	6	0	0	00					
Decorating Revenue										
Purchases	38	0	0	0	00					
Purchases Returns and Allowances						2	2	0	0	00
Purchases Discounts						1	7	0	0	00
Freight-In	1	9	0	0	00					
Wages Expense	38	0	0	0	00					
Advertising Expense	4	2	0	0	00					
Supplies Expense										
Telephone Expense	1	8	7	0	00					
Utilities Expense	8	4	0	0	00					
Insurance Expense										
Depreciation Expense —Building										
Depreciation Expense —Store Equipment										
Miscellaneous Expense		7	8	0	00					
	314	5	5	0	00	314	5	5	0	00

W & D

PROBLEM 14B-2 (LO 1/2/3/4) COMPLETION OF A WORK SHEET SHOWING A NET LOSS The trial balance for Oregon Bike Company, a business owned by Craig Moody, is shown on page 530. Year-end adjustment information is provided below.

(a, b)   Merchandise inventory costing $26,000 is on hand as of December 31, 20--.

(c)   Supplies remaining at the end of the year, $2,500.

(d)   Unexpired insurance on December 31, $1,820.

(continued)

(e)   Depreciation expense on the building for 20--, $6,400.

(f)   Depreciation expense on the store equipment for 20--, $2,800.

(g)   Unearned rent revenue as of December 31, $2,350.

(h)   Wages earned but not paid as of December 31, $1,100.

REQUIRED   1.   Complete the Adjustments columns, identifying each adjustment with its corresponding letter.

2.   Complete the work sheet.

3.   Enter the adjustments in a general journal.

Oregon Bike Company
Trial Balance
December 31, 20 - -

ACCOUNT TITLE	DEBIT BALANCE	CREDIT BALANCE
Cash	27 0 0 0 00	
Accounts Receivable	12 0 0 0 00	
Merchandise Inventory	39 0 0 0 00	
Supplies	6 2 0 0 00	
Prepaid Insurance	5 8 0 0 00	
Land	32 0 0 0 00	
Building	58 0 0 0 00	
Accumulated Depreciation—Building		27 0 0 0 00
Store Equipment	31 0 0 0 00	
Accumulated Depreciation—Store Equipment		14 0 0 0 00
Accounts Payable		4 9 0 0 00
Wages Payable		2 9 0 0 00
Sales Tax Payable		
Unearned Rent Revenue		6 1 0 0 00
Mortgage Payable		49 0 0 0 00
Craig Moody, Capital		169 5 0 0 00
Craig Moody, Drawing	36 0 0 0 00	
Income Summary		
Sales		58 0 0 0 00
Sales Returns and Allowances	3 3 0 0 00	
Rent Revenue		
Purchases	19 0 0 0 00	
Purchases Returns and Allowances		9 0 0 00
Purchases Discounts		1 4 5 0 00
Freight-In	8 0 0 00	
Wages Expense	47 0 0 0 00	
Advertising Expense	6 2 0 0 00	
Supplies Expense		
Telephone Expense	1 8 6 0 00	
Utilities Expense	8 1 0 0 00	
Insurance Expense		
Depreciation Expense —Building		
Depreciation Expense —Store Equipment		
Miscellaneous Expense	4 9 0 00	
	333 7 5 0 00	333 7 5 0 00

PROBLEM 14B-3 (LO 1/2/4) WORKING BACKWARD FROM ADJUSTED TRIAL BALANCE TO DETERMINE ADJUSTING ENTRIES The partial work sheet shown below is taken from the books of Burnside Auto Parts, a business owned by Barbara Davis, for the year ended December 31, 20--.

REQUIRED   1. Determine the adjusting entries by analyzing the difference between the adjusted trial balance and the trial balance.

2. Journalize the adjusting entries in a general journal.

Burnside Auto Parts
Work Sheet (Partial)
For Year Ended December 31, 20 - -

	ACCOUNT TITLE	TRIAL BALANCE DEBIT	TRIAL BALANCE CREDIT	ADJUSTMENTS DEBIT	ADJUSTMENTS CREDIT	ADJUSTED TRIAL BALANCE DEBIT	ADJUSTED TRIAL BALANCE CREDIT	
1	Cash	21 0 0 0 00				21 0 0 0 00		1
2	Accounts Receivable	8 3 0 0 00				8 3 0 0 00		2
3	Merchandise Inventory	32 0 0 0 00				36 0 0 0 00		3
4	Supplies	6 1 5 0 00				1 8 6 5 00		4
5	Prepaid Insurance	5 9 2 5 00				1 8 3 5 00		5
6	Land	41 7 5 0 00				41 7 5 0 00		6
7	Building	43 0 0 0 00				43 0 0 0 00		7
8	Accum. Depr.—Building		24 0 0 0 00				27 5 0 0 00	8
9	Store Equipment	25 4 0 0 00				25 4 0 0 00		9
10	Accum. Depr.—Store Equipment		12 4 0 0 00				14 7 5 0 00	10
11	Accounts Payable		8 1 0 0 00				8 1 0 0 00	11
12	Wages Payable						9 8 0 00	12
13	Sales Tax Payable		5 2 0 0 00				5 2 0 0 00	13
14	Unearned Rent-A-Junk Revenue		7 9 5 0 00				2 3 5 0 00	14
15	Mortgage Payable		26 0 0 0 00				26 0 0 0 00	15
16	Barbara Davis, Capital		109 1 3 0 00				109 1 3 0 00	16
17	Barbara Davis, Drawing	40 0 0 0 00				40 0 0 0 00		17
18	Income Summary					32 0 0 0 00	36 0 0 0 00	18
19	Sales		123 5 0 0 00				123 5 0 0 00	19
20	Sales Returns and Allowances	2 8 6 0 00				2 8 6 0 00		20
21	Rent-A-Junk Revenue						5 6 0 0 00	21
22	Purchases	32 5 2 5 00				32 5 2 5 00		22
23	Purchases Returns and Allowances		2 1 5 0 00				2 1 5 0 00	23
24	Purchases Discounts		2 4 0 0 00				2 4 0 0 00	24
25	Freight-In	3 1 7 5 00				3 1 7 5 00		25
26	Wages Expense	44 1 7 5 00				45 1 5 5 00		26
27	Advertising Expense	3 2 7 5 00				3 2 7 5 00		27
28	Supplies Expense					4 2 8 5 00		28
29	Telephone Expense	2 2 0 0 00				2 2 0 0 00		29
30	Utilities Expense	8 2 5 0 00				8 2 5 0 00		30
31	Insurance Expense					4 0 9 0 00		31
32	Depr. Expense—Building					3 5 0 0 00		32
33	Depr. Expense—Store Equipment					2 3 5 0 00		33
34	Miscellaneous Expense	8 4 5 00				8 4 5 00		34
35		320 8 3 0 00	320 8 3 0 00			363 6 6 0 00	363 6 6 0 00	35

PROBLEM 14B-4 (LO 1/2/3/4) WORKING BACKWARD FROM THE INCOME STATEMENT AND BALANCE SHEET COLUMNS OF THE WORK SHEET TO DETERMINE ADJUSTED TRIAL BALANCE AND ADJUSTING ENTRIES The partial work sheet shown on page 533 is taken from the books of Diamond Music Store, a business owned by Ned Diamond, for the year ended December 31, 20--.

REQUIRED
1. Analyze the work sheet and determine the adjusted trial balance and the adjusting entries by working backward from the Income Statement and Balance Sheet columns.

2. Journalize the adjusting entries in a general journal.

3. Prepare the cost of goods sold section of the income statement for Diamond Music Store.

MASTERY PROBLEM

John Neff owns and operates the Waikiki Surf Shop. A year-end trial balance is provided on page 534. Year-end adjustment data for the Waikiki Surf Shop is shown below.

(a, b) A physical count shows merchandise inventory costing $45,000 on hand as of December 31, 20--.

(c)   Supplies remaining at the end of the year, $600.

(d)   Unexpired insurance on December 31, $900.

(e)   Depreciation expense on the building for 20--, $6,000.

(f)   Depreciation expense on the store equipment for 20--, $4,500.

(g)   Wages earned but not paid as of December 31, $675.

(h)   Unearned boat rental revenue as of December 31, $3,000.

REQUIRED
1. Prepare a year-end work sheet.

2. Journalize the adjusting entries.

PROBLEM 14B-4

Diamond Music Store
Work Sheet
For Year Ended December 31, 20--

#	Account Title	Trial Balance Debit	Trial Balance Credit	Adjustments Debit	Adjustments Credit	Adjusted Trial Balance Debit	Adjusted Trial Balance Credit	Income Statement Debit	Income Statement Credit	Balance Sheet Debit	Balance Sheet Credit
1	Cash	31 0 0 0 00								31 0 0 0 00	
2	Accounts Receivable	11 9 8 0 00								11 9 8 0 00	
3	Merchandise Inventory	33 6 0 0 00								39 1 0 0 00	
4	Supplies	7 1 4 0 00								1 9 6 5 00	
5	Prepaid Insurance	5 9 8 5 00								1 2 3 5 00	
6	Land	36 2 0 0 00								36 2 0 0 00	
7	Building	51 8 5 0 00								51 8 5 0 00	
8	Accum. Depr.—Building		13 5 9 0 00								18 8 7 5 00
9	Store Equipment	32 6 7 5 00								32 6 7 5 00	
10	Accum. Depr.—Store Equipment		10 2 9 0 00								14 7 5 5 00
11	Accounts Payable		5 8 9 5 00								5 8 9 5 00
12	Wages Payable										1 2 5 0 00
13	Sales Tax Payable		6 3 7 5 00								6 3 7 5 00
14	Unearned Rent Revenue		8 8 5 0 00								2 9 3 0 00
15	Mortgage Payable		42 4 0 0 00								42 4 0 0 00
16	Ned Diamond, Capital		116 3 5 0 00								116 3 5 0 00
17	Ned Diamond, Drawing	39 5 0 0 00								39 5 0 0 00	
18	Income Summary							33 6 0 0 00	39 1 0 0 00		
19	Sales		148 0 0 0 00						148 0 0 0 00		
20	Sales Returns and Allowances	2 8 0 0 00						2 8 0 0 00			
21	Rent Revenue								5 9 2 0 00		
22	Purchases	40 7 0 0 00						40 7 0 0 00			
23	Purchases Returns and Allowances		2 7 7 5 00						2 7 7 5 00		
24	Purchases Discounts		2 3 2 5 00						2 3 2 5 00		
25	Freight-In	1 8 7 5 00						1 8 7 5 00			
26	Wages Expense	47 0 0 0 00						48 2 5 0 00			
27	Advertising Expense	4 6 9 5 00						4 6 9 5 00			
28	Supplies Expense							5 1 7 5 00			
29	Telephone Expense	2 2 5 0 00						2 2 5 0 00			
30	Utilities Expense	6 8 2 5 00						6 8 2 5 00			
31	Insurance Expense							4 7 5 0 00			
32	Depr. Expense—Building							5 2 8 5 00			
33	Depr. Expense—Store Equipment							4 4 6 5 00			
34	Miscellaneous Expense	7 7 5 00						7 7 5 00			
35		356 8 5 0 00	356 8 5 0 00					161 4 4 5 00	198 1 2 0 00	245 5 0 5 00	208 8 3 0 00
36	Net Income							36 6 7 5 00			36 6 7 5 00
37								198 1 2 0 00	198 1 2 0 00	245 5 0 5 00	245 5 0 5 00

MASTERY PROBLEM

Waikiki Surf Shop
Trial Balance
December 31, 20 - -

ACCOUNT TITLE	DEBIT BALANCE	CREDIT BALANCE
Cash	30 0 0 0 00	
Accounts Receivable	22 5 0 0 00	
Merchandise Inventory	57 0 0 0 00	
Supplies	2 7 0 0 00	
Prepaid Insurance	3 6 0 0 00	
Land	15 0 0 0 00	
Building	135 0 0 0 00	
Accumulated Depreciation—Building		24 0 0 0 00
Store Equipment	75 0 0 0 00	
Accumulated Depreciation—Store Equipment		22 5 0 0 00
Notes Payable		7 5 0 0 00
Accounts Payable		15 0 0 0 00
Wages Payable		
Unearned Boat Rental Revenue		33 0 0 0 00
John Neff, Capital		233 7 0 0 00
John Neff, Drawing	30 0 0 0 00	
Income Summary		
Sales		300 7 5 0 00
Sales Returns and Allowances	1 8 0 0 00	
Boat Rental Revenue		
Purchases	157 5 0 0 00	
Purchases Returns and Allowances		1 2 0 0 00
Purchases Discounts		1 5 0 0 00
Freight-In	4 5 0 00	
Wages Expense	63 0 0 0 00	
Advertising Expense	11 2 5 0 00	
Supplies Expense		
Telephone Expense	5 2 5 0 00	
Utilities Expense	18 0 0 0 00	
Insurance Expense		
Depreciation Expense —Building		
Depreciation Expense —Store Equipment		
Miscellaneous Expense	10 8 7 5 00	
Interest Expense	2 2 5 00	
	639 1 5 0 00	639 1 5 0 00

Self-Study Test Questions

True/False

1. The beginning inventory is removed from the merchandise inventory account with a credit to Merchandise Inventory and a debit to Income Summary. _____

2. The ending inventory is entered by debiting Merchandise Inventory and crediting Income Summary. _____

3. The cash received in advance before delivering a product or performing a service is called unearned revenue. _____

4. Unearned revenue is adjusted into an expense account at the end of the accounting period. _____

5. Sales Returns and Allowances is classified as a contra-expense account on the income statement. _____

Multiple Choice

1. Purchases Returns and Allowances and Purchases Discounts are classified as _____ on the income statement. _____

   (a) expense accounts
   (b) contra-cost accounts
   (c) revenue accounts
   (d) contra-revenue accounts

2. The first step in preparing a work sheet is to _____

   (a) prepare the trial balance.
   (b) prepare the income statement.
   (c) prepare the adjustments.
   (d) prepare the balance sheet.

3. The last step in preparing a work sheet is to _____

   (a) prepare the adjusted trial balance.
   (b) total the Income Statement and Balance Sheet columns to compute net income or net loss.
   (c) prepare the adjustments.
   (d) extend the Adjusted Trial Balance columns.

4. Unearned Revenue is extended into the _____ on the work sheet. _____

   (a) Adjustments columns
   (b) Balance Sheet columns
   (c) Income Statement columns
   (d) Trial Balance columns

5. The most useful tool in preparing end-of-period adjustments and financial statements is the _____

   (a) general ledger.
   (b) work sheet.
   (c) general journal.
   (d) physical inventory.

The answers to the Self-Study Test Questions are at the end of the text.

Expense Method of Accounting for Prepaid Expenses

LEARNING OBJECTIVES:
Careful study of this appendix should enable you to:

LO 1 Use the expense method of accounting for prepaid expenses.

LO 2 Make the appropriate adjusting entries when the expense method is used for prepaid expenses.

THE EXPENSE METHOD

LO 1 Use the expense method of accounting for prepaid expenses.

Under the **expense method** of accounting for prepaid expenses, supplies and other prepaid items are entered as expenses when purchased. Under this method, we must adjust the accounts at the end of each accounting period to record the unused portions as assets. To illustrate, let's assume that the following entry was made when office supplies were purchased.

4		Office Supplies Expense			4	2	5	00						4
5		Cash								4	2	5	00	5
6		Purchased office supplies												6

In the next section, we will illustrate the proper adjusting entry when using the expense method.

ADJUSTING ENTRIES UNDER THE EXPENSE METHOD

LO 2 Make the appropriate adjusting entries when the expense method is used for prepaid expenses.

Office Supplies Expense was debited for a total of $425 during the period. An inventory taken at the end of the period shows that supplies on hand amounted to $150. The following adjusting entry is made for supplies on hand:

8		Office Supplies		1	5	0	00			8
9		Office Supplies Expense						1	5	0	00	9
10										10

As shown in the T accounts below, after this entry is posted, the office supplies expense account has a debit balance of $275. This amount is reported on the income statement as an operating expense. The office supplies account has a debit balance of $150. It is reported on the balance sheet as a current asset.

Office Supplies	Office Supplies Expense
	425
Adj. 150	Adj. 150
	Bal. 275

Let's consider another example of the use of the expense method. The following entry was made for the payment of $6,000 for a three-year insurance policy:

11		Insurance Expense		6	0	0	0	00		11
12		Cash						6	0	0	0	00	12
13		Paid insurance premium								13

At the end of the first year, one-third of the premium has expired and two-thirds remains. Thus, $2,000 for insurance expense should be reported on the income statement and $4,000 in prepaid insurance should be reported on the balance sheet. The following adjusting entry is made:

15		Prepaid Insurance		4	0	0	0	00		15
16		Insurance Expense						4	0	0	0	00	16
17										17

As shown in the T accounts below, after this entry is posted, the prepaid insurance account has a debit balance of $4,000. The insurance expense account has a debit balance of $2,000.

Prepaid Insurance	Insurance Expense
	6,000
Adj. 4,000	Adj. 4,000
	Bal. 2,000

The asset and expense methods of accounting for prepaid expenses give the same final result. In the **asset method**, the prepaid item is first debited to an asset account. At the end of each period, the amount consumed is debited to an expense account. In the expense method, the original amount is debited to an expense account. At the end of each accounting period, the portion not consumed is debited to an asset account.

	Learning Objectives	Key Points to Remember
1	**Use the expense method of accounting for prepaid expenses.**	Under the expense method, an expense account is debited when prepaid items are acquired.
2	**Make the appropriate adjusting entries when the expense method is used for prepaid expenses.**	At the end of the accounting period, an asset must be recognized for the amount of the prepaid item remaining. The expense account must be credited so that the ending balance represents the amount of the item consumed.

KEY TERMS

asset method, (537)   Under this method, the acquisition of a prepaid item is debited to an asset account.

expense method, (536)   Under this method, the acquisition of a prepaid item is debited to an expense account.

EXERCISES

EX14ApxA-1 (LO 2) EXPENSE METHOD OF ACCOUNTING FOR PREPAID EXPENSES Davidson's Food Mart paid $1,200 in advance to the local newspaper for advertisements that will appear monthly. The following entry was made:

4		Advertising Expense			1	2	0	0	00							4
5		Cash									1	2	0	0	00	5
6		Paid prepaid advertising														6

At the end of the year, December 31, 20--, Davidson received notification that advertisements costing $800 had been run. Prepare the adjusting entry.

EX14ApxB-1 (LO 2) EXPENSE METHOD OF ACCOUNTING FOR PREPAID EXPENSES Ryan's Fish House purchased supplies costing $3,000 for cash. This amount was debited to the supplies expense account. At the end of the year, December 31, 20--, an inventory showed that supplies costing $500 remained. Prepare the entry for the purchase and year-end adjustment.

15

Financial Statements and Year-End Accounting for a Merchandising Business

LEARNING OBJECTIVES:
Careful study of this chapter should enable you to:

LO 1   Prepare a single-step and multiple-step income statement for a merchandising business.

LO 2   Prepare a statement of owner's equity.

LO 3   Prepare a classified balance sheet.

LO 4   Compute standard financial ratios.

LO 5   Prepare closing entries for a merchandising business.

LO 6   Prepare reversing entries.

Betty Jenkins, John's bookkeeper, went to Florida to visit her parents after closing the books for the year. She plans to return during the second week of January. She has given John careful instructions on how to enter basic transactions while she is gone. Unfortunately, John is a bit confused about the proper entry for the first payroll of the new year. He knows that those first paychecks of the year cover wages earned last year, but not yet paid, as well as wages earned this year. Thus, it seems like he should check to get the proper allocation before recording the paychecks for the new year. Although he didn't want to interrupt Betty's vacation, he called her in Florida to get the proper allocations. Surprisingly, Betty said, "Don't worry about it. Just make the 'normal' entry by debiting Wages Expense and crediting Cash." Why is Betty not concerned about the proper allocation for the first payroll period?

The first six chapters of this text illustrated the accounting cycle for a service business. Chapter 7 demonstrated accounting procedures for a professional enterprise. In this chapter we complete the accounting cycle for a merchandising business.

In Chapter 14, we prepared the year-end work sheet and adjusting entries for Northern Micro. In this chapter, we will prepare financial statements, closing and reversing entries, and look briefly at financial statement analysis.

THE INCOME STATEMENT

LO 1   Prepare a single-step and multiple-step income statement for a merchandising business.

As you know, a primary purpose of the work sheet is to serve as an aid in preparing the financial statements. Figure 15-1 shows the completed work sheet for Northern Micro. We will use it to prepare financial statements.

The purpose of an income statement is to summarize the results of operations during an accounting period. The income statement shows the sources of revenue, types of expenses, and the amount of the net income or net loss for the period. Two forms of the income statement commonly used are the single step and the multiple step. The **single-step income statement** lists all revenue items and their total first, followed by all expense items and their total. The difference, which is either net income or net loss, is then calculated. A single-step income statement for Northern Micro is illustrated in Figure 15-2 below.

FIGURE 15-2 Single-Step Income Statement

Northern Micro									
Income Statement									
For Year Ended December 31, 20 - -									
Revenues:									
Net sales	$212	8	0	0	00				
Interest revenue		9	0	0	00				
Rent revenue	8	0	0	0	00				
Subscriptions revenue	10	0	0	0	00				
Total revenues						$231	7	0	0	00
Expenses:									
Cost of goods sold	$111	5	0	0	00				
Wages expense	42	4	5	0	00				
Advertising expense	2	5	0	0	00				
Bank credit card expense	1	5	0	0	00				
Rent expense	20	0	0	0	00				
Supplies expense	1	4	0	0	00				
Telephone expense	3	5	0	0	00				
Utilities expense	12	0	0	0	00				
Insurance expense	1	8	0	0	00				
Depreciation expense—building	4	0	0	0	00				
Depreciation expense—store equipment	3	0	0	0	00				
Miscellaneous expense	2	2	5	0	00				
Interest expense	3	1	5	0	00				
Total expenses						209	0	5	0	00
Net income						$ 22	6	5	0	00

FIGURE 15-1 Northern Micro Work Sheet

Northern Micro
Work Sheet
For Year Ended December 31, 20--

Account Title	Trial Balance Debit	Trial Balance Credit	Adjustments Debit	Adjustments Credit	Adjusted Trial Balance Debit	Adjusted Trial Balance Credit	Income Statement Debit	Income Statement Credit	Balance Sheet Debit	Balance Sheet Credit
1 Cash	20 0 0 0 00				20 0 0 0 00				20 0 0 0 00	
2 Accounts Receivable	15 0 0 0 00				15 0 0 0 00				15 0 0 0 00	
3 Merchandise Inventory	26 0 0 0 00		(b) 18 0 0 0 00	(a) 26 0 0 0 00	18 0 0 0 00				18 0 0 0 00	
4 Supplies	1 8 0 0 00			(c) 1 4 0 0 00	4 0 0 00				4 0 0 00	
5 Prepaid Insurance	2 4 0 0 00			(d) 1 8 0 0 00	6 0 0 00				6 0 0 00	
6 Land	10 0 0 0 00				10 0 0 0 00				10 0 0 0 00	
7 Building	90 0 0 0 00				90 0 0 0 00				90 0 0 0 00	
8 Accum. Depr.—Building		16 0 0 0 00		(e) 4 0 0 0 00		20 0 0 0 00				20 0 0 0 00
9 Store Equipment	50 0 0 0 00				50 0 0 0 00				50 0 0 0 00	
10 Accum. Depr.—Store Equipment		15 0 0 0 00		(f) 3 0 0 0 00		18 0 0 0 00				18 0 0 0 00
11 Notes Payable		5 0 0 0 00				5 0 0 0 00				5 0 0 0 00
12 Accounts Payable		10 0 0 0 00				10 0 0 0 00				10 0 0 0 00
13 Wages Payable				(g) 4 5 0 00		4 5 0 00				4 5 0 00
14 Sales Tax Payable		1 5 0 0 00				1 5 0 0 00				1 5 0 0 00
15 Unearned Subscriptions Revenue		12 0 0 0 00	(h) 10 0 0 0 00			2 0 0 0 00				2 0 0 0 00
16 Mortgage Payable		30 0 0 0 00				30 0 0 0 00				30 0 0 0 00
17 Gary L. Fishel, Capital		114 4 0 0 00				114 4 0 0 00				114 4 0 0 00
18 Gary L. Fishel, Drawing	20 0 0 0 00				20 0 0 0 00				20 0 0 0 00	
19 Income Summary			(a) 26 0 0 0 00	(b) 18 0 0 0 00	26 0 0 0 00	18 0 0 0 00	26 0 0 0 00	18 0 0 0 00		
20 Sales		214 0 0 0 00				214 0 0 0 00		214 0 0 0 00		
21 Sales Returns and Allowances	1 2 0 0 00				1 2 0 0 00		1 2 0 0 00			
22 Interest Revenue		9 0 0 00				9 0 0 00		9 0 0 00		
23 Rent Revenue		8 0 0 0 00				8 0 0 0 00		8 0 0 0 00		
24 Subscriptions Revenue				(h) 10 0 0 0 00		10 0 0 0 00		10 0 0 0 00		
25 Purchases	105 0 0 0 00				105 0 0 0 00		105 0 0 0 00			
26 Purchases Returns and Allowances		8 0 0 0 00				8 0 0 0 00		8 0 0 0 00		
27 Purchases Discounts		1 0 0 0 00				1 0 0 0 00		1 0 0 0 00		
28 Freight-In	3 0 0 0 00				3 0 0 0 00		3 0 0 0 00			
29 Wages Expense	42 0 0 0 00		(g) 4 5 0 00		42 4 5 0 00		42 4 5 0 00			
30 Advertising Expense	2 5 0 0 00				2 5 0 0 00		2 5 0 0 00			
31 Bank Credit Card Expense	1 5 0 0 00				1 5 0 0 00		1 5 0 0 00			
32 Rent Expense	20 0 0 0 00				20 0 0 0 00		20 0 0 0 00			
33 Supplies Expense			(c) 1 4 0 0 00		1 4 0 0 00		1 4 0 0 00			
34 Telephone Expense	3 5 0 0 00				3 5 0 0 00		3 5 0 0 00			
35 Utilities Expense	12 0 0 0 00				12 0 0 0 00		12 0 0 0 00			
36 Insurance Expense			(d) 1 8 0 0 00		1 8 0 0 00		1 8 0 0 00			
37 Depr. Expense—Building			(e) 4 0 0 0 00		4 0 0 0 00		4 0 0 0 00			
38 Depr. Expense—Store Equipment			(f) 3 0 0 0 00		3 0 0 0 00		3 0 0 0 00			
39 Miscellaneous Expense	2 2 5 0 00				2 2 5 0 00		2 2 5 0 00			
40 Interest Expense	3 1 5 0 00				3 1 5 0 00		3 1 5 0 00			
41	428 6 0 0 00	428 6 0 0 00	64 6 5 0 00	64 6 5 0 00	454 0 5 0 00	454 0 5 0 00	230 0 5 0 00	252 7 0 0 00	224 0 0 0 00	201 3 5 0 00
42 Net Income							22 6 5 0 00			22 6 5 0 00
43							252 7 0 0 00	252 7 0 0 00	224 0 0 0 00	224 0 0 0 00

The **multiple-step income statement** is commonly used for merchandising businesses. The term "multiple-step" is used because the final net income is calculated on a step-by-step basis. Gross sales is shown first, less sales returns and allowances and sales discounts. This difference is called **net sales**. (Many published income statements begin with the amount of net sales.) Cost of goods sold is subtracted next to arrive at **gross profit** (sometimes called **gross margin**).

Operating expenses are then listed and subtracted from the gross profit to compute **income from operations** (sometimes called **operating income**). Operating expenses are directly associated with providing the primary goods and services of the business. Some companies divide operating expenses into the following subcategories.

Selling expenses. These expenses are directly associated with selling activities. Examples include:

▶ Sales Salaries Expense

▶ Sales Commissions Expense

▶ Advertising Expense

▶ Bank Credit Card Expense

▶ Delivery Expense

▶ Depreciation Expense—Store Equipment and Fixtures

General expenses. These expenses are associated with administrative, office, or general operating activities. Examples include:

▶ Rent Expense

▶ Office Salaries Expense

▶ Office Supplies Expense

▶ Telephone Expense

▶ Utilities Expense

▶ Insurance Expense

▶ Depreciation Expense—Office Equipment

> By showing other revenues and other expenses separately, it is possible to show income from operations. This makes it easier for the reader to see how the business is doing in its main activity.

Finally, other revenues are added and other expenses are subtracted to arrive at net income (or net loss). A multiple-step income statement for Northern Micro is shown in Figure 15-3. Note that the operating expenses are arranged according to the order given in the chart of accounts. They could also be listed by descending amount, with Miscellaneous Expense last.

FIGURE 15-3 Multiple-Step Income Statement

Northern Micro					
Income Statement					
For Year Ended December 31, 20 - -					
Revenue from sales:					
Sales				$214 0 0 0 00	
Less sales returns and allowances				1 2 0 0 00	
Net sales					$212 8 0 0 00
Cost of goods sold:					
Merchandise inventory, January 1, 20- -				$ 26 0 0 0 00	
Purchases			$105 0 0 0 00		
Less: Purchases returns and allowances	$ 8 0 0 00				
Purchases discounts	1 0 0 0 00		1 8 0 0 00		
Net purchases			$103 2 0 0 00		
Add freight-in			3 0 0 00		
Cost of goods purchased				103 5 0 0 00	
Goods available for sale				$129 5 0 0 00	
Less merchandise inventory, December 31, 20- -				18 0 0 0 00	
Cost of goods sold					111 5 0 0 00
Gross profit					$101 3 0 0 00
Operating expenses:					
Wages expense				$ 42 4 5 0 00	
Advertising expense				2 5 0 0 00	
Bank credit card expense				1 5 0 0 00	
Rent expense				20 0 0 0 00	
Supplies expense				1 4 0 0 00	
Telephone expense				3 5 0 0 00	
Utilities expense				12 0 0 0 00	
Insurance expense				1 8 0 0 00	
Depreciation expense—building				4 0 0 0 00	
Depreciation expense—store equipment				3 0 0 0 00	
Miscellaneous expense				2 2 5 0 00	
Total operating expenses					94 4 0 0 00
Income from operations					$ 6 9 0 0 00
Other revenues:					
Interest revenue				$ 9 0 0 00	
Rent revenue				8 0 0 0 00	
Subscriptions revenue				10 0 0 0 00	
Total other revenues				$ 18 9 0 0 00	
Other expenses:					
Interest expense				3 1 5 0 00	15 7 5 0 00
Net income					$ 22 6 5 0 00

LEARNING KEY: Although the format for the single-step and multiple-step income statements are different, the reported net income is the same.

THE STATEMENT OF OWNER'S EQUITY

LO 2 Prepare a statement of owner's equity.

The statement of owner's equity summarizes all changes in the owner's equity during the period. It includes the net income or loss and any additional investments or withdrawals by the owner. These changes result in the end-of-period balance shown on this statement and the balance sheet.

To prepare the statement of owner's equity for Northern Micro, two sources of information are needed: (1) the work sheet, and (2) Gary Fishel's capital account (no. 311) in the general ledger. The work sheet (Figure 15-1) shows net income of $22,650 and withdrawals of $20,000 during the year. Fishel's capital account (Figure 15-4) shows a beginning balance of $104,400. An additional $10,000 was invested in the business in February of the current year. The statement of owner's equity for Northern Micro for the year ended December 31, 20--, is shown in Figure 15-5.

FIGURE 15-4 Capital Account for Gary L. Fishel

ACCOUNT: Gary L. Fishel, Capital								ACCOUNT NO. 311	
						BALANCE			
DATE	ITEM	POST REF.	DEBIT	CREDIT		DEBIT		CREDIT	
20--Jan. 1	Balance	✓						104 4 0 0 00	
Feb. 12		CR7		10 0 0 0 00				114 4 0 0 00	

FIGURE 15-5 Statement of Owner's Equity

> The statement of owner's equity is the same for service and merchandising businesses.

Northern Micro Statement of Owner's Equity For Year Ended December 31, 20 - -				
Gary L. Fishel, capital, January 1, 20 - -			$104 4 0 0 00	
Add additional investments			10 0 0 0 00	
Total investment			$114 4 0 0 00	
Net income for the year	$22 6 5 0 00			
Less withdrawals for the year	20 0 0 0 00			
Increase in capital			2 6 5 0 00	
Gary L. Fishel, capital, December 31, 20 - -			$117 0 5 0 00	

THE BALANCE SHEET

LO 3 Prepare a classified balance sheet.

The report form of a classified balance sheet is illustrated in Figure 15-6. The balance sheet classifications used by Northern Micro are explained below.

LEARNING KEY: Note the use of the ending balance for merchandise inventory. It is reported on the income statement as part of the calculation of cost of goods sold. It also is reported on the balance sheet as a current asset.

FIGURE 15-6 Balance Sheet for Northern Micro

Northern Micro Balance Sheet December 31, 20 - -																		
Assets																		
Current assets:																		
Cash						$20	0	0	0	00								
Accounts receivable						15	0	0	0	00								
Merchandise inventory						18	0	0	0	00								
Supplies							4	0	0	00								
Prepaid insurance							6	0	0	00								
Total current assets											$ 54	0	0	0	00				
Property, plant, and equipment:																		
Land						$10	0	0	0	00								
Building	$90	0	0	0	00													
Less accumulated depreciation	20	0	0	0	00	70	0	0	0	00								
Store equipment	$50	0	0	0	00													
Less accumulated depreciation	18	0	0	0	00	32	0	0	0	00								
Total property, plant, and equipment											112	0	0	0	00				
Total assets											$166	0	0	0	00				
Liabilities																		
Current liabilities:																		
Notes payable	$ 5	0	0	0	00													
Accounts payable	10	0	0	0	00													
Wages payable		4	5	0	00													
Sales tax payable	1	5	0	0	00													
Unearned subscriptions revenue	2	0	0	0	00													
Mortgage payable (current portion)		5	0	0	00													
Total current liabilities						$19	4	5	0	00								
Long-term liabilities:																		
Mortgage payable	$30	0	0	0	00													
Less current portion		5	0	0	00	29	5	0	0	00								
Total liabilities											$ 48	9	5	0	00				
Owner's Equity																		
Gary L. Fishel, capital											117	0	5	0	00				
Total liabilities and owner's equity											$166	0	0	0	00				

Current Assets

Current assets include cash and all other assets expected to be converted into cash or consumed within one year or the normal operating cycle of the business, whichever is longer. The **operating cycle** is the length of time generally required for a business to buy inventory, sell it, and collect the cash. This time period is generally less than a year. Thus, most firms use one year for classifying current assets. In a merchandising business, the current assets usually include cash, receivables (such as accounts receivable and notes receivable), and merchandise inventory. Since prepaid expenses, such as unused supplies and unexpired insurance, are likely to be consumed within a year, they also are reported as current assets.

Current assets are listed on the balance sheet from the most liquid to least liquid. **Liquidity** refers to the speed with which the company can convert the asset to cash. Cash is the most liquid asset and is always listed first. Notes Receivable, Accounts Receivable, and Merchandise Inventory often follow it on the balance sheet.

Property, Plant, and Equipment

Assets that are expected to be used for more than one year in the operation of a business are called **property, plant, and equipment**. Examples include land, buildings, office equipment, store equipment, and delivery equipment. Of these assets, only land is permanent; however, all of these assets have useful lives that are comparatively long. Typically, assets with longer useful lives are listed first.

The balance sheet of Northern Micro shows Land, Building, and Store Equipment. Land is not depreciated. Accumulated depreciation amounts are shown as deductions from the costs of the building and store equipment. The difference represents the **undepreciated cost**, or **book value**, of the assets. This amount less any salvage value will be written off as depreciation expense in future periods.

Current Liabilities

The current portion of long-term debt, the amount due within one year, is reported as a current liability. The remainder is reported under long-term liabilities.

Current liabilities include those obligations that are due within one year or the normal operating cycle of the business, whichever is longer, and will require the use of current assets. As of December 31, the current liabilities of Northern Micro consist of Notes Payable, Accounts Payable, Wages Payable, Sales Tax Payable, Unearned Subscriptions Revenue, and the portion of Mortgage Payable that is due within the next year.

Long-Term Liabilities

Long-term liabilities include those obligations that will extend beyond one year or the normal operating cycle, whichever is longer. A common long-term liability is a mortgage payable.

A **mortgage** is a written agreement specifying that if the borrower does not repay a debt, the lender has the right to take over specific property to satisfy the debt. When the debt is paid, the mortgage becomes void. **Mortgage Payable** is an account that is used to reflect an obligation that is secured by a mortgage on certain property.

Owner's Equity

The permanent owner's equity accounts reported on the balance sheet are determined by the type of organization. The accounts for a sole proprietorship, a partnership, and a corporation differ. Northern Micro is a sole proprietorship and reports one owner's equity account, Gary L. Fishel, Capital. The balance of this account is taken from the statement of owner's equity. Partnerships are illustrated in Chapter 20 and corporations are discussed in Chapters 21 and 22.

FINANCIAL STATEMENT ANALYSIS

LO 4   Compute standard financial ratios.

Both management and creditors are interested in using the financial statements to evaluate the financial condition and profitability of the firm. This can be done by making a few simple calculations.

Balance Sheet Analysis

Recall the following:

1. Current assets include cash, items that will be converted to cash, and items that will be consumed within one year.

2. Current liabilities are obligations that will require the use of current assets.

Thus, the difference between current assets and current liabilities represents the amount of capital the business has available for current operations. This is called **working capital**.

$$\text{Working Capital} = \text{Current Assets} - \text{Current Liabilities}$$

The balance sheet in Figure 15-6 shows that Northern Micro has current assets of $54,000 and current liabilities of $19,450. Thus, the working capital at year end is $34,550 ($54,000 − $19,450). This amount should be more than adequate to satisfy current operating requirements.

Two measures of the firm's ability to pay its current liabilities are the **current ratio** and **quick ratio**. The formulas for calculating these ratios are as follows:

						Northern Micro		
Current Ratio	=	$\dfrac{\text{Current Assets}}{\text{Current Liabilities}}$	=	$\dfrac{\$54,000}{\$19,450}$	=	2.8 to 1
Quick Ratio	=	$\dfrac{\text{Quick Assets}}{\text{Current Liabilities}}$	=	$\dfrac{\$35,000}{\$19,450}$	=	1.8 to 1

Northern Micro's current ratio of 2.8 to 1 is quite high, which indicates a favorable financial position. The traditional "rule of thumb" has been that a current ratio should be about 2 to 1, but many businesses operate successfully on a current ratio of 1.5 to 1. Although a rule of thumb is helpful, it is better to compare an individual company to industry averages, which are available in most public libraries.

> *Information on industry averages is available in various publications from Dun & Bradstreet, Standard & Poor's, and Moody's.*

Quick assets include cash and all other current assets that can be converted into cash quickly, such as accounts receivable and temporary investments. Temporary investments are discussed in more advanced textbooks. The balance sheet in Figure 15-6 shows total quick assets of $35,000 ($20,000 in cash + $15,000 in accounts receivable). This produces a quick ratio of 1.8 to 1. Quick assets appear to be more than adequate to meet current obligations. The traditional rule of thumb has been that a quick ratio should be about 1 to 1, but many businesses operate successfully on a quick ratio of 0.6 to 1.

Interstatement Analysis

Interstatement analysis provides a comparison of the relationships between selected income statement and balance sheet amounts. A good example of interstatement analysis is the ratio of net income to owner's equity in the business. This ratio is known as **return on owner's equity**.

$$\text{Return on Owner's Equity} = \frac{\text{Net Income}}{\text{Average Owner's Equity}} = \frac{\text{Northern Micro}}{(\$104,400 + \$117,050) \div 2}$$

$$= \frac{\$22,650}{\$110,725}$$

$$= 20.5\%$$

The statement of owner's equity in Figure 15-5 shows that the owner's equity of Northern Micro was $104,400 on January 1 and $117,050 on December 31. The net income for the year of $22,650 is 20.5% of the average owner's equity. A comparison of this ratio with the return on owner's equity in prior years should be of interest to the owner. It may also be of interest to compare the return on owner's equity of Northern Micro with the same ratio for other businesses of comparable nature and size.

A second ratio involving both income statement and balance sheet accounts is a measure of the time required to collect cash from credit customers. This financial measure is often computed in two ways. The **accounts receivable turnover** is the number of times the accounts receivable "turned over," or were collected, during the accounting period. Of course, a higher number indicates that cash is collected more quickly. This ratio is calculated as follows:

> *Net credit sales is generally not reported in the financial statements. Use net sales, instead. As long as the proportion of cash and credit sales is reasonably stable over time, this ratio will provide a reasonable measure of the business's ability to collect receivables in a timely manner from year to year.*

$$\text{Accounts Receivable Turnover} = \frac{\text{Net Credit Sales for the Period}}{\text{Average Accounts Receivable}}$$

The accounts receivable turnover for Northern Micro for the year ended December 31 is computed as follows.

Net *credit* sales for the year (determined from the accounting records)	$110,000
Accounts receivable balance, January 1, 20-- (taken from last year's balance sheet)	10,000
Accounts receivable balance, December 31, 20--	15,000

Average Accounts Receivable	$=$	$\dfrac{\text{Beginning Balance + Ending Balance}}{2}$	$=$	Northern Micro $\dfrac{\$10,000 + \$15,000}{2}$
			$=$	$\$12,500$
Accounts Receivable Turnover	$=$	$\dfrac{\text{Net Credit Sales for the Period}}{\text{Average Accounts Receivable}}$	$=$	$\dfrac{\$110,000}{\$12,500}$
			$=$	8.8

The **average collection period** is calculated by dividing the number of days in the year (365) by the rate of turnover to determine the number of days credit customers take to pay for their purchases. Northern Micro's customers are taking about 42 days.

$$365 \text{ days} \div 8.8 = 41.5 \text{ days}$$

Comparing the average collection period with a business's credit terms offers an indication of whether customers are paying within the terms. If Northern Micro allows credit terms of n/45, an average collection period of 41.5 days would suggest that customers are paying on a timely basis.

A BROADER VIEW

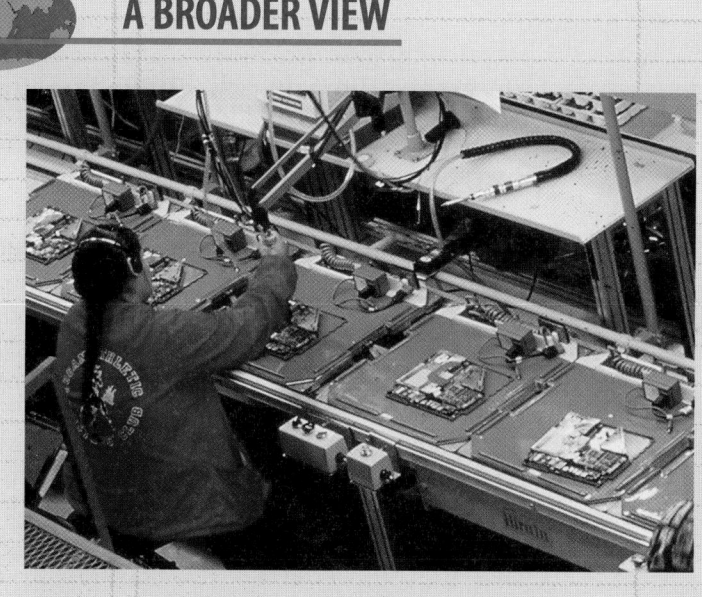

WHO CARES ABOUT TRACKING FINANCIAL RATIOS?

Tracking a business's average collection period for receivables can help investors avoid making poor investments. Take the case of Kendall Square, a super-computer maker. In an effort to increase sales and profits, Kendall Square recognized large amounts of revenues that had not actually been earned. Since no cash was received for these sales, accounts receivable increased dramatically (by 57%). Similarly, the average collection period increased to 157 days. Large increases in the average collection period should warn potential investors that something might be wrong. What happened at Kendall Square? Over $10 million of sales on account was never collected. This was equal to almost half of the revenues reported for the year. When eventually discovered, Kendall Square's stock price fell from $24.25 to $2.28 a share.

A third ratio involving both income statement and balance sheet accounts is the rate of **inventory turnover**. This is the number of times the merchandise inventory turned over, or was sold, during the accounting period. This ratio is calculated as follows:

$$\text{Inventory Turnover} = \frac{\text{Cost of Goods Sold for the Period}}{\text{Average Inventory}}$$

If inventory is taken only at the end of each accounting period, the average inventory for the period can be calculated by adding the beginning and ending inventories and dividing their sum by two. Northern Micro's turnover for the year ended December 31 is computed as follows:

Cost of goods sold for the period	$111,500
Beginning inventory	26,000
Ending inventory	18,000

Northern Micro

$$\text{Average Inventory} = \frac{\text{Beginning Inventory} + \text{Ending Inventory}}{2} = \frac{\$26,000 + \$18,000}{2}$$
$$= \$22,000$$

$$\text{Inventory Turnover} = \frac{\text{Cost of Goods Sold for the Period}}{\text{Average Inventory}} = \frac{\$111,500}{\$22,000}$$
$$= 5.1$$

The **average days to sell inventory** can be computed by dividing the number of days in the year (365) by the inventory turnover. For Northern Micro it takes about two months.

$$365 \text{ days} \div 5.1 = 71.6 \text{ days}$$

The higher the rate of inventory turnover, the smaller the profit required on each dollar of sales to produce a satisfactory gross profit. This is because the increase in the number of units sold offsets the smaller amount of gross profit earned per unit. For example, grocery stores have a very small gross profit on each item sold, but make up for this with a rapid inventory turnover. Other types of businesses, jewelers for example, need a high gross profit on each item because their inventory turnover is quite slow. Evaluations of Northern Micro's rate of inventory turnover would require comparison with prior years, other companies, or its industry.

CLOSING ENTRIES

LO 5 Prepare closing entries for a merchandising business.

Closing entries for a service business were illustrated in Chapter 6. The process is essentially the same for a merchandising business. All revenues and expenses reported on the income statement must be closed to Income Summary. Then, the income summary and drawing accounts are closed to the owner's capital account. Keep in mind, however, that a few new accounts were needed for a merchandising business. These include Sales Returns and Allowances, Sales Discounts, Purchases Returns and Allowances, and Purchases Discounts. Since these are temporary accounts reported on the income statement, they also must be closed. The easiest way to complete the closing process is by using the work sheet to prepare the closing entries in four basic steps, as illustrated in Figures 15-7 and 15-8.

FIGURE 15-7 Closing Entries for a Merchandising Business

Northern Micro
Work Sheet (Partial)
For Year Ended December 31, 20- -

	ACCOUNT TITLE	INCOME STATEMENT DEBIT	INCOME STATEMENT CREDIT	BALANCE SHEET DEBIT	BALANCE SHEET CREDIT
17	Gary L. Fishel, Capital				114 4 0 0 00
18	Gary L. Fishel, Drawing			20 0 0 0 00	
19	Income Summary	26 0 0 0 00	18 0 0 0 00		
20	Sales		214 0 0 0 00		
21	Sales Returns and Allowances	12 0 0 0 00			
22	Interest Revenue		9 0 0 0 00		
23	Rent Revenue		8 0 0 0 00		
24	Subscriptions Revenue		10 0 0 0 00		
25	Purchases	105 0 0 0 00			
26	Purchases Returns and Allow.		8 0 0 0 00		
27	Purchases Discounts		1 0 0 0 00		
28	Freight-In	3 0 0 0 00			
29	Wages Expense	42 4 5 0 00			
30	Advertising Expense	2 5 0 0 00			
31	Bank Credit Card Expense	1 5 0 0 00			
32	Rent Expense	20 0 0 0 00			
33	Supplies Expense	1 4 0 0 00			
34	Telephone Expense	3 5 0 0 00			
35	Utilities Expense	12 0 0 0 00			
36	Insurance Expense	1 8 0 0 00			
37	Depr. Expense—Building	4 0 0 0 00			
38	Depr. Expense—Store Equip.	3 0 0 0 00			
39	Miscellaneous Expense	2 2 5 0 00			
40	Interest Expense	3 1 5 0 00			
41		230 0 5 0 00	252 7 0 0 00	224 0 0 0 00	201 3 5 0 00
42	Net Income	22 6 5 0 00			22 6 5 0 00
43		252 7 0 0 00	252 7 0 0 00	224 0 0 0 00	224 0 0 0 00
44					

GENERAL JOURNAL   PAGE 6

	DATE	DESCRIPTION	POST REF.	DEBIT	CREDIT	
1	20--	**Closing Entries**				1
2	Dec. 31	Sales		214 0 0 0 00		2
3		Subscriptions Revenue		10 0 0 0 00		3
4		Interest Revenue		9 0 0 0 00		4
5		Rent Revenue		8 0 0 0 00		5
6		Purchases Returns and Allowances		8 0 0 0 00		6
7		Purchases Discounts		1 0 0 0 00		7
8		Income Summary			234 7 0 0 00	8
9						9
10	31	Income Summary		204 0 5 0 00		10
11		Sales Returns and Allowances			12 0 0 0 00	11
12		Purchases			105 0 0 0 00	12
13		Freight-In			3 0 0 0 00	13
14		Wages Expense			42 4 5 0 00	14
15		Advertising Expense			2 5 0 0 00	15
16		Bank Credit Card Expense			1 5 0 0 00	16
17		Rent Expense			20 0 0 0 00	17
18		Supplies Expense			1 4 0 0 00	18
19		Telephone Expense			3 5 0 0 00	19
20		Utilities Expense			12 0 0 0 00	20
21		Insurance Expense			1 8 0 0 00	21
22		Depreciation Exp.—Building			4 0 0 0 00	22
23		Depreciation Exp.—Store Equip.			3 0 0 0 00	23
24		Miscellaneous Expense			2 2 5 0 00	24
25		Interest Expense			3 1 5 0 00	25
26						26
27	31	Income Summary		22 6 5 0 00		27
28		Gary L. Fishel, Capital			22 6 5 0 00	28
29						29
30	31	Gary L. Fishel, Capital		20 0 0 0 00		30
31		Gary L. Fishel, Drawing			20 0 0 0 00	31
32						32

FIGURE 15-8 The Closing Process

THE CLOSING PROCESS FOR A MERCHANDISING BUSINESS

STEP 1   All income statement accounts with credit balances are debited, with an offsetting credit to Income Summary.

STEP 2   All income statement accounts with debit balances are credited, with an offsetting debit to Income Summary.

STEP 3   The resulting balance in Income Summary, which is the net income or loss for the period, is transferred to the owner's capital account.

ACCOUNT: Income Summary   ACCOUNT NO. 331

DATE	ITEM	POST REF.	DEBIT	CREDIT	BALANCE DEBIT	BALANCE CREDIT	Adjustments to:
Dec. 31	Adjusting	J5	26 0 0 0 00		26 0 0 0 00		Remove Beg. Inventory
31	Adjusting	J5		18 0 0 0 00	8 0 0 0 00		Enter End. Inventory
31	Closing	J6		234 7 0 0 00		226 7 0 0 00	Closing Step 1
31	Closing	J6	204 0 5 0 00			22 6 5 0 00	Closing Step 2
31	Closing	J6	22 6 5 0 00				Closing Step 3

STEP 4   The balance in the owner's drawing account is transferred to the owner's capital account.

Post-Closing Trial Balance

A trial balance of the general ledger accounts taken after the temporary owner's equity accounts have been closed is called a **post-closing trial balance**. The purpose of the post-closing trial balance is to prove that the general ledger is in balance at the beginning of a new accounting period, before any transactions for the new accounting period are entered. Figure 15-9 shows a post-closing trial balance for Northern Micro.

REVERSING ENTRIES

LO 6   Prepare reversing entries.

Numerous adjusting entries are needed at the end of the accounting period to bring the account balances up to date for presentation in the financial statements. Although not required, some of these adjusting entries should be reversed at the beginning of the next accounting period. This is done to simplify the recording of transactions in the new accounting period. As its name implies, a **reversing entry** is the reverse or opposite of the adjusting entry.

ADJUSTING ENTRY

| 4 | Dec. | 31 | Wages Expense | | 4 5 0 00 | | 4 |
| 5 | | | Wages Payable | | | 4 5 0 00 | 5 |

REVERSING ENTRY (OPPOSITE)

| 7 | Jan. | 1 | Wages Payable | | 4 5 0 00 | | 7 |
| 8 | | | Wages Expense | | | 4 5 0 00 | 8 |

FIGURE 15-9 Post-Closing Trial Balance

The post-closing
trial balance must be
prepared by taking
the balances from
the general ledger
accounts. It should
not be prepared from
the balances on the
work sheet. Using
the general ledger
accounts makes sure
that all adjusting
and closing entries
were entered and
posted correctly.

Northern Micro
Post-Closing Trial Balance
December 31, 20 - -

ACCOUNT TITLE	ACCOUNT NO.	DEBIT BALANCE	CREDIT BALANCE
Cash	101	20 0 0 0 00	
Accounts Receivable	122	15 0 0 0 00	
Merchandise Inventory	131	18 0 0 0 00	
Supplies	141	4 0 0 00	
Prepaid Insurance	145	6 0 0 00	
Land	161	10 0 0 0 00	
Building	171	90 0 0 0 00	
Accumulated Depreciation—Building	171.1		20 0 0 0 00
Store Equipment	181	50 0 0 0 00	
Accumulated Depreciation—Store Equipment	181.1		18 0 0 0 00
Notes Payable	201		5 0 0 0 00
Accounts Payable	202		10 0 0 0 00
Wages Payable	219		4 5 0 00
Sales Tax Payable	231		1 5 0 0 00
Unearned Subscriptions Revenue	241		2 0 0 0 00
Mortgage Payable	251		30 0 0 0 00
Gary L. Fishel, Capital	311		117 0 5 0 00
		204 0 0 0 00	204 0 0 0 00

To see the advantage of using reversing entries, let's consider the effect of reversing Northern Micro's adjusting entry for wages earned, but not paid, at the end of the year. Figure 15-10 shows that accrued wages on December 31 were $450. These wages are for work performed by the employees on the last three days of the accounting period (150 × 3 = $450). The employees will be paid on Friday, January 2, the normal payday.

Note that the adjusting and closing entries are the same, regardless of whether a reversing entry is made. However, the reversing entry on January 1 has an impact on the entry made when the employees are paid. *Without* a reversing entry, the payment on January 2, 20-2, must be split between reduction of the Wages Payable account for wages earned in 20-1 and Wages Expense for wages earned in 20-2. *With* a reversing entry, the bookkeeper simply debits Wages Expense and credits Cash, as is done on every other payday. Thus, the likelihood of error is reduced. Reversing entries are particularly important in large businesses where the individual recording the entry for wages may not even know what adjusting entries were made.

Not all adjusting entries should be reversed. To determine which adjusting entries to reverse, follow this rule: *Except for the first year of operations, reverse all adjusting entries that increase an asset or liability account from a zero balance.*

LEARNING KEY: Reverse all adjusting entries that increase an asset or liability account from a zero balance.

FIGURE 15-10 Adjusting, Closing, and Reversing Entries for Wages

| | 20-1 | | | 20-2 | |
	12/29/-1 Monday	12/30/-1 Tuesday	12/31/-1 Wednesday	1/1/-2 Thursday	1/2/-2 Friday
Wages Earned	150	150	150	150	150
Wages Paid	0	0	0	0	750
Total Earned			450		300
Total Paid			0		750
Accrued Wages on 12/31/-1			450		

Date	Without Reversing Entry		With Reversing Entry	

12/31/-1 Adj. Entry	Wages Expense 450
	    Wages Payable 450
			Wages Expense 450
			    Wages Payable 450	

12/31/-1 Closing Entry	Income Summary 42,450
	    Wages Expense 42,450
			Income Summary 42,450
			    Wages Expense 42,450	

1/1/-2 Rev. Entry	No Entry		Wages Payable 450 Wages Expense 450	

1/2/-2 Payment of Payroll	Wages Expense 300
	Wages Payable 450
	    Cash 750
			Wages Expense 750
			    Cash 750	

Description	Wages Expense		Description
Bal.	42,000		
12/31/-1 Adj.	450		
		42,450	12/31/-1 Close
1/2/-2 Payroll	300		

Description	Wages Expense		Description
Bal.	42,000		
12/31/-1 Adj.	450		
		42,450	12/31/-1 Close
		450	1/1/-2 Reversing
1/2/-2 Payroll	750		
Bal.	300		

	Wages Payable		
		450	12/31/-1 Adj.
1/2/-2 Payroll	450		

	Wages Payable		
		450	12/31/-1 Adj.
1/1/-2 Reverse	450		

	Cash		
		750	1/2/-2 Payroll

	Cash		
		750	1/2/-2 Payroll

Except for the first year of operation, merchandise inventory, and contra-assets like accumulated depreciation, will have existing balances. Thus, they should never be reversed. The adjusting entries for Northern Micro are shown in Figure 15-11. Note that only the adjustment for accrued wages is reversed in Figure 15-12.

FIGURE 15-11 Which Adjusting Entries to Reverse?

	DATE		DESCRIPTION	POST REF.	DEBIT	CREDIT		SHOULD THE ADJUSTMENT BE REVERSED?
			GENERAL JOURNAL			PAGE 5		
1			Adjusting Entries				1	
2	20-- Dec.	31	Income Summary		26 0 0 0 00		2	Never reverse adjustments for merchandise inventory.
3			Merchandise Inventory			26 0 0 0 00	3	
4							4	
5		31	Merchandise Inventory		18 0 0 0 00		5	Never reverse adjustments for merchandise inventory.
6			Income Summary			18 0 0 0 00	6	
7							7	
8		31	Supplies Expense		1 4 0 0 00		8	No. No asset or liability with a zero balance has been increased.
9			Supplies			1 4 0 0 00	9	
10							10	
11		31	Insurance Expense		1 8 0 0 00		11	No. No asset or liability with a zero balance has been increased.
12			Prepaid Insurance			1 8 0 0 00	12	
13							13	
14		31	Depr. Expense—Building		4 0 0 0 00		14	Never reverse adjustments for depreciation.
15			Accum. Depr.—Building			4 0 0 0 00	15	
16							16	
17		31	Depr. Expense—Store Equipment		3 0 0 0 00		17	Never reverse adjustments for depreciation.
18			Accum. Depr.—Store Equipment			3 0 0 0 00	18	
19							19	
20		31	Wages Expense		4 5 0 00		20	Yes. A liability account with a zero balance has been increased.
21			Wages Payable			4 5 0 00	21	
22							22	
23		31	Unearned Subscriptions Revenue		10 0 0 0 00		23	No. No asset or liability with a zero balance has been increased.
24			Subscriptions Revenue			10 0 0 0 00	24	
25							25	

FIGURE 15-12 Reversing Entry for Northern Micro

	DATE		DESCRIPTION	POST REF.	DEBIT	CREDIT	
			GENERAL JOURNAL			PAGE 7	
1			Reversing Entries				1
2	20-- Jan.	1	Wages Payable		4 5 0 00		2
3			Wages Expense			4 5 0 00	3
4							4
5							5

Learning Objectives	Key Points to Remember
1 Prepare a single-step and multiple-step income statement for a merchandising business.	The general format for a single-step and multiple-step income statement is shown below.

Single-Step
Income Statement
For Year Ended December 31, 20--

Revenues:		
List all revenues	$xxx	
Total revenues		$xxx
Expenses:		
Cost of goods sold	$xxx	
List all other expenses	xxx	
Total expenses		xxx
Net income		$xxx

Multiple-Step
Income Statement
For Year Ended December 31, 20--

Revenue from sales:			
Sales		$xxx	
Less sales returns and allowances		xxx	
Net sales			$xxx
Cost of goods sold			xxx
Gross profit			$xxx
Operating expenses:			
List all operating expenses		$xxx	
Total operating expenses			xxx
Income from operations			$xxx
Other revenue:			
List all other revenue		$xxx	
Total other revenue		$xxx	
Other expenses:			
List all other expenses	$xxx		
Total other expenses		xxx	xxx
Net income			$xxx

Learning Objectives	Key Points to Remember
2 Prepare a statement of owner's equity.	A statement of owner's equity has the following format:

Business Name
Statement of Owner's Equity
For Year Ended December 31, 20--

Capital, January 1, 20--		$xxx
Add additional investments		xxx
Total investment		$xxx
Net income for the year	$xxx	
Less withdrawals	xxx	
Increase in capital		xxx
Capital, December 31, 20--		$xxx

Learning Objectives	Key Points to Remember

| 3 **Prepare a classified balance sheet.** | A classified balance sheet has the following major headings: |

Business Name
Balance Sheet
December 31, 20--

Assets

Current assets:			
All are listed		$xxx	
Total current assets			$xxx
Property, plant, and equipment:			
All are listed	$xxx		
Less accumulated depreciation (if appropriate)	xxx	$xxx	
Total property, plant, and equipment			xxx
Total assets			$xxx

Liabilities

Current liabilities:		
All are listed	$xxx	
Total current liabilities		$xxx
Long-term liabilities:		
All are listed	$xxx	
Total long-term liabilities		xxx
Total liabilities		$xxx

Owner's Equity

Owner's capital	xxx
Total liabilities and owner's equity	$xxx

| 4 **Compute standard financial ratios.** | The following measures of financial condition may be computed from financial statement information. |

Working Capital	=	Current Assets − Current Liabilities
Current Ratio	=	Current Assets ÷ Current Liabilities
Quick Ratio	=	Quick Assets ÷ Current Liabilities
Return on Owner's Equity	=	Net Income ÷ Average Owner's Equity
Accounts Receivable Turnover	=	$\dfrac{\text{Net Credit Sales for the Period}}{\text{Average Accounts Receivable}}$
Average Collection Period	=	$\dfrac{365}{\text{Accounts Receivable Turnover}}$
Inventory Turnover	=	$\dfrac{\text{Cost of Goods Sold for the Period}}{\text{Average Inventory}}$
Average Days to Sell Inventory	=	$\dfrac{365}{\text{Inventory Turnover}}$

Learning Objectives	Key Points to Remember
5 **Prepare closing entries for a merchandising business.**	There are four steps in the closing process for a merchandising business: STEP 1 All income statement accounts with credit balances are debited, with an offsetting credit to Income Summary. STEP 2 All income statement accounts with debit balances are credited, with an offsetting debit to Income Summary. STEP 3 The resulting balance in Income Summary, which is the net income or loss for the period, is transferred to the owner's capital account. STEP 4 The balance in the owner's drawing account is transferred to the owner's capital account.
6 **Prepare reversing entries.**	Use the following rule to determine which adjusting entries to reverse: Except for the first year of operations, reverse all adjusting entries that increase an asset or liability account from a zero balance.

Reflection: Answering the Opening Question

As discussed in this chapter, Betty has made reversing entries for the payroll. Thus, it is not necessary for Betty to be concerned about the proper allocation of the payroll between last year's and this year's financial statements.

KEY TERMS

accounts receivable turnover, (548)   The number of times the accounts receivable turned over, or were collected, during the accounting period. When 365 is divided by the turnover, this measure can be expressed in terms of the average number of days required to collect receivables.

average collection period, (549)   The number of days in the year (365) divided by the accounts receivable turnover. Provides an indication of the number of days credit customers take to pay for their purchases.

average days to sell inventory, (550)   The number of days in the year (365) divided by the inventory turnover. Provides an indication of the average number of days required to sell inventory.

book value, (546)   See undepreciated cost.

current assets, (546)   Cash and all other assets expected to be converted into cash or consumed within one year or the normal operating cycle of the business, whichever is longer.

current liabilities, (546)   Those obligations that are due within one year or the normal operating cycle of the business, whichever is longer, and will require the use of current assets.

current ratio, (547)   Current assets divided by current liabilities.

general expenses, (542)   Those expenses associated with administrative, office, or general operating activities.

gross margin, (540)   See gross profit.

gross profit, (540)   Net sales minus cost of goods sold.

income from operations, (540)   Gross profit minus operating expenses on a multiple-step income statement.

interstatement analysis, (548)   Compares the relationship between certain amounts in the income statement and balance sheet.

inventory turnover, (550)   The number of times the merchandise inventory turned over, or was sold, during the accounting period. When 365 is divided by the turnover, this measure can be expressed in terms of the average number of days required to sell inventory.

liquidity, (546)   Refers to the speed with which an asset can be converted to cash.

long-term liabilities, (546)   Those obligations that will extend beyond one year or the normal operating cycle, whichever is longer.

mortgage, (546)   A written agreement specifying that if the borrower does not repay a debt, the lender has the right to take over specific property to satisfy the debt.

Mortgage Payable, (546)   An account that is used to reflect an obligation that is secured by a mortgage on certain property.

multiple-step income statement, (540)   This statement shows a step-by-step calculation of net sales, cost of goods sold, gross profit, operating expenses, income from operations, other revenues and expenses, and net income.

net sales, (540)   Gross sales less sales returns and allowances and less sales discounts.

operating cycle, (546)   The length of time generally required for a business to buy inventory, sell it, and collect the cash.

operating income, (540)   See income from operations.

post-closing trial balance, (552)   A trial balance taken after the temporary owner's equity accounts have been closed.

property, plant, and equipment, (546)   Assets that are expected to be used for more than one year in the operation of a business.

quick assets, (548)   Cash and all other current assets that can be converted into cash quickly, such as accounts receivable and temporary investments.

quick ratio, (547)   Quick assets divided by current liabilities.

return on owner's equity, (548)   Net income divided by average owner's equity.

reversing entry, (552)   The opposite of the adjusting entry. It is made on the first day of the next accounting period and simplifies recording transactions in the new period.

selling expenses, (540)   Those expenses directly associated with selling activities.

single-step income statement, (540)   This statement lists all revenue items and their total first, followed by all expense items and their total.

undepreciated cost, (546)   Cost of plant and equipment less the accumulated depreciation amounts. Also called book value.

working capital, (547)   The difference between current assets and current liabilities, which represents the amount of capital the business has available for current operations.

DEMONSTRATION PROBLEM

W & D

Tom McKinney owns and operates McK's Home Electronics. He has a store where he sells and repairs televisions and stereo equipment. A completed work sheet for 20-1 is provided on the next page. McKinney made a $20,000 additional investment during 20-1. The current portion of Mortgage Payable is $1,000. Credit sales for 20-1 were $200,000, and the balance of Accounts Receivable on January 1 was $26,000.

REQUIRED
1. Prepare a multiple-step income statement.

2. Prepare a statement of owner's equity.

3. Prepare a balance sheet.

4. Compute the following measures of performance and financial condition for 20-1:

   a. current ratio

   b. quick ratio

   c. working capital

   d. return on owner's equity

   e. accounts receivable turnover and the average number of days required to collect receivables

   f. inventory turnover and the average number of days required to sell inventory

5. Prepare adjusting entries and indicate which should be reversed and why.

6. Prepare closing entries.

7. Prepare reversing entries for the adjustments where appropriate.

McK's Home Electronics
Work Sheet
For Year Ended December 31, 20-1

#	Account Title	TB Debit	TB Credit	Adj. Debit	Adj. Credit	ATB Debit	ATB Credit	IS Debit	IS Credit	BS Debit	BS Credit
1	Cash	10 0 0 0 00				10 0 0 0 00				10 0 0 0 00	
2	Accounts Receivable	22 5 0 0 00				22 5 0 0 00				22 5 0 0 00	
3	Merchandise Inventory	39 0 0 0 00		(b) 45 0 0 0 00	(a) 39 0 0 0 00	45 0 0 0 00				45 0 0 0 00	
4	Supplies	2 7 0 0 00			(c) 2 1 0 0 00	6 0 0 00				6 0 0 00	
5	Prepaid Insurance	3 6 0 0 00			(d) 2 7 0 0 00	9 0 0 00				9 0 0 00	
6	Land	15 0 0 0 00				15 0 0 0 00				15 0 0 0 00	
7	Building	135 0 0 0 00				135 0 0 0 00				135 0 0 0 00	
8	Accum. Depr.—Building		24 0 0 0 00		(e) 6 0 0 0 00		30 0 0 0 00				30 0 0 0 00
9	Store Equipment	75 0 0 0 00				75 0 0 0 00				75 0 0 0 00	
10	Accum. Depr.—Store Equipment		22 5 0 0 00		(f) 4 5 0 0 00		27 0 0 0 00				27 0 0 0 00
11	Notes Payable		7 5 0 0 00				7 5 0 0 00				7 5 0 0 00
12	Accounts Payable		15 0 0 0 00				15 0 0 0 00				15 0 0 0 00
13	Wages Payable				(g) 6 7 5 00		6 7 5 00				6 7 5 00
14	Sales Tax Payable		2 2 5 0 00				2 2 5 0 00				2 2 5 0 00
15	Unearned Repair Fees		18 0 0 0 00	(h) 15 0 0 0 00			3 0 0 0 00				3 0 0 0 00
16	Mortgage Payable		45 0 0 0 00				45 0 0 0 00				45 0 0 0 00
17	Tom McKinney, Capital		151 6 0 0 00				151 6 0 0 00				151 6 0 0 00
18	Tom McKinney, Drawing	30 0 0 0 00				30 0 0 0 00				30 0 0 0 00	
19	Income Summary			(a) 39 0 0 0 00	(b) 45 0 0 0 00	39 0 0 0 00	45 0 0 0 00	39 0 0 0 00	45 0 0 0 00		
20	Sales		300 7 5 0 00				300 7 5 0 00		300 7 5 0 00		
21	Sales Returns and Allowances	1 8 0 0 00				1 8 0 0 00		1 8 0 0 00			
22	Repair Fees				(h) 15 0 0 0 00		15 0 0 0 00		15 0 0 0 00		
23	Interest Revenue		1 3 5 0 00				1 3 5 0 00		1 3 5 0 00		
24	Purchases	157 5 0 0 00				157 5 0 0 00		157 5 0 0 00			
25	Purchases Returns and Allowances		1 2 0 0 00				1 2 0 0 00		1 2 0 0 00		
26	Purchases Discounts		1 5 0 0 00				1 5 0 0 00		1 5 0 0 00		
27	Freight-In	4 5 0 00				4 5 0 00		4 5 0 00			
28	Wages Expense	63 0 0 0 00		(g) 6 7 5 00		63 6 7 5 00		63 6 7 5 00			
29	Advertising Expense	3 7 5 0 00				3 7 5 0 00		3 7 5 0 00			
30	Supplies Expense			(c) 2 1 0 0 00		2 1 0 0 00		2 1 0 0 00			
31	Telephone Expense	5 2 5 0 00				5 2 5 0 00		5 2 5 0 00			
32	Utilities Expense	18 0 0 0 00				18 0 0 0 00		18 0 0 0 00			
33	Insurance Expense			(d) 2 7 0 0 00		2 7 0 0 00		2 7 0 0 00			
34	Depr. Expense—Building			(e) 6 0 0 0 00		6 0 0 0 00		6 0 0 0 00			
35	Depr. Expense—Store Equipment			(f) 4 5 0 0 00		4 5 0 0 00		4 5 0 0 00			
36	Miscellaneous Expense	3 3 7 5 00				3 3 7 5 00		3 3 7 5 00			
37	Interest Expense	4 7 2 5 00				4 7 2 5 00		4 7 2 5 00			
38		590 6 5 0 00	590 6 5 0 00	114 9 7 5 00	114 9 7 5 00	646 8 2 5 00	646 8 2 5 00	312 8 2 5 00	364 8 0 0 00	334 0 0 0 00	282 0 2 5 00
39	Net Income							51 9 7 5 00			51 9 7 5 00
40								364 8 0 0 00	364 8 0 0 00	334 0 0 0 00	334 0 0 0 00

Solution

1.

	McK's Home Electronics Income Statement For Year Ended December 31, 20 -1																				
Revenue from sales:																				
Sales									$300	7	5	0	00					
Less sales returns and allowances									1	8	0	0	00					
Net sales														$298	9	5	0	00
Cost of goods sold:																		
Merchandise inventory, January 1, 20-1									$ 39	0	0	0	00					
Purchases					$157	5	0	0	00									
Less: Purchases returns and allowances	$1	2	0	0	00													
Purchases discounts	1	5	0	0	00	2	7	0	0	00								
Net purchases					$154	8	0	0	00									
Add freight-in						4	5	0	00									
Cost of goods purchased									155	2	5	0	00					
Goods available for sale									$194	2	5	0	00					
Less merchandise inventory, December 31, 20- 1									45	0	0	0	00					
Cost of goods sold														149	2	5	0	00
Gross profit														$149	7	0	0	00
Operating expenses:																		
Wages expense									$ 63	6	7	5	00					
Advertising expense									3	7	5	0	00					
Supplies expense									2	1	0	0	00					
Telephone expense									5	2	5	0	00					
Utilities expense									18	0	0	0	00					
Insurance expense									2	7	0	0	00					
Depreciation expense—building									6	0	0	0	00					
Depreciation expense—store equipment									4	5	0	0	00					
Miscellaneous expense									3	3	7	5	00					
Total operating expenses														109	3	5	0	00
Income from operations														$ 40	3	5	0	00
Other revenues:																		
Repair fees									$ 15	0	0	0	00					
Interest revenue									1	3	5	0	00					
Total other revenues									$ 16	3	5	0	00					
Other expenses:																		
Interest expense									4	7	2	5	00	11	6	2	5	00
Net income														$ 51	9	7	5	00

2.

	McK's Home Electronics Statement of Owner's Equity For Year Ended December 31, 20 -1												
Tom McKinney, capital, January 1, 20-1							$131	6	0	0	00
Add additional investments							20	0	0	0	00
Total investment							$151	6	0	0	00
Net income for the year	$51	9	7	5	00						
Less withdrawals	30	0	0	0	00						
Increase in capital							21	9	7	5	00
Tom McKinney, capital, December 31, 20-1							$173	5	7	5	00

3.

McK's Home Electronics Balance Sheet December 31, 20 -1					
Assets					
Current assets:					
Cash			$ 10 0 0 0 00		
Accounts receivable			22 5 0 0 00		
Merchandise inventory			45 0 0 0 00		
Supplies			6 0 0 00		
Prepaid insurance			9 0 0 00		
Total current assets				$ 79 0 0 0 00	
Property, plant and equipment:					
Land			$ 15 0 0 0 00		
Building	$135 0 0 0 00				
Less accumulated depreciation	30 0 0 0 00	105 0 0 0 00			
Store equipment	$ 75 0 0 0 00				
Less accumulated depreciation	27 0 0 0 00	48 0 0 0 00			
Total property, plant and equipment				168 0 0 0 00	
Total assets				$247 0 0 0 00	
Liabilities					
Current liabilities:					
Notes payable	$ 7 5 0 0 00				
Accounts payable	15 0 0 0 00				
Wages payable	6 7 5 00				
Sales tax payable	2 2 5 0 00				
Unearned repair fees	3 0 0 0 00				
Mortgage payable (current portion)	1 0 0 0 00				
Total current liabilities		$ 29 4 2 5 00			
Long-term liabilities:					
Mortgage payable	$45 0 0 0 00				
Less current portion	1 0 0 0 00	44 0 0 0 00			
Total liabilities				$ 73 4 2 5 00	
Owner's Equity					
Tom McKinney, capital				173 5 7 5 00	
Total liabilities and owner's equity				$247 0 0 0 00	

4. a. Current Ratio   = Current Assets ÷ Current Liabilities
        = $79,000 ÷ $29,425 = 2.68 to 1

    b. Quick Ratio   = Quick Assets ÷ Current Liabilities
        = $32,500 ÷ $29,425 = 1.10 to 1

    c. Working Capital   = Current Assets − Current Liabilities
        = $79,000 − $29,425 = $49,575

    d. Return on Owner's Equity   = Net Income ÷ Average Owner's Equity

        $$= \frac{\$51,975}{(\$131,600 + \$173,575) \div 2}$$

        = $51,975 ÷ $152,587.50

        = 34%

e.
$$\text{Accounts Receivable Turnover} = \frac{\text{Net Credit Sales for the Period}}{\text{Average Accounts Receivable}}$$

$$= \frac{\$200,000}{(\$26,000 + \$22,500) \div 2}$$

$$= \$200,000 \div \$24,250$$

$$= 8.25$$

Average number of days to collect an account receivable:
365 ÷ 8.25 = 44.24 days

f.
$$\text{Inventory Turnover} = \frac{\text{Cost of Goods Sold for the Period}}{\text{Average Inventory}}$$

$$= \frac{\$149,250}{(\$39,000 + \$45,000) \div 2}$$

$$= \$149,250 \div \$42,000$$

$$= 3.6$$

Average number of days to sell inventory:
365 ÷ 3.6 = 101.39 days

5.

	DATE	DESCRIPTION	POST REF.	DEBIT	CREDIT	
1		Adjusting Entries				1
2	20-1 Dec. 31	Income Summary		39 0 0 0 00		2
3		Merchandise Inventory			39 0 0 0 00	3
4						4
5	31	Merchandise Inventory		45 0 0 0 00		5
6		Income Summary			45 0 0 0 00	6
7						7
8	31	Supplies Expense		2 1 0 0 00		8
9		Supplies			2 1 0 0 00	9
10						10
11	31	Insurance Expense		2 7 0 0 00		11
12		Prepaid Insurance			2 7 0 0 00	12
13						13
14	31	Depr. Expense—Building		6 0 0 0 00		14
15		Accum. Depr.—Building			6 0 0 0 00	15
16						16
17	31	Depr. Expense—Store Equipment		4 5 0 0 00		17
18		Accum. Depr.—Store Equipment			4 5 0 0 00	18
19						19
20	31	Wages Expense		6 7 5 00		20
21		Wages Payable			6 7 5 00	21
22						22
23	31	Unearned Repair Fees		15 0 0 0 00		23
24		Repair Fees			15 0 0 0 00	24
25						25

GENERAL JOURNAL   PAGE 3

SHOULD THE ADJUSTMENT BE REVERSED?

Never reverse adjustments for merchandise inventory.

Never reverse adjustments for merchandise inventory.

No. No asset or liability with a zero balance has been increased.

No. No asset or liability with a zero balance has been increased.

Never reverse adjustments for depreciation.

Never reverse adjustments for depreciation.

Yes. A liability account with a zero balance has been increased.

No. No asset or liability with a zero balance has been increased.

6.

	DATE		DESCRIPTION	POST REF.	DEBIT					CREDIT					
			GENERAL JOURNAL									PAGE 4			
			Closing Entries												1
1	20-1														
2	Dec.	31	Repair Fees		15	0	0	0	00						2
3			Sales		300	7	5	0	00						3
4			Interest Revenue		1	3	5	0	00						4
5			Purchases Returns and Allowances		1	2	0	0	00						5
6			Purchases Discounts		1	5	0	0	00						6
7			Income Summary							319	8	0	0	00	7
8															8
9		31	Income Summary		273	8	2	5	00						9
10			Sales Returns and Allowances							1	8	0	0	00	10
11			Purchases							157	5	0	0	00	11
12			Freight-In								4	5	0	00	12
13			Wages Expense							63	6	7	5	00	13
14			Advertising Expense							3	7	5	0	00	14
15			Supplies Expense							2	1	0	0	00	15
16			Telephone Expense							5	2	5	0	00	16
17			Utilities Expense							18	0	0	0	00	17
18			Insurance Expense							2	7	0	0	00	18
19			Depr. Expense—Building							6	0	0	0	00	19
20			Depr. Expense—Store Equipment							4	5	0	0	00	20
21			Miscellaneous Expense							3	3	7	5	00	21
22			Interest Expense							4	7	2	5	00	22
23															23
24		31	Income Summary		51	9	7	5	00						24
25			Tom McKinney, Capital							51	9	7	5	00	25
26															26
27		31	Tom McKinney, Capital		30	0	0	0	00						27
28			Tom McKinney, Drawing							30	0	0	0	00	28
29															29

7.

	DATE		DESCRIPTION	POST REF.	DEBIT				CREDIT				
			GENERAL JOURNAL									PAGE 5	
1			Reversing Entries										1
2	20-2												
	Jan.	1	Wages Payable		6	7	5	00					2
3			Wages Expense						6	7	5	00	3
4													4

REVIEW QUESTIONS

1. Describe the nature of the two forms of an income statement.

2. Name and describe the calculation of two measures that provide an indication of a business's ability to pay current obligations.

3. Describe how to calculate the following ratios:

   a. return on owner's equity

   b. accounts receivable turnover

   c. inventory turnover

4. Where is the information obtained that is needed in journalizing the closing entries?

5. Explain the function of each of the four closing entries made by Northern Micro.

6. What is the purpose of a post-closing trial balance?

7. What is the primary purpose of reversing entries?

8. What is the customary date for reversing entries?

9. What adjusting entries should be reversed?

MANAGING YOUR WRITING

A friend of yours has the opportunity to invest in a small business. She has come to you for advice on how she might determine whether this would be a good investment. In particular, she is concerned about how long it takes to sell the merchandise and collect receivables. Draft a memo suggesting various ratios that should be computed to evaluate the business's profitability, ability to pay its current obligations, and time required to sell inventory and collect receivables.

ETHICS CASE

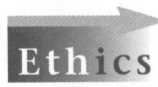

Brian Marlow recently was hired to prepare Louise Michener Consulting's year-end financial statements. Brian just earned his CPA certificate, and Louise Michener was one of his first clients. Louise employs a bookkeeper, Martha Halling, who does the daily journal entries and prepares a year-to-date trial balance at the end of each month. Martha gives the December 31 trial balance to a CPA to make the adjustments and generate the financial statements. As Brian was looking through Louise Michener's books he noticed two things. First, in each of the last three years a different CPA had prepared the financial statements. Second, the amount shown on the December 31 trial balance for miscellaneous expense was quite high this year compared to prior years. Brian called Martha to find out if she knew why miscellaneous expense had such a high balance. Martha's response was "I just do what Louise tells me to do. If she wants to charge personal expenses to the company, it's none of my business."

1. What should Brian do?

2. How might Brian's decision affect Martha? Has Martha done anything unethical?

3. Write a short letter from Brian to Louise explaining why personal items should not be charged to a business.

4. In small groups, discuss the ethical responsibilities of an accountant relating to a client's books.

WEB WORK

Annual reports show a variety of financial statements. Find two companies you are interested in, merchandising or otherwise, and study the formats used for their financial statements. Be prepared to discuss your findings in class. As a starting point, go to

http://www.reportgallery.com/bigaz.htm.
(http://heintz.swcollege.com)

SERIES A EXERCISES

EXERCISE 15A-1 (LO 1) REVENUE SECTION, MULTIPLE-STEP INCOME STATE-MENT Based on the information that follows, prepare the revenue section of a multiple-step income statement.

Sales	$140,000
Sales Returns and Allowances	3,500
Sales Discounts	2,800

EXERCISE 15A-2 (LO 1) COST OF GOODS SOLD SECTION, MULTIPLE-STEP INCOME STATEMENT Based on the information that follows, prepare the cost of goods sold section of a multiple-step income statement.

Merchandise Inventory, January 1, 20--	$ 34,000
Purchases	102,000
Purchases Returns and Allowances	4,200
Purchases Discounts	2,040
Freight-In	800
Merchandise Inventory, December 31, 20--	28,000

EXERCISE 15A-3 (LO 1) MULTIPLE-STEP INCOME STATEMENT Use the following information to prepare a multiple-step income statement, including the revenue section and the cost of goods sold section, for Rau Office Supplies for the year ended December 31, 20--.

Sales	$148,300
Sales Returns and Allowances	1,380
Sales Discounts	2,166
Interest Revenue	240
Merchandise Inventory, January 1, 20--	26,500
Purchases	98,000
Purchases Returns and Allowances	2,180

(continued)

Purchases Discounts	1,960
Freight-In	750
Merchandise Inventory, December 31, 20--	33,250
Wages Expense	23,800
Supplies Expense	900
Telephone Expense	1,100
Utilities Expense	7,000
Insurance Expense	1,000
Depreciation Expense—Equipment	3,100
Miscellaneous Expense	720
Interest Expense	3,880

EXERCISE 15A-4 (LO 5) CLOSING ENTRIES From the work sheet on page 569, prepare closing entries for Gimbel's Gifts and Gadgets in a general journal.

EXERCISE 15A-5 (LO 6) REVERSING ENTRIES From the work sheet used in Exercise 15A-4, identify the adjusting entry(ies) that should be reversed and prepare the reversing entry(ies).

EXERCISE 15A-6 (LO 5/6) ADJUSTING, CLOSING, AND REVERSING ENTRIES Based on the information that follows, prepare two sets of entries—one that will have a reversing entry and the other without a reversing entry. Enter existing balances and post all entries to two sets of T accounts for Wages Expense and Wages Payable.

a. Wages paid during 20-1 are $20,800.

b. Wages earned but not paid (accrued) as of December 31, 20-1, are $300.

c. On January 3, 20-2, payroll of $800 is paid, which includes the $300 of wages earned but not paid in December.

EXERCISE 15A-4

Gimbel's Gifts and Gadgets
Work Sheet
For Year Ended December 31, 20 - -

	ACCOUNT TITLE	TRIAL BALANCE Debit	TRIAL BALANCE Credit	ADJUSTMENTS Debit	ADJUSTMENTS Credit	ADJUSTED TRIAL BALANCE Debit	ADJUSTED TRIAL BALANCE Credit	INCOME STATEMENT Debit	INCOME STATEMENT Credit	BALANCE SHEET Debit	BALANCE SHEET Credit	
1	Cash	8 2 1 4 00				8 2 1 4 00				8 2 1 4 00		1
2	Accounts Receivable	6 7 2 0 00				6 7 2 0 00				6 7 2 0 00		2
3	Merchandise Inventory	14 2 1 0 00		(b) 16 8 0 0 00	(a) 14 2 1 0 00	16 8 0 0 00				16 8 0 0 00		3
4	Supplies	6 8 0 00			(c) 3 8 0 00	3 0 0 00				3 0 0 00		4
5	Prepaid Insurance	8 0 0 00			(d) 2 0 0 00	6 0 0 00				6 0 0 00		5
6	Building	80 0 0 0 00				80 0 0 0 00				80 0 0 0 00		6
7	Accum. Depr.—Building		13 6 0 0 00		(e) 4 0 0 0 00		17 6 0 0 00				17 6 0 0 00	7
8	Accounts Payable		5 2 8 0 00				5 2 8 0 00				5 2 8 0 00	8
9	Wages Payable				(f) 2 8 0 00		2 8 0 00				2 8 0 00	9
10	Sales Tax Payable		3 2 6 00				3 2 6 00				3 2 6 00	10
11	J. M. Gimbel, Capital		87 8 8 3 00				87 8 8 3 00				87 8 8 3 00	11
12	J. M. Gimbel, Drawing	8 0 0 0 00				8 0 0 0 00				8 0 0 0 00		12
13	Income Summary			(a) 14 2 1 0 00	(b) 16 8 0 0 00	14 2 1 0 00	16 8 0 0 00	14 2 1 0 00	16 8 0 0 00			13
14	Sales		86 0 0 0 00				86 0 0 0 00		86 0 0 0 00			14
15	Sales Returns and Allowances	1 8 4 0 00				1 8 4 0 00		1 8 4 0 00				15
16	Purchases	54 2 0 0 00				54 2 0 0 00		54 2 0 0 00				16
17	Purchases Returns and Allowances		2 8 1 3 00				2 8 1 3 00		2 8 1 3 00			17
18	Purchases Discounts		1 0 8 4 00				1 0 8 4 00		1 0 8 4 00			18
19	Freight-In	8 0 0 00				8 0 0 00		8 0 0 00				19
20	Wages Expense	16 8 0 0 00		(f) 2 8 0 00		17 0 8 0 00		17 0 8 0 00				20
21	Advertising Expense	7 8 4 00				7 8 4 00		7 8 4 00				21
22	Supplies Expense			(c) 3 8 0 00		3 8 0 00		3 8 0 00				22
23	Telephone Expense	2 1 0 0 00				2 1 0 0 00		2 1 0 0 00				23
24	Utilities Expense	1 3 1 0 00				1 3 1 0 00		1 3 1 0 00				24
25	Insurance Expense			(d) 2 0 0 00		2 0 0 00		2 0 0 00				25
26	Depr. Expense—Building			(e) 4 0 0 0 00		4 0 0 0 00		4 0 0 0 00				26
27	Miscellaneous Expense	3 8 6 00				3 8 6 00		3 8 6 00				27
28	Interest Expense	1 4 2 00				1 4 2 00		1 4 2 00				28
29		196 9 8 6 00	196 9 8 6 00	35 8 7 0 00	35 8 7 0 00	218 0 6 6 00	218 0 6 6 00	97 4 3 2 00	106 6 9 7 00	120 6 3 4 00	111 3 6 9 00	29
30	Net Income							9 2 6 5 00			9 2 6 5 00	30
31								106 6 9 7 00	106 6 9 7 00	120 6 3 4 00	120 6 3 4 00	31

EXERCISE 15A-7 (LO 4) FINANCIAL RATIOS Based on the financial statements for Jackson Enterprises (income statement, statement of owner's equity, and balance sheet) shown below and on the next page, prepare the following financial ratios. All sales are credit sales. The Accounts Receivable balance on January 1, 20--, was $21,600.

1. Working capital

2. Current ratio

3. Quick ratio

4. Return on owner's equity

5. Accounts receivable turnover and average number of days required to collect receivables

6. Inventory turnover and average number of days required to sell inventory

Jackson Enterprises Income Statement For Year Ended December 31, 20 - -					
Revenue from sales:					
Sales			$184 2 0 0 00		
Less sales returns and allowances			2 1 0 0 00		
Net sales				$182 1 0 0 00	
Cost of goods sold:					
Merchandise inventory, January 1, 20- -			$ 31 3 0 0 00		
Purchases		$92 8 0 0 00			
Less: Purchases returns and allowances	$ 1 8 0 0 00				
Purchases discounts	1 8 5 6 00	3 6 5 6 00			
Net purchases		$89 1 4 4 00			
Add freight-in		9 3 3 00			
Cost of goods purchased			90 0 7 7 00		
Goods available for sale			$121 3 7 7 00		
Less merchandise inventory, December 31, 20- -			28 1 7 7 00		
Cost of goods sold				93 2 0 0 00	
Gross profit				$ 88 9 0 0 00	
Operating expenses:					
Wages expense			$ 38 0 0 0 00		
Advertising expense			1 1 8 0 00		
Supplies expense			3 8 0 00		
Telephone expense			2 2 1 0 00		
Utilities expense			11 0 0 0 00		
Insurance expense			9 0 0 00		
Depreciation expense—building			4 0 0 0 00		
Depreciation expense—equipment			3 8 0 0 00		
Miscellaneous expense			5 3 0 00		
Total operating expenses				62 0 0 0 00	
Income from operations				$ 26 9 0 0 00	
Other revenues:					
Interest revenue			$ 1 8 0 0 00		
Other expenses:					
Interest expense			9 0 0 00	9 0 0 00	
Net income				$ 27 8 0 0 00	

Jackson Enterprises Statement of Owner's Equity For Year Ended December 31, 20 - -											
J. B. Gray, capital, January 1, 20- -							$ 88	0	0	0	00
Net income for the year	$27	8	0	0	00						
Less withdrawals for the year	11	6	0	0	00						
Increase in capital							16	2	0	0	00
J. B. Gray, capital, December 31, 20- -							$104	2	0	0	00

Jackson Enterprises Balance Sheet December 31, 20 - -																
Assets																
Current assets:																
Cash							$20	8	0	0	00					
Accounts receivable							18	9	0	0	00					
Merchandise inventory							28	1	7	7	00					
Supplies							1	3	2	3	00					
Prepaid insurance								9	0	0	00					
Total current assets												$ 70	1	0	0	00
Property, plant, and equipment:																
Building	$90	0	0	0	00											
Less accumulated depreciation	28	0	0	0	00	$62	0	0	0	00						
Equipment	$33	0	0	0	00											
Less accumulated depreciation	7	5	0	0	00	25	5	0	0	00						
Total property, plant, and equipment												87	5	0	0	00
Total assets												$157	6	0	0	00
Liabilities																
Current liabilities:																
Accounts payable	$12	6	0	0	00											
Wages payable		5	0	0	00											
Sales tax payable	1	2	0	0	00											
Mortgage payable (current portion)		8	0	0	00											
Total current liabilities						$15	1	0	0	00						
Long-term liabilities:																
Mortgage payable	$39	1	0	0	00											
Less current portion		8	0	0	00	38	3	0	0	00						
Total liabilities												$53	4	0	0	00
Owner's Equity																
J. B. Gray, capital												104	2	0	0	00
Total liabilities and owner's equity												$157	6	0	0	00

SERIES A PROBLEMS

PROBLEM 15A-1 (LO 5/6) WORK SHEET, ADJUSTING, CLOSING AND REVERS-ING ENTRIES Ellis Fabric Store shows the following trial balance as of December 31, 20--.

At the end of the year, the following adjustments need to be made:

(a, b) Merchandise Inventory as of December 31, $28,900.

(continued)

Ellis Fabric Store
Trial Balance
For Year Ended December 31, 20 - -

ACCOUNT TITLE	ACCOUNT NO.	DEBIT BALANCE	CREDIT BALANCE
Cash		28 0 0 0 00	
Accounts Receivable		14 2 0 0 00	
Merchandise Inventory		33 0 0 0 00	
Supplies		1 6 0 0 00	
Prepaid Insurance		9 0 0 00	
Equipment		6 6 0 0 00	
Accumulated Depreciation—Equipment			1 0 0 0 00
Accounts Payable			16 6 2 0 00
Wages Payable			
Sales Tax Payable			8 5 0 00
W. P. Ellis, Capital			71 2 0 0 00
W. P. Ellis, Drawing		21 6 1 0 00	
Income Summary			
Sales			78 5 0 0 00
Sales Returns and Allowances		1 8 5 0 00	
Interest Revenue			1 2 0 0 00
Purchases		41 5 0 0 00	
Purchases Returns and Allowances			1 8 0 0 00
Purchases Discounts			8 3 0 00
Freight-In		6 6 0 00	
Wages Expense		14 8 8 0 00	
Advertising Expense		8 1 0 00	
Supplies Expense			
Telephone Expense		1 2 1 0 00	
Utilities Expense		3 2 4 0 00	
Insurance Expense			
Depreciation Expense—Equipment			
Miscellaneous Expense		9 2 0 00	
Interest Expense		1 0 2 0 00	
		172 0 0 0 00	172 0 0 0 00

(c) Unused supplies on hand, $1,350.

(d) Insurance expired, $300.

(e) Depreciation expense for the year, $500.

(f) Wages earned but not paid (Wages Payable), $480.

REQUIRED
1. Prepare a work sheet.

2. Prepare adjusting entries.

3. Prepare closing entries.

4. Prepare a post-closing trial balance.

5. Prepare reversing entries.

PROBLEM 15A-2 (LO 1/2/3) INCOME STATEMENT, STATEMENT OF OWNER'S EQUITY, AND BALANCE SHEET Paulson's Pet Store completed the work sheet on page 574 for the year ended December 31, 20--. Owner's equity as of January 1, 20--, was $21,900. The current portion of Mortgage Payable is $500.

REQUIRED   1. Prepare a multiple-step income statement.

2. Prepare a statement of owner's equity.

3. Prepare a balance sheet.

PROBLEM 15A-3 (LO 4) FINANCIAL RATIOS Use the work sheet and financial statements prepared in Problem 15A-2. All sales are credit sales. The Accounts Receivable balance on January 1, 20--, was $3,800.

REQUIRED   Prepare the following financial ratios:

a. Working capital

b. Current ratio

c. Quick ratio

d. Return on owner's equity

e. Accounts receivable turnover and average number of days required to collect receivables

f. Inventory turnover and average number of days required to sell inventory

SERIES B EXERCISES

EXERCISE 15B-1 (LO 1) REVENUE SECTION, MULTIPLE-STEP INCOME STATE-MENT Based on the information that follows, prepare the revenue section of a multiple-step income statement.

Sales	$86,200
Sales Returns and Allowances	2,280
Sales Discounts	1,724

EXERCISE 15B-2 (LO 1) COST OF GOODS SOLD SECTION, MULTIPLE-STEP INCOME STATEMENT Based on the information that follows, prepare the cost of goods sold section of a multiple-step income statement.

Merchandise Inventory, January 1, 20--	$13,800
Purchases	71,300
Purchases Returns and Allowances	3,188
Purchases Discounts	1,460
Freight-In	390
Merchandise Inventory, December 31, 20--	21,400

PROBLEM 15A-2

Paulson's Pet Store
Work Sheet
For Year Ended December 31, 20 - -

ACCOUNT TITLE	TRIAL BALANCE DEBIT	TRIAL BALANCE CREDIT	ADJUSTMENTS DEBIT	ADJUSTMENTS CREDIT	ADJUSTED TRIAL BALANCE DEBIT	ADJUSTED TRIAL BALANCE CREDIT	INCOME STATEMENT DEBIT	INCOME STATEMENT CREDIT	BALANCE SHEET DEBIT	BALANCE SHEET CREDIT	
1 Cash	15 8 6 0 00				15 8 6 0 00				15 8 6 0 00		1
2 Accounts Receivable	2 3 4 0 00				2 3 4 0 00				2 3 4 0 00		2
3 Merchandise Inventory	15 0 0 0 00		(b) 16 5 0 0 00	(a) 15 0 0 0 00	16 5 0 0 00				16 5 0 0 00		3
4 Supplies	8 0 0 00			(c) 2 0 0 00	6 0 0 00				6 0 0 00		4
5 Prepaid Insurance	6 0 0 00			(d) 1 5 0 00	4 5 0 00				4 5 0 00		5
6 Equipment	5 0 0 0 00				5 0 0 0 00				5 0 0 0 00		6
7 Accum. Depr.—Equipment		4 5 0 00		(e) 4 5 0 00		9 0 0 00				9 0 0 00	7
8 Accounts Payable		4 8 9 0 00				4 8 9 0 00				4 8 9 0 00	8
9 Wages Payable				(f) 3 0 0 00		3 0 0 00				3 0 0 00	9
10 Sales Tax Payable		8 6 0 00				8 6 0 00				8 6 0 00	10
11 Mortgage Payable		4 0 0 0 00				4 0 0 0 00				4 0 0 0 00	11
12 B. Paulson, Capital		23 9 0 0 00				23 9 0 0 00				23 9 0 0 00	12
13 B. Paulson, Drawing	1 2 0 0 00				1 2 0 0 00				1 2 0 0 00		13
14 Income Summary			(a) 15 0 0 0 00	(b) 16 5 0 0 00	15 0 0 0 00	16 5 0 0 00	15 0 0 0 00	16 5 0 0 00			14
15 Sales		71 5 1 0 00				71 5 1 0 00		71 5 1 0 00			15
16 Sales Returns and Allowances	1 3 4 0 00				1 3 4 0 00		1 3 4 0 00				16
17 Purchases	40 6 6 0 00				40 6 6 0 00		40 6 6 0 00				17
18 Purchases Returns and Allowances		1 0 2 0 00				1 0 2 0 00		1 0 2 0 00			18
19 Purchases Discounts		8 0 0 00				8 0 0 00		8 0 0 00			19
20 Freight-In	4 0 0 00				4 0 0 00		4 0 0 00				20
21 Wages Expense	22 3 0 0 00		(f) 3 0 0 00		22 6 0 0 00		22 6 0 0 00				21
22 Advertising Expense	3 0 0 00				3 0 0 00		3 0 0 00				22
23 Supplies Expense			(c) 2 0 0 00		2 0 0 00		2 0 0 00				23
24 Telephone Expense	6 8 4 00				6 8 4 00		6 8 4 00				24
25 Utilities Expense	7 1 6 00				7 1 6 00		7 1 6 00				25
26 Insurance Expense			(d) 1 5 0 00		1 5 0 00		1 5 0 00				26
27 Depr. Expense—Equipment			(e) 4 5 0 00		4 5 0 00		4 5 0 00				27
28 Miscellaneous Expense	1 5 0 00				1 5 0 00		1 5 0 00				28
29 Interest Expense	8 0 00				8 0 00		8 0 00				29
30	107 4 3 0 00	107 4 3 0 00	32 6 0 0 00	32 6 0 0 00	124 6 8 0 00	124 6 8 0 00	82 7 3 0 00	89 8 3 0 00	41 9 5 0 00	34 8 5 0 00	30
31 Net Income							7 1 0 0 00			7 1 0 0 00	31
32							89 8 3 0 00	89 8 3 0 00	41 9 5 0 00	41 9 5 0 00	32

EXERCISE 15B-3 (LO 1) MULTIPLE-STEP INCOME STATEMENT Use the following information to prepare a multiple-step income statement, including the revenue section and the cost of goods sold section, for Aeito's Plumbing Supplies for the year ended December 31, 20--.

Sales	$166,000
Sales Returns and Allowances	1,620
Sales Discounts	3,320
Interest Revenue	3,184
Merchandise Inventory, January 1, 20--	33,200
Purchases	111,300
Purchases Returns and Allowances	3,600
Purchases Discounts	2,226
Freight-In	640
Merchandise Inventory, December 31, 20--	29,600
Wages Expense	22,000
Supplies Expense	650
Telephone Expense	1,100
Utilities Expense	9,000
Insurance Expense	1,000
Depreciation Expense—Building	4,600
Depreciation Expense—Equipment	2,800
Miscellaneous Expense	214
Interest Expense	1,126

EXERCISE 15B-4 (LO 5) CLOSING ENTRIES From the work sheet on page 576, prepare closing entries for Balloons and Baubbles in a general journal.

EXERCISE 15B-5 (LO 6) REVERSING ENTRIES From the work sheet in Exercise 15B-4, identify the adjusting entry(ies) that should be reversed and prepare the reversing entry(ies).

EXERCISE 15B-6 (LO 5/6) ADJUSTING, CLOSING, AND REVERSING ENTRIES Based on the information that follows, prepare two sets of entries—one that will have a reversing entry and the other without a reversing entry. Enter existing balances and post all entries to two sets of T accounts for Wages Expense and Wages Payable.

a. Wages paid during 20-1 are $20,080.

b. Wages earned but not paid (accrued) as of December 31, 20-1, are $280.

c. On January 3, 20-2, payroll of $840 is paid, which includes the $280 of wages earned but not paid in December.

EXERCISE 15B-4

Balloons and Baubbles
Work Sheet
For Year Ended December 31, 20 - -

	ACCOUNT TITLE	TRIAL BALANCE DEBIT	TRIAL BALANCE CREDIT	ADJUSTMENTS DEBIT	ADJUSTMENTS CREDIT	ADJUSTED TRIAL BALANCE DEBIT	ADJUSTED TRIAL BALANCE CREDIT	INCOME STATEMENT DEBIT	INCOME STATEMENT CREDIT	BALANCE SHEET DEBIT	BALANCE SHEET CREDIT	
1	Cash	2 8 0 0 00				2 8 0 0 00				2 8 0 0 00		1
2	Accounts Receivable	4 2 0 0 00				4 2 0 0 00				4 2 0 0 00		2
3	Merchandise Inventory	8 6 0 0 00		(b) 7 5 0 0 00	(a) 8 6 0 0 00	7 5 0 0 00				7 5 0 0 00		3
4	Supplies	7 8 0 00			(c) 2 8 0 00	5 0 0 00				5 0 0 00		4
5	Prepaid Insurance	6 2 0 00			(d) 1 2 0 00	5 0 0 00				5 0 0 00		5
6	Equipment	3 0 0 0 00				3 0 0 0 00				3 0 0 0 00		6
7	Accum. Depr.—Equipment		6 0 0 00		(e) 3 0 0 00		9 0 0 00				9 0 0 00	7
8	Accounts Payable		1 8 0 0 00				1 8 0 0 00				1 8 0 0 00	8
9	Wages Payable				(f) 2 0 0 00		2 0 0 00				2 0 0 00	9
10	Sales Tax Payable		8 0 00				8 0 00				8 0 00	10
11	L. Marlow, Capital		12 2 0 0 00				12 2 0 0 00				12 2 0 0 00	11
12	L. Marlow, Drawing	2 0 0 0 00				2 0 0 0 00				2 0 0 0 00		12
13	Income Summary			(a) 8 6 0 0 00	(b) 7 5 0 0 00	8 6 0 0 00	7 5 0 0 00	8 6 0 0 00	7 5 0 0 00			13
14	Sales		31 0 0 0 00				31 0 0 0 00		31 0 0 0 00			14
15	Sales Returns and Allowances	8 0 0 00				8 0 0 00		8 0 0 00				15
16	Purchases	22 0 0 0 00				22 0 0 0 00		22 0 0 0 00				16
17	Purchases Returns and Allowances		1 8 0 0 00				1 8 0 0 00		1 8 0 0 00			17
18	Purchases Discounts		4 0 7 00				4 0 7 00		4 0 7 00			18
19	Freight-In	2 0 0 00				2 0 0 00		2 0 0 00				19
20	Wages Expense	1 2 0 0 00		(f) 2 0 0 00		1 4 0 0 00		1 4 0 0 00				20
21	Advertising Expense	3 0 0 00				3 0 0 00		3 0 0 00				21
22	Supplies Expense			(c) 2 8 0 00		2 8 0 00		2 8 0 00				22
23	Telephone Expense	7 0 0 00				7 0 0 00		7 0 0 00				23
24	Utilities Expense	4 8 0 00				4 8 0 00		4 8 0 00				24
25	Insurance Expense			(d) 1 2 0 00		1 2 0 00		1 2 0 00				25
26	Depr. Expense—Equipment			(e) 3 0 0 00		3 0 0 00		3 0 0 00				26
27	Miscellaneous Expense	1 1 0 00				1 1 0 00		1 1 0 00				27
28	Interest Expense	9 7 00				9 7 00		9 7 00				28
29		47 8 8 7 00	47 8 8 7 00	17 0 0 0 00	17 0 0 0 00	55 8 8 7 00	55 8 8 7 00	35 3 8 7 00	40 7 0 7 00	20 5 0 0 00	15 1 8 0 00	29
30	Net Income							5 3 2 0 00			5 3 2 0 00	30
31								40 7 0 7 00	40 7 0 7 00	20 5 0 0 00	20 5 0 0 00	31

EXERCISE 15B-7 (LO 4) FINANCIAL RATIOS Based on the financial statements shown on pages 577–578 for McDonald Carpeting Co. (income statement, statement of owner's equity, and balance sheet), prepare the following financial ratios. All sales are credit sales. The balance of accounts receivable on January 1, 20--, was $6,800.

1. Working capital

2. Current ratio

3. Quick ratio

4. Return on owner's equity

5. Accounts receivable turnover and the average number of days required to collect receivables

6. Inventory turnover and the average number of days required to sell inventory

McDonald Carpeting Co. Income Statement For Year Ended December 31, 20 - -					
Revenue from sales:					
Sales				$122 8 0 0 00	
Less sales returns and allowances				1 1 0 0 00	
Net sales					$121 7 0 0 00
Cost of goods sold:					
Merchandise inventory, January 1, 20- -				$ 19 3 0 0 00	
Purchases			$62 8 0 0 00		
Less: Purchases returns and allowances	$2 8 0 0 00				
Purchases discounts	1 9 4 4 00		4 7 4 4 00		
Net purchases			$58 0 5 6 00		
Add freight-in			9 4 4 00		
Cost of goods purchased				59 0 0 0 00	
Goods available for sale				$ 78 3 0 0 00	
Less merchandise inventory, December 31, 20- -				16 7 0 0 00	
Cost of goods sold					61 6 0 0 00
Gross profit					$ 60 1 0 0 00
Operating expenses:					
Wages expense				$ 18 0 0 0 00	
Advertising expense				9 8 0 00	
Supplies expense				3 2 0 00	
Telephone expense				1 2 0 0 00	
Utilities expense				8 0 0 0 00	
Insurance expense				8 0 0 00	
Depreciation expense—building				3 5 0 0 00	
Depreciation expense—equipment				2 5 0 0 00	
Miscellaneous expense				2 0 0 00	
Total operating expenses					35 5 0 0 00
Income from operations					$ 24 6 0 0 00
Other revenues:					
Interest revenue				$ 2 8 0 0 00	
Other expenses:					
Interest expense				2 1 0 0 00	7 0 0 00
Net income					$ 25 3 0 0 00

(EXERCISE 15B-7)

McDonald Carpeting Co. Statement of Owner's Equity For Year Ended December 31, 20 - -								
C. S. McDonald, capital, January 1, 20- -						$52	0 0 0	00
Net income for the year	$25	3 0 0	00					
Less withdrawals for the year	10	4 0 0	00					
Increase in capital						14	9 0 0	00
C. S. McDonald, capital, December 31, 20- -						$66	9 0 0	00

McDonald Carpeting Co. Balance Sheet December 31, 20 - -									
Assets									
Current assets:									
Cash				$10	4 0 0	00			
Accounts receivable				8	9 0 0	00			
Merchandise inventory				16	7 0 0	00			
Supplies				1	2 0 0	00			
Prepaid insurance					7 0 0	00			
Total current assets							$37	9 0 0	00
Property, plant, and equipment:									
Building	$60	0 0 0	00						
Less accumulated depreciation—building	18	0 0 0	00	42	0 0 0	00			
Equipment	$22	0 0 0	00						
Less accumulated depreciation—equipment	6	2 0 0	00	15	8 0 0	00			
Total property, plant, and equipment							57	8 0 0	00
Total assets							$95	7 0 0	00
Liabilities									
Current liabilities:									
Accounts payable				$ 8	4 0 0	00			
Wages payable					3 0 0	00			
Sales tax payable				1	0 0 0	00			
Mortgage payable (current portion)					6 0 0	00			
Total current liabilities							$10	3 0 0	00
Long-term liabilities:									
Mortgage payable	$19	1 0 0	00						
Less current portion		6 0 0	00	18	5 0 0	00			
Total liabilities							$28	8 0 0	00
Owner's Equity									
C. S. McDonald, capital							66	9 0 0	00
Total liabilities and owner's equity							$95	7 0 0	00

SERIES B PROBLEMS

W & D

PROBLEM 15B-1 (LO 5/6) WORK SHEET, ADJUSTING, CLOSING AND REVERSING ENTRIES The trial balance for Darby Kite Store as of December 31, 20-- is shown on the next page.

At the end of the year, the following adjustments need to be made:

(a, b)   Merchandise inventory as of December 31, $23,600.

(c)   Unused supplies on hand, $1,050.

(d)   Insurance expired, $250.

(continued)

Darby Kite Store
Trial Balance
For Year Ended December 31, 20 - -

ACCOUNT TITLE	ACCOUNT NO.	DEBIT BALANCE	CREDIT BALANCE
Cash		11 7 0 0 00	
Accounts Receivable		11 2 0 0 00	
Merchandise Inventory		25 0 0 0 00	
Supplies		1 2 0 0 00	
Prepaid Insurance		8 0 0 00	
Equipment		5 4 0 0 00	
Accumulated Depreciation—Equipment			8 0 0 00
Accounts Payable			7 6 0 0 00
Wages Payable			
Sales Tax Payable			2 5 0 00
M. D. Akins, Capital			50 0 0 0 00
M. D. Akins, Drawing		10 5 0 0 00	
Income Summary			
Sales			57 9 9 0 00
Sales Returns and Allowances		1 4 5 0 00	
Purchases		34 5 0 0 00	
Purchases Returns and Allowances			1 1 0 0 00
Purchases Discounts			6 3 0 00
Freight-In		3 6 0 00	
Wages Expense		10 8 8 0 00	
Advertising Expense		7 4 0 00	
Supplies Expense			
Telephone Expense		1 1 0 0 00	
Utilities Expense		2 3 0 0 00	
Insurance Expense			
Depreciation Expense—Equipment			
Miscellaneous Expense		3 2 0 00	
Interest Expense		9 2 0 00	
		118 3 7 0 00	118 3 7 0 00

(e)   Depreciation expense for the year, $400.

(f)   Wages earned but not paid (Wages Payable), $360.

REQUIRED   1.   Prepare a work sheet.

2.   Prepare adjusting entries.

3.   Prepare closing entries.

4.   Prepare a post-closing trial balance.

5.   Prepare reversing entries.

PROBLEM 15B-2 (LO 1/2/3) INCOME STATEMENT, STATEMENT OF OWNER'S EQUITY, AND BALANCE SHEET Backlund Farm Supply completed the work sheet on page 580 for the year ended December 31, 20--. Owner's equity as of January 1, 20--, was $50,000. The current portion of Mortgage Payable is $1,000.

REQUIRED   1.   Prepare a multiple-step income statement.

2.   Prepare a statement of owner's equity.

3.   Prepare a balance sheet.

PROBLEM 15B-2

Backlund Farm Supply
Work Sheet
For Year Ended December 31, 20 - -

	ACCOUNT TITLE	TRIAL BALANCE DEBIT	TRIAL BALANCE CREDIT	ADJUSTMENTS DEBIT	ADJUSTMENTS CREDIT	ADJUSTED TRIAL BALANCE DEBIT	ADJUSTED TRIAL BALANCE CREDIT	INCOME STATEMENT DEBIT	INCOME STATEMENT CREDIT	BALANCE SHEET DEBIT	BALANCE SHEET CREDIT	
1	Cash	10 1 8 0 00				10 1 8 0 00				10 1 8 0 00		1
2	Accounts Receivable	26 4 2 0 00				26 4 2 0 00				26 4 2 0 00		2
3	Merchandise Inventory	42 1 6 0 00		(b) 44 3 0 0 00	(a) 42 1 6 0 00	44 3 0 0 00				44 3 0 0 00		3
4	Supplies	4 3 6 0 00			(c) 8 6 0 00	3 5 0 0 00				3 5 0 0 00		4
5	Prepaid Insurance	3 0 0 0 00			(d) 7 5 0 00	2 2 5 0 00				2 2 5 0 00		5
6	Equipment	38 0 0 0 00				38 0 0 0 00				38 0 0 0 00		6
7	Accum. Depr.—Equipment		6 0 0 0 00		(e) 9 0 0 00		6 9 0 0 00				6 9 0 0 00	7
8	Accounts Payable		41 2 0 0 00				41 2 0 0 00				41 2 0 0 00	8
9	Wages Payable				(f) 4 2 0 00		4 2 0 00				4 2 0 00	9
10	Sales Tax Payable		8 0 0 0 00				8 0 0 0 00				8 0 0 0 00	10
11	Mortgage Payable		8 0 0 0 00				8 0 0 0 00				8 0 0 0 00	11
12	J. Backlund, Capital		57 0 0 0 00				57 0 0 0 00				57 0 0 0 00	12
13	J. Backlund, Drawing	6 8 0 0 00				6 8 0 0 00				6 8 0 0 00		13
14	Income Summary			(a) 42 1 6 0 00	(b) 44 3 0 0 00	42 1 6 0 00	44 3 0 0 00	42 1 6 0 00	44 3 0 0 00			14
15	Sales		141 8 0 0 00				141 8 0 0 00		141 8 0 0 00			15
16	Sales Returns and Allowances	1 3 1 0 00				1 3 1 0 00		1 3 1 0 00				16
17	Purchases	81 3 0 0 00				81 3 0 0 00		81 3 0 0 00				17
18	Purchases Returns and Allowances		2 9 0 0 00				2 9 0 0 00		2 9 0 0 00			18
19	Purchases Discounts		1 5 1 0 00				1 5 1 0 00		1 5 1 0 00			19
20	Freight-In	6 0 0 00				6 0 0 00		6 0 0 00				20
21	Wages Expense	41 3 0 0 00		(f) 4 2 0 00		41 7 2 0 00		41 7 2 0 00				21
22	Advertising Expense	4 0 0 0 00				4 0 0 0 00		4 0 0 0 00				22
23	Supplies Expense			(c) 8 6 0 00		8 6 0 00		8 6 0 00				23
24	Telephone Expense	8 0 0 00				8 0 0 00		8 0 0 00				24
25	Utilities Expense	1 3 0 0 00				1 3 0 0 00		1 3 0 0 00				25
26	Insurance Expense			(d) 7 5 0 00		7 5 0 00		7 5 0 00				26
27	Depr. Expense—Equipment			(e) 9 0 0 00		9 0 0 00		9 0 0 00				27
28	Miscellaneous Expense	2 0 0 0 00				2 0 0 0 00		2 0 0 0 00				28
29	Interest Expense	1 0 8 0 00				1 0 8 0 00		1 0 8 0 00				29
30		259 2 1 0 00	259 2 1 0 00	89 3 9 0 00	89 3 9 0 00	304 8 3 0 00	304 8 3 0 00	173 3 8 0 00	190 5 1 0 00	131 4 5 0 00	114 3 2 0 00	30
31	Net Income							17 1 3 0 00			17 1 3 0 00	31
32								190 5 1 0 00	190 5 1 0 00	131 4 5 0 00	131 4 5 0 00	32

PROBLEM 15B-3 (LO 4) FINANCIAL RATIOS Use the work sheet and financial statements prepared in Problem 15B-2. All sales are credit sales. The Accounts Receivable balance on January 1 was $38,200.

REQUIRED   Prepare the following financial ratios:

a. Working capital

b. Current ratio

c. Quick ratio

d. Return on owner's equity

e. Accounts receivable turnover and the average number of days required to collect receivables

f. Inventory turnover and the average number of days required to sell inventory

MASTERY PROBLEM

Dominique Fouque owns and operates Dominique's Doll House. She has a small shop in which she sells new and antique dolls. She is particularly well known for her collection of antique Ken and Barbie dolls. A completed work sheet for 20-3 is shown on the next page. Fouque made no additional investments during the year and the long-term note payable is due in 20-9. No portion of the long-term note is due within the next year. Net credit sales for 20-3 were $35,300 and receivables on January 1 were $2,500.

REQUIRED   1. Prepare a multiple-step income statement.

2. Prepare a statement of owner's equity.

3. Prepare a balance sheet.

4. Compute the following measures of performance and financial condition for 20-3:

a. Current ratio

b. Quick ratio

c. Working capital

d. Return on owner's equity

e. Accounts receivable turnover and average number of days required to collect receivables

f. Inventory turnover and the average number of days required to sell inventory

5. Prepare adjusting entries and indicate which should be reversed and why.

6. Prepare closing entries.

7. Prepare reversing entries for the adjustments where appropriate.

MASTERY PROBLEM

Dominique's Doll House
Work Sheet
For Year Ended December 31, 20-3

	Account Title	Trial Balance Debit	Trial Balance Credit	Adjustments Debit	Adjustments Credit	Adjusted Trial Balance Debit	Adjusted Trial Balance Credit	Income Statement Debit	Income Statement Credit	Balance Sheet Debit	Balance Sheet Credit	
1	Cash	5 2 0 0 00				5 2 0 0 00				5 2 0 0 00		1
2	Accounts Receivable	3 2 0 0 00				3 2 0 0 00				3 2 0 0 00		2
3	Merchandise Inventory	22 3 0 0 00		(b) 24 6 0 0 00	(a) 22 3 0 0 00	24 6 0 0 00				24 6 0 0 00		3
4	Office Supplies	8 0 0 00			(c) 6 0 0 00	2 0 0 00				2 0 0 00		4
5	Prepaid Insurance	1 2 0 0 00			(d) 4 0 0 00	8 0 0 00				8 0 0 00		5
6	Store Equipment	85 0 0 0 00				85 0 0 0 00				85 0 0 0 00		6
7	Accum. Depr.—Store Equipment		15 0 0 0 00		(e) 5 0 0 0 00		20 0 0 0 00				20 0 0 0 00	7
8	Notes Payable		6 0 0 0 00				6 0 0 0 00				6 0 0 0 00	8
9	Accounts Payable		5 5 0 0 00				5 5 0 0 00				5 5 0 0 00	9
10	Wages Payable				(g) 2 0 0 00		2 0 0 00				2 0 0 00	10
11	Sales Tax Payable		8 5 0 0 00				8 5 0 0 00				8 5 0 0 00	11
12	Unearned Rent Revenue		1 0 0 0 00	(f) 7 0 0 00			3 0 0 00				3 0 0 00	12
13	Long-Term Note Payable		10 0 0 0 00				10 0 0 0 00				10 0 0 0 00	13
14	Dominique Fouque, Capital		75 8 0 0 00				75 8 0 0 00				75 8 0 0 00	14
15	Dominique Fouque, Drawing	21 0 0 0 00				21 0 0 0 00				21 0 0 0 00		15
16	Income Summary			(a) 22 3 0 0 00	(b) 24 6 0 0 00	22 3 0 0 00	24 6 0 0 00	22 3 0 0 00	24 6 0 0 00			16
17	Sales		130 5 0 0 00				130 5 0 0 00		130 5 0 0 00			17
18	Sales Returns and Allowances	9 0 0 0 00				9 0 0 0 00		9 0 0 0 00				18
19	Rent Revenue		25 0 0 0 00		(f) 7 0 0 00		25 7 0 0 00		25 7 0 0 00			19
20	Purchases	72 0 0 0 00				72 0 0 0 00		72 0 0 0 00				20
21	Purchases Discounts		7 5 0 00				7 5 0 00		7 5 0 00			21
22	Freight-In	1 2 0 0 00				1 2 0 0 00		1 2 0 0 00				22
23	Wages Expense	42 0 0 0 00		(g) 2 0 0 00		42 2 0 0 00		42 2 0 0 00				23
24	Rent Expense	6 0 0 0 00				6 0 0 0 00		6 0 0 0 00				24
25	Office Supplies Expense			(c) 6 0 0 00		6 0 0 00		6 0 0 00				25
26	Telephone Expense	1 5 0 0 00				1 5 0 0 00		1 5 0 0 00				26
27	Utilities Expense	7 6 0 0 00				7 6 0 0 00		7 6 0 0 00				27
28	Insurance Expense			(d) 4 0 0 00		4 0 0 00		4 0 0 00				28
29	Depr. Expense—Store Equipment			(e) 5 0 0 0 00		5 0 0 0 00		5 0 0 0 00				29
30	Interest Expense	5 0 0 00				5 0 0 00		5 0 0 00				30
31		270 4 0 0 00	270 4 0 0 00	53 8 0 0 00	53 8 0 0 00	300 2 0 0 00	300 2 0 0 00	160 2 0 0 00	181 5 5 0 00	140 0 0 0 00	118 6 5 0 00	31
32	Net Income							21 3 5 0 00			21 3 5 0 00	32
33								181 5 5 0 00	181 5 5 0 00	140 0 0 0 00	140 0 0 0 00	33

Self-Study Test Questions

True/False

1. A multiple-step form of income statement calculates gross profit, before subtracting operating expenses. _____

2. Current assets include cash, items expected to convert into cash, and items that will be consumed during a year or the normal operating cycle, whichever is shorter. _____

3. Current assets are listed on the balance sheet in order of liquidity. _____

4. Working capital is the difference between current assets and current liabilities. _____

5. Accounts receivable turnover is the number of times merchandise inventory turned over or was sold during the accounting period. _____

Multiple Choice

1. Which of these assets is *not* a current asset? _____

   (a) Cash
   (b) Accounts Receivable
   (c) Office Equipment
   (d) Merchandise Inventory

2. Which of these would be listed *first* on a balance sheet? _____

   (a) Accounts Receivable
   (b) Delivery Equipment
   (c) Accounts Payable
   (d) Prepaid Insurance

3. Which of these is considered a *quick asset*?

   (a) Merchandise Inventory
   (b) Accounts Receivable
   (c) Office Equipment
   (d) Prepaid Insurance

4. To calculate the accounts receivable turnover ratio, _____ is divided by average accounts receivable. _____

   (a) Net sales
   (b) Cost of goods sold
   (c) Total sales
   (d) Net credit sales

5. Inventory turnover is calculated by dividing cost of goods sold by _____

   (a) average accounts receivable.
   (b) average owner's equity.
   (c) average inventory.
   (d) accounts receivable turnover.

The answers to the Self-Study Test Questions are at the end of the text.

COMPREHENSIVE PROBLEM 2: ACCOUNTING CYCLE WITH SUBSIDIARY LEDGERS

During the month of December, 20-1, TJ's Specialty Shop engaged in the following transactions:

Dec. 1 Sold merchandise on account to Anne Clark, $2,000 plus tax of $100. Sale no. 637.

2 Issued check no. 806 to Owen Enterprises in payment of December 1 balance of $1,600, less 2% discount.

3 Issued check no. 807 to Nathen Co. in payment of December 1 balance of $3,000, less 2% discount.

4 Purchased merchandise on account from Owen Enterprises, $1,550. Invoice no. 763, dated December 4, terms 2/10, n/30.

4 Issued check no. 808 in payment of telephone expense for the month of November, $180.

6 Purchased merchandise on account from Evans Essentials, $2,350. Invoice no. 764, dated December 5, terms net 30.

8 Sold merchandise for cash, $4,840, plus tax of $242.

9 Received payment from Heather Waters in full settlement of account, $490.

9 Sold merchandise on account to Lucy Greene, $800 plus tax of $40. Sale no. 638.

10 Issued check no. 809 to West Wholesalers in payment of December 1 balance of $1,000.

11 Issued check no. 810 in payment of advertising expense for the month of December, $400.

12 Sold merchandise on account to Martha Boyle, $1,260 plus tax of $63. Sale no. 639.

12 Received payment from Anne Clark on account, $1,340.

13 Issued check no. 811 to Owen Enterprises in payment of December 4 purchase. Invoice no. 763, less 2% discount.

13 Martha Boyle returned merchandise for a credit, $740 plus sales tax of $37.

15 Issued check no. 812 in payment of wages (Wages Expense) for the two-week period ending December 14, $1,100.

15 Received payment from Lucy Greene on account, $1,960.

16 Sold merchandise on account to Kim Fields, $160 plus sales tax of $8. Sale no. 640.

17 Returned merchandise to Evans Essentials for credit, $150.

18 Issued check no. 813 to Evans Essentials in payment of December 1 balance of $1,250 less the credit received on December 17.

19 Sold merchandise on account to Lucy Greene, $620 plus tax of $31. Sale no. 641.

22 Received payment from John Dempsey on account, $1,560.

23 Issued check no. 814 for the purchase of supplies, $120. (Debit Supplies)

24 Purchased merchandise on account from West Wholesalers, $1,200. Invoice no. 765, dated December 24, terms net 30.

26   Purchased merchandise on account from Nathen Co., $800. Invoice no. 766, dated December 26, terms 2/10, n/30.

27   Issued check no. 815 in payment of utilities expense for the month of November, $630.

27   Sold merchandise on account to John Dempsey, $2,020 plus tax of $101. Sale no. 642.

29   Received payment from Martha Boyle on account, $2,473.

29   Issued check no. 816 in payment of wages (Wages Expense) for the two-week period ending December 28, $1,100.

30   Issued check no. 817 to Meyers Trophy Shop for a cash purchase of merchandise, $200.

As of December 1, TJ's account balances were as follows:

Account	Account No.	Debit	Credit
Cash	101	$ 11,500	
Accounts Receivable	122	8,600	
Merchandise Inventory	131	21,800	
Supplies	141	1,035	
Prepaid Insurance	145	1,380	
Land	161	8,700	
Building	171	52,000	
Accum. Depr.—Building	171.1		$ 9,200
Store Equipment	181	28,750	
Accum. Depr.—Store Equipment	181.1		9,300
Accounts Payable	202		6,850
Wages Payable	219		
Sales Tax Payable	231		970
Mortgage Payable	251		12,525
Tom Jones, Capital	311		90,000
Tom Jones, Drawing	312	8,500	
Income Summary	313		
Sales	401		116,000
Sales Returns and Allowances	401.1	690	
Purchases	501	60,500	
Purchases Returns and Allowances	501.1		460
Purchases Discounts	501.2		575
Freight-In	502	175	
Wages Expense	511	25,000	
Advertising Expense	512	4,300	
Supplies Expense	524		
Telephone Expense	525	2,000	
Utilities Expense	533	6,900	
Insurance Expense	535		
Depr. Expense—Building	540		
Depr. Expense—Store Equipment	541		
Miscellaneous Expense	549	2,700	
Interest Expense	551	1,350	
		$245,880	$245,880

TJ also had the following subsidiary ledger balances as of December 1:

Accounts Receivable:

Customer	Accounts Receivable Balance
Martha Boyle 12 Jude Lane Hartford, CT 06117	$3,250
Anne Clark 52 Juniper Road Hartford, CT 06118	1,340
John Dempsey 700 Hobbes Dr. Avon, CT 06108	1,560
Kim Fields 5200 Hamilton Ave. Hartford, CT 06117	—
Lucy Greene 236 Bally Lane Simsbury, CT 06123	1,960
Heather Waters 447 Drury Lane West Hartford, CT 06107	490

Accounts Payable:

Vendor	Accounts Payable Balance
Evans Essentials 34 Harry Ave. East Hartford, CT 05234	$1,250
Nathen Co. 1009 Drake Rd. Farmington, CT 06082	3,000
Owen Enterprises 43 Lucky Lane Bristol, CT 06007	1,600
West Wholesalers 888 Anders Street Newington, CT 06789	1,000

At the end of the year, the following adjustments need to be made:

(a, b) Merchandise inventory as of December 31, $19,700.

(c)   Unused supplies on hand, $525.

(d)   Unexpired insurance on December 31, $1,000.

(e)   Depreciation expense on the building for the year, $800.

(f)   Depreciation expense on the store equipment for the year, $450.

(g)   Wages earned but not paid as of December 31, $330.

REQUIRED

1. If you are not using the working papers, open a general ledger, an accounts receivable ledger, and an accounts payable ledger as of December 1. Enter the December 1 balance of each of the accounts, with a check mark in the Post. Ref. Column.

2. Enter the transactions for the month of December in the proper journals. Post immediately to the accounts receivable and accounts payable ledgers.

3. Post from the journals to the general ledger. Post the journals in the following order: general, sales, purchases, cash receipts, and cash payments.

4. Prepare schedules of accounts receivable and accounts payable.

5. Prepare a year-end work sheet, an income statement, a statement of owner's equity, and a balance sheet. The mortgage payable includes $600 that is due within one year.

6. Journalize and post adjusting entries.

7. Journalize and post closing entries. (Hint: Close all expense and revenue account balances listed in the Income Statement columns of the work sheet. Then, close Income Summary and Tom Jones, Drawing to Tom Jones, Capital.)

8. Prepare a post-closing trial balance.

9. Journalize and post reversing entries for the adjustments where appropriate, as of January 2, 20-2.

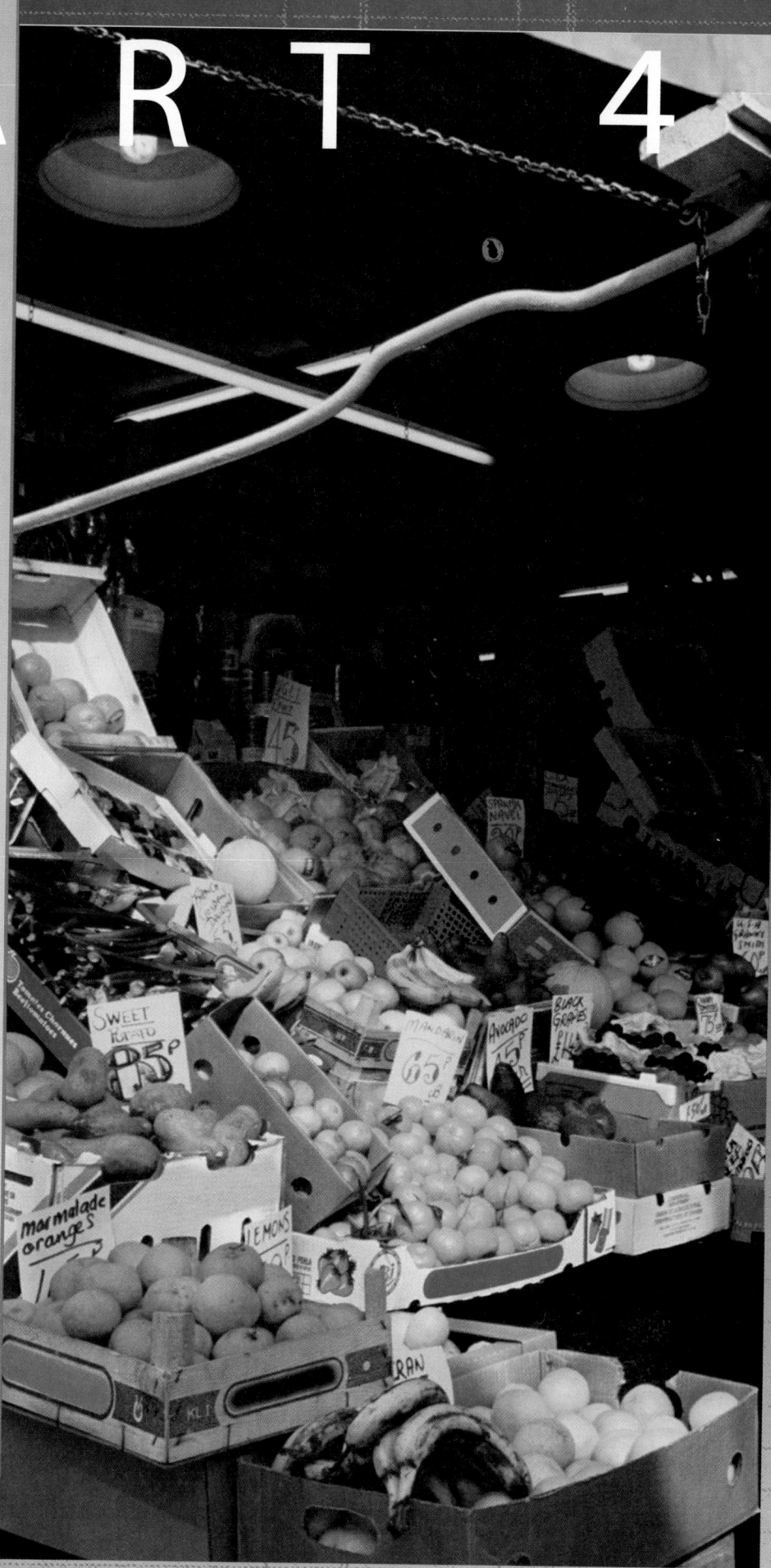

PART 4

Specialized Accounting Procedures for Merchandising Businesses and <u>Partnerships</u>

16

Accounting for Accounts Receivable

LEARNING OBJECTIVES:
Careful study of this chapter should enable you to:

LO 1 Apply the allowance method of accounting for uncollectible accounts.

LO 2 Estimate and write off uncollectible accounts using the percentage of sales method and the percentage of receivables method.

LO 3 Apply the direct write-off method of accounting for uncollectible accounts.

John Zenith's sports equipment and clothing business grew rapidly for several years. He opened a second store and is making sales on account. This has provided a further boost to his sales. When John makes these sales, he knows that some portion of the customers will not pay their accounts. John is puzzled as to how to account for this expense. The matching principle says expenses should be matched with the revenues they helped to produce. This implies he should write off some accounts receivable in the current period, so that the expenses are matched with the related sales. But he doesn't know which accounts will prove uncollectible. How can he write them off before he knows which ones they are? He could wait until he knows which ones are uncollectible, but this seems to violate the matching principle. What should John do?

Businesses generally are willing to sell goods and services on account. A major reason for doing so is to increase sales. Most of us simply tend to buy more if we can "charge it" rather than pay cash. In fact, one way a business can increase sales is to have easy credit policies and sell on account to virtually anyone. Unfortunately, some businesses and individuals who "charge it" then are unwilling or unable to "pay for it." Thus a cost to a business of selling goods and services on account is that some of the accounts receivable will be uncollectible or bad debts. The more willing a business is to make sales on account, the more uncollectible accounts it is likely to have.

There are two methods of accounting for uncollectible accounts: (1) the allowance method and (2) the direct write-off method. The purpose of this chapter is to learn how to use these methods.

ALLOWANCE METHOD

LO 1 Apply the allowance method of accounting for uncollectible accounts.

Bad debt expense is a loss from failure to collect an account receivable. The **allowance method** is a technique that attempts to recognize bad debt expense in the same period that the related credit sales are made. This method is consistent with the **matching principle**, which states that expenses should be matched with the revenues they helped to produce.

Under the accrual basis of accounting, the allowance method is generally required for financial reporting purposes. To use the allowance method, three steps are followed:

STEP 1   At the end of each accounting period, the amount of uncollectible accounts is estimated.

STEP 2   An adjusting entry is made to recognize the bad debt expense and reduce reported receivables for the amount of estimated uncollectible accounts. For example, if the estimated amount is $900, the entry is:

4			Bad Debt Expense			9 0 0 00			4
5			Allowance for Bad Debts				9 0 0 00		5
6									6

Note that the credit is not to Accounts Receivable. This is because at this time we do not know which specific customers will fail to pay. Instead, a contra-asset account, Allowance for Bad Debts (also known as Allowance for Uncollectible Accounts or Allowance for Doubtful Accounts), is credited. The balance of this account is deducted from Accounts Receivable on the balance sheet. The remaining amount is known as the **net receivables** or **net realizable value** of accounts receivable because it is the amount the business expects to collect. Accounts receivable of $30,000 with an allowance of $900 would appear as follows:

Current assets:
Accounts receivable $30,000
Less allowance for bad debts   900 $29,100

STEP 3   In a subsequent period, when a specific uncollectible account is identified, an entry is made to write off the account and reduce the balance in Allowance for

Bad Debts. For example, if the uncollectible account is $250, the entry is:

8		Allowance for Bad Debts				2	5	0	00									8
9		Accounts Receivable/Customer Name									2	5	0	00				9
10		Wrote off uncollectible account																10

 LEARNING KEY: In accounting for bad debts, Accounts Receivable is credited only when we can identify which customers are not going to pay.

ESTIMATING AND WRITING OFF UNCOLLECTIBLES

LO 2 Estimate and write off uncollectible accounts using the percentage of sales method and the percentage of receivables method.

To use the allowance method, we need a way to estimate the amount of uncollectibles. Two basic methods are used: the percentage of sales method and the percentage of receivables method. A company chooses one method or the other and uses it consistently over time.

Percentage of Sales Method

> *If a business is new and has no prior credit experience, industry averages or percentages for similar companies may be used for making estimates in initial years of operation.*

The **percentage of sales method** is based on the relationship between the amount of credit sales and the amount of uncollectible accounts. Assume that during 20-1 and 20-2, Chris Co. had total credit sales of $200,000 and that $2,000 of those credit sales had become uncollectible. Based on this experience, Chris could estimate its uncollectible accounts at 1% of credit sales.

$$\frac{\text{Uncollectible Accounts}}{\text{Credit Sales}} = \frac{\$2,000}{\$200,000} = 1\%$$

If during 20-3 Chris had credit sales of $120,000, the estimate of uncollectible accounts would be made as follows:

Credit sales	$120,000
Estimated % uncollectible	× 1%
Estimated uncollectible accounts	$ 1,200

Thus, the following adjusting entry would be made on December 31, 20-3:

4		Bad Debt Expense				1	2	0	0	00								4
5		Allowance for Bad Debts									1	2	0	0	00			5
6																		6

In T account form, Allowance for Bad Debts would appear as follows:

Allowance for Bad Debts

	20-3
	12/31 1,200

Assume that during 20-4, uncollectible accounts totaling $1,100 were written off as follows:

8		Allowance for Bad Debts		1	1	0	0	00							8
9		Accounts Receivable/Customer Names								1	1	0	0	00	9
10		Wrote off uncollectible accounts													10

After posting this entry, Allowance for Bad Debts would have a credit balance of $100.

Allowance for Bad Debts

				20-3		
				12/31		1,200
20-4		1,100				
				20-4	Bal.	100

Assume that during 20-4, Chris had credit sales of $130,000. Based on experience, Chris would still estimate its uncollectible accounts at 1% of credit sales. This would yield estimated uncollectible accounts of $1,300 (1% × $130,000), and the following adjusting entry would be made on December 31, 20-4:

4		Bad Debt Expense		1	3	0	0	00							4
5		Allowance for Bad Debts								1	3	0	0	00	5
6															6

This would increase the Allowance for Bad Debts balance to $1,400.

Allowance for Bad Debts

				20-3		
				12/31		1,200
20-4		1,100				
				20-4	Bal.	100
				12/31	Adj.	1,300
				12/31	Bal.	1,400

This demonstrates an important feature of the percentage of sales method. Allowance for Bad Debts may have a debit or credit balance prior to adjustment. This is a normal result of underestimating or overestimating uncollectible accounts. Under the percentage of sales method, any balance in Allowance for Bad Debts prior to adjustment is generally *ignored* in making the current period's adjusting entry.

LEARNING KEY: Percentage of Sales Method: When making the adjusting entry, ignore any balance in Allowance for Bad Debts.

This is because the percentage of sales method focuses on the *current year's* credit sales. Any previous balance in the allowance account relates to credit sales and uncollectible accounts from *prior years*. In the above illustration, the balance was a credit of $100. This balance could have been a credit of $300 or a debit of $200, and it would not have mattered. The adjusting entry for uncollectible accounts would have been the same—$1,300.

There is one exception to ignoring the balance in Allowance for Bad Debts in making the adjustment. When a large debit or credit balance accumulates in the allowance account, the percentage of credit sales used to estimate uncollectible accounts should be increased or decreased. This provides a better estimate based on recent experience.

Percentage of Receivables Method

The **percentage of receivables method** is based on the relationship between the amount of accounts receivable and the amount of uncollectible accounts. The simplest form of this method involves computing uncollectible accounts as a percentage of the Accounts Receivable balance. Assume that Craft Co. had an average Accounts Receivable balance at the end of the past two years of $110,000. If a total of $4,400 of these accounts had become uncollectible, Craft would estimate its percentage of uncollectible accounts as follows:

$$\frac{\text{Uncollectible Accounts}}{\text{Average Accounts Receivable}} = \frac{\$4,400}{\$110,000} = 4\%$$

Assume that the Accounts Receivable balance at the end of the current year was $120,000. The estimate of uncollectible accounts would be made as follows:

Accounts receivable	$120,000
Estimated % uncollectible	× 4%
Estimated uncollectible accounts	$ 4,800

Assuming Allowance for Bad Debts has a zero balance prior to adjustment, the following adjusting entry would be made at year end:

4		Bad Debt Expense			4 8 0 0 00			4
5		Allowance for Bad Debts				4 8 0 0 00		5
6								6

Although the above approach is simple, the estimate of uncollectible accounts is not very precise. Therefore, the percentage of receivables method usually is applied in a way that yields a better estimate. Instead of using the total accounts receivable in making the estimate, each customer's balance is analyzed to determine how long it has been outstanding. The probability that a customer's account will not be collected usually increases with the length of time the account has been outstanding. Because of the emphasis on the length of time the accounts have been outstanding, this process is called **aging the receivables**.

An aging schedule similar to the one in Figure 16-1 is often used to analyze the receivables and estimate the uncollectible amount. The following steps are used in preparing the aging schedule:

STEP 1 Categorize each account receivable according to the length of time the amounts have been outstanding.

STEP 2 Multiply the amount of receivables in each category by an estimate of the percent that will be uncollectible. This percentage is based on past experience and increases as the number of days past due increases.

STEP 3 Total the estimates for each category to determine the amount that is not expected to be collected.

FIGURE 16-1 Aging Schedule

CUSTOMER	TOTAL	NOT YET DUE	1–30	31–60	61–90	91–180	181–365	OVER 365
					NUMBER OF DAYS PAST DUE			
W. Billiard	$ 3,000.00	$ 2,500.00	$ 500.00					
K. Campbell	950.00			$ 650.00		$ 300.00		
J. Farley	4,325.00	3,800.00			$ 525.00			
L. Gilbert	1,900.00	1,500.00		400.00				
E. Rome	3,950.00	3,170.00					$ 780.00	
B. Zimmerman	200.00					200.00		
Total	$100,500.00	$65,000.00	$18,000.00	$8,250.00	$6,310.00	$1,810.00	$ 780.00	$ 3,500.00
Estimated percent uncollectible		2 %	5 %	10 %	20 %	30 %	50 %	80 %
Total est. uncollectible accounts	$ 5,500.00	$ 1,300.00	$ 900.00	$ 825.00	$1,262.00	$ 543.00	$ 390.00	$ 280.00
	($ 5,500.00	= 1,300.00	+ 900.00	+ 825.00	+ 1,262.00	+ 543.00	+ 390.00	+ 280.00)

AGING SCHEDULE OF ACCOUNTS RECEIVABLE — December 31, 20-1

Based on the aging schedule in Figure 16-1, uncollectible accounts would be estimated as $5,500. Thus, the following adjusting entry would be made at December 31, 20-1:

4		Bad Debt Expense	5,500.00		4
5		Allowance for Bad Debts		5,500.00	5
6					6

In T account form, Allowance for Bad Debts would appear as follows:

Allowance for Bad Debts

	20-1
	12/31 Adj. 5,500

Assume that during 20-2, uncollectible accounts totaling $5,200 were written off as follows:

8		Allowance for Bad Debts	5,200.00		8
9		Accounts Receivable/Customer Names		5,200.00	9
10		Wrote off uncollectible accounts			10

Allowance for Bad Debts now would have a credit balance of $300.

Allowance for Bad Debts

	20-1
	12/31 Adj. 5,500
20-2 5,200	
	20-2 Bal. 300

Assume that at the end of 20-2 another aging schedule like the one in Figure 16-1 is prepared, and that the estimated uncollectible amount is $5,700. To bring the credit balance in the allowance account to $5,700, an adjustment of $5,400 is needed.

Estimated uncollectible amount	$5,700
Current credit balance in account	– 300
Adjustment needed	$5,400

Thus the following adjusting entry would be made on December 31, 20-2:

4		Bad Debt Expense		5 4 0 0 00			4
5		Allowance for Bad Debts			5 4 0 0 00		5
6							6

This would increase the Allowance for Bad Debts balance to $5,700.

Allowance for Bad Debts

			20-1		
			12/31	Adj.	5,500
20-2		5,200			
			20-2	Bal.	300
			12/31	Adj.	5,400
			12/31	Bal.	5,700

This demonstrates an important feature of the percentage of receivables method. Allowance for Bad Debts may have a debit or credit balance prior to adjustment. Under the percentage of receivables method, this balance must be considered in making the current period's adjusting entry.

> **LEARNING KEY:** Percentage of receivables method: Unlike the percentage of sales method, consider the balance in Allowance for Bad Debts prior to adjustment when making the current period's adjusting entry.

This is because the percentage of receivables method focuses on the Accounts Receivable balance at the end of the year. That balance contains receivables from the current year and any remaining from prior years. The total Accounts Receivable balance consisting of current and prior year receivables is analyzed to determine the proper allowance account balance. The adjusting entry is then made to achieve that balance in the allowance account. In the above illustration, the balance was a credit of $300. Therefore, the adjustment to bring the balance to $5,700 was $5,400 ($5,700 – $300). If the balance prior to adjustment had been a debit of $100, the necessary adjusting entry would have been $5,800:

Estimated uncollectible amount	$5,700
Current debit balance in account	+ 100
Adjustment needed	$5,800

Notice that the resulting credit balance in Allowance for Bad Debts after adjustment would once again be $5,700:

Allowance for Bad Debts

20-2	Bal.	100	20-2		
			12/31	Adj.	5,800
			12/31	Bal.	5,700

Comparison of Methods

Let's summarize the differences between the percentage of sales and percentage of receivables methods of estimating uncollectibles. Figure 16-2 identifies the key features of the two methods.

FIGURE 16-2 Key Features of Allowance Methods

	FEATURE	PERCENTAGE OF SALES	PERCENTAGE OF RECEIVABLES
1	Basis for estimate	% of credit sales	Aging (%) of accounts receivable
2	Amount of year-end adjustment	Amount calculated in 1	Amount calculated in 1 **Plus** debit balance in allowance account before adjustment or **Minus** credit balance in allowance account before adjustment
3	Balance after adjustment	Amount calculated in 1 **Plus** credit balance in allowance account before adjustment or **Minus** debit balance in allowance account before adjustment	Amount calculated in 1

Write-off of Uncollectible Accounts

Recall that to write off a $250 uncollectible account, the following entry is made:

4		Allowance for Bad Debts		2 5 0 00		4
5		Accounts Receivable/Customer Name			2 5 0 00	5
6		Wrote off uncollectible account				6

This entry is the same under both the percentage of sales and percentage of receivables methods.

Note the effect of this entry on the income statement and balance sheet. No income statement accounts are used in the entry, so clearly there is no effect on the income statement. Not so obviously, the balance sheet is not affected either. Since Allowance for Bad Debts is a contra-asset and Accounts Receivable is an asset, the effects offset each other. Let's look more closely at this perhaps surprising situation.

LEARNING KEY: Under the allowance method, the write-off of an account as uncollectible does not affect either the income statement or the balance sheet.

A BROADER VIEW

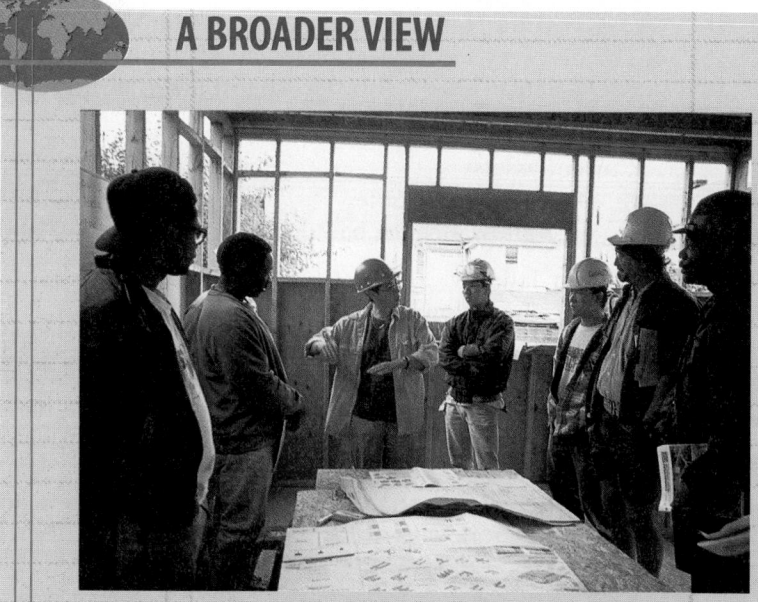

ACCOUNTS RECEIVABLE AND MANAGEMENT OF CASH FLOWS

It is important to be aware of the difference between sales on account and cash inflows, particularly in running a small business. Green Co., a construction contractor in Connecticut, learned this distinction the hard way.

During a period of rapid growth, Green bid successfully on several municipal contracts. This led to major increases in revenue. Unfortunately, accounts receivable also increased dramatically because municipalities tend to be slow in paying their bills, particularly on construction contracts. Thus, Green found itself facing payroll expenses and major bills from its suppliers that required prompt payment, but its cash was tied up in the accounts receivable.

Fortunately, with help from the Small Business Development Center, Green was able to obtain financing to make it through this "cash crunch." But it will long remember that accounts receivable are not the same as cash inflows.

Effect of Entry on the Income Statement. First, how can we write off an account as uncollectible and have no income statement effect? The answer lies in the adjusting entry we made at year end for the estimated uncollectibles. Assume the entry was for $900.

9		Bad Debt Expense		9	0	0	00						9
10			Allowance for Bad Debts						9	0	0	00	10
11													11

The expense was already recognized with this adjusting entry. It would be double counting to recognize the expense again when the specific account is written off.

Effect of Entry on the Balance Sheet. Second, why is the balance sheet not affected? The best way to answer is with an example. Assume that on December 31, 20-1, the balance sheet showed the following information concerning Accounts Receivable:

Current assets:

Accounts receivable	$100,500	
Less allowance for bad debts	5,500	$95,000

On January 15, 20-2, Bill McDonald's account for $500 is written off by making the following entry:

14	Jan.	15	Allowance for Bad Debts		5 0 0 00			14
15			Accounts Receivable/B. McDonald			5 0 0 00		15
16			Wrote off uncollectible account					16

If the balance sheet was prepared immediately after posting the above transaction, the following information would be reported for Accounts Receivable:

Current assets:

Accounts receivable	$100,000	
Less allowance for bad debts	5,000	$95,000

Note that both Accounts Receivable and Allowance for Bad Debts have been reduced by $500. Thus, the reported net receivables are not changed. The business expected to collect $95,000 before writing off McDonald's account and still expects to collect $95,000 after writing off his account. Management knew that there would be some uncollectible accounts. Now they know that McDonald is one of them.

Recovery of Accounts Previously Written Off—Allowance Method

Occasionally an account that was written off is collected. For example, assume that a check for $500 was received on February 1 from Bill McDonald, whose account was written off on January 15. This requires two entries:

1. Reinstate the account.

2. Record the collection.

To reinstate an account, simply reverse the entry made to write off the account, as follows:

5	Feb.	1	Accounts Receivable/B. McDonald		5 0 0 00			5
6			Allowance for Bad Debts			5 0 0 00		6
7			Reinstated account receivable					7

To record the collection, the following entry is made:

9	Feb.	1	Cash		5 0 0 00			9
10			Accounts Receivable/B. McDonald			5 0 0 00		10
11			Collection on account					11

It might be simpler to debit Cash and credit Allowance for Bad Debts. However, this shortcut should not be taken. Without the reinstatement, the subsidiary ledger will only report that McDonald's account was written off as uncollectible. With the reinstatement, the subsidiary ledger will reflect the fact that McDonald has paid his account. This information will be important to McDonald and the business should he desire credit in the future.

DIRECT WRITE-OFF METHOD

LO 3   Apply the direct write-off method of accounting for uncollectible accounts.

Under the **direct write-off method** the bad debt expense is not recognized until it has been determined that an account is uncollectible. For example, assume that on August 15, John Lafollette's account for $500 is judged to be uncollectible. The following entry would be made:

5	Aug.	15	Bad Debt Expense			5	0	0	00						5
6			Accounts Receivable/J. Lafollette							5	0	0	00		6
7			Wrote off uncollectible account												7

Advantage and Disadvantages of Direct Method

The direct write-off method has one advantage. It is very simple to apply. However, there are three disadvantages of using this method. First, efforts to collect the account often extend over many months. Thus, the revenue from the sale might be recognized in one period and the bad debt expense recognized in another. This violates the matching principle.

Second, the amount of bad debt expense recognized in a given period can be manipulated by management. This occurs because there is no general rule for deciding when an account becomes uncollectible. Thus, management can use its subjective judgment in deciding when to recognize bad debt expense.

Third, the amount of accounts receivable reported on the balance sheet does not represent the amount of cash actually expected to be collected. Thus the assets are overstated by the amount of uncollectible accounts included in accounts receivable. For these reasons, the direct write-off method is generally not acceptable for financial reporting purposes. It is acceptable only if the amount of uncollectible accounts cannot be reasonably estimated or if the estimated amount is very small. This method is required, however, for income tax purposes.

Recovery of Accounts Previously Written Off—Direct Write-off Method

Occasionally an account that was written off is collected. The proper entries for the recovery depend on the period in which the cash is collected.

Write-off and Recovery in Same Accounting Period. Assume the write-off and recovery are made in the same accounting period. In this case, first reinstate the account by reversing the entry for the write-off. Then record the collection in the usual manner as shown below.

To write off account:

5	Aug.	15	Bad Debt Expense			5	0	0	00							5
6			Accounts Receivable/J. Lafollette								5	0	0	00	6
7			Wrote off uncollectible account												7

To reinstate account:

35	Jan.	20	Accounts Receivable/J. Lafollette			5	0	0	00							35
36			~~Uncollectible Accounts Recovered~~ *Bad debt exp.*								5	0	0	00	36
37			Reinstated account receivable												37

To record collection:

39	Jan.	20	Cash			5	0	0	00							39
40			Accounts Receivable/J. Lafollette								5	0	0	00	40
41			Collection on account												41

Write-off and Recovery in Different Accounting Periods. Now assume that the write-off is made in one period and the recovery in the following accounting period. In this case, first reinstate the account by debiting Accounts Receivable and crediting Uncollectible Accounts Recovered. This account is credited instead of Bad Debt Expense because a credit to the expense account would understate bad debt expense for the current year. Uncollectible Accounts Recovered is reported on the income statement as other revenue. The entries for the write-off and recovery are shown below.

To write off account:

5	Aug.	15	Bad Debt Expense			5	0	0	00							5
6			Accounts Receivable/J. Lafollette								5	0	0	00	6
7			Wrote off uncollectible account												7

To reinstate account:

35	Jan.	20	Accounts Receivable/J. Lafollette			5	0	0	00							35
36			Uncollectible Accounts Recovered								5	0	0	00	36
37			Reinstated account receivable												37

To record collection:

39	Jan.	20	Cash			5	0	0	00							39
40			Accounts Receivable/J. Lafollette								5	0	0	00	40
41			Collection on account												41

Learning Objectives	Key Points to Remember
1 Apply the allowance method of accounting for uncollectible accounts.	To use the allowance method, apply three steps: STEP 1 At the end of the period, estimate the uncollectible amount. STEP 2 Make the following adjusting entry:

4		Bad Debt Expense			x	x	x	xx							4
5		Allowance for Bad Debts								x	x	x	xx		5

STEP 3   When an uncollectible account is identified, make the following entry:

8		Allowance for Bad Debts			x	x	x	xx							8
9		Accounts Receivable/Customer Name								x	x	x	xx		9
10		Wrote off uncollectible account													10

2 Estimate and write off uncollectible accounts using the percentage of sales method and the percentage of receivables method.	The *percentage of sales method* is based on the relationship between the amount of credit sales and the amount of uncollectible accounts. Any balance in Allowance for Bad Debts prior to adjustment is ignored in making the current period's adjusting entry. The *percentage of receivables method* is based on the relationship between the amount of accounts receivable and the amount of uncollectible accounts. The estimate of uncollectibles is usually based on an aging of receivables. Any balance in Allowance for Bad Debts prior to adjustment is considered in making the current period's adjusting entry. Under the allowance method, the actual write-off of an uncollectible account does not affect either the income statement or the balance sheet. When an account is collected that has been written off, the account is reinstated and then the collection is recorded.
3 Apply the direct write-off method of accounting for uncollectible accounts.	Under the direct write-off method, bad debt expense is not recognized until an account is written off as uncollectible. The entries for collection of an account previously written off depend on when the collection occurs. If the collection is in the same period as the write-off, the credit is to Bad Debt Expense. If the collection is in the following period, the credit is to Uncollectible Accounts Recovered.

Reflection: Answering the Opening Questions

Until John has experience to provide a basis for estimating the percentage of his credit sales that will be uncollectible, he might want to use the direct write-off method. This method is not consistent with the matching principle, but it would be acceptable for John's situation. Alternatively, John could seek advice from owners of similar businesses. They might be able to share their experience with uncollectible accounts.

As soon as John is able to make a reasonable estimate of his uncollectible accounts, he should adopt the allowance method of accounting for uncollectible accounts. He could use either the percentage of sales or the percentage of receivables method.

KEY TERMS

aging the receivables, (595)   The process of estimating the uncollectible amount by analyzing account balances according to the length of time the accounts have been outstanding.

allowance method, (592)   A technique that attempts to recognize bad debt expense in the same period that the related credit sales are made.

bad debt expense, (592)   A loss from failure to collect an account receivable.

direct write-off method, (601)   A method in which the bad debt expense is not recognized until it has been determined that an account is uncollectible.

matching principle, (592)   A concept that requires expenses to be matched with the revenues they helped to produce.

net realizable value, (592)   The amount a business expects to collect from its accounts receivable; calculated as Accounts Receivable less Allowance for Bad Debts. Also called net receivables.

net receivables, (592)   See net realizable value.

percentage of receivables method, (595)   A method in which the current year's uncollectible accounts are estimated based on the relationship between the amount of accounts receivable and the amount of uncollectible accounts in prior years.

percentage of sales method, (593)   A method in which the current year's uncollectible accounts are estimated based on the relationship between the amount of credit sales and the amount of uncollectible accounts in prior years.

DEMONSTRATION PROBLEM

Budke and Budke, a landscaping service, uses the allowance method to record the following transactions related to accounts receivable. Adjusting and closing entries also completed during the current year ended December 31, 20--, are described below.

Mar. 6   Received 50% of the $12,000 balance owed by Columbia Gardens, a bankrupt business, and wrote off the remainder as uncollectible.

June 12   Reinstated the account of Ramon Burgos, which had been written off in the previous year, and received $2,250 cash in full settlement.

Sept. 19   Wrote off the $13,800 balance owed by Kelly Richeson, who has no assets.

Nov. 9   Reinstated the account of Jackie Kwas, which had been written off in the preceding year, and received $2,175 cash in full settlement.

Dec. 27   Wrote off the following accounts as uncollectible, in compound entry form: Blair & Smith, $10,480; Landscapes Unlimited, $8,570; Beekman Brothers, $22,500; B. J. McKay, $9,300.

31   Based on an aging analysis of $1,460,000 of accounts receivable, it was estimated that $73,500 will be uncollectible. Made the adjusting entry.

31   Made the entry to close the appropriate account to Income Summary.

Selected accounts and beginning balances on January 1, 20--, are as follows:

122.1	Allowance for Bad Debts	$95,000 credit
313	Income Summary	—
532	Bad Debt Expense	—

REQUIRED   1.   Open the three selected accounts.

2.   Enter the transactions and the adjusting and closing entries described above in general journal form (page 12 for the first 2 entries; page 13 for all others). After each entry, post to the three accounts named.

3.   Determine the net realizable value as of December 31, 20--.

Solution

1, 2.

GENERAL LEDGER

ACCOUNT: Allowance for Bad Debts   ACCOUNT NO. 122.1

DATE		ITEM	POST REF.	DEBIT	CREDIT	BALANCE DEBIT	BALANCE CREDIT
20-- Jan.	1	Balance	✓				95 0 0 0 00
Mar.	6		J12	6 0 0 0 00			89 0 0 0 00
June	12		J13		2 2 5 0 00		91 2 5 0 00
Sept.	19		J13	13 8 0 0 00			77 4 5 0 00
Nov.	9		J13		2 1 7 5 00		79 6 2 5 00
Dec.	27		J13	50 8 5 0 00			28 7 7 5 00
	31		J13		44 7 2 5 00		73 5 0 0 00

ACCOUNT: Income Summary   ACCOUNT NO. 313

DATE		ITEM	POST REF.	DEBIT	CREDIT	BALANCE DEBIT	BALANCE CREDIT
20-- Dec.	31		J13	44 7 2 5 00		44 7 2 5 00	

ACCOUNT: Bad Debt Expense   ACCOUNT NO. 532

DATE		ITEM	POST REF.	DEBIT	CREDIT	BALANCE DEBIT	BALANCE CREDIT
20-- Dec.	31		J13	44 7 2 5 00		44 7 2 5 00	
	31		J13		44 7 2 5 00	—	

GENERAL JOURNAL   PAGE 12

	DATE		DESCRIPTION	POST REF.	DEBIT	CREDIT	
1	20-- Mar.	6	Cash		6 0 0 0 00		1
2			Accounts Receivable/Columbia Gardens			6 0 0 0 00	2
3			Collection on account				3
4							4
5		6	Allowance for Bad Debts	122.1	6 0 0 0 00		5
6			Accounts Receivable/Columbia Gardens			6 0 0 0 00	6
7			Wrote off uncollectible account				7
8							8

	DATE		DESCRIPTION	POST REF.	DEBIT	CREDIT	
			GENERAL JOURNAL			PAGE 13	
1	20-- June	12	Accounts Receivable/R. Burgos		2 2 5 0 00		1
2			Allowance for Bad Debts	122.1		2 2 5 0 00	2
3			Reinstated account receivable				3
4							4
5		12	Cash		2 2 5 0 00		5
6			Accounts Receivable/R. Burgos			2 2 5 0 00	6
7			Collection on account				7
8							8
9	Sept.	19	Allowance for Bad Debts	122.1	13 8 0 0 00		9
10			Accounts Receivable/K. Richeson			13 8 0 0 00	10
11			Wrote off uncollectible account				11
12							12
13	Nov.	9	Accounts Receivable/J. Kwas		2 1 7 5 00		13
14			Allowance for Bad Debts	122.1		2 1 7 5 00	14
15			Reinstated account receivable				15
16							16
17		9	Cash		2 1 7 5 00		17
18			Accounts Receivable/J. Kwas			2 1 7 5 00	18
19			Collection on account				19
20							20
21	Dec.	27	Allowance for Bad Debts	122.1	50 8 5 0 00		21
22			Accounts Receivable/Blair & Smith			10 4 8 0 00	22
23			Accounts Receivable/Landscapes Unl.			8 5 7 0 00	23
24			Accounts Receivable/Beekman Bros.			22 5 0 0 00	24
25			Accounts Receivable/B. J. McKay			9 3 0 0 00	25
26			Wrote off uncollectible accounts				26
27							27
28			Adjusting Entry				28
29		31	Bad Debt Expense	532	44 7 2 5 00		29
30			Allowance for Bad Debts	122.1		44 7 2 5 00	30
31							31
32			Closing Entry				32
33		31	Income Summary	313	44 7 2 5 00		33
34			Bad Debt Expense	532		44 7 2 5 00	34
35							35

3.

Accounts receivable, December 31, 20--	$1,460,000
Less allowance for bad debts	73,500
Net realizable value	$1,386,500

REVIEW QUESTIONS

1. What method of accounting for uncollectible accounts is generally required for financial reporting purposes?

2. Describe the steps to follow when using the allowance method to account for uncollectible accounts.

3. Explain how to compute net realizable value.

4. Describe the process followed when estimating uncollectible accounts under the percentage of sales method.

5. Describe the process followed when estimating uncollectible accounts under the percentage (aging) of receivables method.

6. How does the balance in Allowance for Bad Debts before adjustment affect the amount of the year-end adjustment under the percentage of sales method? under the percentage of receivables method?

7. Under the allowance method, what impact does the write-off of a customer's account have on the financial statements?

8. Under the allowance method, what journal entries are made if an account is collected that was previously written off?

9. Describe the accounting procedures when using the direct write-off method to account for uncollectible accounts.

10. What are three disadvantages of using the direct write-off method?

MANAGING YOUR WRITING

The heads of the marketing and finance areas at your business are arguing about tight versus easy credit policies. One feels the policy should be tightened and the other feels it should be eased. The division manager is concerned about which approach to use and asks for your advice. Prepare a memo to the division manager stating arguments for and against tight and easy credit policies. The manager will use this information to decide on which policy to establish.

ETHICS CASE

Preston Enterprises uses the direct write-off method of accounting for uncollectible accounts. On October 12 a very large account was written off. The amount was subsequently recovered on December 15. Ray Preston, the owner of the company, instructed the accountant to not make a journal entry for the recovery and to hold the check in his desk until after the first of the year "for tax purposes."

1. If you were the accountant, what would you think of Preston's request?

2. If the December 15 entry is not made, how will it affect Preston's current year financial statements?

3. Assume the amount of the charge-off and the subsequent recovery was $10,000. Prepare the proper journal entries for October 12 and December 15.

4. In groups of two or three, discuss the possible consequences for the accountant holding the check in his desk drawer for a couple of weeks.

WEB WORK

Although all businesses that give credit should expect some uncollectible accounts, there are ways to cut down on the number of such accounts. What strategies can businesses employ to minimize the number of accounts that become uncollectible? Inc. Magazine offers some suggestions at

http://www.inc.com/incmagazine/archives/18951062.html.

(http://heintz.swcollege.com)

SERIES A EXERCISES

EXERCISE 16A-1 (LO 1) CALCULATION OF NET REALIZABLE VALUE J. B. Bucks owns a department store that has a $45,000 balance in Accounts Receivable and a $3,000 credit balance in Allowance for Bad Debts.

1. Determine the net realizable value of the accounts receivable.

2. Assume that an account receivable in the amount of $400 was written off using the allowance method. Determine the net realizable value of the accounts receivable after the write-off.

EXERCISE 16A-2 (LO 2) UNCOLLECTIBLE ACCOUNTS—PERCENTAGE OF SALES Ryan's Express has total credit sales for the year of $180,000 and estimates that 3% of its credit sales will be uncollectible. Record the end-of-period adjusting entry on December 31, in general journal form, to enter the estimate for bad debt expense. Assume the following independent conditions existed prior to the adjustment:

1. Allowance for Bad Debts has a credit balance of $925.

2. Allowance for Bad Debts has a debit balance of $385.

EXERCISE 16A-3 (LO 2) UNCOLLECTIBLE ACCOUNTS—PERCENTAGE OF RECEIVABLES Tammie's Toyota Sales and Service estimates the amount of uncollectible accounts using the percentage of receivables method. After aging the accounts, it is estimated that $4,250 will not be collected. Record the end-of-period adjusting entry on December 31, in general journal form, to enter the estimate for bad debt expense. Assume the following independent conditions existed prior to the adjustment:

1. Allowance for Bad Debts has a credit balance of $690.

2. Allowance for bad Debts has a debit balance of $275.

EXERCISE 16A-4 (LO 2) UNCOLLECTIBLE ACCOUNTS—ALLOWANCE METHOD Julia Alvarez, owner of Alvarez Rentals, uses the allowance method in accounting for uncollectible accounts. Record the following transactions in general journal form.

July 7   Wrote off $5,350 owed by Randy Dalzell, who has no assets.

Aug. 12   Wrote off $2,870 owed by Jason Flint, who declared bankruptcy.

Sept. 27   Reinstated the account of Randy Dalzell, which had been written off on July 7, and received $5,350 cash in full settlement.

EXERCISE 16A-5 (LO 2) UNCOLLECTIBLE ACCOUNTS—PERCENTAGE OF SALES AND PERCENTAGE OF RECEIVABLES At the end of the current year, the accounts receivable account of Glenn's Nursery Supplies has a debit balance of $390,000. Credit sales are $2,800,000. Record the end-of-period adjusting entry on December 31, in general journal form, to enter the estimate for bad debt expense. Assume the following independent conditions existed prior to the adjustment:

1. Allowance for Bad Debts has a credit balance of $1,760.

   a. The percentage of sales method is used and bad debt expense is estimated to be 1% of credit sales.

   b. The percentage of receivables method is used and an analysis of the accounts produces an estimate of $30,330 in uncollectible accounts.

2. Allowance for Bad Debts has a debit balance of $1,900.

   a. The percentage of sales method is used and bad debt expense is estimated to be ¾ of 1% of credit sales.

   b. The percentage of receivables method is used and an analysis of the accounts produces an estimate of $29,890 in uncollectible accounts.

EXERCISE 16A-6 (LO 3) DIRECT WRITE-OFF METHOD Maria Rivera, owner of Rivera Pharmacy, uses the direct write-off method in accounting for uncollectible accounts. Record the following transactions in general journal form.

July 20   Wrote off $2,325 owed by Joe Balouka, who has no assets.

Oct. 15   Wrote off $1,675 owed by Alice Rose, who declared bankruptcy.

EXERCISE 16A-7 (LO 3) COLLECTION OF ACCOUNT WRITTEN OFF—DIRECT WRITE-OFF METHOD Como's Music Store uses the direct write-off method in accounting for uncollectible accounts. Record the following transactions in general journal form.

20-1

May 8   Wrote off $1,745 owed by Vickie Lawrence, who has no assets.

July 15   Wrote off $1,300 owed by Dan Utter, who declared bankruptcy.

Sept. 2   Reinstated the account of Vickie Lawrence, which had been written off on May 8, and received $1,745 cash in full settlement.

20-2

May 15   Reinstated the account of Dan Utter, which had been written off in the previous year, and received $1,300 cash in full settlement.

SERIES A PROBLEMS

PROBLEM 16A-1 (LO 1/2) UNCOLLECTIBLE ACCOUNTS—ALLOWANCE METHOD Emery Nurseries used the allowance method to record the following transactions, adjusting entries, and closing entries during the year ended December 31, 20--.

(continued)

Feb. 9   Received 60% of the $5,000 balance owed by Patty's Petunias, a bankrupt business, and wrote off the remainder as uncollectible.

May 28   Reinstated the account of Danielle Bell, which had been written off in the preceding year, and received $2,400 cash in full settlement.

Aug. 16   Wrote off the $8,200 balance owed by Rich Bouie as uncollectible.

Oct. 5   Reinstated the account of Bonnie McCelland, which had been written off in the preceding year, and received $3,600 cash in full settlement.

Dec. 28   Wrote off the following accounts as uncollectible, in compound entry form: Bloudeck & Rhodes, $14,450; Creative Landscapers, $16,100; Ramona Randol, $12,750.

31   Based on an aging analysis of the $980,000 of accounts receivable, it was estimated that $58,700 will be uncollectible. Made the adjusting entry.

31   Made the entry to close the appropriate account to Income Summary.

Selected accounts and beginning balances on January 1, 20--, are as follows:

122.1	Allowance for Bad Debts	$52,000 credit
313	Income Summary	—
532	Bad Debt Expense	—

REQUIRED

1. Open the three selected accounts.

2. Enter the transactions and the adjusting and closing entries described above in a general journal (page 6). After each entry, post to the three accounts named.

3. Determine the net realizable value as of December 31.

PROBLEM 16A-2 (LO 2) UNCOLLECTIBLE ACCOUNTS—PERCENTAGE OF SALES AND PERCENTAGE OF RECEIVABLES At the completion of the current fiscal year ending December 31, the balance of Accounts Receivable for Yang's Gift Shop was $30,000. Credit sales for the year were $355,200.

REQUIRED

Make the necessary adjusting entry in general journal form under each of the following assumptions. Show calculations for the amount of each adjustment and the resulting net realizable value.

1. Allowance for Bad Debts has a credit balance of $330.

   a. The percentage of sales method is used and bad debt expense is estimated to be 2.0% of credit sales.

   b. The percentage of receivables method is used and an analysis of the accounts produces an estimate of $6,950 in uncollectible accounts.

2. Allowance for Bad Debts has a debit balance of $400.

   a. The percentage of sales method is used and bad debt expense is estimated to be 1.5% of credit sales.

   b. The percentage of receivables method is used and an analysis of the accounts produces an estimate of $5,685 in uncollectible accounts.

PROBLEM 16A-3 (LO 2) AGING ACCOUNTS RECEIVABLE An analysis of the accounts receivable of Johnson Company as of December 31, 20--, reveals the following.

Age Interval	Balance	Estimated Percent Uncollectible
Not yet due	$65,000	2%
1–30 days past due	4,500	5
31–60 days past due	3,550	10
61–90 days past due	1,650	25
91–180 days past due	1,200	35
181–365 days past due	650	55
Over 365 days past due	400	85
Total	$76,950	

REQUIRED

1. Prepare an aging schedule as of December 31, 20--, by adding the following column to the three columns shown above: Estimated Amount Uncollectible.

2. Assuming that Allowance for Bad Debts had a credit balance of $620 before adjustment, record the end-of-period adjusting entry in general journal form to enter the estimate for the bad debt expense.

PROBLEM 16A-4 (LO 3) DIRECT WRITE-OFF METHOD Williams & Hendricks Distributors uses the direct write-off method in accounting for uncollectible accounts.

W & D

20-1

Feb. 18   Sold merchandise on account to Merry Merchants, $17,500.

Mar. 22   Sold merchandise on account to Utter Unicorns, $14,300.

June 3   Received $10,000 from Merry Merchants and wrote off the remainder owed on the sale of February 18 as uncollectible.

Sept. 9   Received $8,000 from Utter Unicorns and wrote off the remainder owed on the sale of March 22 as uncollectible.

Nov. 13   Reinstated the account of Merry Merchants, which had been written off on June 3, and received $7,500 cash in full settlement.

20-2

Jan. 17   Reinstated the account of Utter Unicorns, which had been written off on September 9 of the previous year, and received $6,300 cash in full settlement.

REQUIRED   Record the above transactions in general journal form.

SERIES B EXERCISES

EXERCISE 16B-1 (LO 1) CALCULATION OF NET REALIZABLE VALUE Mary Martin owns a department store that has a $65,200 balance in Accounts Receivable and a $5,175 credit balance in Allowance for Bad Debts.

1. Determine the net realizable value of the accounts receivable.

2. Assume that an account receivable in the amount of $900 was written off using the allowance method. Determine the net realizable value of the accounts receivable after the write-off.

EXERCISE 16B-2 (LO 2) UNCOLLECTIBLE ACCOUNTS—PERCENTAGE OF SALES
Nicole's Neckties has total credit sales for the year of $380,000 and estimates that 2% of its credit sales will be uncollectible. Record the end-of-period adjusting entry on December 31, in general journal form, to enter the estimate for bad debt expense. Assume the following independent conditions existed prior to the adjustment:

1. Allowance for Bad Debts has a credit balance of $430.

2. Allowance for Bad Debts has a debit balance of $295.

EXERCISE 16B-3 (LO 2) UNCOLLECTIBLE ACCOUNTS—PERCENTAGE OF RECEIVABLES Charlie's Chevy Sales and Service estimates the amount of uncollectible accounts using the percentage of receivables method. After aging the accounts, it is estimated that $3,935 will not be collected. Record the end-of-period adjusting entry on December 31, in general journal form, to enter the estimate for bad debt expense. Assume the following independent conditions existed prior to the adjustment:

1. Allowance for Bad Debts has a credit balance of $245.

2. Allowance for Bad Debts has a debit balance of $560.

EXERCISE 16B-4 (LO 2) UNCOLLECTIBLE ACCOUNTS—ALLOWANCE METHOD Raynette Ramos, owner of Ramos Rentals, uses the allowance method in accounting for uncollectible accounts. Record the following transactions in general journal form.

July 9   Wrote off $6,040 owed by Sue Sanchez, who has no assets.

Aug. 15   Wrote off $4,790 owed by Lonnie Jones, who declared bankruptcy.

Sept. 23 Reinstated the account of Sue Sanchez, which had been written off on July 9, and received $6,040 cash in full settlement.

EXERCISE 16B-5 (LO 2) UNCOLLECTIBLE ACCOUNTS—PERCENTAGE OF SALES AND PERCENTAGE OF RECEIVABLES At the end of the current year, the accounts receivable account of Parker's Nursery Supplies has a debit balance of $350,000. Credit sales are $2,300,000. Record the end-of-period adjusting entry on December 31, in general journal form, to enter the estimate for bad debt expense. Assume the following independent conditions existed prior to the adjustment:

1. Allowance for Bad Debts has a credit balance of $1,920.

   a. The percentage of sales method is used and bad debt expense is estimated to be 1% of credit sales.

   b. The percentage of receivables method is used and an analysis of the accounts produces an estimate of $24,560 in uncollectible accounts.

2. Allowance for Bad Debts has a debit balance of $1,280.

   a. The percentage of sales method is used and bad debt expense is estimated to be ¾ of 1% of credit sales.

   b. The percentage of receivables method is used and an analysis of the accounts produces an estimate of $22,440 in uncollectible accounts.

EXERCISE 16B-6 (LO 3) DIRECT WRITE-OFF METHOD Brent Mussellman, owner of Brent's Barbells, uses the direct write-off method in accounting for uncollectible accounts. Record the following transactions in general journal form.

July 19   Wrote off $1,935 owed by Arnold Swartz, who has no assets.

Oct. 12   Wrote off $2,125 owed by Janice Strong, who declared bankruptcy.

EXERCISE 16B-7 (LO 3) COLLECTION OF ACCOUNT WRITTEN OFF—DIRECT WRITE-OFF METHOD Madonna's Music Store uses the direct write-off method in accounting for uncollectible accounts. Record the following transactions in general journal form.

20-1

May 5   Wrote off $2,360 owed by Neal Dammond, who has no assets.

July 18   Wrote off $1,255 owed by Maxine Mouse, who declared bankruptcy.

Sept. 20   Reinstated the account of Neal Dammond, which had been written off on May 5, and received $2,360 cash in full settlement.

20-2

May 11   Reinstated the account of Maxine Mouse, which had been written off in the previous year, and received $1,255 cash in full settlement.

SERIES B PROBLEMS

PROBLEM 16B-1 (LO 1/2) UNCOLLECTIBLE ACCOUNTS—ALLOWANCE METHOD Lewis Warehouse used the allowance method to record the following transactions, adjusting entries, and closing entries during the year ended December 31, 20--.

Feb. 7   Received 70% of the $8,000 balance owed by Luxury Sofas, a bankrupt business, and wrote off the remainder as uncollectible.

May 26   Reinstated the account of Sandy Johnson, which had been written off in the preceding year, and received $3,725 cash in full settlement.

Aug. 15   Wrote off the $9,350 balance owed by Izumi Goto as uncollectible.

Oct. 6   Reinstated the account of Doreen Woods, which had been written off in the preceding year, and received $4,320 cash in full settlement.

Dec. 29   Wrote off the following accounts as uncollectible, in compound entry form: Schmidt & Yeager, $13,945; Economy Homes, $15,830; Davis Industries, $11,865.

31   Based on an aging analysis of the $1,175,000 of accounts receivable, it was estimated that $67,150 will be uncollectible. Made the adjusting entry.

31   Made the entry to close the appropriate account to Income Summary.

Selected accounts and beginning balances on January 1, 20--, are as follows:

122.1	Allowance for Bad Debts	$49,850 credit
313	Income Summary	—
532	Bad Debt Expense	—

(continued)

1.   Open the three selected accounts.

2.   Enter the transactions and the adjusting and closing entries described above in a general journal (page 6). After each entry, post to the three accounts named.

3.   Determine the net realizable value as of December 31, 20--.

PROBLEM 16B-2 (LO 2) UNCOLLECTIBLE ACCOUNTS—PERCENTAGE OF SALES AND PERCENTAGE OF RECEIVABLES At the completion of the current fiscal year ending December 31, the balance of Accounts Receivable for Anderson's Greeting Cards was $180,000. Credit sales for the year were $1,950,000.

Make the necessary adjusting entry in general journal form under each of the following assumptions. Show calculations for the amount of each adjustment and the resulting net realizable value.

1.   Allowance for Bad Debts has a credit balance of $2,600.

a.   The percentage of sales method is used and bad debt expense is estimated to be 1.5% of credit sales.

b.   The percentage of receivables method is used and an analysis of the accounts produces an estimate of $30,250 in uncollectible accounts.

2.   Allowance for Bad Debts has a debit balance of $1,900.

a.   The percentage of sales method is used and bad debt expense is estimated to be 1.0% of credit sales.

b.   The percentage of receivables method is used and an analysis of the accounts produces an estimate of $20,500 in uncollectible accounts.

PROBLEM 16B-3 (LO 2) AGING ACCOUNTS RECEIVABLE An analysis of the accounts receivable of Matsushita Company as of December 31, 20--, reveals the following.

Age Interval	Balance	Estimated Percent Uncollectible
Not yet due	$250,000	1.5%
1–30 days past due	17,000	4
31–60 days past due	12,800	9
61–90 days past due	8,200	20
91–180 days past due	4,600	30
181–365 days past due	4,200	45
over 365 days past due	1,400	75
Total	$298,200	

1.   Prepare an aging schedule as of December 31, 20--, by adding the following column to the three columns shown above: Estimated Amount Uncollectible.

2.   Assuming that Allowance for Bad Debts had a credit balance of $1,750 before adjustment, record the end-of-period adjusting entry in general journal form to enter the estimate for the bad debt expense.

PROBLEM 16B-4 (LO 3) DIRECT WRITE-OFF METHOD Lee and Chen Distributors uses the direct write-off method in accounting for uncollectible accounts.

20-1

Feb. 16   Sold merchandise on account to Biggs and Daughters, $16,000.

Mar. 23   Sold merchandise on account to Lloyd Place, $12,800.

June 8   Received $12,000 from Biggs and Daughters and wrote off the remainder owed on the sale of February 16 as uncollectible.

Sept. 27   Received $7,000 from Lloyd Place and wrote off the remainder owed on the sale of March 23 as uncollectible.

Nov. 18   Reinstated the account of Biggs and Daughters, which had been written off on June 8, and received $4,000 cash in full settlement.

20-2

Jan. 11   Reinstated the account of Lloyd Place, which had been written off on September 27 of the previous year, and received $5,800 cash in full settlement.

REQUIRED   Record the above transactions in general journal form.

MASTERY PROBLEM

Sam and Robert are identical twins. They opened identical businesses and experienced identical transactions. However, they decided to estimate uncollectible accounts in different ways. Sam elected to use the percentage of sales method and Robert elected to use the percentage of receivables method. Listed below are the summary transactions and other relevant information for both businesses for 20--. Remember, both businesses experienced the same events: credit sales, collections of receivables, and write-offs. The only difference between the businesses is the method of estimating uncollectible accounts.

	Sam	**Robert**
(a) Balance of Cash, January 1, 20--	$300,000	$300,000
(b) Balance of Accounts Receivable, January 1	50,000	50,000
(c) Balance of Allowance for Bad Debts, January 1	5,000	5,000
(d) Sales on account during 20--	550,000	550,000
(e) Collections on account during 20--	530,000	530,000
(f) Uncollectible accounts written off during 20--	4,500	4,500
(g) Collections made on accounts written off during 20--	500	500

REQUIRED   1. Enter items (a) through (c) in two sets of general ledger accounts: one for Sam and one for Robert.

2. Prepare entries in a general journal (page 4) for summary transactions (d) through (g) for Sam.

3. Post the entries to a general ledger for Sam, using the following accounts and numbers:

(continued)

Cash	101
Accounts Receivable	122
Allowance for Bad Debts	122.1
Sales	401
Bad Debt Expense	532

4. Sam estimates that 1% of all sales on account will be uncollectible. Calculate the estimated bad debt expense and make the appropriate adjusting entry in a general journal. Post the entry to the general ledger accounts on December 31, 20--.

5. Compute the net realizable value of Sam's accounts receivable on December 31, 20--.

6. Prepare entries in a general journal (page 4) for summary transactions (d) through (g) for Robert.

7. Post the entries to a general ledger for Robert, using the same accounts and numbers as were used for Sam.

8. Robert bases the estimate of uncollectible accounts on an aging schedule of accounts receivable. Using the following information, compute the estimated uncollectible amounts and make the appropriate adjusting entry in a general journal. Post the entry to the general ledger accounts on December 31, 20--.

Customers	Invoice Dates and Amounts for Unpaid Invoices					
Beets, D.	10/7	$2,300	11/15	$1,200	12/18	$8,500
Cook, L.	6/1	1,200	8/15	2,500		
Hylton, D.	9/23	4,300	10/22	2,500	12/23	2,800
Martin, D.	10/15	5,400	11/12	3,200	12/15	1,500
Stokes, D.	9/9	200	12/15	9,500		
Taylor, T.	11/20	400	12/10	1,400		
Thomas, O.	12/2	5,500				
Tower, R.	12/15	2,300				
Williams, G.	11/18	2,800	12/8	8,000		

All sales are billed n/30. The following aging chart is used to estimate the uncollectibles using the percentage of receivables method.

Age Interval	Estimated Percent Uncollectible
Not yet due	2%
1–30 days	5
31–60 days	10
61–90 days	25
91–120 days	50
Over 120 days	80

9. Calculate the net realizable value for Robert on December 31, 20--.

Self-Study Test Questions

True/False

1. There are two methods of accounting for uncollectible accounts: the allowance method and the direct write-off method. _____ *T*

2. The matching principle states that debits should be matched with credits. _____ *F*

3. Using the percentage of sales method, the balance in Allowance for Bad Debts must be taken into consideration before making the adjusting entry. _____ *F* *is ignored*

4. When an account is written off under the allowance method, there should be a debit to Bad Debt Expense. _____ *F* *debit to a allow. debit bad. debit*

5. Each time an account is written off under the direct write-off method, Bad Debt Expense is debited. _____ *T*

Multiple Choice

1. The dollar difference between Accounts Receivable and Allowance for Bad Debts is called _____ *d*

   (a) book value.
   (b) interest value.
   (c) carrying value.
   (d) net realizable value.

2. A business has an ending balance in Accounts Receivable of $35,000; credit sales for the year of $300,000; and a credit balance in Allowance for Bad Debts of $800. If the percentage of sales method is used and the percentage is estimated at 1% of credit sales, what is the amount to be entered for the adjusting entry? _____ *a*

   (a) $3,000
   (b) $3,800
   (c) $2,200
   (d) $1,150

3. A business has an ending balance in Accounts Receivable of $35,000; credit sales for the year of $300,000; and a credit balance in Allowance for Bad Debts of $800. If the percentage of sales method is used and the percentage is estimated at 1% of credit sales, what is the ending balance in Allowance for Bad Debts *after* the adjusting entry? _____ *b*

   (a) $3,000
   (b) $3,800
   (c) $2,200
   (d) $1,150

4. A business has an ending balance in Accounts Receivable of $40,000; credit sales for the year of $500,000; and a debit balance in Allowance for Bad Debts of $300. If an aging analysis indicates that $4,800 should be the balance in Allowance for Bad Debts, the amount to be entered for the adjusting entry is   *d*

   (a) $4,800.
   (b) $4,500.
   (c) $5,000.
   (d) $5,100.

5. Under the allowance method, when an account is determined to be worthless, the journal entry to write off the account will include a _____ *a*

   (a) debit to Allowance for Bad Debts.
   (b) debit to Bad Debt Expense.
   (c) credit to Allowance for Bad Debts.
   (d) debit to Accounts Receivable.

The answers to the Self-Study Test Questions are at the end of the text.

17

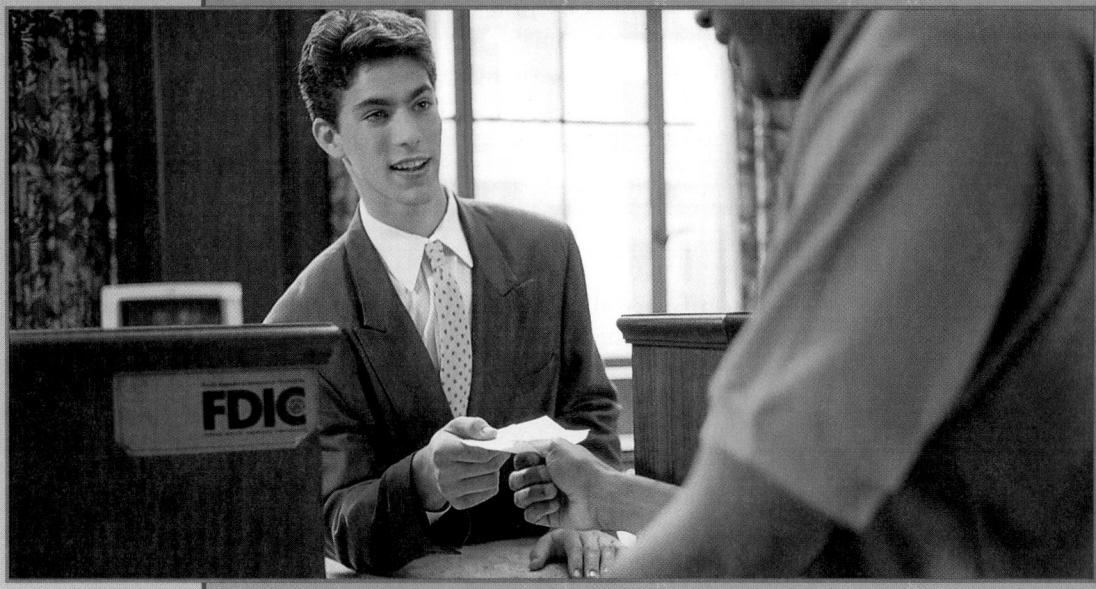

Accounting for Notes and Interest

LEARNING OBJECTIVES:
Careful study of this chapter should enable you to:

LO 1 Describe a promissory note.

LO 2 Calculate interest on and determine the due date of promissory notes.

LO 3 Account for notes receivable transactions and accrued interest.

LO 4 Account for notes payable transactions and accrued interest.

John Zenith recently arranged to borrow $3,000 at the bank so he could add new counters and shelving in one of his stores. The term of the loan was 12 months and the interest rate was set at 9%. At the closing meeting on the loan, John signed a note for $3,000 but was given only $2,730. The loan officer explained that the bank had "deducted the interest of $270 in advance." Is the bank trying to cheat John? What interest rate is John really paying to borrow the $2,730 (rather than the $3,000 he had wanted)?

In Chapter 16, we learned how to account for accounts receivable. Recall that an account receivable is an unwritten promise by a customer to pay for goods or services. In this chapter, we will learn how to account for a more formal, written type of receivable called a promissory note.

After completing our study of notes receivable, we will learn to account for notes payable. You will see that a note payable is very similar to a note receivable. Both are promissory notes. We simply look at the note from two different points of view. A note receivable is someone's promise to pay you. A note payable is your promise to pay someone else.

THE PROMISSORY NOTE

LO 1 Describe a promissory note.

A **promissory note** (usually called a note) is a written promise to pay a specific sum at a definite future date. The note must be signed by the person or business agreeing to make the payment, known as the **maker** of the note. The note must be payable to a specific person or business, known as the **payee**.

Notes are often used when credit is extended for 60 days or more, or when large amounts of money are involved. Figure 17-1 shows one form of promissory note. Paul DeBruke, the maker of the note, promises to pay a specific amount of money ($1,500) at a definite future time (90 days after June 9). Sarah Morney, the payee of the note, is to receive the specified amount of money. Notice that to DeBruke it is a note payable while to Morney it is a note receivable.

FIGURE 17-1 Promissory Note

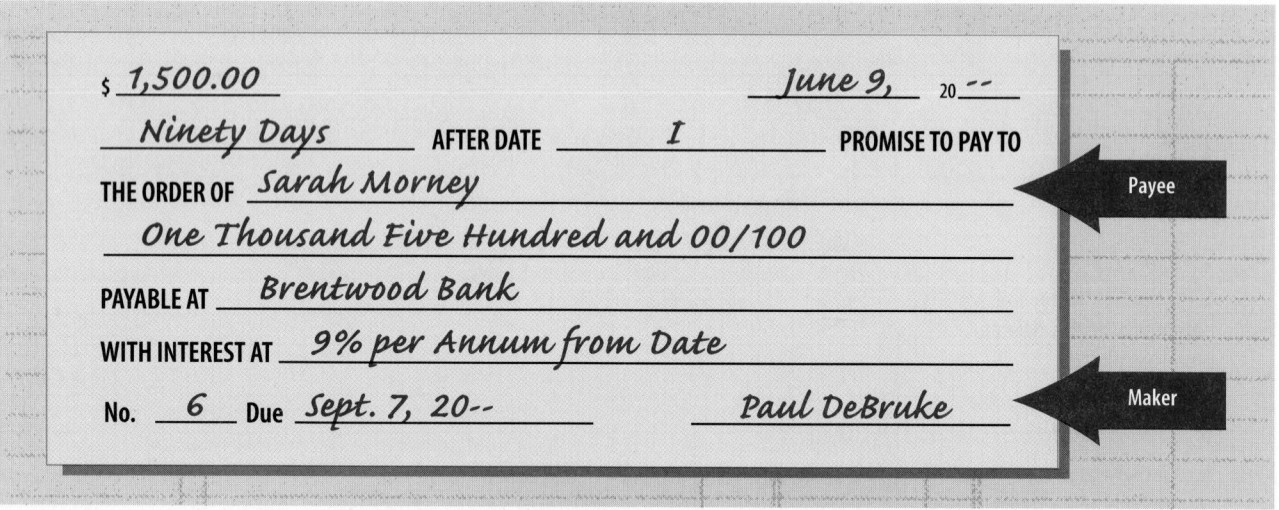

Notes may be interest bearing or non-interest bearing. An **interest-bearing note** is one with an explicit interest rate stated on the face of the note. The note in Figure 17-1 is a 9% interest-bearing note. A **non-interest-bearing note** is one on which no rate of interest is specified, although the note does include an interest component. Notes signed when borrowing from a bank often are of this type. This type of transaction is illustrated later in the chapter.

CALCULATING INTEREST AND DETERMINING DUE DATE

LO 2   Calculate interest on and determine the due date of promissory notes.

To calculate interest on notes, three factors are used:

1. Principal of the note

2. Rate of interest

3. Term of the note

The **principal of the note** is the face amount of the note that the maker promises to pay at maturity. The principal is the base on which the interest is calculated. The principal of the note in Figure 17-1 is $1,500.

The **rate of interest** usually is expressed as a percentage, such as 8% or 10%. Ordinarily an annual rate is used, but in some cases a monthly rate is quoted, such as 1½% a month. A rate of 1½% a month is equivalent to a rate of 18% a year payable monthly (1½% × 12 = 18%). The rate of interest on the note in Figure 17-1 is 9% per year.

The **term of the note** is the months or days from the date of issue to the date of maturity. The term of the note is used to calculate **time**, which is the term of the note stated as a fraction of a year. When the term of the note is specified in months, time is calculated on the basis of months. For example, a 3-month note issued on June 1 is payable on September 1, and time is calculated as follows:

Time
3 mos./12 mos. = 3/12 = ¼ year

When the term of a note is specified in days or when the due date is specified in a note, time is computed using the exact number of days from the date of the note to the date of its maturity. In making this computation, the maturity date is counted but the date of issue is not. For example, for a $1,000, 9% note dated March 1, with a due date of June 1, time is computed as follows:

Days in March	31	
Deduct date of note, March 1	1	
Days remaining in March		30
Add: Days in April		30
Days in May		31
Maturity date, June 1		1
Total time in days		92

Time = 92/360

 LEARNING KEY: To compute the time of a note, count the maturity date; do *not* count the date of issue.

Notice the use of 360 in the denominator in the above calculation. In computing interest, it is common to use 360 days as a year. Most banks and business firms follow this practice, though some banks and all federal government agencies use 365 days as the base in computing daily interest.

The due date of the note in Figure 17-1 is September 7. The term of the note is ninety days, calculated as follows:

Days in June	30	
Deduct date of note, June 9	9	
Days remaining in June		21
Add: Days in July		31
Days in August		31
Maturity date, September 7		7
Total time in days		90

Calculating Interest

The principal, interest rate, and time of the note are used in the following formula to calculate interest:

$$\text{Interest} = \text{Principal} \times \text{Rate} \times \text{Time}$$

LEARNING KEY: $I = P \times R \times T$
I = amount of *interest*
P = amount of *principal*
R = *rate* of interest (annual)
T = *time*

For the $1,000, 9% note described on page 621, interest is calculated as follows:

$$
\begin{aligned}
I &= P &\times& R &\times& T \\
&= \$1{,}000 &\times& .09 &\times& 92/360 \\
&= \underline{\underline{\$23}}
\end{aligned}
$$

For a $2,000, 8% note due in 3 months, interest is calculated as follows:

$$
\begin{aligned}
I &= P &\times& R &\times& T \\
&= \$2{,}000 &\times& .08 &\times& 3/12 \\
&= \underline{\underline{\$40}}
\end{aligned}
$$

For the note in Figure 17-1, interest is calculated as follows:

$$
\begin{aligned}
I &= P &\times& R &\times& T \\
&= \$1{,}500 &\times& .09 &\times& 90/360 \\
&= \underline{\underline{\$33.75}}
\end{aligned}
$$

The principal of the note plus interest equals the **maturity value** of the note. For example, the maturity value of the $1,000 note above is $1,023. Similarly, the maturity value of the $2,000 note is $2,040. Figure 17-2 uses a time line to illustrate the gradual accumulation of interest on the $1,000 note to its $1,023 maturity value.

FIGURE 17-2 Accumulation of Interest Time Line

DATE OF NOTE		DUE DATE
March 1		June 1
Time = 92 Days (92/360)		
	Amount of Interest $23	
Principal $1,000		Maturity Value $1,023

The examples throughout the chapter are for notes of 90 days and less. Notes can be for much longer periods of time—2 to 5 years is common with auto loans.

Determining the Due Date

As explained above, the period of time between the date of issue and the maturity date of a note may be stated in either months or days. If the term of the note is stated in months, the due date is determined by counting the number of months from the date the note was issued. The note is due on the date in the month of maturity that corresponds with the date the note was issued. For example, a three-month note dated August 10 would be due November 10. If there is no date in the month of maturity corresponding to the issue date, the due date is the last day of the month. For example, a three-month note dated January 31 would be due April 30.

If the term of the note is stated in days, the due date is the specified number of days after the issue date. To determine the due date, apply these three steps:

STEP 1   Subtract the date on which the note was issued from the number of days in the month of issuance.

STEP 2   Add to the result of STEP 1 the number of days in as many months as possible without exceeding the time of the note.

STEP 3   Subtract the result of STEP 2 from the time of the note. The result is the date of the month the note is due.

To calculate the due date of the note in Figure 17-1, a 90-day note dated June 9, apply the three steps as follows:

STEP 1
Days in June	30
Less date of note: June	9
Result of STEP 1	**21**

STEP 2
Result of STEP 1	21
Plus days in July	31
Plus days in August	31
Result of STEP 2	**83**

STEP 3   Time of note   90 days
Less result of STEP 2   83
Due date: September 7

ACCOUNTING FOR NOTES RECEIVABLE TRANSACTIONS

LO 3   Account for notes receivable transactions and accrued interest.

Businesses other than banks and savings and loans generally encounter six types of transactions involving notes receivable:

1. Note received from a customer to extend time for payment of an account

2. Note collected at maturity

3. Note renewed at maturity

4. Note discounted before maturity

5. Note dishonored

6. Collection of dishonored note

Note Received from a Customer to Extend Time for Payment

When a customer's account is due, the customer may issue a note for all or part of the amount. A business may be willing to accept the note for two reasons. First, the note is a formal, written promise to pay. This note can be converted to cash at a bank if necessary. Second, the note is likely to bear interest.

Assume that Michael Putter owes Linesch Hardware Co. $2,000 on account. To settle the account, Putter gives Linesch a 90-day, 10% note dated June 8. This transaction is entered by Linesch as follows:

15	June	8	Notes Receivable		2 0 0 0 00			15
16			Accounts Receivable/M. Putter			2 0 0 0 00		16
17			Received note to settle account					17

If instead, Putter gives a check for $250 and a note for $1,750 to settle the account, Linesch makes the following entry:

15	June	8	Cash		2 5 0 00			15
16			Notes Receivable		1 7 5 0 00			16
17			Accounts Receivable/M. Putter			2 0 0 0 00		17
18			Received cash and note to settle account					18

Note Collected at Maturity

When a note receivable matures, it may be collected:

1. By the payee,

2. By the bank named in the note (in Figure 17-1, Brentwood Bank), or

3. By a bank where it was left for collection.

Assume that on September 6, Putter pays Linesch the $2,000 principal plus $50 interest on the note described above. Linesch makes the following entry:

31	Sept.	6	Cash		2 0 5 0 00			31
32			Notes Receivable			2 0 0 0 00		32
33			Interest Revenue			5 0 00		33
34			Received payment of note with interest					34

When a bank makes the collection, it notifies the payee that the net amount has been added to the payee's account. The bank uses a **credit advice** like the one in Figure 17-3 for this purpose.

FIGURE 17-3 Credit Advice

ADVICE OF CREDIT

Planet Bank
Bonne Terre, Missouri

TO Linesch Hardware Co.

Account No. 315   30959   September 6 20 --

WE CREDIT YOUR ACCOUNT BALANCE AS FOLLOWS:

Michael Putter's Note $2,000.00

Interest for 90 Days at 10%   50.00

                                   $2,050.00

Less Collection Charge   10.00 $ $2,040.00

OFFSETTING DR.   Approved R. Shaw

Assume that Linesch left Putter's 90-day, 10% note for $2,000 at Planet Bank for collection. On September 6, the bank notifies Linesch that the note plus $50 interest have been collected. The bank fee for collecting the note was $10. Linesch enters this transaction as follows:

37	Sept.	6	Cash		2 0 4 0 00			37
38			Collection Expense		1 0 00			38
39			Notes Receivable			2 0 0 0 00		39
40			Interest Revenue			5 0 00		40
41			Received payment of note with interest					41
42			less collection fee					42

Note Renewed at Maturity

If the maker of a note is unable to pay the amount due at maturity, the payee may allow the maker to renew all or part of the note. Assume that at maturity of the $2,000 note, Putter pays only the $50 interest and gives a new 60-day, 10% note. Linesch enters this transaction as follows:

31	Sept.	6	Cash			5	0	00					31
32			Notes Receivable (new note)	2	0	0	0	00					32
33			Notes Receivable (old note)						2	0	0	0	00	33
34			Interest Revenue								5	0	00	34
35			Received new note plus interest on old note											35

If Putter pays $50 interest plus $500 on the principal and gives a new 90-day, 11% note for $1,500, Linesch makes the following entry:

31	Sept.	6	Cash			5	5	0	00					31
32			Notes Receivable (new note)	1	5	0	0	00					32
33			Notes Receivable (old note)						2	0	0	0	00	33
34			Interest Revenue								5	0	00	34
35			Received new note plus partial payment											35
36			and interest on old note											36

Note Discounted Before Maturity

> One of the reasons a business might prefer a promissory note from a customer is that the business can obtain cash by discounting the note at the bank.

If a business needs cash before the due date of a note, it can endorse the note and transfer it to a bank. This process is called **discounting a note receivable**. The bank charges an interest fee called a **bank discount** for the time between the date of discounting and the due date of the note. The difference between the maturity value of the note and the bank discount is called the **proceeds**. This is the amount of cash received by the business discounting the note.

> Maturity Value – Discount = Proceeds

Assume that the $2,000, 10%, 90-day note receivable from Putter dated June 8 is discounted by Linesch at the bank on July 8 at a rate of 12%. To calculate the discount and proceeds, apply the following four steps:

STEP 1   Compute the maturity value of the note.

| Face | + | Interest | = | **Maturity Value** |
| $2,000 | + | $50 | = | $2,050 |

STEP 2   Compute the number of days in the discount period—from the discount date to the due date.

Discount date	July 8	
Days in July		31
Less discount date	July	8
Remaining days in July		23
Plus days in August		31
Plus due date	September	6
Days in **discount period**		60

STEP 3   Compute the discount amount.

| Maturity Value* | × | Discount Rate | × | Discount Period | = | **Discount Amount** |
| $2,050 | × | 12% | × | 60/360 | = | $41 |

*Note that in calculating the discount amount, the *maturity value* of the note is used, not the principal.

STEP 4   Compute the proceeds.

Maturity Value	–	Discount Amount	=	**Proceeds**
$2,050	–	$41	=	$2,009

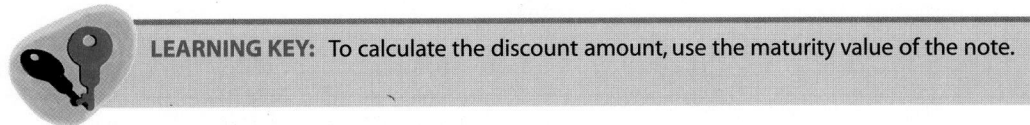

LEARNING KEY: To calculate the discount amount, use the maturity value of the note.

Figure 17-4 shows a time line illustration of this transaction.

FIGURE 17-4 Discounted Note Receivable Time Line

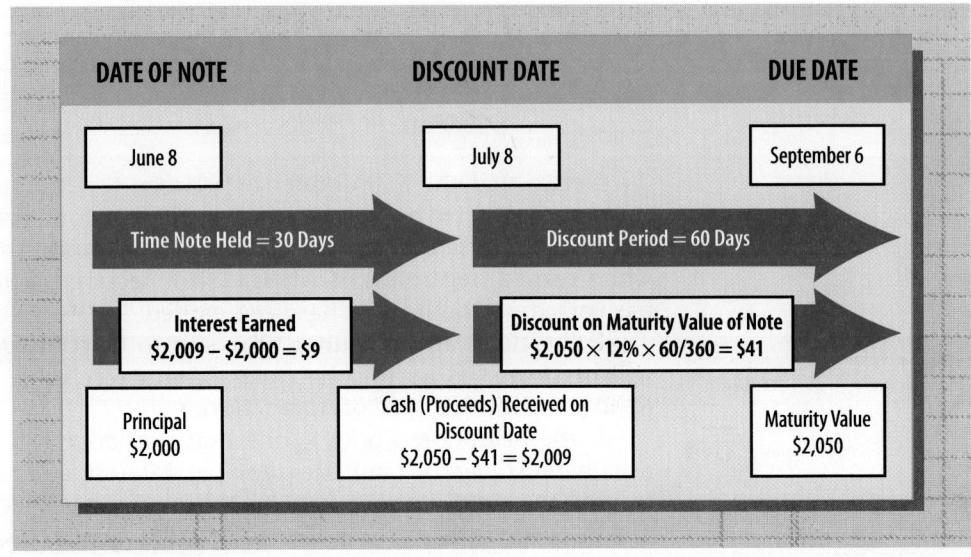

The excess of the $2,009 proceeds over the $2,000 face value of the note represents interest revenue of $9. Linesch enters this transaction as follows:

26	July	8	Cash			2	0	0	9	00							26
27			Notes Receivable									2	0	0	0	00	27
28			Interest Revenue												9	00	28
29			Discounted note receivable														29

If the proceeds from discounting a note are less than the face value of the note, the difference represents interest expense. For example, if the proceeds from discounting Putter's $2,000 note were only $1,992, Linesch would make the following entry:

26	July	8	Cash			1	9	9	2	00							26
27			Interest Expense						8	00							27
28			Notes Receivable									2	0	0	0	00	28
29			Discounted note receivable														29

When a note receivable is discounted, the business that endorses the note becomes potentially liable to the bank. If the maker of the note does not pay it at maturity, the business that discounted the note must pay the maturity value and any bank fees to the bank. This kind of potential liability that may become a real liability, depending on future events, is called a **contingent liability**. A contingent liability does not affect the accounting records. It is disclosed in the notes to the financial statements.

Note Dishonored

If the maker of a note does not pay or renew it at maturity, the note is said to be **dishonored**. The maker of the note is still liable to the payee for the principal amount plus interest. But a dishonored note loses its legal status as a note receivable. Therefore, the payee transfers the amount due from Notes Receivable to Accounts Receivable. For example, if the $2,000, 10%, 90-day note from Putter is dishonored, Linesch makes the following entry:

16	Sept.	6	Accounts Receivable/M. Putter			2 0 5 0 00			16
17			Notes Receivable				2 0 0 0 00		17
18			Interest Revenue				5 0 00		18
19			Note receivable dishonored						19

Notice that the $50 difference between the maturity value and principal of the note is credited to Interest Revenue. This is done even though the amount has not been collected. Recall that under accrual accounting, revenue is recognized when earned, regardless of when cash is received. The time period of the note has passed, so the interest has been earned.

If the claim against Putter turns out to be completely worthless, the $2,050 will be treated as an uncollectible account receivable. Chapter 16 showed how to account for this type of transaction.

If the dishonored note is one that was discounted at a bank, the endorser usually must pay the bank the principal, interest, and any bank fees. The endorser records the total amount paid to the bank as an account receivable from the maker of the note. Assume that the $2,000 note receivable discounted on July 8 for proceeds of $2,009 was dishonored by Putter at maturity. The bank bills Linesch for the $2,000 principal of the note, $50 interest, and a $10 bank fee, a total of $2,060. Linesch pays the bank and makes the following journal entry:

23	Sept.	6	Accounts Receivable/M. Putter			2 0 6 0 00			23
24			Cash				2 0 6 0 00		24
25			Paid bank for dishonored note						25

Note that the $10 bank fee is included in the amount receivable from Putter. This is because the fee was incurred as a result of Putter's dishonoring of the note, and this is not Linesch's expense.

Collection of Dishonored Note

What if a note that has been dishonored eventually is collected? When that occurs, the payee records collection of the account receivable. In addition, interest usually is charged for the period from the due date of the original note to the final collection date. Interest is based on the maturity value of the note plus the bank fee, if any, incurred when the note was dishonored. Let's go back to Putter's $2,000 note that Linesch held until maturity when it was dishonored and transferred to Accounts Receivable on September 6. Assume that on October 16,

Putter pays the original maturity value of the note ($2,050) and interest for the period from September 6 to October 16. Interest would be computed as follows:

Original Maturity Value	×	Rate	×	Time		
$2,050	×	10%	×	40*/360	=	$22.78

*	Days in September				30		
	Less original maturity date of note				6		
	Days remaining in September				24		
	Plus due date in October				16		
	Total days				40		

Linesch would make the following journal entry:

Recall that $50 interest revenue on the $2,000 note was already recorded on September 6 when the note was dishonored.

16	Oct.	16	Cash		2 0 7 2 78			16
17			Accounts Receivable			2 0 5 0 00		17
18			Interest Revenue			2 2 78		18
19			Collected dishonored note with interest					19

Notes Receivable Register

When a business receives many notes, it may keep a **notes receivable register**. This is a detailed auxiliary record of notes receivable. Figure 17-5 shows an abbreviated version of a notes receivable register. A more complete register might also include the number of each note and where the note is payable. The information contained in the register is obtained directly from the notes.

FIGURE 17-5 Notes Receivable Register

NOTES RECEIVABLE REGISTER												PAGE 1
DATE RECEIVED	MAKER	TIME	DUE DATE	AMOUNT	INTEREST		DISCOUNTED		DATE COLLECTED		REMARKS	
					RATE	AMOUNT	BANK	DATE				
20-- Apr. 4	L. Peters	60 day	June 3	4 0 0 00	8%	5 33			June 3			
21	J. Slaw	60 day	June 20	6 0 0 00	9%	9 00			June 20	Renewal for $500		
May 2	S. Alpart	30 day	June 1	7 0 0 00	9%	5 25			June 1	Sent for collection 5/30		
19	L. Shein	90 day	Aug. 17	8 0 0 00	9%	1 8 00						
June 20	J. Slaw	60 day	Aug. 19	5 0 0 00	9%	7 50				Renewal of 4/21 note		

Accrued Interest Receivable

Under accrual accounting, revenue is recognized when it is earned. For notes receivable, interest literally is earned day by day. It would be impractical, however, to record the interest revenue each day. Instead, for notes that are received and due within a single accounting period, no entry is made for interest revenue until the note is due.

For notes that are received in one period and due in the following period, however, accrued interest must be recorded at the end of the period. **Accrued interest on notes receivable** is interest revenue that has been earned but not yet received. The amount of accrued interest can be computed from the notes themselves or from the notes receivable register. The notes receivable register in Figure 17-5 can be used as an example. At June 30, the end of this company's fiscal year, two notes are outstanding. Accrued interest on these notes is calculated as follows:

Principal	Date of Issue	Rate of Interest	Days from Issue Date to June 30	Accrued Interest June 30
$800.00	May 19	9%	42	$8.40
500.00	June 20	9%	10	1.25
Total accrued interest on notes receivable				$9.65

The following adjusting entry is made on June 30 for the accrued interest:

16	June	30	Accrued Interest Receivable				9	65				16
17			Interest Revenue						9	65		17
18			Interest accrued on notes receivable									18

Accrued interest receivable is reported as a current asset on the balance sheet. Interest revenue is reported as other revenue on the income statement.

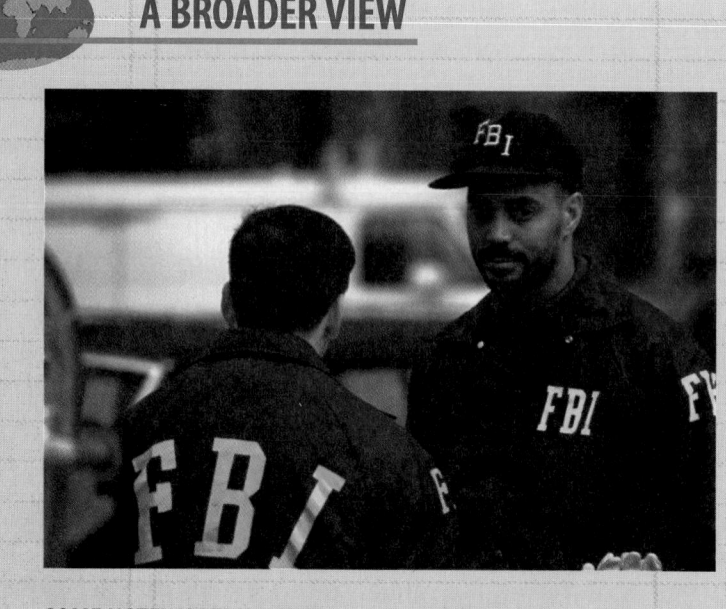

A BROADER VIEW

SOME NOTEWORTHY NOTES

A former branch manager of a bank in Bridgeport, Connecticut, pleaded guilty to defrauding the bank of $142,000 over a three-year period. The manager had approved ten loans to one customer, using notes with varying maturities. Based on these notes, the manager issued checks, money orders, credits, and cash to herself and the customer. The customer's accounts were credited for loan payments never received by the bank. The bogus loan activity was discovered as part of an FBI crackdown on fraud in the banking industry.

ACCOUNTING FOR NOTES PAYABLE TRANSACTIONS

LO 4   Account for notes payable transactions and accrued interest.

Businesses generally encounter four types of transactions involving notes payable:

1.   Note issued to a supplier to extend time for payment of an account

2.   Note issued as security for cash loan

3.   Note paid at maturity

4.   Note renewed at maturity

Note Issued to a Supplier to Extend Time for Payment

When a firm's account with a supplier is due, the supplier may be willing to accept a note for all or part of the amount due. Assume that Linesch Hardware Co. owes Bella & Co. $700 on June 11. If Linesch issues Bella a 90-day, 10% note for $700, Linesch makes the following entry:

26	June	11	Accounts Payable/Bella & Co.			7	0	0	00						26
27			Notes Payable								7	0	0	00	27
28			Issued note to settle account												28

If instead, Linesch gives Bella a check for $200 and a 90-day, 10% note for $500, the entry by Linesch is:

26	June	11	Accounts Payable/Bella & Co.			7	0	0	00						26
27			Cash								2	0	0	00	27
28			Notes Payable								5	0	0	00	28
29			Made partial payment and issued note												29
30			to settle account												30

Note Issued as Security for Cash Loan

Businesses sometimes have brief periods during which receipts from customers are not adequate to finance operations. During such periods, businesses commonly borrow money from banks on short-term notes.

Interest-bearing Notes. Assume that on June 16, Linesch borrows $6,000 from the Planet Bank on a 60-day, 10½% note. This transaction is entered as follows:

38	June	16	Cash			6	0	0	0	00						38
39			Notes Payable									6	0	0	0	00	39
40			Issued note for bank loan														40

Non-interest-bearing Notes. When making a loan, banks often deduct interest in advance, using a procedure known as **discounting**. The nature of this transaction and the procedures for handling it are very similar to those for discounting notes receivable (see pages 626–628). To illustrate, suppose that Linesch borrowed $6,000 on a 60-day, non-interest-bearing note that the bank discounted at 10½%. No interest rate is stated on the face of a non-interest-bearing note, but clearly there is an interest component. In this case, it is the 10½% discount rate. The bank calculates the **bank discount** at 10½% and deducts this amount from the $6,000 face of the note. The amount of the discount and the proceeds to Linesch are calculated using three steps:

STEP 1   Compute the maturity value of the note.

Face	+	Interest	=	**Maturity Value**
$6,000	+	0	=	$6,000

STEP 2   Compute the discount amount.

Maturity Value*	×	Discount Rate	×	Discount Period	=	**Discount Amount**
$6,000	×	10½%	×	60/360	=	$105

* Note that in calculating the discount amount, the *maturity value* of the note is used.

STEP 3   Compute the proceeds.

Maturity Value	–	Discount Amount	=	**Proceeds**
$6,000	–	$105	=	$5,895

 LEARNING KEY: To calculate the discount amount, use the maturity value of the note.

Figure 17-6 shows a time line illustration of this transaction.

FIGURE 17-6 Discounted Note Payable Time Line

Linesch records receipt of the $5,895 proceeds ($6,000 – $105) from the loan as follows:

14	June	16	Cash				5	8	9	5	00						14
15			Discount on Notes Payable				1	0	5	00							15
16			Notes Payable									6	0	0	0	00	16
17			Issued note for bank loan														17

The $105 debit to Discount on Notes Payable is an offset to the $6,000 note payable. Linesch's liability at this time is only $5,895, which is the net amount or **proceeds** received from the bank. Discount on Notes Payable is a contra-liability account. As shown in Figure 17-7, it is reported as a deduction from Notes Payable on the balance sheet.

FIGURE 17-7 Notes Payable and Related Discount on the Balance Sheet

Current liabilities:										
Notes payable	$6	0	0	0	00					
Less: discount on notes payable		1	0	5	00	$5	8	9	5	00

Stated Versus Effective Interest Rate. The stated rate of interest was 10½% on both the interest bearing and discounted notes. Notice, however, that the real interest rates on the two notes are not the same. With the interest-bearing note, Linesch obtained $6,000 for 60 days at a cost of $105—exactly 10½%.

$$\$105 \div \$6,000 = 1.75\% \text{ for 60 days}$$
$$\underline{\times \ 6} \quad (360 \div 60)$$
$$= 10.5\% \text{ for 360 days}$$

With the discounted note, Linesch paid $105 for the use of only $5,895 for 60 days—a rate of nearly 10.7%. This rate is known as the **effective rate** of interest.

$$\$105 \div \$5,895 = 1.781\% \text{ for 60 days}$$
$$\underline{\times \ 6} \quad (360 \div 60)$$
$$= 10.686\% \text{ for 360 days}$$

Note Paid at Maturity

The proper entry to make when a note is paid at maturity depends on whether the note is interest bearing or non-interest bearing. For an interest-bearing note, the same entry is made for payment to a supplier or to a bank. For example, let's reconsider Linesch's $6,000, 60-day, 10½% note due August 15. When the note is paid on August 15, Linesch will make the following entry:

21	Aug.	15	Notes Payable		6	0	0	0	00							21
22			Interest Expense			1	0	5	00							22
23			Cash								6	1	0	5	00	23
24			Paid note with interest at maturity													24

For a non-interest-bearing note from a bank, the entry to record the payment of the note is different. This is because Discount on Notes Payable was debited when the money was borrowed. For example, recall Linesch's $6,000, 60-day, non-interest-bearing note discounted by the bank at 10½%. When the money was borrowed, the following entry was made:

14	June	16	Cash		5	8	9	5	00							14
15			Discount on Notes Payable			1	0	5	00							15
16			Notes Payable								6	0	0	0	00	16
17			Issued note for bank loan													17

The $105 discount gradually becomes interest expense. This expense is recognized when the $6,000 principal amount of the note is repaid on August 15, the due date. Linesch will enter the payment of the note at maturity as follows:

22	Aug.	15	Notes Payable		6	0	0	0	00					22
23			Interest Expense			1	0	5	00					23
24			Cash							6	0	0	0	00	24
25			Discount on Notes Payable								1	0	5	00	25
26			Paid note at maturity												26

Note Renewed at Maturity

The payee of a note may allow the maker to renew all or a part of the note at maturity. For example, let's reconsider the $6,000 interest-bearing note that Linesch issued to Planet Bank on June 16. Assume that on August 15 Linesch pays $105 interest and $1,000 on the principal of this note and gives a new 60-day, 10½% note for $5,000. Linesch enters this transaction as follows:

27	Aug.	15	Notes Payable (old note)		6	0	0	0	00					27
28			Interest Expense			1	0	5	00					28
29			Cash							1	1	0	5	00	29
30			Notes Payable (new note)							5	0	0	0	00	30
31			Paid interest and part of principal on												31
32			old note and issued new note												32

Notes Payable Register

When a business issues many notes, it may keep a **notes payable register**. This is a detailed auxiliary record of notes payable. An abbreviated version of a notes payable register is shown in Figure 17-8. A more complete register might also include the number of each note and where the note is payable. The information contained in the register is obtained directly from the notes.

FIGURE 17-8 Notes Payable Register

NOTES PAYABLE REGISTER													PAGE 1
DATE ISSUED		PAYEE	TIME	DUE DATE		AMOUNT	INTEREST				DATE PAID		REMARKS
							RATE	AMOUNT					
20—Apr.	14	L. Knoop	60 days	June	13	2 0 0 0 00	9%		3 0 00	June	13	Settled 2/14 invoice	
May	13	Apex Bank	90 days	Aug.	11	8 0 0 0 00	10%	2 0 0 00					
June	2	S. Bront	30 days	July	2	1 5 0 0 00	11%		1 3 75			Settled 4/2 invoice	

Accrued Interest Payable

As with notes receivable, it also is necessary to record accrued interest on notes payable at the end of the period. For notes payable issued in one period and due in the following period, accrued interest payable must be recorded. **Accrued interest on notes payable** is interest expense that has been incurred but not paid.

The amount of accrued interest can be computed from the notes themselves or from the notes payable register.

The proper entry for accrued interest on notes payable depends on whether the note is interest-bearing or non-interest-bearing. Assume that a $900, 60-day, 10% note was issued on May 31. On June 30, this company's fiscal year end, an adjusting entry for accrued interest of $7.50 ($900 × 10% × 30/360) is recorded as follows:

19	June	30	Interest Expense				7	50							19
20			Accrued Interest Payable								7	50		20
21			Interest accrued on note payable											21

Assume instead that the $900, 60-day note was non-interest-bearing and discounted at the bank at 10%. When the money was borrowed, the following entry was made:

23	May	31	Cash			8	8	5	00						23
24			Discount on Notes Payable*				1	5	00						24
25			Notes Payable								9	0	0	00	25
26			Issued note for bank loan												26
27															27

* $900 × 10% × 60/360 = $15

On June 30, part of the discount must be transferred from Discount on Notes Payable to Interest Expense. The note was issued on May 31, so 30 days of the 60-day life of the note have passed. Thus, half of the balance in Discount on Notes Payable should be recognized as interest expense. The following adjusting entry is made on June 30:

29	June	30	Interest Expense				7	50							29
30			Discount on Notes Payable								7	50		30
31			Interest accrued on note payable											31

Note that the credit is to Discount on Notes Payable rather than Accrued Interest Payable. This is because the bank already deducted the interest at the time the money was borrowed. Thus, there is no additional interest payable to recognize.

LEARNING KEY: The adjusting entry for accrued interest on an interest-bearing note payable differs from the adjusting entry for accrued interest on a non-interest-bearing note from a bank.

Interest expense is reported as other expense on the income statement. Accrued interest payable is reported as a current liability on the balance sheet. As previously illustrated in Figure 17-7 (page 633), discount on notes payable is reported as a contra-liability to notes payable on the balance sheet.

Learning Objectives	Key Points to Remember
1 Describe a promissory note.	A promissory note is a written promise to pay a specific sum at a future date. Notes are used when credit is extended for periods of 60 days or more, or when large amounts of money are involved. To the maker of a note, the note is a note payable. To the payee of a note, the note is a note receivable.
2 Calculate interest on and determine the due date of promissory notes.	The following formula is used to calculate interest on notes receivable and payable: $$I = P \times R \times T$$ $$\text{Interest} = \text{Principal} \times \text{Rate} \times \text{Time}$$ To determine the due date of a note with a term stated in months, count the number of months from the issue date of the note. To determine the due date of a note with a term stated in days: STEP 1 Subtract the issue date from the number of days in the month of issuance. STEP 2 Add to STEP 1 the number of days in as many months as possible without exceeding the time of the note. STEP 3 Subtract STEP 2 from the time of the note.
3 Account for notes receivable transactions and accrued interest.	Businesses generally encounter six types of transactions involving notes receivable: 1. Note received from a customer to extend time for payment 2. Note collected at maturity 3. Note renewed at maturity 4. Note discounted before maturity 5. Note dishonored 6. Collection of dishonored note When a note receivable is discounted at a bank, four steps are applied to calculate the discount and proceeds: STEP 1 Compute the maturity value of the note. STEP 2 Compute the number of days in the discount period. STEP 3 Compute the discount amount. STEP 4 Compute the proceeds. If a note receivable that was discounted at a bank is dishonored, the endorser of the note is liable to the bank for the maturity value of the note and any bank fees. Notes that are received in one period and due in the following period require an adjustment for accrued interest at the end of the period.

Learning Objectives	Key Points to Remember
4 **Account for notes payable transactions and accrued interest.**	Businesses generally encounter four types of transactions involving notes payable:

1. Note issued to a supplier to extend time for payment

2. Note issued as security for cash loan

3. Note paid at maturity

4. Note renewed at maturity

When money is borrowed at a bank on a non-interest-bearing note that is discounted by the bank, three steps are used to calculate the discount and proceeds:

STEP 1   Compute the maturity value of the note.

STEP 2   Compute the discount amount.

STEP 3   Compute the proceeds.

Notes payable that are issued in one period and due in the following period require an adjustment for accrued interest at the end of the period. The proper entry depends on whether or not the note is interest bearing.

Reflection: Answering the Opening Questions

John apparently signed a non-interest-bearing note that was discounted at 9%. With this type of loan, banks often deduct the interest in advance using a procedure called discounting. The stated rate of interest on the loan is 9%, but the effective rate is 9.89%, calculated as follows:
$270 ÷ $2,730 = 9.89%

KEY TERMS

accrued interest on notes payable, (634)   Interest expense that has been incurred but not paid.

accrued interest on notes receivable, (629)   Interest revenue that has been earned but not yet received.

bank discount (note payable), (632)   The amount that the bank deducts from the face of a note.

bank discount (note receivable), (626)   An interest fee that the bank charges for the time between the date of discounting and the due date of the note.

contingent liability, (628)   A potential liability that may become a real liability depending on future events. In the case of a note discounted at a bank, the business that discounted the note must pay the maturity value and any bank fees if the maker of the note does not pay it at maturity.

credit advice, (625)   A notification to the payee that the bank has collected interest on a note and added the amount to the payee's account.

discounting (note payable), (631)   The procedure, which banks often use, of deducting interest in advance when making a loan.

discounting a note receivable, (626)   Transferring a note receivable to a bank for cash.

dishonored, (628)   A note which the maker does not pay or renew at maturity.

effective rate, (633)   The interest amount paid divided by the proceeds received on a discounted note. This amount will differ from the stated rate on a discounted note.

interest-bearing note, (620)   A note with an explicit interest rate stated on the face of the note.

maker, (620)   The person or business agreeing to make the payment on a note.

maturity value, (622)   The principal of the note plus interest equals the maturity value of the note.

non-interest-bearing note, (620)   A note on which no rate of interest is specified, although the note does include an interest component.

notes payable register, (634)   A detailed auxiliary record of notes payable.

notes receivable register, (629)   A detailed auxiliary record of notes receivable.

payee, (620)   The specific person or business to whom a note is payable.

principal of the note, (621)   The face amount of the note that the maker promises to pay at maturity. The principal is the base on which the interest is calculated.

proceeds (note payable), (633)   The net amount received from the bank.

proceeds (note receivable), (626)   The difference between the maturity value of the note and the bank discount. This is the amount of cash received by the business discounting the note.

promissory note, (620)   A written promise to pay a specific sum at a definite future date.

rate of interest, (621)   The rate at which interest is charged, usually expressed as an annual percentage, but in some cases a monthly rate is quoted.

term of the note, (621)   The months or days from the date of issue to the date of maturity.

time, (621)   The term of the note stated as a fraction of a year.

DEMONSTRATION PROBLEM

Barbar Brothers, partners in a wholesale hardware business, completed the following transactions involving notes and interest during the first half of 20--:

Jan. 11   Received a $900, 60-day, 10% note from Paul Heinsius in payment of an account receivable.

18   Borrowed $10,000 from Landmark Bank issuing a 90-day, 11% note.

Feb. 6   Received an $875, 30-day, 9% note from Ana Fuentes in payment of an account receivable.

21   Issued a $650, 60-day, 11% note to Swanson & Johnson, a supplier, in payment of an account payable.

Mar. 1   Received a $1,000, 90-day, 10% note from Steve Roberts, a customer, in payment of an account receivable.

9   Received a check for $881.56 from Ana Fuentes in payment of note due March 8, including interest.

12   Paul Heinsius dishonored his $900 note due March 12.

31   Discounted the $1,000 note from Steve Roberts at Manchester Bank at a discount rate of 12%.

Apr. 11   Paul Heinsius paid the original maturity value of his note due March 12, plus interest at 10% on the maturity value for the 30 days from March 12 to April 11.

18   Paid Landmark Bank for $10,000 note due today, including interest. (See January 18 transaction.)

22   Paid Swanson & Johnson $61.92 on the note due today (interest of $11.92 plus $50 toward the principal), and issued a new $600, 60-day, 11% note.

May 31   Steve Roberts dishonored his $1,000 note due at the Manchester Bank yesterday. Paid Manchester Bank $1,000, plus interest, plus a $10 bank fee, for the dishonored note.

June 20   Issued a $750, 90-day, 9% note to Greene Acres, a supplier, in payment of an account payable.

REQUIRED   Record each transaction in a general journal.

(continued)

Solution

	DATE		DESCRIPTION	POST REF.	DEBIT					CREDIT					
1	20-- Jan.	11	Notes Receivable			9	0	0	00						1
2			Accounts Receivable/P. Heinsius								9	0	0	00	2
3			60-day, 10% note												3
4															4
5		18	Cash		10	0	0	0	00						5
6			Notes Payable							10	0	0	0	00	6
7			90-day, 11% note—Landmark Bank												7
8															8
9	Feb.	6	Notes Receivable			8	7	5	00						9
10			Accounts Receivable/A. Fuentes								8	7	5	00	10
11			30-day, 9% note												11
12															12
13		21	Accounts Payable/Swanson & Johnson			6	5	0	00						13
14			Notes Payable								6	5	0	00	14
15			60-day, 11% note												15
16															16
17	Mar.	1	Notes Receivable		1	0	0	0	00						17
18			Accounts Receivable/S. Roberts							1	0	0	0	00	18
19			90-day, 10% note												19
20															20
21		9	Cash			8	8	1	56						21
22			Notes Receivable								8	7	5	00	22
23			Interest Revenue										6	56	23
24			Principal and interest—A. Fuentes note												24
25															25
26		12	Accounts Receivable/P. Heinsius			9	1	5	00						26
27			Notes Receivable								9	0	0	00	27
28			Interest Revenue										1	5	00	28
29			Note dishonored												29
30															30
31															31
32															32
33															33
34															34
35															35

GENERAL JOURNAL   PAGE 5

	DATE		DESCRIPTION	POST REF.	DEBIT					CREDIT					
	20- -		GENERAL JOURNAL										PAGE 6		
1	Mar.	31	Cash		1	0	0	4	50						1
2			Notes Receivable							1	0	0	0	00	2
3			Interest Revenue										4	50	3
4			Discounted Steve Roberts's note												4
5			at Manchester Bank												5
6															6
7			Principal	$1,000.00											7
8			Interest to maturity	25.00											8
9			Maturity value	$1,025.00											9
10			Less: Discount												10
11			($1,025 x 12% x 60/360)	20.50											11
12			Cash Proceeds	$1,004.50											12
13															13
14	Apr.	11	Cash			9	2	2	63						14
15			Accounts Receivable/P. Heinsius								9	1	5	00	15
16			Interest Revenue										7	63	16
17			Collection of dishonored note												17
18															18
19		18	Notes Payable		10	0	0	0	00						19
20			Interest Expense			2	7	5	00						20
21			Cash							10	2	7	5	00	21
22			Paid Landmark Bank note due today												22
23															23
24		22	Notes Payable (old note)			6	5	0	00						24
25			Interest Expense				1	1	92						25
26			Cash									6	1	92	26
27			Notes Payable (new note)								6	0	0	00	27
28			Partial payment and issuance of new note												28
29			to Swanson & Johnson												29
30															30
31	May	31	Accounts Receivable/S. Roberts		1	0	3	5	00						31
32			Cash							1	0	3	5	00	32
33			Paid Manchester Bank for dishonored note												33
34															34
35			Principal	$1,000.00											35
36			Interest	25.00											36
37			Bank fee	10.00											37
38				$1,035.00											38
39															39
40	June	20	Accounts Payable/Greene Acres			7	5	0	00						40
41			Notes Payable								7	5	0	00	41
42			90-day, 9% note												42

REVIEW QUESTIONS

1. What is the formula for calculating interest on notes?

2. In the formula for calculating interest, how is time computed?

3. What number of days is considered as a year by most banks and businesses in computing interest?

4. What six types of transactions involving notes receivable do businesses generally encounter?

5. If a note receivable is discounted at a bank, on what amount and for what time period does the bank compute the discount?

6. If a note receivable that was discounted at a bank is dishonored by its maker, what is the responsibility of the person or business discounting the note?

7. On which notes receivable and notes payable is it necessary to record accrued interest at the end of the period?

8. What four types of transactions involving notes payable do businesses generally encounter?

9. When a business borrows money from a bank on a non-interest-bearing note, how are the bank discount and proceeds calculated?

10. What kind of account is Discount on Notes Payable and how is it reported on the balance sheet?

11. What is the appropriate entry for accrued interest on notes payable for an interest-bearing note? for a non-interest-bearing note from a bank?

12. How are accrued interest receivable and accrued interest payable reported on the balance sheet?

MANAGING YOUR WRITING

You are purchasing a new car and plan to finance it through your employee credit union. The credit union has offered you two different promissory note plans, as follows:

Option 1: Three years at 9%, with interest payable annually.
Option 2: One year at 8%, renewable each year for up to three more years, at the then current interest rate. Interest is payable at the end of each year.

Prepare a written report summarizing the advantages and disadvantages of each of these options.

ETHICS CASE

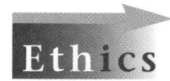

Rochelle needed to borrow $3,000 for three months in order to pay for college expenses while waiting for her scholarship to arrive. After Rochelle filled out the loan application, the loan officer at the bank asked her if she would like to pay the interest up front or at the maturity of the note. He went on to explain that it didn't make a difference, but he preferred that she pay it up front because it would make his paperwork easier. He also told Rochelle that the interest rate and amount would be the same. Rochelle agreed, signed the three-month, 12 percent, discounted note and left with a check for $2,910.

1. Did the loan officer offer Rochelle an acceptable explanation of the interest rate? Justify your answer.

2. What is the effective rate of interest on Rochelle's loan? Round to the nearest tenth of a percent.

3. In a short paragraph, explain the difference between an "interest-bearing" note and a "discounted" note.

4. In groups of two or three, discuss some common situations where the average person might misunderstand interest rate quotations.

WEB WORK

How could promissory notes be used to finance the start-up or improvement of your business? For some ideas, read the article at

http://www.nolo.com/ChunkSB/Borrowing.html

(http://heintz.swcollege.com)

SERIES A EXERCISES

EXERCISE 17A-1 (LO 2) TERM OF A NOTE Calculate total time in days for the following notes. (Assume there are 28 days in February.)

Date of Note	Due Date	Time in Days
May 4	July 17	74
August 17	October 1	_____
July 5	September 5	_____
December 11	February 5	_____
March 24	May 16	_____
January 6	March 18	_____

EXERCISE 17A-2 (LO 2) CALCULATING INTEREST Using 360 days as the denominator, calculate interest for the following notes using the formula $I = P \times R \times T$.

Principal	Rate	Time	Interest
$5,000	6.00%	30 days	_____
1,000	7.50	60	_____
4,500	8.00	120	_____
950	6.80	95	_____
1,250	7.25	102	_____
2,900	7.00	90	_____

W & D

EXERCISE 17A-3 (LO 2) DETERMINING DUE DATE Determine the due date for the following notes. (Assume there are 28 days in February.)

Date of Note	Term of Note	Due Date
August 12	90 days	_____
September 1	60	_____
January 3	120	_____
March 18	88	_____
June 11	200	_____
May 17	38	_____

EXERCISE 17A-4 (LO 3) JOURNAL ENTRIES (NOTE RENEWED, THEN COLLECTED) Prepare general journal entries for the following transactions.

Jan. 15   Received a 30-day, 9% note in payment for accounts receivable balance of $20,000.

Feb. 15   Received $150 (interest) on the old (January 15) note; the old note is renewed for 30 days at 11%.

Mar. 17   Received principal and interest on the new (February 15) note.

19   Received a 60-day, 9% note in payment for accounts receivable balance of $10,000.

May 6   Received $120 (interest) plus $1,000 principal on the old (March 19) note; the old note is renewed for 60 days (from May 6) at 9%.

July 5   Received principal and interest on the new (May 6) note.

EXERCISE 17A-5 (LO 3) JOURNAL ENTRIES (NOTE DISCOUNTED, NOTE DISHONORED) Prepare general journal entries for the following transactions.

Apr. 6   Received 120-day, 11% note in payment for accounts receivable balance of $3,000.

26   Discounted the note at a rate of 12%.

May 3   Received a 30-day, 10% note in payment for accounts receivable balance of $900.

June 2   The $900, 30-day, 10% note is dishonored.

5   The dishonored note is paid, plus interest at 10% on the maturity value.

EXERCISE 17A-6 (LO 3) JOURNAL ENTRIES (ACCRUED INTEREST RECEIVABLE) At the end of the year the following interest is earned, but not yet received. Record the adjusting entry in a general journal.

Interest on $4,000, 90-day, 12% note (for 15 days)	$20.00
Interest on $7,000, 60-day, 11% note (for 18 days)	38.50
	$58.50

EXERCISE 17A-7 (LO 4) JOURNAL ENTRIES (NOTE ISSUED, RENEWED) Prepare general journal entries for the following transactions.

May 1   Purchased $5,000 worth of equipment from a supplier on account.

June 1   Gave a $5,000, 30-day, 10% note in payment of the account payable.

July 1   Paid $500 cash plus interest to the supplier, extending the note for 30 days from July 1.

　　31   Paid the note in full.

EXERCISE 17A-8 (LO 4) JOURNAL ENTRIES (NOTE DISCOUNTED) Prepare general journal entries for the following transactions.

July 15   Borrowed $5,000 cash from the bank, giving a 60-day non-interest-bearing note. The note is discounted 12% by the bank.

Sept. 13 Paid the $5,000 note, recognizing the discount as interest expense.

EXERCISE 17A-9 (LO 4) JOURNAL ENTRIES (ACCRUED INTEREST PAYABLE) At the end of the year the following interest is payable, but not yet paid. Record the adjusting entry in the general journal.

Interest on $5,000, 60-day, 9% note (for 12 days)	$15.00
Interest on $2,500, 30-day, 12% note (for 9 days)	7.50
	$22.50

SERIES A PROBLEMS

PROBLEM 17A-1 (LO 2/3) NOTES RECEIVABLE ENTRIES J. K. Pratt Co. had the following transactions:

20-1

July 1   Sold merchandise on account to J. Akita, $750.

　　20   J. Akita gave a $750, 30-day, 10% note to extend time for payment on merchandise purchased on account.

Aug. 21   J. Akita paid note issued July 20 plus interest.

　　25   Sold merchandise on account to L. Beene, $1,100.

Sept. 5   L. Beene paid $100 and gave a $1,000, 30-day, 12% note to extend time for payment.

Oct. 5   L. Beene paid note issued September 5, plus interest.

　　10   Sold merchandise to R. Harris for $750: $50 plus a $700, 30-day, 11% note.

Nov. 9   R. Harris paid $200 plus interest on note issued October 10, and extended the note ($500) for 30 days.

Dec. 9   R. Harris paid note extended on November 9, plus interest.

　　10   Sold merchandise on account to B. Kraus, $1,500.

　　15   B. Kraus paid $150 on merchandise purchased on account, and gave a $1,350, 30-day, 12% note to extend time for payment.

(continued)

20-2

Jan. 14 B. Kraus' note of December 15 is dishonored.

Feb. 13 Collected B. Kraus' dishonored note, plus interest at 12% on the maturity value.

REQUIRED Record the transactions in a general journal.

PROBLEM 17A-2 (LO 2/3) NOTES RECEIVABLE DISCOUNTING Movado Suppliers had the following transactions:

Mar. 1 Sold merchandise on account to R. Sticca, $5,000.

20 R. Sticca gave a $5,000, 90-day, 12% note to extend time for payment.

30 R. Sticca's note is discounted at Commerce Bank at a discount rate of 15%.

Apr. 1 Sold merchandise on account to K. Jones, $3,600.

20 K. Jones paid $600 and gave a $3,000, 60-day, 10% note to extend time for payment.

May 5 K. Jones' note is discounted at Commerce Bank at a discount rate of 12%.

June 19 K. Jones' note is dishonored. The bank bills Movado for the maturity value of the note plus a $40 bank fee.

July 31 K. Jones' dishonored note is collected; Jones pays Movado the maturity value of the note, the $40 bank fee, and interest at 10% on the maturity value plus the bank fee.

Aug. 1 Sold merchandise on account to R. Brown, $5,600.

12 R. Brown paid $400 and gave a $5,200, 30-day, 12% note to extend time for payment.

Sept. 11 R. Brown paid $400, plus interest, and gave a new $4,800, 60-day, 14% note to extend time for payment.

26 R. Brown's note is discounted at Commerce Bank at a discount rate of 16%.

Nov. 10 R. Brown's note is dishonored. The bank bills Movado for the maturity value of the note plus a $40 bank fee.

Dec. 15 R. Brown's dishonored note is collected. Brown pays Movado the maturity value of the note, the $40 bank fee, and interest at 14% on the maturity value plus the bank fee.

REQUIRED Record the above transactions in a general journal.

PROBLEM 17A-3 (LO 3) ACCRUED INTEREST RECEIVABLE The following is a list of outstanding notes receivable as of December 31, 20--:

Maker	Date of Note	Principal	Interest	Term	No. of Days
K. Savelin	12/15/--	$1,000	10%	60 days	16
R. Hillier	12/3/--	5,000	12	90	28
B. Miranda	11/30/--	2,800	8	90	31
R. Hansen	11/18/--	7,500	9	120	43

REQUIRED 1. Compute the accrued interest at the end of the year.

2. Prepare the adjusting entry in the general journal.

PROBLEM 17A-4 (LO 4) NOTES PAYABLE Milo Radio Shop had the following notes payable transactions:

Apr. 1   Borrowed $5,000 from the Builder's Bank, signing a 90-day, 8% note.

5   Gave a $2,000, 60-day, 10% note to Breaker Parts Co. in full payment of an account payable.

10   Paid $500 cash and gave a $1,500, 30-day, 12% note to M. K. Reynolds in payment of an account payable.

May 10   Paid $500 cash, plus interest, and issued a new $1,000, 30-day, 14% note to M. K. Reynolds.

20   Borrowed $3,500 for 60 days from the Builder's Bank on a non-interest-bearing note. The discount rate is 12%.

June 4   Paid $500 cash, plus interest, to Breaker Parts Co. (see April 5) and gave a new $1,500, 30-day, 12% note to extend time for payment.

9   Paid the principal and interest due on the $1,000 note to M. K. Reynolds. (See May 10.)

30   Paid the principal and interest due on the $5,000 note to the Builder's Bank. (See April 1.)

July 4   Paid the principal and interest due on the $1,500 note to Breaker Parts Co. (See June 4.)

19   Paid the $3,500 non-interest-bearing note to Builder's Bank. (See May 20.)

REQUIRED   Record the above transactions in a general journal.

PROBLEM 17A-5 (LO 4) ACCRUED INTEREST PAYABLE The following is a list of outstanding notes payable as of December 31, 20--:

Maker	Date of Note	Principal	Interest	Term	No. of Days
B. Jones	12/1/--	$1,000	11%	90 days	30
M. Aguilor	11/25/--	2,500	9	80	36
T. Plant	12/14/--	3,800	12	120	17
W. Brand	11/19/--	1,900	10	180	42

REQUIRED   1.   Compute the accrued interest at the end of the year.

2.   Prepare the adjusting entry in the general journal.

SERIES B EXERCISES

EXERCISE 17B-1 (LO 2) TERM OF A NOTE Calculate total time in days for the following notes. (Assume there are 28 days in February.)

Date of Note	Due Date	Time in Days
August 17	October 10	_____
January 12	March 10	_____
July 15	September 13	_____
December 3	February 1	_____
April 11	July 6	_____
October 6	December 18	_____

EXERCISE 17B-2 (LO 2) CALCULATING INTEREST Using 360 days as the denominator, calculate interest for the following notes using the formula I = P × R × T.

Principal	Rate	Time	Interest
$4,000	7.00%	60 days	_____
3,000	9.50	30	_____
7,500	8.00	150	_____
850	7.90	99	_____
2,250	7.55	122	_____
1,900	8.80	82	_____

EXERCISE 17B-3 (LO 2) DETERMINING DUE DATE Determine the due date for the following notes. (Assume there are 28 days in February.)

Date of Note	Term of Note	Due Date
July 11	45 days	_____
December 23	90	_____
April 18	120	_____
October 3	77	_____
January 1	180	_____
August 13	65	_____

EXERCISE 17B-4 (LO 3) JOURNAL ENTRIES (NOTE RENEWED, THEN COLLECTED) Prepare general journal entries for the following transactions.

May 22   Received a 30-day, 9% note in payment for accounts receivable balance of $22,000.

June 21   Received $165.00 cash (interest) on the old (May 22) note; the old note is renewed for 30 days at 10%.

July 21   Received principal and interest on the new (June 21) note.

28   Received a 45-day, 7% note in payment for accounts receivable balance of $11,600.00.

Sept. 11   Received $101.50 cash (interest) plus $1,600 principal on the old (July 28) note; the old note is renewed for 60 days (from September 11) at 9%.

Nov. 10   Received principal and interest on the new (September 11) note.

EXERCISE 17B-5 (LO 3) JOURNAL ENTRIES (NOTE DISCOUNTED, NOTE DISHONORED) Prepare general journal entries for the following transactions.

Aug. 4   Received a 120-day, 12% note in payment for accounts receivable balance of $4,000.

14   Discounted the note at a rate of 14%.

Sept. 6   Received a 30-day, 11% note in payment for accounts receivable balance of $1,200.

Oct. 5   The $1,200, 30-day, 11% note is dishonored.

Nov. 4   The dishonored note is paid, plus interest at 11% on the maturity value.

EXERCISE 17B-6 (LO 3) JOURNAL ENTRIES (ACCRUED INTEREST RECEIVABLE) At the end of the year the following interest is earned, but not yet received. Record the adjusting entry in a general journal.

Interest on $6,000, 60-day, 11% note (for 24 days)	$44.00
Interest on $9,000, 90-day, 12% note (for 12 days)	36.00
	$80.00

EXERCISE 17B-7 (LO 4) JOURNAL ENTRIES (NOTE ISSUED, RENEWED) Prepare general journal entries for the following transactions.

June 15 Purchased $6,000 worth of equipment from a supplier on account.

July 15 Gave a $6,000, 30-day, 12% note in payment of the account payable.

Aug. 14 Paid $600 cash plus interest to the supplier, extending the note for 30 days from August 14.

Sept. 13 Paid the note in full.

EXERCISE 17B-8 (LO 4) JOURNAL ENTRIES (NOTE DISCOUNTED) Prepare general journal entries for the following transactions.

Sept. 15 Borrowed $7,000 cash from the bank, giving a 60-day non-interest-bearing note. The note is discounted 12% by the bank.

Nov. 14 Paid the $7,000 note, recognizing the discount as interest expense.

EXERCISE 17B-9 (LO 4) JOURNAL ENTRIES (ACCRUED INTEREST PAYABLE) At the end of the year the following interest is payable, but not yet paid. Record the adjusting entry in the general journal.

Interest on $8,000, 90-day, 8% note (for 18 days)	$32.00
Interest on $4,500, 60-day, 10% note (for 7 days)	8.75
	$40.75

SERIES B PROBLEMS

PROBLEM 17B-1 (LO 2/3) NOTES RECEIVABLE ENTRIES M. L. DiMaurizio had the following notes receivable transactions:

20-3

June 1 Sold merchandise on account to K. Lorenzo, $2,400.

20 K. Lorenzo gave a $2,400, 30-day, 10% note to extend time for payment.

July 20 K. Lorenzo paid the note plus interest.

25 Sold merchandise on account to R. Boone, $5,600.

Aug. 4 R. Boone paid $600 and gave a $5,000, 30-day, 12% note to extend time for payment.

Sept. 3 R. Boone paid the note plus interest.

10 Sold merchandise to T. Akins for $3,000: $400 plus a $2,600, 30-day, 11% note.

(continued)

Oct. 10   T. Akins paid $600, plus interest, and extended the note ($2,000) for 30 days.

Nov. 9   T. Akins paid the note plus interest.

10   Sold merchandise on account to J. Brown, $5,000.

25   J. Brown paid $1,000 and gave a $4,000, 30-day, 12% note to extend time for payment.

Dec. 25   J. Brown's note is dishonored.

20-4

Jan. 13   J. Brown's dishonored note is collected, plus interest at 12% on the maturity value.

REQUIRED   Record the transactions in a general journal.

PROBLEM 17B-2 (LO 2/3) NOTES RECEIVABLE DISCOUNTING Madison Graphics had the following notes receivable transactions:

May 1   Sold merchandise on account to L. Carney, $5,600.

20   L. Carney gave a $5,600, 90-day, 12% note to extend time for payment.

30   L. Carney's note is discounted at Commercial Bank at a discount rate of 15%.

June 1   Sold merchandise on account to P. Arnst, $2,800.

20   P. Arnst paid $400 and gave a $2,400, 60-day, 10% note to extend time for payment.

July 5   P. Arnst's note is discounted at Commercial Bank at a discount rate of 12%.

Aug. 19   P. Arnst's note is dishonored. The bank bills Madison Graphics for the maturity value of the note plus a $30 bank fee.

31   P. Arnst's dishonored note is collected; Arnst pays Madison the maturity value of the note, the $30 bank fee, and interest at 10% on the maturity value plus the bank fee.

Sept. 1   Sold merchandise on account to B. Faust, $6,400.

12   B. Faust paid $400 and gave a $6,000, 30-day, 12% note to extend time for payment.

Oct. 12   B. Faust paid $400, plus interest, and gave a new $5,600, 60-day, 14% note to extend time for payment.

26   B. Faust's note is discounted at Commercial Bank at a discount rate of 14%.

Dec. 11   B. Faust's note is dishonored. The bank bills Madison Graphics for the maturity value of the note plus a $30 bank fee.

Dec. 27   B. Faust's dishonored note is collected. Faust pays Madison the maturity value of the note, the $30 bank fee, and interest at 14% on the maturity value plus the bank fee.

REQUIRED   Record the above transactions in a general journal.

PROBLEM 17B-3 (LO 3) ACCRUED INTEREST RECEIVABLE The following is a list of outstanding notes receivable as of December 31, 20--:

Maker	Date of Note	Principal	Interest	Term	No. of Days
P. Harrison	12/17/--	$1,200	11.0%	60 days	14
T. Rieber	12/3/--	4,000	12.0	90	28
K. Burke	12/1/--	2,200	9.0	90	30
A. Pai	11/28/--	4,500	8.5	120	33

REQUIRED   1. Compute the accrued interest at the end of the year.

2. Prepare the adjusting entry in the general journal.

PROBLEM 17B-4 (LO 4) NOTES PAYABLE Mary's Travel Agency had the following notes payable transactions:

Apr. 1   Borrowed $4,000 from the Finance Bank, signing a 90-day, 8% note.

5   Gave a $3,000, 60-day, 10% note to Krenshaw Airline in full payment of an account payable.

10   Paid $400 cash and issued a $1,600, 30-day, 12% note to Andrew Adams in payment of an account payable.

May 10   Paid $400, plus interest, and gave a new $1,200, 30-day, 14% note to Andrew Adams.

20   Borrowed $4,500 for 60 days from Finance Bank on a non-interest-bearing note. The discount rate is 14%.

June 4   Paid $500, plus interest, to Krenshaw Airline (see April 5) and gave a new $2,500, 30-day, 12% note to extend time for payment.

9   Paid the principal and interest due on the $1,200 note to Andrew Adams. (See May 10.)

30   Paid the principal and interest due on the $4,000 note to Finance Bank. (See April 1.)

July 4   Paid the principal and interest due on the $2,500 note to Krenshaw Airline (See June 4.)

19   Paid the $4,500 non-interest-bearing note to Finance Bank. (See May 20.)

REQUIRED   Record the above transactions in a general journal.

PROBLEM 17B-5 (LO 4) ACCRUED INTEREST PAYABLE The following is a list of outstanding notes payable as of December 31, 20--:

Payee	Date of Note	Principal	Interest	Term	No. of Days
X. Rayal	12/1/--	$1,200	11%	90 days	30
G. Richards	11/28/--	2,300	8	80	33
A. Gray	12/16/--	3,400	12	120	15
O. Hankins	11/13/--	2,900	10	180	48

REQUIRED   1. Compute the accrued interest at the end of the year.

2. Prepare the adjusting entry in the general journal.

MASTERY PROBLEM

Eddie Edwards and Phil Bell own and operate The Second Hand Equipment Shop. The following transactions involving notes and interest were completed during the last three months of 20--.

Oct. 1 Issued $6,800, 60-day, 10% note to Mac Farm Equipment in payment of an account payable.

15 Received a $2,000, 60-day, 12% note from R. Chambers in payment of an account receivable.

Nov. 1 Discounted the note received from R. Chambers on October 15 at Merchants National Bank. The discount rate is 14%.

1 Borrowed $5,000 from First National Bank on a three-month, non-interest-bearing note that was discounted at 10%.

20 Received a $4,000, 90-day, 9% note from L. Revsine in payment of an account receivable.

30 Issued a check to Mac Farm Equipment in payment of the note issued on October 1, including interest.

Dec. 10 Issued a $3,000, 90-day, 9% note to Remak Tractors to extend time for payment of an account payable.

16 Received notification from Merchants National Bank that R. Chambers has dishonored his note. A check is issued to cover the note plus a $20 bank fee that must be paid to the bank.

REQUIRED 1. Prepare general journal entries for the above transactions.

2. Prepare necessary adjusting entries for the notes outstanding on December 31.

Self-Study Test Questions

True/False

1. The maturity value of a note includes both principal and interest.

2. When a note is renewed at maturity, the old note is cancelled and a new note is issued.

3. The difference between the maturity value of a note and the net proceeds is called discounting.

4. When a note is dishonored, the interest is not credited to Interest Revenue because it is not earned.

5. When a dishonored note is collected, interest is collected for the time between date of maturity and date of collection.

Multiple Choice

1. Which account is debited for interest earned but not yet received?

   (a) Interest Revenue
   (b) Accrued Interest Receivable
   (c) Accrued Interest Payable
   (d) Interest Expense

2. When a note payable is paid at maturity, what account is debited for the amount of the interest?

   (a) Interest Revenue
   (b) Notes Payable
   (c) Interest Expense
   (d) Discount on Notes Payable

3. Accrued interest payable is reported as a _____ on the balance sheet.

   (a) current asset
   (b) long-term asset
   (c) current liability
   (d) long-term liability

4. Principal plus interest equals _____ of a note.

   (a) discount
   (b) net proceeds
   (c) interest rate
   (d) maturity value

5. The discount amount is calculated by multiplying the maturity value times _____ times the discount period.

   (a) discount rate
   (b) interest rate
   (c) term of note
   (d) net proceeds

The answers to the Self-Study Test Questions are at the end of the text.

18

Accounting for Merchandise Inventory

LEARNING OBJECTIVES:
Careful study of this chapter should enable you to:

LO 1 Explain the impact of merchandise inventory on the financial statements.

LO 2 Describe the two principal systems of accounting for merchandise inventory—the periodic system and the perpetual system.

LO 3 Compute the costs allocated to the ending inventory and cost of goods sold using different inventory methods.

LO 4 Estimate the ending inventory and cost of goods sold by using the gross profit and retail inventory methods.

As you walk through a grocery store, have you ever wondered what the store paid for each item? It would be nice to know which items were really "good buys" and which were "overpriced." What happens when management pays different amounts for identical units on the shelf? The selling price is the same. Otherwise, we could have customers arguing over the item marked with the lower price. John Zenith has the same problem with his inventory of sports equipment and clothing. Many of the units are identical, but he paid different prices for them. If the units are identical, how does he know which unit was sold: the one with the higher, or lower, purchase price? Does it matter?

One of the major reasons for keeping accounting records is to determine the net income (or net loss) of a business. For a merchandising business, the cost of goods available for sale during the accounting period must be divided between the cost of goods (merchandise) sold and the ending merchandise inventory. (Recall that the terms "goods" and "merchandise" mean the same thing and are used interchangeably.) End-of-period adjustments for merchandise inventory were illustrated in earlier chapters. In those illustrations, the costs assigned to the cost of goods sold and ending inventory were provided. In this chapter, you will learn how to determine the dollar amounts assigned to the cost of goods sold and ending merchandise inventory.

THE IMPACT OF MERCHANDISE INVENTORY ON FINANCIAL STATEMENTS

LO 1   Explain the impact of merchandise inventory on the financial statements.

> This year's ending inventory becomes next year's beginning inventory.

A company's ending inventory must be reported accurately. An error in the reported inventory will cause errors on the income statement, statement of owner's equity, and balance sheet. In addition, since this year's ending inventory becomes next year's beginning inventory, financial statements for the following year will also contain errors.

Figure 18-1 illustrates the impact of an error in the *ending inventory*. The first pair of columns presents partial financial statements when the ending inventory is correct. For this illustration, sales, cost of goods sold, and operating expenses are assumed to be the same for 20-1 and 20-2. Thus, the same net income of $30,000 and beginning and ending merchandise inventories of $20,000 are reported for both years.

The second pair of columns in Figure 18-1 illustrates the effects of understating the ending inventory. Understating the ending inventory for 20-1 by $5 causes the cost of goods sold to be overstated by $5 and net income to be understated by $5. Since net income is reported on the statement of owner's equity, Erv Bultman's capital on December 31 is understated by $5. The understated capital also appears in the owner's equity section of the balance sheet. The understated ending inventory is reported in the current assets section of the balance sheet.

Even if the ending inventory for 20-2 is accurately reported, we still have a problem with the income statement. Since the ending inventory for 20-1 was understated, the beginning inventory for 20-2 is understated also ($15 instead of $20). This error causes cost of goods sold to be understated by $5 and net income to be overstated by $5.

At this point, we can see that this inventory error "washes out" over the two-year period. The understated net income for 20-1 is offset by overstated net income in 20-2. Thus, Bultman's capital account as of December 31, 20-2, is reported accurately on the statement of owner's equity and balance sheet at $160. Assuming no future inventory errors, the financial statements for 20-3 and thereafter will be correct.

LEARNING KEY: If the ending inventory for 20-1 is understated, net income for 20-1 is understated and net income for 20-2 is overstated.

FIGURE 18-1 Effect of Inventory Errors on Net Income

	ENDING INVENTORY FOR 20-1 IS CORRECT		ENDING INVENTORY FOR 20-1 IS UNDERSTATED		ENDING INVENTORY FOR 20-1 IS OVERSTATED	
	20-1	20-2	20-1	20-2	20-1	20-2
Income Statement						
Sales	80	80	80	80	80	80
Cost of goods sold:						
Beginning merchandise inventory	20	20	20	15	20	25
Add purchases (net)	40	40	40	40	40	40
Cost of goods available for sale	60	60	60	55	60	65
Less ending merchandise inventory	(20)	(20)	(15)	(20)	(25)	(20)
Cost of goods sold		(40)	(40)	(45)	(35)	(35)	(45)
Gross profit	40	40	35	45	45	35
Operating expenses	(10)	(10)	(10)	(10)	(10)	(10)
Net income	30	30	25	35	35	25
Statement of Owner's Equity						
Erv Bultman, capital, January 1	100	130	100	125	100	135
Net income	30	30	25	35	35	25
Erv Bultman, capital, December 31	130	160	125	160	135	160
Balance Sheet (Partial)						
Current assets:						
Merchandise inventory	20	20	15	20	25	20
Owner's equity:						
Erv Bultman, capital	130	160	125	160	135	160

The third pair of columns in Figure 18-1 illustrates the effects of overstating the ending inventory in 20-1. This causes net income to be overstated in 20-1 and understated in 20-2. As discussed above, these errors "wash out" by the end of 20-2. Thus, Bultman's capital account is correct in the 20-2 financial statements.

LEARNING KEY: If the ending inventory for 20-1 is overstated, net income for 20-1 is overstated and net income for 20-2 is understated.

It is very important to have an accurate count and valuation for the ending inventory. Since errors in the ending inventory have a direct effect on net income for the period, managers may be tempted to manipulate this amount to achieve a desired result: to either increase net income to make the company look good, or decrease net income to reduce taxes or smooth earnings. For this reason, observing and verifying the ending inventory is an important aspect of an external auditor's job.

TYPES OF INVENTORY SYSTEMS: PERIODIC AND PERPETUAL

LO 2   Describe the two principal systems of accounting for merchandise inventory—the periodic system and the perpetual system.

The two principal systems of accounting for merchandise inventory are the periodic and the perpetual systems. The previous chapters discussed the **periodic inventory system** without identifying it by name. Under this system, the balance in the merchandise inventory account is merely a record of the most recent count of the physical inventory. The purchases account is debited for the cost of all goods purchased. The sales account is credited for the selling prices of all goods sold. Under this system, the current merchandise inventory and the cost of goods sold are not determined until the end of the accounting period, when a physical inventory is taken. At that time, the following formula is applied to calculate cost of goods sold:

	Beginning Inventory (last year's ending physical count)
+	Net Purchases (account balance at end of this year)
=	Cost of Goods Available for Sale
−	Ending Inventory (this year's ending physical count)
=	Cost of Goods Sold (for this year)

 LEARNING KEY: Under the periodic inventory system, the ending inventory and cost of goods sold are determined at the end of the accounting period, when a physical inventory is taken.

Recall that adjusting entries are needed at the end of the fiscal year to update the merchandise inventory account. These entries are illustrated as Transaction 7 for the periodic system in Figure 18-2.

Under the **perpetual inventory system**, the merchandise inventory account is debited for the cost of all goods purchased, including freight charges, and credited for the cost of all goods sold. In addition, this account is debited when customers return merchandise and is credited when suppliers grant returns, allowances, and discounts. Thus, the balance of the account represents the cost of goods on hand at all times. When goods are sold, the cost of goods sold account is debited for the same amount that the merchandise inventory account is credited. No year-end adjusting entry is necessary as long as the physical inventory agrees with the amount reported in the merchandise inventory account. Figure 18-2 compares entries made under the periodic and perpetual inventory systems.

 LEARNING KEY: Under the perpetual inventory system, cost of goods sold and the amount of merchandise inventory on hand are continually updated as merchandise is bought and sold.

FIGURE 18-2 Entries for Periodic and Perpetual Inventory Systems

TRANSACTION	PERIODIC SYSTEM		PERPETUAL SYSTEM	

1. Purchased merchandise on account, $100.	Purchases
	    Accounts Payable
		100
		    100
			Merchandise Inventory
			    Accounts Payable
				100
				    100

2. Paid freight charge, $30.	Freight-In
	    Cash
		30
		    30
			Merchandise Inventory
			    Cash
				30
				    30

3. Sold merchandise on account, $80. The cost of the merchandise was $50.	Accounts Receivable
	    Sales
		80
		    80
			Accounts Receivable
			    Sales
			Cost of Goods Sold
			    Merchandise Inventory
				80
				    80
				50
				    50

4. Merchandise costing $10 was returned to the supplier.	Accounts Payable
	    Purchases Ret. & Allow.
		10
		    10
			Accounts Payable
			    Merchandise Inventory
				10
				    10

5. Customers returned merchandise sold for $20. The cost of the merchandise was $15.	Sales Ret. and Allow.
	    Accounts Receivable
		20
		    20
			Sales Ret. and Allow.
			    Accounts Receivable
			Merchandise Inventory
			    Cost of Goods Sold
				20
				    20
				15
				    15

6. Paid for merchandise costing $100. The supplier granted a 2% discount for prompt payment.	Accounts Payable
	    Purchases Discounts
	    Cash
		100
		    2
		    98
			Accounts Payable
			    Merchandise Inventory
			    Cash
				100
				    2
				    98

7. Adjusting entries made at the end of the accounting period.	Income Summary
	    Merchandise Inventory
	
	Merchandise Inventory
	    Income Summary
		xx
		    xx
		
		xx
		    xx
			Not necessary if physical inventory agrees with amount reported in merchandise inventory account.	

Figure 18-3 provides a summary of the transactions that affect the merchandise inventory account during the year and adjustments made at year end under the periodic and perpetual systems.

FIGURE 18-3 Transactions and Adjustments Affecting Merchandise Inventory

PERIODIC INVENTORY SYSTEM		PERPETUAL INVENTORY SYSTEM	
Merchandise Inventory		**Merchandise Inventory**	

Entries made during year:
    NONE
		Entries made during year:
		    Purchases
			Purchases Returns
			    & Allowances

		Freight-In Sales Returns	Purchases Discounts Cost of Goods Sold

Year-end adjustments:
    (2) Enter ending
          inventory
	(1) Remove beginning
	       inventory
		Year-end adjustments:
		    Adjust for differences
		    between physical count
		    and amount in account.
		    Debit if physical
		          inventory > Books
			Credit if physical inventory
			    < Books

ASSIGNING COST TO INVENTORY AND COST OF GOODS SOLD

LO 3 Compute the costs allocated to the ending inventory and cost of goods sold using different inventory methods.

To determine the cost of goods sold and ending inventory, it is important to understand:

1. the purpose of a physical inventory,

2. the specific calculations used under the periodic and perpetual systems, and

3. the role of the lower-of-cost-or-market rule.

Taking a Physical Inventory

Even under the perpetual inventory system, there will be differences between the actual inventory on the floor and the amount on the books. These differences are the result of breakage, spoilage, and theft. Thieves rarely yell "Debit Loss Due to Theft and credit Merchandise Inventory" as they attempt to leave the store with merchandise under their coats.

Under the periodic system, the goods on hand at the end of the period are counted to allocate merchandise costs between sold and unsold goods. This process is called taking a **physical inventory.** A physical inventory is also important under the perpetual system. It verifies that the amount of merchandise actually held agrees with what is reported in the accounting records.

Taking a physical inventory can be a sizable task. Frequently, it is done after regular business hours. Some companies even close for a few days to take inventory. The ideal time to count the goods is when the quantity on hand is at its lowest level. A fiscal year that starts and ends at the time the stock of goods is normally at its lowest level is known as a **natural business year.** Such a year is used by many businesses for accounting purposes.

Various procedures are followed in taking an inventory to be sure that no items are missed and that no items are included more than once. Frequently, persons taking inventory work in pairs: one counts the items and the other records the information. Usually this information is entered on a special form called an **inventory sheet**, like the one illustrated in Figure 18-4. The inventory sheet has columns for recording the description of each item, the quantity on hand, the cost per unit, and the extension.

FIGURE 18-4 Inventory Sheet

INVENTORY Aug. 31 20 -- Page 1

Sheet No. 1
Called by L.M.M.
Entered by K.N.

Department A
Location Storeroom

Costed by C.M.H.
Extended by C.M.H.
Examined by C.J.C.

Description	Quantity	Unit	Unit Cost	Extensions	
Table Lamp	20	ea.	62.80	1,256.00	
Wall Rack	18	ea.	19.70	354.60	
Bookcase	7	ea.	88.10	616.70	
End Table	13	ea.	53.20	691.60	
Desk	6	ea.	158.30	949.80	
Total					6,465.10

A BROADER VIEW

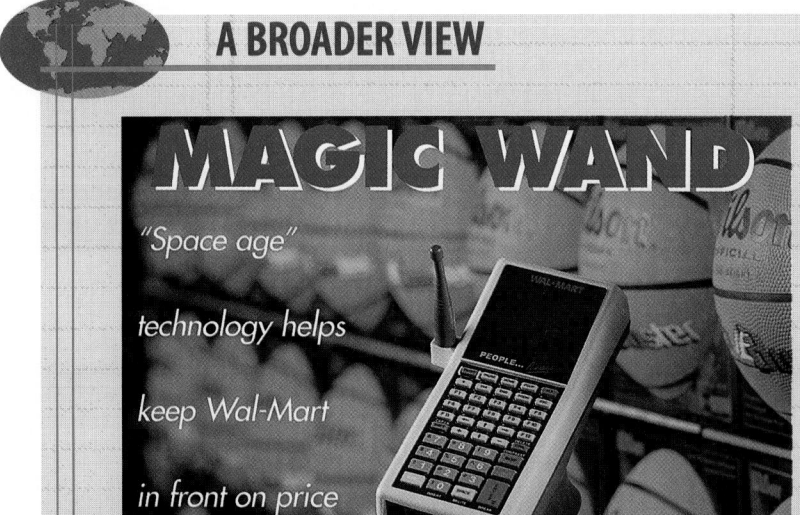

MAGIC WAND

"Space age"

technology helps

keep Wal-Mart

in front on price

and service

THE "MAGIC WAND" AT WAL-MART

At any given time, a typical Wal-Mart discount store has more than 70,000 standard items in stock. Every item must be inventoried and replenished in a timely way to avoid having too much or too little stock. Wal-Mart associates have the aid of the "Magic Wand," a handheld computer, linked by a radio-frequency network to in-store terminals. These high-tech devices provide up-to-the-minute information on inventory on hand, upcoming deliveries, and stock at Wal-Mart distribution centers.

Only goods that are the property of the company should be included in a physical inventory. Two special situations that require care to determine ownership are (1) goods held for sale on **consignment** and (2) goods **in transit**. Sometimes one business will try to sell merchandise for another business or individual on a commission basis. This is called selling goods on consignment. Goods held on consignment remain the property of the shipper **(consignor)**. They should not be included in the inventory of the company holding the goods **(consignee)**.

To determine whether goods in transit at year end should be included in inventory, we must know the FOB (free on board) terms. If goods are shipped FOB shipping point, the buyer pays for shipping and the goods belong to the buyer as soon as they are shipped. If goods are shipped FOB destination, the seller pays for shipping and the goods belong to the seller until they are received by the buyer.

LEARNING KEY: Under FOB shipping point, the goods belong to the buyer as soon as they are shipped. Under FOB destination, the goods belong to the seller until they are received by the buyer.

After calculating the quantities of goods owned at the end of the period, the proper cost must be assigned to the inventory. In addition to the purchase price, we include delivery costs (freight-in), insurance, and, occasionally, storage fees.

Therefore, cost means all necessary and reasonable costs incurred to get the goods to the buyer's place of business.

If all purchases of the same item were made at the same price per unit, computing the cost of the ending inventory would be simple. We would multiply the number of units by the cost per unit. In a world of changing prices, however, identical items are purchased at different times and at different costs per unit. Of the goods available for sale, how do we decide which units were sold and which units remain on the shelf? As shown in Figure 18-5, this decision affects the income statement and balance sheet. The four inventory methods listed below have become generally accepted for answering this question.

1. Specific identification
2. First-in, first-out (FIFO)
3. Weighted-average
4. Last-in, first-out (LIFO)

These methods may be applied under the periodic or perpetual inventory systems.

FIGURE 18-5 Allocation of Goods Available for Sale to Cost of Goods Sold and Ending Inventory

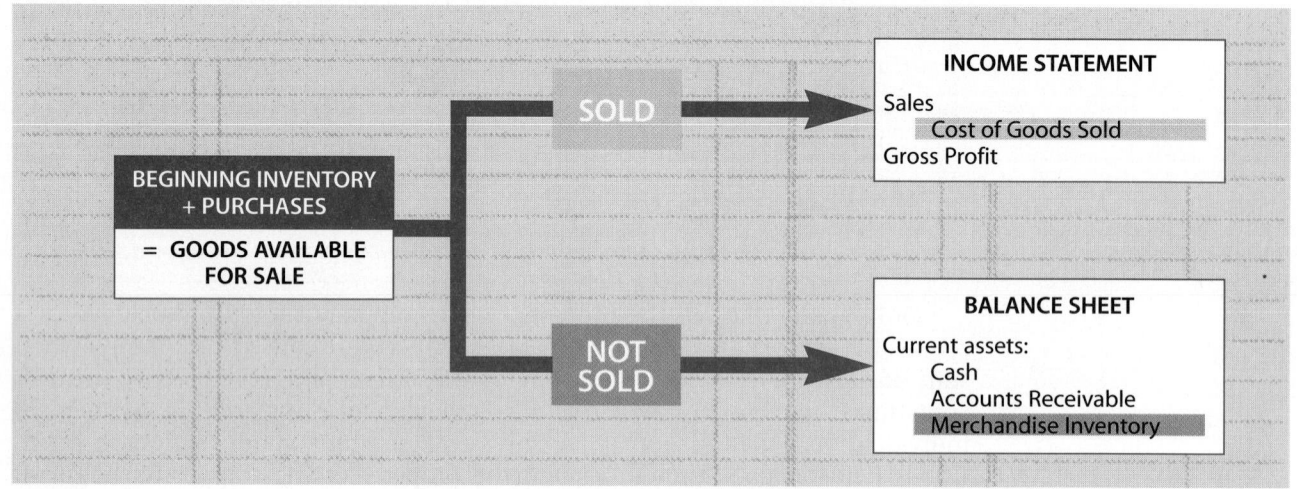

The Periodic Inventory System

Specific Identification Method. When each unit of inventory can be specifically identified, the **specific identification method** can be used. To use this method, inventory items must be physically different from each other, or they must have serial numbers. Examples include cars, motorcycles, furniture, appliances, and fine jewelry. When a unit is sold, its cost is determined from the supplier's invoice. This method is practical only for businesses in which sales volume is relatively low and inventory unit value is relatively high. Otherwise, record keeping becomes expensive and time consuming.

LEARNING KEY: The specific identification method requires that each inventory item have a distinguishing feature or marking to assure proper identification.

To illustrate how specific identification costing works, assume the following data for an inventory of one specific model of children's bicycles:

Children's Bicycles (Model ZX007)

	Units	Unit Price	Total Cost
On hand at start of period	40	$62	$ 2,480
Purchased during period:			
1st purchase	60	65	3,900
2nd purchase	80	67	5,360
3rd purchase	70	68	4,760
Number of units available for sale	250		$16,500
On hand at end of period	50		
Number of units sold during period	200		

Of the 200 units sold during the period, the bicycle serial numbers show that 30 were from the beginning inventory, 50 were from the first purchase, 60 were from the second purchase, and 60 were from the last purchase. The cost of goods sold and the cost of inventory at the end of the period are determined as shown in Figure 18-6.

FIGURE 18-6 Specific Identification Inventory Method

	COST OF GOODS SOLD			COST OF ENDING INVENTORY		
	Units	Unit Price	Total	Units	Unit Price	Total
Beginning inventory	30	$62	$ 1,860	10	$62	$ 620
1st purchase	50	65	3,250	10	65	650
2nd purchase	60	67	4,020	20	67	1,340
3rd purchase	60	68	4,080	10	68	680
Total	200		$13,210	50		$ 3,290
Alternative calculation given goods available for sale and cost of goods sold or ending inventory.	Cost of goods available for sale $16,500 Less cost of ending inventory (3,290) Cost of goods sold $13,210			Cost of goods available for sale $16,500 Less cost of goods sold (13,210) Cost of ending inventory $ 3,290		

First-In, First-Out (FIFO) Method. Another widely used method of allocating merchandise cost is called the **first-in, first-out**, or **FIFO, method**. This costing method assumes that the first goods purchased were the first goods sold. Therefore, the latest goods purchased remain in inventory.

LEARNING KEY: FIFO means First-In, First-Out.

Whenever possible, a business will attempt to sell the older goods first. This is particularly true of businesses that sell perishable items or merchandise that may become obsolete. Grocery stores, fresh fruit stands, and computer software businesses are good examples. These businesses must rotate their stock forward. They pull the oldest bread, milk, fruit, and vegetables to the front of the shelves and try to sell all copies of the current software before a new version arrives. FIFO costing is, therefore, widely used because it often follows the actual movement of goods. It assumes that the oldest units have been sold and the newest or freshest units are in the ending inventory.

Applying FIFO to the bicycle inventory data, the cost of goods sold and the cost of inventory at the end of the period are determined as shown in Figure 18-7.

FIGURE 18-7 FIFO Inventory Method

	COST OF GOODS SOLD			COST OF ENDING INVENTORY		
	Units	Unit Price	Total	Units	Unit Price	Total
Beginning inventory	40	$62	$ 2,480		$62	$ 0
1st purchase	60	65	3,900		65	0
2nd purchase	80	67	5,360		67	0
3rd purchase	20	68	1,360	50	68	3,400
Total	200		$13,100	50		$ 3,400
Alternative calculation given goods available for sale and cost of goods sold or ending inventory.	Cost of goods available for sale $16,500 Less cost of ending inventory (3,400) Cost of goods sold $13,100			Cost of goods available for sale $16,500 Less cost of goods sold (13,100) Cost of ending inventory $ 3,400		

Note that the 50 items on hand at the end of the period are considered to be those most recently purchased.

FIFO costing is widely used because businesses have used this method for a long time. Accountants are reluctant to change a long-followed method of accounting when such a change would affect the comparability of their income calculations over a period of years. **Consistency** based on comparability is an important accounting principle.

 LEARNING KEY: The consistency principle of accounting suggests that a business should use the same accounting techniques from year to year.

Weighted-Average Method. Another method of allocating merchandise cost is called the **weighted-average method**, or **average cost method**. This costing method is based on the average cost of identical units.

Consider the bicycle inventory data again. The average cost of identical units is determined by dividing the total cost of units available for sale ($16,500) by the total number of units available for sale (250).

$$\frac{\$16,500 \text{ (cost of units available for sale)}}{250 \text{ (units available for sale)}} = \$66 \text{ weighted-average cost per unit}$$

The cost of goods sold and the cost of the end-of-period inventory are calculated as follows:

Cost of goods sold	200	units @ $66 =	$13,200
Cost of ending inventory	50	units @ $66 =	3,300
Total	250	units	$16,500

There is a logical appeal to the weighted-average method of allocating cost between goods sold and goods on hand. In this example, one-fifth (50) of the total units available (250) were unsold. The weighted-average method assigns one-fifth ($3,300) of the total cost ($16,500) to these goods.

Last-In, First-Out (LIFO) Method. A fourth method of allocating merchandise cost is called the **last-in, first-out,** or **LIFO, method.** It assumes that the sales in the period were made from the most recently purchased goods. Therefore, the earliest goods purchased remain in inventory.

LEARNING KEY: LIFO means Last-In, First-Out.

This physical flow is associated with businesses selling products that are not perishable or likely to become obsolete, and may be difficult to handle. Imagine a large barrel of nails at a lumberyard. Customers take nails from the top of the barrel. When the supply gets low, new nails are simply piled on top of the old ones. There is no need to rotate the nails from the bottom to the top of the barrel.

Applying LIFO to the bicycle inventory data, the cost of goods sold and the cost of inventory at the end of the period are determined as shown in Figure 18-8.

FIGURE 18-8 LIFO Inventory Method

	COST OF GOODS SOLD			COST OF ENDING INVENTORY		
	Units	Unit Price	Total	Units	Unit Price	Total
Beginning inventory	0	$62	$ 0	40	$62	$ 2,480
1st purchase	50	65	3,250	10	65	650
2nd purchase	80	67	5,360		67	0
3rd purchase	70	68	4,760		68	0
Total	200		$13,370	50		$ 3,130
Alternative calculation given goods available for sale and cost of goods sold or ending inventory.	Cost of goods available for sale $16,500 Less cost of ending inventory (3,130) Cost of goods sold $13,370			Cost of goods available for sale $16,500 Less cost of goods sold (13,370) Cost of ending inventory $ 3,130		

Note that the 50 units on hand at the end of the period are considered to be the 40 units in the beginning inventory plus 10 of the units from the first purchase.

The LIFO method has been justified on the grounds that the physical movement of goods in some businesses is actually last-in, first-out. This is rarely the case, but the method has become popular for other reasons. One persuasive argument for the use of the LIFO method is that it matches the most current cost of items purchased against the current sales revenue. When the most current costs of purchases are subtracted from sales revenue, the impact of changing prices on the resulting gross profit figure is minimized. In the opinion of many accountants, this is proper and desirable.

Another major reason for the popularity of the LIFO method is its effect on income taxes. When prices are rising, net income calculated under the LIFO method is less than net income calculated under either the FIFO or the weighted-average method. Since the net income amount under LIFO is less, the related income tax will be less. The reverse would be true if prices were falling. However, periods of falling prices over the past two centuries have been few and very brief.

Opponents of the LIFO method contend that its use causes old, out-of-date inventory costs to be shown on the balance sheet. The theoretical and practical merits of FIFO versus LIFO are the subject of much professional debate.

Physical Flows and Cost Flows. Of the four inventory costing methods described, only the specific identification costing method will necessarily reflect cost flows that match physical flows of goods. Each of the other three methods—FIFO, weighted-average, and LIFO—is based on assumed cost flows. The assumed cost flows *are not required to reflect the actual physical movement of goods* within the company. Any one of the three assumed cost flow methods could be used under any set of physical flow conditions. For example, a fresh fruit stand with an actual FIFO flow of inventory may use LIFO for accounting purposes. Similarly, a supplier of building materials that sells nails, lumber, and sand off the top of the pile may use FIFO even though the physical flow of goods is LIFO.

 LEARNING KEY: The inventory method used does not have to match the physical flow of goods.

Comparison of Methods. To compare the results of the four inventory methods, let's assume that the 200 bicycle units in our example were sold for $18,000. Figure 18-9 contrasts the ending inventory, cost of goods sold, and gross profit under each of the four methods.

FIGURE 18-9 Comparison of Inventory Methods

	SPECIFIC IDENTIFICATION		FIFO		WEIGHTED-AVERAGE		LIFO	
Sales		$18,000		$18,000		$18,000		$18,000
Cost of goods sold:								
Beginning inventory	$ 2,480		$ 2,480		$ 2,480		$ 2,480	
Purchases	14,020		14,020		14,020		14,020	
Goods available for sale	$16,500		$16,500		$16,500		$16,500	
Less ending inventory	3,290		3,400		3,300		3,130	
Cost of goods sold		13,210		13,100		13,200		13,370
Gross profit		$ 4,790		$ 4,900		$ 4,800		$ 4,630

Note that in all cases the total cost of goods available for sale ($16,500) is the same. It is the allocation between goods sold and goods on hand at the end of the period that differs. For example, under FIFO, $13,100 is assigned to cost of goods sold and $3,400 to ending inventory. Under conditions of rising prices, the gross profit is lowest if LIFO is used. This is because the most recent, and therefore the highest, purchase costs are matched against sales revenue.

LEARNING KEY: In periods of rising prices, LIFO produces the lowest net income and FIFO produces the highest net income.

The Perpetual Inventory System

Under the perpetual inventory system, a continuous record is maintained for the quantities and costs of goods on hand at all times. The general ledger account for Merchandise Inventory under such a system is somewhat like the account for Cash. It provides a chronological record of each addition (purchase) and subtraction (sale). The balance of the account at any time shows the cost of goods that should be on hand.

When perpetual inventory records are kept, the merchandise inventory account in the general ledger is usually a controlling account. A subsidiary ledger is maintained with an account for each type of merchandise. These accounts are often recorded on cards or in computer files. As shown in Figure 18-10, the subsidiary accounts are designed to handle additions and subtractions and determine the new balance after each change. Goods sold usually are assigned cost on either a FIFO, weighted-average, or LIFO basis. Procedures for applying the FIFO method in a perpetual inventory system are similar to those illustrated for a periodic system. The first merchandise purchased is treated as the first merchandise sold. The illustration in Figure 18-10 is based on the FIFO method. The specific techniques used to apply the weighted-average and LIFO methods in a perpetual system are more complicated. They are illustrated in more advanced texts.

LEARNING KEY: A controlling account and subsidiary ledger are maintained for inventory in much the same way as for accounts receivable and accounts payable.

FIGURE 18-10 Perpetual Inventory Record: FIFO Method

CHILDREN'S BICYCLES

Date	Purchases Quantity	Cost Per Unit	Total	Cost of Goods Sold Quantity	Cost Per Unit	Total	Cum. Total	Inventory Quantity	Cost Per Unit	Subtotal	Total
1/1/--								40	62	2,480	2,480
2/15/--				30	62	1,860	1,860	10	62	620	620
3/1/--	60	65	3,900					10	62	620	
								60	65	3,900	4,520
4/1/--				10	62	620					
				30	65	1,950	4,430	30	65	1,950	1,950
5/15/--	80	67	5,360					30	65	1,950	
								80	67	5,360	7,310
6/30/--				30	65	1,950					
				60	67	4,020	10,400	20	67	1,340	1,340
8/28/--	70	68	4,760					20	67	1,340	
								70	68	4,760	6,100
10/30/--				20	67	1,340					
				20	68	1,360	13,100	50	68	3,400	3,400

Perpetual inventories do not eliminate the need for taking periodic physical inventories. The perpetual records must be compared with the physical inventory to discover and correct any errors or losses of merchandise from theft or breakage. If a difference is found between the physical count and the amount in the perpetual inventory records, the records must be corrected by an adjusting entry. Normally an account called **Inventory Short and Over** is used. For example, if the book balance is $3,840 and the physical count shows $3,710 worth of merchandise, the $130 shortage would be entered as follows:

4		Inventory Short and Over			1 3 0 00				4
5		Merchandise Inventory					1 3 0 00		5
6		To adjust inventory per physical count							6

 LEARNING KEY: A physical inventory is still important under the perpetual inventory method. It is used to verify the accuracy of the inventory records.

Similarly, if the book balance is $3,840 and the physical count shows $3,900 worth of merchandise, this $60 overage would be entered as follows:

4		Merchandise Inventory			6 0 00				4
5		Inventory Short and Over					6 0 00		5
6		To adjust inventory per physical count							6

If Inventory Short and Over has a debit balance, the account is listed with other expenses on the income statement. If it has a credit balance, the account is listed with other revenues on the income statement.

 LEARNING KEY: Inventory Short and Over is reported as other expense or other revenue on the income statement.

A business that sells a wide selection of low-cost goods may not find it practical to keep a perpetual inventory. In contrast, a business that sells a few high-cost items (cars, fine jewelry, stereo equipment) can maintain such a record without incurring excessive processing costs. The increasing use of computers and optical scanning devices at the point of sale has enabled more businesses to switch from the periodic to the perpetual inventory method.

Lower-of-Cost-or-Market Method of Inventory Valuation

It is a well-established tradition in accounting that gains should not be recognized unless a sale has occurred. If the value of an asset increases while it is being held, no formal entry of the gain is made on the books. On the other hand, if an asset's value declines while it is being held, it is generally considered proper to recognize a loss. This is in keeping with the accounting practice of **conservatism**, which states that when in doubt, the lower asset value and net income measure should

 LEARNING KEY: The accounting practice of conservatism states that when in doubt, the lower asset value and net income measure should be used. Thus, when in doubt, we should not record gains, but we should record losses.

be used. Thus, we should never anticipate gains, but we should always anticipate and account for losses.

As applied to inventory, conservatism means that if the value of inventory declines while it is being held, the loss should be recognized in the period of the decline. The purpose of the **lower-of-cost-or-market method** is to recognize such losses on the income statement and to report the lower inventory valuation on the balance sheet.

In applying the lower-of-cost-or-market method, "**cost**" means the dollar amount calculated using one of the four inventory costing methods. "**Market**" means the cost to replace the inventory. It is the price in the market in which goods are purchased by the business—not the price in the market in which they are normally sold by the business. The lower-of-cost-or-market method assumes that a decline in the purchase (replacement) price of inventory is accompanied by a decline in the selling price. In this sense, a decline in the purchase (replacement) price signals a decline in the value of the inventory.

LEARNING KEY: Under lower-of-cost-or-market, market represents the cost to replace the inventory item, not the selling price.

To illustrate the lower-of-cost-or-market method, assume the following end-of-period inventory data for three items:

Item	Recorded Purchase Cost	End-of-Period Market Value	Lower-of-Cost-or-Market
1	$ 8,000	$ 7,000	$ 7,000
2	9,000	10,000	9,000
3	7,000	6,500	6,500
	$24,000	$23,500	$22,500

The illustration shows two ways to calculate the lower-of-cost-or-market. First, the lower-of-cost-or-market method can be applied to the total inventory. This involves comparing the $24,000 total cost with the $23,500 *total end-of-period market value*. Under the second approach, the method is applied to each item in inventory. This involves comparing the $24,000 total cost with the $22,500 lower-of-cost-or-market value determined by comparing cost with market value for *each item*. Either approach is acceptable, but the one chosen should be applied consistently across periods.

The difference between the cost and market value is considered a loss due to holding inventory. Normally it is charged to an account such as Loss on Write-Down of Inventory. For example, based on application of the method to the total inventory in the above illustration, a $500 loss ($24,000 − $23,500) is recognized as follows:

14		Loss on Write-Down of Inventory		5 0 0 00			14
15		Merchandise Inventory			5 0 0 00		15
16		To recognize loss in value of inventory held					16

The loss due to write-down of inventory should be reported on the income statement as an expense. Although not a preferred treatment, some businesses include it in cost of goods sold if the amounts are small.

Lower-of-cost-or-market may not be used with LIFO costing for tax purposes.

ESTIMATING ENDING INVENTORY AND COST OF GOODS SOLD

LO 4 Estimate the ending inventory and cost of goods sold by using the gross profit and retail inventory methods.

Many businesses prepare monthly or quarterly financial statements. To do this, the business must estimate the inventory at the end of the month or quarter and the cost of goods sold for the period. This is not a problem for businesses using the perpetual inventory method. Although these amounts need to be verified by a physical inventory at the end of the year, the unverified amounts are generally reliable estimates and can be used for these "interim" statements.

Businesses using the periodic inventory method must use other methods to estimate the ending inventory and cost of goods sold. Two generally accepted methods are the gross profit method and the retail inventory method.

Gross Profit Method of Estimating Inventory

Under the **gross profit method**, a business's normal gross profit (Net Sales – Cost of Goods Sold) is used to estimate the cost of goods sold and ending inventory. To illustrate the gross profit method, assume the following data with respect to Groomer Company:

Inventory, start of period	$80,000
Net purchases, first month	$70,000
Net sales, first month	$110,000
Normal gross profit as a percentage of sales	40%

The estimated cost of goods sold for the month and the estimated merchandise inventory at the end of the month would be determined as shown in Figure 18-11.

FIGURE 18-11 Steps for the Gross Profit Method

STEP 1	Compute the cost of goods available for sale	Cost of goods available for sale:		
		Inventory, start of period	$ 80,000	
		Net purchases, first month	70,000	
		Cost of goods available for sale		$150,000
STEP 2	Estimate cost of goods sold by deducting the normal gross profit from net sales.	Estimated cost of goods sold:		
		Net sales	$110,000	
		Normal gross profit	44,000	
		($110,000 × 40%)		
		Estimated cost of goods sold		66,000
STEP 3	Estimate the ending inventory by deducting cost of goods sold from the cost of goods available for sale.	Estimated end-of-month inventory		$ 84,000

This calculation is appropriate only if the firm's normal gross profit as a percentage of net sales has been relatively stable over time. This type of calculation also can be used to test the reasonableness of the amount of inventory that was computed on the basis of a physical count. A large difference between the two amounts might indicate a mistake in the count, a mistake in the costing of the items, or a marked change in the gross profit rate. The gross profit procedure also can be used to estimate the cost of an inventory that was destroyed by fire or other casualty.

Retail Method of Estimating Inventory

Many retail businesses, such as department and clothing stores, use a variation of the gross profit method to calculate cost of goods sold and ending inventory. The procedure used, called the **retail method** of inventory, requires keeping records of both the cost and selling (retail) prices of all goods purchased. This information can be used to estimate cost of goods sold and ending inventory, as shown in Figure 18-12.

FIGURE 18-12 Steps in the Retail Inventory Method

			COST	RETAIL
STEP 1	Compute the cost of goods available for sale at cost and retail.	Inventory, start of period Net purchases during period Goods available for sale	$ 60,000 126,000 $186,000	$ 85,000 163,000 $248,000
STEP 2	Compute the ending inventory at retail by subtracting sales at retail from goods available for sale at retail.	Less net sales for period Inventory, end of period, at retail		180,000 $ 68,000
STEP 3	Compute the cost-to-retail ratio by dividing the cost of goods available for sale by retail value of the goods available for sale.	Ratio of cost-to-retail prices of goods available for sale ($186,000 ÷ $248,000)		75%
STEP 4	Estimate the cost of the ending inventory by multiplying the ending inventory at retail (Step 2) by the cost-to-retail ratio.	Inventory, end of period, at estimated cost (75% of $68,000)	(51,000)	
STEP 5	Estimate cost of goods sold by a. multiplying sales at retail by the cost-to-retail ratio, or b. subtracting the estimated ending inventory from the cost of goods available for sale.	Estimated cost of goods sold (or, sales of $180,000 × 75% = $135,000)	$135,000	

PROFILES in ACCOUNTING

Jim Bentley, Pantry/Grocery Manager

Jim Bentley began working part-time at Big K-Mart in 1993. While working, Jim attended Copper Mountain Campus in Joshua Tree, California. He earned an Associate Degree in Business Administration, graduating in the Spring of 1995 with a 4.0 GPA. He continues his employment with Big K-Mart and was recently promoted into management. He is currently the manager of the Pantry/Grocery department in Yucca Valley, California.

While at Copper Mountain Campus, Jim, showed a keen interest in accounting and computers. The skills that he learned have helped him be successful in evaluating and maintaining the inventory of products that attract customers.

His future plans include more schooling in Business Administration and moving up the management ladder at Big K-Mart. He admits that hard work really does pay off.

Source: Rosemarie D. Afflick, College of the Desert, Copper Mountain Campus.

Learning Objectives	Key Points to Remember

1 **Explain the impact of merchandise inventory on the financial statements.**

The cost of goods available for sale during the accounting period must be divided between the cost of goods sold and the ending merchandise inventory. Cost of goods sold is reported on the income statement and used to determine the gross profit for the period. The ending merchandise inventory is reported as a current asset on the balance sheet. Figure 18-13 illustrates the allocation of cost of goods available for sale into cost of goods sold and ending inventory.

FIGURE 18-13 Allocation of Goods Available for Sale to Cost of Goods Sold and Ending Inventory

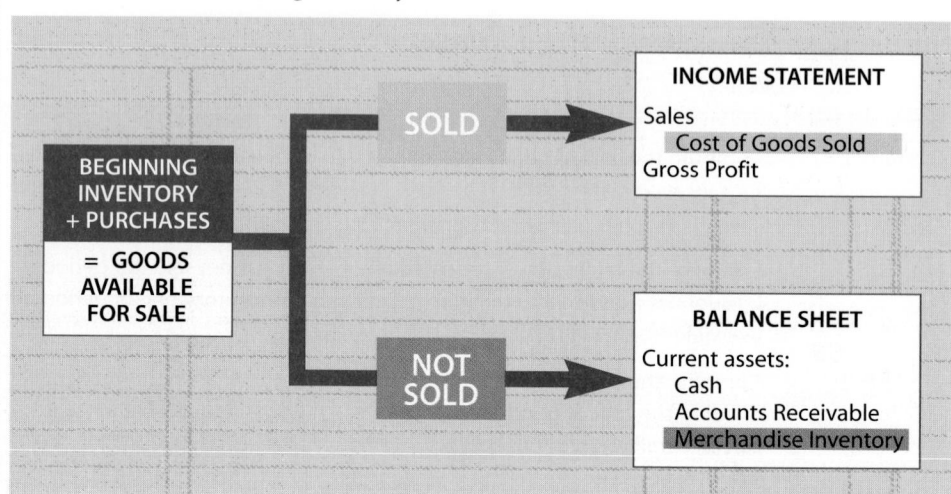

2 **Describe the two principal systems of accounting for merchandise inventory—the periodic system and the perpetual system.**

There are two systems of accounting for merchandise.

Periodic Inventory System
1. The purchases account is debited for the cost of all goods purchased.
2. The sales account is credited for the selling prices of all goods sold.
3. At the end of the accounting period, a physical inventory is taken and the following formula is applied to calculate cost of goods sold.

	Beginning Inventory (last year's ending physical count)
+	Net Purchases (account balance at end of this year)
=	Cost of Goods Available for Sale
−	Ending Inventory (this year's ending physical count)
=	Cost of Goods Sold (for this year)

Perpetual Inventory System
1. The merchandise inventory account is debited for all purchases.
2. The cost of goods sold account is debited and the merchandise inventory account is credited for all sales.
3. Thus, the merchandise inventory account provides a running balance of the goods on hand.

Learning Objectives	Key Points to Remember
3 **Compute the costs allocated to the ending inventory and cost of goods sold using different inventory methods.**	One of four inventory methods is generally used to determine the costs assigned to the goods sold and ending inventory: ▶ Specific identification ▶ FIFO: first-in, first-out ▶ Weighted-average ▶ LIFO: last-in, first-out The actual physical flow of inventory does not have to match the method used. During periods of rising prices, LIFO produces the lowest net income and FIFO produces the highest net income.

4 **Estimate the ending inventory and cost of goods sold by using the gross profit and retail inventory methods.**	Firms using the periodic inventory method often need to estimate their inventory. Two methods are used for this purpose:
	
	▶ **Gross Profit Method**—The firm's normal gross profit as a percentage of net sales is used to estimate cost of goods sold and ending inventory in three steps:
	  1. Compute cost of goods available for sale.
	  2. Estimate cost of goods sold by deducting the normal gross profit (net sales × normal gross profit as percentage of net sales) from net sales.
	  3. Estimate the ending inventory by deducting cost of goods sold from the cost of goods available for sale.
	
	▶ **Retail Inventory Method**—The firm's ratio of cost-to-retail prices of goods available for sale is used to estimate ending inventory and cost of goods sold in five basic steps:
	  1. Compute the cost of goods available for sale at cost and retail.
	  2. Compute the ending inventory at retail by subtracting sales at retail from goods available for sale at retail.
	  3. Compute the cost-to-retail ratio by dividing the cost of goods available for sale by the retail value of the goods available for sale.
	  4. Estimate the cost of ending inventory by multiplying the ending inventory at retail by the cost-to-retail ratio.
	  5. Estimate cost of goods sold by:
	    a. multiplying sales at retail by the cost-to-retail ratio, or
	    b. subtracting the estimated ending inventory from the cost of goods available for sale.

Reflection: Answering the Opening Questions

When a business sells many identical units with different costs, it can be difficult to determine which units were sold and which are still in inventory. Yes, it matters which units were sold. As discussed in the chapter, the cost of goods sold is deducted from net sales to compute gross profit. If all of the less costly units were sold, gross profit would be higher than if all of the more costly units were sold. Thus, John must make an assumption about the flow of inventory through the business. This assumption (FIFO, LIFO, etc.) does not have to match the actual physical flow of the inventory, but must be followed consistently from year to year.

KEY TERMS

average cost method, (664)   See weighted-average method.

conservatism, (668)   The accounting practice of conservatism states that we should never anticipate gains, but always anticipate and account for losses. As applied to inventory, conservatism means that if the value of inventory declines while it is being held, the loss should be recognized in the period of the decline.

consignee, (661)   The company holding the merchandise of another business to be sold.

consignment, (661)   Goods that are held by one business for sale but that are owned by another business.

consignor, (661)   The owner of the merchandise that is held by another business.

consistency, (664)   The principle that states that a business should use the same accounting methods from period to period. This improves the comparability of the financial statements over time.

cost, (669)   In applying the lower-of-cost-or-market method, cost means the dollar amount calculated using one of the four inventory costing methods.

first-in, first-out (FIFO) method, (663)   A method of allocating merchandise cost which assumes that the first goods purchased were the first goods sold and, therefore, that the latest goods purchased remain in inventory.

gross profit method, (670)   A method of estimating inventory in which a business's normal gross profit percentage is used to estimate the cost of goods sold and ending inventory.

in transit, (661)   Goods that are in the process of being shipped between the seller and the buyer.

inventory sheet, (660)   A form used for recording inventory items. It has columns for recording the description of each item, the quantity on hand, the cost per unit, and the extension.

Inventory Short and Over, (668)   An account used to adjust the perpetual inventory records when a difference exists between the physical count and the amount in the perpetual inventory records.

last-in, first-out (LIFO) method, (665)   A method of allocating merchandise cost which assumes that the sales in the period were made from the most recently purchased goods. Therefore, the earliest goods purchased remain in inventory.

lower-of-cost-or-market method, (669)   An inventory valuation method under which inventory is valued at the lower of cost or market value (replacement cost).

market, (669)   In applying the lower-of-cost-or-market method, market means the cost to replace the inventory. It is the prevailing price in the market in which goods are purchased—not the prevailing price in the market in which they are normally sold.

natural business year, (660)   A fiscal year that starts and ends at the time the stock of goods is normally at its lowest level.

periodic inventory system, (658)   Under this system, the ending inventory and cost of goods sold are determined at the end of the accounting period, when a physical inventory is taken.

perpetual inventory system, (658)   Under this system, cost of goods sold and the amount of merchandise inventory on hand are updated when merchandise is bought and sold.

physical inventory, (660)   Counting the goods on hand at the end of the period to allocate merchandise costs between sold and unsold goods.

retail method, (671)   A variation of the gross profit method that is used by many retail businesses, such as department and clothing stores, to estimate the cost of goods sold and ending inventory.

specific identification method, (662)   A method of allocating merchandise cost in which each unit of inventory is specifically identified.

weighted-average method, (664)   A method of allocating merchandise cost based on the average cost of identical units. The average cost of identical units is determined by dividing the total cost of units available for sale by the total number of units available for sale.

DEMONSTRATION PROBLEM

The Fialka Company's beginning inventory and purchases during the fiscal year ended October 31, 20-2, were as follows:

		Units	Unit Price	Total Cost
November 1, 20-1	Beginning inventory	500	$25.00	$ 12,500
November 12, 20-1	1st purchase	600	26.25	15,750
December 28, 20-1	2nd purchase	400	27.50	11,000
March 29, 20-2	3rd purchase	1,000	28.00	28,000
May 31, 20-2	4th purchase	750	28.50	21,375
July 29, 20-2	5th purchase	350	29.00	10,150
August 30, 20-2	6th purchase	675	30.00	20,250
October 21, 20-2	7th purchase	225	31.00	6,975
		4,500		$126,000

There are 1,600 units of inventory on hand on October 31, 20-2.

REQUIRED   1.   Calculate the total amount to be assigned to cost of goods sold for the fiscal year and ending inventory on October 31, 20-2, under each of the following methods:

a.   FIFO

b.   LIFO

c.   Weighted-average cost (round calculations to two decimal places)

2.   Assume that the market price per unit (cost to replace) of Fialka's inventory on October 31, 20-2, was $29. Calculate the total amount to be assigned to the ending inventory on October 31, 20-2, under each of the following methods:

a.   FIFO lower-of-cost-or-market

b.   Weighted-average lower-of-cost-or-market

3.   Now let's assume that a fire destroyed Fialka's store and all inventory on October 31, just prior to taking a physical inventory. Thus, Fialka must estimate the ending inventory and cost of goods sold. During the fiscal year ended October 31, 20-2, net sales of $134,000 were made. The normal gross profit rate is 40%. Use the gross profit method to estimate the cost of goods sold for the fiscal year ended October 31, 20-2, and the inventory on October 31, 20-2.

Solution

1a.

DATE		FIFO INVENTORY METHOD COST OF GOODS SOLD			COST OF ENDING INVENTORY		
20-1/-2		Units	Unit Price	Total	Units	Unit Price	Total
Nov. 1	Beginning inventory	500	$25.00	$ 12,500		$25.00	$ 0
Nov. 12	1st purchase	600	26.25	15,750		26.25	0
Dec. 28	2nd purchase	400	27.50	11,000		27.50	0
Mar. 29	3rd purchase	1,000	28.00	28,000		28.00	0
May 31	4th purchase	400	28.50	11,400	350	28.50	9,975
July 29	5th purchase		29.00	0	350	29.00	10,150
Aug. 30	6th purchase		30.00	0	675	30.00	20,250
Oct. 21	7th purchase		31.00	0	225	31.00	6,975
	Total	2,900		$ 78,650	1,600		$ 47,350

Alternative calculation given goods available for sale and cost of goods sold or ending inventory.	Cost of goods available for sale $126,000 Less cost of ending inventory (47,350) Cost of goods sold $ 78,650	Cost of goods available for sale $126,000 Less cost of goods sold (78,650) Cost of ending inventory $ 47,350

1b.

DATE		LIFO INVENTORY METHOD COST OF GOODS SOLD			COST OF ENDING INVENTORY		
20-1/-2		Units	Unit Price	Total	Units	Unit Price	Total
Nov. 1	Beginning inventory		$25.00	$ 0	500	$25.00	$ 12,500
Nov. 12	1st purchase		26.25	0	600	26.25	15,750
Dec. 28	2nd purchase		27.50	0	400	27.50	11,000
Mar. 29	3rd purchase	900	28.00	25,200	100	28.00	2,800
May 31	4th purchase	750	28.50	21,375		28.50	0
July 29	5th purchase	350	29.00	10,150		29.00	0
Aug. 30	6th purchase	675	30.00	20,250		30.00	0
Oct. 21	7th purchase	225	31.00	6,975		31.00	0
	Total	2,900		$ 83,950	1,600		$ 42,050

Alternative calculation given goods available for sale and cost of goods sold or ending inventory.	Cost of goods available for sale $126,000 Less cost of ending inventory (42,050) Cost of goods sold $ 83,950	Cost of goods available for sale $126,000 Less cost of goods sold (83,950) Cost of ending inventory $ 42,050

1c.   Weighted-average method:
       Average cost per unit: $126,000 ÷ 4,500 units = $28.
       Inventory, October 31, 20-2:
                  1,600 units @ $28 = $44,800
       Cost of goods sold for 20-1/-2:
                  2,900 units @ $28 = $81,200

2a.   FIFO lower-of-cost-or-market:
       FIFO cost $47,350
       Market 1,600 @ $29 $46,400
       Choose market $46,400

2b.   Weighted-average lower-of-cost-or-market:
       Weighted-average cost $44,800
       Market 1,600 @ $29 $46,400
       Choose weighted-average cost $44,800

3. Estimated inventory on October 31, 20-2:
       Inventory, November 1, 20-1 $ 12,500
       Net purchases, November 1, 20-1
          through October 31, 20-2   113,500
       Cost of goods available for sale $126,000
       Estimated cost of goods sold:
          Net sales $134,000
          Normal gross profit ($134,000 × 40%)   53,600
       Estimated cost of goods sold   80,400
       Estimated inventory on October 31, 20-2 $ 45,600

REVIEW QUESTIONS

1. What financial statements are affected by an error in the ending inventory?

2. What is the main difference between the periodic system of accounting for inventory and the perpetual system of accounting for inventory?

3. Is a physical inventory necessary under the periodic method? Why or why not?

4. Is a physical inventory necessary under the perpetual method? Why or why not?

5. In a period of rising prices, which inventory method will result in:

    a.   the highest cost of goods sold?

    b.   the lowest cost of goods sold?

    c.   the highest ending inventory?

    d.   the lowest ending inventory?

    e.   the highest gross profit?

    f.   the lowest gross profit?

6. What two factors are taken into account by the weighted-average method of merchandise cost allocation?

7. Which inventory method always follows the actual physical flow of merchandise?

8. When lower-of-cost-or-market is assigned to the items that comprise the ending merchandise inventory, what does "cost" mean? What does "market" mean?

9. List the three steps followed under the gross profit method of estimating inventory.

10. List the five steps followed under the retail method of estimating inventory.

MANAGING YOUR WRITING

Does your local grocery store have optical scanning devices at the checkout stands? Most major grocery chains have them and they certainly reduce the time required to check out. What benefits do they provide to the business? Next time you go to the grocery store, take a few minutes to chat with the manager. Ask the manager to describe the benefits of the scanning devices over the old machines that required the clerk to key-in each purchase. Pay particular attention to the linkage between the scanning devices and the inventory systems. Be sure to ask whether the grocery store is on a periodic or perpetual system.

After your visit, write a memo to your instructor describing the benefits of the scanning devices and how they are linked with the inventory system.

ETHICS CASE

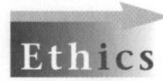

Electronics, Inc., is a high-volume, wholesale merchandising company. Most of its inventory turns over four or five times a year. The company has had 50 units of a particular brand of computers on hand for over a year. These computers have not sold and probably will not sell unless they are discounted 60–70 percent. The accountant is carrying them on the books at cost and intends to recognize the loss when they are sold. This way, she can avoid a significant write-down in inventory on the current year's financial statements.

1. Is the accountant correct in her treatment of the inventory? Why or why not?

2. If the computers cost $1,000 each and their market value is 40 percent of their cost, journalize the entry necessary for the write-down.

3. In a short paragraph, explain what is meant by conservatism and how it ties in with the lower-of-cost-or-market method of accounting for inventory.

4. In groups of three or four, make a list of reasons why inventories of electronic equipment might have to be written down.

WEB WORK

How big a difference in sales can a computerized inventory system make? These two articles offer some insight:

http://www.inc.com/incmagazine/archives/15941021.html
http://www.inc.com/incmagazine/archives/02910811.html
(http://heintz.swcollege.com)

SERIES A EXERCISES

EXERCISE 18A-1 (LO 1) INVENTORY ERRORS Assume that in year 1, the ending merchandise inventory is overstated by $50,000. If this is the only error in years 1 and 2, indicate which items will be understated, overstated, or correctly stated for years 1 and 2.

	Year 1	Year 2
Ending merchandise inventory	Over 50,000	50,000
Beginning merchandise inventory	correct	overstated
Cost of goods sold	over	overs
Gross profit	overstated	understated
Net income	overst.	Understated
Ending owner's capital	overst	OK

EXERCISE 18A-2 (LO 2) JOURNAL ENTRIES—PERIODIC INVENTORY Bill Diamond owns a business called Diamond Distributors. The following transactions took place during January of the current year. Journalize the transactions in a general journal using the periodic inventory method.

Jan. 5 Purchased merchandise on account from Prestigious Jewelers, $3,700.

8 Paid freight charge on merchandise purchased, $200.

12 Sold merchandise on account to Diamonds Unlimited, $4,900.

15 Received a credit memo from Prestigious Jewelers for merchandise returned, $600.

22 Issued a credit memo to Diamonds Unlimited for merchandise returned, $800.

EXERCISE 18A-3 (LO 2) JOURNAL ENTRIES—PERPETUAL INVENTORY Sandy Johnson owns a small variety store. The following transactions took place during March of the current year. Journalize the transactions in a general journal using the perpetual inventory method.

Mar. 3 Purchased merchandise on account from City Galleria, $2,700.

7 Paid freight charge on merchandise purchased, $175.

13 Sold merchandise on account to Amber Specialties, $3,000. The cost of the merchandise was $1,800.

18 Received a credit memo from City Galleria for merchandise returned, $500.

22 Issued a credit memo to Amber Specialties for merchandise returned, $400. The cost of the merchandise was $240.

EXERCISE 18A-4 (LO 3) ENDING INVENTORY COSTS Sandy Chen owns a small specialty store, named Chen's Chattel, whose year end is June 30. Determine the total amount that should be included in Chen's Chattel's year-end inventory. A physical inventory taken on June 30 reveals the following:

Cost of merchandise on the showroom floor and in warehouse	$37,800
Goods held on consignment (consignor is National Manufacturer)	6,400
Goods that Chen's Chattel, as the consignor, has for sale at the location of the Grand Avenue Vista	4,600
Sales invoices indicate that merchandise was shipped on June 29, terms FOB shipping point, delivered at buyer's receiving dock on July 3	3,800
Sales invoices indicate that merchandise was shipped on June 25, terms FOB destination, delivered at buyer's receiving dock on July 5	3,100

EXERCISE 18A-5 (LO 3) JOURNAL ENTRY—INVENTORY SHORT AND OVER Tiger Industries uses the perpetual inventory method in accounting for inventory. Prepare the necessary adjusting entry for each of the following independent cases, using the account Inventory Short and Over. How would Inventory Short and Over be reported on the income statement for each independent case?

Case 1:

Physical count as of April 30	$48,300
Perpetual inventory records as of April 30	46,800

Case 2:

Physical count as of April 30	$43,600
Perpetual inventory records as of April 30	45,200

EXERCISE 18A-6 (LO 3) LOWER-OF-COST-OR-MARKET Stalberg Company's beginning inventory and purchases during the fiscal year ended December 31, 20--, were as follows:

		Units	Unit Price	Total Cost
Jan. 1	Beginning inventory	10	$20	$200
Mar. 5	1st purchase	10	22	220
Sept. 9	2nd purchase	10	25	250
Dec. 8	3rd purchase	10	30	300
		40		$970

There are 10 units of inventory on hand on December 31.

1. Calculate the total amount to be assigned to the ending inventory under each of the following methods:

   a. FIFO

   b. Weighted-average (round calculations to two decimal places)

2. Assume that the market price per unit (cost to replace) of Stalberg's inventory on December 31, 20--, was $26. Calculate the total amount to be assigned to the ending inventory on December 31 under each of the following methods:

   a. FIFO lower-of-cost-or-market

   b. Weighted-average lower-of-cost-or-market

SERIES A PROBLEMS

PROBLEM 18A-1 (LO 3) SPECIFIC IDENTIFICATION, FIFO, LIFO, AND WEIGHTED-AVERAGE The Hamilton Company's beginning inventory and purchases during the fiscal year ended September 30, 20-2, were as follows:

		Units	Unit Price	Total Cost
October 1, 20-1	Beginning inventory	300	$20.00	$ 6,000
October 18	1st purchase	500	21.50	10,750
November 25	2nd purchase	400	22.00	8,800
January 12, 20-2	3rd purchase	800	23.00	18,400
March 17	4th purchase	900	23.50	21,150
June 2	5th purchase	600	24.00	14,400
August 21	6th purchase	500	25.00	12,500
September 27	7th purchase	400	25.75	10,300
		4,400		$102,300

There are 1,000 units of inventory on hand on September 30, 20-2. Of these 1,000 units:

100 are from the October 18, 20-1	1st purchase
300 are from the January 12, 20-2	3rd purchase
100 are from the March 17	4th purchase
200 are from the June 2	5th purchase
100 are from the August 21	6th purchase
200 are from the September 27	7th purchase

REQUIRED Calculate the total amount to be assigned to cost of goods sold for 20-2 and ending inventory on September 30, 20-2, under each of the following methods:

1. FIFO

2. LIFO

3. Weighted-average (round calculations to two decimal places)

4. Specific identification

PROBLEM 18A-2 (LO 3) COST ALLOCATION AND LOWER-OF-COST-OR-MARKET The Douglas Company's beginning inventory and purchases during the fiscal year ended December 31, 20--, were as follows:

		Units	Unit Price	Total Cost
January 1, 20--	Beginning inventory	1,100	$ 8.00	$ 8,800
March 5	1st purchase	900	9.00	8,100
April 16	2nd purchase	400	9.50	3,800
June 3	3rd purchase	700	10.25	7,175
August 18	4th purchase	600	11.00	6,600
September 13	5th purchase	800	12.00	9,600
November 14	6th purchase	400	14.00	5,600
December 3	7th purchase	500	14.05	7,025
		5,400		$56,700

There are 1,000 units of inventory on hand on December 31.

(continued)

REQUIRED

1. Calculate the total amount to be assigned to the ending inventory and cost of goods sold on December 31 under each of the following methods:

   a. FIFO

   b. LIFO

   c. Weighted-average (round calculations to two decimal places)

2. Assume that the market price per unit (cost to replace) of Douglas' inventory on December 31 was $13. Calculate the total amount to be assigned to the ending inventory on December 31 under each of the following methods:

   a. FIFO lower-of-cost-or-market

   b. Weighted-average lower-of-cost-or-market

PROBLEM 18A-3 (LO 4) GROSS PROFIT METHOD A fire completely destroyed all the inventory of Glisan Lumber Yard on August 5, 20--. Fortunately, the books were not destroyed in the fire. The following information is taken from the books of Glisan Lumber Yard for the time period January 1 through August 5:

Beginning inventory, January 1, 20--	$100,000
Net purchases, January 1 through August 5	420,000
Net sales, January 1 through August 5	732,000
Normal gross profit as a percentage of sales	40%

REQUIRED Estimate the amount of merchandise inventory destroyed in the fire on August 5 using the gross profit method.

PROBLEM 18A-4 (LO 4) RETAIL INVENTORY METHOD The following information is taken from the books of Raynette's Pharmacy for the last quarter of its fiscal year ending on March 31, 20--:

	Cost	Retail
Inventory, start of period, January 1, 20--	$ 32,000	$ 52,000
Net purchases during the period	176,000	268,000
Net sales for the period		260,000

REQUIRED

1. Estimate the ending inventory as of March 31 using the retail inventory method.

2. Estimate the cost of goods sold for the time period January 1 through March 31 using the retail inventory method.

SERIES B EXERCISES

EXERCISE 18B-1 (LO 1) INVENTORY ERRORS Assume that in year 1, the ending merchandise inventory is understated by $40,000. If this is the only error in years 1 and 2, indicate which items will be understated, overstated, or correctly stated for years 1 and 2.

	Year 1	Year 2
Ending merchandise inventory	_____	_____
Beginning merchandise inventory	_____	_____
Cost of goods sold	_____	_____
Gross profit	_____	_____
Net income	_____	_____
Ending owner's capital	_____	_____

EXERCISE 18B-2 (LO 2) JOURNAL ENTRIES—PERIODIC INVENTORY Amy Douglas owns a business called Douglas Distributors. The following transactions took place during January of the current year. Journalize the transactions in a general journal using the periodic inventory method.

Jan. 5 Purchased merchandise on account from Elite Warehouse, $4,100.

8 Paid freight charge on merchandise purchased, $300.

12 Sold merchandise on account to Memories Unlimited, $5,200.

15 Received a credit memo from Elite Warehouse for merchandise returned, $700.

22 Issued a credit memo to Memories Unlimited for merchandise returned, $400.

EXERCISE 18B-3 (LO 2) JOURNAL ENTRIES—PERPETUAL INVENTORY Doreen Woods owns a small variety store. The following transactions took place during March of the current year. Journalize the transactions in a general journal using the perpetual inventory method.

Mar. 3 Purchased merchandise on account from Corner Galleria, $3,500.

7 Paid freight charge on merchandise purchased, $200.

13 Sold merchandise on account to Sonya Specialties, $4,250. The cost of the merchandise was $2,550.

18 Received a credit memo from Corner Galleria for merchandise returned, $900.

22 Issued a credit memo to Sonya Specialties for merchandise returned, $500. The cost of the merchandise was $300.

EXERCISE 18B-4 (LO 3) ENDING INVENTORY COSTS Danny Steele owns a small specialty store, named Steele's Storeroom, whose year end is June 30. Determine the total amount that should be included in Steele's Storeroom's year-end inventory. A physical inventory taken on June 30 reveals the following:

Cost of merchandise on the showroom floor and in warehouse	$42,600
Goods held on consignment (consignor is Quality Manufacturer)	7,600

(continued)

Goods that Steele's Storeroom, as the consignor, has for sale at the location of the Midtown Galleria	8,300
Sales invoices indicate that merchandise was shipped on June 28, terms FOB shipping point, delivered at buyer's receiving dock on July 6	4,350
Sales invoices indicate that merchandise was shipped on June 26, terms FOB destination, delivered at buyer's receiving dock on July 1	2,800

EXERCISE 18B-5 (LO 3) JOURNAL ENTRY—INVENTORY SHORT AND OVER Hanson Industries uses the perpetual inventory method in accounting for inventory. Prepare the necessary adjusting entry for each of the following independent cases, using the account Inventory Short and Over. How would Inventory Short and Over be reported on the income statement for each independent case?

Case 1:

Physical count as of April 30	$44,150
Perpetual inventory records as of April 30	47,300

Case 2:

Physical count as of April 30	$38,400
Perpetual inventory records as of April 30	36,200

EXERCISE 18B-6 (LO 3) LOWER-OF-COST-OR-MARKET Bouie Company's beginning inventory and purchases during the fiscal year ended December 31, 20--, were as follows:

		Units	Unit Price	Total Cost
Jan. 1	Beginning inventory	20	$30	$ 600
Mar. 5	1st purchase	22	34	748
Sept. 9	2nd purchase	24	35	840
Dec. 8	3rd purchase	22	40	880
		88		$3,068

There are 20 units of inventory on hand on December 31.

1. Calculate the total amount to be assigned to the ending inventory under each of the following methods:

   a. FIFO

   b. Weighted-average (round calculations to two decimal places)

2. Assume that the market price per unit (cost to replace) of Bouie's inventory on December 31, 20--, was $39. Calculate the total amount to be assigned to the ending inventory on December 31 under each of the following methods:

   a. FIFO lower-of-cost-or-market

   b. Weighted-average lower-of-cost-or-market

SERIES B PROBLEMS

PROBLEM 18B-1 (LO 3) SPECIFIC IDENTIFICATION, FIFO, LIFO, AND WEIGHTED-AVERAGE The Boyce Company's beginning inventory and purchases during the fiscal year ended September 30, 20-2, were as follows:

		Units	Unit Price	Total Cost
October 1, 20-1	Beginning inventory	400	$15.00	$ 6,000
October 18	1st purchase	300	16.50	4,950
November 25	2nd purchase	600	17.00	10,200
January 12, 20-2	3rd purchase	700	17.25	12,075
March 17	4th purchase	800	18.00	14,400
June 2	5th purchase	400	19.00	7,600
August 21	6th purchase	300	21.00	6,300
September 27	7th purchase	500	21.75	10,875
		4,000		$72,400

There are 900 units of inventory on hand on September 30, 20-2. Of these 900 units:

50 are from the October 18, 20-1	1st purchase
300 are from the January 12, 20-2	3rd purchase
100 are from the March 17	4th purchase
200 are from the June 2	5th purchase
50 are from the August 21	6th purchase
200 are from the September 27	7th purchase

REQUIRED Calculate the total amount to be assigned to the cost of goods sold for 20-2 and ending inventory on September 30, 20-2, under each of the following methods:

1. FIFO

2. LIFO

3. Weighted-average (round calculations to two decimal places)

4. Specific identification

PROBLEM 18B-2 (LO 3) COST ALLOCATION AND LOWER-OF-COST-OR-MARKET The Hall Company's beginning inventory and purchases during the fiscal year ended December 31, 20--, were as follows:

		Units	Unit Price	Total Cost
January 1	Beginning inventory	800	$11.00	$ 8,800
March 5	1st purchase	600	12.00	7,200
April 16	2nd purchase	500	12.50	6,250
June 3	3rd purchase	700	14.00	9,800
August 18	4th purchase	800	15.00	12,000
September 13	5th purchase	900	17.00	15,300
November 14	6th purchase	400	18.00	7,200
December 3	7th purchase	500	20.30	10,150
		5,200		$76,700

There are 1,100 units of inventory on hand on December 31.

(continued)

REQUIRED 1. Calculate the total amount to be assigned to the ending inventory and cost of goods sold on December 31 under each of the following methods:

a. FIFO

b. LIFO

c. Weighted-average (round calculations to two decimal places)

2. Assume that the market price per unit (cost to replace) of Hall's inventory on December 31 was $16. Calculate the total amount to be assigned to the ending inventory on December 31 under each of the following methods:

a. FIFO lower-of-cost-or-market

b. Weighted-average lower-of-cost-or-market

PROBLEM 18B-3 (LO 4) GROSS PROFIT METHOD A flood completely destroyed all the inventory of Bayside Waterworks Company on July 1, 20--. Fortunately, the books were not destroyed in the flood. The following information is taken from the books of Bayside Waterworks for the time period January 1 through July 1, 20--:

Beginning inventory, January 1, 20--	$ 60,000
Net purchases, January 1 through July 1	380,000
Net sales, January 1 through July 1	650,000
Normal gross profit as a percentage of sales	45%

REQUIRED Estimate the amount of merchandise inventory destroyed in the flood on July 1 using the gross profit method.

PROBLEM 18B-4 (LO 4) RETAIL INVENTORY METHOD The following information is taken from the books of Beverly's Basket Corner for the last quarter of its fiscal year ending on March 31, 20--.

	Cost	Retail
Inventory, start of period, January 1, 20--	$ 50,000	$ 80,000
Net purchases during the period	220,000	352,000
Net sales for the period		310,000

REQUIRED 1. Estimate the ending inventory as of March 31 using the retail inventory method.

2. Estimate the cost of goods sold for the time period January 1 through March 31 using the retail inventory method.

MASTERY PROBLEM

The Tiller Company's beginning inventory and purchases during the fiscal year ended December 31, 20-2, were as follows:

		Units	Unit Price	Total Cost
January 1, 20-2	Beginning inventory	1,500	$10.00	$15,000
January 12	1st purchase	500	11.50	5,750
February 28	2nd purchase	600	14.50	8,700
June 29	3rd purchase	1,200	15.00	18,000
August 31	4th purchase	800	16.50	13,200
October 29	5th purchase	300	18.00	5,400
November 30	6th purchase	700	18.50	12,950
December 21	7th purchase	400	20.00	8,000
		6,000		$87,000

There are 1,200 units of inventory on hand on December 31, 20-2.

REQUIRED

1. Calculate the total amount to be assigned to the cost of goods sold for 20-2 and ending inventory on December 31 under each of the following methods:

   a. FIFO

   b. LIFO

   c. Weighted-average (round calculations to two decimal places)

2. Assume that the market price per unit (cost to replace) of Tiller's inventory on December 31 was $18. Calculate the total amount to be assigned to the ending inventory on December 31 under each of the following methods:

   a. FIFO lower-of-cost-or-market

   b. Weighted-average lower-of-cost-or-market

3. In addition to taking a physical inventory on December 31, Tiller decides to estimate the ending inventory and cost of goods sold. During the fiscal year ended December 31, 20-2, net sales of $100,000 were made at a normal gross profit rate of 35%. Use the gross profit method to estimate the cost of goods sold for the fiscal year ended December 31 and the inventory on December 31.

Self-Study Test Questions

True/False

1. An overstatement of ending inventory in the year 20-1 will cause net income to be overstated in the year 20-1. _____

2. An understatement of ending inventory in the year 20-1 will cause net income to be overstated in the year 20-2, assuming no other errors. _____

3. Under the perpetual system of accounting for inventory, the current merchandise inventory and the cost of goods sold are not determined until the end of the accounting period when a physical inventory is taken. _____

4. A fiscal year that starts and ends at the time the stock of goods is normally at its lowest level is known as a natural business year. _____

5. If goods are shipped FOB shipping point, the seller pays for the shipping costs. _____

Multiple Choice

1. Goods held on consignment remain the property of the _____

   (a) consignee.   (c) buyer.
   (b) consignor.   (d) seller.

2. In times of rising prices, the inventory cost method that will yield the lowest net income is _____

   (a) FIFO.   (c) LIFO.
   (b) weighted-average.   (d) none of the above.

3. In times of rising prices, the inventory cost method that will yield the highest cost of goods sold is _____

   (a) LIFO.   (c) FIFO.
   (b) weighted-average.   (d) none of the above.

4. In the application of "lower-of-cost-or-market," market is _____

   (a) lowest sales price.   (c) replacement cost.
   (b) highest sales price.   (d) average sales price.

5. An understatement of ending inventory in the year 20-1 will cause the owner's equity account at the end of the year 20-2, assuming no other errors, to be _____

   (a) understated.   (c) overstated.
   (b) correctly stated.   (d) none of the above.

The answers to the Self-Study Test Questions are at the end of the text.

19

Accounting for Long-Term Assets

LEARNING OBJECTIVES:

Careful study of this chapter should enable you to:

LO 1 Determine the cost of property, plant, and equipment.

LO 2 Explain the nature and purpose of depreciation.

LO 3 Compute depreciation using the straight-line, declining-balance, sum-of-the-years'-digits, and units-of-production methods.

LO 4 Account for repairs, maintenance, additions, and improvements to plant and equipment.

LO 5 Account for the disposition of property, plant, and equipment.

LO 6 Explain the nature, purpose, and accounting for depletion.

LO 7 Explain the nature of and account for intangible assets.

John Zenith believes his business could be more profitable if he had a delivery van to pick up merchandise and make deliveries. In fact, he thinks the business needs two delivery vans, but he can afford only one at this time. The expected useful life of the van is four years, but it will be used especially heavily during the first year or two until John can purchase a second van. Betty Jenkins, his bookkeeper, has described straight-line depreciation to him, but he does not believe that this pattern of depreciation will match the way he plans to use the van. Are there other depreciation methods that could be used?

Assets that are expected to provide benefits for a number of accounting periods are called **long-term assets**. Long-term assets that are **tangible** (have physical substance) and that are used in the operations of the business are called **property, plant, and equipment; plant assets;** or **fixed assets**. Examples include land, buildings, furniture, and equipment. Assets whose physical substance consists of natural resources that are consumed in the operation of the business are often called **wasting assets**. Examples include mines (coal, salt, and gold), stands of timber, and oil and gas wells. Long-term assets that have no physical substance are called **intangible assets**. Common examples include patents, copyrights, and trademarks.

All long-term assets except land gradually wear out or are used up as time passes. As an asset's useful life expires, a portion of the asset's cost is recognized as an expense. This is often referred to as "writing off" the asset. A different term is used to describe this expense for the different types of long-term assets. For plant assets, the expense is called **depreciation**; for natural resources, it is called **depletion**; and for intangible assets, it is called **amortization**. In this chapter, proper accounting for property, plant, and equipment; natural resources; and intangible assets is described and illustrated.

 LEARNING KEY: Since land does not wear out, no depreciation is recognized.

ACQUISITION COST OF PROPERTY, PLANT, AND EQUIPMENT

LO 1 Determine the cost of property, plant, and equipment.

The cost of a long-term asset includes all amounts spent to acquire the asset and prepare it for its intended use. Purchases of long-term assets are entered by debiting the proper asset account and crediting either the cash or the proper liability account.

Land

All costs incurred to purchase land and prepare it for its intended use are debited to the land account. These costs include legal and real estate fees as well as the cost of removing old buildings and grading the land to prepare it for its intended use. Special tax assessments for streets, sewers, or parks also are debited to the land account, because these items are viewed as permanent.

Land Improvements

Costs related to land that are not permanent in nature are normally debited to the land improvements account. Common examples include the costs of planting trees and shrubs, installing fences, and paving parking areas. Items debited to the land improvements account are depreciated over their expected useful lives.

Buildings

The cost of buildings that are purchased includes the purchase price, realtor and legal fees, and related taxes on the purchase. If the purchase price includes land, the cost of the land and building must be determined and accounted for separately. If the building is constructed, costs include all normal construction costs for material and labor and architectural and engineering fees. In addition, insurance premiums and interest on loans *while the building is being constructed* are considered part of the cost of the asset.

Equipment

The cost of equipment includes the purchase price, transportation charges, insurance while in transit, installation costs, and any other costs that are incurred up to the point of placing the asset in service.

Treatment of Interest when Acquiring or Constructing Assets

The proper treatment of interest depends on whether the asset is being purchased or constructed. Often, businesses must borrow money to buy major long-term assets. The method used to finance the *acquisition* of an asset should not affect its cost. For example, interest on a mortgage to purchase a building should not be included in the cost of the asset. We always use the **cash equivalent price**, which is the amount of cash that could have been paid for the asset on the date of purchase.

Interest costs are treated differently for assets being constructed. Interest incurred *while an asset is being constructed* should be included as part of the cost of the asset. Since the asset is not operational during the construction period, it is not generating revenues against which the interest could be matched. Thus, the interest is included in the cost of the asset and recognized as part of depreciation expense when the asset is placed in operation and begins generating revenues.

DEPRECIATION

LO 2   Explain the nature and purpose of depreciation.

The purpose of depreciation is to match a plant asset's cost with the revenues it helps to produce. As discussed in earlier chapters, the following is a typical adjusting entry made at the end of each accounting period.

5	Dec.	31	Depr. Expense—Delivery Equipment	541	1	0	0	00						5
6			Accum. Depr.—Delivery Equipment	185.1						1	0	0	00	6
7														7

LEARNING KEY: Depreciation matches an asset's cost with the revenues it helps generate.

Recall that Depreciation Expense is reported on the income statement and Accumulated Depreciation is reported on the balance sheet as a contra-asset. Accumulated Depreciation is deducted from the asset account to report the book value, or undepreciated cost, of the asset.

Keep in mind that depreciation is a process of *cost allocation*, not a process of valuation. Many factors cause the market values of plant assets to change over time. The recognition of depreciation is not intended to make the assets reflect their market values on the balance sheet. The net amounts reported on the balance sheet (book values) are merely the portions of the original costs that have not yet been allocated to expense.

LEARNING KEY: Market Value = Amount Asset Can Be Sold For
Book Value   = Cost – Accumulated Depreciation
The recognition of depreciation is not intended to represent market values on the balance sheet.

The two major types of depreciation are physical and functional. **Physical depreciation** is the loss of usefulness because of deterioration from age and wear. **Functional depreciation** is the loss of usefulness because of inadequacy or obsolescence. As a business grows, some of its plant assets may become inadequate to handle the increased workload. As new manufacturing methods are developed, assets may become obsolete because there are faster, more efficient, or more effective assets that may be used to perform this work.

DEPRECIATION METHODS

LO 3   Compute depreciation using the straight-line, declining-balance, sum-of-the-years'-digits, and units-of-production methods.

Before we discuss the methods of calculating depreciation, there are several terms to be defined.

Cost   The sum of all amounts spent to acquire an asset and prepare it for its intended use.

Useful Life   The amount of service expected to be obtained from an asset. It can be expressed in years, hours of operation, units of production, or miles driven. There is no way of knowing exactly how long an asset will last or exactly what its output will be. Therefore, estimates must be made based on past experience and information from trade associations and engineers.

LEARNING KEY: Recall the concepts of physical and functional depreciation. The useful life is based on an estimate of the period of time that an asset *will be useful* to the business, not necessarily the actual life of the asset.

Salvage Value   The estimated **scrap**, or market, **value** for the asset on its expected disposal date. This amount can be difficult to predict. Often a zero salvage value is used if the asset is expected to have little or no value at the end of its useful life.

Depreciable Cost (Base)   The original cost less salvage (or scrap) value.

> **Depreciable Cost = Original Cost – Salvage Value**

Book Value   The undepreciated cost of the asset.

> **Book Value = Cost – Accumulated Depreciation**

There are several different ways of calculating the amount of depreciation for each period. The most commonly used methods for financial reporting purposes are the following:

1. Straight-line method

2. Declining-balance method

3. Sum-of-the-years'-digits method

4. Units-of-production method

Straight-Line Method

Under the **straight-line method**, the depreciable cost of an asset is allocated equally over the years of the asset's useful life according to the following formula:

Straight-Line Method

$$\text{Annual Depreciation} = \frac{(\text{Cost} - \text{Salvage Value})}{\text{Estimated Useful Life}}$$

To illustrate, assume that a new asset costs $10,000, has an expected life of four years, and has a $1,000 estimated salvage value. Using the straight-line method, the amount of depreciation allocated to each year would be $2,250, computed as follows:

Original Cost	–	Salvage Value	=	Depreciable Cost
$10,000	–	$1,000	=	$9,000

$$\frac{\text{Depreciable Cost}}{\text{Estimated Useful Life}} = \frac{\$9,000}{4 \text{ years}} = \$2,250 \text{ annual depreciation}$$

The annual *rate* of depreciation is 25% (100% ÷ 4 years) of the depreciable cost.

LEARNING KEY: Under the straight-line method, the same amount of depreciation is recorded each period.

A month is usually the shortest period that is used in depreciation accounting. An asset purchased on or before the fifteenth of the month is considered to have been owned for the full month. An asset purchased after the fifteenth of the month is considered to have been acquired the first of the next month.

LEARNING KEY: An asset purchased on or before the fifteenth of the month is depreciated for the full month. An asset purchased after the fifteenth of the month is not depreciated until the next month.

With the straight-line method, the book value of the asset decreases uniformly period by period. As shown in Figure 19-1, the book value over several periods is a downward-sloping, perfectly straight line. That is how the method got its name.

FIGURE 19-1 Comparison of Depreciation Methods

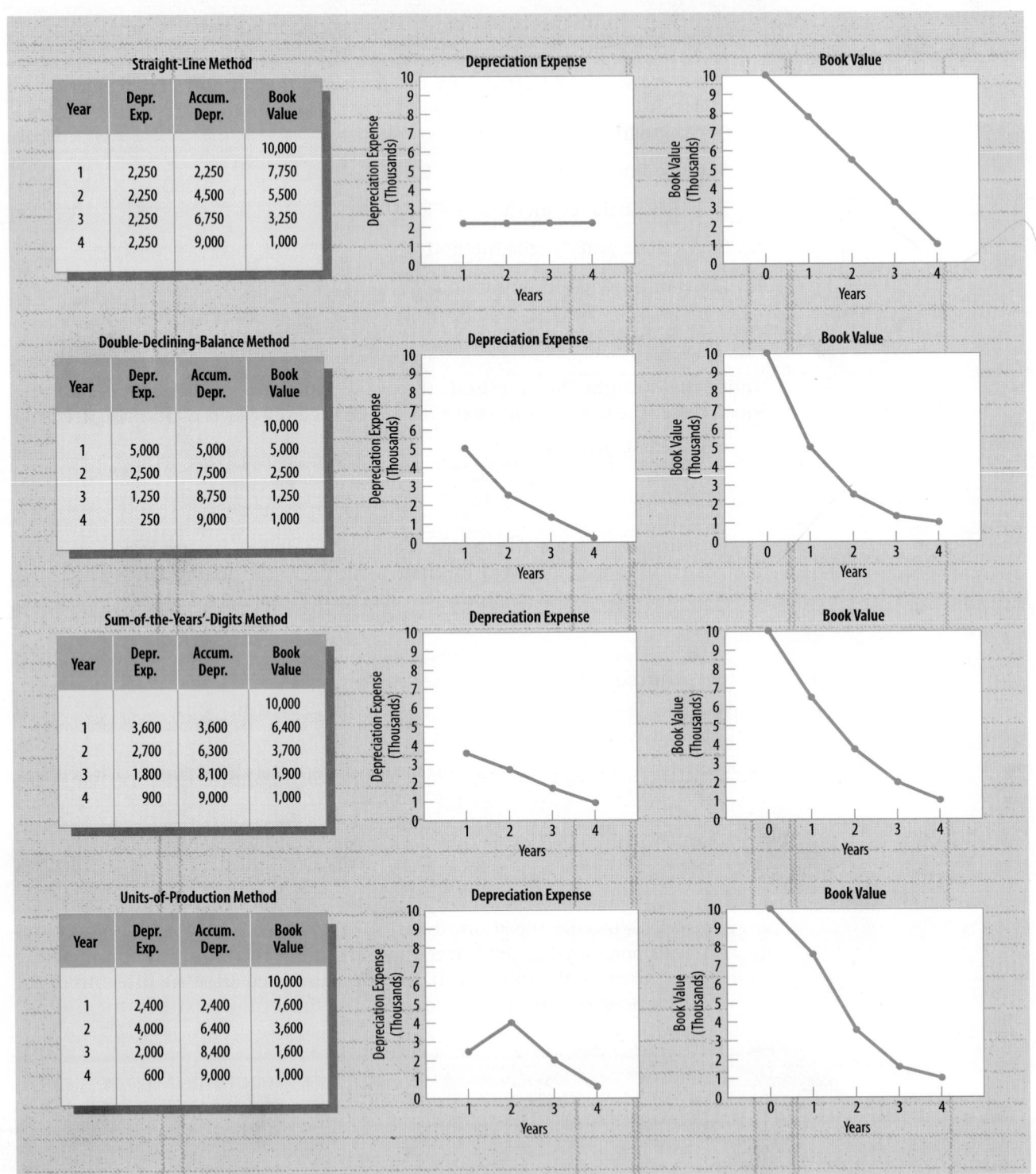

Declining-Balance Method

Many plant assets require repairs and replacement of parts to keep them in service. Such expenses usually increase as the assets get older. Some accountants believe that depreciation expense, therefore, should be higher in the early years to offset the higher repair and maintenance expenses of the later years. Others suggest that assets contribute more to the business when they are comparatively new. For these reasons, it may be desirable to calculate depreciation in a way that will give larger write-offs in the early years of the asset's life. Depreciation methods that provide for a higher depreciation charge in the first year of an asset's life and gradually decreasing charges in subsequent years are called **accelerated depreciation methods**.

One popular accelerated method is the **declining-balance method**. As shown in the formula below, under this method, the book value is multiplied by a fixed rate.

Declining-Balance Method

Annual Depreciation = Depreciation Rate × Book Value at Beginning of Year

This method results in successively smaller depreciation charges as the book value declines year by year. The most common rate used is double the straight-line rate. For this reason, this technique is sometimes referred to as the **double-declining-balance method**.

 LEARNING KEY: "Double" means double the straight-line rate. "Declining balance" means that we should multiply the rate by the declining beginning book value balance.

To illustrate, let's use the same asset as for the straight-line method. The asset cost $10,000, has an expected life of four years, and has a $1,000 estimated salvage value. Using the double-declining-balance method, the depreciation rate to be applied to the book value of the asset each year is 50%, computed as follows:

Straight-line rate = 25% (100% ÷ 4 years)

Double-declining-balance rate = 50% (2 × 25%)

The annual depreciation and the book value at the end of each year are as follows:

Year	Book Value Beginning of Year	Rate	Annual Depreciation	Accumulated Depreciation End of Year	Book Value End of Year
1	$10,000	50%	$5,000	$5,000	$5,000
2	5,000	50	2,500	7,500	2,500
3	2,500	50	1,250	8,750	1,250
4	1,250	—	250	9,000	1,000

The salvage value is not considered in determining the annual depreciation. However, the asset's book value should not be allowed to fall below its estimated salvage value. Thus, the amount of depreciation actually recorded in the final year (year 4) is limited to $250 ($1,250 − $1,000).

LEARNING KEY: Do not subtract the salvage value from the original cost before multiplying by the declining-balance rate.

As shown in Figure 19-1, with the declining-balance method, the book value declines rapidly in the early years and more slowly in the later years of an asset's life. If the asset was acquired at some time other than the beginning of the year, a change would be necessary in the computation of depreciation for the year. For example, if the asset was acquired on April 1, the depreciation for year 1 would be calculated as follows:

> **Year 1: $10,000 × 50% = $5,000 × 9/12 = $3,750**

Depreciation for years 2 through 4 would then be calculated by applying the 50% depreciation rate to the book value of the asset at the beginning of each year, as follows:

Year	Book Value Beginning of Year	Rate	Annual Depreciation	Accumulated Depreciation End of Year	Book Value End of Year
2	$6,250*	50%	$3,125	$6,875	$3,125
3	3,125	50	1,563	8,438	1,562
4	1,562	—	562	9,000	1,000

*$6,250 = $10,000 (cost) − $3,750 (Depreciation for year 1)

Depreciation in year 4 is limited to $562 because the asset should not be depreciated below its estimated salvage value. If the asset continued to be used in year 5, no depreciation would be recorded.

LEARNING KEY: An asset should not be depreciated below its estimated salvage value.

Sum-of-the-Years'-Digits Method

As shown in the following formula, under the **sum-of-the-years'-digits method**, the depreciation each year is determined by multiplying the depreciable cost by a schedule of fractions.

Sum-of-the-Years'-Digits Method

$$\text{Annual Depreciation} = (\text{Cost} - \text{Salvage Value}) \times \frac{\text{Remaining Useful Life}}{\text{Sum-of-the-Years'-Digits}}$$

The numerator in any year is the number of years of remaining life for the asset, measured from the beginning of the year. The denominator for all fractions is determined by listing the digits that represent the years of the estimated life of the asset and adding these digits. For example, suppose that the estimated life of an asset is four years. The sum of the digits (4 + 3 + 2 + 1) equals 10 (the denominator). The following formula can also be used to determine the denominator:

Calculating the Sum-of-the-Years'-Digits

$$S = N \times \frac{(N + 1)}{2}$$

S = sum of the digits
N = number of years of estimated life

If the life of the asset is four years:

$$S = 4 \times \frac{(4 + 1)}{2} = 4 \times (2.5) = 10$$

The denominator equals 10. Therefore, the fractions used for an asset with a four-year life would be 4/10, 3/10, 2/10, and 1/10. Applying these fractions to the asset in our illustration, the results are as follows:

Year	Depreciable Cost	Rate	Annual Depreciation	Accumulated Depreciation End of Year	Book Value End of Year
1	$9,000	4/10	$3,600	$3,600	$6,400
2	9,000	3/10	2,700	6,300	3,700
3	9,000	2/10	1,800	8,100	1,900
4	9,000	1/10	900	9,000	1,000

As shown in Figure 19-1, the pattern of decline in the book value using the sum-of-the-years'-digits method is accelerated. However, the write-off is not as rapid as it is with the double-declining-balance method.

If the asset is acquired at some time other than the beginning of the year, a modification is necessary in the calculation. For example, if the asset is acquired on April 1, the depreciation for years 1 through 3 is calculated as follows:

Year 1: $9,000 × 4/10   = $3,600 × 9/12   =   *$2,700*

Year 2: $9,000 × 4/10   = $3,600 × 3/12   = $ 900
           9,000 × 3/10   =   2,700 × 9/12   =   <u>2,025</u>
                                       $2,925

Year 3: $9,000 × 3/10   = $2,700 × 3/12   = $ 675
           9,000 × 2/10   =   1,800 × 9/12   =   <u>1,350</u>
                                       $2,025

Depreciation for years 4 and 5 is calculated in a similar manner.

Units-of-Production Method

Under the **units-of-production method**, depreciation is based on the extent to which the asset was used during the year. As shown below, annual depreciation is computed in two steps. First, a depreciation charge per unit produced or consumed is computed. Second, this unit rate is multiplied by the number of units produced or consumed during the year.

Units-of-Production Method

Step 1:   Depreciation per Unit   = $\dfrac{\text{(Cost – Salvage Value)}}{\text{Estimated Useful Life in Units}}$

Step 2:   Annual Depreciation = Depreciation per Unit × Number of Units Produced or Consumed this Year

This method can be used for certain types of machinery, equipment, and vehicles. It is most appropriate for assets that receive varying amounts of use over time. For example, assume that a company purchases a car at a cost of $10,000 and expects that it can be sold for $1,000 after 90,000 miles of service. The calculation of depreciation for the first year when the car was driven 24,000 miles is shown below.

Depreciable cost = $10,000 Original Cost − $1,000 Salvage Value = $9,000

$$\text{Depreciation per mile} = \frac{\$9,000 \text{ Depreciable Cost}}{90,000 \text{ Total Miles}} = \$.10$$

First-year depreciation = 24,000 miles × $.10/mile = $2,400

As shown in Figure 19-1, the depreciation expense and book value for each year do not follow a particular pattern. They are a function of the miles driven each year (24,000; 40,000; 20,000; and 6,000 in this illustration).

Depreciation for Federal Income Tax Purposes

A business is allowed to deduct depreciation expenses in calculating taxable income. Allowable depreciation methods for tax purposes vary depending on when the asset was acquired. For plant assets acquired before 1981, any of the four methods described in the previous sections is permitted. For plant assets acquired between 1981 and 1986, either the straight-line method or the **Accelerated Cost Recovery System (ACRS)** must be used. ACRS classifies all business plant assets into four different useful life categories. Most business assets fall into one of three categories: 3-year, 5-year, or 18-year property. For plant assets acquired after 1986, either the straight-line method or the **Modified Accelerated Cost Recovery System (MACRS)** must be used. MACRS identifies eight categories of useful life for plant assets. Most business assets other than real estate fall into one of two categories: 5-year or 7-year property. ACRS and MACRS define depreciation rates for various categories. For example, the rates for 5-year property are shown below. In using these rates, salvage value is ignored. Note that depreciation under MACRS for a 5-year asset must be spread over 6 years. This is because MACRS assumes one-half year's depreciation in year 1 and one-half year's depreciation in year 6. Note that MACRS offers an accelerated "write-off" of the asset and that both methods permit depreciating 100% of the cost of the asset.

Depreciation Rates for Five-Year Assets
ACRS and MACRS Depreciation

Year	ACRS	MACRS
1	15%	20.0%
2	22	32.0
3	21	19.2
4	21	11.5
5	21	11.5
6		5.8
	100%	100.0%

 LEARNING KEY: Under ACRS and MACRS, salvage value is ignored when computing the asset's depreciable cost.

REPAIRS, MAINTENANCE, ADDITIONS, AND IMPROVEMENTS TO PLANT AND EQUIPMENT

LO 4 Account for repairs, maintenance, additions, and improvements to plant and equipment.

Plant and equipment require normal repairs and maintenance for proper operating efficiency and quality. Replacement of minor parts, lubrication, and cleaning are typical examples of normal repairs and maintenance. These expenditures are debited to Repairs Expense, as shown below.

5		Repairs Expense			x	x	x	xx						5
6		Cash or Supplies Inventory							x	x	x	xx		6
7		Made repairs												7

LEARNING KEY: Repairs Expense is debited for normal repair and maintenance costs that do not extend the life of the asset or improve its usefulness.

Additions or improvements to plant and equipment are accounted for in two ways. All additions and some improvements increase the usefulness of the buildings or equipment and will provide benefits in future periods. For example, the addition of a wing to a building and improvements like the installation of partitions, shelving, sprinkler systems, or air conditioning systems enhance the quality and efficiency of the building. These expenditures are debited to the building account and credited to either the cash or a liability account, as shown below.

9		Building or Equipment			x	x	x	xx						9
10		Cash or Liability							x	x	x	xx		10
11		Made addition												11

Since these improvements will benefit future periods, depreciation will be recognized in future periods.

Some improvements extend the useful life of the asset, but do not increase its usefulness or efficiency. For example, a business may replace the engine in a truck. This extends the life of the truck, but it does not improve the truck's usefulness or efficiency. This expenditure is debited to Accumulated Depreciation and credited to either the cash or a liability account, as shown below.

14		Accum. Depr.—Building or Equipment			x	x	x	xx						14
15		Cash or Liability							x	x	x	xx		15
16		Made improvement												16

Accumulated Depreciation is debited because the depreciation taken on the original engine has been recaptured by replacing it with a new one. The debit to Accumulated Depreciation increases the book value of the asset. Since the new engine will benefit future periods, additional depreciation will be taken in future periods.

LEARNING KEY: Expenditures on plant and equipment are accounted for in the following ways:

- If the expenditures simply maintain the asset's operating condition, debit the expense account.
- If the expenditures increase the asset's usefulness or efficiency, debit the asset account.
- If the expenditures extend the asset's useful life, but do not increase its usefulness or efficiency, debit the accumulated depreciation account.

Notice that the book value of the asset is increased regardless of whether we debit the asset account or the accumulated depreciation account. This increase in book value leads to an increase in the amount of depreciation recognized in future periods. To illustrate, assume that a business owns the following two computers that were purchased on January 1, 20-1.

	Computer A	Computer B
Cost	$6,500	$6,500
Salvage value	500	500
Depreciable base	$6,000	$6,000
Estimated life	3 years	3 years
Depreciation method	Straight-line	Straight-line
Depreciation expense		
20-1	$2,000	$2,000

At the beginning of 20-2, a disk drive is replaced on computer A and a new tape drive backup unit is added to computer B. Let's assume that the disk drive and tape backup units cost $400 each. The entries for the improvement to computer A, which extends its life but does not increase its usefulness, and the addition to computer B are shown in T account form below.

Computer A	
6,500	

Computer B	
6,500	
Jan. 1, 20-2 400	
Bal. 6,900	

Accum. Depr.—Computer A	
	Dec. 31, 20-1 2,000
Jan. 1, 20-2 400	
	Bal. 1,600

Accum. Depr.—Computer B	
	Dec. 31, 20-1 2,000

Note that after recording the expenditures on January 1, 20-2, computers A and B both have book values of $4,900 as shown below.

	Computer A	Computer B
Asset account balance	$6,500	$6,900
Accumulated depreciation	(1,600)	(2,000)
Book value	$4,900	$4,900

To compute depreciation expense for 20-2:

1. Compute the new depreciable base by deducting the salvage value from the book value of the computers after recording the expenditures.

2. Divide the new depreciable base by the remaining useful life, two years.

	Computer A	Computer B
Book value	$4,900	$4,900
Salvage value	(500)	(500)
New depreciable cost	$4,400	$4,400
Remaining useful life	2 years	2 years
Depreciation expense ($4,400/2)	$2,200	$2,200

Thus, depreciation expense is $2,200 for each computer in 20-2 and 20-3.

DISPOSAL OF PLANT ASSETS

LO 5   Account for the disposition of property, plant, and equipment.

A plant asset can be disposed of in several ways:

1. It may be discarded or retired.

2. It may be sold.

3. It may be exchanged or traded in for another asset.

Regardless of the method of disposal, any gain or loss that occurred on the disposal must be determined. This is done by comparing the market and book values of the asset on the date of disposal. *To determine the book value on the date of disposal, an adjusting entry must be made to record depreciation from the end of the previous period to the disposal date.* Gains and losses are determined as shown below.

Determining Gains and Losses on Disposal of Assets

Gain = Market Value greater than Book Value

Loss = Market Value less than Book Value

Gains are similar to revenue and increase net income. Losses are similar to expenses and reduce net income. They are reported on the income statement under Other Revenues and Other Expenses.

Discarding or Retiring Plant Assets

A plant asset may be discarded or retired at any time. If its book value on the disposal date is zero, no gain or loss will be realized. If it is greater than zero, the book value of the discarded asset will represent a loss.

To illustrate, assume that a printer with a cost of $800 and accumulated depreciation of $800 is discarded. Because the printer is fully depreciated, its book value is zero and no gain or loss results from this transaction. The removal of the asset and related accumulated depreciation is recorded as follows:

5		Accum. Depr.—Office Equipment			8	0	0	00			5
6		Office Equipment							8	0 0 00	6
7		Discarded printer									7

However, if at the time the printer is discarded, the accumulated depreciation is $720, the book value is $80 and a loss results. In this case, the discard of the asset and recognition of the loss are recorded as follows:

9		Accum. Depr.—Office Equipment			7	2	0	00			9
10		Loss on Discarded Office Equipment				8	0	00			10
11		Office Equipment							8	0 0 00	11
12		Discarded printer									12

Selling Plant Assets

Now let's assume that this same printer is sold for $80 at the time its book value is $80. This transaction is entered as follows:

5		Cash				8	0	00						5
6		Accum. Depr.—Office Equipment			7	2	0	00						6
7		Office Equipment								8	0	0	00	7
8		Sold printer												8

No gain or loss results from this transaction because the printer's selling price, or market value, is equal to its book value.

If the printer is sold for $120 at the time its book value is $80, there is a gain of $40. In this case, the journal entry is as follows:

5		Cash			1	2	0	00						5
6		Accum. Depr.—Office Equipment			7	2	0	00						6
7		Office Equipment								8	0	0	00	7
8		Gain on Sale of Printer									4	0	00	8
9		Sold printer												9

If, instead, the printer is sold for $50, there is a loss of $30. This transaction is recorded as follows:

5		Cash				5	0	00						5
6		Accum. Depr.—Office Equipment			7	2	0	00						6
7		Loss on Sale of Printer				3	0	00						7
8		Office Equipment								8	0	0	00	8
9		Sold printer												9

LEARNING KEY: Gains and losses are always computed by comparing the market and book values of the asset being sold or exchanged.

Exchange or Trade-In of Plant Assets

If one asset is traded in on the purchase of another similar asset, a **trade-in allowance** may be granted. This trade-in allowance may be greater than, less than, or equal to the book value of the asset traded in.

If you have ever traded in a car for a newer model, you know that trade-in allowances frequently are not equal to the fair market value. Therefore, the fair market value of the asset traded in must be determined to calculate the gain or loss on the exchange. For simplicity, however, we will assume in our illustrations that the trade-in allowance is equal to the market value of the old asset being traded.

A BROADER VIEW

VALUE? WHICH VALUE?

Determining the market value of an asset is not always easy. For example, if you have ever traded your car for a newer one, you probably learned that the trade-in allowance is often different from what the dealer would "pay" for the car and different from what you might sell it for by advertising in the newspaper. To test this concept, try it. Next time you are shopping for a car, ask the dealer two questions. First, ask the dealer what trade-in allowance he or she would offer on your car. Then, ask what he or she would accept for the new car if you paid cash. The difference between the "cash price" and the cash that you must pay with a trade-in offers a measure of what the dealer is paying you for your old car. (See illustration below.) This amount probably is not the same as the trade-in allowance offered by the dealer and may not be the same as the amount you could sell the car for by advertising in the paper. Of course, you need this information to make a good decision on whether to trade your car or sell it yourself.

Sticker price of new car	$20,000		
Trade-in allowance	5,000		
Cash that must be paid	$15,000	Cash price for new car	$18,000

The value of your old car to the dealer is $3,000. Compare this with what you might sell it for by advertising in the paper.

To illustrate accounting for the exchange of similar assets, let's assume that an old delivery truck is traded for a new one. Relevant information for this transaction is provided below.

Old Delivery Truck		New Delivery Truck	
Cost	$8,000	Market value (new truck)	$30,000
Accumulated depreciation	6,900	Trade-in allowance (old truck)	1,000
Book value	$1,100	Cash required	$29,000

Gain or Loss on Exchange	
$1,100	Book value
(1,000)	Market value (trade-in allowance)
$ 100	Loss

If the new truck has a fair market value of $30,000 and the **trade-in value** of the old truck is $1,000, then $29,000 is due in cash ($30,000 − $1,000). As discussed earlier, the gain or loss on the exchange is determined by comparing the market value of the old asset ($1,000) with its book value ($1,100). In this case, there is a $100 loss. The transaction is entered as follows:

5			Delivery Equipment (new truck)	30	0	0	0	00						5
6			Accum. Depr.—Delivery Equipment	6	9	0	0	00						6
7			Loss on Exchange of Delivery Equipment	1	0	0	00							7
8			Delivery Equipment (old truck)						8	0	0	0	00	8
9			Cash						29	0	0	0	00	9
10			Purchased a new truck											10

The above entry has the following effects on the accounting records:

1. The original cost ($8,000) and accumulated depreciation ($6,900) for the old truck are removed from the books.

2. Cash is credited to show the amount paid ($29,000).

3. The new delivery equipment is entered on the books at its market value ($30,000).

4. The loss on the exchange is recognized ($100).

Now let's assume the same event, except that the market value and trade-in allowance for the old truck is $1,500. As shown below, this means that only $28,500 in cash is required and there is a $400 gain on the exchange ($1,500 − $1,100 = $400).

Old Delivery Truck		New Delivery Truck	
Cost	$8,000	Market value (new truck)	$30,000
Accumulated depreciation	6,900	Trade-in allowance (old truck)	1,500
Book value	$1,100	Cash required	$28,500

Gain or Loss on Exchange	
$1,500	Market value (Trade-in allowance)
(1,100)	Book value
$ 400	Gain

Because of the practice of conservatism, we are not allowed to recognize this gain for financial reporting purposes. **Conservatism** states that *when in doubt* we should *choose the reporting technique that is least likely to overstate assets or net income.* Since an old delivery truck was replaced with a new delivery truck, the company intends to continue earning revenues by making deliveries. Thus, the earnings process of the delivery service has not been completed. This raises doubt about the amount of earnings to recognize at this time. As noted in Chapter 18, conservatism states that we should never anticipate gains. Thus, no gain should be recognized when recording this transaction. The proper entry is shown below:

5		Delivery Equipment (new truck)		29	6	0	0	00									5
6		Accum. Depr.—Delivery Equipment		6	9	0	0	00									6
7		Delivery Equipment (old truck)								8	0	0	0	00	7
8		Cash								28	5	0	0	00	8
9		Purchased a new truck													9

The above entry has the following effects on the accounting records:

1. The original cost ($8,000) and accumulated depreciation ($6,900) for the old truck are removed from the books.

2. Cash is credited to show the amount paid ($28,500).

3. The new delivery equipment is entered on the books at its market value less the amount of the gain ($30,000 – $400). This must be done to avoid the recognition of the gain.

For tax purposes, neither gains nor losses are recognized on the exchange of similar assets ("like-kind" exchanges).

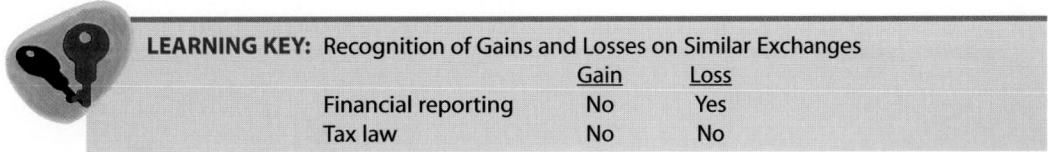

LEARNING KEY: Recognition of Gains and Losses on Similar Exchanges

	Gain	Loss
Financial reporting	No	Yes
Tax law	No	No

Property, Plant, and Equipment Records

If a business has many depreciable assets, a summary general ledger account will be kept for each major class of assets. For example, separate accounts might be kept for buildings, equipment, and furniture. Each summary account has a related accumulated depreciation account. Subsidiary records in the form of cards or computer files support these summary accounts. A typical property, plant, and equipment record is shown in Figure 19-2.

Fully Depreciated Plant Assets

A plant asset is fully depreciated when the book value is equal to the salvage value. When an asset is fully depreciated, no further depreciation should be entered. Since the rate of depreciation is based on its *estimated* useful life, an asset may still be used after it is fully depreciated. In this case, the cost of the asset and the accumulated depreciation are left in the accounts. When the asset eventually is disposed of, the cost and accumulated depreciation should be removed from the accounts, as illustrated in previous sections.

FIGURE 19-2 Property, Plant, and Equipment Record

PROPERTY, PLANT, AND EQUIPMENT RECORD

Description	Computer	Account	Office Equipment
Age when acquired	New	Estimated salvage value	$500
Estimated life	5 years	Rate of annual depreciation based on cost less salvage value	20%

COST				DEPRECIATION RECORD			
Date Purchased	Description	Amount		Year	Rate	Amount	Total To Date
20-2 Jan. 9	ABC DE/3 MODEL 50	5,000 00		20-2	20%	900 00	900 00
	Serial No. 8403637			20-3	20%	900 00	1800 00
	American Micro			20-4	20%	450 00	2250 00
	Less estimated salvage value	500 00		20			
	Depreciable cost	4,500 00		20			
				20			
				20			
				20			
				20			

SOLD, EXCHANGED, OR DISCARDED					
Date	Explanation	Amount Realized	Book Value on Disposal Date	Gain (Loss)	20
20-4 July 1	Sold	2,500 00	2,250 00	250 00	20
					20
					20
					20

NATURAL RESOURCES

LO 6   Explain the nature, purpose, and accounting for depletion.

The consumption or exhaustion of *natural resources* is called *depletion*. The purpose of depletion is to allocate the cost of these assets to the periods in which they are consumed. Computing *cost depletion* is similar to computing depreciation using the units-of-production method. The cost of the property, less the estimated salvage or residual value, is divided by the estimated number of units that the property contains. The result is the depletion expense per unit. This amount times the number of units removed and sold during the period is the depletion expense for the period.

LEARNING KEY: Depletion is the consumption or exhaustion of natural resources.

To illustrate, assume a coal mine is acquired at a cost of $1,000,000. No salvage value is expected. The estimated recoverable amount of coal in the mine is 1,000,000 tons. During the current year, 180,000 tons of coal are mined and sold. The computation of the amount of depletion expense is as follows:

$$\frac{\$1,000,000}{1,000,000 \text{ tons}} = \$1 \text{ per ton}$$

$$180,000 \text{ tons} \times \$1 \text{ per ton} = \$180,000 \text{ depletion expense}$$

An adjusting entry is made at the end of the accounting period to recognize the depletion expense. For the coal mine, this entry is as follows:

11		Depletion Expense—Coal Mine	180 0 0 0 00		11
12		Accum. Depletion—Coal Mine		180 0 0 0 00	12
13					13

The difference between the cost of the mine and the amount of the accumulated depletion is the undepleted cost of the property:

Cost of coal mine	$1,000,000
Less: Accumulated depletion	180,000
Undepleted cost of mine	$ 820,000

Depletion Expense is reported as an operating expense on the income statement. Accumulated Depletion is reported on the balance sheet as a deduction from the related asset account, with the difference identified as undepleted cost of the asset. As was explained for depreciation, this undepleted cost of the wasting asset simply represents the cost not yet charged to operations. It is not intended to reflect the market value of the asset.

INTANGIBLE ASSETS

LO 7   Explain the nature of and account for intangible assets.

In an accounting sense, the term "intangible" has come to have a very restricted meaning. Intangible assets refers to a limited group of valuable legal or economic rights that a firm may acquire. All items classified as intangibles are considered to be long-term assets. Major examples of intangibles include patents, copyrights, and trademarks.

Patents

A **patent** is a grant by the federal government to an inventor giving the exclusive right to produce, use, and sell an invention for a period of twenty years. A firm may purchase a patent from a prior patent owner or may develop its own and acquire an original patent from the government. If purchased, the amount paid represents the cost of the patent.

If a company carries on regular research and development activities to develop its own patents, the costs of such activities are treated as current expenses. If the government grants a patent on an invention the company develops, the cost of this patent includes only the fees paid to the government and to patent attorneys for their services. This amount is debited to an asset account and amortized over the patent's useful life.

Since the life of a patent is specifically limited, any cost assigned to it is allocated over no more than the number of years that the patent right will exist. The greatest number of years would be twenty if the firm developed and applied for the patent. If the expected useful or economic life of a patent is less than its legal life, the cost should be allocated over the shorter period.

With the straight-line method, the amortization each year is determined by dividing the cost of the patent by its expected life. Let's assume that a patent with thirteen years to run is purchased at a cost of $12,000, and that the buyer expects the useful life of the patent to be only ten years. In that event, $1,200 ($12,000 ÷ 10 years) would be amortized as expense for each of the ten years. The adjusting entry for the amortization at the end of each year is as follows:

6			Adjusting Entry																6
7			Patent Amortization				1	2	0	0	00								7
8				Patents										1	2	0	0	00	8

Patent amortization is usually treated as an operating expense. Since patents are assets, their unamortized cost is reported on the balance sheet as an intangible long-term asset.

Copyrights

A **copyright** is similar in many respects to a patent. It consists of a federal grant of the exclusive right to the reproduction and sale of a literary, artistic, or musical composition. A copyright is granted for life plus 50 years after the death of the holder. The cost of obtaining the initial copyright on a composition is nominal. It is treated as an ordinary expense. However, if an existing copyright is purchased, the cost may be large enough and the expected future value sufficient to warrant charging the cost to an asset account entitled Copyrights.

It is a rare case in which a copyright would have an economic life as long as its legal life. In most cases the cost of a copyright is written off in a very few years. The write-off can be on a straight-line basis or in the proportion of the actual sales of the copyrighted item during the period to the total expected sales of the item. The amount of the write-off for each period is debited to Copyright Amortization (or Copyright Expense) and credited to Copyrights. Copyright amortization is treated as an operating expense. Any unamortized portion of the cost of copyrights is reported on the balance sheet as an intangible long-term asset.

Trademarks

The practice of using a **trademark** or registered trade name to identify a firm's merchandise is widespread. Such designations can be legally protected by registering them with the United States Patent Office. As long as the trademark or trade name is continuously used, the trademark is legally enforceable.

Research and development costs incurred to develop a trademark are expensed as incurred. However, costs incurred to register a trademark are debited to an asset account and amortized over the trademark's useful life. These costs include attorney and registration fees.

If a trademark is acquired by purchase, its cost is debited to an asset account entitled Trademarks. The future value of a trademark or a trade name is highly uncertain. Conservatism suggests that any cost incurred in purchasing a trademark should be written off within a few years.

The amount written off each period is debited to Trademark Amortization and credited to Trademarks. The amount written off is reported as an operating expense in the income statement. Any unamortized portion of the cost of trademarks or trade names is reported on the balance sheet as an intangible long-term asset.

Learning Objectives	Key Points to Remember
1 **Determine the cost of property, plant, and equipment.**	The cost to acquire an asset includes the purchase price and all costs incurred to prepare the asset for its intended use.
2 **Explain the nature and purpose of depreciation.**	The purpose of depreciation is to match a plant asset's cost with the revenues it helps to produce.
3 **Compute depreciation using the straight-line, declining-balance, sum-of-the-years'-digits, and units-of-production methods.**	Depreciation methods for financial reporting purposes: *Straight-Line Method* $$\text{Annual Depreciation} = \frac{\text{(Cost} - \text{Salvage Value)}}{\text{Estimated Useful Life}}$$ *Declining-Balance Method* $$\text{Annual Depreciation} = \text{Depreciation Rate} \times \text{Book Value at Beginning of Year}$$ *Sum-of-the-Years'-Digits Method* $$\text{Annual Depreciation} = \text{(Cost} - \text{Salvage Value)} \times \frac{\text{Remaining Useful Life}}{\text{Sum-of-the-Years'-Digits}}$$ *Units-of-Production Method* $$\text{Depreciation per Unit} = \frac{\text{(Cost} - \text{Salvage Value)}}{\text{Estimated Useful Life in Units}}$$ $$\text{Annual Depreciation} = \text{Depreciation per Unit} \times \text{Number of Units Produced or Consumed this Year}$$
4 **Account for repairs, maintenance, additions, and improvements to plant and equipment.**	Entry for additions and improvements that increase the usefulness of equipment: Building or Equipment xxx Cash or Liability account xxx Entry for improvements that extend the life of the asset, but do not improve usefulness or efficiency: Accumulated Depreciation—Building or Equipment xxx Cash or Liability account xxx To compute straight-line depreciation expense for the year following an addition or improvement: 1. Compute the new depreciable base by deducting the salvage value from the book value of the asset following the expenditures for the addition or improvement. 2. Divide the new depreciable base by the remaining useful life.
5 **Account for the disposition of property, plant, and equipment.**	Disposal of Plant Assets When an asset is discarded: 1. Remove cost and accumulated depreciation from accounting records. 2. If book value is greater than zero, recognize loss. When an asset is sold: 1. Remove cost and accumulated depreciation from accounting records. 2. Debit cash for amount received. 3. Recognize gain or loss (Market Value − Book Value of asset sold).

Learning Objectives	Key Points to Remember
	When an asset is traded in for another similar asset:
	1. Remove cost and accumulated depreciation for asset traded in from accounting records.
	2. Credit cash for amount paid.
	3. Treatment of gain or loss (Market Value – Book Value of asset traded in):
	a. Always recognize losses.
	b. Do not recognize gains on the exchange of similar assets.
	4. Valuation of new asset:
	a. When exchanged at a loss,
	Cost = Market Value of new asset.
	b. When similar assets are exchanged at a gain,
	Cost = Market Value of new asset – Gain.
6 **Explain the nature, purpose, and accounting for depletion.**	The consumption or exhaustion of natural resources is called depletion. The purpose of accounting for depletion is to allocate the cost of these assets to the periods in which they are consumed.
7 **Explain the nature of and account for intangible assets.**	The term intangible assets is used to refer to a limited group of valuable legal or economic rights (patent, copyright, and trademark) that a firm may acquire. Since the life of an intangible asset is limited, any cost assigned to it is allocated over no more than the number of years that the asset will exist.

Reflection: Answering the Opening Question

Yes, there are three additional methods that may be used for financial reporting purposes: declining-balance, sum-of-the-years'-digits, and units-of-production. The most appropriate for the van would probably be the units-of-production method. Under this method the depreciation would be based on the number of miles driven.

KEY TERMS

Accelerated Cost Recovery System (ACRS), (698)   A method of depreciation used for federal income tax purposes for plant assets acquired between 1981 and 1986.

accelerated depreciation methods, (695)   Depreciation methods that provide for a higher depreciation charge in the first year of an asset's life and gradually decreasing charges in subsequent years.

amortization, (690)   The portion of an intangible asset's cost that is recognized as expense.

book value, (693)   The undepreciated cost of the asset (Cost – Accumulated Depreciation).

cash equivalent price, (691)   The amount of cash that could have been paid for the asset on the date of purchase.

conservatism, (704)   The practice stating that when in doubt, choose the reporting technique that is least likely to overstate assets or net income.

copyright, (708)   Similar to a patent, a copyright consists of a federal grant of the exclusive right to the reproduction and sale of a literary, artistic, or musical composition.

cost, (692)   The sum of all amounts spent to acquire an asset and prepare it for its intended use.

declining-balance method, (695)   An accelerated depreciation method in which the book value is multiplied by a fixed rate. A common rate is double the straight-line rate (the double-declining-balance method).

depletion, (690)   The consumption or exhaustion of natural resources.

depreciable cost (base), (693)   The original cost less salvage (or scrap) value.

depreciation, (690)   The portion of a plant asset's cost that is recognized as expense.

double-declining-balance method, (695)   An accelerated depreciation method in which the book value is multiplied by double the straight-line rate.

fixed assets, (690)   See property, plant, and equipment.

functional depreciation, (692)   The loss of usefulness because of inadequacy or obsolescence.

intangible assets, (690)   Long-term assets that have no physical substance (patents, copyrights, and trademarks).

long-term assets, (690)   Assets that are expected to provide benefits for a number of accounting periods.

Modified Accelerated Cost Recovery System (MACRS), (698)   A method of depreciation used for federal income tax purposes for plant assets acquired after 1986.

patent, (707)   A grant by the federal government to an inventor giving the exclusive right to produce, use, and sell an invention for a period of twenty years.

physical depreciation, (692)   The loss of usefulness because of deterioration from age and wear.

plant assets, (690)   See property, plant, and equipment.

property, plant, and equipment, (690)   Long-term tangible assets that are used in the operations of the business. Also called plant assets or fixed assets.

salvage value, (692)   The estimated market value of an asset on its expected disposal date.

scrap value, (692)   See salvage value.

straight-line method, (693)   A depreciation method in which the depreciable cost of an asset is allocated equally over the years of the asset's useful life.

sum-of-the-years'-digits method, (696)   A depreciation method in which the annual depreciation is determined by multiplying the depreciable cost by a schedule of fractions.

tangible assets, (690)   Long-term assets that have physical substance.

trade-in allowance, (702)   If one asset is traded in on the purchase of another similar asset, an allowance may be granted.

trade-in value, (704)   See trade-in allowance.

trademark, (708)   A registered trade name or symbol that identifies a firm's merchandise.

units-of-production method, (697)   A depreciation method in which depreciation is based on the extent to which the asset was used during the year.

useful life, (692)   The amount of service expected to be obtained from an asset.

wasting assets, (690)   Assets whose physical substance consists of natural resources that are consumed in the operation of the business.

DEMONSTRATION PROBLEM

The Stillman Company purchased a new machine at the start of their current year at a cost of $37,500. The machine is expected to serve for five years and to have a salvage value of $3,000. Ronald L. Stillman, the Chief Executive Officer, has asked for information as to the effects of alternative depreciation methods.

REQUIRED

1. Calculate the annual depreciation expense for each of the five years of expected life of the machine, the accumulated depreciation at the end of each year, and the book value at the end of each year using the:

   a. Straight-line method

   b. Double-declining-balance method

   c. Sum-of-the-years'-digits method

2. Assume that in year 2 and year 4 of the five-year life of this machine, revenues are $45,000 and costs and expenses other than depreciation are $25,000. Calculate the net income for year 2 and year 4 using the same three depreciation methods used in Requirement 1.

3. Assume that Stillman chose the double-declining-balance method of depreciation for this machine. Then, in the first week of year 5, the machine was exchanged (traded in) for similar equipment costing $45,000. The market value and trade-in allowance on the old machine was $4,000 and cash was paid for the balance. Prepare the necessary journal entry to record this exchange.

Solution

1.

	Year	Annual Depreciation Expense	Accumulated Depreciation End of Year	Book Value End of Year
a.	1	$6,900	$ 6,900	$30,600
	2	6,900	13,800	23,700
	3	6,900	20,700	16,800
	4	6,900	27,600	9,900
	5	6,900	34,500	3,000
b.	1	$15,000	$15,000	$22,500
	2	9,000	24,000	13,500
	3	5,400	29,400	8,100
	4	3,240	32,640	4,860
	5	1,860*	34,500	3,000
c.	1	$11,500	$11,500	$26,000
	2	9,200	20,700	16,800
	3	6,900	27,600	9,900
	4	4,600	32,200	5,300
	5	2,300	34,500	3,000

*The machine is not depreciated below its estimated salvage value of $3,000.

2.

Year 2	(a) Straight-Line Method	(b) Double-Declining-Balance Method	(c) Sum-of-the-Years'-Digits Method
Revenue	$45,000	$45,000	$45,000
Costs and expenses other than depreciation	25,000	25,000	25,000
Depreciation	6,900	9,000	9,200
Net income	$13,100	$11,000	$10,800
Year 4			
Revenue	$45,000	$45,000	$45,000
Costs and expenses other than depreciation	25,000	25,000	25,000
Depreciation	6,900	3,240	4,600
Net income	$13,100	$16,760	$15,400

3.

5	Equipment (new machine)	45 0 0 0 00			5
6	Accum. Depr.—Equipment	32 6 4 0 00			6
7	Loss on Exchange of Equipment	8 6 0 00			7
8	Equipment (old machine)		37 5 0 0 00		8
9	Cash		41 0 0 0 00		9
10	Purchased a new machine				10

Old Equipment		New Equipment	
Cost of old equipment	$37,500	Market Value (new)	$45,000
Accumulated Depreciation	32,640	Trade-in Allowance (old)	4,000
Book Value	$ 4,860	Cash required	$41,000
Book Value	$ 4,860		
Trade-in (Market Value)	(4,000)		
Loss	$ 860		

REVIEW QUESTIONS

1. What costs should be included when measuring the total cost to acquire a long-term asset?

2. How should additions or improvements representing an increase in the usefulness of plant assets be entered?

3. How should the cost of such activities as planting trees and shrubs be entered?

4. What are the two major types of depreciation?

5. What is meant by the "depreciable cost" of a plant asset?

6. What are the four most commonly used methods of calculating depreciation for financial reporting purposes? How do they differ in their application?

7. Which depreciation method provides the fastest write-off of an asset?

8. Explain how the depreciation method selected affects the balance sheet and income statement.

9. For assets acquired after 1986, what depreciation methods are allowed for federal income tax purposes?

10. Explain what is meant by additions and identify the two types of improvements.

11. What are the three major ways of disposing of a plant asset?

12. For what time interval should depreciation be entered on the date of an asset's disposal?

13. When a plant asset is sold, what must be known about the asset in order to determine the proper amount of gain or loss on the sale?

14. What details about a particular asset are provided by a property, plant, and equipment record?

15. What is the purpose of depletion?

16. Which depreciation method is similar to the method used to compute depletion expense?

17. Over what period of time should the cost of a patent be allocated if its economic life is expected to be less than its legal life?

18. How should the unamortized portion of the cost of a copyright be reported on the balance sheet?

19. How does conservatism suggest that the cost of a trademark or trade name be accounted for subsequent to acquisition?

MANAGING YOUR WRITING

A friend owns and operates her own business and is concerned about completing her tax return. She owns several assets and uses straight-line depreciation for business purposes. She intended to use straight-line depreciation for tax purposes also, but recently heard about another method called MACRS. She has asked for your advice on which method to use on her tax return. Write a brief memo recommending a depreciation method and explaining why you believe it should be used.

ETHICS CASE

Creative Solutions purchased a patent from Russell Lazarus, an inventor. At the time of the purchase, the patent had two years remaining. The president of Creative Solutions decided to have the accountant amortize the cost of the patent, $200,000, over ten years rather than two years. His reasoning was that the $200,000 has already been spent and stockholders might ask a lot of questions about a $100,000 expense showing up on the income statement but probably wouldn't pay much attention to a $20,000 expense.

1. What is Russell's ethical responsibility to the company's stockholders?

2. According to GAAP, how should the amortization of patents be treated?

3. Write a short paragraph explaining similarities and differences between plant assets and intangible assets.

4. In groups of two or three, determine an appropriate method of depreciation, depletion, or amortization of the following assets for financial reporting purposes: (1) a car used as a taxi, (2) a parcel of land that will be resold in a few years, (3) a computer that has a very short life and loses most of its value in the first year or two, (4) an ore mine, (5) research and development costs incurred to develop a trademark.

WEB WORK

Intellectual property is one of the most valuable resources a company can have. Whether it is the name "Coke," or the movie *Star Wars*, companies have many ways of using and protecting their properties. What problems come up with the Internet and fair use policies?

Paramount's open letter to Star Trek Fans about Copyright can be found at

http://www.paramount.com/openletter/.

Replies and responses to Paramount can be found on the following pages and their links:

http://www.youth.net/frpg/ceviacom.htm and
http://www.wired.com/news/politics/story/7564.html.
(http://heintz.swcollege.com)

SERIES A EXERCISES

EXERCISE 19A-1 (LO 1) COST OF PROPERTY, PLANT, AND EQUIPMENT Consider the following list of expenditures and indicate whether each would be debited to Land, Building, or Equipment as part of the cost to purchase these assets. Place a check mark in the appropriate column.

	Yes	No
Debit Land?		
Real estate fees	✓	
Cost to remove old buildings	✓	
Cost to pave parking areas		✓
Tax assessment for streets	✓	

(continued)

	Yes	No
Debit Building?		
Cost of land on which the building is located		✓
Legal fees related to purchase	✓	
Taxes related to purchase	✓	
Realtor fees	✓	
Interest on construction loan while building was under construction	✓	
Debit Equipment?		
Transportation charges	✓	
Insurance while in transit	✓	
Installation costs	✓	
Interest on loan to buy equipment		✓

EXERCISE 19A-2 (LO 3) STRAIGHT-LINE, DECLINING-BALANCE, AND SUM-OF-THE-YEARS'-DIGITS METHODS A light truck is purchased on January 1 at a cost of $27,000. It is expected to serve for eight years and have a salvage value of $3,000. Calculate the depreciation expense for the first and third years of the truck's life using the:

1. Straight-line method

2. Double-declining-balance method (round to two decimal places)

3. Sum-of-the-years'-digits method (round to two decimal places)

EXERCISE 19A-3 (LO 3) UNITS-OF-PRODUCTION METHOD The truck purchased in Exercise 19A-2 is expected to be used for 96,000 miles over its eight-year useful life. Using the units-of-production method, calculate the depreciation expense for the first and third years of use if the truck is driven 20,000 miles in year 1 and 18,000 miles in year 3.

EXERCISE 19A-4 (LO 4) JOURNAL ENTRIES: REPAIRS, MAINTENANCE, ADDITIONS, AND IMPROVEMENTS Prepare the entries for the following transactions for Stepanski's Food Mart using a general journal.

1. Replaced the checkout computer in checkout stand A for $2,000 cash. The computer is part of the checkout stand.

2. Added a laser scanner to checkout stand B for $3,000 cash to decrease checkout time.

3. Cleaned scanner window on checkout stand A for $20 cash (normal maintenance).

EXERCISE 19A-5 (LO 5) JOURNAL ENTRIES: DISPOSITION OF PLANT ASSETS Prepare the entries for the following transactions using a general journal.

1. Discarding an asset.

   a. On January 4, shelving units, which had cost $6,400 and had accumulated depreciation of $5,900, were discarded.

   b. On June 15, a hand cart, which had cost $1,500 and had accumulated depreciation of $1,350, was sold for $150.

c. On October 1, a copy machine, which had cost $7,200 and had accumulated depreciation of $6,800, was sold for $450.

2. Exchange or trade-in of assets.

a. On December 31, a drill press, which had cost $60,000 and had accumulated depreciation of $48,000, was traded in for a new drill press with a fair market value of $75,000. The old drill press and $65,000 in cash were given for the new drill press.

b. On December 31, the old drill press in (a) above and $60,000 in cash were given for the new drill press.

EXERCISE 19A-6 (LO 6) DEPLETION Prepare the following entries using a general journal.

1. A coal mine was acquired at a cost of $1,500,000 and estimated to contain 6,000,000 tons of ore. During the year, 100,000 tons were mined and sold. Prepare the journal entry for the year's depletion expense.

2. A silver mine was acquired at a cost of $3,000,000 and estimated to contain 750,000 tons of ore. During the year, 125,000 tons were mined and sold. Prepare the journal entry for the year's depletion expense.

SERIES A PROBLEMS

PROBLEM 19A-1 (LO 3) STRAIGHT-LINE, DECLINING-BALANCE, AND SUM-OF-THE-YEARS'-DIGITS METHODS A machine is purchased January 1 at a cost of $59,000. It is expected to serve for eight years and have a salvage value of $3,000.

REQUIRED Prepare a schedule showing depreciation for each year and the book value at the end of each year using the:

a. Straight-line method

b. Double-declining-balance method (round to two decimal places)

c. Sum-of-the-years'-digits method (round to two decimal places)

PROBLEM 19A-2 (LO 3) UNITS-OF-PRODUCTION METHOD A machine is purchased January 1 at a cost of $59,000. It is expected to produce 130,000 units and have a salvage value of $3,000 at the end of its useful life.

Units produced are as follows:

Year 1	10,000
Year 2	8,000
Year 3	12,000
Year 4	16,000
Year 5	11,000

REQUIRED Prepare a schedule showing depreciation for each year and the undepreciated cost at the end of each year using the units-of-production method (round calculations to two decimal places).

PROBLEM 19A-3 (LO 3) CALCULATING AND JOURNALIZING DEPRECIATION Equipment records for Johnson Machine Co. for the year are given below. Johnson Machine uses the straight-line method of depreciation. In the case of assets acquired before the fifteenth day of the month, depreciation should be computed for the entire month. In the case of assets acquired after the fifteenth day of the month, no depreciation should be considered for the month in which the asset was acquired.

Asset	Purchase Price	Useful Life	Salvage Value	Date Purchased
Truck #1	$20,000	8 years	$4,000	January 1
Truck #2	24,000	8	4,000	April 10
Tractor #1	18,000	5	3,000	May 1
Tractor #2	14,000	6	2,000	June 18
Fork Lift	40,000	10	4,000	September 1

REQUIRED

1. Calculate the depreciation expense for Johnson Machine as of December 31, 20--.

2. Prepare the entry for depreciation expense using a general journal.

PROBLEM 19A-4 (LO 4) IMPACT OF IMPROVEMENTS ON THE CALCULATION OF DEPRECIATION On January 1, 20-1, two flight simulators were purchased by a space camp for $68,000 each with a salvage value of $4,000 each and estimated useful lives of eight years. On January 1, 20-2, the jacks supporting simulator A were replaced for $3,000 cash and an updated computer for more advanced students was installed in simulator B for $10,000 cash.

REQUIRED

1. Using the straight-line method, prepare general journal entries for depreciation on December 31, 20-1, for simulators A and B.

2. Enter the transactions for January 20-2 in a general journal.

3. Assuming no other additions or improvements, calculate the depreciation expense for each simulator for 20-2 through 20-8.

PROBLEM 19A-5 (LO 5) DISPOSITION OF ASSETS: JOURNALIZING Mitchell Parts Co. had the following plant asset transactions during the year:

1. Assets discarded or sold:

Jan. 1   Motor #12, which had cost $2,800 and had accumulated depreciation of $2,800, was discarded.

8   Motor #8, which had cost $4,400 and had accumulated depreciation of $4,000, was sold for $200.

14   Motor #16, which had cost $5,600 and had accumulated depreciation of $5,400, was sold for $450.

2. Assets exchanged or traded-in:

Feb. 1   Motor #6, which had cost $6,000 and had accumulated depreciation of $4,800, was traded in for a new motor (#22) with a fair market value of $7,000. The old motor and $5,600 in cash were given for the new motor.

9   Motor #9, which had cost $5,500 and had accumulated depreciation of $5,000,

was traded in for a new motor (#23) with a fair market value of $6,500. The old motor and $6,200 in cash were given for the new motor.

REQUIRED   Prepare general journal entries for the above transactions.

PROBLEM 19A-6 (LO 6) DEPLETION: CALCULATING AND JOURNALIZING Mineral Works Co. acquired a salt mine at a cost of $1,700,000. The estimated number of units available for production from the mine is 3,400,000 tons.

a.   During the first year, 200,000 tons are mined and sold.

b.   During the second year, 600,000 tons are mined and sold.

REQUIRED   1.   Calculate the amount of depletion expense for both years.

2.   Prepare general journal entries for depletion expense.

PROBLEM 19A-7 (LO 7) INTANGIBLE LONG-TERM ASSETS Track Town Co. had the following transactions involving intangible assets:

Jan. 1   Purchased a patent for leather soles for $10,000 and estimated its useful life to be 10 years.

Apr. 1   Purchased a copyright for a design for $15,000 with a life left on the copyright of 25 years. The estimated remaining (economic) life of the copyright is 5 years.

July 1   Purchased a trademark at a cost of $50,000. The estimated economic life of the trademark is 25 years. However, conservatism suggests it should be written off in 5 years.

REQUIRED   1.   Using the straight-line method, calculate the amortization of the patent, copyright, and trademark.

2.   Prepare general journal entries to record the end-of-year amortizations.

SERIES B EXERCISES

EXERCISE 19B-1 (LO 1) COST OF PROPERTY, PLANT, AND EQUIPMENT The Lam Company purchased the following long-term assets. Determine the purchase cost of each asset.

a.   Ten computers:

Purchase price	$60,000
Transportation costs	500
Insurance during transportation	100
Installation	800
Interest on loan to purchase computers	3,000

b.   Three acres of land:

Purchase price	$30,000
Grading of land in preparation to build	10,000
Planting of trees around border	5,000
Fence on southern border	3,000
Tax assessment for sewer	1,000
Legal fees related to purchase	900

(continued)

c. Five-thousand square foot building:

Purchase price	$102,000
Real estate fees	5,000
Land on which building is located	10,000
Legal fees related to purchase	600
Taxes related to purchase	800
Interest on mortgage to buy building	300

EXERCISE 19B-2 (LO 3) STRAIGHT-LINE, DECLINING-BALANCE, AND SUM-OF-THE-YEARS'-DIGITS METHODS A light truck is purchased on January 1 at a cost of $19,000. It is expected to serve for five years and have a salvage value of $1,000. Calculate the depreciation expense for the first and third years of the truck's life using the:

1. Straight-line method

2. Double-declining-balance method

3. Sum-of-the-years'-digits method

EXERCISE 19B-3 (LO 3) UNITS-OF-PRODUCTION METHOD The truck purchased in Exercise 19B-2 is expected to be used for 100,000 miles over its five-year useful life. Using the units-of-production method, calculate the depreciation expense for the first and third years of use if the truck is driven 18,000 miles in year 1 and 22,000 miles in year 3.

EXERCISE 19B-4 (LO 4) JOURNAL ENTRIES: REPAIRS, MAINTENANCE, ADDITIONS, AND IMPROVEMENTS Enter the following transactions for Larry's Lawn Service in a general journal.

1. Added a second mower deck to tractor A for $550 cash to decrease mowing time.

2. Replaced the engine in mower D for $200 cash.

3. Lubricated engine of tractor A for $25 cash (normal maintenance).

EXERCISE 19B-5 (LO 5) JOURNAL ENTRIES: DISPOSITION OF PLANT ASSETS Prepare the entries for the following transactions using a general journal.

1. Discarding an asset.

   a. On January 4, shelving units, which had cost $7,200 and had accumulated depreciation of $6,900, were discarded.

   b. On June 15, a hand cart, which had cost $2,500 and had accumulated depreciation of $2,250, was sold for $250.

   c. On October 1, a copy machine, which had cost $5,200 and had accumulated depreciation of $4,800, was sold for $500.

2. Exchange or trade-in of assets.

   a. On December 31, a drill press, which had cost $50,000 and had accumulated depreciation of $37,500, was traded in for a new drill press with a fair market value of $55,000. The old drill press and $40,000 in cash were given for the new drill press.

b. On December 31, the old drill press in (a) above and $45,000 in cash were given for the new drill press.

EXERCISE 19B-6 (LO 6) DEPLETION Prepare the following entries using a general journal.

1. A coal mine was acquired at a cost of $1,750,000 and estimated to contain 2,500,000 tons of ore. During the year, 110,000 tons were mined and sold. Prepare the journal entry for the year's depletion expense.

2. A silver mine was acquired at a cost of $2,000,000 and estimated to contain 500,000 tons of ore. During the year, 75,000 tons were mined and sold. Prepare the journal entry for the year's depletion expense.

SERIES B PROBLEMS

PROBLEM 19B-1 (LO 3) STRAIGHT-LINE, DECLINING-BALANCE, AND SUM-OF-THE-YEARS'-DIGITS METHODS A machine is purchased January 1 at a cost of $77,000. It is expected to serve for eight years and have a salvage value of $5,000.

REQUIRED   Prepare a schedule showing depreciation for each year and the book value at the end of each year using the:

a. Straight-line method

b. Double-declining-balance method (round to two decimal places)

c. Sum-of-the-years'-digits method (round to two decimal places)

PROBLEM 19B-2 (LO 3) UNITS-OF-PRODUCTION METHOD A machine is purchased January 1 at a cost of $58,000. It is expected to produce 110,000 units and have a salvage value of $3,000 at the end of its useful life.

Units produced are as follows:

Year 1	18,000
Year 2	16,000
Year 3	20,000
Year 4	16,000
Year 5	12,000

REQUIRED   Prepare a schedule showing depreciation for each year and the undepreciated cost at the end of each year using the units-of-production method.

PROBLEM 19B-3 (LO 3) CALCULATING AND JOURNALIZING DEPRECIATION Equipment records for Byerly Construction Co. for the year are given on the next page. Byerly Construction uses the straight-line method of depreciation. In the case of assets acquired before the fifteenth day of the month, depreciation should be computed for the entire month. In the case of assets acquired after the fifteenth day of the month, no depreciation should be considered for the month in which the asset was acquired.

(continued)

Asset	Purchase Price	Useful Life	Salvage Value	Date Purchased
Truck #1	$22,000	7 years	$1,000	January 17
Truck #2	24,000	5	4,000	March 23
Molding #1	18,000	5	3,000	May 14
Molding #2	24,000	6	6,000	July 1
Fork Lift	35,000	8	3,000	September 19

REQUIRED

1. Calculate the depreciation expense for Byerly Construction as of December 31, 20--.

2. Prepare the entry for depreciation expense using a general journal.

PROBLEM 19B-4 (LO 4) IMPACT OF IMPROVEMENTS ON THE CALCULATION OF DEPRECIATION On January 1, 20-1, Dan's Demolition purchased two jack-hammers for $2,500 each with a salvage value of $100 each and estimated useful lives of four years. On January 1, 20-2, a stronger blade to improve performance was installed in jackhammer A for $800 cash and the compressor was replaced in jackhammer B for $200 cash.

REQUIRED

1. Using the straight-line method, prepare general journal entries for depreciation on December 31, 20-1, for jackhammers A and B.

2. Enter the transactions for January 20-2 in a general journal.

3. Assuming no other additions or improvements, calculate the depreciation expense for each jackhammer for 20-2 through 20-4.

PROBLEM 19B-5 (LO 5) DISPOSITION OF ASSETS: JOURNALIZING Mayer Delivery Co. had the following plant asset transactions during the year:

1. Assets discarded or sold:

Jan. 1 Van #11, which had cost $8,800 and had accumulated depreciation of $8,800, was discarded.

8 Van #7, which had cost $9,400 and had accumulated depreciation of $9,000, was sold for $200.

14 Van #13, which had cost $7,600 and had accumulated depreciation of $7,400, was sold for $250.

2. Assets exchanged or traded-in:

Feb. 1 Van #8, which had cost $11,000 and had accumulated depreciation of $8,800, was traded in for a new van (#20) with a fair market value of $13,000. The old van and $10,500 in cash were given for the new van.

9 Van #3, which had cost $7,500 and had accumulated depreciation of $7,000, was traded in for a new van (#21) with a fair market value of $9,500. The old van and $9,200 in cash were given for the new van.

REQUIRED Prepare general journal entries for the above transactions.

PROBLEM 19B-6 (LO 6) DEPLETION: CALCULATING AND JOURNALIZING Mining Works Co. acquired a copper mine at a cost of $1,200,000. The estimated number of units available for production from the mine is 3,000,000 tons.

a. During the first year, 400,000 tons are mined and sold.

b.   During the second year, 700,000 tons are mined and sold.

REQUIRED   1.   Calculate the amount of depletion expense for both years.

2.   Prepare general journal entries for depletion expense.

PROBLEM 19B-7 (LO 7) INTANGIBLE LONG-TERM ASSETS B. J. Bakery had the following transactions involving intangible assets:

Jan. 1   Purchased a patent for a new pastry for $10,000 and estimated its useful life to be 10 years.

Apr. 1   Purchased a copyright for a cookie cutter design for $5,000 with a life left on the copyright of 15 years. Estimated that the future remaining (economic) life of the copyright is 5 years.

July 1   Purchased a trademark at a cost of $40,000. The estimated economic life on the trademark is 20 years. However, conservatism suggests it should be written off in 5 years.

REQUIRED   1.   Using the straight-line method, calculate the amortization of the patent, copyright, and trademark.

2.   Prepare journal entries to record the end-of-year amortizations using a general journal.

MASTERY PROBLEM

On April 1, 20-3, Kwik Kopy Printing purchased a copy machine for $50,000. The estimated life of the machine is five years and it has an estimated salvage value of $5,000. The machine was used until July 1, 20-6.

REQUIRED   1.   Assume that Kwik Kopy uses straight-line depreciation and prepare the following entries.

a.   Adjusting entries for depreciation on December 31 of 20-3 through 20-5.

b.   Adjusting entry for depreciation on June 30, 20-6, just prior to trading in the asset.

c.   On July 1, 20-6, the copy machine was traded in for a new copy machine. The market value of the new machine is $38,000. Kwik Kopy must trade in the old copy machine and pay $22,000 for the new machine.

2.   Assume that Kwik Kopy uses sum-of-the-years'-digits depreciation and prepare the following entries.

a.   Adjusting entries for depreciation on December 31, 20-3 through 20-5.

b.   Adjusting entry for depreciation on June 30, 20-6, just prior to trading in the asset.

c.   On July 1, 20-6, the copy machine was traded in for a new copy machine. The market value of the new machine is $38,000. Kwik Kopy must trade in the old copy machine and pay $22,000 for the new machine.

Self-Study Test Questions

True/False

1. All long-term assets wear out gradually or are gradually used up entirely. _____

2. Intangible assets are depreciated; plant assets are amortized. _____

3. Depreciation is a process of asset valuation; that is, book value is the same as true asset value. _____

4. The straight-line method of depreciation allocates the cost of an asset more rapidly than the sum-of-the-years'-digits method. _____

5. The units-of-production method of depreciation allocates the cost of an asset equally over each year of the useful life. _____

Multiple Choice

1. Using the sum-of-the-years'-digits method, the denominator for a 5-year useful life would be _____

   (a) 5.   (c) 12.
   (b) 7.   (d) 15.

2. A machine that cost $100 and had accumulated depreciation of $80 was sold for $20. _____

   (a) There was a $20 gain.   (c) There was no gain or loss.
   (b) There was a $20 loss.   (d) There was a $60 loss.

3. A computer was sold on April 1, 20-2, for $575. Its cost was $3,000, and accumulated depreciation as of December 31, 20-1, was $2,100 ($700 a year). _____

   (a) There was a gain of $150.   (c) There was a gain of $325.
   (b) There was a loss of $150.   (d) There was a loss of $325.

4. Cost depletion of natural resources is most like which of these depreciation methods? _____

   (a) straight-line   (c) declining balance
   (b) units-of-production   (d) sum-of-the-years'-digits

5. Which of these is granted for life plus 50 years after the death of the holder? _____

   (a) patent   (c) copyright
   (b) mineral rights   (d) trademark

The answers to the Self-Study Test Questions are at the end of the text.

20

Accounting for Partnerships

LEARNING OBJECTIVES:
Careful study of this chapter should enable you to:

LO 1 Explain how a partnership is formed and account for the formation.

LO 2 Explain how partners are compensated and account for the allocation of net income.

LO 3 Prepare financial statements reporting the allocation of net income and partnership equity.

LO 4 Describe the actions that result in the dissolution of a partnership and account for the dissolution.

LO 5 Describe how a partnership is liquidated and prepare associated entries and a statement of partnership liquidation.

John Zenith was approached by a colleague in the athletic shoe business and asked to consider forming a partnership by combining their businesses. John has heard about partnerships, but he does not know the advantages and disadvantages of this form of ownership structure. Will he need to make an additional cash investment? Or, will each partner simply invest the assets from their current businesses? How will the assets be valued to measure each partner's investment? How will the profits be distributed? Will John have a regular salary to live on? Should any of these issues be placed in writing?

When two or more individuals engage in an enterprise as co-owners, the organization is known as a **partnership**. This form of organization is common to practically all types of enterprises. However, it is more popular among personal service enterprises than among merchandising businesses. For example, the partnership form of organization is quite common in the legal and public accounting professions. In this chapter, the important features of and accounting procedures for partnerships will be discussed and illustrated.

A BROADER VIEW

PARTNERSHIPS: HOW LARGE CAN THEY GO?

When we think of partnerships, we often picture small businesses with a few partners. This is often the case. However, some partnerships are quite large. Take Ernst & Young, an international accounting firm, as an example. This partnership has over 6,000 partners guiding the efforts of over 72,000 personnel in 660 offices located in 130 countries. Worldwide revenues exceed $7.8 billion. This is not what you might call a "mom and pop" operation.

PARTNERSHIP FORMATION

LO 1 Explain how a partnership is formed and account for the formation.

The Uniform Partnership Act states that "a partnership is an association of two or more persons who carry on, as co-owners, a business for profit." Partnerships are formed for many reasons. Primarily, however, they are formed on the belief that individuals with complementary resources and abilities can operate more profitably together than as individuals.

The Partnership Agreement

A written agreement containing the various provisions for operating a partnership is known as a **partnership agreement**. There is no standard form of partnership agreement, but the following provisions are essential:

1. Date of agreement
2. Names of the partners
3. Kind of business to be conducted
4. Length of time the partnership is to run
5. Name and location of the business
6. Investment of each partner
7. Basis on which profits or losses are to be shared by the partners
8. Limitation of partners' rights and activities
9. Salary allowances to partners
10. Division of assets upon dissolution of the partnership
11. Signatures of the partners

Figure 20-1 on the next page is an example of a partnership agreement.

LEARNING KEY: Forming a partnership may lead to a great working relationship where partners can pool their assets, talents, and enthusiasm for the business. However, it is important to have a clear understanding of the key elements of the partnership: expectations for each partner, payments to partners in various forms, sharing of profits and losses, and dissolution of the partnership. The best way to ensure a clear understanding is to put everything in writing.

Characteristics of Partnerships

The characteristics of a partnership are different from those of the sole proprietorships we have accounted for in previous chapters. Some of the more important of these characteristics are listed as follows.

Co-Ownership of Assets. All assets held by a partnership are co-owned by all partners. If one partner contributes an asset to the business, the asset is jointly owned by all partners.

Mutual Agency. Any partner can bind the other partners to a contract if he or she is acting within the general scope of the business. Thus, if Mitchell signs a contract to purchase merchandise for the business, Jenkins is bound by that contract. On the other hand, if Mitchell contracts to buy a personal automobile, this is not part of normal business operations, and Jenkins would not be bound by it.

Limited Life. A partnership has a limited life. It may be dissolved as the result of any change in the ownership. These include death, bankruptcy, incapacity, withdrawal of a partner, addition of a new partner, or expiration of the time specified in the partnership agreement.

FIGURE 20-1 Partnership Agreement

PARTNERSHIP AGREEMENT

THIS CONTRACT, made and entered into on the first day of January 20--, by and between Sam Mitchell of Indianapolis, Indiana, and Lisa Jenkins of the same city and state.

WITNESSETH: That the said parties have this day formed a partnership for the purpose of engaging in and conducting a wholesale and retail business in the city of Indianapolis under the following stipulations which are a part of this contract:

FIRST: The said partnership is to continue for a term of twenty-five years from January 1, 20--.

SECOND: The business is to be conducted under the firm name of Mitchell & Jenkins, at 2200 East Washington Street, Indianapolis, Indiana.

THIRD: The investments are as follows: Sam Mitchell, cash, $350,000; Lisa Jenkins, cash, $200,000. These invested assets are partnership property.

FOURTH: Each partner is to devote his/her entire time and attention to the business and to engage in no other business enterprise without the written consent of the other partner.

FIFTH: During the operation of the partnership, neither partner is to become surety or bonding agent for anyone without the written consent of the other partner.

SIXTH: Sam Mitchell is to receive a salary allowance of $36,000 a year, payable $1,500 in cash on the fifteenth day and last business day of each month. Lisa Jenkins is to receive a salary allowance of $48,000 a year, payable $2,000 in cash on the fifteenth day and last business day of each month. At the end of each annual fiscal period, the net income or the net loss shown by the income statement after the salaries of the two partners have been allowed is to be shared as follows: Sam Mitchell, 60 percent; Lisa Jenkins, 40 percent.

SEVENTH: Neither partner is to withdraw assets in excess of his/her salary, any part of the assets invested, or assets in anticipation of net income to be earned, without the written consent of the other partner.

EIGHTH: In the case of the death or the legal disability of either partner, the other partner is to continue the operations of the business until the close of the annual fiscal period on the following June 30. At that time the continuing partner is to be given an option to buy the interest of the deceased or incapacitated partner at not more than 10 percent above the value of the deceased or incapacitated partner's proprietary interest as shown by the balance of his/her capital account after the books are closed on December 31. It is agreed that this purchase price is to be paid one half in cash and the balance in four equal installments payable quarterly.

NINTH: At the conclusion of this contract, unless it is mutually agreed to continue the operation of the business under a new contract, the assets of the partnership, after the liabilities are paid, are to be divided in proportion to the net credit of each partner's capital account on that date.

IN WITNESS WHEREOF, the parties aforesaid have hereunto set their hands and affixed their seals on the day and year above written.

Sam Mitchell   (Seal)
Sam Mitchell

Lisa Jenkins   (Seal)
Lisa Jenkins

Unlimited Liability. Each partner is personally liable for all debts incurred by the partnership. If the partnership cannot pay a bill, creditors will expect payment from the personal assets of the partners.

Federal Income Taxes. Partnerships are not subject to federal income taxes. However, partnerships file federal income tax returns for informational purposes and notify partners of the amount of partnership income that must be reported on their individual federal (and state if appropriate) income tax returns. Note that partners are taxed on their share of net income, not the amount withdrawn.

Advantages and Disadvantages

In comparison with the sole proprietorship, the partnership form of business offers certain advantages.

1.   The ability and experience of the partners are combined in one enterprise.

2.   More capital may be raised because the resources of the partners are combined.

3.   Credit may be improved because each general partner is personally liable for partnership debts.

    There also are some disadvantages of the partnership form of organization.

1.   Unlimited liability is a major disadvantage of the partnership form of ownership. This means that a partner could lose not only the amount invested, but also personal assets. Although this is also true for a sole proprietorship, it is not true for the corporate form of ownership, which will be introduced in Chapters 21 and 22. Under the laws of some states, certain partners may limit their liability. At least one partner, however, must be a general partner who has unlimited liability.

2.   Mutual agency can lead to serious problems if all partners do not act responsibly and consult each other before signing contracts. Yes, unwitting partners could be liable for swamp land purchased by another partner.

3.   The interest of a partner in the partnership cannot be transferred without the consent of the other partners.

4.   Termination of the partnership agreement, bankruptcy of the firm, death of one of the partners, or any change in partner membership dissolves the partnership.

Accounting for Initial Investments

Accounting for a partnership is basically the same as accounting for a sole proprietorship. The main difference is that separate capital and drawing accounts are maintained for each partner. Care should be used when preparing the opening entry and entering any transactions that affect the respective interests of the partners.

Cash Investments. A partnership may be formed by the investment of cash by the partners. In opening the books for a partnership, a separate journal entry is made for each partner's investment. The opening entries for Mitchell & Jenkins based on the partnership agreement shown in Figure 20-1 are as follows:

5		Cash		350	0	0	0	00						5
6		Sam Mitchell, Capital								350	0	0	0	00	6
7		S. Mitchell invested $350,000 in cash													7
8															8
9		Cash		200	0	0	0	00							9
10		Lisa Jenkins, Capital								200	0	0	0	00	10
11		L. Jenkins invested $200,000 in cash													11

> Accountants generally focus on historical costs and book values. However, when forming a partnership, market values are used to measure the investment of each partner. This is reasonable. Investing $1,000 in cash is equivalent to investing an asset that could be sold for $1,000. The book value of the asset is not useful in this situation.

Investment of Cash and Other Assets. A partnership may also be formed by the investment of cash and other assets by the partners. Certain liabilities also may be assumed by the partnership. Each partner's capital account should be credited for the difference between the market value of the assets invested and liabilities assumed.

Instead of investing $200,000 in cash, assume that Jenkins invested:

1. inventory valued at $47,500 on which $10,500 was owed,

2. office equipment valued at $40,000,

3. delivery equipment valued at $92,000, on which $19,000 was owed on a note, and

4. $50,000 in cash.

The following opening entry would be made:

5		Cash	4	50	0	0	0	00							5
6		Inventory	1	47	5	0	0	00							6
7		Office Equipment	2	40	0	0	0	00							7
8		Delivery Equipment	3	92	0	0	0	00							8
9		Notes Payable							3	19	0	0	0	00	9
10		Accounts Payable							1	10	5	0	0	00	10
11		Lisa Jenkins, Capital								200	0	0	0	00	11
12		L. Jenkins' investment in partnership													12

Partnerships Formed from Existing Businesses. Two or more sole proprietors may combine their businesses to form a partnership. Their respective balance sheets serve as the basis for the opening entries for the investments of such partners. For example, assume that on April 1, Donna Morning and Larry Knight form a partnership under the firm name of Morning & Knight Sports. The balance sheets shown in Figure 20-2 are made a part of the partnership agreement. They agree to invest their assets and that the partnership will assume the liabilities shown in their respective balance sheets. Each partner's investment is measured by the difference between the assets invested and the liabilities assumed. The profits and losses are to be shared on a 50-50 basis. In case of dissolution, the assets are to be distributed between the partners in the ratio of their capital interests at the time of dissolution.

LEARNING KEY: The difference between the assets invested and the liabilities assumed is each partner's investment.

FIGURE 20-2 Balance Sheets for Morning Sports and Knight Athletics Prior to the Formation of the Partnership

Morning Sports
Balance Sheet
March 31, 20 - -

Assets					Liabilities				
Cash			$ 6 3 4 4	00	Notes payable	$4 6 0 0	00		
Accounts receivable	$5 5 2 4	00			Accounts payable	9 0 8 2	00		
Less allowance for bad debts	4 3 0	00	5 0 9 4	00	Total liabilities			$13 6 8 2	00
Merchandise inventory			24 5 7 4	00					
Store equipment	$3 8 4 0	00			**Owner's Equity**				
Less accumulated depreciation	1 0 0 0	00	2 8 4 0	00	Donna Morning, capital			25 1 7 0	00
Total assets			$38 8 5 2	00	Total liabilities and owner's equity			$38 8 5 2	00

Knight Athletics
Balance Sheet
March 31, 20 - -

Assets					Liabilities				
Cash			$ 3 5 4 4	00	Notes payable	$ 6 0 0 0	00		
Accounts receivable	$5 2 8 0	00			Accounts payable	13 2 3 8	00		
Less allowance for bad debts	7 2 0	00	4 5 6 0	00	Total liabilities			$19 2 3 8	00
Merchandise inventory			29 6 9 2	00					
Supplies			2 8 6	00					
Office equipment	$4 3 2 0	00							
Less accumulated depreciation	1 1 0 0	00	3 2 2 0	00					
Store equipment	$4 8 0 0	00			**Owner's Equity**				
Less accumulated depreciation	1 2 0 0	00	3 6 0 0	00	Larry Knight, capital			25 6 6 4	00
Total assets			$44 9 0 2	00	Total liabilities and owner's equity			$44 9 0 2	00

When two sole proprietors decide to combine their businesses, assets should be recorded at their fair market values as of the date of formation of the partnership. For Morning and Knight, any accounts receivable known to be uncollectible as of March 31, 20--, should be written off. None were considered uncollectible in this case. The balance in Accounts Receivable is debited and the amount of the Allowance for Bad Debts is credited in the books of the partnership. In this way, the accounts receivable are entered at their approximate fair market value.

 LEARNING KEY: Assets should be recorded at their fair market values as of the date a partnership is formed.

Both Morning and Knight had been using the first-in, first-out (FIFO) method of inventory costing. Recall that under FIFO, the most recently purchased inventory is considered to be on hand. Thus, the values shown for merchandise inventories on their respective balance sheets are close to their fair market values as of March 31, 20--. If Morning or Knight had been using some other inventory costing method, the merchandise inventory amounts might have required restatement to reflect fair market value.

The fair market value of Morning's store equipment as of March 31, 20--, is $3,600. This amount should be entered on the books of the new partnership, rather than the book value of $2,840 shown on Morning's balance sheet in Figure 20-2. In like manner, the fair market values of Knight's office equipment and store equipment as of March 31, 20--, are $3,850 and $4,200, respectively. These amounts should be entered on the books of the new partnership, rather than the respective book values of $3,220 and $3,600 shown on Knight's balance sheet. Once again, the difference between assets invested and liabilities assumed is credited to each partner's capital account. The opening entries for Morning & Knight Sports are shown below.

	DATE		DESCRIPTION	POST. REF.	DEBIT	CREDIT	
1	20-- Apr.	1	Cash		6 3 4 4 00		1
2			Accounts Receivable		5 5 2 4 00		2
3			Merchandise Inventory		24 5 7 4 00		3
4			Store Equipment		3 6 0 0 00		4
5			Allowance for Bad Debts			4 3 0 00	5
6			Notes Payable			4 6 0 0 00	6
7			Accounts Payable			9 0 8 2 00	7
8			Donna Morning, Capital			25 9 3 0 00	8
9			D. Morning's investment in partnership				9
10							10
11		1	Cash		3 5 4 4 00		11
12			Accounts Receivable		5 2 8 0 00		12
13			Merchandise Inventory		29 6 9 2 00		13
14			Supplies		2 8 6 00		14
15			Office Equipment		3 8 5 0 00		15
16			Store Equipment		4 2 0 0 00		16
17			Allowance for Bad Debts			7 2 0 00	17
18			Notes Payable			6 0 0 0 00	18
19			Accounts Payable			13 2 3 8 00	19
20			Larry Knight, Capital			26 8 9 4 00	20
21			L. Knight's investment in partnership				21
22							22

GENERAL JOURNAL   PAGE 1

PARTNER COMPENSATION AND THE ALLOCATION OF NET INCOME

LO 2 Explain how partners are compensated and account for the allocation of net income.

The basis on which reported profits and losses are shared is a matter of agreement between the partners, and not necessarily the same as their investment ratio. Factors other than the assets invested may enter into a profit-and-loss sharing agreement. For example, one partner may contribute most of the assets but render no services, while the other partner may contribute less in assets but devote full time to the partnership.

In the absence of any agreement between the partners, profits and losses must be shared equally regardless of the ratio of the partners' investments. If the partnership agreement specifies how profits are to be shared, the losses must be shared on the same basis as profits.

 LEARNING KEY: The partnership agreement should define the basis on which profits and losses are shared between the partners. The sharing of profits is not necessarily based on the investment ratio.

In calculating partnership profits and losses, it is important to remember that partners are not employees. Thus, their compensation is not considered an expense. This means that their salaries, for example, are not included on the income statement and are not part of the calculation of net income. Salaries and other forms of compensation are treated as withdrawals and closed to each partner's capital account at the end of the accounting period. Thus, it is important to keep in mind that net income reported on the income statement excludes partner compensation.

Profits and Losses Shared Equally

If the Mitchell and Jenkins partnership agreement shown in Figure 20-1 did not specify how the partners would be compensated, the profits and losses would be shared equally. If net income for the year was $190,800, the allocation would be reported on the income statement as shown in Figure 20-3.

FIGURE 20-3 Allocation of Profit and Loss (Equal Division)

Mitchell and Jenkins Income Statement (Partial) For Year Ended December 31, 20 - -			
	S. MITCHELL	L. JENKINS	TOTAL
Net income			$190 8 0 0 00
Allocation of net income	$95 4 0 0 00	$95 4 0 0 00	$190 8 0 0 00

Maintaining a record of each partner's share of net income and the amount of drawing each year requires a minor change in the way closing entries are made. Recall that four closing entries are made for sole proprietorships at the end of the accounting period. For a partnership, separate capital and drawing accounts are maintained for each partner. Thus, entries three and four must be changed as shown in Figure 20-4 on the next page.

FIGURE 20-4 Closing Entries

CLOSING ENTRIES—SOLE PROPRIETOR	CLOSING ENTRIES—PARTNERSHIP
1. Close all revenues to Income Summary.	1. Close all revenues to Income Summary.
2. Close all expenses to Income Summary.	2. Close all expenses to Income Summary.
3. Close Income Summary to the owner's capital account.	3. Close Income Summary *by allocating each partner's share of net income or loss to the individual capital accounts.*
4. Close Drawing to the owner's capital account.	4. Close *each partner's drawing account to the individual capital accounts.*

Based on the net income allocation shown in Figure 20-3, the third closing entry is:

5	Income Summary	190	8	0	0	00							5
6	S. Mitchell, Capital						95	4	0	0	00	6
7	L. Jenkins, Capital						95	4	0	0	00	7

If Mitchell and Jenkins withdrew $36,000 and $48,000, respectively, the fourth closing entry would be:

9	S. Mitchell, Capital	36	0	0	0	00							9
10	S. Mitchell, Drawing						36	0	0	0	00	10
11													11
12	L. Jenkins, Capital	48	0	0	0	00							12
13	L. Jenkins, Drawing						48	0	0	0	00	13

The four closing entries for a partnership are summarized in T account form in Figure 20-5 on the next page.

Allocation of Profits and Losses with Salary Allowances

Net Income Exceeds Salary Allowances. The partnership agreement in Figure 20-1 specifies that after providing for salary allowances of $36,000 for Mitchell and $48,000 for Jenkins, the remaining net income or loss is divided on a 60-40 basis. Recall that salary payments (or allowances) are debited to the partners' drawing accounts. They are not considered an expense and not included in the calculation of net income. Under these conditions, the allocation of net income would be reported on the income statement as shown in Figure 20-6 on the next page.

LEARNING KEY: If net income is greater than the salary allowances, the remaining income is allocated according to the ratio specified in the partnership agreement.

Net income	$190,800
Less total allowances	84,000
Remaining income	$106,800
60% of $106,800 = $64,080	
40% of $106,800 = $42,720	

FIGURE 20-5 Closing Process for a Partnership

FIGURE 20-6 Allocation of Profit and Loss on Income Statement (60-40 Basis)

Mitchell and Jenkins
Income Statement (Partial)
For Year Ended December 31, 20 - -

	S. MITCHELL	L. JENKINS	TOTAL
Net income			$190 8 0 0 00
Allocation of net income:			
Salary allowances	$ 36 0 0 0 00	$ 48 0 0 0 00	$ 84 0 0 0 00
Remaining income	64 0 8 0 00	42 7 2 0 00	106 8 0 0 00
Allocation of net income	$100 0 8 0 00	$ 90 7 2 0 00	$190 8 0 0 00

Based on the net income allocation shown above, the closing entry is:

5	Dec.	31	Income Summary	190 8 0 0 00		5
6			S. Mitchell, Capital		100 0 8 0 00	6
7			L. Jenkins, Capital		90 7 2 0 00	7

Assuming that Mitchell and Jenkins withdrew their salaries as described in the partnership agreement, the balances in the drawing accounts at year end would be $36,000 and $48,000, respectively. The drawing accounts would be closed to the partners' capital accounts at year end as follows:

9	Dec.	31	S. Mitchell, Capital	36 0 0 0 00			9
10			S. Mitchell, Drawing		36 0 0 0 00		10
11							11
12			L. Jenkins, Capital	48 0 0 0 00			12
13			L. Jenkins, Drawing		48 0 0 0 00		13

Net Income Is Less Than Salary Allowances. If the salary allowances are greater than net income, the excess is allocated to the partners according to the ratio specified in the partnership agreement. If net income for Mitchell and Jenkins is $44,000, the allocation is made as shown in Figure 20-7.

FIGURE 20-7 Allocation of Profit and Loss on Income Statement when Salary Allowances are Greater than Net Income

It may be helpful to think of the excess of salary allowances over net income as an economic loss to the partnership. Although net income of $44,000 is reported on the income statement, the partnership did not generate enough revenues to cover expenses and the salary allowances for the partners. It is this economic loss ($40,000) that is being allocated according to the profit/loss sharing ratio to determine the proper allocation of the reported net income.

Salary allowances	$84,000
Less net income	44,000
Excess of salary allowances over net income	$40,000
60% of $40,000 = $24,000	
40% of $40,000 = $16,000	

Mitchell and Jenkins
Income Statement (Partial)
For Year Ended December 31, 20 - -

	S. MITCHELL	L. JENKINS	TOTAL
Net income			$ 44 0 0 0 00
Allocation of net income:			
Salary allowances	$ 36 0 0 0 00	$ 48 0 0 0 00	$ 84 0 0 0 00
Excess of salary allowances over net income	(24 0 0 0 00)	(16 0 0 0 00)	(40 0 0 0 00)
Allocation of net income	$ 12 0 0 0 00	$ 32 0 0 0 00	$ 44 0 0 0 00

Based on the preceding net income allocations in Figure 20-7, the closing entries are:

5	Dec.	31	Income Summary		44	0	0	0	00							5
6			S. Mitchell, Capital								12	0	0	0	00	6
7			L. Jenkins, Capital								32	0	0	0	00	7
8																8
9			S. Mitchell, Capital		36	0	0	0	00							9
10			S. Mitchell, Drawing								36	0	0	0	00	10
11																11
12			L. Jenkins, Capital		48	0	0	0	00							12
13			L. Jenkins, Drawing								48	0	0	0	00	13

Allocation of Profits and Losses with Salary and Interest Allowances

Net Income Exceeds Allowances. Partners may agree that the best method of allocating profits and losses is to base salaries on the services rendered by each partner and to provide interest on capital investments. The remainder is then shared equally, or according to a predefined ratio. Assume that B. K. Kelly and S. B. Arthur form a partnership on January 1 of the current year. Kelly will devote full time to operating the business, invest $50,000, and draw a salary of $35,000 per year. Arthur will devote about 10 hours per week, invest $150,000, and draw a salary of $10,000 per year. The partners will be allowed interest of 10% on capital balances on January 1 of each year and the balance of earnings will be divided equally. Net income of $80,000 in the first year of operation would be allocated as reported in Figure 20-8.

FIGURE 20-8 Allocation of Profit and Loss on Income Statement (Interest and Salary Allowances)

Kelly and Arthur Income Statement (Partial) For Year Ended December 31, 20 - -					
Net income				$80 0 0 0 00
	B. K. KELLY	S. B. ARTHUR	TOTAL	
Allocation of net income:				
Salary allowances	$35 0 0 0 00	$10 0 0 0 00	$45 0 0 0 00
Interest allowances	5 0 0 0 00	15 0 0 0 00	20 0 0 0 00
Remaining income	7 5 0 0 00	7 5 0 0 00	15 0 0 0 00
Allocation of net income	$47 5 0 0 00	$32 5 0 0 00	$80 0 0 0 00

LEARNING KEY: Interest allowances: Kelly: $50,000 × 10% = $5,000
                                           Arthur: $150,000 × 10% = $15,000

Net income $80,000
Less total allowances   65,000
Remaining income $15,000

$15,000 ÷ 2 = $7,500 allocated to each partner

Based on the net income allocation shown in Figure 20-8, the closing entry is:

5	Dec.	31	Income Summary		80 0 0 0 00		5
6			B. K. Kelly, Capital			47 5 0 0 00	6
7			S. B. Arthur, Capital			32 5 0 0 00	7

Net Income Is Less Than Total Allowances. If Kelly and Arthur incurred a net loss of $20,000 in year 1, the allocation would be made as shown in Figure 20-9.

FIGURE 20-9 Allocation of Net Loss on Income Statement

Kelly and Arthur Income Statement (Partial) For Year Ended December 31, 20 - -			
Net income			$(20 0 0 0 00)
	B. K. KELLY	S. B. ARTHUR	TOTAL
Allocation of net loss:			
Salary allowances	$ 35 0 0 0 00	$ 10 0 0 0 00	$ 45 0 0 0 00
Interest allowances	5 0 0 0 00	15 0 0 0 00	20 0 0 0 00
Excess of allowances over income allocated equally	(42 5 0 0 00)	(42 5 0 0 00)	(85 0 0 0 00)
Allocation of net loss	$ (2 5 0 0 00)	$(17 5 0 0 00)	$(20 0 0 0 00)

LEARNING KEY:	Net loss	$20,000
	Plus total allowances	65,000
	Excess of allowances over income	$85,000

$85,000 ÷ 2 = $42,500 allocated to each partner

The following closing entry would be made to allocate the loss of $20,000.

5	Dec.	31	B. K. Kelly, Capital		2 5 0 0 00		5
6			S. B. Arthur, Capital		17 5 0 0 00		6
7			Income Summary			20 0 0 0 00	7

STATEMENTS FOR PARTNERSHIPS

LO 3 Prepare financial statements reporting the allocation of net income and partnership equity.

The allocation of net income and its impact on the partners' capital balances should be disclosed in the financial statements. All three financial statements are affected: the income statement, statement of owners' (partners') equity, and balance sheet. As illustrated in the preceding section, the allocation is often reported in the lower portion of the income statement. In addition, the statement of partners' equity reflects the equity of each partner and summarizes the allocation of net income for the year.

 LEARNING KEY: The allocation of net income and its impact on the partners' capital balances should be disclosed in the financial statements.

Recall that the capital balances for Kelly and Arthur on January 1, 20--, were $50,000 and $150,000, respectively. Let's assume that Arthur invested an additional $10,000, net income was $80,000 and allocated as reported in Figure 20-8, and the partners withdrew only the salary portion of their compensation ($35,000 and $10,000, respectively) during the first year of operation. As shown in Figure 20-10, the statement of partners' equity reports this information and the income allocations reported on the income statement.

FIGURE 20-10   Statement of Partners' Equity

	B. K. KELLY	S. B. ARTHUR	TOTAL
Kelly and Arthur Statement of Partners' Equity For Year Ended December 31, 20 - -			
Capital, January 1, 20 --	$50 0 0 0 00	$150 0 0 0 00	$200 0 0 0 00
Additional investments during the year	————	10 0 0 0 00	10 0 0 0 00
	$50 0 0 0 00	$160 0 0 0 00	$210 0 0 0 00
Net income for the year	47 5 0 0 00	32 5 0 0 00	80 0 0 0 00
	$97 5 0 0 00	$192 5 0 0 00	$290 0 0 0 00
Withdrawals (salaries during the year)	35 0 0 0 00	10 0 0 0 00	45 0 0 0 00
Capital, December 31, 20 --	$62 5 0 0 00	$182 5 0 0 00	$245 0 0 0 00

 LEARNING KEY: Interest allowances for year 2 would be computed as follows:

Kelly: $62,500 × 10% = $6,250
Arthur: $182,500 × 10% = $18,250

The additional investment is reported in the same manner as for a sole proprietorship.

Finally, the partners' equity section of the balance sheet reports the equity of each partner, as illustrated below.

Kelly and Arthur Balance Sheet (Partial) December 31, 20 - -		
Partners' Equity		
B. K. Kelly, capital	$ 62 5 0 0 00	
S. B. Arthur, capital	182 5 0 0 00	
Total partners' equity		$245 0 0 0 00

DISSOLUTION OF A PARTNERSHIP

LO 4 Describe the actions that result in the dissolution of a partnership and account for the dissolution.

One of the primary characteristics of the partnership form of organization is its limited life. Any change in the members of the partnership results in **dissolution**. Dissolution of a partnership may occur because of the addition of a new partner, the death or withdrawal of one of the partners, or bankruptcy.

 LEARNING KEY: The partnership is dissolved if there is any change in the members of the partnership.

Dissolution of the partnership does not necessarily imply that business operations will halt. It simply means that the partnership is dissolved. The business may continue with a new group of partners, or a different form of ownership.

Admitting a New Partner

A new partner may be admitted by agreement among the existing partners. When this happens, the old partnership is dissolved and a new one is created. A new partner may buy into the business in three ways: (1) by purchasing an interest directly from existing partners, (2) by making a cash investment in the business, or (3) by contributing assets from an existing business.

Assume that Morning and Knight admit Sunny Noon as a new partner as of July 1, 20--, when Morning and Knight have capital interests of $30,000 and $20,000, respectively. Noon pays $12,000 to Morning for one-third of her interest and $12,000 to Knight for one-half of his interest. These cash payments go to the partners directly, not to the business. Thus, the following entry is made by the partnership:

	20--															
1	July	1	Donna Morning, Capital	10	0	0	0	00 *								1
2			Larry Knight, Capital	10	0	0	0	00 **								2
3			Sunny Noon, Capital						20	0	0	0	00			3
4			S. Noon admitted to partnership													4
5			*$30,000 × 1/3 = $10,000													5
6			**$20,000 × 1/2 = $10,000													6

The extra $2,000 ($12,000 – $10,000) paid to both Morning and Knight represents profit to them, but it has no effect on the *partnership's* financial statements.

Now, assume instead that Noon invested $25,000 cash in the new partnership. In this case, the following entry would be made to admit Noon.

	20--														
1	July	1	Cash	25	0	0	0	00							1
2			Sunny Noon, Capital						25	0	0	0	00		2
3			S. Noon admitted to partnership												3
4															4

Finally, let's assume that Noon had been operating her own business, which was then taken over by the new partnership. In this case the balance sheet for Sunny Noon's Golf, shown in Figure 20-11, would serve as a basis for preparing the opening entry. The assets listed in the balance sheet are taken over, the liabilities are assumed, and Noon's capital account is credited for the difference.

FIGURE 20-11 Balance Sheet for Sunny Noon's Golf

Sunny Noon's Golf
Balance Sheet
June 30, 20 - -

Assets									Liabilities									
Cash						$ 5	0	0	0	00	Notes payable	$9	0	4	8	00		
Accounts receivable	$14	2	9	0	00						Accounts payable	7	5	5	0	00		
Less allowance for bad debts	1	0	7	8	00	13	2	1	2	00	Total liabilities						$16	5	9	8	00
Merchandise inventory						27	2	9	0	00	Owner's Equity							
											Sunny Noon, capital						28	9	0	4	00
Total assets						$45	5	0	2	00	Total liabilities and owner's equity						$45	5	0	2	00

Noon has no knowledge of any uncollectible accounts receivable as of June 30, 20--, and has been using the FIFO method of inventory costing. Thus, the amounts reported on the balance sheet are reasonable approximations of market values. The entry to admit Noon as a partner, therefore, is as follows:

	20- -													
1	July	1	Cash	5	0	0	0	00						1
2			Accounts Receivable	14	2	9	0	00						2
3			Merchandise Inventory	27	2	9	0	00						3
4			Allowance for Bad Debts						1	0	7	8	00	4
5			Notes Payable						9	0	4	8	00	5
6			Accounts Payable						7	5	5	0	00	6
7			Sunny Noon, Capital						28	9	0	4	00	7
8			S. Noon admitted to partnership											8
9														9

Withdrawal of Partner

By agreement, a partner may retire and be permitted to withdraw assets equal to, less than, or greater than the amount of his or her interest in the partnership. The book value of a partner's interest is shown by the credit balance of the partner's capital account. The balance is computed after all profits or losses have been allocated in accordance with the partnership agreement and the books closed. If a retiring partner withdraws cash or other assets equal to the credit balance of his or her capital account, the transaction will have no effect on the capital of the remaining partners.

To illustrate, assume that several years after the formation of Morning, Noon, and Knight Sports, Sunny Noon decided to retire. The partners agreed to the withdrawal of cash equal to the amount of Noon's equity in the assets of the partnership. After bringing all accounts up to date, assume that the partners' capital accounts had credit balances as follows:

Donna Morning	$55,000
Sunny Noon	40,000
Larry Knight	45,000

If Noon withdraws $40,000 in cash, the entry on the books of the partnership is as follows:

12		Sunny Noon, Capital	40	0	0	0	00						12
13		Cash						40	0	0	0	00	13
14		S. Noon retired, withdrawing											14
15		$40,000 in equity settlement											15

Note that this transaction decreases cash and decreases the total capital of the partnership, but it does not affect the equity of the remaining partners. Morning still has an equity of $55,000 and Knight an equity of $45,000 in the partnership assets.

If a retiring partner agrees to withdraw less than the amount in his or her capital account, the transaction will increase the capital accounts of the remaining partners. For example, if Noon withdraws only $30,000 in settlement of the interest, the entry in the books of the partnership is as follows:

12		Sunny Noon, Capital	40	0	0	0	00						12
13		Cash						30	0	0	0	00	13
14		Donna Morning, Capital						5	5	0	0	00	14
15		Larry Knight, Capital						4	5	0	0	00	15
16		S. Noon retired, withdrawing											16
17		$30,000 in equity settlement											17

The difference between Noon's equity in the assets of the partnership and the amount of cash withdrawn is $10,000 ($40,000 − $30,000). This difference is divided between the remaining partners on the basis stated in the partnership agreement. In this case it is divided according to the ratio of their capital interests after allocating net income and closing their drawing accounts. On this basis, Morning's capital account is credited for $5,500 and Knight's is credited for $4,500. The calculations are shown below.

Remaining Equity in Partnership

Morning	$55,000
Knight	45,000
Total	$100,000

Allocation to Morning: ($55,000 ÷ $100,000) × $10,000 = $5,500
Allocation to Knight: ($45,000 ÷ $100,000) × $10,000 = $4,500

If a retiring partner withdraws more than the amount in his or her capital account, the transaction will decrease the capital accounts of the remaining partners. Thus, if Morning and Knight allow Noon to withdraw $45,000 in settlement of Noon's interest, the entry in the books of the partnership is as follows:

12		Sunny Noon, Capital	40	0	0	0	00						12
13		Donna Morning, Capital	2	7	5	0	00						13
14		Larry Knight, Capital	2	2	5	0	00						14
15		Cash						45	0	0	0	00	15
16		S. Noon retired, withdrawing											16
17		$45,000 in equity settlement											17

The excess of the amount of cash withdrawn over Noon's equity in the partnership ($5,000) is divided between the remaining partners on the basis stated in the partnership agreement. Thus, Morning, Capital is debited for $2,750 (55/100 of $5,000), while Knight, Capital is debited for $2,250 (45/100 of $5,000).

When a partner retires from the business, the partner's interest may be purchased directly by one or more of the remaining partners or by an outside party. If the retiring partner's interest is sold to one of the remaining partners, the retiring partner's equity is merely transferred to the other partner. For example, assume that Noon's equity is sold to Morning. The entry for the transaction on the books of the partnership is as follows:

12		Sunny Noon, Capital	40 0 0 0 00		12
13		Donna Morning, Capital		40 0 0 0 00	13
14		D. Morning purchased S. Noon's			14
15		interest in partnership			15

The amount paid to Noon by Morning is a personal transaction and has no effect on the above entry. Any gain or loss resulting from the transaction is a personal gain or loss of the withdrawing partner and not of the business. Thus, whatever amount is involved, the credit in Noon's account is transferred to Morning's account.

Death of a Partner

The death of a partner dissolves the partnership. On the date of death, the accounts are closed and the net income for the year to date is allocated to the partners' capital accounts. Most agreements call for an audit and revaluation of the assets at this time. The balance of the deceased partner's capital account is then transferred to a liability account with the deceased's estate. The surviving partners may continue the business or liquidate. If the business continues, the procedures for settling with the estate are the same as those described earlier for the withdrawal of a partner. Liquidation procedures are described in the following section.

LIQUIDATION OF A PARTNERSHIP

LO 5   Describe how a partnership is liquidated and prepare associated entries and a statement of partnership liquidation.

Liquidation of a partnership generally means that the assets are sold, liabilities are paid, and the remaining cash or other assets are distributed to the partners. When normal operations are discontinued, adjusting and closing entries are made. Thus, only the assets, liabilities, and partners' equity accounts remain open. As the assets are sold, the cash realized is applied first to the claims of creditors. Once all liabilities are paid, the remaining cash and other assets are distributed to the partners according to their ownership interests as indicated by their capital accounts.

LEARNING KEY: When a partnership is liquidated, the assets are sold, liabilities are paid, and the remaining cash or other assets are distributed to the partners.

To illustrate, assume that after several years of operations, the partnership of Morning, Noon, and Knight Sports is to be liquidated. After making closing entries on May 31, 20--, the accounts listed below remain open. For simplicity, "Other Assets" and "Liabilities" are used as account titles. In actual practice, several asset, contra-asset, and liability accounts would be involved.

	Account Balance	
Account Title	**Debit**	**Credit**
Cash	$ 10,000	
Inventory	120,000	
Other Assets	220,000	
Liabilities		$ 80,000
Donna Morning, Capital		95,000
Larry Knight, Capital		120,000
Sunny Noon, Capital		55,000

Using these account balances, accounting for the liquidation of the partnership is illustrated in Figure 20-12. For convenience, let's assume that all assets are sold in one transaction on June 1, 20--, and all liabilities are paid at once on June 15, 20--. On June 18, cash settlements are made with the partners who share equally in all profits and losses.

Gain on Sale of Assets

Assume that the noncash assets are sold for $370,000. Since these assets have a book value of $340,000, a gain of $30,000 on the sale is recognized. The gain is allocated to the partners' capital accounts according to the profit-and-loss sharing ratio. In this case, the gain is shared equally. Next, the liabilities are paid and the remaining cash distributed to the partners according to their capital account balances. A statement of partnership liquidation summarizing these transactions is provided in Figure 20-12.

FIGURE 20-12 Statement of Partnership Liquidation

	CASH	INVENTORY	OTHER ASSETS	LIABILITIES	CAPITAL		
Morning, Noon, and Knight Sports Statement of Partnership Liquidation For Period June 1–18, 20 - -					D. MORNING	L. KNIGHT	S. NOON
Balance before sale of assets	$ 10 0 0 0 00	$120 0 0 0 00	$220 0 0 0 00	$ 80 0 0 0 00	$ 95 0 0 0 00	$120 0 0 0 00	$ 55 0 0 0 00
Sale of noncash assets and							
allocation of gain	370 0 0 0 00	(120 0 0 0 00)	(220 0 0 0 00)		10 0 0 0 00	10 0 0 0 00	10 0 0 0 00
Balance after sale	$380 0 0 0 00	0	0	$ 80 0 0 0 00	$105 0 0 0 00	$130 0 0 0 00	$ 65 0 0 0 00
Payment of liabilities	(80 0 0 0 00)			(80 0 0 0 00)			
Balance after payment of liabilities	$300 0 0 0 00	0	0	0	$105 0 0 0 00	$130 0 0 0 00	$ 65 0 0 0 00
Distribution of cash to partners	(300 0 0 0 00)				(105 0 0 0 00)	(130 0 0 0 00)	(65 0 0 0 00)
Final balance	0	0	0	0	0	0	0

The entries for these transactions are illustrated below.

	20- -					
1	June	1	Cash	370 0 0 0 00		1
2			Inventory		120 0 0 0 00	2
3			Other Assets		220 0 0 0 00	3
4			Gain on Sale of Assets		30 0 0 0 00	4
5			Sale of assets			5
6						6
7		1	Gain on Sale of Assets	30 0 0 0 00		7
8			Donna Morning, Capital		10 0 0 0 00	8
9			Larry Knight, Capital		10 0 0 0 00	9
10			Sunny Noon, Capital		10 0 0 0 00	10
11			Allocation of gain			11
12						12
13		15	Liabilities	80 0 0 0 00		13
14			Cash		80 0 0 0 00	14
15			Payment of liabilities			15
16						16
17		18	Donna Morning, Capital	105 0 0 0 00		17
18			Larry Knight, Capital	130 0 0 0 00		18
19			Sunny Noon, Capital	65 0 0 0 00		19
20			Cash		300 0 0 0 00	20
21			Distribution of cash to partners			21

Loss on Sale of Assets

Using the same information for Morning, Noon, and Knight as given on page 744, assume that the noncash assets are sold for $295,000, resulting in a loss of $45,000. A statement of partnership liquidation reflecting the equal allocation of the loss on the sale of assets, payment of the liabilities, and distribution of the cash to the partners is illustrated in Figure 20-13.

FIGURE 20-13 Statement of Partnership Liquidation

Morning, Noon, and Knight Sports Statement of Partnership Liquidation For Period June 1–18, 20 - -							
	CASH	INVENTORY	OTHER ASSETS	LIABILITIES	CAPITAL		
					D. MORNING	L. KNIGHT	S. NOON
Balance before sale of assets	$ 10 0 0 0 00	$120 0 0 0 00	$220 0 0 0 00	$ 80 0 0 0 00	$ 95 0 0 0 00	$120 0 0 0 00	$ 55 0 0 0 00
Sale of noncash assets and							
allocation of loss	295 0 0 0 00	(120 0 0 0 00)	(220 0 0 0 00)		(15 0 0 0 00)	(15 0 0 0 00)	(15 0 0 0 00)
Balance after sale	$305 0 0 0 00	0	0	$ 80 0 0 0 00	$ 80 0 0 0 00	$105 0 0 0 00	$ 40 0 0 0 00
Payment of liabilities	(80 0 0 0 00)			(80 0 0 0 00)			
Balance after payment of liabilities	$225 0 0 0 00	0	0	0	$ 80 0 0 0 00	$105 0 0 0 00	$ 40 0 0 0 00
Distribution of cash to partners	(225 0 0 0 00)				(80 0 0 0 00)	(105 0 0 0 00)	(40 0 0 0 00)
Final balance	0	0	0	0	0	0	0

The entries for these transactions are as follows:

	20- -							
1	June	1	Cash	295 0 0 0 00		1
2			Loss on Sale of Assets	45 0 0 0 00		2
3			Inventory		120 0 0 0 00	3
4			Other Assets		220 0 0 0 00	4
5			Sale of assets			5
6						6
7		1	Donna Morning, Capital	15 0 0 0 00		7
8			Larry Knight, Capital	15 0 0 0 00		8
9			Sunny Noon, Capital	15 0 0 0 00		9
10			Loss on Sale of Assets		45 0 0 0 00	10
11			Allocation of loss			11
12						12
13		15	Liabilities	80 0 0 0 00		13
14			Cash		80 0 0 0 00	14
15			Payment of liabilities			15
16						16
17		18	Donna Morning, Capital	80 0 0 0 00		17
18			Larry Knight, Capital	105 0 0 0 00		18
19			Sunny Noon, Capital	40 0 0 0 00		19
20			Cash		225 0 0 0 00	20
21			Distribution of cash to partners			21

Learning Objectives	Key Points to Remember

1 **Explain how a partnership is formed and account for the formation.**

The proper accounting for the formation of a partnership depends on the type of investment made by each partner. Cash investments are recorded by recognizing the cash and an equal amount of partnership capital as shown below.

5		Cash	50 0 0 0 00						5
6		Katherine Meisenheimer, Capital			50 0 0 0 00				6
7		K. Meisenheimer invested $50,000 in cash							7

If a partner invests cash and other assets, the assets are entered at their market values. The partner's capital account is credited for the sum of the cash and the market value of assets contributed as shown below.

5		Cash	10 0 0 0 00						5
6		Inventory (market value)	20 0 0 0 00						6
7		Office Equipment (market value)	8 0 0 0 00						7
8		Delivery Equipment (market value)	15 0 0 0 00						8
9		Sara Bates, Capital			53 0 0 0 00				9
10		S. Bates investment in partnership							10

If existing sole proprietorships are combined, the balance sheets of the proprietorships are used to prepare the entry for the formation of the partnership. Each partner's investment is measured by the difference between the market value of the assets invested and the liabilities assumed by the partnership as shown below. Before transferring receivables to the partnership, any known bad debts must be written off by the proprietorship.

	20--									
1	Apr.	1	Cash	5 0 0 0 00						1
2			Accounts Receivable	20 0 0 0 00						2
3			Merchandise Inventory (market value)	50 0 0 0 00						3
4			Store Equipment (market value)	30 0 0 0 00						4
5			Allowance for Bad Debts			2 0 0 00				5
6			Notes Payable			10 0 0 0 00				6
7			Accounts Payable			12 0 0 0 00				7
8			Alex Von Rosenberger, Capital			82 8 0 0 00				8
9			A. Von Rosenberger's investment							9
10			in partnership							10

2 **Explain how partners are compensated and account for the allocation of net income.**

Partner compensation may be based on salary and interest allowances as well as an allocation of remaining profits as stated in the partnership agreement.

3 **Prepare financial statements reporting the allocation of net income and partnership equity.**

Partnership financial statements report the allocation of net income and partnership equity as shown in the statements on the next page.

4 **Describe the actions that result in the dissolution of a partnership and account for the dissolution.**

Any change in the members of the partnership results in its dissolution. Accounting for the dissolution varies depending on whether a new partner is admitted or a partner withdraws and whether an additional investment is made in the partnership or payments are made directly to existing partners.

Learning Objectives	Key Points to Remember
5 **Describe how a partnership is liquidated and prepare associated entries and a statement of partnership liquidation.**	The steps in the liquidation process are: 1. Assets are sold. 2. Gains or losses are allocated to the partners. 3. Liabilities are paid. 4. Remaining cash and other assets are distributed to the partners according to their capital accounts.
3 **(continued)** **Prepare financial statements reporting the allocation of net income and partnership equity.**	(table below)

Kelly and Arthur
Income Statement (Partial)
For Year Ended December 31, 20 - -

	B. K. KELLY		
Net income			$80 0 0 0 00
Allocation of net income:			
Salary allowances	$35 0 0 0 00	$10 0 0 0 00	0 0 0 0 00
Interest allowances	5 0 0 0 00	15 0 0 0 00	0 0 0 0 00
Remaining income	7 5 0 0 00	7 5 0 0 00	0 0 0 0 00
	$47 5 0 0	$32 5 0 0 00	0 0 0 0 00

Kelly and Arthur
Statement of Partners' Equity
For Year Ended December 31, 20 - -

	B. K. KELLY	S. B. ARTHUR	TOTAL
Capital, January 1, 20 --	$50 0 0 0 00	$150 0 0 0 00	$200 0 0 0 00
Additonal investments during the year		10 0 0 0 00	10 0 0 0 00
	$50 0 0 0 00	$160 0 0 0 00	$210 0 0 0 00
Net income for the year	47 5 0 0 00	32 5 0 0 00	80 0 0 0 00
	$97 5 0 0 00	$192 5 0 0 00	$290 0 0 0 00
Withdrawals (salaries during the year)	35 0 0 0 00	10 0 0 0 00	45 0 0 0 00
Capital, December 31, 20 --	$62 5 0 0 00	$182 5 0 0 00	$245 0 0 0 00

Kelly and Arthur
Balance Sheet (Partial)
December 31, 20 - -

Partners' Equity		
B. K. Kelly, capital	$ 62 5 0 0 00	
S. B. Arthur, capital	182 5 0 0 00	
Total partners' equity		$245 0 0 0 00

Reflection: Answering the Opening Questions

As discussed in the chapter, advantages of a partnership include the increased capital and credit available to a partnership as well as the combined knowledge and experience that the partners bring to the operation of the business. Disadvantages include personal liability for each partner, non-transferability of a partnership interest without the consent of other partners, and the fact that a partnership dissolves with the termination of the partnership agreement, bankruptcy, or a change in the partners. John may be asked to make a cash investment. However, since the plan is to combine two existing businesses, he will probably be contributing his firm's assets. The assets are valued at market value. Distribution of profits and salary allowances will be determined through a negotiation between John and his potential partner. Of course, all of the essential aspects of the partnership should be clearly and openly discussed and then placed in writing in the form of a partnership agreement.

KEY TERMS

dissolution, (740)   Dissolving of the partnership resulting from any change in the members of the partnership.

liquidation, (743)   The process of selling the assets, paying the liabilities, and distributing the remaining cash or other assets to the partners.

partnership, (726)   The form of organization in which two or more individuals engage in an enterprise as co-owners.

partnership agreement, (727)   A written agreement containing the various provisions for operating a partnership.

DEMONSTRATION PROBLEM

Mascha Schuurmans, Jolijn Brouwer, and Mirjam van Tuil are partners in Holland Law. They share profits and losses in a 50-30-20 ratio. The partnership agreement calls for annual salaries of $40,000, $35,000, and $30,000, respectively, and interest of 12% on their January 1 capital balances.* Any remaining net income (or net loss) is to be divided in accordance with the ratios used for sharing profits and losses.

The partners' capital balances as of January 1, 20-1, were Schuurmans, $120,000; Brouwer, $75,000; and van Tuil, $50,000. No additional investments were made during the year. The net income of the partnership for the year 20-1 was $160,000. Partners' withdrawals for the year were Schuurmans, $50,000; Brouwer, $40,000; and van Tuil, $35,000.

On March 4, 20-2, the partners decide to liquidate their law firm. On that date, the firm has a cash balance of $46,000, noncash assets of $274,000, and liabilities of $40,000. No additional investments or withdrawals were made in 20-2. Between March 5 and March 31, the noncash assets are sold for

$290,000, the gain is divided according to the profit and loss sharing ratio, and the liabilities are paid. The remaining cash is then distributed to the partners.

*Salaries and interest are not recognized as expenses in the determination of net income.

REQUIRED

1. Prepare the lower portion of the income statement of Holland Law for the year ended December 31, 20-1, showing the division of the partnership net income for the year.

2. Prepare the general journal entry to close Income Summary to the partners' capital accounts as of December 31, 20-1.

3. Prepare a statement of partners' equity for Holland Law for the year ended December 31, 20-1.

4. Prepare a statement of partnership liquidation for Holland Law for the period March 5 through March 31, 20-2.

5. Prepare the general journal entries as of March 31, 20-2, for:

   a. The sale of the noncash assets of the partnership

   b. The division of any loss or gain on realization

   c. The payment of partnership liabilities

   d. The distribution of remaining cash to the partners

Solution

1.

Holland Law
Income Statement (Partial)
For Year Ended December 31, 20 - -

	M. SCHUURMANS	J. BROUWER	M. VAN TUIL	TOTAL
Net income				$160 0 0 0 00
Allocation of net income:				
Salary allowances	$40 0 0 0 00	$35 0 0 0 00	$30 0 0 0 00	$105 0 0 0 00
Interest allowances	14 4 0 0 00	9 0 0 0 00	6 0 0 0 00	29 4 0 0 00
Remaining income	12 8 0 0 00	7 6 8 0 00	5 1 2 0 00	25 6 0 0 00
	$67 2 0 0 00	$51 6 8 0 00	$41 1 2 0 00	$160 0 0 0 00

2.

4							4
5	Dec.	31	Income Summary	160 0 0 0 00			5
6			Mascha Schuurmans, Capital		67 2 0 0 00		6
7			Jolijn Brouwer, Capital		51 6 8 0 00		7
8			Mirjam van Tuil, Capital		41 1 2 0 00		8
9							9

3.

Holland Law Statement of Partners' Equity For Year Ended December 31, 20 -1				
	M. SCHUURMANS	J. BROUWER	M. VAN TUIL	TOTAL
Capital, January 1, 20 -1	$120 0 0 0 00	$ 75 0 0 0 00	$50 0 0 0 00	$245 0 0 0 00
Net income for the year	67 2 0 0 00	51 6 8 0 00	41 1 2 0 00	160 0 0 0 00
	$187 2 0 0 00	$126 6 8 0 00	$91 1 2 0 00	$405 0 0 0 00
Withdrawals	50 0 0 0 00	40 0 0 0 00	35 0 0 0 00	125 0 0 0 00
Capital, December 31, 20 -1	$137 2 0 0 00	$ 86 6 8 0 00	$56 1 2 0 00	$280 0 0 0 00

4.

Holland Law Statement of Partnership Liquidation For Period March 5–31, 20 - 2				CAPITAL		
	CASH	NONCASH ASSETS	LIABILITIES	M. SCHUURMANS	J. BROUWER	M. VAN TUIL
Balance before sale of assets	$ 46 0 0 0 00	$274 0 0 0 00	$ 40 0 0 0 00	$137 2 0 0 00	$ 86 6 8 0 00	$ 56 1 2 0 00
Sale of noncash assets and allocation of gain	290 0 0 0 00	(274 0 0 0 00)	0	8 0 0 0 00	4 8 0 0 00	3 2 0 0 00
Balance after sale	$336 0 0 0 00	0	$ 40 0 0 0 00	$145 2 0 0 00	$ 91 4 8 0 00	$ 59 3 2 0 00
Payment of liabilities	(40 0 0 0 00)	0	(40 0 0 0 00)	0	0	0
Balance after payment of liabilities	$296 0 0 0 00	0	0	$145 2 0 0 00	$ 91 4 8 0 00	$ 59 3 2 0 00
Distribution of cash to partners	(296 0 0 0 00)	0	0	(145 2 0 0 00)	(91 4 8 0 00)	(59 3 2 0 00)
Final balance	0	0	0	0	0	0

5.

	DATE		DESCRIPTION	POST REF.	DEBIT	CREDIT	
	20- 2		GENERAL JOURNAL			PAGE 1	
a.	Mar.	31	Cash		290 0 0 0 00		1
			Noncash Assets			274 0 0 0 00	2
			Gain on Sale of Assets			16 0 0 0 00	3
			Sale of assets				4
							5
b.		31	Gain on Sale of Assets		16 0 0 0 00		6
			Mascha Schuurmans, Capital			8 0 0 0 00	7
			Jolijn Brouwer, Capital			4 8 0 0 00	8
			Mirjam van Tuil, Capital			3 2 0 0 00	9
			Allocation of gain				10
							11
c.		31	Liabilities		40 0 0 0 00		12
			Cash			40 0 0 0 00	13
			Payment of liabilities				14
							15
d.		31	Mascha Schuurmans, Capital		145 2 0 0 00		16
			Jolijn Brouwer, Capital		91 4 8 0 00		17
			Mirjam van Tuil, Capital		59 3 2 0 00		18
			Cash			296 0 0 0 00	19
			Distribution of cash to partners				20

REVIEW QUESTIONS

1. Identify eleven essential provisions of a partnership agreement.

2. Identify three advantages of a partnership as compared with a sole proprietorship.

3. Identify four disadvantages of a partnership form of business organization.

4. When two sole proprietors decide to combine their businesses, at what values should the noncash assets be taken over by the partnership?

5. In the absence of any agreement between the partners, how must profits and losses be shared? If the partnership agreement specifies how profits are to be shared, but there is no agreement as to how losses are to be shared, what must be true with respect to losses?

6. What factors generally are considered in determining the allocation of profits and losses?

7. Identify three ways in which a partnership may be dissolved.

8. When a new partner who has been the sole owner of a business is admitted to a partnership by having the partnership take over the old business, what usually serves as the basis for preparing the opening entry?

9. Describe the four accounting entries for the liquidation of a partnership.

MANAGING YOUR WRITING

A friend, Joan Mellencamp, has mentioned that she is thinking about forming a partnership with a small group of colleagues. She is interested in learning about the advantages and disadvantages of the partnership form of ownership. In addition, she has asked for your advice on the kinds of issues that should be agreed upon in advance of the formation of the partnership. Write a memo to your friend explaining the advantages and disadvantages of a partnership and offer your advice on the issues that should be settled in advance.

ETHICS CASE

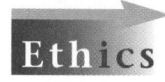

Kathy Lentz, Rob Snyder, and Tom Rohm were all general partners in a consulting business. Each partner owned one-third of the business. The partnership agreement stated that all three partners must approve vouchers for payments in amounts exceeding $5,000. While Tom was on vacation, Kathy and Rob decided to purchase a new computer system costing $6,800. A voucher was prepared and Rob signed both his and Tom's name. Kathy signed her name and gave the voucher to the accounts payable clerk who wrote the check for $6,800.

1. Why would a partnership agreement specify that all purchases over a certain amount be approved by all partners? Are there any circumstances that would warrant deviation from this policy?

2. What are the disadvantages of the partnership form of business ownership?

3. Write a short memo from Tom Rohm to Kathy Lentz and Rob Snyder expressing disapproval of the situation.

4. In groups of three or four, discuss some of the possible outcomes of this situation.

WEB WORK

 Partnerships that go bad have been a mainstay of American cinema, from "The Wild Bunch" to "Reservoir Dogs." What happens when your business partners go astray? Read this article to find out:

http://www.tcp.ca/Oct95/OnYourOwn.html.
(http://heintz.swcollege.com)

SERIES A EXERCISES

EXERCISE 20A-1 (LO 1) PARTNERSHIP OPENING ENTRIES Lisa Morris and Joyce Laski agreed on September 1 to go into business as partners. According to the agreement, Morris is to contribute $45,000 cash and Laski is to contribute $65,000 cash. Provide a separate journal entry for the investment of each partner.

EXERCISE 20A-2 (LO 2) ENTRIES FOR ALLOCATION OF NET INCOME Karen Rhea and Wayne Sellevaeg decided to form a partnership on July 1, 20-1. Rhea invested $100,000 and Sellevaeg invested $50,000. For the fiscal year ended June 30, 20-2, a net income of $90,000 was earned. Determine the amount of net income that Rhea and Sellevaeg would receive under each of the following independent assumptions:

1. There is no agreement concerning the distribution of net income.

2. Each partner is to receive 10% interest on their original investment. The remaining net income is to be divided equally.

3. Rhea and Sellevaeg are to receive a salary allowance of $30,000 and $40,000, respectively. The remaining net income is to be divided equally.

4. Each partner is to receive 10% interest on their original investment. Rhea and Sellevaeg are to receive a salary allowance of $30,000 and $40,000, respectively. The remaining net income is to be divided as follows: Rhea 40% and Sellevaeg 60%.

EXERCISE 20A-3 (LO 3) PARTIAL FINANCIAL STATEMENTS Karen Cooper and Alex Orme formed a partnership on May 1, 20-1. Cooper contributed $80,000 and Orme contributed $50,000. During the year, Cooper contributed an additional $20,000. The partnership agreement states that Cooper is to receive $30,000 and Orme is to receive $60,000 as a salary allowance. Any remaining net income is to be divided as follows: Cooper 20% and Orme 80%. The partnership earned net income of $140,000 for the fiscal year ending April 30, 20-2. The partners withdrew only the salary portion of their compensation during the first year of operation.

(continued)

1. Prepare the lower portion of the income statement showing the allocation of net income between Cooper and Orme for the fiscal year ended April 30, 20-2.

2. Prepare a statement of partners' equity showing each individual partner's equity for the fiscal year ended April 30, 20-2.

EXERCISE 20A-4 (LO 4) ADMITTING NEW PARTNERS Jeff Bowman and Kristi Emery, who have ending capital balances of $100,000 and $60,000, respectively, agree to admit two new partners to their business on August 18, 20--. Dan Bridges will buy one-fifth of Bowman's capital interest for $30,000 and one-fourth of Emery's capital interest for $20,000. Payments will be made directly to the partners. Anna Terrell will invest $50,000 in the business for which she will receive a $50,000 capital interest.

1. Prepare general journal entries showing the transactions admitting Bridges and Terrell to the partnership.

2. Calculate the ending capital balances of all four partners after the transactions.

EXERCISE 20A-5 (LO 5) ENTRIES: PARTNERSHIP LIQUIDATION On liquidation of the partnership of J. Hui and K. Cline, as of November 1, 20--, inventory with a book value of $180,000 is sold for $230,000. Given that Hui and Cline share profits and losses equally, prepare the entries for the sale and the allocation of gain.

SERIES A PROBLEMS

PROBLEM 20A-1 (LO 1) PARTNERSHIP OPENING ENTRIES On July 1, 20--, Susan Woodworth and Barbara Holly combined their two businesses to form a partnership under the firm name of Woodworth and Holly. The balance sheets of the two sole proprietorships are shown below.

Woodworth's Antiques
Balance Sheet
June 30, 20 - -

Assets						Liabilities						
Cash				$ 7 1 0 0	00	Notes payable	$2 5 0 0	00				
Accounts receivable	$4 5 0 0	00				Accounts payable	8 4 0 0	00				
Less allowance for bad debts	6 2 0	00	3 8 8 0	00		Total liabilities				$10 9 0 0	00	
Merchandise inventory			21 4 3 0	00								
Store equipment	$8 2 0 0	00				Owner's Equity						
Less accumulated depreciation	1 3 0 0	00	6 9 0 0	00		Susan Woodworth, capital				28 4 1 0	00	
Total assets			$39 3 1 0	00		Total liabilities and owner's equity				$39 3 1 0	00	

Holly's Unfinished Furniture
Balance Sheet
June 30, 20 - -

Assets										Liabilities									
Cash						$ 4 5 2 0 00		Notes payable			$8 0 0 0 00				
Accounts receivable	$3 2 7 5 00							Accounts payable			6 3 0 0 00				
Less allowance for bad debts	4 7 5 00			2 8 0 0 00				Total liabilities						$14 3 0 0 00	
Merchandise inventory				28 1 9 0 00										
Supplies				9 6 0 00										
Office equipment	$7 4 0 0 00													
Less accumulated depreciation	1 8 0 0 00			5 6 0 0 00										
Store equipment	$7 7 0 0 00							Owner's Equity						
Less accumulated depreciation	1 5 0 0 00			6 2 0 0 00				Barbara Holly, capital						33 9 7 0 00	
Total assets				$48 2 7 0 00				Total liabilities and owner's equity						$48 2 7 0 00	

The balance sheets reflect fair market values except for the following:

a. The fair market value of Woodworth's store equipment is $7,500.

b. The fair market value of Holly's office equipment and store equipment are $6,100 and $6,800, respectively.

REQUIRED Prepare the opening entry for the formation of the Woodworth and Holly partnership as of July 1, 20--, using fair market values. The difference between assets invested and liabilities assumed should be credited to each partner's capital account. Neither partner has knowledge of any uncollectible accounts receivable.

PROBLEM 20A-2 (LO 3) PREPARING PARTIAL FINANCIAL STATEMENTS AND CLOSING ENTRIES The partnership of Hiller and Roundtree, CPAs, showed revenues of $195,000 and expenses of $52,000 on their year-end work sheet. Their capital balances as of January 1, 20--, were $52,000 for B. Hiller and $48,000 for O. Roundtree. No additional investments were made during the year. As stated in their partnership agreement, after withdrawing salary allowances of $60,000 for Hiller and $40,000 for Roundtree, the partners each withdrew 5% interest on their January 1 capital balances. No additional withdrawals were made. Any remaining net income is to be divided on a 45-55 basis.

REQUIRED 1. Prepare the lower portion of the income statement of the partnership for the year ended December 31, 20--, showing the division of the partnership net income for the year.

2. Prepare a statement of partners' equity for the year ended December 31, 20--, and the partners' equity section of the balance sheet on that date.

3. Prepare closing entries for the partnership as of December 31, 20--. (For simplicity, use the account titles "Revenues" for all revenues and "Expenses" for all expenses.)

PROBLEM 20A-3 (LO 4) ENTRIES FOR DISSOLUTION OF PARTNERSHIP The Kelly and Kelly Wrecking Company, a partnership, operates a general demolition business. Ownership of the company is divided among the partners, Mike Kelly, Kim Kelly, Larry Dennis, and Jim Wheeles. Profits and losses are shared equally. The books are kept on a calendar year basis.

(continued)

On September 15, after the business had been in operation for several years, Dennis died. Mrs. Dennis wished to sell her husband's interest in the partnership for $25,000. After the books were closed, the partners' capital accounts had credit balances as follows:

Mike Kelly	$50,000
Kim Kelly	25,000
Larry Dennis	35,000
Jim Wheeles	25,000

REQUIRED

1. Prepare the general journal entry required to enter the check issued to Mrs. Dennis in payment of her deceased husband's interest in the partnership. According to the partnership agreement, the difference between the amount paid to Mrs. Dennis and the book value of Larry Dennis' capital account is allocated to the remaining partners based on their ending capital account balances.

2. Instead of the foregoing, assume that Mrs. Dennis is paid $50,000 for the book value of Larry Dennis' capital account. Prepare the necessary journal entry.

3. Instead of the foregoing, assume that Jim Wheeles (with the consent of the remaining partners) purchased Dennis' interest for $40,000 and gave Mrs. Dennis a personal check for that amount. Prepare the general journal entry for the partnership only.

PROBLEM 20A-4 (LO 5) STATEMENT OF PARTNERSHIP LIQUIDATION WITH GAIN After several years of operations, the partnership of Baldwin, Cowan, and Stewart is to be liquidated. After making closing entries on June 30, 20--, the following accounts remain open:

	Account Balance	
Account Title	**Debit**	**Credit**
Cash	$ 5,000	
Inventory	55,000	
Other Assets	180,000	
Liabilities		$40,000
R. J. Baldwin, Capital		50,000
N. R. Cowan, Capital		90,000
K. M. Stewart, Capital		60,000

The noncash assets are sold for $250,000. Profits and losses are shared equally.

REQUIRED

1. Prepare a statement of partnership liquidation for the period July 1–20, 20--, showing the following:

    a. The sale of noncash assets on July 1

    b. The allocation of any gain or loss to the partners on July 1

    c. The payment of the liabilities on July 15

    d. The distribution of cash to the partners on July 20

2. Journalize these four transactions in a general journal.

PROBLEM 20A-5 (LO 5) STATEMENT OF PARTNERSHIP LIQUIDATION WITH LOSS After several years of operations, the partnership of Nelson, Pope, and Williams is to be liquidated. After making closing entries on March 31, 20--, the following accounts remain open:

	Account Balance	
Account Title	**Debit**	**Credit**
Cash	$ 15,000	
Inventory	40,000	
Other Assets	220,000	
Liabilities		$ 75,000
C. W. Nelson, Capital		40,000
J. R. Pope, Capital		60,000
M. L. Williams, Capital		100,000

The noncash assets are sold for $230,000. Profits and losses are shared equally.

REQUIRED

1. Prepare a statement of partnership liquidation for the period April 1–15, 20--, showing the following:

   a. The sale of the noncash assets on April 1

   b. The allocation of any gain or loss to the partners on April 1

   c. The payment of the liabilities on April 12

   d. The distribution of cash to the partners on April 15

2. Journalize these four transactions in a general journal.

SERIES B EXERCISES

EXERCISE 20B-1 (LO 1) PARTNERSHIP OPENING ENTRIES Sharon Usher and Leann Gomez agreed on September 1 to go into business as partners. According to the agreement, Usher is to contribute $30,000 cash and Gomez is to contribute $50,000 cash. Provide a separate journal entry for the investment of each partner.

EXERCISE 20B-2 (LO 2) ENTRIES FOR ALLOCATION OF NET INCOME John Clark and David Haase decided to form a partnership on July 1, 20-6. Clark invested $60,000 and Haase invested $40,000. For the fiscal year ended June 30, 20-7, a net income of $80,000 was earned. Determine the amount of net income that Clark and Haase would receive under each of the following independent assumptions:

1. There is no agreement concerning the distribution of net income.

2. Each partner is to receive 10% interest on their original investment. The remaining net income is to be divided equally.

3. Clark and Haase are to receive a salary allowance of $25,000 and $30,000, respectively. The remaining net income is to be divided equally.

4. Each partner is to receive 10% interest on their original investment. Clark and Haase are to receive a salary allowance of $25,000 and $30,000, respectively. The remaining net income is to be divided as follows: Clark 30% and Haase 70%.

EXERCISE 20B-3 (LO 3) PARTIAL FINANCIAL STATEMENTS Randy Nolan and Jill Brenton formed a partnership on May 1, 20-1. Nolan contributed $50,000 and Brenton contributed $25,000. During the year Nolan contributed an additional $10,000. The partnership agreement states that Nolan is to receive $15,000 and Brenton is to receive $50,000 as a salary allowance. Any remaining net income is to be divided as follows: Nolan 40% and Brenton 60%. The partnership earned net income of $110,000 for the fiscal year ending April 30, 20-2. The partners withdrew only the salary portion of their compensation during the first year of operation.

1. Prepare the lower portion of the income statement showing the allocation of net income between Nolan and Brenton for the fiscal year ended April 30, 20-2.

2. Prepare a statement of partners' equity, showing each individual partner's equity for the fiscal year ended April 30, 20-2.

EXERCISE 20B-4 (LO 4) ADMITTING NEW PARTNERS Maria Rhodes and Craig Blair, who have ending capital balances of $90,000 and $40,000, respectively, agree to admit two new partners to their business on September 1, 20--. Lori Kinder will buy one-third of Rhodes' capital interest for $40,000 and one-fifth of Blair's capital interest for $12,000. Payments will be made directly to the partners. Todd Gilbert will invest $30,000 in the business for which he will receive a $30,000 capital interest.

1. Prepare general journal entries showing the above transactions admitting Kinder and Gilbert to the partnership.

2. Calculate the ending capital balances of all four partners after the above transactions.

EXERCISE 20B-5 (LO 5) ENTRIES: PARTNERSHIP LIQUIDATION On liquidation of the partnership of L. Straw and M. Maury, as of February 9, 20--, assets with a book value of $156,000 are sold for $140,000. Given that the profit-and-loss ratio is 60% for Straw and 40% for Maury, prepare the entries for the sale and the allocation of loss.

SERIES B PROBLEMS

PROBLEM 20B-1 (LO 1) PARTNERSHIP OPENING ENTRIES On July 1, 20--, Lisa Bush and Wally Dodge combined their two businesses to form a partnership under the firm name of Bush and Dodge. The balance sheets of the two sole proprietorships are shown on the next page.

The balance sheets reflect fair market values except for the following:

a. The fair market value of Bush's store equipment is $7,350.

b. The fair market values of Dodge's office equipment and store equipment are $5,875 and $6,100, respectively.

REQUIRED   Prepare the opening entry for the formation of the Bush and Dodge partnership as of July 1, 20--, using fair market values. The difference between assets invested and liabilities assumed should be credited to each partner's capital account. Neither partner has knowledge of any uncollectible accounts receivable.

Bush's Grooming & Pet Supplies
Balance Sheet
June 30, 20 - -

Assets						Liabilities								
Cash				$ 4 6 0 0	00	Notes payable	$3 6 0 0	00				
Accounts receivable	$4 2 0 0	00				Accounts payable	7 6 9 0	00				
Less allowance for bad debts	4 8 0	00	3 7 2 0	00	Total liabilities			$11 2 9 0	00
Merchandise inventory			28 5 8 0	00					
Store equipment	$9 2 6 0	00				Owner's Equity				
Less accumulated depreciation	2 4 0 0	00	6 8 6 0	00	Lisa Bush, capital			32 4 7 0	00
Total assets			$43 7 6 0	00	Total liabilities and owner's equity			$43 7 6 0	00

Wally's Pet World
Balance Sheet
June 30, 20 - -

Assets						Liabilities								
Cash				$ 3 3 5 0	00	Notes payable	$6 0 0 0	00				
Accounts receivable	$4 1 5 0	00				Accounts payable	5 5 0 0	00				
Less allowance for bad debts	2 5 0	00	3 9 0 0	00	Total liabilities			$11 5 0 0	00
Merchandise inventory			27 2 4 0	00					
Supplies			8 4 5	00					
Office equipment	$8 8 3 0	00								
Less accumulated depreciation	3 4 0 0	00	5 4 3 0	00					
Store equipment	$9 1 7 5	00				Owner's Equity				
Less accumulated depreciation	4 2 5 0	00	4 9 2 5	00	Wally Dodge, capital			34 1 9 0	00
Total assets			$45 6 9 0	00	Total liabilities and owner's equity			$45 6 9 0	00

PROBLEM 20B-2 (LO 3) PREPARING PARTIAL FINANCIAL STATEMENTS AND CLOSING ENTRIES The partnership of Rummel and Kang, Stonecutters, showed revenues of $133,000 and expenses of $41,000 on their year-end work sheet. Their capital balances as of January 1, 20--, were $41,000 for C. Rummel and $25,000 for V. Kang. No additional investments were made during the year. As stated in their partnership agreement, after withdrawing salary allowances of $43,000 for Rummel and $34,000 for Kang, the partners each withdrew 10% interest on their January 1 capital balances. No additional withdrawals were made. Any remaining net income is to be divided on a 60-40 basis.

REQUIRED
1. Prepare the lower portion of the income statement of the partnership for the year ended December 31, 20--, showing the division of the partnership net income for the year.

2. Prepare a statement of partners' equity for the year ended December 31, 20--, and the partners' equity section of the balance sheet on that date.

3. Prepare closing entries for the partnership as of December 31, 20--. (For simplicity, use the account titles "Revenues" for all revenues and "Expenses" for all expenses.)

PROBLEM 20B-3 (LO 4) ENTRIES FOR DISSOLUTION OF PARTNERSHIP The Cummings and Stickel Construction Company, a partnership, is operating a general contracting business. Ownership of the company is divided among the partners, Katie Cummings, Julie Stickel, Roy Hewson, and Patricia Weber. Profits and losses are shared equally. The books are kept on the calendar year basis.

On August 10, after the business had been in operation for several years, Patricia Weber died. Mr. Weber wished to sell his wife's interest for $30,000. After the books were closed, the partners' capital accounts had credit balances as follows:

Katie Cummings	$90,000
Julie Stickel	60,000
Roy Hewson	50,000
Patricia Weber	40,000

REQUIRED

1. Prepare the general journal entry required to enter the check issued to Mr. Weber in payment of his deceased wife's interest in the partnership. According to the partnership agreement, the difference between the amount paid to Mr. Weber and the book value of Patricia Weber's capital account is allocated to the remaining partners based on their ending capital account balances.

2. Instead of the foregoing, assume that Mr. Weber is paid $60,000 for the book value of Patricia Weber's capital account. Prepare the necessary journal entry.

3. Instead of the foregoing, assume that Julie Stickel (with the consent of the remaining partners) purchased Weber's interest for $70,000 and gave Mr. Weber a personal check for that amount. Prepare the general journal entry for the partnership only.

PROBLEM 20B-4 (LO 5) STATEMENT OF PARTNERSHIP LIQUIDATION WITH GAIN After several years of operations, the partnership of Leonard, Mitchell, and Swanson is to be liquidated. After making closing entries on June 30, 20--, the following accounts remain open:

	Account Balance	
Account Title	**Debit**	**Credit**
Cash	$ 4,000	
Inventory	40,000	
Other Assets	150,000	
Liabilities		$44,000
B. J. Leonard, Capital		60,000
W. T. Mitchell, Capital		15,000
J. C. Swanson, Capital		75,000

The noncash assets are sold for $211,000. Profits and losses are shared equally.

REQUIRED

1. Prepare a statement of partnership liquidation for the period July 1–20, 20--, showing the following:

   a. The sale of noncash assets on July 1

   b. The allocation of any gain or loss to the partners on July 1

   c. The payment of the liabilities on July 15

   d. The distribution of cash to the partners on July 20

2. Journalize these four transactions in a general journal.

PROBLEM 20B-5 (LO 5) STATEMENT OF PARTNERSHIP LIQUIDATION WITH LOSS After several years of operations, the partnership of Delco, Smith, and Walker is to be liquidated. After making closing entries on March 31, 20--, the following accounts remain open.

	Account Balance	
Account Title	**Debit**	**Credit**
Cash	$ 7,000	
Inventory	25,000	
Other Assets	185,000	
Liabilities		$17,000
D. W. Delco, Capital		30,000
C. S. Smith, Capital		90,000
T. R. Walker, Capital		80,000

The noncash assets are sold for $165,000. Profits and losses are shared equally.

REQUIRED
1. Prepare a statement of partnership liquidation for the period April 1–15, 20--, showing the following:

   a. The sale of noncash assets on April 1

   b. The allocation of any gain or loss to the partners on April 1

   c. The payment of the liabilities on April 12

   d. The distribution of cash to the partners on April 15

2. Journalize these four transactions in a general journal.

MASTERY PROBLEM

Jim Bond, a plumber, has been working for Fleming's Plumbing Supplies for several years. Based on his hard work and the fact that he recently married Ivan Fleming's daughter, Jim has been invited to enter into a partnership with Fleming. The new partnership will be called Fleming and Bond's Plumbing Supplies. The terms of the partnership are as follows:

a. Fleming will invest the assets of Fleming's Plumbing Supplies and the partnership will assume all liabilities. The market values of the office and store equipment are estimated to be $18,000 and $8,000, respectively. All other values reported on the balance sheet are reasonable approximations of market values. Fleming has no knowledge of any uncollectible accounts receivable.

b. Bond will invest $50,000 cash.

c. Fleming will draw a salary allowance of $50,000 per year and Bond will receive $30,000.

d. Each partner will receive 10% interest on the January 1 balance of his capital account.

e. Profits or losses remaining after allocating salaries and interest will be distributed as follows: Fleming 60% and Bond 40%.

(continued)

Fleming's Plumbing Supplies
Balance Sheet
December 31, 20-1

Assets						Liabilities					
Cash			$ 13 5 4 4 00	Notes payable	$36 0 0 0 00	
Accounts receivable	$15 2 8 0 00			Accounts payable	18 0 8 2 00	
Less allowance for bad debts	1 7 2 0 00	13 5 6 0 00	Total liabilities		$ 54 0 8 2 00
Merchandise inventory		89 6 9 2 00			
Supplies		1 2 8 6 00			
Office equipment	$14 3 2 0 00				
Less accumulated depreciation	1 1 0 0 00	13 2 2 0 00			
Store equipment	$ 8 8 0 0 00		Owner's Equity		
Less accumulated depreciation	2 2 0 0 00	6 6 0 0 00	Ivan Fleming, capital		83 8 2 0 00
Total assets		$137 9 0 2 00	Total liabilities and owner's equity		$137 9 0 2 00

REQUIRED

1. Prepare the entries on January 1, 20-2, for the formation of the partnership.

2. Net income for the partnership for 20-2 was $150,000. Prepare the lower portion of the income statement reporting the allocation of the profits to each partner.

3. In December, 20-4, Fleming's daughter, Penny, graduated from business college and asked to join the business as a partner. She has $30,000 to invest and it is agreed that Penny will be given a capital interest of $30,000. Profits and losses will be shared as follows: I. Fleming, 50%; J. Bond, 30%; P. Fleming, 20%. Prepare the entry for Penny's investment on January 1, 20-5.

4. After several years of operations it is decided to liquidate the partnership. After making closing entries on July 31, 20-9, the following accounts remain open.

Cash	$ 20,000	
Inventory	150,000	
Office Equipment	30,000	
Accum. Depreciation—Office Equipment		$18,000
Store Equipment	22,000	
Accum. Depreciation—Store Equipment		15,000
Notes Payable		20,000
Ivan Fleming, Capital		80,000
Jim Bond, Capital		50,000
Penny Fleming, Capital		39,000

a. On August 1, 20-9, the inventory is sold for $130,000.

b. On August 3, the office equipment is sold for $10,000.

c. On August 5, the store equipment is sold for $12,000.

d. On August 10, the notes payable are paid.

e. On August 15, the remaining cash is distributed to the partners according to the balances in their capital accounts.

Prepare a statement of partnership liquidation and related journal entries for the period August 1–15, 20-9.

Self-Study Test Questions

True/False

1. When two or more individuals engage in an enterprise as co-owners, the organization is known as a proprietorship. _____

2. Mutual agency is a characteristic of a partnership in which any partner can bind the other partners to a contract if he or she is acting within the general scope of the business. _____

3. Limited life is a characteristic of a partnership in which each partner is personally liable for all debts incurred by the partners. _____

4. One advantage of a partnership is that the interest of a partner cannot be transferred without the consent of the other partners. _____

5. When two or more sole proprietors form a partnership, their respective balance sheets serve as the basis for the opening entries for the investments of such partners. _____

Multiple Choice

1. The basis on which profits and losses are to be shared among partners is _____

   (a) a matter of agreement among the partners.
   (b) the same as their withdrawal ratio.
   (c) the same as their investment ratio.
   (d) always equal among all partners.

2. In the absence of any agreement among partners, profits and losses must be shared _____

   (a) equally among all partners.
   (b) on the basis of their withdrawals.
   (c) on the basis of their investment ratio.
   (d) in accordance with the Uniform Partnership Act.

3. If the partnership agreement specifies how profits are to be shared but does not specify how losses are to be shared, the losses must be shared _____

   (a) equally among all partners.
   (b) on the basis of their withdrawals.
   (c) on the basis of their investment ratio.
   (d) none of the above.

4. After closing the temporary owner's equity accounts into Income Summary and after allocating the net income and closing the partners' drawing accounts, assume the partners' capital accounts had credit balances as follows: Abbott, $20,000; Barnes, $30,000; Costello, $45,000. _____

   If Abbott retired and withdrew $25,000 in settlement of her equity, the debit to her capital account would be in the amount of

   (a) $25,000.   (c) $20,000.
   (b) $55,000.   (d) $45,000.

(continued)

5. After closing the temporary owner's equity accounts into Income Summary and after allocating the net income and closing the partners' drawing accounts, assume the partners' capital accounts had credit balances as follows: Abbott, $20,000; Barnes, $30,000; Costello, $45,000. The difference between the withdrawing partner's equity and amount of cash withdrawn is divided according to the ratio of the remaining partners' capital interests.

    If Costello retired and withdrew $40,000 in settlement of his equity, the amount entered in Abbott's capital account would be a

    (a) $2,000 credit.
    (b) $2,000 debit.

    (c) $3,000 credit.
    (d) $3,000 debit.

The answers to the Self-Study Test Questions are at the end of the text.

PART 5

Accounting for Corporations and Manufacturing Businesses

21

Corporations: Organization and Capital Stock

Mike Finbar has produced upper-end, specialty acoustic guitars for ten years. Starting out as a small operation in Mike's basement, the business now produces a range of acoustic guitars, mandolins, and banjos at three production facilities. In response to customer inquiries, Mike is considering expanding by adding acoustic-electric and electric instruments. The problem is that this will require a major increase in capital for new kinds of production equipment. His new accountant, who just completed his college degree, suggests that Mike consider incorporating. He says this will solve the problem of raising capital and also provide other benefits. What would be the advantages and disadvantages for Mike to incorporate?

For most of this text we have studied accounting for sole proprietorships. In Chapter 20, we focused on the partnership form of business. In this chapter, we turn our attention to the third type of business organization—the corporation.

It is important to learn about corporations because they play a major role in the economy. More businesses are organized as sole proprietorships and partnerships than as corporations in the United States. But corporations sell more goods and services in total than do sole proprietorships and partnerships combined.

THE CORPORATION

LO 1   Describe the characteristics, formation, and organization of a corporation.

A corporation is a legal entity that exists separate and distinct from its owners. This is the key difference between corporations, sole proprietorships, and partnerships. The assets of sole proprietorships and partnerships legally belong to the owners. The liabilities of such businesses are legal liabilities of the owners. In contrast, a corporation's assets and liabilities are those of the business, not the owners. A corporation can own property, enter into contracts, and incur debt in its own name. It can sue and be sued.

Advantages and Disadvantages

"Incorporation Terms"
(http://heintz.swcollege.com)
Search a database for information about 70 terms related to incorporation.

In comparison with sole proprietorships and partnerships, the corporate form of organization offers five advantages:

1. *Limited liability of owners.* The owners of a corporation generally have no personal liability for the debts of the corporation. Their financial responsibility is limited to the amount they have invested. The limited liability feature is a major reason for the popularity of the corporate form of organization.

2. *Transferable ownership units.* The owners' equity in a corporation is called **capital stock.** The capital stock is divided into **shares** representing ownership rights in the corporation. These shares can be transferred from one person to another without the consent of the other owners and without disturbing the corporation's normal activities.

3. *Ease of raising capital.* The limited liability and transferable ownership characteristics make the corporation an attractive investment for many people. Therefore, a corporation generally can obtain capital by selling additional shares of stock.

4. *No mutual agency.* **Mutual agency** means that each owner has the power to act as an agent and engage in contracts for a business. In a corporation, individual owners do *not* have such power, unless the other owners have granted it to them.

5. *Unlimited life.* A corporation's life is specified in its charter. The charter either states the life as perpetual or provides for renewal if a limit is indicated. Changes of ownership through transfer of shares or death of owners have no effect on the life of a corporation.

Two disadvantages of the corporate form of organization are:

1. *Taxation of earnings.* A major disadvantage is that corporations must pay income taxes. In contrast, sole proprietorships and partnerships do not pay income taxes. The earnings of sole proprietorships and partnerships are taxed only as the personal income of the owners.

    In addition to the corporate income tax, the corporation's owners pay personal income tax on dividends they receive. **Dividends** are distributions of corporate income to the owners. Taxing corporate income both to the company that earns it and to the owners who receive it is called **double taxation**.

2. *Government regulation.* The corporation's activities may be regulated by federal, state, and local laws. These laws may restrict the corporation's ownership of real property, the purchase of its own stock, and the retention of its earnings. If a corporation does business in several states, each state may impose its own financial and tax reporting requirements.

Forming a Corporation

In the United States, the power to create corporations rests largely with the states. To form a corporation, the **incorporators** file an application with the state in which the company is to be incorporated. After the application is approved, a legal document called a **charter**, or **certificate of incorporation**, is prepared. The contents of the charter may vary, but it typically includes:

1. Name of the corporation

2. Location of the principal office

3. Purpose of the business

4. Description of the capital stock

5. Names and addresses of the incorporators

    After the state approves the charter, the incorporators meet to elect a temporary board of directors and to prepare the corporation **bylaws**. The charter and bylaws provide the general guidelines for conducting the business.

    Next, the corporation issues capital stock. Those who buy the stock become owners, and are known as **stockholders**. Each stockholder receives a form called a **stock certificate** that shows the name of the stockholder and the number of shares owned.

Organization of a Corporation

The stockholders elect a **board of directors**. The board of directors determines corporate policies and selects the corporate officers. The officers generally manage the corporation and are responsible to the board. The officers usually consist of the president, one or more vice presidents, a secretary, and a treasurer. Figure 21-1 on the next page illustrates a common corporate organization, from the owners/stockholders through the employees.

FIGURE 21-1 Corporate Organization

Organization Costs

The costs of organizing a corporation, such as incorporation fees, attorneys' fees, and promotion expenses, are called **organization costs**. Organization costs are viewed as benefiting the entire life of a corporation. Therefore, these costs are recorded as intangible assets rather than expensed in the first year of operations.

Like other long-term assets, organization costs are written off over some period of time. The matching principle would call for writing off these costs over the period benefited, but the corporation has an unlimited life. As a compromise position, an accepted practice is to amortize (write off) organization costs over a period of five years.

Assume that Neo Company charged $8,000 to Organization Costs. These costs would be written off over a five-year period by the following adjusting entry at the end of each year.

4		Amortization of Organization Costs		1 6 0 0 00*		4
5		Organization Costs			1 6 0 0 00	5
6						6
7		* $8,000 ÷ 5 years = $1,600				7

Amortization of organization costs is reported under Other Expenses on the income statement.

STOCKHOLDERS' EQUITY AND TYPES OF CAPITAL STOCK

LO 2 Describe stockholders' equity and the types of capital stock.

A corporation's asset, liability, revenue, and expense accounts are generally the same as those for a sole proprietorship or partnership. The owners' equity accounts, however, are quite different, as shown in T account form in Figure 21-2.

In sole proprietorships and partnerships, the owners' capital accounts are affected by three types of events, identified by number in Figure 21-2.

1. Initial and subsequent investments in the business

2. Net income or losses during the life of the business

3. Withdrawals by the owners

The only difference between the sole proprietorship and partnership accounts is that the partnership has multiple capital and drawing accounts. The drawing accounts represent the amount withdrawn from the business during a given accounting period. Recall that each partner's drawing account is closed to his or her capital account.

FIGURE 21-2 Owners' Equity Accounts

In a corporation, owners' equity is called **stockholders' equity**. More importantly, a distinction is made between capital invested by the owners and earnings retained in the business. The amount paid by the stockholders for their shares of stock is called **paid-in capital** and is generally recorded in two new types of accounts: Capital Stock and Additional Paid-In Capital. Both accounts are reported as part of stockholders' equity. These accounts will be explained in the following sections.

A corporation's net income or net loss is credited or debited to Retained Earnings. Dividends are equivalent to withdrawals in a sole proprietorship or partnership. They are debited to Retained Earnings. Thus, **retained earnings** represents the accumulated earnings of the corporation that have not been paid out to stockholders as dividends.

We will look at a complete illustration of the stockholders' equity section of the corporate balance sheet near the end of the chapter. But to help you picture the paid-in capital and retained earnings accounts described here, Figure 21-3 on the next page illustrates the general format of the stockholders' equity section.

FIGURE 21-3 Stockholders' Equity Section Format

Paid-in capital:			
Capital stock	$xxx		
Additional paid-in capital:			
Paid-in capital in excess of par	xxx		
Total paid-in capital		$xxx	
Retained earnings		xxx	
Total stockholders' equity		$xxx	

Capital Stock

> A corporation must maintain detailed records of who owns all shares of its stock.

Ownership rights in a corporation are represented by shares of capital stock issued by the corporation to the owners. The total number of shares the corporate charter authorizes a corporation to issue is called **authorized stock**. Capital stock that has been sold and issued is called **issued stock**. A corporation may buy back some of its own stock. This stock is known as **treasury stock**. The issued stock less treasury stock equals **outstanding stock**, which is the number of shares in the hands of stockholders.

Shares of stock commonly have a dollar amount per share printed on the stock certificate. This dollar amount is known as the **par value** of the stock. Par value is strictly a legal matter and has no direct relationship to the market value per share. **Market value** is the amount for which the stock can be sold on the open market. The par value has accounting importance, however, because it must be recorded in the capital stock account when stock is issued. If the stock is issued for more than its par value, the excess is credited to the paid-in capital in excess of par account.

Stock that has no dollar amount printed on it is called **no-par stock**. No-par stock sometimes is assigned a value per share by the board of directors. This amount is known as the **stated value** of the stock. From an accounting standpoint, par value and stated value stock are virtually the same.

Common Stock

If a corporation issues only one class or type of stock, each share gives its owner the right to:

1. Vote at stockholders' meetings

2. Share in earnings distributions

3. Purchase additional shares in proportion to the owner's present holding, if more shares are issued by the corporation. (This is called a **preemptive right**.)

4. Share in the assets if the corporation liquidates

Such stock is called **common stock**.

Preferred Stock

Corporations sometimes issue two classes of stock—common stock and preferred stock. **Preferred stock** is stock that gives its owner certain preferences or rights superior to those of common stock. Usually these preferences pertain to dividends or to distribution of assets at liquidation. To obtain these preferences, owners of preferred stock usually do not have one or more of the four rights stated previously. For example, preferred stock owners typically have no voting rights.

The owners of preferred stock usually have the right to dividends of a certain amount before owners of common stock can receive any dividends. The dividend preference is usually stated as a dollar amount per share or as a percentage of par value. For example, preferred stock might be described as "$50 par, $4 preferred stock," or "$50 par, 8% preferred stock."

To illustrate, assume that Pref Company has 2,000 shares of $50 par, $4 preferred stock, and 2,000 shares of $10 par common stock outstanding. The amount available for dividends for the year is $14,000. This $14,000 would be allocated between the preferred and common shares as follows:

1. Total amount available for dividends $14,000
2. Dividend to preferred stock:
   2,000 shares × $4   8,000
3. Amount available for common stock $ 6,000

   Dividends per share:
     Preferred stock $4
     Common stock ($6,000 ÷ 2,000 shares) $3

Cumulative and Noncumulative Preferred Stock. Preferred stock on which any unpaid dividends accumulate from year to year is called **cumulative preferred stock**. The accumulated amounts and the current year preferred dividends must be paid to the preferred stockholders before the common stockholders can receive any dividends.

Preferred stock on which dividend claims do not accumulate from year to year is called **noncumulative preferred stock**. If in one year dividends are not declared, there is no carryover of dividends to the following years.

Assume that the Pref Company described in the previous illustration declared no dividends in Year 1 of operation and $22,000 in Year 2. Neither the preferred stock nor the common stock owners would receive any dividends in Year 1. The dividends in Year 2 for the cumulative and noncumulative preferred stock situations would be as follows:

	Year 2			
	Cumulative		Noncumulative	
Total amount available for dividends		$22,000		$22,000
Cumulative preferred dividend from prior year (2,000 shares x $4)	$8,000		$ 0	
Preferred dividend—current year (2,000 shares x $4)	8,000	16,000	8,000	8,000
Amount available for common stock		$ 6,000		$14,000
Dividends per share:				
Preferred		$8		$4
Common ($6,000 ÷ 2,000 shares)		$3		
($14,000 ÷ 2,000 shares)				$7

The cumulative feature of preferred stock is an important preference. Most preferred stock issued today is cumulative.

Participating and Nonparticipating Preferred Stock. Participating preferred stock gives its owners the right to share with common stock owners in dividends in excess of a stated dividend rate. If preferred dividends are limited to the stated dividend rate, the stock is called **nonparticipating**. It is very unusual to find the participation feature in preferred stock today.

A BROADER VIEW

DID YOU SAY COMPANY OR COUNTRY?

This chapter introduces the corporate form of business. Corporations tend to be the largest business enterprises. In fact, the size of some corporations can be difficult to imagine. One way to appreciate the magnitude of some of the largest corporations is to compare them with countries.

In economic terms, the gross national product of a country is comparable to the sales of a corporation. Based on these yardsticks, consider the following:

1. General Motors is about the 20th largest "country" in the world. Its sales are larger than the gross national product of Finland or Denmark.
2. Ford ranks in the top 25. Its sales are larger than the gross national product of Norway or Saudi Arabia.
3. Exxon is in the top 30, with sales larger than the gross national product of South Africa or Turkey.
4. IBM and GE are in the top 40. Both have sales larger than the gross national product of Greece, Venezuela, or Israel.

These comparisons give real meaning to the expression "big business."

CAPITAL STOCK TRANSACTIONS

LO 3   Account for capital stock transactions.

Corporations issue capital stock in exchange for cash and noncash assets. Issuance for cash is the most common transaction.

Issuing Par Value Stock at Par

If capital stock is issued at par for cash, Cash is debited and Common Stock or Preferred Stock is credited for the amount received. Assume that Linc Corp. issues 10,000 shares of $5 par common stock at par for $50,000 cash. The journal entry for this transaction is:

5		Cash			50	0	0	0	00						5
6		Common Stock								50	0	0	0	00	6
7		Issued common stock at par													7

Issuing Par Value Stock at a Premium

If stock is issued at a price above par, the amount received above par is known as a **premium**. Enter this transaction as follows:

1. Debit Cash for the amount received.

2. Credit Common Stock or Preferred Stock for the par amount.

3. Credit Paid-In Capital in Excess of Par for the amount above par.

LEARNING KEY: Record the sale of par value stock at a price above par by debiting Cash and by crediting Capital Stock and Paid-In Capital in Excess of Par.

Assume that Linc Corp. issues 10,000 shares of $5 par common stock for $60,000 cash. The journal entry for this transaction is:

5		Cash			60	0	0	0	00						5
6		Common Stock*								50	0	0	0	00	6
7		Paid-In Capital in Excess of Par—													7
8		Common Stock**								10	0	0	0	00	8
9		Issued common stock at a premium													9
10															10
11		* 10,000 shares × $5 par													11
12		**$60,000 cash received − $50,000 par value of stock													12

As shown in Figure 21-3 on page 770, Paid-In Capital in Excess of Par is reported as an addition to paid-in capital on the balance sheet.

Issuing Par Value Stock at a Discount

If par value stock is issued at a price below par, the difference between the par amount and the amount received is called a **discount**. Enter this transaction as follows:

1. Debit Cash for the amount received.

2. Debit Discount on Common Stock or Discount on Preferred Stock for the difference between the par amount and the amount received.

3. Credit Common Stock or Preferred Stock for the par amount.

 LEARNING KEY: Record the sale of par value stock at a price below par by debiting Cash and Discount on Capital Stock, and by crediting Capital Stock.

Assume that Linc Corp. issues 2,000 shares of $50 par, 8% preferred stock for $96,000 cash. The journal entry for this transaction is:

5		Cash		96	0	0	0	00									5
6		Discount on Preferred Stock*		4	0	0	0	00									6
7		Preferred Stock**								100	0	0	0	00			7
8		Issued preferred stock at a discount															8
9																	9
10		* $100,000 par value – $96,000 cash received															10
11		** 2,000 shares × $50 par															11

Discount on Preferred Stock is reported as a deduction from paid-in capital on the balance sheet.

Stock is seldom issued at a discount for three reasons:

1. Firms generally set very low par values.

2. The purchaser is liable to the corporation's creditors for the difference between the par value and the amount paid.

3. This practice is illegal in many states.

Issuing Stock with a Stated Value

If no-par stock has a stated value, this value is treated virtually the same as par value in the accounts. Only a slight change in account titles is needed.

 LEARNING KEY: Record the sale of no-par stock with a stated value in virtually the same manner as the sale of par value stock.

Assume that Stat Company issues 5,000 shares of no-par common stock with a stated value of $10 per share for $70,000 cash. The journal entry for this transaction is:

5	Cash	70 0 0 0 00				5
6	Common Stock*		50 0 0 0 00			6
7	Paid-In Capital in Excess of Stated Value—					7
8	Common Stock**		20 0 0 0 00			8
9	Issued common stock at a premium					9
10						10
11	* 5,000 shares × $10 per share stated value					11
12	** $70,000 cash received − $50,000 stated					12
13	value of stock					13

Like Paid-In Capital in Excess of Par, Paid-In Capital in Excess of Stated Value is reported as an addition to paid-in capital on the balance sheet.

Issuing No-Par Stock

Accounting for the issuance of no-par stock is generally simpler than for stock with a par or stated value. If no-par stock is issued, Cash is debited and Common Stock or Preferred Stock is credited for the amount received. No premium or discount is entered, regardless of the amount received.

 LEARNING KEY: Record the sale of no-par stock by debiting Cash and crediting Capital Stock.

Assume that Noll Company issues 5,000 shares of no-par common stock for $70,000 cash. The journal entry for this transaction is:

5	Cash	70 0 0 0 00		5
6	Common Stock		70 0 0 0 00	6
7	Issued common stock			7

Similarly, if Noll issues 5,000 shares of no-par common stock for $40,000 cash, the journal entry is:

5	Cash	40 0 0 0 00		5
6	Common Stock		40 0 0 0 00	6
7	Issued common stock			7

Issuing Stock for Noncash Assets

Each transaction illustrated thus far has involved issuance of stock for cash. Corporations also sometimes issue stock for noncash assets. The accounting for this transaction can be more complicated because the value of the noncash assets received may need to be determined.

If stock is issued for noncash assets, follow this guideline:

The assets received are recorded at the fair market value of the assets or of the stock, whichever can be more clearly determined.

Once the value of the noncash assets or the stock is determined, the journal entry for the stock issuance is very similar to those involving cash. Assume that Linc Corp. issues 5,000 shares of $5 par common stock for a truck. Linc's stock is not actively traded, so its market value is difficult to determine, but the truck has a known fair market value of $30,000. Thus, the fair market value of the truck is used to record this transaction. The journal entry is:

11		Truck	30	0	0	0	00									11
12		Common Stock*							25	0	0	0	00	12
13		Paid-In Capital in Excess of Par—												13
14		Common Stock**							5	0	0	0	00	14
15		Issued common stock at a premium												15
16														16
17		* 5,000 shares × $5 par												17
18		**$30,000 fair market value of truck												18
19		received – $25,000 par value of stock												19

Assume instead that Linc Corp. issues 10,000 shares of $5 par common stock for a building with several different appraisal values. Linc's stock is actively traded and has a fair market value of $7 per share. In this case, the fair market value of the stock, $70,000 (10,000 shares × $7), is used to record this transaction. The journal entry is:

15		Building	70	0	0	0	00									15
16		Common Stock*							50	0	0	0	00	16
17		Paid-In Capital in Excess of Par—												17
18		Common Stock**							20	0	0	0	00	18
19		Issued common stock at a premium												19
20														20
21		* 10,000 shares × $5 par												21
22		**$70,000 fair market value of stock												22
23		– $50,000 par value of stock												23

Capital Stock Subscriptions

Corporations sometimes accept subscriptions for capital stock. A **capital stock subscription** is an agreement in which a buyer (**subscriber**) contracts to buy shares of stock from a corporation at a specific price. The subscriber generally agrees to pay the amount in full on a specified date or in installments. The corporation does not issue the stock until the subscriber makes the full payment.

Accounting for stock subscriptions requires the use of some new accounts. Assume that Linc Corp. received subscriptions for 10,000 shares of its $5 par common stock for $60,000. The journal entry for this transaction is:

8		Common Stock Subscriptions Receivable		60	0	0	0	00									8
9		Common Stock Subscribed*								50	0	0	0	00		9
10		Paid-In Capital in Excess of Par—														10
11		Common Stock**								10	0	0	0	00		11
12		Received subscriptions for common stock														12
13																13
14		* 10,000 shares × $5 par														14
15		**$60,000 subscription amount −														15
16		$50,000 par value of stock														16

Common Stock Subscriptions Receivable is an asset account, normally classified as a current asset. Common Stock Subscribed and Paid-In Capital in Excess of Par are reported as additions to paid-in capital on the balance sheet.

As the subscriber makes payments on the stock, the Common Stock Subscriptions Receivable balance is decreased. If the subscriber to Linc Corp.'s shares makes a payment of $40,000, the following journal entry is made.

25		Cash		40	0	0	0	00									25
26		Common Stock Subscriptions Receivable								40	0	0	0	00		26
27		Received subscription payment														27

> Controversy exists regarding the proper balance sheet presentation of Common Stock Subscriptions Receivable. Some sources say it is an asset; others say it is contra-owners' equity. We prefer the asset treatment.

When the stock subscription has been fully paid, the corporation issues the stock. At this point, Common Stock Subscribed is debited and Common Stock is credited for the par amount of $50,000. The $10,000 premium on the stock issuance was already credited to Paid-In Capital in Excess of Par—Common Stock at the time the subscription was recorded. Assume the subscriber to Linc Corp.'s shares makes the final payment of $20,000 and Linc issues the 10,000 shares. The following journal entries are made.

5		Cash		20	0	0	0	00									5
6		Common Stock Subscriptions Receivable								20	0	0	0	00		6
7		Received subscription payment														7
8																8
9		Common Stock Subscribed		50	0	0	0	00									9
10		Common Stock								50	0	0	0	00		10
11		Issued common stock														11

Subscriptions at par or below par, for no-par stock, and for stated value stock are accounted for in a similar manner. The only new accounts that require special care are the same in each instance: Common (or Preferred) Stock Subscriptions Receivable and Common (or Preferred) Stock Subscribed.

Treasury Stock

When a company buys back some of its own shares of stock, these shares are called treasury stock. When a corporation purchases its own stock, Treasury Stock is debited for the cost of the stock, regardless of any par or stated value. Assume that Linc Corp. purchases 3,000 shares of its $5 par common stock for $6 per share, a total of $18,000. The journal entry for this transaction is:

5	Common Treasury Stock	18 0 0 0 00						5
6	Cash			18 0 0 0 00				6
7	Purchased treasury stock							7

If treasury stock is subsequently sold, the transaction is handled as follows:

1. Cash is debited for the amount received.

2. Treasury Stock is credited for its cost.

3. Any difference between the amount received and the cost is debited or credited to Paid-In Capital from Sale of Treasury Stock.

Assume that Linc Corp. sells 2,000 of the 3,000 treasury shares described above for $7 per share, a total of $14,000. The journal entry is:

15	Cash	14 0 0 0 00						15
16	Common Treasury Stock*			12 0 0 0 00				16
17	Paid-In Capital from Sale of Treasury Stock**			2 0 0 0 00				17
18	Sold treasury stock							18
19								19
20	* 2,000 shares × $6 cost per share							20
21	** $14,000 cash received − $12,000 cost							21
22	of treasury shares							22

Assume that Linc Corp. subsequently sells the remaining 1,000 treasury shares for $5.50 per share, a total of $5,500. The journal entry for this transaction is:

8	Cash	5 5 0 0 00						8
9	Paid-In Capital from Sale of Treasury Stock**	5 0 0 00						9
10	Common Treasury Stock*			6 0 0 0 00				10
11	Sold treasury stock							11
12								12
13	* 1,000 shares × $6 cost per share							13
14	** $6,000 cost of treasury shares							14
15	− $5,500 cash received							15

If treasury stock is sold for less than its cost and Paid-In Capital from Sale of Treasury Stock has a zero balance, the difference is debited to Retained Earnings.

Note that no gain or loss is recognized on treasury stock transactions. A corporation cannot realize a gain or incur a loss by dealing in its own shares.

Be careful in presenting treasury stock on the balance sheet. Treasury stock is *not* an asset. It is a contra-stockholders' equity account and is reported as a deduction from the total of paid-in capital and retained earnings. Paid-In Capital from Sale of Treasury Stock is reported as an addition to paid-in capital on the balance sheet.

Summary of Capital Stock Transaction Accounts

In recording capital stock transactions, we have been introduced to many new accounts. Figure 21-4 summarizes these new accounts by type, purpose, and balance sheet presentation. Refer to this figure as you work the exercises and problems for this chapter.

FIGURE 21-4 Summary of Capital Stock Transaction Accounts

ACCOUNT	TYPE	PURPOSE	BALANCE SHEET PRESENTATION
Common Stock and Preferred Stock	Stockholders' Equity	If stock has par or stated value: Credited for par or stated value of stock issued. If stock has no par or stated value: Credited for amount received for stock issued	Part of paid-in capital
Paid-In Capital in Excess of Par —Common and Preferred Stock. Paid-In Capital in Excess of Stated Value —Common and Preferred Stock	Stockholders' Equity	Credited for amount by which issue price exceeds par or stated value of stock (Used only for stock with par or stated value)	Addition to paid-in capital
Discount on Common Stock and Preferred Stock	Stockholders' Equity	Debited for amount by which par or stated value exceeds issue price of stock	Deduction from paid-in capital
Common and Preferred Stock Subscriptions Receivable	Asset	Debited for subscription price of stock	Usually current asset
Common and Preferred Stock Subscribed	Stockholders' Equity	If stock has par or stated value: Credited for par or stated value of stock subscribed. If stock has no par or stated value: Credited for amount of stock subscription	Addition to paid-in capital
Treasury Stock—Common and Preferred	Stockholders' Equity	Debited for cost of stock purchased	Deduction from total of paid-in capital and retained earnings
Paid-In Capital from Sale of Treasury Stock	Stockholders' Equity	Credited for excess of selling price over cost of treasury stock or Debited for excess of cost over selling price of treasury stock (if a credit balance)	Addition to paid-in capital

STOCKHOLDERS' EQUITY SECTION

LO 4 Prepare the stockholders' equity section of a corporation balance sheet.

Now that we have seen the various accounts used in capital stock transactions, let's bring them together in a stockholders' equity section of the balance sheet. We will use the Roland Company for this purpose.

After closing its books on December 31, Roland Company's stockholders' equity accounts have the following balances.

Account	Balance	Additional Information
Preferred Stock Subscribed	$ 60,000	7%, $10 par, 6,000 shares
Common Stock Subscribed	40,000	no-par, 4,000 shares
Preferred Stock	140,000	7%, $10 par, 20,000 shares authorized, 14,000 shares issued
Common Stock	163,000	no-par, 40,000 shares authorized, 16,300 shares issued

Paid-In Capital in Excess of Par—Preferred Stock	56,000	
Paid-In Capital from Sale of Treasury Stock	600	
Common Treasury Stock	22,000 (Dr.)	no par, 2,000 shares, at cost
Retained Earnings	60,000	

Figure 21-5 shows the stockholders' equity section prepared from these accounts.

FIGURE 21-5 Stockholders' Equity Section

Stockholders' Equity			
Paid-in capital:			
Preferred stock, 7%, $10 par			
(20,000 shares authorized; 14,000 shares issued)	$140 0 0 0 00		
Preferred stock subscribed (6,000 shares)	60 0 0 0 00	$200 0 0 0 00	
Common stock, no par			
(40,000 shares authorized; 16,300 shares issued)	$163 0 0 0 00		
Common stock subscribed (4,000 shares)	40 0 0 0 00	203 0 0 0 00	
Additional paid-in capital:			
Paid-in capital in excess of par—preferred stock	$ 56 0 0 0 00		
Paid-in capital from sale of treasury stock	6 0 0 00	56 6 0 0 00	
Total paid-in capital		$459 6 0 0 00	
Retained earnings		60 0 0 0 00	
		$519 6 0 0 00	
Less common treasury stock (2,000 shares at cost)		22 0 0 0 00	
Total stockholders' equity		$497 6 0 0 00	

Note the following characteristics of this stockholders' equity presentation.

1. Stockholders' equity is separated by source:
   Paid-in capital—amounts contributed by owners
   Retained earnings—accumulated, undistributed earnings

2. Paid-in capital is separated by source:
   Preferred stock
   Common stock
   Stock subscriptions
   Paid-in capital in excess of par
   Paid-in capital from sale of treasury stock

3. Stock characteristics are indicated:
   Dividend rate for preferred stock—7%
   Par or no-par value

4. Numbers of shares authorized, subscribed, issued, and held as treasury stock are indicated.

5. Preferred stock is listed first. (This is because of its preferred claim to dividends and assets.)

6. Retained earnings is listed after all paid-in capital.

7. Treasury stock is subtracted from the total of paid-in capital and retained earnings.

Learning Objectives	Key Points to Remember
1 Describe the characteristics, formation, and organization of a corporation.	A corporation exists independently of its owners. Its assets and liabilities are those of the business. A corporation is formed according to the laws of the state in which it incorporates. It normally has a board of directors and four officers. Organization costs are capitalized and generally written off over a five-year period.
2 Describe stockholders' equity and the types of capital stock.	A key characteristic of owners' equity in a corporation is the distinction between paid-in capital and retained earnings. Paid-in capital is the amount paid in by stockholders. Retained earnings is the accumulated earnings not paid out as dividends.

Owners of capital stock generally have the right to:

1. Vote at stockholders' meetings
2. Share in earnings distributions
3. Purchase additional shares if more shares are issued by the corporation
4. Share in the assets if the corporation liquidates

Owners of preferred stock generally give up the right to vote in order to have a preferential right to dividends and assets.

3 Account for capital stock transactions.	The accounting for par value and stated value stock is virtually the same. In each case, the difference between the par or stated value and the amount received at issuance is recorded as a premium or discount.

▶ There is no premium or discount to account for when no-par stock is issued.

▶ If stock is issued for noncash assets, the assets received are recorded at the fair market value of the assets or of the stock, whichever can be more clearly determined.

▶ If capital stock subscriptions are received, the corporation does not issue the stock until the subscription is paid in full.

▶ No gains or losses are recognized on treasury stock transactions.

4 Prepare the stockholders' equity section of a corporation balance sheet.	The stockholders' equity section of the corporate balance sheet has the following characteristics:

1. Stockholders' equity is separated into paid-in capital and retained earnings.
2. Paid-in capital is separated into preferred stock, common stock, stock subscriptions, paid-in capital in excess of par, and paid-in capital from sale of treasury stock.
3. The dividend rate for preferred stock and par or no-par value are indicated.
4. Numbers of shares authorized, subscribed, issued, and held as treasury stock are indicated.
5. Preferred stock is listed first.
6. Retained earnings is listed after all paid-in capital.
7. Treasury stock is subtracted from the total of paid-in capital and retained earnings.

Reflection: Answering the Opening Question

Mike should consider the following advantages:

1. He would have limited liability rather than being personally liable for the debts of his business.
2. The ownership units would be transferable among the owners without affecting the operation of the business.
3. It would be easier to raise capital by selling additional ownership shares in the business.
4. There would be no mutual agency, so owners would not be able to engage in contracts for the business unless they were given specific power to do so.
5. The business would have unlimited life, so that death of an owner or transfer of ownership would not affect the business.

Mike also should be aware of the following disadvantages:

1. The earnings of the corporation are taxable to the corporation, and any dividends paid to Mike are also taxable to him.
2. The corporation is subject to federal, state, and local regulation.

KEY TERMS

authorized stock, (772)   The total number of shares the corporate charter authorizes a corporation to issue.

board of directors, (769)   A group elected by the stockholders to determine corporate policies and to select corporate officers.

bylaws, (769)   Together with the charter, the bylaws provide the general guidelines for conducting the business.

capital stock, (768)   Represents ownership rights in a corporation. Generally broken down into common and preferred stock.

capital stock subscription, (778)   An agreement in which a buyer contracts to buy shares of a corporation at a specific price.

certificate of incorporation, (769)   See charter.

charter, (769)   Legal document which includes the name of the corporation, the location of the principal office, the purpose of the business, the description of the capital stock, and the names and addresses of the incorporators.

common stock, (772)   Stock that gives its owner the right to vote at stockholders' meetings, share in earnings distributions, purchase additional shares if more shares are issued by the corporation, and share in the assets if the corporation liquidates.

cumulative preferred stock, (773)   Preferred stock on which unpaid dividends accumulate from year to year.

discount, (776)   The difference between the par amount and the amount received when the par value stock is issued at a price below par.

dividends, (769)   The distributions of corporate income to the owners.

double taxation, (769)   The process of taxing corporate income both to the company that earns it and to the owners who receive it.

incorporators, (769)   Those who form a corporation by filing an application with the state in which the company is to be incorporated.

issued stock, (772)   Capital stock that has been sold and issued.

market value, (772)   The amount for which the stock can be sold on the open market.

mutual agency, (768)   The power of each owner to act as an agent and engage in contracts for a business.

no-par stock, (772)   Stock that has no dollar amount printed on it.

noncumulative preferred stock, (773)   Preferred stock on which dividend claims do not accumulate from year to year.

nonparticipating, (774)   Preferred stock on which the dividends are limited to the stated dividend rate.

organization costs, (770)   The costs of organizing a corporation, such as incorporation fees, attorneys' fees, and promotion expenses.

outstanding stock, (772)   The number of shares in the hands of stockholders.

paid-in capital, (771)   The amount paid by stockholders for their shares of stock.

par value, (772)   The dollar amount printed on the share of stock.

participating, (774)   Preferred stock that has a right to share with common stock in dividends in excess of a stated dividend rate.

preemptive right, (772)   The right to purchase additional shares in proportion to the owner's present holding, if more shares are issued by the corporation.

preferred stock, (772)   Stock that has certain preferences or rights superior to common stock.

premium, (775)   The difference between the par value and the price of a stock when the stock is issued at a price above par.

retained earnings, (771)   The accumulated earnings of the corporation that have not been paid out to stockholders as dividends.

shares, (768)   Capital stock is divided into shares that represent ownership rights in the corporation.

stated value, (772)   Value per share assigned to no-par stock by the board of directors.

stock certificate, (769)   A form received by each stockholder that shows the name of the stockholder and the number of shares owned.

stockholders, (769)   Owners of the corporation.

stockholders' equity, (771)   Owners' equity within a corporation.

subscriber, (778)   A buyer who contracts to purchase shares of stock from a corporation at a specific price.

treasury stock, (772)   Shares of stock that have been bought back by the issuing company.

DEMONSTRATION PROBLEM

W & D

Stockholders' equity accounts and other related accounts of the JKL Manufacturing Corporation as of October 1, 20-1, the beginning of its fiscal year, are shown below.

Preferred Stock Subscriptions Receivable	$ 80,000
Preferred Stock, 8%, $10 par (200,000 shares authorized, 50,000 shares issued)	500,000
Preferred Stock Subscribed (10,000 shares)	100,000
Paid-In Capital in Excess of Par—Preferred Stock	50,000
Common Stock, $10 par (1,000,000 shares authorized, 200,000 shares issued)	2,000,000
Paid-In Capital in Excess of Par— Common Stock	500,000
Retained Earnings	2,250,000

During the fiscal year ended September 30, 20-2, JKL Manufacturing completed the following transactions affecting stockholders' equity:

(a) Received the balance due on preferred stock subscriptions and issued the necessary certificates.

(b) Purchased 10,000 shares of common treasury stock for $120,000.

(c) Received subscriptions for 8,000 shares of 8% preferred stock at $12 each, collecting one-fourth of the subscription price.

(d) Sold 6,000 shares of common treasury stock for $78,000.

(e) Issued 80,000 shares of common stock at $15, receiving cash.

(f) Sold 2,000 shares of common treasury stock for $22,000.

(g) Issued 100,000 shares of common stock with a market value of $15 per share in exchange for land for business expansion.

REQUIRED   1. Prepare general journal entries for the above transactions, identifying each transaction by the appropriate letter.

2. Prepare the stockholders' equity section of the balance sheet as of September 30, 20-2. The beginning retained earnings balance must be increased by the net income for the year, $720,000. The preferred stock was paid dividends at 8% on $600,000 par value of stock, and the common stock was paid dividends of $.80 per share on 378,000 outstanding shares.

Solution

1.

	DATE	DESCRIPTION	POST REF.	DEBIT					CREDIT					
1	(a)	Cash		80	0	0	0	00						1
2		Preferred Stock Subscriptions Rec.							80	0	0	0	00	2
3		Received subscription payments												3
4														4
5		Preferred Stock Subscribed		100	0	0	0	00						5
6		Preferred Stock							100	0	0	0	00	6
7		Issued preferred stock												7
8														8
9	(b)	Common Treasury Stock		120	0	0	0	00						9
10		Cash							120	0	0	0	00	10
11		Purchased treasury stock												11
12														12
13	(c)	Cash		24	0	0	0	00						13
14		Preferred Stock Subscriptions Rec.		72	0	0	0	00						14
15		Preferred Stock Subscribed							80	0	0	0	00	15
16		Paid-In Capital in Excess of Par—												16
17		Preferred Stock							16	0	0	0	00	17
18		Received subscriptions for preferred stock												18
19														19
20	(d)	Cash		78	0	0	0	00						20
21		Common Treasury Stock							72	0	0	0	00	21
22		Paid-In Capital from Sale of Treasury Stock							6	0	0	0	00	22
23		Sold treasury stock												23
24														24
25	(e)	Cash		1,200	0	0	0	00						25
26		Common Stock							800	0	0	0	00	26
27		Paid-In Capital in Excess of Par—												27
28		Common Stock							400	0	0	0	00	28
29		Issued common stock at a premium												29
30														30
31	(f)	Cash		22	0	0	0	00						31
32		Paid-In Capital from Sale of Treasury Stock		2	0	0	0	00						32
33		Common Treasury Stock							24	0	0	0	00	33
34		Sold treasury stock												34
35														35
36	(g)	Land		1,500	0	0	0	00						36
37		Common Stock							1,000	0	0	0	00	37
38		Paid-In Capital in Excess of Par—												38
39		Common Stock							500	0	0	0	00	39
40		Issued common stock at a premium												40

GENERAL JOURNAL — PAGE 1

2.

Stockholders' Equity										
Paid-in capital:										
Preferred stock, 8%, $10 par (200,000 shares authorized; 60,000 shares issued)	$ 600	0	0	0	00					
Preferred stock subscribed (8,000 shares)	80	0	0	0	00	$ 680	0	0	0	00
Common stock, $10 par (1,000,000 shares authorized; 380,000 shares issued)						3,800	0	0	0	00
Additional paid-in capital:										
Paid-in capital in excess of par—preferred stock	$ 66	0	0	0	00					
Paid-in capital in excess of par—common stock	1,400	0	0	0	00					
Paid-in capital from sale of treasury stock	4	0	0	0	00	1,470	0	0	0	00
Total paid-in capital						$5,950	0	0	0	00
Retained earnings*						2,619	6	0	0	00
						$8,569	6	0	0	00
Less: Common treasury stock (2,000 shares at cost)						24	0	0	0	00
Total stockholders' equity						$8,545	6	0	0	00

* $2,250,000 + $720,000 − $48,000 − $302,400 = $2,619,600

REVIEW QUESTIONS

1. Briefly describe five advantages of the corporate form of business organization. Describe two disadvantages.

2. What information usually is included in the charter?

3. Who elects the permanent board of directors?

4. Describe how to account for organization costs.

5. How do owners' equity accounts in a corporation differ from those in a sole proprietorship or partnership?

6. If a corporation issues only one class of stock, what four rights does each stockholder have?

7. How is Paid-In Capital in Excess of Par usually reported on the balance sheet? How is Discount on Capital Stock usually reported?

8. If stock is issued for noncash assets, at what amount should the assets be recorded?

9. How is Common Stock Subscriptions Receivable usually reported on the balance sheet?

10. How is Treasury Stock usually shown on the balance sheet?

11. How is Paid-In Capital from Sale of Treasury Stock usually shown on the balance sheet?

MANAGING YOUR WRITING

Your boss started a construction company as a partnership with several other contractors 20 years ago. Twelve years later, the partners incorporated to gain access to additional capital by issuing common stock. Forty percent of the shares were sold to the general public and 60 percent were acquired by the partners. In this way, the partners kept voting control of the business.

Now the company has an opportunity for a major expansion. To obtain additional capital to fund the expansion, the company is considering another stock offering. But the original partners do not want to lose voting control of the business. Your boss knows you are taking college business courses and asks whether there is a way the company can sell additional stock without the partners losing control of the business. Prepare a report for him describing the kinds of capital stock the company could issue that would accomplish his purpose.

ETHICS CASE

Tyler Corporation started its operations in March. During the first year of operation, a significant amount of money was spent on attorneys' fees and promotional expenses connected with organizing the corporation. The amount of revenue Tyler Corporation earned for the year was much higher than expected. Because of this, the accountant decided to charge the attorneys' fees and promotional expenses to advertising expense in the current year.

1. If the accountant simply was not aware of the proper treatment of these expenditures, were any ethical principles violated? Why or why not?

2. How would you have treated these expenditures?

3. Write a short memo from the accountant to the Board of Directors of Tyler Corporation explaining how costs of organizing a corporation are treated for accounting purposes.

4. In groups of two or three, discuss the difference between making unethical decisions and making careless decisions.

WEB WORK

What are some ways, other than the traditional, to raise money for a small business? This site has some suggestions:

http://www.webcom.com/seaquest/sbrc/raisemny.html.

(http://heintz.swcollege.com)

SERIES A EXERCISES

EXERCISE 21A-1 (LO 1) AMORTIZATION OF ORGANIZATION COSTS B&B Electric decided to incorporate and has incurred the following costs of organizing:

Incorporation fees	$ 400
Attorneys' fees	4,800
Promotion expenses	5,700

These costs will be written off over five years. Prepare the entry to record payment of organization costs for cash on January 1, and the adjusting entry for the first full year of operation.

EXERCISE 21A-2 (LO 2) DIVIDEND ALLOCATIONS
Situation 1

Akimoto Company has the following stock outstanding:

Common Stock	Preferred Stock
50,000 shares	5,000 shares
$1 par value	$40 par, $2 dividend

The amount available for dividends this year is $40,000. Prepare the dividend allocation between the preferred and common shares.

Situation 2

Benitez Company has the following stock outstanding:

Common Stock	Preferred Stock
70,000 shares	Cumulative: 1,500 shares
$1 par value	$50 par, $2 dividend
	Noncumulative: 4,000 shares
	$50 par, $2 dividend

No dividends were declared in year 1 of operation. In year 2, there is $28,000 available for dividends. Prepare the dividend allocation between the preferred and common shares.

EXERCISE 21A-3 (LO 3) STOCK ISSUANCE (PAR, NO-PAR, AND STATED VALUE)
The following stock transactions occurred during January 20-- for the Bremer Corporation.

(a) Issued 5,000 shares of $10 par common stock for $50,000 cash.

(b) Issued 4,000 shares of $10 par common stock for $45,000 cash.

(c) Issued 4,000 shares of $10 par common stock for $37,500 cash.

(d) Issued 5,000 shares of no-par common stock for $60,000 cash.

(e) Issued 3,000 shares of no-par common stock for $40,000 cash.

(f) Issued 5,000 shares of no-par common stock with a stated value of $8 per share for $40,000 cash.

(g) Issued 2,000 shares of no-par common stock with a stated value of $8 per share for $15,000 cash.

(h) Issued 3,000 shares of no-par common stock with a stated value of $8 per share for $26,000 cash.

Prepare general journal entries to record the above stock transactions, identifying each transaction by letter.

EXERCISE 21A-4 (LO 3) STOCK ISSUANCE (NONCASH ASSETS, SUBSCRIPTION, AND TREASURY STOCK) Smith & Cline had the following stock transactions during the year:

(a) Issued 5,000 shares of common stock with a $5 par value in exchange for real estate (land) with a fair market value of $27,500.

(b) Issued 7,500 shares of common stock with a $5 par value and $6 fair market value in exchange for a building with an uncertain fair market value.

(c) Received subscriptions for 10,000 shares of $6 par common stock for $65,000.

(d) Received subscriptions for 5,000 shares of $6 par common stock for $28,000.

(e) Received a payment of $30,000 on the stock subscription in (c).

(f) Received the balance in full for the stock subscription in (c) and issued the stock.

(g) Received the balance in full for the stock subscription in (d) and issued the stock.

(h) Purchased 1,000 shares of its own $6 par common stock for $7 a share ($7,000).

(i) Sold 500 shares of the treasury stock in (h) for $7.50 a share.

(j) Sold 500 shares of the treasury stock in (h) for $6.75 a share.

Prepare general journal entries to record the above transactions, identifying each by letter.

EXERCISE 21A-5 (LO 4) STOCKHOLDERS' EQUITY SECTION After closing its books on December 31, Pro Parts' stockholders' equity accounts had the following balances:

Common stock, $5 par, 10,000 shares	$50,000
Preferred stock, $10 par, 5%, 5,000 shares	50,000
Common stock subscribed, $5 par, 2,000 shares	10,000
Retained earnings	25,000

Prepare the stockholders' equity section of the balance sheet.

SERIES A PROBLEMS

PROBLEM 21A-1 (LO 3) PAR AND NO-PAR, COMMON AND PREFERRED STOCK
Hernandez Company had the following stock transactions during the year.

(a) Issued 25,000 shares of $1 par common stock for $25,000 cash.

(b) Issued 20,000 shares of $1 par common stock for $22,000 cash.

(c) Issued 22,000 shares of $1 par common stock for $21,000 cash.

(d) Issued 2,000 shares of $50 par, 8% preferred stock for $100,000 cash.

(e) Issued 1,000 shares of $50 par, 8% preferred stock for $49,000 cash.

(f) Issued 1,000 shares of $50 par, 8% preferred stock for $51,500 cash.

(g) Issued 2,500 shares of no-par common stock for $11,875.

(h) Issued 1,500 shares of no-par, 7% preferred stock for $72,000.

REQUIRED   Prepare general journal entries to record the above transactions, identifying each transaction by letter.

PROBLEM 21A-2 (LO 3) STATED VALUE, COMMON AND PREFERRED STOCK AND NONCASH ASSETS Kris Kraft Stores had the following stock transactions during the year.

(a) Issued 4,000 shares of no-par common stock with a stated value of $10 per share for $40,000 cash.

(b) Issued 6,000 shares of no-par common stock with a stated value of $8 per share for $50,000 cash.

(c) Issued 5,000 shares of no-par, 6% preferred stock with a stated value of $15 per share for $75,000 cash.

(d) Issued 3,000 shares of no-par, 6% preferred stock with a stated value of $20 per share for $58,000 cash.

(e) Issued 10,000 shares of $5 par common stock for land with a fair market value of $50,000.

(f) Issued 10,000 shares of $8 par common stock with a $9 fair market value for a building with an uncertain fair market value.

(g) Issued 8,000 shares of $50 par, 8% preferred stock for land with a fair market value of $405,000.

REQUIRED   Prepare general journal entries to record the above transactions, identifying each transaction by letter.

PROBLEM 21A-3 (LO 3) STOCK SUBSCRIPTIONS Juneau & Associates had the following stock transactions during the year.

(a) Issued 100,000 shares of $1 par common stock for $105,000 cash.

(b) Issued 12,000 shares of $10 par, 8% preferred stock for $128,000 cash.

(c) Received subscriptions for 10,000 shares of $10 par common stock for $105,000.

(d) Received subscriptions for 5,000 shares of $15 par, 8% preferred stock for $80,000.

(e) Received a payment of $55,000 on the common stock subscription.

(f) Received a payment of $40,000 on the preferred stock subscription.

(g) Issued 40,000 shares of $1 par common stock in exchange for a truck with a fair market value of $48,000.

(h) Received the balance in full for the common stock subscription and issued the stock.

(i) Issued 2,500 shares of no-par common stock with a stated value of $8 per share for $21,500 cash.

(j) Received the balance in full for the preferred stock subscription and issued the stock.

REQUIRED   Prepare general journal entries to record the above transactions, identifying each transaction by letter.

PROBLEM 21A-4 (LO 1/3) STOCK SUBSCRIPTIONS AND TREASURY STOCK Brown & Brown formed a corporation and had the following stock transactions during the year:

June 30   Incurred the following costs of incorporation:

Incorporation fees	$ 800
Attorneys' fees	5,000
Promotion fees	7,000

July 15   Issued 5,000 shares of $10 par common stock for $52,000 cash.

21   Issued 4,000 shares of $20 par, 8% preferred stock for $79,500 cash.

Aug. 1   Received subscriptions for 10,000 shares of $10 par common stock for $103,500.

15   Issued 10,000 shares of $10 par common stock in exchange for a building and fixtures with a fair market value of $110,000.

31   Received a payment of $53,500 for the common stock subscription.

Sept. 3   Purchased 1,000 shares of its own $10 par common stock for $11 a share.

12   Issued 3,500 shares of no-par common stock with a stated value of $8 per share for $30,000.

18   Received the balance in full for the common stock subscription and issued the stock.

30   Sold 500 shares of its treasury stock for $11.50 a share.

(continued)

Oct. 15   Issued 5,000 shares of $20 par, 8% preferred stock in exchange for land with a fair market value of $108,000.

31   Sold 500 shares of its treasury stock for $10.75 a share.

Dec. 31   Recorded this year's (6 months) amortization of organization costs (written off over five years).

REQUIRED   Prepare journal entries to record the above transactions.

PROBLEM 21A-5 (LO 4) STOCKHOLDERS' EQUITY SECTION After closing its books on December 31, 20--, the Jackson Corporation's stockholders' equity accounts had the following balances:

Account	Balance	Additional Information
Preferred Stock Subscribed	$ 50,000	$4 dividend, $5 par, 10,000 shares
Common Stock Subscribed	30,000	$10 par, 3,000 shares
Preferred Stock	150,000	$4 dividend, $5 par, 30,000 shares
Common Stock	250,000	$10 par, 25,000 shares
Paid-In Capital in Excess of Par—Preferred Stock	10,000	
Paid-In Capital from Sale of Treasury Stock	1,000	
Common Treasury Stock	10,000	
Retained Earnings	75,000	

REQUIRED   Prepare the stockholders' equity section of the balance sheet for Jackson for the year ended December 31, 20--.

SERIES B EXERCISES

EXERCISE 21B-1 (LO 1) AMORTIZATION OF ORGANIZATION COSTS T&R TrackTown has decided to incorporate and has incurred the following costs of organizing:

Incorporation fees	$ 500
Attorneys' fees	6,800
Promotion fees	4,700

These costs will be written off over five years. Prepare the entry to record payment of organization costs for cash on January 1, and the adjusting entry for the first full year of operation.

EXERCISE 21B-2 (LO 2) DIVIDEND ALLOCATIONS
Situation 1

Espino Company has the following stock outstanding:

Common Stock	**Preferred Stock**
100,000 shares	9,000 shares
$.50 par value	$20 par, $2 dividend

The amount available for dividends this year is $50,000. Prepare the dividend allocation between the preferred and common shares.

Situation 2

Chiola Corporation has the following stock outstanding:

Common Stock	**Preferred Stock**
40,000 shares	Cumulative: 4,000 shares
$1 par value	$40 par, $2 dividend
	Noncumulative: 5,000 shares
	$40 par, $2 dividend

No dividends were declared in year 1 of operation. In year 2, there is $56,000 available for dividends. Prepare the dividend allocation between the preferred and common shares.

EXERCISE 21B-3 (LO 3) STOCK ISSUANCE (PAR, NO-PAR, AND STATED VALUE)
The following stock transactions occurred during January 20-- for Drexel Corporation.

(a) Issued 4,000 shares of $10 par common stock for $40,000 cash.

(b) Issued 5,000 shares of $10 par common stock for $45,000 cash.

(c) Issued 5,000 shares of $10 par common stock for $53,500 cash.

(d) Issued 6,000 shares of no-par common stock for $60,000 cash.

(e) Issued 4,000 shares of no-par common stock for $40,000 cash.

(f) Issued 6,000 shares of no-par common stock with a stated value of $8 per share for $48,000 cash.

(g) Issued 3,000 shares of no-par common stock with a stated value of $8 per share for $25,000 cash.

(h) Issued 4,000 shares of no-par common stock with a stated value of $8 per share for $30,500 cash.

Prepare general journal entries to record the above stock transactions, identifying each transaction by letter.

EXERCISE 21B-4 (LO 3) STOCK ISSUANCE (NONCASH ASSETS, SUBSCRIPTION, AND TREASURY STOCK) Brant & Evans had the following stock transactions during the year:

(a) Issued 6,000 shares of common stock with a $5 par value in exchange for real estate (land) with a fair market value of $33,500.

(b) Issued 5,500 shares of common stock with a $6 par value and $7 fair market value in exchange for a building with an uncertain fair market value.

(c) Received subscriptions for 11,000 shares of $5 par common stock for $58,000.

(d) Received subscriptions for 8,000 shares of $5 par common stock for $38,000.

(e) Received a payment of $29,000 on the stock subscription in (c).

(f) Received the balance in full for the stock subscription in (c) and issued the stock.

(continued)

(g) Received the balance in full for the stock subscription in (d) and issued the stock.

(h) Purchased 2,000 shares of its own $5 par common stock for $6 a share ($12,000).

(i) Sold 1,000 shares of the treasury stock in (h) for $6.50 a share.

(j) Sold 1,000 shares of the treasury stock in (h) for $5.75 a share.

Prepare general journal entries to record the above transactions, identifying each transaction by letter.

EXERCISE 21B-5 (LO 4) STOCKHOLDERS' EQUITY SECTION After closing its books on December 31, Mel Brothers' stockholders' equity accounts have the following balances:

Common stock, $6 par, 15,000 shares	$ 90,000
Preferred stock, $10 par, 8%, 10,000 shares	100,000
Common stock subscribed, $6 par, 5,000 shares	30,000
Retained earnings	50,000

Prepare the stockholders' equity section of the balance sheet.

SERIES B PROBLEMS

PROBLEM 21B-1 (LO 3) PAR AND NO-PAR, COMMON AND PREFERRED STOCK Valdez Company had the following stock transactions during the year:

(a) Issued 24,000 shares of $1 par common stock for $26,000 cash.

(b) Issued 20,000 shares of $1 par common stock for $19,000 cash.

(c) Issued 18,000 shares of $1 par common stock for $18,000 cash.

(d) Issued 3,000 shares of $10 par, 7% preferred stock for $30,000 cash.

(e) Issued 4,000 shares of $15 par, 7% preferred stock for $57,000 cash.

(f) Issued 4,500 shares of $10 par, 7% preferred stock for $46,500 cash.

(g) Issued 1,800 shares of no-par common stock for $10,475.

(h) Issued 1,100 shares of no-par, 7% preferred stock for $32,000.

REQUIRED Prepare general journal entries to record the above transactions, identifying each transaction by letter.

PROBLEM 21B-2 (LO 3) STATED VALUE, COMMON AND PREFERRED STOCK, AND NONCASH ASSETS Dan's Hobby Stores had the following stock transactions during the year:

(a) Issued 5,000 shares of no-par common stock with a stated value of $10 per share for $50,000 cash.

(b) Issued 6,000 shares of no-par common stock with a stated value of $7 per share for $43,000 cash.

(c) Issued 5,000 shares of no-par, 6% preferred stock with a stated value of $18 per share for $88,600 cash.

(d) Issued 3,500 shares of no-par, 6% preferred stock with a stated value of $22 per share for $77,000 cash.

(e) Issued 10,000 shares of $9 par common stock for land with a fair market value of $90,000.

(f) Issued 11,000 shares of $8 par common stock with a $9 fair market value for a building with an uncertain fair market value.

(g) Issued 8,000 shares of $30 par, 6% preferred stock for land with a fair market value of $243,000.

REQUIRED   Prepare general journal entries to record the above transactions, identifying each transaction by letter.

PROBLEM 21B-3 (LO 3) STOCK SUBSCRIPTIONS Athletics West had the following stock transactions during the year:

(a) Issued 140,000 shares of $1 par common stock for $145,000 cash.

(b) Issued 9,000 shares of $18 par, 7% preferred stock for $162,800 cash.

(c) Received subscriptions for 10,000 shares of $12 par common stock for $118,000.

(d) Received subscriptions for 5,000 shares of $18 par, 7% preferred stock for $92,000.

(e) Received a payment of $59,000 on the common stock subscription.

(f) Received payment of $46,000 on the preferred stock subscription.

(g) Issued 60,000 shares of $1 par common stock in exchange for a truck with a fair market value of $66,000.

(h) Received the balance in full for the common stock subscription and issued the stock.

(i) Issued 3,500 shares of no-par common stock with a stated value of $6 per share for $21,500 cash.

(j) Received the balance in full for the preferred stock subscription and issued the stock.

REQUIRED   Prepare general journal entries to record the above transactions, identifying each transaction by letter.

PROBLEM 21B-4 (LO 1/3) STOCK SUBSCRIPTIONS AND TREASURY STOCK Rogers & Hart formed a corporation and had the following stock transactions during the year:

June 30   Incurred the following costs of incorporation:

Incorporation fees	$ 900
Attorneys' fees	6,000
Promotion fees	8,000

July 15	Issued 8,000 shares of $10 par common stock for $82,000 cash.
21	Issued 5,000 shares of $25 par, 8% preferred stock for $124,500 cash.
Aug. 1	Received subscriptions for 10,000 shares of $10 par common stock for $101,500.
15	Issued 10,000 shares of $10 par common stock in exchange for a building and fixtures with a fair market value of $104,800.
31	Received a payment of $51,500 for the common stock subscription.
Sept. 3	Purchased 1,000 shares of its own $10 par common stock for $11 a share.
12	Issued 2,800 shares of no-par common stock with a stated value of $8 per share for $21,400.
18	Received the balance in full for the common stock subscription and issued the stock.
30	Sold 500 shares of its treasury stock for $11.50 a share.
Oct. 15	Issued 4,000 shares of $25 par, 8% value preferred stock in exchange for land with a fair market value of $105,000.
31	Sold 500 shares of its treasury stock for $10.75 a share.
Dec. 31	Recorded this year's (6 months) amortization of organization costs (written off over five years).

REQUIRED   Prepare journal entries to record the above transactions.

PROBLEM 21B-5 (LO 4) STOCKHOLDERS' EQUITY SECTION After closing its books on December 31, 20--, the Merrill Corporation's stockholders' equity accounts have the following balances:

Account	Balance	Additional Information
Preferred Stock Subscribed	$ 40,000	$4 dividend, $5 par, 8,000 shares
Common Stock Subscribed	80,000	$10 par, 8,000 shares
Preferred Stock	120,000	$4 dividend, $5 par, 24,000 shares
Common Stock	280,000	$10 par, 28,000 shares
Paid-In Capital in Excess of Par—Preferred Stock	12,000	
Paid-In Capital from Sale of Treasury Stock	1,150	
Common Treasury Stock	24,000	
Retained Earnings	88,000	

REQUIRED   Prepare the stockholders' equity section of the balance sheet for the Merrill Corporation for the year ended December 31, 20--.

MASTERY PROBLEM

W & D

Stockholders' equity accounts and other related accounts of the Gonzales Company as of January 1, 20--, the beginning of its fiscal year, are shown below.

Preferred Stock Subscriptions Receivable	$ 50,000
Preferred Stock, $10 par, 9%, (200,000 shares authorized; 20,000 shares issued)	200,000
Preferred Stock Subscribed (10,000 shares)	100,000
Paid-In Capital in Excess of Par—Preferred Stock	40,000
Common Stock, $10 par (100,000 shares authorized, 60,000 shares issued)	600,000
Paid-In Capital in Excess of Par— Common Stock	250,000
Retained Earnings	750,000

During 20--, the Gonzales Company completed the following transactions affecting stockholders' equity:

(a) Received $20,000 for the balance due on subscriptions for preferred stock with a par value of $40,000 and issued the stock.

(b) Purchased 10,000 shares of common treasury stock for $18 per share.

(c) Received subscriptions for 10,000 shares of common stock at $19 per share, collecting down payments of $45,000.

(d) Issued 15,000 shares of common stock in exchange for land with a fair market value of $290,000.

(e) Sold 5,000 shares of common treasury stock for $100,000.

(f) Issued 10,000 shares of preferred stock at $11.50 per share, receiving cash.

(g) Sold 3,000 shares of common treasury stock for $17 per share.

REQUIRED

1. Prepare general journal entries for the above transactions, identifying each transaction by letter.

2. Post the journal entries to appropriate T accounts. The cash account has a beginning balance of $300,000.

3. Prepare the stockholders' equity section of the balance sheet as of December 31, 20--. Net income for the year was $825,000 and dividends of $400,000 were paid.

Self-Study Test Questions

True/False

1. Corporations do more dollar volume of business than sole proprietorships and partnerships combined. _____

2. Owners of corporations have no personal liability for debts of the corporation. _____

3. In a corporation, individual owners have mutual agency power. _____

4. Dividends are not taxable because these earnings have already been taxed to the corporation. _____

5. Organizations costs are recorded as an intangible asset and are generally amortized over a period of five years. _____

Multiple Choice

1. When par value stock is issued at a price above par, the amount above par is called a _____

   (a) discount.   (c) stated value.
   (b) market value.   (d) premium.

2. When par value stock is issued at a price below par, the amount below par is called a _____

   (a) discount.   (c) stated value.
   (b) market value.   (d) premium.

3. Shares of stock reacquired by the issuing company are called _____

   (a) par value stock.   (c) treasury stock.
   (b) no-par value stock.   (d) stock subscription.

4. Stock subscriptions receivable are listed as _____ on the balance sheet. _____

   (a) current liabilities   (c) long-term assets
   (b) current assets   (d) owners' equity

5. Treasury stock is listed as a(n) _____ on the balance sheet. _____

   (a) current liability   (c) deduction from stockholders' equity
   (b) current asset   (d) addition to stockholders' equity

The answers to the Self-Study Test Questions are at the end of the text.

22

Corporations: Earnings and Distributions

LEARNING OBJECTIVES:

Careful study of this chapter should enable you to:

LO 1 Explain the use of the retained earnings account and account for corporate income taxes.

LO 2 Account for dividends and stock splits.

LO 3 Account for appropriations of retained earnings.

LO 4 Prepare a retained earnings statement.

Mike Finbar incorporated the business described in Chapter 21, calling it Finny Co. The additional resources provided by the issuance of stock enabled the business to expand into electric instruments. With the new lines of instruments, the business has continued to grow in the four years since incorporating. In spite of its profitable operations, however, the business often is short of cash as it seeks to expand. Mike's accountant says the problem is that too much of the profits are paid out as cash dividends. He argues that the profits need to be retained in the business to finance the growth. If stockholders want distributions, he suggests issuing a stock dividend. How will issuing stock dividends instead of cash dividends enable Finny Co. to have more cash to expand? How will a stock dividend affect the stockholders' ownership in the business?

In Chapter 21 we learned that stockholders' equity is separated into paid-in capital (amounts contributed by owners) and retained earnings (amounts of accumulated earnings not paid out to stockholders). The emphasis in Chapter 21 was on accounting for paid-in capital, primarily the issuance of capital stock. In this chapter, we focus on retained earnings.

THE RETAINED EARNINGS ACCOUNT

LO 1   Explain the use of the retained earnings account and account for corporate income taxes.

Two major sources of capital for every type of business are:

1. Capital that results from investments by the owners

2. Capital that results from earnings retained in the business

In a corporation, capital resulting from the retention of earnings is entered in the retained earnings account. A corporation usually distributes only a portion of its earnings to stockholders. The balance is retained as additional capital to help finance the growth of the business.

Generally there are very few debits and credits to the retained earnings account. Typically the only credit to the account is for the net income of a period. The only debits are for a net loss, declarations of dividends, and appropriations (special restrictions) of retained earnings.

In this section, we will learn how to enter the net income or net loss for a period in the retained earnings account. But first, we need to know how to account for corporate income taxes.

Corporate Income Taxes

In accounting for sole proprietorships and partnerships, we did not need to deal with income taxes. Sole proprietorships and partnerships, as businesses, do not pay taxes. But, as noted in Chapter 21, a disadvantage of corporations is that they must pay income taxes.

Most corporations must estimate their annual income taxes and make quarterly payments. To illustrate, assume Boot Corp. estimates that its income taxes for 20-1 will be \$160,000. Based on this estimate, Boot will have to pay \$40,000 (\$160,000 ÷ 4) on April 15, June 15, September 15, and December 15. The journal entry for each payment is:

5	Income Tax Expense	40	0	0	0	00					5
6	Cash						40	0	0	0	00	6
7	Made quarterly estimated tax payment											7

> Corporations are subject to specific corporate tax rates different from those for individuals. Currently there are eight tax brackets ranging from 15% to 35%.

The actual amount of income taxes typically differs from the estimated amount. Thus, at year end, an adjusting entry is necessary to recognize the correct amount of income taxes for the year. Assume that as part of the year-end adjusting and closing process at Boot Corp., actual income taxes for the year are calculated as \$163,000. The following adjusting journal entry would be made at December 31, 20-1:

5	Dec.	31	Income Tax Expense		3	0	0	0	00*						5
6			Income Tax Payable								3	0	0	0	00	6
7															7
8			* $163,000 actual − $160,000 estimated = $3,000												8

On March 15, 20-2, Boot Corp. would file its income tax return for the year ended December 31, 20-1, and pay the $3,000 income taxes due. The following entry would be made:

15	Mar.	15	Income Tax Payable		3	0	0	0	00						15
16			Cash								3	0	0	0	00	16
17			Made final 20-1 tax payment												17

Income taxes normally are reported as a separate expense item on the income statement, and are subtracted from income before income taxes. Assuming that Boot Corp. had income of $500,000 before considering income taxes, the bottom portion of Boot's income statement would appear as follows:

Income before income taxes	$500,000
Income tax expense	163,000
Net income	$337,000

The Adjusting and Closing Process

The adjusting and closing process at the end of the period is virtually the same for corporations as for sole proprietorships and partnerships. The accounts are adjusted and all revenue and expense accounts (including Income Tax Expense) are closed to Income Summary. A credit balance in Income Summary represents net income; a debit balance signifies a net loss. Beyond this point, however, the closing procedures for corporations differ from those for sole proprietorships and partnerships. The balance of the income summary account of a corporation is transferred to the retained earnings account. For example, if the corporation has net income of $337,000 for the period, the following closing entry is made:

18			Income Summary		337	0	0	0	00						18
19			Retained Earnings								337	0	0	0	00	19

If the corporation has a net loss of $52,000 for the period, the closing entry is:

18			Retained Earnings		52	0	0	0	00						18
19			Income Summary								52	0	0	0	00	19

LEARNING KEY: In a corporation, close Income Summary to Retained Earnings.

A BROADER VIEW

WHEN CORPORATE EARNINGS GET TOO IMPORTANT

Earnings are important in virtually any business, but corporate managers sometimes become so focused on earnings growth that they "create" earnings that do not exist. This apparently is what happened at Kurzweil Applied Intelligence, Inc., a computerized speech recognition company based in Waltham, MA. Under pressure to produce consistently improving results, key executives at the company engaged in a scheme to regularly record fraudulent sales.

According to generally accepted accounting principles, a sale should be counted when goods are shipped from the company to the customer. Kurzweil took a different approach. Millions of dollars of sales were recorded based on shipments of goods to local warehouses for storage until "real" sales could occur. Most of these "real" sales never happened. The fraud was uncovered when Kurzweil's auditor investigated bills from the warehouses for storage of goods supposedly sold nine months previously.

ACCOUNTING FOR DIVIDENDS AND STOCK SPLITS

LO 2   Account for dividends and stock splits.

"Is It a Loan or a Dividend?"
(http://heintz.swcollege.com)
What are the potential effects of borrowing money from a company you own? (Also access "301 Great Management Ideas.")

A distribution of earnings by a corporation to its stockholders is known as a **dividend**. In this section, we consider two types of dividends: cash dividends and stock dividends.

Cash Dividends

A dividend payable in cash is known as a **cash dividend.** For a corporation to issue a cash dividend, three conditions are necessary.

1. Unrestricted retained earnings. In general, corporations can legally declare cash dividends only if the retained earnings balance is sufficient to cover the dividends.

2. Adequate cash balance. The retained earnings balance indicates whether a corporation can legally declare a dividend. But a corporation can pay a cash dividend only if an adequate amount of cash is available. Remember: retained earnings is not the same as cash.

3. Declaration of dividend. Only the board of directors can declare a dividend. Regardless of the amount of cash or other assets accumulated by a corporation, no dividend can be paid unless so declared by the board of directors.

Three dates are involved in the declaration and payment of dividends.

1. **Date of declaration**—the date on which the board of directors decides (declares) that a dividend is to be paid.

2. **Date of record**—the date on which the names of stockholders entitled to receive the dividend are determined.

3. **Date of payment**—the date on which the dividend is actually paid by the corporation.

For example, assume that on January 26 the board of directors declares a dividend of $2 a share on common stock, payable on February 16 to stockholders of record on February 6. In this case, the date of declaration, date of record, and date of payment are as shown in Figure 22-1. To be eligible to receive the dividend, a stockholder's ownership of stock must be entered in the records of the corporation not later than February 6.

FIGURE 22-1 Dividend Dates

> The most important dividend date is the date of declaration. This is the date when the corporation commits to paying the dividend.

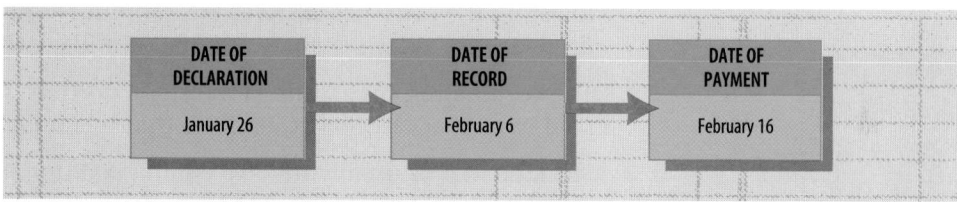

DATE OF DECLARATION	DATE OF RECORD	DATE OF PAYMENT
January 26	February 6	February 16

Dividends on different classes of capital stock should be accounted for separately. To illustrate, assume that on February 1 the board of directors declares a dividend of $4 per share on 4,000 shares of preferred stock and a dividend of $2 per share on 10,000 shares of common stock. Both dividends are payable on February 20 to stockholders of record on February 10. These dividends are accounted for as follows:

Date of Declaration:

4	Feb.	1	Retained Earnings	16 0 0 0 00		4
5			Preferred Dividends Payable		16 0 0 0 00	5
6			Declared preferred stock dividend			6
7						7
8		1	Retained Earnings	20 0 0 0 00		8
9			Common Dividends Payable		20 0 0 0 00	9
10			Declared common stock dividend			10

Date of Record:

Feb. 10 No journal entry is made. The date of record has no effect on the corporation accounts. This date simply determines which stockholders receive the dividends.

Date of Payment:

18	Feb.	20	Preferred Dividends Payable		16	0	0	0	00							18
19			Cash								16	0	0	0	00		19
20			Paid preferred stock dividend														20
21																	21
22			Common Dividends Payable		20	0	0	0	00								22
23			Cash								20	0	0	0	00		23
24			Paid common stock dividend														24

If a balance sheet is prepared between the date of declaration and date of payment, dividends payable accounts are reported as current liabilities.

Note that cash dividends reduce the stockholders' equity in the corporation. A cash dividend is a distribution of corporate assets to the stockholders. The retained earnings portion of stockholders' equity is reduced accordingly.

Stock Dividends

A **stock dividend** is a proportionate distribution of shares of a corporation's own stock to its stockholders. Corporations may distribute this type of dividend for several reasons:

1. The company may be short of cash.

2. The company may want to increase the marketability of its shares by lowering the price per share. A greater number of shares outstanding decreases the price per share and makes wider ownership possible.

3. The corporation may want to transfer a portion of retained earnings to a paid-in capital category to indicate that it is unavailable for dividends.

> Note that this 10% stock dividend does not give the stockholder any increased ownership in the corporation. <u>All</u> stockholders receive the 10% dividend, so everyone still owns the same portion of the corporation. Each stockholder owns 10% more shares, but each individual share is worth less.

Stock dividends usually involve issuing additional common shares to current common stockholders. Stock dividends typically are stated as a percentage of common stock outstanding. For example, a 10% stock dividend means that a stockholder receives one additional share for each 10 shares owned. Thus, the owner of 100 shares of common stock receives an additional 10 shares (10% × 100 shares = 10 shares).

When a stock dividend is declared, the proper journal entry depends on the dividend percentage. If the stock dividend is for less than 20–25% of the outstanding shares, Retained Earnings is debited for the *market value* of the stock to be distributed. If the stock has neither par nor stated value, Stock Dividends Distributable is credited for the market value of the shares. If the stock has a par or stated value, Stock Dividends Distributable is credited for the par or stated value of the shares. The excess of the market value over par or stated value is credited to Paid-In Capital in Excess of Par (or Stated) Value—Common Stock.

LEARNING KEY: To record a stock dividend of less than 20–25%, debit Retained Earnings for the *market value* of the shares distributed.

To illustrate, assume that Diven Corp. has 4,000 shares of $5 par common stock outstanding. Diven declares a 10% stock dividend on March 5, payable on March 27 to stockholders of record on March 14. The market value of Diven's common stock on the date of declaration is $12 per share. This means that Diven will issue a total of 400 shares of common stock (4,000 shares × 10% = 400 shares) with a market value of $4,800 (400 shares × $12 = $4,800).

We account for this stock dividend as follows.

Date of Declaration:

22	Mar.	5	Retained Earnings		4	8	0	0	00								22
23			Stock Dividends Distributable*								2	0	0	0	00		23
24			Paid-In Capital in Excess of Par—														24
25			Common Stock**								2	8	0	0	00		25
26			Declared Stock Dividend														26
27			* 400 shares × $5 par														27
28			** $4,800 market value − $2,000 par value														28

Date of Record:

Mar. 14   No journal entry. As with cash dividends, the date of record has no effect on the corporation accounts.

Date of Distribution:

14	Mar.	27	Stock Dividends Distributable		2	0	0	0	00								14
15			Common Stock								2	0	0	0	00		15
16			Distributed stock dividend														16

Stock Dividends Distributable is reported as an addition to common stock in the stockholders' equity section of the balance sheet. Stock Dividends Distributable is not a liability since no assets or services are owed.

If a stock dividend is more than 20–25% of the outstanding shares, Retained Earnings is debited for the *par or stated value* rather than the market value of the shares to be distributed. Otherwise, the accounting is the same as that illustrated for stock dividends of less than 20–25%.

Note that stock dividends do not affect the assets, liabilities, or total stockholders' equity of the corporation. Stock dividends merely transfer part of the balance of the retained earnings account to one or more paid-in capital accounts.

Stock Splits

> For stock with no par or stated value, Retained Earnings usually is debited for the average amount of paid-in capital per share of outstanding stock.

An exchange of one share of an old issue of stock for multiple shares of a new issue with a reduced par or stated value is known as a **stock split**. The usual purpose of a stock split is to improve the marketability of the shares by reducing the market price per share. Having a greater number of shares outstanding also makes it possible to have a wider ownership of the stock.

Accounting for a stock split differs from accounting for a stock dividend. A stock split requires no formal journal entry and may be recognized simply by a memorandum notation in the general journal and in the appropriate capital stock accounts. Thus, stock splits do not affect the assets, liabilities, or any component of stockholders' equity of a corporation.

LEARNING KEY: No formal journal entry is made for a stock split.

To illustrate, assume that Splice Corp. has 10,000 shares of $10 par common stock outstanding. Splice declares a two-for-one stock split. This means that Splice will issue a total of 20,000 shares of $5 par common stock in exchange for the 10,000 shares of $10 par common stock currently outstanding. Each stockholder will receive two shares of the new $5 par stock in exchange for one share of the old $10 par stock. The memorandum entry in the journal is as follows:

22		Declared two-for-one stock split. Exchanged										22
23		20,000 shares of $5 par common stock for 10,000										23
24		shares of $10 par common stock.										24

Summary of Dividend and Stock Split Transactions

We have seen that cash dividends, stock dividends, and stock splits affect stockholders' equity differently. Figure 22-2 briefly describes and summarizes the effects of these three transactions on the assets, paid-in capital, and retained earnings of the corporation. Refer to this figure as you work the exercises and problems for this chapter.

FIGURE 22-2 Summary of Dividend and Split Transactions

TRANS-ACTION	DESCRIPTION	JOURNAL ENTRIES	ASSETS	PAID-IN CAPITAL	RETAINED EARNINGS

Cash Dividend	Distribution of cash to stockholders	At declaration:
		Retained Earnings xxx
		   Dividends Payable xxx
		At payment:
		Dividends Payable xxx
		   Cash xxx
			Decrease by amount of dividend distributed	No effect	Decrease by amount of dividend distributed

Stock Dividend Less than 20–25%	Distribution of corporation's stock to stockholders	At declaration:
		Retained Earnings xxx
		   Stock Div. Distributable xxx
		   Paid-In Capital in
		   Excess of Par xxx
		At distribution:
		Stock Div. Distributable xxx
		   Common Stock xxx
			No effect	Increase by market value of stock distributed	Decrease by market value of stock distributed

More than 20–25%	Distribution of corporation's stock to stockholders	At declaration:
		Retained Earnings xxx
		   Stock Div. Distributable xxx
		At distribution:
		Stock Div. Distributable xxx
		   Common Stock xxx
			No effect	Increase by par value of stock distributed	Decrease by par value of stock distributed

Stock Split	Exchange of old stock for multiple shares of new stock	Memo notation	No effect	No effect	No effect

APPROPRIATIONS OF RETAINED EARNINGS

LO 3   Account for appropriations of retained earnings.

Thus far we have examined how net income, net loss, cash dividends, and stock dividends affect retained earnings. One other event that affects retained earnings is an appropriation. A **retained earnings appropriation** is a restriction of retained earnings by the board of directors for a specific purpose. Recall that corporations may pay dividends only if the retained earnings balance is sufficient to do so. A retained earnings appropriation is used primarily to limit the availability of retained earnings for paying dividends.

To illustrate, assume that Chem Corp. has decided to build a new waste treatment plant. Chem Corp. has a retained earnings balance of $900,000. To finance a portion of the plant (and to inform people of its concern for the environment), the board of directors decides to appropriate $600,000 of retained earnings over a three-year period. At the end of each year for three years, the following journal entry would be made:

1	Retained Earnings*	200 0 0 0 00			1
2	Retained Earnings Appropriated				2
3	for Treatment Plant		200 0 0 0 00		3
4	Appropriated retained earnings for				4
5	treatment plant				5
6	* $600,000 ÷ 3 = $200,000				6

Notice two important things about the appropriation of retained earnings. First, total retained earnings is unaffected. Retained earnings is simply separated into two categories: appropriated and unappropriated. Retained earnings would appear in the Chem Corp. balance sheet at the end of Year 1 as shown in Figure 22-3. The total retained earnings is $900,000, the same as it would be without the appropriation. Second, cash and other assets of the corporation are unaffected. Retained earnings is just a form of ownership interest in the assets of the corporation. All that a retained earnings appropriation does is restrict the corporation's ability to pay out its assets as dividends. In that sense, the *use* of corporate assets is restricted.

LEARNING KEY: The appropriation of retained earnings does not affect either total retained earnings or the cash and other assets of the corporation.

FIGURE 22-3 Retained Earnings Section of the Balance Sheet

Retained earnings:		
Appropriated for treatment plant	$200 0 0 0 00	
Unappropriated	700 0 0 0 00	
Total retained earnings		$900 0 0 0 00

After the retained earnings appropriation has served its purpose, the appropriated amount can be returned to retained earnings. To illustrate, let's return to the Chem Corp. example. At the end of three years, Retained Earnings Appropriated for Treatment Plant would have a balance of $600,000. Assume that the treatment plant is completed and that in Year 4 the board of directors decides that the appropriation is no longer needed. The following journal entry would be made:

11		Retained Earnings Appropriated												11
12		for Treatment Plant	600	0	0	0	00						12
13		Retained Earnings						600	0	0	0	00	13
14		Returned appropriation to											14
15		retained earnings											15

The practice of appropriating retained earnings is unusual today. Stockholders generally do not regard the retained earnings balance as the total amount likely to be distributed as dividends. Thus, it generally is unnecessary to make appropriations to advise balance sheet readers that retained earnings is not all available for dividends. Restrictions on dividends can be described just as well in a footnote to the financial statements.

RETAINED EARNINGS STATEMENT

LO 4 Prepare a retained earnings statement.

A **retained earnings statement** explains the change in the amount of retained earnings during the year. All of the information necessary to prepare the retained earnings statement is contained in the unappropriated and appropriated retained earnings accounts in the general ledger. If there are no appropriated retained earnings, the statement begins with the beginning of the year retained earnings balance. Net income for the year is added (or net loss is subtracted). Any cash and stock dividends are then subtracted to yield the end of the year retained earnings balance. This balance is the same amount that appears in the stockholders' equity section of the year-end balance sheet. Figure 22-4 shows the format for a retained earnings statement with no appropriated retained earnings.

FIGURE 22-4 Retained Earnings Statement without Appropriated Retained Earnings

Sample Corporation														
Retained Earnings Statement														
For Year Ended December 31, 20 - -														
Retained earnings, January 1							$1,100	0	0	0	00			
Add net income for the year							280	0	0	0	00			
							$1,380	0	0	0	00			
Less: Cash dividends	$30	0	0	0	00									
Stock dividends	20	0	0	0	00		50	0	0	0	00			
Retained earnings, December 31							$1,330	0	0	0	00			

If there are both appropriated and unappropriated retained earnings, each is shown separately in the retained earnings statement. To illustrate the preparation of this type of retained earnings statement, let's look again at Chem Corp. Assume that it is the end of the second year after beginning appropriations for the treatment plant. The appropriated and unappropriated retained earnings accounts from Chem's general ledger are shown as follows:

Retained Earnings Appropriated for Treatment Plant				**Retained Earnings—Unappropriated**			
Jan. 1	Bal.	200,000	Mar. 15	30,000[3]	Jan. 1	Bal.	700,000
Dec. 31		200,000[1]	June 15	20,000[4]	Dec. 31		280,000[2]
	Bal.	400,000	Dec. 31	200,000[1]			
						Bal.	730,000

[1] Current year appropriation for treatment plant
[2] Net income for the year
[3] Cash dividend
[4] Stock dividend

Figure 22-5 shows a retained earnings statement prepared from these accounts.

FIGURE 22-5 Retained Earnings Statement with Appropriated and Unappropriated Retained Earnings

Chem Corporation Retained Earnings Statement For Year Ended December 31, 20 -2				
Appropriated:				
Appropriated for treatment plant, January 1			$200 0 0 0 00	Current year appropriation (shown twice)
Current year appropriation (see below)			200 0 0 0 00	
Retained earnings appropriated, December 31				$ 400 0 0 0 00 *Appropriated shown first*
Unappropriated:				
Balance, January 1	$700 0 0 0 00			
Add net income for the year	280 0 0 0 00	$980 0 0 0 00		
Less: Cash dividends	$ 30 0 0 0 00			
Stock dividends	20 0 0 0 00			
Transfer to appropriated for treatment plant	200 0 0 0 00	250 0 0 0 00		
Retained earnings unappropriated, December 31			*Current year appropriation (shown twice)*	730 0 0 0 00
Total retained earnings, December 31				$1,130 0 0 0 00

Note the following characteristics of this retained earnings statement.

1. Appropriated retained earnings is presented first, followed by unappropriated retained earnings.

2. Changes in appropriated and unappropriated retained earnings are shown separately.

3. Current year appropriations of retained earnings are shown twice: as an increase in appropriated retained earnings and as a decrease in unappropriated retained earnings.

4. The ending unappropriated retained earnings balance is computed by adding net income for the year to the beginning-of-the-year balance, and then subtracting any dividends and current year appropriations.

5. Appropriated, unappropriated, and total retained earnings are shown separately.

Learning Objectives	Key Points to Remember
1 Explain the use of the retained earnings account and account for corporate income taxes.	Earnings retained in a corporation are entered in the retained earnings account by closing the income summary account to the retained earnings account at the end of the period. Corporations must pay income taxes. Most corporations must estimate their annual income taxes and make quarterly payments.
2 Account for dividends and stock splits.	Three important dates in the declaration and payment of dividends are: 1. Date of declaration 2. Date of record 3. Date of payment Journal entries are necessary on the date of declaration and date of payment. For stock dividends of less than 20–25%, Retained Earnings is debited for the market value of the shares to be distributed. For stock dividends of more than 20–25%, Retained Earnings is debited for the par or stated value of the shares. A stock split requires no formal journal entry. A memorandum notation in the general journal and capital stock accounts is all that is necessary.
3 Account for appropriations of retained earnings.	A retained earnings appropriation has no effect on total retained earnings or on the assets of the corporation. An appropriation simply restricts the corporation's ability to pay out its assets as dividends.
4 Prepare a retained earnings statement.	A retained earnings statement explains the change in the amount of retained earnings during the year. If there are both appropriated and unappropriated retained earnings, each is shown separately on the retained earnings statement.

Reflection: Answering the Opening Questions

With a cash dividend, cash is transferred from the business to the stockholders. In contrast, stock dividends involve distributing additional shares of stock rather than cash. The cash stays in the business and can be used for purposes such as expansion. As long as the stockholders do not sell the additional shares they receive, their ownership in the business is unaffected. They would have the same percentage ownership before and after the stock dividend.

KEY TERMS

cash dividend, (804)   A dividend payable in cash.

date of declaration, (805)   The date on which the board of directors declares that a dividend is to be paid.

date of payment, (805)   The date on which the dividend is actually paid by the corporation.

date of record, (805)   The date on which the names of stockholders entitled to receive the dividend are determined.

dividend, (804)   A distribution of earnings by a corporation to its stockholders.

retained earnings appropriation, (809)   A restriction of retained earnings by the board of directors for a specific purpose.

retained earnings statement, (810)   A statement that explains the change in the amount of retained earnings during the year.

stock dividend, (806)   A proportionate distribution of shares of a corporation's own stock to its stockholders.

stock split, (807)   An exchange of one share of an old issue of stock for multiple shares of a new issue with a reduced par or stated value.

DEMONSTRATION PROBLEM

On January 1, 20-1, Grant Company's retained earnings account had the following balances:

Appropriated for warehouse	$ 25,000
Unappropriated retained earnings	650,000
	$675,000

During the year ended December 31, 20-1, Grant completed the following selected transactions:

Apr. 15   Estimated that its 20-1 income tax will be $40,000. Based on this estimate, it will make four quarterly payments of $10,000 each on April 15, June 15, September 15, and December 15.

20   Declared semiannual dividend of $.30 per share on common stock to shareholders of record on May 5, payable May 15. Currently, 50,000 shares of $3 par stock are outstanding.

May 15   Paid the cash dividend.

June 15   Made estimated tax payment of $10,000.

Sept. 15   Made estimated tax payment of $10,000.

Oct. 20   Declared a semiannual dividend of $.30 per share on common stock to shareholders of record on November 5, payable on November 15.

Nov. 4   Last year, Grant's board of directors appropriated $50,000 for a warehouse over a two-year period. Made this year's appropriation for $25,000.

15   Paid the cash dividend.

16   Declared a 10% stock dividend to shareholders of record on December 2, distributable on December 10. Market value of the common stock was estimated at $7 per share.

(continued)

Dec. 10 Issued certificates for common stock dividend.

15 Made estimated tax payment of $10,000.

On December 31, the following adjusting and closing entries were made:

Dec. 31 Grant's actual 20-1 income tax is $44,000. This amount will be paid by March 15, 20-2. Made adjustment for the additional amount owed.

31 Net income for 20-1 was $98,000. Closed the income summary account.

REQUIRED 1. Prepare journal entries for the above transactions and for the adjusting and closing process.

2. Post all entries affecting the appropriated and unappropriated retained earnings accounts to T accounts.

3. Prepare a retained earnings statement for the year ended December 31, 20-1.

Solution

1.

GENERAL JOURNAL
PAGE 1

	DATE		DESCRIPTION	POST REF.	DEBIT	CREDIT	
1	20-1 Apr.	15	Income Tax Expense		10 0 0 0 00		1
2			Cash			10 0 0 0 00	2
3			Made quarterly estimated tax payment				3
4							4
5		20	Retained Earnings		15 0 0 0 00		5
6			Common Dividends Payable			15 0 0 0 00	6
7			Declared common stock dividend				7
8							8
9	May	15	Common Dividends Payable		15 0 0 0 00		9
10			Cash			15 0 0 0 00	10
11			Paid common stock dividend				11
12							12
13	June	15	Income Tax Expense		10 0 0 0 00		13
14			Cash			10 0 0 0 00	14
15			Made quarterly estimated tax payment				15
16							16
17	Sept.	15	Income Tax Expense		10 0 0 0 00		17
18			Cash			10 0 0 0 00	18
19			Made quarterly estimated tax payment				19
20							20
21	Oct.	20	Retained Earnings		15 0 0 0 00		21
22			Common Dividends Payable			15 0 0 0 00	22
23			Declared common stock dividend				23
24							24
25	Nov.	4	Retained Earnings		25 0 0 0 00		25
26			Retained Earnings Appropriated for Warehouse			25 0 0 0 00	26
27			Appropriated retained earnings for warehouse				27
28							28
29		15	Common Dividends Payable		15 0 0 0 00		29
30			Cash			15 0 0 0 00	30
31			Paid common stock dividend				31

GENERAL JOURNAL PAGE 2

	DATE		DESCRIPTION	POST. REF.	DEBIT	CREDIT	
1	20-1 Nov.	16	Retained Earnings		35 0 0 0 00		1
2			Stock Dividends Distributable ($3 ×5,000)			15 0 0 0 00	2
3			Paid-In Capital in Excess of Par—				3
4			Common Stock ($4 × 5,000)			20 0 0 0 00	4
5			Declared stock dividend				5
6							6
7	Dec.	10	Stock Dividends Distributable		15 0 0 0 00		7
8			Common Stock			15 0 0 0 00	8
9			Distributed stock dividend				9
10							10
11		15	Income Tax Expense		10 0 0 0 00		11
12			Cash			10 0 0 0 00	12
13			Made quarterly estimated tax payment				13
14							14
15			**Adjusting**				15
16		31	Income Tax Expense		4 0 0 0 00		16
17			Income Tax Payable			4 0 0 0 00	17
18							18
19			**Closing**				19
20		31	Income Summary		98 0 0 0 00		20
21			Retained Earnings			98 0 0 0 00	21
22							22
23							23
24							24
25							25
26							26
27							27
28							28
29							29

2.

Retained Earnings—Appropriated

	Bal.	25,000
	Nov. 4	25,000
	Bal.	50,000

Retained Earnings—Unappropriated

Apr. 20	15,000	Bal.	650,000
Oct. 20	15,000	Dec. 31	98,000
Nov. 4	25,000		
Nov. 16	35,000		
		Bal.	658,000

3.

Grant Company Retained Earnings Statement For Year Ended December 31, 20-1					
Appropriated:					
Appropriated for warehouse, January 1		$ 25 0 0 0 00		
Current year appropriation (see below)		25 0 0 0 00		
Retained earnings appropriated, December 31			$ 50 0 0 0 00	
Unappropriated:				
Balance, January 1	$650 0 0 0 00			
Add net income for the year	98 0 0 0 00	$748 0 0 0 00		
Less: Cash dividends	$ 30 0 0 0 00			
Stock dividends	35 0 0 0 00			
Transfer to appropriated for warehouse	25 0 0 0 00	90 0 0 0 00		
Retained earnings unappropriated, December 31			658 0 0 0 00	
Total retained earnings, December 31			$708 0 0 0 00	

REVIEW QUESTIONS

1. What are the two major sources of capital for every type of business?

2. For what reason do corporations retain earnings in the business?

3. What expense do corporations incur that sole proprietorships and partnerships do not?

4. How do the procedures for closing Income Summary of a corporation differ from those of a sole proprietorship or partnership?

5. What are the three dates involved in the declaration and payment of dividends? What is the meaning of each date?

6. What is the effect of a cash dividend on the corporation accounts?

7. Give three reasons why a corporation may distribute a stock dividend.

8. Where should stock dividends distributable be reported on the balance sheet? Why?

9. What effect does a stock dividend have on the accounts of the corporation? a stock split?

10. What is the primary reason for appropriating retained earnings?

11. How are appropriated and unappropriated retained earnings shown on the retained earnings statement?

MANAGING YOUR WRITING

The investments committee of your church has come to you for advice. One of the stocks held by the church has paid cash dividends for years. This year the company issued a 10% stock dividend, so that the church received additional shares rather than cash. The committee is concerned about whether this stock dividend is really worth anything. One committee member argues the stock dividend is as good as cash; another argues that the dividend is worthless.

Write a brief report to the committee explaining the difference between a cash dividend and a stock dividend. Evaluate the value of the stock dividend compared with the cash dividend the church has received in prior years.

ETHICS CASE

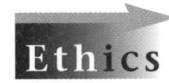

Richard Petri is the chief financial officer at Computer Electronics, Inc. In this capacity he attends all monthly Board of Directors meetings. A special meeting of the Board of Directors was called to discuss substantially increasing the amount of cash dividends paid to stockholders this year. The Board voted unanimously to increase the dividend. Later that night Richard called his uncle and hinted around that Computer Electronics, Inc., was going to make its stockholders very happy. His uncle didn't own any stock in Computer Electronics but went out and purchased 500 shares the next day.

1.   Did Richard do anything unethical? Would your answer be different if Richard specifically stated that the dividends on Computer Electronic, Inc., were being increased substantially?

2.   What should Richard's boss do if he finds out what Richard said to his uncle?

3.   Write a short paragraph explaining the difference between cash dividends and stock dividends.

4.   In groups of two or three, discuss possible reasons why a corporation might want to pay a very low or high dividend in any given year.

WEB WORK

Wendy's International, Inc. went public in 1975 and since then has had seven stock splits.

1.   Read about the history of Wendy's stock at **http://www.wendys.com/officef.htm.** Choose Investor Information, then Stock Price Information.

2.   If you purchased 100 shares of Wendy's stock in 1975, how many would you have today?

(http://heintz.swcollege.com)

SERIES A EXERCISES

EXERCISE 22A-1 (LO 1) CORPORATE INCOME TAX Stanton Company estimates that its 20-1 income tax will be $80,000. Based on this estimate, it will make four quarterly payments of $20,000 each on April 15, June 15, September 15, and December 15.

1. Prepare the journal entry for April 15.

2. Assume that all four quarterly payments have been entered in the general journal. On December 31, Stanton's actual income tax amounts to $86,000. This amount will be paid by March 15, 20-2. Prepare the journal entry to record the additional income tax owed.

EXERCISE 22A-2 (LO 1) CLOSING INCOME SUMMARY TO RETAINED EARNINGS Davidson Company had a net income of $120,000 for 20--. Wilson and Picket Company had a net loss of $30,000.

1. Prepare the journal entry for Davidson as of December 31, 20--, to close Income Summary into Retained Earnings.

2. Prepare the journal entry for Wilson and Picket as of December 31, 20--, to close Income Summary into Retained Earnings.

EXERCISE 22A-3 (LO 2) COMMON AND PREFERRED STOCK DIVIDENDS Wakui Company currently has 100,000 shares of $1 par common stock outstanding and 1,000 shares of $100 par preferred stock outstanding. On July 10, the board of directors declared a semiannual dividend of $.40 per share on common stock to shareholders of record on August 1, payable on August 5.

On July 15, the board of directors declared a semiannual dividend of $10 per share on preferred stock to shareholders of record on August 5, payable on August 10.

Prepare journal entries for the declaration and payment of the common and preferred stock cash dividends.

EXERCISE 22A-4 (LO 2) STOCK DIVIDENDS Cruz Company currently has 100,000 shares of $1 par common stock outstanding. On March 15, a 10% stock dividend was declared to shareholders of record on April 2, distributable on April 14. Market value of the common stock was estimated at $6 per share.

1. Prepare journal entries for the declaration and distribution of the 10% common stock dividend.

2. Assume Cruz Company declared a stock dividend of 30% rather than 10%. Prepare journal entries for the declaration and distribution of the 30% common stock dividend.

EXERCISE 22A-5 (LO 2) STOCK SPLIT Goldstein Company has 100,000 shares of $10 par common stock outstanding. On July 1, the board of directors declared a two-for-one stock split.

Prepare a memorandum entry in the general journal indicating the new par value and the total number of outstanding shares of common stock.

EXERCISE 22A-6 (LO 3) RETAINED EARNINGS APPROPRIATION On October 2, 20-1, the board of directors of Foxworth Company appropriated $80,000 of retained earnings for the purpose of buying a new sailboat (used for entertaining clients). On July 15, 20-2, the sailboat was purchased and the board of directors decided that the appropriation was no longer needed.

Prepare journal entries for the appropriation on October 2, 20-1, and the subsequent return on July 15, 20-2.

EXERCISE 22A-7 (LO 4) RETAINED EARNINGS STATEMENT McGregor Company had the following balances as of December 31, 20--:

Retained earnings, January 1	$60,000
Cash dividends declared	5,000
Net income for the year	20,000

Prepare a retained earnings statement for the year ended December 31, 20--.

SERIES A PROBLEMS

PROBLEM 22A-1 (LO 1/2) CASH DIVIDENDS AND INCOME TAXES During the year ended December 31, 20-2, Bebeto Company completed the following selected transactions:

Apr. 15   Estimated that its 20-2 income tax will be $30,000. Based on this estimate, it will make four quarterly payments of $7,500 each on April 15, June 15, September 15, and December 15. Made the first payment.

25   Declared a semiannual dividend of $.45 per share on common stock to shareholders of record on May 10, payable May 20. Currently, 80,000 shares of $1 par common stock are outstanding.

May 20   Paid the cash dividends.

June 15   Made estimated tax payment of $7,500.

Sept. 15   Made estimated tax payment of $7,500.

Oct. 25   Declared semiannual dividend of $.45 per share on common stock to shareholders of record on November 10, payable on November 20.

Nov. 20   Paid the cash dividends.

Dec. 15   Made estimated tax payment of $7,500.

31   Bebeto's actual 20-2 income tax is $35,000. This amount will be paid by March 15, 20-3. Made adjustment for the additional amount owed.

31   Net income for 20-2 was $100,000. Closed the income summary account.

REQUIRED   Prepare journal entries for the above transactions.

PROBLEM 22A-2 (LO 2) CASH DIVIDENDS, STOCK DIVIDEND, AND STOCK SPLIT During the year ended December 31, 20--, Kuang-fu Company completed the following transactions:

Apr. 15   Declared a semiannual dividend of $.80 per share on preferred stock and $.50 per share on common stock to shareholders of record on May 5, payable on May 10. Currently, 4,000 shares of $100 par preferred stock and 50,000 shares of $1 par common stock are outstanding.

(continued)

May 10   Paid the cash dividends.

Oct. 15   Declared semiannual dividend of $.80 per share on preferred stock and $.50 per share on common stock to shareholders of record on November 5, payable on November 20.

Nov. 20   Paid the cash dividends.

22   Declared a 10% stock dividend to shareholders of record on December 8, distributable on December 16. Market value of the common stock was estimated at $8 per share.

Dec. 16   Issued certificates for common stock dividend.

20   Board of directors declared a two-for-one common stock split.

REQUIRED   Prepare journal entries for the above transactions.

PROBLEM 22A-3 (LO 2/3) CASH DIVIDEND AND APPROPRIATION OF RETAINED EARNINGS On January 1, 20--, MacMillan Company's retained earnings accounts had the following balances:

Appropriated for computer	$ 25,000
Appropriated for warehouse	80,000
Unappropriated retained earnings	600,000
	$705,000

During the year ended December 31, 20--, MacMillan completed the following selected transactions:

Mar. 16   Last year, MacMillan's board of directors appropriated $75,000 for a mainframe computer over a three-year period. Made this year's appropriation for $25,000.

Nov. 5   Purchased a new warehouse for $80,000, paying cash for the total amount.

5   The board of directors returned the amount of retained earnings set aside for the warehouse to unappropriated retained earnings.

12   Declared a cash dividend of $.65 per share on common stock to shareholders of record on December 8, payable on December 19. Currently, 30,000 shares of common stock are outstanding.

Dec. 19   Paid the cash dividends.

REQUIRED   Prepare journal entries for the above transactions.

PROBLEM 22A-4 (LO 1/2/3/4) RETAINED EARNINGS ACCOUNTS AND STATEMENT On January 1, 20--, Glover Company's retained earnings accounts had the following balances:

Appropriated for land acquisition	$ 60,000
Unappropriated retained earnings	900,000
	$960,000

During the year ended December 31, 20--, Glover completed the following selected transactions:

Mar. 20   Declared a semiannual dividend of $.80 per share on preferred stock and $.25 per share on common stock to shareholders of record on April 10, payable on

April 15. Currently, 10,000 shares of $50 par preferred stock and 100,000 shares of $5 par common stock are outstanding.

Apr. 15   Paid the cash dividends.

June 16   Last year, Glover's board of directors appropriated $180,000 for the purchase of land for a future building site over a three-year period. Made this year's appropriation for $60,000.

Oct. 10   Declared semiannual dividend of $.80 per share on preferred stock and $.25 per share on common stock to shareholders of record on November 5, payable on November 10.

Nov. 10   Paid the cash dividends.

17   Declared a 5% stock dividend to shareholders of record on December 8, distributable on December 15. Market value of the common stock was estimated at $18 per share.

Dec. 15   Issued certificates for common stock dividend.

31   Net income for 20-- was $290,000. Closed the income summary account.

REQUIRED   1. Prepare journal entries for the above transactions.

2. Post all entries affecting the appropriated and unappropriated retained earnings accounts to T accounts.

3. Prepare a retained earnings statement for the year ended December 31, 20--.

SERIES B EXERCISES

EXERCISE 22B-1 (LO 1) CORPORATE INCOME TAX Regis Company estimates that its 20-1 income tax will be $100,000. Based on this estimate, it will make four quarterly payments of $25,000 each on April 15, June 15, September 15, and December 15.

1. Prepare the journal entry for April 15.

2. Assume that all four quarterly payments have been entered in the general journal. On December 31, Regis' actual income tax amounts to $112,000. This amount will be paid by March 15, 20-2. Prepare the journal entry to record the additional income tax owed.

EXERCISE 22B-2 (LO 1) CLOSING INCOME SUMMARY TO RETAINED EARNINGS Kennington Company had a net income for 20-- of $90,000. Mueller and Hanson Company had a net loss of $20,000.

1. Prepare the journal entry for Kennington as of December 31, 20--, to close Income Summary into Retained Earnings.

2. Prepare the journal entry for Mueller and Hanson as of December 31, 20--, to close Income Summary into Retained Earnings.

EXERCISE 22B-3 (LO 2) COMMON AND PREFERRED STOCK DIVIDENDS Ramirez Company currently has 100,000 shares of $1 par common stock outstanding and 5,000 shares of $50 par preferred stock outstanding. On July 10, the board of

(continued)

directors declared a semiannual dividend of $.30 per share on common stock to shareholders of record on August 1, payable on August 5.

On July 15, the board of directors declared a semiannual dividend of $5 per share on preferred stock to shareholders of record on August 5, payable on August 10.

Prepare journal entries for the declaration and payment of the common and preferred stock cash dividends.

EXERCISE 22B-4 (LO 2) STOCK DIVIDENDS Martinez Company currently has 200,000 shares of $1 par common stock outstanding. On March 15, a 5% stock dividend was declared to shareholders of record on April 2, distributable on April 14. Market value of the common stock was estimated at $13 per share.

1. Prepare journal entries for the declaration and distribution of the 5% common stock dividend.

2. Assume Martinez Co. declared a stock dividend of 30% rather than 5%. Prepare journal entries for the declaration and distribution of the 30% common stock dividend.

EXERCISE 22B-5 (LO 2) STOCK SPLIT Rogerson Company has 40,000 shares of $2 par common stock outstanding. On July 1, the board of directors declared a two-for-one stock split.

Prepare a memorandum entry in the general journal indicating the new par value and the total number of outstanding shares of common stock.

EXERCISE 22B-6 (LO 3) RETAINED EARNINGS APPROPRIATION On October 2, 20-1, the board of directors of Carr Company appropriated $400,000 of retained earnings for the purpose of buying a new yacht (used for entertaining clients). On July 15, 20-2, the yacht was purchased and the board of directors decided that the appropriation was no longer needed.

Prepare journal entries for the appropriation on October 2, 20-1, and the subsequent return on July 15, 20-2.

EXERCISE 22B-7 (LO 4) RETAINED EARNINGS STATEMENT Womack Company had the following balances as of December 31, 20--:

Retained earnings, January 1	$80,000
Cash dividends declared	15,000
Net income for the year	40,000

Prepare a retained earnings statement for the year ended December 31, 20--.

SERIES B PROBLEMS

PROBLEM 22B-1 (LO 1/2) CASH DIVIDENDS AND INCOME TAXES During the year ended December 31, 20-2, Tatu Company completed the following selected transactions:

Apr. 15   Estimated that its 20-2 income tax will be $160,000. Based on this estimate, it will make four quarterly payments of $40,000 each on April 15, June 15, September 15, and December 15. Made the first payment.

    25   Declared a semiannual dividend of $.50 per share on common stock to share-

holders of record on May 10, payable May 20. Currently, 90,000 shares of $1 par common stock are outstanding.

May 20   Paid the cash dividends.

June 15   Made estimated tax payment of $40,000.

Sept. 15   Made estimated tax payment of $40,000.

Oct. 25   Declared semiannual dividend of $.50 per share on common stock to shareholders of record on November 10, payable on November 20.

Nov. 20   Paid the cash dividends.

Dec. 15   Made estimated tax payment of $40,000.

31   Tatu's actual 20-2 income tax amounts to $174,000. This amount will be paid by March 15, 20-3. Made adjustment for the additional amount owed.

31   Net income for 20-2 was $196,000. Closed the income summary account.

REQUIRED   Prepare journal entries for the above transactions.

PROBLEM 22B-2 (LO 2) CASH DIVIDENDS, STOCK DIVIDEND, AND STOCK SPLIT During the year ended December 31, 20--, Baggio Company completed the following transactions:

Apr. 15   Declared a semiannual dividend of $.65 per share on preferred stock and $.45 per share on common stock to shareholders of record on May 5, payable on May 10. Currently, 6,000 shares of $50 par preferred stock and 70,000 shares of $1 par common stock are outstanding.

May 10   Paid the cash dividends.

Oct. 15   Declared semiannual dividend of $.65 per share on preferred stock and $.45 per share on common stock to shareholders of record on November 5, payable on November 20.

Nov. 20   Paid the cash dividends.

22   Declared a 10% stock dividend to shareholders of record on December 8, distributable on December 16. Market value of the common stock was estimated at $15 per share.

Dec. 16   Issued certificates for common stock dividend.

20   Board of directors declared a two-for-one common stock split.

REQUIRED   Prepare journal entries for the above transactions.

PROBLEM 22B-3 (LO 2/3) CASH DIVIDEND AND APPROPRIATION OF RETAINED EARNINGS On January 1, 20--, Krausert Company's retained earnings accounts had the following balances:

Appropriated for computer	$ 50,000
Appropriated for warehouse	70,000
Unappropriated retained earnings	800,000
	$920,000

(continued)

During the year ended December 31, 20--, Krausert completed the following selected transactions:

Mar. 16   Last year, Krausert's board of directors appropriated $100,000 for a mainframe computer over a two-year period. Made this year's appropriation for $50,000.

Nov. 5   Purchased a warehouse for $70,000, paying cash for the total amount.

5   The board of directors returned the amount of retained earnings set aside for the warehouse to unappropriated retained earnings.

12   Declared a cash dividend of $.90 per share on common stock to shareholders of record on December 8, payable on December 19. Currently, 40,000 shares of common stock are outstanding.

Dec. 19   Paid the cash dividends.

REQUIRED   Prepare journal entries for the above transactions.

W & D

PROBLEM 22B-4 (LO 1/2/3/4) RETAINED EARNINGS ACCOUNTS AND STATEMENT On January 1, 20--, Nguyen Company's retained earnings accounts had the following balances:

Appropriated for land acquisition	$ 75,000
Unappropriated retained earnings	825,000
	$900,000

During the year ended December 31, 20--, Nguyen completed the following selected transactions:

Mar. 20   Declared a semiannual dividend of $.75 per share on preferred stock and $.20 per share on common stock to shareholders of record on April 10, payable on April 15. Currently, 12,000 shares of $50 par preferred stock and 90,000 shares of $2 par common stock are outstanding.

Apr. 15   Paid the cash dividends.

June 16   Last year, Nguyen's board of directors appropriated $150,000 for the purchase of land for a future building site over a two-year period. Made this year's appropriation for $75,000.

Oct. 10   Declared semiannual dividend of $.75 per share on preferred stock and $.20 per share on common stock to shareholders of record on November 5, payable on November 10.

Nov. 10   Paid the cash dividends.

17   Declared a 10% stock dividend to shareholders of record on December 8, distributable on December 15. Market value of the common stock was estimated at $13 per share.

Dec. 15   Issued certificates for common stock dividend.

31   Net income for 20-- was $260,000. Closed the income summary account.

REQUIRED   1. Prepare journal entries for the above transactions.

2. Post all entries affecting the appropriated and unappropriated retained earnings accounts to T accounts.

3. Prepare a retained earnings statement for the year ended December 31, 20--.

MASTERY PROBLEM

W & D

On January 1, 20-1, Dover Company's retained earnings accounts had the following balances:

Appropriated for printing press	$ 50,000
Unappropriated retained earnings	800,000
	$850,000

During the year ended December 31, 20--, Dover completed the following selected transactions:

Mar. 15   Declared a semiannual dividend of $.30 per share on preferred stock and $.40 per share on common stock to shareholders of record on April 5, payable on April 10. Currently, 5,000 shares of $10 par preferred stock and 30,000 shares of $2 par common stock are outstanding.

Apr. 10   Paid the cash dividend.

July 2   Last year, Dover's board of directors appropriated $100,000 for a printing press over a two-year period. Made this year's appropriation for $50,000.

Sept. 15   Declared semiannual dividend of $.30 per share on preferred stock and $.40 per share on common stock to shareholders of record on October 5, payable on October 10.

Oct. 10   Paid the cash dividend.

Nov. 10   Board of directors declared a two-for-one common stock split.

Dec. 31   Net income for 20-- was $135,000. Closed the income summary account.

REQUIRED   1.   Prepare journal entries for the above transactions.

2.   Post all entries affecting the appropriated and unappropriated retained earnings accounts to T accounts.

3.   Prepare a retained earnings statement for the year ended December 31, 20--.

Self-Study Test Questions

True/False

1. Income taxes are a unique expense of the corporate form of business. _____

2. The adjusting and closing process at the end of the period is virtually the same for corporations as for sole proprietorships and partnerships. _____

3. A distribution of earnings by a corporation to its stockholders is known as a dividend. _____

4. A dividend payable in cash is known as a stock dividend. _____

5. When accounting for the declaration and payment of dividends, the date of record requires a journal entry. _____

Multiple Choice

1. A proportionate distribution of shares of a corporation's own stock to its stockholders is called a _____

   (a) stock dividend.   (c) stock split.
   (b) cash dividend.   (d) appropriation.

2. When a stock dividend is declared, the journal entry will include a credit to _____

   (a) Retained Earnings.   (c) Stock Dividends Payable.
   (b) Stock Dividends Distributable. (d) Stock Dividends Declared.

3. Stock Dividends Distributable is classified on the balance sheet as a(n) _____

   (a) asset.   (c) expense.
   (b) liability.   (d) stockholders' equity.

4. The payment of a cash dividend will include a _____

   (a) debit to Dividends Declared.   (c) credit to Cash.
   (b) credit to Dividends Payable.   (d) debit to Retained Earnings.

5. When retained earnings is appropriated, total retained earnings _____

   (a) remains the same.   (c) decreases.
   (b) increases.   (d) increases or decreases, depending on the amount.

The answers to the Self-Study Test Questions are at the end of the text.

Corporations: Bonds

Several years have passed since Chapter 22, and Finny Co. has an opportunity to expand its operations into nearby states. To do so, it needs substantial additional resources. After his experience dealing with stockholders who wanted too much of the company's profits paid out as cash dividends, Mike Finbar is reluctant to issue additional stock. Finny Co. has used promissory notes to borrow necessary funds several times, but the amount and duration of these are not what the company needs now.

Mike's accountant suggests that the company consider issuing bonds to obtain the additional resources. He says that bonds are different from notes. He warns that bonds can be riskier than stock, but that the risk should not be a problem for a successful company like Finny. How are bonds different from notes? How are bonds riskier than stock?

In Chapters 21 and 22 we learned how to account for two major sources of funds for a corporation—capital stock and retained earnings. In this chapter, we turn our attention to a third major source of funds—bonds.

Bonds are similar to the promissory notes payable we saw in Chapter 17. Both are formal, written promises to pay an amount of money at a specified date. The main differences are that bonds are usually for larger sums of money and for longer time periods.

TYPES OF BONDS AND DETERMINATION OF SALES PRICE

LO 1   Describe the types of bonds and how their sales price is determined.

A **bond** is a written promise to pay a specific sum of money at a specific future date. Bonds and stock often are mentioned in the same breath, but they are quite different. A bond is a debt of the corporation—a promise to pay certain amounts of money. If these payments are not made, the creditors can force the company into bankruptcy. Stock represents corporate ownership or equity; there is no promise to pay any definite amount of money. Bondholders are creditors of a corporation; stockholders are owners.

Bonds usually are issued in denominations of $1,000 each. For example, if a corporation issues $300,000 of bonds, this usually means it issues 300 individual bonds, each worth $1,000. This enables the issuing corporation to obtain large amounts of money by selling the bonds to many investors.

Classification of Bonds

"Anatomy of a Deal: Finance Growth with Debt" (http://heintz.swcollege.com) Learn about two important concepts related to debt.

To appeal to different types of investors, bonds come with many different features. Based on some of these features, bonds can be classified as to (1) security, (2) timing of payment of principal, and (3) identification of ownership.

Security.   All bonds are either secured or unsecured. A **secured bond** is one that is backed by specific corporate assets. A common type of secured bond is a **mortgage bond**—a bond secured by a mortgage on corporate property such as real estate or equipment.

An **unsecured bond** is backed solely by the general credit of the corporation, rather than by any specific assets. These bonds are called **debenture bonds**.

Timing of Payment of Principal.   The **principal** of a bond is the amount to be paid to the bondholder at maturity. Based on the provisions made for payment of the principal, four types of bonds can be identified.

1. **Term bonds**—bonds that all have the same maturity date.

2. **Serial bonds**—bonds issued in a series so that a specified amount of the bonds matures each year.

3. **Convertible bonds**—bonds that give the holder the option of exchanging the bonds for capital stock of the corporation.

4. **Callable bonds**—bonds that give the issuing corporation the option of calling the bonds for redemption before the maturity date.

Identification of Ownership. There are two types of bonds according to identification of ownership.

1. **Registered bonds**—bonds whose ownership is recorded (registered) in the corporate records. The corporation maintains a record of the name and address of each owner. Any change of ownership must be registered with the corporation.

2. **Coupon bonds (bearer bonds)**—bonds whose ownership generally is not recorded by the corporation. Change of ownership is accomplished simply by delivering the bond. A coupon bond has interest coupons attached, one for each interest period during the life of the bond. As each coupon comes due, the holder of the bond removes the coupon and presents it to a bank for payment. Corporations no longer issue coupon bonds, but many old ones are still in circulation.

Determining Sales Price

At first glance, you would expect a $1,000 bond to sell for $1,000, its **face value**. But, for various reasons, bonds often do not sell at their face value. Two of the more important factors in determining the price at which bonds will sell are:

1. the rate of interest (**contract** or **coupon rate**) on the bonds.

2. the current **market rate** of interest on similar investments.

To illustrate, assume that Watkin Corp. wants to sell $400,000 of 10%, 10-year bonds. If the current market rate on similar investments is 10%, the bonds will sell at their face value of $400,000. But if the current market rate is 11%, Watkin's bonds will sell at a **discount**, or at a price less than their face value of $400,000. This is because the lower interest rate (10% vs. 11%) on Watkin's bonds makes them less valuable. In simple terms, investors will not pay full price for Watkin's bonds with a 10% interest rate if they can get a similar investment with an 11% interest rate.

What if the current market rate is 9%? In this case, Watkin's bonds will sell at a **premium**, or at a price in excess of their face value of $400,000. This is because the higher interest rate (10% vs. 9%) on the bonds makes them more valuable.

Figure 23-1 summarizes the conditions in which bonds will sell at face value, premium, and discount.

> **LEARNING KEY:** To determine whether a bond will sell at a price equal to, greater than, or less than face value, compare the contract and market interest rates.

FIGURE 23-1 Interest Rates and Bond Selling Prices

INTEREST RATE				SELLING PRICE
Contract rate	=	Market rate	=	Face value
Contract rate	>	Market rate	>	Face value (Premium)
Contract rate	<	Market rate	<	Face value (Discount)

Bond prices usually are stated using numbers such as 95, 99, or 102. These numbers are percentages of the face values of bond issues. Thus, a $100,000 bond issue sold at 95 has a market price of $95,000 ($100,000 × .95). A similar issue sold at 102 has a market price of $102,000. Numbers below 100 indicate discount issues. Numbers above 100 indicate premium issues.

A BROADER VIEW

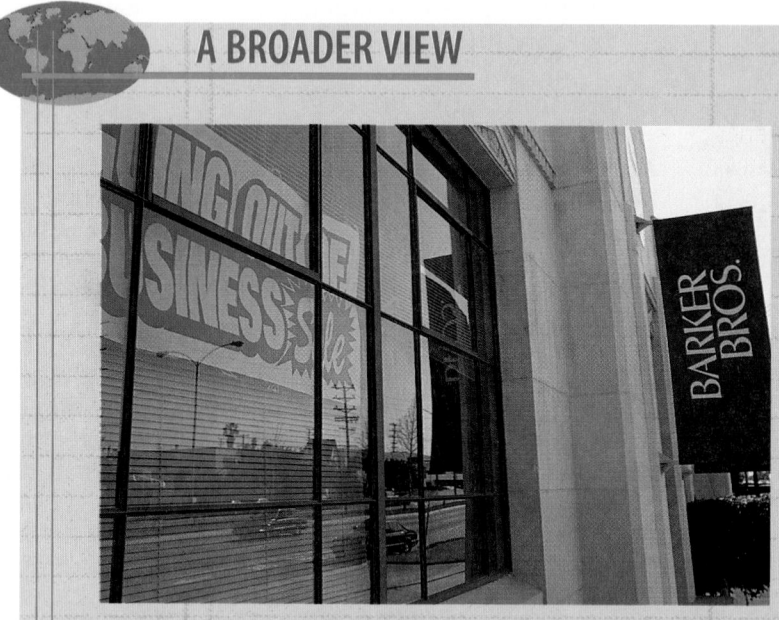

DEBT CAN BE DANGEROUS

The independent auditors' report on the recent financial statements of Hammers Plastic Recycling Corp. of Iowa Falls, Iowa, included the following passage: "…The company's … inability to satisfy debt obligations as they become due … raise substantial doubt about the entity's ability to continue as a going concern." In other words, the independent auditors doubted that Hammers would be able to survive as a business, in part because the company could not make its debt payments.

This is a good example of the risk dimension of debt. By issuing stock, a company gives up ownership interest in the business. But when bonds are issued, a company runs the risk of going bankrupt if it cannot make the payments on its debts. Careful analysis and planning are needed in deciding how to finance a business.

Chapter 23   Corporations: Bonds   **831**

ACCOUNTING FOR BONDS ISSUED AT FACE VALUE

LO 2   Account for bonds issued at face value.

To illustrate the accounting for bonds, we will use bonds issued by Watkin Corp. Assume the following facts regarding these bonds:

Date of issue and sale:	April 1, 20-1
Principal amount:	$400,000
Denomination of each bond:	$1,000
Life of bonds:	10 years
Contract rate:	10%, payable semiannually each April 1 and October 1

Issuance

Assume that on April 1, 20-1, the contract rate of 10% on Watkin's bonds is the same as the current market rate. In this case, the bonds will sell at their face value. The journal entry for the sale and issuance of Watkin's bonds at face value on April 1, 20-1 is:

5	Apr.	1	Cash		400 0 0 0 00		5
6			Bonds Payable			400 0 0 0 00	6
7			Issued bonds at face value				7

Bonds payable is reported as a long-term liability on the corporation balance sheet.

Interest Expense

The journal entry for the first semiannual interest payment of $20,000 (10% × $400,000 × ½ year) on October 1, 20-1 is:

18	Oct.	1	Bond Interest Expense		20 0 0 0 00		18
19			Cash			20 0 0 0 00	19
20			Paid semiannual interest on bonds				20

On December 31, an adjusting entry is needed for interest accrued on the bonds since the last interest payment date, October 1, 20-1. Three months' interest has accrued (October 1–December 31), which amounts to $10,000 (10% × $400,000 × ¼ year). The adjusting entry therefore is:

25	Dec.	31	Bond Interest Expense		10 0 0 0 00		25
26			Bond Interest Payable			10 0 0 0 00	26

After the October 1 and December 31 entries are posted, Bond Interest Expense and Bond Interest Payable appear in T account form as follows:

Bond Interest Expense			Bond Interest Payable	
20-1			20-1	
Oct. 1	20,000		Dec. 31	10,000
Dec. 31	10,000			
	30,000			

The balance in the bond interest expense account is the total interest expense incurred from April 1 to December 31. Bond Interest Expense is reported as other expense on the income statement. The balance in the bond interest payable account is the accrued liability on December 31. Bond Interest Payable is reported as a current liability on the balance sheet.

The December 31, 20-1, adjusting entry normally is reversed as of January 1, 20-2, as follows:

| 8 | Jan. | 1 | Bond Interest Payable | | 10 | 0 | 0 | 0 | 00 | | | | | | | 8 |
| 9 | | | Bond Interest Expense | | | | | | | | 10 | 0 | 0 | 0 | 00 | 9 |

The next semiannual interest payment on April 1, 20-2, is made exactly like the entry on October 1, 20-1. After posting the reversing entry and the April 1 interest payment entry, Bond Interest Expense and Bond Interest Payable appear in T account form as follows:

Bond Interest Expense				**Bond Interest Payable**	
20-1					20-1	
Oct. 1	20,000				Dec. 31	10,000
Dec. 31	10,000	Dec. 31 Close 30,000	20-2			
20-2		20-2	Jan. 1 Rev. 10,000			
Apr. 1	20,000	Jan. 1 Rev. 10,000				

ACCOUNTING FOR BONDS ISSUED AT A PREMIUM

LO 3 Account for bonds issued at a premium.

Recall that if the contract rate on bonds is greater than the current market rate, the bonds will sell at a premium. When bonds are issued at a premium, both bonds payable on the balance sheet and interest expense on the income statement are affected.

Issuance

Assume that on April 1, 20-1, the contract rate of 10% on Watkin's bonds is greater than the current market rate, so that the bonds sell for 106. This means that the bonds sell for $424,000 ($400,000 × 106%), a premium of $24,000. The journal entry for the sale and issuance of Watkin's bonds at a premium on April 1, 20-1, is:

5	Apr.	1	Cash		424	0	0	0	00							5
6			Bonds Payable								400	0	0	0	00	6
7			Premium on Bonds Payable								24	0	0	0	00	7
8			Issued bonds at a premium													8

Premium on Bonds Payable is an adjunct-liability account. It is added to bonds payable on the corporate balance sheet. On Watkin's balance sheet immediately after issuing the $400,000 of bonds for $424,000, the bonds payable and premium would appear as follows:

Long-term liabilities:													
Bonds payable		$400	0	0	0	00							
Premium on bonds payable		24	0	0	0	00	$424	0	0	0	00		

The sum of bonds payable and premium on bonds payable is called the **carrying value** of the bonds.

Interest Expense and Premium Amortization

When bonds are issued at a premium, the amount of interest actually paid is not the true interest expense. This is because the premium received when the bonds are issued effectively reduces the cost of borrowing. For example, Watkin received $424,000 for its bonds but will have to pay back only $400,000, the face value of the bonds. This $24,000 reduction ($424,000 – $400,000) in the cost of borrowing is spread over the life of the bond issue by adjusting interest expense on a regular basis.

The process of adjusting the bond interest expense account for any premium or discount is called **amortization** of the premium or discount. Two commonly used methods of amortizing premium (or discount) over the life of a bond are (1) effective interest and (2) straight-line. The effective interest method is recommended, but the straight-line method is much simpler to apply and generally provides acceptable results. We will use the straight-line method. The effective interest method is covered in more advanced courses.

Using the straight-line method, $1,200 of the premium on Watkin's bonds is amortized each semiannual interest period, calculated as follows:

$$\frac{\text{Premium}}{\text{Life of Bonds}} \times \tfrac{1}{2}\,\text{Year} = \frac{\$24,000}{10\,\text{Years}} \times \tfrac{1}{2}\,\text{Year} = \$1,200$$

The entry for the first semiannual interest payment and amortization of bond premium on October 1, 20-1, is:

18	Oct.	1	Bond Interest Expense		18	8	0	0	00						18
19			Premium on Bonds Payable		1	2	0	0	00						19
20			Cash							20	0	0	0	00	20
21			Paid semiannual interest and												21
22			amortized premium on bonds												22

Note that the premium amortization does not affect the amount of cash paid. The amortization simply reduces the bond interest expense for the period and the carrying value of the bonds.

LEARNING KEY: Premium amortization reduces the interest expense and carrying value of the bonds but has no effect on the amount of cash paid.

On December 31, an adjusting entry is needed both for accrued interest and for premium amortization for the period from October 1 through December 31. Three months' interest of $10,000 (10% × $400,000 × ¼ year) has accrued. Three months' premium of $600 ($24,000 ÷ 10 × ¼ year) should be amortized. The adjusting entry is:

25	Dec.	31	Bond Interest Expense		9 4 0 0 00			25
26			Premium on Bonds Payable		6 0 0 00			26
27			Bond Interest Payable			10 0 0 0 00		27

After the October 1 and December 31 entries are posted, Bond Interest Expense, Bond Interest Payable, and Premium on Bonds Payable appear in T account form as follows:

Bond Interest Expense			**Bond Interest Payable**	
Oct. 1	18,800		Dec. 31	10,000
Dec. 31	9,400			
	28,200			

Premium on Bonds Payable			
Oct. 1	1,200	Apr. 1	24,000
Dec. 31	600		
		Dec. 31 Bal.	22,200

The December 31, 20-1, adjusting entry normally is reversed as of January 1, 20-2. The next semiannual interest and premium amortization entry on April 1, 20-2, is made exactly like the entry on October 1, 20-1. Columns 2, 3, and 4 in Figure 23-2 summarize the semiannual interest and premium amortization entries for the life of the bonds.

FIGURE 23-2 Premium Amortization Schedule

BOND PREMIUM AMORTIZATION SCHEDULE STRAIGHT-LINE METHOD						
(1)	(2)	(3)	(4)	(5)	(6)	(7)
Date	Interest Expense Debit	Premium on Bonds Payable Debit	Cash Credit	Bonds Payable Balance	Premium on Bonds Payable Balance	Carrying Value of Bonds [(5) + (6)]
4/1/-1				$400,000	$24,000	$424,000
10/1/-1	$18,800	$1,200	$20,000	400,000	22,800	422,800
4/1/-2*	18,800	1,200	20,000	400,000	21,600	421,600
10/1/-2	18,800	1,200	20,000	400,000	20,400	420,400
–	–	–	–	–	–	–
–	–	–	–	–	–	–
–	–	–	–	–	–	–
4/1/10	18,800	1,200	20,000	400,000	2,400	402,400
10/1/10	18,800	1,200	20,000	400,000	1,200	401,200
3/31/11	18,800	1,200	20,000	400,000	0	400,000

* The entry for the first interest payment each year assumes that the adjusting entry at December 31 of the preceding year was reversed.

Note that the effect of the premium amortization is to reduce both the interest expense for the period and the balance in the premium on bonds payable account. In fact, the premium on bonds payable account balance is gradually reduced to zero over the life of the bonds, as shown in column 6 of Figure 23-2. Recall that Premium on Bonds Payable is an adjunct-liability account. It is added to bonds payable on the balance sheet. The amount that Watkin will have to pay at maturity is $400,000. By amortizing the premium on bonds payable over the life of the bonds, the carrying value of the bonds decreases to $400,000 at maturity, as shown in column 7 of Figure 23-2.

> Consistent with the matching concept, note that the premium is spread over the period benefited—the ten-year life of the bonds.

ACCOUNTING FOR BONDS ISSUED AT A DISCOUNT

LO 4 Account for bonds issued at a discount.

If the contract rate on bonds is less than the current market rate, the bonds will sell at a discount. When bonds are issued at a discount, both bonds payable on the balance sheet and interest expense on the income statement are affected.

Issuance

Assume that on April 1, 20-1, the contract rate on Watkin's bonds is less than the current market rate, so that the bonds sell for 96. This means that the bonds sell for $384,000 ($400,000 × 96%), a discount of $16,000. The journal entry for the sale and issuance of Watkin's bonds at a discount on April 1, 20-1, is:

5	Apr.	1	Cash		384	0	0	0	00						5
6			Discount on Bonds Payable		16	0	0	0	00						6
7			Bonds Payable							400	0	0	0	00	7
8			Issued bonds at a discount												8

Discount on Bonds Payable is a contra-liability account. It is deducted from bonds payable on the corporate balance sheet. On Watkin's balance sheet immediately after issuing the $400,000 of bonds for $384,000, the bonds payable and discount would appear as follows:

Long-term liabilities:													
Bonds payable	$400	0	0	0	00								
Discount on bonds payable	16	0	0	0	00	$384	0	0	0	00			

> In a sense, Discount on Bonds Payable is a "loss." Watkin received only $384,000 in exchange for a promise to pay $400,000, a "loss" of $16,000. This loss is spread as an "interest expense increase" over the life of the bonds. As the discount is waiting to be spread, it is stored as a debit balance in a contra-liability account.

Bonds payable less the discount on bonds payable is called the **carrying value** of the bonds.

Interest Expense and Discount Amortization

When bonds are sold at a discount, we have a situation similar to what we saw in the case of bonds sold at a premium. The interest actually paid is not the true interest expense. This is because the discount given when the bonds are issued effectively increases the cost of borrowing. For example, Watkin received only $384,000 for its bonds but will have to pay back $400,000, the face value of the bonds. This $16,000 increase ($400,000 – $384,000) in the cost of borrowing is amortized over the life of the bond issue by adjusting interest expense on a regular basis.

Using the straight-line method, $800 of the discount on Watkin's bonds is amortized each semiannual interest period, calculated as follows:

$$\frac{\text{Discount}}{\text{Life of Bonds}} \times \text{½ Year} = \frac{\$16,000}{10\text{ years}} \times \text{½ Year} = \$800$$

The entry for the first semiannual interest payment and amortization of bond discount on October 1, 20-1, is:

				Debit	Credit	
18	Oct.	1	Bond Interest Expense	20 8 0 0 00		18
19			Discount on Bonds Payable		8 0 0 00	19
20			Cash		20 0 0 0 00	20
21			Paid semiannual interest and			21
22			amortized discount on bonds			22

Note that the discount amortization does not affect the amount of cash paid. The amortization simply increases the bond interest expense for the period and the carrying value of the bonds.

 LEARNING KEY: Discount amortization increases the interest expense and carrying value of the bonds but has no effect on the amount of cash paid.

On December 31, an adjusting entry is needed both for accrued interest and for discount amortization for the period from October 1 through December 31. Three months' interest of $10,000 (10% × $400,000 × ¼ year) has accrued. Three months' discount of $400 ($16,000 ÷ 10 × ¼ year) should be amortized. The adjusting entry is:

				Debit	Credit	
25	Dec.	31	Bond Interest Expense	10 4 0 0 00		25
26			Bond Interest Payable		10 0 0 0 00	26
27			Discount on Bonds Payable		4 0 0 00	27

After the October 1 and December 31 entries are posted, Bond Interest Expense, Bond Interest Payable, and Discount on Bonds Payable appear in T account form as follows:

Bond Interest Expense			Bond Interest Payable	
Oct. 1	20,800		Dec. 31	10,000
Dec. 31	10,400			
	31,200			

Discount on Bonds Payable			
20-1		20-1	
Apr. 1	16,000	Oct. 1	800
		Dec. 31	400
Dec. 31 Bal.	14,800		

The December 31 adjusting entry normally is reversed as of January 1, 20-2. The next semiannual interest and discount amortization entry on April 1, 20-2, is made exactly like the entry on October 1, 20-1. Columns 2, 3, and 4 in Figure

23-3 summarize the semiannual interest and discount amortization entries for the life of the bonds.

FIGURE 23-3 Discount Amortization Schedule

BOND DISCOUNT AMORTIZATION SCHEDULE **STRAIGHT-LINE METHOD**						
(1)	(2)	(3)	(4)	(5)	(6)	(7)
Date	Interest Expense Debit	Discount on Bonds Payable Credit	Cash Credit	Bonds Payable Balance	Discount on Bonds Payable Balance	Carrying Value of Bonds [(5) – (6)]
4/1/-1				$400,000	$16,000	$384,000
10/1/-1	$20,800	$800	$20,000	400,000	15,200	384,800
4/1/-2*	20,800	800	20,000	400,000	14,400	385,600
10/1/-2	20,800	800	20,000	400,000	13,600	386,400
–	–	–	–	–	–	–
–	–	–	–	–	–	–
–	–	–	–	–	–	–
4/1/10	20,800	800	20,000	400,000	1,600	398,400
10/1/10	20,800	800	20,000	400,000	800	399,200
3/31/11	20,800	800	20,000	400,000	0	400,000

*The entry for the first interest payment each year assumes that the adjusting entry at December 31 of the preceding year was reversed.

> Consistent with the matching concept, note that the discount is spread over the period benefited—the ten-year life of the bonds.

Note that the effect of the discount amortization is to increase the interest expense for the period and to decrease the balance in the discount on bonds payable account. In fact, the discount on bonds payable account balance is gradually reduced to zero over the life of the bonds, as shown in column 6 of Figure 23-3. Recall that Discount on Bonds Payable is a contra-liability account. It is subtracted from bonds payable on the balance sheet. The amount that Watkin will have to pay at maturity is $400,000. By amortizing the discount on bonds payable over the life of the bonds, the carrying value of the bonds increases to $400,000 at maturity, as shown in column 7 of Figure 23-3.

ACCOUNTING FOR BOND REDEMPTION AND SINKING FUNDS

LO 5   Account for bond redemption and bond sinking funds.

Usually, bonds issued by a corporation are redeemed at face value at their maturity. By that date, the entire amount of any premium or discount should have been amortized. To enter the redemption, Bonds Payable is debited and Cash is credited for the face value of the bonds. For example, if the $400,000 of Watkin bonds are redeemed at maturity, the following journal entry is made:

22	Bonds Payable	400 0 0 0 00		22
23	Cash		400 0 0 0 00	23
24	Redeemed bonds at face value			24

Corporations may redeem part or all of a bond issue before maturity. If the bonds are callable, a corporation may call in the bonds before they mature. The call price is defined in the original bond agreement. If the bonds are not callable, a corporation can purchase its bonds in the open market at the market price. When bonds are redeemed before maturity, any accrued interest must be paid and the premium or discount amortization must be brought up to date. Entries for doing so are the same as those illustrated in previous sections of the chapter.

Redemption of Bonds at a Loss

Usually, there is a gain or loss involved when bonds are redeemed before maturity. The gain or loss is the difference between the amount paid to redeem the bonds and the carrying value of the bonds. When bonds are issued at face value, the carrying value equals the face value throughout the life of the bonds. When bonds are issued at a premium or discount, the carrying value changes over the life of the bonds, as the premium or discount is amortized.

 LEARNING KEY: To determine the amount of gain or loss on redemption of bonds, compare the redemption price with the carrying value of the bonds.

To illustrate, consider the Watkin Corp. $400,000, 10% bonds that were sold at face value. If $40,000 of the bonds are redeemed at 103, there is a loss of $1,200 on redemption of the bonds, calculated as follows:

Cash paid ($40,000 × 103%)	$41,200
Less carrying value (= face value) of bonds	40,000
Loss on redemption	$ 1,200

The journal entry for this transaction is:

31		Bonds Payable	40 0 0 0 00		31
32		Loss on Bonds Redeemed	1 2 0 0 00		32
33		Cash		41 2 0 0 00	33
34		Redeemed bonds at a loss			34

Loss on Bonds Redeemed is reported as an extraordinary item near the bottom of the income statement. Extraordinary Loss on Early Extinguishment of Debt is an appropriate title.

Now consider the Watkin Corp. bonds that were sold at a premium (106) for $424,000. Assume that eight years after the issuance, Watkin redeems $40,000 of this issue at 103. The carrying value of these bonds is calculated as follows:

Issue price ($40,000 × 106)	$42,400	
Face value	40,000	
Premium received at issuance		$ 2,400
Premium amortized per year ($2,400 ÷ 10 yrs) $	240	
Number of years since issuance	× 8	
Total premium amortized in 8 years		1,920
Unamortized premium		$ 480
Face value		40,000
Carrying value		$40,480

Thus, after the interest payment and premium amortization have been entered on April 1, 20-9, the carrying value of the $40,000 of bonds is $40,480. There is a loss of $720 on redemption of the bonds, calculated as follows:

Cash paid ($40,000 × 103)	$41,200
Less carrying value	40,480
Loss on redemption	$ 720

The journal entry for this transaction is:

5	Apr.	1	Bonds Payable				40	0	0	0	00							5
6			Premium on Bonds Payable					4	8	0	00							6
7			Loss on Bonds Redeemed					7	2	0	00							7
8			Cash									41	2	0	0	00		8
9			Redeemed bonds at a loss															9

Redemption of Bonds at a Gain

To illustrate the redemption of bonds at a gain, let's look again at two examples. Assume that $40,000 of Watkin's bonds that were issued at face value are redeemed at 97. In this case, Watkin has a gain of $1,200 on redemption of the bonds, calculated as follows:

Carrying value (= face value) of bonds	$40,000
Less cash paid ($40,000 × 97)	38,800
Gain on bonds redeemed	$ 1,200

The journal entry for this transaction is:

31			Bonds Payable				40	0	0	0	00						31
32			Gain on Bonds Redeemed						1	2	0	0	00				32
33			Cash						38	8	0	0	00				33
34			Redeemed bonds at a gain														34

Gain on Bonds Redeemed is reported as an extraordinary item on the income statement.

Now consider the Watkin Corp. bonds that were sold at a discount (96) for $384,000. Assume that six years after issuance, Watkin redeems $40,000 of this issue at 97. The carrying value of these bonds is calculated as follows:

Face value	$40,000	
Issue price ($40,000 × 96)	38,400	
Discount at issuance		$1,600
Discount amortized per year ($1,600 ÷ 10 yrs.) $	160	
Number of years since issuance	× 6	
Total discount amortized in 6 years		960
Unamortized discount		$ 640
Face value		$40,000
Less unamortized discount		640
Carrying value		$39,360

Thus, after the interest payment and discount amortization have been entered on April 1, 20-7, the carrying value of the $40,000 of bonds is $39,360. There is a gain of $560 on redemption of the bonds, calculated as follows:

Carrying value of bonds	$39,360
Less cash paid ($40,000 × 97)	38,800
Gain on redemption	$ 560

The journal entry for this redemption is:

5	Apr.	1	Bonds Payable	40 0 0 0 00		5
6			Discount on Bonds Payable		6 4 0 00	6
7			Gain on Bonds Redeemed		5 6 0 00	7
8			Cash		38 8 0 0 00	8
9			Redeemed bonds at a gain			9

Bond Sinking Funds

The formal written agreement for issuing bonds is called the **bond indenture**. Bond indentures for term bonds frequently require the accumulation and investment of money over a period of years. This is to provide the amount needed to redeem the bonds at maturity. Such accumulations are known as **bond sinking funds**. The sinking fund usually is administered by a trustee. The corporation makes periodic cash deposits with the trustee. The trustee is responsible for investing the cash and accumulating amounts necessary to redeem the bonds at maturity.

To illustrate, assume that the bond indenture for the Watkin bonds required Watkin to make deposits of $30,000 to a trustee each year. The entry for each deposit is:

12			Bond Sinking Fund	30 0 0 0 00		12
13			Cash		30 0 0 0 00	13
14			Made sinking fund deposit			14

The trustee invests the cash and adds any earnings on these investments to the sinking fund. Assume that Watkin's trustee reports sinking fund earnings of $2,800 for the year. The following entry is made:

26			Bond Sinking Fund	2 8 0 0 00		26
27			Sinking Fund Earnings		2 8 0 0 00	27
28			Annual sinking fund earnings			28

When the bonds mature, the trustee sells all of the sinking fund investments. The corporation then deposits additional cash with the trustee so that the sum of the periodic deposits, the sinking fund earnings, and the additional cash is sufficient to redeem the bonds. When the Watkin bonds are redeemed at maturity by the trustee, the following entry is made:

5			Bonds Payable	400 0 0 0 00		5
6			Bond Sinking Fund		400 0 0 0 00	6
7			Redeemed bonds at face value			7

If any cash is left in the sinking fund after all of the bonds are redeemed, the cash is returned to the corporation. Assume that the sinking fund has a balance of $960 after all the bonds are redeemed. The following entry is made:

18		Cash			9	6	0	00							18
19		Bond Sinking Fund								9	6	0	00		19
20		Received sinking fund balance													20

Sinking fund earnings are reported as other revenue on the corporation income statement. The bond sinking fund is reported under Investments on the corporation balance sheet.

Learning Objectives	Key Points to Remember
1 **Describe the types of bonds and how their sales price is determined.**	Bonds can be classified as to (1) security, (2) timing of payment of principal, and (3) identification of ownership. If the bond and market interest rates are equal, bonds will sell at face value. If the bond interest rate is greater than the market rate, bonds will sell at a premium. If the bond interest rate is less than the market rate, bonds will sell at a discount.
2 **Account for bonds issued at face value.**	The journal entries for bond issuance, interest payments, premium or discount amortization, and redemption can be summarized as follows:
3 **Account for bonds issued at a premium.**	
4 **Account for bonds issued at a discount.**	

	BONDS ISSUED AT		
	FACE	**PREMIUM**	**DISCOUNT**

Issuance	Cash
	  Bonds Payable
		Cash
		  Bonds Payable
		  Premium on Bonds Payable
			Cash
			Discount on Bonds Payable
			  Bonds Payable

Interest Payment and Amortization	Interest Expense
	  Cash
		Interest Expense
		Premium on Bonds Payable
		  Cash
			Interest Expense
			  Discount on Bonds Payable
			  Cash

Redemption at:
  Carrying Value
	Bonds Payable
	  Cash
		Bonds Payable
		Premium on Bonds Payable
		  Cash
			Bonds Payable
			  Discount on Bonds Payable
			  Cash

< Carrying Value	Bonds Payable
	  Gain on Redemption
	  Cash
		Bonds Payable
		Premium on Bonds Payable
		  Gain on Redemption
		  Cash
			Bonds Payable
			  Discount on Bonds Payable
			  Gain on Redemption
			  Cash

> Carrying Value	Bonds Payable
	  Loss on Redemption
	  Cash
		Bonds Payable
		Premium on Bonds Payable
		  Loss on Redemption
		  Cash
			Bonds Payable
			  Loss on Redemption
			  Discount on Bonds Payable
			  Cash

5 **Account for bond redemption and bond sinking funds.**	The gain or loss on redemption of bonds is the difference between the amount paid to redeem the bonds and the carrying value of the bonds. Gains and losses on bonds redeemed are reported as extraordinary items on the income statement. Bond sinking funds are used to accumulate the money needed for bond redemption. The sum of the amounts deposited in the sinking fund, sinking fund earnings, and any additional cash deposited in the sinking fund by the company when the bonds mature is used to redeem the bonds.

Bonds are usually for larger sums of money and for longer periods of time than notes. Bonds are riskier than stock in the sense that bonds are debts of the company rather than ownership interests. The company promises to pay certain amounts of money to bondholders. If the payments are not made, the creditors can force the company into bankruptcy.

KEY TERMS

amortization, (833)   The process of adjusting the bond interest expense account for any premium or discount.

bearer bonds, (829)   See coupon bonds.

bond, (828)   A written promise to pay a specific sum of money at a specific future date.

bond indenture, (840)   The formal written agreement for issuing bonds.

bond sinking funds, (840)   The accumulation and investment of money over a period of years to provide the amount needed for the redemption of bonds.

callable bonds, (828)   Bonds that give the issuing corporation the option of calling the bonds for redemption before the maturity date.

carrying value, (833)   Bonds payable plus the premium or less the discount on bonds payable.

contract rate, (829)   The rate of interest that the bonds pay based on face value.

convertible bonds, (828)   Bonds that give the holder the option of exchanging the bonds for capital stock of the corporation.

coupon bonds, (829)   Bonds whose ownership generally is not recorded by the corporation. These bonds have interest coupons attached.

coupon rate, (829)   See contract rate.

debenture bonds, (828)   See unsecured bonds.

discount, (829)   The difference between the face value and the price of a bond when the current market interest rate is greater than the coupon rate of that bond.

face value, (829)   The amount written on the face of the bond certificate.

market rate, (829)   The interest rate that can be earned on investments similar to the specific bond issue.

mortgage bonds, (828)   Bonds secured by a mortgage on corporate property such as real estate or equipment.

premium, (829)   The difference between the face value and the price of a bond when the current market interest rate is less than the coupon rate of that bond.

principal, (828)   The amount to be paid to the bondholder at maturity.

registered bonds, (829)   Bonds whose ownership is recorded in the corporate records.

secured bonds, (828)   Bonds that are backed by specific corporate assets.

serial bonds, (828)   Bonds issued in a series so that a specified amount of the bonds matures each year.

term bonds, (828)   Bonds that all have the same maturity date.

unsecured bonds, (828)   Bonds backed solely by the general credit of the corporation issuing the bonds.

DEMONSTRATION PROBLEM

Brooks Inc.'s fiscal year ends December 31. Selected transactions for the period 20-1 through 20-8 involving bonds payable issued by Brooks are as follows:

20-1

Nov. 30 Issued $800,000 of ten-year, 9%, callable bonds dated November 30, 20-1, for $776,000. Interest is payable semiannually on November 30 and May 31. The bond indenture provides that Brooks is to pay to the trustee bank $30,000 by June 15 of each year (except the tenth year) as a sinking fund for the retirement of the bonds on call or at maturity.

Dec. 31 Made the adjusting entry for interest payable and amortized one month's discount on the bonds (straight-line method).

20-2

Jan. 2 Reversed the adjusting entry for interest payable and bond discount amortization.

May 31 Paid the semiannual interest on the bonds and amortized six months' discount.

June 15 Paid the sinking fund trustee $30,000.

Nov. 30 Paid the semiannual interest on the bonds and amortized six months' discount.

Dec. 31 Made the adjusting entry for interest payable and amortized one month's discount on the bonds.

31 Sinking fund earnings for the year were $1,100.

20-8

June 15 Paid the sinking fund trustee $30,000.

Nov. 30 Paid the semiannual interest on the bonds and amortized six months' discount.

30 Redeemed the bonds, which were called at 102.
The balance in the bond discount account is $7,200 after the payment of interest and amortization of discount have been entered. The cash balance in the sinking fund is $320,000 which is applied to the redemption. Paid the sinking fund trustee the additional cash needed to pay off the bonds. [Hint: First make the entry for payment to the sinking fund, then make the entry for redemption of the bonds.]

REQUIRED
1. Enter the preceding transactions in general journal form.
2. Calculate the carrying value of the bonds as of December 31, 20-2.

Solution

1.

	DATE		DESCRIPTION	POST REF.	DEBIT					CREDIT					
			GENERAL JOURNAL											PAGE 1	
1	20-1 Nov.	30	Cash		776	0	0	0	00						1
2			Discount on Bonds Payable		24	0	0	0	00						2
3			Bonds Payable							800	0	0	0	00	3
4			Issued bonds at a discount												4
5															5
6			Adjusting Entry												6
7	Dec.	31	Bond Interest Expense		6	2	0	0	00						7
8			Bond Interest Payable							6	0	0	0	00	8
9			Discount on Bonds Payable*								2	0	0	00	9
10															10
11			Reversing Entry												11
12	20-2 Jan.	2	Bond Interest Payable		6	0	0	0	00						12
13			Discount on Bonds Payable			2	0	0	00						13
14			Bond Interest Expense							6	2	0	0	00	14
15															15
16	May	31	Bond Interest Expense		37	2	0	0	00						16
17			Discount on Bonds Payable							1	2	0	0	00	17
18			Cash							36	0	0	0	00	18
19			Paid semiannual interest and												19
20			amortized discount on bonds												20
21															21
22	June	15	Bond Sinking Fund		30	0	0	0	00						22
23			Cash							30	0	0	0	00	23
24			Made sinking fund deposit												24
25															25
26	Nov.	30	Bond Interest Expense		37	2	0	0	00						26
27			Discount on Bonds Payable							1	2	0	0	00	27
28			Cash							36	0	0	0	00	28
29			Paid semiannual interest and												29
30			amortized discount on bonds												30
31															31
32															32

*Amortization rate = $24,000 original discount ÷ 10 years = $2,400/year ÷ 12 months = $200/month

	DATE		DESCRIPTION	POST REF.	DEBIT					CREDIT					
1			Adjusting Entry												1
2	20-2 Dec.	31	Bond Interest Expense		6	2	0	0	00						2
3			Bond Interest Payable							6	0	0	0	00	3
4			Discount on Bonds Payable								2	0	0	00	4
5															5
6		31	Bond Sinking Fund		1	1	0	0	00						6
7			Sinking Fund Earnings							1	1	0	0	00	7
8			Annual sinking fund earnings												8
9															9
10	20-8 June	15	Bond Sinking Fund		30	0	0	0	00						10
11			Cash							30	0	0	0	00	11
12			Made sinking fund deposit												12
13															13
14	Nov.	30	Bond Interest Expense		37	2	0	0	00						14
15			Discount on Bonds Payable							1	2	0	0	00	15
16			Cash							36	0	0	0	00	16
17			Paid semiannual interest and												17
18			amortized discount on bonds												18
19															19
20		30	Bond Sinking Fund		496	0	0	0	00						20
21			Cash							496	0	0	0	00	21
22			[(800,000 × 102%) − 320,000]												22
23			Made sinking fund deposit												23
24															24
25		30	Bonds Payable		800	0	0	0	00						25
26			Loss on Bonds Redeemed		23	2	0	0	00						26
27			Discount on Bonds Payable*							7	2	0	0	00	27
28			Bond Sinking Fund							816	0	0	0	00	28
29			Redeemed bonds at a loss												29

* Original discount on bonds payable	$24,000
Amortization for 7 years at $2,400/year	(16,800)
Unamortized discount on November 30, 20-8	$ 7,200

2. | Face value of bonds | | $800,000 |
    |---|---|---|
    | Original discount on bonds payable | $24,000 | |
    | Less: | | |
    | Discount amortized on December 31, 20-1 | (200) | |
    | Discount amortized during 20-2 | (2,400) | |
    | Balance of discount on bonds payable at December 31, 20-2 | | 21,400 |
    | Carrying value of bonds, December 31, 20-2 | | $778,600 |

REVIEW QUESTIONS

1. Explain the difference between corporate bonds and stock from the standpoint of the issuing corporation.

2. Will a bond sell at a discount or at a premium if the contract rate is greater than the market rate on the bond? If the contract rate is less than the market rate?

3. Explain the meaning of a bond price quotation of 95. Of 102.

4. What accounts are affected when bonds are issued at face value?

5. How is Premium on Bonds Payable shown on the balance sheet? How is Discount on Bonds Payable shown?

6. How is the amount of bond premium or discount to be amortized in a period determined using the straight-line method?

7. How is the periodic interest expense affected by the amortization of the premium on bonds payable?

8. How is the periodic interest expense affected by the amortization of the discount on bonds payable?

9. When bonds are redeemed before maturity, how is the gain or loss on redemption determined? Why does the calculation differ for bonds issued at face value, at a premium, and at a discount?

10. Who usually administers a bond sinking fund?

11. How should sinking fund earnings be reported on the corporation income statement?

12. How should the bond sinking fund be reported on the corporation balance sheet?

MANAGING YOUR WRITING

The business where you work is considering issuing bonds to finance a major expansion. Your boss has just come from a lengthy meeting regarding the bonds, including the interest rate the bonds should carry. This has irritated your boss, who feels that the interest rate to use is obvious—the lowest one possible. This would yield the lowest interest expense to borrow the money. It seems stupid to pay big fees to financial advisors and lawyers when the question is so simple.

Write a report to your boss explaining how the issue price of the bonds (the net amount borrowed) is affected by the contract interest rate on the bonds. Include an explanation of how interest costs consist of more than just periodic interest payments.

ETHICS CASE

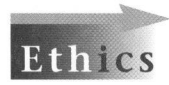

Alva Reese is 65 years old and getting ready to retire. She called her investment broker to help her decide what to do with the $50,000 that she has in the stock market. Alva told him that she didn't want any risky investments but hoped for an investment that was relatively safe and offered steady income. She had heard that bonds were safer than stocks and asked the broker how he felt about bonds. Her broker said bonds were a good safe choice and the ones he had in mind would offer her a high yield. He recommended that she invest all $50,000 in corporate callable bonds. Alva asked him to explain what callable bonds were and he told her the explanation was too technical but they were a safe investment that would serve her needs.

1. What information should the investment broker have given Alva?

2. Are all bonds safe? Why or why not?

3. Write a short paragraph describing how to determine the sales (trading) price of a bond.

4. In groups of three or four, make a list of the factors that Alva and the investment broker should consider before deciding how to invest the $50,000.

WEB WORK

Bonds are commonly used to raise capital for expansion or to purchase new facilities. But what value do bonds offer investors? Why would an investor want a lower interest bond rather than a higher paying stock? For information on bonds and their uses, go to **http://www.finpipe.com** and choose Bonds.

(http://heintz.swcollege.com)

SERIES A EXERCISES

EXERCISE 23A-1 (LO 2) BONDS ISSUED AT FACE VALUE R & R Collectibles issued the following bonds.

Date of issue and sale:	April 1, 20-1
Principal amount:	$500,000
Sale price of bonds:	100
Denomination of bonds:	$1,000
Life of bonds:	10 years
Contract rate:	8%, payable semiannually on September 30 and March 31

Prepare journal entries for:

(a) Issuance of the bonds.

(b) Interest payment on the bonds on September 30.

(c) Year-end adjustment on the bonds.

EXERCISE 23A-2 (LO 3) BONDS ISSUED AT A PREMIUM Velez Entertainment Co. issued the following bonds at a premium.

Date of issue and sale:	April 1, 20-1
Principal amount:	$500,000
Sale price of bonds:	104
Denomination of bonds:	$1,000
Life of bonds:	10 years
Contract rate:	10%, payable semiannually on September 30 and March 31

Prepare journal entries for:

(a) Issuance of the bonds at a premium.

(b) Interest payment and premium amortization on the bonds on September 30.

(c) Year-end adjustment on the bonds.

EXERCISE 23A-3 (LO 4) BONDS ISSUED AT A DISCOUNT Brenner's Home Club issued the following bonds at a discount.

Date of issue and sale:	April 1, 20-1
Principal amount:	$500,000
Sale price of bonds:	98
Denomination of bonds:	$1,000
Life of bonds:	10 years
Contract rate:	7%, payable semiannually on September 30 and March 31

Prepare journal entries for:

(a) Issuance of the bonds at a discount.

(b) Interest payment and discount amortization on the bonds on September 30.

(c) Year-end adjustment on the bonds.

EXERCISE 23A-4 (LO 2/5) REDEMPTION OF BONDS ISSUED AT FACE VALUE Levesque Lumber Co. issued $800,000 in bonds at face value ten years ago and has paid semiannual interest payments through the years.

(a) Assume the bonds are redeemed at face value.

(b) Assume that $80,000 of the bonds are redeemed at 104.

(c) Assume that $80,000 of the bonds are redeemed at 96.

Prepare journal entries to record (a), (b), and (c).

EXERCISE 23A-5 (LO 3/5) REDEMPTION OF BONDS ISSUED AT A PREMIUM Brighton Unlimited sold bonds at a premium for $630,000 (premium of $30,000) eight years ago.

(a) The corporation redeems $60,000 of this issue at 98. The unamortized premium is $600.

(b) The corporation redeems $90,000 of this issue at 102. The unamortized premium is $900.

Prepare journal entries to record the redemption in (a) and (b).

EXERCISE 23A-6 (LO 4/5) REDEMPTION OF BONDS ISSUED AT A DISCOUNT
Martinez Manufacturing sold bonds at a discount for $240,000 (discount of
$10,000) seven years ago.

(a) The corporation redeems $25,000 of this issue at 96. The unamortized
discount is $375.

(b) The corporation redeems $20,000 of this issue at 99. The unamortized
discount is $300.

Prepare journal entries to record the redemption in (a) and (b).

EXERCISE 23A-7 (LO 5) BOND SINKING FUNDS M. J. Adams Corporation pays
$40,000 into a bond sinking fund each year for the future redemption of bonds.
At the end of the first year, earnings on the sinking fund are $3,200. When the
bonds mature, there is a balance in the sinking fund of $301,800, of which
$300,000 is used to redeem the bonds.

Prepare journal entries to record:

(a) The initial sinking fund deposit.

(b) The first year's earnings.

(c) The redemption of the bonds.

(d) The return of excess cash to the corporation.

SERIES A PROBLEMS

PROBLEM 23A-1 (LO 2) BONDS ISSUED AT FACE VALUE Ito Co. issued the
following bonds.

Date of issue and sale:	April 1, 20-1
Principal amount:	$300,000
Sale price of bonds:	100
Denomination of bonds:	$5,000
Life of bonds:	5 years
Contract rate:	10%, payable semiannually on September 30 and March 31

REQUIRED Prepare journal entries for:

(a) Issuance of the bonds.

(b) Interest payment on the bonds on September 30, 20-1.

(c) Year-end adjustment on the bonds for 20-1.

(d) Reversing entry for the beginning of 20-2.

(e) Interest payments on the bonds for 20-2 (March 31 and September 30).

(f) Redemption at maturity.

PROBLEM 23A-2 (LO 3) BONDS ISSUED AT A PREMIUM Bunkichi Corporation issued the following bonds at a premium.

Date of issue and sale:	March 1, 20-1
Principal amount:	$800,000
Sale price of bonds:	103
Denomination of bonds:	$1,000
Life of bonds:	10 years
Contract rate:	8%, payable semiannually on August 31 and February 28

REQUIRED

1. Prepare journal entries for:

   (a) Issuance of the bonds at a premium.

   (b) Interest payment and premium amortization on the bonds on August 31, 20-1.

   (c) Year-end adjustment on the bonds for 20-1.

   (d) Reversing entry for the beginning of 20-2.

   (e) Interest payments and premium amortization on the bonds for 20-2 (February 28 and August 31).

2. Calculate the carrying value of the bonds on August 31, 20-2.

PROBLEM 23A-3 (LO 4) BONDS ISSUED AT A DISCOUNT Emerald, Inc., issued the following bonds at a discount.

Date of issue and sale:	April 1, 20-1
Principal amount:	$500,000
Sale price of bonds:	97
Denomination of bonds:	$1,000
Life of bonds:	10 years
Contract rate:	8%, payable semiannually on September 30 and March 31

REQUIRED

1. Prepare journal entries for:

   (a) Issuance of the bonds at a discount.

   (b) Interest payment and discount amortization on the bonds on September 30, 20-1.

   (c) Year-end adjustment on the bonds for 20-1.

   (d) Reversing entry for the beginning of 20-2.

   (e) Interest payments and discount amortization on the bonds for 20-2 (March 31 and September 30).

2. Calculate the carrying value of the bonds on September 30, 20-2.

PROBLEM 23A-4 (LO 3/5) BONDS ISSUED AT A PREMIUM, REDEEMED AT A LOSS Perez Company issued the following bonds at a premium.

Date of issue and sale: March 1, 20-1
Principal amount: $400,000
Sale price of bonds: 103
Denomination of bonds: $1,000
Life of bonds: 10 years
Contract rate: 12%, payable semiannually on August 31
                                            and February 28

REQUIRED   Prepare journal entries for:

(a) Issuance of the bonds.

(b) Interest payment and premium amortization on the bonds on August 31, 20-1.

(c) Year-end adjustment on the bonds for 20-1.

(d) Reversing entry for the beginning of 20-2.

(e) Redemption of $50,000 of the bonds on March 1, 20-6, at 106.

PROBLEM 23A-5 (LO 4/5) BONDS ISSUED AT A DISCOUNT, REDEEMED AT A GAIN Cline & Co. issued the following bonds at a discount.

Date of issue and sale: April 1, 20-1
Principal amount: $500,000
Sale price of bonds: 98
Denomination of bonds: $1,000
Life of bonds: 10 years
Contract rate: 9%, payable semiannually on September
                                            30 and March 31

REQUIRED   Prepare journal entries for:

(a) Issuance of the bonds.

(b) Interest payment and discount amortization on the bonds on September 30, 20-1.

(c) Year-end adjustment on the bonds for 20-1.

(d) Reversing entry for the beginning of 20-2.

(e) Redemption of $50,000 of the bonds on April 1, 20-4, at 96.

W & D

PROBLEM 23A-6 (LO 2/5) BONDS ISSUED AT FACE VALUE WITH SINKING FUND
Martin Manufacturing issued the following bonds.

Date of issue and sale: April 1, 20-1
Principal amount: $500,000
Sale price of bonds: 100
Denomination of bonds: $10,000
Life of bonds: 10 years
Contract rate: 10%, payable semiannually on September
                                            30 and March 31

Annual sinking fund
requirement: $34,000, payable June 1

(continued)

REQUIRED   Prepare journal entries for:

(a) Issuance of the bonds.

(b) Deposit to sinking fund on June 1.

(c) Interest payment on the bonds on September 30, 20-1.

(d) Earnings of $2,400 on the sinking fund in 20-1.

(e) Year-end adjustment on the bonds for 20-1.

(f) Reversing entry for the beginning of 20-2.

(g) Interest payments on the bonds for 20-2 (March 31 and September 30).

(h) Redemption at maturity from the sinking fund.

(i) Return of excess cash of $1,050 from the sinking fund to the corporation.

SERIES B EXERCISES

EXERCISE 23B-1 (LO 2) BONDS ISSUED AT FACE VALUE L & L Underwriters issued the following bonds.

Date of issue and sale:	April 1, 20-1
Principal amount:	$400,000
Sale price of bonds:	100
Denomination of bonds:	$1,000
Life of bonds:	10 years
Contract rate:	9%, payable semiannually on September 30 and March 31

Prepare journal entries for:

(a) Issuance of the bonds.

(b) Interest payment on the bonds on September 30.

(c) Year-end adjustment on the bonds.

EXERCISE 23B-2 (LO 3) BONDS ISSUED AT A PREMIUM Bryant and Nelson Company issued the following bonds at a premium.

Date of issue and sale:	May 1, 20-1
Principal amount:	$500,000
Sale price of bonds:	103
Denomination of bonds:	$1,000
Life of bonds:	10 years
Contract rate:	12%, payable semiannually on October 31 and April 30

Prepare journal entries for:

(a) Issuance of the bonds at a premium.

(b) Interest payment and premium amortization on the bonds on October 31.

(c) Year-end adjustment on the bonds.

EXERCISE 23B-3 (LO 4) BONDS ISSUED AT A DISCOUNT Beilke's Supply Stores issued the following bonds at a discount.

Date of issue and sale:	April 1, 20-1
Principal amount:	$400,000
Sale price of bonds:	97
Denomination of bonds:	$1,000
Life of bonds:	10 years
Contract rate:	8%, payable semiannually on September 30 and March 31

Prepare journal entries for:

(a) Issuance of the bonds at a discount.

(b) Interest payment and discount amortization on the bonds on September 30.

(c) Year-end adjustment on the bonds.

EXERCISE 23B-4 (LO 2/5) REDEMPTION OF BONDS ISSUED AT FACE VALUE Okano Medical Lab issued $300,000 in bonds at face value ten years ago and has paid semiannual interest payments through the years.

(a) Assume the bonds are redeemed at face value.

(b) Assume that $25,000 of the bonds are redeemed at 103.

(c) Assume that $25,000 of the bonds are redeemed at 97.

Prepare the journal entries to record (a), (b), and (c).

EXERCISE 23B-5 (LO 3/5) REDEMPTION OF BONDS ISSUED AT A PREMIUM Miller & Miller sold bonds at a premium for $525,000 (premium of $25,000) eight years ago.

(a) The corporation redeems $50,000 of this issue at 95. The unamortized premium is $500.

(b) The corporation redeems $75,000 of this issue at 103. The unamortized premium is $750.

Prepare journal entries to record the redemption in (a) and (b).

EXERCISE 23B-6 (LO 4/5) REDEMPTION OF BONDS ISSUED AT A DISCOUNT Medina Optical Supply sold bonds at a discount for $420,000 (discount of $20,000) eight years ago.

(a) The corporation redeems $25,000 of this issue at 94. The unamortized discount is $250.

(b) The corporation redeems $30,000 of this issue at 101. The unamortized discount is $300.

Prepare journal entries to record the redemption in (a) and (b).

EXERCISE 23B-7 (LO 5) BOND SINKING FUNDS Sheng Corporation pays $50,000 into a bond sinking fund each year for the future redemption of bonds. At the end of the first year, earnings on the sinking fund are $4,750. When the bonds mature, there is a balance in the sinking fund of $502,125, of which $500,000 is used to redeem the bonds.

(continued)

Prepare journal entries to record:

(a) The initial sinking fund deposit.

(b) The first year's earnings.

(c) The redemption of the bonds.

(d) The return of excess cash to the corporation.

SERIES B PROBLEMS

PROBLEM 23B-1 (LO 2) BONDS ISSUED AT FACE VALUE Ramona Arroyo Co. issued the following bonds.

Date of issue and sale:	April 1, 20-1
Principal amount:	$250,000
Sale price of bonds:	100
Denomination of bonds:	$5,000
Life of bonds:	10 years
Contract rate:	9%, payable semiannually on September 30 and March 31

REQUIRED   Prepare journal entries for:

(a) Issuance of the bonds.

(b) Interest payment on the bonds on September 30, 20-1.

(c) Year-end adjustment on the bonds for 20-1.

(d) Reversing entry for the beginning of 20-2.

(e) Interest payments on the bonds for 20-2 (March 31 and September 30).

(f) Redemption at maturity.

PROBLEM 23B-2 (LO 3) BONDS ISSUED AT A PREMIUM Wang Corporation issued the following bonds at a premium.

Date of issue and sale:	March 1, 20-1
Principal amount:	$250,000
Sale price of bonds:	103
Denomination of bonds:	$500
Life of bonds:	10 years
Contract rate:	12%, payable semiannually on August 31 and February 28

REQUIRED   1. Prepare journal entries for:

(a) Issuance of the bonds at a premium.

(b) Interest payment and premium amortization on the bonds on August 31, 20-1.

(c) Year-end adjustment on the bonds for 20-1.

(d) Reversing entry for the beginning of 20-2.

(e) Interest payments and premium amortization on the bonds for 20-2 (February 28 and August 31).

2. Calculate the carrying value of the bonds on August 31, 20-2.

PROBLEM 23B-3 (LO 4) BONDS ISSUED AT A DISCOUNT Brandon, Inc., issued the following bonds at a discount.

Date of issue and sale:	April 1, 20-1
Principal amount:	$600,000
Sale price of bonds:	96
Denomination of bonds:	$1,000
Life of bonds:	10 years
Contract rate:	7%, payable semiannually on September 30 and March 31

REQUIRED 1. Prepare journal entries for:

(a) Issuance of the bonds at a discount.

(b) Interest payment and discount amortization on the bonds on September 30, 20-1.

(c) Year-end adjustment on the bonds for 20-1.

(d) Reversing entry for the beginning of 20-2.

(e) Interest payments and discount amortization on the bonds for 20-2 (March 31 and September 30).

2. Calculate the carrying value of the bonds on September 30, 20-2.

PROBLEM 23B-4 (LO 3/5) BONDS ISSUED AT A PREMIUM, REDEEMED AT A LOSS Blackwell Company issued the following bonds at a premium.

Date of issue and sale:	March 1, 20-1
Principal amount:	$500,000
Sale price of bonds:	103
Denomination of bonds:	$1,000
Life of bonds:	10 years
Contract rate:	12%, payable semiannually on August 31 and February 28

REQUIRED Prepare journal entries for:

(a) Issuance of the bonds.

(b) Interest payment and premium amortization on the bonds on August 31, 20-1.

(c) Year-end adjustment on the bonds for 20-1.

(d) Reversing entry for the beginning of 20-2.

(e) Redemption of $50,000 of the bonds on March 1, 20-6, at 106.

PROBLEM 23B-5 (LO 4/5) BONDS ISSUED AT A DISCOUNT, REDEEMED AT A GAIN Ellis & Co. issued the following bonds at a discount.

Date of issue and sale:	April 1, 20-1
Principal amount:	$400,000
Sale price of bonds:	97
Denomination of bonds:	$1,000
Life of bonds:	10 years
Contract rate:	8%, payable semiannually on September 30 and March 31

REQUIRED   Prepare journal entries for:

(a) Issuance of the bonds.

(b) Interest payment and discount amortization on the bonds on September 30, 20-1.

(c) Year-end adjustment on the bonds for 20-1.

(d) Reversing entry for the beginning of 20-2.

(e) Redemption of $50,000 of the bonds on April 1, 20-4, at 96.

W & D

PROBLEM 23B-6 (LO 2/5) BONDS ISSUED AT FACE VALUE WITH SINKING FUND Creswell Entertainment issued the following bonds.

Date of issue and sale:	April 1, 20-1
Principal amount:	$600,000
Sale price of bonds:	100
Denomination of bonds:	$10,000
Life of bonds:	10 years
Contract rate:	8%, payable semiannually on September 30 and March 31
Annual sinking fund requirement:	$40,000, payable on June 1

REQUIRED   Prepare journal entries for:

(a) Issuance of the bonds.

(b) Deposit to sinking fund on June 1.

(c) Interest payment on the bonds on September 30, 20-1.

(d) Earnings of $3,000 on the sinking fund in 20-1.

(e) Year-end adjustment on the bonds for 20-1.

(f) Reversing entry for the beginning of 20-2.

(g) Interest payments on the bonds for 20-2 (March 31 and September 30).

(h) Redemption at maturity from the sinking fund.

(i) Return of excess cash of $1,900 from the sinking fund to the corporation.

MASTERY PROBLEM

Jackson, Inc.'s fiscal year ends December 31. Selected transactions for the period 20-1 through 20-8 involving bonds payable issued by Jackson are as follows:

20-1

Oct. 30 Issued $600,000 of ten-year, 10%, callable bonds dated October 31, 20-1, for $612,000. Interest is payable semiannually on October 31 and April 30. The bond indenture provides that Jackson is to pay to the trustee bank $20,000 by May 15 of each year (except the tenth year) as a sinking fund for the retirement of the bonds on call or at maturity.

Dec. 31 Made the adjusting entry for interest payable and amortized two months' premium on the bonds (straight-line method).

20-2

Jan. 2 Reversed the adjusting entry for interest payable and bond premium amortization.

Apr. 30 Paid the semiannual interest on the bonds and amortized six months' premium.

May 15 Paid the sinking fund trustee $20,000.

Oct. 31 Paid the semiannual interest on the bonds and amortized six months' premium.

Dec. 31 Made the adjusting entry for interest payable and amortized two months' premium on the bonds.

31 Sinking fund earnings for the year were $900.

20-8

May 15 Paid the sinking fund trustee $20,000.

Oct. 31 Paid the semiannual interest on the bonds and amortized six months' premium.

31 Redeemed the bonds, which were called at 97.
    The balance in the bond premium account is $3,600 after the payment of interest and amortization of premium have been entered. The cash balance in the sinking fund is $200,000, which is applied to the redemption. Paid the sinking fund trustee the additional cash needed to pay off the bonds. [Hint: First make the entry for payment to the sinking fund, then make the entry for redemption of the bonds.]

REQUIRED   1. Enter the preceding transactions in general journal form.

2. Calculate the carrying value of the bonds as of December 31, 20-2.

Self-Study Test Questions

True/False

1. A secured bond is one that is backed by specific corporate assets. _____

2. If the contract rate of interest on a bond is 9% and the current market rate on similar investments is 10%, the bond will sell at a premium. _____

3. When bonds are issued at face value, the debit to Cash and credit to Bonds Payable are for the same amount. _____

4. Amortization of the premium on bonds payable increases the bond interest expense and the carrying value of the bonds. _____

5. To determine the amount of gain or loss on redemption of bonds, compare the redemption price with the carrying value of the bonds. _____

Multiple Choice

1. Bonds that give the holder the option of exchanging the bonds for capital stock in the corporation are called _____

   (a) debenture bonds.
   (b) serial bonds.
   (c) convertible bonds.
   (d) callable bonds.

2. If bonds with a face value of $200,000 are sold at 102, Cash is debited for _____

   (a) $200,000.
   (b) $202,000.
   (c) $204,000.
   (d) $196,000.

3. Ten-year bonds with a face value of $300,000 are sold at a premium of $6,000. If the premium is amortized using the straight-line method, each semiannual interest payment and amortization of bond premium will include a _____

   (a) debit to Premium on Bonds Payable.
   (b) credit to Premium on Bonds Payable.
   (c) debit to Cash.
   (d) credit to Bond Interest Expense.

4. If bonds are issued at a discount, the amortization of the discount over the life of the bonds causes the _____

   (a) interest expense to decrease each period.
   (b) interest expense to increase each period.
   (c) carrying value of the bonds to decrease.
   (d) carrying value of the bonds to increase.

5. Bond sinking fund earnings are _____

   (a) subtracted from the bond sinking fund.
   (b) added to the bond sinking fund.
   (c) subtracted from the current year interest expense.
   (d) added to the current year interest expense.

The answers to the Self-Study Test Questions are at the end of the text.

24

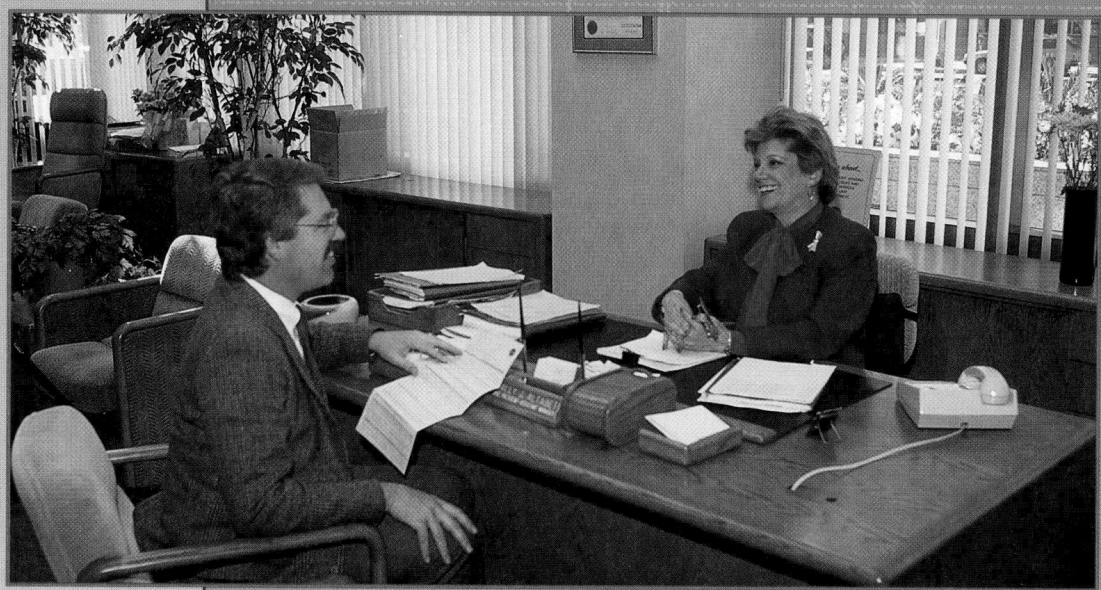

Statement of Cash Flows

Mike Finbar was puzzled after reading the recent income statement prepared by the company's accountant. For months the company has had difficulty meeting the payroll and paying suppliers within the discount periods. The company just never seems to have enough cash. Yet, the most recent income statement shows that the company is exceeding profit expectations. How can the company be highly profitable and not have enough cash to pay its bills on time?

A business must have an adequate amount of cash to operate. Without sufficient cash, suppliers and employees cannot be paid, debt cannot be retired, and dividends cannot be paid to stockholders. Managers, creditors, stockholders, and others pay close attention to a company's cash position and the economic events and transactions leading to changes in that position. The statement of cash flows provides information about the events that affect the cash position of a company.

NATURE AND PURPOSE OF THE STATEMENT OF CASH FLOWS

LO 1   Explain the purpose of the statement of cash flows.

Inc.
ONLINE

"The Cash-Flow Quagmire"
(http://heintz.swcollege.com)
Why is a thriving company
failing?

The managers of a business must generate net income (profitability) and keep the enterprise solvent (liquidity). The income statement reports on the company's profitability by matching revenues and expenses on an accrual basis. Revenues are recognized when earned, regardless of when the cash is received. Expenses are recognized as incurred, regardless of when the cash is paid. Although the accrual basis of accounting is an excellent method for measuring profitability, it does not explain why a company's liquidity has improved or worsened. The income statement does not explain, for example, why a company reporting substantial profits can have difficulty paying its bills on time.

It would seem logical that a profitable company would have plenty of cash. Net income brings in cash, either immediately or as soon as receivables are collected. However, the cash inflow resulting from profitable operations may be used to acquire long-term assets, to pay off long-term debt, or to pay stockholders in the form of dividends. Thus, an increase or decrease in cash results from a combination of operating, investing, and financing activities by management. The income statement alone does not adequately reflect all of these activities.

Management and outside users of the financial statements want to know how cash was generated and used during the period. The purpose of the **statement of cash flows** is to provide this information.

OPERATING, INVESTING, AND FINANCING ACTIVITIES

LO 2   Define operating, investing, and financing activities and describe transactions for each type of activity.

The statement of cash flows categorizes all cash flows into three major types of activities: operating, investing, and financing.

Operating Activities

Operating activities include transactions and events associated with selling a product or providing a service and are related to the revenues and expenses reported on the income statement. Since interest revenue, interest expense, and dividend revenue are reported on the income statement, they are also considered cash flows from operating activities. Figure 24-1 shows cash inflows and outflows from operating activities.

Operating activities represent the company's primary source of cash over the life of the business. Ultimately, net cash inflows from operating activities must be used to purchase plant and equipment, repay loans, and pay dividends to stockholders.

LEARNING KEY: Cash flows from operating activities are primarily related to the revenues and expenses reported on the income statement.

The proper reporting of dividends and interest on the statement of cash flows can be confusing. Here's an easy way to keep it straight. If the item is reported on the income statement (interest _expense_, interest _revenue_, and dividend _revenue_), it is classified as an operating activity on the statement of cash flows. If not (dividends), it is classified as a financing activity.

FIGURE 24-1 Cash Flows from Operating Activities

OPERATING ACTIVITIES	
Cash Inflows	**Cash Outflows**
1. Cash receipts from the sale of goods or services.	1. Payments for the acquisition of inventory.
2. Interest received on loans made to outside entities.	2. Payments to employees and the government.
3. Dividends received on investments made in the stock of other corporations.	3. Payments for interest on loans.
	4. Payments to other suppliers and for other expenses.

Investing Activities

Investing activities are those transactions involving the purchase and sale of long-term assets, investments in debt and equity securities, and lending money and collecting the principal on the related loans. Figure 24-2 shows typical transactions for cash inflows and outflows from investing activities.

LEARNING KEY: Investing activities include buying and selling long-term assets, investing in debt and equity securities, and lending money and collecting the principal on the related loans.

FIGURE 24-2 Cash Flows from Investing Activities

INVESTING ACTIVITIES	
Cash Inflows	**Cash Outflows**
1. Proceeds from collection of principal amount of loans made to borrowers.*	1. Loans made by the company to other parties.
2. Proceeds from the sale of property, plant, and equipment; intangibles; and other productive assets.	2. Payments to acquire property, plant, and equipment; intangibles; and other productive assets.
3. Proceeds from the sale of investments in debt and equity securities.	3. Payments to acquire investments in debt and equity securities.
4. Proceeds from discounting notes receivable.	

* Note that interest received on loans is not included with investing activities. It is included with cash inflows from operating activities.

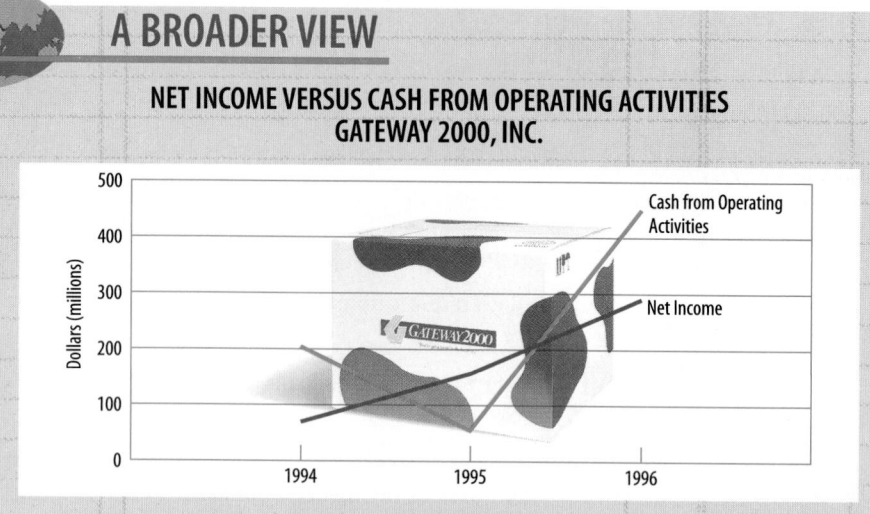

A BROADER VIEW

NET INCOME VERSUS CASH FROM OPERATING ACTIVITIES GATEWAY 2000, INC.

Since cash from operating activities is related to revenues and expenses on the income statement, many financial statement users assume that these measures of performance are similar in value and move in the same direction. As shown above for Gateway 2000, Inc., this is not always true. Note that net income increased dramatically each year. At the same time, cash from operating activities first dipped and then increased even more dramatically than net income. The drop in cash from operating activities in 1995 was caused primarily by major increases in accounts receivable and inventory. The financial statements can tell us a lot about a business, if we read them carefully.

Financing Activities

Financing activities are those transactions dealing with the exchange of cash between the company and its owners (stockholders) and creditors. Cash inflows and outflows include the types of transactions listed in Figure 24-3.

LEARNING KEY: Financing activities deal with the exchange of cash between the company and its stockholders and creditors.

FIGURE 24-3 Cash Flows from Financing Activities

FINANCING ACTIVITIES	
Cash Inflows	**Cash Outflows**
1. Proceeds from additional investments by the owners or the issuance of stock.	1. Payments of dividends to stock-holders or withdrawals by the owners.
2. Proceeds from borrowing money through the signing of a mortgage, issuing a bond, or other long- or short-term loans.	2. Payments to purchase treasury stock.
	3. Repayment of the principal on loans.*

* Note that interest payments on loans are not reported under financing activities. They are reported as cash outflows under operating activities.

Note: Amounts owed to suppliers of goods and services are not considered financing activities. They are used in the calculation of cash from operating activities.

INFORMATION NEEDED TO PREPARE A STATEMENT OF CASH FLOWS

LO 3   Describe the information needed to prepare a statement of cash flows.

To prepare a statement of cash flows, the following statements are needed:

1. Balance sheets for the beginning and end of the period.

2. Income statement for the period.

3. Statement of retained earnings for the period.

Additional information on major cash transactions is useful. This information and an analysis of all noncash balance sheet accounts are used to identify transactions involving cash flows during the year.

The statement of cash flows is divided into three sections:

1. cash flows from operating activities,

2. cash flows from investing activities, and

3. cash flows from financing activities.

LEARNING KEY:	The three major sections of the statement of cash flows focus on: operating activities investing activities financing activities

The sum of the cash generated or used by each of the three activities should equal the difference between the beginning and ending balance of the cash account. For example, if $5,000 was generated from operations, $2,000 used for investing activities, and $3,000 provided by financing activities, the cash balance must have increased by $6,000 ($5,000 − $2,000 + $3,000) during the year. The accuracy of the statement can be verified by computing the change in the balance of the cash account.

LEARNING KEY: Change in cash balance:

	Cash from operating activities
±	Cash from investing activities
±	Cash from financing activities
=	Change in cash balance

To illustrate the preparation of a simple statement of cash flows, the Simplex Company is used. Figure 24-4 shows the financial statements and additional information for Simplex.

FIGURE 24-4 Financial Statements and Additional Information for Simplex

Simplex Company Income Statement For Year Ended December 31, 20-3					
Sales				$900 0 0 0 00
Cost of goods sold				600 0 0 0 00
Gross margin				$300 0 0 0 00
Operating expenses				220 0 0 0 00
Net income				$ 80 0 0 0 00

Simplex Company Statement of Retained Earnings For Year Ended December 31, 20-3					
Retained earnings, January 1, 20-3				$ 50 0 0 0 00
Net income	$ 80 0 0 0 00			
Less dividends	20 0 0 0 00			
Net increase in retained earnings				60 0 0 0 00
Retained earnings, December 31, 20-3				$110 0 0 0 00

PREPARING A STATEMENT OF CASH FLOWS: SIMPLEX

LO 4   Prepare a schedule for the calculation of cash from operating activities under the direct method.

> *Most major corporations use the indirect method. However, the Financial Accounting Standards Board is encouraging these companies to switch to the direct method.*

A sure sign of financial difficulty for a business is the continuing need to sell assets or issue long-term debt to pay operating expenses. Therefore, an important factor in evaluating a company's financial condition is the ability to generate positive cash flows from operating activities. Cash generated from operating activities may be computed and reported using one of two methods. Under the **direct method**, revenues and expenses reported on the income statement are adjusted to reflect the amount of cash received or paid for each item. Under the **indirect method**, net income is adjusted for transactions that affect net income and cash flows in different ways. For example, depreciation expense reduces net income, but has no effect on cash flows. The direct method is presented in this chapter. The indirect method is illustrated in the appendix to this chapter.

Cash Flows from Operating Activities: The Direct Method

To compute the cash generated from operating activities for the Simplex Company, a schedule like the one shown in Figure 24-5 is prepared. Revenues and expenses reported on the income statement are converted to cash received or paid for operating purposes. Column 1 reports the revenue or expense as reported on the income statement. Columns 2 and 3 are used to make additions or subtractions necessary to reflect the associated cash flows in column 4.

FIGURE 24-4 Financial Statements and Additional Information for Simplex (continued)

Simplex Company Comparative Balance Sheet December 31, 20-3 and 20-2	20-3	20-2	INCREASE (DECREASE)
Assets			
Current assets:			
Cash	$ 90 0 0 0 00	$200 0 0 0 00	$(110 0 0 0 00)
Accounts receivable	160 0 0 0 00	190 0 0 0 00	(30 0 0 0 00)
Merchandise inventory	180 0 0 0 00	200 0 0 0 00	(20 0 0 0 00)
Total current assets	$430 0 0 0 00	$590 0 0 0 00	(160 0 0 0 00)
Property, plant, and equipment:			
Land	$ 40 0 0 0 00	$ 40 0 0 0 00	0 00
Building	140 0 0 0 00		140 0 0 0 00
Equipment	100 0 0 0 00		100 0 0 0 00
Total property, plant, and equipment	$280 0 0 0 00	$ 40 0 0 0 00	240 0 0 0 00
Total assets	$710 0 0 0 00	$630 0 0 0 00	80 0 0 0 00
Liabilities			
Current liabilities:			
Notes payable	$ 60 0 0 0 00	$ 50 0 0 0 00	10 0 0 0 00
Accounts payable	120 0 0 0 00	180 0 0 0 00	(60 0 0 0 00)
Total liabilities	$180 0 0 0 00	$230 0 0 0 00	(50 0 0 0 00)
Stockholders' Equity			
Common stock ($5 par, 100,000 shares authorized;			
Issued: 58,000 in 20-3, 50,000 in 20-2)	$290 0 0 0 00	$250 0 0 0 00	40 0 0 0 00
Paid-in capital in excess of par—common stock	130 0 0 0 00	100 0 0 0 00	30 0 0 0 00
Retained earnings	110 0 0 0 00	50 0 0 0 00	60 0 0 0 00
Total stockholders' equity	$530 0 0 0 00	$400 0 0 0 00	130 0 0 0 00
Total liabilities and stockholders' equity	$710 0 0 0 00	$630 0 0 0 00	80 0 0 0 00

Additional information for 20-3:

1. A building and equipment were acquired for cash just before the year end.

2. Issued 8,000 shares of common stock for $8.75 per share.

3. Declared and paid cash dividends of $20,000.

FIGURE 24-5 Schedule for the Calculation of Cash Generated from Operating Activities for Simplex

Simplex Company
Schedule for the Calculation of Cash Generated from Operating Activities
For Year Ended December 31, 20-3

INCOME STATEMENT		ADDITIONS		DEDUCTIONS	CASH FLOWS	
Sales	$900,000	**1** $30,000			$930,000	Cash received from customers
Cost of goods sold	600,000	**3** 60,000		**2** $(20,000)	640,000	Cash paid for merchandise
Gross profit	$300,000				$290,000	
Operating expenses	220,000				220,000	Cash paid for operating expenses
Net income	$ 80,000				$ 70,000	Cash generated from operating activities

1 The $30,000 reduction in receivables is added to sales to compute cash received from customers.

2 The $20,000 reduction in inventory is subtracted from cost of goods sold to compute the cost of merchandise purchased ($600,000 − $20,000 = $580,000).

3 Reducing the amount owed to suppliers (Accounts Payable) required the expenditure of additional cash. By adding the reduction in Accounts Payable to the cost of merchandise purchased, cash paid for merchandise is determined ($580,000 + $60,000 = $640,000).

Cash Received from Customers. The income statement for Simplex reports $900,000 in sales during the year. Remember that revenues are recognized when earned, regardless of the amount of cash actually received. To prepare the statement of cash flows, these revenues must be converted to the amount of *cash received from customers during the year*.

If all sales were made for cash, it would not be necessary to adjust the sales reported on the income statement. However, the presence of Accounts Receivable on the balance sheet indicates that Simplex extends credit to its customers. The rate at which credit customers pay their bills affects the cash received from sales during the year. This relationship is most easily understood by observing changes in the balance of Accounts Receivable.

For example, assume that a company's sales for the year were $100 and the balance of Accounts Receivable went from $0 to $10. Since the amount owed by customers increased by $10, the company received only $90 in cash during the year. On the other hand, if the beginning balance of the receivables account was $10 and the ending balance was $0, cash of $110 was actually received, even though sales for the year were only $100. The latter situation indicates that cash was received for all sales made during the current year and $10 was received from sales made on account in prior years. Thus, an increase in accounts receivable represents a reduction in the cash generated from sales and a decrease in accounts receivable represents an increase in the cash generated from sales.

LEARNING KEY: Cash received from customers:
Sales
(− ↑) or (+ ↓) in Accounts Receivable
= Cash received from customers

The balance sheet for Simplex shows that the receivables decreased during 20-3 by $30,000 ($190,000 − $160,000). From this decrease, we know that the cash received from customers was $30,000 greater than the $900,000 in current sales reported on the income statement. Thus, on the schedule in Figure 24-5, $30,000 is added to the $900,000 in sales reported on the income statement to show that $930,000 was received from customers during the past year.

T accounts also may be used to compute the cash received from customers as shown below.

BB: Beginning Balance
EB: Ending Balance
(1): Entry for sales assuming that all were made on account.
(2): Credit required to balance Accounts Receivable. This represents the amount of cash collected from customers.

(1) Accounts Receivable   900,000
      Sales   900,000
(2) Cash   930,000
      Accounts Receivable   930,000

Cash Paid for Merchandise. Simplex reports cost of goods sold of $600,000 on the income statement. To determine cash generated from operating activities, cost of goods sold is adjusted to reflect cash paid to suppliers for merchandise. To do so, two steps are required:

STEP 1   Examine changes in the inventory account to determine the amount of merchandise purchased during the year.

STEP 2   Examine changes in the accounts payable account to determine the amount of cash actually paid to suppliers.

To determine the amount of inventory purchased during the year, examine the cost of goods sold and inventory accounts. An increase in inventory during the year indicates that merchandise purchases were greater than the cost of the merchandise sold. A decrease in inventory indicates that the company did not replace all of the inventory sold, and purchases were less than the cost of goods sold. Thus, purchases for the year can be determined by adjusting the cost of goods sold for changes in the inventory level.

For example, assume that the cost of goods sold is $80. If the inventory increased by $20, purchases would equal $100. If the inventory decreased by $20, purchases would equal $60.

Cost of goods sold	$ 80
Add increase in inventory	20
Cost of merchandise purchased	$100

Cost of goods sold	$ 80
Less decrease in inventory	(20)
Cost of merchandise purchased	$ 60

To determine the cash paid to suppliers, examine the cost of *merchandise* purchased, as computed above, and accounts payable. Accounts Payable is used primarily to record purchases of merchandise on account. When this is true, an increase in Accounts Payable indicates that the company has not yet paid for all of the goods purchased during the year. A decrease in Accounts Payable indicates that the company has paid for purchases made this year plus purchases made in prior years. Let's continue with the above example for cost of merchandise purchased of $60. If Accounts Payable increased by $10, cash paid for merchandise would equal $50.

Cost of goods sold	$80
Less decrease in inventory	(20)
Cost of merchandise purchased	$60
Less increase in accounts payable	(10)
Cash paid for merchandise	$50

If Accounts Payable decreased by $10, cash paid for merchandise would equal $70.

Cost of goods sold	$80
Less decrease in inventory	(20)
Cost of merchandise purchased	$60
Add decrease in accounts payable	10
Cash paid for merchandise	$70

LEARNING KEY: Cash paid for merchandise:
Cost of goods sold
$(+\uparrow)$ or $(-\downarrow)$ in Inventory
= Cost of merchandise purchased
$(-\uparrow)$ or $(+\downarrow)$ in Accounts Payable
= Cash paid for merchandise

To compute the cash paid for merchandise by Simplex, consider the following three factors:

1. the cost of goods sold,

2. the change in Merchandise Inventory, and

3. the change in Accounts Payable.

Cost of goods sold, as reported on the income statement in Figure 24-4, was $600,000. However, the balance sheet reports that inventory decreased by $20,000 ($200,000 – $180,000). The cost of merchandise purchased by Simplex, therefore, was $580,000 ($600,000 – $20,000 [the decrease in inventory]). Thus, $20,000 is *deducted* from the cost of goods sold in column 3 of Figure 24-5.

The balance sheet shows that Accounts Payable decreased by $60,000 ($180,000 – $120,000). This indicates that in addition to paying for the purchases made this period, Simplex paid $60,000 for merchandise purchased in prior periods. Thus $60,000 must be *added* to the cost of goods sold in column 2 of Figure 24-5 to compute the cash paid for merchandise of $640,000.

LEARNING KEY: Cash Paid for Merchandise—Simplex

Cost of goods sold	$600,000
Less decrease in inventory	(20,000)
Cost of merchandise purchased	$580,000
Add decrease in accounts payable	60,000
Cash paid for merchandise	$640,000

T accounts also may be used to compute cash paid for merchandise as shown below.

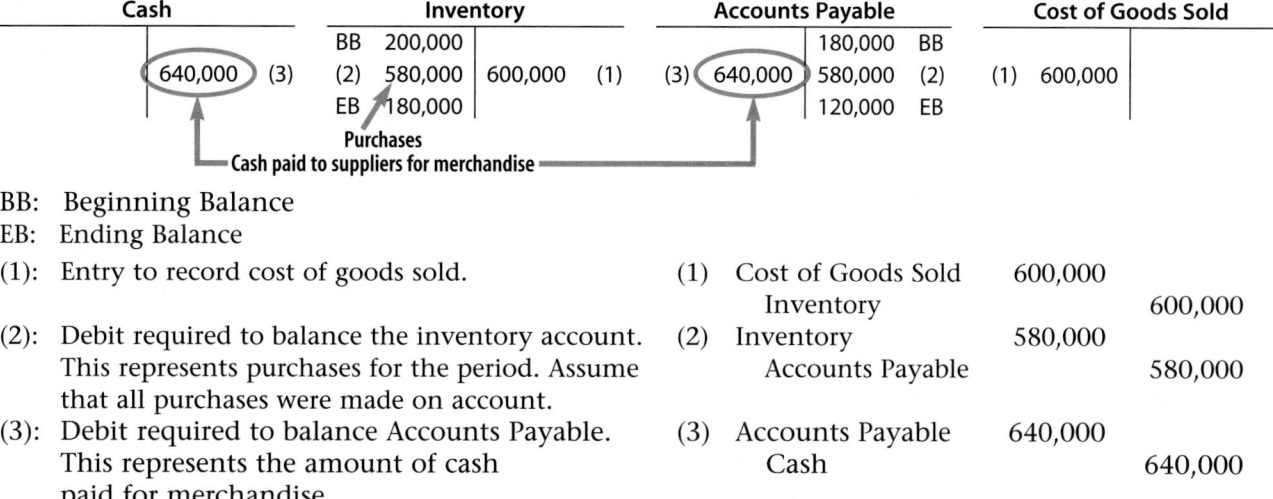

BB: Beginning Balance
EB: Ending Balance

(1): Entry to record cost of goods sold.

(2): Debit required to balance the inventory account. This represents purchases for the period. Assume that all purchases were made on account.

(3): Debit required to balance Accounts Payable. This represents the amount of cash paid for merchandise.

(1)	Cost of Goods Sold	600,000	
	Inventory		600,000
(2)	Inventory	580,000	
	Accounts Payable		580,000
(3)	Accounts Payable	640,000	
	Cash		640,000

Cash Paid for Operating Expenses. Adjustments to operating expenses generally are necessary for items such as prepaid expenses, accrued liabilities, or depreciation on plant and equipment. Simplex does not have any of these items, so there is no need to adjust operating expenses. The entire $220,000 of operating expenses is reported as a cash outflow. It is assumed that all of these expenses required cash outflows.

The schedule in Figure 24-5 demonstrates that net income was $80,000, but only $70,000 in cash was generated from operating activities. All of the information in column 4 is reported on the statement of cash flows illustrated in Figure 24-6.

FIGURE 24-6 Statement of Cash Flows for Simplex

Simplex Company Statement of Cash Flows For Year Ended December 31, 20-3										
Cash flows from operating activities:										
Cash received from customers						$930	0	0	0	00
Cash paid for merchandise	$(640	0	0	0	00)					
Cash paid for operating expenses	(220	0	0	0	00)					
Total cash disbursed for operating activities						(860	0	0	0	00)
Net cash provided by operating activities						$ 70	0	0	0	00
Cash flows from investing activities:										
Purchased building	$(140	0	0	0	00)					
Purchased equipment	(100	0	0	0	00)					
Net cash used by investing activities						(240	0	0	0	00)
Cash flows from financing activities:										
Issued note payable	$ 10	0	0	0	00					
Issued common stock	70	0	0	0	00					
Paid cash dividends	(20	0	0	0	00)					
Net cash provided by financing activities						60	0	0	0	00
Net increase (decrease) in cash						$(110	0	0	0	00)
Cash balance, January 1, 20-3						200	0	0	0	00
Cash balance, December 31, 20-3						$ 90	0	0	0	00

Cash Flows from Investing Activities

The second major section of the statement of cash flows reports investing activities. This section includes the purchase and sale of long-term assets as well as investments in the debt and equity securities of other businesses. Making loans and collecting the principal on loans are also reported in this section.

The balance sheet for Simplex reports that the building account increased from $0 to $140,000 and the equipment account increased from $0 to $100,000. As noted in the additional information in Figure 24-4, the building and equipment were acquired just before year end. As shown in Figure 24-6, the acquisition of the building and equipment are reported under investing activities. The amounts are reported in parentheses ( ) to indicate an outflow of cash. Since these are the only investing activities for the year, the net cash used by investing activities is $240,000.

Cash Flows from Financing Activities

This section of the statement reports exchanges of cash between the company and its stockholders and creditors. For Simplex, the only transaction with creditors is the $10,000 increase in Notes Payable. The proceeds from this financing activity are reported as a cash inflow from financing activities.

The balance sheet in Figure 24-4 shows that total stockholders' equity increased by $130,000. This can be broken down by analyzing the changes in the retained earnings and the capital stock accounts as follows:

Stockholders' equity, January 1, 20-3		$400,000
Retained earnings		
Net income	$80,000	
Less dividends	(20,000)	
Capital stock		
Issuance of common stock	70,000	
Increase in stockholders' equity		130,000
Stockholders' equity, December 31, 20-3		$530,000

As reported on the statement of retained earnings, Simplex earned $80,000 in net income and declared and paid cash dividends of $20,000. The cash flows associated with the net income have already been reported in the section on operating activities. However, the cash paid for dividends must be reported as a cash outflow under financing activities.

The additional information, reported in Figure 24-4, indicated that Simplex issued 8,000 shares of common stock for $70,000. This can be verified by examining the common stock and paid-in capital in excess of par—common stock accounts, as shown below in T account form.

Common Stock		Paid-In Capital in Excess of Par—Common Stock	
	20-3		20-3
	Jan. 1 Bal. 250,000		Jan. 1 Bal. 100,000
	Issuance 40,000		Issuance 30,000
	Dec. 31 Bal. 290,000		Dec. 31 Bal. 130,000

40,000 + 30,000 = $70,000 cash received for common stock

The $70,000 in cash received from the issuance of common stock is reported as a cash inflow from financing activities.

Verifying the Accuracy of the Statement

The sum of the net cash inflow of $70,000 from operating activities, the net cash outflow of $240,000 from investing activities, and the net cash inflow of $60,000 from financing activities results in a net decrease in cash of $110,000. Simplex's balance sheet reports that cash decreased by $110,000 ($200,000 − $90,000) during the year. The fact that these numbers agree provides some assurance that all cash flow activities have been included in the statement. This reconciliation is generally reported at the bottom of the statement of cash flows.

PREPARING A STATEMENT OF CASH FLOWS: MULTIPLEX

LO 5   Prepare a statement of cash flows under the following conditions:
   a. the company defines cash as "cash and cash equivalents,"
   b. the company reports depreciation expense,
   c. the company has prepaid and accrued expenses, and
   d. the company has noncash investing and financing activities.

This section of the chapter shows how to prepare a statement of cash flows for a more complex business. Because of the increased complexity, a methodical approach is needed to identify all cash flows and to prepare the statement. This section provides step-by-step procedures for the preparation of the statement. In addition, four other aspects of a more complex environment are addressed. First, a more precise definition of cash is developed. Second, the treatment of depreciation expense is illustrated. Third, the effect of prepaid and accrued expenses is explained. Fourth, the reporting of noncash investing and financing activities is discussed.

To prepare a statement of cash flows under the direct method, use the information provided in Figure 24-7 and follow these steps:

Steps in Preparing the Statement of Cash Flows

STEP 1   Compute the change in cash and cash equivalents (defined in the following section) as reported on the balance sheet.

STEP 2   Prepare a schedule to calculate cash generated from operating activities by adjusting all income statement items for changes in current asset, current liability, and other related accounts as reported on the balance sheet.

STEP 3   Identify cash flows from investing activities by analyzing any additional information, as illustrated in Figure 24-7, and by reconciling balance sheet accounts related to long-term assets, investments in debt and equity securities, and loans made to parties outside the company.

STEP 4   Identify cash flows from financing activities by analyzing any additional information and reconciling balance sheet accounts related to transactions with stockholders and creditors.

NOTE: Upon completion of STEPS 2–4, all noncash balance sheet accounts should have been analyzed in an attempt to identify cash flows. When performing the steps, check off each account to ensure that none is overlooked.

STEP 5   Sum the cash flows from operating, investing, and financing activities to determine the net increase or decrease in cash and cash equivalents. Compare this amount with the change in cash and cash equivalents computed in STEP 1.

STEP 6   Prepare a schedule of noncash investing and financing activities.

FIGURE 24-7 Financial Statements and Additional Information for Multiplex

Multiplex Corporation Income Statement For Year Ended December 31, 20-2					
Net sales				$460 1 0 0 00	
Cost of goods sold				270 1 0 0 00	
Gross profit on sales				$190 0 0 0 00	
Operating expenses				144 7 5 0 00	
Operating income				$ 45 2 5 0 00	
Other revenues and expenses:					
Interest revenue	$ 1 5 5 00				
Interest expense	(6 5 0 00)		(4 9 5 00)		
Net income				$ 44 7 5 5 00	

Multiplex Corporation Statement of Retained Earnings For Year Ended December 31, 20-2			
Retained earnings, January 1, 20-2			$23 6 6 0 00
Net income	$44 7 5 5 00		
Less dividends	22 8 0 0 00		
Net increase in retained earnings			21 9 5 5 00
Retained earnings, December 31, 20-2			$45 6 1 5 00

Additional information:

1. Depreciation expense for the year was $10,400.

2. No equipment was sold during the period. The following cash purchases were made:

    Store equipment $ 9,200
    Office equipment   4,000
                        $13,200

3. A $13,000, three-year note was issued to acquire delivery equipment with a market value of $13,000.

4. Declared and paid cash dividends of $22,800.

5. Issued 200 shares of common stock for $15 per share.

FIGURE 24-7 Financial Statements and Additional Information for Multiplex (continued)

Multiplex Corporation
Comparative Balance Sheet
December 31, 20-2 and 20-1

	20-2		20-1		INCREASE (DECREASE)
Assets					
Current assets:					
Cash	$ 22 9 8 0 00		$20 0 0 0 00		$ 2 9 8 0 00
Government notes	1 8 0 0 00		3 2 0 0 00		(1 4 0 0 00)
Accrued interest receivable	1 0 0 00		3 0 0 00		(2 0 0 00)
Accounts receivable (net)	60 2 1 5 00		51 5 1 0 00		8 7 0 5 00
Merchandise inventory	64 5 7 0 00		67 5 0 0 00		(2 9 3 0 00)
Supplies and prepayments	4 0 0 0 00		2 7 5 0 00		1 2 5 0 00
Total current assets		$153 6 6 5 00		$145 2 6 0 00	8 4 0 5 00
Property, plant, and equipment:					
Store equipment	$ 48 0 0 0 00		$38 8 0 0 00		9 2 0 0 00
Less accumulated depreciation—Store equipment	18 0 0 0 00	30 0 0 0 00	14 0 0 0 00	24 8 0 0 00	4 0 0 0 00
Delivery equipment	$ 45 0 0 0 00		$32 0 0 0 00		13 0 0 0 00
Less accumulated depreciation—Delivery equip.	12 5 0 0 00	32 5 0 0 00	8 0 0 0 00	24 0 0 0 00	4 5 0 0 00
Office equipment	$ 38 0 0 0 00		$34 0 0 0 00		4 0 0 0 00
Less accumulated depreciation—Office equipment	8 0 0 0 00	30 0 0 0 00	6 1 0 0 00	27 9 0 0 00	1 9 0 0 00
Total property, plant, and equipment		$ 92 5 0 0 00		$ 76 7 0 0 00	15 8 0 0 00
Total assets		$246 1 6 5 00		$221 9 6 0 00	24 2 0 5 00
Liabilities					
Current liabilities:					
Notes payable	$ 10 0 0 0 00		$11 8 0 0 00		(1 8 0 0 00)
Accounts payable	36 5 0 0 00		47 9 0 0 00		(11 4 0 0 00)
Accrued and withheld payroll taxes	9 5 0 00		1 5 2 0 00		(5 7 0 00)
Accrued interest payable	1 0 0 00		8 0 00		2 0 00
Total current liabilities		$ 47 5 5 0 00		$ 61 3 0 0 00	(13 7 5 0 00)
Long-term liabilities:					
Note payable (3-year)		13 0 0 0 00			13 0 0 0 00
Total liabilities		$ 60 5 5 0 00		$ 61 3 0 0 00	(7 5 0 00)
Stockholders' Equity					
Common stock ($10 par, 100,000 shares authorized;					
Issued: 10,000 in 20-2 and 9,800 in 20-1)	$100 0 0 0 00		$98 0 0 0 00		2 0 0 0 00
Paid-in capital in excess of par—Common stock	40 0 0 0 00		39 0 0 0 00		1 0 0 0 00
Retained earnings	45 6 1 5 00		23 6 6 0 00		21 9 5 5 00
Total stockholders' equity		185 6 1 5 00		160 6 6 0 00	24 9 5 5 00
Total liabilities and stockholders' equity		$246 1 6 5 00		$221 9 6 0 00	24 2 0 5 00

Definition of Cash Equivalents

To earn a return on idle cash, many companies invest in short-term, highly liquid investments known as **cash equivalents**. To qualify as cash equivalents, the investments must be readily convertible to a *known* amount of cash, so that when cash is needed, the investments can be easily liquidated. Examples of cash equivalents include short-term investments in government notes and money market funds. These investments are considered the same as cash when preparing the statement of cash flows. Thus, the statement should explain the change in the amount of cash *and* cash equivalents held at the beginning and at the end of an accounting period.

> **LEARNING KEY:** A cash equivalent is a short-term, highly liquid investment that can be readily converted to a known amount of cash.

Multiplex has cash equivalents (government notes) of $1,800 and $3,200 on December 31, 20-2 and 20-1, respectively. Thus, the statement of cash flows must explain why cash and government notes increased by $1,580 during the year.

	20-2 Dec. 31	20-1 Dec. 31	Increase (Decrease)
Cash	$22,980	$20,000	$2,980
Government notes	1,800	3,200	(1,400)
Cash and cash equivalents	$24,780	$23,200	$1,580

Cash Flows from Operating Activities: The Direct Method

To compute the cash flows from operating activities, prepare a schedule converting the accrual basis income statement to cash flows, as shown in Figure 24-8. Following the same procedure used for Simplex, column 1 shows revenues and expenses as reported on the income statement. Columns 2 and 3 show additions and deductions to convert the accrual basis figures to the associated cash flows reported in column 4.

Cash Received from Customers. The abbreviated income statement for Multiplex in Figure 24-7 reports net sales of $460,100. The $8,705 increase in net receivables ($60,215 – $51,510) reported on the balance sheet means that cash was not received for all of the sales made during the year. As shown on the schedule in Figure 24-8, the increase in net receivables must be deducted from net sales to compute cash received from customers of $451,395.

Cash Paid for Merchandise. As discussed earlier, cost of goods sold must be adjusted for changes in Merchandise Inventory and Accounts Payable to compute cash paid for merchandise.

Merchandise Inventory. The balance sheet shows that inventory decreased by $2,930. This means that the cost of the goods sold exceeded the cost of the goods purchased during the year. Deduct the decrease in inventory from the cost of goods sold to compute net purchases, as shown in column 3 in Figure 24-8.

FIGURE 24-8 Schedule for the Calculation of Cash Generated from Operating Activities for Multiplex

Multiplex Corporation								
Schedule for the Calculation of Cash Generated from Operating Activities								
For Year Ended December 31, 20-2								

INCOME STATEMENT		ADDITIONS		DEDUCTIONS		CASH FLOWS	
Net sales	$460,100			**1**	$(8,705)	$451,395	Cash received from customers
Cost of goods sold	270,100	**3**	$11,400	**2**	(2,930)	278,570	Cash paid for merchandise
Gross profit	$190,000					$172,825	
Operating expenses	144,750	**4**	1,250	**5**	(10,400)		
		6	570			136,170	Cash paid for operating expenses
Operating income	$ 45,250					$ 36,655	
Interest revenue	155	**7**	200			355	Interest received
Interest expense	650			**8**	(20)	630	Interest paid
Net income	$ 44,755					$ 36,380	Cash generated from operating activities

1 The increase in Accounts Receivable reduced the amount of cash received from sales. Subtract this $8,705 increase from Sales to compute cash received from customers.

2 The $2,930 decrease in inventory indicates that Multiplex purchased less inventory than it sold. Subtract this decrease from cost of goods sold to compute the cost of merchandise purchased for the year ($270,100 − $2,930 = $267,170).

3 The $11,400 decrease in Accounts Payable means that Multiplex paid cash to suppliers in excess of amounts purchased. Add the decrease in the amount owed to suppliers to the cost of merchandise purchased to compute cash paid for merchandise ($267,170 + $11,400 = $278,570).

4 The increase in supplies and prepayments indicates that Multiplex not only replenished these items for the amounts used during the period, but also increased the supplies on hand and prepayments. Thus, the cash paid for these items is greater than the expense recognized for the period. Add the increase of $1,250 to compute cash paid for operating expenses.

5 Depreciation is an operating expense but requires no cash outflow. Subtract the $10,400 ($4,000 + $4,500 + $1,900) in depreciation expense from operating expenses to compute cash paid for operating expenses.

6 By making payments to the government and reducing Accrued and Withheld Payroll Taxes, the amount of cash paid to the government this period was increased. Add the reduction of $570 to operating expenses to compute cash paid for operating expenses.

7 Add the reduction in Accrued Interest Receivable of $200 to Interest Revenue to compute the amount of interest received in cash.

8 Deduct the increase in Accrued Interest Payable of $20 from Interest Expense to compute the amount of interest paid in cash.

Accounts Payable. Multiplex reports a decrease in Accounts Payable of $11,400. This means that Multiplex paid for merchandise purchased this period *and* for merchandise purchased on account in prior periods. As shown in column 2 in Figure 24-8, add the $11,400 decrease in the amount owed to suppliers to cost of goods sold. The adjustments for inventory and accounts payable result in $278,570 cash paid to suppliers for merchandise.

Cash Paid for Operating Expenses. The income statement shown in Figure 24-7 reports $144,750 in operating expenses. The balance sheet and additional information provided in Figure 24-7 are reviewed to identify necessary adjustments to compute cash paid for operating expenses.

Supplies and Prepayments. The balance sheet shows that Supplies and Prepayments increased by $1,250. Thus, the cash paid for these items was greater than the expense reported on the income statement. As shown in Figure 24-8, add the increase of $1,250 to operating expenses to compute cash paid for operating expenses.

LEARNING KEY: Cash paid for supplies and prepayments:
Expense reported for supplies and prepayments
$(+\uparrow)$ or $(-\downarrow)$ in supplies or prepayments
= Cash paid for supplies and prepayments

Depreciation Expense. Accumulated depreciation on the various types of equipment increased by $10,400. The additional information in Figure 24-7 explains that this increase is the depreciation expense for the year. To recognize depreciation expense, Multiplex made the following adjusting entries at the end of the year:

4	Dec.	31	Depr. Expense—Store Equipment		4	0	0	0	00									4
5			Accum. Depr.—Store Equipment								4	0	0	0	00		5
6																		6
7		31	Depr. Expense—Delivery Equipment		4	5	0	0	00									7
8			Accum. Depr.—Delivery Equipment								4	5	0	0	00		8
9																		9
10		31	Depr. Expense—Office Equipment		1	9	0	0	00									10
11			Accum. Depr.—Office Equipment								1	9	0	0	00		11

The above entries increase operating expenses and reduce net income, but do not require an outflow of cash. Therefore, the amount of depreciation expense must be deducted from the operating expenses to determine the cash paid for operating expenses, as shown in column 3 of Figure 24-8.

LEARNING KEY: Depreciation Expense increases operating expenses, but requires no cash outflow. Therefore, deduct this amount from operating expenses to compute cash paid.

Accrued and Withheld Payroll Taxes. The balance sheet shows that Accrued and Withheld Payroll Taxes decreased by $570. This decrease means that payments made to the government by Multiplex exceeded the Payroll Tax Expense by $570. Thus, the $570 decrease in the accrued and withheld payroll taxes account must be added to operating expenses to compute cash paid for operating expenses.

As reported in column 4 of Figure 24-8, after completing the above adjustments, cash paid for operating expenses is $136,170.

> **LEARNING KEY:** Cash paid for accrued expenses:
> Accrued expenses reported on income statement (e.g., Payroll Tax Expense)
> ($-\uparrow$) or ($+\downarrow$) in accrued liabilities (e.g., Payroll Tax Payable)
> = Cash paid for accrued expenses

Cash Received from Interest. Review the balance sheet to determine whether Interest Revenue must be adjusted to reflect interest received in cash. Accrued Interest Receivable decreased by $200. This means that Multiplex received $200 in cash for interest earned in prior periods in addition to the cash received for interest earned this period. Add this amount to Interest Revenue to compute cash received from interest.

> **LEARNING KEY:** Cash received from interest:
> Interest revenue reported on income statement
> ($-\uparrow$) or ($+\downarrow$) in Interest Receivable
> = Cash received from interest

Cash Paid for Interest. A similar procedure is applied for Interest Expense. As reported on the balance sheet, Accrued Interest Payable increased by $20. This means that Multiplex did not pay for all of the $650 of interest expense incurred this period. The $20 increase in the liability is deducted from Interest Expense to compute cash paid for interest.

> **LEARNING KEY:** Cash paid for interest:
> Interest expense reported on income statement
> ($-\uparrow$) or ($+\downarrow$) in Interest Payable
> = Cash paid for interest

Once the accrual basis revenues and expenses are adjusted, cash from operating activities is determined to be $36,380. This amount is shown at the bottom of column 4. All of the information from column 4 is presented on the statement of cash flows, shown in Figure 24-9, under cash flows from operating activities.

Cash Flows from Investing Activities

Investing activities are transactions involving the purchase and sale of long-term assets, investments in debt and equity securities, and the lending of money and subsequent collection of the principal on those loans. Investing activities by Multiplex this past year included the purchase of store, delivery, and office equipment as disclosed under the additional information in Figure 24-7. These acquisitions explain the increase in store equipment of $9,200, delivery equipment of $13,000, and office equipment of $4,000 as reported on the balance sheet. Since cash was paid for the store and office equipment, these acquisitions are reported in parentheses on the statement of cash flows in Figure 24-9 to indicate a total outflow of cash for investing activities of $13,200. Since the delivery equipment was acquired by issuing a note payable, no cash outflow was required. This

FIGURE 24-9 Statement of Cash Flows for Multiplex

Multiplex Corporation Statement of Cash Flows For Year Ended December 31, 20-2										
Cash flows from operating activities:										
Cash received from customers	$451	3	9	5	00					
Interest received		3	5	5	00					
Cash provided by operating activities						$451	7	5	0	00
Cash paid for merchandise	$(278	5	7	0	00)					
Cash paid for operating expenses	(136	1	7	0	00)					
Interest paid		(6	3	0	00)					
Total cash disbursed for operating activities						(415	3	7	0	00)
Net cash provided by operating activities						$ 36	3	8	0	00
Cash flows from investing activities:										
Purchased store equipment	$ (9	2	0	0	00)					
Purchased office equipment	(4	0	0	0	00)					
Net cash used by investing activities						(13	2	0	0	00)
Cash flows from financing activities:										
Issued common stock	$ 3	0	0	0	00					
Paid cash dividends	(22	8	0	0	00)					
Retired note payable	(1	8	0	0	00)					
Net cash used by financing activities						(21	6	0	0	00)
Net increase (decrease) in cash and cash equivalents						$ 1	5	8	0	00
Cash and cash equivalents, January 1, 20-2						23	2	0	0	00
Cash and cash equivalents, December 31, 20-2						$ 24	7	8	0	00
Schedule of noncash investing and financing activities:										
Acquired delivery equipment by issuing a 3-year note.						$ 13	0	0	0	00

noncash investing and financing activity is reported in a separate schedule at the bottom of the statement.

Cash Flows from Financing Activities

Financing activities include transactions with owners and creditors. The additional information in Figure 24-7 indicates that 200 shares of $10 par common stock were issued for $3,000. This explains the increases in Common Stock of $2,000 and in Paid-In Capital in Excess of Par—Common Stock of $1,000 as reported on the balance sheet. The $3,000 cash inflow is reported under financing activities.

The statement of retained earnings and additional information provided in Figure 24-7 indicate that $22,800 in dividends were declared and paid. These dividends represent an outflow of cash from financing activities and are reported in parentheses.

The reduction in the notes payable account (current) on the balance sheet indicates that a note of $1,800 was paid off. This additional outflow of cash is also reported in parentheses.

These three transactions resulted in a net cash outflow of $21,600 from financing activities. This amount also is reported on the statement of cash flows.

The long-term note payable was issued for the acquisition of delivery equipment, so no cash was received. This noncash investing and financing transaction is reported in the separate schedule at the bottom of the statement.

Schedule of Noncash Investing and Financing Activities

Some investing and financing activities involve no cash flows, but represent a significant change in the company's financial position. These events are called **noncash investing and financing activities**. An example of this type of transaction is the issuance of the $13,000 note payable to acquire delivery equipment. Multiplex entered this transaction as shown below.

15		Delivery Equipment	13	0	0	0	00						15
16		Note Payable						13	0	0	0	00	16
17		Purchased delivery equipment by											17
18		issuing a note payable											18

LEARNING KEY: Noncash investing and financing activities are investing and financing activities that involve no cash flows, but represent a significant change in the company's financial position.

Since no cash is involved in the above transaction, it should not be included in any of the three main sections of the statement of cash flows. However, the acquisition of the delivery equipment is an investing activity and signing the note payable is a financing activity. Since this event is important in understanding changes in the company's financial position, it should be reported in a separate section of the statement as follows:

Schedule of noncash investing and financing activities:
    Acquired delivery equipment by issuing a note payable $13,000

Verifying the Accuracy of the Statement

At this point, the impact of changes in all noncash (and noncash equivalent) balance sheet accounts is reflected on the statement of cash flows. Therefore, the statement's accuracy should be verified. Summing the cash flows from operating, investing, and financing activities indicates that there was a net increase in cash and cash equivalents of $1,580. Since this agrees with the increase in the sum of the cash and government notes reported on the balance sheet in Figure 24-7, there is some assurance of the accuracy of the statement. Generally, this reconciliation is reported at the bottom of the statement of cash flows.

It is important to review all balance sheet accounts to identify transactions impacting cash. In more complex settings, it may be helpful to reconcile the balance of each account and record any impact on cash flows. This approach is illustrated in the appendix to this chapter.

INTERPRETING THE STATEMENT OF CASH FLOWS

LO 6 Interpret the statement of cash flows.

The purpose of the statement of cash flows is to provide information on the sources and uses of cash. To do this, all cash-related activities are grouped into three categories: operating, investing, and financing. Probably the most important indicator of the financial health of a business is the net cash used or provided by operating activities. Both Simplex and Multiplex had positive cash flows from operations. This is important because these funds are needed to purchase property, plant, and equipment to upgrade or expand operations. Expansion and renewal can be financed through borrowing or through the issuance of capital stock. However, loans must be repaid with interest, and dividends will be paid to stockholders in proportion to the amount invested. Ultimately, these funds must be generated from operations. A chronic inability to generate positive cash flows from operations is a sure sign of financial instability.

LEARNING KEY: Probably the most important indicator of the financial health of a business is the net cash used or provided by operating activities.

Information on investing and financing activities is also useful in evaluating the financial health of the company. For example, the statement of cash flows in Figure 24-9 shows that Multiplex generated $36,380 from operating activities. Of this amount, $15,000 ($13,200 + $1,800) was used to buy equipment and pay off debt. An additional $22,800 was paid out in dividends. Approximately 63% ($22,800 ÷ $36,380) of the cash generated from operating activities went to the stockholders. If dividends begin to exceed the cash generated from operating activities, it could imply that the company is planning to go out of business.

Modest increases or decreases in cash balances are normal. Major fluctuations should be investigated and can generally be explained by current and expected future investment and financing activities.

Learning Objectives	Key Points to Remember
1 Explain the purpose of the statement of cash flows.	The purpose of the statement of cash flows is to report how cash was generated and used throughout the accounting period.
2 Define operating, investing, and financing activities and describe transactions for each type of activity.	The statement has three major sections that report on cash flows from operating, investing, and financing activities. Operating activities include transactions and events associated with selling a product or providing a service and are related to the revenues and expenses reported on the income statement. Investing activities are those transactions involving the purchase and sale of long-term assets, investments in debt and equity securities, and lending money and collecting the principal on the related loans. Financing activities are those transactions dealing with the exchange of cash between the company and its stockholders and creditors. The inflows and outflows associated with these types of activities are shown below.

OPERATING ACTIVITIES

Cash Inflows	Cash Outflows
1. Cash receipts from the sale of goods or services.	1. Payments for the acquisition of inventory.
2. Interest received on loans made to outside entities.	2. Payments to employees and the government.
3. Dividends received on investments made in the stock of other corporations.	3. Payments for interest on loans.
	4. Payments to other suppliers and for other expenses.

INVESTING ACTIVITIES

Cash Inflows	Cash Outflows
1. Proceeds from collection of principal amount of loans made to borrowers.*	1. Loans made by the company to other parties.
2. Proceeds from the sale of property, plant, and equipment; intangibles; and other productive assets.	2. Payments to acquire property, plant, and equipment; intangibles; and other productive assets.
3. Proceeds from the sale of investments in debt and equity securities.	3. Payments to acquire investments in debt and equity securities.
4. Proceeds from discounting notes receivable.	

* Note that interest received on loans is not included with investing activities. It is included with cash inflows from operating activities.

Learning Objectives	Key Points to Remember

FINANCING ACTIVITIES	
Cash Inflows	**Cash Outflows**
1. Proceeds from additional investments by the owners or the issuance of stock.	1. Payments of dividends to stockholders or withdrawals by the owners.
2. Proceeds from borrowing money through the signing of a mortgage, issuing a bond, or other long- or short-term loans.	2. Payments to purchase treasury stock.
	3. Repayment of the principal on loans.*

* Interest payments on loans are not reported under financing activities. They are reported as cash outflows under operating activities.

Note: Amounts owed to suppliers of goods and services are not considered financing activities. They are used in the calculation of cash from operating activities.

---

3 **Describe the information needed to prepare a statement of cash flows.**

To prepare a statement of cash flows, the following information is needed:
1. balance sheets for the beginning and end of the period,
2. income statement,
3. statement of retained earnings, and
4. any additional information on major cash transactions.

---

4 **Prepare a schedule for the calculation of cash generated from operating activities under the direct method.**

Steps in preparing a schedule for the calculation of cash flows from operating activities under the direct method are as follows:

STEP 1   Convert sales to cash received from customers by adjusting for changes in accounts receivable.

STEP 2   Convert cost of goods sold to cash paid for merchandise by adjusting for changes in inventory and accounts payable.

STEP 3   Convert operating expenses to cash paid for operating expenses by adjusting for changes in current assets and current liabilities related to operating expenses and for noncash expenses.

STEP 4   Convert interest revenue and interest expense to cash received and paid for interest by adjusting for changes in interest receivable and interest payable.

---

5 **Prepare a statement of cash flows under the following conditions:**

a. the company defines cash as "cash and cash equivalents,"

b. the company reports depreciation expense,

c. the company has prepaid and accrued expenses, and

d. the company has noncash investing and financing activities.

Steps in preparing a statement of cash flows are as follows:

STEP 1   Compute the change in cash and cash equivalents. Many companies define cash as "cash and cash equivalents" on the statement of cash flows. Cash equivalents are short-term, highly liquid investments that can be readily converted to a known amount of cash.

STEP 2   Prepare a schedule to calculate cash generated from operating activities under the direct method.

STEP 3   Identify cash flows from investing activities.

STEP 4   Identify cash flows from financing activities.

NOTE: All noncash balance sheet accounts should have been analyzed to identify cash flows. Check off each account so that none is overlooked.

STEP 5   Sum the cash flows from operating, investing, and financing activities to determine the net increase or decrease in cash and cash equivalents.

Learning Objectives	Key Points to Remember
	Compare this amount with the change in the cash and cash equivalents computed in STEP 1.
	STEP 6 Prepare a schedule of noncash investing and financing activities. An example is the purchase of a machine by signing a note payable. Since no cash is exchanged, this transaction is reported in a separate section on the statement of cash flows.
6 Interpret the statement of cash flows.	Probably the most important indicator of the financial health of a company is the net cash used or provided by operating activities. These funds are needed to purchase property, plant, and equipment. Borrowing or the issuance of capital stock can be used to finance expansion, but loans must be repaid with interest and dividends must be paid to stockholders. These funds must ultimately be generated from operations.

Reflection: Answering the Opening Question

The income statement is prepared under the accrual basis of accounting. Revenues are reported when earned, regardless of when cash is received, and expenses are reported when incurred, regardless of when paid. If customers are slow in paying and creditors expect prompt payment, cash balances may get low, even when the company reports adequate profits. In addition, the company may invest cash in additional plant and equipment, or repay loans faster than it is able to collect cash from customers. When this happens, it will be necessary for Mike to borrow cash from a bank or other creditor.

KEY TERMS

cash equivalents, (874)   Short-term, highly liquid investments that are considered the same as cash when preparing the statement of cash flows.

direct method, (864)   A method of preparing the statement of cash flows in which the revenues and expenses reported on the income statement are adjusted to reflect the amount of cash received or paid for each item.

financing activities, (862)   Transactions dealing with the exchange of cash between the company and its owners (stockholders) and creditors.

indirect method, (864)   A method of reporting cash from operating activities in which net income is adjusted for transactions that affect both net income and cash from operating activities, but in different ways.

investing activities, (861)   Transactions involving the purchase and sale of long-term assets, investments in debt and equity securities, and lending money and collecting the principal on the related loans.

noncash investing and financing activities, (879)   Investing and financing activities that involve no cash flows, but represent a significant change in the company's financial position.

operating activities, (860)   Transactions and events associated with selling a product or providing a service. They are related to the revenues and expenses reported on the income statement.

statement of cash flows, (860)   Statement of the cash flows associated with the operating, investing, and financing activities of the company.

DEMONSTRATION PROBLEM

Financial statements and additional information for Megaproducts are provided below and on page 885.

Megaproducts, Inc.
Income Statement
For Year Ended December 31, 20-3

Net sales		$4,601 0 0 0 00
Cost of goods sold		2,701 0 0 0 00
Gross profit on sales		$1,900 0 0 0 00
Operating expenses		1,447 5 0 4 00
Operating income		$ 452 4 9 6 00
Other revenues and expenses:		
Interest revenue	$1 5 5 0 00	
Interest expense	(6 4 4 0 00)	(4 8 9 0 00)
Net income		$ 447 6 0 6 00

Megaproducts, Inc.
Statement of Retained Earnings
For Year Ended December 31, 20-3

Retained earnings, January 1, 20-3		$236 6 2 2 00
Net income	$447 6 0 6 00	
Less dividends	128 0 0 0 00	
Net increase in retained earnings		319 6 0 6 00
Retained earnings, December 31, 20-3		$556 2 2 8 00

Additional information:

1. Depreciation expense for the year was $104,000.

2. No equipment was sold during the period. The following cash purchases were made:

Store equipment	$ 92,000
Delivery equipment	130,000
Office equipment	40,100
	$262,100

3. Declared and paid cash dividends of $128,000.

4. Issued 2,000 shares of $10 par common stock for $15 per share.

5. Retired notes payable for $17,200 and acquired additional office equipment by issuing a note payable for $12,000.

Megaproducts, Inc.
Comparative Balance Sheet
December 31, 20-3 and 20-2

	20-3		20-2		INCREASE (DECREASE)
Assets					
Current assets:					
Cash	$ 211 7 8 6 00		$ 212 0 0 0 00		$ (2 1 4 00)
Government notes	26 0 0 0 00		20 0 0 0 00		6 0 0 0 00
Accrued interest receivable	3 0 0 00		7 0 0 00		(4 0 0 00)
Accounts receivable (net)	544 0 0 0 00		506 0 0 0 00		38 0 0 0 00
Merchandise inventory	645 6 7 8 00		675 1 2 0 00		(29 4 4 2 00)
Supplies and prepayments	40 1 5 0 00		27 3 5 6 00		12 7 9 4 00
Total current assets		$1,467 9 1 4 00		$1,441 1 7 6 00	26 7 3 8 00
Property, plant, and equipment:					
Store equipment	$ 480 0 0 0 00		$ 388 0 0 0 00		92 0 0 0 00
	180 0 0 0 00	300 0 0 0 00	140 0 0 0 00	248 0 0 0 00	40 0 0 0 00
Delivery equipment	$ 450 0 0 0 00		$ 320 0 0 0 00		130 0 0 0 00
Less accumulated depreciation—delivery equip.	125 0 0 0 00	325 0 0 0 00	80 0 0 0 00	240 0 0 0 00	45 0 0 0 00
Office equipment	$ 392 0 0 0 00		$ 339 9 0 0 00		52 1 0 0 00
Less accumulated depreciation—office equip.	80 0 0 0 00	312 0 0 0 00	61 0 0 0 00	278 9 0 0 00	19 0 0 0 00
Total property, plant, and equipment		$ 937 0 0 0 00		$ 766 9 0 0 00	170 1 0 0 00
Total assets		$2,404 9 1 4 00		$2,208 0 7 6 00	196 8 3 8 00
Liabilities					
Current liabilities:					
Notes payable	$ 112 8 0 0 00		$ 118 0 0 0 00		(5 2 0 0 00)
Accounts payable	325 1 5 0 00		467 4 5 4 00		(142 3 0 4 00)
Accrued and withheld payroll taxes	9 8 9 6 00		15 2 0 0 00		(5 3 0 4 00)
Accrued interest payable	8 4 0 00		8 0 0 00		4 0 00
Total liabilities		$ 448 6 8 6 00		$ 601 4 5 4 00	(152 7 6 8 00)
Stockholders' Equity					
Common stock ($10 par, 1,000,000 shares authorized;					
Issued: 100,000 in 20-3 and 98,000 in 20-2)	$1,000 0 0 0 00		$ 980 0 0 0 00		20 0 0 0 00
Paid-in capital in excess of par—common stock	400 0 0 0 00		390 0 0 0 00		10 0 0 0 00
Retained earnings	556 2 2 8 00		236 6 2 2 00		319 6 0 6 00
Total stockholders' equity		1,956 2 2 8 00		1,606 6 2 2 00	349 6 0 6 00
Total liabilities and stockholders' equity		$2,404 9 1 4 00		$2,208 0 7 6 00	196 8 3 8 00

REQUIRED

1. Prepare a schedule for the calculation of cash generated from operating activities for the year ended December 31, 20-3.

2. Prepare a statement of cash flows explaining the change in cash and cash equivalents for the year ended December 31, 20-3.

3. Reconcile the cash and cash equivalents at the bottom of the statement of cash flows.

Solution

1.

Megaproducts, Inc.
Schedule for the Calculation of Cash Generated from Operating Activities
For Year Ended December 31, 20-3

INCOME STATEMENT		ADDITIONS		DEDUCTIONS		CASH FLOWS	
Net sales	$4,601,000			**1** $ (38,000)		$4,563,000	Cash received from customers
Cost of goods sold	2,701,000	**3** $142,304		**2** (29,442)		2,813,862	Cash paid for merchandise
Gross profit	$1,900,000					$1,749,138	
Operating expenses	1,447,504	**4** 12,794		**5** $(104,000)			
		6 5,304				1,361,602	Cash paid for operating expenses
Operating income	$ 452,496					$ 387,536	
Interest revenue	1,550	**7** 400				1,950	Cash received from interest revenue
Interest expense	6,440			**8** (40)		6,400	Cash paid for interest expense
Net income	$ 447,606					$ 383,086	

1 The increase in Accounts Receivable reduced the amount of cash received from sales. This $38,000 increase is subtracted from sales to compute cash received from customers.

2 The $29,442 decrease in inventory indicates that Megaproducts purchased less inventory than it sold. This decrease must be subtracted from the cost of goods sold to compute purchases for the year ($2,701,000 – $29,442 = $2,671,558).

3 The $142,304 decrease in Accounts Payable is added to the cost of merchandise purchased to compute cash paid for merchandise ($2,671,558 + $142,304 = $2,813,862).

4 The increase in Supplies and Prepayments indicates that Megaproducts not only replenished these items for the amounts used during the period, but also increased the supplies on hand and prepayments. Thus, the cash paid for these items is greater than the expense recognized for the period. The increase of $12,794 must be added in the calculation of cash paid for operating expenses.

5 Depreciation is an operating expense but requires no cash outflow. The $104,000 in Depreciation Expense is subtracted from operating expenses to compute cash paid for operating expenses.

6 By making payments to the government and reducing Accrued and Withheld Payroll Taxes, the amount of cash paid to the government this period was increased. This reduction of $5,304 is added to operating expenses to compute cash paid for operating expenses.

7 The $400 reduction in Accrued Interest Receivable is added to Interest Revenue to determine the amount of interest received.

8 The $40 increase in Accrued Interest Payable is deducted from Interest Expense to compute the amount of interest paid.

2 and 3. Megaproducts, Inc.'s statement of cash flows is shown below.

Megaproducts, Inc. Statement of Cash Flows For Year Ended December 31, 20-3										
Cash flows from operating activities:										
Cash received from customers	$4,563	0	0	0	00					
Interest received	1	9	5	0	00					
Cash provided by operating activities						$4,564	9	5	0	00
Cash paid for merchandise	$(2,813	8	6	2	00)					
Cash paid for operating expenses	(1,361	6	0	2	00)					
Interest paid	(6	4	0	0	00)					
Total cash disbursed for operating activities						(4,181	8	6	4	00)
Net cash provided by operating activities						$ 383	0	8	6	00
Cash flows from investing activities:										
Purchased store equipment	$ (92	0	0	0	00)					
Purchased delivery equipment	(130	0	0	0	00)					
Purchased office equipment	(40	1	0	0	00)					
Net cash used by investing activities						(262	1	0	0	00)
Cash flows from financing activities:										
Paid cash dividends	$ (128	0	0	0	00)					
Issued common stock	30	0	0	0	00					
Retired note payable	(17	2	0	0	00)					
Net cash used by financing activities						(115	2	0	0	00)
Net increase (decrease) in cash and cash equivalents						$ 5	7	8	6	00
Cash and cash equivalents, January 1, 20-3						232	0	0	0	00
Cash and cash equivalents, December 31, 20-3						$ 237	7	8	6	00
Schedule of noncash investing and financing activities:										
Acquired office equipment by issuing a note payable.						$ 12	0	0	0	00

Note that Office Equipment and Notes Payable are affected by two transactions as shown below.

Cash				Office Equipment			Notes Payable			
			BB	339,900				118,000	BB	
	17,200	(5a)	(5b)	12,000		(5a)	17,200	12,000	(5b)	
	40,100			40,100						
			EB	392,000				112,800	EB	

REVIEW QUESTIONS

1. What is the primary purpose of the statement of cash flows?

2. Name the four principal financial statements comprising a full set of financial statements.

3. What are the three categories of cash flows shown on a statement of cash flows?

4. Name the types of cash flows associated with financing activities.

5. Name the types of cash flows associated with investing activities.

6. Name the types of cash flows associated with operating activities under the direct method.

7. What information is needed to prepare a statement of cash flows?

8. What is meant by the direct method of reporting cash flows from operating activities?

9. What is meant by the indirect method of reporting cash flows from operating activities?

10. If a company pays cash dividends, where on the statement of cash flows should the payment be reported?

11. What are cash equivalents?

12. Provide an illustration of a noncash investing and financing activity.

13. Jones Company reported depreciation expense of $45,000 on its income statement. How much cash was paid for this expense?

14. Explain the step-by-step procedures to be followed when preparing a statement of cash flows.

15. Where is cash received for interest reported on the statement of cash flows?

16. Explain the procedure for verifying the accuracy of the statement of cash flows.

MANAGING YOUR WRITING

A friend of yours was reading a statement of cash flows and saw that Depreciation Expense was added when computing cash from operating activities. She is curious why depreciation is considered a source of cash. Write a brief memo that explains why Depreciation Expense is added to net income on the statement of cash flows and why it certainly is not a source of cash.

ETHICS CASE

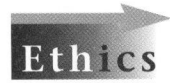

Lyle McGee had been the chief accountant at L & B Corporation for well over 20 years. He routinely omitted noncash investing and financing activities from the statement of cash flows, even when they were significant events. When a junior accountant who had just been hired questioned this practice, Lyle told her that it doesn't make any difference how significant an item is "if it doesn't involve cash. Besides, we're a small company and our stockholders are only interested in the bottom line."

1. Is it possible that Lyle thinks he is treating the significant noncash investing and financing activities properly?

2. If you were the junior accountant, what would you do?

3. Suppose that Lyle wants the junior accountant to give him a refresher course on the statement of cash flows. Write a brief memo to Lyle explaining the purpose of the statement of cash flows. Include a description of both the direct and indirect methods. Also, explain the importance of including significant noncash investing and financing activities.

4. In groups of two or three, discuss which method of preparing the statement of cash flows is easier for you to understand, the direct or the indirect, and why.

WEB WORK

Cash flow is tricky to predict in the best of situations, and for a seasonal business like beekeeping it is even more difficult. Look at a beekeeper's cash flow statements at

http://hammock.ifas.ufl.edu/txt/fairs/609.

What problems can you foresee in managing the cash flow of a seasonal business?

(http://heintz.swcollege.com)

SERIES A EXERCISES

EXERCISE 24A-1 (LO 2) IDENTIFICATION OF OPERATING, INVESTING, AND FINANCING ACTIVITIES The following activities took place during the current year. Indicate whether each activity is a cash inflow (+) or cash outflow (–), and whether it is an operating activity (O), investing activity (I), or financing activity (F).

a. Proceeds from collection of principal amount of loans made to borrowers

b. Cash receipts from the sale of goods

c. Payments for interest on loans

d. Payments of dividends to stockholders

e. Payments to acquire investments in debt securities

f. Dividends received on investments made in the stock of other corporations

(continued)

g. Repayment of the principal on loans

h. Interest received on loans made to outside entities

i. Salaries paid to employees

j. Payments to acquire property, plant, and equipment and other productive assets

k. Payments to purchase treasury stock

l. Proceeds from the sale of equity securities

EXERCISE 24A-2 (LO 4) CASH RECEIVED FROM CUSTOMERS Potts Company's sales for 20-2 were $800,000. The accounts receivable balance as of December 31, 20-1, was $90,000. This same account had a balance of $75,000 as of December 31, 20-2. Compute the amount of cash received from customers in 20-2.

EXERCISE 24A-3 (LO 4) CASH PAID FOR MERCHANDISE Douglas Company's cost of goods sold for 20-2 was $400,000. Compute the amount of cash paid for merchandise in 20-2. The December 31, 20-2 and 20-1, balances of Merchandise Inventory and Accounts Payable were as follows:

	20-2	20-1
Merchandise Inventory	$60,000	$80,000
Accounts Payable	30,000	70,000

EXERCISE 24A-4 (LO 5) CASH FLOWS FROM INVESTING AND FINANCING ACTIVITIES Rogerson Company's comparative balance sheet as of December 31, 20-2 and 20-1, showed the following with regard to investing and financing activities.

	20-2	20-1
Building	$130,000	$ 0
Equipment	90,000	0
Notes payable	30,000	20,000
Common stock at par	300,000	250,000
Paid-in capital in excess of par	80,000	50,000
Retained earnings	260,000	200,000

Net income for 20-2 was $90,000 and cash dividends of $30,000 were declared and paid. Determine the amount of cash received and paid for financing and investing activities and the cash flows as they would appear on Rogerson's statement of cash flows for the year ended December 31, 20-2.

EXERCISE 24A-5 (LO 5) CHANGE IN CASH AND CASH EQUIVALENTS Himes Company's balance sheets as of December 31, 20-4 and 20-3, showed the following with regard to cash and cash equivalents.

	20-4	20-3
Cash	$70,000	$50,000
Government notes	2,000	5,000

Compute the amount of change in cash and cash equivalents and indicate whether it represented an increase or a decrease.

EXERCISE 24A-6 (LO 5) CASH PAID FOR OPERATING EXPENSES The following information was obtained from Knox Company's income statement for 20-4, balance sheets as of December 31, 20-4 and 20-3, and auxiliary records.

Operating expenses for 20-4 $350,400
Depreciation expense for 20-4   22,000

	20-4	20-3
Supplies and prepayments	$9,600	$6,700
Accrued and withheld payroll taxes	2,900	3,800

Compute the amount of cash paid for operating expenses in 20-4.

EXERCISE 24A-7 (LO 5) CASH PAID FOR INTEREST Ball Company's income statement for 20-4 reported interest expense of $1,540. The comparative balance sheet as of December 31, 20-4 and 20-3, reported the following:

	20-4	20-3
Accrued interest payable	$260	$220

Compute the amount of cash paid for interest in 20-4.

EXERCISE 24A-8 (LO 5) CASH RECEIVED FOR INTEREST Eary Company's income statement for 20-4 reported interest revenue of $430. The comparative balance sheet as of December 31, 20-4 and 20-3, reported the following:

	20-4	20-3
Accrued interest receivable	$150	$190

Compute the amount of cash received for interest in 20-4.

EXERCISE 24A-9 (LO 5) NONCASH INVESTING AND FINANCING ACTIVITIES Norton's sign shop issued a $10,000, three-year note payable to acquire a new framing machine. Show how this transaction is reported on a statement of cash flows.

SERIES A PROBLEMS

PROBLEM 24A-1 (LO 4) SCHEDULE FOR CALCULATION OF CASH GENERATED FROM OPERATING ACTIVITIES Mueller Company's condensed income statement for the year ended December 31, 20-2, was as follows:

Net sales	$900,000
Cost of goods sold	500,000
Gross profit	$400,000
Operating expenses	260,000
Net income	$140,000

Additional information obtained from Mueller's comparative balance sheets as of December 31, 20-2 and 20-1, was as follows:

	20-2	20-1
Cash and cash equivalents	$ 50,000	$ 10,000
Accounts receivable	80,000	90,000
Merchandise inventory	120,000	150,000
Accounts payable	60,000	80,000

(continued)

REQUIRED   Prepare a schedule for the calculation of cash generated from operating activities for the year ended December 31, 20-2.

W & D

PROBLEM 24A-2 (LO 5) STATEMENT OF CASH FLOWS Refer to Problem 24A-1. The following additional information was obtained from Mueller's financial statements and auxiliary records for the year ended December 31, 20-2.

Acquired a new warehouse	$120,000
Bought new warehouse equipment	80,000
Issued a note to the bank	40,000
Issued additional common stock:	
Par value	50,000
Paid-in capital in excess of par	20,000
Declared and paid cash dividends	30,000

REQUIRED   Prepare a statement of cash flows for Mueller for the year ended December 31, 20-2.

PROBLEM 24A-3 (LO 5) SCHEDULE FOR CALCULATION OF CASH GENERATED FROM OPERATING ACTIVITIES Horn Company's condensed income statement for the year ended December 31, 20-4, was as follows:

Net sales		$1,220,000
Cost of goods sold		740,000
Gross profit		$ 480,000
Operating expenses		260,000
Operating income		$ 220,000
Other revenues and expenses:		
Interest revenue	$ 420	
Interest expense	(1,200)	(780)
Net income		$ 219,220

Additional information obtained from Horn's comparative balance sheet and auxiliary records as of December 31, 20-4 and 20-3, was as follows:

	20-4	20-3
Accounts receivable	$135,000	$122,600
Merchandise inventory	145,300	158,900
Accounts payable	47,000	88,100
Supplies and prepayments	11,300	6,800
Accrued and withheld payroll taxes	2,750	3,700
Accrued interest receivable	90	210
Accrued interest payable	240	160

Depreciation expense for 20-4, included in operating expenses on the income statement, was $32,000.

REQUIRED   Prepare a schedule for the calculation of cash generated from operating activities for the year ended December 31, 20-4.

PROBLEM 24A-4 (LO 5) EXPANDED STATEMENT OF CASH FLOWS Financial statements for the McDowell Company as well as additional information relevant to cash flows during the period are as follows:

McDowell Company Income Statement For Year Ended December 31, 20-4			
Net sales			$1,890 0 0 0 00
Cost of goods sold			940 0 0 0 00
Gross profit			$ 950 0 0 0 00
Operating expenses			705 3 0 0 00
Operating income			$ 244 7 0 0 00
Other revenues and expenses:			
Interest revenue	$ 3 9 0 0 00		
Interest expense	(8 9 0 00)	3 0 1 0 00	
Net income			$ 247 7 1 0 00

McDowell Company Statement of Retained Earnings For Year Ended December 31, 20-4		
Retained earnings, January 1, 20-4		$360 0 0 0 00
Net income	$ 247 7 1 0 00	
Less dividends	60 0 0 0 00	
Net increase in retained earnings		187 7 1 0 00
Retained earnings, December 31, 20-4		$547 7 1 0 00

Additional information:

1. Depreciation expense for the year was $112,000.

2. No equipment was sold during the period. The following purchases were made for cash:

Store equipment	$ 64,000
Delivery equipment	140,000
Office equipment	30,000
	$234,000

3. Declared and paid cash dividends of $60,000.

4. Issued 10,000 shares of $10 par common stock for $14 per share.

5. Acquired additional store equipment by issuing a note payable for $16,000.

(continued)

McDowell Company
Comparative Balance Sheet
December 31, 20-4 and 20-3

	20-4					20-3					INCREASE (DECREASE)				
Assets															
Current assets:															
Cash	$ 50	3	6	5	00	$ 40	3	2	5	00	$ 10	0	4	0	00
Government notes	6	8	0	0	00	18	0	0	0	00	(11	2	0	0	00)
Accrued interest receivable		7	2	0	00		6	1	0	00		1	1	0	00
Accounts receivable (net)	310	7	0	0	00	325	8	0	0	00	(15	1	0	0	00)
Merchandise inventory	685	4	0	0	00	540	2	0	0	00	145	2	0	0	00
Supplies and prepayments	27	0	0	0	00	39	0	0	0	00	(12	0	0	0	00)
Total current assets	$1,080	9	8	5	00	$ 963	9	3	5	00	117	0	5	0	00
Property, plant, and equipment:															
Store equipment	$ 540	0	0	0	00	$ 460	0	0	0	00	80	0	0	0	00
Less accumulated depreciation—store equipment	(210	0	0	0	00)	(150	0	0	0	00)	60	0	0	0	00
Delivery equipment	530	0	0	0	00	390	0	0	0	00	140	0	0	0	00
Less accumulated depreciation—delivery equipment	(140	0	0	0	00)	(100	0	0	0	00)	40	0	0	0	00
Office equipment	430	0	0	0	00	400	0	0	0	00	30	0	0	0	00
Less accumulated depreciation—office equipment	(88	0	0	0	00)	(76	0	0	0	00)	12	0	0	0	00
Total property, plant, and equipment	$1,062	0	0	0	00	$ 924	0	0	0	00	138	0	0	0	00
Total assets	$2,142	9	8	5	00	$1,887	9	3	5	00	255	0	5	0	00
Liabilities															
Current liabilities:															
Notes payable	$ 118	0	0	0	00	$ 102	0	0	0	00	16	0	0	0	00
Accounts payable	130	0	0	0	00	220	0	0	0	00	(90	0	0	0	00)
Accrued and withheld payroll taxes	16	4	0	0	00	14	9	0	0	00	1	5	0	0	00
Accrued interest payable		8	7	5	00	1	0	3	5	00		(1	6	0	00)
Total liabilities	$ 265	2	7	5	00	$ 337	9	3	5	00	(72	6	6	0	00)
Stockholders' Equity															
Common stock ($10 par, 300,000 shares authorized;															
Issued: 90,000 in 20-4 and 80,000 in 20-3)	$ 900	0	0	0	00	$ 800	0	0	0	00	100	0	0	0	00
Paid-in capital in excess of par—common stock	430	0	0	0	00	390	0	0	0	00	40	0	0	0	00
Retained earnings	547	7	1	0	00	360	0	0	0	00	187	7	1	0	00
Total stockholders' equity	$1,877	7	1	0	00	$1,550	0	0	0	00	327	7	1	0	00
Total liabilities and stockholders' equity	$2,142	9	8	5	00	$1,887	9	3	5	00	255	0	5	0	00

REQUIRED

1. Prepare a schedule for the calculation of cash generated from operating activities for the year ended December 31, 20-4.

2. Prepare a statement of cash flows for the year ended December 31, 20-4.

3. Verify the accuracy of the statement of cash flows.

SERIES B EXERCISES

EXERCISE 24B-1 (LO 2) IDENTIFICATION OF OPERATING, INVESTING, AND FINANCING ACTIVITIES The following activities took place in the Tomberlin Company during the most recent year. Indicate whether each activity is a cash inflow (+) or cash outflow (–), and whether it is an operating activity (O), investing activity (I), or financing activity (F).

a. Payments to acquire productive assets

b. Proceeds from the issuance of stock

c. Interest received on loans made to outside entities

d. Proceeds from the sale of productive assets

e. Dividends received on investments made in the stock of other corporations

f. Payments to other suppliers and for other expenses

g. Payments of dividends to stockholders

h. Payments to acquire investments in debt securities

i. Payments for interest on loans

j. Cash receipts from the sale of services

k. Repayment of the principal on loans

l. Payments for the acquisition of inventory

EXERCISE 24B-2 (LO 4) CASH RECEIVED FROM CUSTOMERS Boyd Company's sales for 20-2 were $760,000. The accounts receivable balance as of December 31, 20-1, was $60,000. This same account had a balance of $85,000 as of December 31, 20-2. Compute the amount of cash received from customers in 20-2.

EXERCISE 24B-3 (LO 4) CASH PAID FOR MERCHANDISE Guild Company's cost of goods sold for 20-2 was $500,000. Compute the amount of cash paid for merchandise in 20-2. The December 31, 20-2 and 20-1, balances of Merchandise Inventory and Accounts Payable were as follows:

	20-2	20-1
Merchandise Inventory	$70,000	$50,000
Accounts Payable	60,000	90,000

EXERCISE 24B-4 (LO 5) CASH FLOWS FROM INVESTING AND FINANCING ACTIVITIES Hansen Company's comparative balance sheets as of December 31, 20-2 and 20-1, showed the following with regard to investing and financing activities.

	20-2	20-1
Building	$160,000	$ 0
Equipment	70,000	0
Notes payable	20,000	30,000
Common stock at par	260,000	200,000
Paid-in capital in excess of par	60,000	40,000
Retained earnings	220,000	160,000

(continued)

Net income for 20-2 was $80,000 and cash dividends of $20,000 were declared and paid. Determine the amount of cash received and paid for financing and investing activities and the cash flows as they would appear on Hansen's statement of cash flows for the year ended December 31, 20-2.

EXERCISE 24B-5 (LO 5) CHANGE IN CASH AND CASH EQUIVALENTS Pike Company's balance sheets as of December 31, 20-4 and 20-3, showed the following with regard to cash and cash equivalents:

	20-4	20-3
Cash	$90,000	$60,000
Government notes	4,000	8,000

Compute the amount of change in cash and cash equivalents and indicate whether it represented an increase or a decrease.

EXERCISE 24B-6 (LO 5) CASH PAID FOR OPERATING EXPENSES The following information was obtained from Busby Company's income statement for 20-4, balance sheets as of December 31, 20-4 and 20-3, and auxiliary records.

Operating expenses for 20-4	$290,500
Depreciation expense for 20-4	30,000

	20-4	20-3
Supplies and prepayments	$7,100	$8,300
Accrued and withheld payroll taxes	3,800	2,700

Compute the amount of cash paid for operating expenses in 20-4.

EXERCISE 24B-7 (LO 5) CASH PAID FOR INTEREST Mulligan Company's income statement for 20-4 reported interest expense of $2,190. The comparative balance sheet as of December 31, 20-4 and 20-3, reported the following:

	20-4	20-3
Accrued interest payable	$340	$410

Compute the amount of cash paid for interest in 20-4.

EXERCISE 24B-8 (LO 5) CASH RECEIVED FOR INTEREST Dowling Company's income statement for 20-4 reported interest revenue of $670. The comparative balance sheet as of December 31, 20-4 and 20-3, reported the following:

	20-4	20-3
Accrued interest receivable	$320	$240

Compute the amount of cash received for interest in 20-4.

EXERCISE 24B-9 (LO 5) NONCASH INVESTING AND FINANCING ACTIVITIES Murry's consulting services issued a two-year, $5,000 note payable to acquire new office furniture. Show how this transaction is reported on the statement of cash flows.

SERIES B PROBLEMS

PROBLEM 24B-1 (LO 4) SCHEDULE FOR CALCULATION OF CASH GENERATED FROM OPERATING ACTIVITIES Kennington Company's condensed income statement for the year ended December 31, 20-2 was as follows:

Net sales	$800,000
Cost of goods sold	475,000
Gross profit	$325,000
Operating expenses	110,000
Net income	$215,000

Additional information obtained from Kennington's comparative balance sheet as of December 31, 20-2 and 20-1, was as follows:

	20-2	20-1
Cash and cash equivalents	$175,000	$20,000
Accounts receivable	50,000	75,000
Merchandise inventory	70,000	110,000
Accounts payable	25,000	50,000

REQUIRED   Prepare a schedule for the calculation of cash generated from operating activities for the year ended December 31, 20-2.

W & D

PROBLEM 24B-2 (LO 5) STATEMENT OF CASH FLOWS Refer to Problem 24B-1. The following additional information was obtained from Kennington's financial statements and auxiliary records for the year ended December 31, 20-2.

Acquired a new warehouse	$90,000
Bought new warehouse equipment	60,000
Issued a note to the bank	30,000
Issued additional common stock:	
Par value	30,000
Paid-in capital in excess of par	10,000
Declared and paid cash dividends	20,000

REQUIRED   Prepare a statement of cash flows for Kennington for the year ended December 31, 20-2.

PROBLEM 24B-3 (LO 5) SCHEDULE FOR CALCULATION OF CASH GENERATED FROM OPERATING ACTIVITIES Powell Company's condensed income statement for the year ended December 31, 20-4, was as follows:

Net sales		$1,160,000
Cost of goods sold		690,000
Gross profit		$ 470,000
Operating expenses		310,100
Operating income		$ 159,900
Other revenues and expenses:		
Interest revenue	$ 560	
Interest expense	(1100)	(540)
Net income		$ 159,360

Additional information obtained from Powell's comparative balance sheet and auxiliary records as of December 31, 20-4 and 20-3, was as follows:

(continued)

	20-4	20-3
Accounts receivable	$122,700	$118,200
Merchandise inventory	116,800	139,300
Accounts payable	41,500	62,400
Supplies and prepayments	10,900	5,200
Accrued and withheld payroll taxes	1,960	2,490
Accrued interest receivable	130	175
Accrued interest payable	230	110

Depreciation expense for 20-4, included in operating expenses on the income statement, was $29,000.

REQUIRED Prepare a schedule for the calculation of cash generated from operating activities for the year ended December 31, 20-4.

PROBLEM 24B-4 (LO 5) EXPANDED STATEMENT OF CASH FLOWS Financial statements for the McGinnis Company as well as additional information relevant to cash flows during the period are as follows:

McGinnis Company Income Statement For Year Ended December 31, 20-4			
Net sales			$1,750 0 0 0 00
Cost of goods sold			890 0 0 0 00
Gross profit			$ 860 0 0 0 00
Operating expenses			685 6 0 0 00
Operating income			$ 174 4 0 0 00
Other revenues and expenses:			
Interest revenue	$2 7 0 0 00		
Interest expense	(7 5 0 00)	1 9 5 0 00	
Net income			$ 176 3 5 0 00

McGinnis Company Statement of Retained Earnings For Year Ended December 31, 20-4			
Retained earnings, January 1, 20-4			$320 0 0 0 00
Net income	$176 3 5 0 00		
Less dividends	40 0 0 0 00		
Net increase in retained earnings			136 3 5 0 00
Retained earnings, December 31, 20-4			$456 3 5 0 00

Additional information:

1. Depreciation expense for the year was $70,000.

2. No equipment was sold during the period. The following purchases were made for cash:

Store equipment	$140,000
Delivery equipment	100,000
Office equipment	32,000
	$272,000

McGinnis Company
Comparative Balance Sheet
December 31, 20-4 and 20-3

	20-4	20-3	INCREASE (DECREASE)
Assets			
Current assets:			
Cash	$ 68 420 00	$ 50 520 00	$ 17 900 00
Government notes	5 400 00	16 000 00	(10 600 00)
Accrued interest receivable	8 30 00	5 80 00	2 50 00
Accounts receivable (net)	300 600 00	309 200 00	(8 600 00)
Merchandise inventory	580 300 00	495 800 00	84 500 00
Supplies and prepayments	65 000 00	32 000 00	33 000 00
Total current assets	$1,020 550 00	$ 904 100 00	116 450 00
Property, plant, and equipment:			
Store equipment	$ 560 000 00	$ 420 000 00	140 000 00
Less accumulated depreciation—store equipment	(120 000 00)	(90 000 00)	30 000 00
Delivery equipment	430 000 00	330 000 00	100 000 00
Less accumulated depreciation—delivery equipment	(150 000 00)	(120 000 00)	30 000 00
Office equipment	420 000 00	380 000 00	40 000 00
Less accumulated depreciation—office equipment	(110 500 00)	(100 500 00)	10 000 00
Total property, plant, and equipment	$1,029 500 00	$ 819 500 00	210 000 00
Total assets	$2,050 050 00	$1,723 600 00	326 450 00
Liabilities			
Current liabilities:			
Notes payable	$ 117 000 00	$ 109 000 00	8 000 00
Accounts payable	160 000 00	200 000 00	(40 000 00)
Accrued and withheld payroll taxes	15 800 00	13 400 00	2 400 00
Accrued interest payable	9 00 00	1 200 00	(3 00 00)
Total liabilities	$ 293 700 00	$ 323 600 00	(29 900 00)
Stockholders' Equity			
Common stock ($10 par, 400,000 shares authorized;			
Issued: 80,000 in 20-4 and 70,000 in 20-3)	$ 800 000 00	$ 700 000 00	100 000 00
Paid-in capital in excess of par—common stock	500 000 00	380 000 00	120 000 00
Retained earnings	456 350 00	320 000 00	136 350 00
Total stockholders' equity	$1,756 350 00	$1,400 000 00	356 350 00
Total liabilities and stockholders' equity	$2,050 050 00	$1,723 600 00	326 450 00

3. Declared and paid cash dividends of $40,000.

4. Issued 10,000 shares of $10 par common stock for $22 per share.

5. Acquired additional office equipment by issuing a note payable for $8,000.

REQUIRED
1. Prepare a schedule for the calculation of cash generated from operating activities for the year ended December 31, 20-4.

2. Prepare a statement of cash flows for the year ended December 31, 20-4.

3. Verify the accuracy of the statement of cash flows.

MASTERY PROBLEM

Financial statements for the Peachfield Corporation as well as additional information relevant to cash flows during the period are provided below.

Peachfield Corporation
Income Statement
For Year Ended December 31, 20-2

Net sales								$985	0	0	0	00
Cost of goods sold								515	0	0	0	00
Gross profit								$470	0	0	0	00
Operating expenses								359	9	0	0	00
Operating income								$110	1	0	0	00
Other revenues and expenses:												
Interest revenue	$2	1	0	0	00							
Interest expense	(4	3	6	00)		1	6	6	4	00
Net income								$111	7	6	4	00

Peachfield Corporation
Statement of Retained Earnings
For Year Ended December 31, 20 -2

Retained earnings, January 1, 20-2								$141	9	7	3	00
Net income	$111	7	6	4	00							
Less dividends	20	0	0	0	00							
Net increase in retained earnings								91	7	6	4	00
Retained earnings, December 31, 20-2								$233	7	3	7	00

Additional information:

1. Depreciation expense for the year was $62,400.

2. No equipment was sold during the year. The following purchases were made for cash:

Store equipment	$ 55,200
Delivery equipment	78,000
Office equipment	24,060
	$157,260

3. Declared and paid cash dividends of $20,000.

4. Issued 11,200 shares of $10 par common stock for $118,000.

5. Issued a note payable for $10,700.

6. Additional store equipment was acquired by issuing a long-term note payable for $20,000.

Peachfield Corporation
Comparative Balance Sheet
December 31, 20-2 and 20-1

	20-2		20-1		INCREASE (DECREASE)
Assets					
Current assets:					
Cash	$ 27,072 00		$ 27,200 00		$ (128 00)
Government notes	3,600 00		12,000 00		(8,400 00)
Accrued interest receivable	320 00		250 00		70 00
Accounts receivable (net)	152,945 00		140,905 00		12,040 00
Merchandise inventory	355,490 00		295,400 00		60,090 00
Supplies and prepayments	14,500 00		21,500 00		(7,000 00)
Total current assets		$ 553,927 00		$497,255 00	56,672 00
Property, plant, and equipment:					
Store equipment	$308,000 00		$232,800 00		75,200 00
Less accumulated depreciation—store equipment	108,000 00	200,000 00	84,000 00	148,800 00	24,000 00
Delivery equipment	$270,000 00		$192,000 00		78,000 00
Less accumulated depreciation—delivery equipment	75,000 00	195,000 00	48,000 00	144,000 00	27,000 00
Office equipment	$228,000 00		$203,940 00		24,060 00
Less accumulated depreciation—office equipment	48,000 00	180,000 00	36,600 00	167,340 00	11,400 00
Total property, plant, and equipment		$ 575,000 00		$460,140 00	114,860 00
Total assets		$1,128,927 00		$957,395 00	171,532 00
Liabilities					
Current liabilities:					
Notes payable	$ 65,480 00		$ 54,780 00		10,700 00
Accounts payable	60,500 00		130,473 00		(69,973 00)
Accrued and withheld payroll taxes	8,760 00		7,644 00		1,116 00
Accrued interest payable	450 00		525 00		(75 00)
Total current liabilities		$ 135,190 00		$193,422 00	(58,232 00)
Long-term liabilities:					
Notes payable		20,000 00		0	20,000 00
Total liabilities		$ 155,190 00		$193,422 00	(38,232 00)
Stockholders' Equity					
Common stock ($10 par, 100,000 shares authorized;					
Issued: 50,000 in 20-2 and 38,800 in 20-1)	$500,000 00		$388,000 00		112,000 00
Paid-in capital in excess of par—common stock	240,000 00		234,000 00		6,000 00
Retained earnings	233,737 00		141,973 00		91,764 00
Total stockholders' equity		973,737 00		763,973 00	209,764 00
Total liabilities and stockholders' equity		$1,128,927 00		$957,395 00	171,532 00

REQUIRED

1. Prepare a schedule for the calculation of cash generated from operating activities.

2. Prepare a statement of cash flows explaining the change in cash and cash equivalents.

3. Reconcile cash and cash equivalents at the bottom of the statement of cash flows.

Self-Study Test Questions

True/False

1. The purpose of the statement of cash flows is to provide information about total revenue and expenses. _____

2. Investing activities are those transactions dealing with the exchange of cash between the company and its stockholders and creditors. _____

3. A decrease in Accounts Receivable is added to Sales to determine the amount of cash received from customers. _____

4. A decrease in Inventory is added to Cost of Goods Sold to determine the amount of cash paid for purchases. _____

5. An increase in Accrued Interest Payable is deducted from Interest Expense to compute the cash paid for interest expense. _____

Multiple Choice

1. The acquisition of a building by signing a mortgage note payable is included on the statement of cash flows as a(n) _____

   (a) operating activity.
   (b) investing activity.
   (c) financing activity.
   (d) schedule of noncash investing and financing activities.

2. The receipt of dividends on an investment is included on the statement of cash flows as a(n) _____

   (a) operating activity.
   (b) investing activity.
   (c) financing activity.
   (d) schedule of noncash investing and financing activities.

3. The purchase of new equipment is included on the statement of cash flows as a(n) _____

   (a) operating activity.
   (b) investing activity.
   (c) financing activity.
   (d) schedule of noncash investing and financing activities.

4. The payment of interest on a note payable is classified on the statement of cash flows as a(n) _____

   (a) operating activity.
   (b) investing activity.
   (c) financing activity.
   (d) schedule of noncash investing and financing activities.

5. The payment of a cash dividend to stockholders is classified on the statement of cash flows as a(n) _____

   (a) operating activity.
   (b) investing activity.
   (c) financing activity.
   (d) schedule of noncash investing and financing activities.

Answers to the Self-Study Test Questions are at the end of the text.

CHAPTER 24 APPENDIX

Statement of Cash Flows: The Indirect Method

LEARNING OBJECTIVES:
Careful study of this appendix should enable you to:

LO 1 Describe the indirect method of reporting cash flows from operating activities.

LO 2 Prepare a statement of cash flows using the indirect method and a work sheet for reconciling balance sheet accounts.

This appendix illustrates the indirect method of reporting cash flows from operating activities. We also will show how to use a work sheet to prepare the statement of cash flows.

CASH FLOWS FROM OPERATING ACTIVITIES: INDIRECT METHOD

LO 1 Describe the indirect method of reporting cash flows from operating activities.

The two methods of reporting *cash flows from operating activities* are the direct and indirect methods. The *direct method* was illustrated earlier in Chapter 24. Under the **indirect method**, net income is considered the primary source of cash from operating activities. Thus, net income is reported on the statement of cash flows under operating activities.

As you know, net income is measured using the accrual basis of accounting. Since increases and decreases in net income do not always increase or decrease cash, the following adjustments must be made to net income to report the cash flows from operating activities:

1. Changes in current assets related to operating activities.

2. Changes in current liabilities related to operating activities.

3. Noncash expenses.

4. Gains and losses on transactions not related to operating activities.

LEARNING KEY: Under the indirect method, net income is considered the primary source of cash from operating activities. However, it must be adjusted for transactions that affect both net income and cash from operating activities, but in different ways.

Although the direct and indirect methods result in different formats for reporting cash flows from operating activities, the two methods report the same amount. In addition, investing and financing activities are reported in the same manner under the direct and indirect methods. Thus, only the operating activities section is different.

Changes in Current Assets Related to Operating Activities

Accounts receivable, prepaid expenses, and inventories are examples of current assets related to operating activities. Increases in these assets reduce the cash generated from operating activities; decreases have the opposite effect. For example, if accounts receivable increased, the cash received from customers was less than the sales revenue reported on the income statement. This increase is deducted from net income when computing cash generated from operating activities. Similar adjustments are made for prepaid expenses. If prepaid expenses increased, the cash paid during the period exceeded the expense reported on the income statement. Again, the increase is deducted from net income. On the other hand, decreases in these assets increase cash from operating activities. Thus, decreases in current assets must be added to net income when computing cash flows from operating activities.

LEARNING KEY: If sales were $100,000 and Accounts Receivable increased by $5,000, think of the following entry.

Cash	95,000	
Accounts Receivable	5,000	
Sales		100,000

Since the revenue used to calculate net income is $5,000 greater than the cash received, $5,000 must be subtracted from net income to compute cash from operating activities.

LEARNING KEY: Adjustment for changes in current assets.
Net income
$(-\uparrow)$ or $(+\downarrow)$ in current assets related to operating activities
= Cash from operating activities

Changes in Current Liabilities Related to Operating Activities

Accounts Payable, Income Taxes Payable, and Salaries Payable are examples of current liabilities related to operating activities. Not all current liabilities are related to operating activities. The declaration of dividends, for example, is not an operating activity and has no effect on net income. Therefore, changes in Dividends Payable do not require an adjustment to net income.

Changes in current liabilities require an adjustment opposite that of current assets. By increasing the amount owed to others, the company increases cash from operating activities in the current period. Thus, increases in current liabilities are added to net income to compute cash from operating activities. Decreases in current liabilities are deducted from net income to compute cash from operating activities.

For example, an increase in Salaries Payable indicates that the expense recognized on the income statement for salaries is greater than the cash paid to employees. Thus, the increase in Salaries Payable must be added to net income to compute cash from operating activities. On the other hand, decreases in this account and other current liabilities reduce cash from operating activities and must be deducted from net income.

LEARNING KEY: If Salaries Expense was $5,000 and Salaries Payable increased by $500, think of the following entry.

Salaries Expense	5,000	
Salaries Payable		500
Cash		4,500

Since the expense is $500 greater than the cash paid, $500 must be added to net income to compute cash from operating activities.

LEARNING KEY: Adjustment for changes in current liabilities
Net income
$(+ \uparrow)$ or $(- \downarrow)$ in current liabilities related to operating activities
= Cash from operating activities

Noncash Expenses

Depreciation expense and the amortization of intangible assets are examples of **noncash expenses**. These expenses reduce net income, but do not require an outflow of cash during the period. Thus, they are added to net income to compute cash flows from operating activities.

LEARNING KEY: Adjustment for noncash expenses
Net income
+ Noncash expenses
= Cash from operating activities

Gains and Losses on the Sale of Long-Term Assets

Gains and losses on the sale of long-term assets are reported on the income statement and included in the calculation of net income. However, since these cash flows are not considered operating activities, the gains and losses should not be included in the calculation of cash from operating activities. Thus, net income must be adjusted on the statement of cash flows to compute cash from operating activities.

To illustrate, consider the financial statements for Stevie B's, shown in Figure 24A-1. Let's assume that all revenues and expenses for the period were for cash. This means that the $300 of operating income reported on the income statement also reflects the net inflow of cash from operating activities. During the accounting period, Stevie B's sold land that cost $200 for $250. Since this is not an operating activity, the gain of $50 is reported separately on the income statement.

FIGURE 24A-1 Treatment of a Gain on the Statement of Cash Flows

Stevie B's
Income Statement
For Year Ended December 31, 20-2

Sales (all cash)	$ 1 0 0 0	00
Wages expense (all cash)	7 0 0	00
Operating income	$ 3 0 0	00
Gain on sale of land	5 0	00
Net income	$ 3 5 0	00

Stevie B's
Balance Sheet
December 31, 20-2

Assets	12/31/-2		1/1/-2	
Cash	$ 9 5 0	00	$ 4 0 0	00
Land	8 0 0	00	1 0 0 0	00
Total Assets	$1 7 5 0	00	$1 4 0 0	00
Stockholders' Equity				
Common stock	$1 2 0 0	00	$1 2 0 0	00
Retained earnings	5 5 0	00	2 0 0	00
Total Stockholders' Equity	$1 7 5 0	00	$1 4 0 0	00

Additional information:
  Sold land that cost $200 for $250.

Stevie B's
Statement of Cash Flows
For Year Ended December 31, 20-2

Cash flows from operating activities:				
Net income	$ 3 5 0	00		
Less gain on sale of land	(5 0	00)		
Net cash provided by operating activities			$ 3 0 0	00
Investing activities:				
Sold land			2 5 0	00
Net increase in cash			$ 5 5 0	00

On the statement of cash flows, this gain must be deducted from net income to compute cash from operating activities, $300. The entire amount of cash received from the sale of the land, $250, is reported as a cash inflow under investing activities.

LEARNING KEY: Adjustment for gains and losses
Net income
  − Gains on the sale of plant and equipment
  + Losses on the sale of plant and equipment
  = Cash from operating activities

STATEMENT OF CASH FLOWS: MULTIPLEX CORPORATION

LO 2 Prepare a statement of cash flows using the indirect method and a work sheet for reconciling balance sheet accounts.

Follow these steps to prepare the statement of cash flows under the indirect method.

STEP 1   Compute the change in cash and cash equivalents reported on the comparative balance sheet.

STEP 2   Prepare a work sheet to identify all transactions affecting cash.

STEP 3   Compute cash flows from operating activities under the indirect method by adjusting net income for the following:

(a) Changes in current assets related to operating activities.

(b) Changes in current liabilities related to operating activities.

(c) Noncash expenses.

(d) Gains and losses on transactions not related to operating activities.

STEP 4   Identify cash flows from investing activities by analyzing any additional information and by reconciling balance sheet accounts related to long-term assets, investments in debt and equity securities, and loans made to parties outside the company.

STEP 5   Identify cash flows from financing activities by analyzing any additional information and by reconciling balance sheet accounts related to transactions with stockholders and creditors.

STEP 6   Sum cash flows from operating, investing, and financing activities to determine the net increase or decrease in cash. Compare this amount with the change in cash and cash equivalents computed in STEP 1.

STEP 7   Prepare a schedule of noncash investing and financing activities.

Figure 24-7 on pages 872–873 shows an income statement, statement of retained earnings, comparative balance sheet, and additional information about the cash flows for the period for Multiplex Corporation. This information is needed to prepare a statement of cash flows.

The purpose of the statement of cash flows is to report all transactions that resulted in cash receipts or payments. To provide a systematic method of searching for these transactions, all noncash (or cash equivalent) balance sheet accounts should be reconciled. The work sheet shown in Figure 24A-2 is helpful in accomplishing this task. Figure 24A-3 shows the statement of cash flows for Multiplex.

The beginning and ending balances reported on the comparative balance sheet in Figure 24-7 are inserted in columns 1 and 4 on the work sheet. The transactions and account changes for the year are entered in the reconciling columns. Once all transactions have been identified, the debits and/or credits in the reconciling columns should explain the difference between the beginning and ending balances. For example, Store Equipment had a beginning balance of $38,800. During the year, additional equipment of $9,200 was purchased (reconciling item number **10**). The beginning balance plus the equipment purchased during the year equals the ending balance of $48,000. The purchase of equipment is reported on the statement of cash flows under investing activities.

FIGURE 24A-2 Work Sheet for the Preparation of the Statement of Cash Flows for Multiplex

Multiplex Corporation
Work Sheet for Preparation of Statement of Cash Flows
December 31, 20-2 and 20-1

	DECEMBER 31, 20-1		20-2 RECONCILING DEBIT		20-2 RECONCILING CREDIT		DECEMBER 31, 20-2	
Assets								
Current assets:								
Cash		$ 20,000	15	$ 2,980				$ 22,980
Government notes		3,200			15	$ 1,400		1,800
Accrued interest receivable		300			2	200		100
Accounts receivable		51,510	3	8,705				60,215
Merchandise inventory		67,500			4	2,930		64,570
Supplies and prepayments		2,750	5	1,250				4,000
Total current assets		$145,260						$153,665
Long-term assets:								
Property, plant, and equipment								
Store equipment	$38,800		10	9,200			$48,000	
Less accumulated depreciation	(14,000)	24,800			9	4,000	(18,000)	30,000
Delivery equipment	$32,000		16	13,000			$45,000	
Less accumulated depreciation	(8,000)	24,000			9	4,500	(12,500)	32,500
Office equipment	$34,000		11	4,000			$38,000	
Less accumulated depreciation	(6,100)	27,900			9	1,900	(8,000)	30,000
Total property, plant, and equipment		$ 76,700						$ 92,500
Total assets		$221,960						$246,165
Liabilities								
Current liabilities:								
Notes payable	$11,800		14	1,800			$10,000	
Accounts payable	47,900		6	11,400			36,500	
Accrued and withheld payroll taxes	1,520		7	570			950	
Accrued interest payable	80				8	20	100	
Total current liabilities		$ 61,300						$ 47,550
Long-term liabilities:								
Note payable (3-year)					16	13,000		13,000
Total liabilities		$ 61,300						$ 60,550
Stockholders' Equity								
Common stock	$98,000				12	2,000	$100,000	
Paid-in capital in excess of par	39,000				12	1,000	40,000	
Retained earnings	23,660		13	22,800	1*	44,755	45,615	
Total stockholders' equity		$160,660						$185,615
Total liabilities and stockholders' equity		$221,960						$246,165

* Note: Numbers show the relationship between the reconciling entries on the work sheet and the items on the statement of cash flows.

FIGURE 24A-3 Statement of Cash Flows for Multiplex

Multiplex Corporation
Statement of Cash Flows
For Year Ended December 31, 20-2

Cash flows from operating activities:			
Net income	$44,755	1*	
Adjustments for changes in current assets and liabilities			
related to operating activities:			
Decrease in interest receivable	200	2	
Increase in accounts receivable	(8,705)	3	
Decrease in merchandise inventory	2,930	4	
Increase in supplies and prepayments	(1,250)	5	
Decrease in accounts payable	(11,400)	6	
Decrease in accrued and withheld payroll taxes	(570)	7	
Increase in accrued interest payable	20	8	
Noncash expenses and other adjustments:			
Depreciation expense	10,400	9	
Net cash provided by operating activities			$36,380
Cash flows from investing activities:			
Purchase of store equipment	$ (9,200)	10	
Purchase of office equipment	(4,000)	11	
Total cash used by investing activities			(13,200)
Cash flows from financing activities:			
Issued common stock	$ 3,000	12	
Paid cash dividends	(22,800)	13	
Retired notes payable	(1,800)	14	
Total cash used by financing activities			(21,600)
Net decrease in cash and cash equivalents		15	$ 1,580
Cash and cash equivalents, January 1, 20-2			23,200
Cash and cash equivalents, December 31, 20-2			$24,780
Schedule of noncash investing and financing activities:			
Purchased delivery equipment by issuing a 3-year note.		16	$13,000

* Note: Numbers show the relationship between the reconciling entries on the work sheet and the items on the statement of cash flows.

Each reconciling item has a debit and a credit. If a debit is made on the work sheet, an offsetting credit must be made either on the work sheet or on the statement of cash flows. Financial statements do not have debits and credits. However, cash receipts or additions to net income can be viewed as debits and cash payments or subtractions from net income as credits. Using this technique may help prevent errors when preparing the statement.

Cash Flows from Operating Activities

Under the indirect method, net income is considered the primary source of cash. Therefore, it is listed first on the statement of cash flows, followed by any necessary additions or subtractions. Since net income increases retained earnings, $44,755 is credited to the retained earnings account on the work sheet (see item number **1**). The credit on the work sheet (Figure 24A-2) is offset by a debit (cash inflow or addition to net income) on the statement of cash flows (Figure 24A-3).

Changes in Current Assets Related to Operating Activities. Items **2** and **4** represent decreases in current assets related to operating activities. These decreases represent increases in cash from operating activities. They are reported as credits on the work sheet to reconcile each account and as additions to net income (debits) on the statement of cash flows.

Items **3** and **5** represent increases in current assets related to operating activities. These increases represent reductions in cash from operating activities. They are reported as debits on the work sheet to reconcile each account and as subtractions from net income (credits) on the statement of cash flows.

Changes in Current Liabilities Related to Operating Activities. Items **6** and **7** represent decreases in current liabilities related to operating activities. These decreases reduce cash from operating activities. They are reported as debits on the work sheet to reconcile each account and as subtractions from net income (credits) on the statement of cash flows.

Item **8** , the increase in Accrued Interest Payable, indicates that Multiplex did not pay all interest expense incurred during the period. Thus, the increase is reported as an addition to net income (debit) in the calculation of cash flows from operating activities and as a credit on the work sheet to reconcile the account.

Noncash Expenses. Item **9** is for Depreciation Expense and represents noncash expenses. These expenses reduce net income on the income statement, but require no cash payments. Thus, they are added back to net income (debit) on the statement of cash flows. They are also entered as credits to Accumulated Depreciation—Store Equipment, Delivery Equipment, and Office Equipment to reconcile these accounts on the work sheet.

Cash Flows from Investing Activities

Items **10** and **11** are for purchases of equipment. These amounts are entered as debits on the work sheet to reconcile the equipment accounts and as outflows of cash (credits) under investing activities on the statement of cash flows.

Cash Flows from Financing Activities

Item **12** is for the issuance of common stock. Common Stock and Paid-In Capital are credited on the work sheet ($2,000 and $1,000, respectively) and the $3,000 is shown as an inflow of cash (debit) from financing activities on the statement of cash flows.

 LEARNING KEY: Investing and financing activities are reported in the same manner under the direct and indirect methods.

The statement of retained earnings in Figure 24-7 shows cash dividends of $22,800 were declared and paid during the year. Since dividends reduce retained earnings, $22,800 is debited to Retained Earnings on the work sheet. The outflow of cash (credit) is reported under financing activities as item **13**

Item **14** represents the decrease of $1,800 in current notes payable. Therefore, Notes Payable is debited on the work sheet and the $1,800 cash outflow (credit) is reported under financing activities on the statement of cash flows.

After accounting for the changes in all noncash balance sheet accounts, the net increase or decrease in cash as reported on the statement of cash flows is computed. This is done by taking the sum of net cash flows provided by operating activities ($36,380), cash used by investing activities ($13,200), and cash used by financing activities ($21,600). To verify the accuracy of the statement, sum the increase of $2,980 in Cash (item **15**) and decrease of $1,400 in Government Notes (item **15**) reported on the work sheet. This amount is the same as the $1,580 increase in cash and cash equivalents (item **15**) reported on the statement of cash flows.

Noncash Investing and Financing Activities

Item **16** represents the issuance of the $13,000, three-year note for the acquisition of delivery equipment. Since there is no cash involved in this transaction, no entries are made in the investing or financing sections of the statement of cash flows. Delivery Equipment is debited and Notes Payable is credited on the work sheet to reconcile these accounts. Note that all debits and credits are made on the work sheet. In addition, this event is noted in the schedule of noncash investing and financing activities on the statement of cash flows.

Learning Objectives	Key Points to Remember
1 **Describe the indirect method of reporting cash flows from operating activities.**	Under the indirect method, net income is considered the primary source of cash from operating activities. Thus, it is reported on the statement of cash flows under operating activities.
	Since increases and decreases in net income do not always increase or decrease cash, the following adjustments must be made to net income to report the cash flows from operating activities:
	1. Changes in current assets related to operating activities.
	2. Changes in current liabilities related to operating activities.
	3. Noncash expenses.
	4. Gains and losses on transactions not related to operating activities.
2 **Prepare a statement of cash flows using the indirect method and a work sheet for reconciling balance sheet accounts.**	Follow these steps to prepare the statement of cash flows under the indirect method:
	STEP 1 Compute the change in cash and cash equivalents reported on the comparative balance sheet.
	STEP 2 Prepare a work sheet to identify all transactions affecting cash.
	STEP 3 Compute cash flows from operating activities under the indirect method by adjusting net income for the following:
	(a) Changes in current assets related to operating activities.
	(b) Changes in current liabilities related to operating activities.
	(c) Noncash expenses.
	(d) Gains and losses on transactions not related to operating activities.
	STEP 4 Identify cash flows from investing activities by analyzing any additional information and by reconciling balance sheet accounts related to long-term assets, investments in debt and equity securities, and loans made to parties outside the company.
	STEP 5 Identify cash flows from financing activities by analyzing any additional information and by reconciling balance sheet accounts related to transactions with stockholders and creditors.
	STEP 6 Sum cash flows from operating, investing, and financing activities to determine the net increase or decrease in cash. Compare this amount with the change in the cash and cash equivalents computed in STEP 1.
	STEP 7 Prepare a schedule of noncash investing and financing activities.

KEY TERMS

indirect method, (903)   A method of reporting cash from operating activities in which net income is adjusted for transactions that affect both net income and cash from operating activities, but in different ways.

noncash expenses, (905)   Expenses that reduce net income, but do not require an outflow of cash during the period.

REVIEW QUESTIONS

1. Describe the indirect method of reporting cash flows from operating activities.

2. List the four major types of adjustments that must be made to net income when computing cash flows from operating activities.

3. What is the purpose of the work sheet for the preparation of the statement of cash flows?

4. List the six major steps followed when preparing a statement of cash flows under the indirect method.

SERIES A EXERCISE

EXERCISE 24ApxA-1 (LO 2) GAINS AND LOSSES ON THE SALE OF LONG-TERM ASSETS The income statement for Hubbard's Professional Edge Tennis Shop is shown below. Assume that all revenues and expenses were for cash and that land was sold for $500. There were no other investing or financing activities during the year. The cash balances at the beginning and end of the year were $100 and $1,000, respectively. Prepare a statement of cash flows.

Hubbard's Professional Edge Tennis Camp Income Statement For Year Ended December 31, 20-2									
Sales (all cash)							$2	0	0	0	00
Wages expense (all cash)							1	6	0	0	00
Operating income							$	4	0	0	00
Gain on sale of land								1	0	0	00
Net income							$	5	0	0	00

SERIES A PROBLEMS

PROBLEM 24ApxA-1 (LO 2) CASH FLOWS FROM OPERATING ACTIVITIES Using the information provided in Problem 24A-1, compute net cash provided (used) by operating activities under the indirect method.

PROBLEM 24ApxA-2 (LO 2) CASH FLOWS FROM OPERATING ACTIVITIES Using the information provided in Problem 24A-3, compute net cash provided (used) by operating activities under the indirect method.

PROBLEM 24ApxA-3 (LO 2) CASH FLOWS FROM OPERATING ACTIVITIES Using the information provided in Problem 24A-4, compute net cash provided (used) by operating activities under the indirect method.

SERIES B EXERCISE

EXERCISE 24ApxB-1 (LO 2) GAINS AND LOSSES ON THE SALE OF LONG-TERM ASSETS The income statement for Leadbetter's Golf Camp is shown below. Assume that all revenues and expenses were for cash and that land was sold for $600. There were no other investing or financing activities during the year. The cash balances at the beginning and end of the year were $1,000 and $3,600, respectively. Prepare a statement of cash flows.

Leadbetter's Golf Camp Income Statement For Year Ended December 31, 20-2									
Sales (all cash)						$5	0	0	0	00
Wages expense (all cash)						3	0	0	0	00
Operating income						$2	0	0	0	00
Loss on sale of land						(2	0	0	00)
Net income						$1	8	0	0	00

SERIES B PROBLEMS

PROBLEM 24ApxB-1 (LO 2) CASH FLOWS FROM OPERATING ACTIVITIES Using the information provided in Problem 24B-1, compute net cash provided (used) by operating activities under the indirect method.

PROBLEM 24ApxB-2 (LO 2) CASH FLOWS FROM OPERATING ACTIVITIES Using the information provided in Problem 24B-3, compute net cash provided (used) by operating activities under the indirect method.

PROBLEM 24ApxB-3 (LO 2) CASH FLOWS FROM OPERATING ACTIVITIES Using the information provided in Problem 24B-4, compute net cash provided (used) by operating activities under the indirect method.

25

Analysis of Financial Statements

Fiona Nairn has been working at The Finny Co. for the past several years. Recently, Finny initiated an employee stock purchase program. All employees are given the opportunity to purchase a certain number of shares of stock at a price slightly below market. Given the company's excellent performance, and her support for employee ownership of the company, Fiona is considering buying stock. She has a copy of the most recent financial statements. The company reported net income of $300,000. This looks good to Fiona. What other factors should she consider when evaluating the financial health of the company?

This chapter demonstrates how to analyze financial statements to better understand the information obtained from them. Comparisons of financial statement variables over time and the calculation and interpretation of selected ratios will be presented.

COMPARATIVE ANALYSIS

LO 1   Perform horizontal and vertical analyses of the income statement and balance sheet.

A business' financial statements supply information to management, present and potential owners and creditors, employees and their unions, government agencies, and sometimes the general public. Normally, interest centers on three aspects of the business.

1. **Liquidity**—the ability to pay current debts when they come due. Liquidity measures focus primarily on current liabilities.

2. **Profitability**—the ability to earn a satisfactory return on the investments in the business.

3. **Leverage**—the proportion of debt to stockholders' equity.

The financial statements can be much more informative if they are analyzed on a comparative basis. The following are four possible types of comparison:

1. with one or more previous periods

2. with data for the industry as a whole

3. with similar information for other businesses in the industry

4. with preset plans or goals (normally in the form of budgets)

We will use the financial statements of French Connection Importers (FCI) for the years ended December 31, 20-4 and 20-3, to illustrate the first type of analysis.

Horizontal Analysis

Comparing the amounts for the same item in the financial statements of two or more periods is called **horizontal analysis**. Figure 25-1 illustrates a horizontal analysis of the condensed comparative income statement of FCI for the two years under review, showing the amount and the percentage change in each item. In calculating the percentage change, the amount for the earlier year serves as the base. For example, to compute the percentage change in net sales, the increase or decrease in net sales for 20-4 is divided by net sales for 20-3.

LEARNING KEY: Horizontal analysis tracks the dollar and percentage change in financial statement amounts for the same company across accounting periods. Use the amount for the earlier year as the base when calculating the percentage change from year to year.

FIGURE 25-1 Comparative Income Statement—Horizontal Analysis

French Connection Importers
Comparative Income Statement
For Years Ended December 31, 20-4 and 20-3

	20-4	20-3	INCREASE (DECREASE)	PERCENT
Net sales	$835,950	$708,800	$127,150	17.9
Cost of goods sold	602,380	520,260	82,120	15.8
Gross profit	$233,570	$188,540	$ 45,030	23.9
Operating expenses	113,000	100,250	12,750	12.7
Operating income	$120,570	$ 88,290	$ 32,280	36.6
Other revenue	525	100	425	425.0
Other expenses	12,650	14,420	(1,770)	−12.3
Income before income taxes	$108,445	$ 73,970	$ 34,475	46.6
Corporate income tax	36,600	19,210	17,390	90.5
Net income	$ 71,845	$ 54,760	$ 17,085	31.2

Net sales in 20-4 were 17.9% greater than in 20-3. Cost of goods sold increased only 15.8%. Because of the smaller percentage increase in cost of goods sold, the percentage increase in the gross profit (23.9%) was greater than that for sales. Operating expenses increased only 12.7%, which was much less than the growth in sales. These events caused an increase of 36.6% in operating income. Although the percentage increase in other revenue was enormous (425%), the amount of this revenue was small. Because other expenses decreased 12.3%, income before income tax was 46.6% greater. The relative amount of income tax increased significantly (90.5%), and net income increased by 31.2%.

This horizontal analysis of the income statement indicates a major improvement in FCI's operating results. A 17.9% increase in net sales accompanied by apparently successful cost control resulted in a 31.2% increase in net income.

The condensed comparative balance sheet as of December 31, 20-4 and 20-3, presented in Figure 25-2, illustrates horizontal analysis. The most noteworthy changes in the balance sheet are listed below (numbers correspond to those in the margin of Figure 25-2).

1 *Increase (18.4%) in current assets and decrease (38.3%) in current liabilities.*

The increase in current assets is due primarily to the increases in cash (30.4%) and receivables (23.5%). These increases probably were needed to support the higher level of operating activity indicated by the 17.9% increase in net sales noted previously.

The decrease in current liabilities is caused by the reduction in notes payable and accounts payable. FCI apparently used some of the funds from its successful operations during 20-4 to pay off a large portion of its current liabilities.

2 *Increase in building (12.0%) and store equipment (11.1%).*

Increases in building and store equipment are important because they are signs of growth. It is common for long-term asset accounts to *decrease* simply because of depreciation and amortization. The decreases in delivery and office equipment and organization costs are examples of this tendency. *Increases* in the building and store equipment accounts mean that new long-term assets were acquired during 20-4.

FIGURE 25-2 Comparative Balance Sheet—Horizontal Analysis

French Connection Importers
Comparative Balance Sheet
December 31, 20-4 and 20-3

	20-4	20-3	INCREASE (DECREASE)	PERCENT	
Assets					
Current assets:					
Cash	$ 25,695	$ 19,700	$ 5,995	30.4	
Government notes	5,000	1,000	4,000	400.0	
Accounts receivable (net)	61,750	50,000	11,750	23.5	
Merchandise inventory	55,500	54,250	1,250	2.3	
Supplies and prepayments	2,400	2,000	400	20.0	
Total current assets	$150,345	$126,950	$23,395	18.4	**1**
Property, plant, and equipment:					
Land	$ 40,000	$ 40,000	$ 0	0.0	
Building (net)	140,000	125,000	15,000	12.0	**2**
Store equipment (net)	100,000	90,000	10,000	11.1	**2**
Delivery and office equipment (net)	22,000	28,500	(6,500)	−22.8	
Organization costs	1,200	2,400	(1,200)	−50.0	
Total property, plant, and equipment	$303,200	$285,900	$17,300	6.1	
Total assets	$453,545	$412,850	$40,695	9.9	
Liabilities					
Current liabilities:					
Accrued and withheld payroll taxes	$ 2,500	$ 2,750	$ (250)	−9.1	
Notes payable	10,000	37,500	(27,500)	−73.3	
Accounts payable	40,000	59,000	(19,000)	−32.2	
Accrued interest payable	600	1,700	(1,100)	−64.7	
Corporation income tax payable	13,600	13,400	200	1.5	
Dividends payable	7,500	6,000	1,500	25.0	
Total current liabilities	$ 74,200	$120,350	$(46,150)	−38.3	**1**
Long-term liabilities:					
Bonds payable	100,000	100,000	0	0.0	
Total liabilities	$174,200	$220,350	$(46,150)	−20.9	
Stockholders' Equity					
Common stock	$ 75,000	$ 60,000	$15,000	25.0	**3**
Paid-in capital in excess of par	20,000	12,500	7,500	60.0	**3**
Retained earnings	184,345	120,000	64,345	53.6	**4**
Total stockholders' equity	$279,345	$192,500	$86,845	45.1	
Total liabilities and stockholders' equity	$453,545	$412,850	$40,695	9.9	

3 *Increases in common stock (25.0%) and paid-in capital in excess of par (60.0%).*

Increases in common stock and paid-in capital in excess of par also indicate growth. Common stock with a par value of $15,000 was issued for $22,500 ($15,000 par + $7,500 paid-in capital in excess of par). Financing growth by issuing additional common stock is often desirable, particularly for a company carrying as much debt as FCI.

4 *Substantial increase (53.6%) in retained earnings.*

The large increase in retained earnings results from a highly profitable year (net income of $71,845) combined with a moderate dividend policy ($7,500). Retention of large amounts of earnings is another desirable way to finance corporate growth.

Vertical Analysis

Reporting the amount of each item in a statement as a percentage of some designated total is called **vertical analysis**. Vertical analysis is most helpful when statements relating to two or more periods are compared.

LEARNING KEY: Vertical analysis reports each financial statement amount as a percentage of a designated total.

Figure 25-3 shows FCI's condensed comparative income statement for the years ended December 31, 20-4 and 20-3. Each item is shown as a percentage of net sales for the year. This statement reveals that several factors contributed to FCI's increased profitability from 20-3 to 20-4. Both cost of goods sold and operating expenses decreased as a percentage of net sales. This allowed operating income to increase from 12.5% to 14.4% of net sales. Other expenses decreased from 2.0% to 1.5% of net sales, so that income before income taxes jumped from 10.4% to 13.0% of net sales. These positive factors were offset somewhat by the increase in taxes from 2.7% to 4.4% of net sales. However, net income as a percentage of net sales still increased from 7.7% to 8.6%

LEARNING KEY: In vertical analysis of the income statement, each item is shown as a percentage of net sales for the year.

Vertical analysis of income statements automatically provides several important ratios. They include the following (numbers correspond to those in the margin of Figure 25-3).

1 **Cost of goods sold ratio**—ratio of cost of goods sold to net sales

2 **Gross profit ratio**—ratio of gross profit to net sales

3 **Operating expense ratio**—ratio of operating expenses to net sales

4 **Operating income ratio**—ratio of operating income to net sales

5 **Net income ratio**—(also called **profit margin**) ratio of net income to net sales

FIGURE 25-3 Comparative Income Statement—Vertical Analysis

French Connection Importers
Comparative Income Statement
For Years Ended December 31, 20-4 and 20-3

	20-4	PERCENT	20-3	PERCENT	
Net sales	$835,950	100.0	$708,800	100.0	
Cost of goods sold	602,380	72.1	520,260	73.4	**1**
Gross profit	$233,570	27.9	$188,540	26.6	**2**
Operating expenses	113,000	13.5	100,250	14.1	**3**
Operating income	$120,570	14.4	$ 88,290	12.5	**4**
Other revenue	525	0.1	100	0.0	
Other expenses	12,650	1.5	14,420	2.0	
Income before income taxes	$108,445	13.0	$ 73,970	10.4	
Corporate income tax	36,600	4.4	19,210	2.7	
Net income	$ 71,845	8.6	$ 54,760	7.7	**5**

Vertical analysis is also performed on balance sheets. For assets, each item is shown as a percentage of the total assets. For liabilities and stockholders' equity, each item is shown as a percentage of the total equities (liabilities and stockholders' equity). Figure 25-4 shows a comparative balance sheet for FCI using vertical analysis. This statement reveals that current assets were a somewhat larger share (33.1% versus 30.7%) of total assets on December 31, 20-4, than on the same date in 20-3. In addition, current liabilities decreased dramatically (16.4% versus 29.2%) as a percentage of total equities. These two factors reflect a major improvement in FCI's current position. Retained earnings increased significantly in amount and as a percentage of total equities. Finally, the combination of favorable changes in current liabilities, common stock, paid-in capital in excess of par, and retained earnings resulted in total liabilities being a much smaller share (38.4% versus 53.4%) of total equities.

LEARNING KEY: In vertical analysis of the balance sheet, assets are shown as a percentage of total assets. Liabilities and stockholders' equity are shown as a percentage of total liabilities and stockholders' equity.

LIQUIDITY MEASURES

LO 2   Compute and explain liquidity measures.

Liquidity measures indicate a company's ability to meet its current debts. These measures focus primarily on balance sheet amounts and on the company's ability to generate funds to liquidate current obligations.

Working Capital

LEARNING KEY Working Capital = Current Assets – Current Liabilities

FIGURE 25-4 Comparative Balance Sheet—Vertical Analysis

French Connection Importers
Comparative Balance Sheet
December 31, 20-4 and 20-3

	20-4	PERCENT	20-3	PERCENT
Assets				
Current assets:				
Cash	$ 25,695	5.7	$ 19,700	4.8
Government notes	5,000	1.1	1,000	0.2
Accounts receivable (net)	61,750	13.6	50,000	12.1
Merchandise inventory	55,500	12.2	54,250	13.1
Supplies and prepayments	2,400	0.5	2,000	0.5
Total current assets	$150,345	33.1	$126,950	30.7
Property, plant, and equipment:				
Land	$ 40,000	8.8	$ 40,000	9.7
Building (net)	140,000	30.9	125,000	30.3
Store equipment (net)	100,000	22.0	90,000	21.8
Delivery and office equipment (net)	22,000	4.9	28,500	6.9
Organization costs	1,200	0.3	2,400	0.6
Total property, plant, and equipment	$303,200	66.9	$285,900	69.3
Total assets	$453,545	100.0	$412,850	100.0
Liabilities				
Current liabilities:				
Accrued and withheld payroll taxes	$ 2,500	0.6	$ 2,750	0.7
Notes payable	10,000	2.2	37,500	9.1
Accounts payable	40,000	8.8	59,000	14.3
Accrued interest payable	600	0.1	1,700	0.4
Corporation income tax payable	13,600	3.0	13,400	3.2
Dividends payable	7,500	1.7	6,000	1.5
Total current liabilities	$ 74,200	16.4	$120,350	29.2
Long-term liabilities:				
Bonds payable	100,000	22.0	100,000	24.2
Total liabilities	$174,200	38.4	$220,350	53.4
Stockholders' Equity				
Common stock	$ 75,000	16.5	$ 60,000	14.5
Paid-in capital in excess of par	20,000	4.4	12,500	3.0
Retained earnings	184,345	40.6	120,000	29.1
Total stockholders' equity	$279,345	61.6	$192,500	46.6
Total liabilities and stockholders' equity	$453,545	100.0	$412,850	100.0

Working capital is the excess of a company's current assets over current liabilities. This measures whether current assets are sufficient to pay off current liabilities. The calculation of working capital for FCI at the end of each year is shown in Figure 25-5.

FIGURE 25-5 Calculation of Working Capital

Working Capital		20-4	20-3
	Current Assets	$150,345	$126,950
−	Current Liabilities	(74,200)	(120,350)
=	Working Capital	$ 76,145	$ 6,600

FCI's working capital position improved dramatically between 20-3 and 20-4. Current assets were barely sufficient to cover current liabilities on December 31, 20-3, whereas there is a substantial margin of working capital at the end of 20-4.

Current Ratio

LEARNING KEY: Current Ratio $= \dfrac{\text{Current Assets}}{\text{Current Liabilities}}$

The **current ratio**, sometimes called **working capital ratio** because of its obvious linkage to working capital, is calculated by dividing current assets by current liabilities. The calculation of the current ratio for FCI at the end of each year is shown in Figure 25-6.

FIGURE 25-6 Calculation of Current Ratio

Current Ratio			20-4	20-3
	$\dfrac{\text{Current Assets}}{\text{Current Liabilities}}$	=	$150,345	$126,950
			$74,200	$120,350
			2.0 to 1	1.1 to 1

The current position of FCI improved greatly during the year ended December 31, 20-4. The general rule is that a current ratio of 2 to 1 or better is satisfactory, although this rule can be modified for certain types of businesses. FCI's current ratio was not acceptable in 20-3, but it improved to an acceptable level in 20-4.

Quick or Acid-Test Ratio

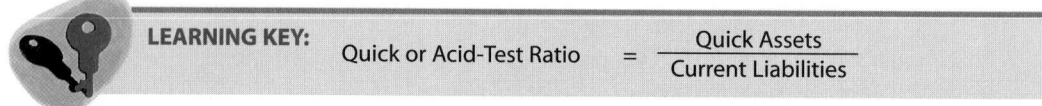

LEARNING KEY: Quick or Acid-Test Ratio $= \dfrac{\text{Quick Assets}}{\text{Current Liabilities}}$

Another frequently used measure of liquidity is the **quick** or **acid-test ratio**. This ratio is calculated by dividing "quick" assets—cash, temporary investments, and receivables—by current liabilities. The calculation of the quick ratio for FCI at the end of each year is shown in Figure 25-7.

FIGURE 25-7 Calculation of Quick Ratio

Quick or Acid-Test Ratio			20-4	20-3
	$\dfrac{\text{Quick Assets}}{\text{Current Liabilities}}$	=	$92,445	$70,700
			$74,200	$120,350
			1.25 to 1	.59 to 1
Quick Assets	Cash		$25,695	$19,700
	Government Notes		5,000	1,000
	Accounts Receivable (net)		61,750	50,000
			$92,445	$70,700

LEARNING KEY: Quick assets include cash, temporary investments, and receivables.

FCI's quick ratio improved during 20-4. As a general rule, the ratio should not be less than 1 to 1. FCI was far below that standard in 20-3, but the company's quick ratio at the end of 20-4 is acceptable.

While it is generally desirable that both the current ratio and the quick or acid-test ratio be high, it is possible for them to be too high. Cash and most receivables are not "earning assets" and the return on most temporary investments is not large. Inventories are expensive to hold. They take up costly space, tie up money, and are subject to loss of value from various causes. Management must try to maintain the ideal amount of each type of asset.

Accounts Receivable Turnover

LEARNING KEY:

$$\text{Accounts Receivable Turnover} = \frac{\text{Net Sales on Account}}{\text{Average Accounts Receivable (net)}}$$

Also expressed in days: 365 ÷ Accounts Receivable Turnover

Net sales on account is used in this ratio. However, this information is not generally available on the financial statements. Net sales may be used if net sales on account is not available. Using net sales will provide a useful measure across time periods as long as the proportion of cash and credit sales remains relatively stable.

Since accounts receivable do not generally earn interest, and some receivables will never be collected, it is important to manage them carefully. The disadvantages of carrying receivables are accepted, however, because selling on account may generate greater sales and net income.

Accounts receivable turnover measures how promptly receivables are collected. It is calculated by dividing net sales on account by the average amount of net accounts receivable. It is preferable to calculate a monthly average of net receivables. However, if monthly figures are not available, averaging the beginning-of-year and end-of-year balances is acceptable if the receivables balance does not fluctuate widely. Only *accounts* receivable are considered. The calculations for FCI are shown in Figure 25-8. Note that beginning balances for 20-3 are not available on the current financial statements. These were taken from last year's financial statements.

FIGURE 25-8 Calculation of Accounts Receivable Turnover

			20-4	20-3
Accounts Receivable Turnover	$\dfrac{\text{Net Sales on Account}}{\text{Average Accounts Receivable}}$	=	$\dfrac{\$668,760}{\$55,875}$	$\dfrac{\$567,040}{\$45,000}$
			11.97	12.6
Average Accounts Receivable	$\dfrac{\text{Beginning Accounts Receivable} + \text{Ending Accounts Receivable}}{2}$	=	$\dfrac{\$50,000 + \$61,750}{2}$	$\dfrac{\$40,000 + \$50,000}{2}$
			$55,875	$45,000
Average Collection Period	$\dfrac{365}{\text{Accounts Receivable Turnover}}$	=	$\dfrac{365}{11.97}$	$\dfrac{365}{12.6}$
			30.5 days	29 days

Another way of examining accounts receivable turnover is to divide 365 days by the turnover figure to get the average collection period. This shows the number of days it takes a business to convert receivables into cash. Fluctuations in the average collection period over time should be investigated.

For FCI, Figure 25-8 shows that the average collection period is 30.5 days and 29 days, respectively, for the years ended December 31, 20-4 and 20-3. Although the accounts receivable turnover decreased slightly, both rates are quite good. The average number of days that receivables are on the books should not be greater than 1½ times the regular length of the credit period. FCI offered 30 days' credit to more customers in 20-4, which probably explains the slight decrease in turnover.

Merchandise Inventory Turnover

LEARNING KEY:

$$\text{Merchandise Inventory Turnover} = \frac{\text{Cost of Goods Sold}}{\text{Average Merchandise Inventory}}$$

Also expressed in days: $365 \div \text{Merchandise Inventory Turnover}$

Every seller of goods would like to have maximum sales and a minimum inventory. **Merchandise inventory turnover** measures the relationship between sales and inventory. It is calculated by dividing cost of goods sold by average merchandise inventory. Again, calculating a monthly average of inventories is preferable. However, if monthly figures are not available, the average of the beginning-of-year and end-of-year inventories can be used. For FCI, the merchandise inventory turnover for each year is shown in Figure 25-9.

FIGURE 25-9 Calculation of Merchandise Inventory Turnover

			20-4	20-3
Merchandise Inventory Turnover	$\dfrac{\text{Cost of Goods Sold}}{\text{Average Merchandise Inventory}}$	=	$\dfrac{\$602,380}{\$54,875}$ 10.98	$\dfrac{\$520,260}{\$52,500}$ 9.91
Average Merchandise Inventory	$\dfrac{\text{Beginning Merchandise Inventory} + \text{Ending Merchandise Inventory}}{2}$	=	$\dfrac{\$54,250 + \$55,500}{2}$ $\$54,875$	$\dfrac{\$50,750 + \$54,250}{2}$ $\$52,500$
Average Number of Days To Sell Inventory	$\dfrac{365}{\text{Merchandise Inventory Turnover}}$	=	$\dfrac{365}{10.98}$ 33.2 days	$\dfrac{365}{9.91}$ 36.8 days

As with accounts receivable turnover, another way of examining merchandise inventory turnover is to divide 365 days by the turnover figure to get the average number of days required to sell the merchandise inventory. If all sales are made on account, this is the average number of days it takes FCI to convert merchandise inventory into accounts receivable. This number of days plus the number of days to collect accounts receivable indicates the number of days to convert inventory into cash. Figure 25-9 shows that merchandise remained in stock an average of 33 days and 37 days, respectively, for the years ended December 31, 20-4 and 20-3.

The turnover increased slightly from 20-3 to 20-4. Both years show acceptable inventory turnover rates. FCI maintained a reasonable inventory turnover while significantly increasing its sales volume.

PROFITABILITY MEASURES

LO 3 Compute and explain profitability measures.

Profitability measures indicate a company's ability to earn income by operating efficiently. These measures focus primarily on the relationship between key income statement and balance sheet amounts.

Ratio of Net Sales to Assets

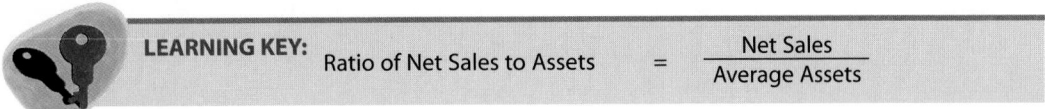

LEARNING KEY: Ratio of Net Sales to Assets $= \dfrac{\text{Net Sales}}{\text{Average Assets}}$

The **ratio of net sales to assets**, or **asset turnover ratio**, measures how efficiently a company used its assets to generate sales. The ratio is calculated by dividing net sales for the year by the average book value of the company's assets. The calculation for FCI is shown in Figure 25-10.

FIGURE 25-10 Calculation of Net Sales to Assets

			20-4	20-3
Ratio of Net Sales to Assets	$\dfrac{\text{Net Sales}}{\text{Average Assets}}$	=	$\dfrac{\$835,950}{\$433,198}$	$\dfrac{\$708,800}{\$406,425}$
			1.9 to 1	1.7 to 1
Average Assets	$\dfrac{\text{Beginning Assets} + \text{Ending Assets}}{2}$	=	$\dfrac{\$412,850 + \$453,545}{2}$	$\dfrac{\$400,000 + \$412,850}{2}$
			$\$433,198$	$\$406,425$

The ratio of net sales to assets increased modestly from 20-3 to 20-4. To evaluate FCI's efficiency in utilizing assets, this ratio can be compared with those of other companies in the same industry.

Return on Total Assets

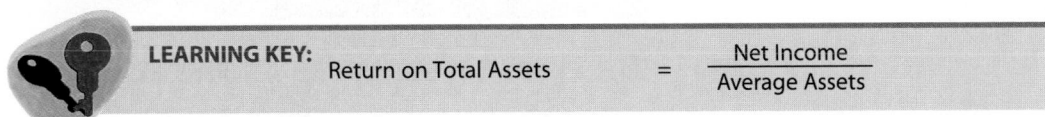

LEARNING KEY: Return on Total Assets $= \dfrac{\text{Net Income}}{\text{Average Assets}}$

Owners or managers of most businesses strive to realize large earnings in relation to the company's resources. The return on total assets measures the success in achieving this objective. The **return on total assets** is calculated by dividing the net income for the year by the average assets for the year. For FCI, the ratio for each year is shown in Figure 25-11.

Inc. ONLINE

"Growing by Numbers" (http://heintz.swcollege.com) Another ratio to think about: What financial ratio is important to a firm that is growing rapidly?

FIGURE 25-11 Calculation of Return on Total Assets

			20-4	20-3
Return on Total Assets	$\dfrac{\text{Net Income}}{\text{Average Assets}}$	=	$\dfrac{\$71,845}{\$433,198}$ 16.6%	$\dfrac{\$54,760}{\$406,425}$ 13.5%
Average Assets	$\dfrac{\text{Beginning Assets} + \text{Ending Assets}}{2}$	=	$\dfrac{\$412,850 + \$453,545}{2}$ $\$433,198$	$\dfrac{\$400,000 + \$412,850}{2}$ $\$406,425$

> Many analysts prefer to add interest expense (net of taxes) to the numerator of return on total assets. This provides a measure of the efficient use of assets regardless of the method used to finance those assets.

Both the horizontal and vertical analyses of the income statement presented in Figures 25-1 and 25-3 showed that FCI's profitability had increased from 20-3 to 20-4. The return on total assets supports the previous analyses. The return on total assets increased from 13.5% in 20-3 to 16.6% in 20-4. This is a sign that management's performance improved during 20-4. To further evaluate management's performance, these results can be compared with those of similar companies or industry results.

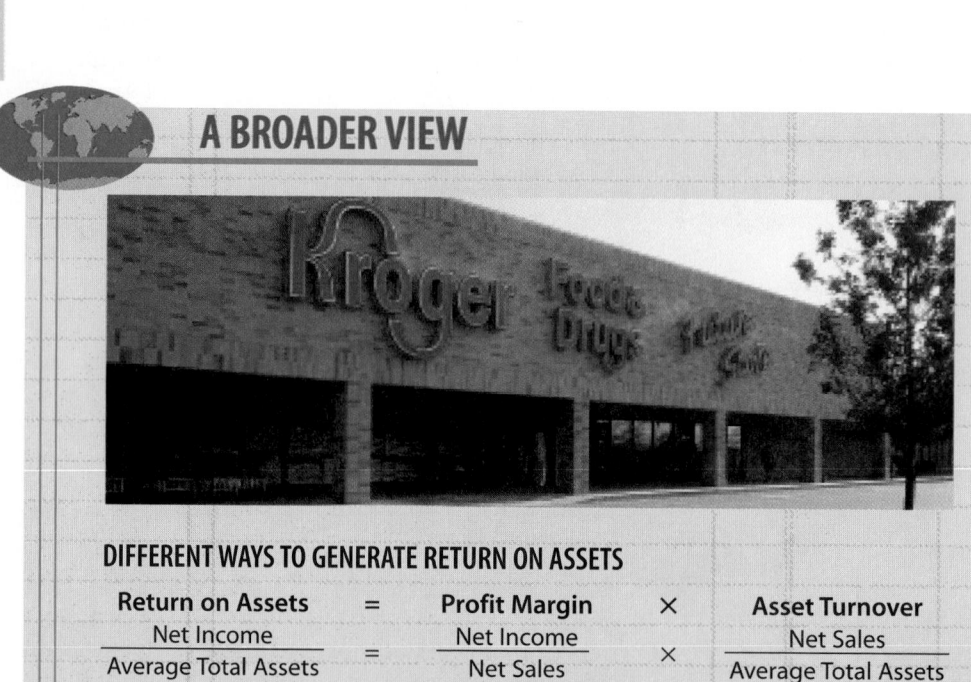

A BROADER VIEW

DIFFERENT WAYS TO GENERATE RETURN ON ASSETS

Return on Assets	=	**Profit Margin**	×	**Asset Turnover**
$\dfrac{\text{Net Income}}{\text{Average Total Assets}}$	=	$\dfrac{\text{Net Income}}{\text{Net Sales}}$	×	$\dfrac{\text{Net Sales}}{\text{Average Total Assets}}$

Return on assets may be broken down into two major ratios, profit margin and asset turnover. This view of ROA helps illustrate that there are different ways to be profitable. Grocery stores, like The Kroger Company, have low profit margins and high asset turnover. For every dollar in net sales, net income is quite small, perhaps just a few cents. However, these businesses are able to generate acceptable profits because they have many customers and must constantly restock the shelves. In contrast, fine jewelry stores, like Tiffany and Company, have high profit margins and low asset turnover. The jeweler may have a very expensive diamond ring in the jewel case for many months before the right customer comes along.

Return on Common Stockholders' Equity

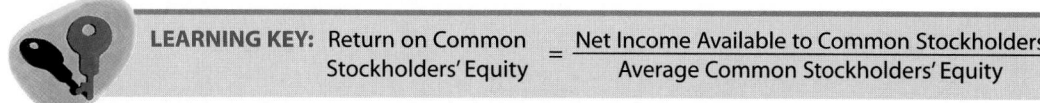

LEARNING KEY: Return on Common Stockholders' Equity $= \dfrac{\text{Net Income Available to Common Stockholders}}{\text{Average Common Stockholders' Equity}}$

Ultimately, the company must provide an adequate return to its common stockholders. Thus, **return on common stockholders' equity** is a very important performance measure. It is calculated by dividing net income available to common stockholders (net income less preferred dividends) for the year by the average common stockholders' equity during the year. For FCI, the calculation of the ratio for each year is shown in Figure 25-12.

FIGURE 25-12   Calculation of Return on Common Stockholders' Equity

			20-4	20-3
Return on Common Stockholders' Equity	$\dfrac{\text{Net Income Available to Common Stockholders}}{\text{Average Common Stockolders' Equity}}$ =		$\dfrac{\$71,845}{\$235,923}$	$\dfrac{\$54,760}{\$183,750}$
			30.5%	29.8%
Average Common Stockholders' Equity	$\dfrac{\text{Beginning Stockholders' Equity + Ending Stockholders' Equity}}{2}$ =		$\dfrac{\$192,500 + \$279,345}{2}$	$\dfrac{\$175,000 + \$192,500}{2}$
			$\$235,923$	$\$183,750$

Net income increased from $54,760 in 20-3 to $71,845 in 20-4, leading to an increase in the return on common stockholders' equity from 29.8% to 30.5%. These rates of return are quite strong.

Earnings Per Share of Common Stock

LEARNING KEY: Earnings Per Share $= \dfrac{\text{Net Income Available to Common Stockholders}}{\text{Average Number of Common Shares Outstanding}}$

Stockholders' equity includes Common Stock, Paid-in Capital in Excess of Par, and Retained Earnings. If FCI had preferred stock, the preferred dividends would be deducted from net income because these funds would not be available to common stockholders.

One of the most important measures of profitability of the company is **earnings per share**. If only common stock is outstanding, earnings per share is calculated by dividing net income for the year by the average number of shares of common stock outstanding during the year. FCI had only common stock outstanding—6,000 shares throughout 20-3, and 6,000 shares at the beginning and 7,500 shares at the end of 20-4. The 1,500 additional shares were issued in the middle of the year, so the average number of shares outstanding during 20-4 was 6,750 ([6,000 + 7,500] ÷ 2). Therefore, FCI's earnings per share for each year is calculated in Figure 25-13 on the next page.

FIGURE 25-13 Calculation of Earnings Per Share of Common Stock

			20-4	20-3
Earnings Per Share	Net Income Available to Common Stockholders / Average Number of Common Shares Outstanding	=	$71,845 / 6,750 = $10.64	$54,760 / 6,000 = $9.13
Average Number of Common Shares Outstanding	Beginning Shares Outstanding + Ending Shares Outstanding / 2	=	6,000 + 7,500 / 2 = 6,750	6,000 + 6,000 / 2 = 6,000

If preferred shares are outstanding, the earnings per share of common stock is calculated after deducting preferred dividend requirements. For example, if a corporation has 40,000 shares of $10 par, 8% preferred stock, $32,000 must be subtracted from net income before dividing by the average number of common shares outstanding. If net income is $310,000, and the average shares of common stock outstanding is 80,000, the earnings per share of common stock is computed as follows:

Net income	$310,000
Less preferred dividend requirements (40,000 × $10 × 8%)	32,000
Earnings available to common stockholders	$278,000
Average number of shares of common stock outstanding	80,000
Earnings per share of common stock	$ 3.48

LEARNING KEY: Earnings per share means *per share of common stock.* Thus, we must focus on earnings available to common stockholders.

Book Value Per Share of Common Stock

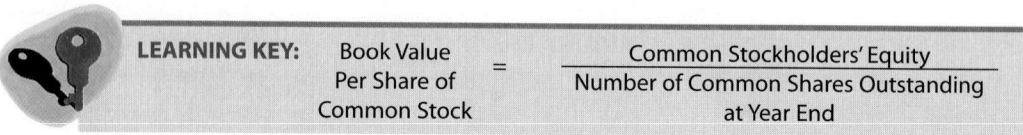

LEARNING KEY: $\dfrac{\text{Book Value Per Share of Common Stock}}{} = \dfrac{\text{Common Stockholders' Equity}}{\text{Number of Common Shares Outstanding at Year End}}$

Book value per share is a measure of the ownership equity represented by each share. If a corporation has only common stock outstanding, book value per share is determined by dividing the total stockholders' equity as reported on the balance sheet by the number of shares outstanding at the end of the year. Book value per share means value per books, not the amount that stockholders would receive for their shares if sold or if the company liquidated.

FCI had 6,000 shares outstanding on December 31, 20-3, and 7,500 shares outstanding on December 31, 20-4. Therefore, the book value per share of common stock is calculated in Figure 25-14.

FIGURE 25-14 Calculation of Book Value Per Share of Common Stock

			20-4	20-3
Book Value Per Share	Common Stockholders' Equity / Number of Common Shares Outstanding	=	$279,345 / 7,500 = $37.25	$192,500 / 6,000 = $32.08

When preferred shares are outstanding, the claims or equity of the preferred stock must be considered. These include liquidation values, dividends in arrears on cumulative preferred stock, and earnings available to participating preferred stock. For example, assume a corporation has 30,000 shares of $10 par, preferred stock with a liquidation value of $10.50 per share, and 60,000 shares of common stock outstanding. The total stockholders' equity in the company is $1,200,000. The book value per share of common stock is calculated as follows:

Total stockholders' equity	$1,200,000
Less liquidation claim of preferred stock ($10.50 × 30,000)	315,000
Balance applicable to common stock	$885,000
Number of shares outstanding	60,000
Book value per share of common stock	$14.75

LEVERAGE MEASURES

LO 4   Compute and explain leverage measures.

Leverage measures indicate the extent to which a company is being financed by debt and the ability of the company to meet its debt obligations. One of these measures focuses on balance sheet relationships and the other focuses on the income statement.

Ratio of Liabilities to Stockholders' Equity

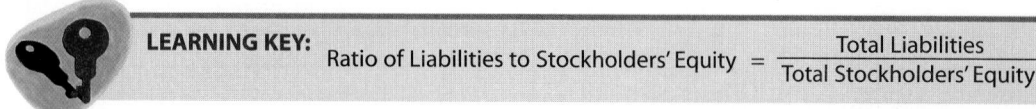

LEARNING KEY: Ratio of Liabilities to Stockholders' Equity $= \dfrac{\text{Total Liabilities}}{\text{Total Stockholders' Equity}}$

The **ratio of liabilities to stockholders' equity**, or **debt-to-equity ratio**, measures the extent of leverage, or proportion of borrowed capital, with which a business operates. This ratio is calculated by dividing total liabilities by total stockholders' equity. For FCI, the calculation of this ratio at the end of each year is shown in Figure 25-15.

FIGURE 25-15   Calculation of the Ratio of Liabilities to Stockholders' Equity

			20-4	20-3
Liabilities to Stockholders' Equity	$\dfrac{\text{Total Liabilities}}{\text{Total Stockholders' Equity}}$ =		$174,200	$220,350
			$279,345	$192,500
			0.62 to 1	1.14 to 1

This ratio was much lower on December 31, 20-4, than it was on December 31, 20-3. The reduction in the ratio appears to have been caused by three factors.

1. Stockholders' equity increased by issuance of common stock for $22,500.

2. Stockholders' equity increased by keeping a large portion of 20-4's earnings.

3. Both notes payable and accounts payable were significantly reduced during 20-4, so that total liabilities decreased.

On December 31, 20-3, the majority of the financing for FCI came from debt. Companies in low-risk industries with fairly stable earnings can operate with a high ratio of liabilities to stockholders' equity. Comparing FCI's ratio with the industry average would be helpful in evaluating the degree of leverage.

Times Interest Earned Ratio

LEARNING KEY: Times Interest Earned Ratio   = $\dfrac{\text{Income before Taxes and Interest}}{\text{Interest Expense}}$

When a business has long-term liabilities such as bonds payable or mortgage payable, creditors want to know the amount of earnings available to pay interest. The ratio of earnings before taxes and interest to the interest expense is called the **times interest earned ratio**.

FCI had bonds payable of $100,000 outstanding on December 31, 20-4 and 20-3. The interest rate on the bonds was 10.5%. Interest expense in each year was $10,500 ($100,000 × 10.5%). The calculation of the times interest earned ratio for each year is shown in Figure 25-16.

FIGURE 25-16   Calculation of Times Interest Earned Ratio

			20-4	20-3
Times Interest Earned	Income before Taxes and Interest	=	$118,945	$84,470
	Interest Expense		$10,500	$10,500
			11.3	8.0
Income before Taxes and Interest	Net Income		$71,845	$54,760
	Add: Income Tax		36,600	19,210
	Bond interest		10,500	10,500
			$118,945	$84,470

These times interest earned ratios would be very satisfactory to the bond holders of FCI. In many businesses, a ratio of 2 or 3 is considered adequate.

LIMITATIONS OF FINANCIAL STATEMENT ANALYSIS

LO 5   Explain the limitations of financial statement analysis.

Financial statement analysis can be a valuable tool in evaluating management performance. However, the methods of analysis need to be used cautiously and with an awareness of their limitations. The accounting system does not measure all aspects of operating a business. For example, the accounting numbers do not reflect the level of customer satisfaction with the company's products or the current employee morale. Further, the reported data are based on many estimates and approximations.

The period of time covered by the financial statements is another consideration. In this chapter, the analysis is based on only two years. A period of two consecutive years is not sufficient to establish a long-term trend. Many companies provide five- and ten-year summaries of operating results in published annual reports.

Comparison of FCI's financial results with other companies and with its industry as a whole can be difficult because generally accepted accounting principles allow different methods of accounting for similar events. For example, the choice of different inventory and depreciation methods can significantly impact both the income statement and the balance sheet. At a minimum, the accounting methods used by the other companies must be identified, so that their possible effects on comparisons can be considered.

Finally, in using ratios, remember that the observed number is simply an expression of the relationship between two other numbers. Either the numerator or the denominator can cause a ratio to provide a distorted message. For example, a company with the same net income in two consecutive years could show a higher rate of return in the second year, simply because the total assets in the second year are lower due to depreciation.

Reflection: Answering the Opening Question

As discussed in this chapter, Fiona needs to consider more than the most recent net income figure. She should compute liquidity, profitability, and leverage measures for the past several years to see if there is an upward or downward trend in the company's financial health. These measures should also be compared with those of other companies in the same type of business.

Learning Objectives	Key Points to Remember
1 Perform horizontal and vertical analyses of the income statement and balance sheet.	The financial statements can be much more informative and meaningful if they are analyzed on a comparative basis. The following are four possible types of comparisons: 1. with one or more previous periods 2. with data for the industry as a whole 3. with similar information for other businesses in the industry 4. with preset plans or goals (normally in the form of budgets) A comparison of the amounts for the same item in the financial statements of two or more periods is called *horizontal analysis*. Reporting the amount of each item in a statement as a percentage of some designated total is called *vertical analysis*.

Learning Objectives	Key Points to Remember
2 3 4 **Compute and explain liquidity, profitability, and leverage measures.**	The following illustration summarizes the liquidity, profitability, and leverage measures.

LIQUIDITY MEASURES

Working Capital	Current Assets − Current Liabilities
Current Ratio	$\dfrac{\text{Current Assets}}{\text{Current Liabilities}}$
Quick Ratio	$\dfrac{\text{Quick Assets}}{\text{Current Liabilities}}$
Accounts Receivable Turnover	$\dfrac{\text{Net Sales on Account}}{\text{Average Accounts Receivable (net)}}$
Also expressed in days	365 ÷ Accounts Receivable Turnover
Merchandise Inventory Turnover	$\dfrac{\text{Cost of Goods Sold}}{\text{Average Merchandise Inventory}}$
Also expressed in days	365 ÷ Merchandise Inventory Turnover

PROFITABILITY MEASURES

Ratio of Net Sales to Assets	$\dfrac{\text{Net Sales}}{\text{Average Assets}}$
Return on Total Assets	$\dfrac{\text{Net Income}}{\text{Average Assets}}$
Return on Common Stockholders' Equity	$\dfrac{\text{Net Income Available to Common Stockholders}}{\text{Average Common Stockholders' Equity}}$
Earnings Per Share of Common Stock	$\dfrac{\text{Net Income Available to Common Stockholders}}{\text{Average Number of Common Shares Outstanding}}$
Book Value Per Share of Common Stock	$\dfrac{\text{Common Stockholders' Equity}}{\text{Number of Common Shares Outstanding at Year End}}$

LEVERAGE MEASURES

Ratio Of Liabilities to Stockholders' Equity	$\dfrac{\text{Total Liabilities}}{\text{Total Stockholders' Equity}}$
Times Interest Earned Ratio	$\dfrac{\text{Income Before Taxes and Interest}}{\text{Interest Expense}}$

Learning Objectives	Key Points to Remember
5 **Explain the limitations of financial statement analysis.**	Limitations of financial statement analysis include the following: 1. Factors not reported on the financial statements are also important in evaluating the financial health of a company. 2. Financial statement information is based on many estimates. 3. Statements from many years should be considered before drawing conclusions about long-term trends. 4. Comparisons across companies are difficult due to the possible use of different accounting techniques. 5. The cause of changes in key ratios must be investigated before drawing conclusions.

KEY TERMS

accounts receivable turnover, (923)   The ratio of net sales on account to the average amount of net accounts receivable.

acid-test ratio, (922)   See quick ratio.

asset turnover ratio, (925)   See ratio of net sales to assets.

book value per share, (928)   The ratio of common stockholders' equity to the number of common shares outstanding at the end of the year.

cost of goods sold ratio, (919)   The ratio of cost of goods sold to net sales.

current ratio, (922)   The ratio of current assets to current liabilities. Also called working capital ratio.

debt-to-equity ratio, (929)   See ratio of liabilities to stockholders' equity.

earnings per share, (927)   The ratio of net income available to common stockholders to the average number of shares of common stock outstanding during the year.

gross profit ratio, (919)   The ratio of gross profit to net sales.

horizontal analysis, (916)   A comparison of the amounts for the same item in the financial statements of two periods.

leverage, (916)   The proportion of debt to stockholders' equity.

leverage measures, (929)   Measures that indicate the extent to which a company is being financed by debt, and the ability of the company to meet its debt obligations.

liquidity, (916)   The ability to pay current debts when they come due.

liquidity measures, (920)   Measures that indicate a company's ability to meet its current debts as they come due.

merchandise inventory turnover, (924)   The ratio of cost of goods sold to the average merchandise inventory.

net income ratio, (919)   The ratio of net income to net sales.

operating expense ratio, (919)   The ratio of operating expenses to net sales.

operating income ratio, (919)   The ratio of operating income to net sales.

profit margin ratio, (919)   See net income ratio.

profitability, (916)   The ability to earn a satisfactory return on the investments in the business.

profitability measures, (925)   Measures that indicate a company's ability to earn income by operating efficiently.

quick ratio, (922)   The ratio of quick assets to current liabilities. Also called the acid-test ratio.

ratio of liabilities to stockholders' equity, (929)   The ratio of total liabilities to total stockholders' equity. It is a measure of the extent of overall leverage, or proportion of borrowed capital, with which a business operates. Also called debt-to-equity ratio.

ratio of net sales to assets, (925)   A measure of how efficiently a company used its assets to generate sales. Also called asset turnover ratio.

return on common stockholders' equity, (927)   The ratio of net income available to common stockholders for the year to the average common stockholders' equity during the year.

return on total assets, (925)   The ratio of net income for the year to the average assets for the year.

times interest earned ratio, (930)   The ratio of earnings before interest and taxes to interest expense.

vertical analysis, (919)   Reporting the amount of each item in a statement as a percentage of some designated total.

working capital, (921)   The excess of a company's current assets over current liabilities.

working capital ratio, (922)   See current ratio.

DEMONSTRATION PROBLEM

W. & D.

Garfinkle Inc.'s comparative financial statements for the years ending December 31, 20-2 and 20-1, are shown on page 935.

REQUIRED

1. Prepare a horizontal analysis of Garfinkle's comparative income statement for 20-2 and 20-1.

2. Prepare a vertical analysis of Garfinkle's comparative income statement for 20-2 and 20-1.

3. Prepare a horizontal analysis of Garfinkle's comparative balance sheet for 20-2 and 20-1.

4. Prepare a vertical analysis of Garfinkle's comparative balance sheet for 20-2 and 20-1.

5. Determine the following measures for 20-2 (round all calculations to two decimal places):

   (a) working capital

   (b) current ratio

   (c) quick ratio

   (d) accounts receivable turnover

   (e) average collection period for accounts receivable

   (f) merchandise inventory turnover

   (g) average number of days required to sell merchandise inventory

   (h) ratio of net sales to assets

   (i) return on total assets

   (j) return on common stockholders' equity

   (k) earnings per share of common stock

   (l) book value per share of common stock

   (m) ratio of liabilities to stockholders' equity

   (n) times interest earned ratio

Garfinkle Inc.
Comparative Income Statement
For Years Ended December 31, 20-2 and 20-1

	20-2	20-1
Sales (all on account)	$10,250,000	$6,515,200
Sales returns and allowances	250,000	115,200
Net sales	$10,000,000	$6,400,000
Cost of goods sold	6,800,000	4,160,000
Gross profit	$ 3,200,000	$2,240,000
Administrative expenses	$ 650,000	$ 448,000
Selling expenses	1,300,000	928,000
Total operating expenses	$ 1,950,000	$1,376,000
Operating income	$ 1,250,000	$ 864,000
Other expense (interest)	160,000	89,600
Income before income taxes	$ 1,090,000	$ 774,400
Corporate income tax	390,000	234,400
Net income	$ 700,000	$ 540,000

Garfinkle Inc.
Comparative Balance Sheet
December 31, 20-2 and 20-1

	20-2	20-1
Assets		
Current assets:		
Cash	$ 350,000	$ 250,000
Accounts receivable (net)	1,150,000	750,000
Inventories	1,440,000	960,000
Supplies and prepayments	60,000	40,000
Total current assets	$3,000,000	$2,000,000
Plant assets (net)	4,686,000	4,346,000
Total assets	$7,686,000	$6,346,000
Liabilities		
Current liabilities	$1,500,000	$1,300,000
Stockholders' Equity		
Common stock, $10 par	$4,500,000	$4,000,000
Retained earnings	1,686,000	1,046,000
Total stockholders' equity	$6,186,000	$5,046,000
Total liabilities and stockholders' equity	$7,686,000	$6,346,000

Solution

1. Horizontal analysis:

Garfinkle Inc.
Comparative Income Statement
For Years Ended December 31, 20-2 and 20-1

	20-2	20-1	INCREASE (DECREASE)	PERCENT
Sales (all on account)	$10,250,000	$6,515,200	$3,734,800	57.3
Sales returns and allowances	250,000	115,200	134,800	117.0
Net sales	$10,000,000	$6,400,000	$3,600,000	56.3
Cost of goods sold	6,800,000	4,160,000	2,640,000	63.5
Gross profit	$ 3,200,000	$2,240,000	$ 960,000	42.9
Administrative expenses	$ 650,000	$ 448,000	$ 202,000	45.1
Selling expenses	1,300,000	928,000	372,000	40.1
Total operating expenses	$ 1,950,000	$1,376,000	$ 574,000	41.7
Operating income	$ 1,250,000	$ 864,000	$ 386,000	44.7
Other expense (interest)	160,000	89,600	70,400	78.6
Income before income taxes	$ 1,090,000	$ 774,400	$ 315,600	40.8
Corporate income tax	390,000	234,400	155,600	66.4
Net income	$ 700,000	$ 540,000	$ 160,000	29.6

2. Vertical analysis:

Garfinkle Inc.
Comparative Income Statement
For Years Ended December 31, 20-2 and 20-1

	20-2	PERCENT	20-1	PERCENT
Sales (all on account)	$10,250,000	102.5	$6,515,200	101.8
Sales returns and allowances	250,000	2.5	115,200	1.8
Net sales	$10,000,000	100.0	$6,400,000	100.0
Cost of goods sold	6,800,000	68.0	4,160,000	65.0
Gross profit	$ 3,200,000	32.0	$2,240,000	35.0
Administrative expenses	$ 650,000	6.5	$ 448,000	7.0
Selling expenses	1,300,000	13.0	928,000	14.5
Total operating expenses	$ 1,950,000	19.5	$1,376,000	21.5
Operating income	$ 1,250,000	12.5	$ 864,000	13.5
Other expense (interest)	160,000	1.6	89,600	1.4
Income before income taxes	$ 1,090,000	10.9	$ 774,400	12.1
Corporate income tax	390,000	3.9	234,400	3.7
Net income	$ 700,000	7.0	$ 540,000	8.4

3. Horizontal analysis:

Garfinkle Inc.
Comparative Balance Sheet
December 31, 20-2 and 20-1

	20-2	20-1	INCREASE (DECREASE)	PERCENT
Assets				
Current assets:				
Cash	$ 350,000	$ 250,000	$ 100,000	40.0
Accounts receivable (net)	1,150,000	750,000	400,000	53.3
Inventories	1,440,000	960,000	480,000	50.0
Supplies and prepayments	60,000	40,000	20,000	50.0
Total current assets	$3,000,000	$2,000,000	$1,000,000	50.0
Plant assets (net)	4,686,000	4,346,000	340,000	7.8
Total assets	$7,686,000	$6,346,000	$1,340,000	21.1
Liabilities				
Current liabilities	$1,500,000	$1,300,000	$ 200,000	15.4
Stockholders' Equity				
Common stock, $10 par	$4,500,000	$4,000,000	$ 500,000	12.5
Retained earnings	1,686,000	1,046,000	640,000	61.2
Total stockholders' equity	$6,186,000	$5,046,000	$1,140,000	22.6
Total liabilities and stockholders' equity	$7,686,000	$6,346,000	$1,340,000	21.1

4. Vertical analysis:

Garfinkle Inc.
Comparative Balance Sheet
December 31, 20-2 and 20-1

	20-2	PERCENT	20-1	PERCENT
Assets				
Current assets:				
Cash	$ 350,000	4.6	$ 250,000	3.9
Accounts receivable (net)	1,150,000	15.0	750,000	11.8
Inventories	1,440,000	18.7	960,000	15.1
Supplies and prepayments	60,000	0.8	40,000	0.6
Total current assets	$3,000,000	39.0	$2,000,000	31.5
Plant assets (net)	4,686,000	61.0	4,346,000	68.5
Total assets	$7,686,000	100.0	$6,346,000	100.0
Liabilities				
Current liabilities	$1,500,000	19.5	$1,300,000	20.5
Stockholders' Equity				
Common stock, $10 par	$4,500,000	58.5	$4,000,000	63.0
Retained earnings	1,686,000	21.9	1,046,000	16.5
Total stockholders' equity	$6,186,000	80.5	$5,046,000	79.5
Total liabilities and stockholders' equity	$7,686,000	100.0	$6,346,000	100.0

(continued)

5. (a) Working capital:

Current assets	$3,000,000
− Current liabilities	(1,500,000)
	$1,500,000

(b) Current ratio:

$$\frac{\text{Current assets}}{\text{Current liabilities}} = \frac{\$3,000,000}{\$1,500,000} = \underline{2.00 \text{ to } 1}$$

(c) Quick ratio:

$$\frac{\text{Quick assets}}{\text{Current liabilities}} = \frac{\$1,500,000}{\$1,500,000} = \underline{1.00 \text{ to } 1}$$

(d) Accounts receivable turnover:

$$\frac{\text{Net sales on account}}{\text{Average accounts receivable}} = \frac{\$10,000,000}{(\$1,150,000 + \$750,000) \div 2} = \underline{10.53}$$

(e) Average collection period: $\frac{365}{10.53} = \underline{34.66 \text{ days}}$

(f) Merchandise inventory turnover:

$$\frac{\text{Cost of goods sold}}{\text{Avg. merchandise inventory}} = \frac{\$6,800,000}{(\$1,440,000 + \$960,000) \div 2} = \underline{5.67}$$

(g) Average number of days to sell inventory:
(365 ÷ 5.67) = <u>64.37 days</u>

(h) Ratio of net sales to assets:

$$\frac{\text{Net sales}}{\text{Average assets}} = \frac{\$10,000,000}{(\$7,686,000 + \$6,346,000) \div 2} = \underline{1.43 \text{ to } 1}$$

(i) Return on total assets:

$$\frac{\text{Net income}}{\text{Average assets}} = \frac{\$700,000}{(\$7,686,000 + \$6,346,000) \div 2} = \underline{9.98\%}$$

(j) Return on stockholders' equity:

$$\frac{\text{Net income}}{\text{Avg. stockholders' equity}} = \frac{\$700,000}{(\$6,186,000 + \$5,046,000) \div 2} = \underline{12.46\%}$$

(k) Earnings per share of common stock

$$\frac{\text{Net income}}{\text{Avg. no. of common shares outstanding}} = \frac{\$700,000}{(450,000 \text{ shares} + 400,000 \text{ shares}) \div 2} = \underline{\$1.65}$$

(l) Book value per share of common stock:

$$\frac{\text{Common stockholders' equity}}{\text{No. of common shares outstanding}} = \frac{\$6,186,000}{450,000 \text{ shares}} = \underline{\$13.75}$$

(m) Ratio of liabilities to stockholders' equity:

$$\frac{\text{Total liabilities}}{\text{Total stockholders' equity}} = \frac{\$1,500,000}{\$6,186,000} = \underline{0.24 \text{ to } 1}$$

(n) Times interest earned ratio:

Net income	$ 700,000
Corporate income taxes	390,000
Interest expense	160,000
Income before interest and taxes	$1,250,000

$$\frac{\text{Income before taxes and interest}}{\text{Interest expense}} = \frac{\$1,250,000}{\$160,000} = \underline{7.81 \text{ times}}$$

REVIEW QUESTIONS

1. Financial statement analysis generally focuses on three main aspects of the business's financial health. What are they?

2. Describe four possible types of comparisons that may be made in financial statement analysis.

3. Why was the increase in FCI's operating income so much greater than the increase in its net sales?

4. What were the main causes of the decrease in FCI's current liabilities?

5. List five ratios that are automatically provided by the vertical analysis of income statements.

6. Identify five measures of liquidity calculated by FCI.

7. Identify five measures of profitability calculated by FCI.

8. Identify two measures of the extent of leverage calculated by FCI.

9. Briefly describe five limitations of financial statement analysis.

MANAGING YOUR WRITING

Many libraries have corporate annual reports and reports on the financial health of companies by financial analysts and rating agencies like Standard and Poor's and Moody's. Go to the library and review financial information on two corporations in your favorite industry. Write a brief memo describing the information available and how it can be used to evaluate the financial health of a company.

ETHICS CASE

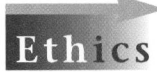

Jim Tennison, L & B Corporation's president, called the company's chief financial officer, Fred Harden, into his office late Friday afternoon. Jim had been reviewing the projected financial statements of L & B Corporation that would be issued as of year end. Jim told Fred he was worried that the company's liquidity position had been declining over the past two years. Fred assured Jim that the company still had sufficient liquidity and they had been steadily decreasing their debt. Jim said that there were three or four major stockholders who were very conservative and would raise lots of questions about the company's declining liquidity ratios. Jim and Fred then decided to take out a two-year loan secured by some land L & B Corporation owned, put the cash in the bank, and pay the loan off after January 1. Jim told Fred to account for the transaction as a long-term liability for financial reporting purposes. They agreed that this measure would solve the problem of liquidity at the annual stockholders' meeting because the company's ratios would be almost identical to last year. Jim was sure that most of the stockholders were only concerned with net income and ratios.

1. If you were a stockholder of L & B Corporation, how would you feel about Jim & Fred's idea? Have any ethical principles been violated?

2. If the transaction is booked as a debit to Cash and a credit to Long-Term Notes Payable, how will it affect the company's key current ratios and debt ratios?

3. Suppose Jim and Fred decide not to take out the loan. Write a brief note to the stockholders justifying a decrease in liquidity measures. Assure them that the company is still in the "safe range."

4. In groups of two or three, list as many reasons as possible, both positive and negative, for a decrease in net working capital.

WEB WORK

Look at the annual report for McDonald's. (Point your browser to **http://www.mcdonalds.com/**; choose Corporate, then Investor Info, then Financial Reports.) Be prepared to discuss both horizontal and vertical analysis of McDonald's financial statements.

(http://heintz.swcollege.com)

SERIES A EXERCISES

EXERCISE 25A-1 (LO 2) ANALYSIS OF LIQUIDITY Based on the comparative income statement and balance sheet of Ace Kitchen Works, Inc., given below, compute the following liquidity measures for 20-2 (round all calculations to two decimal places).

(a) Quick or acid-test ratio

(b) Current ratio

(c) Working capital

(d) Accounts receivable turnover

(e) Merchandise inventory turnover

Ace Kitchen Works, Inc.
Comparative Income Statement
For Years Ended December 31, 20-2 and 20-1

	20-2	20-1
Net sales (on account)	$2,643,000	$2,176,400
Cost of goods sold	1,868,200	1,614,200
Gross profit	$ 774,800	$ 562,200
Operating expenses	244,600	221,800
Other expense (interest)	24,200	24,200
Corporate income tax	161,900	101,200
Net income	$ 344,100	$ 215,000

Ace Kitchen Works, Inc.
Comparative Balance Sheet
December 31, 20-2 and 20-1

	20-2	20-1
Cash	$ 129,000	$ 106,800
Government notes	300,000	300,000
Accounts receivable (net)	892,400	787,400
Merchandise inventory	952,800	866,200
Supplies and prepayments	50,600	46,600
Land	108,200	108,200
Building (net)	330,000	390,600
Office equipment (net)	13,600	15,000
Total assets	$2,776,600	$2,620,800
Current liabilities (accounts payable)	$ 608,000	$ 507,200
Bonds payable	200,000	220,000
Total liabilities	$ 808,000	$ 727,200
Common stock ($10 par, 170,000 shares)	$1,700,000	$1,700,000
Retained earnings	268,600	193,600
Total stockholders' equity	$1,968,600	$1,893,600
Total liabilities and stockholders' equity	$2,776,600	$2,620,800

EXERCISE 25A-2 (LO 3) ANALYSIS OF PROFITABILITY Based on the financial statement data in Exercise 25A-1, compute the following profitability measures for 20-2 (round all calculations to two decimal places).

(a) Ratio of net sales to assets

(b) Return on total assets

(c) Return on common stockholders' equity

(d) Earnings per share of common stock

(e) Book value per share of common stock

EXERCISE 25A-3 (LO 4) ANALYSIS OF LEVERAGE Based on the financial statement data in Exercise 25A-1, compute the following leverage measures (round all calculations to two decimal places).

(a) Ratio of liabilities to stockholders' equity

(b) Times interest earned ratio (Bond interest is $24,200.)

SERIES A PROBLEMS

W & D

PROBLEM 25A-1 (LO 1) HORIZONTAL ANALYSIS OF COMPARATIVE FINANCIAL STATEMENTS Balances from the comparative income statement and balance sheet of Miller Electronics Corporation for the last two years are as follows:

Miller Electronics Corporation
Comparative Income Statement
For Years Ended December 31, 20-2 and 20-1

	20-2	20-1
Net sales (on account)	$650,220	$420,600
Cost of goods sold	395,410	258,668
Gross profit	$254,810	$161,932
Administrative expenses	$ 63,518	$ 42,288
Selling expenses	65,992	43,936
Total operating expenses	$129,510	$ 86,224
Operating income	$125,300	$ 75,708
Interest expense	1,282	1,204
Income before income taxes	$124,018	$ 74,504
Corporate income tax	31,005	13,630
Net income	$ 93,013	$ 60,874

Miller Electronics Corporation
Comparative Balance Sheet
December 31, 20-2 and 20-1

	20-2	20-1
Assets		
Current assets:		
Cash	$ 42,900	$ 22,006
Receivables (net)	73,642	47,510
Merchandise inventory	92,060	50,396
Supplies and prepayments	3,788	1,158
Total current assets	$212,390	$121,070
Property, plant, and equipment:		
Office equipment (net)	12,150	8,490
Factory equipment (net)	105,360	71,190
Total property, plant, and equipment	$117,510	$ 79,680
Total assets	$329,900	$200,750
Liabilities		
Current liabilities:		
Notes payable	$ 10,000	$ 6,000
Accounts payable	43,524	30,242
Accrued and withheld payroll taxes	6,250	5,400
Total current liabilities	$ 59,774	$ 41,642
Stockholders' Equity		
Common stock ($10 par)	100,000	84,000
Retained earnings	170,126	75,108
Total stockholders' equity	$270,126	$159,108
Total liabilities and stockholders' equity	$329,900	$200,750

REQUIRED   Prepare a horizontal analysis. Add columns to show the amount of increase (decrease) and the percentage change. Round percentages to one decimal place.

PROBLEM 25A-2 (LO 1) VERTICAL ANALYSIS OF COMPARATIVE FINANCIAL STATEMENTS Refer to the financial statements in Problem 25A-1.

REQUIRED   Prepare a vertical analysis of the income statement and balance sheet. Show each item on the income statement as a percentage of the net sales for each year. On the balance sheet, show each asset item as a percentage of the total assets and each liability and equity item as a percentage of the total liabilities and stockholders' equity. Round percentages to one decimal place.

PROBLEM 25A-3 (LO 2/3/4) RATIO ANALYSIS OF COMPARATIVE FINANCIAL STATEMENTS Refer to the financial statements in Problem 25A-1.

REQUIRED   Calculate the following ratios and amounts for 20-1 and 20-2 (round all calculations to two decimal places).

(a) Return on total assets (Total assets on January 1, 20-1, were $175,750.)

(b) Return on common stockholders' equity (Total common stockholders' equity on January 1, 20-1, was $106,944.)

(c) Earnings per share of common stock (The average numbers of shares outstanding were 8,400 shares in 20-1 and 9,200 in 20-2.)

(d) Book value per share of common stock

(e) Quick ratio

(f) Current ratio

(g) Working capital

(h) Receivables turnover (Net receivables on January 1, 20-1, were $39,800.)

(i) Merchandise inventory turnover (Merchandise Inventory on January 1, 20-1, was $48,970.)

(j) Ratio of liabilities to stockholders' equity

(k) Ratio of net sales to assets (Assets on January 1, 20-1, were $175,750.)

(l) Times interest earned ratio

SERIES B EXERCISES

EXERCISE 25B-1 (LO 2) ANALYSIS OF LIQUIDITY Based on the comparative income statement and balance sheet for Falcon Designers, Inc., given on the next page, compute the following liquidity measures for 20-2 (round all calculations to two decimal places).

(a) Quick or acid-test ratio

(b) Current ratio

(c) Working capital

(d) Accounts receivable turnover

(e) Merchandise inventory turnover

(continued)

Falcon Designers, Inc.
Comparative Income Statement
For Years Ended December 31, 20-2 and 20-1

	20-2	20-1
Net sales (on account)	$1,850,800	$1,532,600
Cost of goods sold	1,150,400	1,010,500
Gross profit	$ 700,400	$ 522,100
Operating expenses	180,300	156,600
Other expenses (interest)	18,200	18,200
Corporate income tax	160,600	107,600
Net income	$ 341,300	$ 239,700

Falcon Designers, Inc.
Comparative Balance Sheet
December 31, 20-2 and 20-1

	20-2	20-1
Cash	$ 95,500	$ 79,700
Government notes	200,000	200,000
Accounts receivable (net)	639,300	570,600
Merchandise inventory	634,900	639,500
Supplies and prepayments	39,600	29,900
Land	81,900	78,400
Building (net)	227,500	289,300
Office equipment (net)	10,400	10,800
Total assets	$1,929,100	$1,898,200
Current liabilities (accounts payable)	$ 416,000	$ 394,500
Bonds payable	150,000	150,000
Total liabilities	$ 566,000	$ 544,500
Common stock ($10 par, 125,000 shares)	$1,250,000	$1,250,000
Retained earnings	113,100	103,700
Total stockholders' equity	$1,363,100	$1,353,700
Total liabilities and stockholders' equity	$1,929,100	$1,898,200

EXERCISE 25B-2 (LO 3) ANALYSIS OF PROFITABILITY Based on the financial statement data in Exercise 25B-1, compute the following profitability measures for 20-2 (round all calculations to two decimal places).

(a) Ratio of net sales to assets

(b) Return on total assets

(c) Return on common stockholders' equity

(d) Earnings per share of common stock

(e) Book value per share of common stock

EXERCISE 25B-3 (LO 4) ANALYSIS OF LEVERAGE Based on the financial statement data in Exercise 25B-1, compute the following leverage measures for 20-2 (round all calculations to two decimal places).

(a) Ratio of liabilities to stockholders' equity

(b) Times interest earned ratio (bond interest is $18,200)

SERIES B PROBLEMS

W & D

PROBLEM 25B-1 (LO 1) HORIZONTAL ANALYSIS OF COMPARATIVE FINANCIAL STATEMENTS Balances from the comparative income statement and balance sheet of Johnson Stores, Inc., for the last two years are shown below.

REQUIRED   Prepare a horizontal analysis of the statements. Add columns to show the amount of increase (decrease) and the percentage change. Round percentages to one decimal place.

Johnson Stores, Inc.
Comparative Income Statement
For Years Ended December 31, 20-2 and 20-1

	20-2	20-1
Net sales (on account)	$467,865	$305,145
Cost of goods sold	256,955	149,005
Gross profit	$210,910	$156,140
Administrative expenses	$ 43,876	$ 30,617
Selling expenses	44,994	31,293
Total operating expenses	$ 88,870	$ 61,910
Operating income	$122,040	$ 94,230
Interest expense	916	903
Income before income taxes	$121,124	$ 93,327
Corporate income tax	30,280	19,980
Net income	$ 90,844	$ 73,347

Johnson Stores, Inc.
Comparative Balance Sheet
December 31, 20-2 and 20-1

	20-2	20-1
Assets		
Current assets:		
Cash	$ 30,275	$ 15,604
Receivables (net)	42,441	33,565
Merchandise inventory	49,460	34,636
Supplies and prepayments	7,119	6,403
Total current assets	$129,295	$ 90,208
Property, plant, and equipment:		
Office equipment (net)	9,025	6,062
Factory equipment (net)	72,090	52,930
Total property, plant, and equipment	$ 81,115	$ 58,992
Total assets	$210,410	$149,200
Liabilities		
Current liabilities:		
Notes payable	$ 4,000	$ 8,000
Accounts payable	30,233	14,821
Accrued and withheld payroll taxes	6,250	7,600
Total liabilities	$ 40,483	$ 30,421
Stockholders' Equity		
Common stock ($10 par)	75,000	63,000
Retained earnings	94,927	55,779
Total stockholders' equity	$169,927	$118,779
Total liabilities and stockholders' equity	$210,410	$149,200

PROBLEM 25B-2 (LO 1) VERTICAL ANALYSIS OF COMPARATIVE FINANCIAL STATEMENTS Refer to the financial statements in Problem 25B-1.

REQUIRED Prepare a vertical analysis of the income statement and balance sheet. Show each item on the income statement as a percentage of the net sales for each year. On the balance sheet, show each asset item as a percentage of the total assets and each liability and equity item as a percentage of the total liabilities and stockholders' equity. Round percentages to one decimal place.

PROBLEM 25B-3 (LO 2/3/4) RATIO ANALYSIS OF COMPARATIVE FINANCIAL STATEMENTS Refer to the financial statements in Problem 25B-1.

REQUIRED Calculate the following ratios and amounts for 20-1 and 20-2 (round all calculations to two decimal places).

(a) Return on total assets (Total assets on January 1, 20-1, were $111,325.)

(b) Return on common stockholders' equity (Total common stockholders' equity on January 1, 20-1, was $82,008.)

(c) Earnings per share of common stock (The average numbers of shares outstanding were 6,300 shares in 20-1 and 6,900 in 20-2.)

(d) Book value per share of common stock

(e) Quick ratio

(f) Current ratio

(g) Working capital

(h) Receivables turnover (Net receivables on January 1, 20-1, were $28,995.)

(i) Merchandise inventory turnover (Merchandise Inventory on January 1, 20-1, was $32,425.)

(j) Ratio of liabilities to stockholders' equity

(k) Ratio of net sales to assets (Assets on January 1, 20-1, were $111,325.)

(l) Times interest earned ratio

MASTERY PROBLEM

Comparative financial statements for the Na Pali Coast Company for the years ending December 31, 20-1 and 20-2 are provided below.

REQUIRED 1. Perform horizontal analysis of the comparative income statement and balance sheet. Round percentages to one decimal place.

2. Perform vertical analysis of the comparative income statement and balance sheet. Round percentages to one decimal place.

3. Compute the following liquidity measures for 20-2 (round all calculations to two decimal places):

   (a) Working capital

   (b) Current ratio

   (c) Quick or acid-test ratio

   (d) Accounts receivable turnover and average number of days to collect receivables (Assume that sales on account for 20-2 were $120,000.)

   (e) Merchandise inventory turnover and average number of days to sell inventory

4. Compute the following profitability measures for 20-2 (round all calculations to two decimal places):

   (a) Ratio of net sales to assets

   (b) Return on total assets

   (c) Return on common stockholders' equity

   (d) Earnings per share of common stock

   (e) Book value per share of common stock

5. Compute the following leverage measures for 20-2 (round all calculations to two decimal places):

   (a) Ratio of liabilities to stockholders' equity

   (b) Times interest earned ratio (Assume interest expense for 20-2 was $1,200.)

Na Pali Coast Company
Comparative Income Statement
For Years Ended December 31, 20-2 and 20-1

	20-2	20-1
Net sales	$466,451	$291,613
Cost of goods sold	285,889	188,626
Gross profit	$180,562	$102,987
Operating expenses	125,650	78,200
Operating income	$ 54,912	$ 24,787
Other expenses	1,200	500
Income before income taxes	$ 53,712	$ 24,287
Corporate income tax	18,250	7,285
Net income	$ 35,462	$ 17,002

(continued)

Na Pali Coast Company
Comparative Balance Sheet
December 31, 20-2 and 20-1

	20-2	20-1
Assets		
Current assets:		
Cash	$ 8,600	$ 7,500
Government notes	3,000	2,000
Accounts receivable (net)	10,500	8,600
Merchandise inventory	53,600	33,200
Supplies and prepayments	4,500	3,200
Total current assets	$ 80,200	$ 54,500
Property, plant, and equipment:		
Land	$ 40,000	$ 40,000
Building (net)	200,000	150,000
Delivery equipment (net)	13,000	15,000
Office equipment (net)	5,400	6,000
Organization costs	5,000	6,000
Total property, plant, and equipment	$263,400	$217,000
Total assets	$343,600	$271,500
Liabilities		
Current liabilities:		
Notes payable	$ 5,000	$ 3,000
Accounts payable	28,700	22,300
Accrued and withheld payroll taxes	4,200	5,600
Accrued interest payable	500	1,700
Total current liabilities	$ 38,400	$ 32,600
Long-term liabilities:		
Bonds payable	50,000	20,000
Total liabilities	$ 88,400	$ 52,600
Stockholders' Equity		
Common stock ($5 par)	$115,000	$100,000
Paid-in capital in excess of par	65,000	60,000
Retained earnings	75,200	58,900
Total stockholders' equity	$255,200	$218,900
Total liabilities and stockholders' equity	$343,600	$271,500

Self-Study Test Questions

True/False

1. Leverage is the ability to pay debts when they come due. _____

2. A comparison of amounts for the same item in the financial statements of two or more periods is horizontal analysis. _____

3. It is common for long-term asset accounts to show a decrease in the net balance from year to year. _____

4. Working capital is calculated by dividing current assets by current liabilities. _____

5. In calculating accounts receivable turnover, only accounts receivable are considered; others, such as accrued interest receivable, are not included. _____

Multiple Choice

1. The ability to earn a satisfactory return on investments is called _____

   (a) liquidity.   (c) leverage.
   (b) profitability.

2. Working capital is a measure of _____

   (a) liquidity.   (c) leverage.
   (b) profitability.

3. The times interest earned ratio is a measure of _____

   (a) liquidity.   (c) leverage.
   (b) profitability.

4. Financial statements are usually compared with _____

   (a) one or more previous periods.
   (b) data from the industry as a whole.
   (c) similar businesses in the industry.
   (d) all of the above.

5. Which of these is *not* a measure of liquidity? _____

   (a) working capital   (c) quick ratio
   (b) current ratio   (d) return on total assets

The answers to the Self-Study Test Questions are at the end of the text.

26

Departmental Accounting

Finny Co. has continued to enjoy profitable operations. Both the electric and acoustic instruments are known for their high quality. Mike Finbar is happy with the overall success of the business, but he has a gut feeling that the electric instruments are much more profitable than the acoustic. Unfortunately, the accounting reports for the business as a whole give him no evidence to support his feeling. Mike's accountant says that departmental reports could be prepared showing various measures of profitability of different product lines. What measures of departmental profitability can be prepared? Are any judgments and estimates necessary in order to prepare departmental reports? Is there a need for special care in interpreting the departmental profit measures?

Companies often engage in different types of profit-making activities. For example, a merchandiser might sell different products, such as lawn mowers and bicycles. A service business might provide different services, such as auditing and management consulting. Such businesses are often organized into separate segments called departments. In this chapter, we will examine how to account for a business organized into departments.

DEPARTMENTAL ACCOUNTING

LO 1   Explain the nature and purpose of departmental accounting.

"Necessary Losses"
(http://heintz.swcollege.com)
Why does delegating
responsibility to managers
make sense?

When a business sells several products or services, it can be difficult to obtain useful and accurate information about the business. An income statement prepared for the business as a whole might show that the business is reasonably profitable. This statement would not show that one portion of the business is highly successful while another portion is operating at a loss. Departmental accounting overcomes this problem by providing separate information about the revenues and expenses of each department.

Departmental reports are useful to management for three purposes: (1) planning, (2) control, and (3) performance evaluation.

1. Planning—Successful managers set goals and develop plans for achieving these goals. An important part of planning is identifying the strengths and weaknesses of the different parts of the firm. Departmental reports can be very helpful for this purpose.

2. Control—To properly control operations, managers must be able to identify revenues and expenses that are out of line. Departmental reports help management focus attention on problem areas or departments.

3. Performance evaluation—When a business is organized into departments, responsibility for each department can be assigned to a specific manager. Departmental reports can then be used to evaluate each manager's performance.

Departmental reports are usually not part of the basic financial statements. These reports are for internal management use only. This means the accounting rules for external reporting do not apply. Department reports can be prepared in whatever form management finds useful. Generally, only a departmental income statement is prepared. In the following sections, we will look at departmental income statements for Annie's Sporting Goods, which sells golf and tennis equipment. These income statements will be extended through three different levels: gross profit, operating income, and direct operating margin.

DEPARTMENTAL GROSS PROFIT

LO 2　Describe and compute departmental gross profit.

Departmental gross profit is the difference between a department's net sales and cost of goods sold. Each element used to compute gross profit must be determined for each department. Recall that the following elements are used to compute gross profit:

Sales
Sales returns and allowances
Inventory
Purchases
Purchases returns and allowances
Purchases discounts
Freight-in

Two ways of accumulating this information are:

1. Maintain separate general ledger accounts by department for each element (account) making up gross profit.

2. Maintain a single general ledger account for each element. The total in each account is assigned to the appropriate departments at the end of the accounting period.

Departmental Special Journals

Annie's uses departmental accounts for each of the elements of gross profit. Annie's also uses special journals designed to accumulate information by department. Notice that Annie's sales journal (Figure 26-1) provides special columns for golf and tennis sales. Similarly, Annie's purchases journal (Figure 26-2) provides special columns for purchases of golf and tennis merchandise.

FIGURE 26-1　Departmental Sales Journal

| | | | | | | SALES CREDIT | | |
	DATE	SALE NO.	TO WHOM SOLD	POST REF.	ACCOUNTS RECEIVABLE DEBIT	GOLF	TENNIS	SALES TAX PAYABLE CREDIT

FIGURE 26-2　Departmental Purchases Journal

| | | | | PURCHASES DEBIT | | |
DATE	INVOICE NO.	FROM WHOM PURCHASED	POST REF.	GOLF	TENNIS	ACCOUNTS PAYABLE CREDIT

Departmental special journals are posted to general ledger accounts in the same way that we posted from the special journals in Chapters 11 and 12. In this case, however, the postings are to separate departmental general ledger accounts.

Departmental Income Statement Showing Gross Profit

Figure 26-3 shows Annie's departmental income statement for the year 20--. The gross profit section is presented in condensed form. Gross profit is shown by department and in total.

FIGURE 26-3 Income Statement Showing Departmental Gross Profit

<table>
<tr><td colspan="13" align="center">Annie's Sporting Goods
Income Statement
For Year Ended December 31, 20 - -</td></tr>
<tr><td></td><td colspan="4" align="center">GOLF</td><td colspan="4" align="center">TENNIS</td><td colspan="4" align="center">TOTAL</td></tr>
<tr><td>Net sales</td><td>$1,075</td><td>0 0</td><td>0</td><td>00</td><td>$640</td><td>3 0</td><td>0</td><td>00</td><td>$1,715</td><td>3 0</td><td>0</td><td>00</td></tr>
<tr><td>Cost of goods sold</td><td>545</td><td>2 8</td><td>0</td><td>00</td><td>420</td><td>9 0</td><td>0</td><td>00</td><td>966</td><td>1 8</td><td>0</td><td>00</td></tr>
<tr><td>Gross profit</td><td>$ 529</td><td>7 2</td><td>0</td><td>00</td><td>$219</td><td>4 0</td><td>0</td><td>00</td><td>$ 749</td><td>1 2</td><td>0</td><td>00</td></tr>
<tr><td></td><td></td><td></td><td></td><td></td><td></td><td></td><td></td><td></td><td></td><td></td><td></td><td></td></tr>
<tr><td>Operating expenses:</td><td></td><td></td><td></td><td></td><td></td><td></td><td></td><td></td><td></td><td></td><td></td><td></td></tr>
<tr><td>Store clerks wages expense</td><td></td><td></td><td></td><td></td><td></td><td></td><td></td><td></td><td>$ 80</td><td>2 5</td><td>0</td><td>00</td></tr>
<tr><td>Truck drivers wages expense</td><td></td><td></td><td></td><td></td><td></td><td></td><td></td><td></td><td>83</td><td>9 0</td><td>0</td><td>00</td></tr>
<tr><td>Advertising expense</td><td></td><td></td><td></td><td></td><td></td><td></td><td></td><td></td><td>79</td><td>5 0</td><td>0</td><td>00</td></tr>
<tr><td>Store rent expense</td><td></td><td></td><td></td><td></td><td></td><td></td><td></td><td></td><td>22</td><td>8 0</td><td>0</td><td>00</td></tr>
<tr><td>Bad debt expense</td><td></td><td></td><td></td><td></td><td></td><td></td><td></td><td></td><td>17</td><td>9 0</td><td>0</td><td>00</td></tr>
<tr><td>Depreciation expense—delivery equipment</td><td></td><td></td><td></td><td></td><td></td><td></td><td></td><td></td><td>24</td><td>0 0</td><td>0</td><td>00</td></tr>
<tr><td>Other operating expenses</td><td></td><td></td><td></td><td></td><td></td><td></td><td></td><td></td><td>350</td><td>4 3</td><td>0</td><td>00</td></tr>
<tr><td>Total operating expenses</td><td></td><td></td><td></td><td></td><td></td><td></td><td></td><td></td><td>$ 658</td><td>7 8</td><td>0</td><td>00</td></tr>
<tr><td>Operating income</td><td></td><td></td><td></td><td></td><td></td><td></td><td></td><td></td><td>$ 90</td><td>3 4</td><td>0</td><td>00</td></tr>
</table>

This report shows that the golf department provides the majority of Annie's sales and gross profit. The report also reveals a large difference in the gross profit percentages of the two departments.

Golf department gross profit percentage: ($529,720 ÷ $1,075,000)	**49.3%**
Tennis department gross profit percentage: ($219,400 ÷ $640,300)	**34.3%**

Management should determine the causes of this difference and take appropriate action. Perhaps the normal retail markup on golf equipment is higher than that on tennis equipment. If so, management might want to emphasize selling golf equipment. If the normal retail markup on the two products is similar, the pricing policies for tennis equipment should be evaluated. The tennis department may be using an inadequate markup percentage. Another possibility is that the purchase prices for tennis equipment are too high. If so, the purchasing department should try to obtain better prices from vendors.

 LEARNING KEY: An income statement showing departmental gross profit enables management to see whether each of its departments is earning an adequate gross profit.

A higher gross profit or gross profit percentage does not necessarily mean that a department is more profitable overall. Departmental operating expenses must also be considered.

DEPARTMENTAL OPERATING INCOME

LO 3   Describe and compute departmental operating income.

Departmental operating income is the difference between a department's gross profit and its operating expenses. As with departmental gross profit, separate departmental accounts may be maintained for each operating expense. This approach is not common, however, because many operating expenses cannot be directly related to specific departments. Instead, a single general ledger account is maintained for each operating expense. The total is assigned or allocated to departments at the end of the period.

Direct and Indirect Operating Expenses

Departmental operating expenses can be classified as direct and indirect. **Direct expenses** are incurred for the sole benefit of and are traceable directly to a specific department. **Indirect expenses** are incurred for the benefit of the business as a whole and cannot be traced directly to a specific department. Figure 26-4 provides examples of direct and indirect expenses for Annie's Sporting Goods.

FIGURE 26-4 Sample Direct and Indirect Expenses

Direct Expenses	Indirect Expenses
Wages of golf department sales clerk	Cost of renting store space
Cost of advertising tennis equipment	Cost of advertising Annie's Sporting
Wages of driver who delivers golf	Goods store
equipment	Store manager's salary

To compute department operating income, direct expenses are *assigned* to departments based on the actual expenses incurred. If separate departmental accounts are used, the expenses are accumulated there. If separate departmental accounts are not used, the expenses are assigned to departments based on information contained in supporting records. For example, personnel records would show the departments in which employees work, and wages would be assigned accordingly. Indirect expenses are *allocated* to departments on some reasonable basis, such as relative sales, cost of goods sold, or floor space, or the estimated time spent serving a given department. There are no rules like generally accepted accounting principles. The key is to use a "reasonable basis."

Assigning and Allocating Departmental Expenses

To illustrate the computation of departmental operating income, we will assign and allocate the operating expenses of Annie's Sporting Goods. Annie's does not maintain separate general ledger departmental operating expense accounts.

Store Clerks Wages Expense. Annie's employs five store clerks: two work solely in the golf department, one works in the tennis department, and two assist customers in both departments. Their wages are as follows:

Employee Number	Dept.	Wages	
1	Golf	$19,000 }	$36,000
2	Golf	17,000 }	
3	Tennis	15,250	
4	Both	13,000 }	$29,000
5	Both	16,000 }	
Total		$80,250	

Wages of $36,000 ($19,000 + $17,000) for the golf department clerks are assigned to golf. Wages of $15,250 for the tennis department clerk are assigned to tennis. Wages of $29,000 ($13,000 + $16,000) for the other two clerks are allocated between the departments based on the percentage of total net sales represented by each department.

> Another reasonable basis for allocating the clerks' wages might be the percentage of total cost of goods sold. This is a good example of the judgment that must be made any time expenses need to be allocated.

Golf net sales / Total net sales	=	$1,075,000 / $1,715,300	=	62.7%
Tennis net sales / Total net sales	=	$640,300 / $1,715,300	=	37.3%

The total store clerks wages expense is divided between the departments as follows:

	Golf	Tennis	Total
Direct expense	$36,000	$15,250	$51,250
Indirect expense allocation:			
% × Total expense			
62.7% × $29,000	18,183		18,183
37.3% × $29,000		10,817	10,817
	$54,183	$26,067	$80,250

Truck Drivers Wages Expenses. Annie's employs three delivery truck drivers, one of whom delivers only golf equipment. Their wages are as follows:

Driver Number	Product Delivered	Wages	
1	Golf	$29,000	
2	Both	26,500 }	$54,900
3	Both	28,400 }	
Total		$83,900	

> Other reasonable bases for allocating the drivers' wages might be the cost of the equipment delivered or the number of units delivered.

Wages of the driver who delivers only golf equipment ($29,000) are assigned to that department. Wages of the other two drivers ($54,900) are allocated based on the relative dollar amount of golf and tennis equipment delivered by the drivers. Shipping and delivery records are used to estimate the percentages as approximately 70% golf and 30% tennis. The total drivers wages expense is divided between the departments as follows:

	Golf	Tennis	Total
Direct expense	$29,000		$29,000
Indirect expense allocation:			

%	×	Total expense			
70%	×	$54,900	38,430		38,430
30%	×	$54,900		$16,470	16,470
			$67,430	$16,470	$83,900

Advertising Expense. Annie's total advertising expense is $79,500; $45,000 for newspaper advertising and $34,500 for radio. Newspaper advertising is classified as golf, tennis, or "mixed" based on the number of inches of copy space. The $45,000 of newspaper advertising is $17,000 for golf, $12,000 for tennis, and $16,000 mixed. All radio advertising is classified as mixed. The total mixed expense for advertising of $50,500 ($16,000 + $34,500) is allocated between departments based on the percentage of total net sales represented by each department. These percentages are 62.7% golf and 37.3% tennis, as calculated for store clerks wages expense. The total advertising expense is divided between the departments as follows:

	Golf	Tennis	Total
Direct expense	$17,000	$12,000	$29,000
Indirect expense allocation:			

%	×	Total expense			
62.7%	×	$50,500	31,664		31,664
37.3%	×	$50,500		18,836	18,836
			$48,664	$30,836	$79,500

Store Rent Expense. Annie's rents 5,000 square feet of store space for $22,800 per year. This entire expense is an indirect expense, allocated on the basis of the relative number of square feet of floor space occupied by each department. The golf department occupies 3,200 square feet, or 64% of the floor space. The tennis department occupies the remaining 36% of floor space. The rent expense is divided between the departments as follows:

	Golf	Tennis	Total
Indirect expense allocation:			

%	×	Total expense			
64%	×	$22,800	$14,592		$14,592
36%	×	$22,800		$8,208	8,208
			$14,592	$8,208	$22,800

Bad Debt Expense. Annie's bad debt expense of $17,900 is treated as a direct expense. It is assigned to the departments based on experience with accounts written off. For the current year, $9,000 is assigned to golf and $8,900 to tennis.

Depreciation Expense—Delivery Equipment. Annie's has three delivery trucks, one of which is used to deliver only golf equipment. Total depreciation on the delivery equipment is $24,000 for the year, $9,000 of which relates to the golf delivery truck. The other $15,000 of depreciation is allocated on the basis of the relative dollar amount of golf and tennis equipment delivered with the other two trucks. These percentages are 70% golf and 30% tennis, as explained for the truck drivers wages expense. The total depreciation expense on the delivery equipment is divided between the departments as follows:

	Golf	Tennis	Total
Direct expense	$ 9,000		$ 9,000
Indirect expense allocation:			
% × Total expense			
70% × $15,000	10,500		10,500
30% × $15,000		$4,500	4,500
	$19,500	$4,500	$24,000

Other Operating Expenses. Annie's other operating expenses totaled $350,430. This total includes a broad range of expenses, from managers' salaries to postage expense. These expenses are assigned and allocated using methods like those used for the various expenses described above. A summary of the amounts assigned and allocated for other operating expenses is as follows:

	Golf	Tennis	Total
Direct expense	$ 84,420	$ 31,980	$116,400
Indirect expense allocation	159,380	74,650	234,030
	$243,800	$106,630	$350,430

Departmental Operating Expense Summary

The assignment and allocation of departmental operating expenses can be summarized in a **departmental operating expense summary**. The summary in Figure 26-5 shows the following:

1. Classification of each operating expense as direct or indirect

2. Amount assigned or allocated to each department

3. Total operating expenses for each department

FIGURE 26-5 Departmental Operating Expense Summary

Annie's Sporting Goods
Departmental Operating Expense Summary
For Year Ended December 31, 20--

	TOTAL	GOLF DIRECT	GOLF INDIRECT	GOLF TOTAL	TENNIS DIRECT	TENNIS INDIRECT	TENNIS TOTAL
Store clerks wages expense	$ 80 2 5 0 00	$ 36 0 0 0 00	$ 18 1 8 3 00	$ 54 1 8 3 00	$15 2 5 0 00	$ 10 8 1 7 00	$ 26 0 6 7 00
Truck drivers wages expense	83 9 0 0 00	29 0 0 0 00	38 4 3 0 00	67 4 3 0 00		16 4 7 0 00	16 4 7 0 00
Advertising expense	79 5 0 0 00	17 0 0 0 00	31 6 6 4 00	48 6 6 4 00	12 0 0 0 00	18 8 3 6 00	30 8 3 6 00
Store rent expense	22 8 0 0 00		14 5 9 2 00	14 5 9 2 00		8 2 0 8 00	8 2 0 8 00
Bad debt expense	17 9 0 0 00	9 0 0 0 00		9 0 0 0 00	8 9 0 0 00		8 9 0 0 00
Depreciation expense—delivery equipment	24 0 0 0 00	9 0 0 0 00	10 5 0 0 00	19 5 0 0 00		4 5 0 0 00	4 5 0 0 00
Other operating expenses	350 4 3 0 00	84 4 2 0 00	159 3 8 0 00	243 8 0 0 00	31 9 8 0 00	74 6 5 0 00	106 6 3 0 00
Total	$658 7 8 0 00	$184 4 2 0 00	$272 7 4 9 00	$457 1 6 9 00	$68 1 3 0 00	$133 4 8 1 00	$201 6 1 1 00

Departmental Income Statement Showing Operating Income

Figure 26-6 shows Annie's departmental income statement for the year 20--, with operating income by department and in total. Operating expense data on the statement were obtained from the departmental operating expense summary in Figure 26-5.

Compare this income statement with the one in Figure 26-3. Notice that the departmental gross profit, total operating expenses, and total operating income are the same in both statements. The difference is that Figure 26-6 shows operating expenses and operating income for each department.

FIGURE 26-6 Departmental Income Statement Showing Operating Income

Annie's Sporting Goods Income Statement For Year Ended December 31, 20 - -	GOLF					TENNIS					TOTAL				
Net sales	$1,075	0	0	0	00	$640	3	0	0	00	$1,715	3	0	0	00
Cost of goods sold	545	2	8	0	00	420	9	0	0	00	$ 966	1	8	0	00
Gross profit	$ 529	7	2	0	00	$219	4	0	0	00	$ 749	1	2	0	00
Operating expenses:															
Store clerks wages expense	$ 54	1	8	3	00	$ 26	0	6	7	00	$ 80	2	5	0	00
Truck drivers wages expense	67	4	3	0	00	16	4	7	0	00	83	9	0	0	00
Advertising expense	48	6	6	4	00	30	8	3	6	00	79	5	0	0	00
Store rent expense	14	5	9	2	00	8	2	0	8	00	22	8	0	0	00
Bad debt expense	9	0	0	0	00	8	9	0	0	00	17	9	0	0	00
Depreciated expense—delivery equipment	19	5	0	0	00	4	5	0	0	00	24	0	0	0	00
Other operating expenses	243	8	0	0	00	106	6	3	0	00	350	4	3	0	00
Total operating expenses	$ 457	1	6	9	00	$201	6	1	1	00	$ 658	7	8	0	00
Operating income	$ 72	5	5	1	00	$ 17	7	8	9	00	$ 90	3	4	0	00

Management can use this income statement to evaluate the overall performance of the two departments. For example, the income statement shows that the operating income and operating income percentage of the golf department are much higher than those of the tennis department.

Golf department operating income percentage: ($72,551 ÷ $1,075,000)	**6.7%**
Tennis department operating income percentage: ($17,789 ÷ $640,300)	**2.8%**

Remember, however, that the golf department's gross profit and gross profit percentage are much higher than those of the tennis department. The golf department's operating income might be higher simply because the gross profit is higher. Further analysis shows that this is the case. As shown on the next page, the operating expense percentage is lower for the tennis department than for the golf department.

		Golf	Tennis
Operating expenses	=	$457,169	$201,611
Net sales		$1,075,000	$640,300
Operating expense percentage		42.5%	31.5%

Management must be cautious in interpreting departmental operating income results. Most of Annie's operating expenses for both departments are indirect. They therefore are allocated between departments based on estimates. Indirect expenses, by definition, are incurred for the benefit of the business as a whole and cannot be traced directly to any department. Thus the departments have no control over such expenses. Further, it might be possible to reduce some indirect expenses by eliminating a department, but most of these expenses would continue to be incurred. Many accountants argue that to properly evaluate departmental performance, an income measure should be used that considers only the direct expenses of each department.

A BROADER VIEW

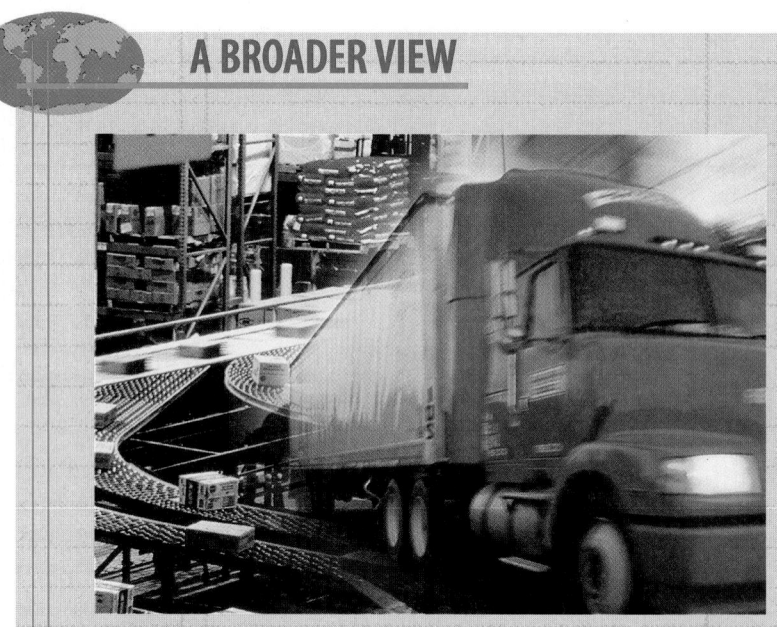

THE SUPPLY CHAIN—REACHING BEYOND YOUR DEPARTMENT OR BUSINESS

Businesses face increasing demands from their customers for higher quality, faster service, and lower costs. One way companies are responding to these demands is through supply-chain management. The supply chain includes all of the purchasing, production, storage, delivery, and sales functions across a set of businesses. Supply-chain management requires focusing on the entire supply chain across businesses instead of just on one's own department or business. By coordinating and participating with other companies, all partners in the chain can operate more efficiently. These arrangements can lead to some new challenges in measuring department performance.

DEPARTMENTAL DIRECT OPERATING MARGIN

LO 4   Describe and compute departmental direct operating margin.

Departmental direct operating margin is the difference between a department's gross profit and its direct operating expenses. To compute departmental direct operating margin, the elements of gross profit and the direct operating expenses are needed for each department. For Annie's, this information was developed in the previous section. We can use it to prepare a departmental income statement showing departmental direct operating margin. The information in the departmental operating expense summary (Figure 26-5) and in the income statement (Figure 26-6) simply needs to be reorganized.

Annie's income statement for the year 20--, showing departmental direct operating margins, appears in Figure 26-7. To determine the departmental direct operating margins, the direct operating expenses listed in the departmental operating expense summary (Figure 26-5) are subtracted from the departmental gross profits.

Departmental Gross Profit – Direct Operating Expenses = Direct Operating Margin

Indirect expenses are then subtracted from the total direct operating margin to calculate total operating income. Note that the indirect expenses that are separated by department in the departmental operating expense summary (Figure 26-5) are combined in Figure 26-7. Indirect expenses are not allocated to specific departments in preparing this departmental income statement.

FIGURE 26-7 Departmental Income Statement Showing Direct Operating Margin

Annie's Sporting Goods — Income Statement — For Year Ended December 31, 20 - -	GOLF	TENNIS	TOTAL
Net sales	$1,075 0 0 0 00	$640 3 0 0 00	$1,715 3 0 0 00
Cost of goods sold	545 2 8 0 00	420 9 0 0 00	966 1 8 0 00
Gross profit	$ 529 7 2 0 00	$219 4 0 0 00	$ 749 1 2 0 00
Direct operating expenses:			
Store clerks wages expense	$ 36 0 0 0 00	$ 15 2 5 0 00	$ 51 2 5 0 00
Truck drivers wages expense	29 0 0 0 00		29 0 0 0 00
Advertising expense	17 0 0 0 00	12 0 0 0 00	29 0 0 0 00
Bad debt expense	9 0 0 0 00	8 9 0 0 00	17 9 0 0 00
Depreciation expense—delivery equipment	9 0 0 0 00		9 0 0 0 00
Other operating expenses	84 4 2 0 00	31 9 8 0 00	116 4 0 0 00
Total direct operating expenses	$ 184 4 2 0 00	$ 68 1 3 0 00	$ 252 5 5 0 00
Departmental direct operating margin	$ 345 3 0 0 00	$151 2 7 0 00	$ 496 5 7 0 00
Indirect operating expenses:			
Store clerks wages expense			$ 29 0 0 0 00
Truck drivers wages expense			54 9 0 0 00
Advertising expense			50 5 0 0 00
Store rent expense			22 8 0 0 00
Depreciation expense—delivery equipment			15 0 0 0 00
Other operating expenses			234 0 3 0 00
Total indirect operating expenses			$ 406 2 3 0 00
Operating income			$ 90 3 4 0 00

Compare this income statement with the one in Figure 26-6. Notice that the departmental gross profit, total operating expenses, and operating income are the same in each statement. The key difference between the statements is that only direct operating expenses are split between departments in Figure 26-7. This permits calculation of the direct operating margin for each department.

Interpretation and Use of Direct Operating Margin

Management can use this form of income statement in several ways.

1. To evaluate departmental performance.

2. To determine the contribution a department makes to the overall operating income of the company.

3. To decide whether to discontinue a department.

Performance Evaluation. Recall that direct expenses are operating expenses that are traceable directly to a specific department. Departmental direct operating margin is calculated by subtracting only direct operating expenses from departmental gross profit. Thus, direct operating margin can be used to evaluate a department on the basis of only those expenses which it can control and for which it is directly responsible. The income statement in Figure 26-7 shows that the golf department's direct operating margin percentage is higher than that of the tennis department.

Golf department direct operating margin percentage: ($345,300 ÷ $1,075,000)	**32.1%**
Tennis department direct operating margin percentage: ($151,270 ÷ $640,300)	**23.6%**

LEARNING KEY: Direct operating margin is a performance measure that focuses on the revenues and expenses that a department can control.

Further analysis, however, shows that this is the case only because of the golf department's higher gross profit. In fact, the tennis department is controlling direct operating expenses more effectively than the golf department. The tennis department's direct operating expenses are only 10.6% ($68,130 ÷ $640,300) of net sales. The golf department's direct operating expenses are 17.2% ($184,420 ÷ $1,075,000) of net sales.

Contribution to Overall Operating Income. Departmental direct operating margin also shows a department's contribution to the company's overall operating income. The conventional operating income in Figure 26-6 implies that the tennis department contributes only $17,789 to overall profits. In contrast, the departmental direct operating margin in Figure 26-7 shows that the tennis department contributes $151,270. This amount is available to cover the company's indirect operating expenses and operating income.

> It can be difficult to determine which expenses will change if a department is discontinued. Part of the plan to discontinue a department might be to expand in some other area. The effects of other changes on departmental expenses must be considered.

Decision to Discontinue. A third possible use of the departmental direct operating margin data is in deciding whether to discontinue a department. In making this decision, management must focus on the revenues and expenses that will be eliminated if a department is discontinued. This means focusing on departmental direct operating margin, not on operating income. Remember that the indirect expenses that are subtracted in calculating conventional operating income are expenses incurred for the business as a whole. Unless management can reduce these expenses by eliminating a department, such expenses will be incurred even if a department is discontinued.

To illustrate, assume that R & R Co. is deciding whether to discontinue one of its three departments. Operating results for the current year for each department, for the business as a whole, and for departments A and B only are shown in Figure 26-8.

FIGURE 26-8 R & R Company

	DEPARTMENT A	DEPARTMENT B	DEPARTMENT C	TOTAL	DEPARTMENTS A & B ONLY
Net sales	$210 0 0 0 00	$185 0 0 0 00	$170 0 0 0 00	$565 0 0 0 00	$395 0 0 0 00
Cost of goods sold	115 0 0 0 00	110 0 0 0 00	96 0 0 0 00	321 0 0 0 00	225 0 0 0 00
Gross margin	$ 95 0 0 0 00	$ 75 0 0 0 00	$ 74 0 0 0 00	$244 0 0 0 00	$170 0 0 0 00
Direct operating expenses	55 0 0 0 00	45 0 0 0 00	54 0 0 0 00	154 0 0 0 00	100 0 0 0 00
Departmental direct operating margin	$ 40 0 0 0 00	$ 30 0 0 0 00	$ 20 0 0 0 00	$ 90 0 0 0 00	$ 70 0 0 0 00
Indirect operating expenses	27 0 0 0 00	22 0 0 0 00	25 0 0 0 00	74 0 0 0 00	74 0 0 0 00
Operating income (loss)	$ 13 0 0 0 00	$ 8 0 0 0 00	$ (5 0 0 0 00)	$ 16 0 0 0 00	$ (4 0 0 0 00)

Operating income results show that Department C is operating at a $5,000 loss. However, eliminating Department C would actually reduce rather than increase R & R's total operating income, as shown in the last column for departments A and B only. This reduction in operating income would occur because Department C's direct operating margin is $20,000. This $20,000 is available to cover the indirect operating expenses and add to the operating income of the firm. If Department C is eliminated, the remaining departments must absorb the indirect operating expenses of $25,000 allocated to Department C. Thus the schedule lists indirect operating expenses as $74,000 both in the total column and in the Departments A and B only column.

Note in Figure 26-8 that the difference between the total operating income of $16,000 and the operating loss of $4,000 for departments A and B only is $20,000. This $20,000 is Department C's departmental direct operating margin. This amount would be lost if the department were eliminated. In general, if a department has a positive departmental direct operating margin, it should not be discontinued. The only exception would be when management has a plan to reduce indirect expenses by at least the amount of that department's direct operating margin.

LEARNING KEY: If a department has a positive direct operating margin, it usually should not be discontinued.

Learning Objectives	Key Points to Remember
1 **Explain the nature and purpose of departmental accounting.**	Departmental reports provide information about the revenues and expenses of each department. These reports are useful to management for planning, control, and performance evaluation.
2 **Describe and compute departmental gross profit.**	Departmental gross profit is the difference between a department's net sales and cost of goods sold. A departmental income statement showing gross profit can help management identify problems with both the sales prices and purchase prices of its products.
3 **Describe and compute departmental operating income.**	Departmental operating income is the difference between a department's gross profit and its operating expenses. Departmental operating expenses are either direct or indirect. Direct expenses are incurred for the sole benefit of a specific department. Indirect expenses are incurred for the benefit of the business as a whole. Direct expenses are assigned to departments based on actual expenses incurred. Indirect expenses are allocated to departments on various reasonable bases. A departmental income statement showing departmental operating income permits evaluation of both the gross profit and operating expense performance of a department.
4 **Describe and compute departmental direct operating margin.**	Departmental direct operating margin is the difference between a department's gross profit and its direct operating expenses. A departmental income statement showing departmental direct operating margin focuses attention on revenues and expenses under the control of a department manager. Such a statement can be very useful for performance evaluation, evaluating contribution to overall operating income, and deciding whether to discontinue a department.

Reflection: Answering the Opening Questions

Three measures of departmental profitability can be prepared: gross profit, operating income, and direct operating margin. To compute direct operating margin, judgment is necessary to classify operating expenses as direct or indirect. Estimates then must be made to allocate the indirect expenses to different departments. Gross profit must be carefully interpreted because it measures the excess of net sales over cost of goods sold, but not the overall profitability of a department. Departmental operating income measures overall profitability but includes indirect expenses that cannot be traced to specific departments and cannot be controlled by the departments.

KEY TERMS

departmental direct operating margin, (961)   The difference between a department's gross profit and its direct operating expenses.

departmental gross profit, (953)   The difference between a department's net sales and cost of goods sold.

departmental operating expense summary, (958)   A summary of the assignment and allocation of departmental operating expenses which shows the classification of each operating expense as direct or indirect, the amount assigned or allocated to each department, and total operating expenses for each department.

departmental operating income, (955)   The difference between a department's gross profit and its operating expenses.

direct expenses, (955)   Operating expenses that are incurred for the sole benefit of and are traceable directly to a specific department.

indirect expenses, (955)   Operating expenses that are incurred for the benefit of the business as a whole.

DEMONSTRATION PROBLEM

Kristen Owen and Stephen Kaplan are partners who own OK Cycling. They sell outdoor bicycles and exercise bicycles. They keep accounts and prepare reports on a departmental basis. Direct expenses are assigned and indirect expenses are allocated to departments by various means. Selected operating information for the year ended December 31, 20--, is given below.

	Outdoor Bicycles	Exercise Bicycles
Net sales	$1,612,500	$1,150,600
Cost of goods sold	935,420	791,800
Direct operating expenses:		
Store clerks wages expense	45,000	19,500
Truck drivers wages expense	26,000	10,000
Advertising expense	16,000	20,000
Depreciation expense—delivery equipment	12,000	0
Bad debt expense	12,000	11,700
Other operating expenses	92,080	44,840
Indirect operating expenses:		
Store clerks wages expense	26,400	14,850
Truck drivers wages expense	62,800	22,250
Advertising expense	48,200	20,500
Depreciation expense—delivery equipment	13,800	5,700
Store rent expense	21,600	14,400
Other operating expenses	197,360	111,190

REQUIRED

1. Prepare an income statement showing departmental operating income.

2. Prepare another income statement showing departmental and total direct operating margins.

3. For the first statement, determine which department has the higher operating income percentage.

4. For the second statement, determine which department has the higher direct operating margin percentage.

5. Which of the two measures is more meaningful for decision-making purposes? Why?

Solution

1.

OK Cycling
Income Statement
For Year Ended December 31, 20 - -

	OUTDOOR BICYCLES	EXERCISE BICYCLES	TOTAL
Net sales	$1,612 5 0 0 00	$1,150 6 0 0 00	$2,763 1 0 0 00
Cost of goods sold	935 4 2 0 00	791 8 0 0 00	1,727 2 2 0 00
Gross profit	$ 677 0 8 0 00	$ 358 8 0 0 00	$1,035 8 8 0 00
Operating expenses:			
Store clerks wages expense	$ 71 4 0 0 00	$ 34 3 5 0 00	$ 105 7 5 0 00
Truck drivers wages expense	88 8 0 0 00	32 2 5 0 00	121 0 5 0 00
Advertising expense	64 2 0 0 00	40 5 0 0 00	104 7 0 0 00
Depreciation expense—delivery equipment	25 8 0 0 00	5 7 0 0 00	31 5 0 0 00
Store rent expense	21 6 0 0 00	14 4 0 0 00	36 0 0 0 00
Bad debt expense	12 0 0 0 00	11 7 0 0 00	23 7 0 0 00
Other operating expenses	289 4 4 0 00	156 0 3 0 00	445 4 7 0 00
Total operating expenses	$ 573 2 4 0 00	$ 294 9 3 0 00	$ 868 1 7 0 00
Operating income	$ 103 8 4 0 00	$ 63 8 7 0 00	$ 167 7 1 0 00

2.

OK Cycling
Income Statement
For Year Ended December 31, 20 - -

	OUTDOOR BICYCLES	EXERCISE BICYCLES	TOTAL
Net sales	$1,612 5 0 0 00	$1,150 6 0 0 00	$2,763 1 0 0 00
Cost of goods sold	935 4 2 0 00	791 8 0 0 00	1,727 2 2 0 00
Gross profit	$ 677 0 8 0 00	$ 358 8 0 0 00	$1,035 8 8 0 00
Direct operating expenses:			
Store clerks wages expense	$ 45 0 0 0 00	$ 19 5 0 0 00	$ 64 5 0 0 00
Truck drivers wages expense	26 0 0 0 00	10 0 0 0 00	36 0 0 0 00
Advertising expense	16 0 0 0 00	20 0 0 0 00	36 0 0 0 00
Depreciation expense—delivery equipment	12 0 0 0 00	0 00	12 0 0 0 00
Bad debt expense	12 0 0 0 00	11 7 0 0 00	23 7 0 0 00
Other operating expenses	92 0 8 0 00	44 8 4 0 00	136 9 2 0 00
Total direct operating expenses	$ 203 0 8 0 00	$ 106 0 4 0 00	$ 309 1 2 0 00
Departmental direct operating margin	$ 474 0 0 0 00	$ 252 7 6 0 00	$ 726 7 6 0 00
Indirect operating expenses:			
Store clerks wages expense			$ 41 2 5 0 00
Truck drivers wages expense			85 0 5 0 00
Advertising expense			68 7 0 0 00
Depreciation expense—delivery equipment			19 5 0 0 00
Store rent expense			36 0 0 0 00
Other operating expenses			308 5 5 0 00
Total indirect operating expenses			$ 559 0 5 0 00
Operating income			$ 167 7 1 0 00

3. Operating income percentage:

    For outdoor bicycles:

    $$\frac{\text{Operating Income}}{\text{Net Sales}} = \frac{\$103,840}{\$1,612,500} = 6.4\%$$

    For exercise bicycles:

    $$\frac{\text{Operating Income}}{\text{Net Sales}} = \frac{\$63,870}{\$1,150,600} = 5.6\%$$

    Outdoor bicycles has the higher operating income percentage.

4. Direct operating margin percentage:

    For outdoor bicycles:

    $$\frac{\text{Direct Operating Margin}}{\text{Net Sales}} = \frac{\$474,000}{\$1,612,500} = 29.4\%$$

    For exercise bicycles:

    $$\frac{\text{Direct Operating Margin}}{\text{Net Sales}} = \frac{\$252,760}{\$1,150,600} = 22.0\%$$

    Outdoor bicycles has the higher direct operating margin percentage.

5. Most accountants believe that the departmental direct operating margin is more meaningful for decision-making purposes than departmental operating income. This is because the direct operating margin takes into account only the direct expenses of operating each department, while departmental operating income is affected by various allocations of indirect operating expenses.

    OK Cycling's results demonstrate the importance of the direct operating margin. The answers to requirements 3 and 4 clearly show that the exercise bicycle department is less profitable than the outdoor bicycle department. Yet, the exercise bicycle department is still making a major contribution to the business. Its operating income is $63,870. More importantly, its direct operating margin is $252,760. Without the exercise bicycle department, OK Cycling would be operating at a loss of $85,050 ($167,710, the present total operating income, minus $252,760, the exercise bicycle department's direct operating margin).

REVIEW QUESTIONS

1. For what purposes are departmental reports useful to management?

2. In what two ways can the information necessary to compute departmental gross profit be accumulated?

3. In what two ways can departmental operating expense data be accumulated?

4. What is the difference between direct and indirect operating expenses?

5. On what basis are direct expenses assigned to departments?

6. On what basis are indirect expenses allocated to departments?

7. What information is contained in a departmental operating expense summary?

8. Why must management be cautious in interpreting departmental operating income results?

9. Distinguish between departmental gross profit, departmental operating income, and departmental direct operating margin.

10. In what ways can an income statement showing departmental direct operating margin be used by management?

MANAGING YOUR WRITING

Two department heads are engaging in an argument. The head of department A argues that department A makes a greater contribution to profits, having produced a higher operating income for three years. The business probably would be better off if department B were discontinued. In fact, department income statements from the last three years show department A had higher operating income than department B. Department B had an operating loss in two of the three years. Write a memo addressing two issues:

1. What are the proper accounting measures to use to determine which department is making a greater contribution to the profits of the business?

2. What are the proper accounting measures to use to decide whether to discontinue one of the departments?

ETHICS CASE

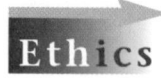

Melanie Sanders and Joyce O'Dell were department heads at Hobgood's Toy and Hobby Store. They had been friends for a long time. Mr. Hobgood, the owner of the store, let the department heads make all decisions relating to the store's operations. During the summer the Hobby Department usually had a higher gross profit, but during the holidays the Toy Department usually caught up. This year the Toy Department wasn't doing well at all mainly because a new discount toy store had opened less than a mile away. In early December Melanie, the Toy Department manager, asked Joyce if she would mind charging all the remaining year's advertising and shipping expenses to the Hobby Department. Melanie went on to explain that she was afraid Mr. Hobgood would get upset if he found out the Toy Department wasn't doing well during the last quarter. She said she had a plan for next year to earn more revenue but was vague on what it involved. Joyce knew the Hobby Department's year-to-date earnings were above average but she felt uncomfortable with what Melanie had asked her to do.

1. What is your reaction to Melanie's idea?

2. If Joyce decides to let Melanie charge all advertising and shipping expenses to the Hobby Department in December, what impact will it have on the financial statements?

3. Write a short paragraph stating both the short- and long-run implications of Melanie's idea.

4. In groups of three or four, make a list of some suggestions to help Hobgood's Toy and Hobby Store earn more revenue.

WEB WORK

Time Warner owns a vast array of cable networks, movie studios, publishers, and other businesses. The information about all of the businesses must be kept separately as well as viewed as one large unit. Look at Time Warner's annual report by visiting the Financial Information section of their homepage at (**http://www.pathfinder.com/corp/**). Try to determine where most of their profit comes from.

(http://heintz.swcollege.com)

SERIES A EXERCISES

EXERCISE 26A-1 (LO 2) GROSS PROFIT SECTION OF DEPARTMENTAL INCOME STATEMENT Bill Walters and Alice Jennings are partners in a business called Walters and Jennings Sportswear that sells athletic footwear. They have organized the business on a departmental basis as follows: Running Shoes, Walking Shoes, and Specialty Shoes. At the end of the first year of operation, the sales and cost of goods sold for the three departments are as shown below.

	Running Shoes	**Walking Shoes**	**Specialty Shoes**
Sales	$36,000	$42,000	$12,000
Cost of goods sold	23,400	23,520	7,680

Prepare the gross profit section of a departmental income statement for the year ended December 31, 20--. Show the gross profit for each department and for the business in total.

EXERCISE 26A-2 (LO 3) ALLOCATING OPERATING EXPENSE—SQUARE FEET
Wray Company rents 10,000 square feet of store space for $32,600 per year. The amount of square footage by department is shown below.

Department A:	1,600 sq. ft.
Department B:	2,200 sq. ft.
Department C:	3,800 sq. ft.
Department D:	2,400 sq. ft.

Allocate the annual rent expense among the four departments on the basis of relative square feet of floor space occupied.

EXERCISE 26A-3 (LO 3) ALLOCATING OPERATING EXPENSE—RELATIVE NET SALES Tina Domingo owns a car stereo store. She has divided her store into three departments. Net sales for the month of July are shown below.

Deluxe:	$36,000
Standard:	30,000
Economy:	54,000

Advertising expense for July amounted to $24,000.

Allocate the advertising expense among the three departments on the basis of relative net sales.

EXERCISE 26A-4 (LO 3) ALLOCATING OPERATING EXPENSE—MILES DRIVEN
Mercado Lopez owns a furniture store that offers free delivery of merchandise delivered within the local area. Mileage records for the three sales departments are shown below.

Department 1:	36,000 miles
Department 2:	48,000 miles
Department 3:	16,000 miles

The cost of using the truck for the last year, including depreciation, amounted to $16,000.

Allocate the cost of the truck among the three departments on the basis of miles driven.

EXERCISE 26A-5 (LO 3) ALLOCATING OPERATING EXPENSE—PURCHASE ORDERS The purchasing department of Brindley Company performs the purchasing function for the entire business. The numbers of purchase orders processed during the most recent month are as follows:

West Division:	33 purchase orders
East Division:	47 purchase orders
Central Division:	20 purchase orders

The monthly cost of operating the purchasing department, including personnel, amounted to $20,000.

Allocate the cost of the purchasing department using the number of purchase orders processed as an allocation base.

EXERCISE 26A-6 (LO 4) DEPARTMENTAL DIRECT OPERATING MARGIN AND DIRECT OPERATING MARGIN PERCENTAGE The sales, gross profit, and condensed direct and indirect operating expenses of Departments A and B of Pan Fei International are as follows:

	Dept. A	Dept. B	Total
Sales	$200,000	$300,000	$500,000
Gross profit	70,000	140,000	210,000
Direct operating expenses	22,000	53,000	75,000
Indirect operating expenses			50,000

Compute the departmental direct operating margin and direct operating margin percentage for each department.

SERIES A PROBLEMS

W & D

PROBLEM 26A-1 (LO 2/3) INCOME STATEMENT WITH DEPARTMENTAL GROSS PROFIT AND OPERATING INCOME Thomas and Hill Distributors have divided their business into two departments: Commercial Sales and Industrial Sales. The following information is provided for the year ended December 31, 20--.

Net sales, Commercial Sales Department	$630,000
Net sales, Industrial Sales Department	470,000
Cost of goods sold, Commercial Sales Department	378,000
Cost of goods sold, Industrial Sales Department	188,000
Warehouse wages expense	99,400
Truck drivers wages expense	88,200
Advertising expense	66,000
Warehouse lease expense	30,000
Depreciation expense—delivery equipment	11,000
Other operating expenses	115,000

REQUIRED
1. Prepare an income statement showing departmental gross profit and total operating income.

2. Calculate departmental gross profit percentages.

PROBLEM 26A-2 (LO 2/3) INCOME STATEMENT WITH DEPARTMENTAL OPERATING INCOME AND TOTAL OPERATING INCOME Carmella Campillo owns a business called Campillo's Bakery. She has divided her business into two departments: Breads and Pastries. The information provided below is for the fiscal year ended June 30, 20--.

	Breads	Pastries
Net sales	$182,000	$98,000
Cost of goods sold	72,800	58,800
Wages expense	30,000	20,000
Advertising expense	16,000	4,000
Other operating expenses	24,000	10,000

REQUIRED
1. Prepare an income statement showing departmental operating income and total operating income.

2. Calculate departmental operating expense and operating income percentages.

PROBLEM 26A-3 (LO 2/3/4) INCOME STATEMENT WITH DEPARTMENTAL DIRECT OPERATING MARGIN AND TOTAL OPERATING INCOME Durwood Thomas operates the business Thomas Security that sells security equipment for commercial property and residential homes. The following information is provided for the year ended December 31, 20--.

	Commercial Property	Residential Homes
Net sales	$465,000	$135,000
Cost of goods sold	279,250	54,000
Direct operating expenses:		
Advertising expense	35,000	20,000
Store clerks wages expense	30,000	18,000
Truck drivers wages expense	15,000	15,000
Bad debt expense	8,000	3,000
Depreciation expense—delivery equipment	6,000	4,000
Other operating expenses	20,000	10,000
Indirect operating expenses:		
Store clerks wages expense	$10,000	
Advertising expense	15,000	
Store rent expense	20,000	
Other operating expenses	10,000	

REQUIRED
1. Prepare an income statement showing departmental direct operating margin and total operating income.

2. Calculate departmental direct operating margin percentages.

PROBLEM 26A-4 (LO 4) WHETHER TO DISCONTINUE A DEPARTMENT Williams and Lloyd Company is trying to decide whether to discontinue department B. Operating results for the year just ended for each of the company's three departments and for the entire operation are given below.

	Dept. A	Dept. B	Dept. C	Total
Net sales	$380,000	$260,000	$290,000	$930,000
Cost of goods sold	210,000	140,000	160,000	510,000
Gross profit	$170,000	$120,000	$130,000	$420,000
Direct operating expenses	100,000	90,000	80,000	270,000
Departmental direct operating margin	$ 70,000	$ 30,000	$ 50,000	$150,000
Indirect operating expenses	40,000	35,000	40,000	115,000
Operating income (loss)	$ 30,000	$ (5,000)	$ 10,000	$ 35,000

REQUIRED
1. Prepare an additional column that combines departments A and C only.

2. Review all data and decide if department B should be discontinued. Defend your decision.

SERIES B EXERCISES

EXERCISE 26B-1 (LO 2) GROSS PROFIT SECTION OF DEPARTMENTAL INCOME STATEMENT Nicole Lawrence and Josh Doyle are partners in a business that sells cheerleading uniforms. They have organized the business, called L and D Uniforms, on a departmental basis as follows: Letters, Sweaters, and Skirts. At the end of the first year of operation, the sales and cost of goods sold for the three departments are as shown below.

	Letters	**Sweaters**	**Skirts**
Sales	$3,000	$12,000	$8,000
Cost of goods sold	1,400	5,900	4,750

Prepare the gross profit section of a departmental income statement for the year ended December 31, 20--. Show the gross profit for each department and for the business in total.

EXERCISE 26B-2 (LO 3) ALLOCATING OPERATING EXPENSE—SQUARE FEET Johnson Company rents 5,000 square feet of store space for $40,000 per year. The amount of square footage by department is shown below.

Department A:	1,200 sq. ft.
Department B:	1,400 sq. ft.
Department C:	1,500 sq. ft.
Department D:	900 sq. ft.

Allocate the annual rent expense among the four departments on the basis of relative square feet of floor space occupied.

EXERCISE 26B-3 (LO 3) ALLOCATING OPERATING EXPENSE—RELATIVE NET SALES Amelia Diaz owns a sporting goods store. She has divided her store into three departments. Net sales for the month of July are shown below.

Football:	$10,000
Basketball:	6,000
Baseball:	9,000

Advertising expense for July amounted to $5,000.

Allocate the advertising expense among the three departments on the basis of relative net sales.

EXERCISE 26B-4 (LO 3) ALLOCATING OPERATING EXPENSE—MILES DRIVEN Herbert Quiong owns a furniture store that offers free delivery of merchandise delivered within the local area. Mileage records for the three sales departments are shown below.

Department 1:	4,000 miles
Department 2:	13,000 miles
Department 3:	8,000 miles

The cost of using the truck for the last year, including depreciation, amounted to $5,000.

Allocate the cost of the truck among the three departments on the basis of miles driven.

EXERCISE 26B-5 (LO 3) ALLOCATING OPERATING EXPENSE—PURCHASE ORDERS The purchasing department of Stokes Company performs the purchasing function for the entire business. The numbers of purchase orders processed during the most recent month are as follows:

West Division:	29 purchase orders
East Division:	37 purchase orders
Central Division:	34 purchase orders

The monthly cost of operating the purchasing department, including personnel, amounted to $30,000.

Allocate the cost of the purchasing department using the number of purchase orders processed as an allocation base.

EXERCISE 26B-6 (LO 4) DEPARTMENTAL DIRECT OPERATING MARGIN AND DIRECT OPERATING MARGIN PERCENTAGE The sales, gross profit, and condensed direct and indirect operating expenses of Departments A and B of Robin Sun Enterprises are as follows:

	Dept. A	Dept. B	Total
Sales	$300,000	$400,000	$700,000
Gross profit	110,000	180,000	290,000
Direct operating expenses	35,000	72,000	107,000
Indirect operating expenses			78,000

Compute the departmental direct operating margin and direct operating margin percentage for each department.

SERIES B PROBLEMS

W & D

PROBLEM 26B-1 (LO 2/3) INCOME STATEMENT WITH DEPARTMENTAL GROSS PROFIT AND OPERATING INCOME Bacon and Hand Distributors have divided their business into two departments: Retail Sales and Wholesale Sales. The following information is provided for the year ended December 31, 20--.

Net sales, Retail Sales Department	$570,000
Net sales, Wholesale Sales Department	830,000
Cost of goods sold, Retail Sales Department	319,200
Cost of goods sold, Wholesale Sales Department	398,400
Warehouse wages expense	110,000
Truck drivers wages expense	90,500
Advertising expense	70,000
Warehouse lease expense	40,000
Depreciation expense—delivery equipment	12,000
Other operating expenses	130,000

REQUIRED

1. Prepare an income statement showing departmental gross profit and total operating income.

2. Calculate departmental gross profit percentages.

PROBLEM 26B-2 (LO 2/3) INCOME STATEMENT WITH DEPARTMENTAL OPERATING INCOME AND TOTAL OPERATING INCOME Sonya McDowell owns a business called The Knitting Chamber. She has divided her business into two departments: Domestic Yarn and International Yarn. The information below is provided for the fiscal year ended June 30, 20--.

	Domestic Yarn	**International Yarn**
Net sales	$60,000	$40,000
Cost of goods sold	37,200	28,000
Wages expense	10,000	5,000
Advertising expense	2,500	1,500
Other operating expenses	4,000	1,000

REQUIRED

1. Prepare an income statement showing departmental operating income and total operating income.

2. Calculate departmental operating expense and operating income percentages.

PROBLEM 26B-3 (LO 2/3/4) INCOME STATEMENT WITH DEPARTMENTAL DIRECT OPERATING MARGIN AND TOTAL OPERATING INCOME Tom Peterson owns the business Peterson's Furniture and Appliances. The following information is provided for the year ended December 31, 20--.

	Furniture Department	**Appliance Department**
Net sales	$390,000	$810,000
Cost of goods sold	234,000	405,000
Direct operating expenses:		
Advertising expense	30,000	60,000
Store clerks wages expense	40,000	90,000
Truck drivers wages expense	35,000	65,000
Bad debt expense	4,000	9,000
Depreciation expense—delivery equipment	4,000	8,000
Other operating expenses	15,000	50,000
Indirect operating expenses:		
Store clerks wages expense	$20,000	
Advertising expense	15,000	
Store rent expense	50,000	
Other operating expenses	25,000	

REQUIRED

1. Prepare an income statement showing departmental direct operating margin and total operating income.

2. Calculate departmental direct operating margin percentages.

PROBLEM 26B-4 (LO 4) WHETHER TO DISCONTINUE A DEPARTMENT Mueller and Kenington Company is trying to decide whether to discontinue department A. Operating results for the year just ended for each of the company's three departments and for the entire operation are given on the next page.

(continued)

	Dept. A	Dept. B	Dept. C	Total
Net sales	$680,000	$730,000	$690,000	$2,100,000
Cost of goods sold	400,000	380,000	360,000	1,140,000
Gross profit	$280,000	$350,000	$330,000	$960,000
Direct operating expenses	230,000	240,000	210,000	680,000
Departmental direct operating margin	$ 50,000	$110,000	$120,000	$280,000
Indirect operating expenses	70,000	70,000	70,000	210,000
Operating income (loss)	$ (20,000)	$ 40,000	$ 50,000	$ 70,000

REQUIRED

1. Prepare an additional column that combines departments B and C only.

2. Review all data and decide if department A should be discontinued. Defend your decision.

MASTERY PROBLEM

Bob's Acme Supermarket has been in operation for many years offering high-quality groceries, produce, and meat at reasonable prices. Accounting records are maintained on a departmental basis with assignment of direct expenses and allocation of indirect expenses through the use of various procedures. Selected operating information for the year ended December 31, 20--, is provided below.

	Grocery	Meat	Produce	Total
Net sales	$2,104,890	$660,500	$345,800	$3,111,190
Cost of goods sold	1,683,912	462,350	207,480	2,353,742
Direct operating expenses:				
Store clerks wages expense	125,000	58,000	38,500	221,500
Advertising expense	25,000	38,500	18,400	81,900
Depreciation expense— store equipment	10,800	15,000	12,000	37,800
Other operating expenses	28,200	28,540	35,600	92,340
Indirect operating expenses:				
Store clerks wages expense	12,000	5,000	4,000	21,000
Advertising expense	7,000	2,000	1,000	10,000
Depreciation expense— store equipment	35,000	10,000	5,000	50,000
Store rent	60,000	20,000	20,000	100,000
Other operating expenses	25,500	4,500	18,450	48,450

REQUIRED

1. a. Prepare an income statement showing departmental operating income.

   b. Compute the gross profit percentage and operating income percentage for each department.

2. a. Prepare an income statement showing departmental and total direct operating margins.

   b. Compute the departmental direct operating margin percentage for each department.

3. Should Bob be concerned about the profitability of the three departments? Should any of the departments be discontinued?

Self-Study Test Questions

True/False

1. Departmental gross profit is the difference between a department's net sales and operating expenses. _____

2. The gross profit percentage can be computed by dividing gross profit by net sales. _____

3. Departmental operating income is the difference between a department's gross profit and its operating expenses. _____

4. Direct expenses are operating expenses incurred for the benefit of the business as a whole and untraceable directly to a specific department. _____

5. Departmental direct operating margin is the difference between a department's gross profit and its direct operating expenses. _____

Multiple Choice

1. The difference between a department's net sales and cost of goods sold is called _____

   (a) departmental gross profit.
   (b) departmental direct operating income.
   (c) departmental operating income.
   (d) net income.

2. Operating expenses incurred for the sole benefit of and traceable directly to a specific department are called _____

   (a) budgeted expenses.
   (b) normal expenses.
   (c) indirect expenses.
   (d) direct expenses.

3. A base used in the text to allocate store rent expense to specific departments is _____

   (a) net sales.
   (b) square footage.
   (c) number of employees.
   (d) number of customers.

4. The difference between a department's gross profit and its direct operating expenses is called _____

   (a) departmental gross profit.
   (b) departmental direct operating margin.
   (c) departmental operating income.
   (d) net income.

5. The difference between a department's gross profit and its operating expenses is called _____

   (a) departmental gross profit.
   (b) departmental direct operating margin.
   (c) departmental operating income.
   (d) net income.

The answers to the Self-Study Test Questions are at the end of the text.

27

Manufacturing Accounting: The Job Order Cost System

LEARNING OBJECTIVES:
Careful study of this chapter should enable you to:

LO 1   Describe the three manufacturing costs.

LO 2   Describe the three inventories of a manufacturing business.

LO 3   Describe and illustrate how manufacturing costs and inventories affect the financial statements of a manufacturing business.

LO 4   Define and describe how to operate a job order cost accounting system.

LO 5   Describe a process cost accounting system.

Finny Co. has obtained a large order to produce a complete set of string instruments for a high school music department. All instruments would have the same face and the school's initials on the neck. Mike Finbar is pleased with this new type of business but is not sure how to estimate the cost for a special order like this. His accountant says a job order cost system ought to work. A few estimates will be necessary, but the basic idea is simply to accumulate the costs of manufacturing that specific order of instruments. Mike is encouraged by his accountant's reaction, but he still has several questions. Exactly what is a job order cost system? What manufacturing costs should be accumulated? What estimates will be necessary?

In the final two chapters of this book, we will study how to account for a manufacturing business. From an accounting standpoint, the key difference between a manufacturing and a merchandising business involves inventory. The manufacturer makes the items it sells; the merchandiser purchases inventory in final form for resale. This makes accounting for a manufacturer more complicated. Special cost accounting systems are needed to accumulate the costs of manufacturing the products. Multiple inventory accounts must be kept. Both the income statement and balance sheet are affected by these accounting changes.

MANUFACTURING COSTS

LO 1   Describe the three manufacturing costs.

The costs incurred to manufacture a product can be classified into three primary elements of manufacturing cost:

1. Materials

2. Labor

3. Factory overhead

As illustrated in Figure 27-1, these costs come together in a conversion process that produces completed products, commonly called finished goods.

FIGURE 27-1 The Manufacturing Process

Materials

Various materials are needed to manufacture a product. A manufacturer of automobiles requires items such as sheet metal, bar steel, fabric, and tires. A manufacturer of electric guitars requires wood, plastic, electrical wire, magnets, nuts, and screws. In many instances, the only distinction between materials and finished goods is their relationship to a particular manufacturer. The finished goods of one manufacturer may be the materials of another. For example, flour is finished goods to a miller but materials to a baker. Similarly, silver may be finished goods to a mining company but materials to a manufacturer of silverware. Materials used in manufacturing are classified as:

1. Direct materials

2. Indirect materials

Direct materials enter into and become a major part of the finished product. Thus the leather and linings used in the manufacture of shoes are direct materials. Similarly, the sheet metal, bar steel, fabric, and many other materials used in the manufacture of an automobile are direct materials.

Indirect materials are used in the manufacturing process but do not become a major part of the finished product. Thus oil and grease used in the operation of machinery are indirect materials. Such materials are often called **factory supplies**. Indirect materials also may include inexpensive items such as nails, screws, and washers. These items may become a part of the finished product, but their small cost is most easily accounted for as part of indirect materials.

Labor

Wages and salaries paid to factory workers and supervisors are part of the cost of manufacturing a product. These wages and salaries are classified as:

1. Direct labor

2. Indirect labor

Direct labor includes the wages of employees who are directly involved in converting materials into finished goods. Such workers may do assembly work or operate factory machinery. These wages are charged directly to the cost of the products being manufactured.

Indirect labor includes the wages and salaries of employees who devote their time to supervision or to work of a general nature. Such workers may include superintendents, inspectors, timekeepers, receiving clerks, and janitors. The costs of these employees cannot be charged directly to the cost of the products being manufactured. They must be included in the indirect costs of the factory operation.

Factory Overhead

All manufacturing costs other than direct materials and direct labor are classified as **factory overhead**. This group of costs is sometimes described as **manufacturing overhead**, **indirect manufacturing cost**, or **factory burden**. Factory overhead consists of:

1. Indirect materials

2. Indirect labor

3. Other factory overhead

Indirect materials and indirect labor have already been discussed. Other factory overhead includes a variety of items, such as:

▶ Depreciation of factory buildings and equipment

▶ Repairs to factory buildings and equipment

▶ Insurance on factory buildings and equipment

▶ Property taxes on factory buildings and equipment

▶ Heat, light, and power

INVENTORIES

LO 2 Describe the three inventories of a manufacturing business.

In accounting for a merchandising business, we used only a single inventory account, Merchandise Inventory. Because a manufacturing business acquires materials in one form and converts them into a different form for final sale, we need three inventory accounts:

1. Materials Inventory

2. Work in Process Inventory

3. Finished Goods Inventory

Materials Inventory consists of the materials acquired to be used in production. This account includes both direct and indirect materials.

Work in Process Inventory consists of products on which work has been started but is not yet finished at the end of the accounting period. Materials, labor, and overhead costs of producing a product are accumulated in this account until the product is completed.

Finished Goods Inventory contains products that have been completed and are ready for sale. All materials, labor, and overhead costs of completed products are accumulated in this account until the products are sold.

Flow of Manufacturing Costs

The flow of the three manufacturing costs through the three inventory accounts is illustrated in Figure 27-2. The figure shows how direct materials and direct labor flow directly into Work in Process. Indirect materials and indirect labor become part of Factory Overhead, which flows into Work in Process.

 LEARNING KEY: Direct materials and direct labor go directly into Work in Process. Indirect materials and indirect labor go through Factory Overhead, and then into Work in Process.

FIGURE 27-2 Flow of Manufacturing Costs

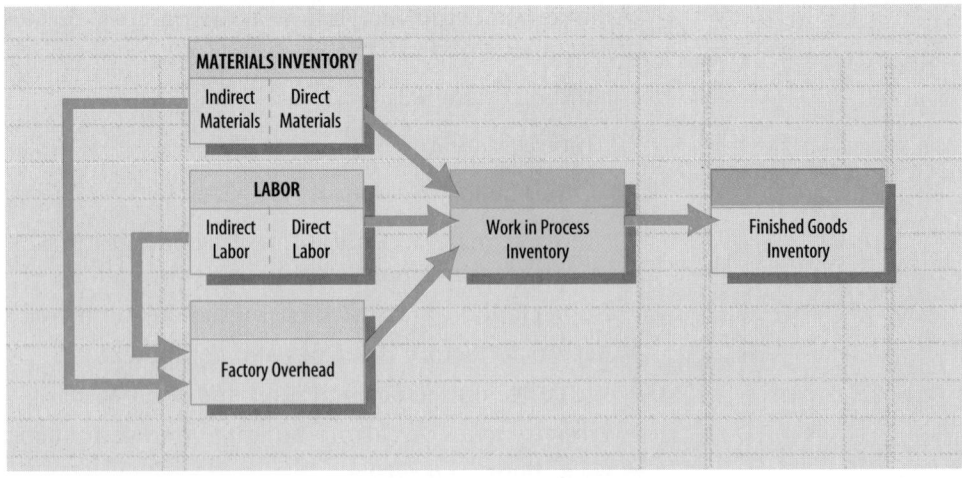

FINANCIAL STATEMENT EFFECTS

LO 3   Describe and illustrate how manufacturing costs and inventories affect the financial statements of a manufacturing business.

The financial statements of a manufacturing business are very similar to those of a merchandiser. The main differences are in the cost of goods sold section of the income statement and the inventories on the balance sheet.

Income Statement

The key difference between the manufacturing and merchandising company income statements is highlighted in Figure 27-3. The purchases made by a merchandiser are the goods that eventually are sold. In contrast, the purchases made by a manufacturer are merely purchases of materials. The cost of manufacturing a product includes not only materials, but also labor and overhead. Thus, *cost of goods manufactured* on the manufacturer's income statement replaces *purchases* on the merchandiser's income statement.

FIGURE 27-3 Cost of Goods Sold Sections

Merchandising Company Partial Income Statement		Manufacturing Company Partial Income Statement	
Cost of goods sold:		Cost of goods sold:	
Merchandise inventory, January 1, 20--	$10,000	Finished goods inventory, January 1, 20--	$10,000
Purchases	42,000	Cost of goods manufactured	42,000
Merchandise available for sale	$52,000	Goods available for sale	$52,000
Merchandise inventory, December 31, 20--	8,000	Finished goods inventory, December 31, 20--	8,000
Cost of goods sold	$44,000	Cost of goods sold	$44,000

The cost of goods sold section of the manufacturer's income statement is commonly supplemented by a schedule of cost of goods manufactured (see Figure 27-4 on the next page). This schedule shows:

1. Beginning work in process.

2. Materials, labor, and overhead costs added to work in process during the period.

3. Ending work in process.

4. Cost of goods manufactured (cost of goods completed during the period).

The *cost of materials used* is calculated in the same way the cost of goods sold is calculated in a merchandiser's income statement. Beginning inventory of materials plus purchases equals materials available. This amount less the ending inventory of materials equals cost of materials used.

The cost of goods manufactured of $42,000 represents:

1. The amount *transferred out* of work in process during the period.

2. The amount *added to* finished goods during the period.

FIGURE 27-4 Schedule of Cost of Goods Manufactured

1 Work in process, Jan. 1, 20--			$ 7 0 0 0 00
Materials inventory, Jan. 1, 20--	$ 3 0 0 0 00		
Materials purchases	15 0 0 0 00		
Materials available for use	$18 0 0 0 00		
Materials inventory, Dec. 31, 20--	2 5 0 0 00		
Cost of materials used		$15 5 0 0 00	
2 Direct labor		16 5 0 0 00	
Overhead		8 0 0 0 00	
Total manufacturing costs			40 0 0 0 00
Total work in process during the period			$47 0 0 0 00
3 Work in process, Dec. 31, 20--			5 0 0 0 00
4 Cost of goods manufactured			$42 0 0 0 00

Balance Sheet

A manufacturer's balance sheet has three inventory accounts rather than the single merchandise inventory account used by a merchandiser. The current assets section of the manufacturer's balance sheet might appear as shown in Figure 27-5. The three inventories are listed in decreasing order of liquidity, with finished goods first and materials last.

FIGURE 27-5 Current Assets Section of Manufacturer's Balance Sheet

Current assets:			
Cash			$17 0 0 0 00
Accounts receivable (net)			12 0 0 0 00
Inventories:			
Finished goods	$8 0 0 0 00		
Work in process	5 0 0 0 00		
Materials	2 5 0 0 00	15 5 0 0 00	
Supplies		2 3 0 0 00	
Total current assets			$46 8 0 0 00

JOB ORDER COST ACCOUNTING

LO 4 Define and describe how to operate a job order cost accounting system.

A **cost accounting system** is a system for accumulating detailed information about the cost of producing a product. Product cost information is needed for three purposes:

1. To assist in setting selling prices. A product's selling price must be sufficient to provide a gross profit and contribute to net income.

2. To assist in controlling production costs. If the actual costs of producing a product exceed the planned costs, management can take corrective action.

3. To assist in determining the net income or loss. When products are manufactured, the manufacturing costs must be accumulated to determine inventories, cost of goods sold, and net income or loss.

The two basic types of inventory cost accounting systems are:

1. Job order cost system.

2. Process cost system.

A **job order cost system** provides a separate record of the cost of producing each individual product or group of products. If products are made to customers' orders or in separately identifiable "lots" or "batches," a job order cost system is appropriate. A printing shop, custom cabinet maker, or consulting firm would use such a system.

A **process cost system** accumulates manufacturing costs by process, such as cutting, painting, or finishing. Each unit of product passing through the process during a period of time is assigned a share of the costs. A business that manufactures cement, chemicals, or flour would use such a system.

A BROADER VIEW

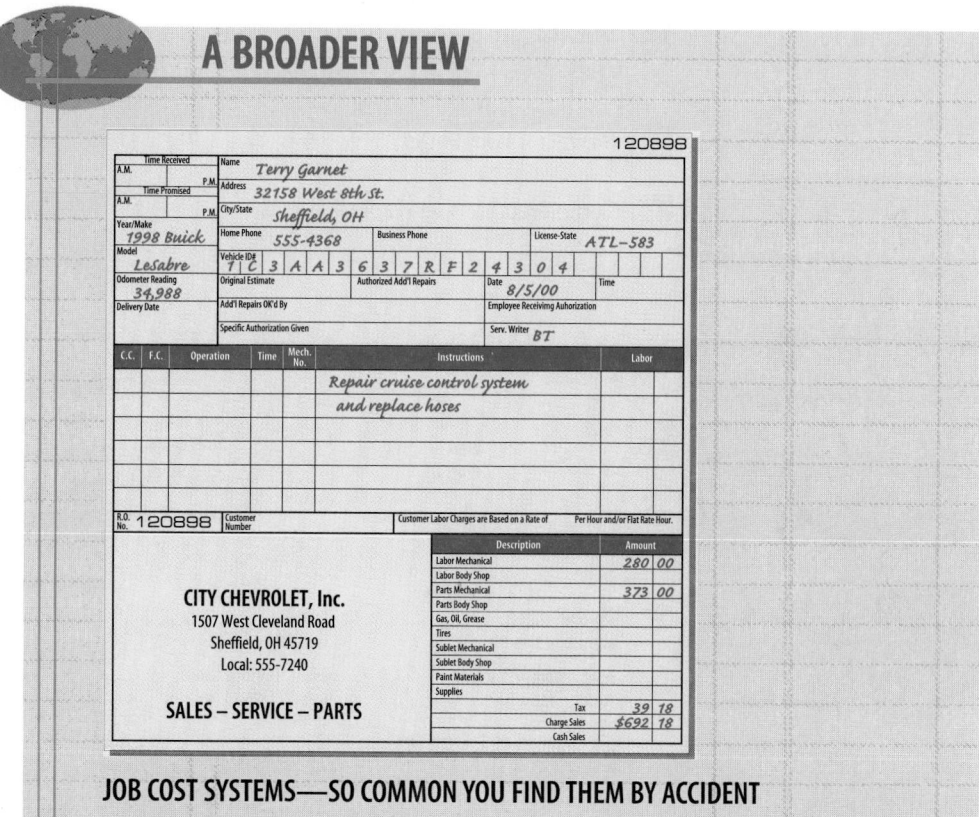

JOB COST SYSTEMS—SO COMMON YOU FIND THEM BY ACCIDENT

Throughout this book we have seen the accounting side of many items we regularly encounter in our everyday lives: managing our checking account, deductions for taxes on our paychecks, purchases we make with our credit cards, and use of promissory notes to borrow money. In this chapter, we see yet another accounting item that is far more common than we probably realize—the job order cost system.

Presented above is Job Order #120898 used by City Chevrolet to repair Terry Garnet's car. If you ever had your car repaired or serviced, even something as minor as an oil change, you probably were a job order. In fact, any repairs or servicing of any kind—on TVs, computers, lawn tractors, etc.—usually are based on a job order system. You can see accounting issues almost everywhere. It is indeed an important language to learn.

Perpetual Inventories

A cost accounting system uses perpetual inventories. To understand the journal entries and flow of information in a cost accounting system, we need to recall how a perpetual inventory system works.

Chapter 18 demonstrated how a perpetual inventory system works for a merchandising business. The merchandise inventory account is increased for each purchase and decreased for each sale.

A manufacturing business has three inventory accounts: Materials, Work in Process, and Finished Goods. This makes a manufacturing business' perpetual inventory system more complex than that of a merchandising business. The following four inventory movements and journal entries are illustrated in Figure 27-6.

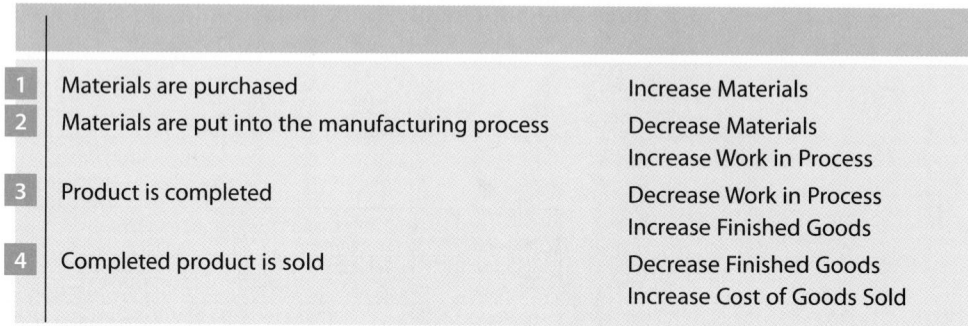

1	Materials are purchased	Increase Materials
2	Materials are put into the manufacturing process	Decrease Materials
		Increase Work in Process
3	Product is completed	Decrease Work in Process
		Increase Finished Goods
4	Completed product is sold	Decrease Finished Goods
		Increase Cost of Goods Sold

FIGURE 27-6 Flow of Costs Through Manufacturing Inventory Accounts

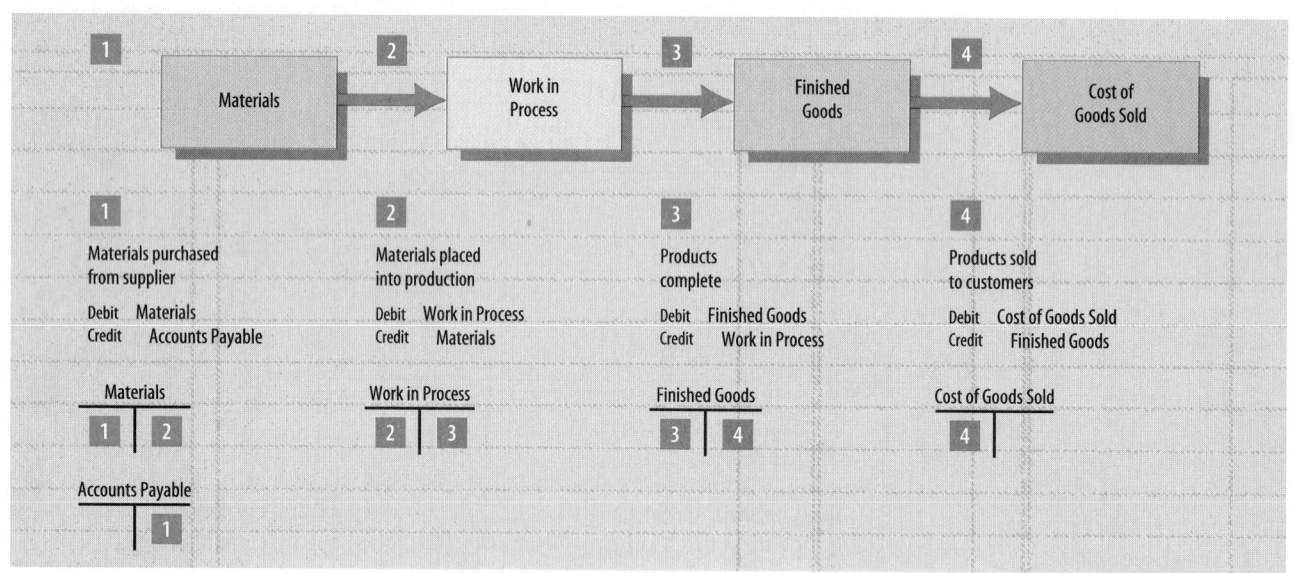

Accounting for Materials

When materials are purchased, their cost is debited to Materials. If materials costing $1,300 are purchased on account, the following journal entry is made:

4		Materials		1 3 0 0 00		4
5		Accounts Payable			1 3 0 0 00	5
6		Purchased materials on account				6

The materials account in the general ledger is a control account. A separate account for each type of material is kept in a subsidiary ledger called a **materials ledger** or **stores ledger**. Each subsidiary account shows the quantity and cost of the material received and issued and the resulting balance.

Materials are issued from the storeroom to production based on a form called a **materials requisition**. This form is both an authorization to the storekeeper to issue materials and a source document showing the movement of materials. Figure 27-7 illustrates one form of materials requisition. If these are direct materials, the following journal entry is made:

8		Work in Process (Job No. 319)	2	1	0	0	00						8
9		Materials						2	1	0	0	00	9
10		Issued direct materials to production											10

Note that the debit to Work in Process also indicates the job to which the materials are charged.

FIGURE 27-7 Materials Requisition

MATERIALS REQUISITION

Requested by: Susan Korman   Req. No. 439
Date: January 19, 20--   Approved: C.D.
Charge to: Job No. 319 Materials

Item No.	Description	Quantity	Unit Cost	Total Cost
SP10	16" Plastic Truck Body	500	$4.20	$2,100.00

Received By: S.K.   Date Received: January 19, 20--

Materials requisitions also are used to issue indirect materials. Since indirect materials are part of overhead, the following journal entry is made to issue $250 of indirect materials to production:

13		Factory Overhead	2	5	0	00							13
14		Materials						2	5	0	00		14
15		Issued indirect materials to production											15

Notice that no job number is indicated for these overhead costs. This is because overhead costs relate to many different jobs. The application of these costs to specific jobs is illustrated later in the chapter.

Accounting for Labor

Chapter 9 showed how to account for employee earnings and payroll deductions. A job order cost accounting system uses the same procedures, except more detail is involved. The earnings of workers whose services are direct labor are charged to the jobs on which they worked. The earnings of workers whose services are indirect labor are charged to the proper factory overhead accounts. This requires keeping a record of the time worked and labor cost incurred on each job. One way of doing so is to require the direct labor employees to complete a **daily time sheet** or **time ticket** like the one in Figure 27-8.

In businesses with computer-based timekeeping systems, a record of time and labor costs on each job can be generated automatically. Employees' barcode time cards (Chapter 9, Figure 9-2) are inserted into a computer at their workstations. The labor costs are then distributed by the computer system.

FIGURE 27-8 Daily Time Sheet

Time sheets normally are summarized by days, weeks, or months to provide the direct labor cost for each job. This summary is used to make the journal entry for the direct labor costs incurred. Based solely on the time sheet in Figure 27-8, the entry is:

4		Work in Process (Job No. 319)		8 0 00			4
5		Wages Payable			8 0 00		5
6		Incurred direct labor costs					6

The debit to Work in Process also indicates the job to which the direct labor is charged.

Employees who perform indirect labor also use time sheets. Since indirect labor is part of overhead, the following journal entry is made if indirect labor costs of $110 are incurred:

8			Factory Overhead			1	1	0	00					8
9			Wages Payable							1	1	0	00	9
10			Incurred indirect labor costs											10

Accounting for Factory Overhead

Factory overhead includes all manufacturing costs other than direct materials and direct labor. The previous two sections showed how to charge indirect materials and indirect labor to Factory Overhead. Similarly, other overhead costs like depreciation of factory buildings, utilities, and repairs are charged to Factory Overhead. For example, the factory lighting bill of $870 is recorded as follows:

12			Factory Overhead			8	7	0	00					12
13			Accounts Payable							8	7	0	00	13
14			Incurred factory lighting costs											14

The factory overhead account generally is a control account in the general ledger. Details of the different types of factory overhead costs are accumulated in a **factory overhead subsidiary ledger**. This ledger would contain separate accounts for indirect materials, indirect labor, utilities, repairs, and other costs.

By using a factory overhead control account and subsidiary ledger, we can readily accumulate factory overhead costs. The major problem in a job order cost accounting system, however, is assigning a reasonable amount of overhead costs to each job. The nature of many factory overhead costs complicates the problem. Most factory overhead costs, such as depreciation of factory buildings, do not vary with the volume of production. Further, some types of overhead, such as heating costs, vacation pay, and repairs, are incurred irregularly throughout the year. These costs do not apply solely to the products manufactured in the months in which the costs occurred.

Predetermined Overhead Rate. Because of the difficulties of relating actual overhead costs to specific jobs, overhead is applied to jobs based on a **predetermined overhead rate**. The basic idea is that we estimate the total overhead costs and total production activity for the year. The overhead is then spread among the jobs based on the amount of production activity on each job. Common measures of production activity are direct labor hours, direct labor costs, and machine hours.

LEARNING KEY: Actual overhead costs are accumulated in factory overhead accounts. Overhead costs are applied to jobs using a predetermined overhead rate.

To illustrate, assume that ToyJoy Manufacturing Co. estimates its factory overhead costs at $366,000 and direct labor costs at $610,000 for the coming year. ToyJoy's predetermined overhead application rate based on direct labor costs would be 60%.

$$\frac{\text{Estimated factory overhead costs}}{\text{Estimated direct labor costs}} = \frac{\$366,000}{\$610,000} = 60\%$$

As each job is completed during the year, 60% of the direct labor cost incurred on the job is added as the job's share of factory overhead. Assume that Job No. 319 had total direct labor costs of $5,040. Factory overhead applied to this job is $3,024.

Direct labor cost	$5,040
Application rate	× 60%
Overhead cost applied	$3,024

The entry to apply the overhead cost to Job No. 319 is:

4		Work in Process (Job No. 319)		3	0	2	4	00					4
5		Factory Overhead							3	0	2	4	00	5
6		Applied overhead to work in process												6

The debit to Work in Process also indicates the job to which the overhead is charged.

Accounting for Work in Process—The Job Cost Sheet

In the three previous sections, we saw materials, labor, and overhead costs charged to a specific job (No. 319) that was part of work in process. In a job order cost accounting system, Work in Process is a control account with a subsidiary ledger (**job cost ledger**). This ledger is made up of job cost sheets. A **job cost sheet** is a document for recording the direct materials and direct labor costs incurred and factory overhead costs applied on a specific job. The job cost sheet for Job No. 319 is illustrated in Figure 27-9. As the direct materials and direct labor costs are incurred on a specific job, they are entered on a cost sheet. When the job is completed, factory overhead is applied at the predetermined rate.

 LEARNING KEY: Direct materials, direct labor, and applied factory overhead costs are accumulated on a job cost sheet.

Accounting for Completed Jobs

After a job has been completed, all of the costs accumulated on the job cost sheet are transferred to finished goods. For Job No. 319 (Figure 27-9), the entry is:

9		Finished Goods (No. R4)		10	1	6	4	00						9
10		Work in Process (Job No. 319)							10	1	6	4	00	10
11		Transferred work in process to finished goods												11

FIGURE 27-9 Job Cost Sheet

The credit to Work in Process indicates the job that has been completed (Job No. 319). The debit to Finished Goods indicates the completed product number (R4). Finished Goods is a control account in the general ledger. A separate account for each product is kept in a subsidiary ledger called a **finished goods ledger.**

In T account form, product R4 would appear in the finished goods ledger as follows:

		Product R4	
Job #297	13,400		
Job #319	10,164		

Notice that the finished goods subsidiary ledger account shows the costs both by product and by job. Remember that in a job cost system, costs are accumulated by job.

At this point, the job has been completed and the costs have been transferred from Work in Process to Finished Goods. Since the costs are no longer in Work in Process, the job cost sheet is removed from the job cost ledger and filed for future reference.

Accounting for Sales

Each time a sale occurs, both the sale and the cost of the goods sold are recorded. Assume that the 500 RC trucks produced in Job No. 319 are sold to RC Time for $13,900 on account. The entry for this sale is

4		Accounts Receivable			13	9	0	0	00									4
5		Sales									13	9	0	0	00			5
6																		6
7		Cost of Goods Sold			10	1	6	4	00									7
8		Finished Goods (No. R4)									10	1	6	4	00			8
9		Made sale on account																9

The credit to Finished Goods also indicates the completed product that was sold (No. R4).

Flow of Job Order Cost Through the Accounts

In the preceding sections, we have made journal entries for events ranging from the purchase of materials through the sale of a finished product. We also used three different subsidiary ledgers. It might be helpful at this point to review the flow of costs in a job order cost system. Figure 27-10 summarizes the journal entries in T account form and ties in the subsidiary ledgers with the related control accounts for the following nine events.

1. Materials purchased from suppliers.

2. Direct materials issued to production (work in process).

3. Indirect materials issued to production (overhead).

4. Direct labor costs incurred (work in process).

5. Indirect labor costs incurred (overhead).

6. Other factory overhead costs incurred (e.g., utilities, depreciation).

7. Overhead applied to completed jobs at predetermined rate.

8. Jobs completed.

9. Finished goods sold to customers.

Note the linkage between each of the control accounts and its related subsidiary ledger. Each time an entry affects one of these control accounts, the related subsidiary ledger must be updated accordingly. All nine events require entries in both a control account and a subsidiary ledger.

Underapplied and Overapplied Factory Overhead

We apply factory overhead to completed jobs based on a predetermined rate. This rate is based on *estimates* of the total factory overhead costs and total production activity for the year. It is unlikely that these estimates will be exactly correct. When either estimate is too high or too low, the amount of factory overhead cost actually incurred will differ from the amount applied. If the amount of applied overhead is greater than actual overhead cost incurred, the difference is called **overapplied overhead**. If the amount applied is less than actual overhead cost incurred, the difference is called **underapplied overhead**.

FIGURE 27-10 Flow of Job Order Costs

Figure 27-11 shows two versions of TJ's factory overhead account after entries for actual and applied overhead have been made for the year. In Case 1, factory overhead is *under*applied by $900 ($185,000 – $184,100). Overhead costs of $900 were incurred that were not applied to goods produced. In Case 2, factory overhead is *over*applied by $1,000 ($185,000 – $186,000). Overhead costs of $1,000 more than were actually incurred were applied to goods produced.

FIGURE 27-11 Factory Overhead Account

CASE 1—Underapplied Overhead

	Factory Overhead			Work in Process	
Actual factory overhead	185,000	184,100	Factory overhead applied	184,100	
	Bal. 900				

CASE 2—Overapplied Overhead

	Factory Overhead			Work in Process	
Actual factory overhead	185,000	186,000	Factory overhead applied	186,000	
		1,000 Bal.			

> If underapplied or overapplied overhead is a large amount, it should be spread among the work in process, finished goods, and cost of goods sold accounts. Usually the amount is small, so the transfer to Cost of Goods Sold is acceptable.

What should we do with the underapplied or overapplied balance in the factory overhead account? Three accounts were affected by the overhead applications during the year: Work in Process, Finished Goods, and Cost of Goods Sold. We could spread the balance among these three accounts. This would require considerable cost and effort, and the accuracy achieved is generally viewed as not worth the trouble. Instead, the underapplied or overapplied overhead commonly is transferred to Cost of Goods Sold by an adjusting entry. The adjusting entries for each case shown in Figure 27-11 would be:

CASE 1—Underapplied Overhead

| 4 | | Cost of Goods Sold | | 9 | 0 | 0 | 00 | | | | | | | 4 |
| 5 | | Factory Overhead | | | | | | | 9 | 0 | 0 | 00 | 5 |

CASE 2—Overapplied Overhead

| 7 | | Factory Overhead | | 1 | 0 | 0 | 0 | 00 | | | | | | 7 |
| 8 | | Cost of Goods Sold | | | | | | | 1 | 0 | 0 | 0 | 00 | 8 |

LEARNING KEY: Underapplied or overapplied overhead normally is transferred to Cost of Goods Sold.

PROCESS COST ACCOUNTING

LO 5   Describe a process cost accounting system.

The job order cost system described above accumulates costs by job. This system is useful for costing separately identifiable products or batches of product. In a process cost system, costs are accumulated by process or department. This system is useful for costing similar or identical products. Good examples include basic models of most automobiles, or wooden bookshelves.

As products move through the manufacturing process in a process cost system, costs of processing "attach" to the products. These costs are then passed on to the next processing operation where additional costs attach to the product. This sequence continues through the final production of finished goods.

LEARNING KEY: In a process cost system, costs attach to products as they are moved from one process to another.

The production of unassembled wooden bookshelves in a process cost system is illustrated in Figure 27-12. Notice how different manufacturing costs are added at different processing stages. Materials, labor, and overhead costs are incurred in Process 1. In Process 2, only labor and overhead costs are added. In Process 3, materials, labor, and overhead costs are incurred again.

Also notice how the costs accumulate from process to process. The costs of the output from Process 1 are the materials, labor, and overhead incurred in Process 1. The costs of the output from Process 2 include both the costs transferred in from Process 1 and the additional costs incurred in Process 2. The costs of the output from Process 3 include the costs transferred in from Processes 1 and 2, plus the additional costs incurred in Process 3. Thus the costs ultimately transferred to Finished Goods include costs incurred in and transferred through three different processing operations.

FIGURE 27-12 Process Cost System

To function effectively, a process cost system must also have the following features:

▶ Work in process accounts. Each processing department has a separate work in process account.

▶ Overhead application rates. Each processing department has a separate predetermined overhead application rate.

▶ Costs per unit. Costs are calculated per unit to allocate costs to products moving through the processes.

The number of units is computed for each process based on:

1. units in process at the beginning of the period,

2. units started and completed during the period, and

3. units still in process at the end of the period.

The cost per unit must be computed separately for materials, labor, and overhead.

In general, process cost systems are more complicated than job order cost systems. Process cost systems are fully explained and illustrated in more advanced texts.

Learning Objectives	Key Points to Remember
1 Describe the three manufacturing costs.	The three primary elements of manufacturing cost are materials, labor, and factory overhead. These three costs come together in a conversion process to produce completed products, as shown in Figure 27-1.
2 Describe the three inventories of a manufacturing business.	Three inventories are needed in a manufacturing business: materials, work in process, and finished goods. Materials inventory consists of materials acquired to be used in production. Work in process inventory consists of products started but not yet finished. Finished goods inventory contains completed products.
3 Describe and illustrate how manufacturing costs and inventories affect the financial statements of a manufacturing business.	There are two main differences in the financial statements of a manufacturer and a merchandiser: (1) cost of goods sold on the income statement and (2) inventories on the balance sheet. Purchases on the merchandiser's income statement is replaced by cost of goods manufactured on the manufacturer's income statement. The manufacturer's balance sheet has three inventory accounts: Finished Goods, Work in Process, and Materials.
4 Define and describe how to operate a job order cost accounting system.	A job order cost system provides a separate record of the cost of each product or group of products that is produced. A cost accounting system with perpetual inventories is used to accumulate information about the cost of producing each product. Under this system, at least one of the three inventory accounts is affected every time (1) materials are purchased, (2) materials are placed in production, (3) products are completed, or (4) products are sold, as shown in Figure 27-6.
	Three important documents used in a job order cost system are the materials requisition, daily time sheet, and job cost sheet.
	Overhead is applied to jobs based on a predetermined overhead rate. Underapplied or overapplied overhead normally is transferred to Cost of Goods Sold.
	Four subsidiary ledgers are used in a job cost system: the materials ledger, factory overhead ledger, job cost ledger, and finished goods ledger. Figure 27-10 shows the use of these four ledgers.
5 Describe a process cost accounting system.	In a process cost system, costs are accumulated by process or department rather than by job.

Reflection: Answering the Opening Questions

A job order cost system is an inventory costing system that provides a separate record of the cost of each product or group of products that is produced. The manufacturing costs to accumulate are the direct materials, direct labor, and overhead. Estimates are required for the total overhead costs and total manufacturing activity for the period. These estimates are important in allocating an appropriate amount of overhead to the job.

KEY TERMS

cost accounting system, (984)   A system for accumulating detailed information regarding the cost of producing a product.

daily time sheet, (988)   A record of the time worked and labor cost incurred on each job.

direct labor, (981)   The wages of employees who are directly involved in converting materials into finished goods.

direct materials , (981)   Those materials that enter into and become a major part of the finished product.

factory burden, (981)   See factory overhead.

factory overhead, (981)   All manufacturing costs other than direct materials and direct labor.

factory overhead subsidiary ledger, (989)   The ledger in which details of the different types of factory overhead costs are accumulated.

factory supplies, (981)   See indirect materials.

Finished Goods Inventory, (982)   The account that contains the costs of products that have been completed and are ready for sale.

finished goods ledger, (991)   The subsidiary ledger in which a separate account for each product is kept.

indirect labor, (981)   The wages and salaries of employees who devote their time to supervision or to work of a general nature.

indirect manufacturing cost, (981)   See factory overhead.

indirect materials, (981)   Those materials used in the manufacturing process that do not become a major part of the finished product.

job cost ledger, (990)   A subsidiary ledger for the work in process control account that is made up of job cost sheets.

job cost sheet, (990)   A document for recording the direct materials, direct labor, and factory overhead costs incurred on a specific job.

job order cost system, (985)   The system that provides a separate record of the cost of each individual product or group of products that is produced.

manufacturing overhead, (981)   See factory overhead.

Materials Inventory, (982)   The account that includes all the materials (both direct and indirect) acquired to be used in production.

materials ledger, (987)   The subsidiary ledger that shows the quantity, cost, material received and issued, and resulting balance for each type of material.

materials requisition, (987)   A form used to issue materials from the storeroom to production.

overapplied overhead, (992)   If the amount of applied overhead is greater than actual overhead cost incurred, the difference is called overapplied overhead.

predetermined overhead rate, (989)   The rate used to apply overhead, based on production activity such as direct labor hours, direct labor costs, or machine hours; used because of the difficulties of relating specific overhead costs to specific jobs.

process cost system, (985)   The system that accumulates manufacturing costs by process, such as cutting, painting, or finishing, and assigns each unit of product passing through the process a share of the costs.

stores ledger, (987)   See materials ledger.

time ticket, (988)   See daily time sheet.

underapplied overhead, (992)   If the amount of applied overhead is less than actual overhead cost incurred, the difference is called underapplied overhead.

Work in Process Inventory, (982)   The account in which materials, labor, and overhead costs of producing a product are accumulated until the product is completed.

DEMONSTRATION PROBLEM

Mantel Manufacturing Company uses a job order cost accounting system. The following is a summary of transactions completed during its first year of operations.

(a)   Purchased materials on account, $435,000.

(b) (1) Issued *direct materials* to production.

Job No. 1	$ 55,000
Job No. 2	76,000
Job No. 3	59,800
Job No. 4	119,000
Job No. 5	65,000
Job No. 6	18,000

(2) Issued *indirect materials* to production, $11,900.

(c) (1) Incurred factory labor costs:

Job No. 1	$34,000
Job No. 2	40,000
Job No. 3	29,000
Job No. 4	76,000
Job No. 5	38,000
Job No. 6	12,000

(2) Incurred indirect labor costs, $10,000.

(d)   Incurred other factory overhead costs, $96,000.

(e)   Depreciation expense on factory equipment, $29,000.

(f)   Applied factory overhead, 65% of direct labor cost incurred on jobs.

(g)   Finished Job Nos. 1, 2, 4, and 5 as products A, B, D, and E, respectively.

(h)   Shipped products A, B, and D and billed customers for $158,000, $210,000, and $362,000, respectively.

REQUIRED

1. Prepare general journal entries for the foregoing transactions. Make compound entries for (b), (c), and (f), but with separate debits for each job. (Use journal page numbers 7 and 8.)

2. Post the entries to the general ledger T accounts for Work in Process and Finished Goods, and determine the ending balances in these accounts.

3. Determine the balances in the job cost ledger to support the balance in the work in process account.

4. Determine the balances in the finished goods ledger to support the balance in the finished goods account.

5. Determine the amount of underapplied or overapplied overhead.

Solution

1.

GENERAL JOURNAL

	DATE	DESCRIPTION	POST REF.	DEBIT					CREDIT					
(a) 1		Materials		435	0	0	0							1
2		Accounts Payable							435	0	0	0	00	2
3														3
(b) 4		Work in Process (Job No. 1)		55	0	0	0	00						4
5		Work in Process (Job No. 2)		76	0	0	0	00						5
6		Work in Process (Job No. 3)		59	8	0	0	00						6
7		Work in Process (Job No. 4)		119	0	0	0	00						7
8		Work in Process (Job No. 5)		65	0	0	0	00						8
9		Work in Process (Job No. 6)		18	0	0	0	00						9
10		Materials							392	8	0	0	00	10
11														11
12		Factory Overhead		11	9	0	0	00						12
13		Materials							11	9	0	0	00	13
14														14
(c) 15		Work in Process (Job No. 1)		34	0	0	0	00						15
16		Work in Process (Job No. 2)		40	0	0	0	00						16
17		Work in Process (Job No. 3)		29	0	0	0	00						17
18		Work in Process (Job No. 4)		76	0	0	0	00						18
19		Work in Process (Job No. 5)		38	0	0	0	00						19
20		Work in Process (Job No. 6)		12	0	0	0	00						20
21		Wages Payable							229	0	0	0	00	21
22														22
23		Factory Overhead		10	0	0	0	00						23
24		Wages Payable							10	0	0	0	00	24
25														25
(d) 26		Factory Overhead		96	0	0	0	00						26
27		Accounts Payable							96	0	0	0	00	27
28														28
(e) 29		Factory Overhead		29	0	0	0	00						29
30		Accumulated Depreciation							29	0	0	0	00	30
31														31
(f) 32		Work in Process (Job No. 1)		22	1	0	0	00						32
33		Work in Process (Job No. 2)		26	0	0	0	00						33
34		Work in Process (Job No. 3)		18	8	5	0	00						34
35		Work in Process (Job No. 4)		49	4	0	0	00						35
36		Work in Process (Job No. 5)		24	7	0	0	00						36
37		Work in Process (Job No. 6)		7	8	0	0	00						37
38		Factory Overhead							148	8	5	0	00	38
39														39
(g) 40		Finished Goods (Product A)		111	1	0	0	00						40
41		Work in Process (Job No. 1)							111	1	0	0	00	41
42														42
43		Finished Goods (Product B)		142	0	0	0	00						43
44		Work in Process (Job No. 2)							142	0	0	0	00	44

		DESCRIPTION		DEBIT					CREDIT				
45													45
46		Finished Goods (Product D)		244	4	0	0	00					46
47		Work in Process (Job No. 4)							244	4	0	0	00	47
48													48
49		Finished Goods (Product E)		127	7	0	0	00					49
50		Work in Process (Job No. 5)							127	7	0	0	00	50

GENERAL JOURNAL

	DATE	DESCRIPTION	POST. REF.	DEBIT					CREDIT					
(h)	1		Accounts Receivable		158	0	0	0	00						1
	2		Sales							158	0	0	0	00	2
	3														3
	4		Cost of Goods Sold		111	1	0	0	00						4
	5		Finished Goods (Product A)							111	1	0	0	00	5
	6														6
	7		Accounts Receivable		210	0	0	0	00						7
	8		Sales							210	0	0	0	00	8
	9														9
	10		Cost of Goods Sold		142	0	0	0	00						10
	11		Finished Goods (Product B)							142	0	0	0	00	11
	12														12
	13		Accounts Receivable		362	0	0	0	00						13
	14		Sales							362	0	0	0	00	14
	15														15
	16		Cost of Goods Sold		244	4	0	0	00						16
	17		Finished Goods (Product D)							244	4	0	0	00	17
	18														18

2.

Work in Process		Finished Goods	
55,000	111,100	111,100	111,100
76,000	142,000	142,000	142,000
59,800	244,400	244,400	244,400
119,000	127,700	127,700	497,500
65,000	625,200	625,200	
18,000		Bal. 127,700	
34,000			
40,000			
29,000			
76,000			
38,000			
12,000			
22,100			
26,000			
18,850			
49,400			
24,700			
7,800			
770,650			
Bal. 145,450			

3. In job cost ledger: Job No. 3 $107,650

                         Job No. 6   37,800

                                         $145,450

4. Product E: $127,700

5.

Factory Overhead

11,900	148,850
10,000	
96,000	
29,000	
146,900	148,850
	1,950 (Overapplied overhead)

REVIEW QUESTIONS

1. Why is the accounting for a manufacturing business more complicated than that for a merchandising business?

2. What are the three primary elements of manufacturing cost?

3. What are the two major types of materials and how do they differ?

4. Distinguish between direct and indirect labor.

5. Describe and give three examples of factory overhead.

6. What are the three inventories needed in a manufacturing business?

7. Describe the flow of materials, labor, and overhead into Work in Process.

8. What are the main differences between the financial statements of a manufacturing and a merchandising business?

9. For what three reasons is product cost information needed by a manufacturing business?

10. What two purposes are served by a materials requisition?

11. What information is provided by the daily time sheet?

12. Explain how to calculate a predetermined overhead rate.

13. What costs are entered on the job cost sheet?

14. Describe underapplied and overapplied overhead. What is commonly done with the underapplied or overapplied balance in the factory overhead account?

15. Briefly describe the difference between a job order cost system and a process cost system.

MANAGING YOUR WRITING

Joan owns a print shop and has a difficult time figuring out what to bid on jobs. She knows how to estimate the cost of materials and labor on different jobs but is confused about how to handle many other costs she knows she incurs to run the shop. These include utilities, cleaning staff, property taxes on the building, and other expenses. Many of these types of costs vary from month to month. In addition, she often does not know the amounts until some time after jobs are completed.

Write a memo to Joan explaining how she should apply her overhead costs in developing bids on her jobs.

ETHICS CASE

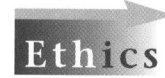

Ben Reese is a painter for a small manufacturing plant. Sometimes he works directly on the product and sometimes he performs routine maintenance on the plant's three buildings. He is paid $11.50 an hour and fills out a time sheet at the end of each week. His supervisor then fills in the specific jobs that will be charged with Ben's time. On Friday afternoon, Ben's supervisor, Ralph Brooks, said he needed Ben to do a job off the plant site. Ralph explained that he had just installed a wooden garage door on his house and needed it painted. He told Ben to leave a couple of hours early and "just sign out as though you had stayed until quitting time." Even though this request made Ben uncomfortable, he did what the boss said.

1. What would you have done if you were Ben? Justify your answer.

2. How do you suppose Ralph will account for Ben's hours away from the plant?

3. Write a short paragraph explaining the difference between direct labor and indirect labor. Include how each is assigned to specific jobs.

4. In groups of two or three, come up with some suggestions on measures a company can take to prevent a situation like this from happening.

WEB WORK

Think of a pair of manufacturing competitors (such as Ford and General Motors or Coke and Pepsi), then look up their annual reports. Find out who is more profitable and who spends more on overhead, labor, and materials. Use the Annual Report Gallery (**http://www.reportgallery.com/bigaz.htm**) as a starting point.

(http://www.heintz.swcollege.com)

SERIES A EXERCISES

EXERCISE 27A-1 (LO 3) COST OF GOODS SOLD SECTION The following information is supplied for R&D Manufacturing Co. and WP West Co. (a merchandising company). Prepare the cost of goods sold sections for the income statements of both companies.

	R&D Manufacturing	WP West
Merchandise inventory, Jan. 1		$57,000
Finished goods inventory, Jan. 1	$57,000	
Merchandise purchases		36,000
Cost of goods manufactured	36,000	
Merchandise inventory, Dec. 31		44,000
Finished goods inventory, Dec. 31	44,000	

EXERCISE 27A-2 (LO 3) SCHEDULE OF COST OF GOODS MANUFACTURED The following information is supplied for Morales Mining and Manufacturing Company. Prepare a schedule of cost of goods manufactured for the year ended December 31, 20--.

Work in Process, Jan. 1	$70,000
Materials inventory, Jan. 1	28,000
Materials purchases	32,000
Materials inventory, Dec. 31	24,000
Direct labor	44,000
Overhead	18,000
Work in Process, Dec. 31	56,000

EXERCISE 27A-3 (LO 4) JOURNAL ENTRIES Jones Manufacturing Corporation had the following transactions for their job order costing operation. Prepare general journal entries to record these transactions.

Jan. 1 Purchased materials on account, $15,000.

15 Issued direct materials to Job No. 101, $10,000.

20 Issued indirect materials (factory overhead), $4,000.

31 Incurred direct labor, Job No. 101, $8,000.

31 Incurred indirect labor (factory overhead), $2,000.

31 Incurred other indirect costs, (factory overhead; credit Accounts Payable), $1,500.

EXERCISE 27A-4 (LO 4) FACTORY OVERHEAD The Huang Company manufactures toys. They keep a factory overhead account where actual factory overhead costs are recorded as a debit and factory overhead applied is recorded as a credit. At the end of the month, underapplied or overapplied factory overhead is calculated and transferred to the cost of goods sold account. For the month of January, Huang had the overhead transactions listed below. Make appropriate general journal entries to record factory overhead and factory overhead applied, and to close the underapplied or overapplied factory overhead to the cost of goods sold account.

Jan. 1 Paid rent, $1,000.

10 Paid electricity bill, $250.

(continued)

15 Paid repair expense, $1,500.

21 Vacation pay for machine operator, $500 (Wages Payable).

31 Depreciation expense for the month, $450.

Factory overhead applied was $3,500.

EXERCISE 27A-5 (LO 4) PREDETERMINED FACTORY OVERHEAD RATE Lovejoy Enterprises calculates a predetermined factory overhead rate so that factory overhead may be applied to production during the month. They calculate the overhead using three different methods and then decide which one to use. Total estimated factory overhead costs are $500,000. Total estimated direct labor hours are 50,000. Total estimated direct labor costs are $800,000. Total machine hours are estimated to be 100,000.

Calculate the predetermined overhead application rates based on (1) direct labor hours, (2) direct labor costs, and (3) machine hours.

EXERCISE 27A-6 (LO 4) JOURNAL ENTRIES Micro Enterprises had the following job order transactions during the month of April. Record the transactions in the general journal, including issuance of materials, labor, and factory overhead applied; completed jobs sent to finished goods inventory; closing of the underapplied or overapplied factory overhead to the cost of goods sold account; and sale of finished goods.

Apr. 1 Purchased materials on account, $35,000.

10 Issued direct materials: to Job No. 33, $10,000

11 Issued direct materials: to Job No. 34, $8,000

12 Issued direct materials: to Job No. 35, $11,000

25 Incurred direct labor:
On Job No. 33, $6,000
On Job No. 34, $4,000
On Job No. 35, $5,000

25 Applied factory overhead:
To Job No. 33, $1,500
To Job No. 34, $1,200
To Job No. 35, $1,600

30 Transferred Job Nos. 33-35 to the finished goods inventory account.

30 Sold Job Nos. 33–35.

30 Actual factory overhead for Job Nos. 33–35, $4,220.

SERIES A PROBLEMS

W & D

PROBLEM 27A-1 (LO 4) JOURNAL ENTRIES Eto Manufacturing had the following transactions during the month.

(a) Purchased raw materials on account, $70,000.

(b) Issued direct materials to Job No. 300, $25,000.

(c) Issued indirect materials to production, $10,000.

(d) Paid biweekly payroll and charged direct labor to Job No. 300, $8,000.

(e) Paid biweekly payroll and charged indirect labor to production, $3,000.

(f) Issued direct materials to Job No. 301, $20,000.

(g) Issued indirect materials to production, $4,000.

(h) Paid miscellaneous factory overhead charges, $6,000.

(i) Paid biweekly payroll and charged direct labor to Job No. 301, $10,000.

(j) Paid biweekly payroll and charged indirect labor to production, $2,000.

REQUIRED Prepare journal entries for transactions (a) through (j) using a general journal.

PROBLEM 27A-2 (LO 4) JOB ORDER COSTING TRANSACTIONS B & L Enterprises makes garage doors. During the month of February, the company had four job orders: 303, 304, 305, and 306. Overhead was applied at predetermined rates, while actual factory overhead was recorded as incurred. All four jobs were completed.

(a) Purchased raw materials on account, $40,000.

(b) Issued direct materials to production:

Job No. 303:	$8,000
Job No. 304:	9,000
Job No. 305:	7,000
Job No. 306:	8,500

(c) Issued indirect materials to production, $5,000.

(d) Incurred direct labor costs:

Job No. 303:	$5,000
Job No. 304:	4,000
Job No. 305:	4,800
Job No. 306:	5,200

(e) Charged indirect labor to production, $3,100.

(f) Paid electricity, heating oil, and repair bills for the factory and charged to production, $4,900.

(g) Applied factory overhead to each of the jobs using a predetermined factory overhead rate as follows:

Job No. 303:	$3,000
Job No. 304:	3,500
Job No. 305:	3,000
Job No. 306:	3,500

(h) Finished Job Nos. 303–306 and transferred to the finished goods inventory account.

(i) Sold Job Nos. 303–306.

REQUIRED 1. Prepare journal entries to record transactions (a) through (i).

2. Post the entries to the work in process and finished goods accounts only.

PROBLEM 27A-3 (LO 4) JOB ORDER COSTING WITH UNDERAPPLIED AND OVERAPPLIED FACTORY OVERHEAD M. Evans & Sons manufactures parts for radios. For each job order, they maintain ledger sheets on which they record direct labor, direct materials, and factory overhead applied. The factory overhead control account contains postings of actual overhead costs. At the end of the month, the underapplied or overapplied factory overhead is charged to the cost of goods sold account.

Factory overhead is applied on the basis of direct labor hours. For Job Nos. 101, 102, 103, and 104, direct labor hours are 12,000, 10,000, 11,000, and 18,000, respectively. The overhead application rate is $1.20/direct labor hour.

(a) Purchased raw materials on account, $50,000.

(b) Issued direct materials:
    Job No. 101: $10,000
    Job No. 102:   8,000
    Job No. 103:   9,000
    Job No. 104:   15,000

(c) Issued indirect materials to production, $8,000.

(d) Incurred direct labor costs:
    Job No. 101: $22,000
    Job No. 102:   19,000
    Job No. 103:   20,500
    Job No. 104:   30,000

(e) Charged indirect labor to production, $15,000.

(f) Paid electricity bill, taxes, and repair fees for the factory and charged to production, $8,000.

(g) Depreciation expense on factory equipment, $30,000.

(h) Applied factory overhead to each of the jobs using the predetermined factory overhead rate (see above).

(i) Finished Job Nos. 101–103 and transferred to the finished goods inventory account.

(j) Sold Job Nos. 101 and 102.

(k) Transferred underapplied or overapplied factory overhead balance to the cost of goods sold account.

REQUIRED
1. Prepare journal entries to record transactions (a) through (k).

2. Post the entries to the work in process and finished goods accounts only and determine the ending balances in these accounts.

3. Compute the balance in the job cost ledger and make certain this balance agrees with that in the work in process control account.

SERIES B EXERCISES

EXERCISE 27B-1 (LO 3) COST OF GOODS SOLD SECTION The following information is supplied for A&B Manufacturing Co. and JC Yoshino Co. (a merchandising company). Prepare the cost of goods sold sections for the income statements of both companies.

	A&B Manufacturing	JC Yoshino
Merchandise inventory, Jan. 1		$15,750
Finished goods inventory, Jan. 1	$15,750	
Merchandise purchases		11,000
Cost of goods manufactured	11,000	
Merchandise inventory, Dec. 31		13,000
Finished goods inventory, Dec. 31	13,000	

EXERCISE 27B-2 (LO 3) SCHEDULE OF COST OF GOODS MANUFACTURED The following information is supplied for Sanchez Welding and Manufacturing Company. Prepare a schedule of cost of goods manufactured for the year ended December 31, 20--.

Work in process, Jan. 1	$20,500
Materials inventory, Jan. 1	11,000
Materials purchases	12,000
Materials inventory, Dec. 31	13,000
Direct labor	9,500
Overhead	5,500
Work in process, Dec. 31	10,500

EXERCISE 27B-3 (LO 4) JOURNAL ENTRIES Rich Manufacturing Corporation had the following transactions for their job order costing operation. Prepare general journal entries to record these transactions.

Jan. 1   Purchased materials on account, $22,000.

15   Issued direct materials to Job No. 1, $18,000.

20   Issued indirect materials (factory overhead), $3,000.

31   Incurred direct labor, Job No. 1, $11,000.

31   Incurred indirect labor (factory overhead), $4,000.

31   Incurred other indirect costs, (factory overhead; credit Accounts Payable), $1,500.

EXERCISE 27B-4 (LO 4) FACTORY OVERHEAD The Bandy Company manufactures toys. They keep a factory overhead account where actual factory overhead costs are recorded as a debit and factory overhead applied is recorded as a credit. At the end of the month, underapplied or overapplied factory overhead is calculated and transferred to the cost of goods sold account. For the month of January, Bandy had the overhead transactions listed below. Make appropriate general journal entries to record factory overhead and factory overhead applied, and to close the underapplied or overapplied factory overhead to the cost of goods sold account.

Jan. 1   Paid rent, $2,000.

10   Paid electricity bill, $500.

(continued)

15 Paid repair expense, $3,000.

21 Vacation pay for machine operator, $500 (Wages Payable).

31 Depreciation expense for the month, $500.

Factory overhead applied was $6,000.

EXERCISE 27B-5 (LO 4) PREDETERMINED FACTORY OVERHEAD RATE Marston Enterprises calculates a predetermined factory overhead rate so that factory overhead may be applied to production during the month. They calculate the overhead using three different methods and then decide which one to use. Total estimated factory overhead costs are $600,000. Total estimated direct labor hours are 30,000. Total estimated direct labor costs are $1,200,000. Total machine hours are estimated to be 200,000.

Calculate the predetermined overhead application rates based on (1) direct labor hours, (2) direct labor costs, and (3) machine hours.

EXERCISE 27B-6 (LO 4) JOURNAL ENTRIES Alert Enterprises had the following job order transactions during the month of April. Record the transactions in the general journal, including issuance of materials, labor, and factory overhead applied; completed jobs sent to finished goods inventory; closing of the underapplied or overapplied factory overhead to the cost of goods sold account; and sale of finished goods.

Apr. 1 Purchased materials on account, $28,000.

10 Issued direct materials: to Job No. 26, $11,000

11 Issued direct materials: to Job No. 27, $9,000

12 Issued direct materials: to Job No. 28, $7,000

25 Incurred direct labor:
On Job No. 26, $6,000
On Job No. 27, $4,000
On Job No. 28, $5,000

25 Applied factory overhead:
To Job No. 26, $1,800
To Job No. 27, $1,500
To Job No. 28, $1,400

30 Transferred Job Nos. 26–28 to the finished goods inventory account.

30 Sold Job Nos. 26–28.

30 Actual factory overhead for Job Nos. 26–28, $4,500.

SERIES B PROBLEMS

PROBLEM 27B-1 (LO 4) JOURNAL ENTRIES Shiar Manufacturing had the following transactions during the month.

(a) Purchased raw materials on account, $22,500.

(b) Issued direct materials to Job No. 200, $11,250.

(c) Issued indirect materials to production, $4,000.

(d) Paid biweekly payroll and charged direct labor to Job No. 200, $4,500.

(e) Paid biweekly payroll and charged indirect labor to production, $1,250.

(f) Issued direct materials to Job No. 201, $10,000.

(g) Issued indirect materials to production, $2,500.

(h) Paid miscellaneous factory overhead charges, $4,500.

(i) Paid biweekly payroll and charged direct labor to Job No. 201, $4,250.

(j) Paid biweekly payroll and charged indirect labor to production, $900.

REQUIRED   Prepare journal entries for transactions (a) through (j) using a general journal.

PROBLEM 27B-2 (LO 4) JOB ORDER COSTING TRANSACTIONS D & K Enterprises makes wicker baskets. During the month of August, the company had four job orders: 501, 502, 503, and 504. Overhead was applied at predetermined rates, while actual factory overhead was recorded as incurred. All four jobs were completed.

(a) Purchased raw materials on account, $44,000.

(b) Issued direct materials to production:

Job No. 501:	$8,200
Job No. 502:	9,100
Job No. 503:	7,300
Job No. 504:	8,500

(c) Issued indirect materials to production, $5,000.

(d) Incurred direct labor costs:

Job No. 501:	$4,800
Job No. 502:	4,100
Job No. 503:	4,800
Job No. 504:	5,000

(e) Charged indirect labor to production, $3,300.

(f) Paid electricity, heating oil, and repair bills for the factory and charged to production, $5,200.

(g) Applied factory overhead to each of the jobs using a predetermined factory overhead rate as follows:

Job No. 501:	$3,100
Job No. 502:	3,300
Job No. 503:	3,300
Job No. 504:	3,800

(h) Finished Job Nos. 501–504 and transferred to the finished goods inventory account.

(i) Sold Job Nos. 501–504.

REQUIRED   1. Prepare journal entries to record transactions (a) through (i).

2. Post the entries to the work in process and finished goods accounts only.

PROBLEM 27B-3 (LO 4) JOB ORDER COSTING WITH UNDERAPPLIED AND OVERAPPLIED FACTORY OVERHEAD J. Bowen & Co. manufactures screen doors. For each job order, they maintain ledger sheets on which they record direct labor, direct materials, and factory overhead applied. The factory overhead control account contains postings of actual overhead costs. At the end of the month, the underapplied or overapplied factory overhead is charged to the cost of goods sold account.

Factory overhead is applied on the basis of direct labor hours. For Job Nos. 201, 202, 203, and 204, direct labor hours are 10,000, 11,000, 11,000, and 12,000, respectively. The overhead application rate is $1.50/direct labor hour.

(a) Purchased raw materials on account, $45,000.

(b) Issued direct materials:

Job No. 201:	$10,000
Job No. 202:	11,000
Job No. 203:	9,500
Job No. 204:	12,200

(c) Issued indirect materials to production, $7,500.

(d) Incurred direct labor costs:

Job No. 201:	$18,000
Job No. 202:	19,000
Job No. 203:	20,500
Job No. 204:	17,500

(e) Charged indirect labor to production, $11,000.

(f) Paid electricity bill, taxes, and repair fees for the factory and charged to production, $7,000.

(g) Depreciation expense on factory equipment, $40,000.

(h) Applied factory overhead to each of the jobs using the predetermined factory overhead rate (see above).

(i) Finished Job Nos. 201–203 and transferred to the finished goods inventory account.

(j) Sold Job Nos. 201 and 202.

(k) Transferred underapplied or overapplied factory overhead balance to the cost of goods sold account.

REQUIRED
1. Prepare journal entries to record transactions (a) through (k).

2. Post the entries to the work in process and finished goods accounts only and determine the ending balances in these accounts.

3. Compute the balance in the job cost ledger and make certain this balance agrees with that in the work in process control account.

MASTERY PROBLEM

The Forester Manufacturing Company uses a job order cost accounting system to keep track of finished jobs and jobs in process. All production is either to customer order or to specification. The following is a summary of transactions completed during the month of August.

(a) Purchased materials (direct and indirect) on account, $158,000.

(b) Requisitioned materials from storerooms, $149,000 (direct materials, $122,000; indirect materials, $27,000). Charged to jobs as follows:

Job No. 805:	$34,000
Job No. 806:	44,000
Job No. 807:	20,000
Job No. 808:	24,000

(c) Incurred factory labor cost for the month, $211,800 (direct labor, $150,000; indirect labor, $61,800). Charged to jobs as follows:

Job No. 805:	$25,500
Job No. 806:	39,800
Job No. 807:	51,400
Job No. 808:	33,300

(d) Incurred other factory overhead costs, $85,000 (depreciation expense, $10,000; miscellaneous factory expense on account, $75,000).

(e) Applied factory overhead, 120% of direct labor cost incurred on jobs. (Make a separate entry for each job.)

(f) Finished Job Nos. 805, 806, and 807 and placed them in stock as products X, Y, and Z, respectively.

(g) Sold products X, Y, and Z on account for $123,000, $150,000, and $168,000, respectively. Costs of products sold were $90,100, $122,000, and $140,000, respectively. (Products Y and Z included some items from the beginning inventory of finished goods and some from the current period's production.)

The beginning balances in the inventory accounts were as follows:

Work in Process	$0
Finished Goods	$76,000 (Product Y, $46,000; Product Z, $30,000).

REQUIRED

1. Prepare general journal entries for the foregoing transactions.

2. Post the entries to the general ledger T accounts for Work in Process and Finished Goods, and compute the ending balances in these accounts.

3. Determine the job cost ledger balance to support the balance in the work in process account.

4. Determine the amount of underapplied or overapplied factory overhead.

Self-Study Test Questions

True/False

1. Both direct and indirect materials enter into and become major parts of the finished product. _____

2. Factory overhead is also known as manufacturing overhead, indirect manufacturing cost, or factory burden. _____

3. Work in Process Inventory consists of three items: materials, labor, and factory overhead. _____

4. Finished Goods Inventory consists of only those items finished and sold during the period. _____

5. Most cost accounting systems use perpetual inventories. _____

Multiple Choice

1. Which of these would most likely be treated as an *indirect* material? (Assume you are manufacturing tables.) _____

   (a) wood   (c) glue
   (b) lacquer   (d) table legs

2. The cost of goods sold section of the income statement for a manufacturing company would contain which of the following? _____

   (a) purchases   (c) direct labor
   (b) cost of goods manufactured   (d) no inventory account

3. When total anticipated factory overhead is $500,000 and budgeted direct labor hours are 200,000, what is the predetermined factory overhead rate based on direct labor hours? _____

   (a) $2.50/hour   (c) $10/hour
   (b) $5.00/hour   (d) It cannot be determined.

4. When direct labor hours for Job 101 are 30 and the predetermined factory overhead rate is $5/direct labor hour, what is the applied factory overhead amount? _____

   (a) $250   (c) $150
   (b) $500   (d) It cannot be determined.

5. Underapplied or overapplied factory overhead is normally charged or credited to which account? _____

   (a) Materials   (c) Finished Goods
   (b) Work in Process   (d) Cost of Goods Sold

The answers to the Self-Study Test Questions are at the end of the text.

28

Manufacturing Accounting: The Work Sheet and Financial Statements

LEARNING OBJECTIVES:
Careful study of this chapter should enable you to:

LO 1 Prepare a ten-column work sheet for a manufacturing company.

LO 2 Prepare adjusting entries to (1) apply factory overhead to ending work in process, (2) record additional actual factory overhead, (3) record underapplied or over-applied overhead, (4) record other expenses not involving overhead, and (5) provide for corporate income taxes.

LO 3 Prepare financial statements for a manufacturing company.

LO 4 Prepare adjusting, closing, and reversing entries for a manufacturing company.

Finny Co. completed the order for the set of instruments for the high school described in Chapter 27. Subsequently, that area of the business has expanded so that special orders are in process for several other high schools and two colleges. According to Mike's accountant, material, labor, and overhead costs will be accumulated for these jobs in the same manner as for the first special order. Mike's understanding of this cost system is that overhead is applied to each job when the job is completed. But it is now the end of the year and Mike once again has an accounting question. Should any overhead costs be applied to the ending work in process, even though these jobs are not finished?

In Chapters 14 and 15, we learned how to use the work sheet to prepare financial statements for a merchandising company. In this chapter, we use a work sheet to prepare financial statements for a manufacturing company. Both the work sheet and financial statements of a manufacturer differ from those of a merchandiser.

THE WORK SHEET FOR A MANUFACTURING COMPANY

LO 1   Prepare a ten-column work sheet for a manufacturing company.

The work sheet for a manufacturing company is similar to the one illustrated in Chapter 14 for a merchandising company. The same five steps are used to prepare both work sheets.

STEP 1   Prepare the trial balance.

STEP 2   Prepare the adjustments.

STEP 3   Prepare the adjusted trial balance.

STEP 4   Extend the adjusted trial balance amounts to the Income Statement and Balance Sheet columns.

STEP 5   Total the Income Statement and Balance Sheet columns to compute the net income or net loss.

Figure 28-1 shows the Trial Balance and Adjustments columns of ToyJoy Manufacturing Company's work sheet. The Trial Balance columns were completed by copying the balances of all accounts from the general ledger (not shown). The following accounts and related adjustments are new and are highlighted in the work sheet:

1   Finished Goods Inventory, Work in Process Inventory, and Materials Inventory

2   Cost of Goods Sold

3   Factory Overhead

4   Income Tax Expense and Corporate Income Tax Payable

Inventories

Instead of a single merchandise inventory account, the manufacturer has three inventory accounts—Finished Goods, Work in Process, and Materials. The manufacturer purchases materials (Materials Inventory) and converts them (Work in Process Inventory) to completed products (Finished Goods Inventory) for sale to customers.

Cost of Goods Sold

The cost of goods sold account is related to the inventory accounts. Cost of Goods Sold appears on the work sheet because ToyJoy uses a perpetual inventory system. With a perpetual inventory system, the movement of goods from materials to work in process to finished goods to cost of goods sold is recorded as the movement occurs. This has two important effects on ToyJoy's work sheet compared

FIGURE 28-1 Partial Work Sheet

ToyJoy Manufacturing Co.
Work Sheet (Partial)
For Year Ended December 31, 20 --

	ACCOUNT TITLE	TRIAL BALANCE DEBIT	TRIAL BALANCE CREDIT	ADJUSTMENTS DEBIT	ADJUSTMENTS CREDIT	
1	Cash	25 7 6 3 00				1
2	Government Notes	5 0 0 0 00				2
3	Accounts Receivable	66 4 8 5 00				3
4	Allowance for Bad Debts		4 6 0 00		(g) 1 4 0 5 00	4
5	Finished Goods Inventory	35 6 1 4 00				5
6	Work in Process Inventory 1	9 9 9 0 00		(a) 2 7 0 0 00		6
7	Materials Inventory	9 2 7 5 00				7
8	Factory Supplies	5 5 4 2 00			(b) 5 0 2 0 00	8
9	Prepaid Insurance	8 0 6 0 00			(c) 6 5 2 0 00	9
10	Land	40 0 0 0 00				10
11	Factory Building	178 0 0 0 00				11
12	Accumulated Depreciation—Factory Building		30 0 0 0 00		(d) 7 5 0 0 00	12
13	Factory Equipment	155 0 0 0 00				13
14	Accumulated Depreciation—Factory Equipment		40 6 4 0 00		(d) 13 5 0 0 00	14
15	Office Equipment	21 3 0 0 00				15
16	Accumulated Depreciation—Office Equipment		4 9 2 5 00		(h) 2 0 0 0 00	16
17	Interest Payable				(f) 8 0 0 00	17
18	Accounts Payable		39 6 8 5 00			18
19	Corporate Income Tax Payable 4				(i) 7 3 0 0 00	19
20	Bonds Payable		100 0 0 0 00			20
21	Capital Stock		75 0 0 0 00			21
22	Paid-In Capital in Excess of Par		20 0 0 0 00			22
23	Retained Earnings		117 6 9 0 00			23
24	Sales		835 9 4 8 00			24
25	Interest Revenue		4 3 0 00			25
26	Factory Overhead 3	155 0 8 0 00	185 9 8 2 00	(b) 5 0 2 0 00	(a) 2 7 0 0 00	26
27				(c) 6 5 2 0 00		27
28				(d) 21 0 0 0 00		28
29				(e) 1 0 6 2 00		29
30	Cost of Goods Sold 2	601 5 8 1 00			(e) 1 0 6 2 00	30
31	Wages Expense	91 3 1 6 00				31
32	Advertising Expense	5 2 6 4 00				32
33	Bad Debt Expense			(g) 1 4 0 5 00		33
34	Utilities Expense—Office	5 6 9 0 00				34
35	Depreciation Expense—Office Equipment			(h) 2 0 0 0 00		35
36	Interest Expense	8 8 0 0 00		(f) 8 0 0 00		36
37	Income Tax Expense 4	23 0 0 0 00		(i) 7 3 0 0 00		37
38		1,450 7 6 0 00	1,450 7 6 0 00	47 8 0 7 00	47 8 0 7 00	38
39						39

with the one presented in Chapter 14 for a business using the periodic inventory method.

1. The costs of goods sold are accumulated in Cost of Goods Sold as sales occur during the year. Thus, Cost of Goods Sold is not computed by means of an adjustment process at the end of the period as we did in Chapter 14.

2. The inventory accounts (Materials, Work in Process, and Finished Goods) reflect ending rather than beginning balances.

LEARNING KEY: Because ToyJoy uses a perpetual inventory system, Cost of Goods Sold contains the costs recorded as sales were made during the year. The inventory accounts reflect the ending balances.

Factory Overhead

The factory overhead account appears solely because ToyJoy is a manufacturer. Factory overhead exists as part of the cost of manufacturing products. Both the debit ($155,080) and credit ($185,982) totals are shown for this account.

The debit represents the actual overhead costs incurred. The credit represents overhead applied to production. Both the debit and credit balances are shown for completeness of presentation, and because both amounts are useful in preparing financial statements.

Income Tax

Income Tax Expense and Corporate Income Tax Payable appear because ToyJoy is a corporation. As explained in Chapter 21, income taxes are an expense of doing business as a corporation.

ADJUSTING ENTRIES

LO 2 Prepare adjusting entries to (1) apply factory overhead to ending work in process, (2) record additional actual factory overhead, (3) record underapplied or overapplied overhead, (4) record other expenses not involving overhead, and (5) provide for corporate income taxes.

The second pair of amount columns in Figure 28-1 contains the adjustments. Data for adjusting the accounts are as follows:

(a) Factory overhead to be applied to work in process ending inventory	$ 2,700
(b) Factory supplies consumed	5,020
(c) Insurance expired on factory building and equipment	6,520
(d) Depreciation on:	
factory building	7,500
factory equipment	13,500
(e) Overapplied factory overhead	1,062
(f) Accrual of interest payable	800

(g) Estimate of uncollectible accounts, based on an aging
of accounts receivable   1,865

(h) Depreciation on office equipment   2,000

(i) Provision for corporate income taxes   7,300

The adjustments that are similar to those illustrated in Chapter 14 will be explained very briefly. Adjustments (a), (b), (c), (d), (e), and (i) are new and will be explained more fully.

Apply Factory Overhead to Ending Work in Process

Adjustment (a)

Adjustment of individual jobs in work in process is unnecessary. This issue is addressed again later in the chapter.

As jobs were completed during the year, factory overhead was applied to them at a rate of 60% of direct labor costs. At the end of the year, several jobs are still in process. To correctly state the work in process ending inventory, factory overhead must be applied to these jobs. The job cost ledger (not shown here) shows total direct labor costs of $4,500 on jobs in process at December 31. An adjustment is needed to apply $2,700 (60% of the direct labor costs) to work in process. Debit Work in Process Inventory and credit Factory Overhead.

> **LEARNING KEY:** Factory overhead must be applied to Work in Process at the end of the year.

Record Additional Actual Factory Overhead

Adjustment (b)

A physical count of factory supplies at the end of the year shows that $5,020 of factory supplies were used during the year. Since factory supplies expense is part of factory overhead, debit Factory Overhead and credit Factory Supplies for $5,020. The factory supplies expense account in the factory overhead ledger (not shown here) also would be debited for this amount.

Adjustment (c)

A review of the insurance policy files shows that $6,520 of insurance on the factory building and equipment has expired. Since factory building and equipment insurance expense is part of factory overhead, debit Factory Overhead and credit Prepaid Insurance for $6,520. Also debit the factory building and equipment insurance expense account in the factory overhead ledger.

Adjustment (d)

Depreciation expense for the year was $7,500 on the factory building and $13,500 on the factory equipment, a total of $21,000. Depreciation expense on the factory building and factory equipment is part of factory overhead. Therefore, debit Factory Overhead for $21,000, and credit Accumulated Depreciation—Factory Building for $7,500 and Accumulated Depreciation—Factory Equipment for $13,500. Also debit the depreciation expense—factory building and equipment account in the factory overhead ledger for $21,000.

Notice that adjustments (b), (c), and (d) are *debited* to Factory Overhead. Recall from Chapter 27 that actual factory overhead expenses are debited to Factory Overhead.

Record Underapplied or Overapplied Overhead

Adjustment (e)

This adjustment is needed because overhead was overapplied during the year. Figure 28-2 shows the factory overhead account in T account form. The amounts shown are:

☐1 debit and credit "balances" from the December 31 trial balance

☐2 debits for adjustments (b), (c), and (d)

☐3 credit for adjustment (a)

☐4 total actual overhead and overhead applied

☐5 debit for adjustment (e), which makes the total debits and credits equal in the account

FIGURE 28-2 Factory Overhead T Account

Factory Overhead

☐1		155,080			185,982	☐1
	(b)	5,020		(a)	2,700	☐3
☐2	(c)	6,520				
	(d)	21,000				
☐4 (Actual overhead)		187,620	(Overhead applied)		188,682	☐4
☐5 Overapplied overhead	(e)	1,062				
Totals		188,682			188,682	

Line ☐4 in Figure 28-2 shows that actual overhead for the year was $187,620 while overhead applied was $188,682. Thus overhead was *overapplied* by $1,062. Debit Factory Overhead and credit Cost of Goods Sold for $1,062 to adjust for overapplied overhead.

> **LEARNING KEY:** After all adjustments are made for actual and applied overhead, an adjustment for underapplied or overapplied overhead is needed.

Record Other Expenses Not Involving Overhead

Adjustment (f)

Interest of $800 is accrued at the end of the year on the bonds payable. Debit Interest Expense and credit Interest Payable.

Adjustment (g)

The estimated amount of uncollectible accounts at the end of the year, based on an aging of accounts receivable, is $1,865. Allowance for Bad Debts had a credit balance of $460, so the necessary adjustment is $1,405 ($1,865 − $460). Debit Bad Debt Expense and credit Allowance for Bad Debts.

Adjustment (h)

Depreciation expense for the year on the office equipment was $2,000. Debit Depreciation Expense—Office Equipment and credit Accumulated Depreciation—Office Equipment.

Provide for Corporate Income Taxes

Adjustment (i)

Corporate income tax for the year is $30,300. Since income tax expense of $23,000 was recorded during the year, an adjustment of $7,300 is needed ($30,300 − $23,000 = $7,300). Debit Income Tax Expense and credit Corporate Income Tax Payable.

A BROADER VIEW

WORK IN PROCESS INVENTORY—THIS STUFF REALLY MATTERS

When you study the year-end accounting procedures for a manufacturing company, you might question whether all the adjustments really matter in the real world. One way to answer that question is to consider the financial statements of a real company.

Gulfstream Aerospace Corp., a leading manufacturer of intercontinental business jets, reported 1996 net income of $47 million. At the end of 1996, Gulfstream's balance sheet showed ending inventory that included $355 million of work in process. Think about the accounting implications of these figures. Gulfstream's work in process inventory is more than 7 times ($355 million ÷ $47 million = 7.55) the size of its net income. This means that a relatively small percentage error in the work in process inventory could have a significant effect on the net income. Clearly, the year-end adjustments can be quite important for a company like Gulfstream.

Completing the Work Sheet

Figure 28-3 on page 1020 shows ToyJoy's full ten-column work sheet. Note the handling of the factory overhead account. The total debits and total credits of $188,682 appear in the Adjusted Trial Balance columns. But neither of these amounts is extended to the Income Statement or Balance Sheet columns. Figure

FIGURE 28-3 Work Sheet

ToyJoy Manufacturing Co.
Work Sheet
For Year Ended December 31, 20--

Account Title	Trial Balance Debit	Trial Balance Credit	Adjustments Debit	Adjustments Credit	Adjusted Trial Balance Debit	Adjusted Trial Balance Credit	Income Statement Debit	Income Statement Credit	Balance Sheet Debit	Balance Sheet Credit
Cash	25 7 6 3 00				25 7 6 3 00				25 7 6 3 00	
Government Notes	5 0 0 0 00				5 0 0 0 00				5 0 0 0 00	
Accounts Receivable	66 4 8 5 00				66 4 8 5 00				66 4 8 5 00	
Allowance for Bad Debts		4 6 0 00		(g) 1 4 0 5 00		1 8 6 5 00				1 8 6 5 00
Finished Goods Inventory	35 6 1 4 00				35 6 1 4 00				35 6 1 4 00	
Work in Process Inventory	9 9 9 0 00		(a) 2 7 0 0 00		12 6 9 0 00				12 6 9 0 00	
Materials Inventory	9 2 7 5 00				9 2 7 5 00				9 2 7 5 00	
Factory Supplies	5 5 4 2 00			(b) 5 0 2 0 00	5 2 2 00				5 2 2 00	
Prepaid Insurance	8 0 6 0 00			(c) 6 5 2 0 00	1 5 4 0 00				1 5 4 0 00	
Land	40 0 0 0 00				40 0 0 0 00				40 0 0 0 00	
Factory Building	178 0 0 0 00				178 0 0 0 00				178 0 0 0 00	
Accum. Depr.—Factory Building		30 0 0 0 00		(d) 7 5 0 0 00		37 5 0 0 00				37 5 0 0 00
Factory Equipment	155 0 0 0 00				155 0 0 0 00				155 0 0 0 00	
Accum. Depr.—Factory Equip.		40 6 4 0 00		(d) 13 5 0 0 00		54 1 4 0 00				54 1 4 0 00
Office Equipment	21 3 0 0 00				21 3 0 0 00				21 3 0 0 00	
Accum. Depr.—Office Equipment		4 9 2 5 00		(h) 2 0 0 0 00		6 9 2 5 00				6 9 2 5 00
Interest Payable				(f) 8 0 0 00		8 0 0 00				8 0 0 00
Accounts Payable		39 6 8 5 00				39 6 8 5 00				39 6 8 5 00
Corporate Income Tax Payable				(i) 7 3 0 0 00		7 3 0 0 00				7 3 0 0 00
Bonds Payable		100 0 0 0 00				100 0 0 0 00				100 0 0 0 00
Capital Stock		75 0 0 0 00				75 0 0 0 00				75 0 0 0 00
Paid-in Capital in Excess of Par		20 0 0 0 00				20 0 0 0 00				20 0 0 0 00
Retained Earnings		117 6 9 0 00				117 6 9 0 00				117 6 9 0 00
Sales		835 9 4 8 00				835 9 4 8 00		835 9 4 8 00		
Interest Revenue		4 3 0 00				4 3 0 00		4 3 0 00		
Factory Overhead	155 0 8 0 00	185 9 8 2 00	(b) 5 0 2 0 00 (c) 6 5 2 0 00 (d) 21 0 0 0 00 (e) 1 0 6 2 00	(a) 2 7 0 0 00	188 6 8 2 00	188 6 8 2 00	Not extended			
Cost of Goods Sold	601 5 8 1 00			(e) 1 0 6 2 00	600 5 1 9 00		600 5 1 9 00			
Wages Expense	91 3 1 6 00				91 3 1 6 00		91 3 1 6 00			
Advertising Expense	5 2 6 4 00				5 2 6 4 00		5 2 6 4 00			
Bad Debt Expense			(g) 1 4 0 5 00		1 4 0 5 00		1 4 0 5 00			
Utilities Expense—Office	5 6 9 0 00				5 6 9 0 00		5 6 9 0 00			
Depr. Expense—Office Equip.			(h) 2 0 0 0 00		2 0 0 0 00		2 0 0 0 00			
Interest Expense	8 8 0 0 00		(f) 8 0 0 00		9 6 0 0 00		9 6 0 0 00			
Income Tax Expense	23 0 0 0 00		(i) 7 3 0 0 00		30 3 0 0 00		30 3 0 0 00			
	1,450 7 6 0 00	1,450 7 6 0 00	47 8 0 7 00	47 8 0 7 00	1,485 9 6 5 00	1,485 9 6 5 00	746 0 9 4 00	836 3 7 8 00	551 1 8 9 00	460 9 0 5 00
Net Income							90 2 8 4 00			90 2 8 4 00
							836 3 7 8 00	836 3 7 8 00	551 1 8 9 00	551 1 8 9 00

28-4 below shows why this is so. Factory overhead costs are (1) incurred, (2) applied to Work in Process, (3) transferred to Finished Goods with completed products, and (4) transferred to Cost of Goods Sold when goods are sold.

LEARNING KEY: The factory overhead account balances are not extended to the Income Statement or Balance Sheet columns.

The factory overhead amounts are not extended because they have already been transferred to Work in Process, Finished Goods, and Cost of Goods Sold. These three account balances are extended to the appropriate Income Statement and Balance Sheet columns.

FIGURE 28-4 Flow of Overhead Costs in a Manufacturing Accounting System

1 Actual overhead costs are accumulated as debits in the factory overhead account.

2 Overhead is applied to products by debiting Work in Process and crediting Factory Overhead. This overhead application *transfers* overhead from Factory Overhead to Work in Process.

3 The portion of factory overhead related to completed products is transferred from Work in Process to Finished Goods.

4 The portion of factory overhead related to products sold is transferred from Finished Goods to Cost of Goods Sold.

FINANCIAL STATEMENTS

LO 3   Prepare financial statements for a manufacturing company.

ToyJoy's financial statements include an income statement, retained earnings statement, balance sheet, and statement of cash flows. The statement of cash flows is essentially the same in format as the one illustrated in Chapter 24, so it is not presented here. We will focus on the statements prepared from the enhanced work sheet for a manufacturing business.

Income Statement

ToyJoy's income statement is presented in Figure 28-5 on page 1022. All income statement data were obtained from the Income Statement columns of the work sheet, except for the cost of goods sold section. To prepare this section, the beginning finished goods inventory was taken from the finished goods account in the general ledger (not shown). The cost of goods manufactured was taken from the schedule of cost of goods manufactured (Figure 28-6, page 1023). The ending finished goods inventory is from the Balance Sheet columns of the work sheet.

A manufacturer's income statement is commonly supported by a schedule of cost of goods manufactured like the one in Figure 28-6. The ending materials and work in process inventories are from the Balance Sheet columns of the work sheet. Other data for this schedule, listed in the order in which they appear, were obtained from the following sources.

Data	Source of Data
Work in process inventory, Jan. 1	Work in process account in general ledger
Materials inventory, Jan. 1	Materials inventory account in general ledger
Purchases	Materials inventory account in general ledger
Direct labor	Work in process account in general ledger
Overhead	Factory overhead account in general ledger
Work in process inventory, Dec. 31	Balance Sheet columns of the work sheet

FIGURE 28-5 Income Statement

ToyJoy Manufacturing Co.
Income Statement
For Year Ended December 31, 20 --

Net sales			$835 9 4 8 00
Less cost of goods sold:			
Finished goods inventory, January 1	$ 24 5 6 9 00		
Cost of goods manufactured	611 5 6 4 00	◁ From Schedule	
Cost of goods available for sale	$636 1 3 3 00		
Finished goods inventory, December 31	35 6 1 4 00		
Cost of goods sold			600 5 1 9 00
Gross profit			$235 4 2 9 00
Operating expenses:			
Wages expense	$ 91 3 1 6 00		
Advertising expense	5 2 6 4 00		
Bad debt expense	1 4 0 5 00		
Utilities expense—office	5 6 9 0 00		
Depreciation expense—office equipment	2 0 0 0 00		
Total operating expenses			105 6 7 5 00
Operating income			$129 7 5 4 00
Other revenue:			
Interest revenue			4 3 0 00
			$130 1 8 4 00
Other expense:			
Interest expense			9 6 0 0 00
Income before income taxes			$120 5 8 4 00
Corporate income tax			30 3 0 0 00
Net income	To Retained Earnings Statement ▷		$ 90 2 8 4 00

FIGURE 28-6　Schedule of Cost of Goods Manufactured

ToyJoy Manufacturing Co.
Schedule of Cost of Goods Manufactured
For Year Ended December 31, 20 --

Work in process, January 1			$ 11 9 4 0 00
Materials inventory, January 1	$ 12 9 9 2 00		
Materials purchases	121 3 8 0 00		
Materials available for use	$134 3 7 2 00		
Materials inventory, December 31	9 2 7 5 00		
Cost of materials used		$125 0 9 7 00	
Direct labor		299 5 9 7 00	
Factory overhead		187 6 2 0 00	
Total manufacturing costs			612 3 1 4 00
Total work in process during the period			$624 2 5 4 00
Work in process, December 31			12 6 9 0 00
Cost of goods manufactured	To Income Statement		$611 5 6 4 00

Retained Earnings Statement

The retained earnings statement appears in Figure 28-7. The net income for the year can be taken from the Income Statement columns of the work sheet or from the income statement. The retained earnings balances at January 1 and December 31 and the cash dividends amount were determined by reviewing the retained earnings account in the general ledger. Note that the January 1 retained earnings balance was obtained from the general ledger, not the work sheet. This is because the retained earnings balance on the work sheet had already been reduced during the year by the $15,000 cash dividend. The only distinctive feature of the retained earnings statement arises from ToyJoy being organized as a corporation. As a corporation, ToyJoy pays dividends, in this case, $15,000.

FIGURE 28-7　Retained Earnings Statement

ToyJoy Manufacturing Co.
Retained Earnings Statement
For Year Ended December 31, 20 --

Retained earnings, January 1	$132 6 9 0 00	
Net income for the year (after provision for income taxes of $30,300)	90 2 8 4 00	From Income Statement
	$222 9 7 4 00	
Less cash dividends ($1.00 per share) Corporate Dividends	15 0 0 0 00	
Retained earnings, December 31	$207 9 7 4 00	To Balance Sheet

Balance Sheet

ToyJoy's balance sheet is presented in Figure 28-8 on the next page. Data for this statement were taken from the Balance Sheet columns of the work sheet, except for the retained earnings. This amount was taken from the retained earnings statement. Note that the retained earnings amount on the balance sheet ($207,974) also can be calculated from the work sheet. It is the sum of the retained earnings balance shown on the work sheet ($117,690) plus the net income for the year ($90,284).

Two main differences in this balance sheet compared with those for merchandising companies are:

1. Since this is a manufacturing company, there are three inventory accounts listed: Finished Goods, Work in Process, and Materials.

2. Since ToyJoy is a corporation, the stockholders' equity section contains information regarding capital stock, paid-in capital in excess of par, and retained earnings.

JOURNAL ENTRIES

LO 4   Prepare adjusting, closing, and reversing entries for a manufacturing company.

Most of ToyJoy's adjusting, closing, and reversing entries are similar to those illustrated in Chapters 14 and 15 for a merchandising company. We will comment only on selected adjustments.

Adjusting Entries

The entries appearing in the Adjustments columns of the work sheet are journalized as shown in Figure 28-9 on page 1026. For ease of identification, each entry includes the coding letter from the work sheet.

Notice two things about these adjusting entries.

> Aggregate work in process must be adjusted so that it is reported correctly on the financial statements. The individual jobs require no adjustment because they are not reported on any financial statements.

1. In adjustment (a), the application of factory overhead to ending work in process, no entries are made to the individual jobs in the job cost ledger. Only the aggregate work in process needs to be adjusted for financial reporting purposes at year end, not the individual jobs in process. The aggregate adjustment will be reversed at the beginning of the following period.

2. In adjustments (b), (c), and (d), the factory overhead account and the related subsidiary accounts are identified. Both the general ledger and subsidiary ledger accounts are adjusted for these actual overhead amounts.

FIGURE 28-8 Balance Sheet

ToyJoy Manufacturing Co.															
Balance Sheet															
December 31, 20--															

Assets									
Current assets:									
Cash				$ 25 7 6 3 00			
Government notes				5 0 0 0 00			
Accounts receivable	$ 66 4 8 5 00					
Less allowance for bad debts	1 8 6 5 00	64 6 2 0 00			
Inventories:						
Finished goods	$ 35 6 1 4 00					
Work in process	12 6 9 0 00					
Materials	9 2 7 5 00	57 5 7 9 00			
Factory supplies		5 2 2 00			
Prepaid insurance		1 5 4 0 00			
Total current assets			$155 0 2 4 00	
Property, plant, and equipment:					
Land		$ 40 0 0 0 00			
Factory building	$178 0 0 0 00				
Less accumulated depreciation	37 5 0 0 00	140 5 0 0 00			
Factory equipment	$155 0 0 0 00				
Less accumulated depreciation	54 1 4 0 00	100 8 6 0 00			
Office equipment	$ 21 3 0 0 00				
Less accumulated depreciation	6 9 2 5 00	14 3 7 5 00			
Total property, plant, and equipment			295 7 3 5 00	
Total assets			$450 7 5 9 00	
Liabilities					
Current liabilities:					
Interest payable		$ 8 0 0 00			
Accounts payable		39 6 8 5 00			
Corporate income tax payable		7 3 0 0 00			
Total current liabilities			$ 47 7 8 5 00	
Long-term liabilities:					
Bonds payable			100 0 0 0 00	
Total liabilities			$147 7 8 5 00	
Stockholders' Equity					
Common stock ($5 par value, 50,000 shares authorized;					
15,000 shares issued)		$ 75 0 0 0 00			
Paid-in capital in excess of par		20 0 0 0 00			
Retained earnings		207 9 7 4 00			
Total stockholders' equity			302 9 7 4 00	
Total liabilities and stockholders' equity			$450 7 5 9 00	

Three inventories ⟶ (Finished goods, Work in process, Materials)

Corporate section ⟶ (Common stock, Paid-in capital in excess of par, Retained earnings)

Retained earnings ⟵ From Retained Earnings Statement

FIGURE 28-9 Adjusting Entries

	DATE		DESCRIPTION	POST REF.	DEBIT	CREDIT		
1			Adjusting Entries				1	
2	20-- Dec.	31	Work in Process Inventory		2 7 0 0 00		2	
3	(a)		Factory Overhead			2 7 0 0 00	3	Aggregate
4							4	
5	(b)	31	Factory Overhead (Factory Supplies Expense)		5 0 2 0 00		5	Identify subsidiary
6			Factory Supplies			5 0 2 0 00	6	
7							7	
8	(c)	31	Factory Overhead (Factory Building and Equipment,				8	
9			Insurance Expense)		6 5 2 0 00		9	Identify subsidiary
10			Prepaid Insurance			6 5 2 0 00	10	
11							11	
12	(d)	31	Factory Overhead (Depreciation Expense—				12	
13			Factory Building and Equipment)		21 0 0 0 00		13	Identify subsidiary
14			Accumulated Depreciation—Factory Equipment			13 5 0 0 00	14	
15			Accumulated Depreciation—Factory Building			7 5 0 0 00	15	
16							16	
17	(e)	31	Factory Overhead		1 0 6 2 00		17	
18			Cost of Goods Sold			1 0 6 2 00	18	
19							19	
20	(f)	31	Interest Expense		8 0 0 00		20	
21			Interest Payable			8 0 0 00	21	
22							22	
23	(g)	31	Bad Debt Expense		1 4 0 5 00		23	
24			Allowance for Bad Debts			1 4 0 5 00	24	
25							25	
26	(h)	31	Depreciation Expense—Office Equipment		2 0 0 0 00		26	
27			Accumulated Depreciation—Office Equipment			2 0 0 0 00	27	
28							28	
29	(i)	31	Income Tax Expense		7 3 0 0 00		29	
30			Corporate Income Tax Payable			7 3 0 0 00	30	
31							31	
32							32	
33							33	
34							34	
35							35	
36							36	
37							37	
38							38	
39							39	

GENERAL JOURNAL

Closing Entries

Five steps are used to close ToyJoy's temporary accounts.

STEP 1   Transfer the debit balance in the factory overhead account to Income Summary and close the subsidiary factory overhead accounts.

STEP 2   Transfer the credit balance in the factory overhead account to Income Summary.

STEP 3   Transfer the balances of the sales and interest revenue accounts to Income Summary.

STEP 4   Transfer the balances of the cost of goods sold and all expense accounts to Income Summary.

STEP 5   Transfer the balance of Income Summary to Retained Earnings.

Figure 28-10 shows the journal entries corresponding to these five steps. Entries (3), (4), and (5) are essentially the same as those for a merchandising company. Entries (1) and (2) require explanation.

FIGURE 28-10   Closing Entries

	DATE		DESCRIPTION	POST REF.	DEBIT	CREDIT		
1			Closing Entries				1	
2	20-- Dec.	31	Income Summary		188 6 8 2 00		2	STEP 1
3	(1)		Factory Overhead (Subsidiary ledger accounts)			188 6 8 2 00	3	
4							4	
5	(2)	31	Factory Overhead		188 6 8 2 00		5	STEP 2
6			Income Summary			188 6 8 2 00	6	
7							7	
8	(3)	31	Sales		835 9 4 8 00		8	STEP 3
9			Interest Revenue		4 3 0 00		9	
10			Income Summary			836 3 7 8 00	10	
11							11	
12	(4)	31	Income Summary		746 0 9 4 00		12	STEP 4
13			Cost of Goods Sold			600 5 1 9 00	13	
14			Wages Expense			91 3 1 6 00	14	
15			Advertising Expense			5 2 6 4 00	15	
16			Bad Debt Expense			1 4 0 5 00	16	
17			Utilities Expense—Office			5 6 9 0 00	17	
18			Depreciation Expense—Office Equipment			2 0 0 0 00	18	
19			Interest Expense			9 6 0 0 00	19	
20			Income Tax Expense			30 3 0 0 00	20	
21							21	
22	(5)	31	Income Summary		90 2 8 4 00		22	STEP 5
23			Retained Earnings			90 2 8 4 00	23	
24							24	

The T account in Figure 28-2 on page 1018 shows that the factory overhead account has a zero balance after all adjustments are entered. This account must still be "closed" to close the factory overhead subsidiary ledger accounts. This is the purpose of entries (1) and (2) in Figure 28-10.

Entry (1) closes the total debit amount in the factory overhead account to Income Summary. At the same time, the related factory overhead subsidiary ledger accounts are closed. (The detail for each subsidiary ledger account is omitted here.) Entry (2) closes the total credit amount in factory overhead to Income Summary.

Reversing Entries

> The purpose of reversing entries is to simplify the recording of routine transactions. Corporate income taxes are a specialized rather than routine transaction, so this adjustment is not reversed.

ToyJoy reverses two of the adjusting entries made on December 31. Entry (1) in Figure 28-11 is related to the accrued interest on bonds payable. The purpose of this type of reversing entry was explained in Chapter 15. Entry (2) is unique to a manufacturing company. This entry reverses the adjusting entry to apply factory overhead to Work in Process. This reversal facilitates applying factory overhead to completed jobs in the following year. Recall that factory overhead is applied at a predetermined rate when a job is completed. If this reversing entry were not made, it would be necessary to keep track of which jobs already had a partial overhead application from a prior year's adjustment.

LEARNING KEY: Reverse the adjusting entry to apply overhead to Work in Process.

FIGURE 28-11   Reversing Entries

	DATE		DESCRIPTION	POST REF.	DEBIT	CREDIT	
1			Reversing Entries				1
2	20-- Jan.	1	Interest Payable		8 0 0 00		2
3	(1)		Interest Expense			8 0 0 00	3
4							4
5	(2)	1	Factory Overhead		2 7 0 0 00		5
6			Work in Process Inventory			2 7 0 0 00	6
7							7

GENERAL JOURNAL

COMPUTERS AND ACCOUNTING

MANUFACTURING INFORMATION SYSTEMS
James Hall

Managers of manufacturing organizations face a range of complex issues such as preparing accurate price quotes for custom projects, scheduling production to meet sales commitments, obtaining raw materials from suppliers, managing inventory flows, and allocating labor resources. Dealing efficiently and effectively with these issues calls for an advanced computerized accounting system. Below we examine three technology approaches that are used in organizations of all sizes: *Manufacturing Resources Planning (MRP); Electronic Data Interchange (EDI);* and *Entity-Wide Information Systems.*

MRP AND MRP II

Manufacturing Resources Planning (MRP II) is an extension of a simpler concept still in use called Materials Requirements Planning (MRP). When a customer work order is entered into the MRP system, it produces a bill of materials (BOM) that lists the inventory requirements in advance of production. This allows the manufacturer to order only the raw materials needed and thus minimize inventory carrying costs.

MRP II is an enhanced concept that goes beyond inventory management. It is used to coordinate several production-related activities of the business, including product design, the production process, sales order entry, and financial and cost accounting. The MRP II system will produce a BOM for the product, fit the production of the product into the master production schedule, determine the machine and labor requirements, produce a material requirements plan that will schedule the delivery of the raw materials just as they are needed in the production process, and manage the raw materials and finished goods inventories. The manufacturer can realize significant benefits from a highly integrated MRP II system, including:

▶ Improved customer service

▶ Reduced inventory investment

▶ Increased productivity

▶ Improved cash flow

▶ Assistance in achieving long-term goals

▶ Help in managing change (that is, new product development or specialized product development for customers or by vendors)

▶ Flexibility in the production process

ELECTRONIC DATA INTERCHANGE (EDI)

Most MRP II systems are capable of external communications through Electronic Data Interchange (EDI). EDI enables the business to automatically receive sales orders and cash receipts from customers, send invoices to customers, send purchase orders and payments to vendors, receive invoices from vendors, and send and receive shipping documents.

To coordinate sales and production operations and to maintain an uninterrupted flow of raw materials, many organizations enter into a trading partner agreement with their suppliers and customers in which they each guarantee certain exclusive business transactions. This agreement is the foundation for a fully automated EDI system. In a pure EDI environment, transactions are processed automatically by the trading partners' computerized information systems with no human to initiate or authorize transactions.

To illustrate EDI, consider the purchase of inventory by customer "A" from supplier "B." When Company A's MRP system identifies the need for raw materials, the purchases system automatically creates a purchase order (PO), which is converted to an electronic message ready for transmission. The message is transmitted to Company B over telephone lines (or the Internet) where the supplier's computer system reads it. The customer order is processed automatically.

BENEFITS OF EDI

Although EDI is often associated with manufacturing, it is not limited to those industries. EDI has made considerable inroads in the food, retail, and health care industries. Below are some typical cost savings that justify EDI.

Data Keying. EDI reduces or even eliminates the need for data entry.

Errors. Firms using EDI see reductions in data keying errors, classification errors, and filing (lost document) errors.

Reduction of Paper. The use of electronic envelopes and documents reduces drastically the paper forms in the system.

Postage. Mailed documents are replaced with much cheaper data transmissions.

Automated Procedures. EDI automates manual activities associated with purchasing, sales order processing, cash disbursements, and cash receipts.

Inventory Reduction. By ordering directly as needed from vendors, EDI reduces the lag time that contributes to inventory build-up.

ENTITY-WIDE INFORMATION SYSTEMS

Basic MRP and EDI systems are available to organizations of all sizes. Even very small businesses can economically take advantage of these technologies. Very large manufacturing businesses, however, face complex issues that cut across functional lines and require entity-wide information. The objective of an entity-wide information system is to integrate information (both accounting and non-accounting) to support the needs of all users in the organization.

Implementing an entity-wide system in a large organization is a multimillion dollar project. SAP, a product from the German firm SAP AG, is currently the market leader in this technology. The SAP system supports over 1,000 different business processes. The heart of SAP is the financial accounting system which is connected to other information system modules. SAP allows customers to place custom orders, reserve inventory, request production of subassemblies, and check the status of orders using EDI or the Internet. Other entity-wide tasks such as payroll, time management, travel expense accounting, employee benefits, recruitment, and workforce planning are also supported by SAP.

Learning Objectives	Key Points to Remember
1 Prepare a ten-column work sheet for a manufacturing company.	Five steps are used to prepare a ten-column work sheet for a manufacturing company: 1. Prepare the trial balance. 2. Prepare the adjustments. 3. Prepare the adjusted trial balance. 4. Extend the adjusted trial balance amounts to the Income Statement and Balance Sheet columns. 5. Total the Income Statement and Balance Sheet columns to compute the net income or net loss. The new accounts and related adjustments on the work sheet are Finished Goods Inventory, Work in Process Inventory, Materials Inventory, Cost of Goods Sold, Factory Overhead, Income Tax Expense, and Corporate Income Tax Payable.
2 Prepare adjusting entries to (1) apply factory overhead to ending work in process, (2) record additional actual factory overhead, (3) record underapplied or overapplied overhead, (4) record other expenses not involving overhead, and (5) provide for corporate income taxes.	Overhead must be applied to work in process at year end. Adjustments for additional amounts of actual overhead are debited to Factory Overhead on the work sheet. After all adjustments are made for actual and applied overhead, an adjustment must be made for underapplied or overapplied overhead. An adjustment also is necessary for corporate income taxes. 　　The factory overhead account balances are extended to the Adjusted Trial Balance columns but not to the Income Statement or Balance Sheet columns on the work sheet.
3 Prepare financial statements for a manufacturing company.	The main differences between a manufacturer's income statement and that of a merchandiser are the cost of goods sold section and the supplementary schedule of cost of goods manufactured. 　　The only distinctive feature of a manufacturer's retained earnings statement is the deduction for dividends. 　　Two main differences in ToyJoy's balance sheet are the three inventory accounts and the stockholders' equity section.
4 Prepare adjusting, closing, and reversing entries for a manufacturing company.	Each of the adjustments on the work sheet must be journalized. 　　All revenue and expense accounts and both the debit and credit totals of the Factory Overhead must be closed to Income Summary. 　　Reverse the adjusting entry for Interest Expense and the adjustment to apply factory overhead to work in process.

Reflection: Answering the Opening Question

To correctly state work in process ending inventory, factory overhead must be applied to jobs in process at the end of the year. The overhead should be applied on the same basis as it is applied to finished jobs.

DEMONSTRATION PROBLEM

The Montgomery Manufacturing Company manufactures and sells a limited line of products per customer order. Nothing is purchased for resale in its original form. The company rents offices and a factory building, and it owns neither real estate nor delivery equipment. It does have its own office and factory equipment. The company uses a perpetual inventory system and keeps its accounts on the calendar year basis. The trial balance of the general ledger as of December 31, 20--, is illustrated below. Data for the year-end adjustment of the accounts follows the trial balance.

Montgomery Manufacturing Co.
Trial Balance
December 31, 20 - -

ACCOUNT TITLE	DEBIT BALANCE	CREDIT BALANCE
Cash	56 1 1 5 00	
Accounts Receivable	90 9 2 8 00	
Allowance for Bad Debts		1 8 0 0 00
Finished Goods Inventory	63 1 8 0 00	
Work in Process Inventory	41 2 5 6 00	
Materials Inventory	46 8 4 5 00	
Office Supplies	2 9 1 6 00	
Factory Supplies	4 6 3 3 00	
Prepaid Insurance	5 5 8 9 00	
Factory Equipment	185 0 2 2 00	
Accumulated Depreciation—Factory Equipment		34 9 5 6 00
Office Equipment	19 5 3 0 00	
Accumulated Depreciation—Office Equipment		2 4 2 1 00
Notes Payable		27 0 0 0 00
Interest Payable		
Accounts Payable		38 5 9 0 00
Corporate Income Tax Payable		
Capital Stock		135 0 0 0 00
Retained Earnings		28 1 3 1 00
Sales		842 1 5 7 00
Factory Overhead	44 2 1 2 00	60 5 8 5 00
Cost of Goods Sold	455 3 9 3 00	
Wages Expense	115 6 6 3 00	
Advertising Expense	24 6 8 0 00	
Office Rent Expense	13 1 8 0 00	
Office Supplies Expense		
Bad Debt Expense		
Insurance Expense—Office Equipment		
Depreciation Expense—Office Equipment		
Interest Expense	1 4 9 8 00	
Income Tax Expense		
	1,170 6 4 0 00	1,170 6 4 0 00

Data for year-end adjustments are as follows:

(a)	Interest payable		$ 168
(b)	Office supplies expense		900
(c)	Factory supplies expense		1,870
(d)	Depreciation of office equipment		960
(e)	Depreciation of factory equipment		22,560
(f)	Insurance expense:		
	On office equipment	$ 120	
	On factory equipment	1,590	$ 1,710
(g)	Provision for uncollectible accounts (based on percentage of sales)		1,000
(h)	Provision for corporate income taxes		60,560
(i)	Factory overhead to be applied to work in process		4,729

Additional information needed to prepare the income statement and schedule of cost of goods manufactured is as follows:

Finished goods inventory, January 1	$219,692
Materials inventory, January 1	23,000
Purchases for the year	110,000
Direct labor	156,897
Work in process inventory, January 1	36,500

REQUIRED

1. Prepare a ten-column work sheet for the year ended December 31, 20--. After the factory overhead account is adjusted, the total debits will differ from the total credits. Enter the underapplied or overapplied overhead on the work sheet by transferring it to Cost of Goods Sold. (Label this adjustment (j).)

2. Prepare an income statement with a supporting schedule of cost of goods manufactured.

3. Journalize the adjusting journal entries from the work sheet. (For parts 3, 4, and 5, use journal page numbers 15–17.)

4. Prepare closing entries.

5. Prepare reversing entries.

Solution

1.

Montgomery Manufacturing Co.
Work Sheet
For Year Ended December 31, 20--

Account Title	Trial Balance Debit	Trial Balance Credit	Adjustments Debit	Adjustments Credit	Adjusted Trial Balance Debit	Adjusted Trial Balance Credit	Income Statement Debit	Income Statement Credit	Balance Sheet Debit	Balance Sheet Credit
Cash	56 115 00				56 115 00				56 115 00	
Accounts Receivable	90 928 00				90 928 00				90 928 00	
Allowance for Bad Debts		1 800 00		(g) 1 000 00		2 800 00				2 800 00
Finished Goods Inventory	63 180 00				63 180 00				63 180 00	
Work in Process Inventory	41 256 00		(i) 4 729 00		45 985 00				45 985 00	
Materials Inventory	46 845 00				46 845 00				46 845 00	
Office Supplies	2 916 00			(b) 900 00	2 016 00				2 016 00	
Factory Supplies	4 633 00			(c) 1 870 00	2 763 00				2 763 00	
Prepaid Insurance	5 589 00			(f) 1 710 00	3 879 00				3 879 00	
Factory Equipment	185 022 00				185 022 00				185 022 00	
Accum. Depr.—Factory Equip.		34 956 00		(e) 22 560 00		57 516 00				57 516 00
Office Equipment	19 530 00				19 530 00				19 530 00	
Accum. Depr.—Office Equip.		2 421 00		(d) 960 00		3 381 00				3 381 00
Notes Payable		27 000 00				27 000 00				27 000 00
Interest Payable				(a) 168 00		168 00				168 00
Accounts Payable		38 590 00				38 590 00				38 590 00
Corp. Income Tax Payable				(h) 60 560 00		60 560 00				60 560 00
Capital Stock		135 000 00				135 000 00				135 000 00
Retained Earnings		28 131 00				28 131 00				28 131 00
Sales		842 157 00				842 157 00		842 157 00		
Factory Overhead	44 212 00		(c) 1 870 00 (e) 22 560 00 (f) 1 590 00	(i) 4 729 00 (j) 4 918 00	70 232 00	70 232 00				
Cost of Goods Sold	455 393 00		(j) 4 918 00		460 311 00		460 311 00			
Wages Expense	115 663 00				115 663 00		115 663 00			
Advertising Expense	24 680 00				24 680 00		24 680 00			
Office Rent Expense	13 180 00				13 180 00		13 180 00			
Office Supplies Expense			(b) 900 00		900 00		900 00			
Bad Debt Expense			(g) 1 000 00		1 000 00		1 000 00			
Insurance Exp.—Office Equip.			(f) 120 00		120 00		120 00			
Depr. Expense—Office Equip.			(d) 960 00		960 00		960 00			
Interest Expense	1 498 00		(a) 168 00		1 666 00		1 666 00			
Income Tax Expense			(h) 60 560 00		60 560 00		60 560 00			
	1,170 640 00	1,170 640 00	99 375 00	99 375 00	1,265 535 00	1,265 535 00	679 040 00	842 157 00	516 263 00	353 146 00
Net Income							163 117 00			163 117 00
							842 157 00	842 157 00	516 263 00	516 263 00

2.

Montgomery Manufacturing Co.
Schedule of Cost of Goods Manufactured
For Year Ended December 31, 20 --

Work in process, January 1				$ 36 5 0 0 00	
Materials inventory, January 1	$ 23 0 0 0 00				
Materials purchases	110 0 0 0 00				
Materials available for use	$133 0 0 0 00				
Materials inventory, December 31	46 8 4 5 00				
Cost of materials used		$ 86 1 5 5 00			
Direct labor		156 8 9 7 00			
Factory overhead		70 2 3 2 00			
Total manufacturing costs				313 2 8 4 00	
Total work in process during the period				$349 7 8 4 00	
Work in process, December 31				45 9 8 5 00	
Cost of goods manufactured				$303 7 9 9 00	

Montgomery Manufacturing Co.
Income Statement
For Year Ended December 31, 20 --

Net sales		$842 1 5 7 00	
Less cost of goods sold:			
Finished goods inventory, January 1	$219 6 9 2 00		
Cost of goods manufactured	303 7 9 9 00		
Cost of goods available for sale	$523 4 9 1 00		
Finished goods inventory, December 31	63 1 8 0 00		
Cost of goods sold		460 3 1 1 00	
Gross profit		$381 8 4 6 00	
Operating expenses:			
Wages expense	$115 6 6 3 00		
Advertising expense	24 6 8 0 00		
Office rent expense	13 1 8 0 00		
Office supplies expense	9 0 0 00		
Bad debt expense	1 0 0 0 00		
Insurance expense—office equipment	1 2 0 00		
Depreciation expense—office equipment	9 6 0 00		
Total operating expenses		156 5 0 3 00	
Operating income		$225 3 4 3 00	
Other expense:			
Interest expense		1 6 6 6 00	
Income before income taxes		$223 6 7 7 00	
Corporate income tax		60 5 6 0 00	
Net income		$163 1 1 7 00	

3.

	DATE		DESCRIPTION	POST REF.	DEBIT					CREDIT					
1			**Adjusting Entries**												1
2	Dec. 20--	31	Interest Expense			1	6	8	00						2
3	(a)		Interest Payable								1	6	8	00	3
4															4
5	(b)	31	Office Supplies Expense			9	0	0	00						5
6			Office Supplies								9	0	0	00	6
7															7
8	(c)	31	Factory Overhead		1	8	7	0	00						8
9			Factory Supplies							1	8	7	0	00	9
10															10
11	(d)	31	Depr. Expense—Office Equipment			9	6	0	00						11
12			Accum. Depr.—Office Equipment								9	6	0	00	12
13															13
14	(e)	31	Factory Overhead (Depr. Expense—Factory Equip.)		22	5	6	0	00						14
15			Accum. Depr.—Factory Equipment							22	5	6	0	00	15
16															16
17	(f)	31	Factory Overhead (Insurance Expense)		1	5	9	0	00						17
18			Insurance Expense—Office Equipment			1	2	0	00						18
19			Prepaid Insurance							1	7	1	0	00	19
20															20
21	(g)	31	Bad Debt Expense		1	0	0	0	00						21
22			Allowance for Bad Debts							1	0	0	0	00	22
23															23
24	(h)	31	Income Tax Expense		60	5	6	0	00						24
25			Corporate Income Tax Payable							60	5	6	0	00	25
26															26
27	(i)	31	Work in Process Inventory		4	7	2	9	00						27
28			Factory Overhead							4	7	2	9	00	28
29															29
30	(j)	31	Cost of Goods Sold		4	9	1	8	00						30
31			Factory Overhead							4	9	1	8	00	31

4.

GENERAL JOURNAL

	DATE		DESCRIPTION	POST REF.	DEBIT	CREDIT	
1			Closing Entries				1
2	20-- Dec.	31	Income Summary		70 2 3 2 00		2
3			Factory Overhead			70 2 3 2 00	3
4							4
5		31	Factory Overhead		70 2 3 2 00		5
6			Income Summary			70 2 3 2 00	6
7							7
8		31	Sales		842 1 5 7 00		8
9			Income Summary			842 1 5 7 00	9
10							10
11		31	Income Summary		679 0 4 0 00		11
12			Cost of Goods Sold			460 3 1 1 00	12
13			Wages Expense			115 6 6 3 00	13
14			Advertising Expense			24 6 8 0 00	14
15			Office Rent Expense			13 1 8 0 00	15
16			Office Supplies Expense			9 0 0 00	16
17			Bad Debt Expense			1 0 0 0 00	17
18			Insurance Expense—Office Equipment			1 2 0 00	18
19			Depr. Expense—Office Equipment			9 6 0 00	19
20			Interest Expense			1 6 6 6 00	20
21			Income Tax Expense			60 5 6 0 00	21
22							22
23		31	Income Summary		163 1 1 7 00		23
24			Retained Earnings			163 1 1 7 00	24
25							25

5.

GENERAL JOURNAL

	DATE		DESCRIPTION	POST REF.	DEBIT	CREDIT	
1			Reversing Entries				1
2	20-- Jan.	1	Interest Payable		1 6 8 00		2
3			Interest Expense			1 6 8 00	3
4							4
5		1	Factory Overhead		4 7 2 9 00		5
6			Work in Process Inventory			4 7 2 9 00	6
7							7

REVIEW QUESTIONS

1. What accounts and related adjustments are new in the work sheet of a manufacturing corporation?

2. How does the use of a perpetual inventory system affect the accounts on the work sheet?

3. Why must the Work in Process Inventory be adjusted for factory overhead applied at year end?

4. What is the relationship between the debit and credit balances in the factory overhead account when the overhead is said to be underapplied? overapplied?

5. Why are the balances in the factory overhead account not extended to the Income Statement and Balance Sheet columns of the work sheet?

6. What are the distinctive features of ToyJoy's income statement? its retained earnings statement? its balance sheet?

7. When the adjustment is made to apply overhead to ending work in process, why are no entries made in the job cost ledger?

8. Describe the procedures for closing the factory overhead account.

9. Which adjusting entries are reversed by ToyJoy?

MANAGING YOUR WRITING

You and a fellow student are arguing about the "value" of Chapter 28. She says that the chapter is mostly review. The work sheet and financial statements were fully covered in Chapter 15. Chapter 28 is a similar story with some cosmetic differences. You have just begun an impressive defense of Chapter 28 when your professor overhears the argument and decides to give the entire class the following assignment.

Prepare a report describing (1) the ways in which the manufacturer's work sheet differs from the merchandiser's and (2) the differences between the merchandiser's financial statements in Chapter 15 and the manufacturer's financial statements in Chapter 28.

ETHICS CASE

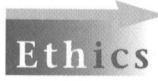

Kevin Ryan is an accountant for Warick Corporation, a medium-size manufacturing firm. One of his responsibilities is to review the adjusting entries at the end of each accounting period. Mary Sellers is a new accountant at Warick Corporation. She is a recent graduate and this is her first accounting job. One of the duties Kevin assigned Mary was to prepare the adjusting entries. After reviewing Mary's work, Kevin came to the conclusion that Mary did not understand the adjusting process for a manufacturing company. During their review meeting, Kevin told Mary that he was concerned about her ability to do the job. Mary admitted not having a sound knowledge of the adjusting and closing process but asked Kevin to give her another month to catch on. Kevin said he would have to think about it over the weekend and he would get back to her on Monday. That weekend, Kevin was offered a much better paying job with a large manufacturing company in the same city. He immediately accepted the position. When he gave his boss notice that he would be leaving Warick, his boss asked him how Mary was doing. Kevin said he thought she'd do just fine.

1. Do you think Kevin should have told his boss about Mary's poor performance? Why or why not?

2. How will Kevin's decision to not say anything affect Mary?

3. Write a short incident report concerning Mary's poor job performance and subsequent conference with Kevin. Assume Kevin writes the report and it will be placed in Mary's personnel file.

4. In groups of two or three, discuss what alternatives Kevin had in this situation. Come to a group consensus on the best alternative.

WEB WORK

Find a major manufacturer (such as GE, Whirlpool, or General Dynamics) and determine what percentage of its assets are tied up in inventory. You can access the financial statements of many corporations at

http://www.reportgallery.com/bigaz.htm.

http://heintz.swcollege.com

SERIES A EXERCISES

EXERCISE 28A-1 (LO 2) ADJUSTING ENTRIES INCLUDING ADJUSTMENT FOR UNDERAPPLIED/OVERAPPLIED FACTORY OVERHEAD Prepare the December 31 adjusting entries in general journal format for Johnson Company. Data are as follows:

(a) Factory overhead is applied at a rate of 60% of direct labor costs. At the end of the year, the direct labor costs associated with the jobs still in process amounted to $6,000.

(b) A physical count of factory supplies at the end of the year shows that $4,630 of factory supplies were used during the year.

(c) A review of the insurance policy files shows that $5,190 of insurance on the factory building and equipment has expired.

(d) Depreciation expense for the year on the factory building was $8,200 and on factory equipment was $12,400, a total of $20,600.

(e) The factory overhead account has a debit balance of $178,300 and a credit balance of $182,700 (after recording adjustments (a) through (d)).

Was factory overhead underapplied or overapplied for the year?

EXERCISE 28A-2 (LO 3) SCHEDULE OF COST OF GOODS MANUFACTURED
Prepare a schedule of cost of goods manufactured for Tomas Company for the year ended June 30, 20-2. Tomas had the following account balances:

Work in process, July 1, 20-1	$ 6,400
Materials inventory, July 1, 20-1	4,875
Materials purchases	65,350
Direct labor	140,300
Factory overhead	85,225
Work in process, June 30, 20-2	7,700
Materials inventory, June 30, 20-2	6,950

EXERCISE 28A-3 (LO 4) ADJUSTING JOURNAL ENTRIES FOR A MANUFACTURING BUSINESS Prepare the December 31 adjusting entries in general journal format for Hanna Company. Data for the end of the year adjustments are as follows:

Factory overhead to be applied to work in process ending inventory	$8,200
Interest receivable	680
Provision for uncollectible accounts	4,100
Office supplies consumed	960
Factory supplies consumed	3,400
Insurance expired on factory building and equipment	2,500
Depreciation on factory building	7,300
Depreciation on factory equipment	3,700

EXERCISE 28A-4 (LO 4) CLOSING JOURNAL ENTRIES Prepare closing journal entries for Medina Company for the year ended December 31. Data for the closing entries are as follows:

Factory overhead, debit and credit balance	$193,460
Sales for the year	840,300
Interest revenue	800
Cost of goods sold	560,400
Salaries expense	93,800
Office supplies expense	2,200
Depreciation expense—office equipment	5,800
Utilities expense—office	6,100
Bad debt expense	1,940
Advertising expense	8,700
Interest expense	9,600
Income tax expense	32,900

EXERCISE 28A-5 (LO 4) REVERSING ENTRIES Prepare reversing entries for Rogerson Company on January 1, 20-2, in general journal format. The following year-end adjustments were made:

20-1

Dec. 31	Interest Receivable		140	
	Interest Revenue			140
31	Interest Expense		930	
	Interest Payable			930
31	Work in Process Inventory		3,180	
	Factory Overhead			3,180

SERIES A PROBLEMS

**PROBLEM 28A-1 (LO 1/2/3) WORK SHEET, ADJUSTING ENTRIES, AND FINAN-
CIAL STATEMENTS** Herrera Company had the following trial balance:

Herrera Company
Trial Balance
December 31, 20 - -

ACCOUNT TITLE	DEBIT BALANCE	CREDIT BALANCE
Cash	30 3 0 0 00	
Government Notes	5 0 0 0 00	
Interest Receivable		
Accounts Receivable	34 0 0 0 00	
Allowance for Bad Debts		5 3 0 00
Finished Goods Inventory	24 0 0 0 00	
Work in Process Inventory	9 0 0 0 00	
Materials Inventory	8 5 0 0 00	
Office Supplies	3 1 0 0 00	
Factory Supplies	3 8 0 0 00	
Land	100 0 0 0 00	
Factory Building	120 0 0 0 00	
Accumulated Depreciation—Factory Building		10 0 0 0 00
Factory Equipment	40 0 0 0 00	
Accumulated Depreciation—Factory Equipment		5 0 0 0 00
Interest Payable		
Accounts Payable		13 8 0 0 00
Corporate Income Tax Payable		
Bonds Payable		80 0 0 0 00
Capital Stock		50 0 0 0 00
Paid-In Capital in Excess of Par		30 0 0 0 00
Retained Earnings		62 4 0 0 00
Sales		405 1 0 0 00
Interest Revenue		3 0 0 00
Factory Overhead	78 6 3 0 00	89 3 0 0 00
Cost of Goods Sold	190 7 0 0 00	
Wages Expense	70 0 0 0 00	
Office Supplies Expense		
Bad Debt Expense		
Utilities Expense—Office	4 4 0 0 00	
Interest Expense	7 0 0 0 00	
Income Tax Expense	18 0 0 0 00	
	746 4 3 0 00	746 4 3 0 00

Data for adjusting the accounts are as follows:

(a) Factory overhead to be applied to work in process
    ending inventory $3,100

(b) Interest receivable   75

(continued)

(c) Interest payable	$ 600
(d) Estimate of uncollectible accounts, based on an aging of accounts receivable	2,930
(e) Office supplies consumed	2,900
(f) Factory supplies consumed	3,300
(g) Factory building depreciation	5,000
(h) Factory equipment depreciation	4,000
(i) Overapplied factory overhead	1,470
(j) Provision for corporate income taxes	6,100

Additional information needed to prepare the financial statements is as follows:

Beginning inventories:

Finished goods, January 1	$18,000
Work in process, January 1	7,300
Materials inventory, January 1	9,500
Materials purchases for the year	48,100
Direct labor	60,000
Actual factory overhead	90,930
Retained earnings, January 1	92,400
Cash dividends declared and paid	30,000

REQUIRED   1.   Prepare a work sheet.

2.   Prepare the following financial statements and schedule:

   (a) income statement

   (b) schedule of cost of goods manufactured

   (c) retained earnings statement

   (d) balance sheet

W & D

PROBLEM 28A-2 (LO 1/3)   FINANCIAL STATEMENTS The Income Statement and Balance Sheet columns of Endo Company's work sheet are shown on the next page.

Additional information needed to prepare the financial statements is as follows:

Materials inventory, January 1	$ 3,760
Work in process inventory, January 1	5,315
Finished goods inventory, January 1	16,225
Materials purchases	130,040
Direct labor	75,000
Actual factory overhead	92,000
Retained earnings, January 1	80,225
Cash dividends declared and paid	25,000

REQUIRED   1.   Prepare an income statement and a schedule of cost of goods manufactured for the year ended December 31, 20--.

2.   Prepare a retained earnings statement for the year ended December 31, 20--.

3.   Prepare a balance sheet as of December 31, 20--.

PR28A-2 *(continued)*

Endo Company
Work Sheet (Partial)
For Year Ended December 31, 20 --

	ACCOUNT TITLE	INCOME STATEMENT				BALANCE SHEET				
		DEBIT	CREDIT	DEBIT	CREDIT	
1	Cash			13 3 5 0 00		1
2	Government Notes			3 5 0 0 00		2
3	Interest Receivable			6 5 00		3
4	Accounts Receivable			24 1 0 0 00		4
5	Allowance for Bad Debts				1 2 2 5 00	5
6	Finished Goods Inventory			18 8 0 0 00		6
7	Work in Process Inventory			6 7 4 0 00		7
8	Materials Inventory			4 3 0 0 00		8
9	Office Supplies			3 2 0 00		9
10	Factory Supplies			4 1 0 00		10
11	Prepaid Insurance			6 0 0 00		11
12	Land			25 0 0 0 00		12
13	Factory Building			80 0 0 0 00		13
14	Accum. Depr.—Factory Building				20 1 5 0 00	14
15	Factory Equipment			90 0 0 0 00		15
16	Accum. Depr.—Factory Equipment				27 0 0 0 00	16
17	Interest Payable				4 5 0 00	17
18	Accounts Payable				16 0 0 0 00	18
19	Corporate Income Tax Payable				3 5 5 0 00	19
20	Bonds Payable				50 0 0 0 00	20
21	Capital Stock				40 0 0 0 00	21
22	Paid-In Capital in Excess of Par				15 0 0 0 00	22
23	Retained Earnings				55 2 2 5 00	23
24	Sales		397 1 1 0 00			24
25	Interest Revenue		3 2 5 00			25
26	Factory Overhead					26
27						27
28	Cost of Goods Sold	292 5 0 0 00				28
29	Wages Expense	44 2 0 0 00				29
30	Office Supplies Expense	1 2 0 0 00				30
31	Bad Debt Expense	2 4 5 0 00				31
32	Utilities Expense—Office	1 5 0 0 00				32
33	Interest Expense	2 5 5 0 00				33
34	Income Tax Expense	14 4 5 0 00				34
35		358 8 5 0 00	397 4 3 5 00	267 1 8 5 00	228 6 0 0 00	35
36	Net Income	38 5 8 5 00			38 5 8 5 00	36
37		397 4 3 5 00	397 4 3 5 00	267 1 8 5 00	267 1 8 5 00	37
38						38
39						39

PROBLEM 28A-3 (LO 1/2/4) ADJUSTING ENTRIES, CLOSING ENTRIES, AND REVERSING ENTRIES A partial work sheet for Baldwin Company is shown on the next page.

Data for adjusting the accounts are as follows:

(a) Factory overhead to be applied to work in process ending inventory	$3,600
(b) Interest receivable	140
(c) Interest payable	1,200
(d) Estimate of uncollectible accounts, based on an aging of accounts receivable	2,370
(e) Office supplies consumed	3,700
(f) Factory supplies consumed	4,200
(g) Insurance on factory building and equipment expired	5,100
(h) Factory building depreciation	5,000
(i) Factory equipment depreciation	4,000
(j) Underapplied factory overhead	1,300
(k) Provision for corporate income taxes	5,900

REQUIRED

1. Journalize the adjusting entries in the general journal.

2. Journalize the closing entries in the general journal.

3. Journalize the reversing entries as of January 1, 20-2, in the general journal.

SERIES B EXERCISES

EXERCISE 28B-1 (LO 2) ADJUSTING ENTRIES INCLUDING ADJUSTMENT FOR UNDERAPPLIED/OVERAPPLIED FACTORY OVERHEAD Prepare the December 31 adjusting entries in general journal format for Keiser Company. Data are as follows:

(a) Factory overhead is applied at a rate of 80% of direct labor costs. At the end of the year, the direct labor costs associated with the jobs still in process amounted to $7,000.

(b) A physical count of factory supplies at the end of the year shows that $3,750 of factory supplies were used during the year.

(c) A review of the insurance policy files shows that $4,360 of insurance on the factory building and equipment has expired.

(d) Depreciation expense for the year on the factory building was $9,400 and on factory equipment was $11,600, a total of $21,000.

(e) The factory overhead account has a debit balance of $146,700 and a credit balance of $143,200 (after recording adjustments (a) through (d)).

Was factory overhead underapplied or overapplied for the year?

PR28A-3 (conituned)

Baldwin Company
Work Sheet (Partial)
For Year Ended December 31, 20-1

#	Account Title	Trial Balance Debit	Trial Balance Credit	Adjustments Debit	Adjustments Credit	Adjusted Trial Balance Debit	Adjusted Trial Balance Credit	Income Statement Debit	Income Statement Credit	Balance Sheet Debit	Balance Sheet Credit
1	Cash	41 2 0 0 00				41 2 0 0 00					
2	Government Notes	6 0 0 0 00				6 0 0 0 00					
3	Interest Receivable			(b) 1 4 0 0 00		1 4 0 0 00					
4	Accounts Receivable	32 0 0 0 00				32 0 0 0 00					
5	Allowance for Bad Debts		9 2 0 00		(d) 1 4 5 0 00		2 3 7 0 00				
6	Finished Goods Inventory	21 0 0 0 00				21 0 0 0 00					
7	Work in Process Inventory	10 2 0 0 00		(a) 3 6 0 0 00		13 8 0 0 00					
8	Materials Inventory	9 1 0 0 00				9 1 0 0 00					
9	Office Supplies	4 2 0 0 00			(e) 3 7 0 0 00	5 0 0 00					
10	Factory Supplies	5 1 0 0 00			(f) 4 2 0 0 00	9 0 0 00					
11	Prepaid Insurance	6 2 0 0 00			(g) 5 1 0 0 00	1 1 0 0 00					
12	Land	80 0 0 0 00				80 0 0 0 00					
13	Factory Building	120 0 0 0 00				120 0 0 0 00					
14	Accum. Depr.—Factory Building		20 0 0 0 00		(h) 5 0 0 0 00		25 0 0 0 00				
15	Factory Equipment	50 0 0 0 00				50 0 0 0 00					
16	Accum. Depr.—Factory Equip.		8 0 0 0 00		(i) 4 0 0 0 00		12 0 0 0 00				
17	Interest Payable				(c) 1 2 0 0 00		1 2 0 0 00				
18	Accounts Payable		16 4 0 0 00				16 4 0 0 00				
19	Corporate Income Tax Payable				(k) 5 9 0 0 00		5 9 0 0 00				
20	Bonds Payable		90 0 0 0 00				90 0 0 0 00				
21	Capital Stock		60 0 0 0 00				60 0 0 0 00				
22	Paid-In Capital in Excess of Par		40 0 0 0 00				40 0 0 0 00				
23	Retained Earnings		46 7 8 0 00				46 7 8 0 00				
24	Sales		410 2 0 0 00				410 2 0 0 00				
25	Interest Revenue		5 0 0 0 00		(b) 1 4 0 0 00		6 4 0 0 00				
26	Factory Overhead	91 8 0 0 00	105 2 0 0 00	(f) 4 2 0 0 00	(a) 3 6 0 0 00	110 1 0 0 00	110 1 0 0 00				
27				(g) 5 1 0 0 00	(j) 1 3 0 0 00						
28				(h) 5 0 0 0 00							
29				(i) 4 0 0 0 00							
30	Cost of Goods Sold	203 5 0 0 00		(j) 1 3 0 0 00		204 8 0 0 00					
31	Salaries Expense	80 0 0 0 00				80 0 0 0 00					
32	Office Supplies Expense			(e) 3 7 0 0 00		3 7 0 0 00					
33	Bad Debt Expense			(d) 1 4 5 0 00		1 4 5 0 00					
34	Utilities Expense—Office	6 7 0 0 00				6 7 0 0 00					
35	Interest Expense	8 0 0 0 00		(c) 1 2 0 0 00		9 2 0 0 00					
36	Income Tax Expense	23 0 0 0 00		(k) 5 9 0 0 00		28 9 0 0 00					
37		798 0 0 0 00	798 0 0 0 00	35 5 9 0 00	35 5 9 0 00	820 5 9 0 00	820 5 9 0 00				
38											

EXERCISE 28B-2 (LO 3) SCHEDULE OF COST OF GOODS MANUFACTURED
Prepare a schedule of cost of goods manufactured for Verdi Company for the year ended June 30, 20-2. Verdi had the following account balances:

Work in process, July 1, 20-1	$ 20,760
Materials inventory, July 1, 20-1	12,348
Materials purchases	154,008
Direct labor	330,576
Factory overhead	201,384
Work in process, June 30, 20-2	17,940
Materials inventory, June 30, 20-2	15,180

EXERCISE 28B-3 (LO 4) ADJUSTING JOURNAL ENTRIES FOR A MANUFACTURING BUSINESS Prepare the December 31 adjusting entries in general journal format for Ortiz Company. Data for the end of the year adjustments are as follows:

Factory overhead to be applied to work in process ending inventory	$7,780
Interest receivable	435
Provision for uncollectible accounts	3,876
Office supplies consumed	750
Factory supplies consumed	4,160
Insurance expired on factory building and equipment	3,200
Depreciation on factory building	6,800
Depreciation on factory equipment	4,200

EXERCISE 28B-4 (LO 4) CLOSING JOURNAL ENTRIES Prepare closing journal entries for Armour Company for the year ended December 31. Data for the closing entries are as follows:

Factory overhead, debit and credit balance	$186,250
Sales for the year	930,600
Interest revenue	920
Cost of goods sold	710,500
Salaries expense	98,100
Office supplies expense	3,500
Depreciation expense—office equipment	6,130
Utilities expense—office	7,460
Bad debt expense	2,275
Advertising expense	9,250
Interest expense	8,300
Income tax expense	41,350

EXERCISE 28B-5 (LO 4) REVERSING ENTRIES Prepare reversing entries for Hendrix Company on January 1, 20-2, in general journal format. The following year-end adjustments were made:

20-1

Dec. 31	Interest Receivable		230	
		Interest Revenue		230
	31	Interest Expense	875	
		Interest Payable		875
	31	Work in Process Inventory	4,250	
		Factory Overhead		4,250

SERIES B PROBLEMS

PROBLEM 28B-1 (LO 1/2/3) WORK SHEET, ADJUSTING ENTRIES, AND FINAN-CIAL STATEMENTS Woods Company's trial balance is shown on the next page. Data for adjusting the accounts are as follows:

(a)	Factory overhead to be applied to work in process ending inventory	$ 4,300
(b)	Interest receivable	100
(c)	Interest payable	700
(d)	Estimate of uncollectible accounts, based on an aging of accounts receivable	4,110
(e)	Office supplies consumed	3,200
(f)	Factory supplies consumed	6,700
(g)	Factory building depreciation	10,000
(h)	Factory equipment depreciation	6,000
(i)	Underapplied factory overhead	7,690
(j)	Provision for corporate income taxes	8,100

Additional information needed to prepare the financial statements is as follows:

Beginning inventories:	
Finished goods, January 1	$ 22,300
Work in process, January 1	12,400
Materials inventory, January 1	7,900
Materials purchases for the year	18,700
Direct labor	90,300
Actual factory overhead	104,290
Retained earnings, January 1	111,400
Cash dividends declared and paid	40,000

REQUIRED

1. Prepare a work sheet.

2. Prepare the following financial statements and schedule:
    - (a) income statement
    - (b) schedule of cost of goods manufactured
    - (c) retained earnings statement
    - (d) balance sheet

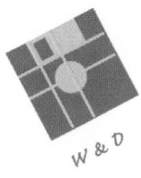

PROBLEM 28B-2 (LO 1/3) FINANCIAL STATEMENTS The Income Statement and Balance Sheet columns of Wen Company's work sheet are shown on page 1049.

Additional information needed to prepare the financial statements is as follows:

Materials inventory, January 1	$ 4,750
Work in process inventory, January 1	3,600
Finished goods inventory, January 1	14,560
Materials purchases	110,990
Direct labor	110,000
Actual factory overhead	96,850
Retained earnings, January 1	83,020
Cash dividends declared and paid	12,500

(continued)

PR28B-1 *(continued)*

<table>
<thead>
<tr><th colspan="11" align="center">Woods Company
Trial Balance
December 31, 20 - -</th></tr>
<tr><th>ACCOUNT TITLE</th><th colspan="5">DEBIT BALANCE</th><th colspan="5">CREDIT BALANCE</th></tr>
</thead>
<tbody>
<tr><td>Cash</td><td>28</td><td>4</td><td>0</td><td>0</td><td>00</td><td></td><td></td><td></td><td></td><td></td></tr>
<tr><td>Government Notes</td><td>6</td><td>0</td><td>0</td><td>0</td><td>00</td><td></td><td></td><td></td><td></td><td></td></tr>
<tr><td>Interest Receivable</td><td></td><td></td><td></td><td></td><td></td><td></td><td></td><td></td><td></td><td></td></tr>
<tr><td>Accounts Receivable</td><td>32</td><td>8</td><td>0</td><td>0</td><td>00</td><td></td><td></td><td></td><td></td><td></td></tr>
<tr><td>Allowance for Bad Debts</td><td></td><td></td><td></td><td></td><td></td><td></td><td>6</td><td>1</td><td>0</td><td>00</td></tr>
<tr><td>Finished Goods Inventory</td><td>26</td><td>1</td><td>0</td><td>0</td><td>00</td><td></td><td></td><td></td><td></td><td></td></tr>
<tr><td>Work in Process Inventory</td><td>10</td><td>2</td><td>0</td><td>0</td><td>00</td><td></td><td></td><td></td><td></td><td></td></tr>
<tr><td>Materials Inventory</td><td>9</td><td>3</td><td>0</td><td>0</td><td>00</td><td></td><td></td><td></td><td></td><td></td></tr>
<tr><td>Office Supplies</td><td>4</td><td>2</td><td>0</td><td>0</td><td>00</td><td></td><td></td><td></td><td></td><td></td></tr>
<tr><td>Factory Supplies</td><td>8</td><td>6</td><td>0</td><td>0</td><td>00</td><td></td><td></td><td></td><td></td><td></td></tr>
<tr><td>Land</td><td>80</td><td>0</td><td>0</td><td>0</td><td>00</td><td></td><td></td><td></td><td></td><td></td></tr>
<tr><td>Factory Building</td><td>160</td><td>0</td><td>0</td><td>0</td><td>00</td><td></td><td></td><td></td><td></td><td></td></tr>
<tr><td>Accumulated Depreciation—Factory Building</td><td></td><td></td><td></td><td></td><td></td><td>30</td><td>0</td><td>0</td><td>0</td><td>00</td></tr>
<tr><td>Factory Equipment</td><td>60</td><td>0</td><td>0</td><td>0</td><td>00</td><td></td><td></td><td></td><td></td><td></td></tr>
<tr><td>Accumulated Depreciation—Factory Equipment</td><td></td><td></td><td></td><td></td><td></td><td>20</td><td>0</td><td>0</td><td>0</td><td>00</td></tr>
<tr><td>Interest Payable</td><td></td><td></td><td></td><td></td><td></td><td></td><td></td><td></td><td></td><td></td></tr>
<tr><td>Accounts Payable</td><td></td><td></td><td></td><td></td><td></td><td>16</td><td>0</td><td>0</td><td>0</td><td>00</td></tr>
<tr><td>Corporate Income Tax Payable</td><td></td><td></td><td></td><td></td><td></td><td></td><td></td><td></td><td></td><td></td></tr>
<tr><td>Bonds Payable</td><td></td><td></td><td></td><td></td><td></td><td>100</td><td>0</td><td>0</td><td>0</td><td>00</td></tr>
<tr><td>Capital Stock</td><td></td><td></td><td></td><td></td><td></td><td>60</td><td>0</td><td>0</td><td>0</td><td>00</td></tr>
<tr><td>Paid-In Capital in Excess of Par</td><td></td><td></td><td></td><td></td><td></td><td>20</td><td>0</td><td>0</td><td>0</td><td>00</td></tr>
<tr><td>Retained Earnings</td><td></td><td></td><td></td><td></td><td></td><td>71</td><td>4</td><td>0</td><td>0</td><td>00</td></tr>
<tr><td>Sales</td><td></td><td></td><td></td><td></td><td></td><td>410</td><td>7</td><td>0</td><td>0</td><td>00</td></tr>
<tr><td>Interest Revenue</td><td></td><td></td><td></td><td></td><td></td><td></td><td>5</td><td>0</td><td>0</td><td>00</td></tr>
<tr><td>Factory Overhead</td><td>81</td><td>5</td><td>9</td><td>0</td><td>00</td><td>92</td><td>3</td><td>0</td><td>0</td><td>00</td></tr>
<tr><td>Cost of Goods Sold</td><td>198</td><td>3</td><td>0</td><td>0</td><td>00</td><td></td><td></td><td></td><td></td><td></td></tr>
<tr><td>Wages Expense</td><td>78</td><td>7</td><td>0</td><td>0</td><td>00</td><td></td><td></td><td></td><td></td><td></td></tr>
<tr><td>Office Supplies Expense</td><td></td><td></td><td></td><td></td><td></td><td></td><td></td><td></td><td></td><td></td></tr>
<tr><td>Bad Debt Expense</td><td></td><td></td><td></td><td></td><td></td><td></td><td></td><td></td><td></td><td></td></tr>
<tr><td>Utilities Expense—Office</td><td>4</td><td>9</td><td>0</td><td>0</td><td>00</td><td></td><td></td><td></td><td></td><td></td></tr>
<tr><td>Interest Expense</td><td>9</td><td>0</td><td>0</td><td>0</td><td>00</td><td></td><td></td><td></td><td></td><td></td></tr>
<tr><td>Income Tax Expense</td><td>23</td><td>4</td><td>2</td><td>0</td><td>00</td><td></td><td></td><td></td><td></td><td></td></tr>
<tr><td></td><td>821</td><td>5</td><td>1</td><td>0</td><td>00</td><td>821</td><td>5</td><td>1</td><td>0</td><td>00</td></tr>
</tbody>
</table>

PR28B-2 *(continued)*

Wen Company
Work Sheet (Partial)
For Year Ended December 31, 20 --

	ACCOUNT TITLE	INCOME STATEMENT DEBIT	INCOME STATEMENT CREDIT	BALANCE SHEET DEBIT	BALANCE SHEET CREDIT	
1	Cash			16 4 5 0 00		1
2	Government Notes			6 0 0 0 00		2
3	Interest Receivable			2 1 0 00		3
4	Accounts Receivable			19 7 0 0 00		4
5	Allowance for Bad Debts				1 6 0 0 00	5
6	Finished Goods Inventory			16 2 5 0 00		6
7	Work in Process Inventory			7 6 0 0 00		7
8	Materials Inventory			4 5 5 0 00		8
9	Office Supplies			4 6 5 00		9
10	Factory Supplies			3 7 5 00		10
11	Prepaid Insurance			7 0 0 00		11
12	Land			30 0 0 0 00		12
13	Factory Building			60 0 0 0 00		13
14	Accum. Depr.—Factory Building				15 2 3 0 00	14
15	Factory Equipment			85 0 0 0 00		15
16	Accum. Depr.—Factory Equipment				23 0 0 0 00	16
17	Interest Payable				6 0 0 00	17
18	Accounts Payable				14 4 5 0 00	18
19	Corporate Income Tax Payable				3 1 5 0 00	19
20	Bonds Payable				40 0 0 0 00	20
21	Capital Stock				30 0 0 0 00	21
22	Paid-In Capital in Excess of Par				20 0 0 0 00	22
23	Retained Earnings				70 5 2 0 00	23
24	Sales		410 1 5 0 00			24
25	Interest Revenue		6 5 0 00			25
26	Factory Overhead					26
27						27
28	Cost of Goods Sold	312 3 5 0 00				28
29	Wages Expense	43 1 0 0 00				29
30	Office Supplies Expense	2 2 5 0 00				30
31	Bad Debt Expense	1 7 5 0 00				31
32	Utilities Expense—Office	4 0 0 0 00				32
33	Interest Expense	3 1 0 0 00				33
34	Income Tax Expense	15 5 0 0 00				34
35		382 0 5 0 00	410 8 0 0 00	247 3 0 0 00	218 5 5 0 00	35
36	Net Income	28 7 5 0 00			28 7 5 0 00	36
37		410 8 0 0 00	410 8 0 0 00	247 3 0 0 00	247 3 0 0 00	37
38						38

REQUIRED

1. Prepare an income statement and a schedule of cost of goods manufactured for the year ended December 31, 20--.

2. Prepare a retained earnings statement for the year ended December 31, 20--.

3. Prepare a balance sheet as of December 31, 20--.

PROBLEM 28B-3 (LO 1/2/4) ADJUSTING ENTRIES, CLOSING ENTRIES, AND REVERSING ENTRIES A partial work sheet for Milnor Company is shown on the next page.

Data for adjusting the accounts are as follows:

(a)	Factory overhead to be applied to work in process ending inventory	$4,400
(b)	Interest receivable	190
(c)	Interest payable	1,420
(d)	Estimate of uncollectible accounts, based on an aging of accounts receivable	4,450
(e)	Office supplies consumed	4,200
(f)	Factory supplies consumed	3,800
(g)	Insurance on factory building and equipment expired	6,800
(h)	Factory building depreciation	8,000
(i)	Factory equipment depreciation	5,000
(j)	Overapplied factory overhead	4,340
(k)	Provision for corporate income taxes	6,400

REQUIRED
1. Journalize the adjusting entries in the general journal.
2. Journalize the closing entries in the general journal.
3. Journalize the reversing entries as of January 1, 20-2, in the general journal.

MASTERY PROBLEM

The Reese Manufacturing Company manufactures and sells a limited line of products made to customer order. The company uses a perpetual inventory system and keeps its accounts on a calendar year basis. A ten-column work sheet is presented on page 1052.

Dividends declared and paid in 20-- were $36,000. (Remember to add this amount back to the retained earnings balance shown on the work sheet to determine the retained earnings balance on January 1, 20--.)

Additional information needed to prepare the income statement and schedule of cost of goods manufactured is as follows:

Finished goods inventory, January 1	$ 85,454
Materials inventory, January 1	11,633
Purchases for the year	93,237
Direct labor	107,740
Work in process inventory, January 1	22,600

REQUIRED
1. Prepare an income statement and schedule of cost of goods manufactured for the year ended December 31, 20--.
2. Prepare a retained earnings statement for the year ended December 31, 20--.
3. Prepare a balance sheet as of December 31, 20--.
4. Prepare the adjusting, closing, and reversing entries.

PR28B-3 *(continued)*

Minor Company
Work Sheet (Partial)
For Year Ended December 31, 20-1

#	ACCOUNT TITLE	TRIAL BALANCE DEBIT	TRIAL BALANCE CREDIT	ADJUSTMENTS DEBIT	ADJUSTMENTS CREDIT	ADJUSTED TRIAL BALANCE DEBIT	ADJUSTED TRIAL BALANCE CREDIT	INCOME STATEMENT DEBIT	INCOME STATEMENT CREDIT	BALANCE SHEET DEBIT	BALANCE SHEET CREDIT
1	Cash	39 6 0 0 00				39 6 0 0 00					
2	Government Notes	8 0 0 0 00				8 0 0 0 00					
3	Interest Receivable			(b) 1 9 0 00		1 9 0 00					
4	Accounts Receivable	40 0 0 0 00				40 0 0 0 00					
5	Allowance for Bad Debts		1 2 5 0 00		(d) 3 2 0 0 00		4 4 5 0 00				
6	Finished Goods Inventory	24 0 0 0 00				24 0 0 0 00					
7	Work in Process Inventory	12 3 0 0 00		(a) 4 4 0 0 00		16 7 0 0 00					
8	Materials Inventory	8 7 0 0 00				8 7 0 0 00					
9	Office Supplies	5 5 0 0 00			(e) 4 2 0 0 00	1 3 0 0 00					
10	Factory Supplies	4 9 5 0 00			(f) 3 8 0 0 00	1 1 5 0 00					
11	Prepaid Insurance	7 4 5 0 00			(g) 6 8 0 0 00	6 5 0 00					
12	Land	90 0 0 0 00				90 0 0 0 00					
13	Factory Building	130 0 0 0 00				130 0 0 0 00					
14	Accum. Depr.—Factory Building		40 0 0 0 00		(h) 8 0 0 0 00		48 0 0 0 00				
15	Factory Equipment	70 0 0 0 00				70 0 0 0 00					
16	Accum. Depr.—Factory Equip.		10 0 0 0 00		(i) 5 0 0 0 00		15 0 0 0 00				
17	Interest Payable				(c) 1 4 2 0 00		1 4 2 0 00				
18	Accounts Payable		17 2 0 0 00				17 2 0 0 00				
19	Corporate Income Tax Payable				(k) 6 4 0 0 00		6 4 0 0 00				
20	Bonds Payable		120 0 0 0 00				120 0 0 0 00				
21	Capital Stock		50 0 0 0 00				50 0 0 0 00				
22	Paid-In Capital in Excess of Par		30 0 0 0 00				30 0 0 0 00				
23	Retained Earnings		72 3 1 0 00				72 3 1 0 00				
24	Sales		395 2 0 0 00				395 2 0 0 00				
25	Interest Revenue		8 0 0 00		(b) 1 9 0 00		9 9 0 00				
26	Factory Overhead	84 5 6 0 00	108 1 0 0 00	(f) 3 8 0 0 00	(a) 4 4 0 0 00	112 5 0 0 00	112 5 0 0 00				
27				(g) 6 8 0 0 00							
28				(h) 8 0 0 0 00							
29				(i) 5 0 0 0 00							
30				(j) 4 3 4 0 00							
31	Cost of Goods Sold	194 6 0 0 00			(j) 4 3 4 0 00	190 2 6 0 00					
32	Wages Expense	90 0 0 0 00				90 0 0 0 00					
33	Office Supplies Expense			(e) 4 2 0 0 00		4 2 0 0 00					
34	Bad Debt Expense			(d) 3 2 0 0 00		3 2 0 0 00					
35	Utilities Expense—Office	7 2 0 0 00				7 2 0 0 00					
36	Interest Expense	9 0 0 0 00		(c) 1 4 2 0 00		10 4 2 0 00					
37	Income Tax Expense	19 0 0 0 00		(k) 6 4 0 0 00		25 4 0 0 00					
38		844 8 6 0 00	844 8 6 0 00	47 7 5 0 00	47 7 5 0 00	873 4 7 0 00	873 4 7 0 00				
39											

MP *(continued)*

The Reese Manufacturing Co.
Work Sheet
For Year Ended December 31, 20 --

#	Account Title	Trial Balance Debit	Trial Balance Credit	Adjustments Debit	Adjustments Credit	Adjusted Trial Balance Debit	Adjusted Trial Balance Credit	Income Statement Debit	Income Statement Credit	Balance Sheet Debit	Balance Sheet Credit
1	Cash	49,423.00				49,423.00				49,423.00	
2	Accounts Receivable	78,096.00				78,096.00				78,096.00	
3	Allowance for Bad Debts		5,074.00		(g) 956.00		6,030.00				6,030.00
4	Finished Goods Inventory	42,675.00				42,675.00				42,675.00	
5	Work in Process Inventory	39,675.00		(i) 1,567.00		41,242.00				41,242.00	
6	Materials Inventory	22,353.00				22,353.00				22,353.00	
7	Office Supplies	3,546.00			(b) 800.00	2,746.00				2,746.00	
8	Factory Supplies	1,878.00			(c) 1,389.00	489.00				489.00	
9	Prepaid Insurance	1,500.00			(f) 1,454.00	46.00				46.00	
10	Factory Equipment	186,674.00				186,674.00				186,674.00	
11	Accum. Depr.—Factory Equip.		23,501.00		(e) 12,553.00		36,054.00				36,054.00
12	Office Equipment	46,986.00				46,986.00				46,986.00	
13	Accum. Depr.—Office Equip.		2,916.00		(d) 923.00		3,839.00				3,839.00
14	Notes Payable		12,470.00				12,470.00				12,470.00
15	Interest Payable				(a) 132.00		132.00				132.00
16	Accounts Payable		10,356.00				10,356.00				10,356.00
17	Corp. Income Tax Payable				(h) 45,725.00		45,725.00				45,725.00
18	Capital Stock		72,000.00				72,000.00				72,000.00
19	Retained Earnings		159,341.00				159,341.00				159,341.00
20	Sales		532,027.00				532,027.00		532,027.00		
21	Factory Overhead	52,356.00	65,446.00	(c) 1,389.00	(i) 1,567.00	67,654.00	67,654.00				
22				(e) 12,553.00	(j) 641.00						
23				(f) 1,356.00							
24	Cost of Goods Sold	281,407.00		(j) 641.00		282,048.00		282,048.00			
25	Wages Expense	58,380.00				58,380.00		58,380.00			
26	Advertising Expense	11,450.00				11,450.00		11,450.00			
27	Office Rent Expense	5,443.00				5,443.00		5,443.00			
28	Office Supplies Expense			(b) 800.00		800.00		800.00			
29	Bad Debt Expense			(g) 956.00		956.00		956.00			
30	Insurance Exp.—Office Equip.			(f) 98.00		98.00		98.00			
31	Depr. Expense—Office Equip.			(d) 923.00		923.00		923.00			
32	Interest Expense	1,289.00		(a) 132.00		1,421.00		1,421.00			
33	Income Tax Expense			(h) 45,725.00		45,725.00		45,725.00			
34		883,131.00	883,131.00	66,140.00	66,140.00	945,628.00	945,628.00	407,244.00	532,027.00	470,730.00	345,947.00
35	Net Income							124,783.00			124,783.00
36								532,027.00	532,027.00	470,730.00	470,730.00
37											
38											
39											

Self-Study Test Questions

True/False

1. Manufacturing companies normally use a periodic inventory system. _____

2. Under the perpetual inventory system, Cost of Goods Sold is debited each time the finished goods inventory is sold. _____

3. On the work sheet, the factory overhead account shows both debit and credit totals in the Trial Balance columns. _____

4. The credit total of Factory Overhead represents actual factory overhead costs. _____

5. The adjustment for factory overhead applied to work in process at the end of the accounting period includes a debit to the factory overhead account. _____

Multiple Choice

1. The adjustment for the amount of factory supplies used during the year includes a _____

   (a) debit to Factory Supplies.   (c) credit to Factory Overhead.
   (b) debit to Factory Overhead.   (d) debit to Supplies Expense.

2. The adjustment for depreciation expense for the year on the factory building includes a _____

   (a) debit to Depreciation Expense.   (c) credit to Accumulated Depreciation.
   (b) credit to Factory Overhead.   (d) debit to Accumulated Depreciation.

3. At the end of the accounting period, a credit balance in the factory overhead account represents _____

   (a) overapplied factory overhead.   (c) underapplied factory overhead.
   (b) actual factory overhead.   (d) revenue earned.

4. During the closing process, the credit total in the factory overhead account is debited to _____

   (a) Work in Process Inventory.   (c) Cost of Goods Sold.
   (b) Factory Overhead Expense.   (d) Income Summary.

5. The adjusting entry to apply factory overhead to Work in Process is reversed at the beginning of the next accounting period and includes a _____

   (a) debit to Work in Process Inventory. (c) credit to Factory Overhead.
   (b) debit to Factory Overhead.   (d) credit to Cost of Goods Sold.

The answers to the Self-Study Test Questions are at the end of the text.

Answers to Self-Study Test Questions

CHAPTER 2

True/False

1. T
2. F (A/P is a liability)
3. T
4. T
5. F (other changes could occur: capital could increase, revenue could increase, etc.)
6. F (net income)   7. T

Multiple Choice

1. c   2. a   3. b   4. d   5. b

CHAPTER 3

True/False

1. T
2. F (liability accounts normally have credit balances)
3. T   4. F (credit balances)
5. T   6. F (increase)

Multiple Choice

1. c   2. c   3. b   4. d   5. a

CHAPTER 4

True/False

1. T   2. T   3. T
4. F (A, L, OE, R, E)   5. T

Multiple Choice

1. b   2. c   3. b   4. a   5. d

CHAPTER 5

True/False

1. F (match revenues and expenses)
2. F (to bring accounts up-to-date)
3. T
4. F (depreciable cost = cost – salvage value)
5. F (to match cost of asset against revenues it will help generate)

Multiple Choice

1. a   2. c   3. d   4. c   5. a

CHAPTER 6

True/False

1. T
2. F (additional investments are added to the beginning balance)
3. F   4. T   5. T

Multiple Choice

1. b   2. d   3. a   4. c   5. b

CHAPTER 7

True/False

1. T
2. F (large businesses use the accrual basis)
3. F (see Figure 7-2) 4. T   5. T

Multiple Choice

1. c   2. b   3. d   4. a   5. b

CHAPTER 8

True/False

1. F (primary purpose is to reconcile book balance with bank balance)

2. F (deducted from book balance)   3. T

4. F (deducted from book balance)

5. F (entries are not posted from petty cash record to general ledger)

Multiple Choice

1. b   2. a   3. c   4. b   5. d

CHAPTER 9

True/False

1. F (does *not* work under control and direction)

2. T   3. F (is called wages)

4. T   5. T

Multiple Choice

1. c   2. b   3. d   4. a   5. d

CHAPTER 10

True/False

1. F (these taxes are paid by the employer)

2. T   3. T

4. F (FUTA tax is levied on employers)

5. F (this form is W-2)

Multiple Choice

1. b   2. d   3. b   4. d   5. a

CHAPTER 11

True/False

1. F (only credit sales are recorded in the sales journal)

2. T   3. T

4. F (the debit *excludes* the sales tax)   5. T

Multiple Choice

1. d   2. c   3. b   4. b   5. a

CHAPTER 12

True/False

1. F (purchase requisition)   2. T

3. T   4. F (credited)   5. F (buyer)

Multiple Choice

1. a   2. c   3. a   4. d   5. b

CHAPTER 13

True/False

1. T   2. F (prepared before check is issued)

3. T   4. T

5. F (used with a check register)

Multiple Choice

1. b   2. d   3. a   4. c   5. b

CHAPTER 14

True/False

1. T   2. T   3. T

4. F (revenue is recognized)

5. F (contra-revenue account)

Multiple Choice

1. b   2. a   3. b   4. b   5. b

CHAPTER 15

True/False

1. T   2. F (whichever is longer)

3. T   4. T

5. F (number of times accounts receivable turned over)

Multiple Choice

1. c   2. a   3. b   4. d   5. c

CHAPTER 16

True/False

1. T   2. F (expenses matched with revenues)

3. F (balance in Allowance for Bad Debts is ignored)

4. F (debit to Allowance for Bad Debts)   5. T

Multiple Choice

1. d   2. a   3. b   4. d   5. a

CHAPTER 17

True/False

1. T   2. T

3. F (Difference is called the *proceeds*.)

4. F (Interest *is* credited to Interest Revenue; time has passed and the interest has been earned.)

5. T

Multiple Choice

1. b   2. c   3. c   4. d   5. a

CHAPTER 18

True/False

1. T   2. T

3. F (this is true for the periodic method)

4. T   5. F (the buyer pays)

Multiple Choice

1. b   2. c   3. a   4. c   5. b

CHAPTER 19

True/False

1. F (land)   2. F (reverse is true)

3. F (depreciation is a method of cost allocation)

4. F (the opposite is true)

5. F (the units-of-production method is based on the usage or output of the asset)

Multiple Choice

1. d   2. c   3. b   4. b   5. c

CHAPTER 20

True/False

1. F (partnership)   2. T

3. F (limited life is a characteristic of a partnership because the partnership is dissolved with any change in the partners)

4. F (this is a disadvantage)   5. T

Multiple Choice

1. a   2. a   3. d   4. c   5. a

CHAPTER 21

True/False

1. T   2. T

3. F (they do not have this power)

4. F (dividends are taxable to the recipients)

5. T

Multiple Choice

1. d   2. a   3. c   4. b   5. c

CHAPTER 22

True/False

1. T   2. T   3. T

4. F (it is known as a cash dividend)

5. F (dates of declaration and payment require journal entries)

Multiple Choice

1. a   2. b   3. d   4. c   5. a

CHAPTER 23

True/False

1. T   2. F (discount)   3. T

4. F (decreases)   5. T

Multiple Choice

1. c   2. c   3. a   4. d   5. b

CHAPTER 24

True/False

1. F (cash flows)

2. F (buying and selling assets)   3. T

4. F (subtracted)   5. T

Multiple Choice

1. d   2. a   3. b   4. a   5. c

CHAPTER 25

True/False

1. F (leverage is a measure of the extent to which debt is used to finance the business)

2. T   3. T

4. F (WC = CA – CL)   5. T

Multiple Choice

1. b   2. a   3. c   4. d   5. d

CHAPTER 26

True/False

1. F (net sales and cost of goods sold)   2. T

3. T   4. F (indirect expenses)   5. T

Multiple Choice

1. a   2. d   3. b   4. b   5. c

CHAPTER 27

True/False

1. F (only direct materials)   2. T   3. T

4. F (items finished and *not* sold)   5. T

Multiple Choice

1. c   2. b   3. a   4. c   5. d

CHAPTER 28

True/False

1. F (perpetual)   2. T   3. T

4. F (debit total)   5. F (credit)

Multiple Choice

1. b   2. c   3. a   4. d   5. b

INDEX

*Page references in bold indicate defined terms.

Note: While for a specific company each account number used would have only one title, titles vary from company to company as needed.

Assets (100–199)

100s—Cash Related Accounts
101 Cash
105 Petty Cash

120s—Receivables
121 Notes Receivable
122 Accounts Receivable
122.1 Allowance for Bad Debts
123 Interest Receivable (Also Accrued Interest Receivable)
125 Common Stock Subscriptions Receivable
126 Preferred Stock Subscriptions Receivable

130s—Inventories
131 Merchandise Inventory
132 Raw Materials
133 Work in Process
134 Finished Goods

140s—Prepaid Items
141 Supplies (Specialty items like Medical, Bicycle, Tailoring, etc.)
142 Office Supplies
144 Food Supplies
145 Prepaid Insurance

150s—Long-Term Investments
153 Bond Sinking Fund

160s—Land
161 Land
162 Natural Resources
162.1 Accumulated Depletion

170s—Buildings
171 Buildings
171.1 Accumulated Depreciation—Buildings

180s—Equipment
181 Office Equipment (Also Store Equipment)
181.1 Accumulated Depreciation—Office Equipment (Also Store Equipment)
182 Office Furniture
182.1 Accumulated Depreciation—Office Furniture
183 Athletic Equipment (Also Tailoring, Lawn, Cleaning)
183.1 Accumulated Depreciation—Athletic Equipment (Also Tailoring, Lawn, Cleaning)
184 Tennis Facilities (Also Basketball Facilities)
184.1 Accumulated Depreciation—Tennis Facilities (Also Basketball Facilities)
185 Delivery Equipment (Also Medical, Van)
185.1 Accumulated Depreciation—Delivery Equipment (Also Medical, Van)
186 Exercise Equipment
186.1 Accumulated Depreciation—Exercise Equipment
187 Computer Equipment
187.1 Accumulated Depreciation—Computer Equipment

190s—Intangibles
191 Patents
192 Copyrights
193 Organization Costs

Liabilities (200–299)

200s—Short-term Payables
201 Notes Payable
201.1 Discount on Notes Payable
202 Accounts Payable (Also Vouchers Payable)
203 United Way Contribution Payable
204 Income Tax Payable
205 Common Dividends Payable
206 Preferred Dividends Payable
207 Interest Payable (Also Bond Interest Payable)

210s—Employee Payroll Related Payables
211 Employee Income Tax Payable
212 Social Security Tax Payable
213 Medicare Tax Payable
215 City Earnings Tax Payable
216 Health Insurance Premiums Payable
217 Credit Union Payable
218 Savings Bond Deductions Payable
219 Wages Payable

220s—Employer Payroll Related Payables
221 FUTA Tax Payable
222 SUTA Tax Payable
223 Workers' Compensation Insurance payable

230s—Sales Tax
231 Sales Tax Payable

240s—Deferred Revenues and Current Portion of Long-Term Debt
241 Unearned Subscription Revenue (Also Unearned Ticket Revenue, Unearned Repair Fees)
242 Current Portion of Mortgage Payable

250s—Long-Term Liabilities
251 Mortgage Payable
252 Bonds Payable
252.1 Discount on Bonds Payable
253 Premium on Bonds Payable